Professional
ASP.NET 2.0

Professional
ASP.NET 2.0

Bill Evjen
Scott Hanselman
Farhan Muhammad
Srinivasa Sivakumar
Devin Rader

WILEY

Wiley Publishing, Inc.

Professional ASP.NET 2.0

Published by
Wiley Publishing, Inc.
10475 Crosspoint Boulevard
Indianapolis, IN 46256
www.wiley.com

Copyright © 2006 by Wiley Publishing, Inc., Indianapolis, Indiana

Published simultaneously in Canada

ISBN-13: 978-0-7645-7610-2
ISBN-10: 0-7645-7610-0

Manufactured in the United States of America

10 9 8 7 6 5

1B/SR/RQ/QV/IN

For general information on our other products and services please contact our Customer Care Department within the United States at (800) 762-2974, outside the United States at (317) 572-3993 or fax (317) 572-4002.

Wiley also publishes its books in a variety of electronic formats. Some content that appears in print may not be available in electronic books.

Library of Congress Cataloging-in-Publication Data

Professional ASP.NET 2.0 / Bill Evjen ... [et al.].
    p. cm.
  Includes index.
  ISBN-13: 978-0-7645-7610-2 (paper/website)
  ISBN-10: 0-7645-7610-0 (paper/website)

  1. Active server pages 2. Microsoft.NET. 3. Web sites—Design. 4. Web servers. 5. Web site development. 6. Internet programming. I. Evjen, Bill.
  TK5105.8885.A26P787 2005
  005.2'76—dc22
                        2005020484

About the Authors

Bill Evjen

Bill Evjen is an active proponent of .NET technologies and community-based learning initiatives for .NET. He has been actively involved with .NET since the first bits were released in 2000. In the same year, Bill founded the St. Louis .NET User Group (www.stlnet.org), one of the world's first such groups. Bill is also the founder and executive director of the International .NET Association (www.ineta.org), which represents more than 375,000 members worldwide.

Based in St. Louis, Missouri, USA, Bill is an acclaimed author and speaker on ASP.NET and XML Web services. He has written or co-written *Professional C#, Third Edition*; *Professional VB.NET, Third Edition*; and *ASP.NET 2.0 Beta Preview* (all Wrox titles), as well as *ASP.NET Professional Secrets, XML Web Services for ASP.NET, Web Services Enhancements: Understanding the WSE for Enterprise Applications, Visual Basic .NET Bible*, and *ASP.NET Professional Secrets* (all published by Wiley). In addition to writing, Bill is a speaker at numerous conferences, including DevConnections, VSLive, and TechEd.

Bill is a Technical Director for Reuters, the international news and financial services company, and he travels the world speaking to major financial institutions about the future of the IT industry. He was graduated from Western Washington University in Bellingham, Washington, with a Russian language degree. When he isn't tinkering on the computer, he can usually be found at his summer house in Toivakka, Finland. You can reach Bill at evjen@yahoo.com. He presently keeps his weblog at www.geekswithblogs.net/evjen.

Scott Hanselman

Scott Hanselman is currently the Chief Architect at the Corillian Corporation (NASDAQ: CORI), an eFinance enabler. He has more than 13 years' experience developing software in C, C++, VB, COM, and certainly in VB.NET and C#. Scott is proud to be both a Microsoft RD as well as an MVP for both ASP.NET and Solutions Architecture. Scott has spoken at dozens of conferences worldwide, including three TechEds and the North African DevCon. He is a primary contributor to "newtelligence DasBlog Community Edition 1.7," the most popular open-source ASP.NET blogging software hosted on SourceForge.

This is the third book Scott has worked on for Wrox and certainly the most fun. His thoughts on the Zen of .NET, programming, and Web Services can be found on his blog at www.computerzen.com. He welcomes email and PayPal'ed money at scott@hanselman.com.

Farhan Muhammad

Farhan Muhammad is the Chief Architect of ILM Professional Service. He is also the Microsoft Regional Director (RD) for the U.S. North Central region. As an RD, he focuses on providing the vital link between Microsoft and the developer community. He has been a board member at the International .NET Association (INETA), where he actively helped support developers' communities worldwide. He leads the Twin Cities .NET User Group, a developers' community of more than 1,200 members in Minnesota dedicated to sharing .NET knowledge among developers. He has also written *Real World ASP.NET Best Practices* (Apress, 2003).

S. Srinivasa Sivakumar

S. Srinivasa Sivakumar is a Solution Architect for Microsoft India. Srinivasa has co-written more than 15 books and more than 40 technical articles for major publications. A list of his published materials is available at `www3.brinkster.com/webguru/`.

Devin Rader

Devin Rader is an Infragistics Technology Evangelist and is responsible for writing Infragistics reference applications and .NET technology articles, as well as the worldwide delivery of Infragistics' technology demonstrations. Devin is an active member and leader for the International .NET Association (INETA) and believes strongly in the software development community. He helped found the St. Louis .NET Users Group in November 2000 and is a frequent speaker at community events nationwide. Devin writes the monthly ASP.NET Tips & Tricks column for *ASP.NET Pro* magazine, as well as .NET technology articles for MSDN Online. He has served as the sole technical editor for a number of works, including *Web Services Enhancements: Understanding the WSE for Enterprise Applications, ASP.NET Professional Secrets*, and *ASP.NET 2.0 Beta Preview* (all published by Wiley).

Credits

Senior Acquisitions Editor
Jim Minatel

Senior Development Editor
Jodi Jensen

Technical Editors
Derek Comingore
Hal Levy
Farhan Muhammad
Jeffrey Palermo
Richard Purchas
Devin Rader
Patrick Santry
Srinivasa Sivakumar
Scott Spradlin

Copy Editor
Mary Lagu

Editorial Manager
Mary Beth Wakefield

Production Manager
Tim Tate

Vice President and Executive Group Publisher
Richard Swadley

Vice President and Executive Publisher
Joseph B. Wikert

Graphics and Production Specialists
Lauren Goddard
Denny Hager
Barbara Moore
Melanee Prendergast
Heather Ryan
Alicia B. South

Quality Control Technicians
Leeann Harney
Jessica Kramer
Carl William Pierce

Proofreading and Indexing
TECHBOOKS Production Services

To Kalle—welcome to the family! —*Bill Evjen*

I dedicate this book to my lovely wife, Luna, whose continuous support and encouragement made this book possible. I also dedicate this book to my parents, who taught me to do my best in everything I start. —*Farhan Muhammad*

I dedicate my work in this book to my dear late father, Mr. V. Sathyanarayanan, whom I miss most in this world. —*S. Srinivasa Sivakumar*

Acknowledgments

Bill Evjen

I have said it before, and I'll say it again: Writing a book may seem like the greatest of solo endeavors, but it requires a large team of people working together to get technical books out the door—and this book is no exception. This time around, the team was incredible. First, and foremost, I thank Jim Minatel of Wrox for giving me the opportunity to work on such a great project. There is nothing better than getting the opportunity to write about your favorite topic for the world's best publisher!

Besides Jim, I dealt with the book's development editor, Jodi Jensen, on a weekly, if not daily, basis. Much of the quality of this book is because of Jodi's attention to detail and her targeted corrections and queries. Jodi was just so dang good that Wiley has decided to promote her to bigger and better things. So I am sad to say that after so many books, this is the last book Jodi and I will be working on together. Good luck, Jodi, in the new job!

I worked closely with both Scott Hanselman and Devin Rader, and these guys deserve a lot of thanks. I appreciate your help and advice throughout this process. Thanks, guys!

I also thank the various editors who worked on the book—Mary Lagu, Tom Dinse, Brian Herrmann, Sara Shlaer, and Maryann Steinhart—as well as the contributing authors Srinivasa Sivakumar, Farhan Muhammad, and Devin Rader (who also worked as technical editors).

Big and ongoing thanks go to the Wrox/Wiley gang, including Joe Wikert (publisher), Katie Mohr (acquisitions editor), and David Mayhew (marketing).

Writing books while the product is still in an alpha or beta format is a difficult task. For this reason, I also thank specific members of the ASP.NET team who helped me immeasurably. Thanks to Kent Sharkey, Thomas Lewis, Brian Goldfarb, and Scott Guthrie. You guys were very helpful!

Finally, thanks to my entire family. I had a new son come into this world while I was writing the book, so things got rather hectic from time to time. The biggest thanks go to my wife, Tuija, who keeps my world together. Thanks, also, to my outstanding children—Sofia, Henri, and now Kalle! You guys are my sunshine.

Scott Hanselman

I want to thank my wife, Ntombenhle ("Mo"), for her infinite patience and understanding as I poked away on the computer into the wee hours when I should have been hanging with her. Thanks to ScottGu and the ASP.NET 2.0 team for making a rocking sweet development platform. Thanks to Ben Miller, the ASP.NET MVP Lead, for brokering my questions all over Redmond and beyond. I thank all the folks at Corillian, including my CTO, Chris Brooks, for his constant mentoring, and especially Patrick Cauldwell for his friendship and technical wisdom over the years. Thanks to Jodi Jensen and Jim Minatel at Wiley/Wrox for all their hard work. Thanks to the folks who read my blog and allow me to bounce code and thoughts off them. Finally, I thank Bill Evjen for his ongoing support, ideas, guidance, and tutelage about the book-writing process.

Contents

Contents

Contents

Contents

Contents

Contents

Contents

Contents

Contents

Contents

Contents

Contents

Introduction

Simply put, ASP.NET 2.0 is an amazing release! When ASP.NET 1.0 was introduced in 2000, many considered it a revolutionary leap forward in the area of Web application development. We believe ASP.NET 2.0 is just as exciting and revolutionary. Although the foundation of ASP.NET was laid with the release of ASP.NET 1.0, ASP.NET 2.0 builds on this foundation by focusing on the area of developer productivity.

ASP.NET 2.0 brings with it a staggering number of new technologies built into the ASP.NET framework. After reading this book, you will see just how busy the ASP.NET team has been in the past few years. The number of classes inside ASP.NET has more than doubled, and this release contains more than 50 new server controls!

This book covers these new built-in technologies. It not only introduces new topics, it also shows you examples of these new technologies in action. So sit back, pull up that keyboard, and let's have some fun!

What You Need for ASP.NET 2.0

You might find it best to install Visual Studio 2005 to work through the examples in this book; you can, however, just use Microsoft's Notepad and the command-line compilers that come with the .NET Framework 2.0. To work through *every* example in this book, you need the following:

- ❏ Windows Server 2003, Windows 2000, or Windows XP
- ❏ Visual Studio 2005
- ❏ SQL Server 2000 or 2005
- ❏ Microsoft Access or SQL Server Express Edition

The nice thing is that you are not required to have Microsoft Internet Information Services (IIS) to work with ASP.NET 2.0 because this release of ASP.NET includes a built-in Web server based on the previously released Microsoft Cassini technology. And if you don't have SQL Server, don't be alarmed. Many examples that use this database can be altered to work with Microsoft Access.

Who Should Read This Book?

This book was written to introduce you to the new features and capabilities that ASP.NET 2.0 offers, as well as to give you an explanation of the foundation that ASP.NET provides. We assume you have a general understanding of Web technologies, such as previous versions of ASP.NET, Active Server Pages 2.0/ 3.0, or JavaServer Pages. If you understand the basics of Web programming, you shouldn't have much trouble following along with this book's content.

If you are brand new to ASP.NET, be sure to check out *Beginning ASP.NET 2.0* by Chris Hart, John Kauffman, Dave Sussman, and Chris Ullman (published by Wiley; ISBN: 0-7645-8850-8) to help you understand the basics.

In addition to working with Web technologies, we also assume that you understand basic programming constructs, such as variables, For Each loops, and object-oriented programming.

You may also be wondering whether this book is for the Visual Basic developer or the C# developer. We're happy to say that it's for both! When the code differs substantially, this book provides examples in both VB and C#.

What This Book Covers

This book spends its time reviewing the big changes that have occurred in the 2.0 release of ASP.NET. Each major new feature included in ASP.NET 2.0 is covered in detail. The following list tells you something about the content of each chapter.

❑   **Chapter 1, "Hello ASP.NET 2.0."** This first chapter gives a good grounding in the new features of ASP.NET 2.0 by taking a look at some of the major new features and capabilities. It starts by providing you with a little bit of the history of ASP.NET and moves on to some of the exciting new additions that this latest version of the technology offers.

❑   **Chapter 2, "Visual Studio 2005."** This chapter introduces the next generation of the major IDE for developing .NET applications: Visual Studio 2005. Previous releases of this IDE included Visual Studio .NET 2003 and Visual Studio .NET 2002. This chapter focuses on the Visual Studio 2005 release and how you can use it to build better ASP.NET applications more quickly.

❑   **Chapter 3, "Application and Page Frameworks."** The third chapter covers the frameworks of ASP.NET applications as well as the structure and frameworks provided for single ASP.NET pages. This chapter shows you how to build ASP.NET applications using IIS or the built-in Web server that now comes with Visual Studio 2005. This chapter also shows you the new folders and files that have been added to ASP.NET. It discusses new ways to compile code and shows you how to perform cross-page posting.

❑   **Chapters 4, 5, 6, and 7.** These four chapters are grouped here because they all deal with server controls. This batch of chapters starts by examining the idea of the server control and its pivotal role in ASP.NET development. In addition to looking at the server control framework, these chapters delve into the plethora of server controls that are at your disposal for ASP.NET development projects. Chapter 4, "Developing with ASP.NET Server Controls and Client-Side Scripts," looks at the basics of working with server controls. Chapter 5, "ASP.NET Web Server Controls," covers the controls that have been part of the ASP.NET technology since its initial release. Chapter 6, "ASP.NET 2.0 Web Server Controls," on the other hand, looks at the new controls that have been added with the 2.0 release. Chapter 7, "Validation Server Controls," describes a special group of server controls: those for validation. You can use these controls to create beginning-to-advanced form validations.

❑   **Chapter 8, "Master Pages."** Master pages are a great new addition to the ASP.NET 2.0 technology. They provide a means of creating templated pages that enable you to work with the entire application, as opposed to single pages. This chapter examines the creation of these templates and how to apply them to your content pages throughout an ASP.NET application.

❑   **Chapter 9, "Themes and Skins."** The Cascading Style Sheet files you are allowed to use in ASP.NET 1.0/1.1 are simply not adequate in many regards, especially in the area of server controls. When using these early versions, the developer can never be sure of the HTML output these files might generate. This chapter takes a look at how to deal with the styles that your applications require and shows you how to create a centrally managed look-and-feel for all the pages of your application by using themes and the skin files that are part of a theme.

❑   **Chapters 10 and 11.** One of the more important tasks of ASP.NET is presenting data, and these two chapters show you how to do that. ASP.NET provides a number of controls to which you can attach data and present it to the end user. Chapter 10, "Collections and Lists," shows you how to take data and attach it to various ASP.NET server controls. Chapter 11, "Data Binding in ASP.NET 2.0," looks at the underlying capabilities that enable you to work with the data programmatically before issuing the data to a control.

❑   **Chapter 12, "Data Management with ADO.NET."** ADO.NET incorporates some radical changes in this release of ASP.NET. This chapter presents the new data model provided by ASP.NET, which allows you to handle the retrieval, updating, and deleting of data quickly and logically. This new data model enables you to use one or two lines of code to get at data stored in everything from SQL Server to XML files.

❑   **Chapter 13, "Working with XML."** Without a doubt, XML has become one of the leading technologies used for data representation. For this reason, the .NET Framework and ASP.NET 2.0 have many capabilities built into their frameworks that enable you to easily extract, create, manipulate, and store XML. This chapter takes a close look at the XML technologies built into ASP.NET and the underlying .NET Framework.

❑   **Chapter 14, "Site Navigation."** It is quite apparent that many developers do not simply develop single pages—they build applications. Therefore, they need mechanics that deal with functionality throughout the entire application, not just the pages. One of the new application capabilities provided by ASP.NET 2.0 is the site navigation system covered in this chapter. The underlying navigation system enables you to define your application's navigation structure through an XML file, and it introduces a whole series of new navigation server controls that work with the data from these XML files.

❑   **Chapter 15, "Personalization."** Developers are always looking for ways to store information pertinent to the end user. After it is stored, this personalization data has to be persisted for future visits or for grabbing other pages within the same application. The ASP.NET team developed a way to store this information—the ASP.NET personalization system. The great thing about this system is that you configure the entire behavior of the system from the `web.config` file.

❑   **Chapter 16, "Membership and Role Management."** This chapter covers the new membership and role management system developed to simplify adding authentication and authorization to your ASP.NET applications. These two new systems are extensive; they make some of the more complicated authentication and authorization implementations of the past a distant memory. This chapter focuses on using the `web.config` file for controlling how these systems are applied, as well as on the new server controls that work with the underlying systems.

❑ **Chapter 17, "Portal Frameworks and Web Parts."** This chapter explains Web Parts—a new way of encapsulating pages into smaller and more manageable objects. The great thing about Web Parts is that they can be made of a larger Portal Framework, which can then enable end users to completely modify how the Web Parts are constructed on the page—including their appearance and layout.

❑ **Chapter 18, "Security."** Chapter 18 discusses security beyond the membership and role management features provided by ASP.NET 2.0. This chapter provides an in-depth look at the authentication and authorization mechanics inherent in the ASP.NET technology, as well as HTTP access types and impersonations.

❑ **Chapter 19, "State Management."** Because ASP.NET is a request-response–based technology, state management and the performance of requests and responses take on significant importance. This chapter introduces these two separate but important areas of ASP.NET development.

❑ **Chapter 20, "Caching."** Because of the request-response nature of ASP.NET, caching (storing previous generated results, images, and pages) on the server becomes rather important to the performance of your ASP.NET applications. This chapter takes a look at some of the advanced caching capabilities provided by ASP.NET, including the new SQL cache invalidation feature introduced by ASP.NET 2.0.

❑ **Chapter 21, "Debugging and Error Handling Techniques."** Being able to handle unanticipated errors in your ASP.NET applications is vital for any application that you build. This chapter tells you how to properly structure error handling within your applications. It also shows you how to use various debugging techniques to find errors that your applications might contain.

❑ **Chapter 22, "File I/O and Streams."** More often than not, you want your ASP.NET applications to work with items that are outside the base application. Examples include files and streams. This chapter takes a close look at working with various file types and streams that might come into your ASP.NET applications.

❑ **Chapter 23, "User Controls, Server Controls, Modules, and HttpHandlers."** Not only can you use the plethora of server controls that come with ASP.NET 2.0, but you can also utilize the same framework these controls use and build your own. This chapter describes building your own server controls and how to use them within your applications. The chapter also delves into building your own HttpHandlers.

❑ **Chapter 24, "Using Business Objects."** Invariably, you are going to have components created with previous technologies that you don't want to rebuild but that you do want to integrate into new ASP.NET applications. If this is the case, the .NET Framework makes it fairly simple and straightforward to incorporate your previous COM components into your applications. Beyond showing you how to integrate your COM components into your applications, this chapter also shows you how to build newer style .NET components instead of turning to the previous COM component architecture.

❑ **Chapter 25, "Mobile Development."** Many people forget that ASP.NET development is not only about building applications for the browser; it is also a great technology for mobile development. This chapter discusses using ASP.NET 2.0 for your mobile application development projects and how ASP.NET can make this process quite simple.

❑ **Chapter 26, "Building and Consuming XML Web Services."** XML Web services have monopolized all the hype for the past few years, and a major aspect of the Web services model within .NET is part of ASP.NET. This chapter reveals the ease not only of building XML Web services, but consuming them in an ASP.NET application. This chapter then ventures further by describing how to build XML Web services that utilize SOAP headers and how to consume this particular type of service.

❑ **Chapter 27, "Configuration."** Configuration in ASP.NET can be a big topic because the ASP.NET team is not into building black boxes; instead, it is building the underlying capabilities of ASP.NET in a fashion that can easily be expanded on later. This chapter teaches you to modify the capabilities and behaviors of ASP.NET using the various configuration files at your disposal.

❑ **Chapter 28, "Administration and Management."** Besides making it easier for the developer to be more productive in building ASP.NET applications, the ASP.NET team also put considerable effort into making it easier to manage applications. In the past, using ASP.NET 1.0/1.1, you managed ASP.NET applications by changing values in an XML configuration file. This chapter provides an overview of the new GUI tools that come with this latest release that enable you to manage your Web applications easily and effectively.

❑ **Chapter 29, "Packaging and Deploying ASP.NET Applications."** So you've built an ASP.NET application—now what? This chapter takes the building process one step further and shows you how to package your ASP.NET applications for easy deployment. Many options are available for working with the installers and compilation model to change what you are actually giving your customers.

❑ **Appendix A, "Visual Basic 8.0 and C# 2.0 Language Enhancements."** In addition to major changes to ASP.NET, considerable change has occurred in Visual Basic 8.0 and C# 2.0. The changes to these two languages, the primary languages used for ASP.NET development, are discussed in this appendix.

❑ **Appendix B, "ASP.NET Resources."** This small appendix points you to some of the more valuable online resources for enhancing your understanding of ASP.NET.

Conventions

This book uses a number of different styles of text and layout to help differentiate among various types of information. Here are examples of the styles used and an explanation of what they mean:

❑ New words being defined are shown in *italics*.

❑ Keys that you press on the keyboard, such as Ctrl and Enter, are shown in initial caps and spelled as they appear on the keyboard.

❑ File and folder names, file extensions, URLs, and code that appears in regular paragraph text are shown in a `monospaced` typeface.

When we show a block of code that you can type as a program and run, it's shown on separate lines, like this:

```
public static void Main()
{
    AFunc(1,2,"abc");
}
```

or like this:

```
public static void Main()
{
    AFunc(1,2,"abc");
}
```

Sometimes you see code in a mixture of styles, like this:

```
// If we haven't reached the end, return true, otherwise
// set the position to invalid, and return false.
pos++;
if (pos < 4)
    return true;
else {
    pos = -1;
    return false;
}
```

When mixed code is shown like this, the code with no background represents code that has been shown previously and that you don't need to examine further. Code with the gray background is what you should focus on in the current example.

We demonstrate the syntactical usage of methods, properties, and so on using the following format:

```
SqlDependency="database:table"
```

Here, the italicized parts indicate *placeholder text:* object references, variables, or parameter values that you need to insert.

Most of the code examples throughout the book are presented as numbered listings that have descriptive titles, like this:

Listing 1-3: Targeting WML devices in your ASP.NET pages

Each listing is numbered (for example: *1-3*) where the first number represents the chapter number and the number following the hyphen represents a sequential number that indicates where that listing falls within the chapter. Downloadable code from the Wrox Web site (`www.wrox.com`) also uses this numbering system so that you can easily locate the examples you are looking for.

All code is shown in both VB and C#, when warranted. The exception is for code in which the only difference is, for example, the value given to the `Language` attribute in the `Page` directive. In such situations, we don't repeat the code for the C# version; the code is shown only once, as in the following example:

```
<%@ Page Language="VB"%>

<html xmlns="http://www.w3.org/1999/xhtml">
<head runat="server">
    <title>DataSetDataSource</title>
</head>
<body>
    <form id="form1" runat="server">
        <asp:DropDownList ID="Dropdownlist1" Runat="server" DataTextField="name"
         DataSourceID="XmlDataSource1">
        </asp:DropDownList>

        <asp:XmlDataSource ID="XmlDataSource1" Runat="server"
         DataFile="~/Painters.xml">
        </asp:DataSetDataSource>
    </form>
</body>
</html>
```

Source Code

As you work through the examples in this book, you may choose either to type all the code manually or to use the source code files that accompany the book. All the source code used in this book is available for download at www.wrox.com. When you get to the site, simply locate the book's title (either by using the Search box or one of the topic lists) and click the Download Code link. You can then choose to download all the code from the book in one large zip file or download just the code you need for a particular chapter.

> Because many books have similar titles, you may find it easiest to search by ISBN; this book's ISBN is 0-7645-7610-0 (changing to 978-0-7645-7610-2 as the new industry-wide 13-digit ISBN numbering system is phased in by January 2007).

After you download the code, just decompress it with your favorite compression tool. Alternatively, you can go to the main Wrox code download page at www.wrox.com/dynamic/books/download.aspx to see the code available for this book and all other Wrox books. Remember, you can easily find the code you are looking for by referencing the listing number of the code example from the book, such as "Listing 1-3." We used these listing numbers when naming the downloadable code files.

Errata

We make every effort to ensure that there are no errors in the text or in the code. However, no one is perfect, and mistakes do occur. If you find an error in one of our books, such as a spelling mistake or faulty piece of code, we would be very grateful if you'd tell us about it. By sending in errata, you may spare another reader hours of frustration; at the same time, you are helping us provide even higher-quality information.

To find the errata page for this book, go to www.wrox.com and locate the title using the Search box or one of the title lists. Then, on the book details page, click the Book Errata link. On this page, you can view all errata that have been submitted for this book and posted by Wrox editors. A complete book list including links to each book's errata is also available at www.wrox.com/misc-pages/booklist.shtml.

If you don't spot "your" error already on the Book Errata page, go to www.wrox.com/contact/techsupport.shtml and complete the form there to send us the error you have found. We'll check the information and, if appropriate, post a message to the book's errata page and fix the problem in subsequent editions of the book.

p2p.wrox.com

For author and peer discussion, join the P2P forums at p2p.wrox.com. The forums are a Web-based system for you to post messages relating to Wrox books and technologies and to interact with other readers and technology users. The forums offer a subscription feature that enables you to receive e-mail on topics of interest when new posts are made to the forums. Wrox authors, editors, other industry experts, and your fellow readers are represented in these forums.

At http://p2p.wrox.com you will find a number of different forums that will help you not only as you read this book but also as you develop your own applications. To join the forums, just follow these steps:

1.   Go to p2p.wrox.com and click the Register link.

2.   Read the terms of use and click Agree.

3.   Supply the information required to join, as well as any optional information you want to provide, and click Submit.

You will receive an e-mail with information describing how to verify your account and complete the joining process.

You can read messages in the forums without joining P2P, but you must join in order to post messages.

After you join, you can post new messages and respond to other users' posts. You can read messages at any time on the Web. If you would like to have new messages from a particular forum e-mailed to you, click the Subscribe to this Forum icon by the forum name in the forum listing.

For more information about how the forum software works, as well as answers to many common questions specific to P2P and Wrox books, be sure to read the P2P FAQs. Simply click the FAQ link on any P2P page.

Professional
ASP.NET 2.0

1

Hello ASP.NET 2.0!

The evolution of ASP.NET continues! The progression from Active Server Pages 3.0 to ASP.NET 1.0 was revolutionary, to say the least; and we are here to tell you that the evolution from ASP.NET 1.0/1.1 to ASP.NET 2.0 is just as exciting and dramatic.

The introduction of ASP.NET 1.0/1.1 changed the Web programming model; but ASP.NET 2.0 is just as revolutionary in the way it increases productivity. The primary goal of ASP.NET 2.0 is to enable you to build powerful, secure, and dynamic applications using the least possible amount of code. Although this book covers the new features provided by ASP.NET 2.0, it also covers most of what the ASP.NET technology offers.

A Little Bit of History

Before organizations were even thinking about developing applications for the Internet, much of the application development focused on thick desktop applications. These thick-client applications were used for everything from home computing and gaming to office productivity and more. No end was in sight for the popularity of this application model.

During that time, Microsoft developed its thick-client applications using mainly Visual Basic (VB). Visual Basic was not only a programming language; it was tied to an IDE that allowed for easy thick-client application development. In the Visual Basic model, developers could drop controls onto a form, set properties for these controls, and provide code behind them to manipulate the events of the control. For example, when an end user clicked a button on one of the Visual Basic forms, the code behind the form handled the event.

Then, in the mid-1990s, the Internet arrived on the scene. Microsoft was unable to move the Visual Basic model to the development of Internet-based applications. The Internet definitely had a lot of power, and right away the problems facing the thick-client application model were revealed. Internet-based applications created a single instance of the application that everyone could access. Having one instance of an application meant that when the application was upgraded or patched, the changes made to this single instance were immediately available to each and every user visiting the application through a browser.

To participate in the Web application world, Microsoft developed Active Server Pages (ASP). ASP was a quick and easy way to develop Web pages. ASP pages consisted of a single page that contained a mix of markup and languages. The power of ASP was that you could include VBScript or JScript code instructions in the page executed on the Web server before the page was sent to the end user's Web browser. This was an easy way to create dynamic Web pages customized based on parameters dictated by the developer.

ASP used script between brackets and percentage signs — <% %> — to control server-side behaviors. A developer could then build an ASP page by starting with a set of static HTML. Any dynamic element needed by the page was defined using a scripting language (such as VBScript or JScript). When a user requested the page from the server by using a browser, the asp.dll (an ISAPI application that provided a bridge between the scripting language and the Web server) would take hold of the page and define all the dynamic aspects of the page on-the-fly based on the programming logic specified in the script. After all the dynamic aspects of the page were defined, the result was an HTML page output to the browser of the requesting client.

As the Web application model developed, more and more languages mixed in with the static HTML to help manipulate the behavior and look of the output page. Over time, such a large number of languages, scripts, and plain text could be placed in a typical ASP page that developers began to refer to pages that utilized these features as *spaghetti code*. For example, it was quite possible to have a page that used HTML, VBScript, JavaScript, Cascading Style Sheets, T-SQL, and more. In certain instances, it became a manageability nightmare.

ASP evolved and new versions were released. ASP 2.0 and 3.0 were popular because the technology made it relatively straightforward and easy to create Web pages. Their popularity was enhanced because they appeared in the late '90s, just as the dotcom era was born. During this time, a mountain of new Web pages and portals were developed, and ASP was one of the leading technologies individuals and companies used to build them. Even today, you can still find a lot of .asp pages on the Internet — including some of Microsoft's own Web pages.

But even at the time of the final release of Active Server Pages in late 1998, Microsoft employees Marc Anders and Scott Guthrie had other ideas. Their ideas generated what they called XSP (an abbreviation with no meaning) — a new way of creating Web applications in an object-oriented manner instead of the procedural manner of ASP 3.0. They showed their idea to many different groups within Microsoft, and were well received. In the summer of 2000, the beta of what was then called ASP+ was released at Microsoft's Professional Developers Conference. The attendees eagerly started working with it. When the technology became available (with the final release of the .NET Framework 1.0), it was renamed ASP.NET — receiving the .NET moniker that most of Microsoft's new products were receiving at that time.

Before the introduction of .NET, the model that classic ASP provided and what developed in Visual Basic were so different that few VB developers also developed Web applications — and few Web application developers also developed the thick-client applications of the VB world. There was a great divide. ASP.NET bridged this gap. ASP.NET brought a Visual Basic–style eventing model to Web application development, providing much-needed state management techniques over stateless HTTP. Its model is much like the earlier Visual Basic model in that a developer can drag and drop a control onto a design surface or form, manipulate the control's properties, and even work with the code behind these controls to act on certain events that occur during their lifecycles. What ASP.NET created is really the best of both models, as you will see throughout this book.

I know you'll enjoy working with this latest release of ASP.NET — 2.0. Nothing is better than getting your hands on a new technology and seeing what's possible. The following section discusses the goals of ASP.NET 2.0 so you can find out what to expect from this new offering!

The Goals of ASP.NET 2.0

ASP.NET 2.0 is a major release of the product and is an integral part of the .NET Framework 2.0. This release of the Framework was code-named *Whidbey* internally at Microsoft. You might hear others referring to this release of ASP.NET as *ASP.NET Whidbey*. ASP.NET 2.0 heralds a new wave of development that should eliminate any of the remaining barriers to adopting this new way of coding Web applications.

When the ASP.NET team started working on ASP.NET 2.0, it had specific goals to achieve. These goals focused around developer productivity, administration and management, as well as performance and scalability. These goals are achieved with this milestone product release. The next sections look at each of these goals.

Developer Productivity

Much of the focus of ASP.NET 2.0 is on productivity. Huge productivity gains were made with the release of ASP.NET 1.*x* — could it be possible to expand further on those gains?

One goal the development team had for ASP.NET 2.0 was to eliminate much of the tedious coding that ASP.NET originally required and to make common ASP.NET tasks easier. The ASP.NET team developing ASP.NET 2.0 had the goal of reducing by two-thirds the number of lines of code required for an ASP.NET application! It succeeded in this release; you will be amazed at how quickly you can create your applications in ASP.NET 2.0.

The new developer productivity capabilities are presented throughout this book. First, take a look at the older ASP.NET technology. Listing 1-1 provides an example of using ASP.NET 1.0 to build a table in a Web page that includes the capability to perform simple paging of the data provided.

Listing 1-1: Showing data in a DataGrid server control with paging enabled (VB only)

```
<%@ Page Language="VB" AutoEventWireup="True" %>
<%@ Import Namespace="System.Data" %>
<%@ Import Namespace="System.Data.SqlClient" %>

<script runat="server">

    Private Sub Page_Load(ByVal sender As System.Object, _
      ByVal e As System.EventArgs)
        If Not Page.IsPostBack Then
            BindData()
        End If
```

(continued)

Listing 1-1: *(continued)*

```
    End Sub

    Private Sub BindData()
        Dim conn As SqlConnection = New SqlConnection("server='localhost';
            trusted_connection=true; Database='Northwind'")
        Dim cmd As SqlCommand = New SqlCommand("Select * From Customers", conn)
        conn.Open()

        Dim da As SqlDataAdapter = New SqlDataAdapter(cmd)
        Dim ds As New DataSet

        da.Fill(ds, "Customers")

        DataGrid1.DataSource = ds
        DataGrid1.DataBind()
    End Sub

    Private Sub DataGrid1_PageIndexChanged(ByVal source As Object, _
      ByVal e As System.Web.UI.WebControls.DataGridPageChangedEventArgs)
        DataGrid1.CurrentPageIndex = e.NewPageIndex
        BindData()
    End Sub

</script>
<html>
<head>
</head>
<body>
    <form runat="server">
        <asp:DataGrid id="DataGrid1" runat="server" AllowPaging="True"
        OnPageIndexChanged="DataGrid1_PageIndexChanged"></asp:DataGrid>
    </form>
</body>
</html>
```

Although quite a bit of code is used here, this is a dramatic improvement over the amount of code required to accomplish this task using classic Active Server Pages 3.0. We won't go into the details of this older code; we just want to demonstrate that in order to add any additional common functionality (such as paging) for the data shown in a table, the developer had to create custom code.

This is one area where the new developer productivity gains are most evident. ASP.NET 2.0 now provides a new control called the GridView server control. This control is much like the DataGrid server control that you may already know and love, but the GridView server control (besides offering many other new features) contains the built-in capability to apply paging, sorting, and editing of data with relatively little work on your part. Listing 1-2 shows you an example of the GridView server control. This example builds a table of data from the Customers table in the Northwind database that includes paging.

Listing 1-2: Viewing a paged dataset with the new GridView server control

```
<%@ Page Language="VB" %>

<script runat="server">

</script>

<html xmlns=http://www.w3.org/1999/xhtml>
<head runat="server">
    <title>GridView Demo</title>
</head>
<body>
    <form runat="server">
        <asp:GridView ID="GridView1" Runat="server" AllowPaging="True"
        DataSourceId="Sqldatasource1" />
        <asp:SqlDataSource ID="SqlDataSource1" Runat="server"
        SelectCommand="Select * From Customers"
        ProviderName="System.Data.OleDb"
        ConnectionString="Provider=SQLOLEDB;Server=localhost;uid=sa;
        pwd=password;database=Northwind" />
    </form>
</body>
</html>
```

That's it! You can apply paging by using a couple of new server controls. You turn on this capability using a server control attribute, the `AllowPaging` attribute of the GridView control:

```
<asp:GridView ID="GridView1" Runat="server" AllowPaging="True"
 DataSourceId="SqlDataSource1" />
```

The other interesting event occurs in the code section of the document:

```
<script runat="server">

</script>
```

These two lines of code aren't actually needed to run the file. They are included here to make a point — *you don't need to write any server-side code to make this all work!* You have to include only some server controls: one control to get the data and one control to display the data. Then the controls are wired together. Running this page produces the results shown in Figure 1-1.

This is just one of thousands of possible examples, so at this point you likely can't grasp how much more productive you can be with ASP.NET 2.0. As you work through the book, however, you will see plenty of examples that demonstrate this new level of productivity.

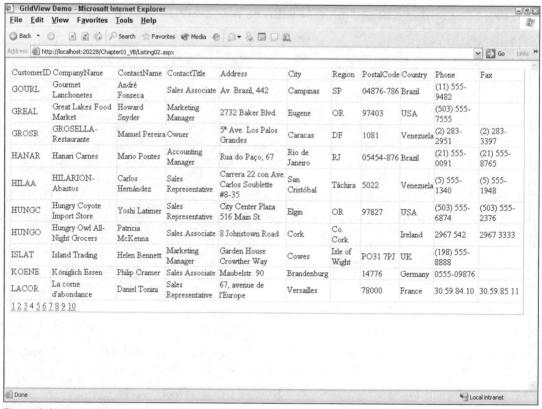

Figure 1-1

Administration and Management

The initial release of ASP.NET focused on the developer, and little thought was given to the people who had to administer and manage all the ASP.NET applications that were built and deployed. Instead of working with consoles and wizards as they did in the past, administrators and managers of these new applications now had to work with unfamiliar XML configuration files such as `machine.config` and `web.config`.

To remedy this situation, ASP.NET 2.0 now includes a Microsoft Management Console (MMC) snap-in that enables Web application administrators to edit configuration settings easily on the fly. Figure 1-2 shows the ASP.NET Configuration Settings dialog open on one of the available tabs.

This dialog allows system administrators to edit the contents of the `machine.config` and the `web.config` files directly from the dialog instead of having them examine the contents of an XML file.

In addition to this dialog, Web or system administrators have a web-based way to administer their ASP.NET 2.0 applications—using the new Web Administration Tool shown in Figure 1-3.

Figure 1-2

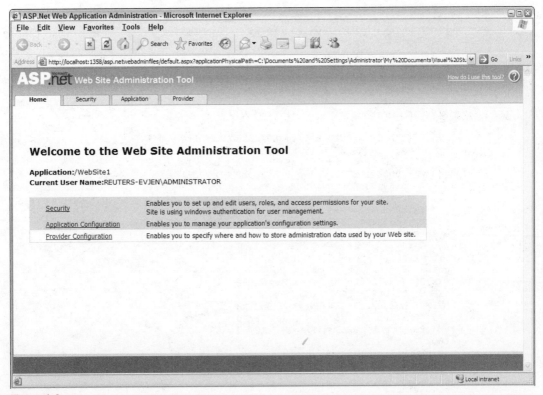

Figure 1-3

You might be asking yourself how you can access these new tools programmatically. Well, that's the exciting part. These tools build off new APIs that are now part of the .NET Framework 2.0 and that are open to developers. These new APIs give you programmatic access to many of the configurations of your Web applications such as reading and writing to .config files. They enable you to create similar tools or even deployment and management scripts.

In addition to these new capabilities, you can now easily encrypt sections of your configuration files. In the past, many programmers stored vital details — such as usernames, passwords, or even their SQL connection strings — directly in the web.config file. With the capability to easily encrypt sections of these files, you can now store these items in a more secure manner. As an example, suppose you have a <connectionStrings> section in your web.config file, like this:

```
<connectionStrings>
   <add name="Northwind"
    connectionString="Server=localhost;Integrated Security=True;Database=Northwind"
    providerName="System.Data.SqlClient" />
</connectionStrings>
```

You could then use the new Configuration class to encrypt this portion of the web.config file. Doing this causes the <connectionStrings> section of the web.config file to be changed to something similar to the following:

```
<connectionStrings configProtectionProvider="RsaProtectedConfigurationProvider">
   <EncryptedData Type="http://www.w3.org/2001/04/xmlenc#Element"
    xmlns="http://www.w3.org/2001/04/xmlenc#">
      <EncryptionMethod
       Algorithm="http://www.w3.org/2001/04/xmlenc#tripledes-cbc" />
      <KeyInfo xmlns="http://www.w3.org/2000/09/xmldsig#">
         <EncryptedKey xmlns="http://www.w3.org/2001/04/xmlenc#">
            <EncryptionMethod
             Algorithm="http://www.w3.org/2001/04/xmlenc#rsa-1_5" />
            <KeyInfo xmlns="http://www.w3.org/2000/09/xmldsig#">
               <KeyName>Rsa Key</KeyName>
            </KeyInfo>
            <CipherData>
               <CipherValue>
                tnbdGPpmif2LOhhzS/fmzCV798XkhdRnK0IrCUrC5q
                AnK8NMqHHVEVYKjIyXvlR/ns7Oofih6YzI+z
                8f5Dh6HrekLS9yR0AxuSeHda/VJA7bmHdL+18
                30nDK0fbrD22BvHTwpYVYNsE6jhYeGEdUBqE1
                oIK9mV3nQSjzqr7GbkI=
               </CipherValue>
            </CipherData>
         </EncryptedKey>
      </KeyInfo>
      <CipherData>
         <CipherValue>
          gnzaR6BRvj76nUO0nsajgnrLwt72qGY6Sw9
          PkM77vk4YTo3816LWDbiVkUuwEpekwN/EPE
          cXGLUxopKVOK97rCqCoLNOQY16jKpPBTTp8
          bY3WGwVhxxGhezdV+EkWaLN8jXpaBSnGYKH
          mY9l4DoWaH9mugrr2a5Y3JB42XPUKJBtrF0
          VZj48Hwkb/zOD7ggWmJujiFH5xQ/FrIC76I
          16QKSInJiZ8dZU
         </CipherValue>
      </CipherData>
   </EncryptedData>
</connectionStrings>
```

Now if some malicious user illegally gets into your machine and gets his hands on your application's `web.config` file, you could prevent him from getting much of value—such as the connection string of your database.

Performance and Scalability

One of the goals for ASP.NET 2.0 set by the Microsoft team was to provide the world's fastest Web application server. This book also addresses a number of performance enhancements available in ASP.NET 2.0.

One of the most exciting performance enhancements is the new caching capability aimed at exploiting Microsoft's SQL Server. ASP.NET 2.0 now includes a feature called *SQL cache invalidation*. Before ASP.NET 2.0, it was possible to cache the results that came from SQL Server and to update the cache based on a time interval—for example, every 15 seconds or so. This meant that the end user might see stale data if the result set changed sometime during that 15-second period.

In some cases, this time interval result set is unacceptable. In an ideal situation, the result set stored in the cache is destroyed if any underlying change occurs in the source from which the result set is retrieved—in this case, SQL Server. With ASP.NET 2.0, you can make this happen with the use of SQL cache invalidation. This means that when the result set from SQL Server changes, the output cache is triggered to change, and the end user always sees the latest result set. The data presented is never stale.

Another big area of change in ASP.NET is in the area of performance and scalability. ASP.NET 2.0 now provides 64-bit support. This means that you can now run your ASP.NET applications on 64-bit Intel or AMD processors.

Because ASP.NET 2.0 is fully backward compatible with ASP.NET 1.0 and 1.1, you can now take any former ASP.NET application, recompile the application on the .NET Framework 2.0, and run it on a 64-bit processor.

Additional New Features of ASP.NET 2.0

You just learned some of the main goals of the ASP.NET team that built ASP.NET 2.0. To achieve these goals, the team built a mountain of new features into ASP.NET. A few of them are described in the following sections.

New Developer Infrastructures

An exciting advancement in ASP.NET 2.0 is that new infrastructures are in place for you to use in your applications. The ASP.NET team selected some of the most common programming operations performed with ASP.NET 1.0 to be built directly into ASP.NET. This saves you considerable time and coding.

Membership and Role Management

In earlier versions, if you were developing a portal that required users to log in to the application to gain privileged access, invariably you had to create it yourself. It can be tricky to create applications with areas that are accessible only to select individuals.

With ASP.NET 2.0, this capability is now built in. You can now validate users as shown in Listing 1-3.

Listing 1-3: Validating a user in code

VB
```
If (Membership.ValidateUser (Username.Text, Password.Text)) Then
    ' Allow access code here
End If
```

C#
```
if (Membership.ValidateUser (Username.Text, Password.Text)) {
    // Allow access code here
}
```

A new series of APIs, controls, and providers in ASP.NET 2.0 enable you to control an application's user membership and role management. Using these APIs, you can easily manage users and their complex roles — creating, deleting, and editing them. You get all this capability by using the APIs or a built-in Web tool called the Web Site Administration Tool.

As far as storing users and their roles, ASP.NET 2.0 uses an .mdb file (the file type for the new SQL Server Express Edition, not to be confused with Microsoft Access) for storing all users and roles. You are in no way limited to just this data store, however. You can expand everything offered to you by ASP.NET and build your own providers using whatever you fancy as a data store. For example, if you want to build your user store in LDAP or within an Oracle database, you can do so quite easily.

Personalization

One advanced feature that portals love to offer their membership base is the capability to personalize their offerings so that end users can make the site look and function however they want. The capability to personalize an application and store the personalization settings is now completely built into the ASP.NET framework.

Because personalization usually revolves around a user and possibly a role that this user participates in, the personalization architecture can be closely tied to the membership and role infrastructures. You have a couple of options for storing the created personalization settings. The capability to store these settings in either Microsoft Access or in SQL Server is built into ASP.NET 2.0. As with the capabilities of the membership and role APIs, you can use the flexible provider model, and then either change how the built-in provider uses the available data store or build your own custom data provider to work with a completely new data store. The personalization API also supports a union of data stores, meaning that you can use more than one data store if you want.

Because it is so easy to create a site for customization using these new APIs, this feature is quite a value-add for any application you build.

The ASP.NET Portal Framework

During the days of ASP.NET 1.0, developers could go to the ASP.NET team's site (found at http://www.asp.net) and download some Web application demos called IBuySpy., These demos were known as Developer Solution Kits and are used as the basis for many of the Web sites on the Internet today. Some were even extended into Open Source frameworks such as DotNetNuke.

The nice thing about IBuySpy was that you could use the code it provided as a basis to build either a Web store or a portal. You simply took the base code as a starting point and extended it. For example, you could change the look and feel of the presentation part of the code or introduce advanced functionality into its modular architecture. Developer Solution Kits were quite popular because they made performing these types of operations so easy. Figure 1-4 shows the INETA (International .NET Association) Web site, which builds on the IBuySpy portal framework.

Because of the popularity of frameworks such as IBuySpy, ASP.NET 2.0 offers built-in capability for using Web Parts to easily build portals. The possibilities for what you can build using the new Portal Framework is astounding. The power of building using Web Parts is that it easily enables end users to completely customize the portal for their own preferences. Figure 1-5 shows an example application built using Web Parts.

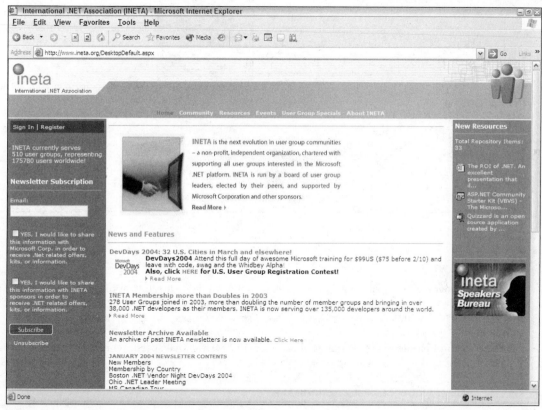

Figure 1-4

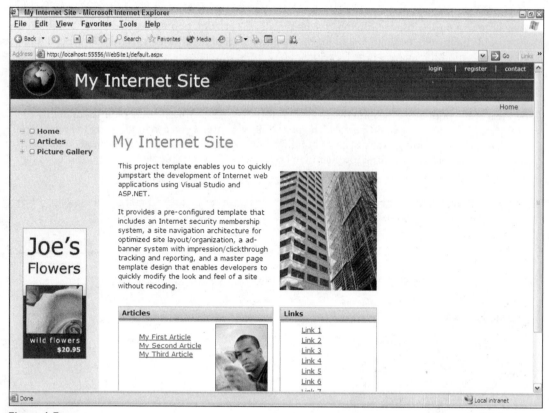

Figure 1-5

Site Navigation

The ASP.NET team members realize that end users want to navigate through applications with ease. The mechanics to make this work in a logical manner is sometimes hard to code. The team solved the problem in ASP.NET 2.0 with a series of navigation-based server controls.

First, you can build a site map for your application in an XML file that specific controls can inherently work from. Listing 1-4 shows a sample site map file.

Listing 1-4: An example of a site map file

```xml
<?xml version="1.0" encoding="utf-8" ?>

<siteMap xmlns="http://schemas.microsoft.com/AspNet/SiteMap-File-1.0">
    <siteMapNode title="Home" description="Home Page" url="default.aspx">
        <siteMapNode title="News" description="The Latest News" url="News.aspx">
            <siteMapNode title="U.S." description="U.S. News"
             url="News.aspx?cat=us" />
            <siteMapNode title="World" description="World News"
             url="News.aspx?cat=world" />
```

```
                <siteMapNode title="Technology" description="Technology News"
                 url="News.aspx?cat=tech" />
                <siteMapNode title="Sports" description="Sports News"
                 url="News.aspx?cat=sport" />
            </siteMapNode>
            <siteMapNode title="Finance" description="The Latest Financial Information"
              url="Finance.aspx">
                <siteMapNode title="Quotes" description="Get the Latest Quotes"
                 url="Quotes.aspx" />
                <siteMapNode title="Markets" description="The Latest Market Information"
                 url="Markets.aspx">
                    <siteMapNode title="U.S. Market Report"
                     description="Looking at the U.S. Market" url="MarketsUS.aspx" />
                    <siteMapNode title="NYSE"
                     description="The New York Stock Exchange" url="NYSE.aspx" />
                </siteMapNode>
                <siteMapNode title="Funds" description="Mutual Funds"
                 url="Funds.aspx" />
            </siteMapNode>
            <siteMapNode title="Weather" description="The Latest Weather"
             url="Weather.aspx" />
        </siteMapNode>
    </siteMap>
```

After you have a site map in place, you can use this file as the data source behind a couple of new site navigation server controls, such as the TreeView and the SiteMapPath server controls. The TreeView server control enables you to place an expandable site navigation system in your application. Figure 1-6 shows you an example of one of the many looks you can give the TreeView server control.

Figure 1-6

The SiteMapPath is a control that provides the capability to place what some call navigation bread-crumbs in your application so that the end user can see the path that he has taken in the application and can easily navigate to higher levels in the tree. Figure 1-7 shows you an example of the SiteMapPath server control at work.

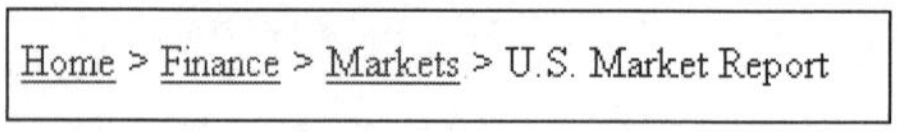

Home > Finance > Markets > U.S. Market Report

Figure 1-7

These new site navigation capabilities provide a great way to get programmatic access to the site layout and even to take into account things like end-user roles to determine which parts of the site to show.

New Compilation System

In ASP.NET 2.0, the code is constructed and compiled in a new way. Compilation in ASP.NET 1.0 was always a tricky scenario. With ASP.NET 1.0, you could build an application's code-behind files using ASP.NET and Visual Studio, deploy it, and then watch as the .aspx files were compiled page by page as each was requested. If you made any changes to the code-behind file in ASP.NET 1.0, it was not reflected in your application until the entire application was rebuilt. That meant that the same page-by-page request had to be done again before the entire application was recompiled.

Everything about how ASP.NET 1.0 worked with classes and compilation changed with the release of ASP.NET 2.0. The mechanics of the new compilation system actually begin with how a page is structured in ASP.NET 2.0. In ASP.NET 1.0, you either constructed your pages using the code-behind model or by placing all the server code inline between <script> tags on your .aspx page. Most pages were constructed using the code-behind model because this was the default when using Visual Studio .NET 2002 or 2003. It was quite difficult to create your page using the inline style in these IDEs. If you did, you were deprived of the use of IntelliSense, which can be quite the lifesaver when working with the tremendously large collection of classes that the .NET Framework offers.

ASP.NET 2.0 offers a new code-behind model because the .NET Framework 2.0 offers the capability to work with *partial classes* (also called partial types). Upon compilation, the separate files are combined into a single offering. This gives you much cleaner code-behind pages. The code that was part of the Web Form Designer Generated section of your classes is separated from the code-behind classes that you create yourself. Contrast this with the ASP.NET 1.0 .aspx file's need to derive from its own code-behind file to represent a single logical page.

ASP.NET 2.0 applications can include an \App_Code directory where you place your class's source. Any class placed here is dynamically compiled and reflected in the application. You do not use a separate build process when you make changes as you did with ASP.NET 1.0. This is a *just save and hit* deployment model like the one in classic ASP 3.0. Visual Studio Web Developer also automatically provides IntelliSense for any objects that are placed in the \App_Code directory, whether you are working with the code-behind model or are coding inline.

ASP.NET 2.0 also provides you with tools that enable you to precompile your ASP.NET applications, both .aspx pages and code behind so that no page within your application has latency when it is retrieved for the first time. It is also a great way to figure out if you have made any errors in the pages without invoking every page yourself.

Precompiling your ASP.NET 2.0 applications is as simple as calling the precompile.axd imaginary file in the application root of your application after it has been deployed. This one call causes your entire application to be precompiled. You receive an error notification if any errors are found anywhere within your application. It is also possible to precompile your application and deliver only the created assembly to the deployment server, thereby protecting your code from snooping, change, and tampering after deployment. You see examples of both of these scenarios later in this book.

Additions to the Page Framework

The ASP.NET page framework has some dramatic new additions that you can include in your applications. One of the most striking ones is the capability to build ASP.NET pages based upon visual inheritance. This was possible in the Windows Forms world, but it was harder to achieve with ASP.NET. You also gain the capability to easily apply a consistent look and feel to the pages of your application by using themes. Many of the difficulties in working with ADO.NET in the past have now been removed with the addition of a new series of data source controls that take care of accessing and retrieving data from a large collection of data stores. Although these are not the only new controls, the many new server controls create a larger ASP.NET page framework.

Master Pages

With the introduction of *master pages* in ASP.NET 2.0, you can now use visual inheritance within your ASP.NET applications. Because many ASP.NET applications have a similar structure throughout their pages, it is logical to build a page template once and use that same template throughout the application.

In ASP.NET 2.0, you do this by creating a `.master` page, as shown in Figure 1-8.

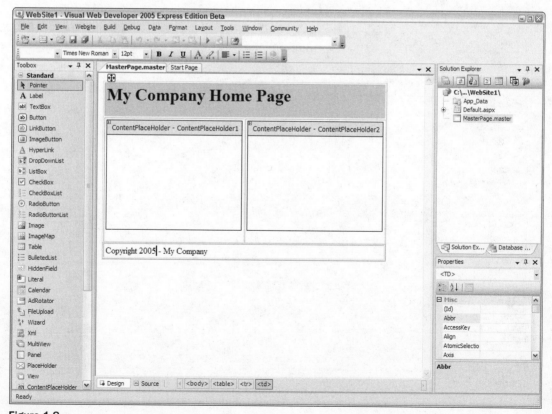

Figure 1-8

An example master page might include a header, footer, and any other elements that all the pages can share. Besides these core elements, which you might want on every page that inherits and uses this template, you can place `<asp:ContentPlaceHolder>` server controls within the master page itself for the subpages (or content pages) to use in order to change specific regions of the master page template. The editing of the subpage is shown in Figure 1-9.

When an end user invokes one of the subpages, he is actually looking at a single page compiled from both the subpage and the master page that the particular subpage inherited from. This also means that the server and client code from both pages are enabled on the new single page.

The nice thing about master pages is that you now have a single place to make any changes that affect the entire site. This eliminates making changes to each and every page within an application.

Themes

The introduction of themes in ASP.NET 2.0 has made it quite simple to provide a consistent look and feel across your entire site. Themes are simple text files where you define the appearance of server controls that can be applied across the site, to a single page, or to a specific server control. You can also easily incorporate graphics and Cascading Style Sheets, in addition to server control definitions.

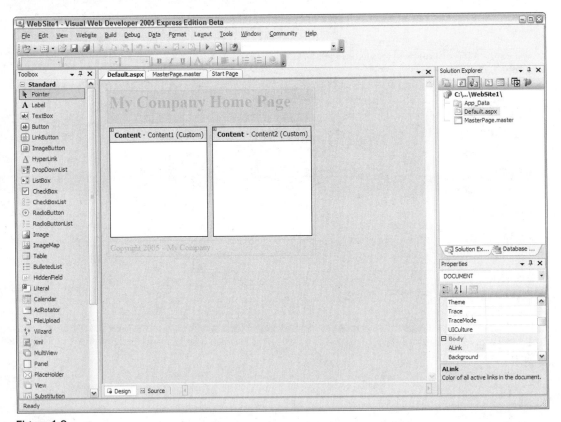

Figure 1-9

Themes are stored in the /App_Theme directory within the application root for use within that particular application. One cool capability of themes is that you can dynamically apply them based on settings that use the new personalization service provided by ASP.NET 2.0. Each unique user of your portal or application can have her own personalized look and feel that she has chosen from your offerings.

New Objects for Accessing Data

One of the more code-intensive tasks in ASP.NET 1.0 was the retrieval of data. In many cases, this meant working with a number of objects. If you have been working with ASP.NET for a while, you know that it was an involved process to display data from a Microsoft SQL Server table within a DataGrid server control. For instance, you first had to create a number of new objects. They included a SqlConnection object followed by a SqlCommand object. When those objects were in place, you then created a SqlDataReader to populate your DataGrid by binding the result to the DataGrid. In the end, a table appeared containing the contents of the data you were retrieving (such as the Customers table from the Northwind database).

ASP.NET 2.0 eliminates this intensive procedure with the introduction of a new set of objects that work specifically with data access and retrieval. These new data controls are so easy to use that you access and retrieve data to populate your ASP.NET server controls without writing any code. You saw an example of this in Listing 1-2, where an <asp:SqlDataSource> server control retrieved rows of data from the Customers table in the Northwind database from SQL Server. This SqlDataSource server control was then bound to the new GridView server control via the use of simple attributes within the GridView control itself. It really couldn't be any easier!

The great news about this new functionality is that it is not limited to just Microsoft's SQL Server. In fact, several data source server controls are at your disposal. You also have the capability to create your own. In addition to the SqlDataSource server control, ASP.NET 2.0 introduces the AccessDataSource, XmlDataSource, ObjectDataSource, and SiteMapDataSource server controls. You use all these new data controls later in this book.

New Server Controls

So far, you have seen a number of new server controls that you can use when building your ASP.NET 2.0 pages. For example, the preceding section talked about all the new data source server controls that you can use to access different kinds of data stores. You also saw the use of the new GridView server control, which is an enhanced version of the previous DataGrid control that you used in ASP.NET 1.0.

Besides the controls presented thus far in this chapter, ASP.NET 2.0 provides more than 50 additional new server controls! In fact, so many new server controls have been introduced that the next IDE for building ASP.NET applications, Visual Studio 2005, had to reorganize the Toolbox where all the server controls are stored. They are now separated into categories instead of being displayed in a straight listing as they were in Visual Studio .NET or the ASP.NET Web Matrix. The new Visual Studio 2005 Toolbox is shown in Figure 1-10.

Figure 1-10

A New IDE for Building ASP.NET 2.0 Pages

With ASP.NET 1.0/1.1, you can build your ASP.NET application using Notepad, Visual Studio .NET 2002 and 2003, as well as the hobbyist-focused ASP.NET Web Matrix. ASP.NET 2.0 comes with another IDE to the Visual Studio family — Visual Studio 2005.

Visual Studio 2005 offers some dramatic enhancements that completely change the way in which you build your ASP.NET applications. Figure 1-11 shows you a screen shot of the new Visual Studio 2005.

The most exciting change to the IDE is that Visual Studio 2005 builds applications using a file-based system, not the project-based system used by Visual Studio .NET. When using Visual Studio .NET, you had to create new projects (for example, an ASP.NET Web Application project). This process created a number of project files in your application. Because everything was based on a singular project, it became very difficult to develop applications in a team environment.

Web projects in Visual Studio 2005, on the other hand, are based on a file system approach. No project files are included in your project, and this makes it very easy for multiple developers to work on a single application together without bumping into each other. Other changes are those to the compilation system discussed earlier. You can now build your ASP.NET pages using the inline model or the new code-behind model. Whether you build pages inline or with the new code-behind model, you have full IntelliSense capabilities. This, in itself, is powerful and innovative. Figure 1-12 shows IntelliSense running from an ASP.NET page that is being built using the inline model.

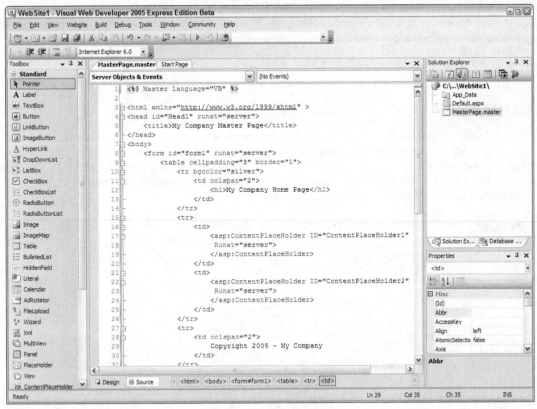

Figure 1-11

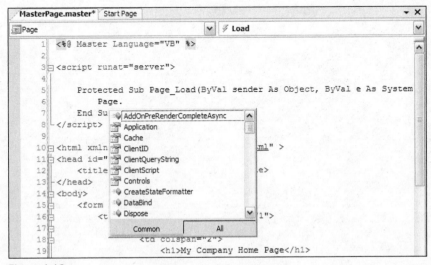

Figure 1-12

Another feature of Visual Studio 2005 that has come over from the ASP.NET Web Matrix is that you don't need IIS on your development machine. Visual Studio 2005 has a built-in Web server that enables you to launch pages from any folder in your system with relative ease. Chapter 2 discusses the new Visual Studio 2005 in detail.

Summary

This whirlwind tour briefly introduced some of the new features in ASP.NET 2.0. This release offers so much that we can't come close to covering it all in this chapter. The new ways of working with data and presentation and the new infrastructure provide effective means to create powerful and secure applications. But this book also gets down and dirty in the underlying architecture and features that have been included in ASP.NET since it was initially released.

ASP.NET 2.0 is so powerful and has so much capability built in that its tremendous benefits to productivity really shine through. Pull up your keyboard and have some fun as you take the journey through this book and this powerful technology.

2

Visual Studio 2005

When you use ASP.NET 2.0, I recommend you also work with Visual Studio 2005 — the latest IDE from Microsoft — to facilitate building .NET components and applications. Visual Studio 2005, building on Visual Studio .NET 2003, provides one of the best development environments for coding your ASP.NET applications.

When learning a new programming language or technology, you spend a lot of time learning the details of the language, as well as how it is structured and used. You must also learn about the environment in which you will code this new language or technology. Understanding the environment is just as important as understanding the programming language itself.

In the past, it seemed that Microsoft had just as many development environments as it had languages or technologies. For example, before the introduction of Visual Studio .NET 2002, Web development required one environment, Visual Basic development another, and C++ development yet another. You had to choose the appropriate development environment for the specific type of programming you were trying to accomplish. With the release of the new Visual Studio Integrated Development Environments (IDEs), you can now build all the possible .NET classes, components, and applications from a single environment — Visual Studio!

Visual Studio 2005 enables you to build any type of .NET component or application. When you use this tool, you can choose any of the Microsoft .NET–compliant languages for building your applications; plus it allows you to create Windows Forms, XML Web services, .NET components, mobile applications, ASP.NET applications, and more. Included in this version are a large number of new wizards and smart tags that simplify the development process for you.

When you pull up Visual Studio 2005 for the first time on your computer, you select the environment in which you wish the IDE to open. This chapter assumes you have selected Web Developer Settings because that environment is the focus of this book.

The next section provides a quick tour of the new Visual Studio 2005 IDE.

The Start Page

The Start Page is the first page you see when you pull up Visual Studio 2005 for the first time. This page guides you as you start projects, as well as search for help or resources.

The Start Page is shown in Figure 2-1.

From this figure, you can see that the latest projects you have worked on are presented in the Recent Projects box. From this box on the Start Page, you can also create a new project or open a project that is not listed. The MSDN: Visual Studio 2005 box shows some of the latest articles available on the public MSDN Web site. The Getting Started box allows you to create new projects from existing code, create new Web sites, import or export Visual Studio settings, or pull up the MSDN help application.

If you close the Start Page from the document window, you can reactivate the Start Page by selecting View ⇨ Start Page from the Visual Studio menu.

The Document Window

The document window is where you create your ASP.NET pages. This section of the IDE enables you to create ASP.NET pages either by dragging and dropping elements onto a design surface or by directly coding them yourself.

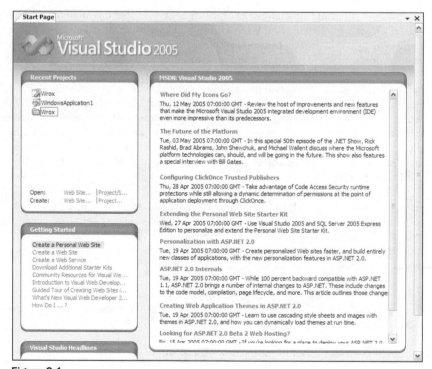

Figure 2-1

Views in the Document Window

Visual Studio .NET 2002 and 2003 both had a Design view and an HTML view of the ASP.NET page. Visual Studio 2005 offers two views of a page: Design and Source. Figure 2-2 shows the document window in Visual Studio 2005.

The document window contains two tabs at the bottom that enable you to switch the view of your page: Design and Source. The Design tab enables you to view your ASP.NET page as it would appear in the browser. You use Design view to create your ASP.NET page visually in a WYSIWYG fashion. Dragging and dropping controls onto the design surface causes Visual Studio to generate code in the page. This is not very different from older versions of Visual Studio. The Source tab shows the complete source of the file and is the default view used by Visual Studio 2005.

By using the Options dialog, you can change the default view Visual Studio uses when a page is opened for the first time. Choose Tools ⇨ Options and navigate to the HTML Designer section. If you highlight this node, you see the option to open pages in either the Design or Source view. Select the view you want and click OK.

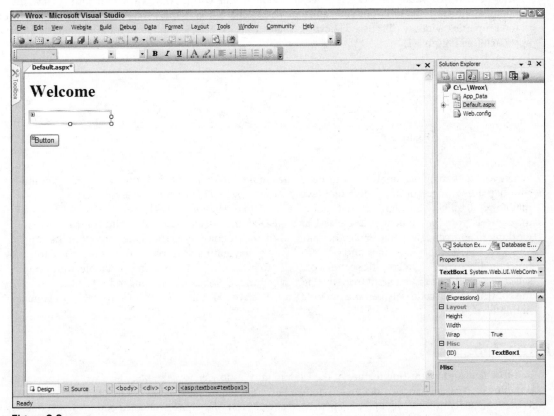

Figure 2-2

23

If you don't see the HTML Designer section in the list of options, be sure to check the Show all settings checkbox in the dialog. By default, this checkbox is unchecked.

Although the document Window is basically the same as in earlier versions of Visual Studio, this section of the IDE does have some new functionality that I describe in the following sections.

The Tag Navigator

When you're working visually with an ASP.NET page, notice that a list of the elements appears on your page at the bottom of the document window. This list of elements is called the *tag navigator* and is illustrated in Figure 2-3.

Figure 2-3

Instead of requiring you to select the element from the design surface or from within Source view, the tag navigator enables you to right-click an element to select it and display the properties for that control in the Properties window (discussed shortly). You can also select the content of the element by using this approach (see Figure 2-4).

Figure 2-4

When you have many elements on your page, the tag navigator is quite helpful. To use its capabilities, simply place your cursor in the document window and use the arrow buttons associated with the display to scroll quickly through elements to find what you are looking for. The tag navigator shows all the controls from the element you selected, as well as all the selected control's child controls. When working in Source view, you can use the same mechanics to jump quickly to the content of the control. This new functionality is a quick and powerful way of navigating your page. You can also use this new functionality to highlight specific sections of code. To highlight everything inside a table, for example, select the `<asp:Table>` element from the tag navigator, right-click the option, and select the content of the control. All the code between the opening `<asp:Table>` and the closing `</asp:Table>` elements is highlighted.

Page Tabs

Another new and interesting feature of the Document Window is how the page tabs work. Whenever you have a page open in the document window, a tab for that page appears at the top of the window. When you have multiple documents open, this tabbed view of the pages enables you to switch quickly from one page to another simply by clicking the tab of the page you want to view. Although page tabs are not new to the IDE, the functionality these tabs provide is certainly new. The following paragraphs explain this new functionality.

Right-clicking the page tab gives you the new options illustrated in Figure 2-5.

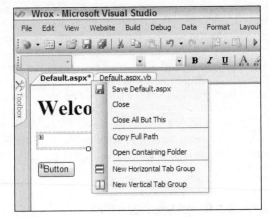

Figure 2-5

By right-clicking the page tab, you can save the file, close the file, close every open document but the one selected, display the full path of the file (such as `C:\Documents and Settings\Billy\My Documents\Visual Studio 2005\WebSites\Wrox\Default.aspx`), and open the containing folder in Windows Explorer (shown in Figure 2-6).

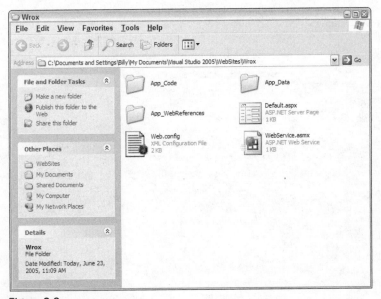

Figure 2-6

Code Change Status Notifications

Some other changes to the document window include a new code-change notification system. When you work with code on your pages, notice that line numbers are now included by default. Clicking any number highlights that line of code. Next to the line numbers is a changing color bar, illustrated in Figure 2-7.

This color bar notifies you of code changes that have occurred on your ASP.NET pages. If no color bar appears on a particular line of code, you have not yet made any changes to that particular line. After you make a change to a particular line of code, a yellow bar appears at the head of that line. After the file is saved, this line changes to green. Yellow code lines indicate that changes have been made but not yet saved to the file. Although you can't see the yellow bar next to lines 13, 14, and 15 in the black-and-white screen shot shown in Figure 2-7, you may be able to see the shading difference. The color difference (when compared to the bar's color next to the rest of the lines of code) indicates that these lines have recently been changed.

Error Notifications and Assistance

In previous versions of Visual Studio, design-time error checking was a great feature of the IDE. As you typed code, Visual Studio checked the code for errors. For instance, if you wrote an If Then statement (in Visual Basic) that didn't include an End If statement, the IDE underlined the If Then statement to remind you that the block of code was not complete. The line disappeared after you corrected the error. With Visual Studio 2005, if you make any design-time errors, a small square appears to the right of the underline (as shown in Figure 2-8).

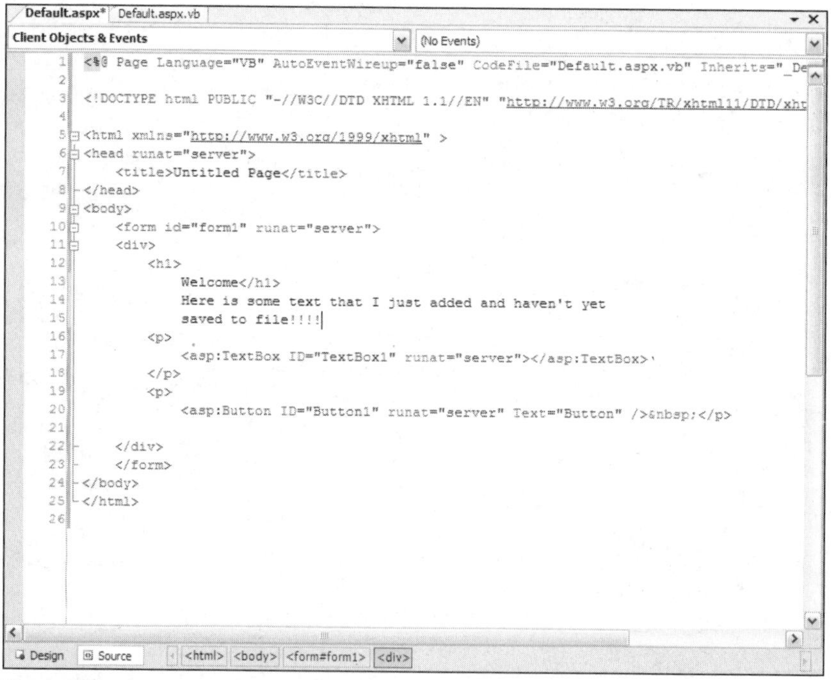

Figure 2-7

```
Sub Button1_Click(ByVal sender
    Dim x As Integer = 3

    If x = 3 Then
End Sub
```

Figure 2-8

Hovering your cursor over the square causes an error sign to appear. Clicking the error sign opens a dialog that gives you options for fixing the error. For example, if you are using an `If Then` statement without the closing `End If` statement in Visual Basic, clicking the Error Notification button provides you with a fix from the IDE, as shown in Figure 2-9.

This pop-up dialog first states the issue. In this case, it says that any opening `If` statement must include a closing `End If` statement. Below this error notification is a link that enables you to apply the fix. Below the link is a code sample showing how the fix will affect your code.

Sometimes, more than one option exists for fixing a design-time error. For example, you might have the following code in your ASP.NET page:

```
Dim x As Integr
```

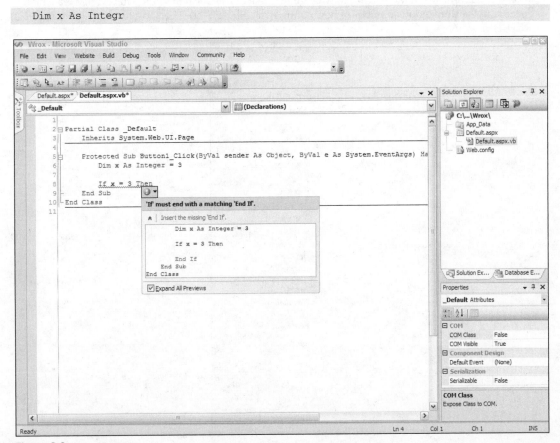

Figure 2-9

In this case, `Integr` is spelled incorrectly; the correct spelling, of course, is `Integer`. The IDE notifies you of this error and opens up the associated error dialog. You have three options for fixing the error (shown in Figure 2-10). To fix it, you simply scroll to the appropriate fix option and click that link.

Figure 2-10

The Toolbox

One of the first changes you notice when you open this latest release of Visual Studio is a change in the Toolbox. The controls in the IDE are now presented in a hierarchical manner. This change was made because of the tremendous number of new controls in ASP.NET 2.0. The Toolbox is shown in Figure 2-11.

Figure 2-11

Because of the number of new controls (somewhere around 50), they have been organized into sections in the Toolbox. The following table shows what all is included in the new control sections.

Control Section	Controls Included in the Section
General	There is nothing in this section, although you are free to use this section for your own custom developed controls. (You can also create a completely new control section if you choose.)
HTML	Includes the HTML server controls that have been a part of ASP.NET since the beginning. The names of these controls, however, have changed.
WebParts	Includes all the controls that deal with the new personalization features provided by ASP.NET 2.0, including all the WebPart controls such as WebPartManager and WebPartZone.
Login	Contains all controls that deal with adding user login and password capabilities to your ASP.NET applications, such as Login, LoginView, and LoginStatus.
Navigation	Includes controls that enable end users to work through a collection of ASP.NET pages, including SiteMapPath, Menu, and TreeView.
Validation	Includes all the validation controls that have always been a part of ASP.NET, such as RequiredFieldValidator and RegularExpressionValidator.
Data	Includes all the controls that deal with the retrieval and display of data that comes from a data store of some kind. Therefore, this section includes all the data source controls (SqlDataSource, AccessDataSource, and more), as well as the data display controls, such as GridView and DetailsView.
Standard	Contains the standard `<asp:>` controls, such as TextBox, Button, and other core controls.

One feature that has always been present in Visual Studio, but makes more sense now that so many new controls have been added, enables you to turn off the List View of the controls. Doing this causes the Toolbox to show the controls simply as icons (see Figure 2-12).

Right-click in the section of the Toolbox you want to change and deselect List View. This changes the view for only those controls in the section where you right-clicked. Each section in the Toolbox maintains its own settings.

Also by right-clicking on the Toolbox, you can select the Show All option. This shows all the possible categories available through the Visual Studio IDE. It is usually not the best option to enable when working with ASP.NET projects because most of the object categories have nothing to do with ASP.NET and, therefore, are not controls you would use in your projects.

Figure 2-12

The Solution Explorer

The Solution Explorer is still located where it was in previous versions of Visual Studio. The Solution Explorer, shown in Figure 2-13, provides you with an organized view of the projects in your application.

Figure 2-13

The toolbar at the top of the Solution Explorer still enables you to do many of the same tasks that you could perform in previous versions of Visual Studio, but this latest release of Visual Studio has some additional buttons on the toolbar. Figure 2-14 shows you the toolbar with a description of the items it contains.

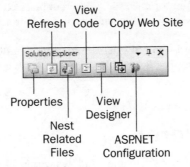

Figure 2-14

The Un-nest/Nest Related Files button is a new feature in the Solution Explorer that enables you to undo the nesting found in ASP.NET pages developed using code-behind files. By default, when working with code-behind files, you can click the plus sign next to the .aspx page to expose the code-behind file (.aspx.vb or .aspx.cs). Un-nesting these files puts them all on the same hierarchical level. Once un-nested, you can then re-nest these files by clicking the same button.

Another new button in the Solution Explorer is the Copy Web Site button. This opens up a new dialog in the document window that enables you to copy your application from one point to another. This dialog is shown in Figure 2-15.

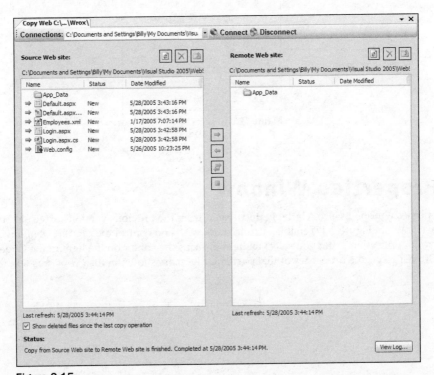

Figure 2-15

Using this dialog, you can copy your projects to a different place on the same server or to an entirely different server. You can now enjoy easy file movements and synchronization between two projects.

A final new button in the toolbar is the ASP.NET Configuration button that pulls up the ASP.NET configuration page for your selected application within the document window. This configuration system is discussed in detail in Chapter 27.

The Server Explorer

The Server Explorer is one of the more valuable windows within Visual Studio. This window can now be found on a separate tab next to the Solution Explorer. The Server Explorer (shown in Figure 2-16) enables you to perform a number of functions such as working with database connectivity, monitoring performance, and interacting with event logs.

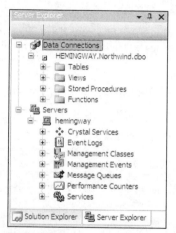

Figure 2-16

The Properties Window

The Properties window is also relatively unchanged from the previous versions of Visual Studio. This window (shown in Figure 2-17) enables you to work with and control the properties of any item that is part of your application. After you select an item or focus the cursor on the item in the Code view of your ASP.NET page, the properties of that particular item are shown in the Properties window.

Figure 2-17

Lost Windows

In the Visual Studio 2005 release, you may not be able to find some familiar windows that were up front in previous versions of Visual Studio. For example, when you open one of your ASP.NET applications in Visual Studio 2005, you do not see the Class View and Dynamic Help windows. Although they are not visible in the default view when the IDE first opens, these windows are still available for use with your applications.

You can find the Class View by choosing View ➪ Other Windows ➪ Class View from the Visual Studio menu. The Class View window opens directly next to the Server Explorer. You can move the window wherever you want within the IDE.

You can find the Dynamic Help window by choosing Help ➪ Dynamic Help. Selecting this option opens the Dynamic Help window next to the Properties window.

Other Common Visual Studio Activities

Visual Studio 2005 is so packed with functionality that it deserves a book of its own. This IDE is mammoth and enables you to do almost anything in the construction and management of your ASP.NET applications. This section takes a look at some of the common tasks that are done somewhat differently or in an altogether new manner in this latest release of Visual Studio.

Creating New Projects

The process of creating new files and projects within Visual Studio 2005 is different from the process using Visual Studio 2002 or 2003. In this latest release of Visual Studio, the focus on project-based applications is gone. Now projects are created in a page-based manner. This means that when you create an ASP.NET application in Visual Studio, you don't find solution or project files. In fact, when you first create the application, the only items created for you by the IDE are the project folder and a single `.aspx` file. If you are creating an ASP.NET page using the code-behind model, you also have an `.aspx.vb` or `.aspx.cs` file.

Visual Studio allows you to create either a new single `.aspx` page or a Web site. To create a single page, simply go to the menu and choose File ⇨ New File. To work on a previous file, choose File ⇨ Open File. To create a new ASP.NET application, choose File ⇨ New Web Site. You can see the dialog of options in Figure 2-18.

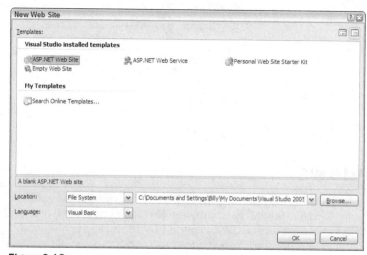

Figure 2-18

In most cases, you select the first option — ASP.NET Web Site. This creates a single folder for your application and a default `.aspx` page.

Making References to Other Objects

When you look at the Solution Explorer of your ASP.NET application, notice that the References and Web References folders are not present. How do you add these references to your file-based applications?

You can add them in a couple of ways, and both ways bring you to the same dialog within the IDE. The first way to add a reference to your application is to highlight the project in the Solution Explorer and then choose Web Site ⇨ Add Reference or Add Web Reference from the Visual Studio menu.

The second option is to right-click the project name in the Solution Explorer and select Property Pages from the list of options (the last option in the menu). This brings up the Property Pages dialog shown in Figure 2-19.

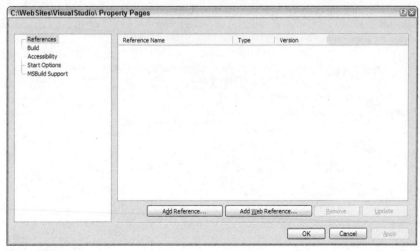

Figure 2-19

The Property Pages dialog allows you to make many modifications to your ASP.NET applications. For now, however, focus only on the first item within the dialog — the References tab. When you have the References item highlighted, two enabled buttons appear in the right-hand portion of the dialog — Add Reference and Add Web Reference.

The Add Reference button invokes the Add Reference dialog so that you can make a reference to a DLL to use in your project. Again in this version of Visual Studio, the objects are divided into categories such as .NET, COM, and others, as shown in Figure 2-20.

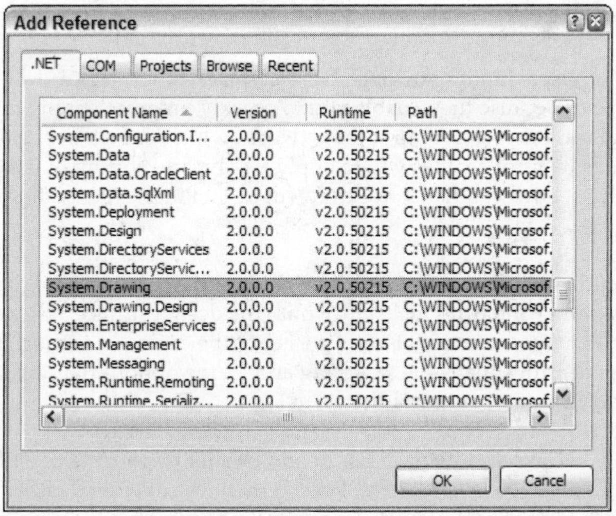

Figure 2-20

The Add Web References button invokes the Add Web Reference dialog (shown in Figure 2-21). Here you can make references to other Web services or .wsdl files found either in the same solution, on the same server, or on some remote server.

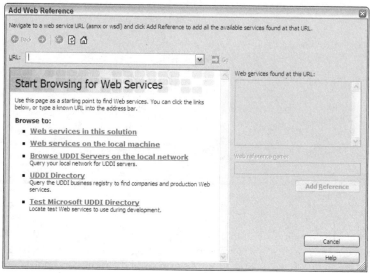

Figure 2-21

Be aware that these buttons have been added because no References or Web References folder appears in the Solution Explorer, which shows the referenced objects.

Using Smart Tags

The visual designer of Visual Studio now includes *smart tags*. Smart tags are a great enhancement to the development experience because they enable you to quickly program common tasks. Each smart tag is different and depends on the server control that it works with. For instance, the smart tag that appears for the GridView server control enables you to apply paging and sorting of the data that the GridView displays. Other controls, however, may have different capabilities exposed through their respective smart tags.

Not every server control has a smart tag associated with it. If a server control has this extra capability, you notice it after you drag and drop the control onto the design surface. After it is on the design surface, an arrow appears in the upper-right-hand corner of the control if a smart tag exists for that particular control. Clicking the arrow opens the smart tag and all the options that the smart tag contains. This is illustrated in the GridView server control shown in Figure 2-22.

From the smart tag, you can select items either to add or alter by clicking one of the available links or by checking one of the available check boxes. When you have completed either of these actions, Visual Studio changes the code in the background—adding the capabilities that you want. You can also see the additions and modifications to the IDE if you change your view to the Code view of the page.

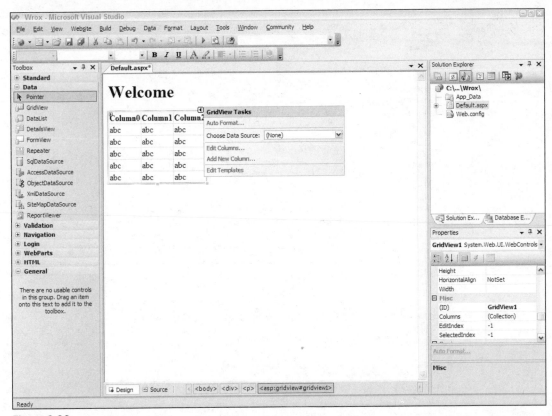

Figure 2-22

Saving and Importing Visual Studio Settings

Visual Studio 2005 allows for a tremendous number of customizations and modifications to the development environment and the development experience. You can do a lot to change Visual Studio either by dragging elements and components to new locations within the IDE, or by choosing Tools ➪ Options in the Visual Studio menu bar to bring up the Options dialog shown in Figure 2-23.

The number of options you can work with from this dialog are staggering and impossible to cover completely in this chapter. In fact, at first you won't see this extensive list of options; the list you see will be rather limited. To see the extensive list presented in Figure 2-23, you must check the Show All Settings check box found in the lower left-hand corner of the dialog. You will find that this Options dialog has many of the same options you worked with in the past, plus some new ones.

After you have Visual Studio set up as you want, you should save these settings so that they can be used again if you rebuild your computer, if you are working with an another instance of Visual Studio elsewhere, or if you want to share your settings with others. To save your settings, choose Tools ➪ Import and Export Settings in the IDE. This pulls up the Import/Export Settings Wizard shown in Figure 2-24.

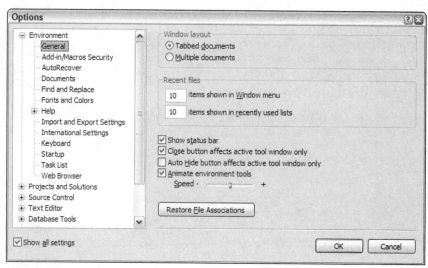

Figure 2-23

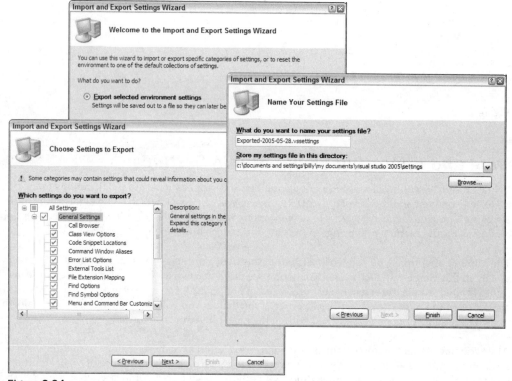

Figure 2-24

From this wizard, you can either save your settings to a file that can be used elsewhere or you can import settings that are stored in the same type of file. You can also just reset Visual Studio to return the settings to the default that existed when Visual Studio was first installed and run.

If you are going to export your settings, select Export Selected Environment Settings. This shows a list of exportable settings in the left-hand pane of the dialog. By default, almost everything is selected. Feel free to uncheck the settings you don't want to export. When this is set up the way you want it, choose the name of the file and the location where you want to save the file. The file has a `.vssettings` extension. If you go back and look at the file, notice that Visual Studio saves the settings as an XML file.

Importing the settings is simply the process of making reference through the Import and Export Settings Wizard to a file of the same type.

Validating Your HTML

When coding your pages in Visual Studio, this IDE provides you with design-time errors it sees in the code you construct. One thing being checked is the structure you apply to the HTML code in your pages. By default, Visual Studio 2005 checks your ASP.NET pages to make sure they are compliant so that they work with Microsoft's Internet Explorer 6.0.

Visual Studio enables you to change this behavior through the use of a drop-down list of available schemas. This drop-down list, found at the top of the document window, is shown in Figure 2-25.

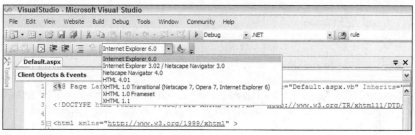

Figure 2-25

The available list of schemas includes the following:

❑   Internet Explorer 6.0

❑   Internet Explorer 3.02/Netscape Navigator 3.0

❑   Netscape Navigator 4.0

❑   HTML 4.01

❑   XHTML 1.0 Transitional (Netscape 7, Opera 7, Internet Explorer 6)

❑   XHTML 1.0 Frameset

❑   XHTML 1.1 Strict

From this, you get different errors for your HTML depending on the schema you are trying to adhere to when developing. For instance, you may be trying to adhere to the XHTML 1.1 schema using a break tag, as shown here:

```
<br>
```

You see a red squiggly line underneath this bit of HTML and an error notification placed in the Error List, which specifies that you should construct the break tag as <br />.

In addition to these specified schemas, by using Visual Studio you can also make sure you follow specific accessibility standards for how the HTML is structured. This is meant for Web surfers with disabilities when it comes to browsing content online. These end users might not be able to see, hear, or move. Therefore, they have special programs on their computers to help them browse Internet content. It is easier to accomplish this, however, if these programs work with pages that follow certain schematic rules.

You can validate your HTML pages using WCAG Priority 1, WCAG Priority 2, or the Access Board Section 508 schemas. You can get to this validation process by clicking the Check Page For Accessibility button in the Visual Studio menu (see Figure 2-26) or by selecting Website ➪ Check Accessibility in Visual Studio.

Figure 2-26

You can get more information on these schemas at the following locations: WCAG Priority 1 —
http://www.w3.org/TR/WAI-WEBCONTENT/; *WCAG Priority2 —*
http://www.w3.org/TR/WAI-WEBCONTENT/full-checklist.html; *Access Board Section*
508 —http://www.access-board.gov/508.htm.

From Visual Studio, clicking the Check Page For Accessibility button gives you the following dialog where you can check the schemas against which you are validating your page (shown here in Figure 2-27).

Figure 2-27

Check the schemas you are interested in working with and click the Validate button to start the validation process. If there are any errors, you see a list of them in the Error List dialog of Visual Studio. A sample page that I ran through this validation process is presented in Figure 2-28.

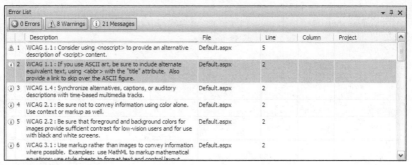

Figure 2-28

Reaching Out to the Community

The Community section adds a new menu bar item in Visual Studio 2005. This section allows you to reach beyond your local computer and your Visual Studio instance to get help and use resources on the Internet. The available options for this menu include the following:

❑ **Ask a Question:** A link to the MSDN Forums

❑ **Send Feedback:** A link to the MSDN Product Feedback Center

❑ **Check Question Status:** A link to the MSDN Forums

❑ **Developer Center:** A link to the Visual Studio 2005 MSDN Developer Center support page

❑ **Codezone Community:** A link to a Microsoft page that describes the Codezone Community

❑ **Community Search:** Perhaps the most useful link from the Community menu. The Community Search section enables you to search for Starter Kits, Item Templates, Code Snippets, Samples, and Controls from your local MSDN, various Microsoft properties, and from the associated member sites.

Working with Snippets

In an effort to help you become a more productive developer, Visual Studio 2005 now includes a rather large collection of code snippets for you to use freely within your code. Snippets are little pieces of code that perform a specific task. Here are some examples of tasks you can perform with snippets:

❑ Generating a random number

❑ Iterating a Hashtable using `For Each`

❑ Encrypting a String

❑ Determining if a folder exists

And the list goes on and on. To get at the list of available snippets, simply place your cursor in the page of code you are working with and right-click directly in the Code view of the page. You are presented with a menu in which you will find the option called Insert Snippet. Selecting this option opens a drop-down list of snippet categories (as shown in Figure 2-29).

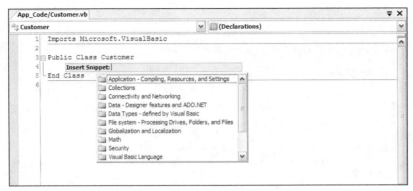

Figure 2-29

To select a snippet, double-click the appropriate folder. Doing this either presents a selection of subfolders, snippets, or both to choose from. You also see the breadcrumb navigation showing where you are in the snippet selection above the drop-down list of items (shown here in Figure 2-30). A single click on one of the linked categories brings you back to this section of the snippets catalog.

Figure 2-30

For an example of using snippets, navigate to and choose Math ⇨ Get a Random Number using the Random class. This produces the following results in your page:

```
Dim generator As New Random
Dim randomValue As Integer
randomValue = generator.Next(10, 100)
```

From here, you can modify this code snippet to get it to perform as you want. In addition to adding code snippets in this manner, all code snippets include a shortcut (found from the ToolTip box when highlighting the snippet). For instance, the previous random number snippet has a shortcut word—mathrand. If you type this word in the IDE and press the Tab key, the snippet appears in your code.

You can also manage the snippets made available to you through Visual Studio. The Visual Studio IDE includes a Code Snippets Manager, which you can find at Tools ⇨ Code Snippets Manager (see Figure 2-31).

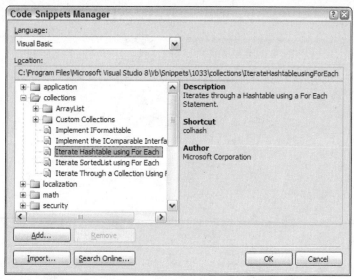

Figure 2-31

From this dialog, you can add or remove snippets used by Visual Studio. Visual Studio includes a My Snippets folder in which you can place your own snippets or snippets you have downloaded from other locations. A snippet is a single `.snippet` file. You can find the `.snippet` files at `C:\Program Files\Microsoft Visual Studio 8\Vb\Snippets\1033`.

From this location, you can add your own categories, but you must be sure you add this new folder to the `SnippetIndex.xml` file found at the same location in order for your folder to be recognized by Visual Studio.

Summary

This chapter took a quick look at the best possible tool for creating ASP.NET 2.0 applications—Visual Studio 2005. This tool is unquestionably packed with functionality and makes you a more productive developer.

Included in this IDE are a number of wizards that make quick work of common programming tasks and allow you to concentrate on getting your applications live as soon as possible. Visual Studio 2005 expands on allowing developers to code to the database, to classes, and to the presentation layer—all from the same IDE.

Illustrated in this chapter were such features as snippets, validations of code, finding answers to problems from the community, and more. This chapter is in no way meant to fully explain this IDE; the intention was to show you some of the newer features you might utilize when building your applications. Delve more deeply into what is shown in the chapter, and you will find new features around every corner.

3

Application and Page Frameworks

If you are new to ASP.NET and building your first set of applications in ASP.NET 2.0, you may be amazed by all the wonderful new server controls it provides. You may marvel at how it enables you to work with data more effectively using the new data providers. You may be impressed at how easily you can build in security and personalization.

The outstanding capabilities of ASP.NET 2.0 don't end there, however. This chapter takes a look at many exciting additions that facilitate working with ASP.NET pages and applications. One of the first steps you, the developer, should take when starting a project is to become familiar with the foundation you are building on and the options available for customizing that foundation.

Application Location Options

With ASP.NET 2.0, you have the option — using Visual Studio 2005 — to create an application with a virtual directory mapped to IIS or a standalone application outside the confines of IIS. Whereas Visual Studio .NET forced developers to use IIS for all Web applications, Visual Studio 2005 (and Visual Web Developer Express Edition, for that matter) includes a built-in Web server that you can use for development, much like the one used in the past with the ASP.NET Web Matrix.

This built-in Web server was previously presented to developers as a code sample called Cassini. In fact, the code for this mini Web server is freely downloadable from the ASP.NET team Web site found at `http://www.asp.net`*.*

The following section shows you how to use this new built-in Web server that comes with ASP.NET 2.0.

Built-In Web Server

By default, Visual Studio 2005 builds applications without the use of IIS. You can see this when you select New Web Site in the IDE. By default, the location provided for your application is in `C:\Documents and Settings\[user]\My Documents\Visual Studio 2005\WebSites` (shown in Figure 3-1). It is not `C:\Inetpub\wwwroot\` as it would have been in Visual Studio .NET 2003/2002. By default, any site that you build and host inside `C:\Documents and Settings\[user]\My Documents\Visual Studio 2005\WebSites` (or any other folder you create) uses the built-in Web server that is part of Visual Studio 2005. If you use the built-in Web server from Visual Studio 2005, you are not locked into the `Websites` folder; you can create any folder you want in your system.

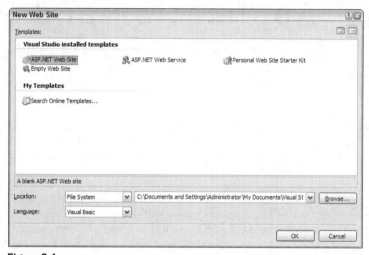

Figure 3-1

To change from this default, you have a handful of options. Click the Browse button in the New Web Site dialog. This brings up the Choose Location dialog, shown in Figure 3-2.

If you continue to use the built-in Web server that Visual Studio 2005 provides, you can choose a new location for your Web application from this dialog. To choose a new location, select a new folder and save your `.aspx` pages and any other associated files to this directory. When using Visual Studio 2005, you can run your application completely from this location. This new way of working with the ASP.NET pages you create is ideal if you don't have access to a Web server because it enables you to build applications that don't reside on a machine with IIS. This means that you can even develop ASP.NET applications on operating systems such as Windows XP Home Edition.

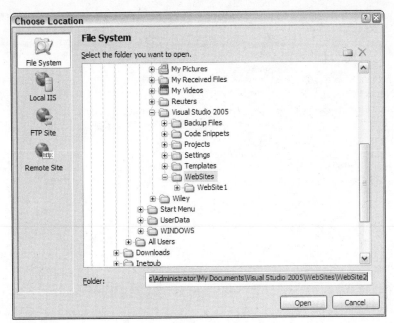

Figure 3-2

IIS

From the Choose Location dialog, you can also change where your application is saved and which type of Web server your application employs. To use IIS (as you probably did when you used Visual Studio .NET 2003/2002), select the Local IIS button in the dialog. This changes the results in the text area to show you a list of all the virtual application roots on your machine.

To create a new virtual root for your application, highlight Default Web Site. Two accessible buttons appear at the top of the dialog (see Figure 3-3). When you look from left to right, the first button in the upper-right corner of the dialog is for creating a new Web application — or a virtual root. This button is shown as a globe inside a box. The second button enables you to create virtual roots for any of the virtual directories you created. The third button is a Delete button, which allows you to delete any selected virtual directories or virtual roots on the server.

After you have created the virtual directory you want, click the Open button. Visual Studio 2005 then goes through the standard process to create your application. Now, however, instead of depending on the built-in Web server from ASP.NET 2.0, your application will use IIS. When you invoke your application, the URL now consists of something like `http://localhost/myweb/default.aspx`, which means it is using IIS.

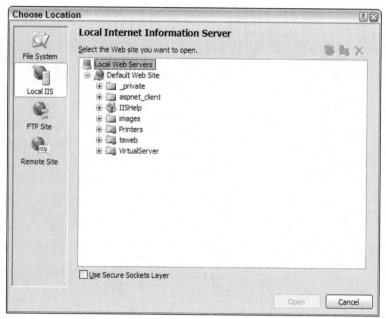

Figure 3-3

FTP

Not only can you decide on the type of Web server for your Web application when you create it using the Choose Location dialog, but you can also decide where your application is going to be located. With the previous options, you built applications that resided on your local server. The FTP option enables you to actually store and even code your applications while they reside on a server somewhere else in your enterprise — or on the other side of the planet. You can also use the FTP capabilities to work on different locations within the same server. Using this new capability provides a wide range of possible options.

The built-in capability giving FTP access to your applications is a major enhancement to the IDE. Although formerly difficult to accomplish, this task is now quite simple, as you can see from Figure 3-4.

To create your application on a remote server using FTP, simply provide the server name, the port to use, and the directory — as well as any required credentials. If the correct information is provided, Visual Studio 2005 reaches out to the remote server and creates the appropriate files for the start of your application, just as if it were doing the job locally. From this point on, you can open your project and connect to the remote server using FTP.

Web Site Requiring FrontPage Extensions

The last option in the Choose Location dialog is the Remote Sites option. Clicking this button provides a dialog that enables you to connect to a remote or local server that utilizes FrontPage Extensions. This option is displayed in Figure 3-5.

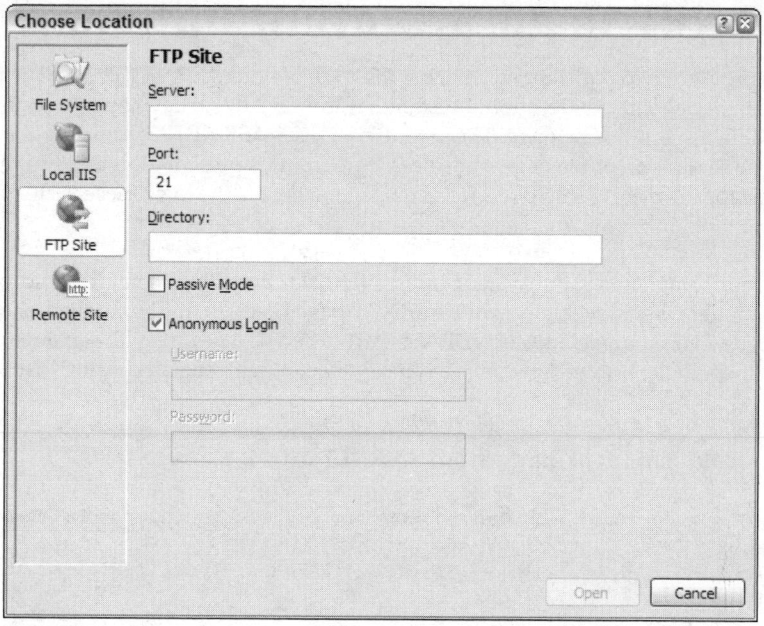

Figure 3-4

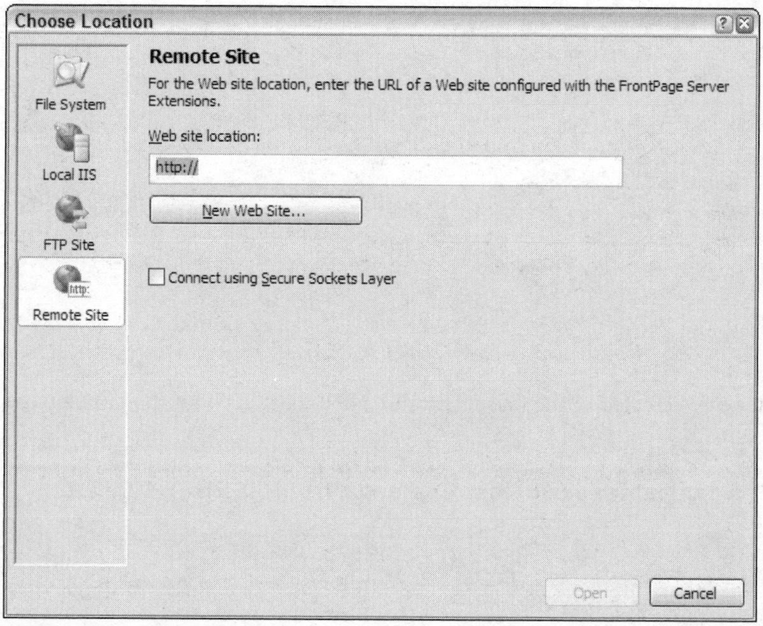

Figure 3-5

The ASP.NET Page Structure Options

ASP.NET 2.0 provides two paths for structuring the code of your ASP.NET pages. The first path utilizes the code-inline model. This model should be familiar to ASP 2.0/3.0 developers because all the code is contained within a single .aspx page. The second path uses ASP.NET's code-behind model, which allows for code separation of the page's business logic from its presentation logic. In this model, the presentation logic for the page is stored in an .aspx page, whereas the logic piece is stored in a separate class file: .aspx.vb or .aspx.cs.

One of the major complaints about Visual Studio .NET 2002 and 2003 is that it forced you to use the code-behind model when developing your ASP.NET pages because it did not understand the code-inline model. The code-behind model in ASP.NET was introduced as a new way to separate the presentation code and business logic. Listing 3-1 shows a typical .aspx page generated using Visual Studio .NET 2002 or 2003.

Listing 3-1: A typical .aspx page from ASP.NET 1.0/1.1

```
<%@ Page Language="vb" AutoEventWireup="false" Codebehind="WebForm1.aspx.vb"
    Inherits="WebApplication.WebForm1"%>
<!DOCTYPE HTML PUBLIC "-//W3C//DTD HTML 4.0 Transitional//EN">
<HTML>
  <HEAD>
    <title>WebForm1</title>
    <meta name="GENERATOR" content="Microsoft Visual Studio .NET 7.1">
    <meta name="CODE_LANGUAGE" content="Visual Basic .NET 7.1">
    <meta name="vs_defaultClientScript" content="JavaScript">
    <meta name="vs_targetSchema"
      content="http://schemas.microsoft.com/intellisense/ie5">
  </HEAD>
<body>
    <form id="Form1" method="post" runat="server">
      <P>What is your name?<br>
      <asp:TextBox id="TextBox1" runat="server"></asp:TextBox><BR>
      <asp:Button id="Button1" runat="server" Text="Submit"></asp:Button></P>
      <P><asp:Label id="Label1" runat="server"></asp:Label></P>
    </form>
  </body>
</HTML>
```

The code-behind file created within Visual Studio .NET 2002/2003 for the .aspx page is shown in Listing 3-2.

Listing 3-2: A typical .aspx.vb/.aspx.cs page from ASP.NET 1.0/1.1

```
Public Class WebForm1
    Inherits System.Web.UI.Page

#Region " Web Form Designer Generated Code "

    'This call is required by the Web Form Designer.
    <System.Diagnostics.DebuggerStepThrough()> Private Sub InitializeComponent()

    End Sub
```

```
    Protected WithEvents TextBox1 As System.Web.UI.WebControls.TextBox
    Protected WithEvents Button1 As System.Web.UI.WebControls.Button
    Protected WithEvents Label1 As System.Web.UI.WebControls.Label

    'NOTE: The following placeholder declaration is required by the Web Form
        Designer.
    'Do not delete or move it.
    Private designerPlaceholderDeclaration As System.Object

    Private Sub Page_Init(ByVal sender As System.Object, ByVal e As
        System.EventArgs) Handles MyBase.Init
            'CODEGEN: This method call is required by the Web Form Designer
            'Do not modify it using the code editor.
            InitializeComponent()
    End Sub

#End Region

    Private Sub Page_Load(ByVal sender As System.Object, ByVal e As
        System.EventArgs) Handles MyBase.Load
            'Put user code to initialize the page here
    End Sub

    Private Sub Button1_Click(ByVal sender As System.Object, ByVal e As
        System.EventArgs) Handles Button1.Click
            Label1.Text = "Hello " & TextBox1.Text
    End Sub
End Class
```

In this code-behind page from ASP.NET 1.0/1.1, you can see that a lot of the code that developers never have to deal with is hidden in the #Region section of the page. Because ASP.NET 2.0 is built on top of .NET 2.0, it can now take advantage of the new .NET Framework capability of partial classes. Partial classes enable you to separate your classes into multiple class files, which are then combined into a single class when the application is compiled. Because ASP.NET 2.0 combines all this page code for you behind the scenes when the application is compiled, the code-behind files you work with in ASP.NET 2.0 are simpler in appearance and the model is easier to use. You are presented with only the pieces of the class that you need. Next, we will take a look at both the inline and code-behind models from ASP.NET 2.0.

Inline Coding

With the .NET Framework 1.0/1.1, developers went out of their way (and outside Visual Studio .NET) to build their ASP.NET pages inline and avoid the code-behind model that was so heavily promoted by Microsoft and others. Visual Studio 2005 (as well as Visual Web Developer 2005 Express Edition) allows you to build your pages easily using this coding style. To build an ASP.NET page inline instead of using the code-behind model, you simply select the page type from the Add New Item dialog and make sure that the Place Code in Separate File check box is unchecked. You can get at this dialog by right-clicking the project or the solution in the Solution Explorer and selecting Add New Item (see Figure 3-6).

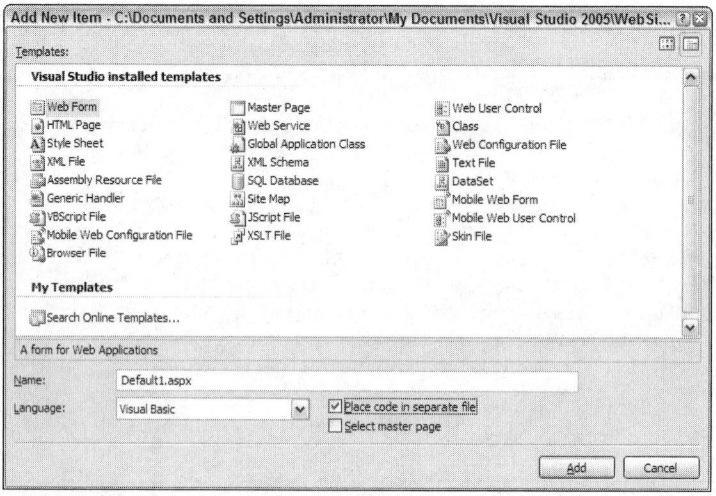

Figure 3-6

From here, you can see the check box you need to unselect if you want to build your ASP.NET pages inline. In fact, many page types have options for both inline and code-behind styles. The following table shows your inline options when selecting files from this dialog.

File Options Using Inline Coding	File Created
Web Form	.aspx file
Master Page	.master file
Web User Control	.ascx file
Web Service	.asmx file

By using the Web Form option with a few controls, you get a page that encapsulates not only the presentation logic, but the business logic as well. This is illustrated in Listing 3-3.

Listing 3-3: A simple page that uses the inline coding model

VB

```
<%@ Page Language="VB" %>

<!DOCTYPE html PUBLIC "-//W3C//DTD XHTML 1.1//EN"
 "http://www.w3.org/TR/xhtml11/DTD/xhtml11.dtd">

<script runat="server">
    Protected Sub Button1_Click(ByVal sender As Object, _
        ByVal e As System.EventArgs)

        Label1.Text = "Hello " & Textbox1.Text
    End Sub
```

```
</script>

<html xmlns="http://www.w3.org/1999/xhtml" >
<head runat="server">
    <title>Simple Page</title>
</head>
<body>
    <form runat="server">
        What is your name?<br />
        <asp:Textbox ID="Textbox1" Runat="server"></asp:Textbox><br />
        <asp:Button ID="Button1" Runat="server" Text="Submit"
         OnClick="Button1_Click" />
        <p><asp:Label ID="Label1" Runat="server"></asp:Label></p>
    </form>
</body>
</html>
```

C#

```
<%@ Page Language="C#" %>

<!DOCTYPE html PUBLIC "-//W3C//DTD XHTML 1.1//EN"
 "http://www.w3.org/TR/xhtml11/DTD/xhtml11.dtd">

<script runat="server">
    protected void Button1_Click(object sender, System.EventArgs e)
    {
        Label1.Text = "Hello " + Textbox1.Text;
    }
</script>
```

From this example, you can see that all the business logic is encapsulated in between <script> tags. The nice feature of the inline model is that the business logic and the presentation logic are contained within the same file. Some developers find that having everything in a single viewable instance makes working with the ASP.NET page easier. Another great thing is that Visual Studio 2005 now provides IntelliSense when working with the inline coding model and ASP.NET 2.0. In the past, this capability didn't exist. Visual Studio forced you to use the code-behind model and, even if you rigged it so your pages were using the inline model, you lost all IntelliSense capabilities.

New Code-Behind Model

The other option for constructing your ASP.NET 2.0 pages is to build your files using the new code-behind model. We say *new* because, even though the idea of the code-behind model is the same as it was in previous versions of ASP.NET, the way in which the code-behind model is used in ASP.NET 2.0 is quite a bit different.

To create a new page in your ASP.NET solution that uses the code-behind model, select the page type you want from the New File dialog. To build a page that uses the code-behind model, you first select the page in the Add New Item dialog and make sure the Place Code in Separate File check box is checked. The following table shows you the options for pages that use the code-behind model.

File Options Using Code-Behind	File Created
Web Form	`.aspx` file `.aspx.vb` or `.aspx.cs` file
Master Page	`.master` file `.master.vb` or `.master.cs` file
Web User Control	`.ascx` file `.ascx.vb` or `.ascx.cs` file
Web Service	`.asmx` file `.vb` or `.cs` file

The idea of using the code-behind model is to separate the business logic and presentation logic into separate files. Doing this makes it easier to work with your pages, especially if you are working in a team environment where visual designers work on the UI of the page and coders work on the business logic that sits behind the presentation pieces. In the earlier Listings 3-1 and 3-2, you saw how pages using the code-behind model in ASP.NET 1.0/1.1 were constructed. To see the difference in ASP.NET 2.0, take a look at how its code-behind pages are constructed. This is illustrated in Listing 3-4 for the presentation piece and Listing 3-5 for the code-behind piece.

Listing 3-4: An .aspx page that uses the ASP.NET 2.0 code-behind model

VB

```
<%@ Page Language="VB" AutoEventWireup="false" CodeFile="Default.aspx.vb"
    Inherits="_Default" %>


<!DOCTYPE html PUBLIC "-//W3C//DTD XHTML 1.1//EN"
 "http://www.w3.org/TR/xhtml11/DTD/xhtml11.dtd">


<html xmlns="http://www.w3.org/1999/xhtml" >
<head runat="server">
    <title>Simple Page</title>
</head>
<body>
    <form runat="server">
        What is your name?<br />
        <asp:Textbox ID="Textbox1" Runat="server"></asp:Textbox><br />
        <asp:Button ID="Button1" Runat="server" Text="Submit"
         OnClick="Button1_Click" />
        <p><asp:Label ID="Label1" Runat="server"></asp:Label></p>
    </form>
</body>
</html>
```

C#

```
<%@ Page Language="C#" CodeFile="Default.aspx.cs" Inherits="_Default" %>
```

Listing 3-5: A code-behind page

VB

```vb
Partial Class _Default
    Inherits System.Web.UI.Page

    Protected Sub Button1_Click(ByVal sender As Object, _
        ByVal e As System.EventArgs) Handles Button1.Click

        Label1.Text = "Hello " & TextBox1.Text
    End Sub
End Class
```

C#

```csharp
using System;
using System.Data;
using System.Configuration;
using System.Collections;
using System.Web;
using System.Web.Security;
using System.Web.UI;
using System.Web.UI.WebControls;
using System.Web.UI.WebControls.WebParts;
using System.Web.UI.HtmlControls;

public partial class _Default : System.Web.UI.Page
{
    protected void Button1_Click(object sender, EventArgs e)
    {
        Label1.Text = "Hello " + Textbox1.Text;
    }
}
```

The `.aspx` page using this new ASP.NET 2.0 code-behind model has some attributes in the `Page` directive different from those you are familiar with from previous versions of ASP.NET. The first is the `CodeFile` attribute. This is a new attribute in the `Page` directive and is meant to point to the code-behind page that is used with this presentation page. In this case, the value assigned is `Default.aspx.vb` or `Default.aspx.cs`. The second attribute needed is the `Inherits` attribute. This attribute was available in previous versions of ASP.NET, but was little used. This attribute specifies the name of the class that is bound to the page when the page is compiled. The directives are simple enough in ASP.NET 2.0. Take another look at the code-behind page from Listing 3-5.

The new code-behind page is rather simple in appearance because of the partial class capabilities that .NET 2.0 provides. You can see that the class created in the code-behind file uses partial classes, employing the new `Partial` keyword in Visual Basic 2005 and the `partial` keyword from C# 2.0. This enables you to simply place the methods that you need in your page class. In this case, you have a button-click event and nothing else.

Later in this chapter, we look at the compilation process for both of these models.

ASP.NET 2.0 Page Directives

ASP.NET directives are something that is a part of every ASP.NET page. You can control the behavior of your ASP.NET pages by using these directives. Here's an example of the `Page` directive:

```
<%@ Page Language="VB" AutoEventWireup="false" CodeFile="Default.aspx.vb"
    Inherits="_Default" %>
```

Eleven directives are at your disposal in your ASP.NET pages or user controls. You use these directives in your applications whether the page uses the code-behind model or the inline coding model.

Basically, these directives are commands that the compiler uses when the page is compiled. Directives are simple to incorporate into your pages. A directive is written in the following format:

```
<%@ [Directive] [Attribute=Value] %>
```

From this, you can see that a directive is opened with a `<%@` and closed with a `%>`. It is best to put these directives at the top of your pages or controls because this is traditionally where developers expect to see them (although the page still compiles if the directives are located at a different place). Of course, you can also add more than a single attribute to your directive statements, as shown in the following:

```
<%@ [Directive] [Attribute=Value] [Attribute=Value] %>
```

The following table describes the directives at your disposal in ASP.NET 2.0.

Directive	Description
Assembly	Links an assembly to the Page or user control for which it is associated.
Control	Page directive meant for use with user controls (.ascx).
Implements	Implements a specified .NET Framework interface.
Import	Imports specified namespaces into the Page or user control.
Master	Enables you to specify master page–specific attributes and values to use when the page parses or compiles. This directive can be used only with master pages (.master).
MasterType	Associates a class name to a Page in order to get at strongly typed references or members contained within the specified master page.
OutputCache	Controls the output caching policies of a Page or user control.
Page	Enables you to specify page specific attributes and values to use when the page parses or compiles. This directive can be used only with ASP.NET pages (.aspx).
PreviousPageType	Enables an ASP.NET page to work with a postback from another page in the application.
Reference	Links a Page or user control to the current Page or user control.
Register	Associates aliases with namespaces and class names for notation in custom server control syntax.

The following sections provide a quick review of each of these directives.

@Page

The `@Page` directive enables you to specify attributes and values for an ASP.NET page (`.aspx`) to be used when the page is parsed or compiled. This is the most frequently used directive of the bunch. Because the ASP.NET page is such an important part of ASP.NET, you have quite a few attributes at your disposal. The following table summarizes the attributes available through the `@Page` directive.

Attribute	Description
AspCompat	Permits the page to be executed on a single-threaded apartment thread when given a value of `True`. The default setting for this attribute is `False`.
Async	Specifies whether the ASP.NET page is processed synchronously or asynchronously.
AutoEventWireUp	Specifies whether the page events are autowired when set to `True`. The default setting for this attribute is `True`.
Buffer	Enables HTTP response buffering when set to `True`. The default setting for this attribute is `True`.
ClassName	Specifies the name of the class that is bound to the page when the page is compiled.
CodeFile	References the code-behind file with which the page is associated.
CodePage	Indicates the code page value for the response.
CompilerOptions	Compiler string that indicates compilation options for the page.
CompileWith	Takes a `String` value that points to the code-behind file used.
ContentType	Defines the HTTP content type of the response as a standard MIME type.
Culture	Specifies the culture setting of the page. ASP.NET 2.0 now includes the capability to give the `Culture` attribute a value of `Auto` to enable automatic detection of the culture required.
Debug	Compiles the page with debug symbols in place when set to `True`.
Description	Provides a text description of the page. The ASP.NET parser ignores this attribute and its assigned value.
EnableSessionState	Session state for the page is enabled when set to `True`. The default setting is `True`.
EnableTheming	Page is enabled to use theming when set to `True`. The default setting for this attribute is `True`.

Table continued on following page

Attribute	Description
EnableViewState	View state is maintained across the page when set to `True`. The default value is `True`.
EnableViewStateMac	Page runs a machine-authentication check on the page's view state when the page is posted back from the user when set to `True`. The default value is `False`.
ErrorPage	Specifies a URL to post to for all unhandled page exceptions.
Explicit	Visual Basic `Explicit` option is enabled when set to `True`. The default setting is `False`.
Language	Defines the language being used for any inline rendering and script blocks.
LCID	Defines the locale identifier for the Web Form's page.
LinePragmas	`Boolean` value that specifies whether line pragmas are used with the resulting assembly.
MasterPageFile	Takes a `String` value that points to the location of the master page used with the page. This attribute is used with content pages.
MaintainScrollPositionOn Postback	Takes a `Boolean` value, which indicates whether the page should be positioned exactly in the same scroll position or if the page should be regenerated in the uppermost position for when the page is posted back to itself.
PersonalizationProvider	Takes a `String` value that specifies the name of the personalization provider used in applying personalization to the page.
ResponseEncoding	Specifies the response encoding of the page content.
SmartNavigation	Specifies whether to activate the ASP.NET Smart Navigation feature for richer browsers. This returns the postback to the current position on the page. The default value is `False`.
Src	Points to the source file of the class used for the code behind of the page being rendered.
Strict	Compiles the page using the Visual Basic `Strict` mode when set to `True`. The default setting is `False`.
Theme	Applies the specified theme to the page using the ASP.NET 2.0 themes feature.
Title	Applies a page's title. This is an attribute mainly meant for content pages that must apply a page title other than what is specified in the master page.
Trace	Page tracing is enabled when set to `True`. The default setting is `False`.

Attribute	Description
TraceMode	Specifies how the trace messages are displayed when tracing is enabled. The settings for this attribute include SortByTime or SortByCategory. The default setting is SortByTime.
Transaction	Specifies whether transactions are supported on the page. The settings for this attribute are Disabled, NotSupported, Supported, Required, and RequiresNew. The default setting is Disabled.
UICulture	The value of the UICulture attribute specifies what UI Culture to use for the ASP.NET page. ASP.NET 2.0 now includes the capability to give the UICulture attribute a value of Auto to enable automatic detection of the UICulture.
ValidateRequest	When this attribute is set to True, the form input values are checked against a list of potentially dangerous values. This helps protect your Web application from harmful attacks such as JavaScript attacks. The default value is True.
WarningLevel	Specifies the compiler warning level at which to stop compilation of the page. Possible values are 0 through 4.

Here is an example of how to use the @Page directive:

```
<%@ Page Language="VB" AutoEventWireup="false" CodeFile="Default.aspx.vb"
    Inherits="_Default" %>
```

@Master

The @Master directive is quite similar to the @Page directive except that the @Master directive is meant for master pages (.master). In using the @Master directive, you specify properties of the templated page that you will be using in conjunction with any number of content pages on your site. Any content pages (built using the @Page directive) can then inherit from the master page all the master content (defined in the master page using the @Master directive). Although they are similar, the @Master directive has fewer attributes available to it than does the @Page directive. The available attributes for the @Master directive are shown in the following table.

Attribute	Description
AutoEventWireup	Specifies whether the master page's events are autowired when set to True. Default setting is True.
ClassName	Specifies the name of the class that is bound to the master page when compiled.
CodeFile	References the code-behind file with which the page is associated.
CompilerOptions	Compiler string that indicates compilation options for the master page.

Table continued on following page

Attribute	Description
CompileWith	Takes a `String` value that points to the code-behind file used for the master page.
Debug	Compiles the master page with debug symbols in place when set to `True`.
Description	Provides a text description of the master page. The ASP.NET parser ignores this attribute and its assigned value.
EnableTheming	Indicates the master page is enabled to use theming when set to `True`. The default setting for this attribute is `True`.
EnableViewState	Maintains view state for the master page when set to `True`. The default value is `True`.
Explicit	Indicates that the Visual Basic `Explicit` option is enabled when set to `True`. The default setting is `False`.
Inherits	Specifies the `CodeBehind` class for the master page to inherit.
Language	Defines the language that is being used for any inline rendering and script blocks.
LinePragmas	`Boolean` value that specifies whether line pragmas are used with the resulting assembly.
MasterPageFile	Takes a `String` value that points to the location of the master page used with the master page. It is possible to have a master page use another master page, which creates a nested master page.
Src	Points to the source file of the class used for the code behind of the master page being rendered.
Strict	Compiles the master page using the Visual Basic `Strict` mode when set to `True`. The default setting is `False`.
WarningLevel	Specifies the compiler warning level at which you want to abort compilation of the page. Possible values are from `0` to `4`.

Here is an example of how to use the `@Master` directive:

```
<%@ Master Language="VB" CodeFile="MasterPage1.master.vb"
    AutoEventWireup="false" Inherits="MasterPage" %>
```

@Control

The `@Control` directive is similar to the `@Page` directive except that `@Control` is used when you build an ASP.NET user control. The `@Control` directive allows you to define the properties to be inherited by the user control. These values are assigned to the user control as the page is parsed and compiled. The available attributes are fewer than those of the `@Page` directive, but quite a few of them allow for the modifications you need when building user controls. The following table details the available attributes.

Attribute	Description
AutoEventWireup	Specifies whether the user control's events are autowired when set to True. Default setting is True.
ClassName	Specifies the name of the class that is bound to the user control when the page is compiled.
CodeFile	References the code-behind file with which the user control is associated.
CompilerOptions	Compiler string that indicates compilation options for the user control.
CompileWith	Takes a String value that points to the code-behind file used for the user control.
Debug	Compiles the user control with debug symbols in place when set to True.
Description	Provides a text description of the user control. The ASP.NET parser ignores this attribute and its assigned value.
EnableTheming	User control is enabled to use theming when set to True. The default setting for this attribute is True.
EnableViewState	View state is maintained for the user control when set to True. The default value is True.
Explicit	Visual Basic Explicit option is enabled when set to True. The default setting is False.
Inherits	Specifies the CodeBehind class for the user control to inherit.
Language	Defines the language used for any inline rendering and script blocks.
LinePragmas	Boolean value that specifies whether line pragmas are used with the resulting assembly.
Src	Points to the source file of the class used for the code behind of the user control being rendered.
Strict	Compiles the user control using the Visual Basic Strict mode when set to True. The default setting is False.
WarningLevel	Specifies the compiler warning level at which to stop compilation of the user control. Possible values are 0 through 4.

The @Control directive is meant to be used with an ASP.NET user control. The following is an example of how to use the directive:

```
<%@ Control Language="VB" Explicit="True"
    CodeFile="WebUserControl.ascx.vb" Inherits="WebUserControl"
    Description="This is the registration user control." %>
```

@Import

The @Import directive allows you to specify a namespace to be imported into the ASP.NET page or user control. By importing, all the classes and interfaces of the namespace are made available to the page or user control. This directive supports only a single attribute: Namespace.

The Namespace attribute takes a String value that specifies the namespace to be imported. The @Import directive cannot contain more than one attribute/value pair. Because of this, you must place multiple namespace imports in multiple lines as shown in the following example:

```
<%@ Import Namespace="System.Data" %>
<%@ Import Namespace="System.Data.SqlClient" %>
```

Several assemblies are already being referenced by your application. You can find a list of these imported namespaces by looking in the web.config.comments file found at C:\Windows\Microsoft.NET\ Framework\v2.0xxxxx\CONFIG. You can find this list of assemblies being referenced from the <assemblies> child element of the <compilation> element. The settings in the web.config.comments file are as follows:

```
<assemblies>
    <add assembly="mscorlib" />
    <add assembly="System, Version=2.0.0.0, Culture=neutral,
     PublicKeyToken=b77a5c561934e089" />
    <add assembly="System.Configuration, Version=2.0.0.0.,Culture=neutral,
     PublicKeyToken=b03f5f7f11d50a3a"/>
    <add assembly="System.Configuration, Version=2.0.0.0.,Culture=neutral,
     PublicKeyToken=b03f57f11d50a3a"/>
    <add assembly="System.Web, Version=2.0.0.0, Culture=neutral,
     PublicKeyToken=b03f5f7f11d50a3a" />
    <add assembly="System.Data, Version=2.0.0.0, Culture=neutral,
     PublicKeyToken=b77a5c561934e089" />
    <add assembly="System.Web.Services, Version=2.0.0.0, Culture=neutral,
     PublicKeyToken=b03f5f7f11d50a3a" />
    <add assembly="System.Xml, Version=2.0.0.0, Culture=neutral,
     PublicKeyToken=b77a5c561934e089" />
    <add assembly="System.Drawing, Version=2.0.0.0, Culture=neutral,
     PublicKeyToken=b03f5f7f11d50a3a" />
    <add assembly="System.EnterpriseServices, Version=2.0.0.0, Culture=neutral,
     PublicKeyToken=b03f5f7f11d50a3a" />
    <add assembly="System.Web.Mobile, Version=2.0.0.0, Culture=neutral,
     PublicKeyToken=b03f5f7f11d50a3a" />
    <add assembly="*" />
</assemblies>
```

Because of this reference in the web.config.comments file, these assemblies need not be referenced in a References folder, as you would have done in ASP.NET 1.0/1.1. You can actually add or delete assemblies that are referenced from this list. For example, if you have a custom assembly referenced continuously by each and every application on the server, you can simply add a similar reference to your custom assembly next to these others. Note that you can perform this same task through the web .config file of your application as well.

Even though assemblies might be referenced, you must still import the namespaces of these assemblies into your pages. The same web.config.comments file contains a list of namespaces automatically imported into each and every page of your application. This is specified through the <namespaces> child element of the <pages> element.

```
<namespaces>
    <add namespace="System" />
    <add namespace="System.Collections" />
    <add namespace="System.Collections.Specialized" />
    <add namespace="System.Configuration" />
    <add namespace="System.Text" />
    <add namespace="System.Text.RegularExpressions" />
    <add namespace="System.Web" />
    <add namespace="System.Web.Caching" />
    <add namespace="System.Web.SessionState" />
    <add namespace="System.Web.Security" />
    <add namespace="System.Web.Profile" />
    <add namespace="System.Web.UI" />
    <add namespace="System.Web.UI.WebControls" />
    <add namespace="System.Web.UI.WebControls.WebParts" />
    <add namespace="System.Web.UI.HtmlControls" />
</namespaces>
```

From this XML list, you can see that quite a number of namespaces are imported into each and every one of your ASP.NET pages. Again, you can feel free to modify this selection in the `web.config.comments` file or even make a similar selection of namespaces from within your application's `web.config` file.

Remember that importing a namespace into your ASP.NET page or user control gives you the opportunity to use the classes without fully identifying the class name. For example, by importing the namespace `System.Data.OleDb` into the ASP.NET page, you can refer to classes within this namespace by using the singular class name (`OleDBConnection` instead of `System.Data.OleDB.OleDBConnection`).

@Implements

The `@Implements` directive gets the ASP.NET page to implement a specified .NET Framework interface. This directive supports only a single attribute: `Interface`.

The `Interface` attribute directly specifies the .NET Framework interface. When the ASP.NET page or user control implements an interface, it has direct access to all its events, methods, and properties.

Here is an example of the `@Implements` directive:

```
<%@ Implements Interface="System.Web.UI.IValidator" %>
```

@Register

The `@Register` directive associates aliases with namespaces and class names for notation in custom server control syntax. You can see the use of the `@Register` directive when you drag and drop a user control onto any of your `.aspx` pages. Dragging a user control onto the `.aspx` page causes Visual Studio 2005 to create an `@Register` directive at the top of the page. This registers your user control on the page so that the control can then be accessed on the `.aspx` page by a specific name.

The `@Register` directive supports five attributes, as described in the following table.

Attribute	Description
Assembly	The assembly you are associating with the `TagPrefix`.
Namespace	The namespace to relate with `TagPrefix`.
Src	The location of the user control.
TagName	The alias to relate to the class name.
TagPrefix	The alias to relate to the namespace.

Here's an example of how to use the `@Register` directive to import a user control to an ASP.NET page:

```
<%@ Register TagPrefix="MyTag" Namespace="MyName.MyNamespace"
    Assembly="MyAssembly" %>
```

@Assembly

The `@Assembly` directive attaches assemblies, the building blocks of .NET applications, to an ASP.NET page or user control as it compiles, thereby making all the assembly's classes and interfaces available to the page. This directive supports two attributes: `Name` and `Src`.

❑   `Name`: Enables you to specify the name of an assembly used to attach to the page files. The name of the assembly should include the filename only, not the file's extension. For instance, if the file is `MyAssembly.vb`, the value of the name attribute should be `MyAssembly`.

❑   `Src`: Enables you to specify the source of the assembly file to use in compilation.

The following provides some examples of how to use the `@Assembly` directive:

```
<%@ Assembly Name="MyAssembly" %>
<%@ Assembly Src="MyAssembly.vb" %>
```

@PreviousPageType

This directive is used to specify the page from which any cross-page postings originate. Cross-page posting between ASP.NET pages is explained later in the section "Cross-Page Posting" and again in Chapter 19.

The `@PreviousPageType` directive is a new directive that works with the new cross-page posting capability that ASP.NET 2.0 provides. This simple directive contains only two possible attributes: `TypeName` and `VirtualPath`:

❑   `TypeName`: Sets the name of the derived class from which the postback will occur.

❑   `VirtualPath`: Sets the location of the posting page from which the postback will occur.

@MasterType

The @MasterType directive associates a class name to an ASP.NET page in order to get at strongly typed references or members contained within the specified master page. This directive supports two attributes:

❑   TypeName: Sets the name of the derived class from which to get strongly typed references or members.

❑   VirtualPath: Sets the location of the page from which these strongly typed references and members will be retrieved.

Details of how to use the @MasterType directive are shown in Chapter 8. Here is an example of its use:

```
<%@ MasterType VirtualPath="~/Wrox.master" %>
```

@OutputCache

The @OutputCache directive controls the output caching policies of an ASP.NET page or user control. This directive supports the ten attributes described in the following table.

Attribute	Description
CacheProfile	Allows for a central way to manage an application's cache profile. Use the CacheProfile attribute to specify the name of the cache profile detailed in the web.config.
Duration	The duration of time in seconds that the ASP.NET page or user control is cached.
Location	Location enumeration value. The default is Any. This is valid for .aspx pages only and does not work with user controls (.ascx). Other possible values include Client, Downstream, None, Server, and ServerAndClient.
NoStore	Specifies whether to send a no-store header with the page.
SqlDependency	Enables a particular page to use SQL Server cache invalidation — a new feature of ASP.NET 2.0.
VaryByControl	Semicolon-separated list of strings used to vary the output cache of a user control.
VaryByCustom	String specifying the custom output caching requirements.
VaryByHeader	Semicolon-separated list of HTTP headers used to vary the output cache.
VaryByParam	Semicolon-separated list of strings used to vary the output cache.

Here is an example of how to use the `@OutputCache` directive:

```
<%@ OutputCache Duration="180" VaryByParam="None" %>
```

Remember that the `Duration` attribute specifies the amount of time in *seconds* during which this page is to be stored in the system cache.

@Reference

The `@Reference` directive declares that another ASP.NET page or user control should be compiled along with the active page or control. This directive supports just a single attribute:

- ❑ `TypeName`: Sets the name of the derived class from which the active page will be referenced.
- ❑ `VirtualPath`: Sets the location of the page or user control from which the active page will be referenced.

Here is an example of how to use the `@Reference` directive:

```
<%@ Reference VirtualPath="~/MyControl.ascx" %>
```

ASP.NET Page Events

ASP.NET developers consistently work with various events in their server-side code. Many of the events that they work with pertain to specific server controls. For instance, if you want to initiate some action when the end user clicks a button on your Web page, you create a button-click event in your server-side code, as shown in Listing 3-6.

Listing 3-6: A sample button-click event shown in VB

```
Protected Sub Button1_Click(sender As Object, e As EventArgs) Handles Button1.Click
    Label1.Text = TextBox1.Text
End Sub
```

In addition to the server controls, developers also want to initiate actions at specific moments when the ASP.NET page is being either created or destroyed. The ASP.NET page itself has always had a number of events for these instances. The following list shows you all the page events you could use in ASP.NET 1.0/1.1:

- ❑ `CommitTransaction`
- ❑ `DataBinding`
- ❑ `Disposed`
- ❑ `Error`
- ❑ `Init`

❑ Load

❑ PreRender

❑ Unload

One of the more popular page events from this list is the Load event, which is used in VB as shown in Listing 3-7.

Listing 3-7: Using the Page_Load event

```
Protected Sub Page_Load(ByVal sender As Object, ByVal e As System.EventArgs)
    Handles Me.Load

    Response.Write("This is the Page_Load event")
End Sub
```

Besides the page events just shown, ASP.NET 2.0 adds the following new events:

❑ InitComplete: Indicates the initialization of the page is completed.

❑ LoadComplete: Indicates the page has been completely loaded into memory.

❑ PreInit: Indicates the moment immediately before a page is initialized.

❑ PreLoad: Indicates the moment before a page has been loaded into memory.

❑ PreRenderComplete: Indicates the moment directly before a page has been rendered in the browser.

You construct these new page events just as you did the previously shown page events. For example, you use the PreInit event as shown in Listing 3-8.

Listing 3-8: Using the new page events

VB
```
<script runat="server" language="vb">
    Protected Sub Page_PreInit(ByVal sender As Object, ByVal e As System.EventArgs)
        Page.Theme = Request.QueryString("ThemeChange")
    End Sub
</script>
```

C#
```
<script runat="server">
    protected void Page_PreInit(object sender, System.EventArgs e)
    {
        Page.Theme = Request.QueryString["ThemeChange"];
    }
</script>
```

If you create an ASP.NET 2.0 page and turn on tracing, you can see the order in which the main page events are initiated. They are fired in the following order:

1. `PreInit`
2. `Init`
3. `InitComplete`
4. `PreLoad`
5. `Load`
6. `LoadComplete`
7. `PreRender`
8. `PreRenderComplete`
9. `Unload`

With the addition of these new choices, you can now work with the page and the controls on the page at many different points in the page-compilation process. You see these useful new page events in code examples throughout the book.

Dealing with PostBacks

When you're working with ASP.NET pages, be sure you understand the page events just listed. They are important because you place a lot of your page behavior inside these events at specific points in a page lifecycle.

In Active Server Pages 3.0, developers had their pages post to other pages within the application. ASP.NET pages typically post back to themselves in order to process events (such as a button-click event).

For this reason, you must differentiate between posts for the first time a page is loaded by the end user and *postbacks*. A postback is just that—a posting back to the same page. The postback contains all the form information collected on the initial page for processing if required.

Because of all the postbacks that can occur with an ASP.NET page, you want to know whether a request is the first instance for a particular page or is a postback from the same page. You can make this check by using the `IsPostBack` property of the `Page` class, as shown in the following example:

VB
```vb
If Page.IsPostBack = True Then
    ' Do processing
End If
```

C#
```csharp
if (Page.IsPostBack == true) {
    // Do processing
}
```

In addition to checking against a `True` or `False` value, you can also find out if the request is not a postback in the following manner:

VB
```
If Not Page.IsPostBack Then
    ' Do processing
End If
```

C#
```
if (!Page.IsPostBack) {
    // Do processing
}
```

Cross-Page Posting

One common feature in ASP 3.0 that is difficult to achieve in ASP.NET 1.0/1.1 is the capability to do cross-page posting. Cross-page posting enables you to submit a form (say, `Page1.aspx`) and have this form and all the control values post themselves to another page (`Page2.aspx`).

Traditionally, any page created in ASP.NET 1.0/1.1 simply posted to itself, and you handled the control values within this page instance. You could differentiate between the page's first request and any post-backs by using the `Page.IsPostBack` property, as shown here:

```
If Page.IsPostBack Then
    ' deal with control values
End If
```

Even with this capability, many developers still wanted to be able to post to another page and deal with the first page's control values on that page. This is now possible in ASP.NET 2.0, and it is quite a simple process.

For an example, create a page called `Page1.aspx` that contains a simple form. This page is shown in Listing 3-9.

Listing 3-9: Page1.aspx

VB
```
<%@ Page Language="VB" %>

<!DOCTYPE html PUBLIC "-//W3C//DTD XHTML 1.1//EN"
 "http://www.w3.org/TR/xhtml11/DTD/xhtml11.dtd">

<script runat="server">
    Protected Sub Button1_Click(ByVal sender As Object, _
        ByVal e As System.EventArgs)

        Label1.Text = "Hello " & TextBox1.Text & "<br />" & _
            "Date Selected: " & Calendar1.SelectedDate.ToShortDateString()
    End Sub
</script>

<html xmlns="http://www.w3.org/1999/xhtml" >
<head runat="server">
```

(continued)

Listing 3-9: *(continued)*

```
        <title>First Page</title>
    </head>
    <body>
        <form id="form1" runat="server">
            Enter your name:<br />
            <asp:Textbox ID="TextBox1" Runat="server">
            </asp:Textbox>
            <p>
            When do you want to fly?<br />
            <asp:Calendar ID="Calendar1" Runat="server"></asp:Calendar></p>
            <br />
            <asp:Button ID="Button1" Runat="server" Text="Submit page to itself"
             OnClick="Button1_Click" />
            <asp:Button ID="Button2" Runat="server" Text="Submit page to Page2.aspx"
             PostBackUrl="Page2.aspx" />
            <p>
            <asp:Label ID="Label1" Runat="server"></asp:Label></p>
        </form>
    </body>
    </html>
```

C#

```
<%@ Page Language="C#" %>

<script runat="server">
    protected void Button1_Click (object sender, System.EventArgs e)
    {
        Label1.Text = "Hello " + TextBox1.Text + "<br />" +
            "Date Selected: " + Calendar1.SelectedDate.ToShortDateString();
    }
</script>
```

The code from `Page1.aspx`, as shown in Listing 3-9, is quite interesting. First, two buttons are shown on the page. Both buttons submit the form, but each submits the form to a different location. The first button submits the form to itself. This is the behavior that has been the default for ASP.NET 1.0/1.1. In fact, nothing is different about `Button1`. It submits to `Page1.aspx` as a postback because of the use of the `OnClick` property in the button control. A `Button1_Click` event on `Page1.aspx` handles the values that are contained within the server controls on the page.

The second button, `Button2`, works quite differently. This button does not contain an `OnClick` event as the first button did. Instead, it uses the `PostBackUrl` property. This property takes a string value that points to the location of the file to which this page should post. In this case, it is `Page2.aspx`. This means that `Page2.aspx` now receives the postback and all the values contained in the `Page1.aspx` controls. Look at the code for `Page2.aspx`, shown in Listing 3-10.

Listing 3-10: Page2.aspx

VB

```
<%@ Page Language="VB" %>

<!DOCTYPE html PUBLIC "-//W3C//DTD XHTML 1.1//EN"
  "http://www.w3.org/TR/xhtml11/DTD/xhtml11.dtd">
```

```
<script runat="server">
    Protected Sub Page_Load(ByVal sender As Object, ByVal e As System.EventArgs)
        Dim pp_Textbox1 As TextBox
        Dim pp_Calendar1 As Calendar

        pp_Textbox1 = CType(PreviousPage.FindControl("Textbox1"), TextBox)
        pp_Calendar1 = CType(PreviousPage.FindControl("Calendar1"), Calendar)

        Label1.Text = "Hello " & pp_Textbox1.Text & "<br />" & _
            "Date Selected: " & pp_Calendar1.SelectedDate.ToShortDateString()
    End Sub
</script>

<html xmlns="http://www.w3.org/1999/xhtml" >
<head runat="server">
    <title>Second Page</title>
</head>
<body>
    <form id="form1" runat="server">
        <asp:Label ID="Label1" Runat="server"></asp:Label>
    </form>
</body>
</html>
```

C#
```
<%@ Page Language="C#" %>

<!DOCTYPE html PUBLIC "-//W3C//DTD XHTML 1.1//EN"
 "http://www.w3.org/TR/xhtml11/DTD/xhtml11.dtd">

<script runat="server">
    protected void Page_Load(object sender, System.EventArgs e)
    {
        TextBox pp_Textbox1;
        Calendar pp_Calendar1;

        pp_Textbox1 = (TextBox)PreviousPage.FindControl("Textbox1");
        pp_Calendar1 = (Calendar)PreviousPage.FindControl("Calendar1");

        Label1.Text = "Hello " + pp_Textbox1.Text + "<br />" + "Date Selected: " +
            pp_Calendar1.SelectedDate.ToShortDateString();
    }
</script>
```

You have a couple of ways of getting at the values of the controls that are exposed from Page1.aspx from the second page. The first option is displayed in Listing 3-10. To get at a particular control's value that is carried over from the previous page, you simply create an instance of that control type and populate this instance using the FindControl method from the PreviousPage property. The String value assigned to the FindControl method is the Id value, which is used for the server control from the previous page. After this is assigned, you can work with the server control and its carried-over values just as if it had originally resided on the current page. You can see from the example that you can extract the Text and SelectedDate properties from the controls without any problem.

Another way of exposing the control values from the first page (Page1.aspx) is to create a Property for the control. This is shown in Listing 3-11.

Listing 3-11: Exposing the values of the control from a Property

VB

```
<%@ Page Language="VB" %>

<!DOCTYPE html PUBLIC "-//W3C//DTD XHTML 1.1//EN"
  "http://www.w3.org/TR/xhtml11/DTD/xhtml11.dtd">

<script runat="server">
    Public ReadOnly Property pp_TextBox1() As TextBox
        Get
            Return TextBox1
        End Get
    End Property

    Public ReadOnly Property pp_Calendar1() As Calendar
        Get
            Return Calendar1
        End Get
    End Property

    Protected Sub Button1_Click(ByVal sender As Object, ByVal e As System.EventArgs)
        Label1.Text = "Hello " & TextBox1.Text & "<br />" & _
            "Date Selected: " & Calendar1.SelectedDate.ToShortDateString()
    End Sub
</script>
```

C#

```
<%@ Page Language="C#" %>

<!DOCTYPE html PUBLIC "-//W3C//DTD XHTML 1.1//EN"
  "http://www.w3.org/TR/xhtml11/DTD/xhtml11.dtd">

<script runat="server">
    public TextBox pp_TextBox1
    {
        get
        {
            return TextBox1;
        }
    }

    public Calendar pp_Calendar1
    {
        get
        {
            return Calendar1;
        }
    }

    protected void Button1_Click (object sender, System.EventArgs e)
    {
        Label1.Text = "Hello " + TextBox1.Text + "<br />" +
            "Date Selected: " + Calendar1.SelectedDate.ToShortDateString();
    }
</script>
```

Now that these properties are exposed on the posting page, the second page (Page2.aspx) can more easily work with the server control properties that are exposed from the first page. Listing 3-12 shows you how Page2.aspx works with these exposed properties.

Listing 3-12: Consuming the exposed properties from the first page

VB
```
<%@ Page Language="VB" %>
<%@ PreviousPageType VirtualPath="Page1.aspx" %>

<!DOCTYPE html PUBLIC "-//W3C//DTD XHTML 1.1//EN"
 "http://www.w3.org/TR/xhtml11/DTD/xhtml11.dtd">

<script runat="server">
    Protected Sub Page_Load(ByVal sender As Object, ByVal e As System.EventArgs)
        Label1.Text = "Hello " & PreviousPage.pp_Textbox1.Text & "<br />" & _
            "Date Selected: " & _
            PreviousPage.pp_Calendar1.SelectedDate.ToShortDateString()
    End Sub
</script>
```

C#
```
<%@ Page Language="C#" %>
<%@ PreviousPageType VirtualPath="Page1.aspx" %>

<!DOCTYPE html PUBLIC "-//W3C//DTD XHTML 1.1//EN"
 "http://www.w3.org/TR/xhtml11/DTD/xhtml11.dtd">

<script runat="server">
    protected void Page_Load(object sender, System.EventArgs e)
    {
        Label1.Text = "Hello " + PreviousPage.pp_TextBox1.Text + "<br />" +
            "Date Selected: " +
            PreviousPage.pp_Calendar1.SelectedDate.ToShortDateStrihg();
    }
</script>
```

In order to be able to work with the properties that Page1.aspx exposes, you have to strongly type the PreviousPage property to Page1.aspx. To do this, you use the PreviousPageType directive. This new directive allows you to specifically point to Page1.aspx with the use of the VirtualPath attribute. When that is in place, notice that you can see the properties that Page1.aspx exposes through IntelliSense from the PreviousPage property. This is illustrated in Figure 3-7.

As you can see, working with cross-page posting is straightforward. Notice that, when you are cross-posting from one page to another, you aren't restricted to working only with the postback on the second page. In fact, you can still create methods on Page1.aspx that work with the postback before moving onto Page2.aspx. To do this, you simply add an OnClick event for the button in Page1.aspx and a method. You also assign a value for the PostBackUrl property. You can then work with the postback on Page1.aspx and then again on Page2.aspx.

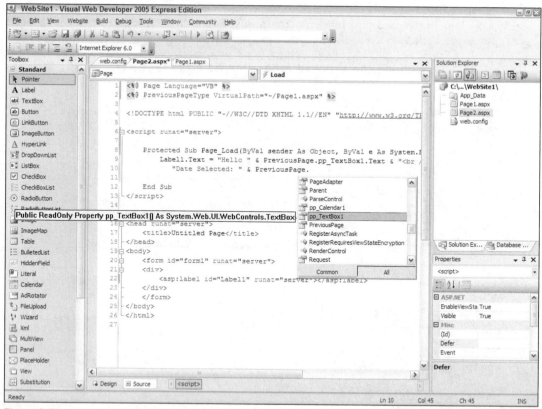

Figure 3-7

What happens if someone requests `Page2.aspx` before she works her way through `Page1.aspx`? It is actually quite easy to determine if the request is coming from `Page1.aspx` or if someone just hit `Page2.aspx` directly. You can work with the request through the use of the `IsCrossPagePostBack` property that is quite similar to the `IsPostBack` property from ASP.NET 1.0/1.1. The `IsCrossPagePostBack` property enables you to check whether the request is from `Page1.aspx`. Listing 3-13 shows an example of this.

Listing 3-13: Using the IsCrossPagePostBack property

VB

```
<%@ Page Language="VB" %>
<%@ PreviousPageType VirtualPath="Page1.aspx" %>

<!DOCTYPE html PUBLIC "-//W3C//DTD XHTML 1.1//EN"
  "http://www.w3.org/TR/xhtml11/DTD/xhtml11.dtd">

<script runat="server">
    Protected Sub Page_Load(ByVal sender As Object, ByVal e As System.EventArgs)
      If PreviousPage.IsCrossPagePostBack Then
        Label1.Text = "Hello " & PreviousPage.pp_Textbox1.Text & "<br />" & _
```

```
                    "Date Selected: " & _
                    PreviousPage.pp_Calendar1.SelectedDate.ToShortDateString()
          Else
              Response.Redirect("Page1.aspx")
          End If
      End Sub
  </script>
```

C#
```
<%@ Page Language="C#" %>
<%@ PreviousPageType VirtualPath="Page1.aspx" %>

<!DOCTYPE html PUBLIC "-//W3C//DTD XHTML 1.1//EN"
  "http://www.w3.org/TR/xhtml11/DTD/xhtml11.dtd">

<script runat="server">
    protected void Page_Load(object sender, System.EventArgs e)
    {
        if (PreviousPage.IsCrossPagePostBack) {
            Label1.Text = "Hello " + PreviousPage.pp_Textbox1.Text + "<br />" +
                "Date Selected: " +
                PreviousPage.pp_Calendar1.SelectedDate.ToShortDateString();
        }
        else
        {
            Response.Redirect("Page1.aspx");
        }
    }
</script>
```

ASP.NET Application Folders

When you create ASP.NET applications, notice that ASP.NET 2.0 now uses a file-based approach. When working with ASP.NET 2.0, you can add as many files and folders as you want within your application without recompiling each and every time a new file is added to the overall solution. ASP.NET 2.0 now includes the capability to automatically precompile your ASP.NET applications dynamically.

ASP.NET 1.0/1.1 compiled everything in your solution into a DLL. This is no longer necessary because ASP.NET 2.0 applications have a defined folder structure. By using the ASP.NET 2.0 defined folders, you can have your code automatically compiled for you, your application themes accessible throughout your application, and your globalization resources available whenever you need them. Take a look at each of these defined folders to see how they work. The first is the \App_Code folder.

\App_Code Folder

The \App_Code folder is meant to store your classes, .wsdl files, and typed datasets. Any of these items stored in this folder are then automatically available to all the pages within your solution. The nice thing about the \App_Code folder is that when you place something inside this folder, Visual Studio 2005 automatically detects this and compiles it if it is a class (.vb or .cs), automatically creates your XML

Web service proxy class (from the `.wsdl` file), or automatically creates a typed dataset for you from your `.xsd` files. After the files are automatically compiled, these items are then instantaneously available to any of your ASP.NET pages that are in the same solution. Look at how to employ a simple class in your solution using the `\App_Code` folder.

The first step is to create an `\App_Code` folder. To do this, simply right-click the solution and choose Add ASP.NET Folder ➪ App_Code. Right away you will notice that Visual Studio 2005 treats this folder differently than the other folders in your solution. The `\App_Code` folder is shown in a different color (gray) with a document pictured next to the folder icon. See Figure 3-8.

Figure 3-8

After the `\App_Code` folder is in place, right-click the folder and select Add New Item. The Add New Item dialog that appears doesn't give you many options for the types of files that you can place within this folder. The available options include a Class file, a Text file, a DataSet, a Report, and a Class Diagram if you are using Visual Studio 2005. Visual Web Developer 2005 Express Edition offers only the Class file, Text file, and DataSet file. For the first example, select the file of type Class and name the class `Calculator.vb` or `Calculator.cs`. Listing 3-14 shows how the `Calculator` class should appear.

Listing 3-14: The Calculator class

VB
```vb
Imports Microsoft.VisualBasic

Public Class Calculator
    Public Function Add(ByVal a As Integer, ByVal b As Integer) As Integer
        Return (a + b)
    End Function
End Class
```

C#

```csharp
using System;

public class Calculator
{
    public int Add(int a, int b)
        {
            return (a + b);
    }
}
```

What's next? Just save this file, and it is now available to use in any pages that are in your solution. To see this in action, create a simple .aspx page that has just a single Label server control. Listing 3-15 shows you the code to place within the Page_Load event to make this new class available to the page.

Listing 3-15: An .aspx page that uses the Calculator class

VB

```vb
<%@ Page Language="VB" %>

<!DOCTYPE html PUBLIC "-//W3C//DTD XHTML 1.1//EN"
 "http://www.w3.org/TR/xhtml11/DTD/xhtml11.dtd">

<script runat="server">
    Protected Sub Page_Load(ByVal sender As Object, ByVal e As System.EventArgs)
        Dim myCalc As New Calculator
        Label1.Text = myCalc.Add(12, 12)
    End Sub
</script>
```

C#

```csharp
<%@ Page Language="C#" %>

<!DOCTYPE html PUBLIC "-//W3C//DTD XHTML 1.1//EN"
 "http://www.w3.org/TR/xhtml11/DTD/xhtml11.dtd">

<script runat="server">
    protected void Page_Load(object sender, System.EventArgs e)
    {
        Calculator myCalc = new Calculator();
        Label1.Text = myCalc.Add(12, 12).ToString();
    }
</script>
```

When you run this .aspx page, notice that it utilizes the Calculator class without any problem, with no need to compile the class before use. In fact, right after saving the Calculator class in your solution or moving the class to the \App_Code folder, you also instantaneously receive IntelliSense capability on the methods that the class exposes (as illustrated in Figure 3-9).

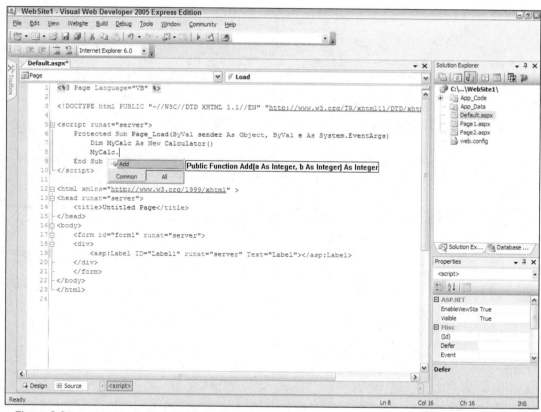

Figure 3-9

To see how Visual Studio 2005 works with the \App_Code folder, open the Calculator class again in the IDE and add a Subtract method. Your class should now appear as shown in Listing 3-16.

Listing 3-16: Adding a Subtract method to the Calculator class

VB
```vb
Imports Microsoft.VisualBasic

Public Class Calculator
    Public Function Add(ByVal a As Integer, ByVal b As Integer) As Integer
        Return (a + b)
    End Function

    Public Function Subtract(ByVal a As Integer, ByVal b As Integer) As Integer
        Return (a - b)
    End Function
End Class
```

C#
```csharp
using System;

public class Calculator
```

```
    {
        public int Add(int a, int b)
        {
            return (a + b);
        }

        public int Subtract(int a, int b)
        {
            return (a - b);
        }
    }
```

After you have added the Subtract method to the Calculator class, save the file and go back to your
.aspx page. Notice that the class has been recompiled by the IDE, and the new method is now available
to your page. You see this directly in IntelliSense. Figure 3-10 shows this in action.

Everything placed in the \App_Code folder is compiled into a single assembly. The class files placed
within the \App_Code folder are not required to use a specific language. This means that even if all the
pages of the solution are written in Visual Basic 2005, the Calculator class in the \App_Code folder of
the solution can be built in C# (Calculator.cs).

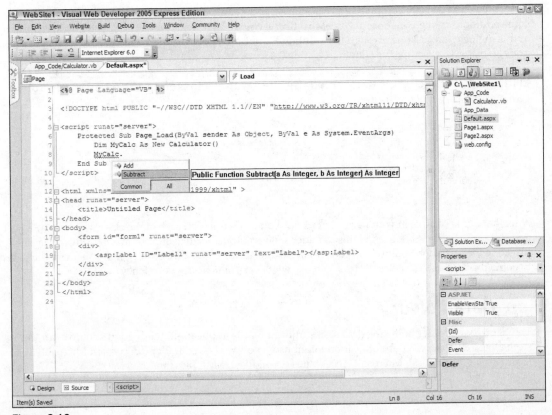

Figure 3-10

Because all the classes contained in this folder are built into a single assembly, you *cannot* have classes of different languages sitting in the root \App_Code folder, as in the following example:

```
\App_Code
   Calculator.cs
   AdvancedMath.vb
```

Having two classes made up of different languages in the \App_Code folder (as shown here) causes an error to be thrown. It is impossible for the assigned compiler to work with two different languages. Therefore, in order to be able to work with multiple languages in your \App_Code folder, you must make some changes to the folder structure and to the web.config file.

The first step is to add two new subfolders to the \App_Code folder—a \VB folder and a \CS folder. This gives you the following folder structure:

```
\App_Code
   \VB
      Add.vb
   \CS
      Subtract.cs
```

This still won't correctly compile these class files into separate assemblies, at least not until you make some additions to the web.config file. Most likely, you don't have a web.config file in your solution at this moment, so add one through the Solution Explorer. After it is added, change the <compilation> node so that it is structured as shown in Listing 3-17.

Listing 3-17: Structuring the web.config file so that classes in the \App_Code folder can use different languages

```
<compilation>
   <codeSubDirectories>
      <add directoryName="VB"></add>
      <add directoryName="CS"></add>
   </codeSubDirectories>
</compilation>
```

Now that this is in place in your web.config file, you can work with each of the classes in your ASP.NET pages. Also, any C# class placed in the CS folder is now automatically compiled just like any of the classes placed in the VB folder. Because you can add these directories in the web.config file, you are not required to name them VB and CS as we did; you can use whatever name tickles your fancy.

\App_Data Folder

The \App_Data folder holds the data stores utilized by the application. It is a good spot to centrally store all the data stores your application might use. The \App_Data folder can contain Microsoft SQL Express files (.mdf files), Microsoft Access files (.mdb files), XML files, and more.

The user account utilized by your application will have read and write access to any of the files contained within the \App_Data folder. By default, this is the ASPNET account. Another reason for storing all your data files in this folder is that much of the ASP.NET system—from the membership and role management systems to the GUI tools such as the ASP.NET MMC snap-in and ASP.NET Web Site Administration Tool—is built to work with the \App_Data folder.

\App_Themes Folder

Themes are a new way of providing a common look-and-feel to your site across every page. You implement a theme by using a .skin file, CSS files, and images used by the server controls of your site. All these elements can make a *theme*, which is then stored in the \App_Themes folder of your solution. By storing these elements within the \App_Themes folder, you ensure that all the pages within the solution can take advantage of the theme and easily apply its elements to the controls and markup of the page. Themes are discussed in great detail in Chapter 9 of this book.

\App_GlobalResources Folder

Resource files are string tables that can serve as data dictionaries for your applications when these applications require changes to content based on things such as changes in culture. You can add Assembly Resource Files (.resx) to this folder, and they are dynamically compiled and made part of the solution for use by all your .aspx pages in the application. When using ASP.NET 1.0/1.1, you had to use the resgen.exe tool and also had to compile your resource files to a .dll or .exe for use within your solution. Now it is considerably easier to deal with resource files in ASP.NET 2.0.

In addition to strings, you can also add images and other files to your resource files. For an example of how to use resource files to create a multilingual ASP.NET 2.0 application, first create the \App_GlobalResources folder in your application. For this example, create two resource files in this folder: Resource.resx and Resource.fi-FI.resx. The first file, Resource.resx, is the default language file using American English. The second file is for the same text, but in the Finnish language. Hence, this file uses fi-FI in its name. When someone with a browser culture of fi-FI invokes the page, he sees the information that comes from this file (Resource.fi-FI.resx). Everyone else who comes to the site gets the information that comes from the other file (Resource.resx).

Notice (as shown in Figure 3-11) that you can actually do a lot with .resx files. The idea is to create a table of the items to be localized (such as text, images, and files). For this example, you can stick to text.

The Resource.resx file should have the following structure:

Name	Value
Answer	Hello there
PageTitle	Sample Page
Question	What is your name?

For the Resource.fi-FI.resx file, use the following structure:

Name	Value
Answer	Hei
PageTitle	Näytesivu
Question	Mikä sinun nimi on?

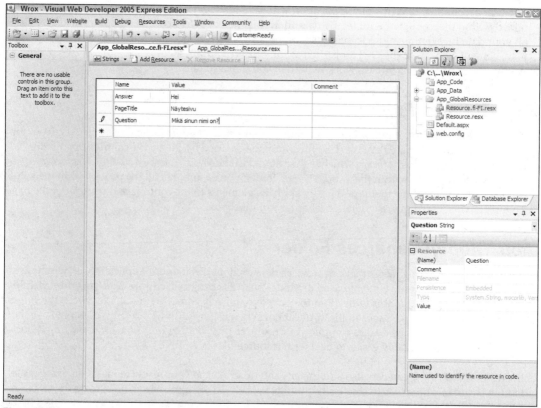

Figure 3-11

To use these files, create a simple `.aspx` page with the code from Listing 3-18.

Listing 3-18: A simple ASP.NET page that uses resource files

VB

```
<%@ Page Language="VB" Culture="Auto" UICulture="Auto" %>

<!DOCTYPE html PUBLIC "-//W3C//DTD XHTML 1.1//EN"
  "http://www.w3.org/TR/xhtml11/DTD/xhtml11.dtd">

<script runat="server">
    Protected Sub Page_Load(ByVal sender As Object, _
        ByVal e As System.EventArgs)

        Page.Title = Resources.Resource.PageTitle
    End Sub

    Protected Sub Button1_Click(ByVal sender As Object, _
        ByVal e As System.EventArgs)

        Label1.Text = Resources.Resource.Answer & " " & Textbox1.Text
    End Sub
```

```
</script>
<html xmlns="http://www.w3.org/1999/xhtml" >
<head id="Head1" runat="server">
    <title></title>
</head>
<body>
    <form id="Form1" runat="server">
        <p><%= Resources.Resource.Question %></p><br />
        <asp:TextBox ID="Textbox1" Runat="server"></asp:TextBox><br />
        <asp:Button ID="Button1" Runat="server" Text="Submit"
         OnClick="Button1_Click" />
        <p><asp:Label ID="Label1" Runat="server"></asp:Label></p>
    </form>
</body>
</html>
```

C#

```
<%@ Page Language="C#" Culture="Auto" UICulture="Auto" %>

<!DOCTYPE html PUBLIC "-//W3C//DTD XHTML 1.1//EN"
 "http://www.w3.org/TR/xhtml11/DTD/xhtml11.dtd">

<script runat="server">
    protected void Page_Load(object sender, System.EventArgs e)
    {
        Page.Title = Resources.Resource.PageTitle;
    }

    protected void Button1_Click(object sender, System.EventArgs e)
    {
        Label1.Text = Resources.Resource.Answer + " " + Textbox1.Text;
    }
</script>
```

When this is run, you get the appropriate text based upon the culture setting in your browser. If this setting is not fi-FI, you get the American English text. The page output is shown in Figure 3-12.

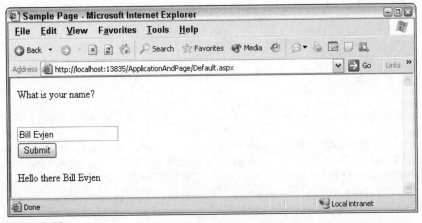

Figure 3-12

In order to see the Finnish text, change your preferred culture in the Microsoft Internet Explorer browser by choosing Tools ➪ Internet Options. This pulls up the Internet Options dialog. From the first tab, General, you can click the Languages button to pull up a dialog that enables you to specify the Finnish language as your preferred language choice. After you have added the Finnish language to the list, be sure that it is the uppermost choice in the dialog. You can do this by highlighting this choice and pressing the Move Up button until it is the uppermost choice.

After this is in place, run the page. You see the Finnish language output shown in Figure 3-13.

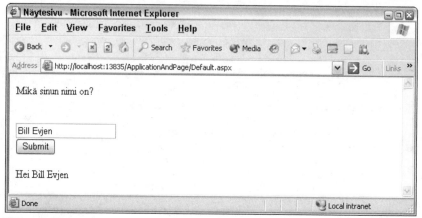

Figure 3-13

\App_LocalResources

As you saw with the \App_GlobalResources folder, it is now pretty simple to incorporate resources that can be used application-wide. If you are not interested in constructing application-wide resources, however, but instead are interested in resources that can be used for a single .aspx page only, you want to turn to the \App_LocalResources folder.

You can add resource files that are page-specific to the \App_LocalResources folder by constructing the name of the .resx file in the following manner:

- ❑ Default.aspx.resx
- ❑ Default.aspx.fi.resx
- ❑ Default.aspx.ja.resx
- ❑ Default.aspx.en-gb.resx

Now, the resource declarations used on the Default.aspx page will be retrieved from the appropriate file found in the \App_LocalResources folder. By default, the Default.aspx.resx resource file will be used if another match is not found. If the client is using a culture specification of fi-FI (Finnish), however, the Default.aspx.fi.resx file will be used instead.

\App_WebReferences

The \App_WebReferences folder is a new name for the previous Web References folder used in previous versions of ASP.NET. Now you can use the \App_WebReferences folder and have automatic access to the remote Web services referenced from your application. Web services in ASP.NET are covered in Chapter 26.

\App_Browsers

The \App_Browsers folder holds .browser files, which are XML files used to identity the browsers making requests to the application and understanding the capabilities these browsers have. You can find a list of globally accessible .browser files at C:\Windows\Microsoft.NET\Framework\v2.0xxxxx\ CONFIG\Browsers. In addition, if you want to change any part of these default browser definition files, just copy the appropriate .browser file from the Browsers folder to your application's \App_Browsers folder and change the definition.

Compilation

You already saw how Visual Studio 2005 compiles pieces of your application as you work with them (for instance, by placing a class in the \App_Code folder). The other parts of the application, such as the .aspx pages, can be compiled just as they were in ASP.NET 1.0/1.1 by referencing the pages in the browser.

When an ASP.NET page is referenced in the browser for the first time, the request is passed to the ASP.NET parser that creates the class file in the language of the page. It is passed to the ASP.NET parser based on the file's extension (.aspx) because ASP.NET realizes that this file extension type is meant for its handling and processing. After the class file has been created, the class file is compiled into a DLL and then written to the disk of the Web server. At this point, the DLL is instantiated and processed, and an output is generated for the initial requester of the ASP.NET page. This is detailed in Figure 3-14.

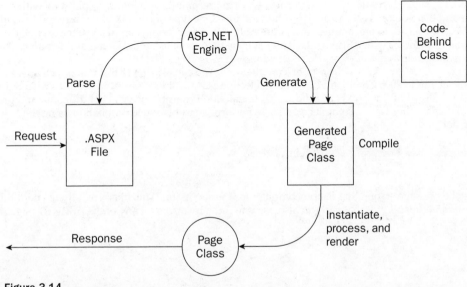

Figure 3-14

On the next request, great things happen. Instead of going through the entire process again for the second and respective requests, the request simply causes an instantiation of the already-created DLL, which sends out a response to the requester. This is illustrated in Figure 3-15.

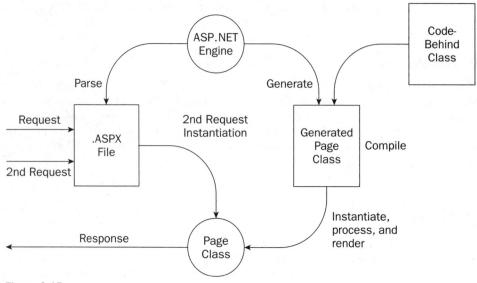

Figure 3-15

Because of the mechanics of this process, if you made changes to your `.aspx` code-behind pages, you found it necessary to recompile your application. This was quite a pain if you had a larger site and didn't want your end users to experience the extreme lag that occurs when an `.aspx` page is referenced for the first time after compilation. Many developers, consequently, began to develop their own tools that automatically go out and hit every single page within their application to remove this first-time lag hit from the end user's browsing experience.

ASP.NET 2.0 introduces the technology a few ways to precompile your entire application with a single command that you can issue through a command line. One type of compilation is referred to as *in-place precompilation*. In order to precompile your entire ASP.NET application, you must use the aspnet_compiler.exe tool that now comes with ASP.NET 2.0. You navigate to the tool using the Command window. Open the Command window and navigate to `C:\Windows\Microsoft.NET\Framework\v2.0.xxxxx\`. When you are there, you can work with the aspnet_compiler tool. You can also get to this tool directly by pulling up the Visual Studio 2005 Command Prompt by selecting Start⇨All Programs⇨Microsoft Visual Studio 2005⇨Visual Studio Tools⇨Visual Studio 2005 Command Prompt. Once you get the command prompt you would then use the aspnet_compiler.exe tool to perform an in-place precompilation using the following command:

```
aspnet_compiler -p "c:\Inetpub\wwwroot\WROX
```

You get a message stating that the precompilation was successful. The other great thing about this precompilation capability is that you can also use it to find any errors on any of the ASP.NET pages in your application. Because it hits each and every page, if one of the pages contains an error that won't be triggered until runtime, you get notification of the error immediately as you employ this precompilation method

The next precompilation option is commonly referred to as *precompilation for deployment*. This is an outstanding new addition to ASP.NET that enables you to compile your application down to some DLLs, which can then be deployed to customers, partners, or elsewhere for your own use. Not only are minimal steps required to do this, but after your application is compiled, you only have to move around the DLL and some placeholder files for the site to work. This means that your Web site code is completely removed and placed in the DLL when deployed.

Before you do, however, create a folder in your root drive called, for example, Wrox. This folder is the one you ask the compiler to output to. When it is in place, you can return to the compiler tool and give the following command:

```
aspnet_compiler -v [Application Name] -p [Physical Location] [Target]
```

So, if you have an application called INETA located at C:\Websites\INETA, you use the following commands:

```
aspnet_compiler -v /INETA -p C:\Websites\INETA C:\Wrox
```

Press the Enter key, and the compiler either tells you that it has a problem with one of the command parameters or that it was successful (shown in Figure 3-16). If it was successful, you can see the output placed in the target directory.

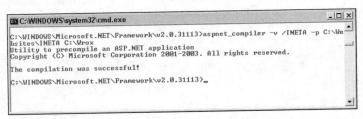

Figure 3-16

In the example just shown, -v is a command for the virtual path of the application — which is provided by using /INETA. The next command is -p, which is pointing to the physical path of the application. In this case, it is C:\Websites\INETA. Finally, the last bit, C:\Wrox, is the location of the compiler output. The following table describes the possible commands for the aspnet_compiler.exe tool.

Command	Description
-m	Specifies the full IIS metabase path of the application. If you use the -m command, you cannot use the -v or -p command.
-v	Specifies the virtual path of the application to be compiled. If you also use the -p command, the physical path is used to find the location of the application.
-p	Specifies the physical path of the application to be compiled. If this is not specified, the IIS metabase is used to find the application.
targetDir	Specifies the target directory where the compiled files should be placed. If this is not specified, the output files are placed in the application directory.

After compiling the application, you can go to C:\Wrox to see the output. Here, you see all the files and the file structures that were in the original application. But if you look at the content of one of the files, notice that the file is simply a placeholder. In the actual file, you find the following comment:

```
This is a marker file generated by the precompilation tool
and should not be deleted!
```

In fact, you find a Code.dll file in the bin folder where all the page code is located. Because it is in a DLL file, it provides great code obfuscation as well. From here on, all you do is move these files to another server using FTP or Windows Explorer, and you can run the entire Web application from these files. When you have an update to the application, you simply provide a new set of compiled files. A sample output is displayed in Figure 3-17.

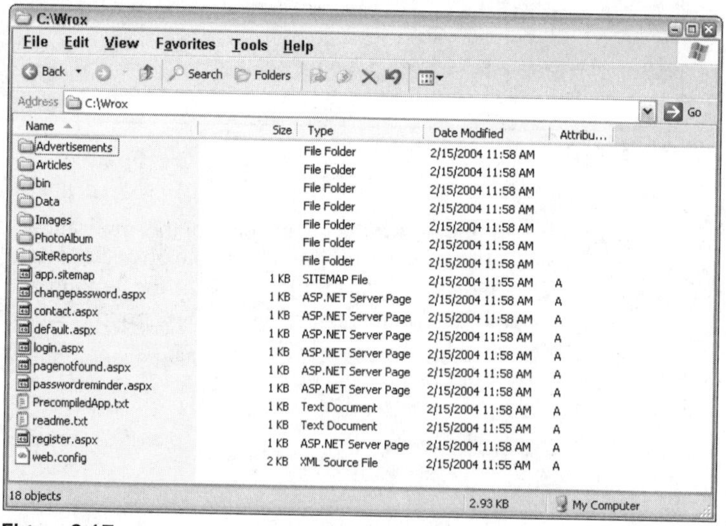

Figure 3-17

Note that this compilation process doesn't compile *every* type of Web file. In fact, it compiles only the ASP.NET-specific file types and leaves out of the compilation process the following types of files:

❑ HTML files

❑ XML files

❑ XSD files

❑ web.config files

❑ Text files

You can't do much to get around this, except in the case of the HTML files and the text files. For these file types, just change the file extension of these file types to .aspx; they are then compiled into the Code.dll like all the other ASP.NET files.

Global.asax

If you add a new item to your ASP.NET application, you get the Add New Item dialog. From here, you can see that you can add a Global Application Class to your applications. This adds a Global.asax file. This file is used by the application to hold application-level events, objects, and variables — all of which are accessible application-wide. Active Server Pages developers had something similar with the Global.asa file.

Your ASP.NET applications can have only a single Global.asax file. This file supports a number of items. When it is created, you are given the following template:

```
<%@ Application Language="VB" %>

<script runat="server">

    Sub Application_Start(ByVal sender As Object, ByVal e As EventArgs)
        ' Code that runs on application startup
    End Sub

    Sub Application_End(ByVal sender As Object, ByVal e As EventArgs)
        ' Code that runs on application shutdown
    End Sub

    Sub Application_Error(ByVal sender As Object, ByVal e As EventArgs)
        ' Code that runs when an unhandled error occurs
    End Sub

    Sub Session_Start(ByVal sender As Object, ByVal e As EventArgs)
        ' Code that runs when a new session is started
    End Sub

    Sub Session_End(ByVal sender As Object, ByVal e As EventArgs)
        ' Code that runs when a session ends.
        ' Note: The Session_End event is raised only when the sessionstate mode
        ' is set to InProc in the Web.config file. If session mode is
        ' set to StateServer
        ' or SQLServer, the event is not raised.
    End Sub

</script>
```

Just as you can work with page-level events in your `.aspx` pages, you can work with overall application events from the `Global.asax` file. In addition to the events listed in this code example, the following list details some of the events you can structure inside this file:

❑ `Application_Start`: Called when the application receives its very first request. It is an ideal spot in your application to assign any application-level variables or state that must be maintained across all users.

❑ `Session_Start`: Similar to the `Application_Start` event except that this event is fired when an individual user accesses the application for the first time. For instance, the `Application_Start` event fires once when the first request comes in, which gets the application going, but the `Session_Start` is invoked for each end user who requests something from the application for the first time.

❑ `Application_BeginRequest`: Although it not listed in the preceding template provided by Visual Studio 2005, the `Application_BeginRequest` event is triggered before each and every request that comes its way. This means that when a request comes into the server, before this request is processed, the `Application_BeginRequest` is triggered and dealt with before any processing of the request occurs.

❑ `Application_AuthenticateRequest`: Triggered for each request and enables you to set up custom authentications for a request.

❑ `Application_Error`: Triggered when an error is thrown anywhere in the application by any user of the application. This is an ideal spot to provide application-wide error handling or an event recording the errors to the server's event logs.

❑ `Session_End`: When running in `InProc` mode, this event is triggered when an end user leaves the application.

❑ `Application_End`: Triggered when the application comes to an end. This is an event that most ASP.NET developers won't use that often because ASP.NET does such a good job of closing and cleaning up any objects that are left around.

In addition to the global application events that the `Global.asax` file provides access to, you can also use directives in this file as you can with other ASP.NET pages. The `Global.asax` file allows for the following directives:

❑ `@Application`

❑ `@Assembly`

❑ `@Import`

These attributes perform in the same way when they are used with other ASP.NET page types.

Summary

This chapter covered a lot of ground. It discussed some of the issues concerning ASP.NET applications as a whole and the choices you have when building and deploying these new applications. With the help of Visual Studio 2005, you now have options about which Web server to use when building your application and whether to work locally or remotely through the new built-in FTP capabilities.

ASP.NET 2.0 and Visual Studio 2005 make it easy to build your pages using an inline coding model or to select a new and better code-behind model that is simpler to use and easier to deploy. You also learned about the new cross-posting capabilities and the new fixed folders that ASP.NET 2.0 has incorporated to make your life easier. These folders make their resources available dynamically with no work on your part. Finally, you saw some of the outstanding new compilation options that you have at your disposal.

As you worked through some of the examples, you may have been thinking, "WOW!" But wait . . . there's plenty more to come!

ASP.NET Server Controls and Client-Side Scripts

As you already know from earlier chapters, ASP.NET evolved from Microsoft's earlier Web technology called Active Server Pages (referred to as *ASP* then and *classic ASP* today). This model was completely different from today's ASP.NET. Classic ASP used interpreted languages to accomplish the construction of the final HTML document before it was sent to the browser. ASP.NET, on the other hand, uses true compiled languages to accomplish the same task. The idea of building Web pages based on objects in a compiled environment is one of the main focuses of this chapter.

This chapter looks at how to use a particular type of object in ASP.NET pages called a *server control*, and how you can profit from using this control. We also introduce a particular type of server control — the HTML server control. The chapter also demonstrates how you can use JavaScript in ASP.NET pages to modify the behavior of server controls.

The rest of this chapter shows you how to use and manipulate server controls, both visually and programmatically, to help with the creation of your ASP.NET pages.

ASP.NET Server Controls

In the past, one of the difficulties of working with classic ASP was that you were completely in charge of the entire HTML output from the browser by virtue of the server-side code you wrote. Although this might seem ideal, it created a problem because each browser interpreted the HTML given to it in a slightly different manner.

The two main browsers out there at the time were Microsoft's Internet Explorer and Netscape Navigator. This meant that not only did developers have to be cognizant of the browser type to which that they were outputting HTML, but they also had to take into account which versions of those particular browsers might be making a request to their application. Some developers resolved the issue by creating two separate applications. When an end user made an initial request to the application, the code made a browser check to see what browser type was making the request.

Then, the ASP page would redirect the request down one path for an IE user, or down another path for a Netscape user.

Because requests came from so many different versions of the same browser, the developer often designed for the lowest possible version that might be used to visit the site. Essentially, everyone lost out by using the lowest common denominator as the target. This technique ensured that the page was rendered properly in most browsers making a request, but it also forced the developer to dummy-down his application. If applications were always built for the lowest common denominator, the developer could never take advantage of some of the more advanced features offered by newer browser versions.

ASP.NET server controls overcome these obstacles. When using the server controls provided by ASP.NET, you are not specifying the HTML to be output from your server-side code. Rather, you are specifying the functionality you want to see in the browser and letting the ASP.NET decide for you on the output to be sent to the browser.

When a request comes in, ASP.NET examines the request to see which browser type is making the request, as well as the version of the browser, and then it produces HTML output specific to that browser. This process is accomplished by a User Agent retrieved from the header of the HTTP Request to *sniff* the browser. This means that you can now build for the best browsers out there without worrying about whether features will work in the browsers making requests to your applications. Because of the previously described capabilities, you will often hear these controls referred to as *smart controls*.

Types of Server Controls

ASP.NET provides two distinct types of server controls — HTML server controls and Web server controls. Each type of control is quite different and, as you work with ASP.NET, you will see that much of the focus is on the Web server controls. This doesn't mean that HTML server controls have no value. They do provide you with many capabilities — some that Web server controls do not give you.

You might be asking yourself which is the better control type to use. The answer is that it really depends on what you are trying to achieve. HTML server controls map to specific HTML elements. You can place an `HtmlTable` server control on your ASP.NET page that works dynamically with a `<table>` element. On the other hand, Web server controls map to specific functionality that you want on your ASP.NET pages. This means an `<asp:Panel>` control might use a `<table>` or an `<IFrame>` element — it really depends on the capability of the browser making the request.

The following table summarizes some advice on when to use HTML server controls and when to use Web server controls.

Control Type	When to Use This Control Type
HTML Server	When converting traditional ASP 3.0 Web pages to ASP.NET Web pages and speed of completion is a concern. It is a lot easier to change your HTML elements to HTML server controls than it is to change them to Web server controls.
	When you prefer a more HTML-type programming model.
	When you want to explicitly control the code that is generated for the browser.

Control Type	When to Use This Control Type
Web Server	When you require a richer set of functionality to perform complicated page requirements.
	When you are developing Web pages that will be viewed by a multitude of browser types and that require different code based upon these types.
	When you prefer a more Visual Basic—type programming model that is based on the use of controls and control properties.

Of course, some developers like to separate certain controls from the rest and place them in their own categories. For instance, you may see references to the following types of controls:

❑ **List controls:** These control types allow data to be bound to them for display purposes of some kind.

❑ **Rich controls:** Controls, such as the Calendar control, that display richer content and capabilities than other controls.

❑ **Validation controls:** Controls that interact with other form controls to validate the data that they contain.

❑ **Mobile controls:** Controls that are specific for output to devices such as mobile phones, PDAs, and more.

❑ **User controls:** These are not really controls, but page templates that you can work with as you would a control on your ASP.NET page.

❑ **Custom controls:** Controls that you build yourself and use in the same manner as the supplied ASP.NET server controls that come with the default install of ASP.NET 2.0.

When you are deciding between HTML server controls and Web server controls, remember that no hard and fast rules exist about which type to use. You might find yourself working with one control type more than another, but certain features are available in one control type that might not be available in the other. If you are trying to accomplish a specific task and you don't see a solution with the control type you are using, take a look at the other control type because it may very well hold the answer. Also realize that you can mix and match these control types. Nothing says that you cannot use both HTML server controls and Web server controls on the same page or within the same application.

Building with Server Controls

You have a couple of ways to use server controls to construct your ASP.NET pages. You can actually use tools that are specifically designed to work with ASP.NET 2.0 that enable you to visually drag and drop controls onto a design surface and manipulate the behavior of the control. You can also work with server controls directly through code input.

Working with Server Controls on a Design Surface

Visual Studio 2005 enables you to visually create an ASP.NET page by dragging and dropping visual controls onto a design surface. You can get to this visual design option by clicking the Design tab at the bottom of the IDE when viewing your ASP.NET page. In this view, you also can place the cursor on the page in the location where you want the control to appear and then double-click the control you want in the Toolbox window of Visual Studio. Unlike previous versions of Visual Studio, Visual Studio 2005 does a really good job of not touching your code when switching between the Design and Source tabs.

In the Design view of your page, you can highlight a control and the properties for the control appear in the Properties window. For example, Figure 4-1 shows a Button control selected in the design panel, and its properties are displayed in the Properties window on the lower right.

Changing the properties in the window changes the appearance or behavior of the highlighted control. Because all controls inherit from a specific base class (`WebControl`), you can also highlight multiple controls at the same time and change the base properties of all the controls at once. You do this by holding down the Ctrl key as you make your control selections.

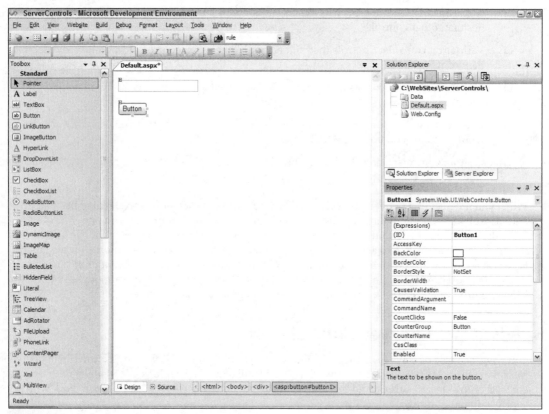

Figure 4-1

Coding Server Controls

You also can work from the Code page directly. Because many developers prefer this, it is the default when you first create your ASP.NET page. Hand-coding your own ASP.NET pages may seem to be a slower approach than simply dragging and dropping controls onto a design surface, but it isn't as slow as you might think. You get plenty of assistance in coding your applications from Visual Studio 2005. As you start typing in Visual Studio, the IntelliSense features kick in and help you with code auto-completion. Figure 4-2, for example, shows an IntelliSense drop-down list of possible code completion statements that appeared as the code was typed.

The IntelliSense focus is on the most commonly used attribute or statement for the control or piece of code that you are working with. Using IntelliSense effectively as you work is a great way to code with great speed.

As with Design view, the Source view of your page lets you drag and drop controls from the Toolbox onto the code page itself. For example, dragging and dropping a TextBox control onto the code page produces the same results as dropping it on the design page:

```
<asp:TextBox ID="TextBox1" Runat="server"></asp:TextBox>
```

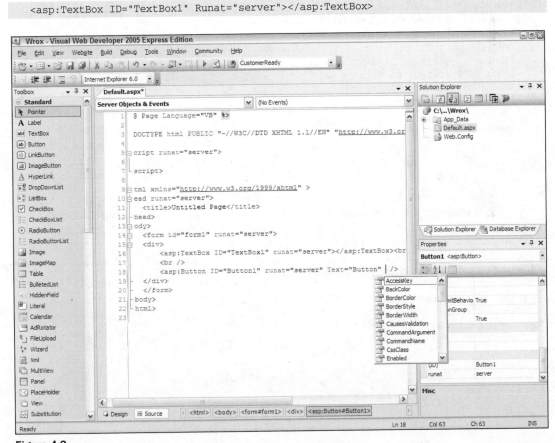

Figure 4-2

You can also highlight a control in Source view or simply place your cursor in the code statement of the control, and the Properties window displays the properties of the control. Now, you can apply properties directly in the Properties window of Visual Studio, and these properties are dynamically added to the code of your control.

Working with Server Control Events

As discussed in Chapter 1, ASP.NET uses more of a traditional Visual Basic event model than classic ASP. Instead of working with interpreted code, you are actually coding an event-based structure for your pages. Classic ASP used an interpreted model — when the server processed the Web page, the code of the page was interpreted line-by-line in a linear fashion where the only "event" implied was the page loading. This meant that occurrences you wanted to get initiated early in the process were placed at the top of the page.

Today, ASP.NET uses an event-driven model. Items or coding tasks get initiated only when a particular event occurs. A common event in the ASP.NET programming model is `Page_Load`, which is illustrated in Listing 4-1.

Listing 4-1: Working with specific page events

VB
```
Protected Sub Page_Load(ByVal sender As Object, ByVal e As System.EventArgs)
    ' Code actions here
End Sub
```

C#
```
protected void Page_Load(object sender, EventArgs e)
{
    // Code actions here
}
```

Not only can you work with the overall page — as well as its properties and methods at particular moments in time through page events — but you can also work with the server controls contained on the page through particular control events. For example, one common event for a button on a form is `Button_Click`, which is illustrated in Listing 4-2.

Listing 4-2: Working with a Button Click event

VB
```
Protected Sub Button1_Click(ByVal sender As Object, ByVal e As System.EventArgs)
    ' Code actions here
End Sub
```

C#
```
protected void Button1_Click(object sender, EventArgs e)
{
    // Code actions here
}
```

The event shown in Listing 4-2 is fired only when the end user actually clicks the button on the form that has an `OnClick` attribute value of `Button1_Click`. So, not only does the event handler exist in the server-side code of the ASP.NET page, but that handler is also hooked up using the OnClick property of the server control in the associated ASP.NET page markup as illustrated in the following code:

```
<asp:Button ID="Button1" Runat="server" Text="Button" OnClick="Button1_Click" />
```

How do you fire these events for server controls? You have a couple of ways to go about it. The first way is to pull up your ASP.NET page in the Design view and double-click the control for which you want to create a server-side event. For instance, double-clicking a Button server control in Design view creates the structure of the Button1_Click event within your server-side code, whether the code is in a code-behind file or inline. This creates a stub handler for that server control's most popular event.

With that said, be aware that a considerable number of additional events are available to the Button control that you cannot get at by double-clicking the control. To access them, pull up the page that contains the server-side code, select the control from the first drop-down list at the top of the IDE, and then choose the particular event you want for that control in the second drop-down list. Figure 4-3 shows the event drop-down list displayed. You might, for example, want to work with the Button control's PreRender event rather than its Click event. The handler for the event you choose is placed in your server-side code.

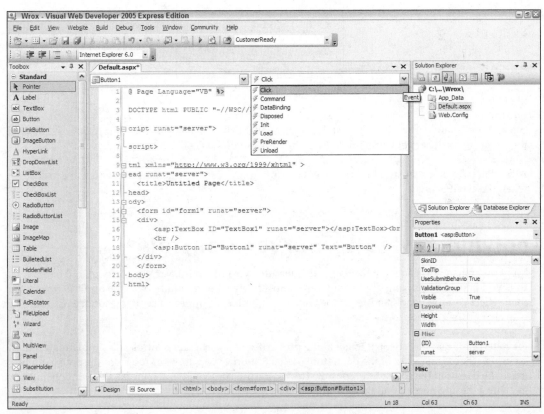

Figure 4-3

The second way is to create server-side events for your server controls from the Properties window of Visual Studio. This works only from Design view of the page. In Design view, highlight the server control that you want to work with. The properties for the control then appear in the Properties window, along with an icon menu. One of the icons, the Events icon, is represented by a lightning bolt (shown in Figure 4-4).

Figure 4-4

Clicking the Events icon pulls up a list of events available for the control. You simply double-click one of the events to get that event structure created in your server-side code.

After you have an event structure in place, you can program specific actions that you want to occur when the event is fired.

Applying Styles to Server Controls

More often than not, you want to change the default style (which is basically no style) to the server controls you implement in your applications. You most likely want to build your Web applications so that they reflect your own look-and-feel. One way to customize the appearance of the controls in your pages is to change the controls' properties.

As stated earlier in this chapter, to get at the properties of a particular control you simply highlight the control in the Design view of the page from Visual Studio. If you are working from the Source view, place the cursor in the code of the control. The properties presented in the Properties window allow you to control the appearance and behavior of the selected control.

Examining the Controls' Common Properties

Many of the default server controls that come with ASP.NET 2.0 are derived from the WebControl class and share similar properties that enable you to alter their appearance and behavior. Not all the derived controls use all the available properties (although many are implemented). Another important point is that not all server controls are implemented from the `WebControl` class. For instance, the Literal, PlaceHolder, Repeater, and XML server controls do not derive from the `WebControl` base class, but instead the `Control` class.

HTML server controls also do not derive from the `WebControl` base class because they are more focused on the set attributes of particular HTML elements. The following table lists the common properties the server controls share.

Property	Description
AccessKey	Enables you to assign a character to be associated with the Alt key so that the end user can activate the control using quick-keys on the keyboard. For instance, you can assign a Button control an `AccessKey` property value of K. Now, instead of clicking the button on the ASP.NET page (using a pointer controlled by the mouse), the end user can simply press Alt+K.
Attributes	Enables you to define additional attributes for a Web server control that are not defined by a public property.
BackColor	Controls the color shown behind the control's layout on the ASP.NET page.
BorderColor	Assigns a color that is shown around the physical edge of the server control.
BorderWidth	Assigns a value to the width of the line that makes up the border of the control. Placing a number as the value assigns the number as a pixel-width of the border. The default border color is black if the `BorderColor` property is not used in conjunction with the `BorderWidth` property setting.
BorderStyle	Enables you to assign the design of the border that is placed around the server control. By default, the border is created as a straight line, but a number of different styles can be used for your borders. Other possible values for the `BorderStyle` property include `Dotted`, `Dashed`, `Solid`, `Double`, `Groove`, `Ridge`, `Inset`, and `Outset`.
CssClass	Assigns a custom CSS (Cascading Style Sheet) class file to the control.
Enabled	Enables you to turn off the functionality of the control by setting the value of this property to `False`. By default, the `Enabled` property is set to `True`.
EnableTheming	Enables you to turn on theming capabilities for the selected server control. The default value is `True`. This is a new property in the .NET Framework 2.0.
Font	Sets the font for all the text that appears anywhere in the control.
ForeColor	Sets the color of all the text that appears anywhere in the control.

Table continued on following page

Property	Description
Height	Sets the height of the control.
SkinID	Sets the skin to use when theming the control. This is a new property in the .NET Framework 2.0.
Style	Enables you to apply CSS styles to the control.
TabIndex	Sets the control's tab position in the ASP.NET page. This property works in conjunction with other controls on the page.
ToolTip	Assigns text that appears in a yellow box in the browser when a mouse pointer is held over the control for a short length of time. This can be used to add more instructions for the end user.
Width	Sets the width of the control.

You can see these common properties in many of the server controls you work with. New properties of the WebControl class in the .NET Framework 2.0 include the EnableTheming and SkinID properties. These properties are covered in more detail in Chapter 9. You also see additional properties that are specific to the control you are viewing. Learning about the properties from the preceding table enables you to quickly work with Web server controls and to modify them to your needs.

Now take a look at some additional methods of customizing the look-and-feel of your server controls.

Changing Styles Using Cascading Style Sheets

One method of changing the look-and-feel of specific elements on your ASP.NET page is to apply a *style* to the element. The most rudimentary method of applying a defined look-and-feel to your page elements is to use various style-changing HTML elements such as <font>, <b>, and <i> directly.

> *All ASP.NET developers should have a good understanding of HTML. For more information on HTML, please read Wrox's* Beginning Web Programming with HTML, XHTML, and CSS *(published by Wiley; ISBN 0-7645-7078-1).*

Using various HTML elements, you can change the appearance of many items contained on your pages. For instance, you can change a string's style as follows:

```
<font face="verdana"><b><i>Pork chops and applesauce</i></b></font>
```

You can go through an entire application and change the style of page elements using any of the appropriate HTML elements. You'll quickly find that this method works, but it is tough to maintain. To make any global style changes to your application, this method requires that you go through your application line-by-line to change each item individually. This can get cumbersome very fast!

Besides applying HTML elements to items to change their style, you can use another method known as *Cascading Style Sheets* (CSS). This alternative, but greatly preferred, styling technique allows you to assign formatting properties to HTML tags throughout your document in a couple of different ways. One way is to apply these styles directly to the HTML elements in your pages using *inline styles*. The other way involves placing these styles in an external stylesheet that can be placed either directly in an ASP.NET page or kept in a separate document that is simply referenced in the ASP.NET page. You explore these methods in the following sections.

Applying Styles Directly to HTML Elements

The first method of using CSS is to apply the styles directly to the tags contained in your ASP.NET pages. For instance, you apply a style to a string, as shown in Listing 4-3.

Listing 4-3: Applying CSS styles directly to HTML elements

```
<p style="color:blue; font-weight:bold">
    Pork chops and applesauce
</p>
```

This text string is changed by the CSS included in the `<p>` element so that the string appears bold and blue. Using the style attribute of the `<p>` element, you can change everything that appears between the opening and closing `<p>` elements. When the page is generated, the first style change applied is to the text between the `<p>` elements. In this example, the text has changed to the color blue because of the `color:blue` command, and then the `font-weight:bold` command is applied. You can separate the styling commands using semicolons, and you can apply as many styles as you want to your elements.

Applying CSS styles in this manner presents the same problem as simply applying various HTML style elements — this is a tough structure to maintain. If styles are scattered throughout your pages, making global style changes can be rather time consuming. Putting all the styles together in a stylesheet is the best approach. A couple of methods can be used to build your stylesheets.

Working with the Visual Studio Style Builder

Visual Studio 2005 includes Style Builder, a tool that makes the building of CSS styles fairly simple. It can be quite a time saver because so many possible CSS definitions are available to you. If you are new to CSS, this tool can make all the difference.

The Visual Studio Style Builder enables you to apply CSS styles to individual elements or to construct your own stylesheets. To access the Style Builder tool when applying a style to a single page element, highlight the page element and then right-click it. From the menu that appears, select Style. Style Builder is shown in Figure 4-5.

You can use Style Builder to change quite a bit about your selected item. After making all the changes you want and clicking OK, you see the styles you chose applied to the selected element.

Now take a look at how to create styles in a stylesheet.

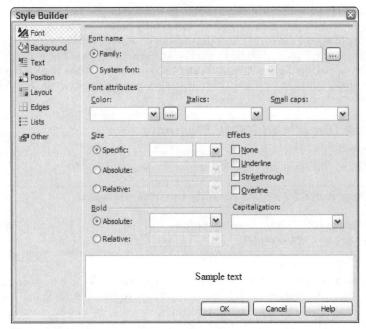

Figure 4-5

Creating External Style Sheets

You can use a couple of different methods to create stylesheets. The most common method is to create an *external* stylesheet—a separate stylesheet file that is referenced in the pages that employ the defined styles. To begin the creation of your external stylesheet, add a new item to your project. From the Add New Item dialog, create a style sheet called `StyleSheet.css`. Add the file to your project by pressing the Add button. Figure 4-6 shows the result.

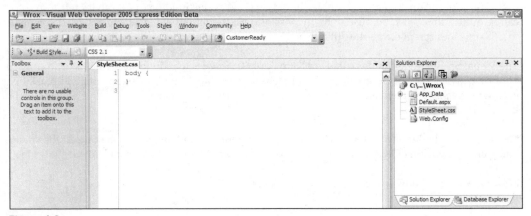

Figure 4-6

Using Visual Studio's CSS Outline window (in the left pane in Figure 4-6), you can apply style rules in any of three ways:

❏ **By element:** You apply styles to specific HTML elements, such as the `<p>`, `<a>`, or `<table>`.

❏ **By class:** You bring your style definitions together as a package, otherwise known as a *class*. Then you apply the selected classes to either specific page elements or to an entire page.

❏ **By element IDs:** This method enables you to say that the selected styles should be applied only to controls with specific ID names, such as Table1 or Button1.

Using Visual Studio, you can construct a stylesheet that looks similar to what is shown in Listing 4-4.

Listing 4-4: An external stylesheet

```
body {
    font-weight: normal;
    font-family: Verdana, Helvetica, sans-serif;
    font-size: .8em;
    letter-spacing: normal;
    text-transform: none;
    word-spacing: normal;
    background-color: white;
}

H1, H2, H3, H4, TH, THEAD, TFOOT {
    color: #003366;
}

H1 {
    font-family: Verdana, Arial, Helvetica, sans-serif;
    font-size: 2em;
    font-weight: 700;
    font-style: normal;
    text-decoration: none;
    word-spacing: normal;
    letter-spacing: normal;
    text-transform: none;
}
```

A stylesheet can go on for quite awhile until each and every possible HTML element is defined (though not required). The first definition in this example is for the entire body of the page (everything between the opening and closing `<body>` elements). The styles are applied in the order in which they appear in the stylesheet. So first, a style is applied to the entire document; then the style is further defined by specific HTML elements. All style definitions follow this pattern:

```
Property: Value;
```

The name of the CSS property is applied first, followed by a colon, and then the value to apply to this property. The definition ends with a semicolon.

The CSS file in Listing 4-4 also shows that it is possible to apply a style to many different elements at the same time by separating the element names with a comma as is done with H1, H2, H3, H4, TH, THEAD, TFOOT.

One wonderful addition to working with CSS files in Visual Studio is that even these allow for IntelliSense features, as illustrated in Figure 4-7.

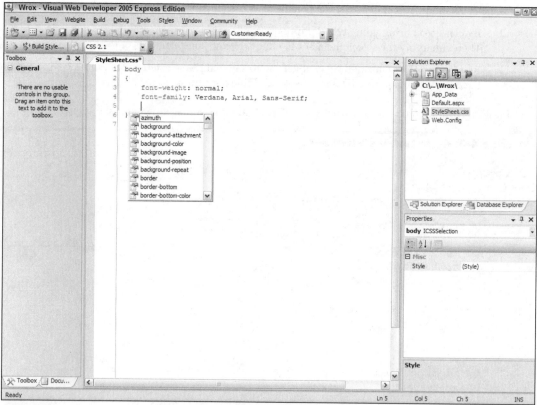

Figure 4-7

After your style file is created, even though it is contained in your project, it is not applied to anything unless you specifically apply the stylesheet to the page itself. You have a couple of approaches to accomplish this task.

One option is to pull up the DOCUMENT properties in the Properties window of Visual Studio and assign a value to the `StyleSheet` property. Assigning the stylesheet shown earlier, `StyleSheet.css`, as a value of the `StyleSheet` property adds the following line to your ASP.NET page within the `<head>` section:

```
<head runat="server">
    <title>My ASP.NET page</title>
    <link type="text/css" rel="stylesheet" href="StyleSheet.css" />
</head>
```

After this line is added to your page, the ASP.NET page applies the styles that are defined in `StyleSheet.css`.

The other method of getting this line into your page is simply to drag and drop the `StyleSheet.css` file from the Solution Explorer to the Design or Source view of the page in the Document window of Visual Studio. The exact same `<link>` element used previously is applied.

Using an external stylesheet within your application enables you to make global changes to the look-and-feel of your application quickly. Simply making a change at this central point cascades the change as defined by the stylesheet to your entire application.

Creating Internal Stylesheets

The second method for applying a stylesheet to a particular ASP.NET page is to bring the defined stylesheet into the actual document by creating an *internal* stylesheet. Instead of making a reference to an external stylesheet file, you bring the style definitions into the document. Note, however, that it is considered best practice to use external, rather than internal, stylesheets.

Consider using an internal stylesheet only if you are applying certain styles to a small number of pages within your application. Listing 4-5 shows the use of an internal stylesheet.

Listing 4-5: Using an internal stylesheet

```
<%@ Page Language="VB" %>

<html xmlns="http://www.w3.org/1999/xhtml" >
<head runat="server">
    <title>My ASP.NET Page</title>

    <style type="text/css">
        <!--
            body {
                font-family: Verdana;
            }

            a:link {
                text-decoration: none;
                color: blue;
            }

            a:visited {
                text-decoration: none;
                color: blue;
            }

            a:hover {
                text-decoration: underline;
                color: red;
            }

        -->
    </style>

</head>
<body>
    <form id="form1" runat="server">
    <div>
        <a href="Default.aspx">Home</a>
    </div>
    </form>
</body>
</html>
```

In this document, the internal stylesheet is set inside the opening and closing <head> elements. Although this is not a requirement, it is considered best practice. The stylesheet itself is placed between <style> tags with a type attribute defined as text/css.

HTML comment tags are included because not all browsers support internal stylesheets (it is generally the older browsers that do not accept them). Putting HTML comments around the style definitions hides these definitions from very old browsers. Except for the comment tags, the style definitions are handled in the same way they are done in an external stylesheet.

HTML Server Controls

ASP.NET enables you to take HTML elements and, with relatively little work on your part, turn them into server-side controls. Afterward, you can use them to control the behavior and actions of elements implemented in your ASP.NET pages.

Of course, you can place any HTML you want in your pages. You have the option of using the HTML placed in the page as a server-side control. You can also find a list of HTML elements contained in the Toolbox of Visual Studio (shown in Figure 4-8).

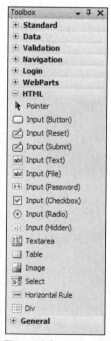

Figure 4-8

Dragging and dropping any of these HTML elements from the Toolbox to the Design or Source view of your ASP.NET page in the Document window simply produces the appropriate HTML element. For instance, placing an HTML Button control on your page produces the following results in your code:

```
<input id="Button1" type="button" value="button" />
```

In this state, the Button control is not a server-side control. It is simply an HTML element and nothing more. You can turn this into an HTML server control in a couple of different ways. In Design view, you can right-click the element and select Run As Server Control from the menu. This causes a few things to happen. The first thing is that a small green triangle appears on the visual element. The Button element, after it has been turned into an HTML server control, looks like Figure 4-9.

Green triangle

Figure 4-9

In Source view, you simply change the HTML element by adding a `runat="server"` to the control:

```
<input id="Button1" type="button" value="button" runat="server" />
```

After it is converted to a server control, you can work with the selected element as you would work with any of the Web server controls. For instance, double-clicking the button from the Design view of the page generates a button-click event for the control. Listing 4-6 shows an example of some HTML server controls.

Listing 4-6: Working with HTML server controls

VB

```
<%@ Page Language="VB" %>

<script runat="server">
    Protected Sub Button1_ServerClick(ByVal sender As Object, _
        ByVal e As System.EventArgs)
        Response.Write("Hello " & Text1.Value)
    End Sub
</script>

<html xmlns="http://www.w3.org/1999/xhtml" >
<head runat="server">
    <title>Using HTML Server Controls</title>
</head>
<body>
    <form id="form1" runat="server">
    <div>
        What is your name?<br />
        <input id="Text1" type="text" runat="server" />
        <input id="Button1" type="button" value="Submit" runat="server"
        onserverclick="Button1_ServerClick" />
    </div>
    </form>
</body>
</html>
```

(continued)

Listing 4-6: *(continued)*

C#

```
<%@ Page Language="C#" %>

<script runat="server">
    protected void Button1_ServerClick(object sender, EventArgs e)
    {
        Response.Write("Hello " + Text1.Value);
    }
</script>
```

In this example, you can see two HTML server controls on the page. Both are simply typical HTML elements with the additional `runat="server"` attribute added. If you are working with HTML elements as server controls, you must include an `id` attribute so that the server control can be identified in the server-side code.

The Button control includes a reference to a server-side event using the `OnServerClick` attribute. This attribute points to the server-side event that is triggered when an end user clicks the button — in this case, `Button1_ServerClick`. Within the `Button1_ServerClick` event, the value placed in the text box is output by using the `Value` property.

Looking at the HtmlControl Base Class

All the HTML server controls use a class that is derived from the `HtmlControl` base class (fully qualified as `System.Web.UI.HtmlControls.HtmlControl`). These classes expose many properties from the control's derived class. The following table details some of the properties available from this base class. Some of these items are themselves derived from the base `Control` class.

Method or Property	Description
Attributes	Provides a collection of name/value of all the available attributes specified in the control, including custom attributes.
Disabled	Allows you to get or set whether the control is disabled using a Boolean value.
EnableTheming	Enables you, using a Boolean value, to get or set whether the control takes part in the page theming capabilities.
EnableViewState	Allows you to get or set a Boolean value that indicates whether the control participates in the page's view state capabilities.
ID	Allows you to get or set the unique identifier for the control.
Page	Allows you to gets a reference to the Page object that contains the specified server control.
Parent	Gets a reference to the parent control in the page control hierarchy.
Site	Provides information about the Web site for which the server control belongs.

Method or Property	Description
SkinID	When the EnableTheming property is set to True, the SkinID property specifies the skin file that should be used in setting a theme.
Style	Makes references to the CSS style collection that applies to the specified control.
TagName	Provides the name of the element that is generated from the specified control.
Visible	Specifies whether the control is visible on the generated page.

You can find a more comprehensive list in the SDK.

Looking at the HtmlContainerControl Class

The HtmlContainerControl base class is used for those HTML classes that are focused on HTML elements that can be contained within a single node. For instance, the <img>, <input>, and <link> elements work from classes derived from the HtmlContainerControl class.

Other HTML elements such as <a>, <form>, and <select>, require an opening and closing set of tags. These elements use classes that are derived from the HtmlContainerControl class — a class specifically designed to work with HTML elements that require a closing tag.

Because the HtmlContainerControl class is derived from the HtmlControl class, you have all the HtmlControl class's properties and methods available to you as well as some new items that have been declared in the HtmlContainerControl class itself. The most important of these are the InnerText and InnerHtml properties:

❑   InnerHtml: Enables you to specify content that can include HTML elements to be placed between the opening and closing tags of the specified control.

❑   InnerText: Enables you to specify raw text to be placed between the opening and closing tags of the specified control.

Looking at All the HTML Classes

It is quite possible to work with every HTML element because a corresponding class is available for each one of them. The .NET Framework documentation shows the following classes for working with your HTML server controls:

❑   HtmlAnchor controls the <a> element.

❑   HtmlButton controls the <button> element.

❑   HtmlForm controls the <form> element.

❑   HtmlHead controls the <head> element. This is new to the .NET Framework 2.0.

❑   HtmlImage controls the <img> element.

- ❑ HtmlInputButton controls the <input type="button"> element.

- ❑ HtmlInputCheckBox controls the <input type="checkbox"> element.

- ❑ HtmlInputFile controls the <input type="file"> element.

- ❑ HtmlInputHidden controls the <input type="hidden"> element.

- ❑ HtmlInputImage controls the <input type="image"> element.

- ❑ HtmlInputPassword controls the <input type="password"> element. This is new to the .NET Framework 2.0.

- ❑ HtmlInputRadioButton controls the <input type="radio"> element.

- ❑ HtmlInputReset controls the <input type="reset"> element. This is new to the .NET Framework 2.0.

- ❑ HtmlInputSubmit controls the <input type="submit"> element. This is new to the .NET Framework 2.0.

- ❑ HtmlInputText controls the <input type="text"> element.

- ❑ HtmlLink controls the <link> element. This is new to the .NET Framework 2.0.

- ❑ HtmlSelect controls the <select> element.

- ❑ HtmlTable controls the <table> element.

- ❑ HtmlTableCell controls the <td> element.

- ❑ HtmlTableRow controls the <tr> element.

- ❑ HtmlTextArea controls the <textarea> element.

- ❑ HtmlTitle controls the <title> element. This is new to the .NET Framework 2.0.

You gain access to one of these classes when you convert an HTML element to an HTML server control. For example, convert the <title> element to a server control this way:

```
<title id="Title1" runat="Server"/>
```

That gives you access to the HtmlTitle class for this particular HTML element. Using this class instance, you can perform a number of tasks including providing a text value for the page title dynamically:

VB
```
Title1.Text = DateTime.Now.ToString()
```

C#
```
Title1.Text = DateTime.Now.ToString();
```

You can get most of the HTML elements you need by using these classes, but a considerable number of other HTML elements are at your disposal that are not explicitly covered by one of these HTML classes. For example, the HtmlGenericControl class provides server-side access to any HTML element you want.

Using the *HtmlGenericControl* Class

You should be aware of the importance of the `HtmlGenericControl` class; it gives you some capabilities that you do not get from any other server control offered by ASP.NET. For instance, using the `HtmlGenericControl` class, you can get server-side access to the `<meta>`, `<p>`, `<span>`, or other elements that would otherwise be unreachable.

Listing 4-7 shows you how to change the `<meta>` element in your page using the `HtmlGenericControl` class.

Listing 4-7: Changing the <meta> element using the HtmlGenericControl class

VB

```
<%@ Page Language="VB" %>

<script runat="server">
    Protected Sub Page_Load(ByVal sender As Object, ByVal e As System.EventArgs)
        Meta1.Attributes("Name") = "description"
        Meta1.Attributes("CONTENT") = "Generated on: " & DateTime.Now.ToString()
    End Sub
</script>

<html xmlns="http://www.w3.org/1999/xhtml" >
<head runat="server">
    <title>Using the HtmlGenericControl class</title>
    <meta id="Meta1" runat="server" />
</head>
<body>
    <form id="form1" runat="server">
    <div>
        The rain in Spain stays mainly in the plains.
    </div>
    </form>
</body>
</html>
```

C#

```
<%@ Page Language="C#" %>

<script runat="server">
    protected void Page_Load(object sender, EventArgs e)
    {
        Meta1.Attributes["Name"] = "description";
        Meta1.Attributes["CONTENT"] = "Generated on: " + DateTime.Now.ToString();
    }
</script>
```

In this example, the page's `<meta>` element is turned into an HTML server control with the addition of the `id` and `runat` attributes. Because the `HtmlGenericControl` class can work with a wide range of HTML elements, you cannot assign values to HTML attributes in the same manner as you do when working with the other HTML classes (such as `HtmlInputButton`). You assign values to the attributes of an HTML element through the use of the `HtmlGenericControl` class's `Attributes` property, specifying the attribute you are working with as a string value.

The following is a partial result of running the example page:

```
<html xmlns="http://www.w3.org/1999/xhtml" >
<head>
    <meta id="Meta1" Name="description"
     CONTENT="Generated on: 6/5/2006 2:42:52 PM"></meta>
    <title>Using the HtmlGenericControl class</title>
</head>
```

By using the `HtmlGenericControl` class, along with the other HTML classes, you can manipulate every element of your ASP.NET pages from your server-side code.

Manipulating Pages and Server Controls with JavaScript

Developers generally like to include some of their own custom JavaScript functions in their ASP.NET pages. You have a couple of ways to do this. The first is to apply JavaScript directly to the controls on your ASP.NET pages. For example, look at a simple Label server control, shown in Listing 4-8, which displays the current date and time.

Listing 4-8: Showing the current date and time

VB
```
Protected Sub Page_Load(ByVal sender As Object, ByVal e As System.EventArgs)
    TextBox1.Text = DateTime.Now.ToString()
End Sub
```

C#
```
protected void Page_Load(object sender, EventArgs e) {
    TextBox1.Text = DateTime.Now.ToString();
}
```

This little bit of code displays the current date and time on the page of the end user. The problem is that the date and time displayed are correct for the Web server that generated the page. If someone sits in the Pacific time zone (PST), and the Web server is in the Eastern time zone (EST), the page won't be correct for that viewer. If you want the time to be correct for anyone visiting the site, regardless of where they reside in the world, you can employ JavaScript to work with the TextBox control, as illustrated in Listing 4-9.

Listing 4-9: Using JavaScript to show the current time for the end user

```
<%@ Page Language="VB" %>

<html xmlns="http://www.w3.org/1999/xhtml" >
<head runat="server">
    <title>Using JavaScript</title>
</head>
```

```
<body onload="javascript:document.forms[0]['TextBox1'].value=Date();">
    <form id="form1" runat="server">
    <div>
        <asp:TextBox ID="TextBox1" Runat="server" Width="300"></asp:TextBox>
    </div>
    </form>
</body>
</html>
```

In this example, even though you are using a standard TextBox server control from the Web server control family, you can get at this control using JavaScript that is planted in the `onload` attribute of the `<body>` element. The value of the `onload` attribute actually points to the specific server control by using the value of the `ID` attribute from the server control: `TextBox1`. You can get at other server controls on your page by employing the same methods. This bit of code produces the result illustrated in Figure 4-10.

Figure 4-10

ASP.NET uses the new `Page.ClientScript` property to register and place JavaScript functions on your ASP.NET pages. Three of these methods are reviewed here. More methods and properties than just these two are available through the `ClientScript` object, but these are the more useful ones. You can find the rest in the SDK documentation.

> *The* `Page.RegisterStartupScript` *and the* `Page.RegisterClientScriptBlock` *methods from the .NET Framework 1.0/1.1 are now considered obsolete. Both of these possibilities for registering scripts required a key/script set of parameters. Because two separate methods were involved, there was an extreme possibility that some key name collisions would occur. The* `Page.ClientScript` *property is meant to bring all the script registrations under one umbrella, making your code less error prone.*

Using Page.ClientScript.RegisterClientScriptBlock

The `RegisterClientScriptBlock` method allows you to place a JavaScript function at the top of the page. This means that the script is in place for the startup of the page in the browser. Its use is illustrated in Listing 4-10.

Listing 4-10: Using the RegisterClientScriptBlock method

VB

```
<%@ Page Language="VB" %>

<script runat="server">
    Protected Sub Page_Load(ByVal sender As Object, ByVal e As System.EventArgs)
        Dim myScript As String = "function AlertHello() { alert('Hello ASP.NET'); }"
        Page.ClientScript.RegisterClientScriptBlock(Me.GetType(), "MyScript", _
            myScript, True)
    End Sub
</script>

<html xmlns="http://www.w3.org/1999/xhtml" >
<head runat="server">
    <title>Adding JavaScript</title>
</head>
<body>
    <form id="form1" runat="server">
    <div>
        <asp:Button ID="Button1" Runat="server" Text="Button"
          OnClientClick="AlertHello()" />
    </div>
    </form>
</body>
</html>
```

C#

```
<%@ Page Language="C#" %>

<script runat="server">
    protected void Page_Load(object sender, EventArgs e)
    {
        string myScript = @"function AlertHello() { alert('Hello ASP.NET'); }";
        Page.ClientScript.RegisterClientScriptBlock(this.GetType(),
            "MyScript", myScript, true);
    }
</script>
```

From this example, you can see that you create the JavaScript function `AlertHello()` as a string called `myScript`. Then using the `Page.ClientScript.RegisterClientScriptBlock` method, you program the script to be placed on the page. The two possible constructions of the `RegisterClientScriptBlock` method are the following:

❑ `RegisterClientScriptBlock` (*type, key, script*)

❑ `RegisterClientScriptBlock` (*type, key, script, script tag specification*)

In the example from Listing 4-10, you are specifying the type as `Me.GetType()`, the key, the script to include, and then a `Boolean` value setting of `True` so that .NET places the script on the ASP.NET page with `<script>` tags automatically. When running the page, you can view the source code for the page to see the results:

```
<html xmlns="http://www.w3.org/1999/xhtml" >
<head><title>
    Adding JavaScript
</title></head>
<body>
    <form method="post" action="JavaScriptPage.aspx" id="form1">
<div>
<input type="hidden" name="__VIEWSTATE"
 value="/wEPDwUKMTY3NzE5MjIyMGRkiyYSRMg+bcXi9DiawYlbxndiTDo=" />
</div>


<script type="text/javascript">
<!--
function AlertHello() { alert('Hello ASP.NET'); }// -->
</script>

    <div>
        <input type="submit" name="Button1" value="Button" onclick="AlertHello();"
         id="Button1" />
    </div>
    </form>
</body>
</html>
```

From this, you can see that the script specified was indeed included on the ASP.NET page before the page code. Not only were the `<script>` tags included, but the proper comment tags were added around the script (so older browsers won't break).

Using Page.ClientScript.RegisterStartupScript

The `RegisterStartupScript` method is not too much different from the `RegisterClientScriptBlock` method. The big difference is that the `RegisterStartupScript` places the script at the bottom of the ASP.NET page instead of at the top. In fact, the `RegisterStartupScript` method even takes the same constructors as the `RegisterClientScriptBlock` method:

❑   `RegisterStartupScript` (*type*, *key*, *script*)

❑   `RegisterStartupScript` (*type*, *key*, *script*, *script tag specification*)

So what difference does it make where the script is registered on the page? A lot, actually!

If you have a bit of JavaScript that is working with one of the controls on your page, in most cases you want to use the `RegisterStartupScript` method instead of `RegisterClientScriptBlock`. For example, you'd use the following code to create a page that includes a simple `<asp:TextBox>` control that contains a default value of `Hello ASP.NET`.

```
<asp:TextBox ID="TextBox1" Runat="server">Hello ASP.NET</asp:TextBox>
```

Then use the `RegisterClientScriptBlock` method to place a script on the page that utilizes the value in the `TextBox1` control, as illustrated in Listing 4-11.

117

Listing 4-11: Improperly using the RegisterClientScriptBlock method

VB

```vb
Protected Sub Page_Load(ByVal sender As Object, ByVal e As System.EventArgs)
    Dim myScript As String = "alert(document.forms[0]['TextBox1'].value);"
    Page.ClientScript.RegisterClientScriptBlock(Me.GetType(), "myKey", myScript, _
        True)
End Sub
```

C#

```csharp
protected void Page_Load(object sender, EventArgs e)
{
    string myScript = @"alert(document.forms[0]['TextBox1'].value);";
    Page.ClientScript.RegisterClientScriptBlock(this.GetType(),
        "MyScript", myScript, true);
}
```

Running this page gives you a JavaScript error, as shown in Figure 4-11.

Figure 4-11

The reason for the error is that the JavaScript function fired before the text box was even placed on the screen. Therefore, the JavaScript function did not find `TextBox1`, and that caused an error to be thrown by the page. Now try the `RegisterStartupScript` method shown in Listing 4-12.

Listing 4-12: Using the RegisterStartupScript method

VB

```vb
Protected Sub Page_Load(ByVal sender As Object, ByVal e As System.EventArgs)
    Dim myScript As String = "alert(document.forms[0]['TextBox1'].value);"
    Page.ClientScript.RegisterStartupScript(Me.GetType(), "myKey", myScript, _
        True)
End Sub
```

C#
```
protected void Page_Load(object sender, EventArgs e)
{
    string myScript = @"alert(document.forms[0]['TextBox1'].value);";
    Page.ClientScript.RegisterStartupScript(this.GetType(),
        "MyScript", myScript, true);
}
```

This approach puts the JavaScript function at the bottom of the ASP.NET page, so when the JavaScript actually starts, it finds the TextBox1 element and works as planned. The result is shown in Figure 4-12.

Figure 4-12

Using Page.ClientScript.RegisterClientScriptInclude

The final method is RegisterClientScriptInclude. Many developers place their JavaScript inside a .js file, which is considered a best practice because it makes it very easy to make global JavaScript changes to the application. You can register the script files on your ASP.NET pages through the use of the RegisterClientScriptInclude method illustrated in Listing 4-13.

Listing 4-13: Using the RegisterClientScriptInclude method

VB
```
Dim myScript As String = "myJavaScriptCode.js"
Page.ClientScript.RegisterClientScriptInclude("myKey", myScript)
```

C#
```
string myScript = "myJavaScriptCode.js";
Page.ClientScript.RegisterClientScriptInclude("myKey", myScript);
```

This creates the following construction on the ASP.NET page:

```
<script src="myJavaScriptCode.js" type="text/javascript"></script>
```

Client-Side Callback

ASP.NET 2.0 includes a new client callback feature that enables you to retrieve page values and populate them to an already-generated page without regenerating the page. This makes it possible to change values on a page without going through the entire postback cycle; that means you can update your pages without completely redrawing the page. End users will not see the page flicker and reposition, and the pages will have a flow more like the flow of a thick-client application.

To work with the new callback capability, you have to know a little about working with JavaScript. This book does not attempt to teach you JavaScript. If you need to get up to speed on this rather large topic, check out Wrox's *Beginning JavaScript, Second Edition*, by Paul Wilton (ISBN: 0-7645-5587-1).

Comparing a Typical Postback to a Callback

Before you jump into some examples of the new callback feature, first look at a comparison to the current postback feature of a typical ASP.NET page.

When a page event is triggered on an ASP.NET page that is working with a typical postback scenario, a lot is going on. The diagram in Figure 4-13 illustrates the process.

In a normal postback situation, an event of some kind triggers an HTTP Post request to be sent to the Web server. An example of such an event might be the end user clicking a button on the form. This sends the HTTP Post request to the Web server, which then processes the request with the IPostbackEventHandler and runs the request through a series of page events. These events include loading the state (as found in the view state of the page), processing data, processing postback events, and finally rendering the page to be interpreted by the consuming browser once again. The process completely reloads the page in the browser, which is what causes the flicker and the realignment to the top of the page.

On the other hand, you have the alternative of using the new callback capabilities, as shown in the diagram in Figure 4-14.

In this case, an event (again, such as a button click) causes the event to be posted to a script event handler (a JavaScript function) that sends off an asynchronous request to the Web server for processing. ICallbackEventHandler runs the request through a pipeline similar to what is used with the postback — but you notice that some of the larger steps (such as rendering the page) are excluded from the process chain. After the information is loaded, the result is returned to the script callback object. The script code then pushes this data into the Web page using JavaScript's capabilities to do this without refreshing the page. To understand how this all works, look at the simple example in the following section.

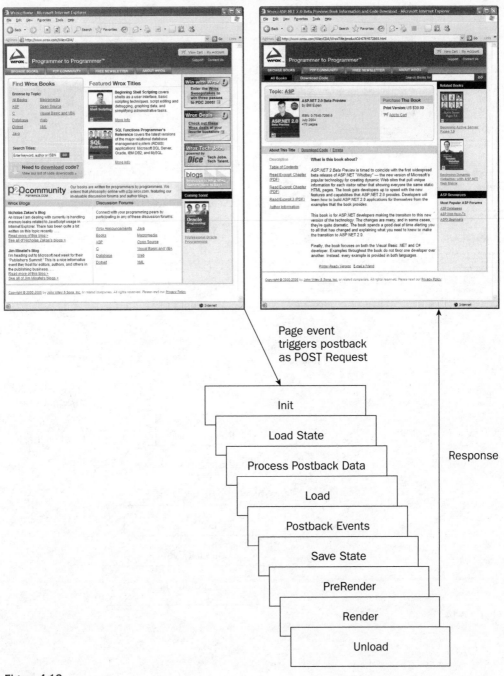

Page event
triggers postback
as POST Request

Response

Init

Load State

Process Postback Data

Load

Postback Events

Save State

PreRender

Render

Unload

Figure 4-13

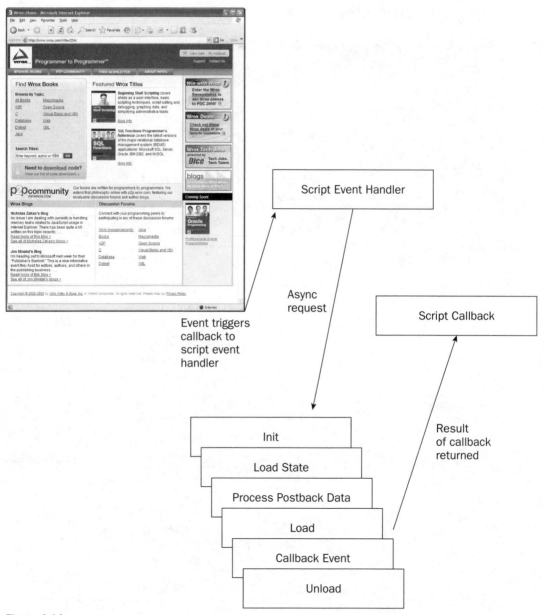

Script Event Handler

Event triggers callback to script event handler

Async request

Script Callback

Init

Load State

Process Postback Data

Load

Callback Event

Unload

Result of callback returned

Figure 4-14

Using the Callback Feature — A Simple Approach

Begin examining the callback feature by looking at how a simple ASP.NET page uses it. For this example, you have only an HTML button control and a TextBox server control (the Web server control version). The idea is that when the end user clicks the button on the form, the callback service is initiated and a random number is populated into the text box. Listing 4-14 shows an example of this in action.

Listing 4-14: Using the callback feature to populate a random value to a Web page

.aspx page (VB version)

```
<%@ Page Language="VB" AutoEventWireup="false" CodeFile="RandomNumber.aspx.vb"
    Inherits="RandomNumber" %>

<html xmlns="http://www.w3.org/1999/xhtml" >
<head runat="server">
    <title>Callback Page</title>

    <script type="text/javascript">
        function GetNumber(){
            UseCallback();
        }

        function GetRandomNumberFromServer(TextBox1, context){
            document.forms[0].TextBox1.value = TextBox1;
        }
    </script>

</head>
<body>
    <form id="form1" runat="server">
    <div>
        <input id="Button1" type="button" value="Get Random Number"
         onclick="GetNumber()" />
        <br />
        <br />
        <asp:TextBox ID="TextBox1" Runat="server"></asp:TextBox>
    </div>
    </form>
</body>
</html>
```

VB (code-behind)

```
Partial Class RandomNumber
    Inherits System.Web.UI.Page
    Implements System.Web.UI.ICallbackEventHandler

    Dim _callbackResult As String = Nothing

    Protected Sub Page_Load(ByVal sender As Object, ByVal e As System.EventArgs) _
        Handles Me.Load

        Dim cbReference As String = Page.ClientScript.GetCallbackEventReference(
            Me, "arg", "GetRandomNumberFromServer", "context")
Dim cbScript As String = "function UseCallback(arg, context)" & _
```

(continued)

123

Listing 4-14: *(continued)*

```vbnet
                "{" & cbReference & ";" & "}"

        Page.ClientScript.RegisterClientScriptBlock(Me.GetType(), _
            "UseCallback", cbScript, True)
    End Sub

Public Sub RaiseCallbackEvent(ByVal eventArgument As String) _
        Implements System.Web.UI.ICallbackEventHandler.RaiseCallbackEvent

        _callbackResult = Rnd().ToString()
    End Sub

    Public Function GetCallbackResult() As String _
        Implements System.Web.UI.ICallbackEventHandler.GetCallbackResult

        Return _callbackResult
    End Function
End Class
```

C# (code-behind)

```csharp
using System;
using System.Data;
using System.Configuration;
using System.Collections;
using System.Web;
using System.Web.Security;
using System.Web.UI;
using System.Web.UI.WebControls;
using System.Web.UI.WebControls.WebParts;
using System.Web.UI.HtmlControls;

public partial class RandomNumber : System.Web.UI.Page,
    System.Web.UI.ICallbackEventHandler
{
    private string _callbackResult = null;

    protected void Page_Load(object sender, EventArgs e)
    {
        string cbReference = Page.ClientScript.GetCallbackEventReference(this,
            "arg", "GetRandomNumberFromServer", "context");
        string cbScript = "function UseCallback(arg, context)" +
            "{" + cbReference + ";" + "}";

        Page.ClientScript.RegisterClientScriptBlock(this.GetType(),
            "UseCallback", cbScript, true);
    }

    public void RaiseCallbackEvent(string eventArg)
    {
        Random rnd = new Random();
        _callbackResult = rnd.Next().ToString();
    }

    public string GetCallbackResult()
```

```
        {
            return _callbackResult;
        }
    }

}
```

When this page is built and run in the browser, you get the results shown in Figure 4-15.

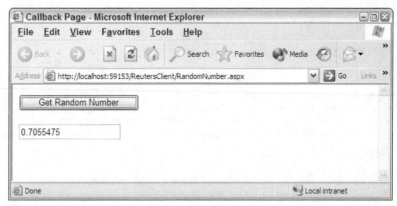

Figure 4-15

Clicking the button on the page invokes the client callback capabilities of the page, and the page then makes an asynchronous request to the code behind of the same page. After getting a response from this part of the page, the client script takes the retrieved value and places it inside the text box — all without doing a page refresh!

Now take a look at the .aspx page, which simply contains an HTML button control and a TextBox server control. Notice that a standard HTML button control is used because a typical <asp:button> control does not work here. No worries. When you work with the HTML button control, just be sure to include an onclick event to point to the JavaScript function that initiates this entire process:

```
<input id="Button1" type="button" value="Get Random Number"
  onclick="GetNumber()" />
```

You don't have to do anything else with the controls themselves. The final thing to include in the page is the client-side JavaScript functions to take care of the callback to the server-side functions. GetNumber() is the first JavaScript function that's instantiated. It starts the entire process by calling the name of the client script handler that is defined in the page's code behind. A string type result from GetNumber() is retrieved using the GetRandomNumberFromServer() function. GetRandomNumberFromServer() simply populates the string value retrieved and makes that the value of the Textbox control—specified by the value of the ID attribute of the server control (TextBox1):

```
<script type="text/javascript">
    function GetNumber(){
        UseCallback();
    }

    function GetRandomNumberFromServer(TextBox1, context){
```

```
                document.forms[0].TextBox1.value = TextBox1;
        }
    </script>
```

Now turn your attention to the code behind.

The `Page` class of the Web page implements the `System.Web.UI.ICallbackEventHandler` interface:

```
Partial Class RandomNumber
    Inherits System.Web.UI.Page
    Implements System.Web.UI.ICallbackEventHandler

    ' Code here

End Class
```

This interface requires you to implement a couple of methods—the `RaiseCallbackEvent` and the `GetCallbackResult` methods, both of which work with the client script request. `RaiseCallbackEvent` enables you to do the work of retrieving the value from the page, but the value can be only of type `string`:

```
Public Sub RaiseCallbackEvent(ByVal eventArgument As String) _
    Implements System.Web.UI.ICallbackEventHandler.RaiseCallbackEvent

    _callbackResult = Rnd().ToString()
End Sub
```

The `GetCallbackResult` is the method that actually grabs the returned value to be used:

```
Public Function GetCallbackResult() As String _
    Implements System.Web.UI.ICallbackEventHandler.GetCallbackResult

        Return _callbackResult
End Function
```

In addition, the `Page_Load` event includes the creation and placement of the client callback script manager (the function that will manage requests and responses) on the client:

```
Dim cbReference As String = Page.GetCallbackEventReference(Me, "arg", _
    "GetRandomNumberFromServer", "context")
Dim cbScript As String = "function UseCallback(arg, context)" & _
    "{" & cbReference & ";" & "}"

Page.ClientScript.RegisterClientScriptBlock(Me.GetType(), _
    "UseCallback", cbScript, True)
```

The function placed on the client for the callback capabilities is called `UseCallback()`. This `string` is then populated to the Web page itself using the `Page.ClientScript.RegisterClientScripBlock` that also puts `<script>` tags around the function on the page. Make sure that the name you use here is the same name you use in the client-side JavaScript function presented earlier.

In the end, you have a page that refreshes content without refreshing the overall page. This opens the door to a whole new area of possibilities. One caveat is that the callback capabilities described here use XmlHTTP and, therefore, the client browser needs to support XmlHTTP (Microsoft's Internet Explorer and FireFox do support this feature). Because of this, the .NET Framework 2.0 introduces the `SupportsCallBack` and the `SupportsXmlHttp` properties. To ensure this support, you could put a check in the page's code behind when the initial page is being generated. It might look similar to the following:

VB

```
If (Page.Request.Browser.SupportsXmlHTTP) Then

End If
```

C#

```
if (Page.Request.Browser.SupportsXmlHTTP == true) {

}
```

Using the Callback Feature with Parameters

Now you'll build a Web page that utilizes the callback feature but requires a parameter to retrieve a returned value. At the top of the page, place a text box that gathers input from the end user, a button, and another text box to populate the page with the result from the callback.

The page asks for a ZIP Code from the user and then uses the callback feature to instantiate an XML Web service request on the server. The Web service returns the latest weather for that particular ZIP Code in a string format. Listing 4-15 shows an example of the page.

Listing 4-15: Using the callback feature with a Web service

.aspx page (VB version)

```
<%@ Page Language="VB" AutoEventWireup="false" CodeFile="WSCallback.aspx.vb"
    Inherits="WSCallback" %>

<html xmlns="http://www.w3.org/1999/xhtml" >
<head runat="server">
    <title>Web Service Callback</title>

    <script type="text/javascript">
        function GetTemp(){
            var zipcode = document.forms[0].TextBox1.value;
            UseCallback(zipcode, "");
        }

        function GetTempFromServer(TextBox2, context){
            document.forms[0].TextBox2.value = "Zipcode: " +
            document.forms[0].TextBox1.value + " | Temp: " + TextBox2;
        }
    </script>
</head>
<body>
    <form id="form1" runat="server">
    <div>
        <asp:TextBox ID="TextBox1" Runat="server"></asp:TextBox>
```

(continued)

Listing 4-15: *(continued)*

```
            <br />
            <input id="Button1" type="button" value="Get Temp" onclick="GetTemp()" />
            <br />
            <asp:TextBox ID="TextBox2" Runat="server" Width="400px">
            </asp:TextBox>
            <br />
            <br />
        </div>
        </form>
    </body>
    </html>
```

VB (code-behind)

```
Partial Class WSCallback
    Inherits System.Web.UI.Page
    Implements System.Web.UI.ICallbackEventHandler

    Dim _callbackResult As String = Nothing

    Protected Sub Page_Load(ByVal sender As Object, ByVal e As System.EventArgs) _
        Handles Me.Load

        Dim cbReference As String = Page.ClientScript.GetCallbackEventReference(
            Me, "arg", "GetTempFromServer", "context")
        Dim cbScript As String = "function UseCallback(arg, context)" & _
            "{" & cbReference & ";" & "}"

        Page.ClientScript.RegisterClientScriptBlock(Me.GetType(), _
            "UseCallback", cbScript, True)
    End Sub

Public Sub RaiseCallbackEvent(ByVal eventArgument As String) _
        Implements System.Web.UI.ICallbackEventHandler.RaiseCallbackEvent

        Dim ws As New Weather.TemperatureService
        _callbackResult = ws.gettemp(eventArgument).ToString()
    End Sub
    Public Function GetCallbackResult() As String _
        Implements System.Web.UI.ICallbackEventHandler.GetCallbackResult

        Return _callbackResult
    End Function
End Class
```

C# (code-behind)

```
using System;
using System.Data;
using System.Configuration;
using System.Collections;
using System.Web;
using System.Web.Security;
using System.Web.UI;
using System.Web.UI.WebControls;
```

```
using System.Web.UI.WebControls.WebParts;
using System.Web.UI.HtmlControls;

public partial class WSCallback : System.Web.UI.Page,
    System.Web.UI.ICallbackEventHandler
{
    string_callbackResult = null;
    protected void Page_Load(object sender, EventArgs e)
    {
        string cbReference = Page.ClientScript.GetCallbackEventReference(this,
            "arg", "GetTempFromServer", "context");
        string cbScript = "function UseCallback(arg, context)" +
            "{" + cbReference + ";" + "}";

        Page.ClientScript.RegisterClientScriptBlock(this.GetType(),
            "UseCallback", cbScript, true);
    }

    public void RaiseCallbackEvent(string eventArg)
    {
        Weather.TemperatureService ws = new Weather.TemperatureService();
        _callbackResult = ws.gettemp(eventArg).ToString();
    }

    public string GetCallbackResult()
    {
        return _callbackResult;
    }
}
```

What you don't see on this page from the listing is that a Web reference has been made to a remote Web service that returns the latest weather to the application based on a ZIP Code the user supplied.

To get at the Web service used in this demo, the location of the WSDL file at the time of this writing is `http://www.xmethods.net/sd/2001/TemperatureService.wsdl`. *For more information on working with Web services in your ASP.NET applications, check out Chapter 26.*

After building and running this page, you get the results illustrated in Figure 4-16.

Figure 4-16

The big difference with the client callback feature is that this example sends in a required parameter. That is done in the `GetTemp()` JavaScript function on the `.aspx` part of the page:

```
function GetTemp(){
    var zipcode = document.forms[0].TextBox1.value;
    UseCallback(zipcode, "");
}
```

The JavaScript function shows the population that the end user input into `TextBox1` and places its value in a variable called `zipcode` that is sent as a parameter in the `UseCallback()` method.

This example, like the previous one, updates the page without doing a complete page refresh.

Summary

This chapter gave you one of the core building blocks of an ASP.NET page — the server control. The server control is an object-oriented approach to page development that encapsulates page elements into modifiable and expandable components.

The chapter also showed you how to customize the look-and-feel of your server controls using Cascading Style Sheets (CSS). Working with CSS in ASP.NET 2.0 is easy and quick, especially if you have Visual Studio 2005 to assist you. Finally, this chapter looked at both HTML server controls and adding JavaScript to your pages to modify the behaviors of your controls.

ASP.NET
Web Server Controls

Of the two types of server controls, HTML server controls and Web server controls, the second is considered the more powerful and flexible. The previous chapter looked at how to use HTML server controls in applications. HTML server controls enable you to manipulate HTML elements from your server-side code. On the other hand, Web server controls are powerful because they are not explicitly tied to specific HTML elements; rather, they are more closely aligned to the specific functionality that you want to generate. As you will see throughout this chapter, Web server controls can be very simple or rather complex depending on the control you are working with.

This chapter introduces some of the available Web server controls. It concentrates on the Web server controls that were around during the ASP.NET 1.0/1.1 days; Chapter 6 explores the server controls that are newly available in ASP.NET 2.0. These chapters do not discuss every possible control because some server controls are introduced and covered in other chapters throughout the book.

The controls that were originally introduced with ASP.NET 1.0/1.1 still work as they did before. ASP.NET 2.0 is backward compatible with the previous two versions of ASP.NET. This means that the control code you wrote in those past versions will work in ASP.NET 2.0, but some of the controls you originally used may now have some additional functionality you may choose to take advantage of. This chapter also looks at some of the new features that make these controls even better today. Some of the improvements are minor, but others are quite dramatic.

An Overview of Web Server Controls

The ASP.NET Web server control is its most-used component. Although you may have been pretty excited by the HTML server controls shown in the previous chapter, Web server controls are definitely a notch higher in capability. They allow for a higher level of functionality that becomes more apparent as you work with them.

The HTML server controls provided by ASP.NET work in that they map to specific HTML elements. You control the output by working with the HTML attributes that the HTML element provides. The attributes can be changed dynamically on the server side before they are finally output to the client. There is a lot of power in this, and you have some HTML server control capabilities that you simply do not have when you work with Web server controls.

Web server controls work differently. They don't map to specific HTML elements, but instead enable you to define functionality, capability, and appearance without the attributes that are available to you through a collection of HTML elements. When constructing a Web page that is made up of Web server controls, you are describing the functionality, the look-and-feel, and the behavior of your page elements. You then let ASP.NET decide how to output this construction. The output, of course, is based on the capabilities of the container that is making the request. This means that each requestor might see a different HTML output because each is requesting the same page with a different browser type or version. ASP.NET takes care of all the browser detection and the work associated with it on your behalf.

Unlike HTML server controls, Web server controls are not only available for working with common Web page form elements (such as text boxes and buttons), but they can also bring some advanced capabilities and functionality to your Web pages. For instance, one common feature of many Web applications is a calendar. No HTML form element places a calendar on your Web forms, but a Web server control from ASP.NET can provide your application with a full-fledged calendar, including some advanced capabilities. In the past, adding calendars to your Web pages was not a small programming task. Today, adding calendars with ASP.NET is rather simple and is achieved with a single line of code!

Remember that when you are constructing your Web server controls, you are actually constructing a control — *a set of instructions* — that is meant for the server (not the client). By default, all Web server controls provided by ASP.NET use an `asp:` at the beginning of the control declaration. The following is a typical Web server control:

```
<asp:Label ID="Label1" runat="server" Text="Hello World"></asp:Label>
```

Like HTML server controls, Web server controls require an `ID` attribute to reference the control in the server-side code, as well as a `Runat="server"` attribute declaration. As you do for other XML-based elements, you need to properly open and close Web server controls. In the preceding example, you can see the `<asp:Label>` control has a closing `</asp:Label>` element associated with it. You could have also closed this element using the following syntax:

```
<asp:Label ID="Label1" Runat="server" Text="Hello World" />
```

The rest of this chapter examines some of the Web server controls available to you in ASP.NET.

The Label Server Control

The Label server control is used to display text in the browser. Because this is a server control, you can dynamically alter the text from your server-side code. As you saw from the preceding examples of using the `<asp:Label>` control, the control uses the `Text` attribute to assign the content of the control as shown here:

```
<asp:Label ID="Label1" Runat="server" Text="Hello World" />
```

Instead of using the `Text` attribute, however, you can place the content to be displayed between the `<asp:Label>` elements like this:

```
<asp:Label ID="Label1" Runat="server">Hello World</asp:Label>
```

You can also provide content for the control through programmatic means, as illustrated in Listing 5-1.

Listing 5-1: Programmatically providing text to the Label control

VB
```
Label1.Text = "Hello ASP.NET"
```

C#
```
Label1.Text = "Hello ASP.NET";
```

The Label server control has always been a control that simply showed text. Now with ASP.NET 2.0, it has a little bit of extra functionality. The big change is that you can now give items in your form hot-key functionality (also known as *accelerator* keys). This causes the page to focus on a particular server control that you declaratively assign to a specific hot-key press (for example, using Alt+N to focus on the first text box on the form).

A hot key is a quick way for the end user to initiate an action on the page. For instance, if you use Microsoft Internet Explorer, you can press Ctrl+N to open a new instance of IE. Hot keys have always been quite common in thick-client applications (Windows Forms), and now you can use them in ASP.NET. Listing 5-2 shows an example of how to give hot-key functionality to two text boxes on a form.

Listing 5-2: Using the Label server control to provide hot-key functionality

```
<%@ Page Language="VB" %>

<html xmlns="http://www.w3.org/1999/xhtml" >
<head runat="server">
    <title>Label Server Control</title>
</head>
<body>
    <form id="form1" runat="server">
        <p>
            <asp:Label ID="Label1" Runat="server" AccessKey="N"
             AssociatedControlID="Textbox1">User<u>n</u>ame</asp:Label>
            <asp:Textbox ID="TextBox1" Runat="server"></asp:Textbox></p>
        <p>
            <asp:Label ID="Label2" Runat="server" AccessKey="P"
             AssociatedControlID="Textbox2"><u>P</u>assword</asp:Label>
            <asp:Textbox ID="TextBox2" Runat="server"></asp:Textbox></p>
        <p>
            <asp:Button ID="Button1" Runat="server" Text="Submit" />
        </p>
    </form>
</body>
</html>
```

Hot keys are assigned with the `AccessKey` attribute. In this case, `Label1` uses N, and `Label2` uses P. The second new attribute for the Label control is the `AssociatedControlID` attribute. The `String` value placed here associates the Label control with another server control on the form. The value must be one of the other server controls on the form. If not, the page gives you an error when invoked.

With these two controls in place, when the page is called in the browser, you can press Alt+N or Alt+P to automatically focus on a particular text box in the form. In Figure 5-1, HTML-declared underlines indicate the letters to be pressed along with the Alt key to create focus on the control adjoining the text. This is not required, but we highly recommend it because it is what the end user expects when working with hot keys. In this example, the letter n in `Username` and the letter P in `Password`. are underlined.

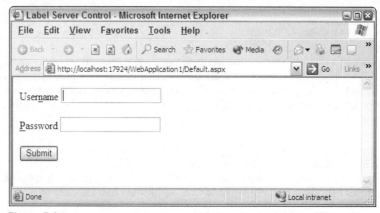

Figure 5-1

When working with hot keys, be aware that not all letters are available to use with the Alt key. Microsoft Internet Explorer already uses Alt+F, E, V, I, O, T, A, W, and H. If you use any of these letters, IE actions supersede any actions you place on the page.

The Literal Server Control

The Literal server control works very much like the Label server control. This control was always used in the past for text that you wanted to push out to the browser, but keep unchanged in the process (a literal state). A Label control alters the output by placing `<span>` elements around the text as shown:

```
<span id="Label1">Here is some text</span>
```

The Literal control just outputs the text without the `<span>` elements. In ASP.NET 2.0, it includes the new attribute `Mode` that enables you to dictate how the text assigned to the control is interpreted by the ASP.NET engine.

If you place some HTML code in the string that is output (for instance, `<b>Here is some text</b>`), the Literal control outputs just that and the consuming browser shows the text as bold:

Here is some text

Try using the Mode attribute as illustrated here:

```
<asp:Literal ID="Literal1" Runat="server" Mode="Encode"
 Text="<b>Here is some text</b>"></asp:Literal>
```

Adding Mode="Encode" encodes the output before it is received by the consuming application:

```
&lt;b&gt;Label&lt;/b&gt;
```

Now, instead of the text being converted to a bold font, the <b> elements are displayed:

```
<b>Here is some text</b>
```

This is ideal if you want to display code in your application. Other values for the Mode attribute include Transform and PassThrough. Transform looks at the consumer and includes or removes elements as needed. For instance, not all devices accept HTML elements so, if the value of the Mode attribute is set to Transform, these elements are removed from the string before it is sent to the consuming application. A value of PassThrough for the Mode property means that the text is sent to the consuming application without any changes being made to the string.

The TextBox Server Control

One of the main features of Web pages is to offer forms that end users can use to submit their information for collection. The TextBox server control is one of the most used controls in this space. As its name suggests, the control provides a text box on the form that enables the end user to input text. You can map the TextBox control to three different HTML elements used in your forms.

First, the TextBox control can be used as a standard HTML text box, as shown in the following code snippet:

```
<asp:TextBox ID="TextBox1" Runat="server"></asp:TextBox>
```

This code creates a text box on the form that looks like the one shown in Figure 5-2.

Figure 5-2

Second, the TextBox control can allow end users to input their passwords into a form. This is done by changing the TextMode attribute of the TextBox control to Password, as illustrated here:

```
<asp:TextBox ID="TextBox1" Runat="server" TextMode="Password"></asp:TextBox>
```

When asking end users for their passwords through the browser, it is best practice to provide a text box that encodes the content placed in this form element. Using an attribute and value of TextMode="Password" ensures that the text is encoded with either a star (*) or a dot, as shown in Figure 5-3.

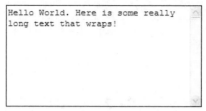

Figure 5-3

Third, the TextBox server control can be used as a multiline text box. The code for accomplishing this task is shown in the following example:

```
<asp:TextBox ID="TextBox1" Runat="server" TextMode="MultiLine"
  Width="300px" Height="150px"></asp:TextBox>
```

Giving the `TextMode` attribute a value of `MultiLine` creates a multilined text box in which the end user can enter a larger amount of text in the form. The `Width` and `Height` attributes set the size of the text area, but these are optional attributes — without them, the text area is produced in its smallest size. Figure 5-4 shows the use of the preceding code.

```
Hello World. Here is some really
long text that wraps!
```

Figure 5-4

When working with a multilined text box, be aware of the `Wrap` attribute. When set to `True` (which is the default), the text entered into the text area wraps to the next line if needed. When set to `False`, the end user can type continuously in a single line until she presses the Enter key, which brings the cursor down to the next line.

Using the Focus() Method

Because the TextBox server control is derived from the base class of `WebControl`, one of the methods available to it is `Focus()` — a new method introduced in version 2.0 of ASP.NET. The `Focus()` method enables you to dynamically place the end user's cursor in an appointed form element (not just the TextBox control, but in any of the server controls derived from the `WebControl` class). With that said, it is probably most often used with the TextBox control, as illustrated in Listing 5-3.

Listing 5-3: Using the Focus() method with the TextBox control

VB
```
Protected Sub Page_Load(ByVal sender As Object, ByVal e As System.EventArgs)
    TextBox1.Focus()
End Sub
```

C#
```
protected void Page_Load(object sender, EventArgs e)
{
    TextBox1.Focus();
}
```

When the page using this method is loaded in the browser, the cursor is already placed inside of the text box, ready for you to start typing. There's no need to move your mouse to get the cursor in place so you can start entering information in the form. This is ideal for those folks who take a keyboard approach to working with forms.

Using AutoPostBack

ASP.NET pages work in an event-driven way. When an action on a Web page triggers an event, server-side code is initiated. One of the more common events is an end user clicking a button on the form. If you double-click the button in Design view of Visual Studio 2005, you can see the code page with the structure of the `Button1_Click` event already in place. This is because `OnClick` is the most common event of the Button control. Double-clicking the TextBox control constructs an `OnTextChanged` event. This event is triggered when the end user moves the cursor focus outside the text box, either by clicking another element on the page after entering something into a text box, or by simply tabbing out of the text box. The use of this event is shown in Listing 5-4.

Listing 5-4: Triggering an event when a TextBox change occurs

VB

```
<%@ Page Language="VB" %>

<script runat="server">
    Protected Sub TextBox1_TextChanged(ByVal sender As Object, _
        ByVal e As System.EventArgs)

        Response.Write("OnTextChanged event triggered")
    End Sub

    Protected Sub Button1_Click(ByVal sender As Object, _
        ByVal e As System.EventArgs)

        Response.Write("OnClick event triggered")
    End Sub
</script>

<html xmlns="http://www.w3.org/1999/xhtml" >
<head runat="server">
    <title>OnTextChanged Page</title>
</head>
<body>
    <form id="form1" runat="server">
    <div>
        <asp:TextBox ID="TextBox1" Runat="server" AutoPostBack="True"
        OnTextChanged="TextBox1_TextChanged"></asp:TextBox>
        <asp:Button ID="Button1" Runat="server" Text="Button"
        OnClick="Button1_Click" />
    </div>
    </form>
</body>
</html>
```

(continued)

137

Listing 5-4: *(continued)*

C#

```
<%@ Page Language="C#" %>

<script runat="server">
    protected void TextBox1_TextChanged(object sender, EventArgs e)
    {
        Response.Write("OnTextChanged event triggered");
    }

    protected void Button1_Click(object sender, EventArgs e)
    {
        Response.Write("OnClick event triggered");
    }
</script>
```

As you build and run this page, notice that you can type something in the text box; but once you tab out of it, the OnTextChanged event is triggered and the code contained in the TextBox1_TextChanged event runs. To make this work, you must add the AutoPostBack attribute to the TextBox control and set it to True. This causes the Web page to look for any text changes prior to an actual page postback. For the AutoPostBack feature to work, the browser viewing the page must support ECMAScript.

Using AutoCompleteType

You want the forms you build for your Web applications to be as simple to use as possible. You want to make them easy and quick for the end user to fill out the information and proceed. If you make a form too time consuming, the people who come to your site may leave without completing it.

One of the great capabilities for any Web form is smart auto-completion. You may have seen this yourself when you visited a site for the first time. As you start to fill out information in a form, a drop-down list appears below the text box as you type showing you a value that you have typed in a previous form. The plain text box you were working with has become a smart text box. Figure 5-5 shows an example of this feature.

Figure 5-5

A great new addition to ASP.NET 2.0 is the AutoCompleteType attribute, which enables you to apply the auto-completion feature to your own forms. You have to help the text boxes on your form to recognize the type of information that they should be looking for. What does that mean? Well, first take a look at the possible values of the AutoCompleteType attribute:

BusinessCity	Disabled	HomeStreetAddress
BusinessCountryRegion	DisplayName	HomeZipCode
BusinessFax	Email	JobTitle
BusinessPhone	FirstName	LastName
BusinessState	Gender	MiddleName

BusinessStateAddress	HomeCity	None
BusinessUrl	HomeCountryRegion	Notes
BusinessZipCode	HomeFax	Office
Cellular	Homepage	Pager
Company	HomePhone	Search
Department	HomeState	

From this list, you can see that if your text box is asking for the end user's home street address, you want to use the following in your TextBox control:

```
<asp:TextBox ID="TextBox1" Runat="server"
  AutoCompleteType="HomeStreetAddress"></asp:TextBox>
```

As you view the source of the text box you created, you can see that the following construction has occurred:

```
<input name="TextBox1" type="text" vcard_name="vCard.Home.StreetAddress"
  id="TextBox1" />
```

This feature makes your forms easier to work with. Yes, it is a simple thing, but sometimes it is the little things that keep the viewers coming back again and again to your Web site.

The Button Server Control

Another common control for your Web forms is a button that can be constructed using the Button server control. Buttons are the usual element used to submit forms. Most of the time you are simply dealing with items contained in your forms through the Button control's OnClick event, as illustrated in Listing 5-5.

Listing 5-5: The Button control's OnClick event

VB
```
Protected Sub Button1_Click(ByVal sender As Object, ByVal e As System.EventArgs)
    ' Code here
End Sub
```

C#
```
protected void Button1_Click(object sender, EventArgs e)
{
    // Code here
}
```

The Button control is one of the easier controls to use, but there are a couple of properties of which you must be aware: CausesValidation and CommandName. They are discussed in the following sections.

The CausesValidation Property

If you have more than one button on your Web page and you are working with the validation server controls, you don't want to fire the validation for each button on the form. Setting the CausesValidation property to False is a way to use a button that will not fire the validation process. This is explained in more detail in Chapter 7.

The CommandName Property

You can have multiple buttons on your form all working from a single event. The nice thing is that you can also tag the buttons so that the code can make logical decisions based on which button on the form was clicked. You must construct your Button controls in the manner illustrated in Listing 5-6 to take advantage of this behavior.

Listing 5-6: Constructing multiple Button controls to work from a single function

```
<asp:Button ID="Button1" Runat="server" Text="Button 1"
 OnCommand="Button_Command" CommandName="DoSomething1" />
<asp:Button ID="Button2" Runat="server" Text="Button 2"
 OnCommand="Button_Command" CommandName="DoSomething2" />
```

Looking at these two instances of the Button control, you should pay attention to several things. The first thing to notice is what isn't present—any attribute mention of an OnClick event. Instead you use the OnCommand event, which points to an event called Button_Command. You can see that both Button controls are working from the same event. How does the event differentiate between the two buttons being clicked? Through the value placed in the CommandName property. In this case, they are indeed separate values—DoSomething1 and DoSomething2.

The next step is to create the Button_Command event to deal with both these buttons by simply typing one out or by selecting the Command event from the drop-down list of available events for the Button control from the code view of Visual Studio. In either case, you should end up with an event like the one shown in Listing 5-7.

Listing 5-7: The Button_Command event

VB
```
Protected Sub Button_Command(ByVal sender As Object, _
   ByVal e As System.Web.UI.WebControls.CommandEventArgs)

   Select Case e.CommandName
      Case "DoSomething1"
         Response.Write("Button 1 was selected")
      Case "DoSomething2"
         Response.Write("Button 2 was selected")
   End Select

End Sub
```

C#
```
protected void Button_Command(Object sender,
   System.Web.UI.WebControls.CommandEventArgs e)
{
   switch (e.CommandName)
   {
      case("DoSomething1"):
         Response.Write("Button 1 was selected");
         break;
      case("DoSomething2"):
         Response.Write("Button 2 was selected");
```

```
            break;
    }
}
```

Notice that this method uses `System.Web.UI.WebControls.CommandEventArgs` instead of the typical `System.EventArgs`. This gives you access to the member `CommandName` used in the `Select Case` (switch) statement as `e.CommandName`. Using this object, you can check for the value of the `CommandName` property used by the button that was clicked on the form and take a specific action based upon the value passed.

You can add some parameters to be passed in to the `Command` event beyond what is defined in the `CommandName` property. You do this by using the Button control's `CommandArgument` property. Adding values to the property enables you to define items a bit more granularly if you want. You can get at this value via server-side code using `e.CommandArgument` from the `CommandEventArgs` object.

Buttons That Work with Client-Side JavaScript

Buttons are frequently used for submitting information and causing actions to occur on a Web page. Before ASP.NET 1.0/1.1, people intermingled quite a bit of JavaScript in their pages to fire JavaScript events when a button was clicked. The process became more cumbersome in ASP.NET 1.0/1.1, but now with ASP.NET 2.0, it is much easier.

You can create a page that has a JavaScript event, as well as a server-side event, triggered when the button is clicked, as illustrated in Listing 5-8.

Listing 5-8: Two types of events for the button

VB

```
<%@ Page Language="VB" %>

<script runat="server">
    Protected Sub Button1_Click(ByVal sender As Object, _
        ByVal e As System.EventArgs)

        Response.Write("Postback!")
    End Sub
</script>

<script language="javascript">
   function AlertHello()
   {
      alert('Hello ASP.NET');
   }
</script>

<html xmlns="http://www.w3.org/1999/xhtml" >
<head runat="server">
    <title>Button Server Control</title>
</head>
<body>
    <form id="form1" runat="server">
```

(continued)

Listing 5-8: *(continued)*

```
            <asp:Button ID="Button1" Runat="server" Text="Button"
            OnClientClick="AlertHello()" OnClick="Button1_Click" />
    </form>
</body>
</html>
```

C#
```
<%@ Page Language="C#" %>

<script runat="server">
    protected void Button1_Click(object sender, EventArgs e)
    {
        Response.Write("Postback!");
    }
</script>
```

The first thing to notice is the new attribute for the Button server control: `OnClientClick`. It points to the client-side function, unlike the `OnClick` attribute that points to the server-side event. This example uses a JavaScript function called `AlertHello()`.

One cool thing about Visual Studio 2005 is that now it can work with server-side script tags that are right alongside client-side script tags. It all works together seamlessly. In the example, after the JavaScript alert dialog is issued (see Figure 5-6) and the end user clicks OK, the page posts back as the server-side event is triggered.

Figure 5-6

Another new and exciting attribute for the button controls is `PostBackUrl`. It enables you to perform cross-page posting, instead of simply posting your ASP.NET pages back to the same page, as shown in the following example:

```
<asp:Button ID="Button2" Runat="server" Text="Submit page to Page2.aspx"
   PostBackUrl="Page2.aspx" />
```

Cross-page posting is covered in greater detail in Chapter 3.

The LinkButton Server Control

The LinkButton server control is a variation of the Button control. It is basically the same except that the LinkButton control takes the form of a hyperlink. But, it isn't a typical hyperlink. When the end user clicks the link, it behaves like a button. This is an ideal control to use if you have a large number of buttons on your Web form.

A LinkButton server control is constructed as follows:

```
<asp:LinkButton ID="LinkButton1" Runat="server" OnClick="LinkButton1_Click">
    Submit your name to our database
</asp:LinkButton>
```

Using the LinkButton control gives you the results shown in Figure 5-7.

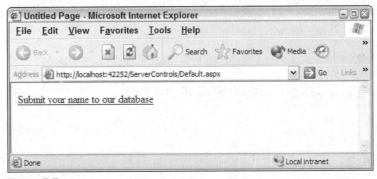

Figure 5-7

The ImageButton Server Control

The ImageButton control is also a variation of the Button control. It is almost exactly the same as the Button control except that it enables you to use a custom image as the form's button instead of the typical buttons used on most forms. This means that you can create your own buttons as images and the end users can click the images to submit form data. A typical construction of the ImageButton is as follows:

```
<asp:ImageButton ID="ImageButton1" Runat="server"
 OnClick="ImageButton1_Click" ImageUrl="MyButton.jpg" />
```

The ImageButton control specifies the location of the image used by using the ImageUrl property. From this example, you can see that the ImageUrl points to MyButton.jpg. The big difference between the ImageButton control and the LinkButton or Button controls is that ImageButton takes a different construction for the OnClick event. It is shown in Listing 5-9.

143

Listing 5-9: The Click event for the ImageButton control

VB

```
Protected Sub ImageButton1_Click(ByVal sender As Object, _
   ByVal e As System.Web.UI.WebControls.ImageClickEventArgs)
   ' Code here
End Sub
```

C#

```
protected void ImageButton1_Click(object sender,
   System.Web.UI.WebControls.ImageClickEventArgs e)
{
   // Code here
}
```

The construction uses the `ImageClickEventArgs` object instead of the `System.EventArgs` object usually used with the LinkButton and Button controls. You can use this object to determine where in the image the end user clicked by using both `e.X` and `e.Y` coordinates.

The GO and PLAY buttons on the page shown in Figure 5-8 are image buttons.

Figure 5-8

The HyperLink Server Control

The HyperLink server control enables you to programmatically work with any hyperlinks on your Web pages. Hyperlinks are links that allow end users to transfer from one page to another. You can set the text of a hyperlink using the control's Text attribute:

```
<asp:HyperLink ID="HyperLink1" Runat="server" Text="Go to this page here"
  NavigateUrl="~/Default2.aspx"></asp:HyperLink>
```

This server control creates a hyperlink on your page with the text Go to this page here. When the link is clicked, the user is redirected to the value that is placed in the NavigateUrl property (in this case, the Default2.aspx page).

The interesting thing about the HyperLink server control is that it can be used for images as well as text. Instead of using the Text attribute, it uses the ImageUrl property:

```
<asp:HyperLink ID="HyperLink1" Runat="server" ImageUrl="~/MyLinkImage.gif"
  NavigateUrl="~/Default2.aspx"></asp:HyperLink>
```

The HyperLink control is a great way to dynamically place hyperlinks on a Web page based either upon user input in a form or on database values that are retrieved when the page is loaded.

The DropDownList Server Control

The DropDownList server control enables you to place an HTML select box on your Web page and program against it. It's ideal when you have a large collection of items from which you want the end user to select a single item. It is usually used for a medium-to-large-sized collection. If the collection size is relatively small, consider using the RadioButtonList server control (described later in this chapter).

The select box generated by the DropDownList control displays a single item and allows the end user to make a selection from a larger list of items. Depending on the number of choices available in the select box, the end user may have to scroll through a list of items. Note that the appearance of the scroll bar in the drop-down list is automatically created by the browser depending on the browser version and the number of items contained in the list.

Here's the code for DropDownList control:

```
<asp:DropDownList ID="DropDownList1" Runat="server">
    <asp:ListItem>Car</asp:ListItem>
    <asp:ListItem>Airplane</asp:ListItem>
    <asp:ListItem>Train</asp:ListItem>
</asp:DropDownList>
```

This code generates a drop-down list in the browser, as shown in Figure 5-9.

Figure 5-9

145

The DropDownList control comes in handy when you start binding it to various data stores. The data stores can either be arrays, database values, XMLfile values, or values found elsewhere. For an example of binding the DropDownList control, look at dynamically generating a DropDownList control to one of two available arrays, as shown in Listing 5-10.

Listing 5-10: Dynamically generating a DropDownList control from an array

VB

```
<%@ Page Language="VB" %>

<script runat="server">
    Protected Sub DropDownList1_SelectedIndexChanged(ByVal sender As Object, _
      ByVal e As System.EventArgs)
        Dim CarArray() As String = {"Ford", "Honda", "BMW", "Dodge"}
        Dim AirplaneArray() As String = {"Boeing 777", "Boeing 747", "Boeing 737"}
        Dim TrainArray() As String = {"Bullet Train", "Amtrack", "Tram"}

        If DropDownList1.SelectedValue = "Car" Then
            DropDownList2.DataSource = CarArray
        ElseIf DropDownList1.SelectedValue = "Airplane" Then
            DropDownList2.DataSource = AirplaneArray
        Else
            DropDownList2.DataSource = TrainArray
        End If

        DropDownList2.DataBind()
        DropDownList2.Visible = True
    End Sub

    Protected Sub Button1_Click(ByVal sender As Object, _
      ByVal e As System.EventArgs)

        Response.Write("You selected <b>" & _
            DropDownList1.SelectedValue.ToString() & ": " & _
            DropDownList2.SelectedValue.ToString() & "</b>")
    End Sub
</script>

<html xmlns="http://www.w3.org/1999/xhtml" >
<head runat="server">
    <title>DropDownList Page</title>
</head>
<body>
    <form id="form1" runat="server">
    <div>
        Select transportation type:<br />
        <asp:DropDownList ID="DropDownList1" Runat="server"
         OnSelectedIndexChanged="DropDownList1_SelectedIndexChanged"
         AutoPostBack="true">
            <asp:ListItem>Select an Item</asp:ListItem>
            <asp:ListItem>Car</asp:ListItem>
            <asp:ListItem>Airplane</asp:ListItem>
            <asp:ListItem>Train</asp:ListItem>
        </asp:DropDownList> 
```

```
            <asp:DropDownList ID="DropDownList2" Runat="server" Visible="false">
            </asp:DropDownList>
            <asp:Button ID="Button1" Runat="server" Text="Select Options"
             OnClick="Button1_Click" />
        </div>
        </form>
</body>
</html>
```

C#

```
<%@ Page Language="C#" %>

<script runat="server">
    protected void DropDownList1_SelectedIndexChanged(object sender, EventArgs e)
    {
        string[] CarArray = new string[4] {"Ford", "Honda", "BMW", "Dodge"};
        string[] AirplaneArray = new string[3] {"Boeing 777", "Boeing 747",
            "Boeing 737"};
        string[] TrainArray = new string[3] {"Bullet Train", "Amtrack", "Tram"};

        if (DropDownList1.SelectedValue == "Car") {
            DropDownList2.DataSource = CarArray; }
        else if (DropDownList1.SelectedValue == "Airplane") {
            DropDownList2.DataSource = AirplaneArray; }
        else {
            DropDownList2.DataSource = TrainArray;
        }

        DropDownList2.DataBind();
        DropDownList2.Visible = true;
    }

    protected void Button1_Click(object sender, EventArgs e)
    {
        Response.Write("You selected <b>" +
            DropDownList1.SelectedValue.ToString() + ": " +
            DropDownList2.SelectedValue.ToString() + "</b>");
    }
</script>
```

In this example, the second drop-down list is generated based upon the value selected from the first drop-down list. For instance, selecting Car from the first drop-down list dynamically creates a second drop-down list on the form that includes a list of available car selections.

This is possible because of the use of the AutoPostBack feature of the DropDownList control. When the AutoPostBack property is set to True, the method provided through the OnSelectedIndexChanged event is fired when a selection is made. In the example, the DropDownList1_SelectedIndexChanged event is fired, dynamically creating the second drop-down list.

In this method, the content of the second drop-down list is created in a string array and then bound to the second DropDownList control through the use of the DataSource property and the DataBind() method.

When built and run, this page looks like the one shown in Figure 5-10.

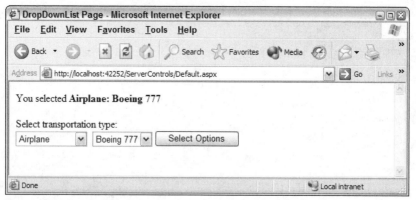

Figure 5-10

Visually Removing Items from a Collection

The DropDownList, ListBox, CheckBoxList, and RadioButtonList server controls give you the capability to visually remove items from the collection displayed in the control, although you can still work with the items that aren't displayed in your server-side code.

The ListBox, CheckBoxList, and RadioButtonList controls are discussed shortly in this chapter.

For a quick example of removing items, create a drop-down list with three items, including one that you won't display. On the postback, however, you can still work with the ListItem's Value or Text property, as illustrated in Listing 5-11.

Listing 5-11: Disabling certain ListItems from a collection

VB

```
<%@ page language="VB" %>

<script runat="server">
    Protected Sub DropDownList1_SelectedIndexChanged(ByVal sender As Object, _
        ByVal e As System.EventArgs)
            Response.Write("You selected item number " & _
                DropDownList1.SelectedValue & "<br>")
            Response.Write("You didn't select item number " & _
                DropDownList1.Items(1).Value)
    End Sub
</script>

<html>
<head runat="server">
    <title>DropDownList Server Control</title>
</head>
```

```
<body>
    <form id="form1" runat="server">
        <asp:DropDownList ID="DropDownList1" Runat="server" AutoPostBack="True"
        OnSelectedIndexChanged="DropDownList1_SelectedIndexChanged">
            <asp:ListItem Value="1">First Choice</asp:ListItem>
            <asp:ListItem Value="2" Enabled="False">Second Choice</asp:ListItem>
            <asp:ListItem Value="3">Third Choice</asp:ListItem>
        </asp:DropDownList>
    </form>
</body>
</html>
```

C#

```
<%@ Page Language="C#" %>

<script runat="server">
    protected void DropDownList1_SelectedIndexChanged(object sender, EventArgs e)
    {
        Response.Write("You selected item number " +
          DropDownList1.SelectedValue + "<br>");
        Response.Write("You didn't select item number " +
          DropDownList1.Items[1].Value);
    }
</script>
```

From the code, you can see that the `<asp:ListItem>` element has a new attribute: `Enabled`. The Boolean value given to this element dictates whether an item in the collection is displayed. If you use `Enabled="False"`, the item is not displayed, but you still have the capability to work with the item in the server-side code displayed in the `DropDownList1_SelectedIndexChanged` event. The result of the output from these `Response.Write` statements is shown in Figure 5-11.

Figure 5-11

The ListBox Server Control

The ListBox server control has a function similar to the DropDownList control. It displays a collection of items. The ListBox control behaves differently from the DropDownList control in that it displays more of the collection to the end user, and it enables the end user to make multiple selections from the collection — something that isn't possible with the DropDownList control.

A typical ListBox control appears in code as follows:

```
<asp:ListBox ID="ListBox1" Runat="server">
    <asp:ListItem>Hematite</asp:ListItem>
    <asp:ListItem>Halite</asp:ListItem>
    <asp:ListItem>Limonite</asp:ListItem>
    <asp:ListItem>Magnetite</asp:ListItem>
</asp:ListBox>
```

This generates the browser display illustrated in Figure 5-12.

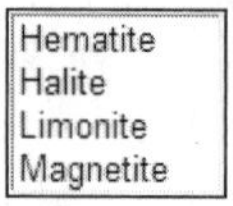

Figure 5-12

Allowing Users to Select Multiple Items

You can use the `SelectionMode` attribute to let your end users make multiple selections from what is displayed by the ListBox control. Here's an example:

```
<asp:ListBox ID="ListBox1" Runat="server" SelectionMode="Multiple">
    <asp:ListItem>Hematite</asp:ListItem>
    <asp:ListItem>Halite</asp:ListItem>
    <asp:ListItem>Limonite</asp:ListItem>
    <asp:ListItem>Magnetite</asp:ListItem>
</asp:ListBox>
```

The possible values of the `SelectionMode` property include `Single` and `Multiple`. Setting the value to `Multiple` allows the end user to make multiple selections in the list box. The user must hold down either the Ctrl or Shift keys while making selections. Holding down the Ctrl key enables the user to make a single selection from the list while maintaining previous selections. Holding down the Shift key enables a range of multiple selections.

An Example of Using the ListBox Control

The ListBox control shown in Listing 5-12 allows multiple selections to be displayed in the browser when a user clicks the Submit button. The form should also have an additional text box and button at the top that enables the end user to add additional items to the ListBox.

Listing 5-12: Using the ListBox control

VB

```
<%@ Page Language="VB" %>

<script runat="server">
    Protected Sub Button1_Click(ByVal sender As Object, _
        ByVal e As System.EventArgs)

        ListBox1.Items.Add(TextBox1.Text.ToString())
    End Sub

    Protected Sub Button2_Click(ByVal sender As Object, _
        ByVal e As System.EventArgs)

        Label1.Text = "You selected from the ListBox:<br>"
        For Each li As ListItem In ListBox1.Items
            If li.Selected = True Then
                label1.Text += li.Text & "<br>"
            End If
        Next
    End Sub
</script>

<html xmlns="http://www.w3.org/1999/xhtml" >
<head runat="server">
    <title>Using the ListBox</title>
</head>
<body>
    <form id="form1" runat="server">
    <div>
        <asp:TextBox ID="TextBox1" Runat="server"></asp:TextBox>
        <asp:Button ID="Button1" Runat="server" Text="Add an additional item"
         OnClick="Button1_Click" />
        <br />
        <br />

        <asp:ListBox ID="ListBox1" Runat="server" SelectionMode="multiple">
            <asp:ListItem>Hematite</asp:ListItem>
            <asp:ListItem>Halite</asp:ListItem>
            <asp:ListItem>Limonite</asp:ListItem>
            <asp:ListItem>Magnetite</asp:ListItem>
        </asp:ListBox>
        <br />
        <br />
        <asp:Button ID="Button2" Runat="server" Text="Submit"
         OnClick="Button2_Click" />
        <br />
        <br />
        <asp:Label ID="Label1" Runat="server"></asp:Label>
    </div>
    </form>
</body>
</html>
```

(continued)

Listing 5-12: *(continued)*

C#

```
<%@ Page Language="C#" %>

<script runat="server">
    protected void Button1_Click(object sender, EventArgs e)
    {
        ListBox1.Items.Add(TextBox1.Text.ToString());
    }

    protected void Button2_Click(object sender, EventArgs e)
    {
        Label1.Text = "You selected from the ListBox:<br>";
        foreach (ListItem li in ListBox1.Items) {
            if (li.Selected == true) {
                Label1.Text += li.Text + "<br>";
            }
        }
    }
</script>
```

This is an interesting example. First, some default items (four common minerals) are already placed inside the ListBox control. However, the text box and button at the top of the form allow the end user to add additional minerals to the list. Users can then make one or more selections from the ListBox, including selections from the items that they dynamically added to the collection. After a user makes his selection and clicks the button, the `Button2_Click` event iterates through the `ListItem` instances in the collection and displays only the items that have been selected.

This control works by creating an instance of a `ListItem` object and using its `Selected` property to see if a particular item in the collection has been selected. The use of the `ListItem` object is not limited to the ListBox control (although that is what is used here). You can dynamically add or remove items from a collection and get at items and their values through the use of the `ListItem` object in the DropDownList, CheckBoxList, and RadioButtonList controls as well. It is a list-control feature.

When this page is built and run, you get the results presented in Figure 5-13.

Adding Items to a Collection

To add items to the collection, you can use the following short syntax:

```
ListBox1.Items.Add(TextBox1.Text)
```

Look at the source code created in the browser, and you should see something similar to the following generated dynamically:

```
<select size="4" name="ListBox1" multiple="multiple" id="ListBox1">
    <option value="Hematite">Hematite</option>
    <option value="Halite">Halite</option>
    <option value="Limonite">Limonite</option>
    <option value="Magnetite">Magnetite</option>
    <option value="Olivine">Olivine</option>
</select>
```

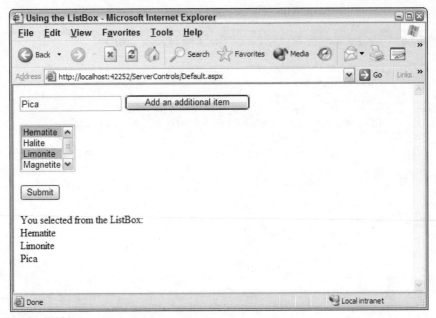

Figure 5-13

You can see that the dynamically added value is a text item, and you can see its value. You can also add instances of the ListItem object to get different values for the item name and value:

VB
```
ListBox1.Items.Add(New ListItem("Olivine", "MG2SIO4"))
```

C#
```
ListBox1.Items.Add(new ListItem("Olivine", "MG2SIO4"));
```

This example adds a new instance of the `ListItem` object — adding not only the textual name of the item, but the value of the item (its chemical formula). It produces the following results in the browser:

```
<option value="MG2SIO4">Olivine</option>
```

The CheckBox Server Control

Check boxes on a Web form enable your users to either make selections from a collection of items or specify a value of an item to be yes/no, on/off, or true/false. Use either the CheckBox control or the CheckBoxList control to include check boxes in your Web forms.

The CheckBox control allows you to place single check boxes on a form; the CheckBoxList control allows you to place collections of check boxes on the form. You can use multiple CheckBox controls on your ASP.NET pages, but then you are treating each check box as its own element with its own associated events. On the other hand, the CheckBoxList control allows you to take multiple check boxes and create specific events for the entire group.

Listing 5-13 shows an example of using the CheckBox control.

Listing 5-13: Using a single instance of the CheckBox control

VB

```
<%@ Page Language="VB" %>

<script runat="server">
    Protected Sub CheckBox1_CheckedChanged(ByVal sender As Object, _
      ByVal e As System.EventArgs)
        Response.Write("Thanks for your donation!")
    End Sub
</script>

<html xmlns="http://www.w3.org/1999/xhtml" >
<head runat="server">
    <title>CheckBox control</title>
</head>
<body>
    <form id="form1" runat="server">
    <div>
        <asp:CheckBox ID="CheckBox1" Runat="server" Text="Donate $10 to our cause!"
          OnCheckedChanged="CheckBox1_CheckedChanged" AutoPostBack="true" />
    </div>
    </form>
</body>
</html>
```

C#

```
<%@ Page Language="C#" %>

<script runat="server">
    protected void CheckBox1_CheckedChanged(object sender, EventArgs e)
    {
        Response.Write("Thanks for your donation!");
    }
</script>
```

This produces a page that contains a single check box asking for a monetary donation. Using the `CheckedChanged` event, `OnCheckedChanged` is used within the CheckBox control. The attribute's value points to the `CheckBox1_CheckedChanged` event, which fires when the user checks the check box. It occurs only if the `AutoPostBack` property is set to `True` (this property is set to `False` by default). Running this page produces the results shown in Figure 5-14.

How to Determine If Check Boxes Are Checked

You might not want to use the `AutoPostBack` feature of the check box, but instead want to determine if the check box is checked after the form is posted back to the server. You can make this check through an `If Then` statement, as illustrated in the following example:

VB

```
If (CheckBox1.Checked = True) Then
    Response.Write("CheckBox is checked!")
End If
```

C#
```
if (CheckBox1.Checked == true) {
    Response.Write("Checkbox is checked!");
}
```

This check is done on the CheckBox value using the control's `Checked` property. The property's value is a Boolean value, so it is either `True` (checked) or `False` (not checked).

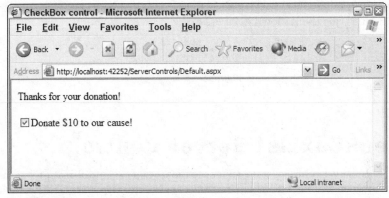

Figure 5-14

Assigning a Value to a Check Box

You can also use the `Checked` property to make sure a check box is checked based on other dynamic values:

VB
```
If (Member = True) Then
    CheckBox1.Checked = True
End If
```

C#
```
if (Member == true) {
    CheckBox1.Checked = true;
}
```

Aligning Text Around the Check Box

In the previous check box example, the text appears to the right of the actual check box, as shown in Figure 5-15.

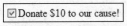

Figure 5-15

Using the CheckBox control's `TextAlign` property, you can realign the text so that it appears on the other side of the check box:

```
<asp:CheckBox ID="CheckBox1" Runat="server" Text="Donate $10 to our cause!"
  OnCheckedChanged="CheckBox1_CheckedChanged" AutoPostBack="true"
  TextAlign="Left" />
```

The possible values of the `TextAlign` property are either `Right` (the default setting) or `Left`. This property is also available to the CheckBoxList, RadioButton, and RadioButtonList controls. Assigning the value `Left` produces the result shown in Figure 5-16.

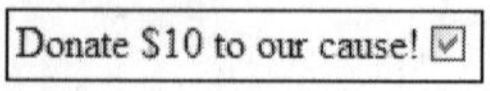

Donate $10 to our cause! ☑

Figure 5-16

The CheckBoxList Server Control

The CheckBoxList server control is quite similar to the CheckBox control, except that the former enables you to work with a collection of items rather than a single item. The idea is that a CheckBoxList server control instance is a collection of related items, each being a check box unto itself.

To see the CheckBoxList control in action, you can build an example that uses Microsoft's SQL Server to pull information from the Customers table of the Northwind example database. An example is presented in Listing 5-14.

Listing 5-14: Dynamically populating a CheckBoxList

VB

```
<%@ Page Language="VB" %>

<script runat="server">
    Protected Sub Button1_Click(ByVal sender As Object, _
        ByVal e As System.EventArgs)

        Label1.Text = "You selected:<br>"
        For Each li As ListItem In CheckBoxList1.Items
            If li.Selected = True Then
                Label1.Text += li.Text & "<br>"
            End If
        Next
    End Sub
</script>

<html xmlns="http://www.w3.org/1999/xhtml" >
<head runat="server">
    <title>CheckBoxList control</title>
</head>
<body>
    <form id="form1" runat="server">
```

```
    <div>
        <asp:Button ID="Button1" Runat="server" Text="Submit Choices"
         OnClick="Button1_Click" />
        <br />
        <br />
        <asp:Label ID="Label1" Runat="server"></asp:Label>
        <br />
        <asp:CheckBoxList ID="CheckBoxList1" Runat="server"
         DataSourceID="SqlDataSource1" DataTextField="CompanyName"
         RepeatColumns="3" BorderColor="Black"
         BorderStyle="Solid" BorderWidth="1px">
        </asp:CheckBoxList>
        <asp:SqlDataSource ID="SqlDataSource1" Runat="server"
         SelectCommand="SELECT [CompanyName] FROM [Customers]"
            ConnectionString="<%$ ConnectionStrings:AppConnectionString1 %>">
        </asp:SqlDataSource>
    </div>
    </form>
</body>
</html>
```

C#
```
<%@ Page Language="C#" %>

<script runat="server">
    protected void Button1_Click(object sender, EventArgs e)
    {
        Label1.Text = "You selected:<br>";
        foreach (ListItem li in CheckBoxList1.Items) {
            if (li.Selected == true) {
                Label1.Text += li.Text + "<br>";
            }
        }
    }
</script>
```

This ASP.NET page has a SqlDataSource control on the page that pulls the information you need from the Northwind database. From the SELECT statement used in this control, you can see that you are retrieving the CompanyName field from each of the listings in the Customers table.

The CheckBoxList control binds itself to the SqlDataSource control using a few properties:

```
<asp:CheckBoxList ID="CheckBoxList1" Runat="server"
 DataSourceID="SqlDataSource1" DataTextField="CompanyName"
 RepeatColumns="3" BorderColor="Black"
 BorderStyle="Solid" BorderWidth="1px">
</asp:CheckBoxList>
```

The DataSourceID property is used to associate the CheckBoxList control with the results that come back from the SqlDataSource control. Then the DataTextField property is used to retrieve the name of the field you want to work with from the results. In this example, it is the only one that is available: the CompanyName. That's it! CheckBoxList generates the results you want.

The remaining code consists of styling properties, which are pretty interesting. The `BorderColor`, `BorderStyle`, and `BorderWidth` properties enable you to put a border around the entire check box list. The most interesting property is the `RepeatColumns` property, which specifies how many columns (three in this example) can be used to display the results.

When you run the page, you get the results shown in Figure 5-17.

The `RepeatDirection` property instructs the CheckBoxList control about how to lay out the items bound to the control on the Web page. Possible values include `Vertical` and `Horizontal`. The default value is `Vertical`. Setting it to `Vertical` with a `RepeatColumn` setting of 3 gives the following results:

```
CheckBox1      CheckBox5      CheckBox9
CheckBox2      CheckBox6      CheckBox10
CheckBox3      CheckBox7      CheckBox11
CheckBox4      CheckBox8      CheckBox12
```

When the `RepeatDirection` property is set to `Horizontal`, you get the check box items laid out in a horizontal fashion:

```
CheckBox1      CheckBox2      CheckBox3
CheckBox4      CheckBox5      CheckBox6
CheckBox7      CheckBox8      CheckBox9
CheckBox10     CheckBox11     CheckBox12
```

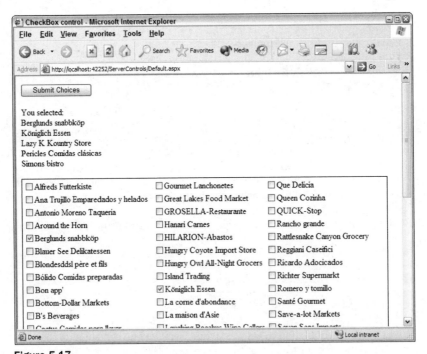

Figure 5-17

The RadioButton Server Control

The RadioButton server control is quite similar to the CheckBox server control. It places a radio button on your Web page. Unlike a check box, however, a single radio button on a form doesn't make much sense. Radio buttons are generally form elements that require at least two options. A typical set of RadioButton controls on a page takes the following construction:

```
<asp:RadioButton ID="RadioButton1" Runat="server" Text="Yes" GroupName="Set1" />
<asp:RadioButton ID="RadioButton2" Runat="server" Text="No" GroupName="Set1"/>
```

Figure 5-18 shows the result.

Figure 5-18

When you look at the code for the RadioButton control, note the standard `Text` property that places the text next to the radio button on the Web form. The more important property here is `GroupName`, which can be set in one of the RadioButton controls to match what it is set to in the other. This enables the radio buttons on the Web form to work together for the end user. How do they work together? Well, when one of the radio buttons on the form is checked, the circle associated with the item selected appears filled in. Any other filled-in circle from the same group in the collection is removed, ensuring that only one of the radio buttons in the collection is selected.

Listing 5-15 shows an example of using the RadioButton control.

Listing 5-15: Using the RadioButton server control

VB

```
<%@ Page Language="VB" %>

<script runat="server">
    Protected Sub RadioButton_CheckedChanged(ByVal sender As Object, _
      ByVal e As System.EventArgs)
        If RadioButton1.Checked = True Then
            Response.Write("You selected Visual Basic 2005")
        Else
            Response.Write("You selected Visual C# 2005")
        End If
    End Sub
</script>

<html xmlns="http://www.w3.org/1999/xhtml" >
<head runat="server">
    <title>RadioButton control</title>
</head>
<body>
    <form id="form1" runat="server">
    <div>
        <asp:RadioButton ID="RadioButton1" Runat="server" Text="Visual Basic 2005"
         GroupName="LanguageChoice" OnCheckedChanged="RadioButton_CheckedChanged"
```

(continued)

Listing 5-15: *(continued)*

```
            AutoPostBack="True" />
        <asp:RadioButton ID="RadioButton2" Runat="server" Text="Visual C# 2005"
        GroupName="LanguageChoice" OnCheckedChanged="RadioButton_CheckedChanged"
        AutoPostBack="True" />
    </div>
    </form>
</body>
</html>
```

C#

```
<%@ Page Language="C#" %>

<script runat="server">
    protected void RadioButton_CheckedChanged(object sender, EventArgs e)
    {
        if (RadioButton1.Checked == true) {
            Response.Write("You selected Visual Basic 2005");
        }
        else {
            Response.Write("You selected Visual C# 2005");
        }
    }
</script>
```

Like the CheckBox, the RadioButton control has a CheckedChanged event that puts an OnCheckedChanged attribute in the control. The attribute's value points to the server-side event that is fired when a selection is made using one of the two radio buttons on the form. Remember that the AutoPostBack property needs to be set to True for this to work correctly.

Figure 5-19 shows the results.

Figure 5-19

One advantage that the RadioButton control has over a RadioButtonList control (which is discussed next) is that it enables you to place other items (text, controls, or images) between the RadioButton controls themselves. RadioButtonList, however, is always a straight list of radio buttons on your Web page.

The RadioButtonList Server Control

The RadioButtonList server control lets you display a collection of radio buttons on a Web page. The RadioButtonList control is quite similar to the CheckBoxList and other list controls in that it allows you to iterate through to see what the user selected, to make counts, or to perform other actions.

A typical RadioButtonList control is written to the page in the following manner:

```
<asp:RadioButtonList ID="RadioButtonList1" Runat="server">
   <asp:ListItem Selected="True">English</asp:ListItem>
   <asp:ListItem>Russian</asp:ListItem>
   <asp:ListItem>Finnish</asp:ListItem>
   <asp:ListItem>Swedish</asp:ListItem>
</asp:RadioButtonList>
```

Like the other list controls, this one uses instances of the `ListItem` object for each of the items contained in the collection. From the example, you can see that if the `Selected` property is set to `True`, one of the `ListItem` objects is selected by default when the page is generated for the first time. This produces the results shown in Figure 5-20.

Figure 5-20

The `Selected` property is not required, but it is a good idea if you want the end user to make some sort of selection from this collection. Using it makes it impossible to leave the collection blank.

You can use the RadioButtonList control to check for the value selected by the end user in any of your page methods. Listing 5-16 shows a `Button1_Click` event that pushes out the value selected in the RadioButtonList collection.

Listing 5-16: Checking the value of the item selected from a RadioButtonList control

VB

```
<%@ Page Language="VB" %>

<script runat="server">
    Protected Sub Button1_Click(ByVal sender As Object, _
        ByVal e As System.EventArgs)

        Label1.Text = "You selected: " & _
            RadioButtonList1.SelectedItem.ToString()
    End Sub
</script>
```

(continued)

Listing 5-16: *(continued)*

C#
```
<%@ Page Language="C#" %>

<script runat="server">
    protected void Button1_Click(object sender, EventArgs e)
    {
        Label1.Text = "You selected: " +
            RadioButtonList1.SelectedItem.ToString();
    }
</script>
```

This bit of code gets at the item selected from the RadioButtonList collection of `ListItem` objects. It is how you work with other list controls that are provided in ASP.NET. The RadioButtonList also affords you access to the `RepeatColumns` and `RepeatDirection` properties (these were explained in the CheckBoxList section). You can bind this control to items that come from any of the data source controls so that you can dynamically create radio button lists on your Web pages.

Image Server Control

The Image server control enables you to work with the images that appear on your Web page from the server-side code. It's a simple server control, but it can give you the power to determine how your images are displayed on the browser screen. A typical Image control is constructed in the following manner:

```
<asp:Image ID="Image1" Runat="server" ImageUrl="~/MyImage1.gif" />
```

The important property here is `ImageUrl`. It points to the file location of the image. In this case, the location is specified as the `MyImage.gif` file.

Listing 5-17 shows an example of how to dynamically change the `ImageUrl` property.

Listing 5-17: Changing the ImageUrl property dynamically

VB
```
<%@ Page Language="VB" %>

<script runat="server">
    Protected Sub Button1_Click(ByVal sender As Object, ByVal e As System.EventArgs)
        Image1.ImageUrl = "~/MyImage2.gif"
    End Sub
</script>

<html xmlns="http://www.w3.org/1999/xhtml" >
<head runat="server">
    <title>Image control</title>
</head>
<body>
    <form id="form1" runat="server">
```

```
            <div>
                <asp:Image ID="Image1" Runat="server" ImageUrl="~/MyImage1.gif" /><br />
                <br />
                <asp:Button ID="Button1" Runat="server" Text="Change Image"
                 OnClick="Button1_Click" />
            </div>
            </form>
    </body>
    </html>
```

C#

```
<%@ Page Language="C#" %>

<script runat="server">
    protected void Button1_Click(object sender, EventArgs e)
    {
        Image1.ImageUrl = "~/MyImage2.gif";
    }
</script>
```

In this example, an image (MyImage1.gif) is shown in the browser when the page is loaded for the first time. When the end user clicks the button on the page, a new image (MyImage2.gif) is loaded in the postback process.

Special circumstances can prevent end users from viewing an image that is part of your Web page. They might be physically unable to see the image, or they might be using a text-only browser. In these cases, their browsers look for the <img> element's longdesc attribute that points to a file containing a long description of the image that is displayed.

For these cases, the Image server control now includes a new DescriptionUrl attribute. The value assigned to it is a text file that contains a thorough description of the image with which it is associated. Here's how to use it:

```
<asp:Image ID="Image1" Runat="server" DescriptionUrl="~/Image01.txt" />
```

This code produces the following results in the browser:

```
<img id="Image1" src="INETA.jpg" longdesc="Image01.txt" alt="" />
```

Remember that the image does not support the user clicking the image. If you want to program events based on button clicks, use the ImageButton server control discussed earlier in this chapter.

Table Server Control

Tables are one of the Web page's more common elements because the HTML <table> element is ideal for controlling the layout of your Web page. The typical construction of the Table server control is as follows:

```
<asp:Table ID="Table1" Runat="server">
  <asp:TableRow Runat="server" Font-Bold="True"
  ForeColor="Black" BackColor="Silver">
     <asp:TableHeaderCell>First Name</asp:TableHeaderCell>
     <asp:TableHeaderCell>Last Name</asp:TableHeaderCell>
  </asp:TableRow>
  <asp:TableRow>
     <asp:TableCell>Bill</asp:TableCell>
     <asp:TableCell>Evjen</asp:TableCell>
  </asp:TableRow>
 <asp:TableRow>
     <asp:TableCell>Devin</asp:TableCell>
     <asp:TableCell>Rader</asp:TableCell>
  </asp:TableRow>
</asp:Table>
```

This produces the simple three-rowed table shown in Figure 5-21.

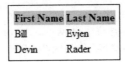

Figure 5-21

You can do a lot with the Table server control. For example, you can dynamically add rows to the table, as illustrated in Listing 5-18.

Listing 5-18: Dynamically adding rows to the table

VB
```
Protected Sub Page_Load(ByVal sender As Object, ByVal e As System.EventArgs)
   Dim tr As New TableRow()

   Dim fname As New TableCell()
   fname.Text = "Scott"
   tr.Cells.Add(fname)

   Dim lname As New TableCell()
   lname.Text = "Hanselman"
   tr.Cells.Add(lname)

   Table1.Rows.Add(tr)
End Sub
```

C#
```
protected void Page_Load(object sender, EventArgs e)
{
   TableRow tr = new TableRow();

   TableCell fname = new TableCell();
   fname.Text = "Scott";
```

```
    tr.Cells.Add(fname);

    TableCell lname = new TableCell();
    lname.Text = "Hanselman";
    tr.Cells.Add(lname);

    Table1.Rows.Add(tr);
}
```

To add a single row to a Table control, you have to create new instances of the `TableRow` and `TableCell` objects. You create the `TableCell` objects first and then place them within a `TableRow` object that is added to a `Table` object.

The Table server control is enhanced with some extra features in ASP.NET 2.0. One of the simpler new features is the capability to add captions to the tables on Web pages. Figure 5-22 shows a table with a caption.

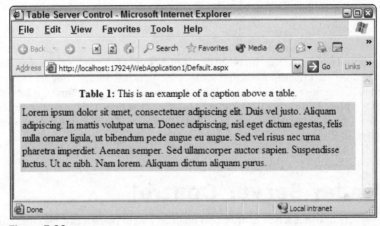

Figure 5-22

To give your table a caption, simply use the new `Caption` attribute in the Table control, as illustrated in Listing 5-19.

Listing 5-19: Using the new Caption attribute

```
<%@ Page Language="VB" %>

<html xmlns="http://www.w3.org/1999/xhtml" ><head runat="server">
    <title>Table Server Control</title>
</head>
<body>
    <form id="form1" runat="server">
        <asp:Table ID="Table1" Runat="server"
         Caption="<b>Table 1:</b> This is an example of a caption above a table."
         BackColor="Gainsboro">
```

(continued)

Listing 5-19: *(continued)*

```
                <asp:TableRow ID="Tablerow1" Runat=server>
                    <asp:TableCell ID="Tablecell1" Runat="server">Lorem ipsum dolor sit
                    amet, consectetuer adipiscing elit. Duis vel justo. Aliquam
                    adipiscing. In mattis volutpat urna. Donec adipiscing, nisl eget
                    dictum egestas, felis nulla ornare ligula, ut bibendum pede augue
                    eu augue. Sed vel risus nec urna pharetra imperdiet. Aenean
                    semper. Sed ullamcorper auctor sapien. Suspendisse luctus. Ut ac
                    nibh. Nam lorem. Aliquam dictum aliquam purus.</asp:TableCell>
                </asp:TableRow>
            </asp:Table>
        </form>
    </body>
</html>
```

By default, the caption is placed at the top center of the table, but you can control where it is placed by using another new attribute — CaptionAlign. Its possible settings include Bottom, Left, NotSet, Right, and Top.

In the past, an <asp:Table> element contained any number of <asp:TableRow> elements. Now you have some additional elements that can be nested within the <asp:Table> element. These new elements include <asp:TableHeaderRow> and <asp:TableFooterRow>. They add either a header or footer to your table, enabling you to use the Table server control to page through lots of data but still retain some text in place to indicate the type of data being handled. This is quite a powerful feature when you work with mobile applications that dictate that sometimes end users can move through only a few records at a time.

The Calendar Server Control

The Calendar server control is a rich control that enables you to place a full-featured calendar directly on your Web pages. It allows for a high degree of customization to ensure that it looks and behaves in a unique manner. The Calendar control, in its simplest form, is coded in the following manner:

```
<asp:Calendar ID="Calendar1" Runat="server">
</asp:Calendar>
```

This code produces a calendar on your Web page without any styles added, as shown in Figure 5-23.

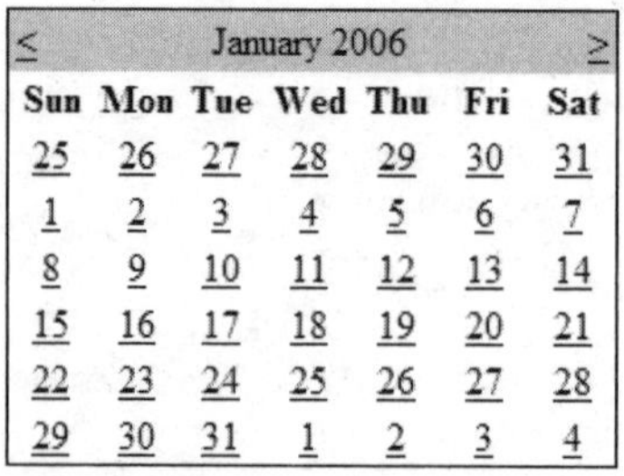

≤	January 2006					≥
Sun	**Mon**	**Tue**	**Wed**	**Thu**	**Fri**	**Sat**
25	26	27	28	29	30	31
1	2	3	4	5	6	7
8	9	10	11	12	13	14
15	16	17	18	19	20	21
22	23	24	25	26	27	28
29	30	31	1	2	3	4

Figure 5-23

Making a Date Selection from the Calendar Control

The calendar allows you to scroll through the months of the year and to select specific days in the exposed month. A simple application that enables the user to select a day of the month is shown in Listing 5-20.

Listing 5-20: Selecting a single day in the Calendar control

VB

```
<%@ Page Language="VB" %>

<script runat="server">
    Protected Sub Calendar1_SelectionChanged(ByVal sender As Object, _
      ByVal e As System.EventArgs)
        Response.Write("You selected: " & _
          Calendar1.SelectedDate.ToShortDateString())
    End Sub
</script>

<html xmlns="http://www.w3.org/1999/xhtml" >
<head id="Head1" runat="server">
    <title>Using the Calendar Control</title>
</head>
<body>
    <form id="form1" runat="server">
    <div>
        <asp:Calendar ID="Calendar1" Runat="server"
         OnSelectionChanged="Calendar1_SelectionChanged">
        </asp:Calendar>
    </div>
    </form>
</body>
</html>
```

C#

```
<%@ Page Language="C#" %>

<script runat="server">
    protected void Calendar1_SelectionChanged(object sender, EventArgs e)
    {
        Response.Write("You selected: " +
          Calendar1.SelectedDate.ToShortDateString());
    }
</script>
```

Running this application pulls up the calendar in the browser. The end user can then select a single date in it. After a date is selected, the Calendar1_SelectionChanged event is triggered, using the OnSelectionChange attribute. This event writes the value of the selected date to the screen. The result is shown in Figure 5-24.

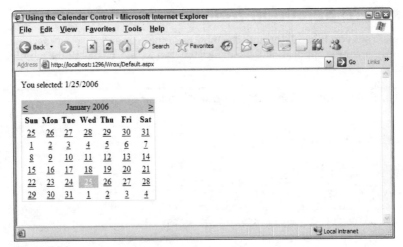

Figure 5-24

Choosing a Date Format to Output from the Calendar

When you use the `Calendar1_SelectionChanged` event, the selected date is written out using the `ToShortDateString()` method. The Calendar control also allows you to write out the date in a number of other formats, as detailed in the following list:

❑ `ToFileTime`: Converts the selection to the local operating system file time: `127473912000000000`.

❑ `ToFileTimeUtc`: Converts the selection to the operating system file time, but instead of using the local time zone, the UTC time is used: `127473696000000000`.

❑ `ToLocalTime`: Converts the current coordinated universal time (UTC) to local time: `12/12/2004 6:00:00 PM`.

❑ `ToLongDateString`: Converts the selection to a human-readable string in a long format: `Monday, December 13, 2004`.

❑ `ToLongTimeString`: Converts the selection to a time value (no date is included) of a long format: `12:00:00 AM`.

❑ `ToOADate`: Converts the selection to an OLE Automation date equivalent: `38334`.

❑ `ToShortDateString`: Converts the selection to a human-readable string in a short format: `12/13/2004`.

❑ `ToShortTimeString`: Converts the selection to a time value (no date is included) in a short format: `12:00 AM`.

❑ `ToString`: Converts the selection to the following: `12/13/2004 12:00:00 AM`.

❑ `ToUniversalTime`: Converts the selection to universal time (UTC): `12/13/2004 6:00:00 AM`.

Making Day, Week, or Month Selections

By default, the Calendar control enables you to make single day selections. You can use the SelectionMode property to change this behavior to allow your users to make week or month selections from the calendar instead. The possible values of this property include Day, DayWeek, DayWeekMonth, and None.

The Day setting enables you to click a specific day in the calendar to highlight it (this is the default). Using the setting of DayWeek still lets you make individual day selections, but it also enables you to click the arrow next to the week (see Figure 5-25) to make selections that consist of an entire week. Using the setting of DayWeekMonth lets users make individual day selections or week selections. A new arrow appears in the upper-left corner of the calendar that enables users to select an entire month (also shown in Figure 5-25). A setting of None means that it is impossible for the end user to make any selections, which is useful for calendars on your site that are informational only.

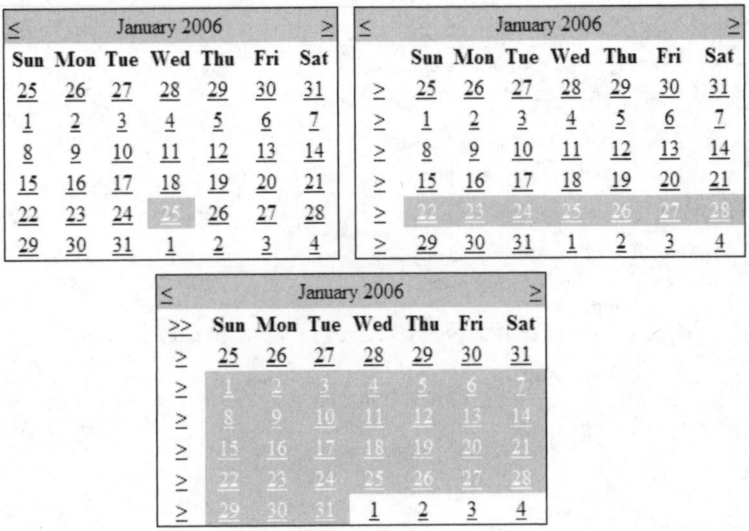

Figure 5-25

Working with Date Ranges

Even if an end user makes a selection that encompasses an entire week or an entire month, you get back from the selection only the first date of this range. If, for example, you allow users to select an entire month and one selects the month of July 2005, what you get back (using ToShortDateString()) is 7/1/2005 — the first date in the date range of the selection. That might work for you, but if you require all the dates in the selected range, Listing 5-21 shows you how to get them.

Listing 5-21: Retrieving a range of dates from a selection

VB

```
<%@ Page Language="VB" %>

<script runat="server">
    Protected Sub Calendar1_SelectionChanged(ByVal sender As Object, _
      ByVal e As System.EventArgs)
        Label1.Text = "<b><u>You selected the following date/dates:</u></b><br>"

        For i As Integer = 0 To (Calendar1.SelectedDates.Count - 1)
            Label1.Text += Calendar1.SelectedDates.Item(i).ToShortDateString() & _
            "<br>"
        Next
    End Sub
</script>

<html xmlns="http://www.w3.org/1999/xhtml" >
<head id="Head1" runat="server">
    <title>Using the Calendar Control</title>
</head>
<body>
    <form id="form1" runat="server">
    <div>
        <asp:Calendar ID="Calendar1" Runat="server"
         OnSelectionChanged="Calendar1_SelectionChanged"
         SelectionMode="DayWeekMonth">
        </asp:Calendar><p>
        <asp:Label ID="Label1" Runat="server"></asp:Label></p>
    </div>
    </form>
</body>
</html>
```

C#

```
<%@ Page Language="C#" %>

<script runat="server">
    protected void Calendar1_SelectionChanged(object sender, EventArgs e)
    {
        Label1.Text = "<b><u>You selected the following date/dates:</u></b><br>";

        for (int i=0; i<Calendar1.SelectedDates.Count; i++) {
            Label1.Text += Calendar1.SelectedDates[i].ToShortDateString() +
            "<br>";
        }
    }
</script>
```

In this example, the Calendar control lets users make selections that can be an individual day, a week, or even a month. Using a For Next loop, you iterate through a selection by using the SelectedDates .Count property. The code produces the results shown in Figure 5-26.

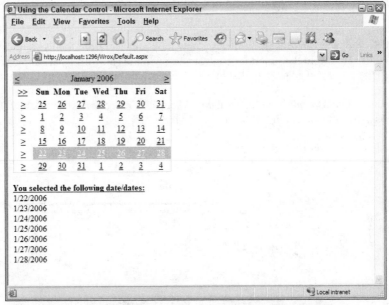

Figure 5-26

You can get just the first day of the selection by using the following:

VB
```
Calendar1.SelectedDates.Item(0).ToShortDateString()
```

C#
```
Calendar1.SelectedDates[0].ToShortDateString();
```

And you can get the last date in the selected range by using:

VB
```
Calendar1.SelectedDates.Item(Calendar1.SelectedDates.Count-1).ToShortDateString()
```

C#
```
Calendar1.SelectedDates[Calendar1.SelectedDates.Count-1].ToShortDateString();
```

As you can see, this is possible using the Count property of the SelectedDates object.

Modifying the Style and Behavior of Your Calendar

There is a lot to the Calendar control—definitely more than can be covered in this chapter. One nice thing about the Calendar control is the ease of extensibility that it offers. Begin exploring new ways to customize this control further by looking at one of the easiest ways to change it—applying a style to the control.

Using Visual Studio, you can give the controls a new look-and-feel from the Design view of the page you are working with. Highlight the Calendar control and open the control's smart tag to see the Auto Format link. That gives you a list of available styles that can be applied to your Calendar control.

The Calendar control isn't alone in this capability. Many other rich controls offer a list of styles. You can always find this capability in the control's smart tag.

Some of the styles are shown in Figure 5-27.

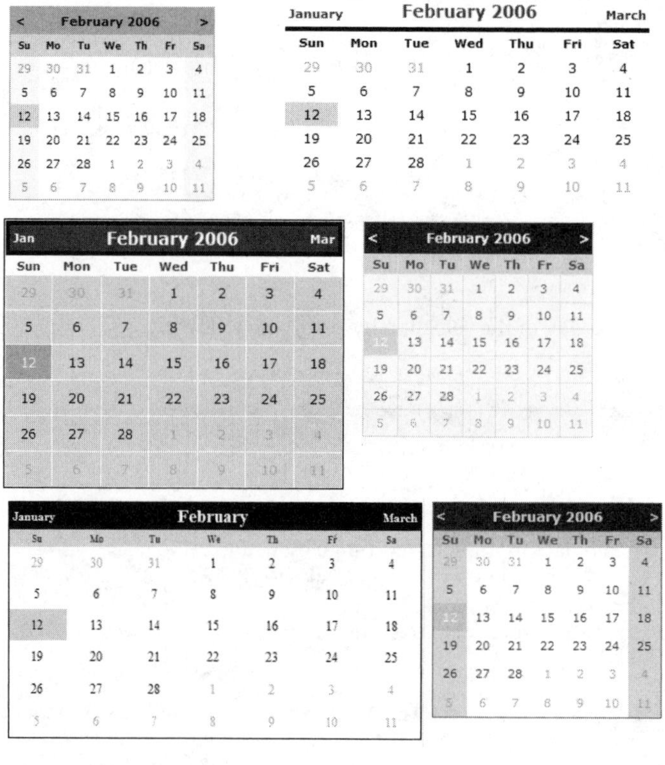

Figure 5-27

In addition to changing the style of the Calendar control, you can work with the control during its rendering process. The Calendar control includes an event called DayRender that allows you to control how a single date or all the dates in the calendar are rendered. Listing 5-22 shows an example of how to change one of the dates being rendered in the calendar.

Listing 5-22: Controlling how a day is rendered in the Calendar

VB

```
<%@ Page Language="VB" %>

<script runat="server">
    Protected Sub Calendar1_DayRender(ByVal sender As Object, _
       ByVal e As System.Web.UI.WebControls.DayRenderEventArgs)
          e.Cell.VerticalAlign = VerticalAlign.Top

       If (e.Day.DayNumberText = "25") Then
             e.Cell.Controls.Add(New LiteralControl("<p>User Group Meeting!</p>"))
             e.Cell.BorderColor = Drawing.Color.Black
             e.Cell.BorderWidth = 1
             e.Cell.BorderStyle = BorderStyle.Solid
             e.Cell.BackColor = Drawing.Color.LightGray
       End If
    End Sub
</script>

<html xmlns="http://www.w3.org/1999/xhtml" >
<head id="Head1" runat="server">
    <title>Using the Calendar Control</title>
</head>
<body>
    <form id="form1" runat="server">
    <div>
        <asp:Calendar ID="Calendar1" Runat="server"
         OnDayRender="Calendar1_DayRender" Height="190px" BorderColor="White"
         Width="350px" ForeColor="Black" BackColor="White" BorderWidth="1px"
         NextPrevFormat="FullMonth" Font-Names="Verdana" Font-Size="9pt">
            <SelectedDayStyle ForeColor="White"
             BackColor="#333399"></SelectedDayStyle>
            <OtherMonthDayStyle ForeColor="#999999"></OtherMonthDayStyle>
            <TodayDayStyle BackColor="#CCCCCC"></TodayDayStyle>
            <NextPrevStyle ForeColor="#333333" VerticalAlign="Bottom"
             Font-Size="8pt" Font-Bold="True"></NextPrevStyle>
            <DayHeaderStyle Font-Size="8pt" Font-Bold="True"></DayHeaderStyle>
            <TitleStyle ForeColor="#333399" BorderColor="Black" Font-Size="12pt"
                Font-Bold="True" BackColor="White" BorderWidth="4px">
            </TitleStyle>
        </asp:Calendar>
    </div>
    </form>
</body>
</html>
```

(continued)

Listing 5-22: *(continued)*

C#

```csharp
<%@ Page Language="C#" %>

<script runat="server">
    protected void Calendar1_DayRender(object sender, DayRenderEventArgs e)
    {
        e.Cell.VerticalAlign = VerticalAlign.Top;

        if (e.Day.DayNumberText == "25")
        {
            e.Cell.Controls.Add(new LiteralControl("<p>User Group Meeting!</p>"));
            e.Cell.BorderColor = System.Drawing.Color.Black;
            e.Cell.BorderWidth = 1;
            e.Cell.BorderStyle = BorderStyle.Solid;
            e.Cell.BackColor = System.Drawing.Color.LightGray;
        }


    }
</script>
```

In this example, you use a Calendar control with a little style to it. When the page is built and run in the browser, you can see that the 25th of every month in the calendar has been changed by the code in the `Calendar1_DayRender` event. The calendar is shown in Figure 5-28.

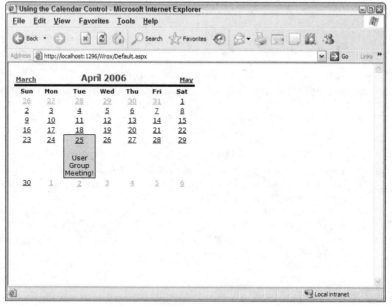

Figure 5-28

The Calendar control in this example adds an `OnDayRender` attribute that points to the `Calendar1_DayRender` event. The method is run for each of the days rendered in the calendar. The class constructor shows that you are not working with the typical `System.EventArgs` class, but instead with the `DayRenderEventArgs` class. It gives you access to each of the days rendered in the calendar.

The two main properties from the `DayRenderEventArgs` class are `Cell` and `Day`. The `Cell` property gives you access to the space in which the day is being rendered, and the `Day` property gives you access to the specific date being rendered in the cell.

From the actions being taken in the `Calendar1_DayRender` event, you can see that both properties are used. First, the `Cell` property sets the vertical alignment of the cell to `Top`. If it didn't, the table might look a little strange when one of the cells has content. Next, a check is made to see if the day being rendered (checked with the `Day` property) is the 25th of the month. If it is, the `If Then` statement runs using the `Cell` property to change the styling of just that cell. The styling change adds a control, as well as makes changes to the border and color of the cell.

As you can see, working with individual dates in the calendar is fairly straightforward. You can easily give them the content and appearance you want.

A nice feature of the `Day` property is that you can turn off the option to select a particular date or range of dates by setting the `Day` property's `IsSelectable` property to `False`:

VB
```
If (e.Day.Date < DateTime.Now) Then
    e.Day.IsSelectable = False
End If
```

C#
```
if (e.Day.Date < DateTime.Now) {
    e.Day.IsSelectable = false;
}
```

AdRotator Server Control

Although Web users find ads rather annoying, advertising continues to be prevalent everywhere on the Web. With the AdRotator control, you can now use advertisement data from sources other than the standard XML file that was used with the previous versions of this control.

If you're using an XML source for the ad information, first create an XML advertisement file. The advertisement file is quite similar to the previous advertisement file, but you can now incorporate some new elements that give you even more control over the appearance and behavior of your ads. Listing 5-23 shows an example of an XML advertisement file.

Listing 5-23: The XML advertisement file

```
<?xml version="1.0" encoding="utf-8" ?>
<Advertisements
  xmlns="http://schemas.microsoft.com/AspNet/AdRotator-Schedule-File">
```

(continued)

Listing 5-23: *(continued)*

```
<Ad>
    <ImageUrl>book1.gif</ImageUrl>
    <NavigateUrl>http://www.wrox.com</NavigateUrl>
    <AlternateText>Visit Wrox Today!</AlternateText>
    <Impressions>50</Impressions>
    <Keyword>VB.NET</Keyword>
</Ad>
<Ad>
    <ImageUrl>book2.gif</ImageUrl>
    <NavigateUrl>http://www.wrox.com</NavigateUrl>
    <AlternateText>Visit Wrox Today!</AlternateText>
    <Impressions>50</Impressions>
    <Keyword>XML</Keyword>
</Ad>
</Advertisements>
```

This XML file, used for storing information about the advertisements that appear in your application, has just a few elements detailed in the following table. Remember that all elements are optional.

Element	Description
ImageUrl	Takes a string value that indicatesthe location of the image to use.
NavigateUrl	Takes a string value that indicates the URL to post to when the image is clicked.
AlternateText	Takes a string value that is used for display if images are either turned off in the client's browser or if the image is not found.
Impressions	Takes a numerical value that indicates the likelihood of the image getting selected for display.
Keyword	Takes a string value that sets the category of the image in order to allow for the filtering of ads.

Now that the XML advertisement file is in place, you can simply use the AdRotator control to read from this file. Listing 5-24 shows an example of this in action.

Listing 5-24: Using the AdRotator control as a banner ad

```
<%@ Page Language="VB" %>

<html xmlns="http://www.w3.org/1999/xhtml" >
<head runat="server">
    <title>AdRotator Page</title>
</head>
<body>
    <form id="form1" runat="server">
        <asp:AdRotator ID="AdRotator1" Runat="server"
          AdvertisementFile="MyAds.xml" />
```

```
        <p>Lorem ipsum dolor sit
        amet, consectetuer adipiscing elit. Duis vel justo. Aliquam
        adipiscing. In mattis volutpat urna. Donec adipiscing, nisl eget
        dictum egestas, felis nulla ornare ligula, ut bibendum pede augue
        eu augue. Sed vel risus nec urna pharetra imperdiet. Aenean
        semper. Sed ullamcorper auctor sapien. Suspendisse luctus. Ut ac
        nibh. Nam lorem. Aliquam dictum aliquam purus.</p>
    </form>
</body>
</html>
```

The example shows the ad specified in the XML advertisement file as a banner ad at the top of the page.

You are not required to place all your ad information in the XML advertisement file. Instead, you can use another data source to which you bind the AdRotator. For instance, you bind the AdRotator to a SqlDataSource object that is retrieving the ad information from SQL Server in the following fashion:

```
<asp:AdRotator ID="AdRotator1" Runat="server"
  DataSourceId="SqlDataSource1" AlternateTextField="AlternateTF"
  ImageUrlField="Image" NavigateUrlField="NavigateUrl" />
```

The AlternateTextField, ImageUrlField, and NavigateUrlField properties point to the column names that are used in SQL Server for those items.

The Xml Server Control

The Xml server control provides a means of getting XML and transforming it using an XSL style sheet. The Xml control can work with your XML in a couple of different ways. The simplest method is by using the construction shown in Listing 5-25. This control is covered in more detail in Chapter 13.

Listing 5-25: Displaying an XML document

```
<asp:Xml ID="Xml1" Runat="server" DocumentSource="~/MyXMLFile.xml"
  TransformSource="MyXSLFile.xslt"></asp:Xml>
```

This method takes only a couple of attributes to make it work: DocumentSource, which points to the path of the XML file, and TransformSource, which provides the XSLT file to use in transforming the XML document.

The other way to use the Xml server control is to load the XML into an object and then pass the object to the Xml control, as illustrated in Listing 5-26.

Listing 5-26: Loading the XML file to an object before providing it to the Xml control

VB
```
Dim MyXmlDoc as XmlDocument = New XmlDocument()
MyXmlDoc.Load(Server.MapPath("Customers.xml"))

Dim MyXslDoc As XslTransform = New XslTransform()
```

(continued)

177

Listing 5-26: *(continued)*

```
MyXslDoc.Load(Server.MapPath("CustomersSchema.xslt"))

Xml1.Document = MyXmlDoc
Xml1.Transform = MyXslDoc
```

C#
```
XmlDocument MyXmlDoc = new XmlDocument();
MyXmlDoc.Load(Server.MapPath("Customers.xml"));

XslTransform MyXsltDoc = new XslTransform();
MyXsltDoc.Load(Server.MapPath("CustomersSchema.xslt"));

Xml1.Document = MyXmlDoc;
Xml1.Transform = MyXslDoc;
```

To make this work, you have to ensure that the `System.Xml` and `System.Xml.Xsl` namespaces are imported into your page. The example loads both the XML and XSL files and then assigns these files as the values of the `Document` and `Transform` properties.

Panel Server Control

The Panel server control encapsulates a set of controls you can use to manipulate or lay out your ASP.NET pages. It is basically a wrapper for other controls, enabling you to take a group of server controls along with other elements (such as HTML and images) and turn them into a single unit.

The advantage of using the Panel control to encapsulate a set of other elements is that you can manipulate these elements as a single unit using one attribute set in the Panel control itself. For example, setting the `Font-Bold` attribute to `True` causes each item within the Panel control to adopt this attribute.

The new addition to the Panel control is the capability to scroll with scrollbars that appear automatically depending on the amount of information that Panel control holds. You can even specify how the scrollbars should appear.

For an example of using scrollbars, look at a long version of the Lorem Ipsum text (found at www .lipsum.com) and place that text within the Panel control, as shown in Listing 5-27.

Listing 5-27: Using the new scrollbar feature with the Panel server control

```
<%@ Page Language="VB" %>

<html>
<head runat="server">
    <title>Panel Server Control Page</title>
</head>
<body>
    <form id="form1" runat="server">
        <asp:Panel ID="Panel1" Runat="server" Height="300" Width="300"
```

```
            ScrollBars="auto">
                <p>Lorem ipsum dolor sit amet...</p>
            </asp:Panel>
        </form>
    </body>
</html>
```

By assigning values to the `Height` and `Width` attributes of the Panel server control and using the `ScrollBars` attribute (in this case, set to `Auto`), you can display the information it contains within the defined area using scrollbars (see Figure 5-29).

As you can see, a single vertical scrollbar has been added to the set area of 300 × 300 pixels. The Panel control wraps the text by default as required. To change this behavior, use the new `Wrap` attribute, which takes a `Boolean` value:

```
<asp:Panel ID="Panel1" Runat="server"
  Height="300" Width="300" ScrollBars="Auto"
  Wrap="False" />
```

Turning off wrapping may cause the horizontal scrollbar to turn on (depending on what is contained in the panel section).

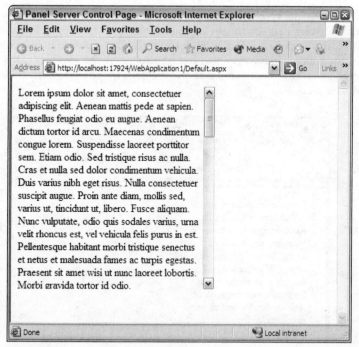

Figure 5-29

If you don't want to let the ASP.NET engine choose which scrollbars to activate, you can actually make that decision through the use of the `ScrollBars` attribute. In addition to `Auto`, its values include `None`, `Horizontal`, `Vertical`, and `Both`.

Another interesting attribute that enables you to change the behavior of the Panel control is `HorizontalAlign`. It enables you to set how the content in the Panel control is horizontally aligned. The possible values of this attribute include `NotSet`, `Center`, `Justify`, `Left`, and `Right`. Figure 5-30 shows a collection of Panel controls with different horizontal alignments.

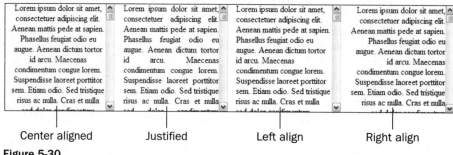

Center aligned   Justified   Left align   Right align

Figure 5-30

It is also possible to move the vertical scrollbar to the left side of the Panel control by using the `Direction` attribute. `Direction` can be set to `NotSet`, `LeftToRight`, and `RightToLeft`. A setting of `RightToLeft` is ideal when you are dealing with languages that are written from right to left (some Asian languages, for example). However, that setting also moves the scrollbar to the left side of the Panel control. If the scrollbar is moved to the left side and the `HorizontalAlign` attribute is set to `Left`, your content resembles Figure 5-31.

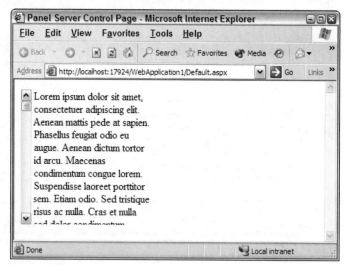

Figure 5-31

The PlaceHolder Server Control

The PlaceHolder server control works just as its name implies — it is a placeholder for you to interject objects dynamically into your page. Think of it as a marker with which you can add other controls. The capability to add controls to a page at a specific point also works with the Panel control.

To see how it works, insert a PlaceHolder control into your page and then add controls to it from your server-side code in the manner shown in Listing 5-28.

Listing 5-28: Using PlaceHolder to add controls to a page dynamically

VB
```
Dim NewLabelControl As New Label()
NewLabelControl.Text = "Hello there"
PlaceHolder1.Controls.Add(NewLabelControl)
```

C#
```
Label NewLabelControl = new Label();
NewLabelControl.Text = "Hello there";
PlaceHolder1.Controls.Add(NewLabelControl);
```

This example creates a new instance of a Label control and populates it with a value before it is added to the PlaceHolder control. You can add more than one control to a single instance of a PlaceHolder control.

Summary

This chapter explored numerous server controls, their capabilities, and the features they provide. With ASP.NET 2.0, you have more than 50 new server controls at your disposal, besides some great changes to the server controls from ASP.NET 1.0/1.1 that you already use on a day-to-day basis.

Because you have so many server controls at your disposal when you are creating your ASP.NET applications, you have to think carefully about which is the best control for the task. Many controls seem similar, but they offer different features. These controls guarantee that you can build the best possible applications for all browsers.

This chapter also covered some of the changes ASP.NET 2.0 brings to the classic server controls. The new features added to classic server controls are, in many ways, just as outstanding as the new controls that appear in ASP.NET 2.0. The new features make it easy to extend the capabilities of your ASP.NET applications.

ASP.NET 2.0
Web Server Controls

When I sat in one of the first review sessions for ASP.NET 2.0 on the Microsoft campus in Redmond, Washington, I remember being amazed by the number of new server controls (in addition to many other new and exciting features) this newest release offered. The core infrastructure was already in place with ASP.NET 1.0/1.1; but with the much-improved 2.0 release, the ASP.NET team was making the lives of developers even simpler.

The purpose of the large collection of new controls is to make you more productive. These controls give you advanced functionality that, in the past, you would have had to laboriously program or simply omit. In the classic ASP days, for example, few calendars were used on Internet Web sites. With the introduction of the Calendar server control in ASP.NET 1.0, calendar creation on a site became a trivial task. Building an image map on top of an image was another task that was difficult to achieve in ASP.NET 1.*x*. Through the use of a new server control, however, this capability is now built into ASP.NET 2.0.

This chapter takes a look at some of these new server controls and explains how to use them in ASP.NET 2.0 applications. It doesn't cover all of the new controls, many of which are discussed in other chapters of this book.

BulletedList Server Control

One common HTML Web page element is a collection of items in a bulleted list. The BulletedList server control is meant to display a bulleted list of items easily in an ordered (using the HTML <ol> element) or unordered (using the HTML <ul> element) fashion. In addition, the control can determine the style used for displaying the list.

The BulletedList control can be constructed of any number of `<asp:ListItem>` controls or can be data-bound to a data source of some kind and populated based upon the contents retrieved. Listing 6-1 shows a bulleted list in its simplest form.

Listing 6-1: A simple BulletedList control

```
<%@ Page Language="VB" %>

<html xmlns="http://www.w3.org/1999/xhtml" >
<head runat="server">
    <title>BulletedList Server Control</title>
</head>
<body>
    <form id="form1" runat="server">
        <asp:BulletedList ID="Bulletedlist1" Runat="server">
            <asp:ListItem>United States</asp:ListItem>
            <asp:ListItem>United Kingdom</asp:ListItem>
            <asp:ListItem>Finland</asp:ListItem>
            <asp:ListItem>Russia</asp:ListItem>
            <asp:ListItem>Sweden</asp:ListItem>
            <asp:ListItem>Estonia</asp:ListItem>
        </asp:BulletedList>
    </form>
</body>
</html>
```

The use of the `<asp:BulletedList>` element, along with `<asp:ListItem>` elements, produces a simple bulleted list output like the one shown in Figure 6-1.

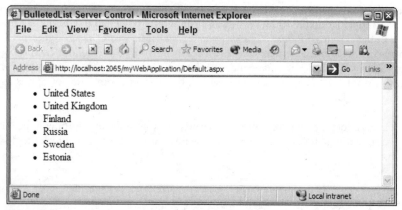

Figure 6-1

The BulletedList control also enables you to easily change the style of the list with just one or two attributes. The `BulletStyle` attribute changes the style of the bullet that precedes each line of the list. It has possible values of `Numbered`, `LowerAlpha`, `UpperAlpha`, `LowerRoman`, `UpperRoman`, `Disc`, `Circle`, `Square`, `NotSet`, and `CustomImage`. Figure 6-2 shows examples of these styles (minus the `CustomImage` setting that enables you to use any image of your choice).

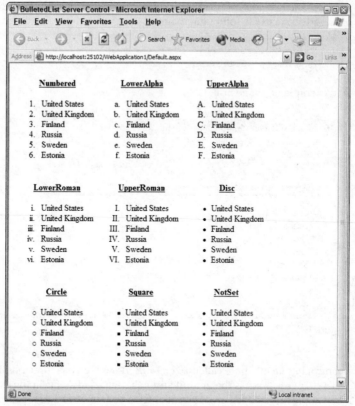

Figure 6-2

You can change the starting value of the first item in any of the numbered styles (Numbered, LowerAlpha, UpperAlpha, LowerRoman, UpperRoman) by using the FirstBulletNumber attribute. If you set the attribute's value to 5 when you use the UpperRoman setting, for example, you get the format illustrated in Figure 6-3.

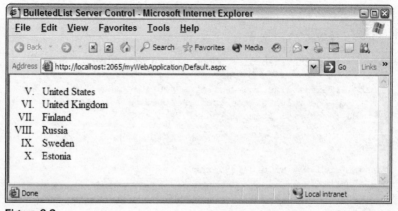

Figure 6-3

To employ images as bullets, use the `CustomImage` setting in the BulletedList control. You must also use the `BulletImageUrl` attribute in the following manner:

```
<asp:BulletedList ID="Bulletedlist1" Runat="server"
  BulletStyle="CustomImage" BulletImageUrl="~/myImage.gif">
```

Figure 6-4 shows an example of image bullets.

Figure 6-4

The BulletedList control has an attribute called `DisplayMode`, which has three possible values: `Text`, `HyperLink`, and `LinkButton`. `Text` is the default and has been used so far in the examples. Using `Text` means that the items in the bulleted list are laid out only as text. `HyperLink` means that each of the items is turned into a hyperlink — any user clicking the link is redirected to another page, which is specified by the `<asp:ListItem>` control's `Value` attribute. A value of `LinkButton` turns each bulleted list item into a hyperlink that posts back to the same page. It enables you to retrieve the selection that the end user makes, as illustrated in Listing 6-2.

Listing 6-2: Using the LinkButton value for the DisplayMode attribute

VB

```
<%@ Page Language="VB"%>
```

```
<script runat="server">
    Protected Sub BulletedList1_Click(ByVal sender As Object, _
        ByVal e As System.Web.UI.WebControls.BulletedListEventArgs)

            Label1.Text = "The index of item you selected: " & e.Index & _
                "<br>The value of the item selected: " & _
                BulletedList1.Items(e.Index).Text
    End Sub
</script>
```

```
<html xmlns="http://www.w3.org/1999/xhtml" >
<head runat="server">
```

```
        <title>BulletedList Server Control</title>
    </head>
    <body>
        <form id="form1" runat="server">
            <asp:BulletedList ID="BulletedList1" Runat="server"
             OnClick="BulletedList1_Click" DisplayMode="LinkButton">
                <asp:ListItem>United States</asp:ListItem>
                <asp:ListItem>United Kingdom</asp:ListItem>
                <asp:ListItem>Finland</asp:ListItem>
                <asp:ListItem>Russia</asp:ListItem>
                <asp:ListItem>Sweden</asp:ListItem>
                <asp:ListItem>Estonia</asp:ListItem>
            </asp:BulletedList>
            <asp:Label ID="Label1" Runat="server">
            </asp:Label>
        </form>
    </body>
</html>
```

C#

```
<%@ Page Language="C#"%>
<script runat="server">
    protected void BulletedList1_Click(object sender,
        System.Web.UI.WebControls.BulletedListEventArgs e)
    {
        Label1.Text = "The index of item you selected: " + e.Index +
            "<br>The value of the item selected: " +
            BulletedList1.Items[e.Index].Text;
    }
</script>
```

In this example, the `DisplayMode` attribute is set to `LinkButton`, and the `OnClick` attribute is used to point to the `BulletedList1_Click` event. `BulletedList1_Click` uses the `BulletedListEventArgs` object, which only exposes the `Index` property. Using that, you can determine the index number of the item selected.

You can directly access the `Text` value of a selected item by using the `Items` property, or you can use the same property to populate an instance of the `ListItem` object. You do that as shown here:

VB

```
Dim blSelectedValue As ListItem = BulletedList1.Items(e.Index)
```

C#

```
ListItem blSelectedValue = BulletedList1.Items[e.Index];
```

Now that you have seen how to create bulleted lists with items that you declaratively place in the code, take a look at how to create dynamic bulleted lists from items that are stored in a data store. The following example shows how to use the BulletedList control to data-bind to results coming from a data store; in it, all information is retrieved from an XML file.

The first step is to create the XML in Listing 6-3.

Listing 6-3: FilmChoices.xml

```
<?xml version="1.0" encoding="utf-8"?>
<FilmChoices>
   <Film
     Title="Close Encounters of the Third Kind"
     Year="1977"
     Director="Steven Spielberg" />
   <Film
     Title="Grease"
     Year="1978"
     Director="Randal Kleiser" />
   <Film
     Title="Lawrence of Arabia"
     Year="1962"
     Director="David Lean" />
</FilmChoices>
```

To populate the BulletedList server control with the `Title` attribute from the `FilmChoices.xml` file, use an XmlDataSource control to access the file, as illustrated in Listing 6-4.

Listing 6-4: Dynamically populating a BulletedList server control

```
<%@ Page Language="VB" %>

<html xmlns="http://www.w3.org/1999/xhtml" >
<head runat="server">
    <title>BulletedList Server Control</title>
</head>
<body>
    <form id="form1" runat="server">
       <asp:BulletedList ID="BulletedList1" Runat="server"
        DataSourceID="XmlDataSource1" DataTextField="Title">
       </asp:BulletedList>
       <asp:XmlDataSource ID="XmlDataSource1" Runat="server"
        DataFile="~/FilmChoices.xml" XPath="FilmChoices/Film">
       </asp:XmlDataSource>
    </form>
</body>
</html>
```

In this example, you use the `DataSourceID` attribute to point to the XmlDataSource control (as you would with any control that can be bound to one of the data source controls). After you are connected to the data source control, you specifically point to the `Title` attribute using the `DataTextField` attribute. After the two server controls are connected and the page is run, you get a bulleted list that is completely generated from the contents of the XML file. Figure 6-5 shows the result.

The XmlDataSource server control has some limitations in that the binding to the BulletedList server control worked in the previous example only because the `Title` value was an XML attribute and not a sub-element. The XmlDataSource control only exposes XML attributes as properties when databinding. If you are going to want to work with sub-elements, then you are going to have to perform an XSLT transform using the XmlDataSource control's `TransformFile` attribute to turn elements into attributes.

Figure 6-5

HiddenField Server Control

For many years now, developers have been using hidden fields in their Web pages to work with state management. The `<input type="hidden">` element is ideal for storing items that have no security context to them. These items are simply placeholders for data points that you want to store in the page itself instead of using the `Session` object or intermingling the data with the view state of the page. View state is another great way to store information in a page, but many developers turn off this feature to avoid corruption of the view state or possibly degradation of page performance.

Any time a hidden field is placed within a Web page, it is not interpreted in the browser in any fashion, although it is completely viewable by end users if they look at the source of the HTML page.

Listing 6-5 is an example of using the HiddenField server control to hold a GUID that can be used from page to page simply by carrying over its value as the end user navigates through your application.

Listing 6-5: Working with the HiddenField server control

VB

```
<%@ Page Language="VB" %>

<script runat="server" language="vb">
    Protected Sub Page_Load(ByVal sender As Object, ByVal e As System.EventArgs)
        HiddenField1.Value = System.Guid.NewGuid().ToString()
    End Sub
</script>

<html xmlns="http://www.w3.org/1999/xhtml" >
<head runat="server">
    <title>HiddenField Server Control</title>
</head>
<body>
    <form id="form1" runat="server">
        <asp:HiddenField ID="HiddenField1" Runat="Server" />
    </form>
</body>
</html>
```

(continued)

Listing 6-5: *(continued)*

C#

```
<%@ Page Language="C#"%>

<script runat="server">
    protected void Page_Load(object sender, EventArgs e)
    {
        HiddenField1.Value = System.Guid.NewGuid().ToString();
    }
</script>
```

In this example, the `Page_Load` event populates the `HiddenField1` control with a GUID. You can see the hidden field and its value by looking at the source of the blank HTML page that is created. You should see a result similar to the following (the GUID will have a different value, of course):

```
<input type="hidden" name="HiddenField1" id="HiddenField1"
  value="a031e77c-379b-4b4a-887c-244ee69584d5" />
```

On the page postback, ASP.NET can detect whether the HiddenField server control has changed its value since the last post. This enables you to change the HiddenField value with client-side script and then work with the changes in a page event.

The HiddenField server control has an event called `ValueChanged` that you can use when the value is changed:

VB

```
Protected Sub HiddenField1_ValueChanged(ByVal sender As Object, _
    ByVal e As System.EventArgs)
    ' Handle event here
End Sub
```

C#

```
protected void HiddenField1_ValueChanged(object sender, EventArgs e)
{
    // Handle event here
}
```

The `ValueChanged` event is triggered when the ASP.NET page is posted back to the server if the value of the HiddenField server control has changed since the last time the page was drawn. If the value has not changed, the method is never triggered. Therefore, the method is useful to act upon any changes to the HiddenField control — such as recording a value to the database or changing a value in the user's profile.

FileUpload Server Control

In ASP.NET 1.0/1.1, you could upload files using the HTML FileUpload server control. This control put an `<input type="file">` element on your Web page to enable the end user to upload files to the server. To use the file, however, you had to make a couple of modifications to the page. For example, you were required to add `enctype="multipart/form-data"` to the page's `<form>` element.

ASP.NET 2.0 introduces a new FileUpload server control that makes the process of uploading files to a server even simpler. When giving a page the capability to upload files, you simply include the new <asp:FileUpload> control and ASP.NET takes care of the rest, including adding the enctype attribute to the page's <form> element.

Uploading Files Using the FileUpload Control

After the file is uploaded to the server, you can also take hold of the uploaded file's properties and either display them to the end user or use these values yourself in your page's code behind. Listing 6-6 shows an example of using the new FileUpload control. The page contains a single FileUpload control, plus a Button and a Label control.

Listing 6-6: Uploading files using the new FileUpload control

VB

```
<%@ Page Language="VB"%>

<script runat="server">
    Protected Sub Button1_Click(ByVal sender As Object, ByVal e As System.EventArgs)
        If FileUpload1.HasFile Then
            Try
                FileUpload1.SaveAs("C:\Uploads\" & _
                    FileUpload1.FileName)
                Label1.Text = "File name: " & _
                    FileUpload1.PostedFile.FileName & "<br>" & _
                    "File Size: " & _
                    FileUpload1.PostedFile.ContentLength & " kb<br>" & _
                    "Content type: " & _
                    FileUpload1.PostedFile.ContentType
            Catch ex As Exception
                Label1.Text = "ERROR: " & ex.Message.ToString()
            End Try
        Else
            Label1.Text = "You have not specified a file."
        End If
    End Sub
</script>

<html xmlns="http://www.w3.org/1999/xhtml" >
<head runat="server">
    <title>FileUpload Server Control</title>
</head>
<body>
    <form id="form1" runat="server">
        <asp:FileUpload ID="FileUpload1" Runat="server" />
        <p>
        <asp:Button ID="Button1" Runat="server" Text="Upload"
         OnClick="Button1_Click" /></p>
        <p>
        <asp:Label ID="Label1" Runat="server"></asp:Label></p>
    </form>
</body>
</html>
```

(continued)

Listing 6-6: *(continued)*

C#

```csharp
<%@ Page Language="C#"%>

<script runat="server">
    protected void Button1_Click(object sender, EventArgs e)
    {
        if (FileUpload1.HasFile)
            try {
                FileUpload1.SaveAs("C:\\Uploads\\" + FileUpload1.FileName);
                Label1.Text = "File name: " +
                    FileUpload1.PostedFile.FileName + "<br>" +
                    FileUpload1.PostedFile.ContentLength + " kb<br>" +
                    "Content type: " +
                    FileUpload1.PostedFile.ContentType;
            }
            catch (Exception ex) {
                Label1.Text = "ERROR: " + ex.Message.ToString();
            }
        else
        {
            Label1.Text = "You have not specified a file.";
        }
    }
</script>
```

From this example, you can see that the entire process is rather simple. The single button on the page initiates the upload process. The FileUpload control itself does not initiate the uploading process. You must initiate it through another event such as `Button_Click`.

After the file is uploaded, the first check examines whether a file reference was actually placed within the `<input type="file">` element. If a file was specified, an attempt is made to upload the referenced file to the server using the `SaveAs` method of the FileUpload control. That method takes a single `String` parameter, which should include the location where you want to save the file. In the `String` parameter used in Listing 6-6, you can see that the file is being saved to a folder called `Uploads`, which is located in the `C:\` drive.

The `PostedFile.FileName` attribute is used to give the saved file the same name as the file it was copied from. If you want to name the file something else, simply use the `SaveAs` method in the following manner:

```
FileUpload1.SaveAs("C:\Uploads\UploadedFile.txt")
```

You could also give the file a name that specifies the time it was uploaded:

```
FileUpload1.SaveAs("C:\Uploads\" & System.DateTime.Now.ToFileTimeUtc() & ".txt")
```

After the upload is successfully completed, the Label control on the page is populated with metadata of the uploaded file. In the example, the file's name, size, and content type are retrieved and displayed on the page for the end user. When the file is uploaded to the server, the page generated is similar to that shown in Figure 6-6.

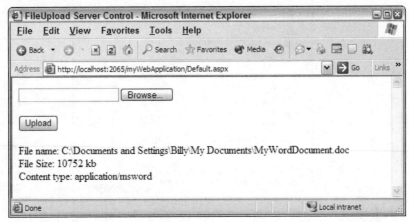

Figure 6-6

Uploading files to another server can be an error-prone affair. It is vital to upload files in your code using proper exception handling. That's why the file in the example is uploaded using a Try Catch statement.

Giving ASP.NET Proper Permissions to Upload Files

You might receive errors when your end users upload files to your Web server through the FileUpload control in your application. These might occur because the destination folder on the server is not writable for the account used by ASP.NET. If ASP.NET is not enabled to write to the folder you want, you can enable it using the folder's properties.

First, right-click the folder into which the ASP.NET files should be uploaded. The Properties dialog for the selected folder opens. Click the Security tab to make sure the ASP.NET Machine Account is included in the list and has the proper permissions to write to disk. If it is enabled, you see something similar to what is presented in Figure 6-7.

If you don't see the ASP.NET Machine Account in the list of users allowed to access the folder, add ASP.NET by clicking the Add button and entering ASPNET (without the period) in the text area provided (see Figure 6-8).

Click OK, and you can then click the appropriate check boxes to provide the permissions needed for your application.

Figure 6-7

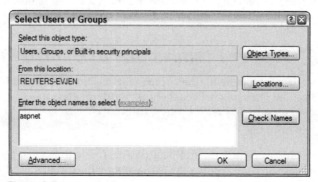

Figure 6-8

Understanding File Size Limitations

Your end users might never encounter an issue with the file upload process in your application, but you should be aware that some limitations exist. When users work through the process of uploading files, a size restriction is actually sent to the server for uploading. The default size limitation is 4MB (4096kb); the transfer fails if a user tries to upload a file that is larger than 4096kb.

A size restriction protects your application. You want to prevent malicious users from uploading numerous large files to your Web server in an attempt to tie up all the available processes on the server. Such an occurrence is called a *denial of service attack*. It ties up the Web server's resources so that legitimate users are denied responses from the server.

The default allowable file size is dictated by the actual request size permitted to the Web server (4096KB). You can change this setting in the web.config file, as shown in Listing 6-7.

Listing 6-7: Changing the file-size limitation setting in the web.config file

```
<httpRuntime
  idleTime="15"
  executionTimeout="90"
  maxRequestLength="4096"
  useFullyQualifiedRedirectUrl="False"
  minFreeThreads="8"
  minLocalRequestFreeThreads="4"
  appRequestQueueLimit="100"
/>
```

You can do a lot with the <httpRuntime> section of the web.config file, but two properties — the maxRequestLength and executionTimeout properties — are especially interesting.

The maxRequestLength property is the setting that dictates the size of the request made to the Web server. When you upload files, the file is included in the request; you alter the size allowed to be uploaded by changing the value of this property. The value presented is in kilobytes. To allow files larger than the default of 4MB, change the maxRequestLength property as in the following:

```
maxRequestLength="11000"
```

This example changes the maxRequestLength property's value to 11,000KB (around 10MB). With this setting in place, your end users can upload 10MB files to the server. When changing the maxRequestLength property, be aware of the setting provided for the executionTimeout property. This property sets the time (in seconds) for a request to attempt to execute to the server before ASP.NET shuts down the request (whether or not it is finished). The default setting is 90 seconds. The end user receives a timeout error notification in the browser if the time limit is exceeded. If you are going to permit larger requests, remember that they take longer to execute than smaller ones. If you increase the size of the maxRequestLength property, you should examine whether to increase the executionTimeout property as well.

> *If you are working with smaller files, it's advisable to reduce the size allotted for the request to the Web server by decreasing the value of the* maxRequestLength *property. This helps safeguard your application from a denial of service attack.*

Placing the Uploaded File into a Stream Object

One nice feature of the FileUpload control is that it not only gives you the capability to save the file to disk, but it also lets you place the contents of the file into a Stream object. You do this by using the FileContent property, as demonstrated in Listing 6-8.

Listing 6-8: Uploading the file contents into a Stream object

VB
```
Dim myStream As System.IO.Stream
myStream = FileUpload1.FileContent
```

(continued)

Listing 6-8: *(continued)*

C#
```
System.IO.Stream myStream;
myStream = FileUpload1.FileContent;
```

In this short example, an instance of the Stream object is created. Then, using the FileUpload control's FileContent property, the content of the uploaded file is placed into the object. This is possible because the FileContent property returns a Stream object.

Moving File Contents from a Stream Object to a Byte Array

Because you have the capability to move the file contents to a Stream object of some kind, it is also fairly simple to move the contents of the file to a Byte array. To do so, first move the file contents to a MemoryStream object and then convert the object to the necessary Byte array object. Listing 6-9 shows the process.

Listing 6-9: Uploading the file contents into a Byte array

VB
```
Dim myByteArray() As Byte
Dim myStream As System.IO.MemoryStream

myStream = FileUpload1.FileContent
myByteArray = myStream.ToArray()
```

C#
```
Byte myByteArray[];
System.IO.Stream myStream;

myStream = FileUpload1.FileContent;
myByteArray = myStream.ToArray();
```

In this example, instances of a Byte array and a MemoryStream object are created. First the MemoryStream object is created using the FileUpload control's FileContent property as you did previously. Then it's fairly simple to use the MemoryStream object's ToArray() method to populate the myByteArray() instance. After the file is placed into a Byte array, you can work with the file contents as necessary.

MultiView and View Server Controls

The MultiView and View server controls work together to give you the capability to turn on/off sections of an ASP.NET page. Turning sections on and off, which means activating or deactivating a series of

View controls within a MultiView control, is similar to changing the visibility of Panel controls. For certain operations, however, you may find that the MultiView control is easier to manage and work with.

The sections, or views, do not change on the client-side; rather, they change with a postback to the server. You can put any number of elements and controls in each view, and the end user can work through the views based upon the sequence numbers that you assign to the views.

You can build these controls (like all server controls) from the source view or design view. If working with Visual Studio 2005, you can drag and drop a MultiView control onto the design surface and then drag and drop any number of View controls inside the MultiView control. Place the elements you want within the View controls. When you're finished, you have something like the view shown in Figure 6-9.

You also can create your controls directly in the code, as shown in Listing 6-10.

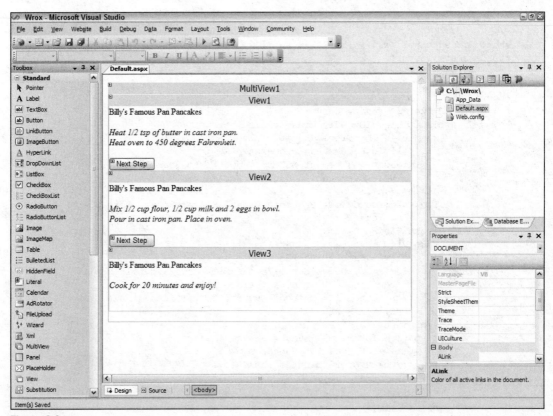

Figure 6-9

Listing 6-10: Using the MultiView and View server controls

VB

```
<%@ Page Language="VB"%>

<script runat="server">
    Protected Sub Page_Load(ByVal sender As Object, ByVal e As System.EventArgs)
        If Not Page.IsPostBack Then
            MultiView1.ActiveViewIndex = 0
        End If
    End Sub

    Sub NextView(ByVal sender As Object, ByVal e As System.EventArgs)
        MultiView1.ActiveViewIndex += 1
    End Sub
</script>

<html xmlns="http://www.w3.org/1999/xhtml" >
<head runat="server">
    <title>MultiView Server Control</title>
</head>
<body>
    <form id="form1" runat="server">
        <asp:MultiView ID="MultiView1" Runat="server">
            <asp:View ID="View1" Runat="Server">
                Billy's Famous Pan Pancakes<p />
                <i>Heat 1/2 tsp of butter in cast iron pan.<br />
                    Heat oven to 450 degrees Fahrenheit.<br />
                </i><p />
                <asp:Button ID="Button1" Runat="Server" Text="Next Step"
                 OnClick="NextView" />
            </asp:View>
            <asp:View ID="View2" Runat="Server">
                Billy's Famous Pan Pancakes<p />
                <i>Mix 1/2 cup flour, 1/2 cup milk and 2 eggs in bowl.<br />
                    Pour in cast iron pan. Place in oven.</i><p />
                <asp:Button ID="Button2" Runat="Server" Text="Next Step"
                 OnClick="NextView" />
            </asp:View>
            <asp:View ID="View3" Runat="Server">
                Billy's Famous Pan Pancakes<p />
                <i>Cook for 20 minutes and enjoy!<br />
                </i><p />
            </asp:View>
        </asp:MultiView>
    </form>
</body>
</html>
```

C#

```
<%@ Page Language="C#"%>

<script runat="server">
    protected void Page_Load(object sender, EventArgs e)
    {
        if (!Page.IsPostBack)
```

```
            {
                MultiView1.ActiveViewIndex = 0;
            }
        }

    void NextView(object sender, EventArgs e)
    {
        MultiView1.ActiveViewIndex += 1;
    }
</script>
```

This example shows three views expressed in the MultiView control. Each view is constructed with an `<asp:View>` server control that also needs `ID` and `Runat` attributes. A button is added to each of the first two views (`View1` and `View2`) of the MultiView control. The buttons point to a server-side event that triggers the MultiView control to progress onto the next view within the series of views.

Before either of the buttons can be clicked, the MultiView control's `ActiveViewIndex` attribute is assigned a value. By default, the `ActiveViewIndex`, which describes the view that should be showing, is set to `-1`. This means that no view shows when the page is generated. To start on the first view when the page is drawn, set the `ActiveViewIndex` property to `0`, which is the first view because this is a zero-based index. Therefore, the code from Listing 6-10 first checks to see if the page is in a postback situation and if not, the `ActiveViewIndex` is assigned to the first View control.

Each of the buttons in the MultiView control triggers the `NextView` method. `NextView` simply adds one to the `ActiveViewIndex` value, thereby showing the next view in the series until the last view is shown. The view series is illustrated in Figure 6-10.

In addition to the Next Step button on the first and second views, you could place a button in the second and third views to enable the user to navigate backward through the views. To do this, create two buttons titled Previous Step in the last two views and point them to the following method in their `OnClick` events:

VB

```
    Sub PreviousView(ByVal sender As Object, ByVal e As System.EventArgs)
        MultiView1.ActiveViewIndex -= 1
    End Sub
```

C#

```
    void PreviousView(object sender, EventArgs e)
    {
        MultiView1.ActiveViewIndex -= 1;
    }
```

Here, the `PreviousView` method subtracts one from the `ActiveViewIndex` value, thereby showing the previous view in the view series.

Another option is to spice up the MultiView control by adding a step counter that displays (to a Label control) which step in the series the end user is currently performing. In the `Page_PreRender` event, you add the following line:

VB

```
    Label1.Text = "Step " & (MultiView1.ActiveViewIndex + 1).ToString() & _
        " of " & MultiView1.Views.Count.ToString()
```

C#

```csharp
Label1.Text = "Step " + (MultiView1.ActiveViewIndex + 1).ToString() +
    " of " + MultiView1.Views.Count.ToString();
```

Now when working through the MultiView control, the end user sees `Step 1 of 3` on the first view, which changes to `Step 2 of 3` on the next view, and so on.

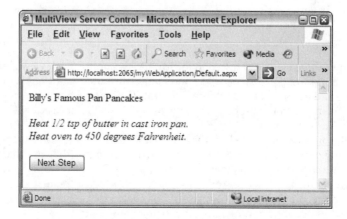

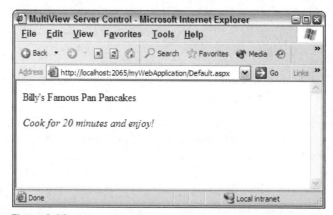

Figure 6-10

Wizard Server Control

Much like the MultiView control, the Wizard server control enables you to build a sequence of steps that is displayed to the end user. Web pages are all about either displaying or gathering information and, in many cases, you don't want to display all the information at once—nor do you always want to gather everything from the end user at once. Sometimes, you want to trickle the information in from or out to the end user.

When you are constructing a step-by-step process that includes logic on the steps taken, use the Wizard control to manage the entire process. The first time you use the Wizard control, notice that it allows for a far greater degree of customization than does the MultiView control.

In its simplest form, the Wizard control can be just an `<asp:Wizard>` element with any number of `<asp:WizardStep>` elements. Listing 6-11 creates a Wizard control that works through three steps.

Listing 6-11: A simple Wizard control

```
<%@ Page Language="VB"%>

<html xmlns="http://www.w3.org/1999/xhtml" >
<head runat="server">
    <title>Wizard server control</title>
</head>
<body>
    <form id="form1" runat="server">
        <asp:Wizard ID="Wizard1" Runat="server" SideBarEnabled="true"
        ActiveStepIndex="0">
            <WizardSteps>
                <asp:WizardStep Runat="server" Title="Step 1">
                    This is the first step.</asp:WizardStep>
                <asp:WizardStep Runat="server" Title="Step 2">
                    This is the second step.</asp:WizardStep>
                <asp:WizardStep Runat="server" Title="Step 3">
                    This is the third and final step.</asp:WizardStep>
            </WizardSteps>
        </asp:Wizard>
    </form>
</body>
</html>
```

In this example, three steps are defined with the `<asp:WizardSteps>` control. Each step contains content—simply text in this case, although you can put in anything you want, such as other Web server controls or even user controls. The order in which the `WizardSteps` are defined is based completely on the order in which they appear within the `<WizardSteps>` element.

The `<asp:Wizard>` element itself contains a couple of important attributes. The first is `SideBarEnabled`. In this example, it is set to `True`—meaning that a side navigation system in the displayed control enables the end user to quickly navigate to other steps in the process. The `ActiveStepIndex` attribute of the Wizard control defines the first wizard step. In this case, it is the first step—0.

The three steps of the example Wizard control are shown in Figure 6-11.

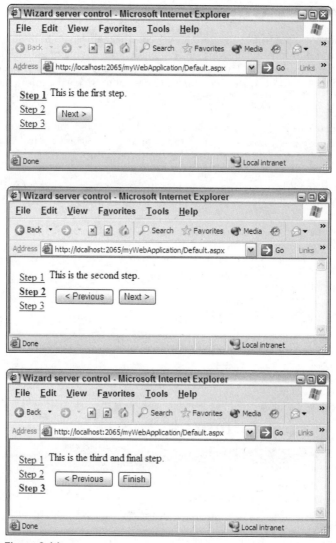

Figure 6-11

The side navigation allows for easy access to the defined steps. The Wizard control adds appropriate buttons to the steps in the process. The first step has simply a Next button, the middle step has Previous and Next buttons, and the final step has Previous and Finish buttons. The user can navigate through the steps using either the side navigation or the buttons on each of the steps. You can customize the Wizard control in so many ways that it tends to remind me of the other rich Web server controls from ASP.NET, such as the Calendar control. Because so much is possible, only a few of the basics are covered — the ones you are most likely to employ in some of the Wizard controls you build.

Customizing the Side Navigation

The steps in the Figure 6-11 example are defined as Step 1, Step 2, and Step 3. The links are created based on the `Title` property's value that you give to each of the `<asp:WizardStep>` elements in the Wizard control:

```
<asp:WizardStep Runat="server" Title="Step 1">
  This is the first step.</asp:WizardStep>
```

By default, each wizard step created in Design view is titled `Step X` (with `X` being the number in the sequence). You can easily change the value of the `Title` attributes of each of the wizard steps to define the steps as you see fit. Figure 6-12 shows the side navigation of the Wizard control with renamed titles.

Figure 6-12

Examining the AllowReturn Attribute

Another interesting point of customization for the side navigation piece of the Wizard control is the `AllowReturn` attribute. By setting this attribute on one of the wizard steps to `False`, you can remove the capability for end users to go back to this step after they have viewed it. The end user cannot navigate backward to any viewed steps that contain the attribute, but he would be able to return to any steps that do not contain the attribute or that have it set to `True`:

```
<asp:WizardStep Runat="server" Title="Step 1" AllowReturn="False">
  This is the first step.</asp:WizardStep>
```

Working with the StepType Attribute

Another interesting attribute in the `<asp:WizardStep>` element is `StepType`. The `StepType` attribute defines the structure of the buttons used on the steps. By default, the Wizard control places only a Next button on the first step. It understands that you don't need the Previous button there. It also knows to use a Next and Previous button on the middle step, and it uses Previous and Finish buttons on the last step. It draws the buttons in this fashion because, by default, the `StepType` attribute is set to `Auto`, meaning that the Wizard control determines the placement of buttons. You can, however, take control of the StepType attribute in the <asp:WizardStep> element to make your own determination about which buttons are used for which steps.

In addition to Auto, StepType value options include Start, Step, Finish, and Complete. Start means that the step defined has only a Next button. It simply allows the user to proceed to the next step in the series. A value of Step means that the wizard step has Next and Previous buttons. A value of Finish means that the step includes a Previous and a Finish button. Complete enables you to give some final message to the end user who is working through the steps of your Wizard control. In the Wizard control shown in Listing 6-11, for example, when the end user gets to the last step and clicks the Finish button, nothing happens and the user just stays on the last page. You can add a final step to give an ending message, as shown in Listing 6-12.

Listing 6-12: Having a complete step in the wizard step collection

```
<WizardSteps>
   <asp:WizardStep Runat="server" Title="Step 1">
    This is the first step.</asp:WizardStep>
   <asp:WizardStep Runat="server" Title="Step 2">
    This is the second step.</asp:WizardStep>
   <asp:WizardStep Runat="server" Title="Step 3">
    This is the third and final step.</asp:WizardStep>
   <asp:WizardStep Runat="server" Title="Final Step" StepType="Complete">
    Thanks for working through the steps.</asp:WizardStep>
</WizardSteps>
```

When you run this Wizard control in a page, you still see only the first three steps in the side navigation. Because the last step has a StepType set to Complete, it does not appear in the side navigation list. When the end user clicks the Finish button in Step 3, the last step — Final Step — is shown and no buttons are shown with it.

Adding a Header to the Wizard Control

The Wizard control enables you to place a header at the top of the control by means of the HeaderText attribute in the main <asp:Wizard> element. Listing 6-13 provides an example.

Listing 6-13: Working with the HeaderText attribute

```
<asp:Wizard ID="Wizard1" Runat="server" SideBarEnabled="true" ActiveStepIndex="0"
 HeaderText=" Step by Step with the Wizard control "
 HeaderStyle-BackColor="DarkGray" HeaderStyle-Font-Bold="true"
 HeaderStyle-Font-Size="20">

   . . .

</asp:Wizard>
```

This code creates a header that appears on each of the steps in the wizard. The result of this snippet is shown in Figure 6-13.

Figure 6-13

Working with the Wizard's Navigation System

As stated earlier, the Wizard control allows for a very high degree of customization—especially in the area of style. You can customize every single aspect of the process, as well as how every element appears to the end user.

Pay particular attention to the options that are available for customization of the navigation buttons. By default, the wizard steps use Next, Previous, and Finish buttons throughout the entire series of steps. From the main `<asp:Wizard>` element, you can change everything about these buttons and how they work.

First, if you look through the long list of attributes available for this element, notice that one available button isn't shown by default: the Cancel button. Set the value of the `DisplayCancelButton` attribute to `True`, and a Cancel button appears within the navigation created for each and every step, including the final step in the series. Figure 6-14 shows a Cancel button in a step.

Figure 6-14

After you decide which buttons to use within the Wizard navigation, you can choose their style. By default, regular buttons appear; you can change the button style with the `CancelButtonType`, `FinishStepButtonType`, `FinishStepPreviousButtonType`, `NextStepButtonType`,

PreviousStepButtonType, and StartStepNextButtonType attributes. If you use any of these button types and want all the buttons consistently styled, you must change each attribute to the same value. The possible values of these button-specific elements include Button, Image, and Link. Button is the default and means that the navigation system uses buttons. A value of Image enables you to use image buttons, and Link turns a selected item in the navigation system into a hyperlink.

In addition to these button-specific attributes of the <asp:Wizard> element, you can also specify a URL to which the user is directed when the he clicks either the Cancel or Finish buttons. To redirect the user with one of these buttons, you use the CancelDestinationPageUrl or the FinishDestinationPageUrl attributes and set the appropriate URL as the destination.

Finally, you are not required to use the default text included with the buttons in the navigation system. You can change the text of each of the buttons with the use of the CancelButtonText, FinishStepButtonText, FinishStepPreviousButtonText, NextStepButtonText, PreviousStepButtonText, and the StartStepNextButtonText attributes.

Utilizing Wizard Control Events

One of the most convenient capabilities of the Wizard control is that it enables you to divide large forms into logical pieces. The end user can then work step-by-step through each section of the form. The developer, dealing with the inputted values of the form, has a few options because of the various events that are available in the Wizard control.

The Wizard control exposes events for each of the possible steps that an end user might take when working with the control. The following table describes each of the available events.

Event	Description
ActiveStepChanged	Triggers when the end user moves from one step to the next It doesn't matter if the step is the middle or final step in the series. This event simply covers each step change generically.
CancelButtonClick	Triggers when the end user clicks the Cancel button in the navigation system.
FinishButtonClick	Triggers when the end user clicks the Finish button in the navigation system.
NextButtonClick	Triggers when the end user clicks the Next button in the navigation system.
PreviousButtonClick	Triggers when the end user clicks the Previous button in the navigation system.
SideBarButtonClick	Triggers when the end user clicks one of the links contained within the sidebar navigation of the Wizard control.

By working with these events, you can create a multi-step form that saves all the end user's input information when he changes from one step to the next. You can also use the FinishButtonClick event to save everything that was stored in each of the steps at the end of the process. The Wizard control remembers all the end user's input in each of the steps by means of the view state in the page, which enables you to work with all these values in the last step. It also gives the end user the capability to go back to previous steps and change values before those values are saved to a data store.

The event appears in your code behind or inline code as shown in Listing 6-14.

Listing 6-14: The FinishButtonClick event

VB

```
<script runat="server">
    Sub Wizard1_FinishButtonClick(ByVal sender As Object, _
        ByVal e As System.Web.UI.WebControls.WizardNavigationEventArgs)

    End Sub
</script>
```

C#

```
<script runat="server">
    void Wizard1_FinishButtonClick(object sender, WizardNavigationEventArgs e)
    {

    }
</script>
```

The OnFinishButtonClick attribute should be added to the main <asp:Wizard> element to point at the new Wizard1_FinishButtonClick event. Listing 6-15 shows how to do this.

Listing 6-15: The <asp:Wizard> Element Changes

```
<asp:Wizard ID="Wizard1" Runat="server" SideBarEnabled="true" ActiveStepIndex="0"
  OnFinishButtonClick="Wizard1_FinishButtonClick">
```

The Wizard control is one of the great new controls that enables you to break up longer workflows into more manageable pieces for your end users. By separating longer Web forms into various wizard steps, you can effectively make your forms easy to understand and less daunting to the end user.

Using the Wizard Control to Show Form Elements

So far, you've learned how to work with each of the Wizard control steps, including how to add steps to the process and how to work with the styling of the control. Now take a look at how you put form elements into the Wizard control to collect information from the end user in a stepped process. This is just as simple as the first examples of the Wizard control that used only text in each of the steps.

One nice thing about putting form elements in the Wizard step process is that the Wizard control remembers each input into the form elements from step to step, enabling you to save the results of the entire form at the last step. It also means that when the end user presses the Previous button, the data that he entered into the form previously is still there and can be changed.

Work through a stepped process that enters form information by building a registration process. The last step of the process saves the results to a database of your choice, although in this example, you just push the results to a Label control on the page. Listing 6-16 shows the first part of the process.

Listing 6-16: Building the form in the Wizard control

```
<asp:Wizard ID="Wizard1" runat="Server">
    <WizardSteps>
        <asp:WizardStep ID="WizardStep1" runat="server"
         Title="Provide Personal Info">
            First name:<br />
            <asp:TextBox ID="fnameTextBox" runat="server"></asp:TextBox><br />
            Last name:<br />
            <asp:TextBox ID="lnameTextBox" runat="server"></asp:TextBox><br />
            Email:<br />
            <asp:TextBox ID="emailTextBox" runat="server"></asp:TextBox><br />
        </asp:WizardStep>
        <asp:WizardStep ID="WizardStep2" runat="server"
         Title="Membership Information">
            Are you already a member of our group?<br />
            <asp:RadioButton ID="RadioButton1" runat="server" Text="Yes"
             GroupName="Member" />
            <asp:RadioButton ID="RadioButton2" runat="server" Text="No"
             GroupName="Member" />
        </asp:WizardStep>
        <asp:WizardStep ID="WizardStep3" runat="server" Title="Provided Information"
         StepType="Complete" OnActivate="WizardStep3_Activate">
            <asp:Label ID="Label1" runat="server" />
        </asp:WizardStep>
    </WizardSteps>
</asp:Wizard>
```

This Wizard control has three steps. The first step asks for the user's personal information, and the second asks for the user's membership information. The third step contains a Label control that pushes out all the information that was input. This is done through the `Activate` event that is specific for the `WizardStep` object on the third WizardStep control. The code for the `WizardStep3_Activate` event is shown in Listing 6-17.

Listing 6-17: Adding an Activate event to a WizardStep object

VB

```
Protected Sub WizardStep3_Activate(ByVal sender As Object, _
   ByVal e As System.EventArgs)

    ' You could save the inputted data to the database here instead
    Label1.Text = "First name: " & fnameTextBox.Text.ToString() & "<br>" & _
        "Last name: " & lnameTextBox.Text.ToString() & "<br>" & _
        "Email: " & emailTextBox.Text.ToString()
End Sub
```

C#

```
protected void WizardStep3_Activate(object sender, EventArgs e)
{
    Label1.Text = "First name: " + fnameTextBox.Text.ToString() + "<br>" +
        "Last name: " + lnameTextBox.Text.ToString() + "<br>" +
        "Email: " + emailTextBox.Text.ToString();
}
```

When the end user comes to the third step in the display, the `WizardStep3_Activate` method from Listing 6-17 is invoked. Using the `OnActivate` attribute in the third WizardStep control, the content provided by the end user in earlier steps is used to populate a Label control. The three steps are shown in Figure 6-15.

This example is simple and straightforward, but you can increase the complexity a little bit. Imagine you want to add another WizardStep control to the process, and you want to display it only if a user specifies that he is a member in `WizardStep2`. If he answers from the radio button selection that he is not a member, you have him skip the new step and go straight to the final step where the results are displayed in the Label control. First, add an additional `WizardStep` to the Wizard control, as shown in Listing 6-18.

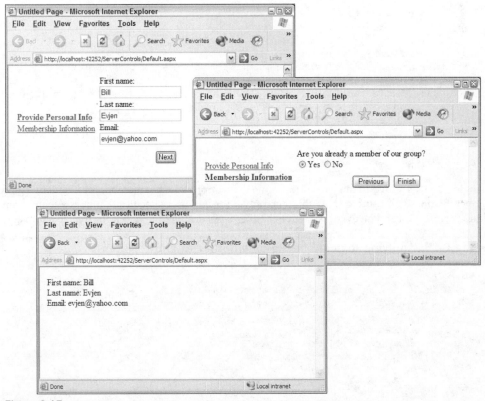

Figure 6-15

Listing 6-18: Adding an additional WizardStep

```
<asp:Wizard ID="Wizard1" runat="Server">
   <WizardSteps>
      <asp:WizardStep ID="WizardStep1" runat="server"
       Title="Provide Personal Info">
         First name:<br />
         <asp:TextBox ID="fnameTextBox" runat="server"></asp:TextBox><br />
         Last name:<br />
         <asp:TextBox ID="lnameTextBox" runat="server"></asp:TextBox><br />
         Email:<br />
         <asp:TextBox ID="emailTextBox" runat="server"></asp:TextBox><br />
      </asp:WizardStep>
      <asp:WizardStep ID="WizardStep2" runat="server"
       Title="Membership Information">
         Are you already a member of our group?<br />
         <asp:RadioButton ID="RadioButton1" runat="server" Text="Yes"
          GroupName="Member" />
         <asp:RadioButton ID="RadioButton2" runat="server" Text="No"
          GroupName="Member" />
      </asp:WizardStep>
      <asp:WizardStep ID="MemberStep" runat="server"
       Title="Provide Membership Number">
         Membership Number:<br />
         <asp:TextBox ID="mNumberTextBox" runat="server"></asp:TextBox>
      </asp:WizardStep>
      <asp:WizardStep ID="WizardStep3" runat="server" Title="Provided Information"
       StepType="Complete" OnActivate="WizardStep3_Activate">
         <asp:Label ID="Label1" runat="server" />
      </asp:WizardStep>
   </WizardSteps>
</asp:Wizard>
```

A single step was added to the workflow — one that simply asks the member for his membership number. Because you want to show this step only if the end user specifies that he is a member in WizardStep2, you add an event (shown in Listing 6-19) designed to check for that specification.

Listing 6-19: Applying logical checks on whether to show a step

VB

```
Sub Wizard1_NextButtonClick(ByVal sender As Object, _
   ByVal e As System.Web.UI.WebControls.WizardNavigationEventArgs)

   If e.NextStepIndex = 2 Then
      If RadioButton1.Checked = True Then
         Wizard1.ActiveStepIndex = 2
      Else
         Wizard1.ActiveStepIndex = 3
      End If
   End If
End Sub
```

C#

```
void Wizard1_NextButtonClick(object sender, WizardNavigationEventArgs e)
{
   if (e.NextStepIndex == 2) {
      if (RadioButton1.Checked == true) {
         Wizard1.ActiveStepIndex = 2; }
      else {
         Wizard1.ActiveStepIndex = 3; }
      }
}
```

To check whether you should show a specific step in the process, use the `NextButtonClick` event from the Wizard control. The event uses the `WizardNavigationEventArgs` class instead of the typical `EventArgs` class that gives you access to the `NextStepIndex` number, as well as to the `CurrentStepIndex` number.

In the example from Listing 6-19, you check whether the next step to be presented in the process is 2. Remember that this is index 2 from a zero-based index (0, 1, 2, and so on). If it is Step 2 in the index, you check which radio button is selected from the previous WizardStep. If the `RadioButton1` control is checked (meaning that the user is a member), the next step in the process is assigned as index 2. If the `RadioButton2` control is selected, the user is not a member, and the index is then assigned as 3 (the final step), thereby bypassing the membership step in the process.

ImageMap Server Control

The ImageMap server control is new to ASP.NET 2.0. It enables you to turn an image into a navigation menu. In the past, many developers would break an image into multiple pieces and put it together again in a table, reassembling the pieces into one image. When the end user clicked a particular piece of the overall image, the application picked out which piece of the image was chosen and based actions upon that particular selection.

With the new ImageMap control, you can take a single image and specify particular hotspots on the image using coordinates. An example is shown in Listing 6-20.

Listing 6-20: Specifying sections of an image that are clickable

VB

```
<%@ Page Language="VB"%>

<script runat="server">
    Protected Sub Imagemap1_Click(ByVal sender As Object, _
        ByVal e As System.Web.UI.WebControls.ImageMapEventArgs)

        Response.Write("You selected: " & e.PostBackValue)
    End Sub
</script>

<html xmlns="http://www.w3.org/1999/xhtml" >
```

(continued)

Listing 6-20: *(continued)*

```
<head runat="server">
    <title>ImageMap Control</title>
</head>
<body>
    <form id="form1" runat="server">
        <asp:ImageMap ID="Imagemap1" Runat="server" ImageUrl="kids.jpg"
        Width="300" OnClick="Imagemap1_Click" HotSpotMode="PostBack">
            <asp:RectangleHotSpot Top="0" Bottom="225" Left="0" Right="150"
            AlternateText="Henri" PostBackValue="Henri">
            </asp:RectangleHotSpot>
            <asp:RectangleHotSpot Top="0" Bottom="225" Left="151" Right="300"
            AlternateText="Sofia" PostBackValue="Sofia">
            </asp:RectangleHotSpot>
        </asp:ImageMap>
    </form>
</body>
</html>
```

C#

```
<%@ page language="C#"%>

<script runat="server">
    protected void Imagemap1_Click(object sender,
        System.Web.UI.WebControls.ImageMapEventArgs e) {

            Response.Write("You selected: " + e.PostBackValue);
    }
</script>
```

This page brings up an image of my children. If you click the left side of the image, you select Henri, and if you click the right side of the image, you select Sofia. You know which child you selected through a `Response.Write` statement, as shown in Figure 6-16.

The ImageMap control enables you to specify hotspots in a couple of different ways. From the example in Listing 6-16, you can see that hotspots are placed in a rectangular fashion using the `<asp:RectangleHotSpot>` element. The control takes the `Top`, `Bottom`, `Left`, and `Right` coordinates of the rectangle that is to be the hotspot. Besides the `<asp:RectangleHotSpot>` control, you can also use the `<asp:CircleHotSpot>` and the `<asp:PolygonHotSpot>` controls. Each control takes coordinates appropriate to its shape.

After you define the hotspots on the image, you can respond to the end-user click of the hotspot in several ways. You first specify how to deal with the hotspot clicks in the root `<asp:ImageMap>` element with the use the `HotSpotMode` attribute.

The `HotSpotMode` attribute can take the values `PostBack`, `Navigate`, or `InActive`. In the previous example, the `HotSpotMode` value is set to `PostBack`—meaning that after the end user clicks the hotspot, you want to postback to the server and deal with the click at that point.

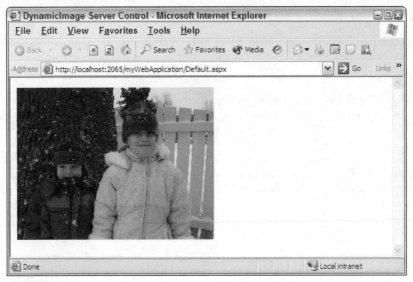

Figure 6-16

Because the `HotSpotMode` is set to `PostBack` and you have created several hotspots, you must determine which hotspot is selected. You make this determination by giving each hotspot (`<asp:RectangleHotSpot>`) a postback value with the `PostBackValue` attribute. The example uses `Henri` as the value of the first hotspot, and `Sofia` as the value for the second.

The `PostBackValue` attribute is also the helper text that appears in the browser (in the yellow box) directly below the mouse cursor when the end user hovers the mouse over the hotspot.

After the user clicks one of the hotspots, the event procedure displays the value that was selected in a `Response.Write` statement.

Instead of posting back to the server, you can also navigate to an entirely different URL when a particular hotspot is selected. To accomplish this, change the `HotSpotMode` attribute in the main `<asp:ImageMap>` element to the value `Navigate`. Then, within the `<asp:RectangleHotSpot>` elements, simply use the `NavigateUrl` attribute and assign the location to which the end user should be directed if that particular hotspot is clicked:

```
<asp:ImageMap ID="Imagemap1" Runat="server" ImageUrl="kids.jpg"
 HotSpotMode="Navigate">
   <asp:RectangleHotSpot Top="0" Bottom="225" Left="0" Right="150"
    AlternateText="Henri" NavigateUrl="HenriPage.aspx">
   </asp:RectangleHotSpot>
   <asp:RectangleHotSpot Top="0" Bottom="225" Left="151" Right="300"
    AlternateText="Sofia" NavigateUrl="SofiaPage.aspx">
   </asp:RectangleHotSpot>
</asp:ImageMap>
```

Summary

New server controls are fun. They're also useful and can save you a lot of time. This chapter introduced you to some of these new controls and to the different ways you might incorporate them into your next projects.

The BulletedList control enables you to create all sorts of bulleted lists either directly from inline items or from items contained in a data store of some kind. The HiddenField control allows for server-side access to a very important HTML element that was formerly far more difficult to work with. Other controls discussed include the FileUpload control, which enables you to upload files easily to the server; the MultiView and View controls for working through processes; the Wizard control for advanced process work; and the ImageMap control for creating hotspots on an image. All these controls are wonderful options to use on any of your ASP.NET pages and make it much easier to develop the functionality that your pages require.

Validation Server Controls

When you look at the Toolbox window in Visual Studio 2005 — especially if you've read Chapters 5 and 6, which cover the various server controls at your disposal — you may be struck by the number of server controls that come with ASP.NET 2.0. This chapter takes a look at a specific type of server control you find in the Toolbox window: the *validation server control*.

Validation server controls are a series of controls that enable you to work with the information your end users input into the form elements of the applications you build. These controls work to ensure the validity of the data being placed in the form.

Before learning how to use these controls, however, take a look at the process of validation to learn what it's all about.

Understanding Validation

People have been constructing Web applications for a number of years. Usually the motivation is to provide or gather information. In this chapter, you focus on the information-gathering aspect of Web applications. If you collect data with your applications, collecting *valid* data should be important to you. If the information isn't valid, there really isn't much point in collecting it.

Validation comes in degrees. Validation is a set of rules that you apply to the data you collect. These rules can be many or few and enforced either strictly or in a lax manner: It really depends on you. No perfect validation process exists because some users may find a way cheat to some degree, no matter what rules you establish. The trick is to find the right balance of the fewest rules and the proper strictness, without compromising the usability of the application.

The data you collect for validation comes from the Web forms you provide in your applications. Web forms are made up of different types of HTML elements that are constructed using raw HTML form elements, ASP.NET HTML server controls, or ASP.NET Web Form server controls.

In the end, your forms are made up of many different types of HTML elements, such as text boxes, radio buttons, check boxes, drop-down lists, and more.

As you work through this chapter, you see the different types of validation rules that you can apply to your form elements. Remember that you have no way to validate the *truthfulness* of the information you collect; instead, you apply rules that respond to such questions as

❑   Is something entered in the text box?

❑   Is the data entered in the text box in the form of an e-mail address?

Notice from these questions that you can apply more than a single validation rule to an HTML form element (you'll see examples of this later in this chapter). In fact, you can apply as many rules to a single element as you want. Applying more rules to elements increases the strictness of the validation applied to the data.

Just remember, data collection on the Internet is one of the Internet's most important features, so you must make sure that the data you collect has value and meaning. You ensure this by eliminating any chance that the information collected does not abide by the rules you outline.

Client-Side versus Server-Side Validation

If you are new to Web application development, you might not be aware of the difference between client-side and server-side validation. Suppose that the end user clicks the Submit button on a form after filling out some information. What happens in ASP.NET is that this form is packaged in a *request* and sent to the server where the application resides. At this point in the request/response cycle, you can run validation checks on the information submitted. If you do this, it is called *server-side validation* because it occurs on the server.

On the other hand, it is also possible to supply a script (usually in the form of JavaScript) in the page that is posted to the end user's browser to perform validations on the data entered in the form *before* the form is posted back to the originating server. If this is the case, *client-side validation* has occurred.

Both types of validation have their pros and cons. Active Server Pages 2.0/3.0 developers are quite aware of these pros and cons because they have probably performed all the validation chores themselves. Many developers spent a considerable amount of their classic ASP programming days coding various validation techniques for performance and security.

Client-side validation is quick and responsive for the end user. It is something end users expect of the forms that they work with. If something is wrong with the form, using client-side validation ensures that the end user knows this as soon as possible. Client-side validation also pushes the processing power required of validation to the client meaning that you don't need to spin CPU cycles on the server to process the same information because the client can do the work for you.

With this said, client-side validation is the more insecure form of validation. When a page is generated in an end user's browser, this end user can look at the code of the page quite easily (simply by right-clicking his mouse in the browser and selecting View Code). When he does this, in addition to seeing the HTML code for the page, he can also see all the JavaScript that is associated with the page. If you are validating your form client-side, it doesn't take much for the crafty hacker to repost a form (containing the values he wants in it) to your server as valid. There are also the cases in which clients have simply disabled the client-scripting capabilities in their browsers — thereby making your validations useless. Therefore, client-side validation should be looked on as a convenience and a courtesy to the end user and never as a security mechanism.

The more secure form of validation is server-side validation. Server-side validation means that the validation checks are performed on the server instead of on the client. It is more secure because these checks cannot be easily bypassed. Instead, the form data values are checked using server code (C# or VB) on the server. If the form isn't valid, the page is posted back to the client as invalid. Although it is more secure, server-side validation can be slow. It is sluggish simply because the page has to be posted to a remote location and checked. Your end user might not be the happiest surfer in the world if, after waiting 20 seconds for a form to post, he is told his e-mail address isn't in the correct format.

So what is the correct path? Well, actually, both! The best approach is always to perform client-side validation first and then, after the form passes and is posted to the server, to perform the validation checks again using server-side validation This approach provides the best of both worlds. It is secure because hackers can't simply bypass the validation. They may bypass the client-side validation, but they quickly find that their form data is checked once again on the server after it is posted. This validation technique is also highly effective — giving you both the quickness and snappiness of client-side validation.

ASP.NET Validation Server Controls

In the classic ASP days, developers could spend a great deal of their time dealing with different form validation schemes. For this reason, with the initial release of ASP.NET, the ASP.NET team introduced a series of validation server controls meant to make it a snap to implement sound validation for forms.

ASP.NET not only introduces form validations as server controls, but it also makes these controls rather smart. As stated earlier, one of the tasks of classic ASP developers was to determine where to perform form validation — either on the client or on the server. The ASP.NET validation server controls eliminate this dilemma because ASP.NET performs browser detection when generating the ASP.NET page and makes decisions based on the information it gleans.

This means that if the browser can support the JavaScript that ASP.NET can send its way, the validation occurs on the client-side. If the client cannot support the JavaScript meant for client-side validation, this JavaScript is omitted and the validation occurs on the server.

The best part about this scenario is that even if client-side validation is initiated on a page, ASP.NET still performs the server-side validation when it receives the submitted page, thereby ensuring security won't be compromised. This decisive nature of the validation server controls means that you can build your ASP.NET Web pages to be the best they can possibly be — rather than dumbing-down your Web applications for the lowest common denominator.

Presently, six validation controls are available to you in ASP.NET 2.0. No new validation server controls have been added to ASP.NET since the initial release of the technology, but the ASP.NET 2.0 validation server controls do have some new features, such as validation groups and new JavaScript capabilities. Both these features are discussed in this chapter. The available validation server controls include

- ❏ RequiredFieldValidator
- ❏ CompareValidator
- ❏ RangeValidator
- ❏ RegularExpressionValidator
- ❏ CustomValidator
- ❏ ValidationSummary

Working with ASP.NET validation server controls is no different from working with any other ASP.NET server controls. Each of these controls allows you to drag and drop it onto a design surface or to work with it directly from the code of your ASP.NET page. These controls can also be modified so that they appear exactly as you wish — ensuring the visual uniqueness that your applications might require. You see some aspects of this throughout this chapter.

> If the ASP.NET Validation controls don't meet your needs, you can certainly write your own custom validation controls. However, there are third-party controls available such as Peter Blum's Validation and More (VAM) from `http://www.peterblum.com/VAM`, which includes over 40 ASP.NET validation controls.

The following table describes the functionality of each of the available validation server controls.

Validation Server Control	Description
RequiredFieldValidator	Ensures that the user does not skip a form entry field
CompareValidator	Allows for comparisons between the user's input and another item using a comparison operator (equals, greater than, less than, and so on)
RangeValidator	Checks the user's input based upon a lower- and upper-level range of numbers or characters
RegularExpressionValidator	Checks that the user's entry matches a pattern defined by a regular expression. This is a good control to use to check e-mail addresses and phone numbers.
CustomValidator	Checks the user's entry using custom-coded validation logic
ValidationSummary	Displays all the error messages from the validators in one specific spot on the page

Validation Causes

Validation doesn't just happen; it occurs in response to an event. In most cases, it is a button click event. The Button, LinkButton, and ImageButton server controls all have the capability to cause a page's form validation to initiate. This is the default behavior. Dragging and dropping a Button server control onto your form will give you the following initial result:

```
<asp:Button ID="Button1" Runat="server" Text="Button" />
```

If you look through the properties of the Button control, you can notice that the `CausesValidation` property is set to `True`. As stated, this is the default behavior — all buttons on the page, no matter how many there are, cause the form validation to fire.

If you have multiple buttons on an ASP.NET page, and you don't want each and every button to initiate the form validation, you can set the `CausesValidation` property to `False` for all the buttons you want to ignore the validation process (for example, a form's Cancel button):

```
<asp:Button ID="Button1" Runat="server" Text="Cancel" CausesValidation="False" />
```

The RequiredFieldValidator Server Control

The RequiredFieldValidator control simply checks to see if *something* was entered into the HTML form element. It is a simple validation control, but it is one of the most frequently used. You must have a RequiredFieldValidator control for each form element on which you wish to enforce a *value-required* rule.

Listing 7-1 shows a simple use of the RequiredFieldValidator control.

Listing 7-1: A simple use of the RequiredFieldValidator server control

VB

```
<%@ Page Language="VB" %>

<script runat="server">
    Protected Sub Button1_Click(ByVal sender As Object, ByVal e As System.EventArgs)
        If Page.IsValid Then
        Label1.Text="Page is valid!"
        End If
    End Sub
</script>

<html xmlns="http://www.w3.org/1999/xhtml" >
<head runat="server" id=Head1">>
    <title>RequiredFieldValidator</title>
</head>
<body>
    <form id="form1" runat="server">
    <div>
        <asp:TextBox ID="TextBox1" Runat="server"></asp:TextBox>
        <asp:RequiredFieldValidator ID="RequiredFieldValidator1"
         Runat="server" ErrorMessage="Required!" ControlToValidate="TextBox1">
        </asp:RequiredFieldValidator>
        <br />
        <asp:Button ID="Button1" Runat="server" Text="Submit"
         OnClick="Button1_Click" />
        <br />
        <br />
        <asp:Label ID="Label1" Runat="server"></asp:Label>
    </div>
    </form>
</body>
</html>
```

(continued)

Listing 7-1: *(continued)*

C#

```
<%@ Page Language="C#" %>

<script runat="server">
    protected void Button1_Click(Object sender, EventArgs e) {
        if (Page.IsValid) { Label1.Text = "Page is valid!";
    }
</script>
```

Build and run this page. You are presented with a simple text box and button on the page. Don't enter any value inside the text box, and click the Submit button. The result is shown in Figure 7-1.

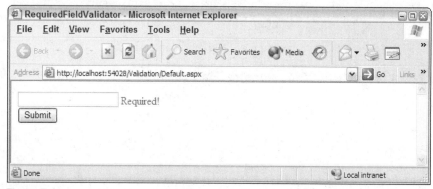

Figure 7-1

Now look at the code from this example. First, nothing is different about the TextBox, Button, or Label controls. They are constructed just as they would be if you were not using any type of form validation. This page does contain a simple RequiredFieldValidator control however. Several properties of this control are especially notable because you will use them in most of the validation server controls you create.

The first property to look at is the `ErrorMessage` property. This property is the value that is shown to the end user via the Web page if the validation fails. In this case, it is a simple `Required!` string. The second property to look at is the `ControlToValidate` property. This property is used to make an association between this validation server control and the ASP.NET form element that requires the validation. In this case, the value specifies the only element in the form — the text box.

As you can see from this example, the error message ID is constructed from an attribute within the `<asp:RequiredFieldValidator>` control. You can also accomplish this same task by using the `Text` attribute, as shown in Listing 7-2.

Listing 7-2: Using the Text attribute

```
<asp:RequiredFieldValidator ID="RequiredFieldValidator1"
  Runat="server" Text="Required!" ControlToValidate="TextBox1">
</asp:RequiredFieldValidator>
```

You can also express this error message between the `<asp:RequiredFieldValidator>` opening and closing nodes as shown in Listing 7-3.

Listing 7-3: Placing values between nodes

```
<asp:RequiredFieldValidator ID="RequiredFieldValidator1"
Runat="server" ControlToValidate="TextBox1">
Required!
</asp:RequiredFieldValidator>
```

Looking at the Results Generated

Again, the RequiredFieldValidator control uses client-side validation if the browser allows for such an action. You can see the client-side validation for yourself (if your browser allows for this) by right-clicking on the page and selecting View Source from the menu. In the page code, you see the JavaScript shown in Listing 7-4. Note that your JavaScript may be slightly different than what is presented in this listing because ASP.NET sends the JavaScript to the appropriate browsers and your browser may be of a different type.

Listing 7-4: The generated JavaScript

```
... page markup removed for clarity here ...

<script type="text/javascript">
<!--
function WebForm_OnSubmit() {
if (ValidatorOnSubmit() == false) return false;
return true;
}
// -->
</script>

... page markup removed for clarity here ...

<script type="text/javascript">
<!--
var Page_Validators =  new
Array(document.getElementById("RequiredFieldValidator1"));// -->
</script>

<script type="text/javascript">
<!--
var RequiredFieldValidator1 = document.all ?
  document.all["RequiredFieldValidator1"] :
  document.getElementById("RequiredFieldValidator1");
RequiredFieldValidator1.controltovalidate = "TextBox1";
RequiredFieldValidator1.errormessage = "Required!";
RequiredFieldValidator1.evaluationfunction =
  "RequiredFieldValidatorEvaluateIsValid";
RequiredFieldValidator1.initialvalue = "";
// -->
</script>
```

(continued)

Listing 7-4: *(continued)*

```
... page markup removed for clarity here ...

<script type="text/javascript">
<!--
var Page_ValidationActive = false;
if (typeof(ValidatorOnLoad) == "function") {
    ValidatorOnLoad();
}

function ValidatorOnSubmit() {
    if (Page_ValidationActive) {
        return ValidatorCommonOnSubmit();
    }
    else {
        return true;
    }
}
// -->
</script>
```

In the page code, you may also notice some changes to the form elements (the former server controls) that deal with the submission of the form and the associated validation requirements.

Using the InitialValue Property

Another important property when working with the RequireFieldValidator control is the `InitialValue` property. Sometimes you have form elements that are populated with some default properties (for example, from a data store), and these form elements might present the end user with values that require changes before the form can be submitted to the server.

When using the `InitialValue` property, you specify to the RequiredFieldValidator control the initial text of the element. The end user is then required to change that text value before he can submit the form. Listing 7-5 shows an example of using this property.

Listing 7-5: Working with the InitialValue property

```
<asp:TextBox ID="TextBox1" Runat="server">My Initial Value</asp:TextBox>
  
<asp:RequiredFieldValidator ID="RequiredFieldValidator1"
 Runat="server" ErrorMessage="Please change the value of the textbox!"
 ControlToValidate="TextBox1" InitialValue="My Initial Value">
</asp:RequiredFieldValidator>
```

In this case, you can see that the `InitialValue` property contains a value of `My Initial Value`. When the page is built and run, the text box contains this value as well. The RequiredFieldValidator control requires a change in this value for the page to be considered valid.

Disallowing Blank Entries and Requiring Changes at the Same Time

In the preceding example of the use of the InitialValue property, an interesting problem arises. First, if you run the associated example, one thing the end user can do to get past the form validation is to submit the page with no value entered in this particular text box. A blank text box does not fire a validation error because the RequiredFieldValidator control is now reconstructed to force the end user only to *change* the default value of the text box (which he did when he removed the old value). When you reconstruct the RequiredFieldValidator control in this manner, nothing in the validation rule requires that *something* be entered in the text box — just that the initial value be changed. It is possible for the user to completely bypass the form validation process by just removing anything entered in this text box.

There is a way around this, however, and it goes back to what we were saying earlier about how a form is made up of multiple validation rules — some of which are assigned to the same form element. To both require a change to the initial value of the text box and to disallow a blank entry (thereby making the element a required element), you must put an additional RequiredFieldValidator control on the page. This second RequiredFieldValidator control is associated with the same text box as the first RequiredFieldValidator control. This is illustrated in the example shown in Listing 7-6.

Listing 7-6: Using two RequiredFieldValidator controls for one form element

```
<asp:TextBox ID="TextBox1" Runat="server">My Initial Value</asp:TextBox> 

<asp:RequiredFieldValidator ID="RequiredFieldValidator1" Runat="server"
 ErrorMessage="Please change value" ControlToValidate="TextBox1"
 InitialValue="My Initial Value"></asp:RequiredFieldValidator>

<asp:RequiredFieldValidator ID="RequiredFieldValidator2" Runat="server"
 ErrorMessage="Do not leave empty" ControlToValidate="TextBox1">
</asp:RequiredFieldValidator>
```

In this example, you can see that the text box does indeed have two RequiredFieldValidator controls associated with it. The first, RequiredFieldValidator1, requires a change to the default value of the text box through the use of the InitialValue property. The second RequiredFieldValidator control, RequiredFieldValidator2, simply makes the TextBox1 control a form element that requires a value. You get the behavior you want by applying two validation rules to a single form element.

Validating Drop-Down Lists with the RequiredFieldValidator Control

So far, you have seen a lot of examples of using the RequiredFieldValidator control with a series of text boxes, but you can just as easily use this validation control with other form elements as well.

For example, you can use the RequiredFieldValidator control with an <asp:DropDownList> server control. To see this, suppose that you have a drop-down list that requires the end user to select her profession from a list of items. The first line of the drop-down list includes instructions to the end user about what to select, and you want to make this a required form element as well. The code to do this is shown in Listing 7-7.

Listing 7-7: Drop-down list validations

```
<asp:DropDownList id="DropDownList1" runat="server">
    <asp:ListItem Selected="True">Select a profession</asp:ListItem>
    <asp:ListItem>Programmer</asp:ListItem>
    <asp:ListItem>Lawyer</asp:ListItem>
    <asp:ListItem>Doctor</asp:ListItem>
    <asp:ListItem>Artist</asp:ListItem>
</asp:DropDownList>
     
<asp:RequiredFieldValidator id="RequiredFieldValidator1"
    runat="server" ErrorMessage="Please make a selection"
    ControlToValidate="DropDownList1"
    InitialValue="Select a profession">
</asp:RequiredFieldValidator>
```

Just as when you work with the text box, the RequiredFieldValidator control in this example associates itself with the DropDownList control through the use of the `ControlToValidate` property. The drop-down list to which the validation control is bound has an initial value — `Select a profession`. You obviously don't want your end user to retain that value when she posts the form back to the server. So again, you use to the `InitialValue` property of the RequiredFieldValidator control. The value of this property is assigned to the initial selected value of the drop-down list. This forces the end user to select one of the provided professions in the drop-down list before she is able to post the form.

The CompareValidator Server Control

The CompareValidator control allows you to make comparisons between two form elements as well as to compare values contained within form elements to constants that you specify. For instance, you can specify that a form element's value must be an integer and greater than a specified number. You can also state that values must be strings, dates, or other data types that are at your disposal.

Validating against Other Controls

One of the more common ways of using the CompareValidator control is to make a comparison between two form elements. For example, suppose that you have an application which requires users to have passwords in order to access the site. You create one text box asking for the user's password and a second text box which asks the user to confirm the password. Because the text box is in password mode, the end user cannot see what she is typing — just the number of characters that she has typed. To reduce the chances of the end user mistyping her password and inputting this incorrect password into the system, you ask her to confirm the password. After the form is input into the system, you simply have to make a comparison between the two text boxes to see if they match. If they match, it is likely that the end user typed the password correctly, and you can input the password choice into the system. If the two text boxes do not match, you want the form to be invalid. The following example, in Listing 7-8, demonstrates this situation.

Listing 7-8: Using the CompareValidator to test values against other control values

VB
```
<%@ Page Language="VB" %>
<script runat="server">

    Protected Sub Button1_Click(sender As Object, e As EventArgs)
```

```
                Label1.Text = "Passwords match"
        End Sub

</script>
<html xmlns="http://www.w3.org/1999/xhtml" >
<head runat="server" id="Head1">>
    <title>CompareFieldValidator</title>
</head>
<body>
    <form runat="server" id="Form1">>
        <p>
            Password<br>
            <asp:TextBox ID="TextBox1" Runat="server"
            TextMode="Password"></asp:TextBox>
             
            <asp:CompareValidator ID="CompareValidator1"
            Runat="server" ErrorMessage="Passwords do not match!"
            ControlToValidate="TextBox2"
            ControlToCompare="TextBox1"></asp:CompareValidator>
        </p>
        <p>
            Confirm Password<br>
            <asp:TextBox ID="TextBox2" Runat="server"
            TextMode="Password"></asp:TextBox>
        </p>
        <p>
            <asp:Button ID="Button1" OnClick="Button1_Click"
            Runat="server" Text="Login"></asp:Button>
        </p>
        <p>
            <asp:Label ID="Label1" Runat="server"></asp:Label>
        </p>
    </form>
</body>
</html>
```

C#

```
<%@ Page Language="C#" %>
<script runat="server">

    protected void Button1_Click(Object sender, EventArgs e) {
        Label1.Text = "Passwords match";
    }

</script>
```

Looking at the CompareValidator control on the form, you can see that it is similar to the RequiredFieldValidator control. The CompareValidator control has a property called ControlToValidate that associates itself with one of the form elements on the page. In this case, you need only a single CompareValidator control on the page because a single comparison is made. In this example, you are making a comparison between the value of TextBox2 and that of TextBox1. Therefore, you use the ControlToCompare property. This specifies what value is compared to TextBox2. In this case, the value is TextBox1.

It's as simple as that. If the two text boxes do not match after the page is posted by the end user, the value of the ErrorMessage property from the CompareValidator control is displayed in the browser. An example of this is shown in Figure 7-2.

Figure 7-2

Validating against Constants

Besides being able to validate values against values in other controls, you can also use the CompareValidator control to make comparisons against constants of specific data types. For example, suppose you have a text box on your registration form that asks for the age of the user. In most cases, you want to get back an actual number and not something such as aa or bb as a value. Listing 7-9 shows you how to ensure that you get back an actual number.

Listing 7-9: Using the CompareValidator to validate against constants

```
Age:
<asp:TextBox ID="TextBox1" Runat="server" MaxLength="3">
</asp:TextBox>
 
<asp:CompareValidator ID="CompareValidator1" Runat="server"
    ErrorMessage="You must enter a number"
    ControlToValidate="TextBox1" Type="Integer"
    Operator="DataTypeCheck"></asp:CompareValidator>
```

In this example, the end user is required to enter in a number into the text box. If she attempts to bypass the validation by entering a fake value that contains anything other than a number, the page is identified as invalid, and the CompareValidator control displays the value of the ErrorMessage property.

To specify the data types that you want to use in these comparisons, you simply use the Type property. The Type property can take the following values:

❑   Currency

❑   Date

- ❑   Double

- ❑   Integer

- ❑   String

Not only can you make sure that what is entered is of a specific data type, but you can also make sure that what is entered is valid when compared to specific constants. For instance, you can make sure what is entered in a form element is greater than, less than, equal to, greater than or equal to, or less than or equal to a specified value. An example of this is illustrated in Listing 7-10.

Listing 7-10: Making comparisons with the CompareValidator control

```
Age:
<asp:TextBox ID="TextBox1" Runat="server"></asp:TextBox>
   
<asp:CompareValidator ID="CompareValidator1" Runat="server"
  Operator="GreaterThan" ValueToCompare="18"
  ControlToValidate="TextBox1"
  ErrorMessage="You must be older than 18 to join" Type="Integer">
</asp:CompareValidator>
```

In this case, the CompareValidator control not only associates itself with the TextBox1 control and requires that the value must be an integer, but it also uses the Operator and the ValueToCompare properties to ensure that the number is greater than 18. Therefore, if the end user enters a value of 18 or less, the validation fails, and the page is considered invalid.

The Operator property can take one of the following values:

- ❑   Equal

- ❑   NotEqual

- ❑   GreaterThan

- ❑   GreaterThanEqual

- ❑   LessThan

- ❑   LessThanEqual

- ❑   DataTypeCheck

The ValueToCompare property is where you place the constant value used in the comparison. In the preceding example, it is the number 18.

The RangeValidator Server Control

The RangeValidator control is quite similar to that of the CompareValidator control, but it makes sure that the end user value or selection provided is between a specified range as opposed to being just greater than or less than a specified constant. For an example of this, go back to the text-box element that asks for the age of the end user and performs a validation on the value provided. This is illustrated in Listing 7-11.

Listing 7-11: Using the RangeValidator control to test an integer value

```
Age:
<asp:TextBox ID="TextBox1" Runat="server"></asp:TextBox>
 
<asp:RangeValidator ID="RangeValidator1" Runat="server"
ControlToValidate="TextBox1" Type="Integer"
ErrorMessage="You must be between 30 and 40"
MaximumValue="40" MinimumValue="30"></asp:RangeValidator>
```

In this example, this page consists of a text box asking for the age of the end user. The RangeValidator control makes an analysis of the value provided and makes sure the value is somewhere in the range of 30 to 40. This is done through the use of the `MaximumValue` and `MinimumValue` properties. The RangeValidator control also makes sure what is entered is an integer data type. It uses the `Type` property, which is set to `Integer`. The collection of screenshots in Figure 7-3 shows this example in action.

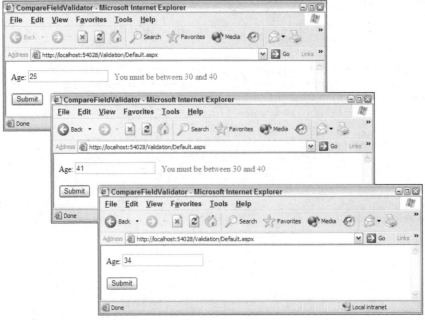

Figure 7-3

As you can see from the screenshots in Figure 7-3, a value of less than 30 causes the RangeValidator control to fire as does a number greater than 40. A value that is somewhere between 30 and 40 (in this case 34) conforms to the validation rule of the control.

The RangeValidator control is not only about validating numbers (although it is most often used in this fashion). It can also be about validating a range of string characters as well as other items, including calendar dates. By default, the `Type` property of any of the validation controls is set to `String`. You can use the RangeValidator control to make sure what is entered in another server control (such as a calendar control) is within a certain range of dates.

For example, suppose that you are building a Web form that asks for a customer's arrival date, and the arrival date needs to be within two weeks of the current date. You can use the RangeValidator control to test for these scenarios quite easily.

Since the date range that you want to check is dynamically generated, you assign the `MaximumValue` and `MinimumValue` attribute programmatically in the `Page_Load` event. In the Designer, your sample page for this example should look like Figure 7-4.

The idea is that the end user will select a date from the Calendar control, which will then populate the TextBox control. Then, when the end user clicks the form's button, he is notified if the date selected is invalid. If the date selected is valid, that date is presented through the Label control on the page. The code for this example is presented in Listing 7-12.

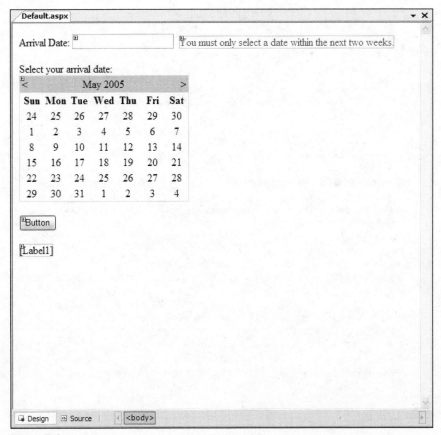

Figure 7-4

Listing 7-12: Using the RangeValidator control to test a string date value

VB

```
<%@ Page Language="VB" %>

<script runat="server">
    Protected Sub Page_Load(ByVal sender As Object, ByVal e As System.EventArgs)
        RangeValidator1.MinimumValue = DateTime.Now.ToShortDateString()
        RangeValidator1.MaximumValue = DateTime.Now.AddDays(14).ToShortDateString()
    End Sub

    Protected Sub Calendar1_SelectionChanged(ByVal sender As Object, _
      ByVal e As System.EventArgs)
        TextBox1.Text = Calendar1.SelectedDate.ToShortDateString()
    End Sub

    Protected Sub Button1_Click(ByVal sender As Object, _
      ByVal e As System.EventArgs)
        If Page.IsValid Then
            Label1.Text = "You are set to arrive on: " & TextBox1.Text
        End If
    End Sub
</script>

<html xmlns="http://www.w3.org/1999/xhtml" >
<head id="Head1" runat="server">
    <title>Date Validation Check</title>
</head>
<body>
    <form id="form1" runat="server">
        Arrival Date:
        <asp:TextBox ID="TextBox1" runat="server"></asp:TextBox> 
        <asp:RangeValidator ID="RangeValidator1" runat="server"
         ErrorMessage="You must only select a date within the next two weeks."
         ControlToValidate="TextBox1" Type="Date"></asp:RangeValidator><br />
        <br />
        Select your arrival date:<br />
        <asp:Calendar ID="Calendar1" runat="server"
         OnSelectionChanged="Calendar1_SelectionChanged"></asp:Calendar>
         
        <br />
        <asp:Button ID="Button1" runat="server" Text="Button"
         OnClick="Button1_Click" />
        <br />
        <br />
        <asp:Label ID="Label1" runat="server"></asp:Label>
    </form>
</body>
</html>
```

C#

```
<%@ Page Language="C#" %>

<script runat="server">
    protected void Page_Load(object sender, EventArgs e)
```

```
    {
        RangeValidator1.MinimumValue = DateTime.Now.ToShortDateString();
        RangeValidator1.MaximumValue =
            DateTime.Now.AddDays(14).ToShortDateString();
    }

    protected void Calendar1_SelectionChanged(object sender, EventArgs e)
    {
        TextBox1.Text = Calendar1.SelectedDate.ToShortDateString();
    }

    protected void Button1_Click(object sender, EventArgs e)
    {
        if (Page.IsValid)
        {
            Label1.Text = "You are set to arrive on: " + TextBox1.Text.ToString();
        }
    }
</script>
```

From this code, you can see that when the page is loaded, the `MinimumValue` and `MaximumValue` attributes are assigned a dynamic value. In this case, the `MinimumValue` gets the `DateTime.Now` `.ToShortDateString()` value, while the `MaximumValue` gets a date of 14 days later.

After the end user selects a date, the selected date is populated in the `TextBox1` control using the `Calendar1_SelectionChanged` event. After a date is selected and the button on the page is clicked, the `Button1_Click` event is fired and the page is checked for form validity using the `Page.IsValid` property. An invalid page will give you the result shown in Figure 7-5.

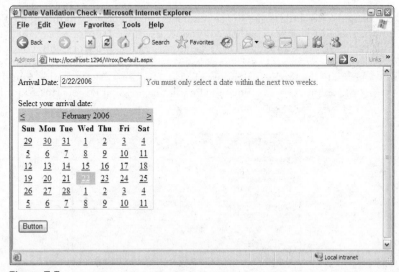

Figure 7-5

The RegularExpressionValidator Server Control

One exciting control that developers like to use is the RegularExpressionValidator control. This control offers a lot of flexibility when you apply validation rules to your Web forms. Using the RegularExpressionValidator control, you can check a user's input based on a pattern that you define using a regular expression.

This means that you can define a structure that a user's input will be applied against to see if its structure matches the one that you define. For instance, you can define that the structure of the user input must be in the form of an e-mail address or an Internet URL; if it doesn't match this definition, the page is considered invalid. Listing 7-13 shows you how to validate what is input into a text box by making sure it is in the form of an e-mail address.

Listing 7-13: Making sure the text-box value is an e-mail address

```
Email:
<asp:TextBox ID="TextBox1" Runat="server"></asp:TextBox>
   
<asp:RegularExpressionValidator ID="RegularExpressionValidator1"
  Runat="server" ControlToValidate="TextBox1"
  ErrorMessage="You must enter an email address"
  ValidationExpression="\w+([-+.]\w+)*@\w+([-.]\w+)*\.\w+([-.]\w+)*">
</asp:RegularExpressionValidator>
```

Just like the other validation server controls, the RegularExpressionValidator control uses the `ControlToValidate` property to bind itself to the TextBox control, and it includes an `ErrorMessage` property to push out the error message to the screen if the validation test fails. The unique property of this validation control is the `ValidationExpression` property. This property takes a string value, which is the regular expression you are going to apply to the input value.

Visual Studio 2005 makes it a little easier to use regular expressions by introducing the Regular Expression Editor. This editor provides a few commonly used regular expressions that you might want to apply to your RegularExpressionValidator. To get at this editor, you work with your page from Design view. Be sure to highlight the `RegularExpressionValidator1` server control in this Design view to see the control's properties. In the Property window of Visual Studio, click the button found next to the `ValidationExpression` property to launch the Regular Expression Editor. This editor is shown in Figure 7-6.

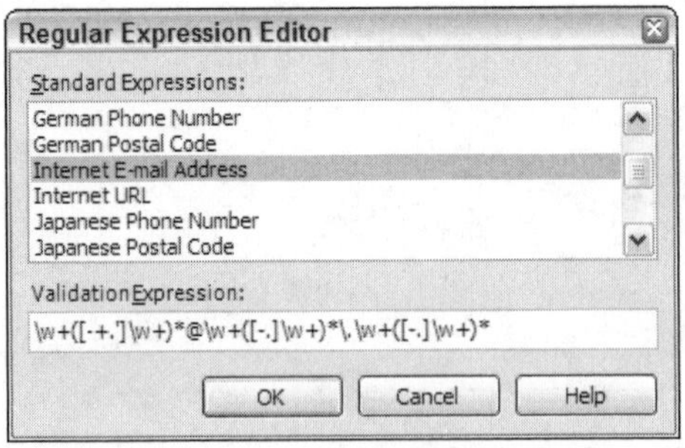

Figure 7-6

Using this editor, you can find regular expressions for things like e-mail addresses, Internet URLs, zip codes, phone numbers, and social security numbers. In addition to working with the Regular Expression Editor to help you with these sometimes complicated regular expression strings, you can also find a good-sized collection of them at an Internet site called RegExLib found at `www.regexlib.com`.

The CustomValidator Server Control

So far, you have seen a wide variety of validation controls that are at your disposal. In many cases, these validation controls address many of the validation rules that you want to apply to your Web forms. Sometime, however, none of these controls work for you, and you have to go beyond what they offer. This is where the CustomValidator control comes into play.

The CustomValidator control allows you to build your own client-side or server-side validations that can then be easily applied to your Web forms. Doing so allows you to make validation checks against values or calculations performed in the data tier (for example, in a database), or to make sure that the user's input validates against some arithmetic validation (for example, determining if a number is even or odd). You can do quite a bit with the CustomValidator control.

Using Client-Side Validation

One of the worthwhile functions of the CustomValidator control is its capability to easily provide custom client-side validations. Many developers have their own collections of JavaScript functions they employ in their applications, and using the CustomValidator control is one easy way of getting these functions implemented.

For example, look at a simple form that asks for a number from the end user. This form uses the CustomValidator control to perform a custom client-side validation on the user input to make sure that the number provided is divisible by 5. This is illustrated in Listing 7-14.

Listing 7-14: Using the CustomValidator control to perform client-side validations

VB

```
<%@ Page Language="VB" %>

<script runat="server">
    Protected Sub Button1_Click(ByVal sender As Object, ByVal e As System.EventArgs)
        Label1.Text = "VALID NUMBER!"
    End Sub
</script>

<html xmlns="http://www.w3.org/1999/xhtml" >
<head id="Head1" runat="server">
    <title>CustomValidator</title>

    <script language="JavaScript">
        function validateNumber(oSrc, args) {
            args.IsValid = (args.Value % 5 == 0);
        }
    </script>

</head>
```

(continued)

Listing 7-14: *(continued)*

```
<body>
    <form id="form1" runat="server">
    <div>
        <p>
            Number:
            <asp:TextBox ID="TextBox1"
             Runat="server"></asp:TextBox>
             
            <asp:CustomValidator ID="CustomValidator1"
             Runat="server" ControlToValidate="TextBox1"
             ErrorMessage="Number must be divisible by 5"
             ClientValidationFunction="validateNumber">
             </asp:CustomValidator>
        </p>
        <p>
            <asp:Button ID="Button1" OnClick="Button1_Click"
             Runat="server" Text="Button"></asp:Button>
        </p>
        <p>
            <asp:Label ID="Label1" Runat="server"></asp:Label>
        </p>
    </div>
    </form>
</body>
</html>
```

C#

```
<%@ Page Language="C#" %>
<script runat="server">

    protected void Button1_Click(Object sender, EventArgs e) {
        Label1.Text = "VALID NUMBER!";
    }

</script>
```

Looking over this Web form, you can see a couple of things happening. First, it is a simple form with only a single text box requiring user input. The user clicks the button that triggers the `Button1_Click` event that, in turn, populates the `Label1` control on the page. It carries out this simple operation only if all the validation checks are performed and the user input passes these tests.

One item that is different about this page is the inclusion of the second `<script>` block found within the `<head>` section. This is the custom JavaScript. Note that Visual Studio 2005 is now very friendly toward these kinds of constructions, even when you are switching between the Design and Code views of the page — something the two previous Visual Studio editions were rather poor at dealing with. This JavaScript function — `validateNumber` — is shown here:

```
<script type="JavaScript">
    function validateNumber(oSrc, args) {
        args.IsValid = (args.Value % 5 == 0);
    }
</script>
```

This second `<script>` section is the client-side JavaScript that you want the CustomValidator control to use when making its validation checks on the information entered into the text box. The JavaScript functions you employ are going to use the `args.IsValid` property and set this property to either `true` or `false` depending on the outcome of the validation check. In this case, the user input (`args.Value`) is checked to see if it is divisible by 5. The Boolean value returned is then assigned to the `args.IsValid` property, which is then used by the CustomValidator control.

The CustomValidator control, like the other controls before it, uses the `ControlToValidate` property to associate itself with a particular element on the page. The property that you are interested in here is the `ClientValidationFunction` property. The string value provided to this property is the name of the client-side function that you want this validation check to employ when the CustomValidator control is triggered. In this case, it is `validateNumber`:

```
ClientValidationFunction="validateNumber"
```

If you run this page and make an invalid entry, you produce the result illustrated in Figure 7-7.

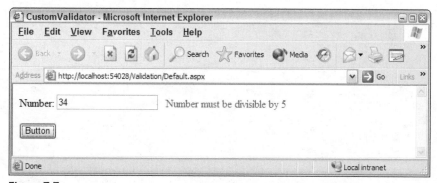

Figure 7-7

Using Server-Side Validation

Now let's move this same validation check from the client to the server. The CustomValidator control allows you to make custom server-side validations a reality as well. You will find that creating your server-side validations is just as easy as creating client-side validations.

If you create your own server-side validations, you can make them as complex as your applications require. For instance, using the CustomValidator for server-side validations is something you do if you want to check the user's input against dynamic values coming from XML files, databases, or elsewhere.

For an example of using the CustomValidator control for some custom server-side validation, you can work with the same example as you did when creating the client-side validation. Now, create a server-side check that makes sure a user-input number is divisible by 5. This is illustrated in Listing 7-15.

Listing 7-15: Using the CustomValidator control to perform server-side validations

VB
```
<%@ Page Language="VB" %>

<script runat="server">
    Protected Sub Button1_Click(ByVal sender As Object, ByVal e As System.EventArgs)
        If Page.IsValid Then
            Label1.Text = "VALID ENTRY!"
        End If
    End Sub

    Sub ValidateNumber(sender As Object, args As ServerValidateEventArgs)
        Try
            Dim num As Integer = Integer.Parse(args.Value)
            args.IsValid = ((num mod 5) = 0)
        Catch ex As Exception
            args.IsValid = False
        End Try
    End Sub
</script>

<html xmlns="http://www.w3.org/1999/xhtml" >
<head runat="server id="Head1" runat="server">">
    <title>CustomValidator</title>
</head>
<body>
    <form id="form1" runat="server">
    <div>
        <p>
            Number:
            <asp:TextBox ID="TextBox1"
             Runat="server"></asp:TextBox>
             
            <asp:CustomValidator ID="CustomValidator1"
             Runat="server" ControlToValidate="TextBox1"
             ErrorMessage="Number must be divisible by 5"
             OnServerValidate="ValidateNumber"></asp:CustomValidator>
        </p>
        <p>
            <asp:Button ID="Button1" OnClick="Button1_Click"
             Runat="server" Text="Button"></asp:Button>
        </p>
        <p>
            <asp:Label ID="Label1" Runat="server"></asp:Label>
        </p>
    </div>
    </form>
</body>
</html>

```

C#
```
<%@ Page Language="C#" %>
```

```
<script runat="server">

    protected void Button1_Click(Object sender, EventArgs e) {
        if (Page.IsValid) {
            Label1.Text = "VALID ENTRY!";
        }
    }

    void ValidateNumber(object source, ServerValidateEventArgs args)
    {
        try
        {
            int num = int.Parse(args.Value);
            args.IsValid = ((num%5) == 0);
        }
        catch(Exception ex)
        {
            args.IsValid = false;
        }
    }

</script>
```

Instead of a client-side JavaScript function in the code, this example includes a server-side function — `ValidateNumber`. The `ValidateNumber` function, as well as all functions that are being constructed to work with the CustomValidator control, must use the `ServerValidateEventArgs` object as one of the parameters in order to get the data passed to the function for the validation check. The `ValidateNumber` function itself is nothing fancy. It simply checks to see if the provided number is divisible by 5.

From within your custom function, which is designed to work with the CustomValidator control, you actually get at the value coming from the form element through the `args.Value` object. Then you set the `args.IsValid` property to either `True` or `False` depending on your validation checks. From the preceding example, you can see that the `args.IsValid` is set to `False` if the number is not divisible by 5 and also that an exception is thrown (which would occur if a string value was input into the form element). After the custom function is established, the next step is to apply it to the CustomValidator control, as shown in the following example:

```
<asp:CustomValidator ID="CustomValidator1"
 Runat="server" ControlToValidate="TextBox1"
 ErrorMessage="Number must be divisible by 5"
 OnServerValidate="ValidateNumber"></asp:CustomValidator>
```

To make the association between a CustomValidator control and a function that you have in your server-side code, you simply use the `OnServerValidate` property. The value assigned to this property is the name of the function — in this case, `ValidateNumber`.

Running this example causes the postback to come back to the server and the validation check (based on the `ValidateNumber` function) to be performed. From here, the page reloads and the `Page_Load` event is called. In the example from Listing 7-15, you can see that a check is done to see whether the page is valid. This is done using the `Page.IsValid` property.

```
If Page.IsValid Then
    Label1.Text = "VALID ENTRY!"
End If
```

Using Client-Side and Server-Side Validation Together

As stated earlier in this chapter, you have to think about the security of your forms and to ensure that the data you are collecting from the forms is valid data. For this reason, when you decide to employ client-side validations (as you did in Listing 7-14), you should take steps to also reconstruct the client-side function as a server-side function. When you have done this, you should associate the CustomValidator control to both the client-side and server-side functions. In the case of the number check validation from Listings 7-14 and 7-15, you can use both validation functions in your page and then change the CustomValidator control to point to both of these functions as shown in Listing 7-16.

Listing 7-16: The CustomValidator control with client- and server-side validations

```
<asp:CustomValidator ID="CustomValidator1"
    Runat="server" ControlToValidate="TextBox1"
    ErrorMessage="Number must be divisible by 5"
    ClientValidationFunction="validateNumber"
    OnServerValidate="ValidateNumber"></asp:CustomValidator>
```

From this example, you can see it is simply a matter of using both the `ClientValidationFunction` and the `OnServerValidate` properties at the same time.

The ValidationSummary Server Control

The ValidationSummary control is not a control that performs validations on the content input into your Web forms. Instead, this control is the reporting control, which is used by the other validation controls on a page. You can use this validation control to consolidate error reporting for all the validation errors that occur on a page instead of leaving this up to each and every individual validation control.

You might want this capability for larger forms, which have a comprehensive form validation process. If this is the case, you may find it rather user-friendly to have all the possible validation errors reported to the end user in a single and easily identifiable manner. These error messages can be displayed in a list, bulleted list, or paragraph.

By default, the ValidationSummary control shows the list of validation errors as a bulleted list. This is illustrated in Listing 7-17.

Listing 7-17: A partial page example of the ValidationSummary control

```
<p>First name
    <asp:TextBox ID="TextBox1" Runat="server"></asp:TextBox>
     
    <asp:RequiredFieldValidator ID="RequiredFieldValidator1"
    Runat="server" ErrorMessage="You must enter your first name"
    ControlToValidate="TextBox1"></asp:RequiredFieldValidator>
</p>
<p>Last name
    <asp:TextBox ID="TextBox2" Runat="server"></asp:TextBox>
     
    <asp:RequiredFieldValidator ID="RequiredFieldValidator2"
    Runat="server" ErrorMessage="You must enter your last name"
    ControlToValidate="TextBox2"></asp:RequiredFieldValidator>
```

```
    </p>
    <p>
       <asp:Button ID="Button1" OnClick="Button1_Click" Runat="server"
        Text="Submit"></asp:Button>
    </p>
    <p>
       <asp:ValidationSummary ID="ValidationSummary1" Runat="server"
        HeaderText="You received the following errors:">
       </asp:ValidationSummary>
    </p>
    <p>
       <asp:Label ID="Label1" Runat="server"></asp:Label>
    </p>
```

This example asks the end user for her first and last name. Each text box in the form has an associated RequiredFieldValidator control assigned to it. When the page is built and run, if the user clicks the Submit button with no values placed in either of the text boxes, it causes both validation errors to fire. This result is shown in Figure 7-8.

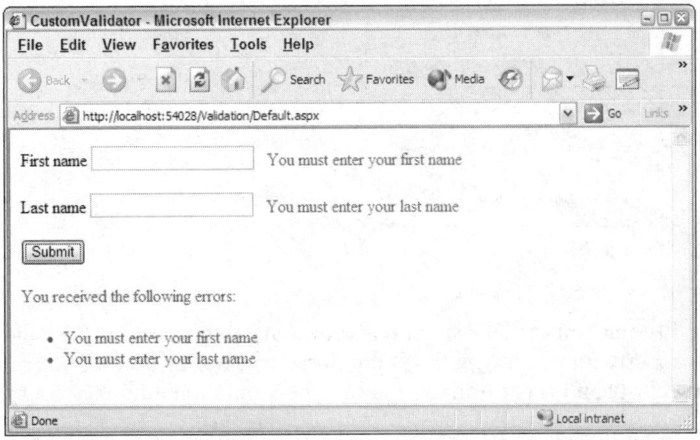

Figure 7-8

As in earlier examples of validation controls on the form, these validation errors appear next to each of the text boxes. You can see, however, that the ValidationSummary control also displays the validation errors as a bulleted list in red at the location of the control on the Web form. In most cases, you do not want these errors to appear twice on a page for the end user. You can change this behavior by using the Text property of the validation controls, in addition to the ErrorMessage property, as you have typically done throughout this chapter. This approach is shown in Listing 7-18.

Listing 7-18: Using the Text property of a validation control

```
<asp:RequiredFieldValidator ID="RequiredFieldValidator1"
 Runat="server" ErrorMessage="You must enter your first name" Text="*"
 ControlToValidate="TextBox1"></asp:RequiredFieldValidator>
```

or

(continued)

Listing 7-18: *(continued)*

```
<asp:RequiredFieldValidator ID="RequiredFieldValidator1"
  Runat="server" ErrorMessage="You must enter your first name"
  ControlToValidate="TextBox1">*</asp:RequiredFieldValidator>
```

Listing 7-18 shows two ways to accomplish the same task. The first is to use the Text property and the second option is to place the provided output between the nodes of the `<asp:RequiredFieldValidator>` elements. Making this type of change to the validation controls produces the results shown in Figure 7-9.

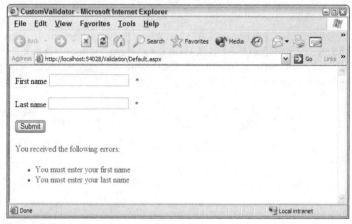

Figure 7-9

To get this result, just remember that the ValidationSummary control uses the validation control's ErrorMessage property for displaying the validation errors if they occur. The Text property is used by the validation control and is not utilized at all by the ValidationSummary control.

In addition to bulleted lists, you can use the DisplayMode property of the ValidationSummary control to change the display of the results to other types of formats. This control has the following possible values:

- ❑ BulletList
- ❑ List
- ❑ SingleParagraph

You can also utilize a dialog box instead of displaying the results to the Web page. Listing 7-19 shows an example of this behavior.

Listing 7-19: Using a dialog box to report validation errors

```
<asp:ValidationSummary ID="ValidationSummary1" Runat="server"
  ShowMessageBox="True" ShowSummary="False"></asp:ValidationSummary>
```

From this code example, you can see that the ShowSummary property is set to False—meaning that the bulleted list of validation errors are not shown on the actual Web page. However, because the ShowMessageBox property is set to True, you now get these errors reported in a message box, as illustrated in Figure 7-10.

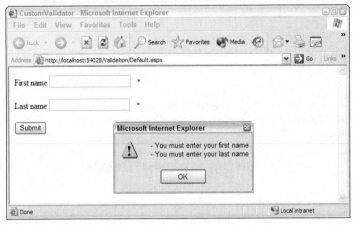

Figure 7-10

Turning Off Client-Side Validation

Because validation server controls provide clients with client-side validations automatically (if the requesting container can properly handle the JavaScript produced), you might, at times, want a way to control this behavior.

It is quite possible to turn off the client-side capabilities of these controls so that they don't independently send client-side capabilities to the requestors. For instance, you might want all validations done on the server, no matter what capabilities the requesting containers offer. You can take a couple of approaches to turning off this functionality.

The first is at the control level. Each of the validation server controls has a property called EnableClientScript. This property is set to True by default, but setting it to False prevents the control from sending out a JavaScript function for validation on the client. Instead, the validation check is done on the server. The use of this property is shown in Listing 7-20.

Listing 7-20: Disabling client-side validations in a validation control

```
<asp:RequiredFieldValidator ID="RequiredFieldValidator1" Runat="server"
  ErrorMessage="*" ControlToValidate="TextBox1" EnableClientScript="false">
```

You can also remove a validation control's client-side capability programmatically (shown in Listing 7-21).

Listing 7-21: Removing the client-side capabilities programmatically

VB

```
Protected Sub Page_Load(ByVal sender As Object, ByVal e As System.EventArgs)
    RequiredFieldValidator1.EnableClientScript = False
End Sub
```

C#

```
protected void Page_Load(Object sender, EventArgs e) {
    RequiredFieldValidator1.EnableClientScript = false;
}
```

Another option is to turn off the client-side script capabilities for all the validation controls on a page from within the Page_Load event. This can be rather helpful if you want to dynamically decide not to allow client-side validation. This is illustrated in Listing 7-22.

Listing 7-22: Disabling all client-side validations from the Page_Load event

VB

```
Protected Sub Page_Load(ByVal sender As Object, ByVal e As System.EventArgs)
    For Each bv As BaseValidator In Page.Validators
        bv.EnableClientScript = False
    Next
End Sub
```

C#

```
protected void Page_Load(Object sender, EventArgs e) {
    foreach(BaseValidator bv in Page.Validators)
    {
        bv.EnableClientScript = false;
    }
}
```

Looking for each instance of a BaseValidator object in the validators contained on an ASP.NET page, this For Each loop turns off client-side validation capabilities for each and every validation control the page contains.

Using Images and Sounds for Error Notifications

So far, we have been displaying simple textual messages for the error notifications that come from the validation server controls. In most instances, you are going to do just that — display some simple textual messages to inform end users that they input something into the form that doesn't pass your validation rules.

An interesting tip regarding the validation controls is that you are not limited to just text — you can also use images and sounds for error notifications.

To do this, you use the `ErrorMessage` property of any of the validation controls. To use an image for the error, you can simply place some appropriate HTML as the value of this property. This is illustrated in Listing 7-23.

Listing 7-23: Using images for error notifications

```
<asp:RequiredFieldValidator ID="RequiredFieldValidator1"
 Runat="server" ErrorMessage='<img src="error.gif">'
 ControlToValidate="TextBox1"></asp:RequiredFieldValidator>
```

As you can see from this example, instead of some text being output to the Web page, the value of the `ErrorMessage` property is an HTML string. This bit of HTML is used to display an image. Be sure to notice the use of the single and double quotation marks so you won't get any errors when the page is generated in the browser. This example produces something similar to what is shown in Figure 7-11.

Figure 7-11

The other interesting twist you can create is to add a sound notification when the end user errs. You can do this the same way you display an image for error notifications. Listing 7-24 shows an example of this.

Listing 7-24: Using sound for error notifications

```
<asp:RequiredFieldValidator ID="RequiredFieldValidator1"
 Runat="server" ErrorMessage='<bgsound src="C:\Windows\Media\tada.wav">'
 ControlToValidate="TextBox1" EnableClientScript="False">
</asp:RequiredFieldValidator>
```

You can find a lot of the Windows system sounds in the `C:\Windows\Media` directory. In this example, the `ErrorMessage` uses the `<bgsound sound>` element to place a sound on the Web form (works only with Internet Explorer). The sound is played only when the end user triggers the validation control.

When working with sounds for error notifications, you have to disable the client-side script capability for that particular control because if you do not, the sound plays when the page is loaded in the browser, whether or not a validation error has been triggered.

Working with Validation Groups

In many instances, developers want to place more than one form on a single page. This was always possible in ASP.NET 1.0/1.1 because different button clicks could be used to perform different server-side events. Some issues related to this type of construction were problematic, however.

One of these issues was the difficulty of having validation controls for each of the forms on the page. Different validation controls were often assigned to two distinct forms on the page. When the end user submitted one form, the validation controls in the other form were fired (because the user was not working with that form), thereby stopping the first form from being submitted.

Figure 7-12, for example, shows a basic page for the St. Louis .NET User Group that includes two forms.

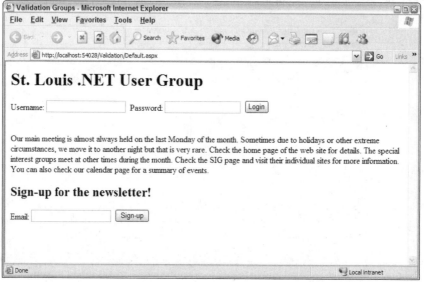

Figure 7-12

One of the forms is for members of the site to supply their usernames and passwords to log into the Members Only section of the site. The second form on the page is for anyone who wishes to sign up for the user group's newsletter. Each form has its own button and some validation controls associated with it. The problem arises when someone submits information for one of the forms. For instance, if you are a member of the group, you would supply your username and password, and click the Login button. The validation controls for the newsletter form would fire because no e-mail address was placed in that particular form. If someone interested in getting the newsletter places an e-mail address in the last text box and clicks the Sign-up button, the validation controls in the first form fire because no username and password were input in that form.

ASP.NET 2.0 now provides you with a `ValidationGroup` property that enables you to separate the validation controls into separate groups. It enables you to activate only the required validation controls when an end user clicks a button on the page. Listing 7-25 shows an example of separating the validation controls on a user group page into different buckets.

Listing 7-25: Using the ValidationGroup property

```
<%@ Page Language="VB" %>

<html xmlns="http://www.w3.org/1999/xhtml" >
<head id="Head1" runat="server">
    <title>Validation Groups</title>
</head>
<body>
    <form id="form1" runat="server">
    <div>
        <h1>St. Louis .NET User Group</h1>
        <p>Username:
        <asp:TextBox ID="TextBox1" Runat="server"></asp:TextBox>  Password:
        <asp:TextBox ID="TextBox2" Runat="server"
         TextMode="Password"></asp:TextBox> 
        <asp:Button ID="Button1" Runat="server" Text="Login"
         ValidationGroup="Login" />
            <br />
            <asp:RequiredFieldValidator ID="RequiredFieldValidator1" Runat="server"
             ErrorMessage="* You must submit a username!"
             ControlToValidate="TextBox1" ValidationGroup="Login">
            </asp:RequiredFieldValidator>
            <br />
            <asp:RequiredFieldValidator ID="RequiredFieldValidator2" Runat="server"
             ErrorMessage="* You must submit a password!"
             ControlToValidate="TextBox2" ValidationGroup="Login">
            </asp:RequiredFieldValidator>
        <p>
            Our main meeting is almost always held on the last Monday of the month.
            Sometimes due to holidays or other extreme circumstances,
            we move it to another night but that is very rare. Check the home page
            of the web site for details. The special
            interest groups meet at other times during the month. Check the SIG
            page and visit their individual sites for more information.
            You can also check our calendar page for a summary of events.<br />
        </p>
        <h2>Sign-up for the newsletter!</h2>
        <p>Email:
        <asp:TextBox ID="TextBox3" Runat="server"></asp:TextBox> 
        <asp:Button ID="Button2" Runat="server" Text="Sign-up"
         ValidationGroup="Newsletter" /> 
            <br />
            <asp:RegularExpressionValidator ID="RegularExpressionValidator1"
             Runat="server"
             ErrorMessage="* You must submit a correctly formatted email address!"
             ControlToValidate="TextBox3" ValidationGroup="Newsletter"
             ValidationExpression="\w+([-+.]\w+)*@\w+([-.]\w+)*\.\w+([-.]\w+)*">
            </asp:RegularExpressionValidator>
            <br />
            <asp:RequiredFieldValidator ID="RequiredFieldValidator3" Runat="server"
             ErrorMessage="* You forgot your email address!"
             ControlToValidate="TextBox3" ValidationGroup="Newsletter">
```

(continued)

Listing 7-25: *(continued)*

```
            </asp:RequiredFieldValidator>
        </p>
    </div>
    </form>
</body>
</html>
```

The `ValidationGroup` property on this page is shown in bold. You can see that this property takes a `String` value. Also note that not only validation controls have this new property. The core server controls also have the `ValidationGroup` property because things like button clicks must be associated with specific validation groups.

In this example, each of the buttons has a distinct validation group assignment. The first button on the form uses `Login` as a value, and the second button on the form uses `Newsletter` as a value. Then each of the validation controls is associated with one of these validation groups. Because of this, when the end user clicks the Login button on the page, ASP.NET recognizes that it should work only with the validation server controls that have the same validation group name. ASP.NET ignores the validation controls assigned to other validation groups.

Using this enhancement, you can now have multiple sets of validation rules that fire only when you want them to fire (see Figure 7-13).

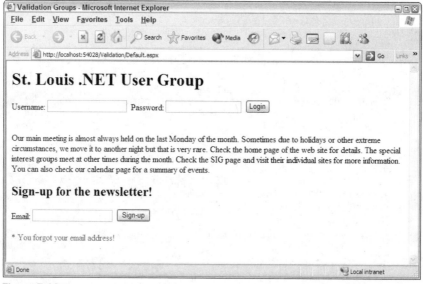

Figure 7-13

Another great feature that has been added to validation controls is a property called `SetFocusOnError`. This property takes a `Boolean` value and, if a validation error is thrown when the form is submitted, the property places the page focus on the form element that receives the error. The `SetFocusOnError` property is used in the following example:

```
<asp:RequiredFieldValidator ID="RequiredFieldValidator1" Runat="server"
 ErrorMessage="* You must submit a username!"
 ControlToValidate="TextBox1" ValidationGroup="Login" SetFocusOnError="True">
</asp:RequiredFieldValidator>
```

If `RequiredFieldValidator1` throws an error because the end user didn't place a value in `TextBox1`, the page is redrawn with the focus on `TextBox1`, as shown in Figure 7-14.

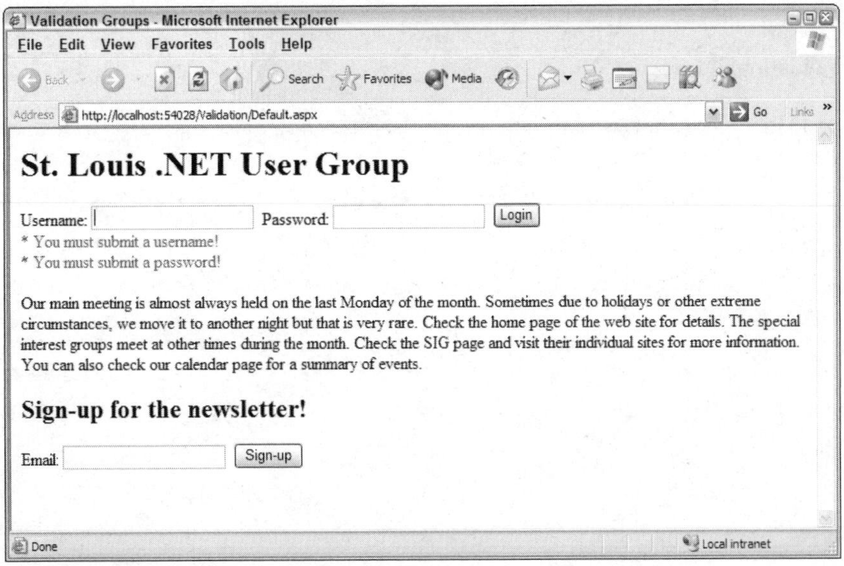

Figure 7-14

Note that if you have multiple validation controls on your page with the `SetFocusOnError` property set to `True`, and more than one validation error occurs, the uppermost form element that has a validation error gets the focus. In the previous example, if both the username text box (`TextBox1`) and the password text box (`TextBox2`) have validation errors associated with them, the page focus is assigned to the username text box because it is the first control on the form with an error.

Summary

Validation controls are a welcome addition for those developers moving from Active Server Pages to ASP.NET. They bring a lot of functionality in a simple-to-use package and, like most things in the .NET world, you can easily get them to look and behave exactly as you want them to.

Remember that the purpose of having forms in your applications is to collect data, but this data collection has no meaning if the data is not valid. This means that you are must establish validation rules that can be implemented in your forms through a series of different controls — the validation server controls.

This chapter took a good look at the various validation controls, including

- ❑ RequiredFieldValidator
- ❑ CompareValidator
- ❑ RangeValidator
- ❑ RegularExpressionValidator
- ❑ CustomValidator
- ❑ ValidationSummary

In addition to looking at the base validation controls, this chapter also discussed how to apply client-side and server-side validations.

Working with Master Pages

Visual inheritance is a great new enhancement to your Web pages provided by new additions to ASP.NET 2.0. In effect, you can create a single template page that can be used as a foundation for any number of ASP.NET content pages in your application. These templates, called *master pages*, increase your productivity by making your applications easier to build and easier to manage after they are built. Visual Studio 2005 includes full designer support for master pages, making the developer experience richer than ever before. This chapter takes a close look at how to utilize master pages to the fullest extent in your applications and begins by explaining the advantages of master pages.

Why Do You Need Master Pages?

Most Web sites today have common elements used throughout the entire application or on a majority of the pages within the application. For instance, if you look at the main page of the Reuters News Web site (found at www.reuters.com), you see common elements that are used throughout the entire Web site. These common areas are labeled in Figure 8-1.

In this screen shot, notice a header section, a navigation section, and a footer section on the page. In fact, nearly every page within the entire application uses these same elements. Even before master pages, you had ways to put these elements into every page; but in most cases, doing so posed difficulties.

Some developers simply copy and paste the code for these common sections to each and every page that requires them. This works, but it's rather labor intensive. But, if you use the copy-and-paste method, whenever a change is required to one of these common sections of the application, you have to go into each and every page and duplicate the change. That's not much fun and an ineffective use of your time!

Header ▶

◀ Ad Space

Secondary
Navigation ▶

Common
Page
Items ▶

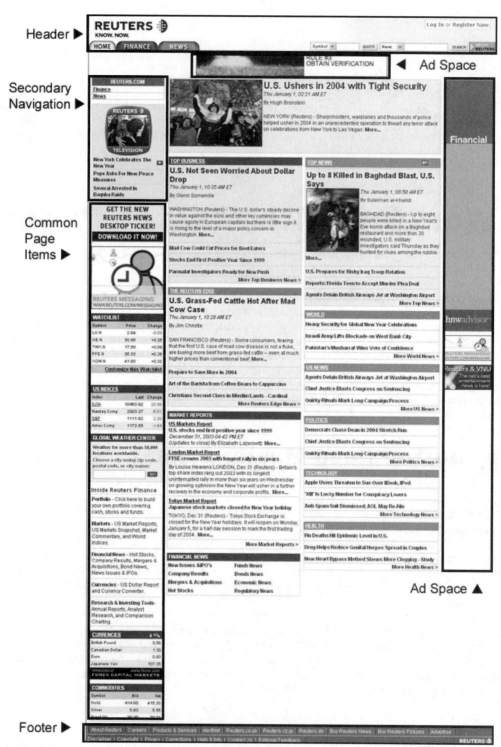

Ad Space ▲

Footer ▶

Figure 8-1

In the days of Classic Active Server Pages, one popular option was to put all the common sections into what was called an *include file*. You could then place this file within your page like this:

```
<!-- #include virtual="/myIncludes/header.asp" -->
```

The problem with using `include` files was that you had to take into account the newly opened HTML tags in the header `include` file. These tags had to be closed in the main document or in the footer `include` file. It was usually difficult to keep all the HTML tags in order, especially if multiple people worked on a project. Web pages sometimes displayed strange results because of inappropriate or nonexistent tag closings or openings. It was also difficult to work with `include` files in a visual designer. Using `include` files didn't allow the developer to see the entire page as it would appear in a browser. The developer ended up developing the page in sections and *hoping* that the pieces would come together as planned. Many hours were wasted "chasing tables" opened in an include file and possibly closed later!

With the introduction of ASP.NET 1.0 in 2000, developers started using *user controls* to encapsulate common sections of their Web pages. For instance, you could build a Web page that included header, navigation, and footer sections by simply dragging and dropping these sections of code onto each page that required them.

This technique worked, but it also raised some issues. Before Visual Studio 2005, user controls caused problems similar to those related to `include` files. When you worked in the design view of your Web page, the common areas of the page displayed only as gray boxes in Visual Studio .NET 2002 and 2003. This made it harder to build a page. You could not visualize what the page you were building actually looked like until you compiled and ran the completed page in a browser. User controls also suffered from the same problem as `include` files — you had to match up the opening and closing of your HTML tags in two separate files. Personally, we prefer user controls over `include` files, but user controls aren't perfect template pieces for use throughout an application. Visual Studio 2005 corrects some of the problems by rendering user-control content in the design view. User controls are ideal if you are including only small sections on a Web page; they are still rather cumbersome, however, when working with larger page templates.

In light of the issues with `include` files and user controls, the ASP.NET team developed the idea of *master pages* — an outstanding new way of applying templates to your applications. They *inverted* the way the developer attacks the problem. Master pages live *outside* the pages you develop, while user controls live within your pages and are doomed to duplication. These master pages draw a more distinct line between the common areas that you carry over from page to page and the content areas that are unique on each page. Working with master pages is easy and fun. Look at some of the basics of master pages in ASP.NET 2.0.

The Basics of Master Pages

Master pages are an easy way to provide a template that can be used by any number of ASP.NET pages in your application. In working with master pages, you create a master file that is the template referenced by a *subpage* or *content page*. Master pages use a `.master` file extension, whereas content pages use the `.aspx` file extension you're used to; but content pages are declared as such within the file's `Page` directive.

Put anything you want to share within the template in the `.master` file. This can include the header, navigation, and footer sections used across the Web application. The content page then contains all the page content except for the master page's elements. At runtime, the ASP.NET engine combines these elements into a single page for the end user. Figure 8-2 shows a diagram of how this process works.

One of the nice things about working with master pages is that you can visually see the template in the IDE when you are creating the content pages. Because you can see the entire page while you are working on it, it is much easier to develop content pages that use a template. While you are working on the content page, all the templated items are shaded gray and are not editable. The only items that are alterable are clearly shown in the template. These workable areas, called *content areas*, originally are defined in the master page itself. Within the master page, you specify the areas of the page that the content pages can use. You can have more than one content area in your master page if you want. Figure 8-3 shows the master page with a couple of content areas shown.

With the release of ASP.NET 2.0, master pages are possible because the .NET Framework 2.0 now supports *partial classes*. This is the capability to take two classes and merge them into a single class at runtime. Using this new capability, the ASP.NET engine takes two page classes and brings them together into a single page class at runtime.

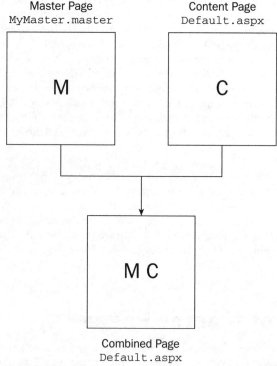

Figure 8-2

Figure 8-3

Companies and organizations will find using master pages ideal, as the technology closely models their typical business requirements. Many companies have a common look and feel that they apply across their intranet. They can now provide the divisions of their company with a `.master` file to use when creating a department's section of the intranet. This process makes it quite easy for the company to keep a consistent look and feel across its entire intranet.

Coding a Master Page

Now look at building the master page shown in Figure 8-3. You can create one in any text-based editor, such as Notepad or Visual Web Developer Express Edition, or you can use the new Visual Studio 2005. In this chapter, you see how to use Visual Web Developer.

Master pages are added to your projects in the same way as regular `.aspx` pages — choose the Master Page option when you add a new file to your application, as shown in Figure 8-4.

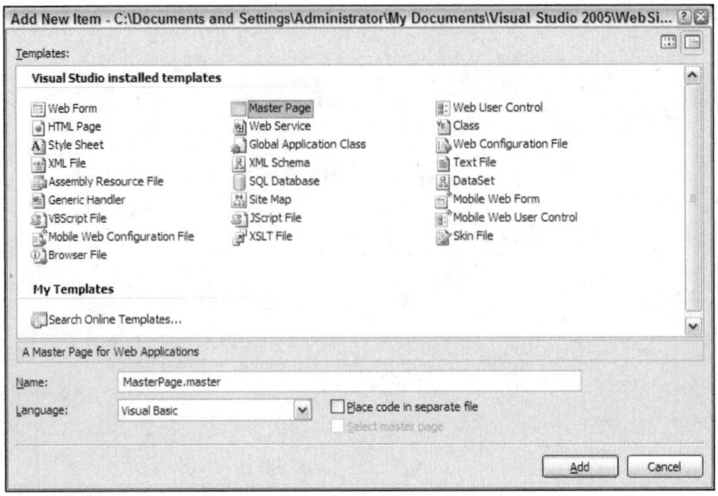

Figure 8-4

Because it's just like any other `.aspx` page, the Add New Item dialog enables you to choose from a master page using the inline coding model or a master page that places its code in a separate file. Not placing your server code in a separate file means that you use the inline code model for the page you are creating. This option creates a single `.master` page. Choosing the option to place your code in a separate file means that you use the new code-behind model with the page you are creating. Selecting the check box Place Code In Separate File creates a single `.master` page, along with an associated `.master` `.vb` or `.master.cs` file.

A sample master page that uses the inline-coding model is shown in Listing 8-1.

Listing 8-1: A sample master page

```
<%@ Master Language="VB" %>

<script runat="server">

</script>

<html xmlns="http://www.w3.org/1999/xhtml" >
<head runat="server">
    <title>My Company Master Page</title>
</head>
<body>
    <form id="form1" runat="server">
        <table cellpadding="3" border="1">
            <tr bgcolor="silver">
                <td colspan="2">
                    <h1>My Company Home Page</h1>
                </td>
            </tr>
            <tr>
```

```
                <td>
                    <asp:ContentPlaceHolder ID="ContentPlaceHolder1"
                     Runat="server">
                    </asp:ContentPlaceHolder>
                </td>
                <td>
                    <asp:ContentPlaceHolder ID="ContentPlaceHolder2"
                     Runat="server">
                    </asp:ContentPlaceHolder>
                </td>
            </tr>
            <tr>
                <td colspan="2">
                    Copyright 2006 - My Company
                </td>
            </tr>
        </table>
    </form>
</body>
</html>
```

This is a simple master page. The great thing about creating master pages in Visual Studio 2005 is that you can work with the master page in code view, but you can also switch over to design view to create your master pages.

Start by reviewing the code for the master page. The first line is the directive:

```
<%@ Master Language="VB" %>
```

Instead of using the Page directive, as you would with a typical .aspx page, you use the Master directive for a master page. This master page uses only a single attribute, Language. The Language attribute's value here is VB, but of course, you could also use C# if you are building a C# master page.

You code the rest of the master page just as you would any other .aspx page. You can use server controls, raw HTML and text, images, events, or anything else you normally would use for any .aspx page. This means that your master page can have a Page_Load event as well or any other event that you deem appropriate.

In the code shown in Listing 8-1, notice the use of a new server control — the <asp:ContentPlaceHolder> control. This control defines the areas of the template where the content page can place its content:

```
<tr>
    <td>
        <asp:ContentPlaceHolder ID="ContentPlaceHolder1"
         Runat="server">
        </asp:ContentPlaceHolder>
    </td>
    <td>
        <asp:ContentPlaceHolder ID="ContentPlaceHolder2"
         Runat="server">
        </asp:ContentPlaceHolder>
    </td>
</tr>
```

In the case of this master page, two defined areas exist where the content page can place content. Our master page contains a header and a footer area. It also defines two areas in the page where any inheriting content page can place its own content. Look at how a content page uses this master page.

Coding a Content Page

Now that you have a master page in place in your application, you can use this new template for any content pages in your application. Right-click the application in the Solution Explorer and choose Add New Item to create a new content page within your application.

To create a content page or a page that uses this master page as its template, you select a typical Web Form from the list of options in the Add New Item dialog. Instead of creating a typical Web Form, however, you check the Select Master Page check box. This gives you the option of associating this Web Form later to some master page. The Add New Item dialog is shown in Figure 8-5.

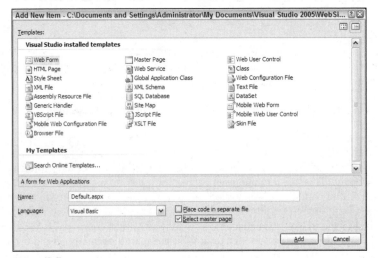

Figure 8-5

After you name your content page and click the Add button in the Add New Item dialog, you are presented with the Select A Master Page dialog, as shown in Figure 8-6.

This dialog allows you to choose the master page from which you want to build your content page. You choose from the available master pages that are contained within your application. For this example, select the new master page that you created in Listing 8-1 and click the OK button. This creates the content page. The created page is a simple .aspx page with only a single line of code contained in the file, as shown in Listing 8-2.

Listing 8-2: The created content page

```
<%@ Page Language="VB" MasterPageFile="~/Wrox.master" Title="Untitled Page" %>
```

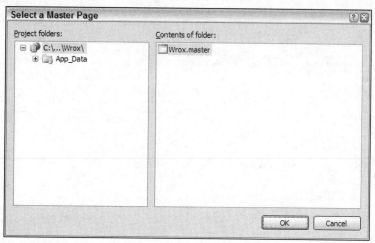

Figure 8-6

This content page is not much different from the typical .aspx page you coded in the past. The big difference is the inclusion of the MasterPageFile attribute within the Page directive. The use of this attribute indicates that this particular .aspx page inherits from another page. The location of the master page within the application is specified as the value of the MasterPageFile attribute.

The other big difference is that it contains neither the <form id="form1" runat="server"> tag nor any opening or closing HTML tags that would normally be included in a typical .aspx page.

This content page may seem simple, but if you switch to the design view within Visual Studio 2005, you see the power of using content pages. What you get with visual inheritance is shown in Figure 8-7.

In this screen shot, you can see that just by using the MasterFilePage attribute in the Page directive, you are able to visually inherit everything that the Wrox.master file exposes. All the common areas defined in the master page are shown in gray, whereas the content areas that you specified in the master page using the <asp:ContentPlaceHolder> server control are shown clearly and available for additional content in the content page. You can add any content to these defined content areas as if you were working with a regular .aspx page. An example of using this .master page for a content page is shown in Listing 8-3.

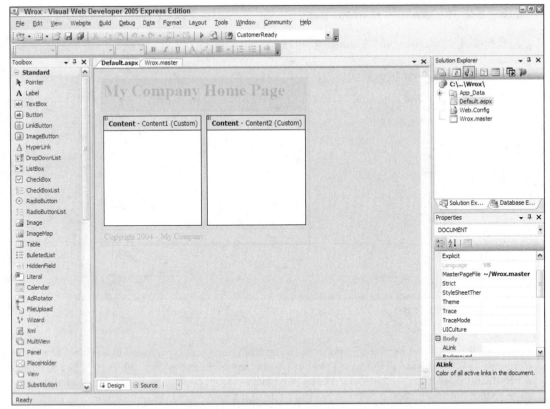

Figure 8-7

Listing 8-3: The content page that uses Wrox.master

VB

```vb
<%@ Page Language="VB" MasterPageFile="~/Wrox.master" %>

<script runat="server" language="vb">
    Protected Sub Button1_Click(ByVal sender As Object, ByVal e As System.EventArgs)
        Label1.Text = "<b>Hello " & TextBox1.Text & "!</b>"
    End Sub
</script>

<asp:Content ID="Content1" ContentPlaceHolderId="ContentPlaceHolder1"
 Runat="server">
    <b>Enter your name:</b><br />
    <asp:Textbox ID="TextBox1" Runat="server" />
    <br />
    <br />
    <asp:Button ID="Button1" Runat="server" Text="Submit"
```

```
        OnClick="Button1_Click" /><br />
    <br />
    <asp:Label ID="Label1" Runat="server" />
</asp:Content>

<asp:Content ID="Content2" ContentPlaceHolderId="ContentPlaceHolder2"
 Runat="server">
        <asp:Image ID="Image1" Runat="server" ImageUrl="wrox.gif" />
</asp:content>
```

C#

```
<%@ Page Language="C#" MasterPageFile="~/Wrox.master" %>

<script runat="server" language="c#">
    protected void Button1_Click(object sender, System.EventArgs e)
    {
        Label1.Text = "<b>Hello " + TextBox1.Text + "!</b>";
    }
</script>
```

Right away you see some differences. As stated before, this page has no `<form id="form1"` `runat="server">` tag nor any opening or closing HTML tags. These tags are not included because they are located in the master page. Also notice a new server control — the `<asp:Content>` server control.

```
<asp:Content ID="Content1" ContentPlaceHolderId="ContentPlaceHolder1"
 Runat="server">
    ...
</asp:Content>
```

The `<asp:Content>` server control is a defined content area that maps to a specific `<asp:ContentPlaceHolder>` server control on the master page. In this example, you can see that the `<asp:Content>` server control maps itself to the `<asp:ContentPlaceHolder>` server control in the master page that has the ID of ContentPlaceHolder1. Within the content page, you don't have to worry about specifying the location of the content because this is already defined within the master page. Therefore, your only concern is to place the appropriate content within the provided content sections, allowing the master page to do most of the work for you.

Just as when you work with any typical .aspx page, you can create any event handlers for your content page. In this case, you are using just a single event handler — the button-click when the end user submits the form. The created .aspx page that includes the master page and content page material is shown in Figure 8-8.

Mixing Page Types and Languages

One interesting point: When you use master pages, you are not tying yourself to a specific coding model (inline or code-behind), nor are you tying yourself to the use of a specific language. You can feel free to mix these elements within your application knowing that they all work well.

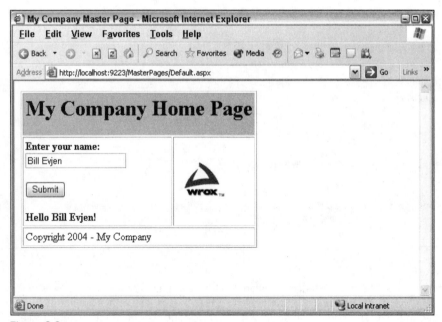

Figure 8-8

You could use the master page created earlier, knowing that it was created using the inline-coding model, and then build your content pages using the code-behind model. Listing 8-4 shows a content page created using a Web Form that uses the code-behind option.

Listing 8-4: A content page that uses that code-behind model

.aspx (VB)

```
<%@ Page Language="VB" MasterPageFile="~/Wrox.master" AutoEventWireup="false"
    CodeFile="MyContentPage.aspx.vb" Inherits="MyContentPage" %>

<asp:Content ID="Content1" ContentPlaceHolderId="ContentPlaceHolder1"
 Runat="server">
    <b>Enter your name:</b><br />
    <asp:Textbox ID="TextBox1" Runat="server" />
    <br />
    <br />
    <asp:Button ID="Button1" Runat="server" Text="Submit"
     OnClick="Button1_Click" /><br />
    <br />
    <asp:Label ID="Label1" Runat="server" />
</asp:Content>

<asp:Content ID="Content2" ContentPlaceHolderId="ContentPlaceHolder2"
 Runat="server">
        <asp:Image ID="Image1" Runat="server" ImageUrl="ineta.JPG" />
</asp:Content>
```

VB Code-Behind
```
Partial Class MyContentPage
    Inherits System.Web.UI.Page

    Protected Sub Button1_Click(ByVal sender As Object, ByVal e As System.EventArgs)
        Label1.Text = "<b>Hello " & TextBox1.Text & "!</b>"
    End Sub

End Class
```

C# Code-Behind
```
public partial class MyContentPage : System.Web.UI.Page
{
    protected void Button1_Click (object sender, System.EventArgs e)
    {
        Label1.Text = "<b>Hello " + TextBox1.Text + "!</b>";
    }
}
```

Even though the master page is using the inline-coding model, you can easily create content pages (such as the page shown in Listing 8-4) that use the code-behind model. The pages will still work perfectly.

Not only can you mix the coding models when using master pages, you can also mix the programming languages you use for the master or content pages. Just because you build a master page in C# doesn't mean that you are required to use C# for all the content pages that use this master page. You can also build content pages in Visual Basic. For a good example, create a master page in C# that uses the Page_Load event handler and then create a content page in Visual Basic. Once it's complete, run the page. It works perfectly well. This means that even though you might have a master page in one of the available .NET languages, the programming teams that build applications from the master page can use whatever .NET language they want. You have to love the openness that the .NET Framework offers!

Specifying Which Master Page to Use

You just observed that it is pretty easy to specify at page level which master page to use. In the Page directive of the content page, you simply use the MasterPageFile attribute:

```
<%@ Page Language="VB" MasterPageFile="~/Wrox.master" %>
```

Besides specifying the master page that you want to use at the page level, you have a second way to specify which master page you want to use in the Web.config file of the application. This is shown in Listing 8-5.

Listing 8-5: Specifying the master page in the Web.config file

```
<configuration>
    <system.web>
        <pages masterPageFile="~/Wrox.master" />
    </system.web>
</configuration>
```

Specifying the master page in the `Web.config` file causes every single content page you create in the application to inherit from the specified master page. If you declare your master page in the `Web.config` file, you can create any number of content pages that use this master page. Once specified in this manner, the content page's `Page` directive can then be constructed in the following manner:

```
<%@ Page Language="VB" %>
```

You can easily override the application-wide master page specification by simply declaring a different master page within your content page:

```
<%@ Page Language="VB" MasterPageFile="~/MyOtherCompany.master" %>
```

By specifying the master page in the `Web.config`, you are really not saying that you want *all* the `.aspx` pages to use this master page. If you create a normal Web Form and run it, ASP.NET will know that the page is not a content page and will run the page as a normal `.aspx` page.

If you want to apply the master page template to only a specific subset of pages (such as pages contained within a specific folder of your application), you can use the `<location>` element within the `Web.config` file, as illustrated in Listing 8-6.

Listing 8-6: Specifying the master page for a specific folder in the Web.config file

```
<configuration>

    <location path="AdministrationArea">
        <system.web>
            <pages masterPageFile="~/WroxAdmin.master" />
        </system.web>
    </location>

</configuration>
```

With the addition of this `<location>` section in the `Web.config` file, you have now specified that a specific folder (`AdministrationArea`) will use a different master file template. This is done using the path attribute of the `<location>` element. The value of the `path` attribute can be a folder name as shown, or it can even be a specific page — such as `AdminPage.aspx`.

Working with the Page Title

When you create content pages in your application, by default all the content pages automatically use the title that is declared in the master page. For instance, you have primarily been using a master page with the title `My Company Master Page`. Every content page that is created using this particular master page also uses the same `My Company Master Page` title. You can avoid this by specifying the page's title using the `Title` attribute in the `@Page` directive in the content page. You can also work with the page title programmatically in your content pages. To accomplish this, in the code of the content page, you use the `Master` object. The `Master` object conveniently has a property called `Title`. The value of this property is the page title that is used for the content page. You code it as shown in Listing 8-7.

Listing 8-7: Coding a custom page title for the content page

VB

```
<%@ Page Language="VB" MasterPageFile="~/Wrox.master" %>

<script runat="server" language="vb">
    Protected Sub Page_LoadComplete(ByVal sender As Object, _
        ByVal e As System.EventArgs)

        Master.Page.Title = "This page was generated on: " & _
            DateTime.Now.ToString()
    End Sub
</script>
```

C#

```
<%@ Page Language="C#" MasterPageFile="~/wrox.master" %>

<script runat="server">
    protected void Page_LoadComplete(object sender, EventArgs e)
    {
        Master.Page.Title = "This page was generated on: " +
            DateTime.Now.ToString();
    }
</script>
```

Working with Controls and Properties from the Master Page

When working with master pages from a content page, you actually have good access to the controls and the properties that the master page exposes. The master page, when inherited by the content page, exposes a property called `Master`. You use this property to get at control values or custom properties that are contained in the master page itself.

To see an example of this, create a GUID (unique identifier) in the master page that you can retrieve on the content page that is using the master. For this example, use the master page that was created in Listing 8-1, but add a Label server control and the `Page_Load` event (see Listing 8-8).

Listing 8-8: A master page that creates a GUID on the first request

VB

```
<%@ Master Language="VB" %>

<script runat="server">
    Protected Sub Page_Load(ByVal sender As Object, ByVal e As System.EventArgs)
        If Not Page.IsPostBack Then
            Label1.Text = System.Guid.NewGuid().ToString()
        End If
    End Sub
</script>

<html xmlns="http://www.w3.org/1999/xhtml" >
```

(continued)

Listing 8-8: *(continued)*

```
<head runat="server">
    <title>My Company Master Page</title>
</head>
<body>
    <form id="form1" runat="server">
        <table cellpadding="3" border="1">
            <tr bgcolor="silver">
                <td colspan="2">
                    <h1>My Company Home Page</h1>
                    <b>User's GUID:  
                        <asp:Label ID="Label1" Runat="server" /></b>
                </td>
            </tr>
            <tr>
                <td>
                    <asp:ContentPlaceHolder ID="ContentPlaceHolder1"
                     Runat="server">
                    </asp:ContentPlaceHolder>
                </td>
                <td>
                    <asp:ContentPlaceHolder ID="ContentPlaceHolder2"
                     Runat="server">
                    </asp:ContentPlaceHolder>
                </td>
            </tr>
            <tr>
                <td colspan="2">
                    Copyright 2006 - My Company
                </td>
            </tr>
        </table>
    </form>
</body>
</html>
```

C#

```
protected void Page_Load(object sender, EventArgs e)
{
    if (!Page.IsPostBack)
    {
        Label1.Text = System.Guid.NewGuid().ToString();
    }
}
```

Now you have a Label control on the master page that you can access from the content page. You have a couple of ways to accomplish this task. The first is to use the `FindControl` method that the master page exposes. This approach is shown in Listing 8-9.

Listing 8-9: Getting at the Label's Text value in the content page

VB

```
<%@ Page Language="VB" MasterPageFile="~/Wrox.master" %>

<script runat="server" language="vb">
    Protected Sub Page_LoadComplete(ByVal sender As Object, _
        ByVal e As System.EventArgs)

        Label1.Text = CType(Master.FindControl("Label1"), Label).Text
    End Sub

    Protected Sub Button1_Click(ByVal sender As Object, _
        ByVal e As System.EventArgs)

        Label2.Text = "<b>Hello " & TextBox1.Text & "!</b>"
    End Sub
</script>

<asp:Content ID="Content1" ContentPlaceHolderId="ContentPlaceHolder1"
 Runat="server">
    <b>Your GUID number from the master page is:<br />
    <asp:Label ID="Label1" Runat="server" /></b><p>
    <b>Enter your name:</b><br />
    <asp:Textbox ID="TextBox1" Runat="server" />
    <br />
    <br />
    <asp:Button ID="Button1" Runat="server" Text="Submit"
     OnClick="Button1_Click" /><br />
    <br />
    <asp:Label ID="Label2" Runat="server" />
</asp:content>

<asp:Content ID="Content2" ContentPlaceHolderId="ContentPlaceHolder2"
 Runat="server">
        <asp:Image ID="Image1" Runat="server" ImageUrl="Wrox.gif" />
</asp:Content>
```

C#

```
<%@ Page Language="C#" MasterPageFile="~/wrox.master" %>

<script runat="server">

    protected void Page_LoadComplete(object sender, EventArgs e)
    {
        Label1.Text = (Master.FindControl("Label1") as Label).Text;
    }

    protected void Button1_Click(object sender, EventArgs e)
    {
        Label2.Text = "<b>Hello " + TextBox1.Text + "!</b>";
    }
</script>
```

In this example, the master page in Listing 8-8 first creates a GUID that it stores as a text value in a Label server control on the master page itself. The ID of this Label control is Label1. The master page generates this GUID only on the first request for this particular content page. From here, you then populate one of the content page's controls with this value.

The interesting thing about the content page is that you put code in the Page_LoadComplete event handler so that you can get at the GUID value that is on the master page. This new event in ASP.NET 2.0 fires immediately after the Page_Load event fires. Event ordering is covered later, but the Page_Load event in the content page always fires before the Page_Load event in the master page. In order to get at the newly created GUID (if it is created in the master page's Page_Load event), you have to get the GUID in an event that comes after the Page_Load event — and that is where the Page_LoadComplete comes into play. So within the content page's Page_LoadComplete event, you populate a Label server control within the content page itself. Note that the Label control in the content page has the same ID as the Label control in the master page, but this doesn't make a difference. You can differentiate between them with the use of the Master property.

Not only can you get at the server controls that are in the master page in this way, you can get at any custom properties that the master page might expose as well. Look at the master page shown in Listing 8-10; it uses a custom property for the <h1> section of the page.

Listing 8-10: A master page that exposes a custom property

VB

```
<%@ Master Language="VB" %>

<script runat="server">
    Protected Sub Page_Load(ByVal sender As Object, ByVal e As System.EventArgs)
        If Not Page.IsPostBack Then
            Label1.Text = Guid.NewGuid().ToString()
        End If
    End Sub

    Dim m_PageHeadingTitle As String = "My Company"

    Public Property PageHeadingTitle() As String
        Get
            Return m_PageHeadingTitle
        End Get
        Set(ByVal Value As String)
            m_PageHeadingTitle = Value
        End Set
    End Property
</script>

<html xmlns="http://www.w3.org/1999/xhtml" >
<head id="Head1" runat="server">
    <title>My Company Master Page</title>
</head>
<body>
    <form id="Form1" runat="server">
        <table cellpadding="3" border="1">
            <tr bgcolor="silver">
                <td colspan="2">
```

```
            <h1><%= PageHeadingTitle() %></h1>
            <b>User's GUID:  
                <asp:Label ID="Label1" Runat="server" /></b>
        </td>
    </tr>
    <tr>
        <td>
            <asp:ContentPlaceHolder ID="ContentPlaceHolder1"
             Runat="server">
            </asp:ContentPlaceHolder>
        </td>
        <td>
            <asp:ContentPlaceHolder ID="ContentPlaceHolder2"
             Runat="server">
            </asp:ContentPlaceHolder>
        </td>
    </tr>
    <tr>
        <td colspan="2">
            Copyright 2004 - My Company
        </td>
    </tr>
</table>
    </form>
</body>
</html>
```

C#

```
<%@ Master Language="C#" %>

<script runat="server">
    protected void Page_Load(object sender, EventArgs e)
    {
        if (!Page.IsPostBack)
        {
            Label1.Text = System.Guid.NewGuid().ToString();
        }
    }

    string m_PageHeadingTitle = "My Company";

    public string PageHeadingTitle
    {
        get
        {
            return m_PageHeadingTitle;
        }
        set
        {
            m_PageHeadingTitle = value;
        }
    }
</script>
```

In this master page example, the master page is exposing the property you created called
PageHeadingTitle(). A default value of "My Company" is assigned to this property. You then place it
within the HTML of the master page file between some <h1> elements. This makes the default value
become the heading used on the page within the master page template. Although the master page
already has a value it uses for the heading, any content page that is using this master page can override
the <h1> title heading. The process is shown in Listing 8-11.

Listing 8-11: A content page that overrides the property from the master page

VB
```vb
<%@ Page Language="VB" MasterPageFile="~/Wrox.master" %>
<%@ MasterType VirtualPath="~/Wrox.master" %>

<script runat="server" language="vb">
    Protected Sub Page_Load(ByVal sender As Object, ByVal e As System.EventArgs)
        Master.PageHeadingTitle = "My Company - Division X"
    End Sub
</script>
```

C#
```csharp
<%@ Page Language="C#" MasterPageFile="~/Wrox.master" %>
<%@ MasterType VirtualPath="~/Wrox.master" %>

<script runat="server">
    protected void Page_Load(object sender, EventArgs e)
    {
        Master.PageHeadingTitle = "My Company - Division X";
    }
</script>
```

From the content page, you can assign a value to the property that is exposed from the master page by
the use of the Master property. As you can see, this is quite simple to do. Remember that not only can
you get at any public properties that the master page might expose, but you can also retrieve any methods that the master page contains as well.

Earlier, we showed you how to get at the server controls that are on the master page by using the
FindControl method. The FindControl method works fine, but it is a late-bound approach, and as
such, the method call may fail if the control was removed from markup. Use defensive coding practices
and always check for null when returning objects from FindControl. Using the mechanics just illustrated (with the use of public properties shown in Listing 8-10), you have another approach to expose
any server controls on the master page. You may find this approach to be more effective.

To do this, you simply expose the server control as a public property as shown in Listing 8-12.

Listing 8-12: Exposing a server control from a master page as a public property

VB
```vb
<%@ Master Language="VB" %>

<script runat="server" language="vb">
    Public Property MasterPageLabel1() As Label
        Get
```

```
                    Return Label1
            End Get
            Set(ByVal Value As Label)
                Label1 = Value
            End Set
        End Property
    </script>
```

C#
```
<%@ Master Language="VB" %>
```

```
<script runat="server" language="C#">
    public Label MasterPageLabel
    {
        get
        {
            return Label1;
        }
        set
        {
            Label1 = value;
        }
    }
</script>
```

In this case, a public property called MasterPageLabel returns an instance of the Label control that uses the ID of Label1. You can now create an instance of the MasterPageLabel property on the content page and override any of the attributes of the Label server control. So if you want to increase the size of the GUID that the master page creates and displays in the Label1 server control, you can simply override the Font.Size attribute of the Label control as shown in Listing 8-13.

Listing 8-13: Overriding an attribute from the Label control that is on the master page

VB
```
<%@ Page Language="VB" MasterPageFile="~/Wrox.master" %>
<%@ MasterType VirtualPath="~/Wrox.master" %>

<script runat="server" language="vb">
    Protected Sub Page_Load(ByVal sender As Object, ByVal e As System.EventArgs)
        Master.MasterPageLabel1.Font.Size = 25
    End Sub
</script>
```

C#
```
<%@ Page Language="C#" MasterPageFile="~/Wrox.master" %>
<%@ MasterType VirtualPath="~/Wrox.master" %>

<script runat="server" language="C#">
    protected void Page_Load(object sender, EventArgs e)
    {
        Master.MasterPageLabel1.Font.Size = 25;
    }
</script>
```

This approach may be the most effective way to get at any server controls that the master page exposes to the content pages.

Specifying Default Content in the Master Page

As you have seen, the master page enables you to specify content areas that the content page can use. Master pages can consist of just one content area, or they can be made up of multiple content areas. The nice thing about content areas is that when you create a master page, you can specify default content for the content area. This default content can then be left in place and utilized by the content page if you choose not to override it. Listing 8-14 shows a master page that specifies some default content within a content area.

Listing 8-14: Specifying default content in the master page

```
<%@ Master Language="VB" %>

<html xmlns="http://www.w3.org/1999/xhtml" >
<head runat="server">
    <title>My Company</title>
</head>
<body>
    <form id="form1" runat="server">
        <asp:ContentPlaceHolder ID="ContentPlaceHolder1" Runat="server">
        Here is some default content
        </asp:ContentPlaceHolder><p>
        <asp:ContentPlaceHolder ID="ContentPlaceHolder2" Runat="server">
        Here is some more default content
        </asp:ContentPlaceHolder></p>
    </form>
</body>
</html>
```

To place default content within one of the content areas of the master page, you simply put it in the ContentPlaceHolder server control on the master page itself. Any content page that inherits this master page also inherits the default content. Listing 8-15 shows a content page that overrides just one of the content areas from this master page.

Listing 8-15: Overriding some default content in the content page

```
<%@ Page Language="VB" MasterPageFile="~/MasterPage.master" %>

<asp:Content ID="Content2" ContentPlaceHolderId="ContentPlaceHolder2"
 Runat="server">
    This is new content
</asp:Content>
```

This code creates a page with one content area that shows content coming from the master page itself, in addition to other content that comes from the content page (see Figure 8-9).

Figure 8-9

The other interesting point when you work with content areas in the design mode of Visual Studio 2005 is that the smart tag allows you to work easily with the default content (shown in Figure 8-10).

When you first start working with the content page, the option in the smart tag is to create new content. This option enables you to override the master page content and insert your own defined content. After you have placed some custom content inside the content area, the smart tag shows a different option — Default to Master's Content. This option enables you to return the default content that the master page exposes to the content area and to erase whatever content you have already placed in the content area — thereby simply returning to the default content.

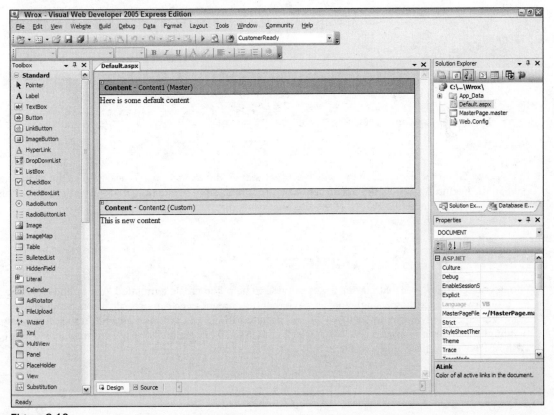

Figure 8-10

Programmatically Assigning the Master Page

From any content page, you can easily assign a master page programmatically. You assign the master page to the content page through the use of the `Page.MasterPageFile` property. This can be used regardless of whether another master page is already assigned in the `@Page` directive.

To accomplish this, you use this property through the `Page_PreInit` event. The `Page_PreInit` event is the earliest point in which you can access the Page lifecycle. For this reason, this is where you need to assign any master page that is used by any content pages. The `Page_PreInit` is an important event to make note of when you are working with master pages, as this is the only point where you can affect both the master and content page before they are combined into a single instance. Listing 8-16 illustrates how to assign the master page programmatically from the content page.

Listing 8-16: Using Page_PreInit to assign the master page programmatically

VB
```
<%@ Page Language="VB" %>

<script runat="server">
    Protected Sub Page_PreInit(ByVal sender As Object, ByVal e As System.EventArgs)
        Page.MasterPageFile = "~/MyMasterPage.master"
    End Sub
</script>
```

C#
```
<%@ Page Language="C#" %>

<script runat="server">
    protected void Page_PreInit(object sender, EventArgs e)
    {
        Page.MasterPageFile = "~/MyMasterPage.master";
    }
</script>
```

In this case, when the page is dynamically being generated, the master page is assigned to the content page in the beginning of the page construction process. It is important to note that the content page must have the expected Content controls; otherwise an error is thrown.

Nesting Master Pages

I hope you see the power that master pages provide to help you create templated Web applications. So far, you have been creating a single master page that the content page can use. Most companies and organizations, however, are not just two layers. Many divisions and groups exist within the organization that might want to use variations of the master by, in effect, having a master page within a master page. With ASP.NET 2.0, this is quite possible.

For example, imagine that Reuters is creating a master page to be used throughout the entire company intranet. Not only does the Reuters enterprise want to implement this master page company-wide, but various divisions within Reuters also want to provide templates for the subsections of the intranet directly under their control. Reuters Europe and Reuters America, for example, each wants its own unique master page, as illustrated in Figure 8-11.

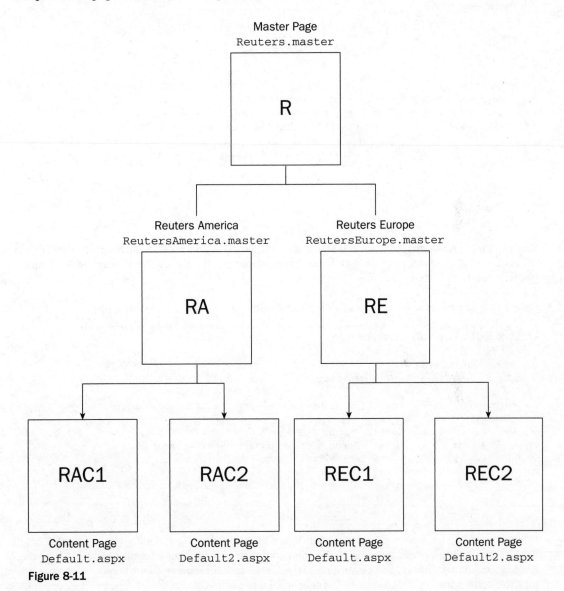

Figure 8-11

To do this, the creators of the Reuters Europe and Reuters America master pages simply create a master page that inherits from the global master page. All the files are shown here, starting with Listing 8-17.

Listing 8-17: The main master page

ReutersMain.master

```
<%@ Master Language="VB" %>

<html xmlns="http://www.w3.org/1999/xhtml" >
<head runat="server">
    <title>Reuters</title>
</head>
<body>
    <form id="form1" runat="server">
        <p><asp:Label ID="Label1" Runat="server" BackColor="LightGray"
            BorderColor="Black" BorderWidth="1px" BorderStyle="Solid"
            Font-Size="XX-Large">Reuters</asp:Label></p>
        <asp:ContentPlaceHolder ID="ContentPlaceHolder1" Runat="server">
        </asp:ContentPlaceHolder>
    </form>
</body>
</html>
```

This is a simple master page, but excellent for showing you how this nesting capability works. The main master page is the master page used globally in the company. It has the ContentPlaceHolder server control with the ID of ContentPlaceHolder1.

Listing 8-18 illustrates how you can work with this main master from a sub-master file.

Listing 8-18: The sub-master page

ReutersEurope.master

```
<%@ Master MasterPageFile="~/ReutersMain.master" %>

<asp:Content ID="Content1" ContentPlaceHolderId="ContentPlaceHolder1"
  Runat="server">
    <asp:Label ID="Label1" Runat="server" BackColor="#E0E0E0" BorderColor="Black"
    BorderStyle="Dotted" BorderWidth="2px" Font-Size="Large">
    Reuters Europe</asp:Label><br /><hr />

        <asp:ContentPlaceHolder ID="ContentPlaceHolder2" Runat="server">
        </asp:ContentPlaceHolder>
</asp:Content>
```

When creating the submaster page, notice that Visual Studio 2005 isn't as friendly when it creates this file for you. This is because Visual Studio 2005 is not expecting the creation of a submaster page. Therefore, to create your submaster page, first create a normal master page and remove all the content in the file except for the directive line. Then you create a Content server control.

The objects that you place in the content area defined with this Content control are actually placed in the defined content area within the master page. You can see this by using the ContentPlaceHolderId attribute of the Content control. This attribute is tying this content area to the content area `ContentPlaceHolder1`, which is defined in the master page.

Within this submaster page, you can also now use as many ContentPlaceHolder server controls as you want. Any content page that uses this master can use these controls. Listing 8-19 shows a content page that uses this submaster page, `ReutersEurope.master`.

Listing 8-19: The content page

Default.aspx

```
<%@ Page Language="VB" MasterPageFile="~/ReutersEurope.master" %>

<asp:Content ID="Content1" ContentPlaceHolderId="ContentPlaceHolder2"
 Runat="server">
    Hello World
</asp:Content>
```

As you can see, in this content page the value of the `MasterPageFile` attribute in the `Page` directive is the sub-master page that you created. Inheriting the `ReutersEurope` master page actually combines both master pages (`ReutersMain.master` and `ReutersEurope.master`) into a single master page. The Content control in this content page points to the content area defined in the submaster page as well. You can see this with the use of the `ContentPlaceHolderId` attribute. In the end, you get a very non-artistic page, as shown in Figure 8-12.

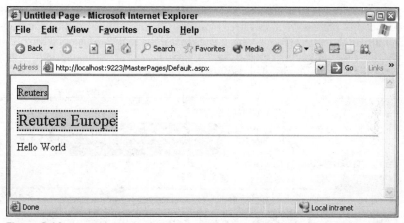

Figure 8-12

Creating a content page that uses a submaster page works pretty well. One negative point is that Visual Studio 2005 has issues with this construct, and you cannot work in the design mode when creating your content page.

Container-Specific Master Pages

In many cases, developers are building applications that will be viewed in a multitude of different containers. Some viewers may view the application in Microsoft Internet Explorer and some might view it using Opera or Netscape Navigator. And still other viewers may call up the application on a Pocket PC or Nokia cell phone.

For this reason, ASP.NET 2.0 allows you to use multiple master pages within your content page. Depending on the viewing container used by the end user, the ASP.NET engine pulls the appropriate master file. Therefore, you want to build container-specific master pages to provide your end users with the best possible viewing experience by taking advantage of the features that a specific container provides. The capability to use multiple master pages is demonstrated in Listing 8-20.

Listing 8-20: A content page that can work with more than one master page

```
<%@ Page Language="VB" MasterPageFile="~/Wrox.master"
        Mozilla:MasterPageFile="~/WroxMozilla.master"
        Opera:MasterPageFile="~/WroxOpera.master" %>

<asp:Content ID="Content1" ContentPlaceHolderId="ContentPlaceHolder1"
  Runat="server">
    Hello World
</asp:Content>
```

As you can see from this example content page, it can work with three different master page files. The first one uses the attribute `MasterPageFile`. This is the default setting used for any page that doesn't fit the criteria for any of the other options. This means that if the requestor is not a Mozilla or Opera browser, the default master page, `Wrox.master`, is used. However, if the requestor is an Opera browser, `WroxOpera.master` is used instead. This is illustrated in Figure 8-13.

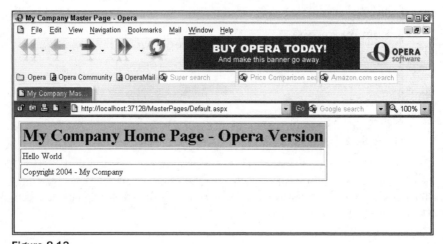

Figure 8-13

You can find a list of available browsers on the production server where the application will be hosted at `C:\Windows\Microsoft.NET\Framework\v2.0.50727\CONFIG\Browsers`. Some of the available options include the following:

- ❑ avantgo
- ❑ cassio
- ❑ Default
- ❑ docomo
- ❑ ericsson
- ❑ EZWap
- ❑ gateway
- ❑ generic
- ❑ goAmerica
- ❑ ie
- ❑ Jataayu
- ❑ jphone
- ❑ legend
- ❑ MME
- ❑ mozilla
- ❑ netscape
- ❑ nokia
- ❑ openwave
- ❑ opera
- ❑ palm
- ❑ panasonic
- ❑ pie
- ❑ webtv
- ❑ winwap
- ❑ xiino

Of course, you can also add any additional .browser files that you deem necessary.

Event Ordering

When you work with master pages and content pages, both can use the same events (such as Page_Load). Be sure you know which events come before others. You are bringing two classes together to create a single page class, and a specific order is required. When an end user requests a content page in the browser, the event ordering is the following:

- ❑ **Master page child controls initialization:** All server controls contained within the master page are first initialized.
- ❑ **Content page child controls initialization:** All server controls contained in the content page are initialized.
- ❑ **Master page initialization:** The master page itself is initialized.
- ❑ **Content page initialization:** The content page is initialized.
- ❑ **Content page load:** The content page is loaded (this is the Page_Load event followed by the Page_LoadComplete event).
- ❑ **Master page load:** The master page is loaded (this is also the Page_Load event followed by the Page_LoadComplete event).
- ❑ **Master page child controls load:** The server controls on the master page are loaded onto the page.
- ❑ **Content page child controls load:** The server controls on the content page are loaded onto the page.

Pay attention to this event ordering when building your applications. If you want to use server control values that are contained on the master page within a specific content page, for example, you can't retrieve the values of these server controls from within the content page's Page_Load event. This is because this event is triggered before the master page's Page_Load event. This problem prompted the creation of the new Page_LoadComplete event. The content page's Page_LoadComplete event follows the master page's Page_Load event. You can, therefore, use this ordering to get at values from the master page even though it isn't populated when the content page's Page_Load event is triggered.

Caching with Master Pages

When working with typical .aspx pages, you can apply output caching to the page by using the following construct (or variation thereof):

```
<%@ OutputCache Duration="10" Varybyparam="None" %>
```

This caches the page in the server's memory for 10 seconds. Many developers use output caching to increase the performance of their ASP.NET pages. It also makes a lot of sense for use on pages with data that doesn't become stale too quickly.

How do you go about applying output caching to ASP.NET pages when working with master pages? First, you cannot apply caching to just the master page. You cannot put the OutputCache directive on the master page itself. If you do so, on the page's second retrieval, you get an error because the application cannot find the cached page.

To work with output caching when using a master page, stick the OutputCache directive in the content page. This caches both the contents of the content page as well as the contents of the master page (remember, it is just a single page at this point). The OutputCache directive placed in the master page does not cause the master page to produce an error, but it won't be cached. This directive works in the content page only.

Summary

When you create applications that use a common header, footer, or navigation section on pretty much every page of the application, master pages are a great solution. Master pages are easy to implement and enable you to make changes to each and every page of your application by changing a single file. Imagine how much easier this makes managing large applications that contain thousands of pages.

This chapter described master pages in ASP.NET 2.0 and explained how you build and use master pages within your Web applications. In addition to the basics, the chapter covered master page event ordering, caching, and specific master pages for specific containers. In the end, when you are working with templated applications, master pages should be your first option — the power of this approach is immense.

Themes and Skins

When you build a Web application, it usually has a similar look-and-feel across all its pages. Not too many applications are designed with each page dramatically different from the next. Generally, for your applications, you use similar fonts, colors, and server control styles across all the pages.

You can apply these common styles individually to each and every server control or object on each page, or you can use a new capability provided by ASP.NET 2.0 to centrally specify these styles. All pages or parts of pages in the application can then access them.

Themes are the text-based style definitions in ASP.NET 2.0 that are the focus of this chapter.

Using ASP.NET 2.0 Themes

Themes are similar to Cascading Style Sheets (CSS) in that they enable you to define visual styles for your Web pages. Themes go further than CSS, however, in that they allow you to apply styles, graphics, and even CSS files themselves to the pages of your applications. You can apply ASP.NET themes at the application, page, or server control level.

Applying a Theme to a Single ASP.NET Page

In order to see how to use one of these themes, create a basic page, which includes some text, a text box, a button, and a calendar. This is shown in Listing 9-1.

Listing 9-1: An ASP.NET page that does not use themes

```
<%@ Page Language="VB" %>

<html xmlns="http://www.w3.org/1999/xhtml" >
<head runat="server">
    <title>INETA</title>
</head>
<body>
    <form id="form1" runat="server">
        <h1>International .NET Association (INETA)</h1><br />
        <asp:Textbox ID="TextBox1" Runat="server" /><br />
        <br />
        <asp:Calendar ID="Calendar1" Runat="server" /><br />
        <asp:Button ID="Button1" Runat="server" Text="Button" />
    </form>
</body>
</html>
```

This simple page shows some default server controls that appear just as you would expect, but that you can change with one of these new ASP.NET themes. When this theme-less page is called in the browser, it should look like Figure 9-1.

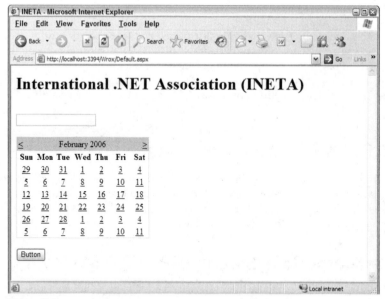

Figure 9-1

You can instantly change the appearance of this page without changing the style of each server control on the page. From within the Page directive, you simply apply an ASP.NET theme that you have either built (shown later in this chapter) or downloaded from the Internet:

```
<%@ Page Language="VB" Theme="SmokeAndGlass" %>
```

Adding the Theme attribute to the Page directive changes the appearance of everything on the page that is defined in an example SmokeAndGlass theme file. Using this theme, when I invoked the page in the browser, I got the result shown in Figure 9-2.

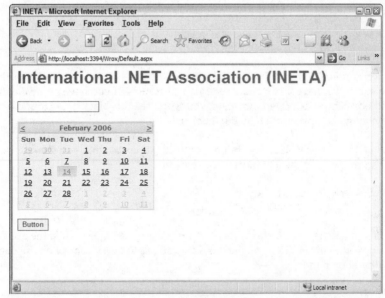

Figure 9-2

From here, you can see that everything — including the font, font color, text box, button, and more — has changed appearance. If you have multiple pages, you may find that it's nice not to have to think about applying styles to everything you do as you build because the styles are already centrally defined for you.

Applying a Theme to an Entire Application

In addition to applying an ASP.NET 2.0 theme to your ASP.NET pages using the Theme attribute within the Page directive, you can also apply it at an application level from the Web.config file. This is illustrated in Listing 9-2.

Listing 9-2: Applying a theme application-wide from the Web.config file

```
<?xml version="1.0" encoding="UTF-8" ?>

<configuration>
    <system.web>
        <pages theme="SmokeAndGlass" />
    </system.web>
</configuration>
```

If you specify the theme in the Web.config file, you don't need to define the theme again in the Page directive of your ASP.NET pages. This theme is applied automatically to each and every page within your application.

Removing Themes from Server Controls

Whether themes are set at the application level or on a page, at times you want an alternative to the theme that has been defined. For example, change the text box server control that you have been working with (from Listing 9-1) by making its background black and using white text:

```
<asp:Textbox ID="TextBox1" Runat="server"
  BackColor="#000000" ForeColor="#ffffff" />
```

The black background color and the color of the text in the text box are specified directly in the control itself with the use of the `BackColor` and `ForeColor` attributes. If you have applied a theme to the page where this text box control is located, however, you won't see this black background or white text because these changes are overridden by the theme itself.

To apply a theme to your ASP.NET page but not to this text box control, you simply use the `EnableTheming` property of the text box server control:

```
<asp:Textbox ID="TextBox1" Runat="server"
  BackColor="#000000" ForeColor="#ffffff" EnableTheming="false" />
```

If you apply this property to the text box server control from Listing 9-1 while the `SmokeAndGlass` theme is still applied to the entire page, the theme is applied to every control on the page *except* the text box. This result is shown in Figure 9-3.

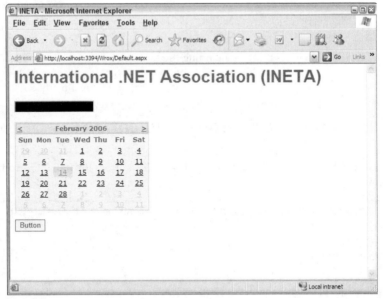

Figure 9-3

If you want to turn off theming for multiple controls within a page, consider using the Panel control to encapsulate a collection of controls and then set the `EnableTheming` attribute of the Panel control to `False`. This disables theming for each control contained within the Panel control.

Removing Themes from Web Pages

Now what if, when you set the theme for an entire application in the `Web.config` file, you want to exclude a single ASP.NET page? It is quite possible to remove a theme setting at the page level, just as it is at the server control level.

The `Page` directive includes an `EnableTheming` attribute that can be used to remove theming from your ASP.NET pages. To remove the theme that would be applied by the theme setting in the `Web.config`, you simply construct your `Page` directive in the following manner:

```
<%@ Page Language="VB" EnableTheming="False" %>
```

This construct sets the theme to nothing—thereby removing any settings that were specified in the `Web.config` file. When this directive is set to `False` at the page or control level, the `Theme` directory is not searched, and no `.skin` files are applied. When it is set to `True` at the page or control level, the `Theme` directory is searched and `.skin` files are applied.

If themes are disabled because the `EnableTheming` attribute is set to `False` at the page level, you can still enable theming for specific controls on this page by setting the `EnableTheming` property for the control to `True` and applying a specific theme at the same time, as illustrated here:

```
<asp:Textbox ID="TextBox1" Runat="server"
  BackColor="#000000" ForeColor="#ffffff" EnableTheming="true" Theme="Summer" />
```

Understanding the StyleSheetTheme Attribute

The `Page` directive also includes the attribute `StylesheetTheme` that you can use to apply themes to a page. So, the big question is: If you have a `Theme` attribute and a `StylesheetTheme` attribute for the `Page` directive, what is the difference between the two?

```
<%@ Page Language="VB" StylesheetTheme="Summer" %>
```

The `StylesheetTheme` attribute works the same as the `Theme` attribute in that it can be used to apply a theme to a page. The difference is that the when attributes are set locally on the page within a particular control, the attributes are overridden by the theme if you use the `Theme` attribute. They are kept in place, however, if you apply the page's theme using the `StylesheetTheme` attribute. Suppose you have a text box control like the following:

```
<asp:Textbox ID="TextBox1" Runat="server"
  BackColor="#000000" ForeColor="#ffffff" />
```

In this example, the `BackColor` and `ForeColor` settings are overridden by the theme if you have applied it using the `Theme` attribute in the `Page` directive. If, instead, you applied the theme using the `StylesheetTheme` attribute in the `Page` directive, the `BackColor` and `ForeColor` settings remain in place, even if they are explicitly defined in the theme.

Creating Your Own Themes

You will find that creating themes in ASP.NET is a rather simple process—although sometimes it does require some artistic capabilities. The themes you create can be applied at the application, page, or server control level. Themes are a great way to easily apply a consistent look-and-feel across your entire application.

Creating the proper folder structure

In order to create your own themes for an application, you first need to create the proper folder structure in your application. To do this, right-click your project and add a new folder. Name the folder App_Themes. You can also create this folder by right-clicking on your project in Visual Studio and selecting Add Folder ⇨ Theme Folder. Notice when you do this that the App_Themes folder does not have the typical folder icon next to it, but instead has a folder icon that includes a paint brush. This is shown in Figure 9-4.

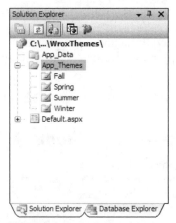

Figure 9-4

Within the App_Themes folder, you create an additional theme folder for each and every theme that you might use in your application. For instance, if you are going to have four themes—Summer, Fall, Winter, and Spring—then you create four folders that are named appropriately.

You might use more than one theme in your application for many reasons—season changes, day/night changes, different business units, category of user, or even user preferences.

Each theme folder must contain the elements of the theme, which can include the following:

❑ A single skin file

❑ CSS files

❑ Images

Creating a Skin

A *skin* is a definition of styles applied to the server controls in your ASP.NET page. Skins can work in conjunction with CSS files or images. To create a theme to use in your ASP.NET applications, you use just a single skin file in the theme folder. The skin file can have any name, but it must have a .skin file extension.

Even though you have four theme folders in your application, concentrate on the creation of the Summer theme for the purposes of this chapter. Right-click the Summer folder, select Add New Item, and select Skin File from the listed options. Name the file **Summer.skin**. Then complete the skin file as shown in Listing 9-3.

Listing 9-3: The Summer.skin file

```
<asp:Label Runat="server" ForeColor="#004000" Font-Names="Verdana"
           Font-Size="X-Small" />

<asp:Textbox Runat="server" ForeColor="#004000" Font-Names="Verdana"
             Font-Size="X-Small" BorderStyle="Solid" BorderWidth="1px"
             BorderColor="#004000" Font-Bold="True" />

<asp:Button Runat="server" ForeColor="#004000" Font-Names="Verdana"
            Font-Size="X-Small" BorderStyle="Solid" BorderWidth="1px"
            BorderColor="#004000" Font-Bold="True" BackColor="#FFE0C0" />
```

This is just a sampling of what the Summer.skin file should contain. To use it in a real application, you should actually make a definition for each and every server control option. In this case, you have a definition in place for three different types of server controls: Label, TextBox, and Button. After saving the Summer.skin file in the Summer folder, your file structure should resemble Figure 9-5 from the Solution Explorer of Visual Studio 2005.

Figure 9-5

Just like the regular server control definitions that you put on a typical `.aspx` page, these control definitions must contain the `Runat="server"` attribute. If you specify this attribute in the skinned version of the control, you also include it in the server control you put on an `.aspx` page that uses this theme. Also notice is that no ID attribute is specified in the skinned version of the control. If you specify an ID attribute here, you get an error when a page tries to use this theme.

As you can see, you supply a lot of different visual definitions to these three controls, and this should give the page a summery look and feel. An ASP.NET page in this project can simply use this custom theme as was shown earlier in this chapter (see Listing 9-4).

Listing 9-4: Using the Summer theme in an ASP.NET page

VB
```
<%@ Page Language="VB" Theme="Summer" %>

<script runat="server">
    Protected Sub Button1_Click(ByVal sender As Object, ByVal e As System.EventArgs)
        Label1.Text = "Hello " & TextBox1.Text
    End Sub
</script>

<html xmlns="http://www.w3.org/1999/xhtml" >
<head runat="server">
    <title>INETA</title>
</head>
<body>
    <form id="form1" runat="server">
        <asp:Textbox ID="TextBox1" Runat="server">
        </asp:Textbox>
        <br />
        <br />
        <asp:Button ID="Button1" Runat="server" Text="Submit Your Name"
         OnClick="Button1_Click" />
        <br />
        <br />
        <asp:Label ID="Label1" Runat="server" />
    </form>
</body>
</html>
```

C#
```
<%@ Page Language="C#" Theme="Summer" %>

<script runat="server">
    protected void Button1_Click(object sender, System.EventArgs e)
    {
        Label1.Text = "Hello " + TextBox1.Text.ToString();
    }
</script>
```

Looking at the server controls on this `.aspx` page, you can see that no styles are associated with them. These are just the default server controls that you drag and drop onto the design surface of Visual Studio 2005. There is, however, the style that you defined in the `Summer.skin` file, as shown in Figure 9-6.

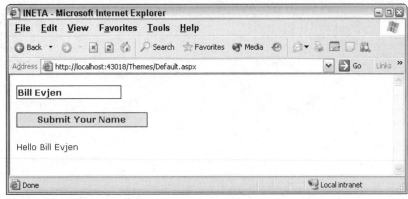

Figure 9-6

Including CSS Files in Your Themes

In addition to the server control definitions that you create from within a `.skin` file, you can make further definitions using Cascading Style Sheets (CSS). You might have noticed, when using a `.skin` file, that you could define only the styles associated with server controls and nothing else. But developers usually use quite a bit more than server controls in their ASP.NET pages. For instance, ASP.NET pages are routinely made up of HTML server controls, raw HTML, or even raw text. At present, the Summer theme has only a `Summer.skin` file associated with it. Any other items have no style whatsoever applied to them.

For a theme that goes beyond the server controls, you must further define the theme style so that HTML server controls, HTML, and raw text are all changed according to the theme. You achieve this with a CSS file within your `Themes` folder.

It is rather easy to create CSS files for your themes when using Visual Studio 2005. Right-click the `Summer` theme folder and select Add New Item. In the list of options, select the option Style Sheet and name it `Summer.css`. The `Summer.css` file should be sitting right next to your `Summer.skin` file. This creates an empty `.css` file for your theme. I won't go into the details of how to make a CSS file using Visual Studio 2005 and the CSS creation tool because this was covered earlier in the book. The process is the same as in previous versions of Visual Studio. Just remember that the dialog that comes with Visual Studio 2005 enables you to completely define your CSS page with no need to actually code anything. A sample dialog is shown in Figure 9-7.

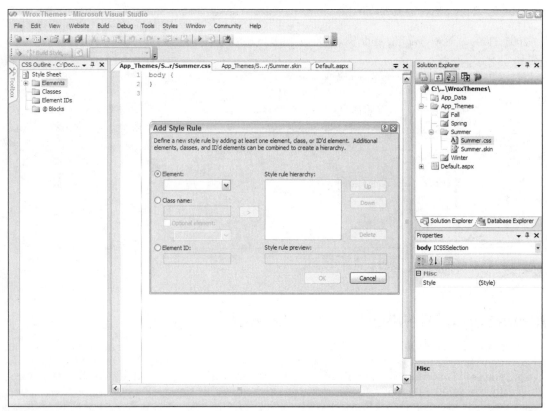

Figure 9-7

To create a comprehensive theme with this dialog, you define each HTML element that might appear in the ASP.NET page. This can be a lot of work, but it's worth it in the end. For now, create a small CSS file that changes some of the non-server control items on your ASP.NET page. This CSS file is shown in Listing 9-5.

Listing 9-5: A CSS file with some definitions

```css
body
{
  font-size: x-small;
  font-family: Verdana;
  color: #004000;
}

A:link {
  color: Blue;
  text-decoration: none;
}

A:visited
{
  color: Blue;
```

```
    text-decoration: none;
}

A:hover {
  color: Red;
  text-decoration: underline overline;
}
```

In this CSS file, four things are defined. First, you define text that is found within the <body> tag of the page (basically all the text). Plenty of text appears in a typical ASP.NET page that is not placed inside an <asp:Label> or <asp:Literal> tag. Therefore, you define how your text should appear; otherwise, your Web page may appear quite odd at times. In this case, a definition is in place for the size, the font family, and the color of the text. You make this definition the same as the one for the <asp:Label> server control in the Summer.skin file.

The next three definitions in this CSS file revolve around the <a> element (for hyperlinks). One cool feature that many Web pages use is responsive hyperlinks — or hyperlinks that change when you hover a mouse over them. The A:link definition defines what a typical link looks like on the page. The A:visited definition defines the look of the link if the end user has clicked on the link previously (without this definition, it is typically purple in IE). Then the A:hover definition defines the appearance of the hyperlink when the end user hovers the mouse over the link. You can see that not only are these three definitions changing the color of the hyperlink, but they are also changing how the underline is used. In fact, when the end user hovers the mouse over a hyperlink on a page using this CSS file, an underline and an overline appear on the link itself.

In CSS files, the order in which the style definitions appear in the .css file is important. This is an interpreted file — the first definition in the CSS file is applied first to the page, next the second definition is applied, and so forth. Some styles might change previous styles, so make sure your style definitions are in the proper order. For instance, if you put the A:hover style definition first, you would never see it. The A:link and A:visited definitions would supersede it because they are defined after it.

In working with your themes that include .css files, you must understand what they can and cannot do for you. For instance, examine an .aspx file that contains two text boxes — one text box created using a server control and another text box created using a typical <input> HTML element:

```
<asp:Textbox ID="TextBox1" Runat="server" /> 
<input type="text" />
```

Suppose you have a definition for the TextBox server control in the .skin file:

```
<asp:Textbox Runat="server" ForeColor="#004000" Font-Names="Verdana"
  BackColor="#ffffff" Font-Size="X-Small" BorderStyle="Solid" BorderWidth="1px"
  BorderColor="#004000" Font-Bold="True" />
```

But, what if you also have a definition in your .css file for each <input> element in the ASP.NET page as shown here:

```
INPUT
{
  background-color: black;
}
```

When you run the `.aspx` page with these kinds of style conflicts, the `.skin` file takes precedence over styles applied to every HTML element that is created using ASP.NET server controls regardless of what the `.css` file says. In fact, this sort of scenario gives you a page in which the `<input>` element that is created from the server control is white as defined in the `.skin` file and the second text box is black as defined in the `.css` file. This is shown in Figure 9-8.

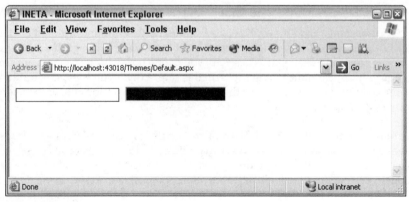

Figure 9-8

Having Your Themes Include Images

Probably one of the coolest reasons why themes, rather than CSS, are the better approach for applying a consistent style to your Web page is that themes enable you to incorporate actual images into the style definitions.

A lot of controls use images to create a better visual appearance. The first step in incorporating images into your server controls that consistently use themes is to create an `Images` folder within the `Themes` folder itself, as illustrated in Figure 9-9.

Figure 9-9

You have a couple of easy ways to use the images that you might place in this folder. The first is to incorporate the images directly from the `.skin` file itself. You can do this with the TreeView server control. The TreeView control can contain images used to open and close nodes for navigation purposes. You can place images in your theme for each and every TreeView control in your application. If you do so, you can then define the TreeView server control in the `.skin` file, as shown in Listing 9-6.

Listing 9-6: Using images from the theme folder in a TreeView server control

```
<asp:TreeView runat="server" BorderColor="#FFFFFF" BackColor="#FFFFFF"
    ForeColor="#585880" Font-Size=".9em" Font-Names="Verdana"
    LeafNodeImageURL="images\summer_iconlevel.gif"
    RootNodeImageURL="images\summer_iconmain.gif"
    ParentNodeImageURL="images\summer_iconmain.gif" NodeIndent="30"
    CollapseImageURL="images\summer_minus.gif"
    ExpandImageURL="images\summer_plus.gif">

    ...
</asp:TreeView>
```

When you run a page containing a TreeView server control, it is populated with the images held in the `Images` folder of the theme.

It's easy to incorporate images into the TreeView control. The control even specifically asks for an image location as an attribute. The new WebParts controls are used to build portals. Listing 9-7 is an example of a Web Part definition from a `.skin` file that incorporates images from the `Images` folder of the theme.

Listing 9-7: Using images from the theme folder in a WebPartZone server control

```
<asp:WebPartZone ID="WebPartZone1" runat="server"
 DragHighlightColor="#6464FE" BorderStyle="double"
 BorderColor="#E7E5DB" BorderWidth="2pt" BackColor="#F8F8FC"
 cssclass="theme_fadeblue" Font-Size=".9em" Font-Names="Verdana">
    <FooterStyle ForeColor="#585880" BackColor="#CCCCCC"></FooterStyle>
    <HelpVerb ImageURL="images/SmokeAndGlass_help.gif"
     checked="False" enabled="True" visible="True"></HelpVerb>
    <CloseVerb ImageURL="images/SmokeAndGlass_close.gif"
     checked="False" enabled="True" visible="True"></CloseVerb>
    <RestoreVerb ImageURL="images/SmokeAndGlass_restore.gif"
     checked="False" enabled="True" visible="True"></RestoreVerb>
    <MinimizeVerb ImageURL="images/SmokeAndGlass_minimize.gif"
     checked="False" enabled="True" visible="True"></MinimizeVerb>
    <EditVerb ImageURL="images/SmokeAndGlass_edit.gif"
     checked="False" enabled="True" visible="True"></EditVerb>
</asp:WebPartZone>
```

As you can see here, this series of toolbar buttons, which is contained in a WebPartZone control, now uses images that come from the aforementioned SmokeAndGlass theme. When this WebPartZone is then generated, the style is defined directly from the `.skin` file, but the images specified in the `.skin` file are retrieved from the `Images` folder in the theme itself.

Not all server controls enable you to work with images directly from the Themes folder by giving you an `image` attribute to work with. If you don't have this capability, you must work with the `.skin` file and the CSS file together. If you do, you can place your theme-based images in any element you want. Next is a good example of how to do this.

Place the image that you want to use in the `Images` folder just as you normally would. Then define the use of the images in the `.css` file. The continued `SmokeAndGlass` example in Listing 9-8 demonstrates this.

Listing 9-8: Part of the CSS file from SmokeAndGlass.css

```
theme_header {
background-image :url( images/smokeandglass_brownfadetop.gif);
}

.theme_highlighted {
background-image :url( images/smokeandglass_blueandwhitef.gif);
}

.theme_fadeblue {
background-image :url( images/smokeandglass_fadeblue.gif);
}
```

These are not styles for a specific HTML element; instead, they are CSS classes that you can put into any HTML element that you want. In this case, each CSS class mentioned here is defining a specific background image to use for the element.

After it is defined in the CSS file, you can utilize this CSS class in the `.skin` file when defining your server controls. Listing 9-9 shows you how.

Listing 9-9: Using the CSS class in one of the server controls defined in the .skin file

```
<asp:Calendar runat="server" BorderStyle="double" BorderColor="#E7E5DB"
 BorderWidth="2" BackColor="#F8F7F4" Font-Size=".9em" Font-Names="Verdana">
    <TodayDayStyle BackColor="#F8F7F4" BorderWidth="1" BorderColor="#585880"
     ForeColor="#585880" />
    <OtherMonthDayStyle BackColor="transparent" ForeColor="#CCCCCC" />
    <SelectedDayStyle ForeColor="#6464FE" BackColor="transparent"
     CssClass="theme_highlighted" />
    <TitleStyle Font-Bold="True" BackColor="#CCCCCC" ForeColor="#585880"
     BorderColor="#CCCCCC" BorderWidth="1pt" CssClass="theme_header" />
    <NextPrevStyle Font-Bold="True" ForeColor="#585880"
     BorderColor="transparent" BackColor="transparent" />
    <DayStyle ForeColor="#000000"
     BorderColor="transparent" BackColor="transparent" />
    <SelectorStyle Font-Bold="True" ForeColor="#696969" BackColor="#F8F7F4" />
    <WeekendDayStyle Font-Bold="False" ForeColor="#000000"
     BackColor="transparent" />
    <DayHeaderStyle Font-Bold="True" ForeColor="#585880"
     BackColor="Transparent" />
</asp:Calendar>
```

This Calendar server control definition from a `.skin` file uses one of the earlier CSS classes in its definition. It actually uses an image that is specified in the CSS file in two different spots within the control (shown in bold). It is first specified in the `<SelectedDayStyle>` element. Here you see the attribute and value `CssClass="theme_highlighted"`. The other spot is within the `<TitleStyle>` element. In this case, it is using `theme_header`. When the control is rendered, these CSS classes are referenced and finally point to the images that are defined in the CSS file.

It is interesting that the images used here for the header of the Calendar control don't really have much to them. For instance, the `smokeandglass_brownfadetop.gif` image that we are using for this example is simply a thin, gray sliver, as shown in Figure 9-10.

Figure 9-10

This very small image (in this case, very thin) is actually repeated as often as necessary to make it equal the length of the header in the Calendar control. The image is lighter at the top and darkens toward the bottom. Repeated horizontally, this gives a three-dimensional effect to the control. Try it out, and you get the result shown in Figure 9-11.

≤	February 2006					≥
Sun	Mon	Tue	Wed	Thu	Fri	Sat
29	30	31	1	2	3	4
5	6	7	8	9	10	11
12	13	14	15	16	17	18
19	20	21	22	23	24	25
26	27	28	1	2	3	4
5	6	7	8	9	10	11

Figure 9-11

Defining Multiple Skin Options

Using the themes technology in ASP.NET 2.0, you can have a single theme; but also, within the theme's `.skin` file, you can have specific controls that are defined in multiple ways. You can frequently take advantage of this feature within your themes. For instance, you might have text box elements scattered throughout your application, but you might not want each and every text box to have the same visual appearance. In this case, you can create multiple versions of the `<asp:Textbox>` server control within your `.skin` file. In Listing 9-10 you see how to create multiple versions of the `<asp:Textbox>` control in the `.skin` file from Listing 9-3.

Listing 9-10: The Summer.skin file, which contains multiple versions of the `<asp:Textbox>` server control

```
<asp:Label Runat="server" ForeColor="#004000" Font-Names="Verdana"
           Font-Size="X-Small" />

<asp:Textbox Runat="server" ForeColor="#004000" Font-Names="Verdana"
           Font-Size="X-Small" BorderStyle="Solid" BorderWidth="1px"
           BorderColor="#004000" Font-Bold="True" />

<asp:Textbox Runat="server" ForeColor="#000000" Font-Names="Verdana"
```

(continued)

Listing 9-10: *(continued)*

```
            Font-Size="X-Small" BorderStyle="Dotted" BorderWidth="5px"
            BorderColor="#000000" Font-Bold="False" SkinID="TextboxDotted" />

  <asp:Textbox Runat="server" ForeColor="#000000" Font-Names="Arial"
            Font-Size="X-Large" BorderStyle="Dashed" BorderWidth="3px"
            BorderColor="#000000" Font-Bold="False" SkinID="TextboxDashed" />

  <asp:Button Runat="server" ForeColor="#004000" Font-Names="Verdana"
            Font-Size="X-Small" BorderStyle="Solid" BorderWidth="1px"
            BorderColor="#004000" Font-Bold="True" BackColor="#FFE0C0" />
```

In this .skin file, you can see three definitions in place for the TextBox server control. The first one is the same as before. Although the second and third definitions have a different style, they also contain a new attribute in the definition—SkinID. To create multiple definitions of a single element, you use the SkinID attribute to differentiate among the definitions. The value used in the SkinID can be anything you want. In this case, it is TextboxDotted and TextboxDashed.

Note that no SkinID attribute is used for the first <asp:Textbox> definition. By not using one, you are saying that this is the default style definition to use for each <asp:Textbox> control on an ASP.NET page that uses this theme but has no pointer to a SkinID.

Take a look at a sample .aspx page that uses this .skin file in Listing 9-11.

Listing 9-11: A simple .aspx page that uses the Summer.skin file with multiple text-box style definitions

```
<%@ Page Language="VB" Theme="Summer" %>

<html xmlns="http://www.w3.org/1999/xhtml" >
<head runat="server">
    <title>Different SkinIDs</title>
</head>
<body>
    <form id="form1" runat="server">
    <p>
        <asp:Textbox ID="TextBox1" Runat="server">Textbox1</asp:Textbox>
    </p><p>
        <asp:Textbox ID="TextBox2" Runat="server"
         SkinId="TextboxDotted">Textbox2</asp:Textbox>
    </p><p>
        <asp:Textbox ID="TextBox3" Runat="server"
         SkinId="TextboxDashed">Textbox3</asp:Textbox>
    </p>
    </form>
</body>
</html>
```

This small .aspx page shows three text boxes, each of a different style. When you run this page, you get the results shown in Figure 9-12.

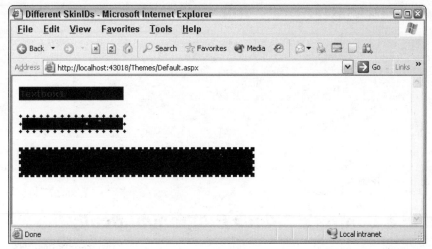

Figure 9-12

The first text box doesn't point to any particular SkinID in the .skin file. Therefore, the default skin is used. As stated before, the default skin is the one in the .skin file that doesn't have a SkinID attribute in it. The second text box then contains skinID="TextboxDotted" and, therefore, inherits the style definition defined in the TextboxDotted skin in the Summer.skin file. The third text box takes the SkinID TextboxDashed and is also changed appropriately.

As you can see, it is quite simple to define multiple versions of a control that can be used throughout your entire application.

Programmatically Working with Themes

So far, you have seen examples of working with ASP.NET 2.0 themes in a declarative fashion, but you can also work with themes programmatically.

Assigning the Page's Theme Programmatically

To programmatically assign the theme to the page, use the construct shown in Listing 9-12.

Listing 9-12: Assigning the theme of the page programmatically

```
VB
<script runat="server">
    Protected Sub Page_PreInit(ByVal sender As Object, ByVal e As System.EventArgs)
        Page.Theme = Request.QueryString("ThemeChange")
    End Sub
</script>
```

(continued)

Listing 9-12: *(continued)*

C#

```
<script runat="server">
    protected void Page_PreInit(object sender, System.EventArgs e)
    {
        Page.Theme = Request.QueryString["ThemeChange"];
    }
</script>
```

You must set the `Theme` of the `Page` property in or before the `Page_PreInit` event for any static controls that are on the page. If you are working with dynamic controls, set the `Theme` property before adding it to the Controls collection.

Assigning a Control's SkinID Programmatically

Another option is to assign a specific server control's `SkinID` property programmatically (see Listing 9-13).

Listing 9-13: Assigning the server control's SkinID property programmatically

VB

```
<script runat="server" language="vb">
    Protected Sub Page_PreInit(ByVal sender As Object, ByVal e As System.EventArgs)
        TextBox1.SkinID = "TextboxDashed"
    End Sub
</script>
```

C#

```
<script runat="server">
    protected void Page_PreInit(object sender, System.EventArgs e)
    {
        TextBox1.SkinID = "TextboxDashed";
    }
</script>
```

Again, you assign this property before or in the `Page_PreInit` event in your code.

Themes and Custom Controls

If you are building custom controls in an ASP.NET 2.0 world, understand that end users can also apply themes to the controls that they use in their pages. By default, your custom controls are theme-enabled whether your custom control inherits from `Control` or `WebControl`.

To disable theming for your control, you can simply use the `Themeable` attribute on your class. This is illustrated in Listing 9-14.

Listing 9-14: Disabling theming for your custom controls

VB

```vb
Imports System.Web.UI

Namespace Wrox.ServerControls

    <Themeable(False)> _
    Public Class SimpleHello
        Inherits System.Web.UI.Control

        Private _name As String

        Public Property Name() As String
            Get
                Return _name
            End Get
            Set(ByVal Value As String)
                _name = Value
            End Set
        End Property

        Protected Overrides Sub Render(ByVal controlOutput As _
           HtmlTextWriter)
                controlOutput.Write("Hello " + Name)
        End Sub

    End Class

End Namespace
```

C#

```csharp
using System.Web.UI;

namespace Wrox.ServerControls
{
    [Themeable(false)]
    public class SimpleHello : Control
    {
        private string _name;

        public string Name
        {
            get { return _name; }
            set { _name = value; }
        }

        protected override void Render(HtmlTextWriter controlOutput)
        {
            controlOutput.Write ("Hello " + Name);
        }
    }
}
```

You can also disable theming for the individual properties that might be in your custom controls. You do this as illustrated in Listing 9-15.

Listing 9-15: Disabling theming for properties in your custom controls

VB

```
Imports System.Web.UI

Namespace Wrox.ServerControls

    Public Class SimpleHello
        Inherits System.Web.UI.Control

        Private _myValue As String

        <Themeable(False)> _
        Public Property MyCustomProperty() As String
            Get
                Return _myValue
            End Get
            Set(ByVal Value As String)
                _myValue = Value
            End Set
        End Property

    End Class

End Namespace
```

C#

```
using System.Web.UI;

namespace Wrox.ServerControls
{
    public class SimpleHello : Control
    {
        private string _myValue;

        [Themeable(false)]
        public string Name
        {
            get { return _myValue; }
            set { _myValue = value; }
        }
    }
}
```

Summary

With the addition of themes and skins in ASP.NET 2.0, it has become quite easy to apply a consistent
look and feel across your entire application. Remember that themes can contain only simple server control definitions in a .skin file or elaborate style definitions, which include not only .skin files, but also
CSS style definitions and even images!

As you will see later in the book, you can use themes in conjunction with the new personalization features that ASP.NET 2.0 provides. This can enable your end users to customize their experiences by selecting their own themes. Your application can present a theme just for them, and it can remember their
choices through the APIs that are offered in ASP.NET 2.0.

10

Collections and Lists

Object-oriented programming (OOP) has been successful because it gives programmers a way to model physical reality in code. The easiest systems to understand are those that effectively model a familiar reality. If you're trying to represent a *person* in real-life, for example, you might create a class Person. After you create a Person class, what's the next most obvious thing for that person to do? Well, have a party and congregate with other *persons*, of course! As soon as you have more than one Person, you need a place to put them all — that's where lists, arrays, hash tables, and other *collections* come in.

This chapter explains the collections made available to you in the .NET Framework 2.0. Although the concept of *collections* is not specific to ASP.NET, this chapter shows you how to use them in the context of an ASP.NET 2.0 application. It also looks at the differences between strongly typed collections and generics, as well as exploring the unusual Microsoft.VisualBasic.Collection class and contrasting it with the System.Collections namespace.

Arrays

Most folks would say that the simplest collection of objects is an *array*. Create some objects and put them into an array. Start with a basic Person class with a simple constructor that initializes the Person's first and surname (last name), as well as a public property that returns the full name (see Listing 10-1).

Listing 10-1: A simple Person class

VB

```
Public Class Person
    Dim FirstName As String
    Dim LastName As String

    Public Sub New(ByVal First As String, ByVal Last As String)
```

(continued)

Listing 10-1: *(continued)*

```
        FirstName = First
        LastName = Last
    End Sub

    Public ReadOnly Property FullName() As String
        Get
            Return FirstName & " " & LastName
        End Get
    End Property
End Class
```

C#

```
public class Person
{
    string FirstName;
    string LastName;

    public Person(string first, string last)
    {
        FirstName = first;
        LastName = last;
    }

    public string FullName
    {
        get
        {
            return FirstName + " " + LastName;
        }
    }
}
```

In Listing 10-2 you put a few of these *people* into an array, iterate over them, and print their names. You iterate twice: once using the `For Each` form, and once using the traditional `For` technique. Then you can put your code in the `Page_Load` of the Default page in a new Web-based project.

> Note that these examples use `Response.Write` for the purpose of illustration. In the next chapter, you see far more appropriate ways to print your collections.

Listing 10-2: Printing people in an array

VB

```
Partial Class _Default
    Inherits System.Web.UI.Page

    Protected Sub Page_Load(ByVal sender As Object, _
            ByVal e As System.EventArgs) Handles Me.Load

        Dim scott As New Person("Scott", "Hanselman")
        Dim bill As New Person("Bill", "Evjen")
```

```vb
        Dim srini As New Person("Srinivasa", "Sivakumar")

        Dim people() As Person = {bill, scott, srini}
        Response.Write("We used foreach.<BR/>")
        For Each p As Person In people
            Response.Write(p.FullName & "<BR/>")
        Next

        Response.Write("We used a for loop.<BR/>")
        For i As Integer = 0 To (people.Length - 1)
            Response.Write(people(i).FullName + "<BR/>")
        Next
    End Sub
End Class
```

C#

```csharp
public partial class _Default : System.Web.UI.Page
{
    protected void Page_Load(object sender, EventArgs e)
    {
        Person scott = new Person("Scott", "Hanselman");
        Person bill = new Person("Bill", "Evjen");
        Person srini = new Person("Srinivasa", "Sivakumar");

        Person[] people = { bill, scott, srini };

        Response.Write("We used foreach.<BR/>");
        foreach(Person p in people)
        {
            Response.Write(p.FullName + "<BR/>");
        }

        Response.Write("We used a for loop.<BR/>");
        for (int i = 0; i < people.Length; i++)
        {
            Response.Write(people[i].FullName + "<BR/>");
        }
    }
}
```

The result of this very simple code from Listing 10-2 is, as expected, a list of the names in the array, printed in the browser:

```
We used foreach.
Bill Evjen
Scott Hanselman
Srinivasa Sivakumar

We used a for loop.
Bill Evjen
Scott Hanselman
Srinivasa Sivakumar
```

Note that the results are the same for both For and For Each. The For loop syntax, although familiar to many, is certainly more difficult to read or write. While writing this sample, we forgot to subtract one from `people.Length`. It was an immediately obvious mistake, but it could have been avoided by using `For Each`.

> When you use `For Each` with an array, as you did here, the compiled Intermediate Language (IL) code is identical to the code you wrote as a `For`. Unless you require more complex behavior, such as iterating in reverse or iterating over every other item, always be sure to use `For Each` to iterate over arrays and most collections. The language-specific compiler handles this expansion and you reap the benefit. Your code will be less prone to *off-by-one bugs*, and it will be much easier to read.

Resizing Arrays

VB can resize an array and keep the existing values using the `ReDim` statement. Here you double the size of the `people` array. Note the use of `ReDim` to redimension the array that has elements 0 through 5, so this array can hold six `Person` objects:

```
ReDim Preserve people(5)
```

C# doesn't support a convenient array-resizing statement such as `ReDim`. Instead, you copy people to a new, larger array. Again, note the syntax here as you create an array with a length of six. It can hold elements 0 through 5:

```
Person[] people2  = new Person[6];
Array.Copy(people, people2, people.Length);
```

Finding Objects in Arrays

Arrays are the simplest form of collection. Indexing into an array is *the* fastest way to get access to your data — if you know the index of the item you want! If you don't know the index of an item in your array, you go looking for it. However, what does it mean to ask an array, "Where is this object?"

Object Identity versus Object Equivalence

Two objects can be compared based on their identity — are these the same objects? Or based on equivalence — do these objects contain the same values? When you look through a collection, you typically already have a reference to that object, and you want to find that same object. Ask yourself whether you are looking for that identical object reference or just an object with values equivalent to yours?

Next, modify Listing 10-2 and look for Bill and Scott in the array. You can add your search right after the initialization of the `people` array (see Listing 10-3).

Listing 10-3: Looking for an object in an array by reference

VB
```
Dim people() As Person = {bill, scott, srini}

Dim indexOfBill As Integer = Array.IndexOf(people, bill)
Response.Write("Bill is at " & indexOfBill & "<BR/>")
```

```
Dim indexOfScott As Integer = Array.IndexOf(people, scott)
Response.Write("Scott is at " & indexOfScott & "<BR/>")
```

C#
```
Person[] people = { bill, scott, srini };
```

```
int indexOfBill = Array.IndexOf(people, bill);
Response.Write("Bill is at " + indexOfBill + "<BR/>");
```

```
int indexOfScott = Array.IndexOf(people, scott);
Response.Write("Scott is at " + indexOfScott + "<BR/>");
```

The output of Listing 10-3 in the Web browser makes sense. Bill is at the zero-eth position in the array, and Scott is at the first position. Remember that arrays are zero-based.

```
Bill is at 0
Scott is at 1
```

Now, look for Scott again, but this time using another object reference in Listing 10-4 that contains the same information as our current `scott` object reference. The `scott2` object is certainly equivalent to the `scott` object because they contain the same information.

Listing 10-4: Searching for a object in an array by reference

VB
```
Dim scott2 As New Person("Scott", "Hanselman")
Dim indexOfScott2 As Integer = Array.IndexOf(people, scott2)
Response.Write("Scott #2 is at " & indexOfScott2 & "<BR/>")
```

C#
```
Person scott2 = new Person("Scott", "Hanselman");
int indexOfScott2 = Array.IndexOf(people, scott2);
Response.Write("Scott #2 is at " + indexOfScott2 + "<BR/>");
```

That's interesting! The output may not be what you expected:

```
Bill is at 1
Scott is at 0
Scott #2 is at -1
```

Listing 10-4 makes sense, however, as `scott2` is not in the array because it is not identical to the object `scott`. They may be equivalent objects, but they are not the same object. If, instead, you want to retrieve the index of the `scott` object while still using `scott2` as the object to search for, just provide a method on the `Person` class that the system can use to establish equivalence.

Overriding Equals

When you have created an object like `Person` that is composed of simple types, you can override the `Equals` method that all objects inherit from `System.Object` and provide an implementation that evaluates object equivalence.

```
public override bool Equals(object obj)
{
        Person other = obj as Person;
        return (other.LastName == this.LastName &&
            other.FirstName == this.FirstName) ;
}
```

Now, two `Person` instances can be compared for equivalence. Add an Equals implementation to the code in Listing 10-4 and see how the results change. `IndexOf` searches for objects linearly and compares them using their implementation of `Equals`.

The Importance of Implementing IComparable

In order to find objects that are like other objects and perform operations like sorting, the `Person` class must be comparable. Specifically, you implement the `IComparable` interface that consists of one method, `CompareTo()`. Return zero from `CompareTo` if the objects are equivalent. Fortunately, the`Person` object has only two string fields, `FirstName` and `LastName`. These fields are both `System.String` objects and, because strings implement `IComparable` themselves, you can aggregate the return `CompareTo` values of the properties. In Listing 10-5, `LastName` is more important than `FirstName` because it's reasonable to sort people with their last names first. Additionally, you may want to use this `IComparable` implementation later to put a `Person` into other collections, and it can also be used when sorting.

Listing 10-5: Adding IComparable to the Person class

VB
```
Public Class Person
    Implements IComparable
    '...The rest of our class here...

    Public Function CompareTo(ByVal obj As Object)
            As Integer Implements IComparable.CompareTo

        If Not TypeOf (obj) Is Person Then
            Throw New ArgumentException("Object is not a Person!")
        End If

        Dim p2 As Person = CType(obj, Person)
        Dim lastNameResult As Integer = Me.LastName.CompareTo(p2.LastName)

        If lastNameResult = 0 Then
            Dim firstNameResult As Integer = Me.FirstName.CompareTo(p2.FirstName)
            Return firstNameResult
        Else
            Return lastNameResult
        End If
    End Function
End Class
```

C#
```
public class Person : IComparable
{
```

```
//...The rest of our class here...
```

```
    int IComparable.CompareTo(object obj)
    {
        Person p2 = obj as Person;
        if (p2 == null) throw new ArgumentException("Object is not a Person!");

        int lastNameResult = this.LastName.CompareTo(p2.LastName);

        if (lastNameResult == 0)
        {
            int firstNameResult = this.FirstName.CompareTo(p2.FirstName);
            return firstNameResult;
        }
        else
        {
            return lastNameResult;
        }
    }
}
```

Now `Person` objects can be compared to each other in order to determine if they are less than, greater than, or equal to each other. Note that Listing 10-5 checks the `FirstName` only if the `LastName` is the same. Otherwise, it just returns the comparison value of the `LastName`.

Additionally, since no support exists for comparing the `Person` class with other kinds of objects, Listing 10-5 throws an `ArgumentException` to alert the developer of this decision. If you choose, you can support comparisons of `Person` to other objects, but it's up to you to decide the semantics of such a comparison.

You can use the `IComparable` `Person` class with any method that takes an `IComparable` object as a parameter. An example is `System.Array`'s static `BinarySearch` method that takes in an array of `IComparable` implementations, along with an object to find within the array, and returns the index where that object was found. `BinarySearch` is just one method among dozens that your `IComparable` implementations can take advantage of.

Using BinarySearch to Find Like Objects in Arrays

The `Array` class includes a `BinarySearch` method with a series of overloads. This method uses the `IComparable` interface of each object to determine if the object you've asked it to look for is the same one it has found. However, `BinarySearch` requires that the array be presorted. Fortunately, this small example array is presorted for Listing 10-6. You'll see alternative ways to retrieve objects from collections later in the chapter.

Listing 10-6: Searching for an equivalent object with Array.BinarySearch

VB
```
Dim indexOfEquivalentScott As Integer = Array.BinarySearch(people, scott2)
Response.Write("An Equivalent Scott is at " & indexOfEquivalentScott & "<BR/>")
```

C#
```
int indexOfEquivalentScott = Array.BinarySearch(people, scott2);
Response.Write("An Equivalent Scott is at " + indexOfEquivalentScott + "<BR/>");
```

Now run the page again and look at the Web browser's output for Listing 10-6:

```
Bill is at 0
Scott is at 1
Scott #2 is at -1
An Equivalent Scott is at 1
```

When you look for the `scott2` object reference using `indexOf` from Listing 10-4, you find nothing and -1 is returned. Now that you can compare `Person` objects and also search for objects that are equivalent but not the same as `scott2`, you find an equivalent at index `1`. That's the index of the first `scott` object.

It's useful to spend time on these concepts of equivalence versus identity so that you, as a programmer, can successfully express your intent in code. Later, when you retrieve objects from more complex collections such as `Hashtables`, you can see what power it gives you to know if the object you're returning is the same reference (and hence the same object) or just an equivalent object (and a different reference).

So far, you have put objects in arrays and iterated over those objects with both the `For` loop and the `For Each` syntax. You've resized arrays both in VB and C#, retrieved the index of an object reference from an array, and searched for equivalent objects in a sorted array.

> Note that the `BinarySearch` **works only with presorted arrays. If you are going to search the array only once, then just iterate over the array checking each object. It is less expensive than sorting the array and *then* calling** `BinarySearch`. **However, if you call** `BinarySearch` **many times on the same array, it may be worth your while to perform the sort. Remember, be sure to measure all your performance assumptions. Don't take the word of anyone (even this book) as the final truth.**

Sorting Objects in Arrays

Now, change the currently hard-coded sort order of the array to a random sort order. Then use the new `IComparable` implementation to sort the array. Also change the initial sort order in the array initializer and add a `For Each` loop just before the sort so that you can see the before and after results of Listing 10-7.

Listing 10-7: Sorting arrays of Person

VB
```vb
Dim people() As Person = {scott, bill, srini}

Response.Write("Unsorted. We used foreach.<BR/>")
For Each p As Person In people
    Response.Write(p.FullName & "<BR/>")
Next

Response.Write("Sort...<BR/>")
Array.Sort(people)

Response.Write("Sorted. We used foreach.<BR/>")
For Each p As Person In people
    Response.Write(p.FullName & "<BR/>")
Next
```

C#

```
Person[] people = { scott, bill, srini };

Response.Write("Unsorted. We used foreach.<BR/>");
foreach (Person p in people)
{
    Response.Write(p.FullName + "<BR/>");
}

Response.Write("Sort...<BR/>");
Array.Sort(people);

Response.Write("Sorted. We used foreach.<BR/>");
foreach(Person p in people)
{
    Response.Write(p.FullName + "<BR/>");
}
```

Look at the partial output of Listing 10-7 in the Web browser:

```
Unsorted. We used foreach.
Scott Hanselman
Bill Evjen
Srinivasa Sivakumar
```

```
Sort...
Sorted. We used foreach.
Bill Evjen
Scott Hanselman
Srinivasa Sivakumar
```

The `Array.Sort` method is a `Shared` method (`static` in C#) that returns a `void`. That means that it sorts the array that you passed in as a parameter in place; the method doesn't return the array. Notice that after the call to the `sort` method, the list is correctly sorted by `LastName` because that's how you wrote the `Person` class's implementation of `IComparable`.

As you can see, arrays can be tricky and a bit of a hassle. You find yourself worrying about issues like the size of the array and the indexes of items in the array. Now explore some higher-level kinds of collections to see how they are more powerful than a simple array.

The System.Collections Namespace

The `System.Array` class is the very core of the .NET Framework and serves as the base class for all simple arrays in the Common Language Runtime. However, the `System.Collection` namespace contains most of the classes and interfaces that you are interested in, and builds on the concepts you learned by examining the simple array.

ArrayList

Think of an ArrayList as everything that is good about an array PLUS automatic sizing, `Add`, `Insert`, `Remove`, `Sort`, `BinarySearch` — you get the idea. All these great helper methods are added when implementing the `IList` interface, the specifics of which are explored in the next section. The downside of an ArrayList is the need to cast objects upon retrieval. New solutions introduced in .NET 2.0 will be covered a little later in this chapter

The `ArrayList` class keeps an array of objects internally but takes care of housekeeping chores such as ensuring there is enough capacity in the array. For example, if you add an item to an `ArrayList`, but there's no room in its internal array, the `ArrayList` doubles the size of the internal array to make room.

Now, reconsider and modify the code from Listings 10-1 through Listing 10-7 using an `ArrayList` instead of an array. Start with a statement including the `System.Collections` namespace, and change the way you add `Person` objects to the collection. Also change the calls to the `Sort` and `BinarySearch` methods (see Listing 10-8).

Listing 10-8: Using an ArrayList instead of an array

VB

```vb
Imports System
Imports System.Collections

Partial Class _Default
    Inherits System.Web.UI.Page

    Protected Sub Page_Load(ByVal sender As Object, _
            ByVal e As System.EventArgs) Handles Me.Load

        Dim scott As New Person("Scott", "Hanselman")
        Dim bill As New Person("Bill", "Evjen")
        Dim srini As New Person("Srinivasa", "Sivakumar")

        Dim people As New ArrayList()
        people.Add(scott)
        people.Add(bill)
        people.Add(srini)

        Response.Write("Unsorted. We used foreach.<BR/>")
        For Each p As Person In people
            Response.Write(p.FullName & "<BR/>")
        Next

        Response.Write("Sort...<BR/>")
        people.Sort()

        Response.Write("Sorted. We used foreach.<BR/>")
        For Each p As Person In people
            Response.Write(p.FullName & "<BR/>")
        Next

        Dim scott2 As New Person("Scott", "Hanselman")
        Dim indexOfScott2 As Integer = people.IndexOf(scott2)
        Response.Write("Scott #2 is at " & indexOfScott2 & "<BR/>")

        Dim indexOfEquivalentScott As Integer = people.BinarySearch(scott2)
        Response.Write("An Equivalent Scott is at " & _
```

```
                    indexOfEquivalentScott & "<BR/>")

            Response.Write("We used a for loop.<BR/>")
            For i As Integer = 0 To people.Count - 1
                Response.Write(CType(people(i), Person).FullName & "<BR/>")
            Next
        End Sub
    End Class
```

C#

```
using System;
using System.Collections;

public partial class _Default : System.Web.UI.Page
{
    protected void Page_Load(object sender, EventArgs e)
    {
        Person scott = new Person("Scott", "Hanselman");
        Person bill = new Person("Bill", "Evjen");
        Person srini = new Person("Srinivasa", "Sivakumar");

        ArrayList people = new ArrayList();
        people.Add(scott);
        people.Add(bill);
        people.Add(srini);

        Response.Write("We used foreach.<BR/>");
        foreach (Person p in people)
        {
            Response.Write(p.FullName + "<BR/>");
        }

        Response.Write("Sort...<BR/>");
        people.Sort();

        Response.Write("We used foreach.<BR/>");
        foreach (Person p in people)
        {
            Response.Write(p.FullName + "<BR/>");
        }

        Person scott2 = new Person("Scott", "Hanselman");
        int indexOfScott2 = people.IndexOf(scott2);
        Response.Write("Scott #2 is at " + indexOfScott2 + "<BR/>");

        int indexOfEquivalentScott = people.BinarySearch(scott2);
        Response.Write("An Equivalent Scott is at " + indexOfEquivalentScott +
        "<BR/>");

        Response.Write("We used a for loop.<BR/>");
        for (int i = 0; i < people.Count; i++)
        {
            Response.Write(((Person)people[i]).FullName + "<BR/>");
        }
    }
}
```

Listing 10-8 includes the `System.Collections` namespace and creates a new `ArrayList`. Then you add the objects to the `ArrayList` with the very intuitive `ArrayList.Add`. The calls to the `Shared` methods (`static` in C#) `Array.Sort`, and `Array.BinarySearch` turn into more natural calls to instance methods on the `people` ArrayList.

It is interesting that you don't have to change the `For Each` loop, but you must change the `For` loop. The `ArrayList` holds `Person` objects, but ultimately it holds objects of the root type from which all objects derive, namely `System.Object`. (Remember that our `Person` class derives automatically from `System.Object`). Because you can store other kinds of objects, not just `Person`, in an `ArrayList`, you have to tell the system what kind of object you expect to get out of the `ArrayList`. You let the system know the object's type via casting. Some people find casting to be a confusing concept; so this book examines how generics—a new feature of the .NET Framework 2.0—helps solve this problem (see the section "System.Collections.Generics" later in this chapter). Until then, you can avoid casting by using `For Each`.

Additionally, an `ArrayList` doesn't have a `Length` property; it has a `Count` property. You change the upper bound expression from `Length` to `Count` in the `For` loop. Your first reaction to this odd semantic change might be negative, but it makes sense when you remember that the intent of your code is to ask the `ArrayList` for the `Count` of `Person` objects, not the `Length` of the `ArrayList`'s internal array! The array's length may well be considerably larger than the number of `Person` objects. You see where this `Count` property comes from in the next section.

Notice that you can index into an `ArrayList` just like an array. Here you pull out the `FullName` of the `Person` at index 2 (the third `Person` in the `ArrayList`):

VB
```
CType(people(2), Person).FullName
```

C#
```
((Person)people[2]).FullName
```

Next, we show you how the `ArrayList` and other collections can be everything an array is and more—using interfaces that make the `For Each` statement and array-like indexing possible. You also learn about dictionaries, a whole new kind of collection that lets you specify the index or *key*.

IEnumerable and IEnumerator

The `System.Collections` namespace has many useful classes. But before digging any farther, you should examine the core interfaces that make all the different collections possible.

When you have a collection of something, inevitably you want to enumerate—move forward over—all the objects in that collection. A collection implements `IEnumerable` if its contents can be enumerated. `IEnumerable` does more than inform you of the collection's capabilities; it gives you access via its one method, `GetEnumerator`, returning that collection's implementation of `IEnumerator`.

`IEnumerator` exposes these capabilities via this interface:

```
Public Interface IEnumerator
     ' Methods
     Function MoveNext() As Boolean
     Sub Reset()
```

```
            ' Properties
            ReadOnly Property Current As Object
    End Interface
```

It is so simple, it's brilliant. `MoveNext` returns `True` if the move succeeded and `False` if not. `Reset` resets the internal "cursor" to the beginning of the collection, and the `Current` property always returns the current object. If you create your own custom collection, that collection can support the very useful `For Each` keyword in VB or `foreach` in C# by implementing these interfaces.

> You were able to use the `For Each` **statement seamlessly with your** `ArrayList` **in Listing 10-8 because the** `ArrayList` **class is** `IEnumerable`!

ICollection

`IEnumerable` and `IEnumerator` let you loop over your collections, but you would probably like to know the count of items in your collection without having to count them yourself. The `ICollection` interface cleverly derives from `IEnumerable` and includes a few new ideas in its interface definition:

```
    Public Interface ICollection
        Implements IEnumerable

        ' Methods
        Sub CopyTo(ByVal array As Array, ByVal index As Integer)

        ' Properties
        ReadOnly Property Count As Integer
        ReadOnly Property IsSynchronized As Boolean
        ReadOnly Property SyncRoot As Object
    End Interface
```

Looks like `ICollection` added a `Count` property that gets the number of items in a collection. Because you know an `ArrayList` implements `ICollection`, you know it also implements `IEnumerable`. Immediately, then, you see that you can enumerate over an `ArrayList` with `ForEach` and easily retrieve the count of items.

Many threads within a multithreaded application may want access to a collection. `ICollection` has chosen to recognize that fact by including a `SyncRoot` object and the `IsSynchronized` property to get a value indicating whether that collection can safely be used by multiple threads.

`ICollection` also adds a `CopyTo` method that bridges the gap between an array of objects and an `ICollection` of objects. A one-dimensional array is passed in along with an index indicating where to start copying items.

To recap, the `ICollection` interface extends `IEnumerable`. Collections keep a count of items, whereas classes that implement `Ienumerable` are iterated again with `ForEach`.

> You were able to use the `Count` **Property in Listing 10-8 because the** `ArrayList` **class is an** `ICollection`.

IDictionary and IList are specific, dedicated interfaces that extend ICollection. An IDictionary implementation is a collection of key/value pairs, like Hashtable. An IList is a collection of values, and its members are accessed by index and also by many helper methods, such as the ArrayList class.

Lists and IList

The IList interface extends ICollection, which extends IEnumerable. Classes that implement IList are easy to use and very powerful. The IList interface adds the intuitive methods such as Add, Remove, Insert, and Clear, among others, to its interface definition:

```
Public Interface IList
        Implements ICollection, IEnumerable

        ' Methods
        Function Add(ByVal value As Object) As Integer
        Sub Clear()
        Function Contains(ByVal value As Object) As Boolean
        Function IndexOf(ByVal value As Object) As Integer
        Sub Insert(ByVal index As Integer, ByVal value As Object)
        Sub Remove(ByVal value As Object)
        Sub RemoveAt(ByVal index As Integer)

        ' Properties
        ReadOnly Property IsFixedSize As Boolean
        ReadOnly Property IsReadOnly As Boolean
        Property Item(ByVal index As Integer) As Object
End Interface
```

Lists (ILists) come in three flavors:

❑ **Read-only** IList: Does not allow modification of its elements after the collection has been created. IsReadOnly always returns True after the collection's initial creation.

❑ **Fixed-size** IList: Allows the modification of elements, but not adding or removing them.

❑ **Variable** IList: Allows adding, removing, and modifying of elements.

The IList interface includes the very powerful Item property that allows you to index into the collection exactly as if it were an array. When you combine that capability with the Count property that ICollection includes, you can now use a For statement to iterate forward, backward, or by steps through collections.

For most medium-size collections, an ArrayList is a great way to go. Later, you learn how to make strongly typed ILists. You do this using a new .NET Framework 2.0 feature called *generics* that, ironically, makes your Lists specific to the classes they contain. Standard ArrayLists from System .Collections can contain any object at all. You can have ArrayLists containing different kinds of objects, but when you want to retrieve a reference to an object in an ArrayList, or any standard collection, you must cast that object to the specific type it is. We had to cast (or use CType in VB) in Listing 10-8. Here's an example of a cast:

VB
```
Dim p as Person = CType(peopleList(1), Person)
```

C#
```
Person p = (Person)peopleList[1];
```

You know that when you put an object of type `Person` in your `ArrayList`, you have to tell the compiler what type the object is every time it's retrieved at runtime. Generics enables you to tell the compiler what type of object your `ArrayList` contains up-front at the time you create and compile it; then you don't have to tell the system every time it's retrieved. You hear more about generics a little later.

> You can add objects easily to the `ArrayList` in Listing 10-8 because an `ArrayList` is an `IList`. You indexed into the `ArrayList` as if it were an array because `IList` implements an `Item` indexing property, and the `ArrayList` class is an `IList`!

So far, you have worked with collections that are either ordered or indexed. Arrays and `ArrayLists` (and anything that implements `IList` or `ICollection`) contain other objects in a specific order. Those objects can be retrieved either by iterating over the collection or by a zero-based numeric index. Now, look at how to store objects in a collection with a unique key that can be used to access the objects later.

Dictionaries and IDictionary

Collections that implement `IEnumerable` let the programmer iterate over them with the `For Each` statement. The `ICollection` interface extends `IEnumerable` by including the `Count` property. `IList` extends `ICollection` and adds public methods such as `Add`, `Insert`, `Remove`, and `Contains`. `IList` also adds the `Item` property, enabling you to access objects in the list as if it were an array.

`IDictionary` extends `ICollection`; but rather than representing a list of objects that can be indexed, it represents a collection of key/value pairs. Notice that the `Add` method includes both a `key` and a `value` as parameters. The `Contains` method, rather than checking for a particular object, checks for a particular `key`; the `Item` property indexer indexes by `key` as well:

```
Public Interface IDictionary
    Implements ICollection, IEnumerable

    ' Methods
    Sub Add(ByVal key As Object, ByVal value As Object)
    Sub Clear()
    Function Contains(ByVal key As Object) As Boolean
    Function GetEnumerator() As IDictionaryEnumerator
    Sub Remove(ByVal key As Object)

    ' Properties
    ReadOnly Property IsFixedSize As Boolean
    ReadOnly Property IsReadOnly As Boolean
    Property Item(ByVal key As Object) As Object
    ReadOnly Property Keys As ICollection
    ReadOnly Property Values As ICollection
End Interface
```

A number of .NET Framework classes implement `IDictionary`; the ones you should be concerned with are the `Hashtable` and the `SortedList`. Later, `IDictionary` is also used by the specialized `ListDictionary` and `HybridDictionary`. This base hierarchy of interfaces is presented in Figure 10-1.

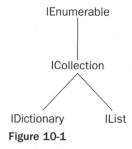

Figure 10-1

Hashtables

Take a few instances of the `Person` class and add them to a `Hashtable`. `Person` is the value, but you must decide on a key. The `Hashtable` class calls the `GetHashCode` method on each object used as a key. All objects have a default implementation of `GetHashCode` that they inherit from the ultimate base class, `object`. `GetHashCode` returns an integer, but that integer isn't a unique identifier for an object reference. The MSDN Documentation says this about `GetHashCode`:

> If two objects of the same type represent the same value, the hash function must return the same constant value for either object. Therefore, two `String` objects return the same hash code if they represent the same string value.

> **Here's a powerful tip to amaze your friends and family. The newest version of Microsoft's online MSDN documentation is called MSDN2 and offers hackable URLs for the first time. Hackable URLs mean that you can guess at the URL for most MSDN documentation. For example, the link to the `System.Collections``.Hashtable` documentation is** `http://msdn2.microsoft.com/library/system``.collections.hashtable.aspx`**. This convention applies to namespaces, class names, members, and methods.**

You'll be using strings as keys to index into the values contained by your `Hashtable` and, for this example, the string keys contain the initials of `Person`. In Listing 10-9, you retrieve the `Person` objects by using the `IDictionary` `Item` property indexer and casting the objects to type `Person`, as shown in Listing 10-8.

Listing 10-9: Retrieving Person objects from a Hashtable

VB

```
Protected Sub Page_Load(ByVal sender As Object, ByVal e As System.EventArgs) _
        Handles Me.Load

    Dim scott As New Person("Scott", "Hanselman")
```

```vb
Dim bill As New Person("Bill", "Evjen")
Dim srini As New Person("Srinivasa", "Sivakumar")

        Dim peopleHashtable As New Hashtable()
        peopleHashtable.Add("sh", scott)
        peopleHashtable.Add("be", bill)
        peopleHashtable.Add("ss", srini)

        Dim found As Person = CType(peopleHashtable("sh"), Person)
        Response.Write(found.FullName & "<BR/>")
        found = CType(peopleHashtable("be"), Person)
        Response.Write(found.FullName & "<BR/>")
        found = CType(peopleHashtable("sh"), Person)
        Response.Write(found.FullName & "<BR/>")

End Sub
```

C#

```csharp
protected void Page_Load(object sender, EventArgs e)
{
    Person scott = new Person("Scott", "Hanselman");
    Person bill = new Person("Bill", "Evjen");
    Person srini = new Person("Srinivasa", "Sivakumar");

    Hashtable peopleHashtable = new Hashtable();
    peopleHashtable.Add("sh", scott);
    peopleHashtable.Add("be", bill);
    peopleHashtable.Add("ss", srini);

    Person found = (Person)peopleHashtable["sh"];
    Response.Write(found.FullName + "<BR/>");
    found = (Person)peopleHashtable["be"];
    Response.Write(found.FullName + "<BR/>");
    found = (Person)peopleHashtable["sh"];
    Response.Write(found.FullName + "<BR/>");
}
```

Notice that you are reusing the object reference named `found`. In Listing 10-9, each time you retrieve a `Person` from the `Hashtable` using a key, you retrieve a reference to the same object added to the `Hashtable` a few lines earlier. Here is the output in the browser:

```
Scott Hanselman
Bill Evjen
Scott Hanselman
```

An Important Point about Hashtables

Inevitably, every programmer runs into a little *gotcha* with hashtables. You've spent this chapter becoming familiar with `System.Collections` and the interfaces that make them work. `Hashtable` implements `IDictionary`, which ultimately inherits from `IEnumerable`. `IEnumerable` is the interface that enables `For Each` behavior, so you may want to iterate over your `Hashtable` and dump its contents. However, when you `foreach` over a `Hashtable`, you're not iterating over the values the `Hashtable` contains, but rather a strange new composite object.

For example, you might try something like this:

VB
```
For Each p As Person In peopleHashtable ' Will compile but not run!
    Response.Write(p.FullName & "<BR/>")
Next
```

C#
```
foreach(Person  p in peopleHashtable) // Will compile but not run!
{
    Response.Write(p.FullName + "<BR/>");
}
```

This code snippet compiles happily, but it won't run. You are greeted with a potentially confusing error message stating that the Specified cast is not valid. The important point is that you should think of Hashtables as containing DictionaryEntry objects. Hashtable implements IEnumerable and returns an IEnumerator to the For Each statement, but that IEnumerator returns a DictionaryEntry. That DictionaryEntry then has a Key property and a Value Property.

> The Hashtable **default implementation of** IEnumerator **returns** DictionaryEntry **objects, not objects of your type. However, you can also iterate over both the** Keys **collection and** Values **collection exposed by** Hashtable.

Armed with this new knowledge, you can output the Person objects and the keys with which they are stored, as shown in Listing 10-10. Remember that Hashtables can contain any objects as their values — you just need to tell the system via a cast (CType in VB) that the Hashtable contains objects of type Person.

Listing 10-10: Using For Each with a Hashtable's default IEnumerator implementation

VB
```
For Each de As DictionaryEntry In peopleHashtable
    Response.Write(de.Key.ToString() & ":" & CType(de.Value, Person).FullName & _
        "<BR/>")
Next
```

C#
```
foreach (DictionaryEntry de in peopleHashtable)
{
    Response.Write(de.Key.ToString() + ":" + ((Person)de.Value).FullName +
        "<BR/>");
}
```

The output in the browser includes both the key and the value for each DictionaryEntry. Note that you have no control over how the Hashtable chooses to order your objects:

```
ss:Srinivasa Sivakumar
sh:Scott Hanselman
be:Bill Evjen
```

In Listing 10-10, you iterated directly over the Hashtable; however, Hashtable also exposes two ICollections: one for Keys and one for Values. Because these properties are ICollections, you can iterate over them with For Each, giving you two more ways to access data from a Hashtable (see Listing 10-11).

Listing 10-11: Using For Each with a Hashtable's Keys and Values member collections

VB
```vb
For Each s As String In peopleHashtable.Keys
    Response.Write(s & "<BR/>")
Next

For Each p As Person In peopleHashtable.Values
    Response.Write(p.FullName & "<BR/>")
Next
```

C#
```csharp
foreach (string s in peopleHashtable.Keys)
{
    Response.Write(s + "<BR/>");
}

foreach (Person p in peopleHashtable.Values)
{
    Response.Write(p.FullName + "<BR/>");
}
```

In Listing 10-11, you iterate twice, once over the Keys and once over the Values. Here's the browser's output:

```
ss
sh
be
Srinivasa Sivakumar
Scott Hanselman
Bill Evjen
```

Note again that you have no control over the ordering of these Keys and Values. In the next section, you look at another potentially more useful collection that has characteristics of both a Hashtable and an ArrayList: SortedList.

SortedList

A SortedList is a collection of key/value pairs like a Hashtable, except that it's sorted by its keys and the values can be manipulated via a numeric index, like an array.

Like many of the collections in System.Collections, SortedList includes a number of overloaded constructors that make creation more convenient. You can take advantage of SortedList's overloaded constructor, which takes an IDictionary. You could certainly create an empty SortedList and then manually iterate over the Hashtable's DictionaryEntries and add them to the SortedList. But why not take advantage of the careful design and expertise that have been put into the .NET Framework?

You've been using initials as the key, so you'd expect *Srinivas* to sort last in a SortedList because his initials are *ss*. The expected sort order would then be *be*, *sh*, and *ss*. Listing 10-12 outputs the Values collection of the new SortedList and then checks the index of Srinivas as if it were an array.

Listing 10-12: Using a SortedList to sort by values by key

VB
```
Dim peopleSortedList As SortedList = New SortedList(peopleHashtable)
For Each p As Person In peopleSortedList.Values
    Response.Write(p.FullName & "<BR/>")
Next
Response.Write("Index of Srinivasa: " & peopleSortedList.IndexOfKey("ss"))
```

C#
```
SortedList peopleSortedList = new SortedList(peopleHashtable);
foreach (Person p in peopleSortedList.Values)
{
    Response.Write(p.FullName + "<BR/>");
}
Response.Write("Index of Srinivasa: " + peopleSortedList.IndexOfKey("ss"));
```

If you compare the output of Listing 10-12 to the output of values from Listing 10-11, notice that the list is sorted and *Srinivas* is at index 2 (the third item in a zero-based array):

```
Bill Evjen
Scott Hanselman
Srinivasa Sivakumar
Index of Srinivas: 2
```

A SortedList can give you the best of both worlds if you need something that's like a Hashtable but is also ordered. The next section looks at the final two collections that round out System.Collections: Queues and Stacks. They just happen to emphasize the order in which their values are stored. Remember that like a Hashtable, the keys in a SortedList have to be unique, or a duplicate's addition will result in a runtime exception.

Queues and Stacks

Queues and Stacks are almost the inverse of each other. Queues are great for storing objects in the order in which they arrive, whereas a Stack is a first-in, last-out structure. Listings 10-13 and 10-14 are two small examples; if you put instances of a Person class in each structure, note the order as you remove them.

Both Stack and Queue implement ICollection and IEnumerable but not IList; that means that each has a Count and can be iterated over with For Each, but they aren't as flexible as IList implementations. Each collection has very explicit behavior as seen in Listing 10-13 that should be appended to the previous listings.

Listing 10-13: Queuing Person objects

VB
```
Dim peopleQueue As New Queue()
peopleQueue.Enqueue(scott)
peopleQueue.Enqueue(bill)
peopleQueue.Enqueue(srini)

Dim x As Person = CType(peopleQueue.Dequeue(), Person)
```

```
Response.Write(x.FullName & "<BR/>")

x = CType(peopleQueue.Dequeue(), Person)
Response.Write(x.FullName & "<BR/>")

x = CType(peopleQueue.Dequeue(), Person)
Response.Write(x.FullName & "<BR/>")
```

C#
```
Queue peopleQueue = new Queue();
peopleQueue.Enqueue(scott);
peopleQueue.Enqueue(bill);
peopleQueue.Enqueue(srini);

Person x = (Person)peopleQueue.Dequeue();
Response.Write(x.FullName + "<BR/>");

x = (Person)peopleQueue.Dequeue();
Response.Write(x.FullName + "<BR/>");

x = (Person)peopleQueue.Dequeue();
Response.Write(x.FullName + "<BR/>");
```

Because a `Queue` is a first-in, first-out structure, the `Person` objects print in the same order that they were *enqueued* into the `Queue`. Here's the output of Listing 10-13:

```
Scott Hanselman
Bill Evjen
Srinivasa Sivakumar
```

`Stacks` are first in, last out. One pushes objects onto a stack and pops them off the stack. If you imagine literally stacking objects on top of each other, you see that the analogy works. `Stacks` also include an extra useful function, `Peek`, that lets you see the object at the top of the `Stack` without removing it.

In Listing 10-14, you pop two objects, being sure to cast them to objects of type `Person`; then you peek at an object without changing the stack. Having peeked at the final object, you pop it off the stack.

Listing 10-14: Pushing, popping, and peeking Person objects in a Stack

VB
```
Dim peopleStack As New Stack()
peopleStack.Push(scott)
peopleStack.Push(bill)
peopleStack.Push(srini)

Dim x As Person = CType(peopleStack.Pop(), Person)
Response.Write(x.FullName & "<BR/>")

x = CType(peopleStack.Pop(), Person)
Response.Write(x.FullName & "<BR/>")

x = CType(peopleStack.Peek(), Person) 'Peek, not Pop
```

(continued)

Listing 10-14: *(continued)*

```
Response.Write(x.FullName & "<BR/>")

x = CType(peopleStack.Pop(), Person)
Response.Write(x.FullName & "<BR/>")
```

C#
```
Stack peopleStack = new Stack();
peopleStack.Push(scott);
peopleStack.Push(bill);
peopleStack.Push(srini);

Person x = (Person)peopleStack.Pop();
Response.Write(x.FullName + "<BR/>");

x = (Person)peopleStack.Pop();
Response.Write(x.FullName + "<BR/>");

x = (Person)peopleStack.Peek(); //Peek, not Pop
Response.Write(x.FullName + "<BR/>");

x = (Person)peopleStack.Pop();
Response.Write(x.FullName + "<BR/>");
```

The output in the browser of Listing 10-14 is the opposite of the output from Listing 10-13, plus it includes the extra output from the call to `Peek`:

```
Srinivasa Sivakumar
Bill Evjen
Scott Hanselman
Scott Hanselman
```

You'll probably use `Stack` and `Queue` less often than `Hashtable` and `ArrayList`, but when you do need them, it's good to know they are waiting.

Specialized Collections

The MSDN Documentation at `http://msdn2.microsoft.com/library/system.collections` `.specialized.aspx` says that `System.Collections.Specialized` contains "specialized and strongly-typed collections." For that reason, this section talks about `System.Collection.BitArray` because it is certainly a very specific kind of collection. The other collections in `System.Collections` `.Specialized` are strongly typed collections that contain only strings, as well as another bit-related collection and an `IDictionary` implementation for tiny collections.

HybridDictionary and ListDictionary

The `ListDictionary` is an implementation of `IDictionary` that works very quickly for lists of items composed of 10 or less. It is not performant for large numbers of items. The `HybridDictionary` is a great compromise that uses a `ListDictionary` until the collection gets larger than 10 items, and then it switches internally to use a `Hashtable`.

Note, however, that none of these collections implements IList, and, therefore, the order of the objects is not guaranteed, like a HashTable. If you need keys and to maintain ordering, refer to the OrderedDictionary in the Specialized namespace.

> **If you code to the methods** IDictionary **provides, implementations of** IDictionary **are interchangeable. Some of the implementations you can choose from are** Hashtable, SortedList, ListDictionary, **and** HybridDictionary **(among others).**

StringCollection, StringDictionary, and NameValueCollection

The StringCollection is like a strongly typed ArrayList that contains only strings. Because it is strongly typed for string, no casting is required when you retrieve strings from it. It implements IList, ICollection, and IEnumerable, so you can iterate over it with For Each and access strings via a numeric index.

The StringDictionary is a Hashtable with the keys and values both strongly typed as strings. Both the Keys and Values collection properties are strings, and the indexing property accessor requires no casting or calls to CType.

A NameValueCollection is a sorted collection of string keys and string values. It behaves like a Hashtable with string keys, and its values can be accessed by numeric index. Its property accessor is overloaded to take both a string and an integer.

BitArray

The BitArray is a very specialized collection that manages a compact list of bit values, but presents those values as Booleans to the programmer. BitArray also includes methods for applying And, Or, and Not methods to other BitArrays. It is very efficient in its use of memory, so if you find yourself managing an array or collection of Booleans, consider using a BitArray instead.

The Microsoft.VisualBasic.Collection Class

The Microsoft.VisualBasic.Collection is a strange animal. It implements both IList and ICollection and usually behaves like an ArrayList. However, its Add method includes optional key parameters that are typed as strings. This Collection class has behavior and method signatures identical to the Visual Basic 6 Collection object, but it cannot be passed over COM interop boundaries. When new .NET code interoperates with legacy VB6 code, data types must be "marshaled," or translated, between the world of .NET and the world of VB6. The space between these two worlds is often called the *COM interoperability boundary*. Some collections lend themselves for easy marshaling and some do not.

If you are attempting to upgrade code from Visual Basic 6 or earlier to Visual Basic 2005 (now called just VB), any automated upgrading your tools are using will map the VB6 Collection to this Microsoft .VisualBasic.Collection. However, stay away from this class for any new .NET development. Think of this collection as a helper for upgrade and COM interop scenarios only.

Strongly Typed Collections

So far, in this chapter, you call CType (or cast in C#) every time you retrieve an object from a System.Collection. Sometimes you might like a collection called PersonList that holds only objects of type Person and that can retrieve Person references without casting.

There are many different ways to create a strongly typed collection class. In Listing 10-15, you use an ArrayList internally, but you present only the Person class to the public. You create your own Add and Remove methods that take a Person class as a parameter, and then you expose the internal ArrayList's IEnumerable implementation in order to support the For Each keyword.

Listing 10-15: A strongly typed PersonList with an internal ArrayList

VB

```vb
Imports System.Collections
Public Class PersonList
    Implements System.Collections.IEnumerable

    Private innerList As ArrayList = New ArrayList()

    Public Sub Add(ByVal aPerson As Person)
        innerList.Add(aPerson)
    End Sub

    Public Sub Remove(ByVal aPerson As Person)
        innerList.Remove(aPerson)
    End Sub

    Public ReadOnly Property Count() As Integer
        Get
            Return innerList.Count
        End Get
    End Property

    'Get/set element at given index
    Default Public Property Item(ByVal index As Integer) As Person
        Get
            Return CType(innerList(index), Person)
        End Get
        Set(ByVal Value As Person)
            innerList(index) = Value
        End Set
    End Property

    Public Function GetEnumerator() As IEnumerator _
            Implements IEnumerable.GetEnumerator
        Return innerList.GetEnumerator()
    End Function
End Class
```

C#

```csharp
using System.Collections;
public class PersonList : System.Collections.IEnumerable
{
    private ArrayList innerList = new ArrayList();

    public void Add(Person aPerson)
    {
        innerList.Add(aPerson);
    }

    public void Remove(Person aPerson)
    {
        innerList.Remove(aPerson);
    }

    public int Count
    {
        get { return innerList.Count; }
    }

    // Get/set element at given index
    public Person this[int index]
    {
        get { return (Person)innerList[index]; }
        set { innerList[index] = value; }
    }

    public IEnumerator GetEnumerator()
    {
        return innerList.GetEnumerator();
    }
}
```

Listing 10-16 uses the custom `PersonList` instead of an `ArrayList`, as you saw earlier in Listing 10-8.

Listing 10-16: Using a custom strongly typed PersonList

VB

```vb
Protected Sub Page_Load(ByVal sender As Object, ByVal e As System.EventArgs) _
        Handles Me.Load

    Dim scott As New Person("Scott", "Hanselman")
    Dim bill As New Person("Bill", "Evjen")
    Dim srini As New Person("Srinivasa", "Sivakumar")

    Dim people As New PersonList()
    people.Add(scott)
    people.Add(bill)
    people.Add(srini)

    For Each p As Person In people
        Response.Write(p.FullName & "<BR/>")
```

(continued)

Listing 10-16: *(continued)*

```
        Next

        For i As Integer = 0 To people.Count -1
            Response.Write(people(i).FullName & "<BR/>")
        Next
    End Sub
```

C#
```
protected void Page_Load(object sender, EventArgs e)
{
    Person scott = new Person("Scott", "Hanselman");
    Person bill = new Person("Bill", "Evjen");
    Person srini = new Person("Srinivasa", "Sivakumar");

    PersonList people = new PersonList();
    people.Add(scott);
    people.Add(bill);
    people.Add(srini);

    foreach (Person p in people)
    {
        Response.Write(p.FullName + "<BR/>");
    }

    for (int i = 0; i < people.Count; i++)
    {
        Response.Write(people[i].FullName + "<BR/>");
    }
}
```

The `For Each` syntax is the same for the custom collection as it is for the `ArrayList` because this custom collection implements `IEnumerable`.

The `For` loop construct becomes even simpler with the removal of the call to `CType` (or casting in C#). Note the use of the `Default` keyword for the VB property accessor and the use of `this` for the C# property accessor. You can see (in Listing 10-15) that the cast is hidden in the property accessor and the return value of the property is strongly typed.

VB
```
Default Public Property Item(ByVal index As Integer) As Person
```

C#
```
public Person this[int index]
```

These constructs enable array-style indexing into the strongly typed collection. Strongly typed custom collections can be extended and customized to your heart's desire. You can create strongly typed HashMaps that enable lookup of objects by both key *and* value, or chains and networks of objects. The public face of your custom collections is up to you.

However, when you just want a simple `PersonHashtable` or `PersonList`, it is a real hassle to write a custom strongly typed collection. In order to help with this problem, the .NET Framework 2.0 has introduced a concept called *generics*.

System.Collections.Generics

Strongly typed collections written by hand are verbose and tied to one type of object by their nature. The `PersonList`, although convenient to use, is inadequate if you introduce an `Employee` class or `Vehicle` class; in those situations, you should write a custom `EmployeeList` and `VehicleList`.

What Are Generics?

When you use *generics*, you are creating classes or methods that use a generic type, rather than a specific type. For example, rather than creating a type-specific (and, therefore, nonreusable) `PersonList`, as shown in Listing 10-16, you could create a reusable `List` class using generics. How is that different from the `ArrayList` class you have already? The `System.Collection.ArrayList` can be used with any object, including `Person`, but no type checking is done when instances of `Person` are passed to methods. You have to manually cast objects back to type `Person` when retrieving; which makes the code not only harder to read, but more fragile at runtime.

Generics aim to promote the following:

❑ **Binary code reuse:** You can use an `ArrayList` with any object, but the custom `PersonList` (from Listing 10-16) can't be easily reused. Generic classes can be used with any type.

❑ **Performance:** You are paying a performance price every time you cast an object during a retrieve, and you pay a price for *boxing up* value types such as `int` (`Integer` in VB) and `bool` (`Boolean` in VB) when they are put into collections. This isn't the case with generics because the knowledge of generics is built directly into the runtime.

❑ **Ease of reading:** Handwritten, strongly typed collections can be tricky to write and hard to read. Generic syntax is intuitive, easy to read, and reduces *code bloat*.

❑ **Type safety:** A standard `ArrayList` takes any object in as a parameter to its `Add` method. The compiler doesn't care, and you won't know if anything has gone wrong until a cast fails when pulling an object out of the collection. Generics have built-in type safety; the compiler complains if any type checking rules are broken going into or coming out of a generic collection class.

Generics are often compared directly to C++ templates and the proposed generics equivalent in the Java language. However, these additions to C++ and Java are largely features of their respective compilers. These compilers construct "extra" code at compile time for each referenced template type. Generics in the .NET 2.0 CLR work differently.

Generics in .NET 2.0 are a first-class feature of the Common Language Runtime and are created and JIT'ed at runtime. Each instance of a generic type, such as `List<Person>` or `Hashtable<int>`, is a first class entity and can be reused by the CLR. If these generic types are referenced in another assembly, they share type equivalency and can be passed back and forth.

Additionally, these types can be used between languages. A List<Person> in C# is a List(Of Person) in VB, but they are the *same type* and can be shared and treated as such. This first class treatment of generics, along with the unique runtime typing and type equivalence, makes .NET 2.0's implementation of generics fantastically powerful.

Generic Lists

All the Generic collections are in System.Collections.Generic. Listing 10-17 creates a Person-specific list using generics in order to illustrate the new generic syntax.

Amazingly, the code from Listing 10-16 works using generics by simply changing a single line in Listing 10-17 and deleting all the custom collection code from Listing 10-15! Instead of creating a specialized and custom PersonList, generics allow us to use a template and create a strongly typed and generic List of type Person that can be operated on exactly as before in Listing 10-16.

Listing 10-17: Creating a list of Person objects using generics

VB

```vb
Imports System.Collections.Generic
Protected Sub Page_Load(ByVal sender As Object, _
    ByVal e As System.EventArgs) Handles Me.Load

    Dim scott As New Person("Scott", "Hanselman")
    Dim bill As New Person("Bill", "Evjen")
    Dim srini As New Person("Srinivasa", "Sivakumar")

    Dim people As New List(Of Person)
    people.Add(scott)
    people.Add(bill)
    people.Add(srini)

    For Each p As Person In people
        Response.Write(p.FullName & "<BR/>")
    Next

    For i As Integer = 0 To people.Count - 1
        Response.Write(people(i).FullName & "<BR/>")
    Next
End Sub
```

C#

```csharp
using System.Collections.Generic;
protected void Page_Load(object sender, EventArgs e)
{
    Person scott = new Person("Scott", "Hanselman");
    Person bill = new Person("Bill", "Evjen");
    Person srini = new Person("Srinivasa", "Sivakumar");

    List<Person> people = new List<Person>();
    people.Add(scott);
    people.Add(bill);
```

```
        people.Add(srini);

        foreach (Person p in people)
        {
            Response.Write(p.FullName + "<BR/>");
        }

        for (int i = 0; i < people.Count; i++)
        {
            Response.Write(people[i].FullName + "<BR/>");
        }
    }
```

Notice the new syntax used for generics. VB adds the intuitive Of keyword to enable you to create a List(Of Person), whereas C# uses the C++-like angle-bracket syntax to create a List<Person>. The documentation shows type declarations for generic types like List<T> in C# and List(Of T) in VB, where T means Type. Dictionaries that take type parameters as a key and a value use TKey and TValue, respectively, to represent those types, as in Dictionary<TKey, TValue> for C# and Dictionary(Of TKey, TValue) for VB.

VB
```
Public Class List(Of T) 'Class Definition
'...
Dim people As New List(Of Person) 'Instance Declaration
```

C#
```
Public class List< T> //Class Definition
//...
List<Person> people = new List<Person>(); //Instance Declaration
```

You can use this syntax for all generics, including those that take multiple generic type parameters. Listing 10-18 extends this concept to create a hashtable-like structure using generics.

Generic Dictionary

Hashtables are dictionaries, and the generic version of a hashtable is Dictionary(Of TKey, TValue). As shown in Listing 10-18, you can change Listing 10-9 to use a generic Dictionary instead of a Hashtable. You'll also need to add the System.Collections.Generics namespace.

Listing 10-18: Using a generic Dictionary instead of a non-generic Hashtable

VB
```
Dim peopleHashtable As New Dictionary(Of String, Person)
peopleHashtable.Add("sh", scott)
peopleHashtable.Add("be", bill)
peopleHashtable.Add("ss", srini)

Dim found As Person = peopleHashtable("sh")
Response.Write(found.FullName & "<BR/>")
found = peopleHashtable("be")
Response.Write(found.FullName & "<BR/>")
found = peopleHashtable("sh")
Response.Write(found.FullName & "<BR/>")
```

(continued)

Listing 10-18: *(continued)*

C#

```
Dictionary<String, Person> peopleHashtable = new Dictionary<string, Person>();
peopleHashtable.Add("sh", scott);
peopleHashtable.Add("be", bill);
peopleHashtable.Add("ss", srini);

Person found = peopleHashtable["sh"];
Response.Write(found.FullName + "<BR/>");
found = peopleHashtable["be"];
Response.Write(found.FullName + "<BR/>");
found = peopleHashtable["sh"];
Response.Write(found.FullName + "<BR/>");
```

Notice that the one-line type declaration changed from Listing 10-9 to Listing 10-18, and you were also able to remove all the casting during retrieval in both languages!

> Generics are completely Common Language Specification (CLS) compliant. They were not in early betas, but the final release of .NET 2.0 finds the C# and VB compilers treating generics as fully supported CLS-compliant code. The CLS dictates what features a .NET language must support — the lowest common denominator, if you will. The capability to consume CLS-compliant types is the minimum that all .NET languages targeting the CLR must meet, not only to use APIs from the Base Class Library, but also for interoperability between each other. This new addition has nothing but upside for the developer. You will be able to use many elegant new generics-based APIs from Microsoft, as well as CLS-compliant libraries from third-party developers. Additionally, third-party languages such as Delphi or Python that choose to target the .NET 2.0 CLR will include generics in their updated language implementation.

Other Generic Collections

There are `Queue(Of T)`, `Stack(Of T)`, and `SortedDictionary(Of TKey, TValue)` generic classes as well. A new collection type addition to the .NET Framework is the `LinkedList(Of T)` class. It is a strongly typed, doubly linked list where each node points both forward to the next node and backward to the previous node.

Collection Changes from .NET 1.1 to .NET 2.0

The big change in the .NET Framework 2.0 is the addition of Generics support in the runtime and the many classes in the `System.Collections.Generics` namespace. However, a few small things have been changed or added in `System.Collections` and `.Specialized` that you should be aware of if you are porting collection-related code from .NET 1.1:

❑ A new interface, `System.Collections.Specialized.IOrderedDictionary` derives from `IDictionary`, but it adds a property indexer that takes an integer, as well as `RemoveAt` and overloads for `Insert`.

❑ All collections, except `BitVector32`, are now marked with the `[Serializable]` attribute.

❑ `IEqualityComparer` is a new interface, and constructor overloads have been added to `Hashtable`. If `IEqualityComparer` is provided, the key objects in the `Hashtable` do not need to override `GetHashCode`. This clever addition means that key comparison is completely pluggable and multiple-key comparison implementations can be provided for the same kind of key object.

❑ The `CollectionBase` class now includes a property called `Capacity`.

Collections and List Guidance

The following table summarizes the collections discussed in this chapter, as well as a few others for you to explore.

Collection	Interfaces	Why It's Special	What It's Useful for
System.Array	IList, ICollection, IEnumerable	Most basic collection type; indexing is wickedly fast	Collections of fixed size
System.Collections. ArrayList	IList, ICollection, IEnumerable	Numeric indexing is fast as Array; grows internal array automatically	Ordered lists of varying kinds of objects
System.Collections. Hashtable	IDictionary, ICollection, IEnumerable	Objects are indexed by key; increases size automatically	Whenever you need a non-ordered, keyed collection
System.Collections. Queue	ICollection, IEnumerable	First in, first out	Implementing Queue-like behavior
System.Collections. Stack	ICollection, IEnumerable	First in, last out	Implementing Stack-like behavior
System.Collections. SortedList	IDictionary, ICollection, IEnumerable	Hybrid of Hashtable and ArrayList; sorts keys with IComparable or IComparer	Smaller Hashtables where order of keys matters
System.Collections. BitArray	ICollection, IEnumerable	Tiny and very fast	Instead of an array of Booleans for efficiency
System.Collections. Specialized. ListDictionary	IDictionary, ICollection, IEnumerable	Faster than Hashtable for small numbers of items	Very small collections, less than 10 items

Table continued on following page

Collection	Interfaces	Why It's Special	What It's Useful for
System.Collections. Specialized. HybridDictionary	IDictionary, ICollection, IEnumerable	Stores objects in a ListDictionary until it gets too big; then switches to a Hashtable	Key collections that may get large
System.Collections. Specialized. StringCollection	IList, ICollection, IEnumerable	A strongly typed ArrayList-like structure for strings	Instead of an ArrayList when you're storing strings
System.Collections. Specialized. StringDictionary	IEnumerable	A strongly typed Hashtable for Strings	Instead of a Hashtable when both key and value are strings
System.Collections. Specialized. NameValueCollection	ICollection, IEnumerable	A Hashtable where the keys are strings	Instead of a Hashtable when the key is a string and the value is an object
Microsoft. VisualBasic. Collection	IList, ICollection, IEnumerable	An indexable array of items that is also keyed with a string like a Hashtable	Visual Basic 6 upgrade compatibility
System.Collections. Generic. Dictionary<TKey, TValue>	IDictionary, ICollection, IEnumerable, IDictionary<TKey, TValue>, ICollection <KeyValuePair<TKey, TValue>, IEnumerable <KeyValuePair<TKey, TValue>>	Generic version of a Hashtable	Strongly typed Hashtable of objects of the same type or with a shared base class with key objects of the same type, or with a shared base class
System.Collections. Generic.List<T>	IList<T>, ICollection<T>, IEnumerable<T>, IList, ICollection, IEnumerable	Generic version of an ArrayList	Strongly typed ordered List of objects of the same type, or with a shared base class
System.Collections. Generic. Queue<T>	ICollection, IEnumerable, ICollection<T>, IEnumerable<T>	Generic version of a Queue	Strongly typed queue of objects of the same type, or with a shared base class

Collection	Interfaces	Why It's Special	What It's Useful for
`System.Collections.Generic.Stack<T>`	`ICollection,` `IEnumerable,` `ICollection<T>,` `IEnumerable<T>`	Generic version of a `Stack`	Strongly typed `Stack` of objects of the same type, or with a shared base class
`System.Collections.Generic.SortedDictionary<TKey,TValue>`	`IDictionary,` `ICollection,` `IEnumerable,` `IDictionary<TKey,` `TValue>, ICollection` `<KeyValuePair<TKey,` `TValue>>,IEnumerable` `<KeyValuePair` `<TKey,TValue>>`	Generic version of a `Hashtable` with Keys sorted using `Icomparer`	Strongly typed `Hashtable` of objects of the same type, or with a shared base class, with sorted key objects of the same type, or with a shared base class
`System.Collections.Generic.Collection<T>`	`IList<T>,` `ICollection<T>,` `IEnumerable<T>,` `IList, ICollection,` `IEnumerable`	An extended version of `List<T>`	Acts as a base class template for custom collections that you create via derivation
`System.Collections.ObjectModel.KeyedCollection<TKyey,TItem>`	`Ilist<T>,` `ICollection<T>,` `IEnumerable<T>,` `IList, ICollection,` `IEnumerable`	Derives from `Collection<T>`, adds `Hashtable`-like support for keys	Similar to a `Hashtable`
`System.Collections.Generic.LinkedList<T>` and `System.Collections.Generic.LinkedListNode<T>`	`ICollection<T>,` `IEnumerable<T>,` `ICollection,` `IEnumerable`	Like a collection, but each node knows about the previous and next nodes	Strongly typed `LinkedList`

Summary

When you understand the building block interfaces `IEnumerable`, `IList`, and `IDictionary` that make up `System.Collections`, you can use any collection class comfortably.

In this chapter, you learned how to store objects in standard `System.Arrays`. You stored objects in traditional collections from the `System.Collection` namespace but cast them back to their specific type upon retrieval. You also explored the advanced techniques available in the specialized collections, and you created custom strongly typed collections that can hide the casting internally and expand the collections with additional functionality. Finally, you delved into `System.Collections.Generic` and discovered how you can have the best of both worlds with strongly typed classes via generics, as well as less code, compile-time checking, and a syntax that is simpler to read.

As you continue to investigate collections, remember that `IEnumerable` and `IEnumerator` enable the `For Each` statement, and `ICollection` adds support for the `Count` property. `IList` adds `Add`, `Remove`, `Contains`, and other helpful methods, whereas `IDictionary` extends the `ICollection` with a default property accessor that takes a key object and a few other methods to support key/value pairs. A clear understanding of the responsibilities of these elemental interfaces will serve you well.

11

Data Binding in ASP.NET 2.0

One of the most exciting features of ASP.NET 1.0/1.1 was its capability to bind entire collections of data to controls at runtime without requiring you to write large amounts of code. The controls understood they were data-bound and would render the appropriate HTML for each item in the data collection. Additionally, you could bind the controls to any type of data sources, from simple arrays to complex Oracle database query results. This was a huge step forward from ASP, in which each developer was responsible for writing all the data access code, looping through a RecordSet, and manually rendering the appropriate HTML code for each record of data.

In ASP.NET 2.0, Microsoft has taken the concept of data binding and expanded it to make data binding even easier to understand and use. ASP.NET 2.0 introduces a new layer of data abstraction called data source controls. This chapter explores all the provided data source controls, as well as describing other ASP.NET 2.0 data-binding changes. It shows how you can use the data source controls to easily and quickly bind data to data-bound controls. This chapter also focuses on the power of the new data-bound List controls included in ASP.NET 2.0, such as the GridView, DetailsView, and FormView controls. Finally, you take a look at changes in the inline data binding syntax and inline XML data binding.

Data Source Controls

In ASP.NET 1.0/1.1, you typically performed a data-binding operation by writing some data access code to retrieve a `DataReader` or a `DataSet` object; then you bound that data object to a server control such as a DataGrid, DropDownList, or ListBox. If you wanted to update or delete the bound data, you were then responsible for writing the data access code to do that. Listing 11-1 shows a typical example of a data-binding operation in ASP.NET 1.0/1.1.

Listing 11-1: Typical data-binding operation in ASP.NET 1.0/1.1

VB

```
Dim conn As New SqlConnection()
Dim cmd As New SqlCommand("SELECT * FROM Customers", conn)

Dim da As New SqlDataAdapter(cmd)

Dim ds As New DataSet()
da.Fill(ds)

DataGrid1.DataSource = ds
DataGrid1.DataBind()
```

C#

```
SqlConnection conn = new SqlConnection();
SqlCommand cmd = new SqlCommand("SELECT * FROM Customers", conn);

SqlDataAdapter da = new SqlDataAdapter(cmd);

DataSet ds = new DataSet();
da.Fill(ds);

DataGrid1.DataSource = ds;
DataGrid1.DataBind();
```

ASP.NET 2.0 introduces an additional layer of abstraction through the use of data source controls. As shown in Figure 11-1, these controls abstract the use of an underlying data provider, such as the SQL Data Provider or the OLE DB Data Provider. This means you no longer need to concern yourself with the hows and whys of using the data providers. Instead, the data source controls do all the heavy lifting for you. You need to know only where your data is and, if necessary, how to construct a query for performing CRUD (Create, Retrieve, Update, and Delete) operations.

Additionally, because the data source controls all derive from the Control class, you can use them much as you would any other Web Server control. For instance, you can define and control the behavior of the data source control either declaratively in your HTML or programmatically. This means you can perform all manner of data access and manipulation without ever having to write one line of code. In fact, although you certainly can control the data source controls from code, the samples in this chapter show you how to perform powerful database queries using nothing more than the Visual Studio 2005 wizards and declarative syntax.

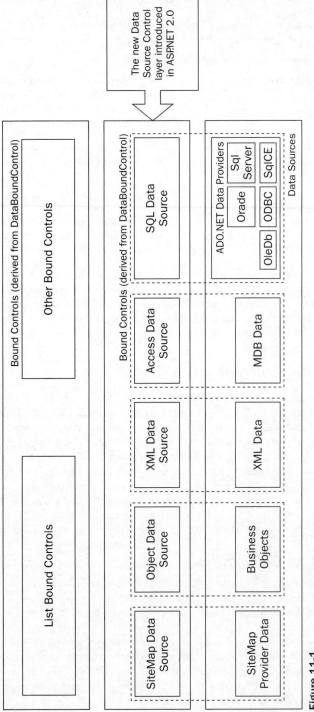

Figure 11-1

The five built-in data source controls in ASP.NET 2.0 are each used for a specific type of data access. The following table lists and describes each data source control included in ASP.NET 2.0.

Control Name	Description
SqlDataSource control	Provides access to any data source that has an ADO.NET Data Provider available; by default, the control has access to the ODBC, OLE DB, SQL Server, Oracle, and SQL Server CE providers
ObjectDataSource control	Provides specialized data access to business objects or other classes that return data
XmlDataSource control	Provides specialized data access to XML documents, either physically or in-memory
SiteMapDataSource control	Provides specialized access to site map data for a Web site that is stored by the site map provider

All the data source controls are derived from the DataSourceControl class, which is derived from Control and implements the IDataSource and IListSource interfaces. This means that although each control is designed for use with specific data sources, all data source controls share a basic set of core functionality. It also means that it is easy for you to create your own custom data source controls based on the structure of your specific data sources.

SqlDataSource Control

The SqlDataSource control is the data source control to use if your data is stored in a SQL Server, Oracle Server, ODBC data source, OLE DB data source, or Windows SQL CE Database. The control provides an easy-to-use wizard that walks you through the configuration process, or you can modify the control manually by changing the control attributes directly in Source view. In the example presented in this section, you walk through creating a SqlDataSource control and configuring it using the wizard. After you complete the configuration, you examine the source code it generates.

Begin using the control by opening an .aspx page inside a Visual Studio Web site project and dragging the SqlDataSource control from the toolbox onto the form. The Visual Studio toolbox has been divided into functional groups so you find all the data-related controls located under the Data section.

Configuring a Data Connection

After the control has been dropped onto the Web page, you tell it what connection it should use. The easiest way to do this is by using the Configure Data Source Wizard, shown in Figure 11-2. Launch this wizard by selecting the Configure Data Source option from the data source control's smart tag menu.

Once the wizard opens, you should create a connection to the Northwind database in SQL Server or MSDE. You will use this connection for most of the demonstrations in this chapter. After the wizard opens, you can select an existing connection from the drop-down list or create a new connection. If you click the New Connection button, the Connection Properties dialog, shown in Figure 11-3, appears. From here, you can set all the properties of a new database connection.

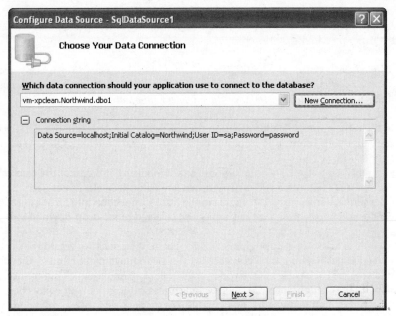

Figure 11-2

Figure 11-3

Click the Change button. From here, you can choose the specific data provider you want this connection to use. By default, the control uses the ADO.NET SQL Data Provider; also available are Oracle, OLE DB, ODBC, and SQL Server Mobile Edition providers.

> *The list of providers is generated from the data contained in the* `DbProviderFactory` *node of the* `machine.config` *file. If you have additional providers to display in the wizard you can modify your* `machine.config` *file to include specific providers' information.*

Next, simply fill in the appropriate information for your database connection. Click the Test Connection button to verify that your connection information is correct, and then click OK to return to the wizard.

After you have returned to the Data Source Configuration wizard, notice that the connection you created is now listed in the available connections drop-down list. After you select a connection string from the drop-down, the connection information shows in the Data Connection info area. This allows you to easily review the connection information for the Connection selected in the drop-down list.

Click the Next button to continue through the wizard. The next step allows you to choose to have the wizard save your connection information in your `web.config` file to make maintenance and deployment of your application easier. This screen allows you to specify the key under which the connection information should be stored in the configuration file. Should you choose not to store your connection information in the `web.config` file, it is stored in the actual `.aspx` page as a property of the `SqlDataSource` control.

The next step in the wizard allows you to configure the SELECT statement your data source control will use to retrieve data from the database. This screen, shown in Figure 11-4, gives you a drop-down list of all the tables and views available in the database that you specified in your connection information. After you select a table or view, the list box allows you to select the column you want to include in the query. You can select all columns available using an asterisk (*), or you can choose specific columns by marking the check box located next to each column name. By clicking the WHERE or ORDER BY button, it is also possible to specify WHERE clause parameters and ORDER BY parameters for your query. For now, do not enter any additional WHERE or ORDER BY parameters.

Finally, the Advanced button contains two advanced options. You can have the wizard generate INSERT, UPDATE, and DELETE statements for your data, based on the SELECT statement you created. You can also configure the data source control to use Optimistic Concurrency to prevent data concurrency issues.

The final screen of the wizard allows you to preview the data selected by your data source control to verify the query is working as you expect it to. Simply click the Finish button to complete the wizard.

Figure 11-4

When you are done configuring your data connection, you can see exactly what the configured SqlDataSource control looks like. Change to Source view in Visual Studio to see how the wizard has generated the appropriate attributes for your control. It should look something like the code in Listing 11-2.

Listing 11-2: Typical SqlDataSource control generated by Visual Studio

```
<asp:SqlDataSource ID="SqlDataSource1" Runat="server"
    SelectCommand="SELECT * FROM [Customers]"
    ConnectionString="<%$ ConnectionStrings:AppConnectionString1 %>">
</asp:SqlDataSource>
```

You can see that the control uses a declarative syntax to configure which connection it should use by creating a ConnectionString attribute, and what query to execute by creating a SelectCommand attribute. A little later in the chapter, you look at how to configure the SqlDataSource control to execute INSERT, UPDATE and DELETE commands as this data changes.

Data Source Mode Property

One of many important properties of the SqlDataSource control is the `DataSourceMode` property. This property enables you to tell the control if it should use a `DataSet` or a `DataReader` internally when retrieving the data. This is important when you are designing data-driven ASP.NET pages. If you choose to use a `DataReader`, data is retrieved using what is commonly known as *fire hose mode*, or a forward-only, read-only cursor. This is the fastest way to read data from your data source because a `DataReader` does not have the memory and processing overhead of a `DataSet`. But choosing to use a `DataSet` makes the data source control more powerful by enabling the control to perform other operations such as inserting, updating, or deleting data as it is changed in the `DataSet`. It also enables the built-in caching capabilities of the control. Each option offers distinct advantages and disadvantages, so consider this property carefully when designing your Web site. The default value for this property is to use a `DataSet` to retrieve data. The code in Listing 11-3 shows how to add the `DataSourceMode` property to your SqlDataSource control.

Listing 11-3: Adding the DataSourceMode property to a SqlDataSource control

```
<asp:SqlDataSource ID="SqlDataSource1" Runat="server"
    SelectCommand="SELECT * FROM [Customers]"
    ConnectionString="<%$ ConnectionStrings:AppConnectionString1 %>"
    DataSourceMode="DataSet">
</asp:SqlDataSource>
```

Filtering Data Using SelectParameters

Of course, when selecting data from your data source, you may not want to get every single row of data from a view or table. You want to be able to specify parameters in your query to limit the data that is returned. The data source control allows you to do this by using the `SelectParameters` collection to create parameters that it can use at runtime to alter the data that is returned from a query.

The `SelectParameters` collection consists of controls that derive from the `Parameters` class. You can combine any number of parameter controls in the collection. The data source control then uses these to create a dynamic SQL query. The following table lists and describes the available parameter controls.

Parameter	Description
ControlParameter	Uses the value of the specified control
CookieParameter	Uses the key value of a cookie
FormParameter	Uses the key value from the Forms collection
QuerystringParameter	Uses a key value from the Querystring collection
ProfileParameter	Uses a key value from the user's profile
SessionParameter	Uses a key value from the current user's session

Because all the parameter controls derive from the `Parameters` class, they all contain several useful common properties. These properties are shown in the following table.

Property	Description
Type	Allows you to strongly type the value of the parameter
ConvertEmptyToNull	Indicates the control should convert the value assigned to it to `Null` if it is equal to `System.String.Empty`
DefaultValue	Allows you to specify a default value for the parameter if it is evaluated as `Null`

The code in Listing 11-4 shows an example of adding a QueryStringParameter control to the `SelectParameters` collection of your SqlDataSource control. As you can see, the `SelectCommand` query has been modified to include a `WHERE` clause. When you run this code, the value of the query string field `ID` is bound to the `@CustomerID` field in your `SelectCommand`, allowing you to select only those customers whose `CustomerID` field matches the value of the query string field.

Listing 11-4: Filtering select data using SelectParameter controls

```
<asp:SqlDataSource ID="SqlDataSource1" Runat="server"
    SelectCommand="SELECT * FROM [Customers] WHERE ([CustomerID] = @CustomerID)"
    ConnectionString="<%$ ConnectionStrings:AppConnectionString1 %>"
    DataSourceMode="DataSet">
    <SelectParameters>
        <asp:QueryStringParameter Name="CustomerID"
            QueryStringField="ID" Type="String">
        </asp:QueryStringParameter>
    </SelectParameters>
</asp:SqlDataSource>
```

In addition to hand-coding your `SelectParameters` collection, you can create parameters using the Command and Parameter Editor dialog, which can be accessed by modifying the `SelectCommand` property of the SqlDataSource control while you are viewing the Web page in design mode. Figure 11-5 shows the Command and Parameter Editor dialog.

This dialog gives you a fast and friendly way to create `SelectParameters` for your query. Simply select the Parameter source from the drop-down list and enter the required parameter data. Figure 11-5 demonstrates how to add the `QuerystringParameter` (based on the value of the `querystring` Field ID) to your SqlDataSource control.

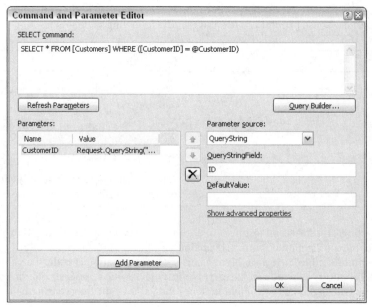

Figure 11-5

Conflict Detection Property

The ConflictDetection property allows you to tell the SqlDataSource control what style of conflict detection to use when updating the data. When the value is set to OverwriteChanges, the control uses a *Last in Wins* style of updating data. In this style, the control overwrites any changes to data that have been made between the time the data was retrieved by the control and the time the update is made.

If the value is set to CompareAllValues, the control compares the original data values (what was retrieved) to the data values currently in the data store. If the data has not changed since it was retrieved, the control allows the changes to be implemented. If the control detects differences between the original data that was retrieved from the data store and what is currently in the data store, it does not allow the update to continue. This could potentially occur when you have multiple users accessing the data store and making changes to the data. In this case, another user could possibly retrieve and change the data well before you send your own changes to the data store. If you don't want to override the previous user's changes, you need to use the CompareAllValues value. Listing 11-5 shows how to add the ConflictDetection property to the SqlDataSource control.

Listing 11-5: Adding the ConflictDetection property to a SqlDataSource control

```
<asp:SqlDataSource ID="SqlDataSource1" Runat="server"
    SelectCommand="SELECT * FROM [Customers] WHERE ([CustomerID] = @CustomerID)"
    ConnectionString="<%$ ConnectionStrings:AppConnectionString1 %>"
    DataSourceMode="DataSet"
```

```
            ConflictDetection="CompareAllValues">
        <SelectParameters>
            <asp:QueryStringParameter Name="CustomerID"
                QueryStringField="id" Type="String">
            </asp:QueryStringParameter>
        </SelectParameters>
    </asp:SqlDataSource>
```

One way to determine whether your update has encountered a concurrency error is by testing the `AffectedRows` property in the SqlDataSources `Updated` event. Listing 11-6 shows one way to do this.

Listing 11-6: Detecting concurrency errors after updating data

VB

```
Protected Sub SqlDataSource1_Updated(ByVal sender as Object, _
    ByVal e As System.Web.UI.WebControls.SqlDataSourceStatusEventArgs)

    If (e.AffectedRows > 0) Then
        Message.Text = "The record has been updated"
    Else
        Message.Text = "Possible concurrency violation"
    End If
End Sub
```

C#

```
protected void SqlDataSource1_Updated(object sender,
    SqlDataSourceStatusEventArgs e)
{
    if (e.AffectedRows > 0)
        Message.Text = "The record has been updated";
    else
        Message.Text = "Possible concurrency violation";
}
```

Although the Sql data source control is powerful, there are a number of other data source controls that might better suite your specific data access scenario.

XmlDataSource Control

The XmlDataSource control provides you with a simple way of binding XML documents, either in-memory or located on a physical drive. The control provides you with a number of properties that make it easy to specify an XML file containing data and an XSLT transform file for converting the source XML into a more suitable format. You can also provide an XPath query to select only a certain subset of data.

You can use the XmlDataSource control's Configure Data Wizard, shown in Figure 11-6, to configure the control.

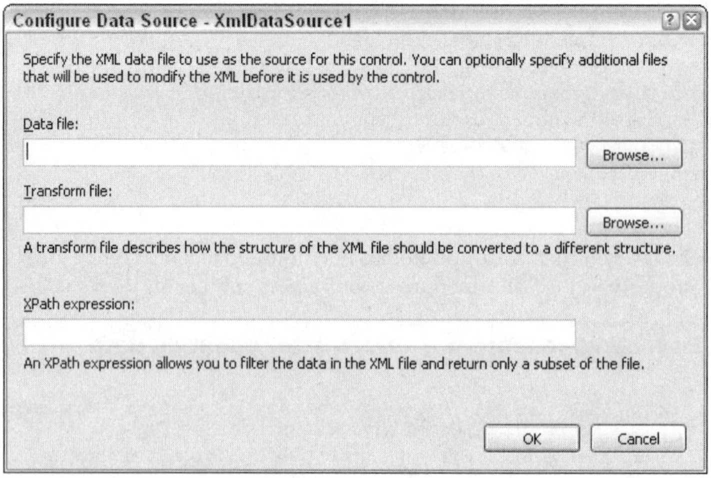

Figure 11-6

Listing 11-7 shows how you might consume an RSS feed from the MSDN Web site, selecting all the item nodes within it for binding to a bound list control such as the GridView.

Listing 11-7: Using the XmlDataSource control to consume an RSS feed

```
<asp:XmlDataSource ID="XmlDataSource1" Runat="server"
    DataFile="http://msdn.microsoft.com/rss.xml"
    XPath="rss/channel/item" >
</asp:XmlDataSource>
```

ObjectDataSource Control

The ObjectDataSource control is one of the most anticipated new data source controls in ASP.NET 2.0. It gives you the power to bind data controls to middle-layer business objects that can be generated from programs like O/R mappers. This was always difficult to achieve in ASP.NET 1.0/1.1, but the ObjectDataSource control makes it easy — while maintaining the powerful features of the data source controls such as caching and paging.

To demonstrate how to use the ObjectDataSource control, create a class in the project that represents a customer. Listing 11-8 shows a class that you can use for this demonstration.

Listing 11-8: Creating a Customer class to demonstrate the ObjectDataSource control

VB
```
Public Class Customer
    Private _customerID As Integer
    Private _companyName As String
    Private _contactName As String
    Private _contactTitle As String

    Public Property CustomerID() As Integer
        Get
```

```vbnet
            Return _customerID
        End Get
        Set
            _customerID = value
        End Set
End Property

Public Property CompanyName() As Integer
    Get
            Return _companyName
    End Get
    Set
            _companyName = value
    End Set
End Property

Public Property ContactName() As Integer
    Get
            Return _contactName
    End Get
    Set
            _contactName = value
    End Set
End Property

Public Property ContactTitle() As Integer
    Get
            Return _contactTitle
    End Get
    Set
            _contactTitle = value
    End Set
End Property

Public Function [Select](ByVal customerID As Integer) As System.Data.DataSet
    ' You would implement logic here to reterive
    ' Customer data based on the customerID parameter

    Dim ds As New System.Data.DataSet()
    ds.Tables.Add(New System.Data.DataTable())
    Return ds
End Function

Public Sub Insert(ByVal c As Customer)
    ' Implement Insert logic
End Sub

Public Sub Update(ByVal c As Customer)
    ' Implement Update logic
```

(continued)

Listing 11-8: *(continued)*

```
        End Sub

        Public Sub Delete(ByVal c As Customer)
                ' Implement Delete logic
        End Sub

End Class
```

C#
```
public class Customer
{
    private int _customerID;
    private string _companyName;
    private string _contactName;
    private string _contactTitle;

    public int CustomerID
    {
        get
        {
            return _customerID;
        }

        set
        {
            _customerID = value;
        }
    }

    public string CompanyName
    {
        get
        {
            return _companyName;
        }

        set
        {
            _companyName = value;
        }
    }

    public string ContactName
    {
        get
        {
            return _contactName;
        }

        set
        {
            _contactName = value;
```

```
        }
    }

    public string ContactTitle
    {
        get
        {
            return _contactTitle;
        }

        set
        {
            _contactTitle = value;
        }
    }

    public Customer()
    {
    }

    public System.Data.DataSet Select(Int32 customerId)
    {
        // Implement logic here to retrieve the Customer
        // data based on the methods customerId parameter

        System.Data.DataSet ds = new System.Data.DataSet();
        ds.Tables.Add(new System.Data.DataTable());
        return ds;
    }

    public void Insert(Customer c)
    {
        // Implement Insert logic
    }

    public void Update(Customer c)
    {
        // Implement Update logic
    }

    public void Delete(Customer c)
    {
        // Implement Delete logic
    }
}
```

To start using the ObjectDataSource, drag the control onto the designer surface. Using the control's smart tag, load the configuration wizard by selecting the Configure Data Source option. After the wizard opens, it asks you to select the business object you want to use as your data source. The drop-down list shows all the classes located in the App_Code folder of your Web site that can be successfully compiled. In this case, you want to use the Customer class shown in Listing 11-8.

Click the Next button, and the wizard asks you to specify which methods it should use for the CRUD operations it can perform: SELECT, INSERT, UPDATE and DELETE. Each tab lets you select a specific method located in your business class to perform the specific action. Figure 11-7 shows that you want the control to use a method called `Select()` to retrieve data.

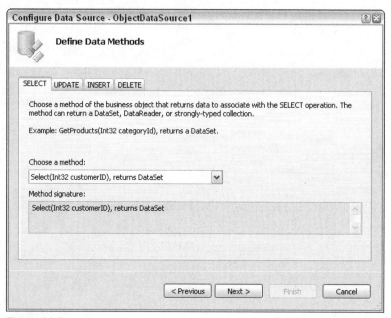

Figure 11-7

The methods the ObjectDataSource uses to perform CRUD operations must follow certain rules in order for the control to understand. For instance, the control's SELECT method must return a `DataSet`, `DataReader`, or a strongly typed collection. Each of the control's operation tabs explains what the control expects of the method you specify for it to use. Additionally, if a method does not conform to the rules that specific operation expects, it is not listed in the drop-down list on that tab.

Finally, if your SELECT method contains parameters, the wizard lets you create `SelectParameters` you can use to provide the method parameter data.

When you have completed configuring the ObjectDataSource, you should have code in your page source like that shown in Listing 11-9.

Listing 11-9: The ObjectDataSource code generated by the configuration wizard

```
<asp:ObjectDataSource ID="ObjectDataSource1" runat="server" DeleteMethod="Delete"
    InsertMethod="Insert" SelectMethod="Select" TypeName="Customer"
    UpdateMethod="Update">
    <SelectParameters>
        <asp:QueryStringParameter Name="customerID" QueryStringField="ID"
            Type="Int32" />
    </SelectParameters>
</asp:ObjectDataSource>
```

As you can see, the wizard has generated the attributes for the SELECT, UPDATE, INSERT and DELETE methods you specified in the wizard. Also notice that it has added the Select parameter. Depending on your application, you could change this to any of the Parameter objects discussed earlier, such as a ControlParameter or QuerystringParameter object.

SiteMapDataSource Control

The SiteMapDataSource enables you to work with data stored in your Web site's SiteMap configuration file if you have one. This can be useful if you are changing your site map data at runtime, perhaps based on user privilege or status.

Note two items regarding the SiteMapDataSource control. First, it does not support any of the data caching options that exist in the other data source controls provided, so you cannot natively cache your sitemap data. Second, the SiteMapDataSource control does not have any configuration wizards like the other data source controls. This is because the SiteMap control can be bound only to the SiteMap configuration data file of your Web site, so no other configuration is possible.

Listing 11-10 shows an example of using the SiteMap control.

Listing 11-10: Using the SiteMapDataSource control

```
<asp:SiteMapDataSource ID="SiteMapDataSource1" Runat="server" />
```

Using the SiteMapDataSource control is discussed in greater detail in Chapter 14.

Configuring Data Source Control Caching

Caching is now automatically built into all the data source controls except the SiteMapDataSource Control. This means that you can easily configure and control data caching using the same declarative syntax. All data source controls (except the SiteMapDataSource control) enable you to create basic caching policies including a cache direction, expiration policies, and key dependencies.

> *Remember that the SqlDataSource control's caching features are available only if you have set the* DataSourceMode *property to* DataSet. *If it is set to* DataReader, *the control throws a* NotSupportedException.

Cache duration can be set to a specific length of time, such as 3600 seconds (60 minutes), or you can set it to Infinite to force the cached data never to expire. Listing 11-11 shows how you can easily add caching features to a data source control.

Listing 11-11: Enabling caching on a SqlDataSource control

```
<asp:SqlDataSource ID="SqlDataSource1" Runat="server"
    SelectCommand="SELECT * FROM [Customers]"
    ConnectionString="<%$ ConnectionStrings:AppConnectionString1 %>"
    DataSourceMode="DataSet"
    ConflictDetection="CompareAllValues"
    EnableCaching="True" CacheKeyDependency="SomeKey" CacheDuration="Infinite">
```

```
    <SelectParameters>
        <asp:QueryStringParameter Name="CustomerID"
            QueryStringField="id" Type="String"></asp:QueryStringParameter>
    </SelectParameters>
</asp:SqlDataSource>
```

Some controls also extend this core set of caching features with additional caching functionality specific to their data sources. For instance, if you are using the SqlDataSource control, you can use the SqlCacheDependacy property to create SQL dependencies. You can learn more about ASP.NET 2.0 caching features in Chapter 20.

Storing Connection Information

In ASP.NET 1.0/1.1, Microsoft introduced the web.config file as a way of storing application configuration data in a readable and portable format. Many people quickly decided that the web.config file was a great place to store things like the database connection information their applications use. It was easy to access from within the application, created a single central location for the configuration data, and it was a cinch to change just by editing the XML.

Although all those advantages were great, several drawbacks existed. First, none of the information in the web.config file can be strongly typed. It was, therefore, difficult to find data type problems within the application until a runtime error occurred. It also meant that developers were unable to use the power of IntelliSense to facilitate development. A second problem was that although the web.config file was secured from access by browsers (it cannot be served up by Internet Information Server), the data within the file was clearly visible to anyone who had file access to the Web server.

In ASP.NET 2.0, Microsoft has tried to address these shortcomings in the web.config file. Because database connection information is so frequently stored in the web.config file, you now have an entirely new configuration section in that file, <connectionStrings>, specifically for storing the connection string information.

If you examine your web.config file, you should see at least one connection string already in the <connectionStrings> section because our example told the Data Connection Wizard to store connections in the web.config file. Listing 11-12 shows how ASP.NET stores a connection string.

Listing 11-12: A typical connection string saved in the web.config file

```
<connectionStrings>
    <add name="AppConnectionString1" connectionString="Server=localhost;
        User ID=sa;Password=password;Database=Northwind;
        Persist Security Info=True" providerName="System.Data.SqlClient" />
</connectionStrings>
```

Using a separate configuration section has several advantages. First, .NET 2.0 now exposes the `ConnectionString` section using the `ConnectionStringSettings` class. This class contains a collection of all the connection strings entered in your `web.config` file and allows you to add, modify, or remove connection strings at runtime. Listing 11-13 shows how you can access and modify connection strings at runtime.

Listing 11-13: Modifying connection string properties at runtime

VB

```vb
<%@ Page Language="VB" %>

<script runat="server">

    Protected Sub Page_Load(ByVal sender As Object, ByVal e As EventArgs)

        If (Not Page.IsPostBack) Then
            ' Create a new ConnectionStringSettings object and populate it
            Dim conn As New ConnectionStringSettings()
            conn.ConnectionString = _
                "Server=localhost;User ID=sa;Password=password" & _
                "Database=Northwind;Persist Security Info=True"
            conn.Name = "AppConnectionString1"
            conn.ProviderName = "System.Data.SqlClient"

            ' Add the new connection string to the web.config
            ConfigurationManager.ConnectionStrings.Add(conn)
        End If

    End Sub

</script>

<html xmlns="http://www.w3.org/1999/xhtml" >
<head runat="server">
    <title>Modifying the Connection String</title>
</head>
<body>
    <form id="form1" runat="server">
    <div>
        <asp:SqlDataSource ID="SqlDataSource1" Runat="server">
        </asp:SqlDataSource>
    </div>
    </form>
</body>
</html>
```

C#

```csharp
<%@ Page Language="C#" %>

<script runat="server">

    protected void Page_Load(object sender, EventArgs e)
```

(continued)

Listing 11-13: *(continued)*

```
    {

        if (!Page.IsPostBack)

        {
            // Create a new ConnectionStringSettings object and populate it
            ConnectionStringSettings conn = new ConnectionStringSettings();
            conn.ConnectionString =

                "Server=localhost;User ID=sa;Password=password; " +
                "Database=Northwind;Persist Security Info=True";
            conn.Name = "AppConnectionString1";
            conn.ProviderName = "System.Data.SqlClient";

            // Add the new connection string to the web.config
            ConfigurationManager.ConnectionStrings.Add(conn);
        }
    }
</script>
```

As you can see, the `ConfigurationManager` class now has a `ConnectionStrings` collection property in addition to the `AppSettings` collection used in ASP.NET 1.0. This new collection contains all the connection strings for your application.

Additionally, ASP.NET 2.0 makes it much easier to build connection strings using strongly typed properties at runtime, and easier to add them to the `web.config` file. Using the new `SqlConnectionStringBuilder` class, you can build connection strings and then add them to your `ConnectionStringSettings` collection. Listing 11-14 shows how you can use the `ConnectionStringBuilder` class to dynamically assemble connection strings at runtime and save them to your `web.config` file.

Listing 11-14: Building connection strings using ConnectionStringBuilder

VB
```
' Retrieve an existing connection string into a Connection String Builder
Dim builder As New System.Data.SqlClient.SqlConnectionStringBuilder()

' Change the connection string properties
builder.DataSource = "localhost"
builder.InitialCatalog = "Northwind1"
builder.UserID = "sa"
builder.Password = "password"
builder.PersistSecurityInfo = true

' Save the connection string back to the web.config
ConfigurationManager.ConnectionStrings("AppConnectionString1").ConnectionString = _
    builder.ConnectionString
```

C#
```
// Retrieve an existing connection string into a Connection String Builder
System.Data.SqlClient.SqlConnectionStringBuilder builder = new
```

```
                System.Data.SqlClient.SqlConnectionStringBuilder();

    // Change the connection string properties
    builder.DataSource = "localhost";
    builder.InitialCatalog = "Northwind1";
    builder.UserID = "sa";
    builder.Password = "password";
    builder.PersistSecurityInfo = true;

    // Save the connection string back to the web.config
    ConfigurationManager.ConnectionStrings["AppConnectionString1"].ConnectionString =
        builder.ConnectionString;
```

Using Bound List Controls with Data Source Controls

The new data source controls really shine when you combine them with the Bound List controls included in ASP.NET 2.0. This combination allows you to declaratively bind your data source to a bound control without ever writing a single line of C# or VB code.

Fear not, those of you who like to write code. You can still use the familiar DataBind() *method to bind data to the list controls. In fact, that method has even been enhanced to include a Boolean overload that allows you to turn the data-binding events on or off. This enables you improve the performance of your application if you are not using any of the binding events.*

GridView

With ASP.NET 1.0/1.1, Microsoft introduced a new set of server controls designed to make developers more productive. One of the most popular controls was the DataGrid. With this one control, you could display an entire collection of data, easily add sorting and paging, and perform inline editing. Although this new functionality was great, many of the tasks still required that the developer write a significant amount of code to take advantage of this advanced functionality.

With ASP.NET 2.0, Microsoft has taken the basic DataGrid and enhanced it, creating a new server control called the GridView. This new control makes it even easier to use those advanced DataGrid features, mostly without having to write one line of code. It even adds a number of new features.

Displaying Data with the GridView

Start using the GridView by dragging the control onto the designer surface of an ASP.NET Web page. You are prompted to select a data source control to bind to the grid. In this sample, you use the SqlDataSource control created earlier in the chapter.

After you assign the GridView a data source, notice a number of changes. First, the GridView changes its design-time display to reflect the data exposed by the data source control assigned to it. Should the schema of the data behind the data source control ever change, you can use the GridView's Refresh Schema option to force the grid to redraw itself based on the new data schema. Second, the GridView's smart tag now has additional options for formatting, paging, sorting, and selection.

Switch the page to Source view in Visual Studio to examine GridView's code. Listing 11-15 shows the code generated by Visual Studio.

Listing 11-15: Using the GridView control in an ASP.NET Web page

```
<html>
<head runat="server">
    <title>Using the GridView server control</title>
</head>
<body>
    <form id="form1" runat="server">
    <div>
        <asp:GridView ID="GridView1" Runat="server" DataSourceID="SqlDataSource1"
            DataKeyNames="CustomerID" AutoGenerateColumns="False">
          <Columns>
              <asp:BoundField ReadOnly="True" HeaderText="CustomerID"
                  DataField="CustomerID"
                  SortExpression="CustomerID"></asp:BoundField>
              <asp:BoundField HeaderText="CompanyName" DataField="CompanyName"
                  SortExpression="CompanyName"></asp:BoundField>
              <asp:BoundField HeaderText="ContactName" DataField="ContactName"
                  SortExpression="ContactName"></asp:BoundField>
              <asp:BoundField HeaderText="ContactTitle" DataField="ContactTitle"
                  SortExpression="ContactTitle"></asp:BoundField>
              <asp:BoundField HeaderText="Address" DataField="Address"
                  SortExpression="Address"></asp:BoundField>
              <asp:BoundField HeaderText="City" DataField="City"
                  SortExpression="City"></asp:BoundField>
              <asp:BoundField HeaderText="Region" DataField="Region"
                  SortExpression="Region"></asp:BoundField>
              <asp:BoundField HeaderText="PostalCode" DataField="PostalCode"
                  SortExpression="PostalCode"></asp:BoundField>
              <asp:BoundField HeaderText="Country" DataField="Country"
                  SortExpression="Country"></asp:BoundField>
              <asp:BoundField HeaderText="Phone" DataField="Phone"
                  SortExpression="Phone"></asp:BoundField>
              <asp:BoundField HeaderText="Fax" DataField="Fax"
                  SortExpression="Fax"></asp:BoundField>
          </Columns>
        </asp:GridView>

        <asp:SqlDataSource ID="SqlDataSource1" Runat="server"
            SelectCommand="SELECT * FROM [Customers]"
            ConnectionString="<%$ ConnectionStrings:AppConnectionString1 %>"
            DataSourceMode="DataSet"
            ConflictDetection="CompareAllValues" EnableCaching="True"
            CacheKeyDependency="MyKey" CacheDuration="Infinite">
        </asp:SqlDataSource>
    </div>
    </form>
</body>
</html>
```

Figure 11-8 shows what your Web page looks like when you execute the code in the browser.

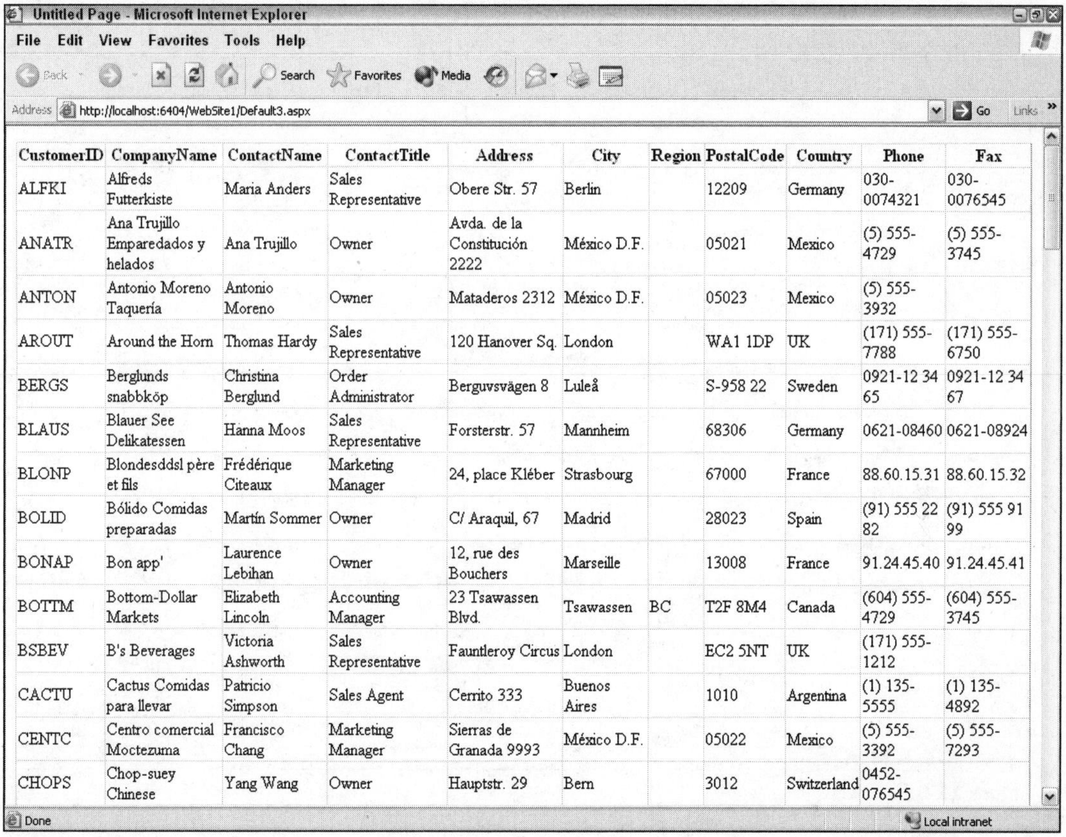

CustomerID	CompanyName	ContactName	ContactTitle	Address	City	Region	PostalCode	Country	Phone	Fax
ALFKI	Alfreds Futterkiste	Maria Anders	Sales Representative	Obere Str. 57	Berlin		12209	Germany	030-0074321	030-0076545
ANATR	Ana Trujillo Emparedados y helados	Ana Trujillo	Owner	Avda. de la Constitución 2222	México D.F.		05021	Mexico	(5) 555-4729	(5) 555-3745
ANTON	Antonio Moreno Taquería	Antonio Moreno	Owner	Mataderos 2312	México D.F.		05023	Mexico	(5) 555-3932	
AROUT	Around the Horn	Thomas Hardy	Sales Representative	120 Hanover Sq.	London		WA1 1DP	UK	(171) 555-7788	(171) 555-6750
BERGS	Berglunds snabbköp	Christina Berglund	Order Administrator	Berguvsvägen 8	Luleå		S-958 22	Sweden	0921-12 34 65	0921-12 34 67
BLAUS	Blauer See Delikatessen	Hanna Moos	Sales Representative	Forsterstr. 57	Mannheim		68306	Germany	0621-08460	0621-08924
BLONP	Blondesddsl père et fils	Frédérique Citeaux	Marketing Manager	24, place Kléber	Strasbourg		67000	France	88.60.15.31	88.60.15.32
BOLID	Bólido Comidas preparadas	Martín Sommer	Owner	C/ Araquil, 67	Madrid		28023	Spain	(91) 555 22 82	(91) 555 91 99
BONAP	Bon app'	Laurence Lebihan	Owner	12, rue des Bouchers	Marseille		13008	France	91.24.45.40	91.24.45.41
BOTTM	Bottom-Dollar Markets	Elizabeth Lincoln	Accounting Manager	23 Tsawassen Blvd.	Tsawassen	BC	T2F 8M4	Canada	(604) 555-4729	(604) 555-3745
BSBEV	B's Beverages	Victoria Ashworth	Sales Representative	Fauntleroy Circus	London		EC2 5NT	UK	(171) 555-1212	
CACTU	Cactus Comidas para llevar	Patricio Simpson	Sales Agent	Cerrito 333	Buenos Aires		1010	Argentina	(1) 135-5555	(1) 135-4892
CENTC	Centro comercial Moctezuma	Francisco Chang	Marketing Manager	Sierras de Granada 9993	México D.F.		05022	Mexico	(5) 555-3392	(5) 555-7293
CHOPS	Chop-suey Chinese	Yang Wang	Owner	Hauptstr. 29	Bern		3012	Switzerland	0452-076545	

Figure 11-8

Enabling GridView Column Sorting

The capability to sort data is one of the most basic tools users have to navigate through a significant amount of data. The DataGrid control made sorting columns in a grid a relatively easy task, but the GridView control takes it one step further. Unlike using the DataGrid, where you are responsible for coding the sort routine, to enable column sorting in this grid, you just set the `AllowSorting` attribute to `True`. The control takes care of all the sorting logic for you internally. Listing 11-16 shows how to add this attribute to your grid.

Listing 11-16: Adding sorting to the GridView control

```
<asp:GridView ID="GridView1" Runat="server" DataSourceID="SqlDataSource1"
    DataKeyNames="CustomerID" AutoGenerateColumns="False"
    AllowSorting="True">
```

After enabling sorting, you see that all grid columns have now become hyperlinks. Clicking a column header sorts that specific column. Figure 11-9 shows your grid after the data has been sorted by country.

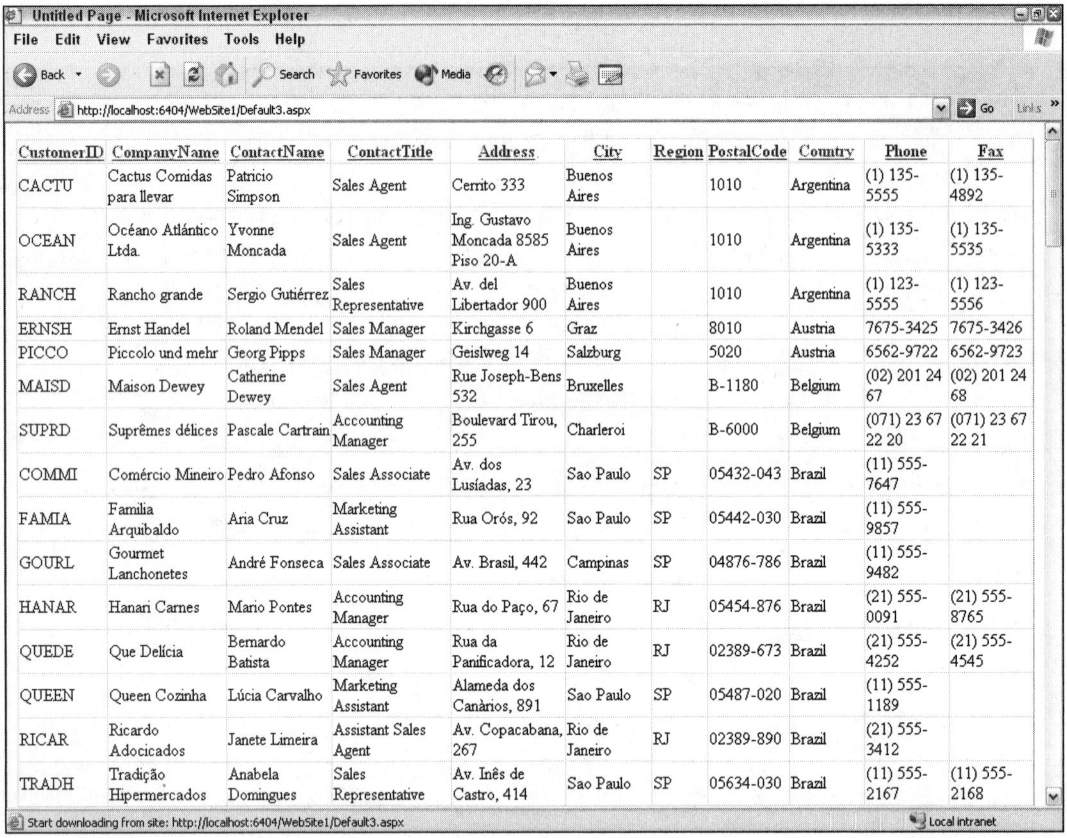

CustomerID	CompanyName	ContactName	ContactTitle	Address	City	Region	PostalCode	Country	Phone	Fax
CACTU	Cactus Comidas para llevar	Patricio Simpson	Sales Agent	Cerrito 333	Buenos Aires		1010	Argentina	(1) 135-5555	(1) 135-4892
OCEAN	Océano Atlántico Ltda.	Yvonne Moncada	Sales Agent	Ing. Gustavo Moncada 8585 Piso 20-A	Buenos Aires		1010	Argentina	(1) 135-5333	(1) 135-5535
RANCH	Rancho grande	Sergio Gutiérrez	Sales Representative	Av. del Libertador 900	Buenos Aires		1010	Argentina	(1) 123-5555	(1) 123-5556
ERNSH	Ernst Handel	Roland Mendel	Sales Manager	Kirchgasse 6	Graz		8010	Austria	7675-3425	7675-3426
PICCO	Piccolo und mehr	Georg Pipps	Sales Manager	Geislweg 14	Salzburg		5020	Austria	6562-9722	6562-9723
MAISD	Maison Dewey	Catherine Dewey	Sales Agent	Rue Joseph-Bens 532	Bruxelles		B-1180	Belgium	(02) 201 24 67	(02) 201 24 68
SUPRD	Suprêmes délices	Pascale Cartrain	Accounting Manager	Boulevard Tirou, 255	Charleroi		B-6000	Belgium	(071) 23 67 22 20	(071) 23 67 22 21
COMMI	Comércio Mineiro	Pedro Afonso	Sales Associate	Av. dos Lusíadas, 23	Sao Paulo	SP	05432-043	Brazil	(11) 555-7647	
FAMIA	Familia Arquibaldo	Aria Cruz	Marketing Assistant	Rua Orós, 92	Sao Paulo	SP	05442-030	Brazil	(11) 555-9857	
GOURL	Gourmet Lanchonetes	André Fonseca	Sales Associate	Av. Brasil, 442	Campinas	SP	04876-786	Brazil	(11) 555-9482	
HANAR	Hanari Carnes	Mario Pontes	Accounting Manager	Rua do Paço, 67	Rio de Janeiro	RJ	05454-876	Brazil	(21) 555-0091	(21) 555-8765
QUEDE	Que Delícia	Bernardo Batista	Accounting Manager	Rua da Panificadora, 12	Rio de Janeiro	RJ	02389-673	Brazil	(21) 555-4252	(21) 555-4545
QUEEN	Queen Cozinha	Lúcia Carvalho	Marketing Assistant	Alameda dos Canàrios, 891	Sao Paulo	SP	05487-020	Brazil	(11) 555-1189	
RICAR	Ricardo Adocicados	Janete Limeira	Assistant Sales Agent	Av. Copacabana, 267	Rio de Janeiro	RJ	02389-890	Brazil	(21) 555-3412	
TRADH	Tradição Hipermercados	Anabela Domingues	Sales Representative	Av. Inês de Castro, 414	Sao Paulo	SP	05634-030	Brazil	(11) 555-2167	(11) 555-2168

Figure 11-9

GridView sorting has also been enhanced in a number of other ways. The grid can handle both ascending and descending sorting. If you repeatedly click the column head, you cause the sort order to switch back and forth between ascending and descending. The GridView's `Sort` method can also accept multiple `SortExpressions` to enable multicolumn sorting. Listing 11-17 shows how you can use the GridView's sorting event to implement a multicolumn sort.

Listing 11-17: Adding multicolumn sorting to the GridView

VB

```
<script runat="server">
    Protected Sub GridView1_Sorting(ByVal sender As Object, _
       ByVal e As GridViewSortEventArgs)

        Dim oldExpression As String = GridView1.SortExpression
        Dim newExpression As String = e.SortExpression

        If (oldExpression.IndexOf(newExpression) < 0) Then
```

```
                If (oldExpression.Length > 0) Then
                    e.SortExpression = newExpression & "," & oldExpression
                Else
                    e.SortExpression = newExpression
                End If
            Else
                e.SortExpression = oldExpression
            End If
        End Sub
    </script>
```

C#

```
<script runat="server">
    protected void GridView1_Sorting(object sender, GridViewSortEventArgs e)
    {
        string oldExpression = GridView1.SortExpression;
        string newExpression = e.SortExpression;

        if (oldExpression.IndexOf(newExpression) < 0)
        {
            if (oldExpression.Length > 0)
                e.SortExpression = newExpression + "," + oldExpression;
            else
                e.SortExpression = newExpression;
        }
        else
        {
            e.SortExpression = oldExpression;
        }
    }
</script>
```

Enabling the GridView Pager

Another common grid navigation feature that the GridView greatly improves on is paging. Although implementing paging using a DataGrid greatly simplified paging (especially in comparison to paging in ASP), the GridView makes it even easier with its AllowPaging attribute. This attribute can be set either by adding the attribute to the GridView control in HTML mode or by checking the Enable Paging check box in the GridView's smart tag. Enabling paging in the GridView control defaults to a page size of 10 records and adds the Pager to the bottom of the grid. Listing 11-18 shows an example of modifying your grid to enable paging.

Listing 11-18: Enabling paging on the GridView control

```
<asp:GridView ID="GridView1" Runat="server" DataSourceID="SqlDataSource1"
    DataKeyNames="CustomerID" AutoGenerateColumns="False"
    AllowSorting="True" AllowPaging="True">
```

Enabling paging in your GridView creates a page that looks like Figure 11-10.

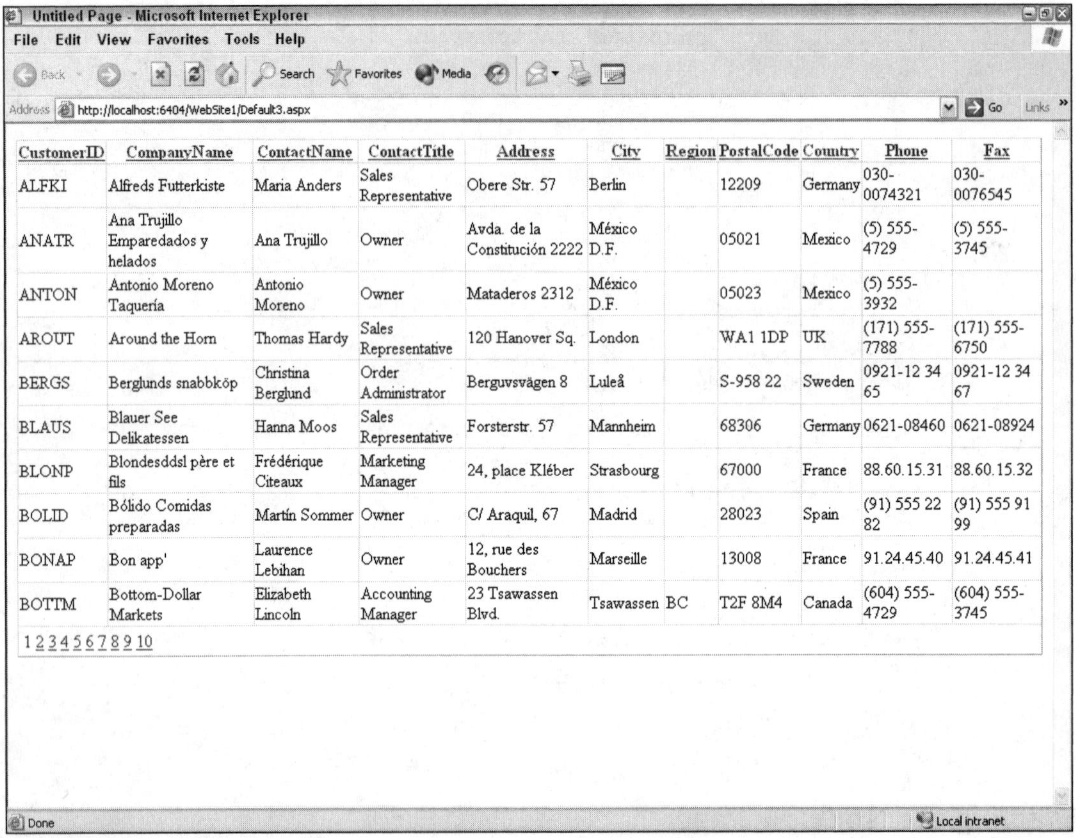

Figure 11-10

As with the DataGrid, the GridView allows most of the paging options to be customized. For instance, the PagersSettings-Mode attribute allows you to dictate how the grid's Pager is displayed using the various Pager modes including NextPrevious, NextPreviousFirstLast, Numeric (the default value), or NumericFirstLast. Additionally, by specifying the PagerStyle element in the GridView, you can customize how the grid displays the Pager text, including font color, size, and type, as well as text alignment and a variety of other style options. Listing 11-19 shows how you might customize your GridView control to use the NextPrevious mode and style the Pager text using the PagerStyle element. Also, you can control the number of records displayed on the page using the GridView's PageSize attribute.

Listing 11-19: Using the PagerStyle and PagerSettings objects in the GridView control

```
<asp:GridView ID="GridView1" Runat="server" DataSourceID="SqlDataSource1"
     DataKeyNames="CustomerID" AutoGenerateColumns="False"
     AllowSorting="True" AllowPaging="True" PageSize="10">
     <PagerStyle HorizontalAlign="Center"></PagerStyle>
     <PagerSettings Position="TopAndBottom"
          FirstPageText="Go to the first page"
          LastPageText="Go to the last page" Mode="NextPreviousFirstLast">
     </PagerSettings>
```

Figure 11-11 shows the grid after you change several style options and set the `PagerSettings-Mode` to `NextPreviousFirstLast`.

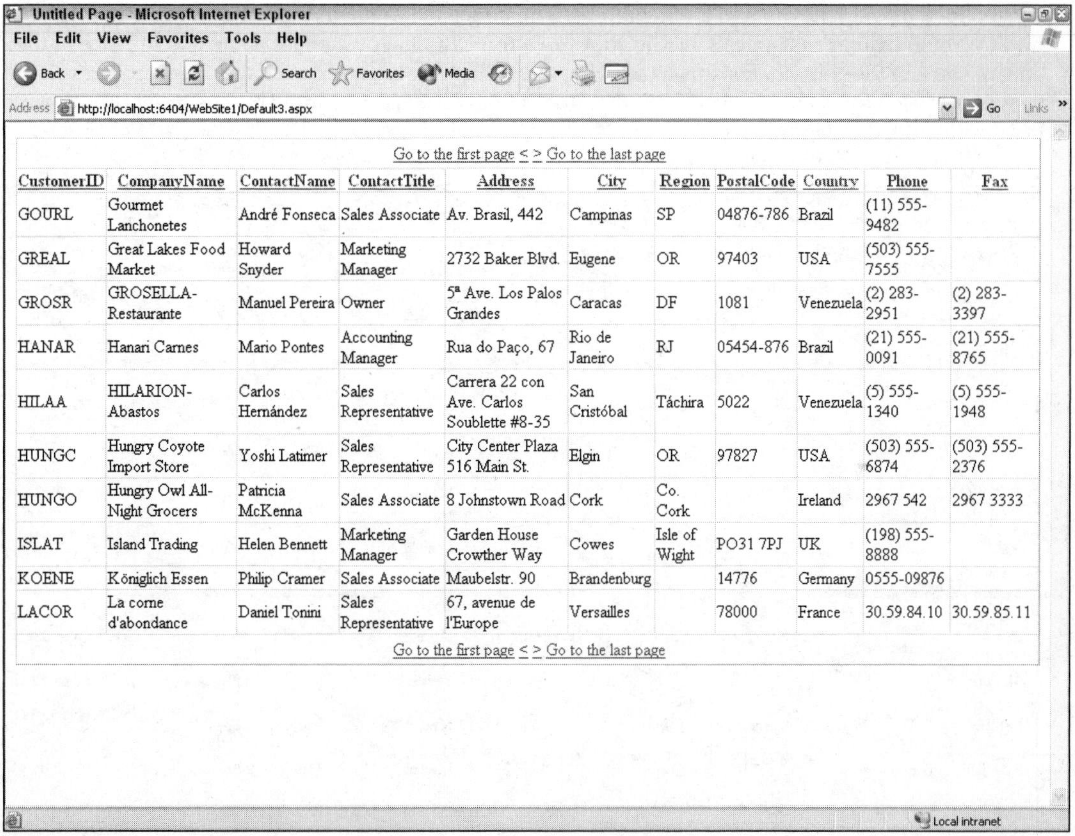

CustomerID	CompanyName	ContactName	ContactTitle	Address	City	Region	PostalCode	Country	Phone	Fax
GOURL	Gourmet Lanchonetes	André Fonseca	Sales Associate	Av. Brasil, 442	Campinas	SP	04876-786	Brazil	(11) 555-9482	
GREAL	Great Lakes Food Market	Howard Snyder	Marketing Manager	2732 Baker Blvd.	Eugene	OR	97403	USA	(503) 555-7555	
GROSR	GROSELLA-Restaurante	Manuel Pereira	Owner	5ª Ave. Los Palos Grandes	Caracas	DF	1081	Venezuela	(2) 283-2951	(2) 283-3397
HANAR	Hanari Carnes	Mario Pontes	Accounting Manager	Rua do Paço, 67	Rio de Janeiro	RJ	05454-876	Brazil	(21) 555-0091	(21) 555-8765
HILAA	HILARION-Abastos	Carlos Hernández	Sales Representative	Carrera 22 con Ave. Carlos Soublette #8-35	San Cristóbal	Táchira	5022	Venezuela	(5) 555-1340	(5) 555-1948
HUNGC	Hungry Coyote Import Store	Yoshi Latimer	Sales Representative	City Center Plaza 516 Main St.	Elgin	OR	97827	USA	(503) 555-6874	(503) 555-2376
HUNGO	Hungry Owl All-Night Grocers	Patricia McKenna	Sales Associate	8 Johnstown Road	Cork	Co. Cork		Ireland	2967 542	2967 3333
ISLAT	Island Trading	Helen Bennett	Marketing Manager	Garden House Crowther Way	Cowes	Isle of Wight	PO31 7PJ	UK	(198) 555-8888	
KOENE	Königlich Essen	Philip Cramer	Sales Associate	Maubelstr. 90	Brandenburg		14776	Germany	0555-09876	
LACOR	La corne d'abondance	Daniel Tonini	Sales Representative	67, avenue de l'Europe	Versailles		78000	France	30.59.84.10	30.59.85.11

Figure 11-11

The GridView has a multitude of other Pager and Pager style options that we encourage you to experiment with. Because the list of `PagerSetting` and `PagerStyle` options is so long, all options are not listed here. You can find a full list of the options in the Visual Studio Help documents.

Another interesting feature of column generation is the capability to specify what the GridView should display when it encounters a `Null` value within the column. For an example of this, add a column using an additional `<asp:BoundField>` control, as shown in Listing 11-20.

Listing 11-20: Using the Null value

```
<asp:BoundField HeaderText="Region" NullDisplayText="N/A"
     DataField="Region" SortExpression="Region"></asp:BoundField>
```

In this example, the `<asp:BoundField>` element displays the Region column from the Customers table. As you look through the data in the Region section, notice that not every row has a value in it. If you don't want to display just a blank box to show an empty value, you can use some text in place of the empty items in the column. For this, you utilize the `NullDisplayText` attribute. The `String` value it provides is used for each and every row that doesn't have a Region value. This construct produces the results illustrated in Figure 11-12.

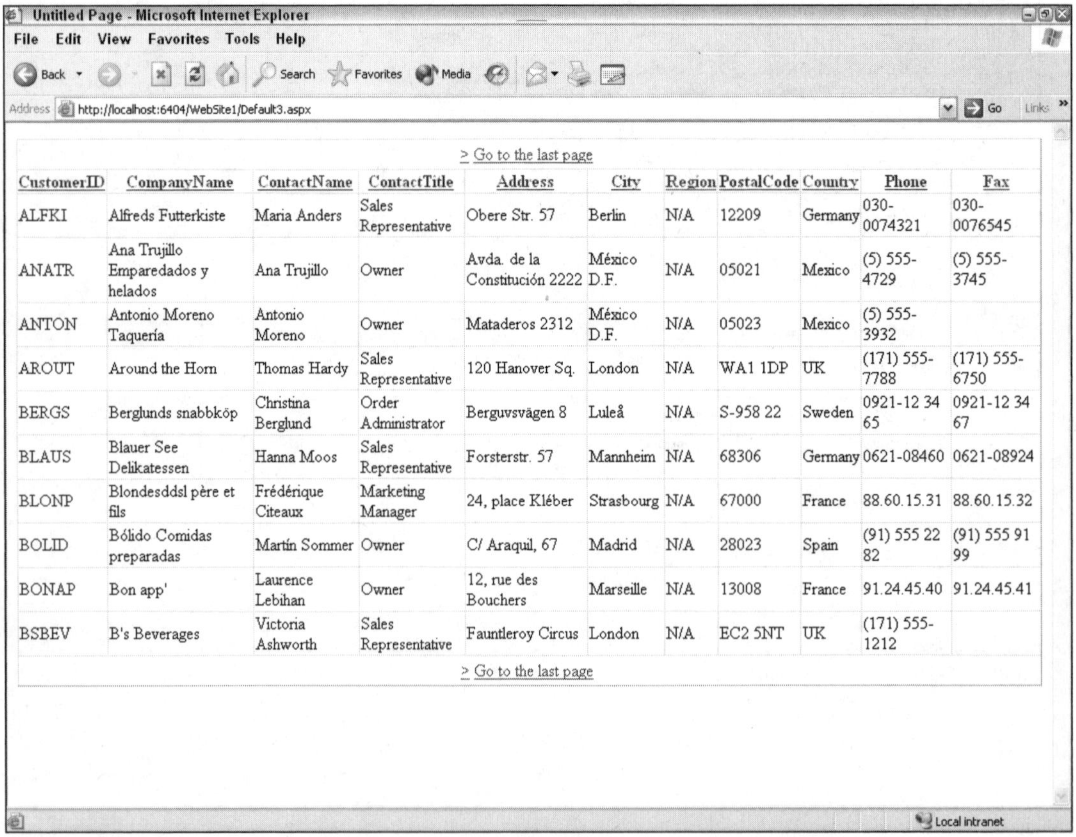

> Go to the last page

CustomerID	CompanyName	ContactName	ContactTitle	Address	City	Region	PostalCode	Country	Phone	Fax
ALFKI	Alfreds Futterkiste	Maria Anders	Sales Representative	Obere Str. 57	Berlin	N/A	12209	Germany	030-0074321	030-0076545
ANATR	Ana Trujillo Emparedados y helados	Ana Trujillo	Owner	Avda. de la Constitución 2222	México D.F.	N/A	05021	Mexico	(5) 555-4729	(5) 555-3745
ANTON	Antonio Moreno Taquería	Antonio Moreno	Owner	Mataderos 2312	México D.F.	N/A	05023	Mexico	(5) 555-3932	
AROUT	Around the Horn	Thomas Hardy	Sales Representative	120 Hanover Sq.	London	N/A	WA1 1DP	UK	(171) 555-7788	(171) 555-6750
BERGS	Berglunds snabbköp	Christina Berglund	Order Administrator	Berguvsvägen 8	Luleå	N/A	S-958 22	Sweden	0921-12 34 65	0921-12 34 67
BLAUS	Blauer See Delikatessen	Hanna Moos	Sales Representative	Forsterstr. 57	Mannheim	N/A	68306	Germany	0621-08460	0621-08924
BLONP	Blondesddsl père et fils	Frédérique Citeaux	Marketing Manager	24, place Kléber	Strasbourg	N/A	67000	France	88.60.15.31	88.60.15.32
BOLID	Bólido Comidas preparadas	Martín Sommer	Owner	C/ Araquil, 67	Madrid	N/A	28023	Spain	(91) 555 22 82	(91) 555 91 99
BONAP	Bon app'	Laurence Lebihan	Owner	12, rue des Bouchers	Marseille	N/A	13008	France	91.24.45.40	91.24.45.41
BSBEV	B's Beverages	Victoria Ashworth	Sales Representative	Fauntleroy Circus	London	N/A	EC2 5NT	UK	(171) 555-1212	

> Go to the last page

Figure 11-12

Customizing Columns in the GridView

Frequently, the data in your grid is not simply text data, but data that you either want to display using other types of controls or don't want to display at all. For instance, you have been retrieving the CustomerID as part of your SELECT query and displaying it in your grid. By default, the GridView control displays all columns returned as part of a query. But rather than automatically displaying the CustomerID, it might be better to hide that data from the end user. Or perhaps you are also storing the corporate URL for all your customers and want the CustomerName column to hyperlink directly to their Web sites. The GridView gives you great flexibility and power regarding how you display the data in your grid.

The GridView automatically converts columns with a data type of bit or Boolean to a CheckBoxField.

You can edit your GridView columns in two ways. You can select the Edit Columns option from the GridView smart tag. This link allows you to edit any existing columns in your grid using the Fields dialog window, shown in Figure 11-13. From here you can change a column's visibility, header text, the usual style options, and many other properties of the column.

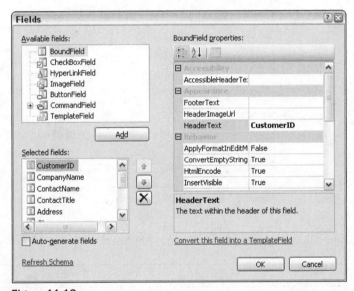

Figure 11-13

Selecting the Add New Column link from the GridView control's smart tag displays another easy form—the Add Field dialog (shown in Figure 11-14)—with options allowing you to add completely new columns to your grid. Depending on which column field type you select from the drop-down list, the dialog presents you with the appropriate options for that column type. In this case, you want to add a hyperlink; so you select the HyperLinkField from the drop-down list. The Add Field dialog changes and lets you enter in the hyperlink information, including the URL, the data field, and a formatter string for the column.

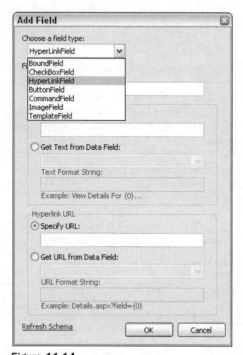

Figure 11-14

The Add Field dialog lets you select one of the Field types described in the following table.

Field Control	Description
BoundField	Displays the value of a field in a data source. This is the default column type of the GridView control.
CheckBoxField	Displays a check box for each item in the GridView control. This column field type is commonly used to display fields with a Boolean value.
HyperLinkField	Displays the value of a field in a data source as a hyperlink. This column field type allows you to bind a second field to the hyperlink's URL.
ButtonField	Displays a command button for each item in the GridView control. This allows you to create a column of custom button controls, such as the Add or the Remove button.

Field Control	Description
CommandField	Represents a special field that displays command buttons to perform select, edit, insert, or delete operations in a data-bound control.
ImageField	Automatically displays an image when the data in the field represents an image.
TemplateField	Displays user-defined content for each item in the GridView control according to a specified template. This column field type allows you to create a custom column field.

You can also change the grid columns in the Source view. Listing 11-21 shows how you can add a HyperLinkField. Note that by providing a comma-delimited list of data field names, you can actually specify multiple data fields to bind to this column. You can then use these fields in your formatting string to pass two query string parameters, which is a new feature in ASP.NET 2.0.

Listing 11-21: Adding a HyperlinkField control to the GridView

```
<asp:HyperLinkField HeaderText="CompanyName"
    DataNavigateUrlFields="CustomerID,Country" SortExpression="CompanyName"
    DataNavigateUrlFormatString=
        "http://www.foo.com/Customer.aspx?id={0}&country={1}"
    DataTextField="CompanyName">
</asp:HyperLinkField>
```

Editing GridView Row Data

Not only do users want to view the data in their browser, but they also want to be able to edit the data and save changes back to the data store. Adding editing capabilities to the DataGrid was never easy, but it was important enough that developers frequently attempted to do so.

The GridView control makes it very easy to edit the data contained in the grid. To demonstrate just how easy it is, you can modify the existing grid so you can edit the customer data it contains. First, modify your existing SqlDataSource control by adding an UpdateCommand attribute. This tells the data source control what SQL it should execute when it is requested to perform an update. Listing 11-22 shows the code to add the UpdateCommand attribute.

Listing 11-22: Adding an UpdateCommand to a SqlDataSource control

```
<asp:SqlDataSource ID="SqlDataSource1" Runat="server"
    SelectCommand="SELECT * FROM [Customers]"
    ConnectionString="<%$ ConnectionStrings:AppConnectionString1 %>"
    DataSourceMode="DataSet"
    UpdateCommand="UPDATE [Customers] SET [CompanyName] = @CompanyName,
        [ContactName] = @ContactName, [ContactTitle] = @ContactTitle,
        [Address] = @Address, [City] = @City, [Region] = @Region,
        [PostalCode] = @PostalCode, [Country] = @Country, [Phone] = @Phone,
        [Fax] = @Fax WHERE [CustomerID] = @original_CustomerID">
```

Notice that the UpdateCommand includes a number of parameters like `@CompanyName`, `@Country`, `@Region`, and `@CustomerID`. These are placeholders for the corresponding information that will come from the selected row in GridView. In order to use the parameters, you must define them using the `UpdateParameters` element of the SqlDataSource control. The `UpdateParameters` element, shown in Listing 11-23, works much like the `SelectParameters` element discussed earlier in the chapter.

Listing 11-23: Adding UpdateParameters to the SqlDataSource control

```
<asp:SqlDataSource ID="SqlDataSource1" Runat="server"
    SelectCommand="SELECT * FROM [Customers]"
    ConnectionString="<%$ ConnectionStrings:AppConnectionString1 %>"
    DataSourceMode="DataSet"
    UpdateCommand="UPDATE [Customers] SET [CompanyName] = @CompanyName,
        [ContactName] = @ContactName, [ContactTitle] = @ContactTitle,
        [Address] = @Address, [City] = @City, [Region] = @Region,
        [PostalCode] = @PostalCode, [Country] = @Country, [Phone] = @Phone,
        [Fax] = @Fax WHERE [CustomerID] = @original_CustomerID">
    <UpdateParameters>
        <asp:Parameter Type="String" Name="CompanyName"></asp:Parameter>
        <asp:Parameter Type="String" Name="ContactName"></asp:Parameter>
        <asp:Parameter Type="String" Name="ContactTitle"></asp:Parameter>
        <asp:Parameter Type="String" Name="Address"></asp:Parameter>
        <asp:Parameter Type="String" Name="City"></asp:Parameter>
        <asp:Parameter Type="String" Name="Region"></asp:Parameter>
        <asp:Parameter Type="String" Name="PostalCode"></asp:Parameter>
        <asp:Parameter Type="String" Name="Country"></asp:Parameter>
        <asp:Parameter Type="String" Name="Phone"></asp:Parameter>
        <asp:Parameter Type="String" Name="Fax"></asp:Parameter>
        <asp:Parameter Type="String" Name="CustomerID"></asp:Parameter>
    </UpdateParameters>
</asp:SqlDataSource>
```

Within the `UpdateParameters` element, each named parameter is defined using the `<asp:Parameter>` element. This element uses two attributes that define the name and the data type of the parameter. In this case, all the parameters are of type `String`. Remember that you can also use any of the Parameter controls mentioned earlier in the chapter, such as the `ControlParameter` or `QuerystringParameter` in the `UpdateParameters` element.

Next, you give the grid a column it can use to trigger editing of a data row. You can do this in several ways. First, you can use the GridView's `AutoGenerateEditButton` attribute. When set to `True`, this attribute tells the grid to add to itself a `ButtonField` column with an Edit button for each data row. Listing 11-24 shows how to add the `AutoGenerateEditButton` attribute to the GridView control.

Listing 11-24: Adding the AutoGenerateEditButton attribute to a SqlDataSource control

```
<asp:GridView ID="GridView1" Runat="server" DataSourceID="SqlDataSource1"
    DataKeyNames="CustomerID" AutoGenerateColumns="False"
    AllowSorting="True" AllowPaging="True"
    AutoGenerateEditButton="true">
```

The GridView control also includes `AutoGenerateSelectButton` and `AutoGenerateDeleteButton` attributes, which allow you to easily add Row Selection and Row Deletion capabilities to the grid.

A second way to add an Edit button is to add a `CommandField` column. This is shown in Listing 11-25.

Listing 11-25: Adding edit functionality using a CommandField control

```
<asp:CommandField ShowHeader="True" HeaderText="Command"
    ShowEditButton="True"></asp:CommandField>
```

Notice that you add the `ShowEditButton` attribute to the `CommandField` to indicate that you want to display the Edit command in this column. You can control how the command is displayed in the grid using the `ButtonType` attribute, which allows you to display the command as a link, a button, or even an image. Figure 11-15 shows what the grid looks like after adding the `CommandField` with the `Edit` command displayed.

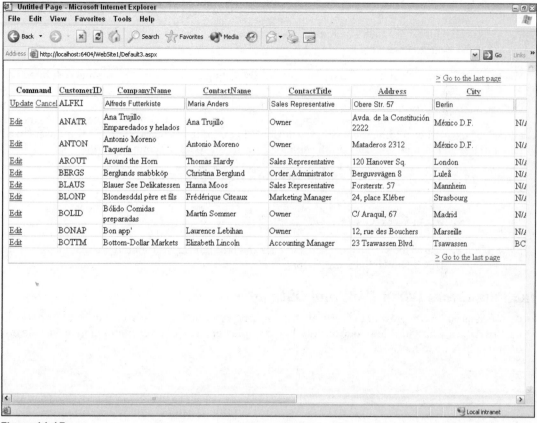

Figure 11-15

Now if you browse to your Web page, you see that a new Edit column has been added. Clicking the Edit link allows the user to edit the contents of that particular data row.

The CommandField element also has attributes that allow you to control exactly what is shown in the column. You can dictate whether the column displays commands like Cancel, Delete, Edit, Insert, and Select.

With the Edit CommandField enabled, you still have one more attribute to be set in order to enable the grid to perform the UPDATE SQL command. You tell the grid which SQL columns are serving as your primary keys. You can accomplish this by using the DataKeyNames attribute, as illustrated in Listing 11-26.

Listing 11-26: Turning off AutoGenerateColumns in the GridView control

```
<asp:GridView ID="GridView1" Runat="server" DataSourceID="SqlDataSource1"
    DataKeyNames="CustomerID" AutoGenerateColumns="False"
    AllowSorting="True" AllowPaging="True"
    AutoGenerateEditButton="true">
```

You can specify more than one primary key column by setting the attribute to a comma-delimited list.

Notice that when you add the edit capabilities to the grid, by default it allows all displayed columns to be edited. You probably won't always want this to be the case. You can control which columns the grid allows to be edited by adding the ReadOnly attribute to the columns that you do not want users to edit. Listing 11-27 shows how you can add the ReadOnly attribute to the ID column.

Listing 11-27: Adding the ReadOnly attribute to a BoundField

```
<asp:BoundField ReadOnly="True" HeaderText="CustomerID" DataField="CustomerID"
    SortExpression="CustomerID" Visible="False"></asp:BoundField>
```

Now if you browse to the Web page again and click the Edit button, you should see that the ID column is not editable. This is shown in Figure 11-16.

Handling Errors When Updating Data

As much as you try to prevent them, errors happen when you save data. If you allow your users to update data in your GridView control, you should implement a bit of error trapping to make sure errors do not bubble up to the user.

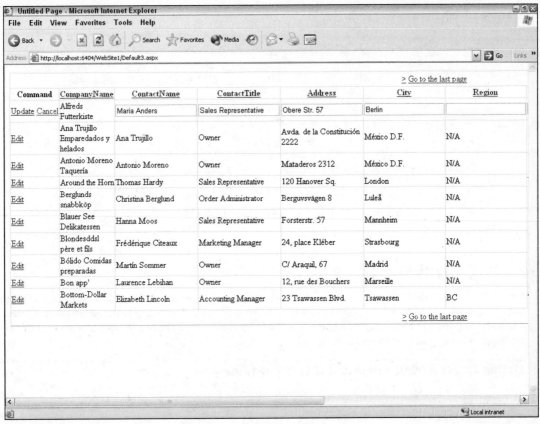

Figure 11-16

To check for errors when updating data through the GridView, you can use the `RowUpdated` event. Listing 11-28 shows how to check for errors after a user has attempted to update data. In this scenario, if an error does occur, you simply display a message to the user in a Label.

Listing 11-28: Checking for Update errors using the RowUpdated event

VB
```
<script runat="server">
    Protected Sub GridView1_RowUpdated(ByVal sender As Object, _
        ByVal e As System.Web.UI.WebControls.GridViewUpdatedEventArgs)

        If (Not IsNothing(e.Exception)) Then
```

(continued)

Listing 11-28: *(continued)*

```
            Me.lblErrorMessage.Text = e.Exception.Message
        End If
    End Sub
</script>
```

C#

```
<script runat="server">
    protected void GridView1_RowUpdated(object sender, GridViewUpdatedEventArgs e)
    {
        if (e.Exception != null)
        {
            this.lblErrorMessage.Text = e.Exception.Message;
        }
    }
</script>
```

Deleting GridView Data

Deleting data from the table produced by the GridView is even easier than editing data. Just a few additions to the code enable you to delete an entire row of data from the table. Much like with the Edit buttons you added earlier, you can easily add a Delete button to the grid by setting the `AutoGenerateDeleteButton` attribute to `True`. This is shown in Listing 11-29.

Listing 11-29: Adding a delete link to the GridView

```
<asp:GridView ID="GridView1" Runat="server" DataSourceID="SqlDataSource1"
    DataKeyNames="CustomerID" AutoGenerateColumns="False"
    AllowSorting="True" AllowPaging="True"
    AutoGenerateEditButton="true" AutoGenerateDeleteButton="true">
```

The addition of the `AutoGenerateDeleteButton` attribute to the GridView is the only change you make to this control. Now look at the SqlDataSource control. Listing 11-30 shows you the root element of this control.

Listing 11-30: Adding delete functionality to the SqlDataSource Control

```
<asp:SqlDataSource ID="SqlDataSource1" Runat="server"
    SelectCommand="SELECT * FROM [Customers]"
    ConnectionString="<%$ ConnectionStrings:AppConnectionString1 %>"
    DataSourceMode="DataSet"
    DeleteCommand="DELETE From Customers WHERE (CustomerID = @CustomerID)"
    UpdateCommand="UPDATE [Customers] SET [CompanyName] = @CompanyName,
        [ContactName] = @ContactName, [ContactTitle] = @ContactTitle,
        [Address] = @Address, [City] = @City, [Region] = @Region,
        [PostalCode] = @PostalCode, [Country] = @Country, [Phone] = @Phone,
        [Fax] = @Fax WHERE [CustomerID] = @original_CustomerID">
```

In addition to the `SelectCommand` and `UpdateCommand` attributes, you also add the `DeleteCommand` attribute to the SqlDataSource and provide the SQL command that deletes the specified row. Just like the `UpdateCommand` attribute, the `DeleteCommand` attribute makes use of named parameters. Because of this, you define this parameter from within the SqlDataSource control. To do this, add a `<DeleteParameters>` section to the SqlDataSource control. This is shown in Listing 11-31.

Listing 11-31: Adding a <DeleteParameters> section to the SqlDataSource control

```
<DeleteParameters>
    <asp:Parameter Name="CustomerID" Type="String">
    </asp:Parameter>
</DeleteParameters>
```

This is the only parameter definition needed for the `<DeleteParameters>` section because the SQL command for this deletion requires only the CustomerID from the row to delete the entire row.

When you run the example with this code in place, you see a Delete link next to the Edit link. Clicking the Delete link completely deletes the selected row. Remember that it is a good idea to check for database errors after you complete the deletion. Listing 11-32 shows how you can use the GridViews `RowDeleted` event and the SqlDataSources `Deleted` event to check for errors that might have occurred during the Delete.

Notice that both events provide Exception properties to you as part of the event arguments. If the properties are not empty, then an exception occurred that you can handle. If you do choose to handle the exception, then you should set the `ExceptionHandled` property to `True`; otherwise, the Exception will continue to bubble up to the end user.

Listing 11-32: Using the RowDeleted event to catch SQL errors

VB

```
<script runat="server">
    Protected Sub GridView1_RowDeleted(ByVal sender As Object, _
        ByVal e As GridViewDeletedEventArgs)

        If (Not IsDBNull(e.Exception)) Then
            Me.lblErrorMessage.Text = e.Exception.Message
            e.ExceptionHandled = True
        End If
    End Sub

    Protected Sub SqlDataSource1_Deleted(ByVal sender As Object, _
        ByVal e As System.Web.UI.WebControls.SqlDataSourceStatusEventArgs)

        If (e.Exception IsNot Nothing) Then
            Me.lblErrorMessage.Text = e.Exception.Message
            e.ExceptionHandled = True
        End If
    End Sub
</script>
```

(continued)

Listing 11-32: *(continued)*

C#

```
<script runat="server">
    protected void GridView1_RowDeleted(object sender, GridViewDeletedEventArgs e)
    {
        if (e.Exception != null)
        {
            this.lblErrorMessage.Text = e.Exception.Message;
            e.ExceptionHandled = true;
        }
    }

    protected void SqlDataSource1_Deleted(object sender,
        SqlDataSourceStatusEventArgs e)
    {
        if (e.Exception != null)
        {
            this.lblErrorMessage.Text = e.Exception.Message;
            e.ExceptionHandled = true;
        }
    }
</script>
```

DetailsView

The DetailsView server control is a new data-bound control that enables you to view a single data record at a time. Although the GridView control is an excellent control for viewing a collection of data, many scenarios demand that you be able to drill down into an individual record. The DetailsView control allows you to do this and provides many of the same data manipulation and display capabilities as the GridView. It allows you to do things such as paging, updating, inserting, and deleting data.

To start using the DetailsView, drag the control onto the design surface. Like the GridView, you can use the DetailsView's smart tag to create and set the data source for the control. For this sample, just use the SqlDataSource control you used for the DataGrid. If you run the page at this point, you see that the control displays one record, the first record returned by your query. Figure 11-17 shows you what the DetailsView looks like in a Web page.

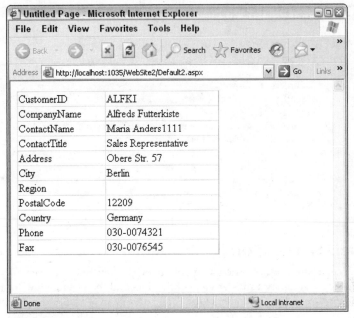

Figure 11-17

If this is all the functionality you want, you probably want to create a new SqlDataSource control and modify the `SelectCommand` so that it returns only one record, rather than returning all records as our query does. For this example, however, you want to be able to page through all the Customer data returned by your query. To do this, simply turn on paging by setting the DetailsView's `AllowPaging` attribute to `True`. You can either check the Enable Paging check box in the DetailsView smart tag or add the attribute to the control in HTML View. Listing 11-33 shows the DetailsView code for the control.

Listing 11-33: Enabling paging on the DetailsView control

```
<asp:DetailsView ID="DetailsView1" Runat="server" DataSourceID="SqlDataSource1"
    AutoGenerateRows="False" DataKeyNames="CustomerID"></asp:DetailsView>
```

Like the GridView, the DetailsView control enables you to customize the control's Pager using the `PagerSettings-Mode`, as well as the `Pager` style.

Customizing the DetailsView Display

You can customize the appearance of the DetailsView control by picking and choosing which fields the control displays. By default, the control displays each column from the table it is working with. Much like the GridView control, however, the DetailsView control enables you to specify that only certain selected columns be displayed, as illustrated in Listing 11-34.

Listing 11-34: Customizing the display of the DetailsView control

```
<asp:DetailsView ID="DetailsView1" Runat="server" DataSourceID="SqlDataSource1"
    AutoGenerateRows="False" DataKeyNames="CustomerID">
    <Fields>
        <asp:BoundField ReadOnly="True" HeaderText="CustomerID"
            DataField="CustomerID" SortExpression="CustomerID"
            Visible="False" />
        <asp:BoundField ReadOnly="True" HeaderText="CompanyName"
            DataField="CompanyName" SortExpression="CompanyName" />
        <asp:BoundField HeaderText="ContactName" DataField="ContactName"
            SortExpression="ContactName" />
        <asp:BoundField HeaderText="ContactTitle" DataField="ContactTitle"
            SortExpression="ContactTitle" />
    </Fields>
</asp:DetailsView>
```

Using the DetailsView and GridView Together

This section looks at a common scenario using both the GridView and the DetailsView. In this example, you use the GridView to display a master view of the data and the DetailsView to show the details of the selected GridView row. The Customers table is the data source. Listing 11-35 shows the code needed for this.

Listing 11-35: Using the GridView and DetailsView together

```
<html>
<head id="Head1" runat="server">
    <title>GridView & DetailsView Controls</title>
</head>
<body>
    <form id="form1" runat="server">
        <p>
            <asp:GridView ID="GridView1" runat="server"
                DataSourceId="SqlDataSource1" AllowPaging="True"
                BorderColor="#DEBA84" BorderStyle="None" BorderWidth="1px"
                BackColor="#DEBA84" CellSpacing="2" CellPadding="3"
                DataKeyNames="CustomerID" AutoGenerateSelectButton="True"
                AutoGenerateColumns="False" PageSize="5">
                <FooterStyle ForeColor="#8C4510"
                    BackColor="#F7DFB5"></FooterStyle>
                <PagerStyle ForeColor="#8C4510"
                    HorizontalAlign="Center"></PagerStyle>
                <HeaderStyle ForeColor="White" BackColor="#A55129"
                    Font-Bold="True"></HeaderStyle>
                <Columns>
                    <asp:BoundField ReadOnly="True" HeaderText="CustomerID"
                        DataField="CustomerID" SortExpression="CustomerID">
                    </asp:BoundField>
```

```
            <asp:BoundField HeaderText="CompanyName"
                DataField="CompanyName" SortExpression="CompanyName">
            </asp:BoundField>
            <asp:BoundField HeaderText="ContactName"
                DataField="ContactName" SortExpression="ContactName">
            </asp:BoundField>
            <asp:BoundField HeaderText="ContactTitle"
                DataField="ContactTitle" SortExpression="ContactTitle">
            </asp:BoundField>
            <asp:BoundField HeaderText="Address" DataField="Address"
                SortExpression="Address"></asp:BoundField>
            <asp:BoundField HeaderText="City" DataField="City"
                SortExpression="City"></asp:BoundField>
            <asp:BoundField HeaderText="Region" DataField="Region"
                SortExpression="Region"></asp:BoundField>
            <asp:BoundField HeaderText="PostalCode" DataField="PostalCode"
                SortExpression="PostalCode"></asp:BoundField>
            <asp:BoundField HeaderText="Country" DataField="Country"
                SortExpression="Country"></asp:BoundField>
            <asp:BoundField HeaderText="Phone" DataField="Phone"
                SortExpression="Phone"></asp:BoundField>
            <asp:BoundField HeaderText="Fax" DataField="Fax"
                SortExpression="Fax"></asp:BoundField>
        </Columns>
        <SelectedRowStyle ForeColor="White" BackColor="#738A9C"
            Font-Bold="True"></SelectedRowStyle>
        <RowStyle ForeColor="#8C4510" BackColor="#FFF7E7"></RowStyle>
    </asp:GridView>
</p>
<p><b>Customer Details:</b></p>
<asp:DetailsView ID="DetailsView1" runat="server"
    DataSourceId="SqlDataSource2"
    BorderColor="#DEBA84" BorderStyle="None" BorderWidth="1px"
    BackColor="#DEBA84" CellSpacing="2" CellPadding="3"
    AutoGenerateRows="False" DataKeyNames="CustomerID">
    <FooterStyle ForeColor="#8C4510" BackColor="#F7DFB5"></FooterStyle>
    <RowStyle ForeColor="#8C4510" BackColor="#FFF7E7"></RowStyle>
    <PagerStyle ForeColor="#8C4510" HorizontalAlign="Center"></PagerStyle>
    <Fields>
        <asp:BoundField ReadOnly="True" HeaderText="CustomerID"
            DataField="CustomerID" SortExpression="CustomerID">
        </asp:BoundField>
        <asp:BoundField HeaderText="CompanyName" DataField="CompanyName"
            SortExpression="CompanyName"></asp:BoundField>
        <asp:BoundField HeaderText="ContactName" DataField="ContactName"
            SortExpression="ContactName"></asp:BoundField>
        <asp:BoundField HeaderText="ContactTitle" DataField="ContactTitle"
            SortExpression="ContactTitle"></asp:BoundField>
        <asp:BoundField HeaderText="Address" DataField="Address"
            SortExpression="Address"></asp:BoundField>
        <asp:BoundField HeaderText="City" DataField="City"
            SortExpression="City"></asp:BoundField>
        <asp:BoundField HeaderText="Region" DataField="Region"
            SortExpression="Region"></asp:BoundField>
```

(continued)

Listing 11-35: *(continued)*

```
                <asp:BoundField HeaderText="PostalCode" DataField="PostalCode"
                    SortExpression="PostalCode"></asp:BoundField>
                <asp:BoundField HeaderText="Country" DataField="Country"
                    SortExpression="Country"></asp:BoundField>
                <asp:BoundField HeaderText="Phone" DataField="Phone"
                    SortExpression="Phone"></asp:BoundField>
                <asp:BoundField HeaderText="Fax" DataField="Fax"
                    SortExpression="Fax"></asp:BoundField>
            </Fields>
            <HeaderStyle ForeColor="White" BackColor="#A55129"
                Font-Bold="True"></HeaderStyle>
            <EditRowStyle ForeColor="White" BackColor="#738A9C"
                Font-Bold="True"></EditRowStyle>
        </asp:DetailsView>
        <asp:SqlDataSource ID="SqlDataSource1" runat="server"
            SelectCommand="SELECT * FROM [Customers]"
            ConnectionString="<%$ ConnectionStrings:AppConnectionString1 %>" />
        <asp:SqlDataSource ID="SqlDataSource2" runat="server"
            SelectCommand="SELECT * FROM [Customers]"
            FilterExpression="CustomerID='{0}'"
            ConnectionString="<%$ ConnectionStrings:AppConnectionString1 %>">
            <FilterParameters>
                <asp:ControlParameter Name="CustomerID" ControlId="GridView1"
                    PropertyName="SelectedValue"></asp:ControlParameter>
            </FilterParameters>
        </asp:SqlDataSource>
    </form>
</body>
</html>
```

When this code is run in your browser, you get the results shown in Figure 11-18.

In this figure, one of the rows in the GridView has been selected (noticeable because of the gray highlighting). The details of the selected row are shown in the DetailsView control directly below the GridView control.

To see how this works, look at the changes that were made to the second SqlDataSource control, SqlDataSource2. Notice that a `FilterExpression` attribute has been added, which is used to modify the `SelectCommand` attribute.

The value given to the `FilterExpression` attribute expresses how you want the SqlDataSource control to filter its `Select` command. In this case, the value of the `FilterExpression` is `CustomerID=@CustomerID`. This tells the SqlDataSource control to filter records that it returns by the CustomerID given to it, as shown in Listing 11-36.

Listing 11-36: Filtering SqlDataSource data with a FilterExpression

```
<asp:SqlDataSource ID="SqlDataSource2" runat="server"
    SelectCommand="SELECT * FROM [Customers]"
    FilterExpression="CustomerID='{0}'"
    ConnectionString="<%$ ConnectionStrings:AppConnectionString1 %>">
    <FilterParameters>
        <asp:ControlParameter Name="CustomerID" ControlId="GridView1"
            PropertyName="SelectedValue"></asp:ControlParameter>
    </FilterParameters>
</asp:SqlDataSource>
```

The parameter specified in the `FilterExpression` attribute, `@CustomerID`, is defined within the SqlDataSource control through the use of the `<FilterParameters>` element. This sample uses an `<asp:ControlParameter>` to specify the name of the parameter, the control that the parameter value is coming from (the GridView control), and the property name that is used to populate the parameter value.

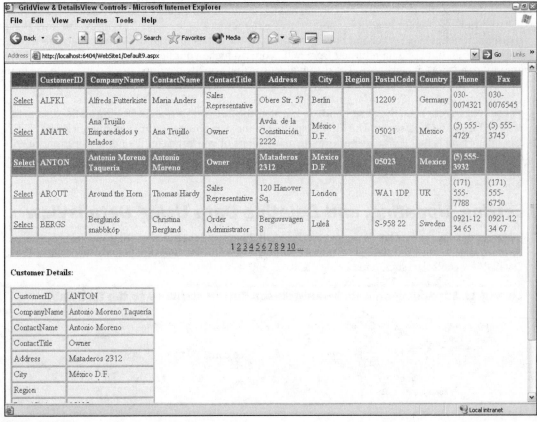

Figure 11-18

Finally, be sure to include the `DataKeyNames` attribute in the GridView control. In this case supply `CustomerID` as the value. This tells the GridView which column(s) are to be used as a primary key. When a user selects a row, the value of that column is then provided to the DetailsView control via the `SelectValue` property. The procedure for adding the DataKeyNames to the GridView is shown in Listing 11-37.

Listing 11-37: Adding the DataKeyNames attribute to the GridView

```
<asp:GridView ID="GridView1" runat="server"
              DataSourceId="SqlDataSource1" AllowPaging="True"
              BorderColor="#DEBA84" BorderStyle="None" BorderWidth="1px"
              BackColor="#DEBA84" CellSpacing="2" CellPadding="3"
              DataKeyNames="CustomerID" AutoGenerateSelectButton="True"
              AutoGenerateColumns="False" PageSize="5">
```

SelectParameters versus FilterParameters

You might have noticed in our last example that the `FilterParameters` seem to provide the same functionality as the `SelectParameters`. Although both produce essentially the same result, they use very different methods. Using a `SelectParameters` modifies the query that is executed against the SQL server by dynamically adding a `WHERE` clause to the `SelectCommand`. This limits the rows that are returned from the SQL Server and held in memory by the data source control. The advantage is that by limiting the amount of data returned from SQL, you can make your application faster and reduce the amount of memory it consumes. The disadvantage is that you are confined to working with the limited subset of data returned by the SQL query.

`FilterParameters`, on the other hand, do not alter the `SelectCommand`, allowing all the data to be returned from the SQL server. The filter is applied to the data source control's in-memory data. The advantage here is that if you are performing many filters of one large chunk of data (for instance, to enable paging in the DetailView), you do not have to call out to SQL Server each time you need the next record. All the data is stored in memory by the data source control.

Inserting, Updating, and Deleting Data Using DetailsView

Inserting data using the DetailsView is similar to all the other data functions that you have performed. To insert data using the DetailsView, simply add the `AutoGenerateInsertButton` attribute to the DetailsView control as shown in Listing 11-38.

Listing 11-38: Adding an AutoGenerateInsertButton attribute to the DetailsView

```
<asp:DetailsView ID="DetailsView1" runat="server"
     DataSourceId="SqlDataSource2"
     BorderColor="#DEBA84" BorderStyle="None" BorderWidth="1px"
     BackColor="#DEBA84" CellSpacing="2" CellPadding="3"
     AutoGenerateRows="False" AutoGenerateInsertButton="true"
     DataKeyNames="CustomerID">
```

Then add the `InsertCommand` and corresponding `InsertParameter` elements to the SqlDataSource control, as shown in Listing 11-39.

Listing 11-39: Adding an InsertCommand to the SqlDataSource control

```
<asp:SqlDataSource ID="sqlDataSource2" runat="server"
    SelectCommand="SELECT * FROM [Customers]"
    InsertCommand="INSERT INTO [Customers] ([CustomerID], [CompanyName],
        [ContactName], [ContactTitle], [Address], [City], [Region], [PostalCode],
        [Country], [Phone], [Fax]) VALUES (@CustomerID, @CompanyName,
        @ContactName, @ContactTitle, @Address, @City, @Region, @PostalCode,
        @Country, @Phone, @Fax)" DeleteCommand="DELETE FROM [Customers] WHERE
        [CustomerID] = @original_CustomerID"
    FilterExpression="CustomerID='@CustomerID'"
    ConnectionString="<%$ ConnectionStrings:AppConnectionString1 %>">
    <FilterParameters>
        <asp:ControlParameter Name="CustomerID" ControlId="GridView1"
            PropertyName="SelectedValue"></asp:ControlParameter>
    </FilterParameters>
    <InsertParameters>
        <asp:Parameter Type="String" Name="CustomerID"></asp:Parameter>
        <asp:Parameter Type="String" Name="CompanyName"></asp:Parameter>
        <asp:Parameter Type="String" Name="ContactName"></asp:Parameter>
        <asp:Parameter Type="String" Name="ContactTitle"></asp:Parameter>
        <asp:Parameter Type="String" Name="Address"></asp:Parameter>
        <asp:Parameter Type="String" Name="City"></asp:Parameter>
        <asp:Parameter Type="String" Name="Region"></asp:Parameter>
        <asp:Parameter Type="String" Name="PostalCode"></asp:Parameter>
        <asp:Parameter Type="String" Name="Country"></asp:Parameter>
        <asp:Parameter Type="String" Name="Phone"></asp:Parameter>
        <asp:Parameter Type="String" Name="Fax"></asp:Parameter>
    </InsertParameters>
</asp:SqlDataSource>
```

Figure 11-19 shows the DetailsView control page loaded in the browser in Insert mode, ready to add a new record.

Figure 11-20 shows the DetailsView control after a new record has been inserted.

Updating and deleting data using the DetailsView control are similar to deleting data from the GridView. Simply specify the `UpdateCommand` or `DeleteCommand` attributes in the DetailView control; then provide the proper `UpdateParameters` and `DeleteParameters` elements.

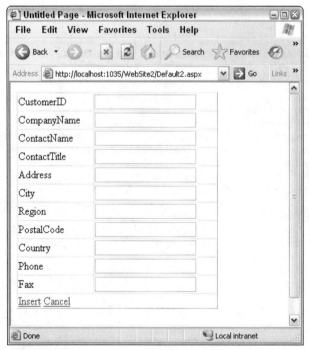

Figure 11-19

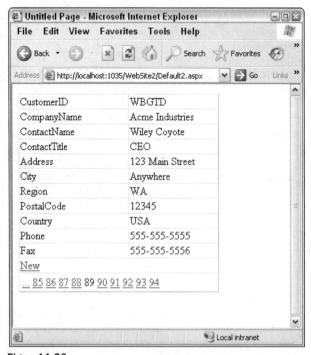

Figue 11-20

FormView

The FormView control is a new control included with the ASP.NET 2.0 toolbox. It basically functions like the DetailsView control in that it displays a single data item from a bound data source control and allows adding, editing, and deleting data. What makes it unique is that it displays the data in custom templates, which gives much greater control over how the data is displayed and edited. Figure 11-21 shows a FormView control ItemTemplate being edited in Visual Studio. You can see that you have complete control over how your data is displayed. The FormView control also contains an EditTemplate that allows you to determine how the control displays when entering Edit or Insert mode.

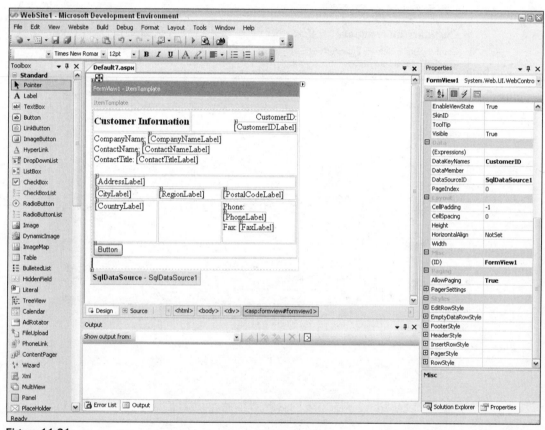

Figure 11-21

Figures 11-20 and 11-21 show the FormView control in action. Figure 11-22 shows the control displaying its ItemTemplate, reflecting the custom layout that was designed in Visual Studio.

In Figure 11-23, you see the control in Edit mode, showing the standard EditTemplate layout.

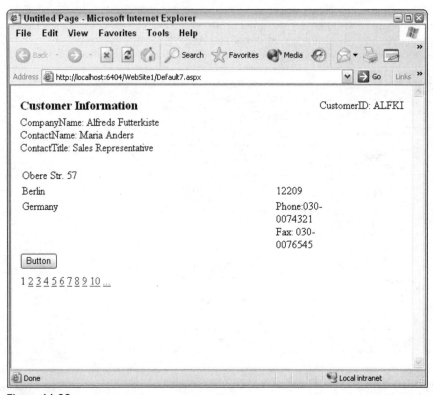

Figure 11-22

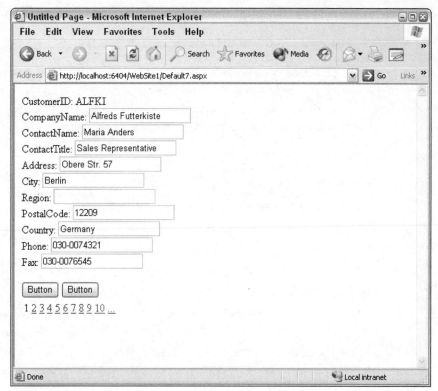

Figure 11-23

Listing 11-40 shows the code that Visual Studio generates when designing the FormView control's customized ItemTemplate.

Listing 11-40: Using a FormView control to display and edit data

```
<%@ Page Language="C#" %>

<html xmlns="http://www.w3.org/1999/xhtml" >
<head runat="server">
    <title>Using the FormView control</title>
</head>
<body>
    <form id="form1" runat="server">
    <div>
        <asp:FormView ID="FormView1" Runat="server" DataSourceID="SqlDataSource1"
            DataKeyNames="CustomerID" AllowPaging="True">
            <EditItemTemplate>
                CustomerID:
                <asp:Label Text='<%# Eval("CustomerID") %>' Runat="server"
                    ID="CustomerIDLabel1">
```

(continued)

Listing 11-40: *(continued)*

```
                </asp:Label><br />
            CompanyName:
            <asp:TextBox Text='<%# Bind("CompanyName") %>' Runat="server"
                ID="CompanyNameTextBox"></asp:TextBox><br />
            ContactName:
            <asp:TextBox Text='<%# Bind("ContactName") %>' Runat="server"
                ID="ContactNameTextBox"></asp:TextBox><br />
            ContactTitle:
            <asp:TextBox Text='<%# Bind("ContactTitle") %>' Runat="server"
                ID="ContactTitleTextBox"></asp:TextBox><br />
            Address:
            <asp:TextBox Text='<%# Bind("Address") %>' Runat="server"
                ID="AddressTextBox"></asp:TextBox><br />
            City:
            <asp:TextBox Text='<%# Bind("City") %>' Runat="server"
                ID="CityTextBox"></asp:TextBox><br />
            Region:
            <asp:TextBox Text='<%# Bind("Region") %>' Runat="server"
                ID="RegionTextBox"></asp:TextBox><br />
            PostalCode:
            <asp:TextBox Text='<%# Bind("PostalCode") %>' Runat="server"
                ID="PostalCodeTextBox"></asp:TextBox><br />
            Country:
            <asp:TextBox Text='<%# Bind("Country") %>' Runat="server"
                ID="CountryTextBox"></asp:TextBox><br />
            Phone:
            <asp:TextBox Text='<%# Bind("Phone") %>' Runat="server"
                ID="PhoneTextBox"></asp:TextBox><br />
            Fax:
            <asp:TextBox Text='<%# Bind("Fax") %>' Runat="server"
                ID="FaxTextBox"></asp:TextBox><br />
            <br />
            <asp:Button ID="Button2" Runat="server" Text="Button"
                CommandName="update" />
            <asp:Button ID="Button3" Runat="server" Text="Button"
                CommandName="cancel" />
        </EditItemTemplate>
        <ItemTemplate>
            <table width="100%">
                <tr>
                    <td style="width: 439px">
                    <b>
                    <span style="font-size: 14pt">Customer Information</span>
                    </b>
                    </td>
                    <td style="width: 439px" align="right">
                        CustomerID:
                        <asp:Label ID="CustomerIDLabel" Runat="server"
                            Text='<%# Bind("CustomerID") %>'>
                            </asp:Label></td>
                </tr>
                <tr>
                    <td colspan="2">
                    CompanyName:
```

```
                              <asp:Label ID="CompanyNameLabel" Runat="server"
                                  Text='<%# Bind("CompanyName") %>'>
                                  </asp:Label><br />
                      ContactName:
                      <asp:Label ID="ContactNameLabel" Runat="server"
                          Text='<%# Bind("ContactName") %>'>
                          </asp:Label><br />
                      ContactTitle:
                      <asp:Label ID="ContactTitleLabel" Runat="server"
                          Text='<%# Bind("ContactTitle") %>'>
                          </asp:Label><br />
                      <br />
                      <table width="100%"><tr>
                              <td colspan="3">
                                  <asp:Label ID="AddressLabel" Runat="server"
                                      Text='<%# Bind("Address") %>'>
                                      </asp:Label></td>
                          </tr>
                          <tr>
                              <td style="width: 100px">
                                  <asp:Label ID="CityLabel" Runat="server"
                                      Text='<%# Bind("City") %>'>
                                      </asp:Label></td>
                              <td style="width: 100px">
                                  <asp:Label ID="RegionLabel" Runat="server"
                                      Text='<%# Bind("Region") %>'>
                                      </asp:Label></td>
                              <td style="width: 100px">
                                  <asp:Label ID="PostalCodeLabel"
                                      Runat="server"
                                      Text='<%# Bind("PostalCode") %>'>
                                      </asp:Label>
                              </td>
                          </tr>
                          <tr>
                              <td style="width: 100px" valign="top">
                                  <asp:Label ID="CountryLabel" Runat="server"
                                      Text='<%# Bind("Country") %>'>
                                      </asp:Label></td>
                              <td style="width: 100px"></td>
                              <td style="width: 100px">
                                  Phone:
                                  <asp:Label ID="PhoneLabel" Runat="server"
                                          Text='<%# Bind("Phone") %>'>
                                          </asp:Label><br />
                                  Fax:
                                  <asp:Label ID="FaxLabel" Runat="server"
                                      Text='<%# Bind("Fax") %>'>
                                      </asp:Label><br />
                              </td>
                          </tr></table>
                      <asp:Button ID="Button1" Runat="server"
                          Text="Button" CommandName="edit" />
                  </td>
          </tr></table>
```

(continued)

Listing 11-40: *(continued)*

```
            </ItemTemplate>
        </asp:FormView>
        <asp:SqlDataSource ID="SqlDataSource1" Runat="server"
            SelectCommand="SELECT * FROM [Customers]"
            ConnectionString="<%$ ConnectionStrings:AppConnectionString1 %>">
        </asp:SqlDataSource>

    </div>
    </form>
</body>
</html>
```

Other Databound Controls

ASP.NET 1.0/1.1 contained many other controls that could be bound to data sources. ASP.NET 2.0 retains these controls, enhances some, and adds several new bound controls to the toolbox.

DropDownList, ListBox, RadioButtonList and CheckBoxList

Although the DropDownList, ListBox and CheckBoxList controls have largely remained the same from ASP.NET 1.0/1.1 to ASP.NET 2.0, they contain several new properties that you might find useful. Additionally ASP.NET 2.0 contains the new RadioButtonList and BulletedList controls.

One of the new properties available in all these controls is the AppendDataBoundItems property. Setting this property to True tells the DropDownList control to append data-bound list items to any existing statically declared items, rather then overwriting them as the ASP.NET 1.0/1.1 version would have done.

Another useful new property available to all these controls is the DataTextFormatString, which allows you to specify a string format for the display text of the DropDownList items.

TreeView

Another exciting new control included in the ASP.NET 2.0 toolbox is the new TreeView control. Because the TreeView can display only hierarchical data, it can be bound only to the XmlDataSource and the SiteMapDataSource controls. Listing 11-41 shows a sample SiteMap file you can use for your SiteMapDataSource control.

Listing 11-41: A SiteMap file for your samples

```
<siteMap>
    <siteMapNode url="page3.aspx" title="Home" description="" roles="">
        <siteMapNode url="page2.aspx" title="Content" description="" roles="" />
        <siteMapNode url="page4.aspx" title="Links" description="" roles="" />
        <siteMapNode url="page1.aspx" title="Comments" description="" roles="" />
    </siteMapNode>
</siteMap>
```

Listing 11-42 shows how you can bind a TreeView control to a SiteMapDataSource control to generate navigation for your Web site.

Listing 11-42: Using the TreeView with a SqlDataSource control

```
<%@ Page Language="C#" %>

<html xmlns="http://www.w3.org/1999/xhtml" >
<head runat="server">
    <title>Using the TreeView control</title>
</head>
<body>
    <form id="form1" runat="server">
    <div>
        <asp:TreeView ID="TreeView1" Runat="server"
            DataSourceID="SiteMapDataSource1">
        </asp:TreeView>
        <asp:SiteMapDataSource ID="SiteMapDataSource1" Runat="server" />

    </div>
    </form>
</body>
</html>
```

Ad Rotator

The familiar Ad Rotator control has been greatly enhanced in ASP.NET 2.0. You can see the control by using the SqlDataSource or XmlDataSource controls. Listing 11-43 shows an example of binding the Ad Rotator to a SqlDataSource control.

Listing 11-43: Using the AdRotator with a SqlDataSource control

```
<asp:AdRotator ID="AdRotator1" runat="server"
    DataSourceId="SqlDataSource1" AlternateTextField="AlternateTF"
    ImageUrlField="Image" NavigateUrlField="NavigateUrl" />
```

For more information on the Ad Rotator control, see Chapter 5.

Menu

The last control in this section is the new Menu control. Like the TreeView control, it is capable of displaying hierarchical data in a vertical *pop-out style* menu. Also like the TreeView control, it can be bound only to the XmlDataSource and the SiteMapDataSource controls. Listing 11-44 shows how you can use the same SiteMap data used earlier in the TreeView control sample, and modify it to display using the new Menu control.

Listing 11-44: Using the Menu control with a SiteMap

```
<%@ Page Language="C#" %>

<html xmlns="http://www.w3.org/1999/xhtml" >
<head runat="server">
    <title>Using the Menu control</title>
</head>
<body>
    <form id="form1" runat="server">
    <div>
        <asp:Menu ID="Menu1" Runat="server" DataSourceID="SiteMapDataSource1">
        </asp:Menu>
        <asp:SiteMapDataSource ID="SiteMapDataSource1" Runat="server" />
    </div>
    </form>
</body>
</html>
```

For more information on using the Menu control, see Chapter 14.

Inline Data-Binding Syntax

Another feature of data binding that has greatly improved in ASP.NET 2.0 is inline data-binding syntax. Inline syntax in ASP.NET 1.0/1.1 was primarily relegated to templated controls such as the DataList or the Repeater controls, and even then it was sometimes difficult and confusing to make it work as you wanted it to. In ASP.NET 1.0/1.1, if you needed to use inline data binding, you might have created something like the procedure shown in Listing 11-45.

Listing 11-45: Using DataBinders in ASP.NET 1.0

```
<asp:Repeater id=Repeater1 runat="server">
    <HeaderTemplate>
        <table>
    </HeaderTemplate>
    <ItemTemplate>
        <tr>
            <td>
                <%# Container.DataItem("Name") %><BR/>
                <%# Container.DataItem("Department") %><BR/>
                <%# DataBinder.Eval(
                        Container.DataItem, "HireDate", "{0:mm dd yyyy}") %><BR/>
            </td>
        </tr>
    </ItemTemplate>
    <FooterTemplate>
        </table>
    </FooterTemplate>
</asp:Repeater>
```

As you can see in this sample, you are using a Repeater control to display a series of Employees. Because the Repeater control is a template control, you use data binding to output the employee-specific data in the proper location of the template. Using the Eval method also allows you to provide formatting information such as Date or Currency formatting at render-time.

In ASP.NET 2.0, the content of inline data binding remains basically the same, but you are given a simpler syntax and several powerful new binding tools to use.

DataBinder Syntax Changes

ASP.NET 2.0 contains three different ways to perform data binding. First, you can continue to use the existing method of binding, using the Container.DataItem syntax:

```
<%# Container.DataItem("Name") %>
```

This is good because it means you won't have to change your existing Web pages if you are migrating from ASP.NET 1.0/1.1 to ASP.NET 2.0. But if you are creating new Web pages, you should probably use the simplest form of binding, using the Eval method directly:

```
<%# Eval("Name") %>
```

You can also continue to format data using the formatter overload of the Eval method:

```
<%# Eval("HireDate", "{0:mm dd yyyy}" ) %>
```

In addition to these changes, ASP.NET 2.0 introduces a new form of data binding called *two-way data binding*. In ASP.NET 1.0/1.1, using the binding syntax was essentially a read-only form of accessing data. In ASP.NET 2.0, two-way data binding allows you to support both read and write operations for bound data. This is done using the Bind method, which, other than using a different method name, works just like the Eval method:

```
<%# Bind("Name") %>
```

The new Bind method should be used in new controls like the GridView, DetailsView, or FormView, where auto-updates to the data source are implemented.

XML Data Binders

Because XML is becoming ever more prevalent in applications, ASP.NET 2.0 also introduces several new ways to bind specifically to XML data sources, called XML Data Binders. These new binders give you powerful ways of working with the hierarchical format of XML. Additionally, except for the different method names, these binding methods work exactly the same as the Eval and Bind methods discussed earlier. These binders should be used when you are using the XmlDataSource control. The first binding format that uses the XPathBinder class is shown in the following code.

```
<% XPathBinder.Eval(Container.DataItem, "employees/employee/Name") %>
```

Notice that rather than specifying a column name as in the `Eval` method, the `XPathBinder` binds the result of an XPath query. Like the standard `Eval` binder, the XML binder also has a shorthand format:

```
<% XPath("employees/employee/Name") %>
```

Also, like the `Eval` method, the XPath binder supports applying formatting to the data:

```
<% XPath("employees/employee/HireDate", "{0:mm dd yyyy}") %>
```

The `XPathBinder` returns a single node using the XPath query provided. Should you want to return multiple nodes from the XmlDataSource Control, you can use the class's `Select` method. This method returns a list of nodes that match the supplied XPath query:

```
<% XPathBinder.Select(Container.DataItem, "employees/employee") %>
```

Or use the shorthand syntax:

```
<% XpathSelect("employees/employee") %>
```

Summary

In this chapter, you examined how data binding in ASP.NET 2.0 has been significantly enhanced and improved. The introduction of data source controls like the SqlDataSource control or the XmlDataSource control makes querying and displaying data from any number of data sources an almost trivial task. Using the data source controls' own wizards, you learned how easy it is to generate powerful data access functionality with almost no code required.

You examined how even a beginning developer can easily combine the data source controls with the new GridView and DetailsView controls to create powerful data manipulation applications with a minimal amount of coding.

You saw how ASP.NET includes a multitude of controls that can be data-bound, specifically examining how many ASP.NET 1.0/1.1 controls have been enhanced, and examining the features of the new Data Bound controls that are included in ASP.NET 2.0, such as the TreeView and Menu controls.

Finally, you looked at how the inline data-binding syntax has been improved and strengthened with the addition of the XML-specific Data Binders.

12

Data Management with ADO.NET

This chapter provides information on programming with data management features that are part of ADO.NET. The discussion begins with the basics of ADO.NET and later dives into the ways you can use the newly added advanced ADO.NET features to manage data contained in a relational database.

ADO.NET was first introduced in version 1.0 of the .NET Framework and provided an extensive array of features to handle data either live — while connected to the database — or when disconnected. With the introduction of ADO.NET 2.0, the already-extensive features list has grown even larger. Some of the newly added features include the capability to bulk load large quantities of data from a variety of sources, to batch process updates to the database with fewer round trips back to the database server, to reuse the same live connection for multiple operations, as well as to achieve asynchronous access to the database.

Basic ADO.NET Features

This chapter covers the basics of ADO.NET and then provides an overview of basic ADO.NET namespaces and classes. It also shows you how to work with `Connection`, `Command`, `DataAdapter`, `DataSet`, and `DataReader` objects.

Basic ADO.NET Namespaces and Classes

The six basic ADO.NET namespaces are shown in the following table. In addition to these namespaces, each new data provider can have its own namespace. As an example, the Oracle .NET data provider adds a namespace of `Microsoft.Data.OracleClient`.

Namespace	Description
System.Data	This namespace is the core of ADO.NET. It contains classes used by all data providers. It contains classes to represent tables, columns, rows, and the DataSet. It also contains several very useful interfaces, such as IDbCommand, IDbConnection, and IDbDataAdapter. These interfaces are used by all managed providers, enabling them to plug into the core of ADO.NET.
System.Data.Common	This namespace defines common classes that are used as base classes for data providers. All data providers share these classes. A few examples are DbConnection and DbDataAdapter.
System.Data.OleDb	This namespace defines classes that work with OLE-DB data sources using the .NET OleDb data provider. It contains classes such as OleDbConnection and OleDbCommand.
System.Data.Odbc	This namespace defines classes that work with the ODBC data sources using the .NET ODBC data provider. It contains classes such as OdbcConnection and OdbcCommand.
System.Data.SqlClient	This namespace defines a data provider for the SQL Server 7.0 or higher database. It contains classes such as SqlConnection and SqlCommand.
System.Data.SqlTypes	This namespace defines a few classes that represent specific data types for the SQL Server database.

ADO.NET has three distinct types of classes commonly referred to as Disconnected, Shared, and Data Providers. The Disconnected classes provide the basic structure for the ADO.NET framework. A good example of this type of class is the DataTable class. The objects of this class are capable of storing data without any dependency on a specific data provider. The Shared classes form the base classes for data providers and are shared among all data providers. The Data Provider classes are meant to work with different kinds of data sources. They are used to perform all data-management operations on specific databases. The SqlClient data provider, for example, works only with the SQL Server database.

A data provider contains Connection, Command, DataAdapter, and DataReader objects. In a typical ADO.NET programming, you first create the Connection object and provide it with the necessary information, such as the connection string. You then create a Command object and provide it with the details of the SQL command that is to be executed. This command can be an inline SQL text command, a stored procedure, or direct table access. You can also provide parameters to these commands if needed. After you create the Connection and the Command objects, you must decide whether the command returns a result set. If the command doesn't return a result set, you can simply execute the command by calling one of its several Execute methods. On the other hand, if the command returns a result set, you must make a decision about whether you want to retain the result set for future uses without maintaining the connection to the database. If you want to retain the result set, you must create a DataAdapter object and use it to fill a DataSet or a DataTable object. These objects are capable of maintaining their information in a disconnected mode. However, if you don't want to retain the result set, but rather to simply process the command in a swift fashion, you can use the Command object to create a DataReader object. The DataReader object needs a live connection to the database, and it works as a forward-only, read-only cursor.

Using the Connection Object

The Connection object creates a link to the data source. This object needs the necessary information to discover the data source and to log in to it properly. This information is provided via a connection string.

The properties for the SqlConnection class are shown in the following table. The SqlConnection is a class that is specific to the SqlClient provider. As discussed earlier in this chapter, the SqlClient provider is built for working with the SQL Server 7.0 and higher databases.

Property	Description
Datasource	This read-only property returns the name of the instance of the SQL Server database used by the SqlConnection object.
Database	This read-only property returns the name of the database to use after the connection is opened.
State	This read-only property returns the current state of the connection. The possible values are Broken, Closed, Connecting, Executing, Fetching, and Open.
ConnectionString	This property allows you to read or provide the connection string that should be used by the SqlConnection object.

Using the Command Object

The Command object uses the Connection object to execute SQL queries. These queries can be in the form of inline text, a stored procedure, or direct table access. If the SQL query uses the SELECT clause, the result set it returns is usually stored in either a DataSet or a DataReader object. The command object provides a number of Execute methods that can be used to perform the SQL queries in a variety of fashions.

First take a look at some useful properties of the SqlCommand class, as shown in the following table.

Property	Description
CommandText	This read-write property allows you to set or retrieve either the T-SQL statement or the stored procedure name.
CommandTimeout	This read-write property gets or sets the number of seconds to wait while attempting to execute a command. The command is aborted after it times out and an exception is thrown. The default is 30 seconds.
CommandType	This read-write property indicates the way the CommandText property should be interpreted. The possible values are StoredProcedure, TableDirect, and Text.
Connection	This read-write property gets or sets the SqlConnection object that should be used by this command object.

Now look at the various Execute methods that can be called on a Command object.

Property	Description
ExecuteNonQuery	This method executes the command and returns the number of rows affected.
ExecuteReader	This method executes the command and returns an object of SqlDataReader class. The data reader is a read-only and forward-only cursor.
ExecuteRow	This method executes the command and returns an object of the SqlRecord class. This object contains a single returned row.
ExecuteScalar	This method executes the command and returns the first column of the first row in the form of a generic object. The remaining rows and columns are ignored.
ExecuteXmlReader	This method executes the command and returns an object of the XmlReader class. This method enables you to use a command that returns the results set in the form of an XML document.

Using the DataReader Object

The `DataReader` object is a simple forward-only and read-only cursor. It requires a live connection with the data source and provides a very efficient way of looping and consuming all or part of the result set. This object cannot be directly instantiated. Instead, you must call the `ExecuteReader` method of the `Command` object to obtain a valid `DataReader` object. Be sure to close the connection when you are done using the data reader. Otherwise, the connection stays alive until it is explicitly closed. You can close the connection after using the data reader in one of two ways. One way is to provide the `CommandBehavior.CloseConnection` enumeration while calling the `ExecuteMethod` of the `Command` object. This approach works only if you loop through the data reader until you reach the end of file, at which point the reader object automatically closes the connection for you. However, if you don't want to keep reading the data reader until the end of file, you can call the `Close` method of the `Connection` object yourself.

Listing 12-1 shows the `Connection`, `Command`, and `DataReader` objects in action. It shows how to connect with the Northwind database, read the Customers table, and show the results in a GridView control.

Listing 12-1: The SqlConnection, SqlCommand, and SqlDataReader objects

VB

```
<%@ Page Language="VB" %>
<%@ Import Namespace="System.Data" %>
<%@ Import Namespace="System.Data.SqlClient" %>
<%@ Import Namespace="System.Configuration" %>

<script runat="server">
    Protected Sub Page_Load(ByVal sender As Object, _
            ByVal e As System.EventArgs)

        If Not Page.IsPostBack Then
            Dim MyConnection As SqlConnection
            Dim MyCommand As SqlCommand
            Dim MyReader As SqlDataReader

            MyConnection = New SqlConnection()
            MyConnection.ConnectionString = _
        ConfigurationManager.ConnectionStrings("DSN_Northwind").ConnectionString

            MyCommand = New SqlCommand()
            MyCommand.CommandText = "SELECT TOP 3 * FROM CUSTOMERS"
            MyCommand.CommandType = CommandType.Text
            MyCommand.Connection = MyConnection

            MyCommand.Connection.Open()
            MyReader = MyCommand.ExecuteReader(CommandBehavior.CloseConnection)

            gvCustomers.DataSource = MyReader
            gvCustomers.DataBind()

            MyCommand.Dispose()
            MyConnection.Dispose()
```

(continued)

Listing 12-1: *(continued)*

```
        End If
    End Sub
</script>

<html>
<body>
    <form id="form1" runat="server">
    <div>
        <asp:GridView ID="gvCustomers" runat="server">
        </asp:GridView>
    </div>
    </form>
</body>
</html>
```

C#

```csharp
<%@ Page Language="C#" %>
<%@ Import Namespace="System.Data" %>
<%@ Import Namespace="System.Data.SqlClient" %>
<%@ Import Namespace="System.Configuration" %>

<script runat="server">
    protected void Page_Load(object sender, EventArgs e)
    {
        if (!Page.IsPostBack)
        {
            SqlConnection MyConnection;
            SqlCommand MyCommand;
            SqlDataReader MyReader;

            MyConnection = new SqlConnection();
            MyConnection.ConnectionString =
        ConfigurationManager.ConnectionStrings["DSN_Northwind"].ConnectionString;

            MyCommand = new SqlCommand();
            MyCommand.CommandText = " SELECT TOP 3 * FROM CUSTOMERS ";
            MyCommand.CommandType = CommandType.Text;
            MyCommand.Connection = MyConnection;

            MyCommand.Connection.Open();
            MyReader = MyCommand.ExecuteReader(CommandBehavior.CloseConnection);

            gvCustomers.DataSource = MyReader;
            gvCustomers.DataBind();

            MyCommand.Dispose();
            MyConnection.Dispose();
        }
    }

</script>
```

The code shown in Listing 12-1 uses the SqlConnection class to create a connection with the Northwind database using the connection string stored in the Web.config file. It then creates a Command object using the SqlCommand class and provides it with command text, command type, and connection properties. After the command and the connection are created, the code opens the connection and executes the command by calling the ExecuteReader method of the MyCommand object. After receiving the data reader from the Command object, you simply data bind it to a GridView control. The result of the code is shown in Figure 12-1.

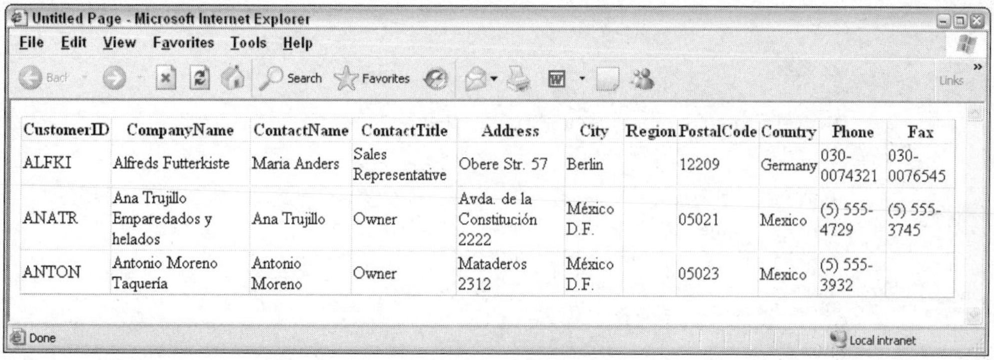

Figure 12-1

Using Data Adapter

The SqlDataAdapter is a special class whose purpose is to bridge the gap between the disconnected DataTable objects and the physical data source. The SqlDataAdapter provides a two-way data transfer mechanism. It is capable of executing a SELECT statement on a data source and transferring the result set into a DataTable object. It is also capable of executing INSERT, UPDATE, and DELETE statements and extracting the input data from a DataTable object.

The commonly used properties offered by the SqlDataAdapter class are shown in the following table.

Property	Description
SelectCommand	This read-write property sets or gets an object of type SqlCommand. This command is automatically executed to fill a DataTable with the result set.
InsertCommand	This read-write property sets or gets an object of type SqlCommand. This command is automatically executed to insert a new record to the SQL Server database.
UpdateCommand	This read-write property sets or gets an object of type SqlCommand. This command is automatically executed to update an existing record on the SQL Server database.
DeleteCommand	This read-write property sets or gets an object of type SqlCommand. This command is automatically executed to delete an existing record on the SQL Server database.

The SqlDataAdapter class also provides a method called `Fill`. Calling the `Fill` method automatically executes the command provided in the SelectCommand property, receives the result set, and copies it to a DataTable object.

The code example in Listing 12-2 illustrates how to use an object of SqlDataAdapter class to fill a DataTable object.

Listing 12-2: Using an object of SqlDataAdapter to fill a DataTable

```vb
VB
<%@ Page Language="VB" %>
<%@ Import Namespace="System.Data" %>
<%@ Import Namespace="System.Data.SqlClient" %>
<%@ Import Namespace="System.Configuration" %>

<script runat="server">
    Protected Sub Page_Load(ByVal sender As Object, _
            ByVal e As System.EventArgs)

        If Not Page.IsPostBack Then
            Dim MyConnection As SqlConnection
            Dim MyCommand As SqlCommand
            Dim MyAdapter As SqlDataAdapter
            Dim MyTable As DataTable = New DataTable()

            MyConnection = New SqlConnection()
            MyConnection.ConnectionString = _
            ConfigurationManager.ConnectionStrings("DSN_Northwind").ConnectionString

            MyCommand = New SqlCommand()
            MyCommand.CommandText = "SELECT TOP 5 * FROM CUSTOMERS"
            MyCommand.CommandType = CommandType.Text
            MyCommand.Connection = MyConnection

            MyAdapter = New SqlDataAdapter()
            MyAdapter.SelectCommand = MyCommand
            MyAdapter.Fill(MyTable)

            gvCustomers.DataSource = MyTable.DefaultView
            gvCustomers.DataBind()

            MyAdapter.Dispose()
            MyCommand.Dispose()
            MyConnection.Dispose()

        End If

    End Sub
</script>
```

C#

```
<%@ Page Language="C#" %>
<%@ Import Namespace="System.Data" %>
<%@ Import Namespace="System.Data.SqlClient" %>
<%@ Import Namespace="System.Configuration" %>

<script runat="server">
    protected void Page_Load(object sender, EventArgs e)
    {
        if (!Page.IsPostBack)
        {
            SqlConnection MyConnection;
            SqlCommand MyCommand;
            SqlDataAdapter MyAdapter;
            DataTable MyTable = new DataTable();

            MyConnection = new SqlConnection();
            MyConnection.ConnectionString =
        ConfigurationManager.ConnectionStrings["DSN_Northwind"].ConnectionString;

            MyCommand = new SqlCommand();
            MyCommand.CommandText = "SELECT TOP 5 * FROM CUSTOMERS";
            MyCommand.CommandType = CommandType.Text;
            MyCommand.Connection = MyConnection;

            MyAdapter = new SqlDataAdapter();
            MyAdapter.SelectCommand = MyCommand;
            MyAdapter.Fill(MyTable);

            gvCustomers.DataSource = MyTable.DefaultView;
            gvCustomers.DataBind();

            MyAdapter.Dispose();
            MyCommand.Dispose();
            MyConnection.Dispose();
        }
    }

</script>
```

The code shown in Listing 12-2 creates a `Connection` and `Command` object and then proceeds to create an object of the `SqlDataAdapter` class. It then fills the `SelectCommand` property of the `DataAdapter` object with the `Command` object it had previously created. After the `DataAdapter` object is ready for executing, the code executes the `Fill` method, passing it an object of the `DataTable` class. The `Fill` method returns a populated `DataTable` object. Figure 12-2 shows the result of executing this code.

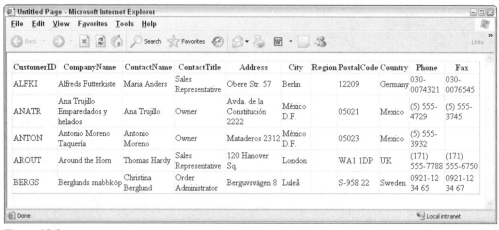

Figure 12-2

Using Parameters

Most serious database programming, regardless of how simple it might be, requires you to configure SQL statements using parameters. Obviously, a discussion on the basics of ADO.NET programming is not complete without covering the use of parameterized SQL statements.

Creating a parameter is as simple as declaring an object of the SqlParameter class and providing it the necessary information, such as parameter name, type, size, direction, and so on. The following table shows the properties of the SqlParameter class.

Property	Description
ParameterName	This read-write property gets or sets the name of the parameter.
SqlDbType	This read-write property gets or sets the SQL Server database type of the parameter value.
Size	This read-write property sets or gets the size of the parameter value.
Direction	This read-write property sets or gets the direction of the parameter, such as Input, Output, or Both
SourceColumn	This read-write property maps a column from a DataTable to the parameter. It enables you to execute multiple commands using the SqlDataAdapter object and pick the correct parameter value from a DataTable column during the command execution.
Value	This read-write property sets or gets the value provided to the parameter object. This value is passed to the parameter defined in the command during runtime.

Listing 12-3 modifies the code shown in Listing 12-1 to use two parameters while retrieving the list of customers from the database.

Listing 12-3: The use of a parameterized SQL statement

```
B
<%@ Page Language="VB" %>
<%@ Import Namespace="System.Data" %>
<%@ Import Namespace="System.Data.SqlClient" %>
<%@ Import Namespace="System.Configuration" %>

<script runat="server">
    Protected Sub Page_Load(ByVal sender As Object, _
            ByVal e As System.EventArgs)
        If Not Page.IsPostBack Then
            Dim MyConnection As SqlConnection
            Dim MyCommand As SqlCommand
            Dim MyReader As SqlDataReader
            Dim CityParam As SqlParameter
            Dim ContactParam As SqlParameter

            MyConnection = New SqlConnection()
            MyConnection.ConnectionString = _

ConfigurationManager.ConnectionStrings("DSN_Northwind").ConnectionString

            MyCommand = New SqlCommand()
            MyCommand.CommandText = _
        "SELECT * FROM CUSTOMERS WHERE CITY = @CITY AND CONTACTNAME = @CONTACT"
            MyCommand.CommandType = CommandType.Text
            MyCommand.Connection = MyConnection

            CityParam = New SqlParameter()
            CityParam.ParameterName = "@CITY"
            CityParam.SqlDbType = SqlDbType.VarChar
            CityParam.Size = 15
            CityParam.Direction = ParameterDirection.Input
            CityParam.Value = "Berlin"

            ContactParam = New SqlParameter()
            ContactParam.ParameterName = "@CONTACT"
            ContactParam.SqlDbType = SqlDbType.VarChar
            ContactParam.Size = 15
            ContactParam.Direction = ParameterDirection.Input
            ContactParam.Value = "Maria Anders"

            MyCommand.Parameters.Add(CityParam)
            MyCommand.Parameters.Add(ContactParam)

            MyCommand.Connection.Open()
            MyReader = MyCommand.ExecuteReader(CommandBehavior.CloseConnection)

            gvCustomers.DataSource = MyReader
```

(continued)

Listing 12-3: *(continued)*

```
            gvCustomers.DataBind()

            MyCommand.Dispose()
            MyConnection.Dispose()

        End If

    End Sub
</script>
```

C#
```
<%@ Page Language="C#" %>
<%@ Import Namespace="System.Data" %>
<%@ Import Namespace="System.Data.SqlClient" %>
<%@ Import Namespace="System.Configuration" %>

<script runat="server">
    protected void Page_Load(object sender, EventArgs e)
    {
        if (!Page.IsPostBack)
        {
            SqlConnection MyConnection;
            SqlCommand MyCommand;
            SqlDataReader MyReader;
            SqlParameter CityParam;
            SqlParameter ContactParam;

            MyConnection = new SqlConnection();
            MyConnection.ConnectionString =

ConfigurationManager.ConnectionStrings["DSN_Northwind"].ConnectionString;

            MyCommand = new SqlCommand();
            MyCommand.CommandText =
        "SELECT * FROM CUSTOMERS WHERE CITY = @CITY AND CONTACTNAME = @CONTACT";
            MyCommand.CommandType = CommandType.Text;
            MyCommand.Connection = MyConnection;
```

```
                    CityParam = new SqlParameter();
                    CityParam.ParameterName = "@CITY";
                    CityParam.SqlDbType = SqlDbType.VarChar;
                    CityParam.Size = 15;
                    CityParam.Direction = ParameterDirection.Input;
                    CityParam.Value = "Berlin";

                    ContactParam = new SqlParameter();
                    ContactParam.ParameterName = "@CONTACT";
                    ContactParam.SqlDbType = SqlDbType.VarChar;
                    ContactParam.Size = 15;
                    ContactParam.Direction = ParameterDirection.Input;
                    ContactParam.Value = "Maria Anders";

                    MyCommand.Parameters.Add(CityParam);
                    MyCommand.Parameters.Add(ContactParam);

                    MyCommand.Connection.Open();
                    MyReader = MyCommand.ExecuteReader(CommandBehavior.CloseConnection);

                    gvCustomers.DataSource = MyReader;
                    gvCustomers.DataBind();

                    MyCommand.Dispose();
                    MyConnection.Dispose();
            }
        }
    </script>
```

The code shown in Listing 12-3 uses a parameterized SQL statement that receives the name of the city and the contact person to narrow the result set. These parameters are provided by declaring the objects of SqlParameter class and filling in the name, type, size, direction, and value properties for each object of SqlParameter class. You then add the parameters to the Command object by calling the Add method of the Parameters collection. The result of executing this code is shown in Figure 12-3.

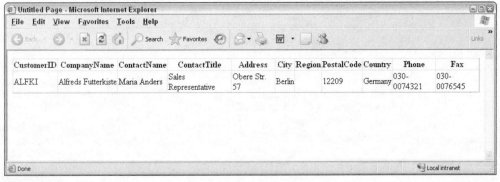

Figure 12-3

Understanding DataSet and DataTable

Most programmers agree that the `DataSet` class is the most commonly used part of ADO.NET in real-world, database-driven applications. This class provides mechanisms for managing data when it is disconnected from the data source. This capability to handle data in a disconnected state was first introduced in .NET during the 1.0 version of ADO.NET. The current 2.0 version of ADO.NET retains all the features of its predecessors and provides a few newer, much-needed features.

An object created from the DataSet class works as a container for other objects that are created from the DataTable class. The DataTable object represents a logical table in memory. It contains rows, columns, primary keys, constraints, and relations with other DataTable objects. Most of the disconnected data-driven programming is actually done using one or more DataTable objects. However, the previous versions of ADO.NET didn't allow you to work directly with the DataTable object for some very important tasks, such as reading and writing data to and from an XML file. It didn't even allow you to serialize the DataTable object independently. This limitation required you to always use the DataSet object to perform any operation on a DataTable. The current version of ADO.NET removes this limitation and enables you to work directly with the DataTable for all your needs. In fact, we recommend that you don't use the DataSet object unless you need to work with multiple DataTable objects and need a container object to manage them.

The current version of ADO.NET provides the capability to load a `DataTable` in memory by consuming a data source using a `DataReader`. In the past, you were sometimes restricted to creating multiple overloads of the same method just to work with both the `DataReader` and the `DataTable` objects. Now you have the flexibility to write the data access code one time and reuse the `DataReader` — either directly or to fill a `DataTable`, as shown in Listing 12-4.

Listing 12-4: How to load a DataTable from a DataReader

VB

```vb
<%@ Page Language="VB" %>
<%@ Import Namespace="System.Data" %>
<%@ Import Namespace="System.Data.SqlClient" %>
<%@ Import Namespace="System.Configuration" %>

<script runat="server">
    Protected Sub Page_Load(ByVal sender As Object, _
            ByVal e As System.EventArgs)

        If Not Page.IsPostBack Then
            Dim MyConnection As SqlConnection
            Dim MyCommand As SqlCommand
            Dim MyDataTable As DataTable
            Dim MyReader As SqlDataReader
            Dim CityParam As SqlParameter

            MyConnection = New SqlConnection()
```

```
        MyConnection.ConnectionString = _
    ConfigurationManager.ConnectionStrings("DSN_Northwind").ConnectionString

        MyCommand = New SqlCommand()
        MyCommand.CommandText = _
                "SELECT * FROM CUSTOMERS WHERE CITY = @CITY"
        MyCommand.CommandType = CommandType.Text
        MyCommand.Connection = MyConnection

        CityParam = New SqlParameter()
        CityParam.ParameterName = "@CITY"
        CityParam.SqlDbType = SqlDbType.VarChar
        CityParam.Size = 15
        CityParam.Direction = ParameterDirection.Input
        CityParam.Value = "London"

        MyCommand.Parameters.Add(CityParam)

        MyCommand.Connection.Open()
        MyReader = MyCommand.ExecuteReader(CommandBehavior.CloseConnection)

        MyDataTable = New DataTable()

        ' Loading DataTable using a DataReader
        MyDataTable.Load(MyReader)

        gvCustomers.DataSource = MyDataTable
        gvCustomers.DataBind()

        MyDataTable.Dispose()
        MyCommand.Dispose()
        MyConnection.Dispose()
    End If

    End Sub

</script>
```

C#
```
<%@ Page Language="C#" %>
<%@ Import Namespace="System.Data" %>
<%@ Import Namespace="System.Data.SqlClient" %>
<%@ Import Namespace="System.Configuration" %>

<script runat="server">
    protected void Page_Load(object sender, EventArgs e)
    {
```

(continued)

Listing 12-4: *(continued)*

```
            if (!Page.IsPostBack )
            {
                SqlConnection MyConnection;
                SqlCommand MyCommand;
                DataTable MyDataTable;
                SqlDataReader MyReader;
                SqlParameter CityParam;

                MyConnection = new SqlConnection();
                MyConnection.ConnectionString =
            ConfigurationManager.ConnectionStrings["DSN_Northwind"].ConnectionString;

                MyCommand = new SqlCommand();
                MyCommand.CommandText =
                    "SELECT * FROM CUSTOMERS WHERE CITY = @CITY";
                MyCommand.CommandType = CommandType.Text;
                MyCommand.Connection = MyConnection;

                CityParam = new SqlParameter();
                CityParam.ParameterName = "@CITY";
                CityParam.SqlDbType = SqlDbType.VarChar;
                CityParam.Size = 15;
                CityParam.Direction = ParameterDirection.Input;
                CityParam.Value = "London";

                MyCommand.Parameters.Add(CityParam);

                MyCommand.Connection.Open();
                MyReader = MyCommand.ExecuteReader(CommandBehavior.CloseConnection);

                MyDataTable = new DataTable();

                // Loading DataTable using a DataReader
                MyDataTable.Load(MyReader);

                gvCustomers.DataSource = MyDataTable;
                gvCustomers.DataBind();

                MyDataTable.Dispose();
                MyCommand.Dispose();
                MyConnection.Dispose();

            }
        }

    </script>
```

Not only can you load a `DataTable` object from a `DataReader` object, you can also retrieve a `DataTableReader` (new to the .NET Framework 2.0) from an existing `DataTable` object. This is accomplished by calling the `CreateDataReader` method of the `DataTable` class. This method returns an instance of the `DataTableReader` object that can be passed to any method that expects to receive a `DataReader`.

Newly Added ADO.NET Features

Now that you have seen the basic features of ADO.NET, let's dig deeper into the advanced features. These advanced features are added to the 2.0 version of ADO.NET and provide a plethora of functionality that simply wasn't available in previous versions.

These features are specific to the database server, and the discussion in this chapter focuses on the SQL Server database server. As we point out in the text, some of these features rely on the 9.0 version of the Microsoft Data Access Components (MDAC).

An exciting feature added to ADO.NET 2.0 enables you to bulk load large quantities of data from virtually any source into a SQL Server database swiftly and easily. If you write code long enough, you are bound to find yourself digging through the trenches of the SQL Server Data Transformation Service (DTS) in order to move bulk quantities of data from one place to another. Although DTS works for most tasks, programmers have always wished for a way to write custom code that retrieves data in custom formats, processes it while applying business rules, and eventually transfers it to a database server. You can certainly write such code with previous versions of ASP.NET, but you are restricted to using the Update method of the DataAdapter object that makes a roundtrip to the database server for every record to be inserted. You can also write a custom command to insert or update these records without using the DataAdapter object, but your program must then make roundtrip calls to the database server for every record. Moving over 100,000 records can easily take hours and can also flood your network with traffic. When your database server is so busy, you lose productivity as you endlessly wait for the update process to finish.

The new Bulk Copy feature of ADO.NET makes it a snap to load large quantities of data to a SQL Server database. This process works so fast that we didn't believe our eyes when we first ran performance tests. After all, it's not every day that programmers like us get to see large quantities of data copied to a database server in mere seconds.

Bulk Loading of Data from a Variety of Sources

Database administrators have been accustomed to a variety of data transfer mechanisms such as DTS, which is a graphical environment, and BCP (Bulk Copy Program), which is a command-line utility. With the advent of ADO.NET 2.0, programmers can now write complete managed code to retrieve data from a variety of sources. They can also bulk copy the data to a SQL Server database — all in the programmer's favorite language.

The SQLClient namespace provides several new classes that help you bulk copy data by consuming either a DataTable or DataReader object. The data source can be virtually any media from a relational database, to an XML file, to the result of a Web service call. Now that you can write managed code, you can utilize all available features in the .NET Framework to access the data source, retrieve the information, process business rules, and clean up the data. After you have processed the data and it is ready to be stored in its destination table on a SQL Server database, you simply use the SqlBulkCopy class to transfer the data to its destination.

SqlBulkCopy class

The SqlBulkCopy class exposes a set of properties and methods that enable you to customize the bulk copy operation by providing information such as the destination table names, batch sizes, time outs, and the column mappings.

Properties

The properties of the SqlBulkCopy class are shown in the following table. These properties define the details of various copy operations, such as the batch size and time outs.

Property	Description
BatchSize	Sets or returns an Integer value specifying the number of records to be copied in each batch. The default value is 0 which indicates that all records will be done in one batch. If the database server supports batch updates, the SqlBulkCopy class leverages the database server to perform batch updates. If the database server doesn't support batch updates, the SqlBulkCopy class manages and executes each batch individually.
BulkCopyTimeOut	Sets or returns an Integer value indicating the time the SqlBulkCopy class will wait for the updates to process before it times out and throws an exception. In the event of a time out, the transaction is not committed, and all copied rows are removed from the server.
ColumnMappings	Returns a reference to a SqlBulkCopyColumnMappingsCollection object. This object is a collection object that maintains a list of column mappings in the form of instances of SqlBulkCopyColumnMapping objects. This property can be used to map the columns from the source data table or data reader with the destination table.
DestinationTableName	Sets or returns a String value indicating the table name of the destination table in the SQL Server database.
NotifyAfter	Sets or returns an Integer value indicating the time after which a SqlRowsCopied event is raised. This event can be used for a variety of purposes, such as showing the progress of the bulk copy operation to the end user.

The SqlBulkCopy class also exposes a few constructors and methods that enable you to alter its behavior to meet your data processing needs. By using one of several overloaded constructors, you can provide a connection to your destination database along with a custom transaction, if one is needed. You can also select from a list of copy options that allow you to check constraints, keep identity fields, keep null values, and use table-level locking.

Constructors

The details of various overloaded constructors of the SqlBulkCopy class are shown in the following table. You can use these constructors to instantiate an object of the SqlBulkCopy class by specifying the connection, copy options, and external transactions.

Constructor	Description
SqlBulkCopy(connectionString)	Takes a String object containing a connection string to the destination SQL Server database.
SqlBulkCopy(connection)	Takes an instance of the SqlConnection object to access the destination SQL Server database.
SqlBulkCopy (connectionString, copyOptions)	Takes a String object containing the connection string for the destination SQL Server as the first parameter. The second parameter is a combination of values from the SqlBulkCopyOptions enumeration. Here are the details of this enumeration: —**Default**: None of the following rules is applied. —**CheckConstraints**: Constraints defined in the destination table are enforced during the copy operation. If any of the constraints fail, the update process is rolled back, and a SqlException is thrown specifying that a constraint is violated. —**KeepIdentity**: This option is helpful if you want to preserve the identity fields defined in the source column; otherwise, the update operation creates new identity fields provided that the destination column is marked as type Identity. If this option is used and a destination column already consists of a value that conflicts with the source, the update process is rolled back and a SqlException is thrown. It specifies that a duplicate key cannot be entered in the table. —**KeepNulls**: This option forces the null values to be stored in the destination table even if a default value is specified. If this option is not specified, all null values are replaced by the column's default value if the column has a default value specified. —**TableLock**: This option causes the update process to obtain a lock on the entire table for the duration of the bulk copy process. If this option is not used, row-level locking is used by default.
SqlBulkCopy (connection, copyOptions, externalTransactions)	Takes an instance of the SqlConnection class, a set of copy options, and a reference to an existing transaction object. All the bulk copy through the update process uses the provided transaction object.

Methods

The `SqlBulkCopy` class provides one method to process the copy operation, as shown in the following table. This method has overloads, which can be used to process a `DataReader`, `DataTable`, or an array of `DataRow` objects.

Method	Description
`WriteToServer(reader)`	This overloaded method copies records from an open `DataReader` object. The `DataReader` doesn't have to be SQL Server specific. The method receives a reference to the IDataReader interface, which enables you to use any database server as the source of the data.
`WriteToServer(table)`	This overloaded method copies records from a `DataTable` object.
`WriteToServer(table, rowState)`	This overloaded method copies records from a `DataTable` object but uses only those records that are marked by the given `RowState` flag. For example, if you want to copy only those records that are updated in the data table after they are retrieved from the source, you pass `DataRowState.Modified` as the value of the second parameter.
`WriteToServer(rows())`	This overloaded method copies records from an array of `DataRow` objects.

While you are trying to bulk copy large quantities of data from one place to another, you may need to map the columns from source to destination. The `SqlBulkCopy` class provides this capability by exposing the `ColumnMappings` property that allows you to specify column-level mappings.

SqlBulkCopyColumnMapping

The `SqlBulkCopyColumnMapping` class enables you to map the columns between the source and the destination tables. It provides a series of overloaded constructors and a list of properties that allow you to specify source and destination columns either by their names or by their indexes. After objects of this class have been instantiated, they can be added to or removed from the object of the `SqlBulkCopyColumnMappingsCollection` class by calling its `Add` method

Properties

The properties of `SqlBulkCopyColumnMapping` class are shown in the following table. These properties allow you to specify the source and column mapping.

Property	Description
SourceColumn	Sets or returns the source column for this mapping using the column name specified as String.
SourceOrdinal	Sets or returns the source column for this mapping using the column index specified as Integer.
DestinationColumn	Sets or returns the destination column for this mapping using the column name specified as String.
DestinationOrdinal	Sets or returns the destination column for this mapping using the column index specified as Integer.

Constructors

The `SqlBulkCopyColumnMapping` class provides five overloaded constructors, as shown in the following table. You can use these constructors instead of or in conjunction with the properties to provide mappings between the source and destination columns.

Constructor	Description
SqlBulkCopyColumnMapping( )	Creates an instance of the class without any column mapping.
SqlBulkCopyColumnMapping (sourceColumn, destinationColumn)	Receives column names of both source and destination columns.
SqlBulkCopyColumnMapping (sourceColumn, destinationColumnOrdinal)	Receives the name of the source column and the index of the destination column.
SqlBulkCopyColumnMapping (sourceColumnOrdinal, destinationColumn)	Receives the index of the source column and the name of the destination column.
SqlBulkCopyColumnMapping (sourceColumnOrdinal, destinationColumnOrdinal)	Receives the indexes of source and destination columns.

Method

The methods for adding column mappings to the bulk copy operation are provided in the `SqlBulkCopyColumnMappingsCollection` class, as shown in the following table. These overloaded methods allow you to provide either the objects of the `SqlBulkCopyColumnMapping` class or simply the source and destination column names or indexes. If you provide the column names or indexes, the method automatically creates an object of the `SqlBulkCopyColumnMapping` class and adds that object to its internal collection.

Method	Description
`Add (bulkCopyColumnMapping)`	Receives an object of the `SqlBulkCopyColumnMapping` class and adds it to the internal collection.
`Add (sourceColumn, destinationColumn)`	Receives source and destination column names. It then creates an object of the `SqlBulkCopyColumnMapping` class and adds it to the internal collection.
`Add (sourceColumnIndex, destinationColumn)`	Receives source column index and destination column names. It then creates an object of the `SqlBulkCopyColumnMapping` class and adds it to the internal collection.
`Add (sourceColumn, destinationColumnIndex)`	Receives source column name and destination column index. It then creates an object of the `SqlBulkCopyColumnMapping` class and adds it to the internal collection.
`Add (sourceColumnIndex, destinationColumnIndex)`	Receives source and destination column indexes. It then creates an object of the `SqlBulkCopyColumnMapping` class and adds it to the internal collection.
`RemoveAt (index)`	Removes an object of the `SqlBulkCopyColumnMapping` at a specified index from the internal collection.
`Clear ( )`	Clears the internal collection.

Now that you have learned the intricacies of the bulk loading feature of ADO.NET 2.0, you can put your knowledge to the test by attempting to load a relatively large quantity of data from a source SQL Server database to a destination table inside another SQL Server database.

A Bulk Copy Example Using a Data Reader

The code shown in Listing 12-5 connects with a database of employees containing over 100MB records. It uses a simple SELECT statement to read all employee data from the source database using an object of type SQLDataReader. After the SELECT statement has been processed successfully, you declare column mappings between the source and the destination tables. While creating these column mappings, you are tasked with storing the name of the data source in the Title column of the destination table. This information can be used later to sort out the records retrieved from various sources that end up being in the same destination table. You satisfy this requirement by creating a dummy column in the source result set and mapping it with the Title column of the destination table.

Note that column mappings are completely optional. If your source and destination tables use the exact same schema, you can simply skip the steps related to creating column-mapping objects. The `SqlBulkCopy` *object, in the absence of column mappings, automatically attempts to map the source and destination columns by their names.*

This example uses a custom-developed ERP database as a source of employee information and uses the Northwind database as the destination.

> On the Wrox.com site you will find an Excel file containing the custom data source used in Listing 12-5. Load this into your SQL Server database and use it to run this sample. You can find the steps for loading this data source into SQL Server in the Readme.txt file bundled with the code for this chapter (Chapter12.zip).

Listing 12-5: Code for bulk loading large quantities of data from a custom source table to the Northwind database

VB

```vb
<%@ Page Language="VB" %>
<%@ Import Namespace="System.Data" %>
<%@ Import Namespace="System.Data.SqlClient" %>
<%@ Import Namespace="System.Configuration" %>

<script runat="server">
    Sub btnBulkCopy_Click(ByVal sender As Object, _
            ByVal e As System.EventArgs) Handles btnBulkCopy.Click

        Dim ShajarConString As String
        Dim NorthWindConString As String
        Dim ShajarCon As SqlConnection = New SqlConnection()
        Dim NorthwindCon As SqlConnection = New SqlConnection()

        Dim ShajarCom As SqlCommand = New SqlCommand()
        Dim ShajarReader As SqlDataReader

        ShajarConString = _
            ConfigurationManager.ConnectionStrings("DSN_Shajar").ConnectionString
        NorthWindConString = _
            ConfigurationManager.ConnectionStrings("DSN_Northwind").ConnectionString

        ShajarCon.ConnectionString = ShajarConString
        ShajarCom.Connection = ShajarCon
        ShajarCom.CommandText = "SELECT ID, First_Name, Last_Name, " & _
                                " 'Shajar' as Source FROM MailingList_Temp"
```

(continued)

Listing 12-5: *(continued)*

```
        ShajarCom.CommandType = CommandType.Text

        ShajarCom.Connection.Open()

        Dim NorthWindBulkOp As SqlBulkCopy
        NorthWindBulkOp = New SqlBulkCopy(NorthWindConString, _
                            SqlBulkCopyOptions.UseInternalTransaction)

        NorthWindBulkOp.DestinationTableName = "Employees"
        NorthWindBulkOp.ColumnMappings.Add("Id", "EmployeeID")
        NorthWindBulkOp.ColumnMappings.Add("First_Name", "FirstName")
        NorthWindBulkOp.ColumnMappings.Add("Last_Name", "LastName")

        Dim JobTitleColMap As SqlBulkCopyColumnMapping
        JobTitleColMap = New SqlBulkCopyColumnMapping("Source", "Title")

        NorthWindBulkOp.ColumnMappings.Add(JobTitleColMap)
        NorthWindBulkOp.BulkCopyTimeout = 500000000

        AddHandler NorthWindBulkOp.SqlRowsCopied, _
                New SqlRowsCopiedEventHandler(AddressOf OnSqlRowsCopied)

        NorthWindBulkOp.NotifyAfter = 1000

        ShajarReader = ShajarCom.ExecuteReader()

        Try
            NorthWindBulkOp.WriteToServer(ShajarReader)
        Catch ex As Exception
            ' Write error handling code here
            lblResult.Text = ex.Message
        Finally
            ShajarReader.Close()
        End Try

    End Sub

    Private Sub OnSqlRowsCopied(ByVal sender As Object, _
            ByVal args As SqlRowsCopiedEventArgs)

        lblCounter.Text += args.RowsCopied.ToString() + " rows are copied<Br>"
    End Sub

</script>

<html xmlns="http://www.w3.org/1999/xhtml" >
<head id="Head1" runat="server">
    <title>Bulk Loading Large Volume Data</title>
</head>
<body>
    <form id="form1" runat="server">
    <div>
        <asp:Button ID="btnBulkCopy" Runat="server" Text="Start Bulk Copy" /> 
```

```
            <br />
            <br />

        <asp:Label ID="lblResult" Runat="server"></asp:Label>
            <br />
            <br />
            <asp:Label ID="lblCounter" Runat="server"></asp:Label>
        </div>
        </form>
</body>
</html>
```

C#

```
<%@ Page Language="C#" %>
<%@ Import Namespace="System.Data" %>
<%@ Import Namespace="System.Data.SqlClient" %>
<%@ Import Namespace="System.Configuration" %>

<script runat="server">
    protected void btnBulkCopy_Click(object sender, EventArgs e)
    {
        String ShajarConString;
        String NorthWindConString;
        SqlConnection ShajarCon = new SqlConnection();
        SqlConnection NorthwindCon = new SqlConnection();

        SqlCommand ShajarCom = new SqlCommand();
        SqlDataReader ShajarReader;

        ShajarConString =
          ConfigurationManager.ConnectionStrings["DSN_Shajar"].ConnectionString;

        NorthWindConString =
          ConfigurationManager.ConnectionStrings["DSN_Northwind"].ConnectionString;

        ShajarCon.ConnectionString = ShajarConString;
        ShajarCom.Connection = ShajarCon;
        ShajarCom.CommandText = "SELECT ID, First_Name, Last_Name, " +
                           " 'Shajar' as Source FROM MailingList_Temp";
        ShajarCom.CommandType = CommandType.Text;

        ShajarCom.Connection.Open();

        SqlBulkCopy NorthWindBulkOp;
        NorthWindBulkOp = new SqlBulkCopy(NorthWindConString,
                           SqlBulkCopyOptions.UseInternalTransaction);

        NorthWindBulkOp.DestinationTableName = "Employees";

        NorthWindBulkOp.ColumnMappings.Add("Id", "EmployeeID");
        NorthWindBulkOp.ColumnMappings.Add("First_Name", "FirstName");
        NorthWindBulkOp.ColumnMappings.Add("Last_Name", "LastName");

        SqlBulkCopyColumnMapping JobTitleColMap;
```

(continued)

Listing 12-5: *(continued)*

```
        JobTitleColMap = new SqlBulkCopyColumnMapping("Source", "Title");

        NorthWindBulkOp.ColumnMappings.Add(JobTitleColMap);
        NorthWindBulkOp.BulkCopyTimeout = 500000000;

        NorthWindBulkOp.SqlRowsCopied +=
            new SqlRowsCopiedEventHandler(OnRowsCopied);

        NorthWindBulkOp.NotifyAfter = 1000;

        ShajarReader = ShajarCom.ExecuteReader();

        try
        {
            NorthWindBulkOp.WriteToServer(ShajarReader);
        }
        catch (Exception ex)
        {
            lblResult.Text = ex.Message;
        }
        finally
        {
            ShajarReader.Close();
        }
    }

    private void OnRowsCopied(object sender, SqlRowsCopiedEventArgs args)
    {
        lblCounter.Text += args.RowsCopied.ToString() + " rows are copied<Br>";
    }
</script>
```

The code example shown in Listing 12-5 uses an internal transaction to process all records. If the bulk operation fails before all records are processed, the transaction is rolled back and all records that were added prior to the failure are retracted from the destination table.

To make sure that you commit all records that were processed successfully before the error occurred, you must provide a custom transaction object to the constructor of the `SqlBulkCopy` object. In this case, you commit the transaction manually using the `Finally` clause, as shown in Listing 12-6.

Listing 12-6: Committing a transaction after successfully completing the bulk copy operation

VB

```
Dim Transaction As SqlTransaction
Transaction = ShajarCom.Connection.BeginTransaction()

Dim NorthWindBulkOp As SqlBulkCopy
NorthWindBulkOp = New SqlBulkCopy(New SqlConnection(NorthWindConString), _
                        SqlBulkCopyOptions.Default, _
                        Transaction)
```

```vb
' ...Code removed for clarity...

ShajarReader = ShajarCom.ExecuteReader()

Try
    NorthWindBulkOp.WriteToServer(ShajarReader)
Catch ex As Exception
    ' Write error handling code here
Finally
    Transaction.Commit()
    ShajarReader.Close()
End Try
```

C#

```csharp
SqlTransaction Transaction;
Transaction = ShajarCom.Connection.BeginTransaction();

SqlBulkCopy NorthWindBulkOp;
NorthWindBulkOp = new SqlBulkCopy(new SqlConnection(NorthWindConString),
                        SqlBulkCopyOptions.Default,
                        Transaction);

// ...Code removed for clarity...

ShajarReader = ShajarCom.ExecuteReader();

try
{
    NorthWindBulkOp.WriteToServer(ShajarReader);
}
catch (Exception ex)
{
    // Write error handling code here
}
finally
{
    Transaction.Commit();
    ShajarReader.Close();
}
```

The advantage of committing the transaction in the `Finally` clause is that the transaction gets committed regardless of whether the error occurs.

SqlRowsCopied Event

Listing 12-5 shows the `OnRowsCopied` event handler. It simply updates a label control to show progress. It is not necessary to do this. However, this event is a good way to show progress while the user is waiting for a large volume of data to finish loading.

The big advantage of using this bulk copy method is that it reduces the number of times the database is accessed during the copy operation. The code shown in Listing 12-5 processes large volumes of data at a very rapid pace. You can see the database trace log in Figure 12-4. This trace log clearly shows that the database copied all records with a few requests. In fact, the number of requests made to the database is affected only by the size of the batch that you specify in the code.

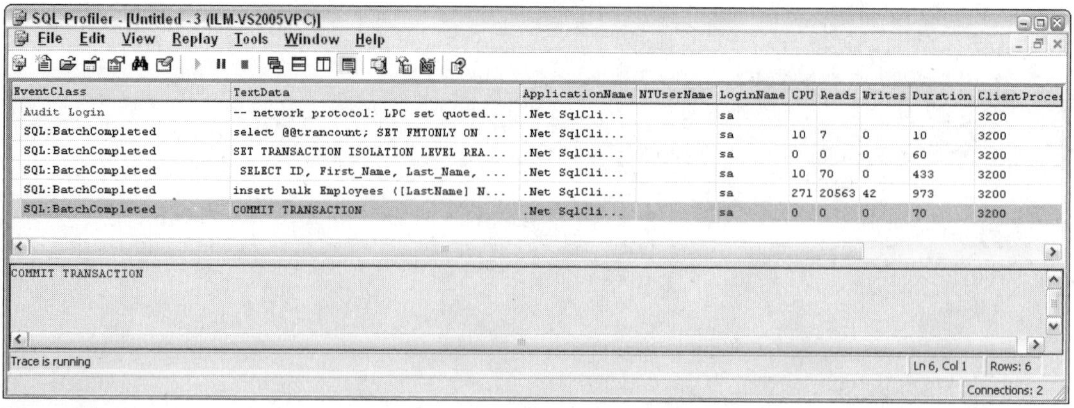

Figure 12-4

Batch Processing Multiple Updates

Even though the bulk copy operation provides the most efficient way of loading data into the destination database, it also provides the fewest opportunities for the customization of the database update processes. For instance, the bulk copy operation is capable of loading the data only to a single table in the destination database. In many real-world cases, the destination database uses multiple tables and data updates that often require executing either a custom SQL statement or a custom Stored Procedure.

ADO.NET provides the `DataAdapter` object for just such cases. You can use the `DataAdapter` object to provide custom `Update`, `Insert`, and `Delete` commands and to consume a `DataTable`. When the `Update` method is called on a `DataAdapter`, it simply iterates through all rows in a `DataTable` and fires the appropriate `Update`, `Insert`, or `Delete` command depending on the `RowState` flag set on each row.

The only problem with using `DataAdapter` in the previous version of ADO.NET was that it was unable to process batch updates. The `DataAdapter` object was capable of executing only one command at a time, and this caused a very significant performance slowdown if you were processing a large volume of updates. This lack of batch processing also put a much greater load on the database server because it had to process each command in a separate request.

With the introduction of ADO.NET 2.0, the `DataAdapter` object now provides a new property called `UpdateBatchSize`. Using the value provided to this property, the `DataAdapter` object is now capable of sending a group of commands to the database server in one batch. As a result, this feature significantly improves performance when compared to the previous processing mechanism that handled each command separately.

The batch updates feature, however, relies on the target database or data source to support batch command execution. If the data source does not, the `DataAdapter` object ignores the `UpdateBatchSize` property and proceeds with processing each command separately.

If you don't provide any value to the `UpdateBatchSize` property, it defaults to a value of 1, which causes the `DataAdapter` to process each command individually. If the `UpdateBatchSize` property is set to 0, the `DataAdapter` processes all commands as one batch. Be careful about making the batch sizes too large because different databases can handle only up to a certain batch size. If the batch size is larger than the capability of the destination database, the `DataAdapter` throws an exception.

Listing 12-7 shows a code example that retrieves all employee records from the Northwind database, updates their addresses, and saves the changes back to the same table. It uses a batch size of 3 to process three commands in each batch. You can change this number to a larger one if you want to process a larger batch of records later. Currently, the Employees table in the Northwind database contains only nine records, and setting a batch size of 3 accomplishes updates to these nine records in three requests to the database server.

Listing 12-7: Batch processing multiple updates to the Northwind database

VB

```vb
<%@ Page Language="VB" %>
<%@ Import Namespace="System.Data" %>
<%@ Import Namespace="System.Data.SqlClient" %>
<%@ Import Namespace="System.Configuration" %>

<script runat="server">
    Sub btnUpdateAddress_Click(ByVal sender As Object, _
      ByVal e As System.EventArgs) Handles btnUpdateAddress.Click

        Dim EmpAdapter As SqlDataAdapter = New SqlDataAdapter()
        Dim EmpDT As DataTable = New DataTable()
        Dim DBConSelect As SqlConnection = New SqlConnection()
        Dim DBConUpdate As SqlConnection = New SqlConnection()
        Dim SelectCommand As SqlCommand = New SqlCommand()
        Dim UpdateCommand As SqlCommand = New SqlCommand()

        ' Using different connection objects for select and updates from the
        ' Northwind database.
        DBConSelect.ConnectionString = _
          ConfigurationManager.ConnectionStrings("DSN_NorthWind").ConnectionString

        DBConUpdate.ConnectionString = _
          ConfigurationManager.ConnectionStrings("DSN_NorthWind").ConnectionString

        ' Reading all records from the Employees table
        SelectCommand.CommandText = "SELECT * FROM EMPLOYEES"
        SelectCommand.CommandType = CommandType.Text
        SelectCommand.Connection = DBConSelect

        UpdateCommand.CommandText = _
        "UPDATE EMPLOYEES SET Address=@Address, " & _
        "City=@City, Region=@Region, Country=@Country"

        UpdateCommand.CommandType = CommandType.Text
        UpdateCommand.Connection = DBConUpdate

        Dim AddressParam As SqlParameter
        AddressParam = New SqlParameter("@Address", _
            SqlDbType.VarChar, 15, "Address")

        Dim CityParam As SqlParameter
        CityParam = New SqlParameter("@City", SqlDbType.VarChar, 15, "City")

        Dim RegionParam As SqlParameter
```

(continued)

Listing 12-7: *(continued)*

```
RegionParam = New SqlParameter("@Region", SqlDbType.VarChar, 15, "Region")

Dim CountryParam As SqlParameter
CountryParam = New SqlParameter("@Country", _
    SqlDbType.VarChar, 15, "Country")

UpdateCommand.Parameters.Add(AddressParam)
UpdateCommand.Parameters.Add(CityParam)
UpdateCommand.Parameters.Add(RegionParam)
UpdateCommand.Parameters.Add(CountryParam)

' Setting up Data Adapter with the Select and Update Commands
' The Select command will be used to retrieve all employee
' information from the Northwind database and the Update command
' will be used to save changes back to the database
EmpAdapter.SelectCommand = SelectCommand
EmpAdapter.UpdateCommand = UpdateCommand

EmpAdapter.Fill(EmpDT)

DBConSelect.Close()

' Looping through all employee records and assigning them the new
' address
For Each DR As DataRow In EmpDT.Rows
    DR("Address") = "4445 W 77th Street, Suite 140"
    DR("City") = "Edina"
    DR("Region") = "Minnesota"
    DR("Country") = "USA"
Next

' Adding an event handler to listen to the RowUpdated event.
' This event will will fire after each batch is executed
AddHandler EmpAdapter.RowUpdated, _
New SqlRowUpdatedEventHandler(AddressOf OnRowUpdated)

lblCounter.Text = ""

EmpAdapter.UpdateBatchSize = 3


' It is important to set this property for batch processing of
' updated records since batch updates are incapable of updating
' the source with changes from the database
UpdateCommand.UpdatedRowSource = UpdateRowSource.None

Try
    DBConUpdate.Open()
    EmpAdapter.Update(EmpDT)
Catch ex As Exception
    lblCounter.Text += ex.Message + "<Br>"
```

```
            Finally
                If DBConUpdate.State = ConnectionState.Open Then
                    DBConUpdate.Close()
                End If
            End Try

        End Sub

        Private Sub OnRowUpdated(ByVal sender As Object, ByVal args As _
            SqlRowUpdatedEventArgs)

            lblCounter.Text += "Batch is processed for " + args.RowCount.ToString() & _
                " rows<br>"

        End Sub

</script>

<html xmlns="http://www.w3.org/1999/xhtml" >
<head id="Head1" runat="server">
    <title>Batch Processing Multiple Updates</title>
</head>
<body>
    <form id="form1" runat="server">
    <div>
        <asp:Button ID="btnUpdateAddress" Runat="server" Text="Update Address"
                OnClick="btnUpdateAddress_Click" />
        <br />
        <br />
        <asp:Label ID="lblCounter" Runat="server"></asp:Label> <br />
        <br />
        <br />
    </div>
    </form>
</body>
</html>
```

C#

```
<%@ Page Language="C#" %>
<%@ Import Namespace="System.Data" %>
<%@ Import Namespace="System.Data.SqlClient" %>
<%@ Import Namespace="System.Configuration" %>

<script runat="server">
    protected void btnUpdateAddress_Click(object sender, EventArgs e)
    {
        SqlDataAdapter EmpAdapter = new SqlDataAdapter();
        DataTable EmpDT = new DataTable();
        SqlConnection DBConSelect = new SqlConnection();
        SqlConnection DBConUpdate = new SqlConnection();
        SqlCommand SelectCommand = new SqlCommand();
```

(continued)

Listing 12-7: *(continued)*

```
SqlCommand UpdateCommand = new SqlCommand();

// Using different connection objects for select and updates from the
// Northwind database.
DBConSelect.ConnectionString =
  ConfigurationManager.ConnectionStrings["DSN_NorthWind"].ConnectionString;
DBConUpdate.ConnectionString =
  ConfigurationManager.ConnectionStrings["DSN_NorthWind"].ConnectionString;

// Reading all records from the Employees table
SelectCommand.CommandText = "SELECT * FROM EMPLOYEES";
SelectCommand.CommandType = CommandType.Text;
SelectCommand.Connection = DBConSelect;

UpdateCommand.CommandText = "UPDATE EMPLOYEES SET Address=@Address, " +
                            "City=@City, Region=@Region, Country=@Country";

UpdateCommand.CommandType = CommandType.Text;
UpdateCommand.Connection = DBConUpdate;

SqlParameter AddressParam;
AddressParam = new SqlParameter("@Address",
   SqlDbType.VarChar, 15, "Address");

SqlParameter CityParam;
CityParam = new SqlParameter("@City", SqlDbType.VarChar, 15, "City");

SqlParameter RegionParam;
RegionParam = new SqlParameter("@Region", SqlDbType.VarChar, 15, "Region");

SqlParameter CountryParam;
CountryParam = new SqlParameter("@Country",
   SqlDbType.VarChar, 15, "Country");

UpdateCommand.Parameters.Add(AddressParam);
UpdateCommand.Parameters.Add(CityParam);
UpdateCommand.Parameters.Add(RegionParam);
UpdateCommand.Parameters.Add(CountryParam);

// Setting up Data Adapter with the Select and Update Commands
// The Select command will be used to retrieve all employee
// information from the Northwind database and the Update command
// will be used to save changes back to the database
EmpAdapter.SelectCommand = SelectCommand;
EmpAdapter.UpdateCommand = UpdateCommand;

EmpAdapter.Fill(EmpDT);

DBConSelect.Close();

// Looping through all employee records and assigning them the new
```

```
        // address
        foreach (DataRow DR in EmpDT.Rows)
        {
            DR["Address"] = "4445 W 77th Street, Suite 140";
            DR["City"] = "Edina";
            DR["Region"] = "Minnesota";
            DR["Country"] = "USA";
        }

        // Adding an event handler to listen to the RowUpdated event.
        // This event will will fire after each batch is executed
        EmpAdapter.RowUpdated +=  new SqlRowUpdatedEventHandler(OnRowUpdated);

        lblCounter.Text = "";

        EmpAdapter.UpdateBatchSize = 3;

        // It is important to set this property for batch processing of
        // updated records since batch updates are incapable of
        // updating the source with changes from the database
        UpdateCommand.UpdatedRowSource = UpdateRowSource.None;

        try
        {
            DBConUpdate.Open();
            EmpAdapter.Update(EmpDT);
        }
        catch (Exception ex)
        {
            lblCounter.Text += ex.Message + "<Br>";
        }
        finally
        {
            if (DBConUpdate.State == ConnectionState.Open)
            {
                DBConUpdate.Close();
            }
        }
    }

    private void OnRowUpdated(object sender, SqlRowUpdatedEventArgs args)
    {
        lblCounter.Text += "Batch is processed till row number = " +
            args.RowCount.ToString() + "<br>";
    }
```

</script>

The batch update operation runs one SQL command for each operation, thereby causing significant performance overhead. The trace log shown in Figure 12-5 shows this fact.

The ADO.NET classes introduced in version 1.0 provided a mechanism for developing cutting-edge, database-driven applications. The features introduced to help manage data in a disconnected manner especially paved the way for creating highly efficient and scalable applications. At the same time, the features for processing data in a connected state using a fast-forward read-only cursor let you create applications that consumed larger quantities of data at a rapid pace.

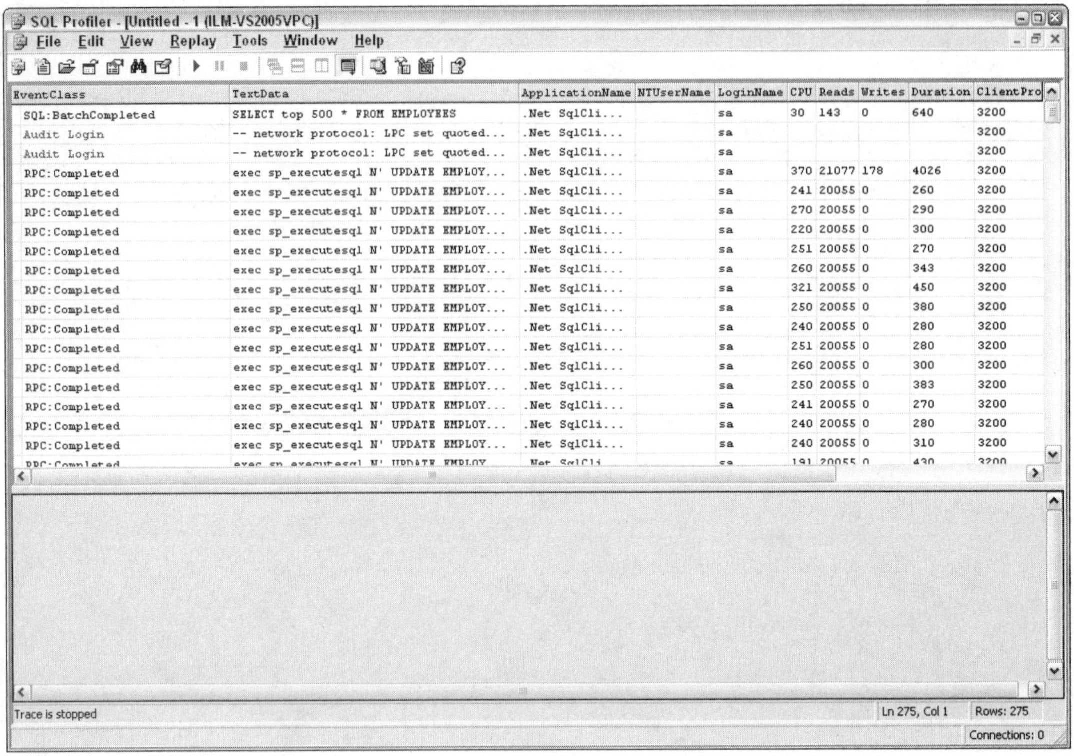

EventClass	TextData	ApplicationName	NTUserName	LoginName	CPU	Reads	Writes	Duration	ClientPro
SQL:BatchCompleted	SELECT top 500 * FROM EMPLOYEES	.Net SqlCli...		sa	30	143	0	640	3200
Audit Login	-- network protocol: LPC set quoted...	.Net SqlCli...		sa					3200
Audit Login	-- network protocol: LPC set quoted...	.Net SqlCli...		sa					3200
RPC:Completed	exec sp_executesql N' UPDATE EMPLOY...	.Net SqlCli...		sa	370	21077	178	4026	3200
RPC:Completed	exec sp_executesql N' UPDATE EMPLOY...	.Net SqlCli...		sa	241	20055	0	260	3200
RPC:Completed	exec sp_executesql N' UPDATE EMPLOY...	.Net SqlCli...		sa	270	20055	0	290	3200
RPC:Completed	exec sp_executesql N' UPDATE EMPLOY...	.Net SqlCli...		sa	220	20055	0	300	3200
RPC:Completed	exec sp_executesql N' UPDATE EMPLOY...	.Net SqlCli...		sa	251	20055	0	270	3200
RPC:Completed	exec sp_executesql N' UPDATE EMPLOY...	.Net SqlCli...		sa	260	20055	0	343	3200
RPC:Completed	exec sp_executesql N' UPDATE EMPLOY...	.Net SqlCli...		sa	321	20055	0	450	3200
RPC:Completed	exec sp_executesql N' UPDATE EMPLOY...	.Net SqlCli...		sa	250	20055	0	380	3200
RPC:Completed	exec sp_executesql N' UPDATE EMPLOY...	.Net SqlCli...		sa	240	20055	0	280	3200
RPC:Completed	exec sp_executesql N' UPDATE EMPLOY...	.Net SqlCli...		sa	251	20055	0	280	3200
RPC:Completed	exec sp_executesql N' UPDATE EMPLOY...	.Net SqlCli...		sa	260	20055	0	300	3200
RPC:Completed	exec sp_executesql N' UPDATE EMPLOY...	.Net SqlCli...		sa	250	20055	0	383	3200
RPC:Completed	exec sp_executesql N' UPDATE EMPLOY...	.Net SqlCli...		sa	241	20055	0	270	3200
RPC:Completed	exec sp_executesql N' UPDATE EMPLOY...	.Net SqlCli...		sa	240	20055	0	280	3200
RPC:Completed	exec sp_executesql N' UPDATE EMPLOY...	.Net SqlCli...		sa	240	20055	0	310	3200
RPC:Completed	exec sp_executesql N' UPDATE EMPLOY	.Net SqlCli		sa	191	20055	0	430	3200

Trace is stopped   Ln 275, Col 1   Rows: 275   Connections: 0

Figure 12-5

Surpassing even these advancements, the latest 2.0 version of ADO.NET provides a newer capability that enables you to create a database-driven application in a manner that was impossible in previous versions. The capability to process Multiple Active Result Sets (MARS) over the same connection not only reduces programming tasks but also significantly enhances performance.

Multiple Active Result Sets

MARS provides the capability to open more than one result set over the same connection and lets you access them all concurrently. MARS is helpful in the scenarios where the application uses a single data source for its needs. You have probably written code where you executed a command to retrieve a result set and then had to execute other commands for each record in the result set to retrieve detailed information related to those records.

A typical master and detailed information scenario is a perfect example of how MARS can provide an elegant programming model and enhance code performance at the same time. In this scenario, your code executes a command to retrieve a set of records such as list of orders for a given day. While you are retrieving orders, you also want to retrieve detailed line items for each order so that you can present a complete report to the user. It is quite common in a relational database to execute a separate command to retrieve all the detailed line items for a given order. When we have found ourselves in such a scenario, we ended up writing code that executed the command for retrieving the detailed information using one loop for each record.

This type of scenario is still programmable in the older versions of ADO.NET. In older versions, however, programmers were limited to opening and closing separate connections for each request to the database servers. Even though the programs ran successfully and produced desired results, programmers often wished for a more elegant mechanism that would enable them to reuse the same connection and reduce the overhead associated with accessing the database. The release of ADO.NET 2.0 and support for MARS allow users to do just that.

Now you can write some code to access the Northwind database that produces a Web report showing all the orders and item details of each order. As some of you already know, the Northwind database provides two tables with the names Order and Order Details. The Orders table contains all the orders ever made and the Order Details table shows the merchandise included as part of each order.

Listing 12-8 shows a GridView control that uses BoundField columns to show selected columns from the database on the screen. The GridView control also uses a template column containing a Label control whose value gets populated with a list of order details when you run a separate SQL query against the Order Details table for each Order record.

> The `OnRowDataBound` event of the GridView control is what executes the SQL query for retrieving order details.

Listing 12-8: GridView control declaration for displaying Orders and Order Details from the Northwind database

VB

```
<%@ Page Language="VB" %>
<%@ Import Namespace="System.Data" %>
<%@ Import Namespace="System.Data.SqlClient" %>
<%@ Import Namespace="System.Configuration" %>

<script runat="server">
    ' Declaring connection here allows us to use it inside all methods
    ' of this class
    Dim DBCon As SqlConnection

    Protected Sub Page_Load(ByVal sender As Object, _
                ByVal e As System.EventArgs)

        Dim Command As SqlCommand = New SqlCommand()
        Dim OrdersReader As SqlDataReader

        DBCon = New SqlConnection()
        DBCon.ConnectionString = _
```

(continued)

Listing 12-8: *(continued)*

```
            ConfigurationManager.ConnectionStrings("DSN_NorthWind").ConnectionString

        Command.CommandText = _
                "SELECT TOP 5 Customers.CompanyName, Customers.ContactName, " & _
                "Orders.OrderID, Orders.OrderDate, " & _
                "Orders.RequiredDate, Orders.ShippedDate " & _
                "FROM Orders, Customers " & _
                "WHERE Orders.CustomerID = Customers.CustomerID " & _
                "ORDER BY Customers.CompanyName, Customers.ContactName "

        Command.CommandType = CommandType.Text
        Command.Connection = DBCon

        ' Opening the connection and executing the SQL query.
        DBCon.Open()
        OrdersReader = Command.ExecuteReader()

        ' Binding the Data Reader to the GridView control
        gvOrders.DataSource = OrdersReader
        gvOrders.DataBind()

        ' Closing connection after we are done processing all order records
        DBCon.Close()

    End Sub

    ' This event handler is called for each record being bound to the
    ' GridView control
    Protected Sub gvOrders_RowDataBound(ByVal sender As Object, _
                ByVal e As System.Web.UI.WebControls.GridViewRowEventArgs)

        Dim OrderRecord As IDataRecord
        Dim lblOrderDetail As Label

        ' Retrieving the currently bound record from the Data Reader
        ' using the IDataRecord interface
        OrderRecord = CType(e.Row.DataItem, IDataRecord)

        ' Retrieving reference to the Label Control inside the current
        ' GridView row. This Label will be populated with Order Details
        lblOrderDetail = CType(e.Row.FindControl("lblOrderDetail"), Label)

        If OrderRecord Is Nothing Or lblOrderDetail Is Nothing Then
            Return
        End If

        Dim Command As SqlCommand = New SqlCommand()
        Dim OrderDetailReader As SqlDataReader

        ' Creating an SQL query to retrieve details
        ' for the currently processed order
        Command.CommandText = _
```

```
            "SELECT Products.ProductName, [Order Details].UnitPrice, " & _
            "[Order Details].Quantity, [Order Details].Discount " & _
            "FROM [Order Details], Products " & _
            "WHERE [Order Details].ProductID = Products.ProductID " & _
            "AND [Order Details].OrderID = " & _
            Convert.ToString(OrderRecord("OrderID"))

        Command.CommandType = CommandType.Text

        ' Reusing the same connection object that was used in retrieving
        ' allorder records from the Orders table
        Command.Connection = DBCon

        ' Executing SQL query without passing CommandBehavior.CloseConnection
        ' as parameter to ExecuteReader. We don't want the connection
        ' to automatically close because we want to reuse it for more operations
        OrderDetailReader = Command.ExecuteReader()

        While OrderDetailReader.Read()
            ' Populating the lable control with the product name field
            lblOrderDetail.Text += OrderDetailReader(0).ToString() + "<Br>"
        End While

    End Sub

</script>

<html xmlns="http://www.w3.org/1999/xhtml" >
<head id="Head1" runat="server">
    <title>Multiple Active Result Sets</title>
</head>
<body>
    <form id="form1" runat="server">
    <div>
        <asp:Label ID="lblCounter" Runat="server"></asp:Label>
        <br />
        <asp:GridView ID="gvOrders" Runat="server" AutoGenerateColumns="False"
                OnRowDataBound="gvOrders_RowDataBound" Width="100%">
        <Columns>
        <asp:BoundField HeaderText="Company Name"
                DataField="CompanyName"></asp:BoundField>
        <asp:BoundField HeaderText="Contact Name"
                DataField="ContactName"></asp:BoundField>
        <asp:TemplateField>
        <HeaderTemplate>
                Order Detail
        </HeaderTemplate>
        <ItemTemplate>
                <asp:Label ID="lblOrderDetail" runat="server"></asp:Label>
        </ItemTemplate>

        </asp:TemplateField>
                <asp:BoundField HeaderText="Order Date" DataField="orderdate"
                    DataFormatString="{0:d}"></asp:BoundField>
```

(continued)

Listing 12-8: *(continued)*

```
                <asp:BoundField HeaderText="Required Date" DataField="requireddate"
                        DataFormatString="{0:d}"></asp:BoundField>
                <asp:BoundField HeaderText="Shipped Date" DataField="shippeddate"
                        DataFormatString="{0:d}"></asp:BoundField>
            </Columns>
        </asp:GridView><br />
        <br />
    </div>
    </form>
</body>
</html>
```

C#

```csharp
<%@ Page Language="C#" %>
<%@ Import Namespace="System.Data" %>
<%@ Import Namespace="System.Data.SqlClient" %>
<%@ Import Namespace="System.Configuration" %>

<script runat="server">
    // Declaring connection here allows us to use it inside all methods
    // of this class
    SqlConnection DBCon;

    protected void Page_Load(object sender, EventArgs e)
    {
        SqlCommand Command = new SqlCommand();
        SqlDataReader OrdersReader;

        DBCon = new SqlConnection();
        DBCon.ConnectionString =
          ConfigurationManager.ConnectionStrings["DSN_NorthWind"].ConnectionString;

        Command.CommandText =
                "SELECT TOP 5 Customers.CompanyName, Customers.ContactName, " +
                "Orders.OrderID, Orders.OrderDate, " +
                "Orders.RequiredDate, Orders.ShippedDate " +
                "FROM Orders, Customers " +
                "WHERE Orders.CustomerID = Customers.CustomerID " +
                "ORDER BY Customers.CompanyName, Customers.ContactName "

        Command.CommandType = CommandType.Text;
        Command.Connection = DBCon;

        // Opening the connection and executing the SQL query.
        DBCon.Open();
        OrdersReader = Command.ExecuteReader();

        // Binding the Data Reader to the GridView control
        gvOrders.DataSource = OrdersReader;
```

```
        gvOrders.DataBind();

        // Closing connection after we are done processing all order records
        DBCon.Close();
    }

    protected void gvOrders_RowDataBound(object sender, GridViewRowEventArgs e)
    {
        IDataRecord OrderRecord;
        Label lblOrderDetail;

        // Retrieving the currently bound record from the Data Reader
        // using the IDataRecord interface
        OrderRecord = e.Row.DataItem as IDataRecord;

        // Retrieving reference to the Label Control inside the current
        // GridView row. This Label will be populated with Order Details
        lblOrderDetail = e.Row.FindControl("lblOrderDetail") as Label;

        if ((OrderRecord == null) || (lblOrderDetail == null))
            return;

        SqlCommand Command = new SqlCommand();
        SqlDataReader OrderDetailReader;

        // Creating an SQL query to retrieve details
        // for the currently processed order
        Command.CommandText =
                "SELECT Products.ProductName, [Order Details].UnitPrice, " +
                "[Order Details].Quantity, [Order Details].Discount " +
                "FROM [Order Details], Products " +
                "WHERE [Order Details].ProductID = Products.ProductID " +
                "AND [Order Details].OrderID = " +
                Convert.ToString(OrderRecord["OrderID"]);

        Command.CommandType = CommandType.Text;

        // Reusing the same connection object that was used in retrieving
        // allorder records from the Orders table
        Command.Connection = DBCon;

        // Executing SQL query without passing CommandBehavior.CloseConnection
        // as parameter to ExecuteReader. We don't want the connection
        // to automatically close because we want to reuse it for more operations
        OrderDetailReader = Command.ExecuteReader();

        while (OrderDetailReader.Read())
        {
            // Populating the lable control with the product name field
            lblOrderDetail.Text += OrderDetailReader[0].ToString() + "<br/>";
        }
    }
</script>
```

Listing 12-8 show a sample of code that runs an inline SQL statement to retrieve all orders from the Orders table. It retrieves the result set using a `SqlDataReader` object and binds the `DataReader` to a GridView control. When the GridView control starts to bind the `DataReader`, it starts firing an `OnRowDataBound` event for each record. The code listens to this event using an event handler. The parameters automatically passed to this event handler contain the record that is currently being bound to the GridView control. To get reference to this record, use the IDataRecord interface. You can use its properties to access the OrderID column for the order record that is currently being data bound. After you know the OrderID, you execute an SQL query against the Order Details table and retrieve items details for the order.

When executing the code shown in the Listings 12-4 and 12-5, you see the result on the screen showing the five orders from the Orders table (see Figure 12-6). Pay close attention to the Order Detail column that shows the list of products within each order. This list is retrieved by running separate SQL query for each order using the same connection to the database.

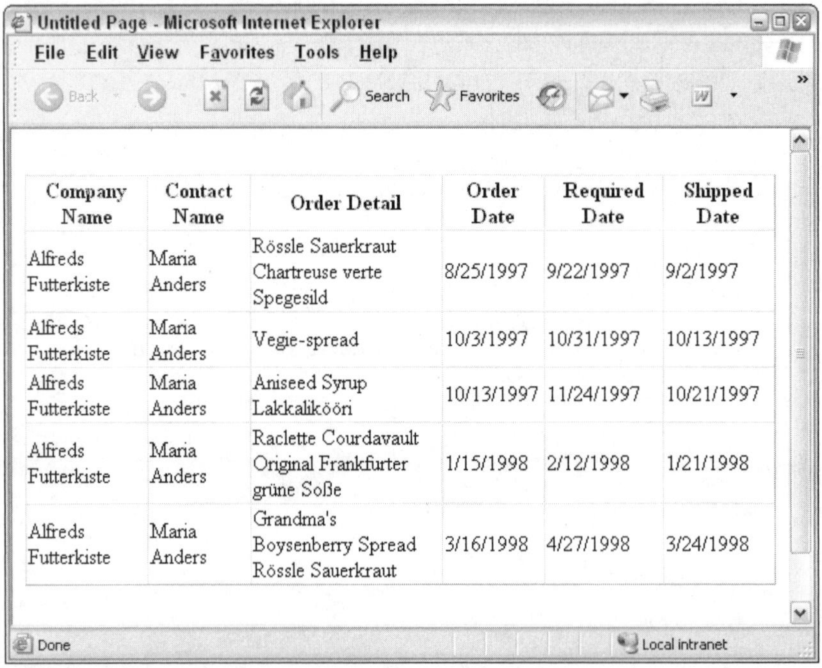

Company Name	Contact Name	Order Detail	Order Date	Required Date	Shipped Date
Alfreds Futterkiste	Maria Anders	Rössle Sauerkraut Chartreuse verte Spegesild	8/25/1997	9/22/1997	9/2/1997
Alfreds Futterkiste	Maria Anders	Vegie-spread	10/3/1997	10/31/1997	10/13/1997
Alfreds Futterkiste	Maria Anders	Aniseed Syrup Lakkalikööri	10/13/1997	11/24/1997	10/21/1997
Alfreds Futterkiste	Maria Anders	Raclette Courdavault Original Frankfurter grüne Soße	1/15/1998	2/12/1998	1/21/1998
Alfreds Futterkiste	Maria Anders	Grandma's Boysenberry Spread Rössle Sauerkraut	3/16/1998	4/27/1998	3/24/1998

Figure 12-6

One of the disadvantages of the previous versions of ADO.NET was its lack of support for asynchronous processing. Each command had to finish executing before the user could issue more commands to the database. Support for asynchronous processing would have allowed users to make multiple, unrelated updates to the database in a parallel fashion. This was especially true if multiple databases were involved. With the release of ADO.NET 2.0, you are now able to process database commands asynchronously, as discussed in the following section.

Asynchronous Command Execution

When you process data using ADO or previous versions of ADO.NET, each command is executed sequentially. The code waits for each command to complete before the next one is processed. When you use a single database, the sequential processing enables you to reuse the same connection object for all commands. However, with the introduction of MARS, you can now use a single connection for multiple, concurrent database access. The 2.0 version of ADO.NET also enables you to process database commands asynchronously. This enables you to not only use same connection, but also to use it in a parallel manner. The real advantage of asynchronous processing becomes apparent when you are accessing multiple data sources—especially when the data access queries across these databases aren't dependent on each other. You can now open a connection to the database in an asynchronous manner. When you are working with multiple databases, you can now open connections to them in a parallel fashion as well.

> The use of asynchronous processing with ADO.NET 2.0 requires that MDAC 9.0 be installed on the machine. Be sure to download and install MDAC 9.0 before attempting to use this feature. Also, be sure to add `Asynchronous Processing=true;` to the connection string.

Asynchronous Methods of the SqlCommand Class

The `SqlCommand` class provides a few additional methods that facilitate executing commands asynchronously. These new methods are summarized in the following table.

Method	Description
`BeginExecuteNonQuery ( )`	This method expects a query that doesn't return any results and starts it asynchronously. The return value is a reference to an object of the `SqlAsyncResult` class that implements the `IAsyncResult` interface. The returned object can be used to monitor the process as it runs and when it is completed.
`BeginExecuteNonQuery (callback, stateObject )`	This overloaded method also starts the process asynchronously, and it expects to receive an object of the `AsynchCallback` instance. The callback method is called after the process is finished running so that you can proceed with other tasks. The second parameter receives any custom-defined object. This object is passed to the callback automatically. It provides an excellent mechanism for passing parameters to the callback method. The callback method can retrieve the custom-defined state object by using the `AsyncState` property of the `IAsyncResult` interface.

Table continued on following page

Method	Description
EndExecuteNonQuery (asyncResult)	This method is used to access the results from the BeginExecuteNonQuery method. This should be called after the process has finished running; otherwise, an exception is thrown. When calling this method, you are required to pass the same SqlAsyncResult object that you received when you called the BeginExecuteNonQuery method. This method returns an Integer value containing the number of rows affected.
BeginExecuteReader	This method expects a query that returns a result set and starts it asynchronously. The return value is a reference to an object of SqlAsyncResult class that implements IAsyncResult interface. The returned object can be used to monitor the process as it runs and as it is completed.
BeginExecuteReader (commandBehavior)	This overloaded method works the same way as the one described previously. It also takes a parameter containing a command behavior enumeration just like the synchronous ExecuteReader method.
BeginExecuteReader (callback, stateObject)	This overloaded method starts the asynchronous process and it expects to receive an object of AsyncCallback instance. The callback method is called after the process finishes running so that you can proceed with other tasks. The second parameter receives any custom-defined object. This object is passed to the callback automatically. It provides an excellent mechanism for passing parameters to the callback method. The callback method can retrieve the custom-defined state object by using the AsyncState property of the IAsyncResult interface.
BeginExecuteReader (callback, stateObject, commandBehavior)	This overloaded method takes an instance of the AsyncCallback class and uses it to fire a callback method when the process has finished running. The second parameter receives a custom object to be passed to the callback method, and the third parameter uses the command behavior enumeration in the same way as the synchronous ExecuteReader method.

Method	Description
EndExecuteReader	This method is used to access the results from the BeginExecuteReader method. This should be called after the process has finished running; otherwise, an exception is thrown. When calling this method, you are required to pass the same SqlAsyncResult object that you receive when you called the BeginExecuteReader method. This method returns a SqlDataReader object containing the result of the SQL query.
BeginExecuteXmlReader	This method expects a query that returns the result set as XML. The return value is a reference to an object of SqlAsyncResult class that implements IAsyncResult interface. The returned object can be used to monitor the process as it runs and as it is completed.
BeginExecuteXmlReader (callback, stateObject)	This overloaded method starts the asynchronous process, and it expects to receive an object of AsyncCallback instance. The callback method is called after the process has finished running so that you can proceed with other tasks. The second parameter receives any custom-defined object. This object is passed to the callback automatically. It provides an excellent mechanism for passing parameters to the callback method. The callback method can retrieve the custom-defined state object by using the AsyncState property of the IAsyncResult interface.
EndExecuteXmlReader	This method is used to access the results from the BeginExecuteXmlReader method. It should be called after the process has finished running; otherwise, an exception is thrown. When calling this method, you are required to pass the same SqlAsyncResult object that you received when you called the BeginExecuteXmlReader method. This method returns an XML Reader object containing the result of the SQL query.

IAsyncResult Interface

All the asynchronous methods for the SqlCommand class return a reference to an object that exposes the IAsyncResult interface. The properties of this interface are shown in the following table.

Property	Description
AsyncState	This read-only property returns an object that describes the state of the process.
AsyncWaitHandle	This read-only property returns an instance of WaitHandle that can be used to set the time out, test whether the process has completed, and force the code to wait for completion.
CompletedSynchronously	This read-only property returns a Boolean value that indicates whether the process was executed synchronously.
IsCompleted	This read-only property returns a Boolean value indicating whether the process has completed.

AsyncCallback

Some of the asynchronous methods of the SqlCommand class receive an instance of the AsyncCallback class. This class is not specific to ADO.NET and is used by many objects in the .NET Framework. It is used to specify those methods that you want to execute after the asynchronous process has finished running. This class uses its constructor to receive the address of the method that you want to use for call-back purposes.

WaitHandle Class

This class is an abstract class used for multiple purposes such as causing the execution to wait for any or all asynchronous processes to finish. To process more than one database command asynchronously, you can simply create an array containing wait handles for each asynchronous process. Using the static properties of WaitHandle class, you can cause the execution to wait for either any or all wait handles in the array to finish processing.

The WaitHandle class exposes a single property with the name WaitTimeout, and it is used to provide an Integer value representing the number of milliseconds the asynchronous has to finish running.

The WaitHandle class also exposes a few methods, as shown in the following table.

Method	Description
WaitOne	This method waits for a single asynchronous process to complete or time out. It returns a Boolean value containing True if the process completed successfully and False if it timed out.

Method	Description
WaitOne (milliseconds, exitContext)	This overloaded method receives an Integer value as the first parameter. This value represents the time out in milliseconds. The second parameter receives a Boolean value specifying whether the method requires asynchronous context and should be set to False for asynchronous processing.
WaitOne (timeSpan, exitContext)	This overloaded method received a TimeSpan object to represent the time-out value. The second parameter receives a Boolean value specifying whether the method requires asynchronous context and should be set to False for Asynchronous processing.
WaitAny (waitHandles)	This is a Static method used if you are managing more than one Wait Handle in the form of an array. Using this method causes the execution to wait for any of the asynchronous processes that have been started and whose wait handles are in the array being passed to it. The WaitAny method must be called repeatedly — once for each Wait Handle you want to process.
WaitAny (waitHandles, milliseconds, exitContext)	This overloaded method receives the time-out value in the form of milliseconds and a Boolean value specifying whether the method requires asynchronous context. It should be set to False for asynchronous processing.
WaitAny (waitHandles, timeSpan, exitContext	This overloaded method receives the time-out value in the form of Time Span object. The second parameter receives a Boolean value specifying whether the method requires asynchronous context. It should be set to False for asynchronous processing.
WaitAll (waitHandles)	This is a Static method and is used to wait for all asynchronous processes to finish running.
WaitAll (waitHandles, milliseconds, exitContext)	This overloaded method receives the time-out value in the form of milliseconds and a Boolean value specifying whether the method requires asynchronous context. It should be set to False for asynchronous processing.
WaitAll (waitHandles, timeSpan, exitContext)	This overloaded method receives the time-out value in the form of Time Span object. The second parameter receives a Boolean value specifying whether the method requires asynchronous context. It should be set to False for asynchronous processing.
Close ( )	This method releases all wait handles and reclaims their resources.

Now that you understand asynchronous methods added to the SqlCommand and how to properly inter-act with them, you can write some code to see the asynchronous processing in action.

Approaches of Asynchronous Processing in ADO.NET

You can process asynchronous commands in three distinct ways. One approach is to start the asynchronous process and start polling the IAsyncResult object to see when the process has finished. The second approach is to provide a callback method while starting the asynchronous process. This approach enables you to perform other tasks in parallel. When the asynchronous process finishes, it fires the callback method that cleans up after the process and notifies other parts of the program that the asynchronous process has finished. The third and most elegant method is to associate a wait handle with the asynchronous process. Using this approach, you can start all the asynchronous processing you want and then wait for all or any of them to finish so that you can process them accordingly.

The Poll Approach

The code shown in Listing 12-9 creates an inline SQL statement to retrieve the top five records from the Orders table of the Northwind database. It starts the asynchronous process by calling the BeginExecuteReader. After the asynchronous process has started, it uses a while loop to wait for the process to finish. While waiting, the main thread sleeps for 10 milliseconds after checking the status of the asynchronous process. After the process has finished, it retrieves the result using the EndExecuteReader method.

Listing 12-9: The Poll approach of working with asynchronous commands

VB

```
<%@ Page Language="VB" %>
<%@ Import Namespace="System.Data" %>
<%@ Import Namespace="System.Data.SqlClient" %>
<%@ Import Namespace="System.Configuration" %>


<script runat="server">

    Protected Sub Page_Load(ByVal sender As Object, ByVal e As System.EventArgs)

        Dim DBCon As SqlConnection
        Dim Command As SqlCommand = New SqlCommand()
        Dim OrdersReader As SqlDataReader
        Dim ASyncResult As IAsyncResult

        DBCon = New SqlConnection()
        DBCon.ConnectionString = _
            ConfigurationManager.ConnectionStrings("DSN_NorthWind").ConnectionString

        Command.CommandText = _
                "SELECT TOP 5 Customers.CompanyName, Customers.ContactName, " & _
                "Orders.OrderID, Orders.OrderDate, " & _
                "Orders.RequiredDate, Orders.ShippedDate " & _
                "FROM Orders, Customers " & _
                "WHERE Orders.CustomerID = Customers.CustomerID " & _
                "ORDER BY Customers.CompanyName, Customers.ContactName "
        Command.CommandType = CommandType.Text
```

```
        Command.Connection = DBCon

        DBCon.Open()

        ' Starting the asynchronous processing
        ASyncResult = Command.BeginExecuteReader()

        ' This loop with keep the main thread waiting until the
        ' asynchronous process is finished
        While Not ASyncResult.IsCompleted
            ' Sleeping current thread for 10 milliseconds
            System.Threading.Thread.Sleep(10)
        End While

        ' Retrieving result from the asynchronous process
        OrdersReader = Command.EndExecuteReader(ASyncResult)

        ' Displaying result on the screen
        gvOrders.DataSource = OrdersReader
        gvOrders.DataBind()

        ' Closing connection
        DBCon.Close()
    End Sub

</script>

<html xmlns="http://www.w3.org/1999/xhtml" >
<head id="Head1" runat="server">
    <title>The Poll Approach</title>
</head>
<body>
    <form id="form1" runat="server">
    <div>
    <asp:GridView ID="gvOrders" Runat="server"
                  AutoGenerateColumns="False" Width="100%">
    <Columns>
        <asp:BoundField HeaderText="Company Name"
            DataField="CompanyName"></asp:BoundField>
        <asp:BoundField HeaderText="Contact Name"
            DataField="ContactName"></asp:BoundField>
        <asp:BoundField HeaderText="Order Date"
            DataField="orderdate" DataFormatString="{0:d}"></asp:BoundField>
        <asp:BoundField HeaderText="Required Date" DataField="requireddate"
            DataFormatString="{0:d}"></asp:BoundField>
        <asp:BoundField HeaderText="Shipped Date" DataField="shippeddate"
            DataFormatString="{0:d}"></asp:BoundField>
    </Columns>
    </asp:GridView>
    </div>
    </form>
</body>
</html>
```

(continued)

435

Listing 12-9: *(continued)*

C#

```csharp
<%@ Page Language="C#" %>
<%@ Import Namespace="System.Data" %>
<%@ Import Namespace="System.Data.SqlClient" %>
<%@ Import Namespace="System.Configuration" %>

<script runat="server">

    protected void Page_Load(object sender, EventArgs e)
    {
        SqlConnection DBCon;
        SqlCommand Command = new SqlCommand();
        SqlDataReader OrdersReader;
        IAsyncResult ASyncResult;

        DBCon = new SqlConnection();
        DBCon.ConnectionString =
          ConfigurationManager.ConnectionStrings["DSN_NorthWind"].ConnectionString;

        Command.CommandText =
                "SELECT TOP 5 Customers.CompanyName, Customers.ContactName, " +
                "Orders.OrderID, Orders.OrderDate, " +
                "Orders.RequiredDate, Orders.ShippedDate " +
                "FROM Orders, Customers " +
                "WHERE Orders.CustomerID = Customers.CustomerID " +
                "ORDER BY Customers.CompanyName, Customers.ContactName"

        Command.CommandType = CommandType.Text;
        Command.Connection = DBCon;

        DBCon.Open();

        // Starting the asynchronous processing
        ASyncResult = Command.BeginExecuteReader();

        // This loop with keep the main thread waiting until the
        // asynchronous process is finished
        while (!ASyncResult.IsCompleted)
        {
            // Sleeping current thread for 10 milliseconds
            System.Threading.Thread.Sleep(10);
        }

        // Retrieving result from the asynchronous process
        OrdersReader = Command.EndExecuteReader(ASyncResult);

        // Displaying result on the screen
        gvOrders.DataSource = OrdersReader;
        gvOrders.DataBind();

        // Closing connection
        DBCon.Close();
    }
</script>
```

If you set a break point at the `while` loop, you will be able to see that the code execution continues after calling the `BeginExecuteReader` method. The code then continues to loop until the asynchronous execution has finished.

The Wait Approach

The most elegant of the three approaches is neither the poll approach nor the callback approach. The approach that provides the highest level of flexibility, efficiency, and (admittedly) a bit more complexity is the wait approach. Using this approach, you can write code that starts multiple asynchronous processes and waits for any or all the processes to finish running. This approach allows you to wait for only those processes that are dependent on each other and to proceed with the ones that don't. This approach, by its design, requires you to think about asynchronous processes in great detail. You must pick a good candidate for running in parallel and, most importantly, determine how different processes depend on each other. The complexity of this approach requires you to understand its details and design the code accordingly. The end result is, typically, a very elegant code design that makes the best use of synchronous and asynchronous processing models.

The code shown in Listing 12-10 uses the `WaitOne` method of the `WaitHandle` class. This method causes the program execution to wait until the asynchronous process has finished running.

Listing 12-10: The wait approach of handling a single asynchronous process

```
VB
<%@ Page Language="VB" %>
<%@ Import Namespace="System.Data" %>
<%@ Import Namespace="System.Data.SqlClient" %>
<%@ Import Namespace="System.Configuration" %>

<script runat="server">
    Protected Sub Page_Load(ByVal sender As Object, ByVal e As System.EventArgs)

        Dim DBCon As SqlConnection
        Dim Command As SqlCommand = New SqlCommand()
        Dim OrdersReader As SqlDataReader
        Dim ASyncResult As IAsyncResult
        Dim WHandle As Threading.WaitHandle

        DBCon = New SqlConnection()
        DBCon.ConnectionString = _

ConfigurationManager.ConnectionStrings("DSN_NorthWind").ConnectionString

        Command.CommandText = _
            "SELECT TOP 5 Customers.CompanyName, Customers.ContactName, " & _
            "Orders.OrderID, Orders.OrderDate, " & _
            "Orders.RequiredDate, Orders.ShippedDate " & _
            "FROM Orders, Customers " & _
            "WHERE Orders.CustomerID = Customers.CustomerID " & _
            "ORDER BY Customers.CompanyName, Customers.ContactName";

        Command.CommandType = CommandType.Text
```

(continued)

Listing 12-10: *(continued)*

```
        Command.Connection = DBCon

        DBCon.Open()

        ' Starting the asynchronous processing
        ASyncResult = Command.BeginExecuteReader()

        WHandle = ASyncResult.AsyncWaitHandle

        If WHandle.WaitOne = True Then
            ' Retrieving result from the asynchronous process
            OrdersReader = Command.EndExecuteReader(ASyncResult)

            ' Displaying result on the screen
            gvOrders.DataSource = OrdersReader
            gvOrders.DataBind()

            ' Closing connection
            DBCon.Close()
        Else
            ' Asynchronous process has timed out. Handle this
            ' situation here.
        End If
    End Sub
</script>

<html xmlns="http://www.w3.org/1999/xhtml" >
<head id="Head1" runat="server">
    <title>The Wait Approach</title>
</head>
<body>
    <form id="form1" runat="server">
    <div>
    <asp:GridView ID="gvOrders" Runat="server"
                  AutoGenerateColumns="False" Width="100%">
    <Columns>
        <asp:BoundField HeaderText="Company Name"
            DataField="CompanyName"></asp:BoundField>
        <asp:BoundField HeaderText="Contact Name"
            DataField="ContactName"></asp:BoundField>
        <asp:BoundField HeaderText="Order Date"
            DataField="orderdate" DataFormatString="{0:d}"></asp:BoundField>
        <asp:BoundField HeaderText="Required Date" DataField="requireddate"
            DataFormatString="{0:d}"></asp:BoundField>
        <asp:BoundField HeaderText="Shipped Date" DataField="shippeddate"
            DataFormatString="{0:d}"></asp:BoundField>
    </Columns>
    </asp:GridView>
    </div>
    </form>
</body>
</html>
```

C#

```
<%@ Page Language="C#" %>
<%@ Import Namespace="System.Data" %>
<%@ Import Namespace="System.Data.SqlClient" %>
<%@ Import Namespace="System.Configuration" %>

<script runat="server">
    protected void Page_Load(object sender, EventArgs e)
    {
        SqlConnection DBCon;
        SqlCommand Command = new SqlCommand();
        SqlDataReader OrdersReader;
        IAsyncResult ASyncResult;
        System.Threading.WaitHandle WHandle;

        DBCon = new SqlConnection();
        DBCon.ConnectionString =

ConfigurationManager.ConnectionStrings["DSN_NorthWind"].ConnectionString;

        Command.CommandText =
                " SELECT TOP 5 Customers.CompanyName, Customers.ContactName, " +
                "Orders.OrderID, Orders.OrderDate, " +
                "Orders.RequiredDate, Orders.ShippedDate " +
                "FROM Orders, Customers " +
                "WHERE Orders.CustomerID = Customers.CustomerID " +
                "ORDER BY Customers.CompanyName, Customers.ContactName";

        Command.CommandType = CommandType.Text;
        Command.Connection = DBCon;

        DBCon.Open();

        // Starting the asynchronous processing
        ASyncResult = Command.BeginExecuteReader();

        WHandle = ASyncResult.AsyncWaitHandle;

        if (WHandle.WaitOne() == true)
        {
            // Retrieving result from the asynchronous process
            OrdersReader = Command.EndExecuteReader(ASyncResult);

            // Displaying result on the screen
            gvOrders.DataSource = OrdersReader;
            gvOrders.DataBind();

            // Closing connection
            DBCon.Close();
        }
        else
        {
            // Asynchronous process has timed out. Handle this
            // situation here.
        }
    }
</script>
```

If you set a break point and step through this code, you will notice that the program execution stops at the `WHandle.WaitOne` method call. The program automatically resumes when the asynchronous commands finishes its execution.

Using Multiple Wait Handles

The real power of the wait approach doesn't become apparent until you start multiple asynchronous processes. The code shown in Listing 12-11 starts two asynchronous processes. One process queries a database to get information about a specific customer and runs another query to retrieve all orders submitted by that the same customer. The code example shown in this listing creates two separate Command objects, Data Reader objects, and wait handles. However, it uses the same connection object for both queries to demonstrate how well multiple Active Result Set (MARS) supports work in conjunction with the asynchronous processing.

Listing 12-11: Use of multiple wait handles in conjunction with MARS

VB

```
<%@ Page Language="VB" %>
<%@ Import Namespace="System.Data" %>
<%@ Import Namespace="System.Data.SqlClient" %>
<%@ Import Namespace="System.Configuration" %>

<script runat="server">
    Protected Sub Page_Load(ByVal sender As Object, ByVal e As System.EventArgs)

        Dim DBCon As SqlConnection
        Dim OrdersCommand As SqlCommand = New SqlCommand()
        Dim CustCommand As SqlCommand = New SqlCommand()
        Dim OrdersReader As SqlDataReader
        Dim CustReader As SqlDataReader
        Dim OrdersASyncResult As IAsyncResult
        Dim CustAsyncResult As IAsyncResult

        Dim WHandles(1) As System.Threading.WaitHandle
        Dim OrdersWHandle As System.Threading.WaitHandle
        Dim CustWHandle As System.Threading.WaitHandle

        DBCon = New SqlConnection()
        DBCon.ConnectionString = _
          ConfigurationManager.ConnectionStrings("DSN_NorthWind").ConnectionString

        CustCommand.CommandText = _
           "SELECT * FROM Customers WHERE CompanyName = 'Alfreds Futterkiste'"

        CustCommand.CommandType = CommandType.Text
        CustCommand.Connection = DBCon

        ' Selecting all orders for a specific customer
        OrdersCommand.CommandText = _
              " SELECT Customers.CompanyName, Customers.ContactName, " & _
              "Orders.OrderID, Orders.OrderDate, " & _
              "Orders.RequiredDate, Orders.ShippedDate " & _
              "FROM Orders, Customers " & _
```

```
                "WHERE Orders.CustomerID = Customers.CustomerID " & _
                "AND Customers.CompanyName = 'Alfreds Futterkiste' " & _
                "ORDER BY Customers.CompanyName, Customers.ContactName "

        OrdersCommand.CommandType = CommandType.Text
        OrdersCommand.Connection = DBCon

        DBCon.Open()

        ' Retrieving customer information asynchronously
        CustAsyncResult = CustCommand.BeginExecuteReader()

        ' Retrieving orders list asynchronously
        OrdersASyncResult = OrdersCommand.BeginExecuteReader()

        CustWHandle = CustAsyncResult.AsyncWaitHandle
        OrdersWHandle = OrdersASyncResult.AsyncWaitHandle

        ' Filling Wait Handles array with the two wait handles we
        ' are going to use in this code
        WHandles(0) = CustWHandle
        WHandles(1) = OrdersWHandle

        System.Threading.WaitHandle.WaitAll(WHandles)

        CustReader = CustCommand.EndExecuteReader(CustAsyncResult)

        OrdersReader = OrdersCommand.EndExecuteReader(OrdersASyncResult)

        gvCustomers.DataSource = CustReader
        gvCustomers.DataBind()

        gvOrders.DataSource = OrdersReader
        gvOrders.DataBind()

        DBCon.Close()
    End Sub

</script>

<html xmlns="http://www.w3.org/1999/xhtml" >
<head id="Head1" runat="server">
    <title>Wait All Approach</title>
</head>
<body>
    <form id="form1" runat="server">
    <div>
    <asp:GridView ID="gvCustomers" Width="100%" Runat="server"></asp:GridView>
    <br /><br />
    <asp:GridView ID="gvOrders" Width="100%" AutoGenerateColumns="False"
        Runat="server">
        <Columns>
        <asp:BoundField HeaderText="Company Name"
            DataField="CompanyName"></asp:BoundField>
```

(continued)

Listing 12-11: *(continued)*

```
            <asp:BoundField HeaderText="Contact Name"
                DataField="ContactName"></asp:BoundField>
            <asp:BoundField HeaderText="Order Date" DataField="orderdate"
                DataFormatString="{0:d}"></asp:BoundField>
            <asp:BoundField HeaderText="Required Date" DataField="requireddate"
                DataFormatString="{0:d}"></asp:BoundField>
            <asp:BoundField HeaderText="Shipped Date" DataField="shippeddate"
                DataFormatString="{0:d}"></asp:BoundField>
        </Columns>
    </asp:GridView>
    </div>
    </form>
</body>
</html>
```

C#

```
<%@ Page Language="C#" %>
<%@ Import Namespace="System.Data" %>
<%@ Import Namespace="System.Data.SqlClient" %>
<%@ Import Namespace="System.Configuration" %>

<script runat="server">
    protected void Page_Load(object sender, EventArgs e)
    {
        SqlConnection DBCon;
        SqlCommand OrdersCommand = new SqlCommand();
        SqlCommand CustCommand = new SqlCommand();
        SqlDataReader OrdersReader;
        SqlDataReader CustReader;
        IAsyncResult OrdersASyncResult;
        IAsyncResult CustAsyncResult;

        System.Threading.WaitHandle[] WHandles = new
            System.Threading.WaitHandle[1];
        System.Threading.WaitHandle OrdersWHandle;
        System.Threading.WaitHandle CustWHandle;

        DBCon = new SqlConnection();
        DBCon.ConnectionString =
          ConfigurationManager.ConnectionStrings["DSN_NorthWind"].ConnectionString;

        CustCommand.CommandText =
            " SELECT * FROM Customers WHERE CompanyName = 'Alfreds Futterkiste' ";

        CustCommand.CommandType = CommandType.Text;
        CustCommand.Connection = DBCon;

        // Selecting all orders for a specific customer
        OrdersCommand.CommandText=
```

```
                    " SELECT Customers.CompanyName, Customers.ContactName, " +
                    "Orders.OrderID, Orders.OrderDate, " +
                    "Orders.RequiredDate, Orders.ShippedDate " +
                    "FROM Orders, Customers " +
                    "WHERE Orders.CustomerID = Customers.CustomerID " +
                    "AND Customers.CompanyName = 'Alfreds Futterkiste' " +
                    "ORDER BY Customers.CompanyName, Customers.ContactName";

        OrdersCommand.CommandType = CommandType.Text;
        OrdersCommand.Connection = DBCon;

        DBCon.Open();

        // Retrieving customer information asynchronously
        CustAsyncResult = CustCommand.BeginExecuteReader();

        // Retrieving orders list asynchronously
        OrdersASyncResult = OrdersCommand.BeginExecuteReader();

        CustWHandle = CustAsyncResult.AsyncWaitHandle;
        OrdersWHandle = OrdersASyncResult.AsyncWaitHandle;

        // Filling Wait Handles array with the two wait handles we
        // are going to use in this code
        WHandles[0] = CustWHandle;
        WHandles[1] = OrdersWHandle;

        System.Threading.WaitHandle.WaitAll(WHandles);

        CustReader = CustCommand.EndExecuteReader(CustAsyncResult);

        OrdersReader = OrdersCommand.EndExecuteReader(OrdersASyncResult);

        gvCustomers.DataSource = CustReader;
        gvCustomers.DataBind();

        gvOrders.DataSource = OrdersReader;
        gvOrders.DataBind();

        DBCon.Close();
    }
</script>
```

When you compile and execute the code shown in Listing 12-11, you see the result on the screen as shown in Figure 12-7. This figure clearly shows two GridView controls that were used in the code example. The Grid View control on the top shows the result of executing a query that retrieved all information related to a specific customer. The Grid View control on the bottom shows the results of executing the second query that retrieved a list of all orders submitted by a specific customer.

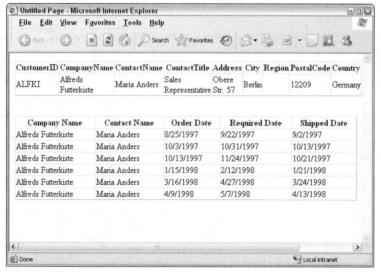

Figure 12-7

The code shown in Listing 12-11 reveals some of the elegance of using the wait approach. However, it is still not the most efficient code you can write with ADO.NET 2.0. The code should allow for a wait until both asynchronous processes finish running before the data binds the result sets to the respective GridView controls.

You can change the code shown in Listing 12-11 just a little to gain even more efficiency. Replace the `WaitAll` method with the `WaitAny` method. The `WaitAny` method enables you to handle the results of each of the asynchronous processes as soon as each is completed without waiting for other processing to finish. To use the `WaitAny` method and still manage the execution of all asynchronous processes, you can also add a loop that makes sure that all asynchronous processes are handled after they are completed.

The `WaitAny` method returns an Integer value that indicates an array index of the wait handle that has finished running. Using this return value, you can easily find the correct wait handle and process the result set retrieved from the query that was executed in that particular process, as shown in Listing 12-12.

Listing 12-12: Use of the WaitAny method of processing multiple asynchronous processes

VB

```
<%@ Page Language="VB" %>
<%@ Import Namespace="System.Data" %>
<%@ Import Namespace="System.Data.SqlClient" %>
<%@ Import Namespace="System.Configuration" %>

<script runat="server">
    Protected Sub Page_Load(ByVal sender As Object, ByVal e As System.EventArgs)
        Dim DBCon As SqlConnection
        Dim OrdersCommand As SqlCommand = New SqlCommand()
```

```vb
Dim CustCommand As SqlCommand = New SqlCommand()
Dim OrdersReader As SqlDataReader
Dim CustReader As SqlDataReader
Dim OrdersASyncResult As IAsyncResult
Dim CustAsyncResult As IAsyncResult

Dim WHIndex As Integer
Dim WHandles(1) As Threading.WaitHandle
Dim OrdersWHandle As Threading.WaitHandle
Dim CustWHandle As Threading.WaitHandle

DBCon = New SqlConnection()
DBCon.ConnectionString = _
    ConfigurationManager.ConnectionStrings("DSN_NorthWind").ConnectionString

CustCommand.CommandText = _
    "SELECT * FROM Customers WHERE CompanyName = 'Alfreds Futterkiste'"

CustCommand.CommandType = CommandType.Text
CustCommand.Connection = DBCon

OrdersCommand.CommandText = _
        "SELECT Customers.CompanyName, Customers.ContactName, " & _
        "Orders.OrderID, Orders.OrderDate, " & _
        "Orders.RequiredDate, Orders.ShippedDate " & _
        "FROM Orders, Customers " & _
        "WHERE Orders.CustomerID = Customers.CustomerID " & _
        "AND Customers.CompanyName = 'Alfreds Futterkiste' " & _
        "ORDER BY Customers.CompanyName, Customers.ContactName"

OrdersCommand.CommandType = CommandType.Text
OrdersCommand.Connection = DBCon

' Opening the database connection
DBCon.Open ()

' Retrieving customer information asynchronously
CustAsyncResult = CustCommand.BeginExecuteReader()

' Retrieving orders list asynchronously
OrdersASyncResult = OrdersCommand.BeginExecuteReader()

CustWHandle = CustAsyncResult.AsyncWaitHandle
OrdersWHandle = OrdersASyncResult.AsyncWaitHandle

' Filling Wait Handles array with the two wait handles we
' are going to use in this code
WHandles(0) = CustWHandle
WHandles(1) = OrdersWHandle

' Looping 2 times because there are 2 wait handles
' in the array
For Index As Integer = 0 To 1
    ' We are only waiting for any of the two
```

(continued)

Listing 12-12: *(continued)*

```
                ' asynchronous process to finish running
                WHIndex = Threading.WaitHandle.WaitAny(WHandles)

                ' The return value from the WaitAny method is
                ' the array index of the Wait Handle that just
                ' finsihed running
                Select Case WHIndex
                    Case 0
                        CustReader = CustCommand.EndExecuteReader(CustAsyncResult)

                        gvCustomers.DataSource = CustReader
                        gvCustomers.DataBind()
                    Case 1
                        OrdersReader = _
                            OrdersCommand.EndExecuteReader(OrdersASyncResult)

                        gvOrders.DataSource = OrdersReader
                        gvOrders.DataBind()

                End Select
            Next

            ' Closing connection
            DBCon.Close()
    End Sub

</script>

<html xmlns="http://www.w3.org/1999/xhtml" >
<head id="Head1" runat="server">
    <title>The Wait Any Approach</title>
</head>
<body>
    <form id="form1" runat="server">
    <div>
    <asp:GridView ID="gvCustomers" Width="100%" Runat="server"></asp:GridView>
    <br /><br />
    <asp:GridView ID="gvOrders" Width="100%" AutoGenerateColumns="False"
        Runat="server">
        <Columns>
        <asp:BoundField HeaderText="Company Name"
            DataField="CompanyName"></asp:BoundField>
        <asp:BoundField HeaderText="Contact Name"
            DataField="ContactName"></asp:BoundField>
        <asp:BoundField HeaderText="Order Date" DataField="orderdate"
            DataFormatString="{0:d}"></asp:BoundField>
        <asp:BoundField HeaderText="Required Date" DataField="requireddate"
            DataFormatString="{0:d}"></asp:BoundField>
        <asp:BoundField HeaderText="Shipped Date" DataField="shippeddate"
            DataFormatString="{0:d}"></asp:BoundField>
        </Columns>
    </asp:GridView>
```

```
    </div>
    </form>
</body>
</html>
```

C#

```
<%@ Page Language="C#" %>
<%@ Import Namespace="System.Data" %>
<%@ Import Namespace="System.Data.SqlClient" %>
<%@ Import Namespace="System.Configuration" %>

<script runat="server">
    protected void Page_Load(object sender, EventArgs e)
    {
        SqlConnection DBCon;
        SqlCommand OrdersCommand = new SqlCommand();
        SqlCommand CustCommand = new SqlCommand();
        SqlDataReader OrdersReader;
        SqlDataReader CustReader;
        IAsyncResult OrdersASyncResult;
        IAsyncResult CustAsyncResult;

        int WHIndex;
        System.Threading.WaitHandle[] WHandles =
            new System.Threading.WaitHandle[1];
        System.Threading.WaitHandle OrdersWHandle;
        System.Threading.WaitHandle CustWHandle;

        DBCon = new SqlConnection();
        DBCon.ConnectionString =
          ConfigurationManager.ConnectionStrings["DSN_NorthWind"].ConnectionString;

        CustCommand.CommandText =
            "SELECT * FROM Customers WHERE CompanyName = 'Alfreds Futterkiste'";

        CustCommand.CommandType = CommandType.Text;
        CustCommand.Connection = DBCon;

        OrdersCommand.CommandText =
                "SELECT Customers.CompanyName, Customers.ContactName, " +
                "Orders.OrderID, Orders.OrderDate, " +
                "Orders.RequiredDate, Orders.ShippedDate " +
                "FROM Orders, Customers " +
                "WHERE Orders.CustomerID = Customers.CustomerID " +
                "AND Customers.CompanyName = 'Alfreds Futterkiste' " +
                "ORDER BY Customers.CompanyName, Customers.ContactName";

        OrdersCommand.CommandType = CommandType.Text;
        OrdersCommand.Connection = DBCon;

        // Opening the database connection
```

(continued)

Listing 12-12: *(continued)*

```
        DBCon.Open();

        // Retrieving customer information asynchronously
        CustAsyncResult = CustCommand.BeginExecuteReader();

        // Retrieving orders list asynchronously
        OrdersASyncResult = OrdersCommand.BeginExecuteReader();

        CustWHandle = CustAsyncResult.AsyncWaitHandle;
        OrdersWHandle = OrdersASyncResult.AsyncWaitHandle;

        // Filling Wait Handles array with the two wait handles we
        // are going to use in this code
        WHandles[0] = CustWHandle;
        WHandles[1] = OrdersWHandle;

        // Looping 2 times because there are 2 wait handles
        // in the array
        for (int Index = 0; Index < 2; Index++ )
        {
            // We are only waiting for any of the two
            // asynchronous process to finish running
            WHIndex = System.Threading.WaitHandle.WaitAny(WHandles);

            // The return value from the WaitAny method is
            // the array index of the Wait Handle that just
            // finsihed running
            switch (WHIndex)
            {
                case 0:
                    CustReader = CustCommand.EndExecuteReader(CustAsyncResult);

                    gvCustomers.DataSource = CustReader;
                    gvCustomers.DataBind();
                    break;
                case 1:
                    OrdersReader =
                        OrdersCommand.EndExecuteReader(OrdersASyncResult);

                    gvOrders.DataSource = OrdersReader;
                    gvOrders.DataBind();
                    break;
            }
        }
        // Closing connection
        DBCon.Close();
    }
</script>
```

Next, look at the callback approach. Using this approach, you assign a callback method to the asynchronous process and use it to display the result returned by executing the SQL query.

The Callback Approach

Listing 12-13 creates an inline SQL statement that retrieves the top five records from the database. It starts the asynchronous process by calling the `BeginExecuteReader` method and passing it the callback delegate. No further processing is needed, and the method ends after the asynchronous process has started. After the callback method is fired, it retrieves the result and displays it on the screen.

Listing 12-13: Asynchronous command processing using the callback approach

VB

```
<%@ Page Language="C#" %>
<%@ Import Namespace="System.Data" %>
<%@ Import Namespace="System.Data.SqlClient" %>
<%@ Import Namespace="System.Configuration" %>

<script runat="server">
    Private Sub Page_Load(ByVal sender As Object, ByVal e As System.EventArgs)
        Dim DBCon As SqlConnection
        Dim Command As SqlCommand = New SqlCommand()
        Dim ASyncResult As SqlAsyncResult

        DBCon = New SqlConnection()
        Command = New SqlCommand()
        DBCon.ConnectionString = _
        ConfigurationManager.ConnectionStrings("DSN_NorthWind").ConnectionString

        ' Selecting top 5 records from the Orders table
        Command.CommandText = _
            "SELECT TOP 5 Customers.CompanyName, Customers.ContactName, " & _
            "Orders.OrderID, Orders.OrderDate, " & _
            "Orders.RequiredDate, Orders.ShippedDate " & _
            "FROM Orders, Customers " & _
            "WHERE Orders.CustomerID = Customers.CustomerID " & _
            "ORDER BY Customers.CompanyName, Customers.ContactName"

        Command.CommandType = CommandType.Text
        Command.Connection = DBCon

        DBCon.Open()

        ' Starting the asynchronous processing
        AsyncResult = Command.BeginExecuteReader(New _
            AsyncCallback(AddressOf CBMethod), CommandBehavior.CloseConnection)
    End Sub

    Public Sub CBMethod(ByVal ar As SQLAsyncResult)
        Dim OrdersReader As SqlDataReader

        ' Retrieving result from the asynchronous process
        OrdersReader = ar.EndExecuteReader(ar)

        ' Displaying result on the screen
        gvOrders.DataSource = OrdersReader
```

(continued)

Listing 12-13: *(continued)*

```
            gvOrders.DataBind()
    End Sub
</script>

<html xmlns="http://www.w3.org/1999/xhtml" >
<head id="Head1" runat="server">
    <title>The Call Back Approach</title>
</head>
<body>
    <form id="form1" runat="server">
    <div>
    <asp:GridView ID="gvOrders" Width="100%" AutoGenerateColumns="False"
        Runat="server">
        <Columns>
        <asp:BoundField HeaderText="Company Name"
            DataField="CompanyName"></asp:BoundField>
        <asp:BoundField HeaderText="Contact Name"
            DataField="ContactName"></asp:BoundField>
        <asp:BoundField HeaderText="Order Date" DataField="orderdate"
            DataFormatString="{0:d}"></asp:BoundField>
        <asp:BoundField HeaderText="Required Date" DataField="requireddate"
            DataFormatString="{0:d}"></asp:BoundField>
        <asp:BoundField HeaderText="Shipped Date" DataField="shippeddate"
            DataFormatString="{0:d}"></asp:BoundField>
        </Columns>
    </asp:GridView>
    </div>
    </form>
</body>
</html>
```

C#

```
<%@ Page Language="C#" %>
<%@ Import Namespace="System.Data" %>
<%@ Import Namespace="System.Data.SqlClient" %>
<%@ Import Namespace="System.Configuration" %>

<script runat="server">
    protected void Page_Load(object sender, EventArgs e)
    {
        SqlConnection DBCon;
        SqlCommand Command = new SqlCommand();
        SqlAsyncResult ASyncResult;

        DBCon = new SqlConnection();
        Command = new SqlCommand();
        DBCon.ConnectionString =
          ConfigurationManager.ConnectionStrings["DSN_NorthWind"].ConnectionString;

        // Selecting top 5 records from the Orders table
        Command.CommandText =
```

```
                        "SELECT TOP 5 Customers.CompanyName, Customers.ContactName, " +
                        "Orders.OrderID, Orders.OrderDate, " +
                        "Orders.RequiredDate, Orders.ShippedDate " +
                        "FROM Orders, Customers " +
                        "WHERE Orders.CustomerID = Customers.CustomerID " +
                        "ORDER BY Customers.CompanyName, Customers.ContactName";

            Command.CommandType = CommandType.Text;
            Command.Connection = DBCon;

            DBCon.Open();

            // Starting the asynchronous processing
            AsyncResult = Command.BeginExecuteReader(new AsyncCallback(CBMethod),
                                        CommandBehavior.CloseConnection);
        }

        public void CBMethod(SQLAsyncResult ar)
        {
            SqlDataReader OrdersReader;

            // Retrieving result from the asynchronous process
            OrdersReader = ar.EndExecuteReader(ar);

            // Displaying result on the screen
            gvOrders.DataSource = OrdersReader;
            gvOrders.DataBind();
        }
    </script>
```

The callback approach enables you to handle the result of a command execution at a different part of your code. This feature is useful in cases where the command execution takes longer than usual and you want to respond to the user without waiting for the command execution to finish.

Canceling Asynchronous Processing

The asynchronous process often takes longer than expected. To alleviate this problem, you can provide an option to the user to cancel the process without waiting for the result. Canceling an asynchronous process is as easy as calling the `Cancel` method on the appropriate `Command` object. This method doesn't return any value. To roll back the work that was already completed by the `Command` object, you must provide a custom transaction to the `Command` object before executing the query. You can also handle the Rollback or the Commit process yourself.

Asynchronous Connections

Now that you understand how to execute multiple database queries asynchronously using the `Command` object, take a quick look at how you can open database connections asynchronously, as well. The principles of working with asynchronous connections are the same as when you work with asynchronous commands. You can still use any of the three approaches you learned previously.

In ADO.NET 2.0, the `SqlConnection` class exposes a couple of new properties needed when working asynchronously. These properties are shown in the following table.

Property	Description
Asynchronous	This read-only property returns a Boolean value indicating whether the connection has been opened asynchronously.
State	This property returns a value from System.Data.ConnectionState enumeration indicating the state of the connection. The possible values are as follows: —Broken —Closed —Connecting —Executing —Fetching —Open

Summary

This chapter covered a range of advanced features that have been added to the 2.0 version of ADO.NET. These features are designed to give you the flexibility to handle database processing in a manner never before possible with either of the previous versions of ADO.NET or ADO.

The Bulk Copy feature is extremely efficient and geared toward loading large quantities of data into a single destination table. You have been using the Data Transformation Services (DTS) to accomplish this purpose. However, DTS lacks some flexibility and control over the retrieval and application of business rules before the data is loaded in the destination table. With the introduction of the Bulk Copy feature in ADO.NET, you have the ultimate control of using a managed runtime to process the data with the same performance as DTS.

The Bulk Copy feature is not without its limitations. The most significant limitation is its inability to store data in multiple destination tables or by leveraging a stored procedure. The creators of ADO.NET 2.0 realized this fact and empowered users with the flexibility of batch processing updated queries. This enables users to create custom UPATE, INSERT, and DELETE queries using the Data Adapter object with previous versions of ADO.NET. However, these previous versions were capable of processing each command only as a separate database request. Loading of large quantities of information in those days was, therefore, extremely slow and counterproductive. The 2.0 version of ADO.NET provides a new property in the Data Adapter object that enables you to specify batch sizes and cause the Data Adapter object to process multiple commands in a single batch.

This chapter also covered the features of Multiple Active Result Sets (MARS), which enables you to reuse a single open connection for multiple accesses to the database, even if the connection is currently processing a result set. This feature becomes even more powerful when it is used in conjunction with the asynchronous command processing.

As you learned in this chapter, the 2.0 version of ADO.NET provides new properties for the SqlCommand and SqlConnection classes. These new properties enable you to start database commands or open database connections in an asynchronous process and manage their execution using a variety of approaches, such as the poll approach, the callback approach, and the wait approach.

13

Working with XML

This is not a book about XML, the eXtensible Markup Language; but XML has become such a part of an ASP.NET programmer's life that the topic deserves its own chapter. Although most of the XML functionality in the .NET Framework appears to be in the `System.Xml` namespace, you can find XML's influence throughout the entire Framework including `System.Data` and `System.Web`.

XML is oft maligned and misunderstood. To some, XML is simply a text-based markup language; to others it is an object serialization format or a document-encoding standard. In fact, XML has become the de facto standard manner in which data passes around the Internet. XML, however, is not really a technology as much as it is a set of standards or guiding principles. It provides a structure within which data can be stored; but the XML specification doesn't dictate how XML processors, parsers, formatters, and data access methods should be written or implemented. `System.Xml` and other namespaces contain the .NET Framework 2.0's view on how programmers should manipulate XML. Some of its techniques, such as XSLT and XML Schema, are standards-based. Others, like `XmlReader` and `XmlWriter`, exist purely in the world of the .NET Framework. The XML consumed and produced by these techniques is standards-based and can be used by other languages that consume XML, but the .NET Framework has its own philosophy about the uses of XML.

This chapter covers all the major techniques for manipulating XML provided by the .NET Framework. `XmlReader` and `XmlWriter` offer incredible speed but require a bit more thought. The XmlDocument or DOM is the most commonly used method for manipulating XML but you'll pay dearly in performance penalties without careful use. ADO DataSets have always provided XML support, and their support improves with .NET 2.0. XML Stylesheet Tree Transformations (XSLT) gain debugging capabilities in Visual Studio 2005, and ASP.NET has some simple yet powerful server controls to manipulate XML.

Its flexibility and room for innovation make XML very powerful and a joy to work with.

> Note that when the acronym XML appears by itself, the whole acronym is capital-
> ized, but when it appears in a function name or namespace, only the X is capitalized,
> as in `System.Xml` or `XmlTextReader`. Microsoft's API Design Guidelines dictate
> that if an abbreviation of three or more characters appears in a variable name, class
> name, or namespace, the first character is capitalized.

The Basics of XML

Listing 13-1, a `Books.xml` document that represents a bookstore's inventory database, is one of the sample
documents used in this chapter. This example document has been used in various MSDN examples for
many years.

Listing 13-1: The Books.xml XML document

```xml
<?xml version='1.0'?>
<!-- This file is a part of a book store inventory database -->
<bookstore xmlns="http://example.books.com">
    <book genre="autobiography" publicationdate="1981" ISBN="1-861003-11-0">
        <title>The Autobiography of Benjamin Franklin</title>
        <author>
            <first-name>Benjamin</first-name>
            <last-name>Franklin</last-name>
        </author>
        <price>8.99</price>
    </book>
    <book genre="novel" publicationdate="1967" ISBN="0-201-63361-2">
        <title>The Confidence Man</title>
        <author>
            <first-name>Herman</first-name>
            <last-name>Melville</last-name>
        </author>
        <price>11.99</price>
    </book>
    <book genre="philosophy" publicationdate="1991" ISBN="1-861001-57-6">
        <title>The Gorgias</title>
        <author>
            <first-name>Sidas</first-name>
            <last-name>Plato</last-name>
        </author>
        <price>9.99</price>
    </book>
</bookstore>
```

The first line of Listing 13-1, starting with `<?xml version='1.0'?>`, is an XML declaration also called
the Prolog. This line should always appear before the first element in the XML document and indicates
the version of XML with which this document is compliant.

The second line is an XML comment and uses the same syntax as an HTML comment. This isn't a coinci-
dence; remember that XML and HTML are both descendants of SGML, the Standard Generalized
Markup Language. Comments are always optional in XML documents

The third line, `<bookstore>`, is the root element or document entity of the XML document. An XML document can have only one root element. The last line in the document is the matching end element `</bookstore>`. No elements of the document can appear after the final closing tag `</bookstore>`. The `<bookstore>` element contains an `xmlns` attribute such as `xmlns="http://example.books.com"`. Namespaces in XML are similar to namespaces in the .NET Framework because they provide *qualification of elements and attributes*. It's very likely that someone else in the world has created a bookstore XML document before, and it's also likely he or she chose an element such as `<book>` or `<bookstore/>`. A namespace is defined to make your `<book>` element different from any others and to deal with the chance that other `<book>` elements might appear with yours in the same document — it's possible with XML.

This namespace is often a URL (Uniform/Universal Resource Locator), but it actually can be a URI (Uniform/Universal Resource Identifier). A namespace can be a GUID or a nonsense string such as `"www-computerzen-com:schema"` as long as it is unique. Recently, the convention has been to use a URL because they are ostensibly unique, thus making the document's associated schema unique. You learn more about schemas and namespaces in the next section.

The fourth line is a little different because the `<book>` element contains some additional attributes such as `genre`, `publicationdate`, and `ISBN`. The order of the elements matters in an XML document, but the order of the attributes does not. These attributes are said to be *on* or *contained within* the book element. Consider the following line of code:

```
<book genre="autobiography" publicationdate="1981" ISBN="1-861003-11-0">
```

Notice that every element following this line has a matching end element, similar to the example that follows:

```
<example>This is a test</example>
```

If no matching end element is used, the XML is not well formed; technically it isn't even XML! These next two example XML fragments are not well formed because the elements don't match up:

```
<example>This is a test
```

```
<example>This is a test</anothertag>
```

If the `<example>` element is empty, it might appear like this:

```
<example></example>
```

Alternatively, it could appear as a shortcut like this:

```
<example/>
```

The syntax is different, but the semantics are the same. The difference between the syntax and the semantics of an XML document is crucial for understanding what XML is trying to accomplish. XML documents are text files by their nature, but the information — the information set — is representable using text that isn't exact. The set of information is the same, but the actual bytes are not.

> Note that attributes appear only within start tags or empty elements such as `<book genre="scifi"></book>` or `<book genre="scifi" />`. Visit the World Wide Web Consortium's (W3C) XML site at `www.w3.org/XML/` for more detailed information on XML.

The XML InfoSet

The XML InfoSet is a W3C concept that describes what is and isn't significant in an XML document. The InfoSet isn't a class, a function, a namespace, or a language — the InfoSet is a concept.

Listing 13-2 describes two XML documents that are syntactically different but semantically the same.

Listing 13-2: XML syntax versus semantics

XML document

```xml
<?xml version='1.0'?>
<book genre="autobiography" publicationdate="1981" ISBN="1-861003-11-0">
    <title>The Autobiography of Benjamin Franklin</title>
    <author>
        <first-name>Benjamin</first-name>
        <last-name>Franklin</last-name>
    </author>
    <price></price>
</book>
```

XML document that differs in syntax, but not in semantics

```xml
<?xml version='1.0'?><book genre="autobiography" publicationdate="1981"
ISBN="1-861003-11-0"><title>The Autobiography of Benjamin
Franklin</title><author><first-name>Benjamin</first-name><last-name>Franklin</last-name></author><price/></book>
```

Certainly, the first document in Listing 13-2 is easier for a human to read, but the second document is just as easy for a computer to read. The second document has insignificant white space removed.

Notice also that the empty `<price/>` element is different in the two documents. The first uses the verbose form, whereas the second element uses the shortcut form to express an empty element. However, *both are empty elements.*

You can manipulate XML as elements and attributes. You can visualize XML as a tree of nodes. You rarely, if ever, have to worry about angle brackets or parse text yourself. A text-based differences (diff) tool would report these two documents are different because their character representations are different. An XML-based differences tool would report (correctly) that they are the same document. Each document contains the same InfoSet.

> You can run an XML Diff Tool online at `http://apps.gotdotnet.com/xmltools/xmldiff/`.

XSD–XML Schema Definition

XML documents must be well formed at the very least. However, just because a document is well formed doesn't assure that its elements are in the right order, have the right name, or are the correct data types. After creating a well-formed XML document, you should ensure that your document is also *valid*. A *valid* XML document is well formed and also has an associated XML Schema Definition (XSD) that describes what elements, simple types, and complex types are allowed in the document.

The schema for the Books.xml file is a glossary or vocabulary for the bookstore described in an XML Schema definition. In programming terms, an XML Schema is a type definition, whereas an XML document is an instance of that type. Listing 13-3 describes one possible XML Schema called Books.xsd that validates against the Books.xml file.

Listing 13-3: The Books.xsd XML Schema

```
<?xml version="1.0" encoding="utf-8" ?>
<xsd:schema xmlns:xsd="http://www.w3.org/2001/XMLSchema"
xmlns:tns="http://example.books.com"
xmlns="http://example.books.com"
targetNamespace="http://example.books.com"
elementFormDefault="qualified">

    <xsd:element name="bookstore" type="bookstoreType"/>

    <xsd:complexType name="bookstoreType">
        <xsd:sequence maxOccurs="unbounded">
            <xsd:element name="book" type="bookType"/>
        </xsd:sequence>
    </xsd:complexType>

    <xsd:complexType name="bookType">
        <xsd:sequence>
            <xsd:element name="title" type="xsd:string"/>
            <xsd:element name="author" type="authorName"/>
            <xsd:element name="price" type="xsd:decimal"/>
        </xsd:sequence>
        <xsd:attribute name="genre" type="xsd:string"/>
        <xsd:attribute name="publicationdate" type="xsd:string"/>
        <xsd:attribute name="ISBN" type="xsd:string"/>
    </xsd:complexType>

    <xsd:complexType name="authorName">
        <xsd:sequence>
            <xsd:element name="first-name" type="xsd:string"/>
            <xsd:element name="last-name" type="xsd:string"/>
        </xsd:sequence>
    </xsd:complexType>
</xsd:schema>
```

The XML Schema in Listing 13-3 starts by including a series of namespace prefixes used in the schema document as attributes on the root element. The prefix xsd: is declared on the root element (xmlns:xsd="http://www.w3.org/2001/XMLSchema") and then used on all other elements of that schema. The default namespace assumed for any elements without prefixes is described by the `xmlns` attribute like this:

```
xmlns=http://example.books.com
```

A namespace-qualified element has a prefix such as `<xsd:element>`. The target namespace for all elements in this schema is declared with the `targetNamespace` attribute.

XML Schema can be daunting at first; but if you read each line to yourself as a *declaration*, it makes more sense. For example, the line

```
<xsd:element name="bookstore" type="bookstoreType"/>
```

declares that an element named `bookstore` has the type `bookstoreType`. Because the `targetNamespace` for the schema is `http://example.books.com`, that is the namespace of each declared type in the `Books.xsd` schema. If you refer to Listing 13-1, you see that the namespace of the `Books.xml` document is also `http://example.books.com`.

For more detailed information on XML Schema, visit the W3C's XML Schema site at `www.w3.org/XML/Schema`.

Editing XML and XML Schema in Visual Studio .NET 2005

If you start up Visual Studio .NET and open the `Books.xml` file into the editor, you notice immediately that the Visual Studio editor provides syntax highlighting and formats the XML document as a nicely indented tree. If you start writing a new XML element anywhere, you don't have access to IntelliSense. Even though the `http://example.books.com` namespace is the default namespace, Visual Studio .NET has no way to find the `Books.xsd` file; it could be located anywhere. Remember that the namespace is *not* a URL; it's a URI — an identifier. Even if it were a URL it wouldn't be appropriate for the editor, or any program you write, to go out on the Web looking for a schema. You have to be explicit when associating XML Schema with instance documents.

Classes and methods are used to validate XML documents when you are working programmatically, but the Visual Studio editor needs a hint to find the `Book.xsd` schema. Assuming the `Books.xsd` file is in the same directory as `Books.xml`, you have three ways to inform the editor:

❑ Open the `Books.xsd` schema in Visual Studio in another window while the `Books.xml` file is also open.

❑ Include a `schemaLocation` attribute in the `Books.xml` file.

❑ If you open at least one XML file with the `schemaLocation` attribute set, Visual Studio uses that schema for any other open XML files that don't include the attribute.

❑ Add the `Books.xsd` schema to the list of schemas that Visual Studio knows about internally by adding it to the `Schemas` property in the document properties window of the `Books.xml` file. When schemas are added in this way, Visual Studio checks the document's namespace and determines if it already knows of a schema that matches.

The `schemaLocation` attribute is in a different namespace, so include the `xmlns` namespace attribute and your chosen prefix for the schema's location, as shown in Listing 13-4.

Listing 13-4: Updating the Books.xml file with a schemaLocation attribute

```
<?xml version='1.0'?>
<!-- This file is a part of a book store inventory database -->
<bookstore xmlns="http://example.books.com"
xmlns:xsi="http://www.w3.org/2001/XMLSchema-instance"
xsi:schemaLocation="http://example.books.com Books.xsd">
    <book genre="autobiography" publicationdate="1981" ISBN="1-861003-11-0">
        <title>The Autobiography of Benjamin Franklin</title>
        ...Rest of the XML document omitted for brevity...
```

The format for the `schemaLocation` attribute is pairs of strings separated by spaces where the first string in each pair is a namespace URI and the second string is the location of the schema. The location can be relative, as shown in Listing 13-4, or it can be an `http://` URL or `file://` location.

When the `Books.xsd` schema can be located for the `Books.xml` document, Visual Studio .NET's XML editor becomes considerably more useful. Not only does the editor underline incorrect elements with blue squiggles, it also includes tooltips and IntelliSense for the entire document, as shown in Figure 13-1.

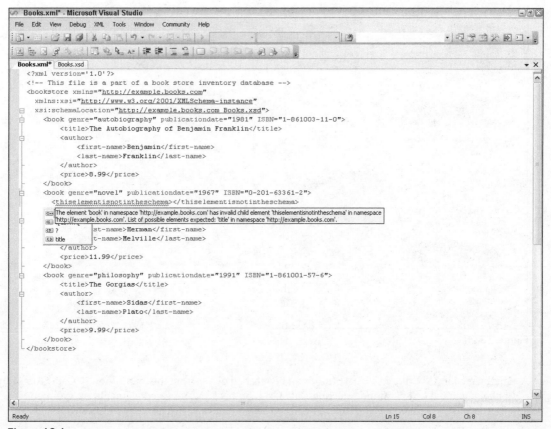

Figure 13-1

When the XML Schema file from Listing 13-3 is loaded into the Visual Studio editor, the default view presents the elements and complex types in a format that is familiar if you've edited database schemas before (see Figure 13-2).

The gray squares in the schema in Figure 13-2 represent references to global entities. For example, the bookType complex type declaration has an author element that is an instance of the authorName complex type. Because the authorName type can be used and reused in many places within the same schema, the visual editor allows you to edit only the global declaration, shown in Figure 13-2 as the white square in the lower-left corner. All the white squares represent elements or composite complex types that are editable.

The visual layout of the schema doesn't relate in any way to the underlying XML Schema document, so you are free to organize the look of your schemas without fear. The layout is stored in a parallel XSD designer layout file with the extension .XSX — in this case, Books.xsx. If this file is deleted, don't worry; it is created automatically with a default layout the next time the schema is opened in the designer.

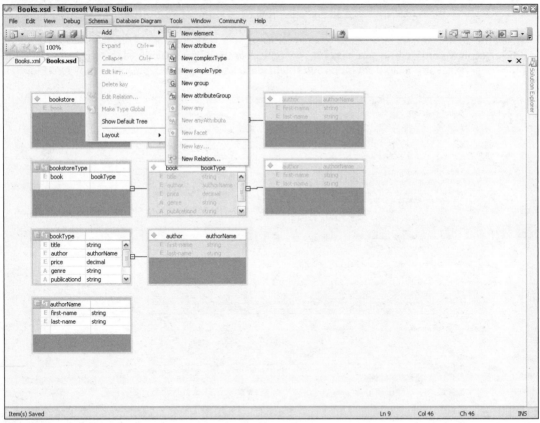

Figure 13-2

A visual view for XML files in Visual Studio can be reached either from the menu View ➪ Data Grid or by right-clicking in the text view and selecting Data Grid. In this view, repeated elements are grouped together in a list box called a Data Table, as you can see in Figure 13-3. This view meshes well with the database-centric view presented by the Schema editor in Figure 13-2 and underlines the point that XML is just a set of information, or InfoSet, and a developer can program quite comfortably without ever seeing an angle bracket.

After you have created an XML Schema that correctly describes an XML document, you're ready to start programmatically manipulating XML. The System.Xml namespace provides a number of ways to access XML. XML Schemas provide valuable typing information for all XML consumers that are type aware.

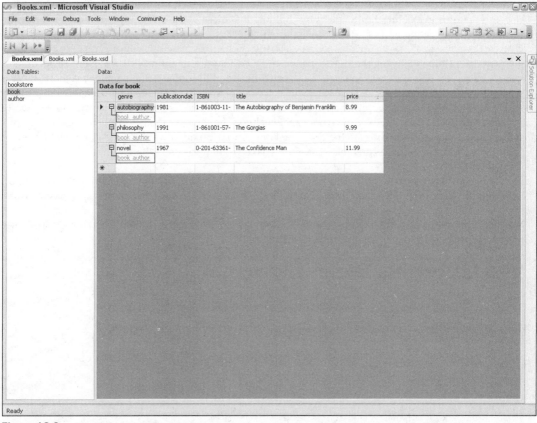

Figure 13-3

XmlReader and XmlWriter

XmlReader offers a *pull-style* API over an XML document that is unique to the .NET Framework. It provides fast, forward-only, read-only access to XML documents. These documents may contain elements in multiple namespaces. XmlReader is actually an abstract class that other classes derive from to provide specific concrete instances like XmlTextReader and XmlNodeReader.

Things have changed slightly with `XmlReader` since .NET Framework 1.1. Convenient new methods have been added, and the way you create `XmlReader` has changed for the better. `XmlReader` has become a factory. The primary way for you to create an instance of an `XmlReader` is by using the Static/Shared `Create` method. Rather than creating concrete implementations of the `XmlReader` class, you create an instance of the `XmlReaderSettings` class and pass it to the `Create` method. You specify the features you want for your `XmlReader` object with the `XmlReaderSettings` class. For example, you might want a specialized `XmlReader` that checks the validity of an XML document with the `IgnoreWhite Space` and `IgnoreComments` properties pre-set. The `Create` method of the `XmlReader` class provides you with an instance of an `XmlReader` without requiring you to decide which implementation to use. You can also add features to existing XmlReaders by chaining instances of the `XmlReader` class with each other because the `Create` method of `XmlReader` takes another `XmlReader` as a parameter.

If you are accustomed to using the `XmlDocument` or DOM to write an entire XML fragment or document into memory, you will find `XmlReader` to be a very different philosophy. A good analogy is that `XmlReader` is to `XmlDocument` what the ADO ForwardOnly recordset is to the ADO Static recordset. Remember that the ADO Static recordset loads the entire results set into memory and holds it there. Certainly, you wouldn't use a Static recordset if you want to retrieve only a few values. The same basic rules apply to the `XmlReader` class. If you're going to run through the document only once, you don't want to hold it in memory; you want the access to be as fast as possible. `XmlReader` is the right decision in this case.

Listing 13-5 creates an `XmlReader` class instance and iterates forward through it, counting the number of books in the `Books.xml` document from Listing 13-1. The `XmlReaderSettings` object specifies the features that are required, rather than the actual kind of `XmlReader` to create. In this example, `IgnoreWhitespace` and `IgnoreComments` are set to `True`. The `XmlReaderSettings` object is created with these property settings and then passed to the `Create` method of `XmlReader`.

Listing 13-5: Processing XML with an XmlReader

VB

```vb
Imports System.IO
Imports System.Xml

Protected Sub Page_Load(ByVal sender As Object, ByVal e As System.EventArgs) _
        Handles Me.Load
    Dim bookcount As Integer = 0
    Dim settings As New XmlReaderSettings()

    settings.IgnoreWhitespace = True
    settings.IgnoreComments = True

    Dim booksFile As String = _
        Path.Combine(Request.PhysicalApplicationPath, "books.xml")
    Using reader As XmlReader = XmlReader.Create(booksFile, settings)
        While (reader.Read())
            If (reader.NodeType = XmlNodeType.Element _
                    And "book" = reader.LocalName) Then
                bookcount += 1
            End If
        End While
    End Using
    Response.Write(String.Format("Found {0} books!", bookcount))
End Sub
```

C#

```
using System.IO;
using System.Xml;

protected void Page_Load(object sender, EventArgs e)
{
    int bookcount = 0;
    XmlReaderSettings settings = new XmlReaderSettings();

    settings.IgnoreWhitespace = true;
    settings.IgnoreComments = true;

    string booksFile = Path.Combine(Request.PhysicalApplicationPath, "books.xml");
    using (XmlReader reader = XmlReader.Create(booksFile, settings))
    {
        while (reader.Read())
        {
            if (reader.NodeType == XmlNodeType.Element &&
                    "book" == reader.LocalName)
            {
                bookcount++;
            }
        }
    }
    Response.Write(String.Format("Found {0} books!", bookcount));
}
```

Notice the use of the XmlReader.Create method in Listing 13-5. You may be used to creating concrete implementations of an XmlReader, but if you try this technique, you should find it much more flexible because you can reuse the XmlReaderSettings objects in the creation of other instances of XmlReader. XmlReader implements IDisposable, so the Using keyword is correct in both VB and C#.

In Listing 13-5 the Books.xml file is in the same directory as this ASPX page, so a call to Path.Combine gets the complete path to the XML file. The file name with full path is then passed into XmlReader.Create, along with the XmlReaderSettings instance from a few lines earlier.

The read method continues to return true if the node was read successfully. It will return false when no more nodes are left to read. From the point of view of an XmlReader, everything is a node including white space, comments, attributes, elements, and end elements. If Listing 13-5 had simply spun through the while loop incrementing the bookcount variable each time reader.LocalName equaled book, the final value for bookcount would have been six. You would have counted both the beginning book element and the ending book element. Consequently, you have to be more explicit, and ensure that the if statement is modified to check not only the LocalName but also the NodeType.

> The Reader.LocalName **property contains the non–namespace qualified name of that node. The** Reader.Name **property is different and contains the fully qualified name of that node including namespace. The** Reader.LocalName **property is used in the example in Listing 13-5 for simplicity and ease. You'll hear more about namespaces a little later in the chapter.**

Using Schema with XmlTextReader

The code in Listing 13-5 reads any XML document regardless of its schema, and if the document contains an element named book, the code counts it. If this code is meant to count books of a particular schema type only, specifically the books from the Books.xml file, it should be validated against the Books.xsd schema.

Now modify the creation of the XmlReader class from Listing 13-5 to validate the XmlDocument against the XML Schema used earlier in the chapter. Note that the XmlValidatingReader class is now considered obsolete because all reader creation is done using the Create method of the XmlReader class.

Listing 13-6 shows a concrete example of how easy it is to add schema validation to code using XmlReaderSettings and the XmlReader Create method.

Listing 13-6: Validating XML with an XmlReader against an XML Schema

VB

```
Imports System.Xml.Schema

Protected Sub Page_Load(ByVal sender As Object, ByVal e As System.EventArgs) _
        Handles Me.Load
    Dim bookcount As Integer = 0
    Dim settings As New XmlReaderSettings()
    Dim booksSchemaFile As String = _
        Path.Combine(Request.PhysicalApplicationPath, "books.xsd")

    settings.Schemas.Add(Nothing, XmlReader.Create(booksSchemaFile))
    settings.ValidationType = ValidationType.Schema
    settings.ValidationFlags = _
        XmlSchemaValidationFlags.ReportValidationWarnings

    AddHandler settings.ValidationEventHandler, _
    AddressOf settings_ValidationEventHandler

    settings.IgnoreWhitespace = True
    settings.IgnoreComments = True

    Dim booksFile As String = _
    Path.Combine(Request.PhysicalApplicationPath, "books.xml")
    Using reader As XmlReader = XmlReader.Create(booksFile, settings)
        While (reader.Read())
            If (reader.NodeType = XmlNodeType.Element _
                    And "book" = reader.LocalName) Then
                bookcount += 1
            End If
        End While
    End Using
    Response.Write(String.Format("Found {0} books!", bookcount))
End Sub

Sub settings_ValidationEventHandler(ByVal sender As Object, _
        ByVal e As System.Xml.Schema.ValidationEventArgs)
    Response.Write(e.Message)
End Sub
```

C#

```csharp
using System.Xml.Schema;

protected void Page_Load(object sender, EventArgs e)
{
    int bookcount = 0;
    XmlReaderSettings settings = new XmlReaderSettings();

    string booksSchemaFile = Path.Combine(Request.PhysicalApplicationPath,
        "books.xsd");

    settings.Schemas.Add(null, XmlReader.Create(booksSchemaFile));
    settings.ValidationType = ValidationType.Schema;
    settings.ValidationFlags =

    XmlSchemaValidationFlags.ReportValidationWarnings;
    settings.ValidationEventHandler +=
            new ValidationEventHandler(settings_ValidationEventHandler);

    settings.IgnoreWhitespace = true;
    settings.IgnoreComments = true;

    string booksFile = Path.Combine(Request.PhysicalApplicationPath, "books.xml");
    using (XmlReader reader = XmlReader.Create(booksFile, settings))
    {
        while (reader.Read())
        {
            if (reader.NodeType == XmlNodeType.Element &&
                    "book" == reader.LocalName)
            {
                bookcount++;
            }
        }
    }
    Response.Write(String.Format("Found {0} books!", bookcount));
}

void settings_ValidationEventHandler(object sender,
        System.Xml.Schema.ValidationEventArgs e)
{
    Response.Write(e.Message);
}
```

When validating XML, the validator uses the schemaLocation hint found in the XML instance document. If an XML instance document does not contain enough information to find an XML Schema, the instance document expects an XmlSchemaSet object on the XmlReaderSettings object. In the interest of being explicit, Listing 13-6 shows this technique. The XmlReaderSettings object has a Schemas collection available as a property and many overloads for the Add method. This listing passes null into the Add method as the first parameter, indicating that the targetNamespace is specified in the schema. Optionally, XML documents can also contain their schemas inline.

The validator needs a way to let you know when validation problems occur. The XmlReaderSettings object has a validation event handler that notifies you as validation events occur. Listing 13-6 also includes a handler for the validation event that writes the message to the browser.

Including NameTable Optimization

XmlReader internally uses a NameTable that lists all the known elements and attributes with name-spaces that are used in that document. This process is called *atomization* — literally meaning that the XML document is broken up into its atomic parts. There's no need to store the string book more than once in the internal structure if you can make book an object reference that is held in a table with the names of other elements.

Although this is an internal implementation detail, it is a supported and valid way that you can measurably speed up your use of XML classes, such as XmlReader and XmlDocument. You add name elements to the NameTable that you know will be in the document. Listings 13-5 and 13-6 use string comparisons to compare a string literal with reader.LocalName. These comparisons can also be optimized by turning them into object reference comparisons that are many, many times faster. Additionally, an XML NameTable can be shared across multiple instances of System.Xml classes and even between XmlReaders and XmlDocuments. This topic is covered shortly.

Because you are counting book elements, create a NameTable including this element (book), and instead of comparing string against string, compare object reference against object reference, as shown in Listing 13-7.

Listing 13-7: Optimizing XmlReader with a NameTable

```vb
VB
Protected Sub Page_Load(ByVal sender As Object, ByVal e As System.EventArgs) _
        Handles Me.Load
    Dim bookcount As Integer = 0
    Dim settings As New XmlReaderSettings()
    Dim nt As New NameTable()
    Dim book As Object = nt.Add("book")

    settings.NameTable = nt
    Dim booksSchemaFile As String = _
        Path.Combine(Request.PhysicalApplicationPath, "books.xsd")
    settings.Schemas.Add(Nothing, XmlReader.Create(booksSchemaFile))
    settings.ValidationType = ValidationType.Schema
    settings.ValidationFlags = _
    XmlSchemaValidationFlags.ReportValidationWarnings

    AddHandler settings.ValidationEventHandler, _
        AddressOf settings_ValidationEventHandler

    settings.IgnoreWhitespace = True
    settings.IgnoreComments = True

    Dim booksFile As String = _
    Path.Combine(Request.PhysicalApplicationPath, "books.xml")
    Using reader As XmlReader = XmlReader.Create(booksFile, settings)
        While (reader.Read())
            If (reader.NodeType = XmlNodeType.Element _
                And book.Equals(reader.LocalName)) Then
                'A subtle, but significant change!
                bookcount += 1
```

```
              End If
          End While
      End Using
      Response.Write(String.Format("Found {0} books!", bookcount))
  End Sub
```

C#

```csharp
protected void Page_Load(object sender, EventArgs e)
{
    int bookcount = 0;
    XmlReaderSettings settings = new XmlReaderSettings();
    NameTable nt = new NameTable();
    object book = nt.Add("book");

    settings.NameTable = nt;
    string booksSchemaFile = Path.Combine(Request.PhysicalApplicationPath,
        "books.xsd");

    settings.Schemas.Add(null, XmlReader.Create(booksSchemaFile));
    settings.ValidationType = ValidationType.Schema;
    settings.ValidationFlags =
        XmlSchemaValidationFlags.ReportValidationWarnings;

    settings.ValidationEventHandler +=
        new ValidationEventHandler(settings_ValidationEventHandler);

    settings.IgnoreWhitespace = true;
    settings.IgnoreComments = true;

    string booksFile = Path.Combine(Request.PhysicalApplicationPath, "books.xml");
    using (XmlReader reader = XmlReader.Create(booksFile, settings))
    {
        while (reader.Read())
        {
            if (reader.NodeType == XmlNodeType.Element &&
                book.Equals(reader.LocalName)) //A subtle, but significant change!
            {
                bookcount++;
            }
        }
    }
    Response.Write(String.Format("Found {0} books!", bookcount));
}
```

The `NameTable` is added to the `XmlSettings` object and the `Add` method of the `NameTable` returns an object reference to the just-added atom that is stored, in this case, in an object reference named `book`. The `book` reference is then used later to make a comparison to the `reader.LocalName` property. We specifically chose to use the `Equals` method that is present on all objects within that .NET Framework in order to emphasize that this is specifically an object identity check for equality. These two objects are either the same identical atoms or they are not. The `book` object that is returned from the `Add` method on the `NameTable` is the identical object that the reader uses when parsing the `book` element from the `Books.xml` XML document.

In the example of Listing 13-7, in which you count a very small number of books, you probably won't have a measurable performance gain. However, for larger XML documents that approach sizes of 1MB, you may see performance gains of as much as 10 to 15 percent — especially for the involved calculations and manipulations of `XmlReader`. Additionally, because the `NameTable` is cached within the `XmlReaderSettings` object, that `NameTable` is reused when the `XmlReaderSettings` object is reused for other `System.Xml` objects. This creates additional potential performance gains.

Retrieving .NET CLR Types from XML

In .NET Framework 2.0, it is considerably simpler to retrieve CLR types from an `XmlReader` than it was previously. If you've used SQL Server data reader objects before, retrieving data types from `XmlReader` may feel very familiar. Previously the Framework used a helper class called `XmlConvert`. When combined with the `ReadElementString` method on `XmlReader`, this helper class retrieved a strong, simple type, as shown in the following code:

```
//Retrieving a double from an XmlReader in the .NET Framework 1.1
Double price = XmlConvert.ToDouble(reader.ReadElementString());
//Has been replaced by and improved in the .NET Framework 2.0
Double price = reader.ReadElementContentAsDouble();
```

You can see the removal of the unnecessary double method call results in much cleaner and easier-to-read code. Listing 13-8 adds not only the counting of books but also prints the total price of all books using `ReadElementContentAs` when your `XmlReader` is currently on an element, or `ReadContentAs` if on text content. If schema information is available to the reader, `ReadElementContentAsObject` returns the value directly as, in this case, a decimal. If the reader does not have any schema information, it attempts to convert the string to a decimal. A whole series of `ReadElementContentAs` and `ReadContentAs` methods, including `ReadElementContentAsBoolean` and `ReadElementContentAsInt`, are available. Note that the code specific to `XmlSchema` has been removed from Listing 13-8 in the interest of brevity.

Listing 13-8: Using XmlReader.ReadElementContentAs

```
VB
Dim bookcount As Integer = 0
Dim booktotal As Decimal = 0
Dim settings As New XmlReaderSettings()
Dim nt As New NameTable()
Dim book As Object = nt.Add("book")
Dim price As Object = nt.Add("price")

settings.NameTable = nt

Dim booksFile As String = _
Path.Combine(Request.PhysicalApplicationPath, "books.xml")
Using reader As XmlReader = XmlReader.Create(booksFile, settings)
    While (reader.Read())
        If (reader.NodeType = XmlNodeType.Element _
            And book.Equals(reader.LocalName)) Then
            bookcount += 1
        End If
```

```
        If (reader.NodeType = XmlNodeType.Element _
            And price.Equals(reader.LocalName)) Then
            booktotal += reader.ReadElementContentAsDecimal ()
        End If
    End While
End Using

Response.Write(String.Format("Found {0} books that total {1:C}!", _
    bookcount, booktotal))
```

C#
```
int bookcount = 0;
decimal booktotal = 0;
XmlReaderSettings settings = new XmlReaderSettings();
string booksSchemaFile = Path.Combine(Request.PhysicalApplicationPath,
"books.xsd");
NameTable nt = new NameTable();
object book = nt.Add("book");
object price = nt.Add("price");

settings.NameTable = nt;

string booksFile = Path.Combine(Request.PhysicalApplicationPath, "books.xml");

using (XmlReader reader = XmlReader.Create(booksFile, settings))
{
    while (reader.Read())
    {
        if (reader.NodeType == XmlNodeType.Element &&
            book.Equals(reader.LocalName))//A subtle, but significant change!
        {
            bookcount++;
        }
        if (reader.NodeType == XmlNodeType.Element &&
        price.Equals(reader.LocalName))
        {
            booktotal +=
                reader.ReadElementContentAsDecimal ();
        }
    }
}

Response.Write(String.Format("Found {0} books that total {1:C}!",
    bookcount, booktotal));
```

The booktotal variable from Listing 13-8 is strongly typed as a decimal so that, in the String.Format call, it can be formatted as currency using the formatting string {1:C}. This results in output from the browser similar to the following:

```
Found 3 books that total $30.97!
```

ReadSubtree and XmlSerialization

Not only does XmlReader help you retrieve simple types from XML, it can help you retrieve more complicated types using XML serialization and ReadSubtree.

XML serialization allows you to add attributes to an existing class that give hints to the XML serialization on how to represent an object as XML. XML serialization serializes only the public properties of an object, not the private ones.

When you create an XmlSerializer, a Type object is passed into the constructor, and the XmlSerializer uses reflection to examine whether the object can create a temporary assembly that knows how to read and write this particular object as XML. The XmlSerializer uses a concrete implementation of XmlReader internally to serialize these objects.

Instead of retrieving the author's first name and last name using XmlReader.ReadAsString, Listing 13-10 uses ReadSubtree and a new strongly typed Author class that has been marked up with XML serialization attributes, as shown in Listing 13-9. ReadSubtree "breaks off" a new XmlReader at the current location, and that XmlReader is passed to an XmlSerializer and a complex type is created. The Author class includes XmlElement attributes that indicate, for example, that although there is a property called FirstName, it should be serialized and deserialized as "first-name."

Listing 13-9: An Author class with XML serialization attributes matching Books.xsd

VB
```
Imports System.Xml.Serialization
<XmlRoot(ElementName:="author", _
Namespace:="http://example.books.com")> Public Class Author
    <XmlElement(ElementName:="first-name")> Public FirstName As String
    <XmlElement(ElementName:="last-name")> Public LastName As String
End Class
```

C#
```
using System.Xml.Serialization;
[XmlRoot(ElementName = "author", Namespace = "http://example.books.com")]
public class Author
{
    [XmlElement(ElementName = "first-name")]
    public string FirstName;

    [XmlElement(ElementName = "last-name")]
    public string LastName;
}
```

Next, this Author class is used along with XmlReader.ReadSubtree and XmlSerializer to output the names of each book's author. Listing 13-10 shows just the additional statements added to the While loop.

Listing 13-10: Reading author instances from an XmlReader using XmlSerialization

VB

```vb
'Create factory early
Dim factory As New XmlSerializerFactory

Using reader As XmlReader = XmlReader.Create(booksFile, settings)
    While (reader.Read())
        If (reader.NodeType = XmlNodeType.Element _
            And author.Equals(reader.LocalName)) Then

            'Then use the factory to create and cache serializers
            Dim xs As XmlSerializer = factory.CreateSerializer(GetType(Author))
            Dim a As Author = CType(xs.Deserialize(reader.ReadSubtree), Author)
            Response.Write(String.Format("Author: {1}, {0}<BR/>", _
                a.FirstName, a.LastName))
        End If
    End While
End Using
```

C#

```csharp
//Create factory early
XmlSerializerFactory factory = new XmlSerializerFactory();

using (XmlReader reader = XmlReader.Create(booksFile, settings))
{
    while (reader.Read())
    {
        if (reader.NodeType == XmlNodeType.Element &&
            author.Equals(reader.LocalName))
        {
            //Then use the factory to create and cache serializers
            XmlSerializer xs = factory.CreateSerializer(typeof(Author));
            Author a = (Author)xs.Deserialize(reader.ReadSubtree());
            Response.Write(String.Format("Author: {1}, {0}<BR/>",
                a.FirstName, a.LastName));
        }
    }
}
```

The only other addition to the code, as you can guess, is the author object atom (used only in the Equals statement) that is added to the NameTable just as the book and price were, via Dim author As Object = nt.Add("author").

When you create an XmlSerializer instance for a specific type, the framework uses reflection to create a temporary type-specific assembly to handle serialization and deserialization. The .NET Framework 2.0 includes a new XmlSerializerFactory that automatically handles caching of these temporary assemblies. This small factory provides an important layer of abstraction that allows you to structure your code in a way that is convenient without worrying about creating XmlSerializer instances ahead of time.

Creating Xml with XmlWriter

`XmlWriter` works exactly like `XmlReader` except in reverse. It's very tempting to use string concatenation to quickly create XML documents or fragments of XML, but you should resist the urge! Remember that the whole point of XML is the representation of the InfoSet, not the angle brackets. If you concatenate string literals together with `StringBuilder` to create XML, you are dropping below the level of the InfoSet to the implementation details of the format. Tell yourself that XML documents are not strings!

> Most people find it helpful (as a visualization tool) to indent the method calls to the `XmlWriter` with the same structure as the resulting XML document. However, VB in Visual Studio is much more aggressive than C# in keeping the code indented a specific way. It does not allow this kind of artificial indentation unless Smart Indenting is changed to either Block or None by using Tools ⇨ Options ⇨ Text Editor ⇨ Basic ⇨ Tabs.

`XmlWriter` also has a settings class called, obviously, `XmlWriterSettings`. This class has options for indentation, new lines, encoding, and XML conformance level. Listing 13-11 uses `XmlWriter` to create a `bookstore` XML document and output it directly to the ASP.NET `Response.OutputStream`. All the HTML tags in the ASPX page must be removed in order for the XML document to be output correctly. Another way to output XML easily is with an ASHX `HttpHandler`.

The unusual indenting in Listing 13-11 is significant and very common when using `XmlWriter`. It helps the programmer visualize the hierarchical structure of an XML document.

Listing 13-11: Writing out a bookstore with XmlWriter

Default.aspx - C#

```
<%@ Page Language="C#" codefile="Default.aspx.cs" Inherits="Default_aspx" %>
```

Default.aspx - VB

```
<%@ Page Language="VB" codefile="Default.aspx.vb" Inherits="Default_aspx" %>
```

VB

```
Protected Sub Page_Load(ByVal sender As Object, ByVal e As System.EventArgs) _
Handles Me.Load

Dim price As Double = 49.99
Dim publicationdate As New DateTime(2005, 1, 1)
Dim isbn As String = "1-057-610-0"
Dim a As New Author()
a.FirstName = "Scott"
a.LastName = "Hanselman"

Dim settings As New XmlWriterSettings()
settings.Indent = True
settings.NewLineOnAttributes = True

Response.ContentType = "text/xml"

Dim factory As New XmlSerializerFactory()

Using writer As XmlWriter = XmlWriter.Create(Response.OutputStream, settings)

    'Note the artificial, but useful, indenting
```

```
        writer.WriteStartDocument()
            writer.WriteStartElement("bookstore")
                writer.WriteStartElement("book")
                    writer.WriteStartAttribute("publicationdate")
                        writer.WriteValue(publicationdate)
                    writer.WriteEndAttribute()
                    writer.WriteStartAttribute("ISBN")
                        writer.WriteValue(isbn)
                    writer.WriteEndAttribute()
                    writer.WriteElementString("title", "ASP.NET 2.0")
                    writer.WriteStartElement("price")
                        writer.WriteValue(price)
                    writer.WriteEndElement() 'price
                    Dim xs As XmlSerializer = _
                        factory.CreateSerializer(GetType(Author))
                    xs.Serialize(writer, a)
                writer.WriteEndElement() 'book
            writer.WriteEndElement() 'bookstore
        writer.WriteEndDocument()
End Using

End Sub
```

C#

```csharp
protected void Page_Load(object sender, EventArgs e)
{
Double price = 49.99;
DateTime publicationdate = new DateTime(2005, 1, 1);
String isbn = "1-057-610-0";
Author a = new Author();
a.FirstName = "Scott";
a.LastName = "Hanselman";

XmlWriterSettings settings = new XmlWriterSettings();
settings.Indent = true;
settings.NewLineOnAttributes = true;

Response.ContentType = "text/xml";

XmlSerializerFactory factory = new XmlSerializerFactory();

using (XmlWriter writer =
        XmlWriter.Create(Response.OutputStream, settings))
{
    //Note the artificial, but useful, indenting
    writer.WriteStartDocument();
        writer.WriteStartElement("bookstore");
            writer.WriteStartElement("book");
                writer.WriteStartAttribute("publicationdate");
                    writer.WriteValue(publicationdate);
                writer.WriteEndAttribute();
                writer.WriteStartAttribute("ISBN");
                    writer.WriteValue(isbn);
                writer.WriteEndAttribute();
                writer.WriteElementString("title", "ASP.NET 2.0");
```

```
                writer.WriteStartElement("price");
                    writer.WriteValue(price);
                writer.WriteEndElement(); //price
                XmlSerializer xs = factory.CreateSerializer(typeof(Author));
                xs.Serialize(writer, a);
            writer.WriteEndElement(); //book
        writer.WriteEndElement(); //bookstore
    writer.WriteEndDocument();
    }


    }
```

The `Response.ContentType` in Listing 13-11 is set to `"text/xml"` to indicate to Internet Explorer that the result is XML. An `XmlSerializer` is created in the middle of the process and serialized directly to `XmlWriter`. The `XmlWriterSettings.Indent` property includes indentation that makes the resulting XML document more palatable for human consumption. Setting both this property and `NewLineOnAttributes` to `false` results in a smaller, more compact document.

Improvements for XmlReader and XmlWriter in 2.0

A few helper methods and changes make using `XmlReader` and `XmlWriter` even simpler in the .NET Framework 2.0:

❏ `ReadSubtree`: This method reads the current node of an `XmlReader` and returns a new `XmlReader` that traverses the current node and all its descendants. It allows you to chop off a portion of the XML InfoSet and process it separately.

❏ `ReadToDescendant` **and** `ReadToNextSibling`: These two methods provide convenient ways to advance the `XmlReader` to specific elements that appear later in the document.

❏ `Dispose`: `XmlReader` and `XmlWriter` are both a disposable level, which means that they support the `Using` keyword. `Using`, in turn, calls `Dispose`, which calls the `Close` method. These methods are now less problematic because you no longer have to remember to call `Close` to release any resources. This simple but powerful technique has been used in the listings in this chapter.

XmlDocument and XPathDocument

In the .NET Framework 1.1, the `XmlDocument` was one of the most common ways to manipulate XML. It is similar to using a static ADO recordset because it parses and loads the entire `XmlDocument` into memory. Often the `XmlDocument` is the first class a programmer learns to use and, consequently, as a solution it becomes the hammer in his toolkit. Unfortunately, not every kind of XML problem is a nail. `XmlDocuments` have been known to use many times their file size in memory. Often an `XmlDocument` is referred to as the DOM or Document Object Model. The `XmlDocument` is compliant with the W3C DOM implementation and should be familiar to anyone who has used a DOM implementation.

Problems with the DOM

There are a number of problems with the XmlDocument class in .NET Framework 1.1. The data model of the XmlDocument is very different from other XML query languages such as XSLT and XPath. The XmlDocument is editable and provides a familiar API for those who used MSXML in Visual Basic 6. Often, however, people use the XmlDocument to search for data within a larger document, but the XmlDocument isn't designed for searching large amounts of information. The XPathDocument is read-only and optimized for XPath queries or XPath-heavy technologies such as XSLT. In .NET Framework 2.0, the XPathDocument is much, much faster than the XmlDocument for loading and querying XML.

The XPathDocument is very focused around the InfoSet because it has a much-optimized internal structure. Be aware, however, that it does throw away insignificant white spaces and CDATA sections, so it is not appropriate if you want the XPathDocument to maintain the identical number of bytes that you originally created. However, if you're focused more on the set of information that is contained within your document, you can be assured that the XPathDocument contains everything that your source document contains.

A rule of thumb for querying data is that you should use the XPathDocument instead of the XmlDocument — except in situations where you must maintain compatibility with previous versions of the .NET Framework. The new XPathDocument supports all the type information from any associated XML Schema and supports the schema validation via the Validate method. The XPathDocument lets you load XML documents to URLs, files, or streams. The XPathDocument is also the preferred class to use for the XSLT transformations covered later in this chapter.

XPath, the XPathDocument, and XmlDocument

The XPathDocument is so named because it is the most efficient way to use XPath expressions over an in-memory data structure. The XPathDocument implements the IXPathNavigable interface, allowing you to iterate over the underlying XML by providing an XPathNavigator. The XPathNavigator class differs from the XmlReader because rather than forward-only, it provides random access over your XML, similar to a read-only ADO Keyset recordset versus a forward-only recordset.

You typically want to use an XPathDocument to move around freely, forward and backward, within a document. XPathDocument is read-only, while XmlDocument allows read-write access.

The XmlDocument in version 2.0 adds in-memory validation. Using the XmlReader, the only way to validate the XML is from a stream or file. The XmlDocument now allows in-memory validation without the file or stream access using Validate(). XmlDocument also adds capability to subscribe to events like NodeChanged, NodeInserting, and the like.

XPath is a query language best learned by example. You must know it to make good use of the XPathDocument. Here are some valid XPath queries that you can use with the Books.xml file. XPath is a rich language in its own right, with many dozens of functions. As such, fully exploring XPath is beyond the scope of this book, but this table should give you a taste of what's possible.

Xpath Function	Result
`//book[@genre = "novel"]/title`	Recursively from the root node, gets all books with the title element whose genre attribute is equal to `novel`
`/bookstore/book[author/last-name = "Melville"]`	Gets all books that are children of `bookstore` whose author's last name is `Melville`
`/bookstore/book/author[last-name = "Melville"]`	Gets all authors that are children of `book` whose last name is `Melville`
`//book[title = "The Gorgias" or title = "The Confidence Man"]`	Recursively from the root node, gets all books whose title is either The Gorgias or The Confidence Man
`//title[contains(., "The")]`	Gets all titles that contain the string The
`//book[not(price[. > 10.00])]`	Gets all books whose prices are not greater than `10.00`

Listing 13-12 queries an XPathDocument for books whose prices are less than $10.00 and outputs the price. In order to illustrate using built-in XPath functions, this example uses a greater-than instead of using a less-than. It then inverts the result using the built-in not() method. XPath includes a number of functions for string concatenation, arithmetic, and many other uses. The XPathDocument returns an XPathNavigator as a result of calling CreateNavigator. The XPathNavigator is queried using an XPath passed to the Select method and returns an XPathNodeIterator. That XPathNodeIterator is foreach enabled via IEnumerable. As Listing 13-12 uses a read-only XPathDocument, it will not update the data in memory.

Listing 13-12: Querying XML with XPathDocument and XPathNodeIterator

VB

```
'Load document
Dim booksFile As String = Path.Combine(Request.PhysicalApplicationPath, _
    "books.xml")

Dim document As New XPathDocument(booksFile)
Dim nav As XPathNavigator = document.CreateNavigator()

'Add a namespace prefix that can be used in the XPath expression
Dim namespaceMgr As New XmlNamespaceManager(nav.NameTable)
namespaceMgr.AddNamespace("b", "http://example.books.com")

'All books whose price is not greater than 10.00
For Each node As XPathNavigator In nav.Select( _
        "//b:book[not(b:price[. > 10.00])]/b:price", namespaceMgr)
    Dim price As Decimal = _
        CType(node.ValueAs(GetType(Decimal)), Decimal)
    Response.Write(String.Format("Price is {0}<BR/>", _
        price))
Next
```

C#

```
//Load document
string booksFile = Path.Combine(Request.PhysicalApplicationPath, "books.xml");

XPathDocument document = new XPathDocument(booksFile);
XPathNavigator nav = document.CreateNavigator();

//Add a namespace prefix that can be used in the XPath expression
XmlNamespaceManager namespaceMgr = new XmlNamespaceManager(nav.NameTable);
namespaceMgr.AddNamespace("b", "http://example.books.com");

//All books whose price is not greater than 10.00
foreach(XPathNavigator node in
    nav.Select("//b:book[not(b:price[. > 10.00])]/b:price",
    namespaceMgr))
{
    Decimal price = (decimal)node.ValueAs(typeof(decimal));
    Response.Write(String.Format("Price is {0}<BR/>",
        price));
}
```

If you then want to modify the underlying XML nodes, in the form of an XPathNavigator, you would use an XmlDocument instead of an XPathDocument. Your XPath expression evaluation may slow you down, but you will gain the capability to edit. Be ware of this tradeoff in performance. Most often, you will want to use the read-only XPathDocument whenever possible. Listing 13-13 illustrates this change with the new or changed portions appearing in gray. Additionally, now that the document is editable, the price is increased 20 percent.

Listing 13-13: Querying and editing XML with XmlDocument and XPathNodeIterator

VB

```
'Load document
Dim booksFile As String = Path.Combine(Request.PhysicalApplicationPath, _
    "books.xml")

Dim document As New XmlDocument()
document.Load(booksFile)
Dim nav As XPathNavigator = document.CreateNavigator()

'Add a namespace prefix that can be used in the XPath expression
Dim namespaceMgr As New XmlNamespaceManager(nav.NameTable)
namespaceMgr.AddNamespace("b", "http://example.books.com")
'All books whose price is not greater than 10.00
For Each node As XPathNavigator In nav.Select( _
        "//b:book[not(b:price[. > 10.00])]/b:price", namespaceMgr)
    Dim price As Decimal = CType(node.ValueAs(GetType(Decimal)), Decimal)
    node.SetTypedValue(price * CDec(1.2))
    Response.Write(String.Format("Price raised from {0} to {1}<BR/>", _
        price, _
        CType(node.ValueAs(GetType(Decimal)), Decimal)))
Next
```

C#

```
//Load document
string booksFile = Path.Combine(Request.PhysicalApplicationPath, "books.xml");

XmlDocument document = new XmlDocument();
document.Load(booksFile);
XPathNavigator nav = document.CreateNavigator();

//Add a namespace prefix that can be used in the XPath expression
XmlNamespaceManager namespaceMgr = new XmlNamespaceManager(nav.NameTable);
namespaceMgr.AddNamespace("b", "http://example.books.com");

//All books whose price is not greater than 10.00
foreach(XPathNavigator node in
    nav.Select("//b:book[not(b:price[. > 10.00])]/b:price",
    namespaceMgr))
{
    Decimal price = (decimal)node.ValueAs(typeof(decimal));
    node.SetTypedValue(price * 1.2M);
    Response.Write(String.Format("Price inflated raised from {0} to {1}<BR/>",
        price,
        node.ValueAs(typeof(decimal))));
}
```

Listing 13-3 changes the XPathDocument to an XmlDocument, and adds a call to XPathNavigator
.SetTypedValue to update the price of the document in memory. The resulting document could then be
persisted to storage as needed. If SetTypedValue was instead called on the XPathNavigator that was
returned by XPathDocument, a NotSupportedException would be thrown as the XPathDocument is
read-only.

The Books.xml document loaded from disk uses http://example.books.com as its default namespace.
Because the Books.xsd XML Schema is associated with the Books.xml document, and it assigns the default
namespace to be http://example.books.com, the XPath must know how to resolve that namespace.
Otherwise, you cannot determine if an XPath expression with the word book in it refers to a book from this
namespace or another book entirely. An XmlNamespaceManager is created, and b is arbitrarily used as the
namespace prefix for the XPath expression.

Namespace resolution can be very confusing because it is easy to assume that your XML file is all alone in
the world and that specifying a node named book is specific enough to enable the system to find it.
However, remember that your XML documents should be thought of as living among all the XML in the
world — this makes providing a qualified namespace all the more important. The XmlNamespaceManager
in Listing 13-12 is passed into the call to SelectNodes in order to associate the prefix with the appropriate
namespace. Remember, the namespace is unique, not the prefix; the prefix is simply a convenience acting
as an alias to the longer namespace. If you find that you're having trouble getting an XPath expression to
work and no nodes are being returned, find out if your source XML has a namespace specified and that it
matches up with a namespace in your XPath.

DataSets

XQuery is an excellent example of how XML is baked into the experience of manipulating data on the .NET Framework. The `System.Data` namespace and `System.Xml` namespace have started mingling their functionality for some time. DataSets are another example of how relational data and XML data meet in a hybrid class library. During the COM and XML heyday, the ADO 2.5 recordset sported the capability to persist as XML. The dramatic inclusion of XML functionality in a class library focused entirely on manipulation of relational data was a boon for developer productivity. XML could be pulled out of SQL Server and manipulated.

Persisting DataSets to XML

Classes within `System.Data` use `XmlWriter` and `XmlReader` in a number of places. Now that you're more familiar with `System.Xml` concepts, be sure to take note of the method overloads provided by the classes within `System.Data`. For example, the `DataSet.WriteXml` method has four overloads, one of which takes in `XmlWriter`. Most of the methods with `System.Data` are very pluggable with the classes from `System.Xml`. Listing 13-14 shows another way to retrieve the XML from relational data by loading a DataSet from a SQL command and writing it directly to the browser with the `Response` object's `TextWriter` property using `DataSet.WriteXml`.

Listing 13-14: Extracting XML from a SQL Server with System.Data.DataSet

VB
```vb
Dim connStr As String = "database=Northwind;Data Source=localhost; " _
        & "User id=sa;pwd=wrox"

Using conn As New SqlConnection(connStr)
    Dim command As New SqlCommand("select * from customers", conn)
    conn.Open()
    Dim ds As New DataSet()
    ds.DataSetName = "Customers"
    ds.Load(command.ExecuteReader(), LoadOption.OverwriteChanges, "Customer")
    Response.ContentType = "text/xml"
    ds.WriteXml(Response.OutputStream)
End Using
```

C#
```csharp
string connStr = "database=Northwind;Data Source=localhost;User id=sa;pwd=wrox";

using (SqlConnection conn = new SqlConnection(connStr))
{
    SqlCommand command = new SqlCommand("select * from customers", conn);
    conn.Open();
    DataSet ds = new DataSet();
    ds.DataSetName = "Customers";
    ds.Load(command.ExecuteReader(), LoadOption.OverwriteChanges, "Customer");
    Response.ContentType = "text/xml";
    ds.WriteXml(Response.OutputStream);
}
```

DataSets have a fairly fixed format, as seen in this example. The root node of the document is `Customers`, which corresponds to the `DataSetName` property. DataSets contain one or more named `DataTable` objects, and the names of these `DataTables` define the wrapper element — in this case, `Customer`. The name of the `DataTable` is passed into the `load` method of the DataSet. The correlation between the DataSet's name, `DataTable`'s name, and the resulting XML is not obvious when using DataSets. The resulting XML is shown in the browser in Figure 13-4.

DataSets present a data model that is very different from the XML way of thinking about data. Much of the XML-style of thinking revolves around the InfoSet or the DOM, whereas DataSets are row- and column-based. The `XmlDataDocument` is an attempt to present these two ways of thinking into one relatively unified model.

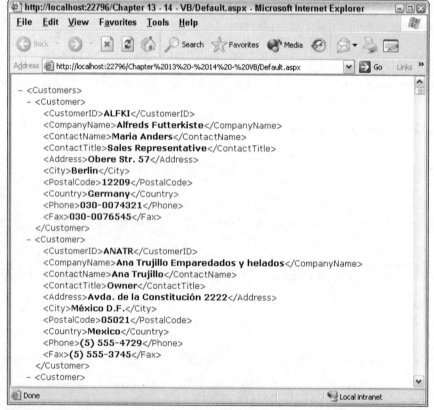

Figure 13-4

XmlDataDocument

Although DataSets have their own relatively inflexible format for using XML, the `XmlDocument` class does not. In order to bridge this gap, an unusual hybrid object, the `XmlDataDocument`, is introduced. This object maintains the full fidelity of all the XML structure and allows you to access XML via the `XmlDocument` API without losing the flexibility of a relational API. An `XmlDataDocument` contains a

DataSet of its own and can be called DataSet-aware. Its internal DataSet offers a relational view of the XML data. Any data contained within the XML data document that does not map into the relational view is not lost, but becomes available to the DataSet's APIs

The `XMLDataDocument` is a constructor that takes a DataSet as a parameter. Any changes made to the `XmlDataDocument` are reflected in the DataSet and vice versa.

Now take the DataSet loaded in Listing 13-14 and manipulate the data with the `XmlDataDocument` and DOM APIs you're familiar with. Next, jump back into the world of `System.Data` and see that the DataSets underlying DataRows have been updated with the new data, as shown in Listing 13-15.

Listing 13-15: Changing DataSets using the DOM APIs from XmlDataDocument

VB

```vb
Dim connStr As String = "database=Northwind;Data Source=localhost; " _
        & "User id=sa;pwd=wrox"

Using conn As New SqlConnection(connStr)
    Dim command As New SqlCommand("select * from customers", conn)
    conn.Open()
    Dim ds As New DataSet()
    ds.DataSetName = "Customers"
    ds.Load(command.ExecuteReader(), LoadOption.OverwriteChanges, "Customer")
    'Response.ContentType = "text/xml"
    'ds.WriteXml(Response.OutputStream)


    'Added in Listing 13-15
    Dim doc As New XmlDataDocument(ds)
    doc.DataSet.EnforceConstraints = False
    Dim node As XmlNode = _
    doc.SelectSingleNode("//Customer[CustomerID = 'ANATR']/ContactTitle")
    node.InnerText = "Boss"
    doc.DataSet.EnforceConstraints = True

    Dim dr As DataRow = doc.GetRowFromElement(CType(node.ParentNode, XmlElement))
    Response.Write(dr("ContactName").ToString() & " is the ")
    Response.Write(dr("ContactTitle").ToString())
End Using
```

C#

```csharp
string connStr = "database=Northwind;Data Source=localhost; "
        + "User id=sa;pwd=wrox";

using (SqlConnection conn = new SqlConnection(connStr))
{
    SqlCommand command = new SqlCommand("select * from customers", conn);
    conn.Open();
    DataSet ds = new DataSet();
    ds.DataSetName = "Customers";
    ds.Load(command.ExecuteReader(), LoadOption.OverwriteChanges,"Customer");
    //Response.ContentType = "text/xml";
    //ds.WriteXml(Response.OutputStream);

    //Added in Listing 13-15
```

```
XmlDataDocument doc = new XmlDataDocument(ds);
doc.DataSet.EnforceConstraints = false;
XmlNode node = doc.SelectSingleNode(@"//Customer[CustomerID
    = 'ANATR']/ContactTitle");
node.InnerText = "Boss";
doc.DataSet.EnforceConstraints = true;

DataRow dr = doc.GetRowFromElement((XmlElement)node.ParentNode);
Response.Write(dr["ContactName"].ToString() + " is the ");
Response.Write(dr["ContactTitle"].ToString());
}
```

Listing 13-15 extends Listing 13-14 by first commenting out changing the HTTP ContentType and the call to DataSet.WriteXml. After the DataSet is loaded from the database, it is passed to the XmlDataDocument constructor. At this point, the XmlDataDocument and the DataSet refer to the same set of information. The EnforceConstraints property of the DataSet is set to false to allow changes to the DataSet. When EnforceConstraints is later set to true, if any constraint rules were broken, an exception is thrown. An XPath expression is passed to the DOM method SelectSingleNode, selecting the ContactTitle node of a particular customer, and its text is changed to Boss. Then by calling GetRowFromElement on the XmlDataDocument, the context jumps from the world of the XmlDocument back to the world of the DataSet. Column names are passed into the indexing property of the returned DataRow, and the output is shown in this line:

```
Ana Trujillo is the Boss
```

The data is loaded from the SQL server and then manipulated and edited with XmlDocument-style methods; a string is then built using a DataRow from the underlying DataSet.

XML is clearly more than just angle brackets. XML data can come from files, from databases, from information sets like the DataSet object, and certainly from the Web. Today, however, a considerable amount of data is stored in XML format, so a specific data source control has been added to ASP.NET 2.0 just for retrieving and working with XML data.

The XmlDataSource Control

The XmlDataSource control enables you to connect to your XML data and to use this data with any of the ASP.NET data-bound controls. Just like the SqlDataSource and the AccessDataSource controls, the XmlDataSource control also enables you not only to retrieve data, but also to insert, delete, and update data items.

> One unfortunate caveat of the new `XmlDataSource` is its `XPath` attribute does not support documents that use namespace qualification. Examples in this chapter use the `Books.xml` file with a default namespace of `http://examples.books.com`. It is very common for XML files to use multiple namespaces, including a default namespace. As you learned when you created an `XPathDocument` and queried it with XPath, the namespace in which an element exists is very important. The regrettable reality is, there is no way to use a namespace qualified XPath expression or to make the XmlDataSource Control aware of a list of prefix/namespace pairs via the `XmlNamespaceManager` class. However, the `XPath` function used in the `ItemTemplate` of the templated `DataList` control *can* take a `XmlNamespaceManager` as its second parameter and query XML returned from the `XmlDataSource` — as long as the control does not include an `XPath` attribute with namespace qualification or you can just omit it all together. That said, in order for these examples to work, you must remove the namespaces from your source XML and use XPath queries that include no namespace qualification, as shown in Listing 13-16.

You can use a `DataList` control or any DataBinding-aware control and connect to an `<asp:XmlDataSource>` control. The technique for binding a control directly to the `Books.xml` file is illustrated in Listing 13-16.

Listing 13-16 Using a DataList control to display XML content

```
<%@ Page Language="VB" AutoEventWireup="false" CodeFile="Default.aspx.vb"
Inherits="Default_aspx" %>
<html xmlns="http://www.w3.org/1999/xhtml" >
    <head id="Head1" runat="server">
        <title>XmlDataSource</title>
    </head>
    <body>
    <form id="form1" runat="server">
        <asp:datalist id="DataList1" DataSourceID="XmlDataSource1" runat="server">
            <ItemTemplate>
                <p><b><%# XPath("author/first-name") %>
                    <%# XPath("author/last-name")%></b>
                    wrote <%# XPath("title") %></p>
            </ItemTemplate>
        </asp:datalist>
        <asp:xmldatasource id="XmlDataSource1" runat="server"
            datafile="~/Books.xml"
            xpath="//bookstore/book"/>
    </form>
    </body>
</html>
```

This is a simple example, but it shows you the ease of using the `XmlDataSource` control. You should focus on two attributes in this example. The first is the `DataFile` attribute. This attribute points to the location of the XML file. Because the file resides in the root directory of the application, it is simply `~/Books.xml`. The next attribute included in the `XmlDataSource` control is the `XPath` attribute. The `XmlDataSource` control uses the `XPath` attribute for the filtering of XML data. In this case, the `XmlDataSource` control is taking everything within the `<book>` set of elements. The value `//bookstore/book` means that the

`XmlDataSource` control navigates to the `<bookstore>` element and then to the `<book>` element within the specified XML file and returns a list of all books.

The `DataList` control then must specify its `DataSourceID` as the `XmlDataSource` control. In the `<ItemTemplate>` section of the `DataList` control, you can retrieve specific values from the XML file by using XPath commands within the template. The XPath commands filter the data from the XML file. The first value retrieved is an element attribute (`author/first-name`) that is contained in the `<book>` element. If you are retrieving an attribute of an element, you preface the name of the attribute with an *at* (@) symbol. The next two XPath commands get the last name and the title of the book. Remember to separate nodes with a forward slash (/). When run in the browser, this code produces the results illustrated in the following list:

```
Benjamin Franklin wrote The Autobiography of Benjamin Franklin
Herman Melville wrote The Confidence Man
Sidas Plato wrote The Gorgias
```

Note that if you wrote the actual code, this entire exercise would be done entirely in the ASPX page itself!

Besides working from static XML files such as the `Books.xml` file shown earlier, the `XmlDataSource` control has the capability to work from dynamic, URL-accessible XML files. One popular XML format that is pervasive on the Internet today is the *weblog*. These *blogs*, or personal diaries, can be viewed either in the browser, through an RSS-aggregator, or as pure XML.

As you look at my blog in Figure 13-5, you can see the XML it produces when visited directly in the browser. (You can find a lot of blogs to play with for this example at `weblogs.asp.net`.)

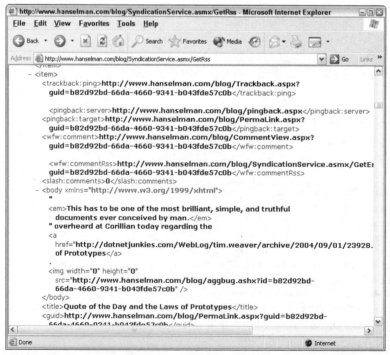

Figure 13-5

Now that you know the location of the XML from the blog, you can use this XML with the XmlDataSource control and display some of the results in a DataList control. The code for this example is shown in Listing 13-17.

Listing 13-17: Displaying an XML RSS blog feed

```
<%@ Page Language="VB"%>
<html xmlns="http://www.w3.org/1999/xhtml" >
    <head runat="server">
        <title>XmlDataSource</title>
    </head>
    <body>
    <form id="form1" runat="server">
        <asp:DataList ID="DataList1" Runat="server" DataSourceID="XmlDataSource1">
            <HeaderTemplate>
                <table border="1" cellpadding="3">
            </HeaderTemplate>
            <ItemTemplate>
                <tr><td><b><%# XPath("title") %></b><br />
                <i><%# XPath("pubDate") %></i><br />
                <%# XPath("description") %></td></tr>
            </ItemTemplate>
            <AlternatingItemTemplate>
                <tr bgcolor="LightGrey"><td><b><%# XPath("title") %></b><br />
                <i><%# XPath("pubDate") %></i><br />
                <%# XPath("description") %></td></tr>
            </AlternatingItemTemplate>
            <FooterTemplate>
                </table>
            </FooterTemplate>
        </asp:DataList>
        <asp:XmlDataSource ID="XmlDataSource1" Runat="server"
        DataFile="http://www.hanselman.com/blog/SyndicationService.asmx/GetRss"
        XPath="rss/channel/item">
        </asp:XmlDataSource>
    </form>
    </body>
</html>
```

Looking at the code in Listing 13-17, you can see that the DataFile points to a URL where the XML is retrieved. The XPath property filters and returns all the <item> elements from the RSS feed. The DataList control creates an HTML table and pulls out specific data elements from the RSS feed, such as the <title>, <pubDate>, and <description> elements.

Running this page in the browser, you get something similar to the results shown in Figure 13-6.

This approach also works with XML Web services, even ones for which you can pass in parameters using HTTP-GET. You just set up the DataFile property value in the following manner:

```
DataFile="http://www.someserver.com/GetWeather.asmx/ZipWeather?zipcode=63301"
```

There is no end to the number of places you can find and use XML: files, databases, Web sites, and services. Sometimes you will want to manipulate the XML via queries or programmatically, and sometimes you will want to take the XML "tree" and transform it into a tree of a different form.

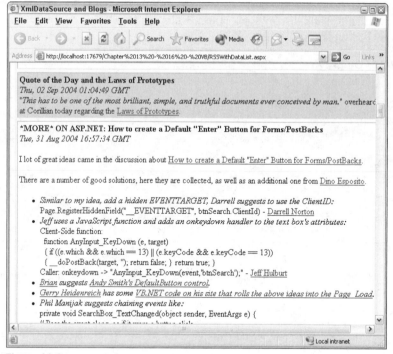

Figure 13-6

XSLT

XSLT is a tree transformation language also written in XML syntax. It's a strange hybrid of a declarative and a programmatic language, and some programmers would argue that it's not a language at all. Others, who use a number of XSLT scripting extensions, would argue that it is a very powerful language. Regardless of the controversy, XSLT transformations are very useful for changing the structure of XML files quickly and easily, often using a very declarative syntax.

The best way to familiarize yourself with XSLT is to look at an example. Remember that the Books.xml file used in this chapter is a list of books and their authors. The XSLT in Listing 13-18 takes that document and transforms it into a document that is a list of authors.

Listing 13-18: Books.xslt

XSLT

```
<?xml version="1.0" encoding="utf-8" ?>
<xsl:stylesheet xmlns:xsl="http://www.w3.org/1999/XSL/Transform" version="1.0">
    <xsl:template match="/">
        <xsl:element name="Authors">
            <xsl:apply-templates select="//book"/>
        </xsl:element>
    </xsl:template>
    <xsl:template match="book">
```

```
        <xsl:element name="Author">
            <xsl:value-of select="author/first-name"/>
            <xsl:text> </xsl:text>
            <xsl:value-of select="author/last-name"/>
        </xsl:element>
    </xsl:template>
</xsl:stylesheet>
```

Remember that XSLT is XML vocabulary in its own right, so it makes sense that it has its own namespace and namespace prefix. XSLT is typically structured with a series of templates that match elements in the source document. The XSLT document doesn't describe what the result looks like as much as it declares what steps must occur for the transformation to succeed. Remembering that your goal is an XML file with a list of authors, you match on the root node of `Books.xml` and output a root element for the resulting document named `<Authors>`. Then `<xsl:apply-templates select="//book"/>` indicates to the processor that it should continue looking for templates that, in this case, match the XPath expression `//book`. Below the first template is a second template that handles all book matches. It outputs a new element named `<Author>`.

XSLT is very focused on context, so it is often helpful to imagine a cursor that is on a particular element of the source document. Immediately after outputting the `<Author>` element, the processor is in the middle of the template match on the `book` element. All XPath expressions in this example are relative to the `book` element. So the `<xsl:value-of select="author/first-name">` directive searches for the author's first name relative to the `book` element. The `<xsl:text> </xsl:text>` directive is interesting to note because it is explicit and a reminder that a difference exists between significant white space and insignificant white space. It is important, for example, that a space is put between the author's first and last names, so it must be called out explicitly.

The resulting document is shown in Figure 13-7.

This example only scratches the surface of XSLT's power. Although a full exploration of XSLT is beyond the scope of this book, other books by Wrox Press cover the topic more fully. Remember that the .NET Framework implements the 1.0 implementation of XSLT.

Figure 13-7 shows the resulting XML as the `Books.xslt` transformation is applied to `Books.xml`. You can apply XSLT transformations in a number of ways, both declarative and programmatic. These are described in the following sections.

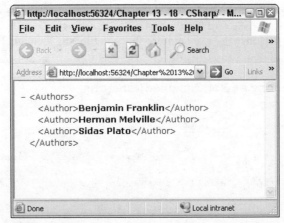

Figure 13-7

XslCompiledTransform

The `XslTransform` class was used in the .NET Framework 1.*x* for XSLT transformation. In the .NET Framework 2.0, the `XsltCompiledTransform` class is the new XSLT processor. It is such an improvement that `XslTransform` is deprecated and marked with the `Obsolete` attribute. The compiler will now advise you to use `XslCompiledTransform`. The system generates MSIL code on the call to `Compile()` and the XSLT executes many times faster than previous techniques. This compilation technique also includes full debugging support from within Visual Studio, which is covered a little later in this chapter.

> The `XPathDocument` **is absolutely optimized for XSLT transformations and should be used instead of the** `XmlDocument` **if you would like a 15- to 30-percent performance gain in your transformations. Remember that XSLT contains XPath, and when you use XPath, use an** `XPathDocument`. **According to the team's numbers, XSLT is 400 percent faster in .NET Framework 2.0.**

`XslCompiledTransform` has only two methods: `Load` and `Transform`. The compilation happens without any effort on your part. Listing 13-19 loads the `Books.xml` file into an `XPathDocument` and transforms it using `Books.xslt` and an `XslCompiledTransform`. Even though there are only two methods, there are *fourteen* overrides for `Transform` and six for `Load`. That may seem a little daunting at first, but there is a simple explanation.

The `Load` method can handle loading a stylesheet from a string, an `XmlReader`, or any class that implements `IXPathNavigable`. An `XsltSettings` object can be passed in optionally with any of the previous three overloads, giving you six to choose from. `XsltSettings` includes options to enable the `document()` XSLT–specific function via the `XsltSettings.EnableDocumentFunction` property or enable embedded script blocks within XSLT via `XsltSettings.EnableScript`. These advanced options are disabled by default for security reasons. Alternatively, you can retrieve a pre-populated `XsltSettings` object via the static property `XsltSettings.TrustedXslt`, which has enabled both these settings.

Note in Listing 13-19 that the `Response.Output` property eliminates an unnecessary string allocation. In the example, `Response.Output` is a `TextWriter` wrapped in an `XmlTextWriter` and passed directly to the `Execute` method.

> **If you think it is odd that the class that does the work is called the** `XslCompiledTransform` **and not the** `XsltCompiledTransform`, **but** `XsltSettings` **includes the** *t*, **remember that the** *t* **in XSLT means** *transformation*.

Listing 13-19: Executing an XsltCompiledTransform

VB

```
Response.ContentType = "text/xml"

Dim xsltFile As String = Path.Combine(Request.PhysicalApplicationPath, _
    "books.xslt")
Dim xmlFile As String = Path.Combine(Request.PhysicalApplicationPath, "books.xml")

Dim xslt As New XslCompiledTransform()
```

```
xslt.Load(xsltFile)

Dim doc As New XPathDocument(xmlFile)
xslt.Transform(doc, New XmlTextWriter(Response.Output))
```

C#
```
Response.ContentType = "text/xml";

string xsltFile = Path.Combine(Request.PhysicalApplicationPath, "books.xslt");
string xmlFile = Path.Combine(Request.PhysicalApplicationPath, "books.xml");

XslCompiledTransform xslt = new XslCompiledTransform();
xslt.Load(xsltFile);

XPathDocument doc = new XPathDocument(xmlFile);
xslt.Transform(doc, new XmlTextWriter(Response.Output));
```

Named arguments may be passed into an XslTransform or XslCompiledTransform if the stylesheet takes parameters. The following code snippet illustrates the use of XslArgumentList:

```
XslTransform transformer = new XslTransform();
transformer.Load("foo.xslt");

XslArgumentList args = new XslArgumentList();
args.Add("ID", "SOMEVALUE");

transformer.Transform("foo.xml", args, Response.OutputStream);
```

The XML resulting from an XSLT transformation can be manipulated with any of the system.XML APIs that have been discussed in this chapter. One common use of XSLT is to flatten hierarchical and, sometimes, relational XML documents into a format that is more conducive to output as HTML. The results of these transformations to HTML can be placed inline within an existing ASPX document.

XML Web Server Control

XSLT transformations can also be a very quick way to get information out to the browser as HTML. Consider this technique as yet another tool in your toolbox. HTML is a tree, and HTML is a cousin of XML, so an XML tree can be transformed into an HTML tree. A benefit of using XSLT transformations to create large amounts of static text, like HTML tables, is that the XSLT file can be kept external to the application. You can make quick changes to its formatting without a recompile. A problem when using XSLT transformations is that they can become large and very unruly when someone attempts to use them to generate the entire user interface experience. The practice was in vogue in the mid-nineties to use XSLT transformations to generate entire Web sites, but the usefulness of this technique breaks down when complex user interactions are introduced. That said, XSLT has a place, not only for transforming data from one format to another, but also for creating reasonable chunks of your user interface — as long as you don't go overboard.

In the next example, the output of the XSLT is HTML rather than XML. Note the use of the <xsl:output method="html"> directive. When this directive is omitted, the default output of an XSLT transformation is XML. This template begins with a match on the root node. It is creating an HTML fragment rather than an entire HTML document. Its first output is the <h3> tag with some static text. Next comes a table tag and the header row, and then the <xsl:apply-template> element selects all books within the source XML document. For every book element in the source document, the second template is invoked with the

489

responsibility of outputting one table row per book. Calls to `<xsl:value-of>` select each of the book's subnodes and outputs them within the `<td>` tags. This is seen in Listing 13-20, which follows.

Listing 13-20: BookstoHTML.xslt used with the XML Web Server Control

XSLT

```
<?xml version="1.0" encoding="utf-8" ?>
<xsl:stylesheet xmlns:xsl="http://www.w3.org/1999/XSL/Transform"
        xmlns:b="http://example.books.com" version="1.0">
    <xsl:output method="html"/>
    <xsl:template match="/">
        <h3>List of Authors</h3>
        <table border="1">
            <tr>
                <th>First</th><th>Last</th>
            </tr>
            <xsl:apply-templates select="//b:book"/>
        </table>
    </xsl:template>
    <xsl:template match="b:book">
        <tr>
            <td><xsl:value-of select="b:author/b:first-name"/></td>
            <td><xsl:value-of select="b:author/b:last-name"/></td>
        </tr>
    </xsl:template>
</xsl:stylesheet>
```

ASPX

```
<%@ Page Language="VB" %>
<html xmlns="http://www.w3.org/1999/xhtml" >
    <head runat="server"><title>HTML/XSLT Transformation</title></head>
    <body>
        <form id="form1" runat="server">
            <div>
                <asp:Xml ID="Xml1" Runat="server"
                    DocumentSource="~/Books.xml"
                    TransformSource="~/bookstoHTML.xslt"/>
            </div>
        </form>
    </body>
</html>
```

Notice the use of namespace prefixes in Listing 13-20. The source namespace is declared with the prefix b as in xmlns:b="http://example.books.com" and the b prefix is subsequently used in XPath expressions like //b:book. The XSLT in Listing 13-20 can use the XSLTCommand to perform this transformation on the server-side because the entire operation is declarative and requires just two inputs — the XML document and the XSLT document. The XML Web server control makes the transformation easy to perform from the ASPX page and does not require any language-specific features. The DocumentSource property of the control holds the path to the Books.xml file, whereas the TransformSource property holds the path to the BookstoHTML.xslt file:

```
<h3>List of Authors</h3>
<table border="1">
    <tr>
        <th>First</th>
        <th>Last</th>
```

```
        </tr>
        <tr>
            <td>Benjamin</td>
            <td>Franklin</td>
        </tr>
        <tr>
            <td>Herman</td>
            <td>Melville</td>
        </tr>
        <tr>
            <td>Sidas</td>
            <td>Plato</td>
        </tr>
    </table>
```

The results of this transformation are output inline to this HTML document and appear between the two <div> tags. You see the results of this HTML fragment in the previous code and in the browser's output shown in Figure 13-8.

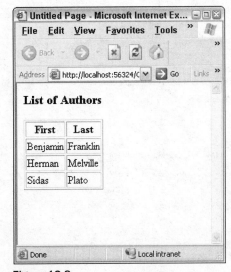

Figure 13-8

XSLT Debugging

By passing the Boolean value true into the constructor of the XslCompiledTransform class, you can step into your XSLT transformations within the Microsoft Development Environment.

```
Dim xslt As New XslCompiledTransform(True)
```

Change the constructor of the `XslCompiledTransform` to `true` in Listing 13-19 and set a breakpoint on the `Transform` method. When you reach that breakpoint, press F11 to step into the transformation. Figure 13-9 shows a debugging session of the `Books.xslt`/`Books.xml` transformation in process.

In the past, debugging XSLT was largely an opaque process that required a third-party application to troubleshoot. The addition of debugging XSLT to Visual Studio means that your XML experience is just that much more integrated and seamless.

Databases and XML

You have seen that XML can come from any source whether it be a Web service, a file on disk, an XML fragment returned from a Web server, or a database. SQL server and ADO have rich support for XML, starting with the `ExecuteXmlReader` method of the `System.Data.SqlCommand` class. Additional support for XML on SQL Server 2000 is included with SQLXML 3.0 and its XML extensions and SQL Server 2005 has native XML data type support built right in.

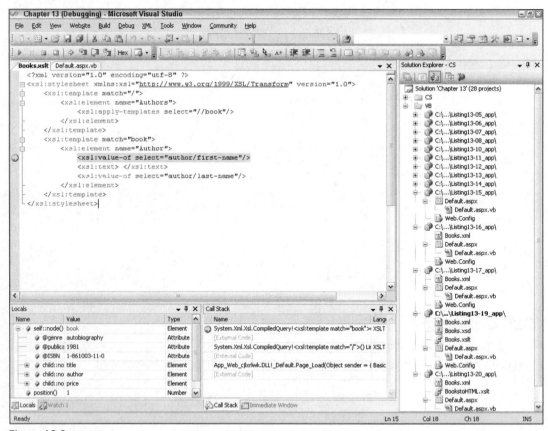

Figure 13-9

FOR XML AUTO

You can modify a SQL query to return XML with the FOR XML AUTO clause. If you take a simple query such as select * from customers, you just change the statement like so:

```
select * from customers as customer FOR XML AUTO
```

XML AUTO returns XML fragments rather than a full XML document with a root node. Each row in the database becomes one element; each column in the database becomes one attribute on the element. Notice that each element in the following result set is named Customers because the select clause is from customers:

```
<Customers CustomerID="ALFKI" CompanyName="Alfreds Futterkiste" ContactName="Maria
Anders" ContactTitle="Sales Representative" Address="Obere Str. 57" City="Berlin"
PostalCode="12209" Country="Germany" Phone="030-0074321" Fax="030-0076545" />
<Customers CustomerID="ANATR" CompanyName="Ana Trujillo Emparedados y helados"
ContactName="Ana Trujillo" ContactTitle="Owner" Address="Avda. de la Constitución
2222" City="México D.F." PostalCode="05021" Country="Mexico" Phone="(5) 555-4729"
Fax="(5) 555-3745" />
```

If you add ELEMENTS to the query like so

```
select * from customers FOR XML AUTO, ELEMENTS
```

you get an XML fragment like this:

```
<Customers>
    <CustomerID>ALFKI</CustomerID>
    <CompanyName>Alfreds Futterkiste</CompanyName>
    <ContactName>Maria Anders</ContactName>
    <ContactTitle>Sales Representative</ContactTitle>
    <Address>Obere Str. 57</Address>
    <City>Berlin</City>
    <PostalCode>12209</PostalCode>
    <Country>Germany</Country>
    <Phone>030-0074321</Phone>
    <Fax>030-0076545</Fax>
</Customers>
<Customers>
    <CustomerID>ANATR</CustomerID>
    <CompanyName>Ana Trujillo Emparedados y helados</CompanyName>
    <ContactName>Ana Trujillo</ContactName>
    <ContactTitle>Owner</ContactTitle>
    <Address>Avda. de la Constitución 2222</Address>
    <City>México D.F.</City>
    <PostalCode>05021</PostalCode>
    <Country>Mexico</Country>
    <Phone>(5) 555-4729</Phone>
    <Fax>(5) 555-3745</Fax>
</Customers>
```

The previous example is just a fragment with no root node. To perform an XSLT transformation, you need a root node, and you probably want to change the <Customers> elements to <Customer>. By using an alias in the select statement, you can affect the name of each row's element. The query select * from Customers as Customer for XML AUTO, ELEMENTS changes the name of the element to <Customer>.

Now, put together all the things you've learned from this chapter and create an XmlDocument, edit and manipulate it, retrieve data from SQL Server as an XmlReader, and style that information with XSLT into an HTML table all in just a few lines of code.

First, add a root node to the document retrieved by the SQL query select * from Customers as Customer for XML AUTO, ELEMENTS as seen in Listing 13-21.

Listing 13-21: Retrieving XML from SQL Server 2000 using FOR XML AUTO

VB

```vb
Dim connStr As String = "database=Northwind;Data Source=localhost;" & _
    " User id=sa;pwd=wrox"
Dim x As New XmlDocument()
Dim xpathnav As XPathNavigator = x.CreateNavigator()
Using conn As New SqlConnection(connStr)
    conn.Open()
    Dim command As New SqlCommand("select * from Customers as Customer " & _
        "for XML AUTO, ELEMENTS", conn)
    Using xw As XmlWriter = xpathnav.PrependChild()
        xw.WriteStartElement("Customers")
        Using xr As XmlReader = command.ExecuteXmlReader()
            xw.WriteNode(xr, True)
        End Using
        xw.WriteEndElement()
    End Using
End Using
Response.ContentType = "text/xml"
x.Save(Response.Output)
```

C#

```csharp
string connStr = "database=Northwind;Data Source=localhost;User id=sa;pwd=wrox";
XmlDocument x = new XmlDocument();
XPathNavigator xpathnav = x.CreateNavigator();
using (SqlConnection conn = new SqlConnection(connStr))
{
    conn.Open();
    SqlCommand command = new SqlCommand(
        "select * from Customers as Customer for XML AUTO, ELEMENTS", conn);
    using (XmlWriter xw = xpathnav.PrependChild())
    {
        xw.WriteStartElement("Customers");
        using (XmlReader xr = command.ExecuteXmlReader())
        {
            xw.WriteNode(xr, true);
        }
        xw.WriteEndElement();
    }
}
```

```
}
Response.ContentType = "text/xml";
x.Save(Response.Output);
```

This code creates an XmlDocument called Customers. Then it executes the SQL command and retrieves the XML data into an XmlReader. An XPathNavigator is created from the XmlDocument, and a child node is prepended to the document. A single call to the WriteNode method of the XmlWriter retrieved from the XPathDocument moves the entire XML fragment into the well-formed XDocument. Because the SQL statement contained from Customers as Customer as a table alias, each XML element is named <Customer>. Then, for this example, the resulting XML document is output directly to the response object. You see the resulting XML in the browser shown in Figure 13-10.

Figure 13-10

Of course, it's nice to see the resulting XML, but it's far more useful to style that information with XSLT. The XML Web Server control mentioned earlier is perfect for this task. However, in Listing 13-22, rather than setting both the TransformSource and DocumentSource properties as in Listing 13-20, you set only the TransformSource property at design time, and the XmlDocument is the one created in the code-behind of Listing 13-21.

Listing 13-22: The ASPX Page and XSLT to style the XML from SQL Server

ASPX

```
<%@ Page Language="C#" CodeFile="Default.aspx.cs" Inherits="Default_aspx" %>
<asp:xml id="Xml1" runat="server" transformsource="~/customersToHtml.xslt"/>
```

XSLT

```
<?xml version="1.0" encoding="utf-8" ?>
<xsl:stylesheet xmlns:xsl="http://www.w3.org/1999/XSL/Transform" version="1.0">
    <xsl:output method="html"/>
    <xsl:template match="/">
        <h3>List of Customers</h3>
        <table border="1">
            <tr>
                <th>Company Name</th><th>Contact Name</th><th>Contact Title</th>
            </tr>
            <xsl:apply-templates select="//Customer"/>
        </table>
    </xsl:template>
    <xsl:template match="Customer">
        <tr>
            <td><xsl:value-of select="CompanyName"/></td>
            <td><xsl:value-of select="ContactName"/></td>
            <td><xsl:value-of select="ContactTitle"/></td>
        </tr>
    </xsl:template>
</xsl:stylesheet>
```

VB

```
'Response.ContentType = "text/xml"
'x.Save(Response.Output)
Xml1.XPathNavigator = xpathnav
```

C#

```
//Response.ContentType = "text/xml";
//x.Save(Response.Output);
Xml1.XPathNavigator = xpathnav;
```

In the code-behind file, the lines that set ContentType and write the XML to the Response object are commented out, and instead the XPathNavigator from the XmlDocument that is manipulated in Listing 13-21 is set as a property of the XML Web Server control. The control then performs the XSLT Stylesheet transformation, and the results are output to the browser as shown in Figure 13-11.

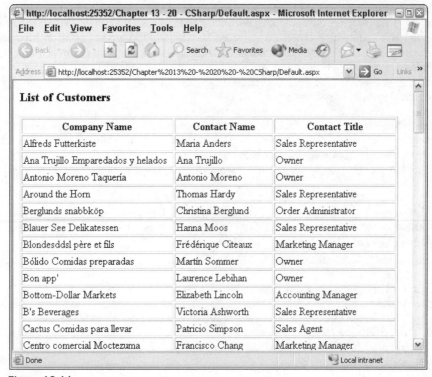

Figure 13-11

You have an infinite amount of flexibility within the `System.Xml` and `System.Data` namespaces. Microsoft has put together a fantastic series of APIs that interoperate beautifully. When you're creating your own APIs that expose or consume XML, compare them to the APIs that Microsoft has provided—if you expose your data over an `XmlReader` or `IXPathNavigable` interface, you are sure to make your users much happier. Passing XML around with these more flexible APIs (rather than as simple and opaque strings) provides a much more comfortable and intuitive expression of the XML information set.

> Remember that the `XmlReader` that is returned from `SqlCommand.ExecuteXmlReader()` is holding its SQL connection open, so you must call `Close()` when you're done using the `XmlReader`. The easiest way to ensure that this is done is the `using` statement. An `XmlReader` implements `IDisposable` and calls `Close()` for you as the variable leaves the scope of the `using` statement.

SQL Server Yukon 2005 and the XML DataType

You've seen that retrieving data from SQL Server 2000 is straightforward, if a little limited. SQL Server 2005, originally codenamed Yukon, includes a number of very powerful XML-based features. Dare Obasanjo, an XML Program Manager at Microsoft has said, "The rise of the ROX [Relational-Object-XML] database has begun." SQL Server 2005 is definitely leading the way.

One of the things that is particularly tricky about mapping XML and the XML information set to the relational structure that SQL Server shares with most databases is that most XML data has a hierarchical structure. Relational databases structure hierarchical data with foreign key relationships. Relational data often has no order, but the order of the elements within XmlDocument is very important. SQL Server 2005 introduces a new data type called, appropriately, XML. Previously, data was stored in an nvarchar or other string-based data type. SQL Server 2005 can now have a table with a column of type XML, and each XML data type can have associated XML Schema.

The FOR XML syntax is improved to include the TYPE directive, so a query that includes FOR XML TYPE returns the results as a single XML-typed value. This XML data is returned with a new class called System.Data.SqlXml. It exposes its data as an XmlReader retrieved by calling Sql.Xml.CreateReader, so you'll find it to be very easy to use because it works like all the other examples you've seen in this chapter.

> **In a DataSet returned from SQL Server 2005, XML data defaults to being a string unless** DataAdapter.ReturnProviderSpecificTypes = true **is set or a schema is loaded ahead of time to specify the column type.**

The XML data type stores data as a new internal binary format that is more efficient to query. The programmer doesn't have to worry about the details of how the XML is stored if it continues to be available on the XQuery or in XmlReader. You can mix column types in a way that was not possible in SQL Server 2000. You're used to returning data as either a DataSet or an XmlReader. With SQL Server 2005, you can return a DataSet where some columns contain XML and some contain traditional SQL Server data types.

Summary

XML and the XML InfoSet is pervasive in the .NET Framework and in ASP.NET 2.0. All ASP.NET 2.0 configuration files now include associated XML Schema, and the Visual Studio Editor is even smarter about XML documents that use XSDs.

XmlReader and XmlWriter provide unique and incredibly fast ways to consume and create XML; they now also include even better support for mapping XML Schema types to CLR types, as well as other improvements. The XmlDocument and XPathDocument return in .NET 2.0 with API additions and numerous performance improvements, while the XmlDataDocument straddles the world of System.Data and System.Xml. ASP.NET 2.0 and .NET 2.0 include support for XSLT via not only the new XslCompiledTransform but also the XML Web Server Controls, and tops it all with XSLT debugging support for compiled stylesheets.

All these ways to manipulate XML via the Base Class Library are married with XML support in SQL Server 2000 and 2005. SQL Server 2005 also includes the new XML data type for storing XML in a first class column type.

14

Site Navigation

The Web applications that you develop generally have more than a single page to them. Usually you create a number of Web pages that are interconnected in some fashion. If you also build the navigation around your pages, you make it easy for the end user to successfully work through your application in a straightforward manner.

Currently, you must choose among a number of different ways to expose the paths through your application to the end user. The difficult task of site navigation is compounded when you continue to add pages to the overall application.

The present method for building navigation within Web applications is to sprinkle pages with hyperlinks. Hyperlinks are generally added to Web pages by using include files or user controls. They can also be directly hard-coded onto a page so that they appear in the header or the sidebar of the page being viewed. The difficulties in working with navigation become worse when you move pages around or change page names. Sometimes developers are forced to go to each and every page in the application just to change some aspect of the navigation.

ASP.NET 2.0 tackles this problem with the introduction of a navigation system that makes it quite trivial to manage how end users work through the applications you create. This new capability in ASP.NET is complex; but the great thing is that it can be as simple as you need it to be, or you can actually get in deep and control every aspect of how it works.

The new site navigation system includes the capability to define your entire site in an XML file that is called a *site map*. After you define a new site map, you can work with it programmatically using the SiteMap class. Another addition in ASP.NET 2.0 is a new data provider that is specifically developed to work with site map files and to bind them to a new series of navigation-based server controls. This chapter looks at all these components in the new ASP.NET 2.0 navigation system. The following section introduces site maps.

XML-Based Site Maps

Although a site map is not a required element (as you see later), one of the common first steps you take in working with the new ASP.NET 2.0 navigation system is building a site map for your application. A site map is an XML description of your site's structure.

You use this site map to define the layout of all the pages in your application and how they relate to one another. If you do this according to the new site map standard, you interact with this navigation information using either the new `SiteMap` class or the new SiteMapDataSource control. By using the SiteMapDataSource control, you can then bind the information in the site map file to a variety of data-binding controls, including the new navigation server controls provided by ASP.NET 2.0.

To create a new site map file for your application, add a site map or an XML file to your application. When asked, you name the XML file `Web.sitemap`; this file is already in place if you select the Site Map option. The file is named `Web` and has the new file extension of `.sitemap`. Take a look at an example of a `.sitemap` file in Listing 14-1.

Listing 14-1: An example of a Web.sitemap file

```xml
<?xml version="1.0" encoding="utf-8" ?>

<siteMap xmlns="http://schemas.microsoft.com/AspNet/SiteMap-File-1.0" >
    <siteMapNode title="Home" description="Home Page" url="Default.aspx">
        <siteMapNode title="News" description="The Latest News" url="News.aspx">
            <siteMapNode title="U.S." description="U.S. News"
             url="News.aspx?cat=us" />
            <siteMapNode title="World" description="World News"
             url="News.aspx?cat=world" />
            <siteMapNode title="Technology" description="Technology News"
             url="News.aspx?cat=tech" />
            <siteMapNode title="Sports" description="Sports News"
             url="News.aspx?cat=sport" />
        </siteMapNode>
        <siteMapNode title="Finance" description="The Latest Financial Information"
         url="Finance.aspx">
            <siteMapNode title="Quotes" description="Get the Latest Quotes"
             url="Quotes.aspx" />
            <siteMapNode title="Markets" description="The Latest Market Information"
             url="Markets.aspx">
                <siteMapNode title="U.S. Market Report"
                 description="Looking at the U.S. Market" url="MarketsUS.aspx" />
                <siteMapNode title="NYSE"
                 description="The New York Stock Exchange" url="NYSE.aspx" />
            </siteMapNode>
            <siteMapNode title="Funds" description="Mutual Funds"
             url="Funds.aspx" />
        </siteMapNode>
        <siteMapNode title="Weather" description="The Latest Weather"
         url="Weather.aspx" />
    </siteMapNode>
</siteMap>
```

So what does this file give you? Well, it gives you a logical structure that ASP.NET 2.0 can now use in the rest of the navigation system it provides. Next, examine how this file is constructed.

The root node of this XML file is a `<siteMap>` element. Only one `<siteMap>` element can exist in the file. Within the `<siteMap>` element, there is a `<siteMapNode>` element. This is generally the start page of the application. In the case of the file in Listing 14-1, the root `<siteMapNode>` points to the `Default.aspx` page, the start page:

```
<siteMapNode title="Home" description="Home Page" url="Default.aspx">
```

The following table describes the most common attributes in the `<siteMapNode>` element.

Attribute	Description
title	The `title` attribute provides a textual description of the link. The `String` value used here is the text used for the link.
description	The `description` attribute not only reminds you what the link is for, but it is also used for the `ToolTip` attribute on the link. The `ToolTip` attribute is the yellow box that shows up next to the link when the end user hovers the cursor over the link for a couple of seconds.
url	The `url` attribute describes where the file is located in the solution. If the file is in the root directory, simply use the filename, such as `"Default.aspx"`. If the file is located in a subfolder, be sure to include the folders in the String value used in this attribute. For example, "`MySubFolder/Markets.aspx`".

After you have the first `<siteMapNode>` in place, you can place as many additional `<siteMapNode>` elements as you need. You can also create additional link-levels by creating child `<siteMapNode>` elements for any parent `<siteMapNode>` in the structure.

The example in Listing 14-1 gives the application the following navigation structure:

```
Home
    News
        U.S.
        World
        Technology
        Sports
    Finance
        Quotes
        Markets
            U.S. Market Report
            NYSE
        Funds
    Weather
```

You can see that this structure goes down three levels in some places. One of the easiest places to use this file is with the new SiteMapPath server control that now comes with ASP.NET 2.0. The new SiteMapPath server control in ASP.NET 2.0 is built to work specifically with the new `.sitemap` files.

SiteMapPath Server Control

It is quite easy to use the `.sitemap` file you just created with the new SiteMapPath server control provided with ASP.NET 2.0. You find this new control in the Navigation section of the Visual Studio 2005 IDE.

The SiteMapPath control creates navigation functionality that you once might have either created yourself or have seen elsewhere in Web pages on the Internet. The SiteMapPath control creates what some refer to as *breadcrumb navigation*. This is a linear path defining where the end user is in the navigation structure. The Reuters.com Web site, shown in Figure 14-1, uses this type of navigation. A black arrow points out the breadcrumb navigation used on the page.

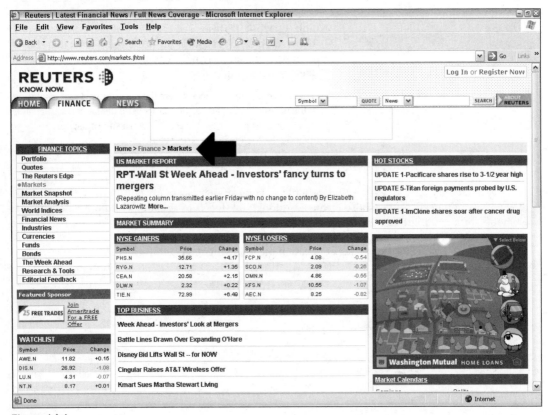

Figure 14-1

The purpose of this type of navigation is to show end users where they are in relation to the rest of the site. Traditionally, coding this kind of navigation has been tricky, to say the least; but now with the introduction of the SiteMapPath server control, you should find coding for this type of navigation a breeze.

You should first create an application that has the Web.sitemap file created in Listing 14-1. From there, create a WebForm called MarketsUS.aspx. This file is defined in the Web.sitemap file as being on the lowest tier of files in the application.

The SiteMapPath control is so easy to work with that it doesn't even require a datasource control to hook it up to the Web.sitemap file where it infers all its information. All you do is drag and drop a SiteMapPath control onto your MarketsUS.aspx page. In the end, you should have a page like the one shown in Listing 14-2.

Listing 14-2: Using the Web.sitemap file with a SiteMapPath server control

```
<%@ Page Language="VB" %>

<html xmlns="http://www.w3.org/1999/xhtml" >
<head runat="server">
    <title>Using the SiteMapPath Server Control</title>
</head>
<body>
    <form id="form1" runat="server">
        <asp:SiteMapPath ID="Sitemappath1" Runat="server">
        </asp:SiteMapPath>
    </form>
</body>
</html>
```

Not much to it, is there? It really is that easy. Run this page and you see the results shown in Figure 14-2.

This screen shot shows that you are on the U.S. Market Report page at MarketsUS.aspx. As an end user, you can see that this page is part of the Markets section of the site; Markets, in turn, is part of the Finance section of the site. With breadcrumb navigation, end users who understand the structure of the site and their place in it can quickly select the links to navigate to any location in the site.

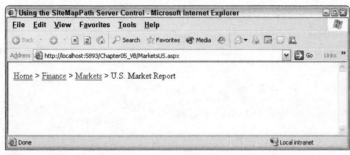

Figure 14-2

If you hover your mouse over the Finance link, you see a tooltip appear after a couple of seconds, as shown in Figure 14-3.

Figure 14-3

This tooltip, which reads The Latest Financial Information, comes from the description attribute of the <siteMapNode> element in the Web.sitemap file.

```
<siteMapNode title="Finance" description="The Latest Financial Information"
   url="Finance.aspx">
```

The SiteMapPath control works automatically requiring very little work on your part. You just add the basic control to your page, and the control automatically creates the breadcrumb navigation you have just seen. However, you can use the properties discussed in the following sections to modify the control's appearance and behavior.

The PathSeparator Property

One important style property for the SiteMapPath control is the PathSeparator property. By default, the SiteMapPath control uses a greater than sign (>) to separate the link elements. You can change this by reassigning a new value to the PathSeparator property. Listing 14-3 illustrates the use of this property.

Listing 14-3: Changing the PathSeparator value

```
<asp:SiteMapPath ID="Sitemappath1" Runat="server" PathSeparator=" | ">
</asp:SiteMapPath>
```

Or

```
<asp:SiteMapPath ID="Sitemappath1" Runat="server">
   <PathSeparatorTemplate> | </PathSeparatorTemplate>
</asp:SiteMapPath>
```

The SiteMapPath control in this example uses the pipe character (|), which is found above the Enter key. When it is rendered, you get the results shown in Figure 14-4.

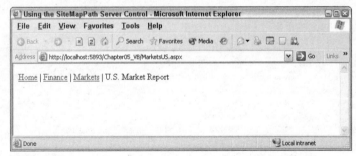

Figure 14-4

As you can see, you can use either the `PathSeparator` property or the `<PathSeparatorTemplate>` element within the SiteMapPath control.

With the use of the `PathSeparator` property or the `<PathSeparatorTemplate>` element, it is quite easy to specify what you want to use to separate the links in the breadcrumb navigation, but you might also want to give this pipe some visual style as well. You can add a `<PathSeparatorStyle>` node to your SiteMapPath control. An example of this is shown in Listing 14-4.

Listing 14-4: Adding style to the PathSeparator property

```
<asp:SiteMapPath ID="Sitemappath1" Runat="server" PathSeparator=" | ">
    <PathSeparatorStyle Font-Bold="true" Font-Names="Verdana" ForeColor="#663333"
    BackColor="#cccc66"></PathSeparatorStyle>
</asp:SiteMapPath>
```

Okay, it may not be pretty (I am not much of a designer), but by using the `<PathSeparatorStyle>` element with the SiteMapPath control, I am able to change the visual appearance of the separator elements. The results are shown in Figure 14-5.

Figure 14-5

Using these constructs, you can also add an image as the separator, as illustrated in Listing 14-5.

Listing 14-5: Using an image as the separator

```
<%@ Page Language="VB" %>

<html xmlns="http://www.w3.org/1999/xhtml" >
<head runat="server">
    <title>Using the SiteMapPath Server Control</title>
</head>
<body>
    <form id="form1" runat="server">
        <asp:SiteMapPath ID="SiteMapPath1" Runat="server">
            <PathSeparatorTemplate>
                <asp:Image ID="Image1" Runat="server" ImageUrl="divider.gif" />
            </PathSeparatorTemplate>
        </asp:SiteMapPath>
    </form>
</body>
</html>
```

To utilize an image as the separator between the links, you use the `<PathSeparatorTemplate>` element and place an Image control within it. In fact, you can place any type of control between the navigation links that the SiteMapPath control produces.

The PathDirection Property

Another interesting property to use with the SiteMapPath control is `PathDirection`. This property changes the direction of the links generated in the output. Only two settings are possible for this property: `RootToCurrent` and `CurrentToRoot`.

The Root link is the first link in the display. This is usually the Home page. The Current link is the link for the page currently being displayed. By default, this property is set to `RootToCurrent`. Changing the example to `CurrentToRoot` produces the results shown in Figure 14-6.

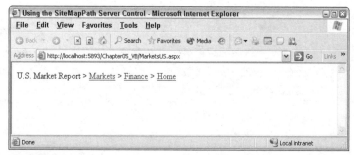

Figure 14-6

The ParentLevelsDisplayed Property

In some cases, your navigation may go quite deep. You can see on the site map, shown in Listing 14-1, that you go three pages deep, which isn't a big deal. Some of you, however, might be dealing with sites that go quite a number of pages deeper. In these cases, it might be bit silly to use the SiteMapPath control. Doing so would display a huge list of pages.

In a case like this, you can turn to the `ParentLevelsDisplayed` property that is part of the SiteMapPath control. When set, this property displays pages only as deep as specified. Therefore, if you are using the SiteMapPath control with the `Web.sitemap`, as shown in Listing 14-1, and you give the `ParentLevelsDisplayed` property a value of 3, you don't notice any change to your page. It already displays the path three pages deep. If you change this value to 2, however, the SiteMapPath control is constructed as follows:

```
<asp:SiteMapPath ID="Sitemappath1" Runat="server" ParentLevelsDisplayed="2">
</asp:SiteMapPath>
```

Notice the result of this change in Figure 14-7. The SiteMapPath control shows links only two pages deep and doesn't show the Home page link.

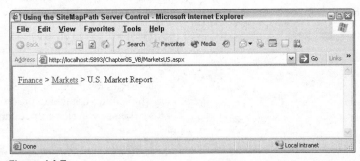

Figure 14-7

By default, no limit is set on the number of links shown, so the SiteMapPath control just generates the specified number of links based on what is labeled in the site map file.

The ShowToolTips Property

By default, the SiteMapPath control generates tooltips for each link if a description property is used within the `Web.sitemap` file. Remember, a tooltip is the text that appears onscreen when an end user hovers the mouse over one of the links in the SiteMapPath control. I showed you this capability earlier in this chapter.

There may be times when you do not want your SiteMapPath control to show any tooltips for the links that it generates. For these situations, you can actually turn off this capability in a couple of ways. The first way is to omit any description attributes in the `.sitemap` file. If you remove these attributes from the file, the SiteMapPath has nothing to display for the tooltips on the page.

The other way to turn off the display of tooltips is to set the ShowToolTips property to False, as shown here:

```
<asp:SiteMapPath ID="Sitemappath1" Runat="server" ShowToolTips="false">
</asp:SiteMapPath>
```

This turns off the tooltips capability but still allows you to use the description property in the .sitemap file. You may still want to use the description attribute because it allows you to keep track of what the links in your file are used for. This is quite advantageous when you are dealing with hundreds or even thousands of links in your application.

The SiteMapPath Control's Child Elements

You already saw the use of the <PathSeparatorStyle> and the <PathSeparatorTemplate> child elements for the SiteMapPath control, but additional child elements exist. The following table covers each of the available child elements.

Child Element	Description
CurrentNodeStyle	Applies styles to the link in the SiteMapPath navigation for the currently displayed page.
CurrentNodeTemplate	Applies a template construction to the link in the SiteMapPath navigation for the currently displayed page.
NodeStyle	Applies styles to all links in the SiteMapPath navigation. The settings applied in the CurrentNodeStyle or RootNodeStyle elements supersede any settings placed here.
NodeStyleTemplate	Applies a template construction to all links in the SiteMapPath navigation. The settings applied in the CurrentNodeStyle or RootNodeStyle elements supersede any settings placed here.
PathSeparatorStyle	Applies styles to the link dividers in the SiteMapPath navigation.
PathSeparatorTemplate	Applies a template construction to the link dividers in the SiteMapPath navigation.
RootNodeStyle	Applies styles to the first link (the root link) in the SiteMapPath navigation.
RootNodeTemplate	Applies a template construction to the first link in the SiteMapPath navigation.

TreeView Server Control

The TreeView server control is another new control that has been introduced with ASP.NET 2.0, and I have to say that I really like this control. The TreeView server control is a rich server control for rendering a of data, so it is quite ideal for displaying what is contained in your `.sitemap` file. Figure 14-8 shows you how it displays the contents of the site map (again from Listing 14-1) that you have been working with thus far in this chapter. This figure first shows a completely collapsed TreeView control at the top of the screen; the second TreeView control has been completely expanded.

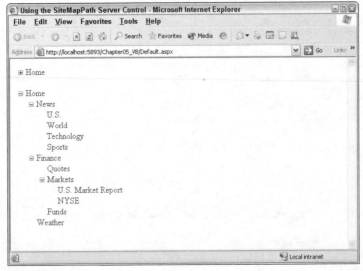

Figure 14-8

This control can preload the nodes to be displayed, even if they are hidden, at first, by the collapsible framework of the control. If the control renders the treeview output using a client-side script, the control doesn't need to make a call back to the server if someone expands one of the nodes in the control. Just the fact that it won't make a postback and redraw the page gives this control a snappiness that will cause your end users to really enjoy using it. Of course, this capability is there only if the browser accepts the client-side code that the TreeView control can generate. If not, the control knows this and renders only what is appropriate. It performs postbacks for those clients who cannot work with this client-side script.

The TreeView control is quite customizable; but first, take a look at how to create a default version of the control using the `.sitemap` file from Listing 14-1. For this example, continue to use the `MarketsUS.aspx` page you created earlier.

The first step is to create a SiteMapDataSource control on the page. When working with the TreeView control that displays the contents of your `.sitemap` file, you must apply one of these datasource controls. The TreeView control doesn't just bind to your site map file automatically as the SiteMapPath control does.

After a basic SiteMapDataSource control is in place, position a TreeView control on the page and set the `DataSourceId` property to `SiteMapDataSource1`. When you have finished, your code should look like Listing 14-6.

Listing 14-6: A basic TreeView control

```
<%@ Page Language="VB" %>

<html xmlns="http://www.w3.org/1999/xhtml" >
<head runat="server">
    <title>Using the TreeView Server Control</title>
</head>
<body>
    <form id="form1" runat="server">
        <asp:SiteMapPath ID="SiteMapPath1" Runat="server">
        </asp:SiteMapPath>
        <br /><p>
        <asp:TreeView ID="TreeView1" Runat="server"
         DataSourceID="SiteMapDataSource1">
        </asp:TreeView>
        <asp:SiteMapDataSource ID="SiteMapDataSource1" Runat="server" /></p>
    </form>
</body>
</html>
```

After the page is run and the TreeView control is expanded, the results are displayed as shown in Figure 14-9.

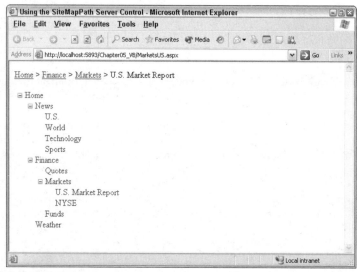

Figure 14-9

This is a very basic TreeView control. The great thing about this control is that it allows for a high degree of customization and even gives you the capability to use some predefined styles that come prepackaged with ASP.NET 2.0.

Identifying the TreeView Control's Built-In Styles

As stated, the TreeView control does come with a number of prebuilt styles right out of the box. The best way to utilize these predefined styles is to do so from the Design view of your page. By right-clicking on the TreeView control on your page from the Design view in Visual Studio 2005, you find the Auto Format option. Click this option and a number of styles become available to you. Selecting one of these styles changes the code of your TreeView control to adapt to that chosen style. For instance, if you choose MSDN from the list of options, the simple one-line TreeView control you created is converted to what is shown in Listing 14-7.

Listing 14-7: A TreeView control with the MSDN style applied to it

```
<asp:TreeView ID="TreeView1" Runat="server" DataSourceID="SiteMapDataSource1"
  ImageSet="Msdn" NodeIndent="10">
    <SelectedNodeStyle BackColor="White" VerticalPadding="1" BorderColor="#888888"
    BorderStyle="Solid" BorderWidth="1px"
    HorizontalPadding="3"></SelectedNodeStyle>
    <NodeStyle VerticalPadding="2" Font-Names="Verdana" Font-Size="8pt"
    NodeSpacing="1" HorizontalPadding="5" ForeColor="Black"></NodeStyle>
    <HoverNodeStyle BackColor="#CCCCCC" BorderColor="#888888" BorderStyle="Solid"
    BorderWidth="1px" Font-Underline="True"></HoverNodeStyle>
</asp:TreeView>
```

As you can see, if you use these built-in styles, it isn't too difficult to completely change the look and feel of the TreeView control. When this bit of code is run, you get the results shown in Figure 14-10.

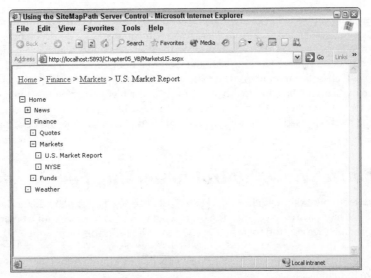

Figure 14-10

Examining the Parts of the TreeView Control

To master working with the TreeView control, you must understand the terminology used for each part of the hierarchical tree that is created by the control.

First, every element or entry in the TreeView control is called a *node*. The uppermost node in the hierarchy of nodes is the *root node*. It is possible for a TreeView control to have multiple root nodes. Any node, including the root node, is also considered a *parent node* if it has any nodes that are directly under it in the hierarchy of nodes. The nodes directly under this parent node are referred to as *child nodes*. Each parent node can have one or more child nodes. Finally, if a node contains no child nodes, it is referred to as a *leaf node*.

The following is based on the site map shown earlier and details the use of this terminology:

```
Home - Root node, parent node
    News - Parent node, child node
        U.S. - Child node, leaf node
        World - Child node, leaf node
        Technology - Child node, leaf node
        Sports - Child node, leaf node
    Finance - Parent node, child node
        Quotes - Child node, leaf node
        Markets - Parent node, child node
            U.S. Market Report - Child node, leaf node
            NYSE - Child node, leaf node
        Funds - Child node, leaf node
    Weather - Child node, leaf node
```

From this listing, you can see what each node is and how it is referred in the hierarchy of nodes. For instance, the U.S. Market Report node is a leaf node — meaning that it doesn't have any child nodes associated with it. However, it is also a child node to the Markets node, which is a parent node to the U.S. Market Report node. If you are working with the Markets node directly, it is also a child node to the Finance node, which is its parent node. The main point to take away from all this is that each node in the site map hierarchy has a relationship to the other nodes in the hierarchy. You must understand these relationships because you can programmatically work with these nodes (as will be demonstrated later in this chapter) and the methods used for working with them include terms like RootNode, CurrentNode and ParentNode.

Binding the TreeView Control to an XML File

You are not limited to working with just a .sitemap file in order to populate the nodes of your TreeView controls. You have many ways to get this done. One cool way is to use the XmlDataSource control (instead of the SiteMapDataSource control) to populate your TreeView controls from your XML files.

For an example of this, create a hierarchical list of items in an XML file called Hardware.xml. An example of this is shown in Listing 14-8.

Listing 14-8: Hardware.xml

```xml
<?xml version="1.0" encoding="utf-8"?>
<Hardware>
    <Item Category="Motherboards">
        <Option Choice="Asus" />
```

```
                <Option Choice="Abit" />
            </Item>
            <Item Category="Memory">
                <Option Choice="128mb" />
                <Option Choice="256mb" />
                <Option Choice="512mb" />
            </Item>
            <Item Category="HardDrives">
                <Option Choice="40GB" />
                <Option Choice="80GB" />
                <Option Choice="100GB" />
            </Item>
            <Item Category="Drives">
                <Option Choice="CD" />
                <Option Choice="DVD" />
                <Option Choice="DVD Burner" />
            </Item>
    </Hardware>
```

As you can see, this list is not meant to be used for site navigation purposes, but instead for allowing the end user to make a selection from a hierarchical list of options. This XML file is divided into four categories of available options: `Motherboards`, `Memory`, `HardDrives`, and `Drives`. To bind your TreeView control to this XML file, use an XmlDataSource control that specifies the location of the XML file you are going to use. Then within the TreeView control itself, use the `<asp:TreeNodeBinding>` element to specify which elements to bind in the XML file to populate the nodes of the TreeView control. This is illustrated in Listing 14-9.

Listing 14-9: Binding a TreeView control to the Hardware.xml file

```
<%@ Page Language="VB" %>

<html xmlns="http://www.w3.org/1999/xhtml" >
<head runat="server">
    <title>Latest Hardware</title>
</head>
<body>
    <form id="form1" runat="server">
        <asp:TreeView ID="Treeview1" Runat="server" DataSourceID="Xmldatasource1">
            <DataBindings>
                <asp:TreeNodeBinding DataMember="Hardware"
                 Text="Computer Hardware" />
                <asp:TreeNodeBinding DataMember="Item" TextField="Category" />
                <asp:TreeNodeBinding DataMember="Option" TextField="Choice" />
            </DataBindings>
        </asp:TreeView>
        <asp:XmlDataSource ID="Xmldatasource1" Runat="server"
         DataFile="Hardware.xml">
        </asp:XmlDataSource>
    </form>
</body>
</html>
```

The first item to look at is the `<asp:XmlDataSource>` control. It is just as simple as the previous `<asp:SiteMapDataSource>` control, but it points at the `Hardware.xml` file using the `DataFile` property.

The next step is to create a TreeView control that binds to this particular XML file. You can bind a default TreeView control directly to the XmlDataSource control like this:

```
<asp:TreeView ID="TreeView1" Runat="server" DataSourceId="XmlDataSource1" />
```

Doing this, you get the *incorrect* result shown in Figure 14-11.

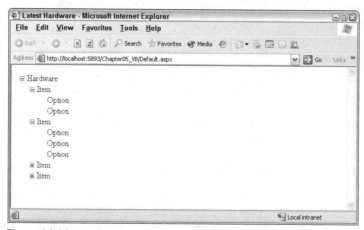

Figure 14-11

As you can see, the TreeView control binds just fine to the `Hardware.xml` file, but looking at the nodes within the TreeView control, you can see that it is simply displaying the names of the actual XML elements from the file itself. Because this isn't what you want, you specify how to bind to the XML file with the use of the `<DataBindings>` element within the TreeView control.

The `<DataBindings>` element encapsulates one or more `TreeNodeBinding` objects. Two of the more important available properties of a `TreeNodeBinding` object are the `DataMember` and `TextField` properties. The `DataMember` property points to the name of the XML element that the TreeView control should look for. The `TextField` property specifies the XML attribute that the TreeView should look for in that particular XML element. If you do this correctly, using the `<DataBindings>` construct, you get the result shown in Figure 14-12.

You can also see from Listing 14-9 that you can override the text value of the root node from the XML file, `<Hardware>`, and have it appear as `Computer Hardware` in the TreeView control:

```
<asp:TreeNodeBinding DataMember="Hardware" Text="Computer Hardware" />
```

Selecting Multiple Options in a TreeView

As I stated earlier, the TreeView control is not meant to be used primarily for navigation purposes. You can use it for all sorts of things. In many cases, you can present a hierarchical list from which you want the end user to select one or more items.

One great built-in feature of the TreeView control is the capability to put check boxes next to nodes within the hierarchical items in the list. These boxes allow end users to make multiple selections. The TreeView control contains a property called ShowCheckBoxes that can be used create check boxes next to many different types of nodes within a list of items.

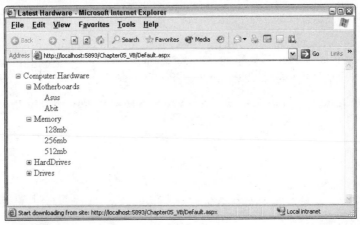

Figure 14-12

The available values for the ShowCheckBoxes property are discussed in the following table.

Value	Description
All	Applies check boxes to each and every node within the TreeView control.
Leaf	Applies check boxes to only the nodes that have no additional child elements.
None	Applies no check boxes to any node within the TreeView control.
Parent	Applies check boxes to only the nodes considered parent nodes within the TreeView control. A parent node has at least one child node associated with it.
Root	Applies a check box to any root node contained within the TreeView control.

When working with the ShowCheckBoxes property, you can set it declaratively in the control itself:

```
<asp:TreeView ID="Treeview1" Runat="server" Font-Underline="false"
 DataSourceID="Xmldatasource1" ShowCheckBoxes="Leaf">
 ...
</asp:TreeViewTreeView>
```

Or you can set it programmatically by using the following code:

VB

```
TreeView1.ShowCheckBoxes = TreeNodeTypes.Leaf
```

C#

```
TreeView1.ShowCheckBoxes = TreeNodeTypes.Leaf;
```

For an example of using check boxes with the TreeView control, let's continue to expand on the computer hardware example from Listing 14-9. Create a hierarchical list that enables people to select multiple items from the list in order to receive additional information about them. Listing 14-10 shows an example of this.

Listing 14-10: Applying check boxes next to the leaf nodes within the hierarchical list of nodes

VB

```
<%@ Page Language="VB" %>

<script runat="server">
    Protected Sub Button1_Click(ByVal sender As Object, ByVal e As System.EventArgs)
        If TreeView1.CheckedNodes.Count > 0 Then
            Label1.Text = "We are sending you information on:<p>"

            For Each node As TreeNode In TreeView1.CheckedNodes
                Label1.Text += node.Text & " " & node.Parent.Text & "<br>"
            Next
        Else
            Label1.Text = "You didn't select anything. Sorry!"
        End If
    End Sub
</script>

<html xmlns="http://www.w3.org/1999/xhtml" >
<head runat="server">
    <title>Latest Hardware</title>
</head>
<body>
    <form runat="server">
    Please select the items you are interested in:
        <p>
        <asp:TreeView ID="TreeView1" Runat="server" Font-Underline="False"
         DataSourceID="XmlDataSource1" ShowCheckBoxes="Leaf">
            <DataBindings>
                <asp:TreeNodeBinding DataMember="Hardware"
                 Text="Computer Hardware" />
                <asp:TreeNodeBinding DataMember="Item" TextField="Category" />
                <asp:TreeNodeBinding DataMember="Option" TextField="Choice" />
            </DataBindings>
        </asp:TreeView>
        <p>
        <asp:Button ID="Button1" Runat="server" Text="Submit Choices"
         OnClick="Button1_Click" />
        </p>
```

```
      <asp:XmlDataSource ID="XmlDataSource1" Runat="server"
       DataFile="Hardware.xml">
      </asp:XmlDataSource>
    </p>
    <asp:Label ID="Label1" Runat="Server" />
  </form>
</body>
</html>
```

C#

```
<%@ Page Language="C#" %>
```

```
<script runat="server">
    protected void Button1_Click(object sender, System.EventArgs e)
    {
        if (TreeView1.CheckedNodes.Count > 0)
        {
            Label1.Text = "We are sending you information on:<p>";
            foreach (TreeNode node in TreeView1.CheckedNodes)
            {
                Label1.Text += node.Text + " " + node.Parent.Text + "<br>";
            }
        }
        else
        {
            Label1.Text = "You didn't select anything. Sorry!";
        }
    }
</script>
```

In this example, you first set the ShowTextBoxes property to Leaf, meaning that you are interested in having check boxes appear only next to items in the TreeView control that do not contain any child nodes. The items with check boxes next to them should be the last items that can be expanded in the hierarchical list.

After this property is set, you then work with the items that are selected by the end user in the Button1_Click event. The first thing you should check is whether any selection at all was made:

```
If TreeView1.CheckedNodes.Count > 0 Then
    ...
End If
```

In this case, the number of checked nodes on the postback needs to be greater than zero, meaning that at least one was selected. If so, you can execute the code within the If statement. The If statement then proceeds to populate the Label control that is on the page. To populate the Label control with data from the selected nodes, you use a For Each statement, as shown in the following:

```
For Each node As TreeNode In TreeView1.CheckedNodes
    ...
Next
```

This creates an instance of a TreeNode object and checks each TreeNode object within the TreeView1 collection of checked nodes.

For each node that is checked, you grab the nodes `Text` value and the `Text` value of this node's parent node to further populate the Label control:

```
Label1.Text += node.Text & " " & node.Parent.Text & "<br>"
```

In the end, you get a page that produces the results shown in Figure 14-13.

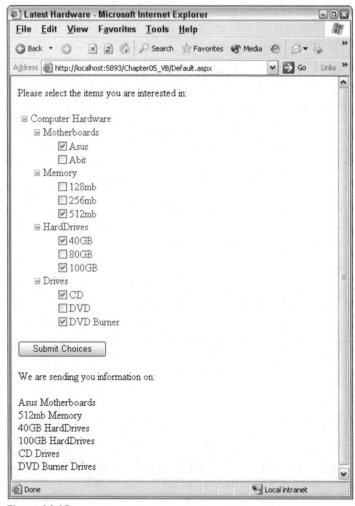

Figure 14-13

Specifying Custom Icons in the TreeView Control

The TreeView control allows for a high degree of customization. You saw earlier in the chapter that you were easily able to customize the look-and-feel of the TreeView control by specifying one of the built-in styles. Applying one of these styles dramatically changes the appearance of the control. One of the most noticeable changes concerns the icons used for the nodes within the TreeView control. Although it is not as easy as just selecting one of the styles built into the TreeView control, you can apply your own icons to be used for the nodes within the hierarchical list of nodes.

The TreeView control contains the properties discussed in the following table. These properties enable you to specify your own images to use for the nodes of the control.

Property	Description
CollapseImageUrl	Applies a custom image next to nodes that have been expanded to show any of their child nodes and have the capability of being collapsed.
ExpandImageUrl	Applies a custom image next to nodes that have the capability of being expanded to display their child nodes.
LeafImageUrl	Applies a custom image next to a node that has no child nodes and is last in the hierarchical chain of nodes.
NoExpandImageUrl	Applies a custom image to nodes that, for programmatic reasons, cannot be expanded or to nodes that are leaf nodes. This is primarily used for spacing purposes to align leaf nodes with their parent nodes.
ParentNodeImageUrl	Applies a custom image only to the parent nodes within the TreeView control.
RootNodeImageUrl	Applies a custom image next to only the root nodes within the TreeView control.

Listing 14-11 shows an example of these properties in use.

Listing 14-11: Applying custom images to the TreeView control

```
<asp:TreeView ID="TreeView1" Runat="server" Font-Underline="False"
  DataSourceId="XmlDataSource1"
  CollapseImageUrl="Images/CollapseImage.gif"
  ExpandImageUrl="Images/ExpandImage.gif"
  LeafImageUrl="Images/LeafImage.gif">
    <DataBindings>
        <asp:TreeNodeBinding DataMember="Hardware" Text="Computer Hardware" />
        <asp:TreeNodeBinding DataMember="Item" TextField="Category" />
        <asp:TreeNodeBinding DataMember="Option" TextField="Choice" />
    </DataBindings>
</asp:TreeView>
```

Specifying these three images to precede the nodes in your control overrides the default values of using a plus (+) sign and a minus (–) sign for the expandable and collapsible nodes. It also overrides simply using an image for any leaf nodes when by default nothing is used. Using the code from Listing 14-11, you get something similar to the results illustrated in Figure 14-14 (depending on the images you use, of course).

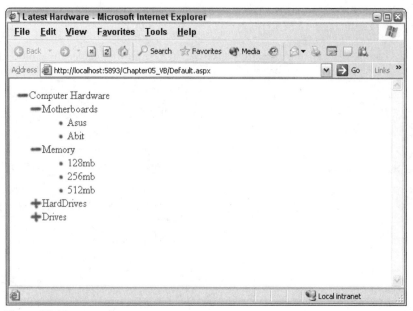

Figure 14-14

Specifying Lines Used to Connect Nodes

Because the TreeView control shows a hierarchical list of items to the end user, you sometimes want to show the relationship between these hierarchical items more explicitly than it is shown by default with the TreeView control. One possibility is to show line connections between parent and child nodes within the display. Simply set the ShowLines property of the TreeView control to True (by default, this property is set to False):

```
<asp:TreeView ID="TreeView1" Runat="server" Font-Underline="False"
  DataSourceId="XmlDataSource1" ShowCheckBoxes="Leaf" ShowLines="True">
    ...
  </asp:TreeView>
```

This code gives the result shown in Figure 14-15.

If the ShowLines property is set to True, you can also define your own lines and images within the TreeView control. This is quite easy to do because Visual Studio 2005 provides you with an ASP.NET TreeView Line Image Generator tool. This tool enables you to visually design how you want the lines and corresponding expanding and collapsing images to appear. After you have it set up as you want, the tool then creates all the necessary files for any of your TreeView controls to use.

To get at the tool, move to the Design view of your file and click the smart tag for the TreeView control that is on your page. Here you find the option Customize Line Images. Click this and you are presented with the ASP.NET TreeView Line Generator dialog (shown in Figure 14-16).

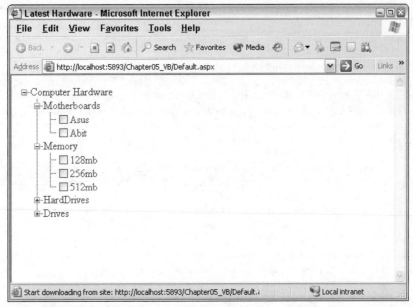

Figure 14-15

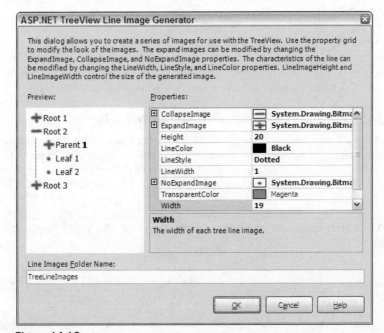

Figure 14-16

From within this dialog, you can select the images used for the nodes that require an Expand, Collapse, or NoCollapse icon. You can also specify the color and style of the lines that connect the nodes. As you create your styles, a sample TreeView control output is displayed for you directly in the dialog based on how your styles are to be applied. The final step is to choose the output of the files that this dialog will create. When you have completed this step, click the OK button. This generates a long list of new files to the folder that you specified in the dialog. By default, the ASP.NET TreeView Line Image Generator wants you to name the output folder `TreeLineImages`, but feel free to name it as you wish. If the folder doesn't exist in the project, you are prompted to allow Visual Studio to create the folder for you. After this is in place, the TreeView control can use your new images and styles by setting the `LineImagesFolderUrl` property as shown here:

```
<asp:TreeView ID="TreeView1" Runat="server" ShowLines="True"
 DataSourceId="SiteMapDataSource1" LineImagesFolderUrl="TreeViewLineImages">
```

The important properties are shown in bold. The `ShowLines` property must be set to `True`. After it is set, it uses the default settings displayed earlier, unless you have specified a location where it can retrieve custom images and styles using the `LineImagesFolderUrl` property. As you can see, this simply points to the new folder, `TreeViewLineImages`, which contains all the new images and styles you created. Take a look in the folder. It is interesting to see what is output by the tool.

Working with the TreeView Control Programmatically

So far with the TreeView control, you have learned how to work with the control declaratively. The great thing about ASP.NET is that you are not simply required to work with its components declaratively, but you can also manipulate these controls programmatically.

The TreeView control has an associated `TreeView` class that enables you to completely manage the TreeView control and how it functions from within your code. The next section takes a look at how to use some of the more common ways to control the `TreeView` programmatically.

Expanding and Collapsing Nodes Programmatically

One thing you can do with your TreeView control is to expand or collapse the nodes within the hierarchy programmatically. You can accomplish this by using either the `ExpandAll` or `CollapseAll` methods from the `TreeView` class. Listing 14-12 shows you one of the earlier TreeView controls that you used in Listing 14-6, but with a couple of buttons above it that you can now use to initiate the expanding and collapsing of the nodes.

Listing 14-12: Expanding and collapsing the nodes of the TreeView control programmatically

VB

```
<%@ Page Language="VB" %>

<script runat="server" language="vb">
    Protected Sub Button1_Click(ByVal sender As Object, ByVal e As System.EventArgs)
        TreeView1.ExpandAll()
    End Sub

    Protected Sub Button2_Click(ByVal sender As Object, ByVal e As System.EventArgs)
        TreeView1.CollapseAll()
```

```
      End Sub
</script>

<html xmlns="http://www.w3.org/1999/xhtml" >
<head runat="server">
    <title>TreeView Control</title>
</head>
<body>
    <form id="Form1" runat="server">
        <p>
            <asp:Button ID="Button1" Runat="server" Text="Expand Nodes"
             OnClick="Button1_Click" />
            <asp:Button ID="Button2" Runat="server" Text="Collapse Nodes"
             OnClick="Button2_Click" />
            <br />
            <br />
        <asp:TreeView ID="TreeView1" Runat="server"
         DataSourceId="SiteMapDataSource1">
        </asp:TreeView>
        <asp:SiteMapDataSource ID="SiteMapDataSource1" Runat="server" /></p>
    </form>
</body>
</html>
```

C#

```
<%@ Page Language="C#" %>

<script runat="server">
    protected void Button1_Click(object sender, System.EventArgs e)
    {
        TreeView1.ExpandAll();
    }

    protected void Button2_Click(object sender, System.EventArgs e)
    {
        TreeView1.CollapseAll();
    }
</script>
```

Running this page gives you two buttons above your TreeView control. Clicking the first button invokes the ExpandAll method and completely expands the entire list of nodes. Clicking the second button invokes the CollapseAll method and completely collapses the list of nodes (see Figure 14-17).

The example shown in Listing 14-12 is nice, but it expands and collapses the nodes only on end user actions (when the end user clicks the button). It would be even nicer if you could initiate this action programmatically.

You might want to simply place the TreeView1.ExpandAll() command within the Page_Load event, but if you try this, you see that it doesn't work. Instead, you use the OnDataBound attribute within the TreeView control:

```
<asp:TreeView ID="TreeView1" Runat="server"
 DataSourceId="SiteMapDataSource1" OnDataBound="TreeView1_DataBound">
</asp:TreeView>
```

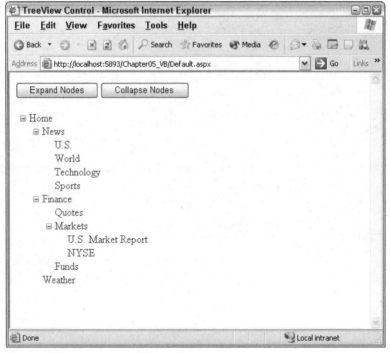

Figure 14-17

The value of this attribute points to a method in your code, as shown here:

VB
```vb
Protected Sub TreeView1_DataBound(ByVal sender As Object, _
  ByVal e As System.EventArgs)
    TreeView1.ExpandAll()
End Sub
```

C#
```csharp
protected void TreeView1_DataBound(object sender, System.EventArgs e)
{
    TreeView1.ExpandAll();
}
```

Now when you run the page, notice that the TreeView control is completely expanded when the page is first loaded in the browser.

You can also expand specific nodes within the tree instead of just expanding the entire list. For this example, use the TreeView1_DataBound method you just created. Using the site map from Listing 14-1, change the TreeView1_DataBound method so that it appears as shown in Listing 14-13.

Listing 14-13: Expanding specific nodes programmatically

VB

```
Protected Sub TreeView1_DataBound(ByVal sender As Object, _
  TreeView1.CollapseAll()
  ByVal e As System.EventArgs)
   TreeView1.FindNode("Home").Expand()
   TreeView1.FindNode("Home/Finance").Expand()
   TreeView1.FindNode("Home/Finance/Markets").Expand()
End Sub
```

C#

```
protected void TreeView1_DataBound(object sender, System.EventArgs e)
{
   TreeView1.CollapseAll()
   TreeView1.FindNode("Home").Expand();
   TreeView1.FindNode("Home//Finance").Expand();
   TreeView1.FindNode("Home//Finance//Markets").Expand();
}
```

In this case, you use the FindNode method and expand the node that is found. The FindNode method takes a String value, which is the node and the path of the node that you want to reference. For instance, TreeView1.FindNode("Home/Finance").Expand() expands the Finance node. To find the node, it is important to specify the entire path from the root node to the node you want to work with (in this case, the Finance node). You separate the nodes within the site map path structure with a forward-slash between each of the nodes in the site map path.

Note that you had to expand each of the nodes individually until you got to the Finance node. If you simply used TreeView1.FindNode("Home/Finance/Markets").Expand() in the TreeView1_DataBound method, the Finance node would indeed be expanded, but the parent nodes above it (the Finance and Home nodes) would not have been expanded and you wouldn't see the expanded Markets node when invoking the page. (Try it; it's interesting.)

Instead of using the Expand method, you can just as easily set the Expanded property to True, as shown in Listing 14-14.

Listing 14-14: Expanding nodes programmatically using the Expanded property

VB

```
Protected Sub TreeView1_DataBound(ByVal sender As Object, _
  ByVal e As System.EventArgs)
   TreeView1.CollapseAll();
   TreeView1.FindNode("Home").Expanded = True
   TreeView1.FindNode("Home/Finance").Expanded = True
   TreeView1.FindNode("Home/Finance/Markets").Expanded = True
End Sub
```

C#

```
protected void TreeView1_DataBound(object sender, System.EventArgs e)
{
   TreeView1.FindNode("Home").Expanded = true;
   TreeView1.FindNode("Home/Finance").Expanded = true;
   TreeView1.FindNode("Home/Finance/Markets").Expanded = true;
}
```

Although you focus on the Expand method and the Expanded property here, you can just as easily programmatically collapse nodes using the Collapse method. No Collapsed property really exists. Instead, you simply set the Expanded property to False.

Adding Nodes

Another interesting thing you can do with the TreeView control is to add nodes to the overall hierarchy programmatically. The TreeView control is made up of a collection of TreeNode objects. So as you see in previous examples, the Finance node is actually a TreeNode object that you can work with programmatically. It includes the capability to add other TreeNode objects.

A TreeNode object typically stores a Text and Value property. The Text property is what is displayed in the TreeView control for the end user. The Value property is an additional data item that you can use to associate with this particular TreeNode object. Another property that you can use (if your TreeView control is a list of navigational links) is the NavigateUrl property. Listing 14-15 demonstrates how to add nodes programmatically to the same site map from Listing 14-1 that you have been using.

Listing 14-15: Adding nodes programmatically to the TreeView control

VB

```
<%@ Page Language="VB" %>
<script runat="server" language="vb">
    Protected Sub Button1_Click(ByVal sender As Object, ByVal e As System.EventArgs)
        TreeView1.ExpandAll()
    End Sub

    Protected Sub Button2_Click(ByVal sender As Object, ByVal e As System.EventArgs)
        TreeView1.CollapseAll()
    End Sub

    Protected Sub Button3_Click(ByVal sender As Object, ByVal e As System.EventArgs)
        Dim myNode As New TreeNode
        myNode.Text = TextBox1.Text
        myNode.NavigateUrl = TextBox2.Text
        TreeView1.FindNode("Home/Finance/Markets").ChildNodes.Add(myNode)
    End Sub
</script>

<html xmlns="http://www.w3.org/1999/xhtml" >
<head runat="server">
    <title>TreeView Control</title>
</head>
<body>
    <form id="Form1" runat="server">
        <p>
            <asp:Button ID="Button1" Runat="server" Text="Expand Nodes"
             OnClick="Button1_Click" />
            <asp:Button ID="Button2" Runat="server" Text="Collapse Nodes"
             OnClick="Button2_Click" /></p>
        <p>
            <strong>Text of new node:</strong>
            <asp:TextBox ID="TextBox1" runat="server">
            </asp:TextBox>
        </p>
```

```
    <p>
        <strong>Desination URL of new node:</strong>
        <asp:TextBox ID="TextBox2" Runat="server">
        </asp:TextBox>
        <br />
        <br />
        <asp:Button ID="Button3" Runat="server" Text="Add New Node"
         OnClick="Button3_Click" />
    </p>
    <p>
    <asp:TreeView ID="TreeView1" runat="server"
     DataSourceId="SiteMapDataSource1">
    </asp:TreeView></p>
    <p>
    <asp:SiteMapDataSource ID="SiteMapDataSource1" Runat="server" /></p>
  </form>
</body>
</html>
```

C#

```
protected void Button3_Click(object sender, System.EventArgs e)
{
    TreeNode myNode = new TreeNode();
    myNode.Text = TextBox1.Text;
    myNode.NavigateUrl = TextBox2.Text;
    TreeView1.FindNode("Home/Finance/Markets").ChildNodes.Add(myNode);
}
```

This page contains two text boxes and a new Button control. The first text box is used to populate the Text property of the new node that is created. The second text box is used to populate the NavigateUrl property of the new node.

If you run the page, you can expand the entire hierarchy by clicking the Expand Nodes button. Then you can add additional child nodes to the Markets node. To add a new node programmatically, use the FindNode method as you did before to find the Markets node. When you find it, you can add additional child nodes by using the ChildNodes.Add method and pass in a TreeNode object instance. Submitting NASDAQ in the first text box and Nasdaq.aspx in the second text box changes your TreeView control as illustrated in Figure 14-18.

After it is added, the node stays added even after the hierarchy tree is collapsed and re-opened. You can also add as many child nodes as you want to the Markets node. Note that, although you are changing nodes programmatically, this in no way alters the contents of the data source (the XML file, or the .sitemap file). These sources remain unchanged throughout the entire process.

Menu Server Control

One of the cooler navigation controls also introduced with ASP.NET 2.0 is the new Menu server control. This control is ideal for allowing the end user to navigate a larger hierarchy of options while utilizing very little browser real estate in the process. Figure 14-19 shows you what the menu control looks like when it is either completely collapsed or completely extended down one of the branches of the hierarchy.

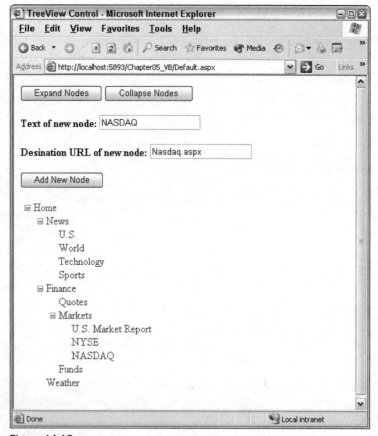

Figure 14-18

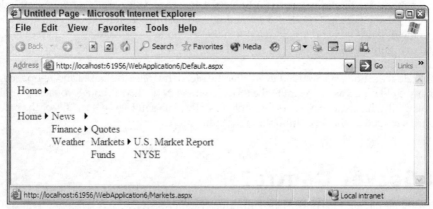

Figure 14-19

From here, you can see that the first Menu control displayed simply shows the Home link with a small arrow to the right of the display. The arrow means that more options are available that relate to this up-most link in the hierarchy. The second Menu control displayed shows what the default control looks like when the end user works down one of the branches provided by the site map.

The Menu control is an ideal control to use when you have lots of options — whether these options are selections the end user can make or navigation points provided by the application in which they are working. The Menu control can provide a multitude of options and consumes little space in the process.

Using the Menu control in your ASP.NET applications is rather simple. The Menu control works with a SiteMapDataSource control. You can drag and drop the SiteMapDataSource control and the Menu control onto the Visual Studio 2005 design surface and connect the two by using the Menu control's `DataSourceId` property. Alternatively, you can create and connect them directly in code. Listing 14-16 shows an example of the Menu control in its simplest form.

Listing 14-16: A simple use of the Menu control

```
<%@ Page Language="VB" %>

<html xmlns="http://www.w3.org/1999/xhtml" >
<head runat="server">
    <title>Menu Server Control</title>
</head>
<body>
    <form id="form1" runat="server">
        <asp:SiteMapDataSource ID="SiteMapDataSource1" Runat="server" />
        <asp:Menu ID="Menu1" Runat="server" DataSourceID="SiteMapDataSource1">
        </asp:Menu>
    </form>
</body>
</html>
```

From this example, you can see that I'm using a SiteMapDataSource control that automatically works with the application's `Web.sitemap` file. The only other item included is the Menu control, which uses the typical `ID` and `Runat` attributes and the `DataSourceID` attribute to connect it with what is retrieved from the SiteMapDataSource control.

Although the default Menu control is pretty simple, you can highly customize how this control looks and works by redefining the properties of the control. The following sections take a look at some examples of how you can modify the appearance and change the behavior of this control.

Applying Different Styles to the Menu Control

By default, the Menu control is pretty plain. If you want to maintain this appearance, you can use what is provided or simply change the font sizes and styles to make it fit in with your site. You actually have quite a number of ways in which you can modify this control so that it appears unique and fits in with the rest of your site. You can either customize this control's appearance yourself, or you can use one of the predefined styles that come with the control.

Using a Predefined Style

Visual Studio 2005 includes some predefined styles that you can use with the Menu control to quickly apply a look-and-feel to the displayed menu of items. Some of the provided styles include `Classic` and `Professional` and more. To apply one of these predefined styles, you work with the Menu control from the Design view of your page. Within the Design view, highlight the Menu control and expand the control's smart tag. From here, you see a list of options for working with this control. To change the look-and-feel of the control, click the Auto Format link and select one of the styles.

Performing this operation changes the code of your control by applying a set of style properties. For example, if you select the `Classic` option, you get the results shown in Listing 14-17.

Listing 14-17: Code changes when a style is applied to the Menu control

```
<asp:Menu ID="Menu1" Runat="server" DataSourceID="SiteMapDataSource1"
  BackColor="#B5C7DE" ForeColor="#284E98"
  Font-Names="Verdana" Font-Size="0.8em" StaticSubMenuIndent="10px"
  DynamicHorizontalOffset="2">
   <StaticSelectedStyle BackColor="#507CD1"></StaticSelectedStyle>
   <StaticMenuItemStyle HorizontalPadding="5"
   VerticalPadding="2"></StaticMenuItemStyle>
   <DynamicMenuStyle BackColor="#B5C7DE"></DynamicMenuStyle>
   <DynamicSelectedStyle BackColor="#507CD1"></DynamicSelectedStyle>
   <DynamicMenuItemStyle HorizontalPadding="5"
   VerticalPadding="2"></DynamicMenuItemStyle>
   <DynamicHoverStyle ForeColor="White" Font-Bold="True"
   BackColor="#284E98"></DynamicHoverStyle>
   <StaticHoverStyle ForeColor="White" Font-Bold="True"
   BackColor="#284E98"></StaticHoverStyle>
</asp:Menu>
```

You can see a lot of added styles that change the menu items that appear in the control. Figure 14-20 shows how this style selection appears in the browser.

Figure 14-20

Changing the Style for Static Items

The Menu control considers items in the hierarchy to be either *static* or *dynamic*. Static items from this example would be the Home link that appears when the page is generated. Dynamic links are the items that appear dynamically when the user hovers the mouse over the Home link in the menu. It is possible to change the styles for both these types of nodes in the menu.

To apply a specific style to the static links that appear, you must add a static style element to the Menu control. The Menu control includes the following static style elements:

- ❑ `<StaticHoverStyle>`
- ❑ `<StaticMenuItemStyle>`
- ❑ `<StaticMenuStyle>`
- ❑ `<StaticSelectedStyle>`
- ❑ `<StaticTemplate>`

The important options from this list include the `<StaticHoverStyle>` and the `<StaticMenuItemStyle>` elements. The `<StaticHoverStyle>` is what you use to define the style of the static item in the menu when the end user hovers the mouse over the option. The `<StaticMenuItemStyle>` is what you use for the style of the static item when the end user is not hovering the mouse over the option.

Listing 14-18 illustrates adding a style that is applied when the end user hovers the mouse over static items.

Listing 14-18: Adding a hover style to static items in the menu control

```
<asp:Menu ID="Menu1" Runat="server" DataSourceID="SiteMapDataSource1">
    <StaticHoverStyle BackColor="DarkGray" BorderColor="Black" BorderStyle="Solid"
    BorderWidth="1"></StaticHoverStyle>
</asp:Menu>
```

This little example adds a background color and border to the static items in the menu when the end user hovers the mouse over the item. The result is shown in Figure 14-21.

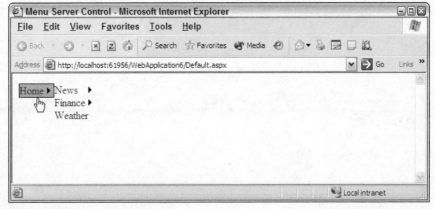

Figure 14-21

Adding Styles to Dynamic Items

Adding styles to the dynamic items of the menu control is just as easy as adding them to static items. The Menu control has a number of different elements for modifying the appearance of dynamic items, including the following:

❑   `<DynamicHoverStyle>`

❑   `<DynamicMenuItemStyle>`

❑   `<DynamicMenuStyle>`

❑   `<DynamicSelectedStyle>`

❑   `<DynamicTemplate>`

These elements change menu items the same way as the static versions of these elements, but they change only the items that dynamically pop-out from the static items. Listing 14-19 shows an example of applying the hover style to dynamic items.

Listing 14-19: Adding a hover style to dynamic items in the menu control

```
<asp:Menu ID="Menu1" Runat="server" DataSourceID="Sitemapdatasource1">
    <StaticHoverStyle BackColor="DarkGray" BorderColor="Black" BorderStyle="Solid"
    BorderWidth="1"></StaticHoverStyle>
    <DynamicHoverStyle BackColor="DarkGray" BorderColor="Black" BorderStyle="Solid"
    BorderWidth="1"></DynamicHoverStyle>
</asp:Menu>
```

This code produces the results shown in Figure 14-22.

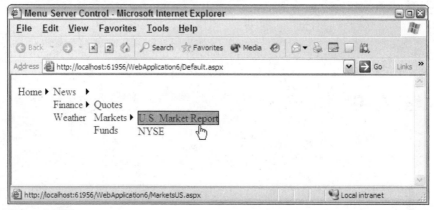

Figure 14-22

Changing the Layout of the Menu Items

By default, the dynamic menu items are displayed from left to right. This means that, as the items in the menu expand, they are continually displayed in a vertical fashion. You can actually control this behavior, but another option is available to you.

The other option is to have the first level of menu items appear directly below the first static item (horizontally). You change this behavior by using the `Orientation` attribute of the Menu control, as shown in Listing 14-20.

Listing 14-20: Forcing the menu items to use a horizontal orientation

```
<asp:Menu ID="Menu1" Runat="server" DataSourceID="SiteMapDataSource1"
  Orientation="Horizontal">
</asp:Menu>
```

This code produces the results shown in Figure 14-23.

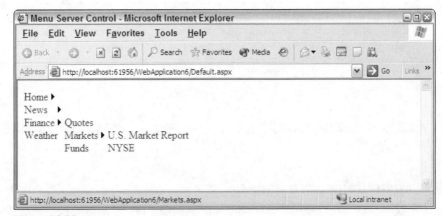

Figure 14-23

The `Orientation` attribute can take a value of `Horizontal` or `Vertical` only. The default value is `Vertical`.

Changing the Pop-Out Symbol

As the default, an arrow is used as the pop-out symbol for the menu items generated, whether they are static or dynamic. This is shown in Figure 14-24.

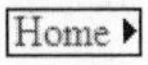

Home ▶

Figure 14-24

You are not forced to use this arrow symbol; in fact, you can change it to an image with relatively little work. Listing 14-21 shows how to accomplish this task.

Listing 14-21: Using custom images

```
<asp:Menu ID="Menu1" Runat="server" DataSourceID="SiteMapDataSource1"
  Orientation="Horizontal" DynamicPopOutImageUrl="myArrow.gif"
  StaticPopOutImageUrl="myArrow.gif">
</asp:Menu>
```

To change the pop-out symbol to an image of your choice, you use the `DynamicPopOutImageUrl` or `StaticPopOutImageUrl` properties. The `String` value these attributes take is simply the path of the image you want to use. Depending on the image used, it produces something similar to what you see in Figure 14-25.

Figure 14-25

Separating Menu Items with Images

Another nice styling option of the Menu control is the capability to add a divider image to the menu items. You use the `StaticBottomSeparatorImageUrl`, `StaticTopSeparatorImageUrl`, `DynamicBottomSeparatorImageUrl`, and `DynamicTopSeparatorImageUrl` properties depending on where you want to place the separator image.

For example, if you wanted to place a divider image under only the dynamic menu items, you use the `DynamicBottomSeparatorImageUrl` property, as shown in Listing 14-22.

Listing 14-22: Applying divider images to dynamic items

```
<asp:Menu ID="Menu1" Runat="server" DataSourceID="SiteMapDataSource1"
  DynamicBottomSeparatorImageUrl="myDivider.gif">
</asp:Menu>
```

All the properties of the Menu control that define the image to use for the dividers take a `String` value that points to the location of the image. The result of Listing 14-22 is shown in Figure 14-26.

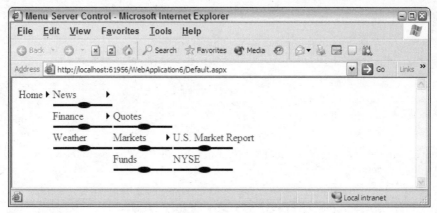

Figure 14-26

Menu Events

The Menu control exposes events such as the following:

❑ DataBinding

❑ DataBound

❑ Disposed

❑ Init

❑ Load

❑ MenuItemClick

❑ MenuItemDataBound

❑ PreRender

❑ Unload

One nice event to be aware of is the MenuItemClick event. This event, shown in Listing 14-23, enables you to take some action when the end user clicks one of the available menu items.

Listing 14-23: Using the MenuItemClick event

VB
```vb
Protected Sub Menu1_MenuItemClick(ByVal sender As Object, _
    ByVal e As System.Web.UI.WebControls.MenuEventArgs)

    ' Code for event here

End Sub
```

(continued)

Listing 14-23: *(continued)*

C#

```
protected void Menu1_MenuItemClick(object sender, MenuEventArgs e)
{

    // Code for event here

}
```

This event uses the `MenuEventArgs` event delegate and provides you access to the text and value of the item selected from the menu.

Binding the Menu Control to an XML File

Just as with the TreeView control, it is possible to bind the Menu control to items that come from other data source controls provided with ASP.NET 2.0. Although most developers are likely to use the Menu control to enable end users to navigate to URL destinations, you can also use the Menu control to enable users to make selections.

As an example, take the previous XML file, `Hardware.xml`, which was used with the TreeView control from Listing 14-8 earlier in the chapter. For this example, the Menu control works with an XmlDataSource control. When the end user makes a selection from the menu, you populate a Listbox on the page with the items selected. The code for this is shown in Listing 14-24.

Listing 14-24: Using the Menu control with an XML file

VB

```
<%@ Page Language="VB" %>

<script runat="server">
    Protected Sub Menu1_MenuItemClick(ByVal sender As Object, _
        ByVal e As System.Web.UI.WebControls.MenuEventArgs)

        Listbox1.Items.Add(e.Item.Parent.Value & " : " & e.Item.Value)
    End Sub
</script>

<html xmlns="http://www.w3.org/1999/xhtml" >
<head runat="server">
    <title>Menu Server Control</title>
</head>
<body>
    <form id="form1" runat="server">
        <asp:Menu ID="Menu1" Runat="server" DataSourceID="XmlDataSource1"
          OnMenuItemClick="Menu1_MenuItemClick">
            <DataBindings>
                <asp:MenuItemBinding DataMember="Item"
                 TextField="Category"></asp:MenuItemBinding>
                <asp:MenuItemBinding DataMember="Option"
```

```
                        TextField="Choice"></asp:MenuItemBinding>
            </DataBindings>
        </asp:Menu>
        <p>
        <asp:ListBox ID="Listbox1" Runat="server">
        </asp:ListBox></p>
        <asp:xmldatasource ID="XmlDataSource1" runat="server"
         datafile="Hardware.xml" />
    </form>
</body>
</html>
```

C#

```
<%@ Page Language="C#" %>

<script runat="server">
    protected void Menu1_MenuItemClick(object sender, MenuEventArgs e)
    {
        Listbox1.Items.Add(e.Item.Parent.Value + " : " + e.Item.Value);
    }
</script>
```

From this example, you can see that instead of using the `<asp:TreeNodeBinding>` elements, as I did with the TreeView control, the Menu control uses the `<asp:MenuItemBinding>` elements to make connections to items listed in the XML file, `Hardware.xml`. In addition, the root element of the Menu control, the `<asp:Menu>` element, now includes the `OnMenuItemClick` attribute, which points to the event delegate `Menu1_MenuItemClick`.

The `Menu1_MenuItemClick` event includes the event delegate `MenuEventArgs`, which enables you to get at both the values of the child and parent elements selected. For this example, both are used and then populated into the Listbox control, as illustrated in Figure 14-27.

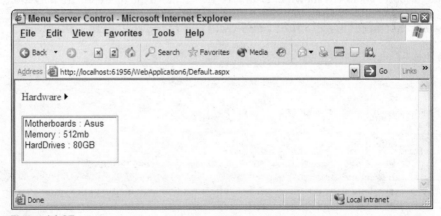

Figure 14-27

SiteMap Data Provider

A whole new series of data providers in the form of DataSource controls have been added to ASP.NET 2.0. One of these new DataSource controls now at your disposal, which you looked at earlier in the chapter, is the SiteMapDataSource control. This new DataSource control was developed to work with site maps and the controls that can bind to them.

Some controls don't need a SiteMapDataSource control in order to bind to the application's site map (which is typically stored in the `Web.sitemap` file). Earlier in the chapter, you saw this in action when using the SiteMapPath control. This control was able to work with the `Web.sitemap` file directly — without the need for this new data provider.

Certain navigation controls, however, such as the TreeView control and the DropDownList control, require an intermediary SiteMapDataSource control to retrieve the site navigation information.

The SiteMapDataSource control is simple to use as demonstrated throughout this chapter. The SiteMapDataSource control in its simplest form is illustrated here:

```
<asp:SiteMapDataSource ID="SiteMapDataSource1" Runat="server" />
```

In this form, the SiteMapDataSource control simply grabs the info as a tree hierarchy (as consistently demonstrated so far). Be aware that a number of properties do change how the data is displayed in any control that binds to the data output.

ShowStartingNode

The `ShowStartingNode` property determines whether the root node of the `.sitemap` file is retrieved with the retrieved collection of node objects. This property takes a `Boolean` value and is set to `True` by default. If you are working with the `Web.sitemap` file shown in Listing 14-1, you construct your SiteMapdataSource control as shown in Listing 14-25 to remove the root node from the collection.

Listing 14-25: Removing the root node from the retrieved node collection

```
<%@ Page Language="VB" %>

<html xmlns="http://www.w3.org/1999/xhtml" >
<head runat="server">
    <title>Menu Server Control</title>
</head>
<body>
    <form id="form1" runat="server">
        <asp:SiteMapDataSource ID="SiteMapDataSource1" Runat="server"
         ShowStartingNode="False" />
        <asp:Menu ID="Menu1" Runat="server" DataSourceID="SiteMapDataSource1">
        </asp:Menu>
    </form>
</body>
</html>
```

This code produces a menu like the one shown in Figure 14-28.

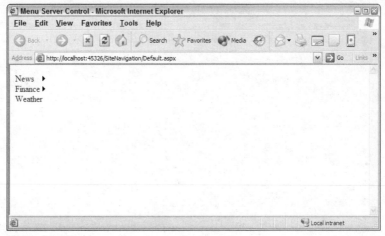

Figure 14-28

From this screen shot, you can see that indeed the root node has been removed, and the menu shown starts by using all the child nodes of the root node.

StartFromCurrentNode

The StartFromCurrentNode property causes the SiteMapDataProvider to retrieve only a node collection that starts from the current node of the page being viewed. By default, this is set to False, meaning that the SiteMapDataProvider always retrieves all the available nodes (from the root node to the current node).

For an example of this, use the .sitemap file from Listing 14-1 and create a page called Markets.aspx. This page in the hierarchy of the node collection is a child node of the Finance node, as well as having two child nodes itself: U.S. Market Report and NYSE. An example of setting the StartFromCurrentNode property to True is shown in Listing 14-26.

Listing 14-26: The MarketsUS.aspx page using the StartFromCurrentNode property

```
<%@ Page Language="VB" %>

<html xmlns="http://www.w3.org/1999/xhtml" >
<head runat="server">
    <title>Menu Server Control</title>
</head>
<body>
    <form id="form1" runat="server">
        <asp:SiteMapDataSource ID="SiteMapDataSource1" Runat="server"
        StartFromCurrentNode="True" />
        <asp:Menu ID="Menu1" Runat="server" DataSourceID="SiteMapDataSource1">
        </asp:Menu>
    </form>
</body>
</html>
```

This simple property addition produces the result shown in Figure 14-29.

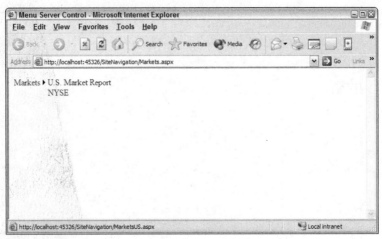

Figure 14-29

StartingNodeOffset

The `StartingNodeOffset` property takes an `Integer` value that determines the starting point of the hierarchy collection. Be default, this property is set to `0`, meaning that the node collection retrieved by the SiteMapDataSource control starts at the root node. From the example provided in Listing 14-1, you know that the collection starts with the Home page found at `Default.aspx`, a page that you have seen in numerous examples in this chapter.

If you set this property's value to `1`, the starting point of the collection is one space off the default starting point (the Home page starting at Default.aspx). For example, if the page using the SiteMapDataSource control is the MarketsUS.aspx page, the node collection starts with the Finance page (Finance.aspx).

```
Home      Offset 0
   News    Offset 1
      U.S.    Offset 2
      World    Offset 2
      Technology    Offset 2
      Sports    Offset 2
   Finance    Offset 1
      Quotes    Offset 2
      Markets    Offset 2
         U.S. Market Report    Offset 3
         NYSE    Offset 3
      Funds    Offset 2
   Weather    Offset 1
```

From this hierarchy, you can see how much each node is offset from the root node. Therefore, if you set the `StartingNodeOffset` property to `1` and you are browsing on the U.S. Market Report page, you can see that the node collection starts with the Finance page (`Finance.aspx`) and the other child nodes of the root node (News and Weather) are not represented in the node collection.

StartingNodeUrl

The `StartingNodeUrl` property allows you to specify the page found in the `.sitemap` file from which the node collection should start. By default, the value of this property is empty; but when set to something like `Finance.aspx`, the collection starts with the Finance page as the root node of the node collection. Listing 14-27 shows an example of using the `StartingNodeUrl` property.

Listing 14-27: Using the StartingNodeUrl property

```
<%@ Page Language="VB" %>

<html xmlns="http://www.w3.org/1999/xhtml" >
<head runat="server">
    <title>Menu Server Control</title>
</head>
<body>
    <form id="form1" runat="server">
        <asp:SiteMapDataSource ID="SiteMapDataSource1" Runat="server"
         StartingNodeUrl="Finance.aspx" />
        <asp:Menu ID="Menu1" Runat="server" DataSourceID="SiteMapDataSource1">
        </asp:Menu>
    </form>
</body>
</html>
```

When the `StartingNodeUrl` property value is encountered, the value is compared against the `url` attributes in the `Web.sitemap` file. When a match is found, the matched page is the one used as the root node in the node collection retrieved by the SiteMapDataSource control.

SiteMap API

The `SiteMap` class is an in-memory representation of the site's navigation structure. This is a great class for programmatically working around the hierarchical structure of your site. The `SiteMap` class comes with a couple of objects that make working with the navigation structure easy. These objects (or public properties) are described in the following table.

Properties	Description
CurrentNode	Retrieves a `SiteMapNode` object for the current page
RootNode	Retrieves a `SiteMapNode` object that starts from the root node and the rest of the site's navigation structure
Provider	Retrieves the default `ISiteMapProvider` for the current site map
Providers	Retrieves a collection of available, named `ISiteMapProvider` objects

Listing 14-28 shows an example of working with some `SiteMap` objects by demonstrating how to use the `CurrentNode` object from the `Markets.aspx` page.

Listing 14-28: Working with the CurrentNode object

VB

```vb
<%@ Page Language="VB" %>

<script runat="server" language="vb">
    Protected Sub Page_Load(ByVal sender As Object, ByVal e As System.EventArgs)
        Label1.Text = SiteMap.CurrentNode.Description & "<br>" & _
            SiteMap.CurrentNode.HasChildNodes & "<br>" & _
            SiteMap.CurrentNode.NextSibling.ToString() & "<br>" & _
            SiteMap.CurrentNode.ParentNode.ToString() & "<br>" & _
            SiteMap.CurrentNode.PreviousSibling.ToString() & "<br>" & _
            SiteMap.CurrentNode.RootNode.ToString() & "<br>" & _
            SiteMap.CurrentNode.Title & "<br>" & _
            SiteMap.CurrentNode.Url
    End Sub
</script>

<html xmlns="http://www.w3.org/1999/xhtml" >
<head runat="server">
    <title>SiteMapDataSource</title>
</head>
<body>
    <form id="form1" runat="server">
        <asp:Label ID="Label1" Runat="server"></asp:Label>
    </form>
</body>
</html>
```

C#

```csharp
<%@ Page Language="C#" %>

<script runat="server">
    protected void Page_Load(object sender, System.EventArgs e)
    {
        Label1.Text = SiteMap.CurrentNode.Description + "<br>" +
            SiteMap.CurrentNode.HasChildNodes + "<br>" +
            SiteMap.CurrentNode.NextSibling.ToString() + "<br>" +
            SiteMap.CurrentNode.ParentNode.ToString() + "<br>" +
            SiteMap.CurrentNode.PreviousSibling.ToString() + "<br>" +
            SiteMap.CurrentNode.RootNode.ToString() + "<br>" +
            SiteMap.CurrentNode.Title + "<br>" +
            SiteMap.CurrentNode.Url;
    }
</script>
```

As you can see from this little bit of code, by using the `SiteMap` class and the `CurrentNode` object you can work with a plethora of information regarding the current page. Running this page, you get the following results printed to the screen:

```
The Latest Market Information
True
Funds
Finance
Quotes
Home
Markets
/Chapter14_VB/Markets.aspx
```

Using the `CurrentNode` property, you can actually create your own style of the SiteMapPath control, as illustrated in Listing 14-29.

Listing 14-29: Creating a custom navigation display using the CurrentNode property

VB

```
<%@ Page Language="VB" %>

<script runat="server" language="vb">
    Protected Sub Page_Load(ByVal sender As Object, ByVal e As System.EventArgs)
        Hyperlink1.Text = SiteMap.CurrentNode.ParentNode.ToString()
        Hyperlink1.NavigateUrl = SiteMap.CurrentNode.ParentNode.Url

        Hyperlink2.Text = SiteMap.CurrentNode.PreviousSibling.ToString()
        Hyperlink2.NavigateUrl = SiteMap.CurrentNode.PreviousSibling.Url

        Hyperlink3.Text = SiteMap.CurrentNode.NextSibling.ToString()
        Hyperlink3.NavigateUrl = SiteMap.CurrentNode.NextSibling.Url
    End Sub
</script>

<html xmlns="http://www.w3.org/1999/xhtml" >
<head runat="server">
    <title>SiteMapDataSource</title>
</head>
<body>
    <form id="form1" runat="server">
        Move Up:
        <asp:Hyperlink ID="Hyperlink1" Runat="server"></asp:Hyperlink><br />
        <-- <asp:Hyperlink ID="Hyperlink2" Runat="server"></asp:Hyperlink> |
        <asp:Hyperlink ID="Hyperlink3" Runat="server"></asp:Hyperlink> -->
    </form>
</body>
</html>
```

(continued)

543

Listing 14-29: *(continued)*

C#
```
<%@ Page Language="C#" %>

<script runat="server">
    protected void Page_Load(object sender, System.EventArgs e)
    {
        Hyperlink1.Text = SiteMap.CurrentNode.ParentNode.ToString();
        Hyperlink1.NavigateUrl = SiteMap.CurrentNode.ParentNode.Url;

        Hyperlink2.Text = SiteMap.CurrentNode.PreviousSibling.ToString();
Hyperlink2.NavigateUrl = SiteMap.CurrentNode.PreviousSibling.Url;

        Hyperlink3.Text = SiteMap.CurrentNode.NextSibling.ToString();
        Hyperlink3.NavigateUrl = SiteMap.CurrentNode.NextSibling.Url;
    }
</script>
```

When run, this page gives you your own custom navigation structure, as shown in Figure 14-30.

Figure 14-30

URL Mapping

The URLs used by Web pages can sometimes get rather complex as your application grows and grows. Sometimes, you could be presenting Web pages that change their content based on querystrings that are provided via the URL, such as:

```
http://www.asp.net/forums/view.aspx?forumid=12&categoryid=6
```

In other cases, your Web page might be so deep within a hierarchy of folders that the URL has become rather cumbersome for an end user to type or remember when they want to pull up the page later in their browser. There are also moments when you want a collection of pages to look like they are the same page or a single destination.

In cases like these, you can take advantage of a new ASP.NET feature called *URL mapping.* URL mapping lets you map complex URLs to simpler ones. You accomplish this through settings you apply in the web.config file using the <urlMappings> element (see Listing 14-30).

Listing 14-30: Mapping URLs using the <urlMappings> element

```
<configuration>


  <system.web>


    <urlMappings>
        <add url="~/Content.aspx" mappedUrl="~/SystemNews.aspx?categoryid=5" />
    </urlMappings>

  </system.web>

</configuration>
```

In this example, we provide a fake URL — Content.aspx — that is mapped to a more complicated URL: SystemNews.aspx?categoryid=5. With this construction in place, when the end user types the URL Content.aspx, the application knows to invoke the more complicated URL SystemNews.aspx?categoryid=5 page. This takes place without the URL even being changed in the browser. Even after the page has completely loaded, the browser will still show the Content.aspx page as the destination — thereby tricking the end user in a sense.

It is important to note that in this situation, the end user is routed to SystemNews.aspx?categoryid=5 no matter what — *even if a* Content.aspx *page exists*! Therefore, it is important to map to pages that aren't actually contained within your application.

Sitemap Localization

The improved resource files (.resx) are a great way to localize ASP.NET applications. This localization of Web applications using ASP.NET was introduced in Chapter 3 of this book. However, this introduction focused on applying localization features to the pages of your applications; we didn't demonstrate how to take this localization capability further by applying it to items such as the Web.sitemap file.

Structuring the Web.sitemap File for Localization

Just as it is possible to apply localization instructions to the pages of your ASP.NET Web applications, you can also use the same framework to accomplish your localization tasks in the Web.sitemap file. To show you this in action, Listing 14-31 constructs a Web.sitemap file somewhat similar to the one presented in Listing 14-1, but much simpler.

Listing 14-31: Creating a basic .sitemap file for localization

```
<?xml version="1.0" encoding="utf-8" ?>

<siteMap xmlns="http://schemas.microsoft.com/AspNet/SiteMap-File-1.0"
 enableLocalization="true">
 <siteMapNode url="Default.aspx" resourceKey="Home">
        <siteMapNode url="News.aspx" resourceKey="News">
               <siteMapNode url="News.aspx?cat=us" resourceKey="NewsUS" />
               <siteMapNode url="News.aspx?cat=world" resourceKey="NewsWorld" />
               <siteMapNode url="News.aspx?cat=tech" resourceKey="NewsTech" />
               <siteMapNode url="News.aspx?cat=sport" resourceKey="NewsSport" />
        </siteMapNode>
 </siteMapNode>
</siteMap>
```

Looking at Listing 14-31, you can see that we have a rather simple `Web.sitemap` file. To enable the localization capability from the `Web.sitemap` file, you have to turn this capability on by using the `enableLocalization` attribute in the `<siteMap>` element and setting it to `true`. Once enabled, you can then define each of the navigation nodes as you would normally through the use of the `<siteMapNode>` element. In this case, however, because you are going to define the contents of these navigation pieces (most notably the `title` and `description` attributes) in various `.resx` files, there is no need to repeatedly define these items in this file. That means you need to define only the `url` attribute for this example. It's important to note, however, that you could also define this attribute through your `.resx` files, thereby forwarding end users to different pages depending on their defined culture settings.

The next attribute to note is the `resourceKey` attribute used in the `<siteMapNode>` elements. This is the key that is used and defined in the various `.resx` files you will implement. Take the following `<siteMapNode>` element as an example:

```
<siteMapNode url="News.aspx" resourceKey="News">
   ...
</siteMapNode>
```

In this case, the value of the `resourceKey` (and the key that will be used in the `.resx` file) is `News`. This means that you are then able to define the values of the `title` and `description` attributes in the `.resx` file through the use of the following syntax:

```
News.Title
News.Description
```

Now that the `Web.sitemap` is in place, the next step is to make some minor modifications to the `Web.config` file, as shown next.

Making Modifications to the Web.config File

Now that the `Web.sitemap` file is in place and ready, the next step is to provide some minor additions to the `Web.config` file. In order for your Web application to make an automatic detection of the culture of the users visiting the various pages you are providing, you need to either set the Culture and UICulture settings in the @Page directive, or set these attributes for automatic detection in the <globalization> element of the Web.config file.

When you are working with navigation and the Web.sitemap file, as we are, it is actually best to make this change in the Web.config file so that it automatically takes effect on each and every page in your application. This makes it much simpler because you won't have to make these additions yourself to each and every page.

To make these changes, open your Web.config file and add a <globalization> element, as shown in Listing 14-32.

Listing 14-32: Adding culture detection to the Web.config file

```
<configuration>
    <system.web>

        <globalization culture="auto" uiCulture="auto" />

    </system.web>
</configuration>
```

For the auto-detection capabilities to occur, you simply need to set the culture and uiCulture attributes to auto. You could have also defined the values as auto:en-US, which means that the automatic culture detection capabilities should occur, but if the culture defined is not found in the various resource files, then use en-US (American English) as the default culture. But because we are going to define a default Web.sitemap set of values, there really is no need for you to bring forward this construction.

Next, you need to create the assembly resources files that define the values used by the Web.sitemap file.

Creating Assembly Resource (.resx) Files

To create a set of assembly resource files that you will use with the Web.sitemap file, create a folder in your project called App_GlobalResources. If you are using Visual Studio 2005 or Visual Web Developer, you can add this folder by right-clicking on the project and selecting Add Folder ⇨ App_GlobalResources Folder.

After the folder is in place, the next step is to add two assembly resource files to this folder. Name the first file Web.sitemap.resx and the second one Web.sitemap.fi.resx. Your goal with these two files is to have a default set of values for the Web.sitemap file that will be defined in the Web.sitemap.resx file, and a version of these values that has been translated to the Finnish language and is contained in the Web.sitemap.fi.resx file.

The fi value used in the name will be the file used by individuals who have their preferred language set to fi-FI. Other variations of these constructions are shown in the following table.

.resx File	Culture Served
Web.sitemap.resx	The default values used when the end user's culture cannot be identified through another .resx file
Web.sitemap.en.resx	The resource file used for all en (English) users
Web.sitemap.en-gb.resx	The resource file used for the English speakers of Great Britain
Web.sitemap.fr-ca.resx	The resource file used for the French speakers of Canada
Web.sitemap.ru.resx	The resource file used for Russian speakers

Now that the Web.sitemap.resx and Web.sitemap.fi.resx files are in place, the next step is to fill these files with values. To accomplish this task, you use the keys defined earlier directly in the Web.sitemap file. Figure 14-31 shows the result of this exercise.

After you have the files in place you can test how this localization endeavor works, as shown in the following section.

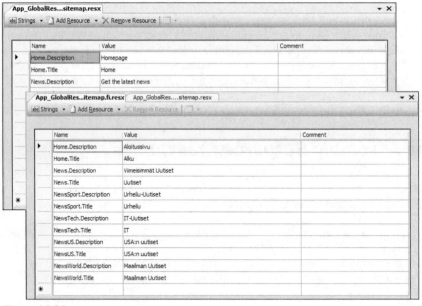

Figure 14-31

Testing the Results

Create a page in your application and place a TreeView server control on the page. In addition to the TreeView control, you also have to include a SiteMapDataSource control to work with the Web.sitemap file you created. Be sure to tie the two controls together by giving the TreeView control the attribute DataSourceID="SiteMapDataSource1", as demonstrated earlier in this chapter.

If you have your language preference in Microsoft's Internet Explorer set to en-us (American English), you will see the results shown in Figure 14-32.

Figure 14-32

When you pull up the page in the browser, the culture of the request is checked. Because the only finely grained preference defined in the example is for users using the culture of fi (Finnish), the default Web.sitemap.resx is used instead. Because of this, the Web.sitemap.resx file is used to populate the values of the TreeView control, as shown in Figure 14-32. If the requestor has a culture setting of fi, however, he gets an entirely different set of results.

To test this out, change the preferred language used in IE by selecting Tools ⇨ Internet Options in IE. On the first tab (General), click the Languages button at the bottom of the dialog. You are presented with the Language Preferences dialog. Click the Add button and add the Finnish language setting to the list of options. The final step is to use the Move Up button to move the Finnish choice to the top of the list. In the end, you should see something similar to what's shown in Figure 14-33.

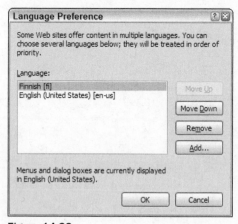

Figure 14-33

With this setting in place, running the page with the TreeView control gives you the result shown in Figure 14-34.

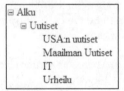

Figure 14-34

Now, when the page is requested, the culture is set to `fi` and correlates to the `Web.sitemap.fi.resx` file instead of to the default `Web.sitemap.resx` file.

Summary

This chapter introduced the new navigation mechanics that ASP.NET 2.0 provides. At the core of the new navigation capabilities is the power to detail the navigation structure in an XML file, which can then be utilized by various navigation controls — such as the new TreeView and SiteMapPath controls.

The powerful functionality that the new navigation capabilities provide saves you a tremendous amount of coding time.

In addition to showing you the core infrastructure for navigation in ASP.NET 2.0, this chapter also described both the new TreeView and SiteMapPath controls and how to use them throughout your applications. The great thing about these new controls is that, right out of the box, they can richly display your navigation hierarchy and enable the end user to work through the site easily. In addition, these controls are easily changeable so that you can go beyond the standard appearance and functionality that they provide.

Finally, this chapter took a look at how to achieve URL mapping, as well as how to localize your `Web.sitemap` files.

Personalization

Many Web applications must be customized with information that is specific to the end user who is presently viewing the page. In the past, the developer usually provided storage of personalization properties for end users viewing the page by means of cookies, the `Session` object, or the `Application` object. Cookies enabled storage of persistent items so that when the end user returned to a Web page, any settings related to him were retrieved. Cookies aren't the best way to approach persistent user data storage, however, because they are not accepted by all computers and also because a crafty end user can easily alter them.

As you will see in Chapter 16, ASP.NET 2.0's membership and role management capabilities are ways that ASP.NET can conveniently store information about the user. How can you, as the developer, use the same mechanics to store custom information?

ASP.NET 2.0 provides you with an outstanding new feature — *personalization*. The ASP.NET personalization engine provided with this latest release can make an automatic association between the end user viewing the page and any data points stored for that user. The personalization properties that are maintained on a per-user basis are stored on the server and not on the client. These items are conveniently placed in a data store of your choice (such as Microsoft's SQL Server) and, therefore, the end user can access these personalization properties on later site visits.

This new feature is an ideal way to start creating highly customizable and user-specific sites without building any of the plumbing beforehand. The new personalization feature is yet another way that the ASP.NET team is making developers more productive and their jobs easier.

The Personalization Model

The personalization model provided with ASP.NET 2.0 is simple and, as with most items that come with ASP.NET, it is an extensible model as well. Figure 15-1 shows a simple diagram that outlines the new personalization model.

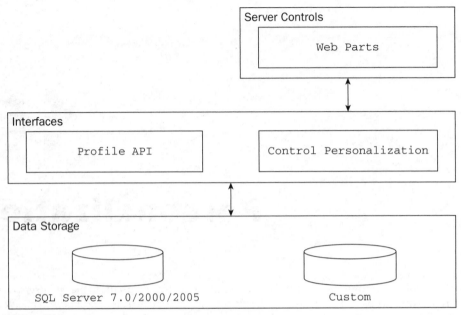

Figure 15-1

From this diagram, you can see the three layers in this model. First, look at the middle layer of the personalization model — the Personalization Services layer. This layer contains the Profile API. This new Profile API layer enables you to program your end user's data points into one of the lower-layer data stores. Also included in this layer are the server control personalization capabilities, which are important for the Portal Framework and the use of Web Parts. The Portal Framework and Web Parts are discussed in Chapter 17.

Although certain controls built into ASP.NET can utilize the new personalization capabilities for storing information about the page settings, you can also use this new engine to store your own data points. Just like Web Parts, these points can be used within your ASP.NET pages.

Below the Personalization Services layer, you find the default personalization data provider for working with Microsoft's SQL Server 2005 or 2000, as well as the new Microsoft SQL Server Express Edition files. You are not limited to just this one data store when applying the new personalization features of ASP.NET 2.0; you can also extend the model and create a custom data provider for the personalization engine.

Now that you have looked briefly at the personalization model, you can begin using it by creating some stored personalization properties that can be used later within your applications.

Creating Personalization Properties

The nice thing about creating custom personalization properties is that you can do it so easily. After these properties are created, you can gain a strongly typed access to them. It is also possible to create personalization properties that are used only by authenticated users, and also some that anonymous users can utilize. These data points are powerful — mainly because you can start using them immediately in your application. The first step is to create some simple personalization properties. Later, you learn how to use these personalization properties within your application.

Adding a Simple Personalization Property

The first step is to decide what data items from the user you are going to store. For this example, create a few items about the user that you can use within your application; assume that you want to store the following information about the user:

❑ First name

❑ Last name

❑ Last visited

❑ Age

❑ Membership Status

ASP.NET has a heavy dependency on storing configurations inside XML files, and the ASP.NET 2.0 personalization engine is no different. All these customization points concerning the end user are defined and stored within the `web.config` file of the application. This is illustrated in Listing 15-1.

Listing 15-1: Creating personalization properties in the web.config file

```
<configuration>
  <system.web>

    <profile>

      <properties>

        <add name="FirstName" />
        <add name="LastName" />
        <add name="LastVisited" />
        <add name="Age" />
        <add name="Member" />

      </properties>

    </profile>

    <authentication mode="Windows" />

  </system.web>
</configuration>
```

Within the `web.config` file and nested within the `<system.web>` section of the file, you create a `<profile>` section in order to work with the ASP.NET 2.0 personalization engine. Within this `<profile>` section of the `web.config` file, you create a `<properties>` section. In this section, you can define all the properties you want the personalization engine to store.

From this code example, you can see that it is rather easy to define simple properties using the `<add>` element. This element simply takes the `name` attribute, which takes the name of the property you want to persist.

We start out with the assumption that accessing the page we will build with these properties is already authenticated using Windows authentication (you can read more on authentication and authorization in the next chapter). Later in this chapter, we look at how to apply personalization properties to anonymous users as well.

It's just as easy to use these personalization properties as it is to define them. The next section looks at how to use these definitions in an application.

Using Personalization Properties

Now that you have defined the personalization properties in the `web.config` file, it's possible to use these items in code. For example, you can create a simple form that asks for some of this information from the end user. On the `Button_Click` event, the data is stored in the personalization engine. Listing 15-2 shows an example of this.

Listing 15-2: Using the defined personalization properties

VB

```
<%@ Page Language="VB" %>

<script runat="server">
    Protected Sub Button1_Click(ByVal sender As Object, ByVal e As System.EventArgs)
        If Page.User.Identity.IsAuthenticated Then
            Profile.FirstName = TextBox1.Text
            Profile.LastName = TextBox2.Text
            Profile.Age = TextBox3.Text
            Profile.Member = Radiobuttonlist1.SelectedItem.Text
            Profile.LastVisited = DateTime.Now().ToString()

            Label1.Text = "Stored information includes:<p>" & _
                "First name: " & Profile.FirstName & _
                "<br>Last name: " & Profile.LastName & _
                "<br>Age: " & Profile.Age & _
                "<br>Member: " & Profile.Member & _
                "<br>Last visited: " & Profile.LastVisited
        Else
            Label1.Text = "You must be authenticated!"
        End If
    End Sub
</script>

<html xmlns="http://www.w3.org/1999/xhtml" >
<head runat="server">
    <title>Storing Personalization</title>
</head>
<body>
    <form id="form1" runat="server">
        <p>First Name:
        <asp:TextBox ID="TextBox1" Runat="server"></asp:TextBox></p>
```

```
        <p>Last Name:
        <asp:TextBox ID="TextBox2" Runat="server"></asp:TextBox></p>
        <p>Age:
        <asp:TextBox ID="TextBox3" Runat="server" Width="50px"
         MaxLength="3"></asp:TextBox></p>
        <p>Are you a member?
        <asp:RadioButtonList ID="Radiobuttonlist1" Runat="server">
            <asp:ListItem Value="1">Yes</asp:ListItem>
            <asp:ListItem Value="0" Selected="True">No</asp:ListItem>
        </asp:RadioButtonList></p>
        <p><asp:Button ID="Button1" Runat="server" Text="Submit"
            OnClick="Button1_Click" />
        </p>
        <hr /><p>
        <asp:Label ID="Label1" Runat="server"></asp:Label></p>
    </form>
</body>
</html>
```

C#

```
<%@ Page Language="C#" %>

<script runat="server">
    protected void Button1_Click(object sender, EventArgs e)
    {
      if (Page.User.Identity.IsAuthenticated)
      {
        Profile.FirstName = TextBox1.Text;
        Profile.LastName = TextBox2.Text;
        Profile.Age = TextBox3.Text;
        Profile.Member = Radiobuttonlist1.SelectedItem.Text;
        Profile.LastVisited = DateTime.Now.ToString();

        Label1.Text = "Stored information includes:<p>" +
            "First name: " + Profile.FirstName +
            "<br>Last name: " + Profile.LastName +
            "<br>Age: " + Profile.Age +
            "<br>Member: " + Profile.Member +
            "<br>Last visited: " + Profile.LastVisited;
      }
      else
      {
        Label1.Text = "You must be authenticated!";
      }
    }
</script>
```

This is similar to the way you worked with the Session object in the past, but note that the personalization properties you are storing and retrieving are not key based. Therefore, when working with them you don't need to remember key names.

By default, these items are stored as type `String`, and you have early-bound access to the items stored. To store an item, you simply populate the personalization property directly using the `Profile` object:

```
Profile.FirstName = TextBox1.Text
```

To retrieve the same information, you simply grab the appropriate property of the `Profile` class as shown here:

```
Label1.Text = Profile.FirstName
```

The great thing about using the `Profile` class and all the personalization properties defined in code is that this method provides IntelliSense. When working with the `Profile` class, all the items you define are listed as available options, as illustrated in Figure 15-2.

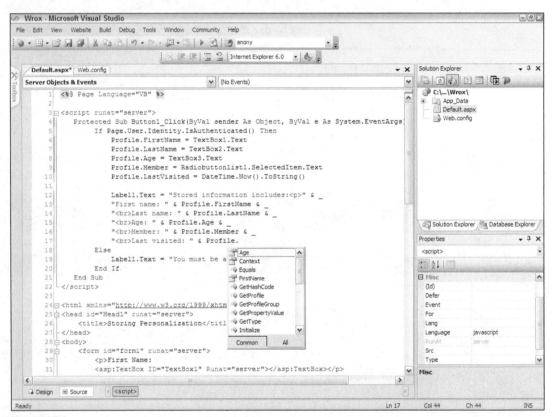

Figure 15-2

All these properties are accessible in IntelliSense because the `Profile` class is hidden and dynamically compiled behind the scenes whenever you save the personalization changes made to the `web.config` file. After these items are saved in the `web.config` file, these properties are available to you throughout your application.

When run, the page from Listing 15-2 produces the results shown in Figure 15-3.

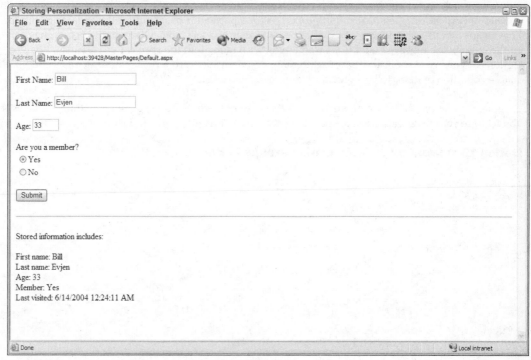

Figure 15-3

In addition to using early-bound access techniques, you can also use late-bound access for the items that you store in the personalization engine. This technique is illustrated in Listing 15-3.

Listing 15-3: Using late-bound access

VB

```
Dim myFirstName As String

myFirstName = Profile.PropertyValues("FirstName").PropertyValue.ToString()
```

C#

```
string myFirstName;

myFirstName = (string) Profile.PropertyValues["FirstName"].PropertyValue;
```

Whether it is early-bound access or late-bound access, you can easily store and retrieve personalization properties for a particular user using this new capability afforded by ASP.NET 2.0. All this is done in the personalization engine's simplest form — now take a look at how you can customize for specific needs in your applications.

Adding a Group of Personalization Properties

If you want to store a large number of personalization properties about a particular user, remember that you are not just storing personalization properties for a particular page, but for the *entire* application. This means that items you have stored about a particular end user somewhere in the beginning of the application can be retrieved later for use on any other page within the application. Because different sections of your Web applications store different personalization properties, you sometimes end up with a large collection of items to be stored and then made accessible.

To make it easier not only to store the items, but also to retrieve them, the personalization engine enables you to store your personalization properties in groups. This is illustrated in Listing 15-4.

Listing 15-4: Creating personalization groups in the web.config file

```
<configuration>
  <system.web>

    <profile>

      <properties>

        <add name="FirstName" />
        <add name="LastName" />
        <add name="LastVisited" />
        <add name="Age" />

        <group name="MemberDetails">
          <add name="Member" />
          <add name="DateJoined" />
          <add name="PaidDuesStatus" />
          <add name="Location" />
        </group>

        <group name="FamilyDetails">
          <add name="MarriedStatus" />
          <add name="DateMarried" />
          <add name="NumberChildren" />
          <add name="Location" />
        </group>

      </properties>

    </profile>

    <authentication mode="Windows" />

  </system.web>
</configuration>
```

From the code in Listing 15-4, which is placed within the web.config file, you can see that two groups are listed. The first group is the MemberDetails group, which has four specific items defined; the second group — FamilyDetails — has three other related items defined. Personalization groups are defined using the <group> element within the <properties> definition. The name of the group is specified using the name attribute, just as you specify the <add> element. You can have as many groups defined as you deem necessary or as have been recommended as good practice to employ.

Using Grouped Personalization Properties

From Listing 15-4, you can also see that some items are not defined in any particular group. It is possible to mix properties defined from within a group with those that are not. The items not defined in a group in Listing 15-4 can still be accessed in the manner illustrated previously:

```
Label1.Text = Profile.FirstName
```

Now, using personalization groups, you can access your defined items in a logical manner using nested namespaces:

```
Label1.Text = Profile.MemberDetails.DateJoined

Label2.Text = Profile.FamilyDetails.MarriedStatus
```

From this example, you can see that two separate items from each of the defined personalization groups were accessed in a logical manner. From the defined properties, you can see that each of the groups has a property with the same name—Location. This is possible because you are using personalization groups. With this structure, it is now possible to get at each of the Location properties by specifying the appropriate group:

```
Label1.Text = Profile.MemberDetails.Location

Label2.Text = Profile.FamilyDetails.Location
```

Defining Types for Personalization Properties

By default, when you store personalization properties, these properties are created as type String. It is quite easy, however, to change the type to something else through configurations within the web.config file. To define the name of the personalization property along with its type, you use the Type attribute, as shown in Listing 15-5.

Listing 15-5: Defining types for personalization properties

```
<properties>

    <add name="FirstName" type="System.String" />
    <add name="LastName" type="System.String" />
    <add name="LastVisited" type="System.DateTime" />
    <add name="Age" type="System.Integer" />
    <add name="Member" type="System.Boolean" />

</properties>
```

The first two properties, FirstName and LastName, are cast as type String. This isn't actually required. Even if you omitted this step, they would still be cast as type String because that is the default type. The next personalization property is the LastVisited property, which is defined as type System.DateTime and used to store the date and time of the end user's last visit to the page. Beyond that, you can see the rest of the personalization properties are defined using a specific .NET data type.

This is the preferred approach because it gives you type-checking capabilities as you code your application and use the personalization properties you have defined.

Using Custom Types

As you can see from the examples that show you how to define types for the personalization properties, it is quite simple to define types that are available in the .NET Framework. Items such as System.Integer, System.String, System.DateTime, System.Byte, and System.Boolean are easily defined within the web.config file. But how do you go about defining complex types?

Personalization properties that utilize custom types are just as easy to define as personalization properties that use simple types. Custom types give you the capability to store complex items such as shopping cart information or other status information from one use of the application to the next. Listing 15-6 first shows a class, ShoppingCart, which you use later in one of the personalization property definitions.

Listing 15-6: Creating a class to use as a personalization type

VB

```vb
<Serializable()> _
Public Class ShoppingCart
    Private PID As String
    Private CompanyProductName As String
    Private Number As Integer
    Private Price As Decimal
    Private DateAdded As DateTime

    Public Property ProductID() As String
        Get
            Return PID
        End Get
        Set(ByVal value As String)
            PID = value
        End Set
    End Property

    Public Property ProductName() As String
        Get
            Return CompanyProductName
        End Get
        Set(ByVal value As String)
            CompanyProductName = value
        End Set
    End Property

    Public Property NumberSelected() As Integer
        Get
            Return Number
        End Get
        Set(ByVal value As Integer)
            Number = value
        End Set
```

```
        End Property

    Public Property ItemPrice() As Decimal
        Get
            Return Price
        End Get
        Set(ByVal value As Decimal)
            Price = value
        End Set
    End Property

    Public Property DateItemAdded() As DateTime
        Get
            Return DateAdded
        End Get
        Set(ByVal value As DateTime)
            DateAdded = value
        End Set
    End Property
End Class
```

C#

```
using System;

[Serializable]
public class ShoppingCart
{
    private string PID;
    private string CompanyProductName;
    private int Number;
    private decimal Price;
    private DateTime DateAdded;

    public ShoppingCart() {}

    public string ProductID
    {
        get { return PID; }
        set { PID = value; }
    }

    public string ProductName
    {
        get { return CompanyProductName; }
        set { CompanyProductName = value; }
    }

    public int NumberSelected
    {
        get { return Number; }
        set { Number = value; }
    }

    public decimal ItemPrice
```

(continued)

Listing 15-6: *(continued)*

```
    {
        get { return Price; }
        set { Price = value; }
    }

    public DateTime DateItemAdded
    {
        get { return DateAdded; }
        set { DateAdded = value; }
    }
}
```

This simple shopping cart construction can now store the end user's shopping cart basket as the user moves around on an e-commerce site. The basket can even be persisted when the end user returns to the site at another time.

Take a look at how you would specify from within the web.config file that a personalization property is this complex type. This is illustrated in Listing 15-7.

Listing 15-7: Using complex types for personalization properties

```
<properties>

    <add name="FirstName" type="System.String" />
    <add name="LastName" type="System.String" />
    <add name="LastVisited" type="System.DateTime" />
    <add name="Age" type="System.Integer" />
    <add name="Member" type="System.Boolean" />
    <add name="Cart" type="ShoppingCart" serializeAs="Binary" />

</properties>
```

Just as the basic data types are stored in the personalization data stores, this construction allows you to easily store custom types and to have them serialized into the end data store in the format you choose. In this case, the ShoppingCart object is serialized into a binary object in the data store. The SerializeAs attribute can take the values defined in the following list:

❑ **Binary:** Serializes and stores the object as binary data within the chosen data store.

❑ **ProviderSpecific:** Stores the object based upon the direction of the provider. This simply means that instead of the personalization engine determining the serialization of the object, it is simply left up to the data store.

❑ **String:** The default setting. Stores the personalization properties as a string inside the chosen data store.

❑ **XML:** Takes the object and serializes it into an XML format before storing it in the chosen data store.

Providing Default Values

In addition to defining the types of personalization properties, you can also define their default values. The personalization properties you create do not have a value, but you can easily change this using the `DefaultValue` attribute of the `<add>` element. Defining default values is illustrated in Listing 15-8.

Listing 15-8: Defining default values for personalization properties

```
<properties>

    <add name="FirstName" type="System.String" />
    <add name="LastName" type="System.String" />
    <add name="LastVisited" type="System.DateTime" />
    <add name="Age" type="System.Integer" />
    <add name="Member" type="System.Boolean" defaultValue="False" />

</properties>
```

From this example, you can see that only one of the personalization properties is provided with a default value. The last personalization property, `Member` in this example, is given a default value of `False`. This means that when you add a new end user to the personalization property database, `Member` is defined instead of remaining a blank value.

Making Personalization Properties Read-Only

It is also possible to make personalization properties read-only. To do this, you simply add the `readOnly` attribute to the `<add>` element:

```
<add name="StartDate" type="System.DateTime" readOnly="True" />
```

To make the personalization property a read-only property, you give the `readOnly` attribute a value of `True`. By default, this property is set to `False`.

Anonymous Personalization

A great new feature in ASP.NET 2.0 enables anonymous end users to utilize the personalization features it provides. This is important if a site requires registration of some kind. In these cases, end users do not always register for access to the greater application until they have first taken advantage of some of the basic services. For instance, many e-commerce sites allow anonymous end users to shop a site and use the site's shopping cart before the shoppers register with the site.

Enabling Anonymous Identification of the End User

By default, anonymous personalization is turned off because it consumes database resources on popular sites. Therefore, one of the first steps in allowing anonymous personalization is to turn on this feature using a setting in the `web.config` file.

As shown in Listing 15-9, you can turn on anonymous identification to enable the personalization engine to identify the unknown end users.

Listing 15-9: Allowing anonymous identification

```
<configuration>
  <system.web>

      <anonymousIdentification enabled="True" />

  </system.web>
</configuration>
```

To enable anonymous identification of the end users who might visit your applications, you add an `<anonymousIdentification>` element to the `web.config` file within the `<system.web>` nodes. Then within the `<anonymousIdentification>` element, you use the `Enabled` attribute and set its value to `True`. Remember that by default, this value is set to `False`.

When anonymous identification is turned on, ASP.NET uses a unique identifier for each anonymous user who comes to the application. This identifier is sent with each and every request, although after the end user becomes authenticated by ASP.NET, the identifier is removed from the process.

For an anonymous user, information is stored by default as a cookie on the end user's machine. Additional information (the personalization properties that you enable for anonymous users) is stored in the specified data store on the server.

Changing the Name of the Cookie for Anonymous Identification

Cookies are used by default under the cookie name `.ASPXANONYMOUS`. You can change the name of this cookie from the `<anonymousIdentification>` element in the `web.config` file by using the `cookieName` attribute, as shown in Listing 15-10.

Listing 15-10: Changing the name of the cookie

```
<configuration>
  <system.web>

      <anonymousIdentification
          enabled="True"
          cookieName=".ASPXEvjenWebApplication" />

  </system.web>
</configuration>
```

Changing the Length of Time the Cookie Is Stored

Also, by default, the cookie stored on the end user's machine is stored for 100,000 minutes (which is almost 70 days). If you want to change this value, you do it within this `<anonymousIdentification>` element through the use of the `cookieTimeout` attribute, as shown in Listing 15-11.

Listing 15-11: Changing the length of time the cookie is stored

```
<configuration>
  <system.web>

      <anonymousIdentification
```

```
        enabled="True"
        cookieTimeout="1440" />

   </system.web>
</configuration>
```

In this case, the `cookieTimeout` value was changed to `1440` — meaning 1,440 minutes (or one day). This would be ideal for a shopping cart when you don't want to persist the identification of the end user too long.

Changing How the Identifiers Are Stored

Although anonymous identifiers are stored through the use of cookies, you can also easily change this. Cookies are, by far, the preferred way to achieve identification, but you can also do it without the use of cookies. Other options include using the URI or device profiles. Listing 15-12 shows an example of using the URI to place the identifiers.

Listing 15-12: Specifying how cookies are stored

```
<configuration>
   <system.web>

      <anonymousIdentification
          enabled="True"
          cookieless="UseUri" />

   </system.web>
</configuration>
```

Besides `UseUri`, other options include `UseCookies`, `AutoDetect`, and `UseDeviceProfile`. The following list reviews each of the options:

❏   `UseCookies`: This is the default setting. If you set no value, ASP.NET assumes this is the value. `UseCookies` means that a cookie is placed on the end user's machine for identification.

❏   `UseUri`: This value means that a cookie *will not* be stored on the end user's machine, but instead the unique identifier will be munged within the URL of the page. This is the same approach used for cookieless sessions in ASP.NET 1.0/1.1. Although this is great if developers want to avoid sticking a cookie on an end user's machine, it does create strange looking URLs and can be an issue when an end user bookmarks pages for later retrieval.

❏   `AutoDetect`: Using this value means that you are letting the ASP.NET engine decide whether to use cookies or use the URL approach for the anonymous identification. This is done on a per-user basis and performs a little worse than the other two options. ASP.NET must check the end user before deciding which approach to use. My suggestion is to use `AutoDetect` instead of `UseUri` if you absolutely must allow for end users who have cookies turned off (which is rare these days).

❏   `UseDeviceProfile`: Configures the identifier for the device or browser that is making the request.

Looking at the Anonymous Identifiers Stored

In order to make the anonymous identifiers unique, a globally unique GUID is used. You can also now grab hold of this unique identifier for your own use. In order to retrieve the GUID, the `Request` object has been enhanced with an `AnonymousId` property. The `AnonymousId` property returns a value of type `String`, which can be used in your code as shown here:

```
Label1.Text = Request.AnonymousId
```

Working with Anonymous Identification Events

In working with the creation of anonymous users, be aware of two important events that can be used for managing the process:

❑   `AnonymousIdentification_OnCreate`

❑   `AnonymousIdentification_OnRemove`

By using the `AnonymousIdentification_OnCreate` event, you can work with the identification of the end user as it occurs. For instance, if you do not want to use GUIDs for uniquely identifying the end user, you can change the identifying value from this event instead.

To do so, create the event using the event delegate of type `AnonymousIdentificationEventArgs`, as illustrated in Listing 15-13.

Listing 15-13: Changing the unique identifier of the anonymous user

VB
```
Public Sub AnonymousIdentification_OnCreate(ByVal sender As Object, _
    ByVal e As AnonymousIdentificationEventArgs)

        e.AnonymousID = "Bubbles " & DateTime.Now()

End Sub
```

C#
```
public void AnonymousIdentification_OnCreate(object sender,
    AnonymousIdentificationEventArgs e)
{
        e.AnonymousID = "Bubbles" + DateTime.Now;
}
```

The `AnonymousIdentificationEventArgs` event delegate exposes an `AnonymousId` property that assigns the value used to uniquely identify the anonymous user. Now, instead of a GUID to uniquely identify the anonymous user as

```
d13fafec-244a-4d21-9137-b213236ebedb
```

the `AnonymousID` property is changed within the `AnonymousIdentification_OnCreate` event to

```
Bubbles 2/10/2006 2:07:33 PM
```

The `AnonymousIdentification_OnRemove` event also employs an event delegate of type `AnonymousIdentificationEventArgs` that is used immediately prior to migrating anonymous users to registered users. Note that the `AnonymousId` property of the `Request` object is still accessible at this point.

Anonymous Options for Personalization Properties

Now that the capability to work with anonymous users is in place, you have to specify which personalization properties you want to enable for anonymous users. This is also done through the `web.config` file by adding the `allowAnonymous` attribute to the `<add>` element (see Listing 15-14).

Listing 15-14: Turning on anonymous capabilities personalization properties

```
<properties>

    <add name="FirstName" type="System.String" />
    <add name="LastName" type="System.String" />
    <add name="LastVisited" type="System.DateTime" allowAnonymous="true" />
    <add name="Age" type="System.Integer" />
    <add name="Member" type="System.Boolean" />

</properties>
```

In this example, the `LastVisited` property is set to allow anonymous users by setting the `allowAnonymous` attribute to `True`. Because this is the only property that works with anonymous users, the rest of the defined properties do not store information for these types of users.

Programmatic Access to Personalization

When an ASP.NET is invoked, ASP.NET creates a class (`ProfileCommon`) by inheriting from the `ProfileBase` class, which it uses to strongly type the profile properties that were defined in the `web.config` file. This created class, meant to deal with the user's profile store, gets and sets profile properties through the use of the `GetPropertyValue` and `SetPropertyValue` methods from the `ProfileBase` class.

As you would expect, ASP.NET provides you with the hooks necessary to get at specific `Profile` events through the use of the `ProfileModule` class. The `ProfileModule` class is what ASP.NET itself uses to create and store profile information in the page's `Profile` object.

The `ProfileModule` class exposes three events that you can use to handle your user's profile situations. These events, `MigrateAnonymous`, `Personalize`, and `ProfileAutoSaving`, are focused around the area of authentication. Because we were just covering how to work with anonymous users in your applications, we first take a look at how to migrate these users from anonymous users to authenticated users — as you are most likely going to want to be moving their profile properties as well.

Migrating Anonymous Users

When working with anonymous users, you must be able to migrate anonymous users to registered users. For example, after an end user fills a shopping cart, he can register on the site to purchase the items. At that moment, the end user switches from being an anonymous user to a registered user.

For this reason, ASP.NET 2.0 provides a Profile_MigrateAnonymous event enabling you to migrate anonymous users to registered users. The Profile_MigrateAnonymous event requires an event delegate of type ProfileMigrateEventArgs. It is placed either in the page that deals with the migration or within the Global.asax file (if it can be used from anywhere within the application). The use of this event is illustrated in Listing 15-15.

Listing 15-15: Migrating anonymous users for particular personalization properties

VB

```
Public Sub Profile_MigrateAnonymous(ByVal sender As Object, _
   ByVal e As ProfileMigrateEventArgs)

    Profile.LastVisited = Profile.GetPropertyValue(e.AnonymousId).LastVisited

End Sub
```

C#

```
public void Profile_MigrateAnonymous(object sender,
   ProfileMigrateEventArgs e)
{
    Profile.GetPropertyValue(e.AnonymousID).LastVisited.ToString();
}
```

From this example, you populate the new Profile property with the old property. You get at the old property of the anonymous user by using the GetPropertyValue property, which takes a parameter of the ID of the anonymous user. From the Profile_MigrateAnonymous event, you still have access to the AnonymousId property, which you can retrieve from the event delegate — ProfileMigrateEventArgs.

Listing 15-15 shows how to migrate a single personalization property from an anonymous user to the new registered user. In addition to migrating single properties, you also can migrate properties that come from personalization groups. This is shown in Listing 15-16.

Listing 15-16: Migrating anonymous users for items in personalization groups

VB

```
Public Sub Profile_MigrateAnonymous(ByVal sender As Object, _
   ByVal e As ProfileMigrateEventArgs)

    Dim au As HttpProfile = Profile.GetProfile(e.AnonymousId)

    If au.MemberDetails.DateJoined <> "" Then
        Profile.MemberDetails.DateJoined = DateTime.Now().ToString()
        Profile.FamilyDetails.MarriedStatus = au.FamilyDetails.MarriedStatus
    End If

    AnonymousIdentificationModule.ClearAnonymousIdentifier()
End Sub
```

C#

```
public void Profile_MigrateAnonymous(object sender,
    ProfileMigrateEventArgs e)
{

        HttpProfile au = Profile.GetProfile(e.AnonymousID);

        if (au.MemberDetails.DateJoined != String.Empty) {
            Profile.MemberDetails.DateJoined = DateTime.Now.ToString();
            Profile.FamilyDetails.MarriedStatus = au.FamilyDetails.MarriedStatus;
            AnonymousIdentificationModule.ClearAnonymousIdentifier()
        }

}
```

Using this event either in the page or in the `Global.asax` file enables you to logically migrate anonymous users as they register themselves with your applications. The migration process also allows you to pick and choose which items you migrate and to change the values as you wish.

Personalizing Profiles

Besides working with anonymous users from the `Global.asax` file, you can also programmatically personalize the profiles retrieved from the personalization store. This is done though the use of the `Profile_Personalize` event. An example use of this event is shown in Listing 15-17.

Listing 15-17: Personalizing a retrieved profile

VB

```
Public Sub Profile_Personalize(sender As Object, args As ProfileEventArgs)
  Dim checkedProfile As ProfileCommon

  If User Is Nothing Then Return

  checkedProfile = CType(ProfileBase.Create(User.Identity.Name), ProfileCommon)

  If (Date.Now.IsDaylightSavingTime()) Then
    checkedProfile = checkedProfile.GetProfile("TimeDifferenceUser")
  Else
    checkedProfile = checkedProfile.GetProfile("TimeUser")
  End If

  If Not checkedProfile Is Nothing Then
    args.Profile = checkedProfile
  End If
End Sub
```

C#

```
public void Profile_Personalize(object sender, ProfileEventArgs args)
{
```

(continued)

Listing 15-17: *(continued)*

```
    ProfileCommon checkedProfile;

    if (User == null) { return; }

    checkedProfile = (ProfileCommon)ProfileBase.Create(User.Identity.Name);

    if (DateTime.Now.IsDaylightSavingTime()) {
      checkedProfile = checkedProfile.GetProfile("TimeDifferenceUser");
    }
    else {
      checkedProfile = checkedProfile.GetProfile("TimeUser");
    }

    if (userProfile != null) {
      args.Profile = userProfile;
    }
  }
```

In this case, based on a specific parameter (whether it is Daylight Savings Time or something else), you are able to assign a specific profile to the user. You do this by using the `ProfileBase.Personalize` event, which you would usually stick inside the `Global.asax` page.

Determining Whether to Continue with Automatic Saves

When you are working with the profile capabilities provided by ASP.NET, the page automatically saves the profile values to the specified data store at the end of the page's execution. This capability, which is turned on (set to `True`) by default, can be set to `False` through the use of the `automaticSaveEnabled` attribute in the `<profile>` node in the `web.config` file.

Listing 15-18: Working with the automaticSaveEnabled attribute

```
    <profile automaticSaveEnabled="False">

      <properties>

        <add name="FirstName" />
        <add name="LastName" />
        <add name="LastVisited" />
        <add name="Age" />
        <add name="Member" />

      </properties>

    </profile>
```

If you have set the `automaticSaveEnabled` attribute value to `False`, you will have to invoke the `ProfileBase.Save()` method yourself. In most cases though, you are going to leave this setting on `True`. Once a page request has been made and finalized, the `ProfileModule.ProfileAutoSaving` event is raised. This is an event that you can also work with, as shown in Listing 15-19.

Listing 15-19: Using the ProfileAutoSaving event to turn off the auto-saving feature

VB
```vb
Public Sub Profile_ProfileAutoSaving(sender As Object, _
 args As ProfileAutoSaveEventArgs)

   If Profile.PaidDueStatus.HasChanged Then
     args.ContinueWithProfileAutoSave = True
   Else
     args.ContinueWithProfileAutoSave = False
   End If
End Sub
```

C#
```csharp
public void Profile_ProfileAutoSaving(object sender, ProfileAutoSaveEventArgs args)
{
   if (Profile.PaidDueStatus.HasChanged)
     args.ContinueWithProfileAutoSave = true;
   else
     args.ContinueWithProfileAutoSave = false;
}
```

In this case, when the `Profile_ProfileAutoSaving` event is triggered, it is then possible to work within this event and change some behaviors. Listing 15-19 looks to see if the `Profile.PaidDueStatus` property has changed. If it has changed, the auto-saving feature of the profile system is continued; if the `Profile.PaidDueStatus` hasn't changed, the auto-saving feature is turned off.

Personalization Providers

As shown in Figure 15-1 earlier in the chapter, the middle tier of the personalization model, the personalization API layer, communicates with a series of default data providers. By default, the personalization model uses Microsoft SQL Server Express Edition files for storing the personalization properties you define. You are not limited to just this type of data store, however. You can also use the Microsoft SQL Server data provider to allow you to work with Microsoft SQL Server 7.0, 2000, and SQL Server 2005. Besides the Microsoft SQL Server data provider, the architecture also allows you to create your own data providers if one of these data stores doesn't fit your requirements.

Working with SQL Server Express Edition

The Microsoft SQL Server data provider does allow you to work with the new SQL Server Express Edition files. The SQL Server data provider is the default provider used by the personalization system provided by ASP.NET. When used with Visual Studio 2005, the IDE places the `ASPNETDB.MDF` file within your application's `App_Data` folder.

As you look through the `machine.config` file, notice the sections that deal with how the personalization engine works with this database. In the first reference to the `LocalSqlServer` file that it works with, you find a connection string to this file (shown in Listing 15-20) within the `<connectionStrings>` section of the file.

Listing 15-20: Adding a connection string to the SQL Server Express file

```
<configuration>

    <connectionStrings>
        <clear />
        <add name="LocalSqlServer"
         connectionString="data source=.\SQLEXPRESS;Integrated Security=SSPI;
         AttachDBFilename=|DataDirectory|aspnetdb.mdf;User Instance=true"
         providerName="System.Data.SqlClient" />
    </connectionStrings>

</configuration>
```

In this example, you see that a connection string with the name `LocalSqlServer` has been defined. The location of the file, specified by the `connectionString` attribute, points to the relative path of the file. This means that in every application you build that utilizes the new personalization capabilities, the default SQL Server provider should be located in the application's `App_Data` folder and have the name of `ASPNETDB.MDF`.

The SQL Server Express file's connection string is specified through the `LocalSqlServer` declaration within this `<connectionStrings>` section. You can see the personalization engine's reference to this in the `<profile>` section within the `machine.config` file. The `<profile>` section includes a subsection listing all the providers available to the personalization engine. This is shown in Listing 15-21.

Listing 15-21: Adding a new SQL Server data provider

```
<configuration>
  <system.web>

        <profile>
            <providers>
                <add name="AspNetSqlProfileProvider"
                 connectionStringName="LocalSqlServer" applicationName="/"
                 type="System.Web.Profile.SqlProfileProvider, System.Web,
                   Version=2.0.0.0, Culture=neutral,
                   PublicKeyToken=b03f5f7f11d50a3a" />
            </providers>
        </profile>

  </system.web>
</configuration>
```

From this, you can see that a provider is added by using the `<add>` element. Within this element, the `connectionStringName` attribute points to what was declared in the `<connectionString>` attribute from Listing 15-20.

You can specify an entirely different Microsoft SQL Server Express Edition file other than the one specified in the `machine.config` file. First, create a connection string that points to a new SQL Server Express file that is a templated version of the ASPNETDB.mdb file. At this point, you can use <connectionString> to point to this new file. If you change these values in the machine.config file, all the ASP.NET applications that reside on the server will then use this specified file. If you make the changes only to the web.config file, however, only the application using this particular web.config file uses this new data store. Other applications on the server remain unchanged.

Working with Microsoft's SQL Server

You will likely find it quite easy to work with the personalization framework using the SQL Server Express files. But when you work with larger applications that require the factors of performance and reliability, you should use the SQL Server personalization provider along with SQL Server 7.0, 2000, or 2005. If this data store is available, you should always try to use this option instead of the default SQL Server Express Edition files.

If you worked with the SQL Server personalization provider using SQL Server Express files as explained earlier, you probably found it easy to use. The personalization provider works right out of the box — without any set up or configuration on your part. Using the SQL Server personalization provider with a full-blown version of SQL Server, however, is a bit of a different story. Although it is not difficult to work with, you must set up and configure your SQL Server before using it.

ASP.NET 2.0 provides a couple of ways to set up and configure SQL Server for the personalization framework. The following sections look at two ways to achieve this task. One way is through the ASP.NET SQL Server Setup Wizard, and the other method is by running some of the SQL Server scripts provided with the .NET Framework 2.0.

Using the ASP.NET SQL Server Setup Wizard

The ASP.NET SQL Server Setup Wizard is an easy-to-use tool that facilitates setup of the SQL Server to work with the personalization framework. The Setup Wizard provides two ways for you to set up the database: using a command-line tool or using a GUI tool.

The ASP.NET SQL Server Setup Wizard Command-Line Tool

The command-line version of the Setup Wizard gives the developer optimal control over how the database is created. Working from the command-line using this tool is not difficult, so don't be intimidated by it.

You can get at the actual tool, aspnet_regsql.exe, from the Visual Studio Command Prompt if you have Visual Studio 2005. You can find this command prompt at Start ⇨ All Programs ⇨ Microsoft Visual Studio 2005 ⇨ Visual Studio Tools ⇨ Visual Studio Command Prompt. At the command prompt, type **aspnet_regsql.exe -?** to get a list of all the available command-line options at your disposal for working this tool.

The following table describes some of the available options for setting up your SQL Server instance to work with the personalization framework.

Command Option	Description
-?	Displays a list of available option commands.
-W	Uses the Wizard mode. This uses the default installation if no other parameters are used.
-S <server>	Specifies the SQL Server instance to work with.
-U <login>	The username to log in to SQL Server. If you use this, you also use the -P command.
-P <password>	The password to use for logging in to SQL Server. If you use this, you also use the -U command.
-E	Provides instructions to use the current Windows credentials for authentication.
-C	Specifies the connection string for connecting to SQL Server. If you use this, you can avoid using the -U and -P commands because they are specified in the connection string itself.
-A all	Adds support for all the available SQL Server operations provided by ASP.NET 2.0 including membership, role management, profiles, site counters, and page/control personalization.
-A p	Adds support for working with profiles.
_R all	Removes support for all the available SQL Server operations that have been previously installed. These include membership, role management, profiles, site counters, and page/control personalization.
-R p	Removes support for the profile capability from SQL Server.
-d <database>	Specifies the database name to use with the application services. If you don't specify a name of a database, aspnetdb is used.
/sqlexportonly <filename>	Instead of modifying an instance of a SQL Server database, use this command in conjunction with the other commands to generate a SQL script that adds or removes the features specified. This command creates the scripts in a file that has the name specified in the command.

To modify SQL Server to work with the personalization provider using this command-line tool, you enter a command such as the following:

```
aspnet_regsql.exe -A p -E
```

After you enter the preceding command, the command-line tool creates the profile features required. The results are shown in the tool itself, as you see in Figure 15-4.

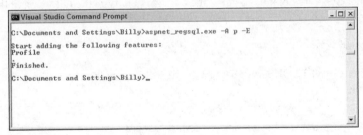

Figure 15-4

When this action is completed, you can see that a new table, `aspnetdb`, has been created in the SQL Server Enterprise Manager. You now have the appropriate tables for working with the personalization framework (see Figure 15-5).

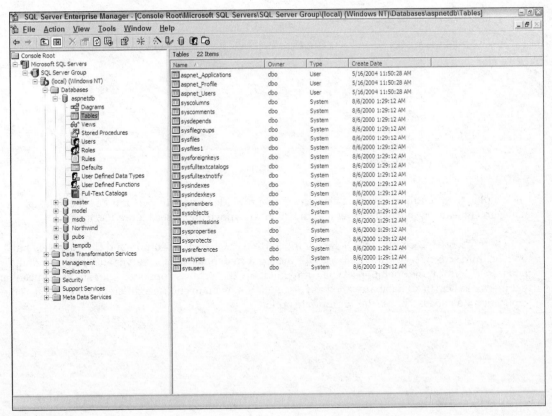

Figure 15-5

The ASP.NET SQL Server Setup Wizard GUI Tool

Instead of working with this tool through the command-line, another option is to work with the same wizard through a GUI version of it. To get at the GUI version, type the following at the Visual Studio Command Prompt:

```
aspnet_regsql.exe
```

At this point, the ASP.NET SQL Server Setup Wizard welcome screen appears, as shown in Figure 15-6.

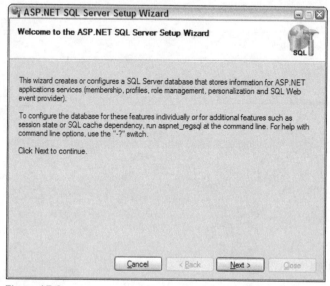

Figure 15-6

Clicking the Next button gives you a new screen that provides you with two options: one to install management features into SQL Server and the other to remove them (see Figure 15-7).

From here, choose the Configure SQL Server for ASP.NET SQL Server Features and click the Next button. The third screen (see Figure 15-8) asks for the login credentials to SQL Server and the name of the database to perform the operations. When you pull it up, the Database option is <default> — meaning that the wizard creates a database called aspnetdb. If you want to choose a different folder, such as the application's database, choose the appropriate option.

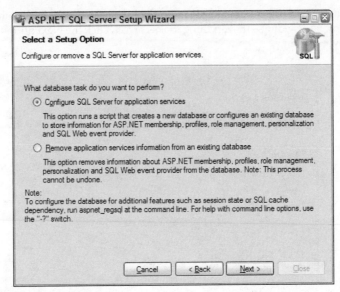

Figure 15-7

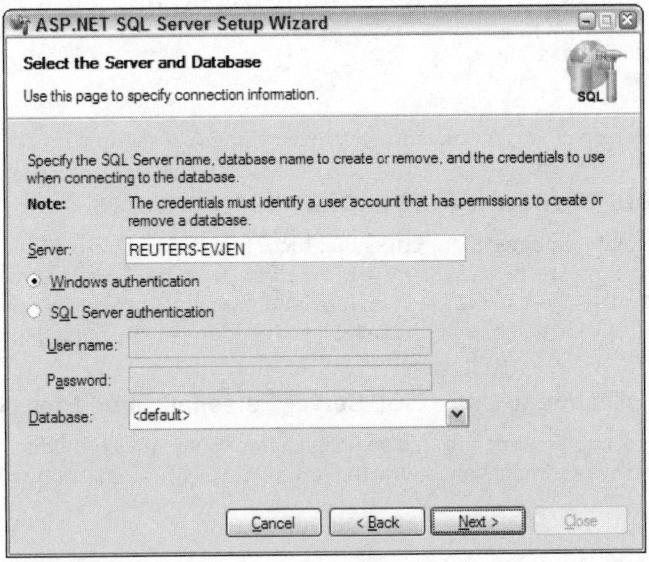

Figure 15-8

After you have made your server and database selections, click Next. The screen shown in Figure 15-9 asks you to confirm your settings. If everything looks correct, click the Next button — otherwise, click Back and correct your settings.

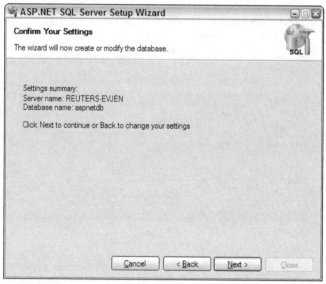

Figure 15-9

When this is complete, you get a notification that everything was set up correctly.

Using SQL Scripts to Install Personalization Features

Another option is to use the same SQL scripts that these tools and wizards use. If you look at `C:\Windows\Microsoft.NET\Framework\v2.0xxxxx\`, from this location, you see the install and remove scripts — `InstallPersonalization.sql` and `UninstallPersonalization.sql`. Running these scripts provides your database with the tables needed to run the personalization framework.

Setting Up Your Application to Use a SQL Server Personalization Provider

Now SQL Server is set up to work with the personalization capabilities provided by ASP.NET 2.0. The personalization framework understands how to work with SQL through settings in the `machine.config` or `web.config` files.

If you look in the machine.config file, you find that the connection string to SQL Server is specified in the <connectionStrings> section of the document. This SQL Server connection string actually is constructed to work with the SQL Server Express Edition files by default. To change it to work with SQL Server 2000 or 2005, you need to implement the code shown in Listing 15-22.

Listing 15-22: Changing the connection string in the machine.config file to work with SQL Server 2000

```
<configuration>

   <connectionStrings>
      <add name="LocalSql2000Server"
       connectionString="data source=127.0.0.1;Integrated Security=SSPI" />
   </connectionStrings>

</configuration>
```

You may want to change the values provided if you are working with a remote instance of SQL Server rather than an instance that resides on the same server as the application. Changing this value in the machine.config file changes how each and every ASP.NET application uses this provider.

After the connection string is set up accordingly, look further in the <providers> section of the <profile> element. You see the settings for SQL Server, as shown in Listing 15-23.

Listing 15-23: Adding a custom SQL Server data provider

```
<configuration>
   <system.web>

      <profile>
         <providers>
            <clear />
            <add name="AspNetSql2000ProfileProvider"
             connectionStringName="LocalSql2000Server" applicationName="/"
             type="System.Web.Profile.SqlProfileProvider, System.Web,
               Version=2.0.0.0, Culture=neutral,
               PublicKeyToken=b03f5f7f11d50a3a" />
         </providers>
      </profile>

   </system.web>
</configuration>
```

With these changes, SQL Server is now added as one of available providers to use with your applications. The name of this provider instance is AspNetSql2000Provider. You can see that this instance also uses the connection string of LocalSql2000Server, which was defined in Listing 15-22.

Now that the SQL Server provider is configured, in place, and ready to use, you can further define that this is the provider to use. You make a minor change to the web.config file of your application to enable it to take advantage of what you have established. Listing 15-24 shows the <profile> section of the web.config file.

Listing 15-24: Specifying SQL Server as the provider in the web.config file

```
<configuration>
  <system.web>

        <profile defaultProvider="AspNetSql2000Provider">

            <properties>

                    <add name="FirstName" />
                    <add name="LastName" />
                    <add name="LastVisited" />
                    <add name="Age" />
                    <add name="Member" />

            </properties>

        </profile>

    </system.web>
</configuration>
```

The only change necessary is to use the defaultProvider attribute and give it a value that is the name of the provider you want to use — in this case the newly created SQL Server provider, AspNetSql2000Provider. You can also make this change to the machine.config file by changing the <profile> element, as shown in Listing 15-25.

Listing 15-25: Using SQL Server as the provider in the machine.config file

```
<configuration>
  <system.web>

    . . .

        <profile enabled="true" defaultProvider="AspNetSql2000ProfileProvider">

            . . .

        </profile>

    . . .

    </system.web>
</configuration>
```

This change forces each and every application that resides on this server to use this new SQL Server provider instead of the default SQL Server provider (unless this command is overridden in the application's web.config file).

Using Multiple Providers

You are not limited to using a single data store or provider. Instead, you can use any number of providers. You can even specify the personalization provider for each property defined. This means that you can use the default provider for most properties, as well as allowing a few of them use an entirely different provider (see Listing 15-26).

Listing 15-26: Using different providers

```
<configuration>
  <system.web>

    <profile
      defaultProvider="AspNetSqlProvider">

          <properties>

              <add name="FirstName" />
              <add name="LastName" />
              <add name="LastVisited" />
              <add name="Age" />
              <add name="Member" provider="AspNetSql2000ProfileProvider" />

          </properties>

      </profile>

  </system.web>
</configuration>
```

From this example, you can see that a default provider is specified — AspNetSqlProvider. Unless specified otherwise, this provider is used. The only property that changes this setting is the property Member. The Member property uses an entirely different personalization provider. In this case, it employs the Access provider (AspNetSql2000Provider) through the use of the provider attribute of the <add> element. With this attribute, you can define a specific provider for each and every property that is defined.

Summary

The new personalization capabilities provided by ASP.NET 2.0 make it incredibly easy to make your Web applications unique for all end users, whether they are authenticated or anonymous. This new system enables you to store everything from basic data types provided by the .NET Framework to custom types that you create. This system is more versatile and extensible than using the Session or Application objects. The data is stored via a couple of built-in personalization providers that ship with ASP.NET. These providers include ones that connect with either Microsoft's SQL Server Express Edition files or Microsoft SQL Server 2005, 2000, or 7.0.

16

Membership and Role Management

The authentication and authorization of users are important functions in many Web sites and browser-based applications. Traditionally, when working with Microsoft's Windows Forms applications (thick-client), you depended on Windows Integrated Authentication; when working with browser-based applications (thin-client), you used forms authentication.

Forms authentication enabled you to take requests that were not yet authenticated and redirect them to an HTML form using HTTP client-side redirection. The user provided his login information and submitted the form. After the application authenticated the request, the user received an HTTP cookie, which was then used on any subsequent requests. This kind of authentication was fine in many ways, but it required developers to build every element and even manage the back-end mechanics of the overall system. This was a daunting task for many developers and, in most cases, it was rather time-consuming.

ASP.NET 2.0 introduces a new authentication and authorization management service that takes care of the login, authentication, authorization, and management of users who require access to your Web pages or applications. This outstanding new *membership and role management service* is an easy-to-implement framework that works out of the box using Microsoft SQL Server as the back-end data store. This new framework also includes a new API that allows for programmatic access to the capabilities of both the membership and role management services. In addition, a number of new server controls make it easy to create Web applications that incorporate everything these services have to offer.

Before you look at the new membership and role management features of ASP.NET 2.0, here's a quick review of authentication and authorization.

Authentication

Authentication is a process that determines the identity of a user. After a user has been authenticated, a developer can determine if the identified user has *authorization* to proceed. It is impossible to give an entity authorization if no authentication process has been applied. Authentication is provided in ASP.NET 2.0 through the use of the new membership service.

Authorization

Authorization is the process determining whether an authenticated user is allowed access to any part of an application, access to specific points of an application, or access only to specific datasets that the application provides. Authenticating and authorizing users or groups enable you to customize a site based on user types or preferences. Authorization is provided in ASP.NET 2.0 through the use of a new role management service.

ASP.NET 2.0 Authentication

ASP.NET 2.0 provides the membership management service to deal with authenticating users to access a page or an entire site. The new ASP.NET management service not only provides a new API suite for managing users, but it also gives you some new server controls. These new server controls work with the end user through the process of authentication. Shortly, you look at the functionality of these controls.

Setting Up Your Web Site for Membership

Before you can use the security controls that are provided with ASP.NET 2.0, you first have to set up your application to work with the new membership service. How you do this depends on how you approach the security framework provided.

By default, ASP.NET 2.0 uses the built-in AspNetSqlProvider for storing details about the registered users of your application. Also, for the initial demonstrations, you work with forms authentication. Let's assume that the application is open to the public for registration and viewing. If it were an intranet-based application (meaning that all the users are on a particular network), you could use Windows Integrated Authentication for authenticating users.

ASP.NET 2.0, as you know, offers a data provider model that handles the detailed management required to interact with multiple types of underlying data stores. Figure 16-1 shows a diagram of the new ASP.NET 2.0 membership service.

From the diagram, you can see that, like the rest of the ASP.NET 2.0 provider models, the membership providers can access a wide variety of underlying data stores. In this diagram, you can see the built-in Microsoft SQL Server data store. You can also build your own membership providers to get at any other custom data stores that work with user credentials. Above the membership providers in the diagram, you can see a list of security server controls that utilize the access granted by providers to work with the users in the authentication process.

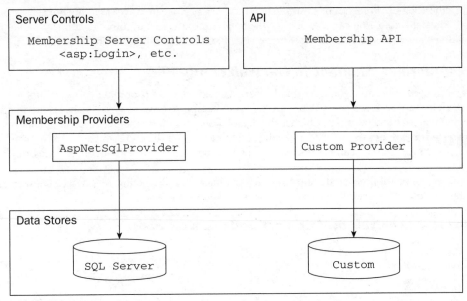

Figure 16-1

Adding an <authentication> Element to the web.config File

To allow forms authentication in your Web application for the new membership service, the first step is to turn on this feature from the web.config file. So create a web.config file if you don't already have one. Then, add the section shown in Listing 16-1 to the file.

Listing 16-1: Adding forms authentication to the web.config file

```
<?xml version="1.0" encoding="utf-8"?>
<configuration>
    <system.web>
        <authentication mode="Forms" />
    </system.web>
</configuration>
```

The simple addition of the <authentication> element to the web.config file turns on everything that you need to start using the membership service provided by ASP.NET 2.0. To turn on the forms authentication using this element, you simply give the value Forms to the mode attribute. This is a forms authentication example, but other possible values of the mode attribute include Windows, Passport, or None.

IIS authentication schemes include basic, digest, and Integrated Windows Authentication. Passport authentication points to a centralized service provided by Microsoft that offers a single login and core profile service for any member sites. It costs money to use Passport, which has recently been depreciated by Microsoft.

Because the mode attribute in our example is set to Forms, you can move on to the next step of adding users to the data store. You can also change the behavior of the forms authentication system at this point by making some modifications to the web.config file. These possibilities are reviewed next.

Adding a <forms> Element to the web.config File

Using forms authentication, you can provide users with access to a site or materials based upon credentials they input into a Web-based form. When an end user attempts to access a Web site, he is entering the site using anonymous authentication, which is the default authentication mode. If he is found to be anonymous, he can be redirected (by ASP.NET) to a specified login page. After the end user passes the authentication process, he is provided with an HTTP cookie, which can be used in any subsequent requests.

You can see the possibilities of the forms authentication setting in Listing 16-2, which shows possible changes to the web.config file.

Listing 16-2: Modifying the forms authentication behavior

```xml
<?xml version="1.0" encoding="utf-8"?>
<configuration>
    <system.web>
        <authentication mode="Forms">
            <forms name=".ASPXAUTH"
                   loginUrl="Login.aspx"
                   protection="All"
                   timeout="30"
                   path="/"
                   requireSSL="false"
                   slidingExpiration="true"
                   cookieless="UseDeviceProfile" />
        </authentication>
    </system.web>
</configuration>
```

You can set these as you wish, and you have plenty of options for values other than the ones that are displayed. Also, as stated earlier, these values are not required. You can use the membership service right away with only what was shown in Listing 16-1.

You can find some interesting settings in Listing 16-2, however. You can change how the forms authentication system works by adding a <forms> element to the web.config file. Make sure that you have the <forms> element nested within the <authentication> elements. The following list describes the possible attributes of the <forms> element:

❑　name: Defines the name used for the cookie sent to end users after they have been authenticated. By default, this cookie is named .ASPXAUTH.

❑　loginUrl: Specifies the page location to which the HTTP request is redirected for login if no valid authentication cookie (.ASPXAUTH or otherwise) is found. By default, it is set to Login.aspx.

❑　protection: Specifies the amount of protection that you want to apply to the cookie that is stored on the end user's machine after he has been authenticated. The possible settings include All, None, Encryption, and Validation. You should always attempt to use All.

❏   `timeout`: Defines the amount of time (in minutes) after which the cookie expires. The default value is 30 minutes.

❏   `path`: Specifies the path for cookies issued by the application.

❏   `requireSSL`: Defines whether you require that credentials be sent over an encrypted wire (SSL) instead of clear text.

❏   `slidingExpiration`: Specifies whether the timeout of the cookie is on a sliding scale. The default value is `True`. This means that the end user's cookie does not expire until 30 minutes (or the time specified in the `timeout` attribute) after the last request to the application has been made. If the value of the `slidingExpiration` attribute is set to `False`, the cookie expires 30 minutes from the first request.

❏   `cookieless`: Specifies how the cookies are handled by ASP.NET. The possible values include `UseDeviceProfile`, `UseCookies`, `Auto`, and `UseUri`. The default value is `UseDeviceProfile`. This value detects whether to use cookies based on the user agent of the device. `UseCookies` requires that all requests have the credentials stored in a cookie. `Auto` auto-determines whether the details are stored in a cookie on the client or within the URI (this is done by sending a test cookie first). Finally, `UseUri` forces ASP.NET to store the details within the URI on all instances.

Now that forms authentication is turned on, the next step is adding users to the Microsoft Access data store.

Adding Users

To add users to the membership service, you can register users into the Microsoft SQL Server Express Edition data store. The first question you might ask is, "Where is this data store?"

The Microsoft SQL Server provider can use a SQL Server Express Edition file that is structured specifically for the membership service (and other ASP.NET systems). Visual Studio 2005 is set to create this particular file for you. To accomplish this task, you work with the ASP.NET server controls that utilize the membership service to force the creation of this file. If a SQL Server Express Edition file is needed by the application, Visual Studio will create this file on your behalf in the `App_Data` folder.

Once the data store is in place, it is time to start adding users to the data store.

Using the CreateUserWizard Server Control

The first server control that utilizes the membership service is the CreateUserWizard server control. You can find this and the other controls mentioned in this chapter under the Login section in the Visual Studio Toolbox. The CreateUserWizard control enables you to plug registered users into your data store for later retrieval. If a page in your application allows end users to register for your site, you want, at a minimum, to retrieve a login and password from the user so that he can use these items later to log in to the site.

To make your life as simple as possible, the CreateUserWizard control takes complete control of doing all these things. Listing 16-3 shows a simple use of the control.

Listing 16-3: Allowing end users to register with the site

```
<%@ Page Language="VB" %>

<html xmlns="http://www.w3.org/1999/xhtml" >
<head runat="server">
    <title>Creating Users</title>
</head>
<body>
    <form id="form1" runat="server">
        <asp:CreateUserWizard ID="CreateUserWizard1" Runat="server"
         BorderWidth="1px" BorderColor="#FFDFAD" BorderStyle="Solid"
         BackColor="#FFFBD6" Font-Names="Verdana">
            <TitleTextStyle Font-Bold="True" BackColor="#990000"
             ForeColor="White"></TitleTextStyle>
        </asp:CreateUserWizard>
    </form>
</body>
</html>
```

This page simply uses the CreateUserWizard control and nothing more. This one control enables you to register end users. This particular CreateUserWizard control has a little style applied to it, but this control can be as simple as:

```
<asp:CreateUserWizard ID="CreateUserWizard1" Runat="server">
</asp:CreateUserWizard>
```

When this code is run, an end user is presented with the form shown in Figure 16-2.

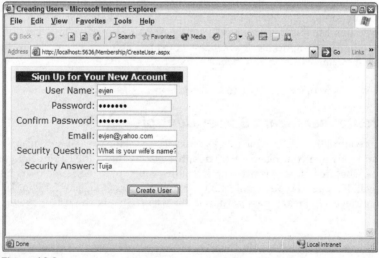

Figure 16-2

This screen shot shows the form as it would appear when filled out by the end user and includes user information such as the username, password, e-mail address, as well as the security question-and-answer section. Clicking the Create User button places this user information into the data store.

The username and password enable the end user to log in to the application through the login server control. A Confirm Password text box is also included in the form to ensure that the password is spelled correctly. An e-mail address is included in case end users forget their login credentials and want the credentials e-mailed to them. Then finally, the security question and answer are used to verify the identity of the end user before any credentials or user information is changed.

After the Create User button is clicked, the end user is presented with a confirmation of the information being stored (see Figure 16-3).

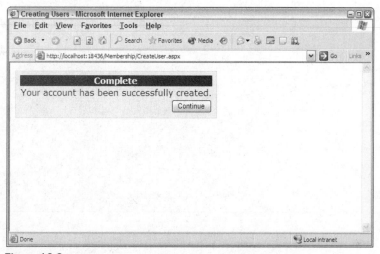

Figure 16-3

Seeing Where Users Are Stored

Now that the CreateUserWizard control has been used to add a user to the membership service, take a look at where this information is stored. If you used Visual Studio to create the Microsoft SQL Server Express Edition file in which you want to store the user information, the file is created when the previous example is run and you complete the form process as shown in the figures. When the example is run and completed, you can click the Refresh button in the Solution Explorer to find the ASPNETDB.MDF file, which is located in the App_Data folder of your project. Many different tables are included in this file, but you are interested in the aspnet_Membership table only.

When you open the aspnet_Membership table (by right-clicking on the table in the Database Explorer and selecting Show Table Data), the users you entered are in the system. This is shown in Figure 16-4.

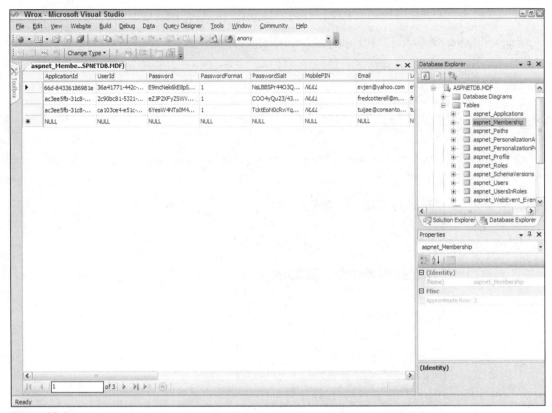

Figure 16-4

The user password in this table is not stored as clear text; instead, it is hashed. When a user logs into an application that is using the ASP.NET 2.0 membership service, his or her password is immediately hashed and then compared to the hashed password stored in the database. If the two hashed strings do not compare, the passwords are not considered a match. Storing clear text passwords is considered a security risk.

Here is a note in regard to the passwords used in ASP.NET 2.0. If you are having difficulty entering users because of a password error, it might be because, by default, ASP.NET requires strong passwords. All passwords input into the system must be at least eight characters, and contain at least one number, one non-alphanumeric character (such as [ ], !, @, #, $), as well as one uppercase and one lowercase letter. Whew! An example password of this combination is

```
Bevjen7777$
```

Although this type of password is a heck of a lot more secure, a password like this is sometimes difficult to remember. You can actually change how the membership provider works so that it doesn't require passwords as difficult as this by reworking the membership provider in the web.config file, as illustrated here in Listing 16-4.

Listing 16-4: Modifying the membership provider in web.config

```
<configuration>
  <system.web>

    <membership>
      <providers>
        <clear />
        <add name="AspNetSqlMembershipProvider"
        type="System.Web.Security.SqlMembershipProvider, System.Web,
        Version=2.0.0.0, Culture=neutral, PublicKeyToken=b03f5f7f11d50a3a"
        connectionStringName="LocalSqlServer"
        requiresQuestionAndAnswer="false"
        requiresUniqueEmail="true"
        passwordFormat="Hashed"
        minRequiredNonalphanumericCharacters="0"
        minRequiredPasswordLength="3" />
      </providers>
    </membership>

  </system.web>
</configuration>
```

In this example, we have reworked the membership provider for SQL Server so that it doesn't actually require any non-alphanumeric characters and allows passwords as small as three characters in length. You do this by using the `minRequiredNonalphanumericCharacters` and `minRequiredPasswordLength` attributes. With these in place, you can now create users with these password rules as set forth in these configuration settings. Modifying the membership provider is covered in more detail later in this chapter.

Working with the CreateUserWizard Control

When you work with the CreateUserWizard control, be aware of the `ContinueButtonClick` and the `CreatedUser` events. The `ContinueButtonClick` event is triggered when the Continue button on the second page is clicked after the user has been successfully created (see Listing 16-5).

Listing 16-5: The ContinueButtonClick event

VB
```
Protected Sub CreateUserWizard1_ContinueButtonClick(ByVal sender As Object, _
   ByVal e As System.EventArgs)

      Response.Redirect("Default.aspx")
End Sub
```

C#
```
protected void CreateUserWizard1_ContinueButtonClick(object sender, EventArgs e)
{
   Response.Redirect("Default.aspx");
}
```

In this example, after the user has been added to the membership service through the form provided by the CreateUserWizard control, she can click the Continue button to be redirected to another page in the application. This is done with a simple `Response.Redirect` statement. Remember when you use this event, that you must add an `OnContinueButtonClick="CreateUserWizard1_ContinueButtonClick"` to the `<asp:CreateUserWizard>` control.

The `CreateUser` event is triggered when a user is successfully created in the data store. The use of this event is shown in Listing 16-6.

Listing 16-6: The CreateUser event

VB
```
Protected Sub CreateUserWizard1_CreateUser(ByVal sender As Object, _
   ByVal e As System.EventArgs)

      ' Code here
End Sub
```

C#
```
protected void CreateUserWizard1_CreateUser(object sender, EventArgs e)
{
   // Code here
}
```

Use this event if you want to take any additional actions when a user is registered to the service.

Incorporating Personalization Properties in the Registration Process

As you saw in the previous chapter on personalization, it's fairly simple to use the new personalization management system that comes with ASP.NET 2.0 and store user-specific details. The registration process provided by the CreateUserWizard control is an ideal spot to retrieve this information from the user to store directly in the personalization system. The retrieval isn't too difficult to incorporate into your code.

The first step, as you learned in the previous chapter on personalization, is to have some personalization points defined in the application's `web.config` file. This is shown in Listing 16-7.

Listing 16-7: Creating personalization properties in the web.config file

```
<configuration>
  <system.web>

    <profile>

      <properties>

          <add name="FirstName" />
          <add name="LastName" />
          <add name="LastVisited" />
          <add name="Age" />
          <add name="Member" />

      </properties>

    </profile>

  </system.web>
</configuration>
```

Now that these properties are defined in the `web.config` file, you can use them to create users in the ASP.NET membership system. Using the CreateUserWizard control, you can create a process that requires the user to enter his preferred username and password in the first step, and then the second step asks for these custom-defined personalization points. Listing 16-8 shows a CreateUserWizard control that incorporates this idea.

Listing 16-8: Using personalization properties with the CreateUserWizard control

VB

```vb
<%@ Page Language="VB" %>

<script runat="server">
    Protected Sub CreateUserWizard1_CreatedUser(ByVal sender As Object, _
        ByVal e As System.EventArgs)

        Profile.FirstName = Firstname.Text
        Profile.LastName = Lastname.Text
        Profile.Age = Age.Text
    End Sub
</script>

<html xmlns="http://www.w3.org/1999/xhtml" >
<head id="Head1" runat="server">
    <title>Creating Users with Personalization</title>
</head>
<body>
    <form id="form1" runat="server">
        <asp:CreateUserWizard ID="CreateUserWizard1" Runat="server"
         BorderWidth="1px" BorderColor="#FFDFAD" BorderStyle="Solid"
         BackColor="#FFFBD6" Font-Names="Verdana"
         LoginCreatedUser="true" OnCreatedUser="CreateUserWizard1_CreatedUser" >
            <WizardSteps>
                <asp:WizardStep ID="WizardStep1" Runat="server"
                 Title="Additional Information" StepType="Start">
                    <table width="100%"><tr><td>
                    Firstname: </td><td>
                    <asp:TextBox ID="Firstname" Runat="server"></asp:TextBox>
                    </td></tr><tr><td>
                    Lastname: </td><td>
                    <asp:TextBox ID="Lastname" Runat="server"></asp:TextBox>
                    </td></tr><tr><td>
                    Age: </td><td>
                    <asp:TextBox ID="Age" Runat="server"></asp:TextBox>
                    </td></tr></table>
                </asp:WizardStep>
                <asp:CreateUserWizardStep Runat="server"
                 Title="Sign Up for Your New Account">
                </asp:CreateUserWizardStep>
                <asp:CompleteWizardStep Runat="server" Title="Complete">
                </asp:CompleteWizardStep>
            </WizardSteps>
            <StepStyle BorderColor="#FFDFAD" Font-Names="Verdana"
             BackColor="#FFFBD6" BorderStyle="Solid"
             BorderWidth="1px"></StepStyle>
```

(continued)

Listing 16-8: *(continued)*

```
            <TitleTextStyle Font-Bold="True" BackColor="#990000"
             ForeColor="White"></TitleTextStyle>
          </asp:CreateUserWizard>
      </form>
 </body>
 </html>
```

C#
```
<%@ Page Language="C#" %>

<script runat="server">
    protected void CreateUserWizard1_CreatedUser(object sender, EventArgs e)
    {
        Profile.FirstName = Firstname.Text;
        Profile.LastName = Lastname.Text;
        Profile.Age = Age.Text;
    }
</script>
```

With this change to the standard registration process as is defined by a default instance of the CreateUserWizard control, your registration system now includes the request for properties stored using the `Profile` object. You can define a custom step within the CreateUserWizard control by using the `<WizardSteps>` element. Within this element, you can construct a series of registration steps in whatever fashion you choose. From the `<WizardSteps>` section, shown in Listing 16-8, you can see that three steps are defined. The first is the custom step in which the end user's personalization properties are requested with the `<asp:WizardStep>` control. Within the `<asp:WizardStep>` control, a table is laid out and a custom form is created.

Two additional steps are defined within Listing 16-7: a step to create the user (using the `<asp:CreateUserWizardStep>` control) and a step to confirm the creation of a new user (using the `<asp:CompleteWizardStep>` control). The order in which these steps appear is the order in which they are presented to the end user.

After the steps are created the way you want, you can then store the custom properties using the CreateUserWizard control's `CreatedUser` event:

```
    Protected Sub CreateUserWizard1_CreatedUser(ByVal sender As Object, _
       ByVal e As System.EventArgs)

       Profile.FirstName = Firstname.Text
       Profile.LastName = Lastname.Text
       Profile.Age = Age.Text
    End Sub
```

You are not limited to having a separate step in which you ask for personal bits of information; you can incorporate these items directly into the `<asp:CreateUserWizardStep>` step itself. An easy way to do this is to switch to the Design view of your page and pull up the smart tag for the CreateUserWizard control. Then click the Customize Create User Step link (shown in Figure 16-5).

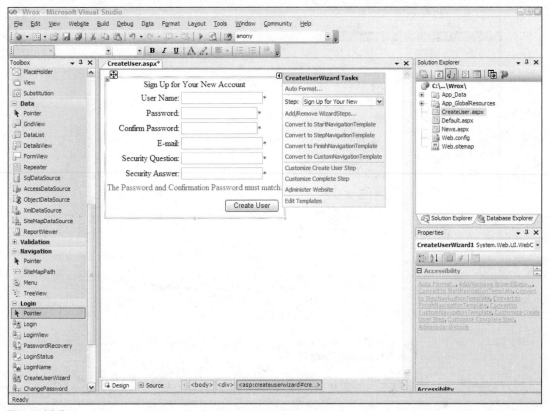

Figure 16-5

Clicking on the Customize Create User Step details the contents of this particular step within a new `<ContentTemplate>` section that is now contained within the `<asp:CreateUserWizardStep>` control. Within the `<ContentTemplate>` element, you can now see the complete default form used for creating a new user. At this point, you are free to change the form by adding your own sections that request the end user's personal information. From this detailed form, you can also remove items. For instance, if you are not interested in asking for the security question and answer, you can remove these two items from the form. By changing this default form, you can completely customize the registration process for your end users (see Figure 16-6).

Adding Users Programmatically

You are not limited to using only server controls to register or add new users to the membership service. ASP.NET 2.0 provides a Membership API for performing this task programmatically. This is ideal to create your own mechanics for adding users to the service—or if you are modifying a Web application that was created using ASP.NET 1.0/1.1.

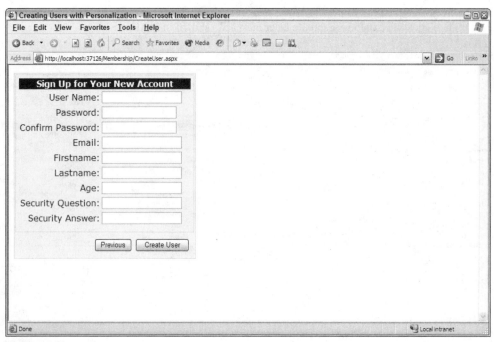

Figure 16-6

The Membership API includes the `CreateUser` method for adding users to the service. The `CreateUser` method includes four possible signatures:

```
Membership.CreateUser(username As String, password As String)

Membership.CreateUser(username As String, password As String,
    email As String)

Membership.CreateUser(username As String, password As String,
    email As String, passwordQuestion As String,
    passwordAnswer As String, isApproved As Boolean,
    ByRef status As System.Web.Security.MembershipCreateStatus)

Membership.CreateUser(username As String, password As String,
    email As String, passwordQuestion As String,
    passwordAnswer As String, isApproved As Boolean, providerUserKey As Object
    ByRef status As System.Web.Security.MembershipCreateStatus)
```

You can use this method to create users. The nice thing about this method is that you aren't required to create an instance of the `Membership` class; you use it directly. A simple use of the `CreateUser` method is illustrated in Listing 16-9.

Listing 16-9: Creating users programmatically

VB

```
<%@ Page Language="VB" %>

<script runat="server">
Protected Sub Button1_Click(ByVal sender As Object, ByVal e As System.EventArgs)
   Try
       Membership.CreateUser(TextBox1.Text, TextBox2.Text)
       Label1.Text = "Successfully created user " & TextBox1.Text
   Catch ex As MembershipCreateUserException
       Label1.Text = "Error: " & ex.ToString()
   End Try
End Sub
</script>

<html xmlns="http://www.w3.org/1999/xhtml" >
<head runat="server">
    <title>Creating a User</title>
</head>
<body>
    <form id="form1" runat="server">
        <h1>Create User</h1>
        <p>Username<br />
            <asp:TextBox ID="TextBox1" Runat="server"></asp:TextBox>
        </p>
        <p>Password<br />
            <asp:TextBox ID="TextBox2" Runat="server"
             TextMode="Password"></asp:TextBox>
        </p>
        <p>
            <asp:Button ID="Button1" Runat="server" Text="Create User"
             OnClick="Button1_Click" />
        </p>
        <p>
            <asp:Label ID="Label1" Runat="server"></asp:Label>
        </p>
    </form>
</body>
</html>
```

C#

```
<%@ Page Language="C#" %>

<script runat="server">
    protected void Button1_Click(object sender, EventArgs e)
    {
        try
        {
            Membership.CreateUser(TextBox1.Text.ToString(),
                TextBox2.Text.ToString());
```

(continued)

597

Listing 16-9: *(continued)*

```
            Label1.Text = "Successfully created user " + TextBox1.Text;
        }
        catch (MembershipCreateUserException ex)
        {
            Label1.Text = "Error: " + ex.ToString();
        }
    }
</script>
```

So, use either the CreateUserWizard control or the `CreateUser` method found in the Membership API to create users for your Web applications with relative ease. This functionality was possible in the past with ASP.NET 1.0/1.1, but it was a labor-intensive task. Now with ASP.NET 2.0, you can create users with either a single control or with a single line of code.

Changing How Users Register with Your Application

You determine how users register with your applications and what is required of them by the membership provider you choose. You will find a default membership provider and its applied settings is established within the `machine.config` file. If you dig down in the `machine.config` file on your server, you find the following code (shown in Listing 16-10).

Listing 16-10: Membership provider settings in the machine.config file

```
<membership>
    <providers>
        <add name="AspNetSqlMembershipProvider"
          type="System.Web.Security.SqlMembershipProvider, System.Web,
              Version=2.0.0.0, Culture=neutral, PublicKeyToken=b03f5f7f11d50a3a"
          connectionStringName="LocalSqlServer"
          enablePasswordRetrieval="false"
          enablePasswordReset="true"
          requiresQuestionAndAnswer="true"
          applicationName="/"
          requiresUniqueEmail="false"
          passwordFormat="Hashed"
          maxInvalidPasswordAttempts="5"
          passwordAttemptWindow="10"
          passwordStrengthRegularExpression="" />
    </providers>
</membership>
```

This section of the `machine.config` file shows the default membership provider that comes with ASP.NET 2.0 — the AspNetSqlProvider. If you are going to add any additional membership providers for use on a server-wide scale, you are going to want to add this provider to this `<membership>` section of the `machine.config` file.

The important attributes of the AspNetSqlMembershipProvider definition include the `enablePasswordRetrieval`, `enablePasswordReset`, `requiresQuestionAndAnswer`, `requiresUniqueEmail`, and `PasswordFormat` attributes. The following table defines these attributes.

Attribute	Description
enablePasswordRetrieval	Defines whether the provider supports password retrievals. This attribute takes a `Boolean` value. The default value is `False`. When it is set to `False`, passwords cannot be retrieved although they can be changed with a new random password.
enablePasswordReset	Defines whether the provider supports password resets. This attribute takes a `Boolean` value. The default value is `True`.
requiresQuestionAndAnswer	Specifies whether the provider should require a question-and-answer combination when a user is created. This attribute takes a `Boolean` value, and the default value is `False`.
requiresUniqueEmail	Defines whether the provider should require a unique e-mail to be specified when the user is created. This attribute takes a `Boolean` value, and the default value is `False`. When set to `True`, only unique e-mail addresses can be entered into the data store.
passwordFormat	Defines the format in which the password is stored in the data store. The possible values include `Hashed`, `Clear`, and `Encrypted`. The default value is `Hashed`. Hashed passwords use SHA1, whereas encrypted passwords use Triple-DES encryption.

In addition to having these items defined in the `machine.config` file, you can also redefine them in the `web.config` file.

Asking for Credentials

After you have users that can access your Web application using the new membership service provided by ASP.NET 2.0, you can then give these users the means to log in to the site. This requires little work on your part. Before you learn the controls that enable users to access your applications, you should make a few more modifications to the `web.config` file.

Turning Off Access with the <authorization> Element

After you make the changes to the `web.config` file by adding the `<authorization>` and `<forms>` elements (Listings 16-1 and 16-2), your Web application is accessible to each and every user that browses to any page your application contains. To prevent open access, you have to deny unauthenticated users access to the pages of your site.

Denying unauthenticated users access to your site is illustrated in Listing 16-11.

Listing 16-11: Denying unauthenticated users

```
<?xml version="1.0" encoding="utf-8"?>
<configuration>
    <system.web>
        <authentication mode="Forms" />
        <authorization>
            <deny users="?" />
        </authorization>
    </system.web>
</configuration>
```

Using the `<authorization>` and `<deny>` elements, you can deny specific users access to your Web application — or (as in this case) simply deny every unauthenticated user (this is what the question mark signifies).

Now that everyone but authenticated users has been denied access to the site, you want to make it easy for viewers of your application to become authenticated users. To do so, use the Login server control.

Using the Login Server Control

The Login server control enables you to turn unauthenticated users into authenticated users by allowing them to provide login credentials that can be verified in a data store of some kind. In the examples so far, you have used Microsoft SQL Server Express Edition as the data store, but you can just as easily use the full-blown version of Microsoft's SQL Server.

The first step in using the Login control is to create a new Web page titled `Login.aspx`. This is the default page to which unauthenticated users are redirected in order to obtain their credentials. Remember that you can change this behavior by changing the value of the `<forms>` element's `loginUrl` attribute in the `web.config` file.

The `Login.aspx` page simply needs an `<asp:Login>` control to give the end user everything he needs to become authenticated, as illustrated in Listing 16-12.

Listing 16-12: Providing a login for the end user using the Login control

```
<%@ Page Language="VB" %>

<html xmlns="http://www.w3.org/1999/xhtml" >
<head runat="server">
    <title>Login Page</title>
</head>
<body>
    <form id="form1" runat="server">
        <asp:Login ID="Login1" Runat="server">
        </asp:Login>
    </form>
</body>
</html>
```

In the situation established here, if the unauthenticated user hits a different page in the application, he is redirected to the Login.aspx page. You can see how ASP.NET tracks the location in the URL from the address bar in the browser:

```
http://localhost:18436/Membership/Login.aspx?ReturnUrl=%2fMembership%2fDefault.aspx
```

The login page, using the Login control, is shown in Figure 16-7.

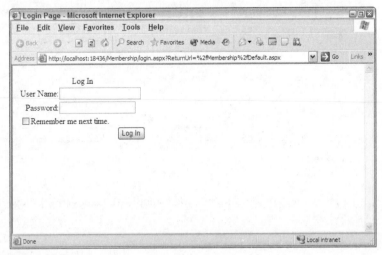

Figure 16-7

From this figure, you can see that the Login control asks the user for a username and password. A check box allows for a cookie to be stored on the client machine. This cookie enables the end user to bypass future logins. You can remove the check box and related text created to remember the user by setting the Login control's DisplayRememberMe property to False.

In addition to the DisplayRememberMe property, you can work with this aspect of the Login control by using the RememberMeText and the RememberMeSet properties. The RememberMeText property is pretty self-explanatory because its value simply defines the text set next to the check box. The RememberMeSet property, however, is fairly interesting. The RememberMeSet property takes a Boolean value (by default, it is set to False) that specifies whether to set a persistent cookie on the client's machine after a user has logged in using the Login control. If set to True when the DisplayRememberMe property is also set to True, the check box is simply checked by default when the Login control is generated in the browser. If the DisplayRememberMe property is set to False (meaning the end user does not see the check box or cannot select the option of persisting the login cookie) and the RememberMeSet is set to True, a cookie is set on the user's machine automatically without the user's knowledge or choice in the matter. This cookie remains on the client's machine until the user logs out of the application (if this option is provided). With the persisted cookie, and assuming the end user has not logged out of the application, the user never needs to log in again when he returns to the application because his credentials are provided by the contents found in the cookie. After the end user has logged in to the application, he is returned to the page he originally intended to access.

You can also modify the look-and-feel of the Login control just as you can for the other controls. One way to do this is by clicking the Auto Format link in the control's smart tag. There you find a list of options for modifying the look-and-feel of the control (see Figure 16-8).

Figure 16-8

Select the `Elegant` option, for example, and the code is modified. Listing 16-13 shows the code generated for this selection.

Listing 16-13: A formatted Login control

```
<asp:Login ID="Login1" Runat="server" BorderWidth="1px" BorderColor="#CCCC99"
  BorderStyle="Solid" BackColor="#F7F7DE" Font-Names="Verdana" Font-Size="10pt">
    <TitleTextStyle Font-Bold="True" BackColor="#6B696B"
    ForeColor="#FFFFFF"></TitleTextStyle>
</asp:Login>
```

From this listing, you can see that the `<TitleTextStyle>` sub-element is used to modify a particular item displayed by the control. The available styling elements for the Login control include the following:

❑   `<CheckboxStyle>`

❑   `<FailureTextStyle>`

❑   `<HyperLinkStyle>`

❑   `<InstructionTextStyle>`

❑   `<LabelStyle>`

❑   `<LoginButtonStyle>`

❑   `<TextBoxStyle>`

❑   `<TitleTextStyle>`

❑   `<ValidatorTextStyle>`

The Login control has numerous properties that allow you to alter how the control appears and behaves. An interesting change you can make is to add some links at the bottom of the control to provide access to additional resources. With these links, you can give users the capability to get help or register for the application so that they can be provided with log-in credentials.

Here are some links you can provide:

❑ The capability to be redirected to a help page using the HelpPageText, HelpPageUrl, and HelpPageIconUrl properties.

❑ The capability to be redirected to a registration page using the CreateUserText, CreateUserUrl, and CreateUserIconUrl properties.

❑ The capability to be redirected to a page that allows end users to recover their forgotten passwords using the PasswordRecoveryText, PasswordRecoveryUrl, and PasswordRecoveryIconUrl properties.

When used, the Login control looks like what's shown in Figure 16-9.

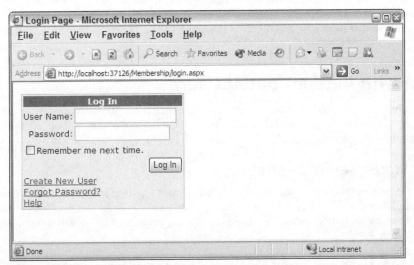

Figure 16-9

Logging In Users Programmatically

Besides using the prebuilt mechanics of the Login control, you can also perform this task programmatically using the Membership class. To validate credentials that you receive, you use the ValidateUser method of this class. The ValidateUser method takes a single signature:

```
ValidateUser(username As String, password As String)
```

This method is illustrated in Listing 16-14.

Listing 16-14: Validating a user's credentials programmatically

VB

```vb
If Membership.ValidateUser(TextBox1.Text, TextBox2.Text) Then
    FormsAuthentication.RedirectFromLoginPage(TextBox1.Text, False)
Else
    Label1.Text = "You are not registered with the site."
End If
```

C#

```csharp
if (Membership.ValidateUser(TextBox1.Text, TextBox2.Text) {
    FormsAuthentication.RedirectFromLoginPage(TextBox1.Text.ToString(), false);
}
else {
    Label1.Text = "You are not registered with the site.";
}
```

The ValidateUser method returns a Boolean value of True if the user credentials pass the test and False if they do not. From the code snippet in Listing 16-14, you can see that end users whose credentials are verified as correct are redirected from the login page using the RedirectFromLoginPage method. This method takes the username and a Boolean value that specifies whether the credentials are persisted through a cookie setting.

Working with Authenticated Users

After users are authenticated, ASP.NET 2.0 provides a number of different server controls and methods that you can use to work with the user details. Included in this collection of tools are the LoginStatus and the LoginName controls.

The LoginStatus Server Control

The LoginStatus server control enables users to click a link to log in or log out of a site. For a good example of this control, remove the <deny> element from the web.config file so that the pages of your site are accessible to unauthenticated users. Then code your Default.aspx page so that it is similar to the code shown in Listing 16-15.

Listing 16-15: Login and logout features of the LoginStatus control

```
<%@ Page Language="VB" %>

<html xmlns="http://www.w3.org/1999/xhtml" >
<head runat="server">
    <title>Login or Logout</title>
</head>
<body>
    <form id="form1" runat="server">
        <asp:LoginStatus ID="LoginStatus1" Runat="server" />
    </form>
</body>
</html>
```

Running this gives you a simple page that contains only a hyperlink titled Login, as shown in Figure 16-10.

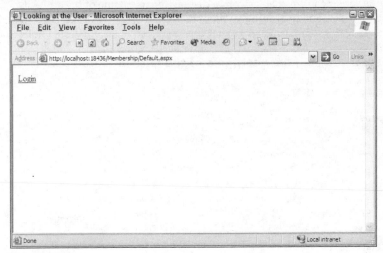

Figure 16-10

Clicking the Login hyperlink forwards you to the Login.aspx page where you provide your credentials. After the credentials are provided, you are redirected to the Default.aspx page — although now the page includes a hyperlink titled Logout (see Figure 16-11). The LinkStatus control displays one link when the user is unauthenticated and another link when the user is authenticated. Clicking the Logout hyperlink logs out the user and redraws the Default.aspx page — but with the Login hyperlink in place.

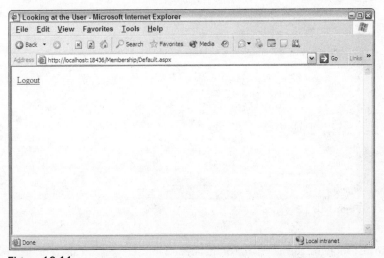

Figure 16-11

The LoginName Server Control

The LoginName server control enables you to display the username of the authenticated user. This is a common practice today. For an example of this, change the `Default.aspx` page so that it now includes the authenticated user's login name when that user is logged in, as illustrated in Listing 16-16.

Listing 16-16: Displaying the username of the authenticated user

```
<%@ Page Language="VB" %>

<html xmlns="http://www.w3.org/1999/xhtml" >
<head runat="server">
    <title>Login or Logout</title>
</head>
<body>
    <form id="form1" runat="server">
        <asp:LoginStatus ID="LoginStatus1" Runat="server" />
        <p><asp:LoginName ID="LoginName1" Runat="server"
            Font-Bold="True" Font-Size="XX-Large" /></p>
    </form>
</body>
</html>
```

When the user logs in to the application and is returned to the `Default.aspx` page, he sees his username displayed, as well as the hyperlink generated by the LoginStatus control (see Figure 16-12).

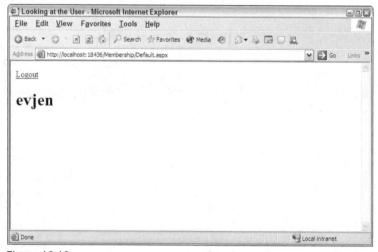

Figure 16-12

In addition to just showing the username of the logged in user, you can also add text by using the LoginName control's `FormatString` property. For instance, to provide a welcome message along with the username, you construct the LoginName control as follows:

```
<asp:LoginName ID="LoginName1" Runat="Server"
  FormatString="Welcome to our Website {0}!" />
```

You can also simply use the following construction in one of the page events. (This is shown in VB; if you are using C#, add a semicolon at the end of the line):

```
LoginName1.FormatString = "Welcome to the site {0}!"
```

When the page is generated, ASP.NET replaces the {0} part of the string with the username of the logged-in user. This provides you with a result similar to the following:

```
Welcome to the site evjen!
```

If you don't want to show the username when using the LoginName control, simply omit the {0} aspect of the string. The control then places the FormatString property's value on the page.

Showing the Number of Users Online

One cool feature of the membership service is that you can display how many users are online at a given moment. This is an especially popular option for a portal or a forum that wishes to impress visitors to the site with its popularity.

To show the number of users online, you use the GetNumberOfUsersOnline method provided by the Membership class. You can add to the Default.aspx page shown in Figure 16-10 with the code illustrated in Listing 16-17.

Listing 16-17: Displaying the number of users online

```
VB
<%@ Page Language="VB" %>

<script runat="server">
    Protected Sub Page_Load(ByVal sender As Object, ByVal e As System.EventArgs)
        Label1.Text = Membership.GetNumberOfUsersOnline().ToString()
    End Sub
</script>

<html xmlns="http://www.w3.org/1999/xhtml" >
<head runat="server">
    <title>Login or Logout</title>
</head>
<body>
    <form id="form1" runat="server">
        <asp:LoginStatus ID="LoginStatus1" Runat="server" />
        <p><asp:LoginName ID="LoginName1" Runat="server"
            Font-Bold="True" Font-Size="XX-Large" /></p>
        <p>There are <asp:Label ID="Label1" Runat="server" Text="0" />
            users online.</p>
    </form>
</body>
</html>
```

(continued)

Listing 16-17: *(continued)*

C#

```
<%@ Page Language="C#" %>

<script runat="server">
   protected void Page_Load(object sender, EventArgs e)
   {
      Label1.Text = Membership.GetNumberOfUsersOnline().ToString();
   }
</script>
```

When the page is generated, it displays the number of users who have logged on in the last 15 minutes. An example of what is generated is shown in Figure 16-13.

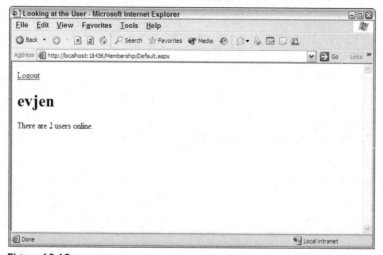

Figure 16-13

You can see that two users have logged on in the last 15 minutes. This 15-minute period is determined in the `machine.config` file from within the `<membership>` element:

```
<membership userIsOnlineTimeWindow="15" >
</membership>
```

By default, the `userIsOnlineTimeWindow` is set to 15. The number is specified here in minutes. To increase the time window, you simply increase this number. In addition to specifying this number from within the `machine.config` file, you can also set this number in the `web.config` file.

Dealing with Passwords

Many of us seem to spend our lives online and have username/password combinations for many different Web sites on the Internet. For this reason, end users forget passwords or want to change them every so often. ASP.NET 2.0 provides a couple of new server controls that work with the membership service so that end users can either change their passwords or retrieve forgotten passwords.

The ChangePassword Server Control

The ChangePassword server control enables end users to change their passwords directly in the browser. Listing 16-18 shows a use of the ChangePassword control.

Listing 16-18: Allowing users to change passwords

```
<%@ Page Language="VB" %>

<html xmlns="http://www.w3.org/1999/xhtml" >
<head runat="server">
    <title>Change Your Password</title>
</head>
<body>
    <form id="form1" runat="server">
        <asp:LoginStatus ID="LoginStatus1" Runat="server" />
        <p><asp:ChangePassword ID="ChangePassword1" Runat="server">
            </asp:ChangePassword><p>
    </form>
</body>
</html>
```

This is a rather simple use of the `<asp:ChangePassword>` control. Running this page produces the results shown in Figure 16-14.

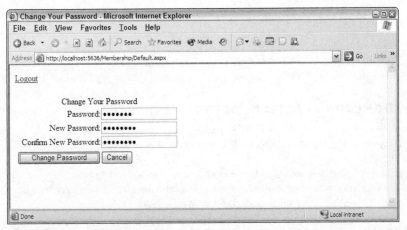

Figure 16-14

The ChangePassword control produces a form that asks for the previous password. It also requires the end user to type the new password twice. Clicking the Change Password button launches an attempt to change the password if the user is logged in. If the end user isn't logged into the application yet, he or she is redirected to the login page. Only a logged-in user can change a password. After the password is changed, the end user is notified (see Figure 16-15).

Remember that end users are allowed to change their passwords because the `enablePasswordReset` attribute of the membership provider is set to `True`. To deny this capability, set the `enablePasswordReset` attribute to `False`.

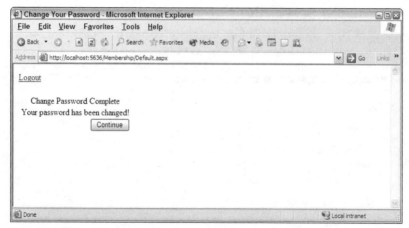

Figure 16-15

You can also specify rules on how the passwords must be constructed when an end user attempts to change her password. For instance, you might want to require that the password contain more than a certain number of characters or that it use numbers and/or special characters in addition to alpha-characters. Using the `NewPasswordRegularExpression` attribute, you can specify the construction required for the new password, as shown here:

```
NewPasswordRegularExpression='@\"(?=.{6,})(?=(.*\d){1,})(?=(.*\W){1,})'
```

Any new passwords created by the end user are checked against this regular expression. If there isn't a match, you can use the `NewPasswordRegularExpressionErrorMessage` attribute (one of the lengthier names for an attribute in ASP.NET) to cause an error message to appear within the control.

The PasswordRecovery Server Control

People simply forget their passwords. For this reason, you should provide the means to retrieve passwords from your data store. The PasswordRecovery server control provides an easy way to accomplish this task.

Password recovery usually means sending the end user's password to him in an e-mail. Therefore, you need to set up an SMTP server (it might be the same as the application server). You configure for this server in the `web.config` file, as illustrated in Listing 16-19.

Listing 16-19: Configuring passwords to be sent via email in the web.config file

```
<configuration>
   <system.web>
      <!-- Removed for clarity -->
   </system.web>

   <system.net>

      <mailSettings>
         <smtp from="evjen@yahoo.com">
            <network host="localhost" port="25"
            defaultCredentials="true" />
         </smtp>
```

```
        </mailSettings>

    </system.net>
</configuration>
```

After you have the `<mailSettings>` element set up correctly, you can start to use the PasswordRecovery control. A simple use of the PasswordRecovery control is shown in Listing 16-20.

Listing 16-20: Using the PasswordRecovery control

```
<%@ Page Language="VB" %>

<html xmlns="http://www.w3.org/1999/xhtml" >
<head runat="server">
    <title>Getting Your Password</title>
</head>
<body>
    <form id="form1" runat="server">
        <asp:PasswordRecovery ID="PasswordRecovery1" Runat="server">
            <MailDefinition From="evjen@yahoo.com">
            </MailDefinition>
        </asp:PasswordRecovery>
    </form>
</body>
</html>
```

The `<asp:PasswordRecovery>` element needs a `<MailDefinition>` subelement. The `<MailDefinition>` element contains details about the e-mail to be sent to the end user. The minimum requirement is that the `From` attribute is used, which provides the e-mail address for the From part of the e-mail. The `String` value of this attribute should be an e-mail address. Other attributes for the `<MailDefinition>` element include the following:

- ❏ BodyFileName
- ❏ CC
- ❏ From
- ❏ IsBodyHtml
- ❏ Priority
- ❏ Subject

When you run this page, the PasswordRecovery control asks for the user's username, as shown in Figure 16-16.

When it has the username, the membership service retrieves the question and answer that was earlier entered by the end user and generates the view shown in Figure 16-17.

If the question is answered correctly, an e-mail containing the password is generated and mailed to the end user. If the question is answered incorrectly, an error message is displayed. Of course, a question will not be used if you have the Question/Answer feature of the membership system disabled.

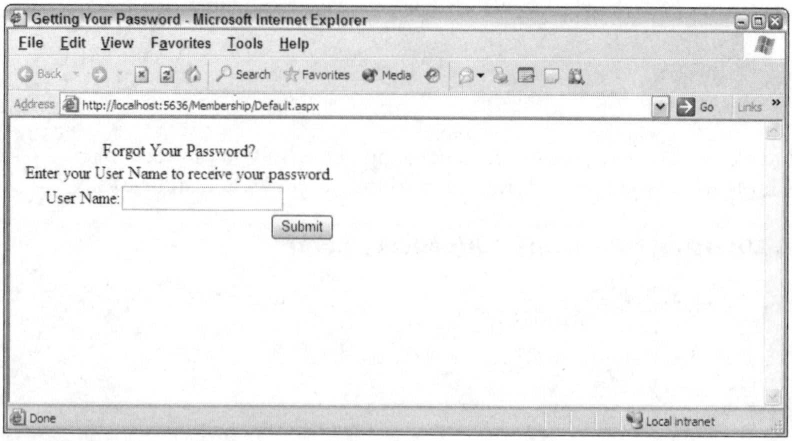

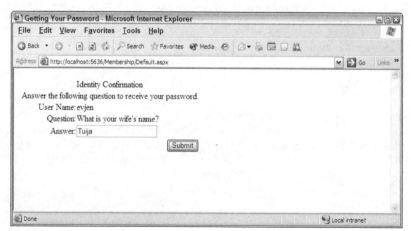

Figure 16-16

Figure 16-17

It is important to change some of your membership service settings in order for this entire process to work. At present, it won't work because of the way in which a user's password is hashed. The membership service data store isn't storing the actual password—just a hashed version of it. Of course, it is useless for an end user to receive a hashed password.

In order for you to be able to send back an actual password to the user, you must change how the passwords are stored in the membership service data store. This is done (as stated earlier in the chapter) by changing `PasswordFormat` attribute of your membership data provider. The other possible values (besides `Hashed`) are `Clear` and `Encrypted`. Changing it to either `Clear` or `Encrypted` makes it possible for the passwords to be sent back to the end user in a readable format.

ASP.NET 2.0 Authorization

Now that you can deal with the registration and authentication of users who want to access your Web applications, the next step is authorization. What are they allowed to see and what roles do they take? These are important questions for any Web application. First, learn how to show only certain items to authenticated users while you show different items to unauthenticated users.

Using the LoginView Server Control

The LoginView server control allows you to control who views what information on a particular part of a page. Using the LoginView control, you can dictate which parts of the pages are for authenticated users and which parts of the pages are for unauthenticated users. Listing 16-21 shows an example of this control.

Listing 16-21: Controlling information viewed via the LoginView control

```
<%@ Page Language="VB" %>

<html xmlns="http://www.w3.org/1999/xhtml" >
<head runat="server">
    <title>Changing the View</title>
</head>
<body>
    <form id="form1" runat="server">
        <asp:LoginStatus ID="LoginStatus1" Runat="server" />
        <p>
        <asp:LoginView ID="LoginView1" Runat="server">
            <LoggedInTemplate>
                Here is some REALLY important information that you should know
                about all those people that are not authenticated!
            </LoggedInTemplate>
            <AnonymousTemplate>
                Here is some basic information for you.
            </AnonymousTemplate>
        </asp:LoginView><p>
    </form>
</body>
</html>
```

The `<asp:LoginView>` control is a templated control that takes two possible subelements — the `<LoggedInTemplate>` and `<AnonymousTemplate>` elements. In this case, the information defined in the `<AnonymousTemplate>` section (see Figure 16-18) is for unauthenticated users.

It is quite different from what authenticated users see defined in the `<LoggedInTemplate>` section (see Figure 16-19).

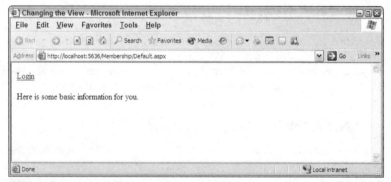

Figure 16-18

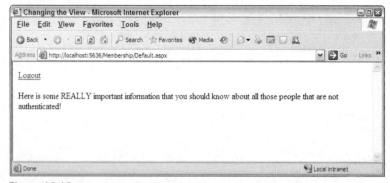

Figure 16-19

Only simple ASCII text is placed inside both of these templates, but you can actually place anything else within the template including additional server controls. This means that you can show entire sections of pages, including forms, from within the templated sections.

Besides using just the `<LoggedInTemplate>` and the `<AnonymousTemplate>` of the LoginView control, you can also enable sections of a page or specific content for entities that are part of a particular role—such as someone who is part of the `Admin` group. You can accomplish this by using the `<RoleGroups>` section of the LoginView control, as shown in Listing 16-22.

Listing 16-22: Providing a view for a particular group

```
<%@ Page Language="VB" %>

<html xmlns="http://www.w3.org/1999/xhtml" >
<head runat="server">
    <title>Changing the View</title>
</head>
<body>
    <form id="form1" runat="server">
        <asp:LoginStatus ID="LoginStatus1" Runat="server" />
        <p>
        <asp:LoginView ID="LoginView1" Runat="server">
            <LoggedInTemplate>
```

```
            Here is some REALLY important information that you should know
            about all those people that are not authenticated!
        </LoggedInTemplate>
        <AnonymousTemplate>
            Here is some basic information for you.
        </AnonymousTemplate>
        <RoleGroups>
            <asp:RoleGroup Roles="Admins">
                <ContentTemplate>
                    You are an Admin!
                </ContentTemplate>
            </asp:RoleGroup>
            <asp:RoleGroup Roles="CoolPeople">
                <ContentTemplate>
                    You are cool!
                </ContentTemplate>
            </asp:RoleGroup>
        </RoleGroups>
    </asp:LoginView><p>
  </form>
</body>
</html>
```

To show content for a particular group of users, you add a `<RoleGroups>` element to the LoginView control. The `<RoleGroups>` section can take one or more RoleGroup controls (you will not find this control in Visual Studio's Toolbox). To provide content to display using the RoleGroup control, you provide a `<ContentTemplate>` element, which enables you to define the content to be displayed for an entity that belongs to the specified role. What is placed in the `<ContentTemplate>` section completely depends on you. You can place raw text (as shown in the example) or even other ASP.NET controls.

Be cautious of the order in which you place the defined roles in the `<RoleGroups>` section. When users log in to a site, they are first checked to see if they match one of the defined roles. The first (uppermost) role matched is the view used for the LoginView control — even if they match more than one role. You can also place more than one role in the `Roles` attribute of the `<asp:RoleGroups>` control, like this:

```
<asp:RoleGroup Roles="CoolPeople, HappyPeople">
    <ContentTemplate>
        You are cool or happy (or both)!
    </ContentTemplate>
</asp:RoleGroup>
```

Setting Up Your Web Site for Role Management

In addition to the membership service just reviewed, ASP.NET 2.0 provides you with the other side of the end-user–management service — the ASP.NET role management service. The membership service covered all the details of authentication for your applications, whereas the role management service covers authorization. Just as the membership service can use any of the data providers listed earlier, the role management service can use the same SQL Server provider plus any custom providers. In fact, this service is comparable to the membership service in many ways. Figure 16-20 shows you a simple diagram that details some the particulars of the role management service.

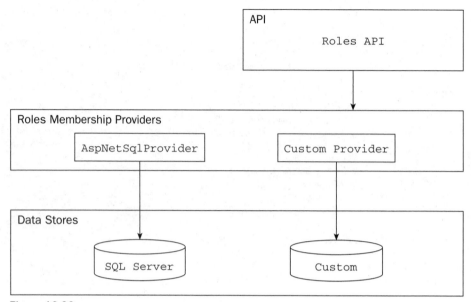

Figure 16-20

Making Changes to the <roleManager> Section

The first step in working with the role management service is to change any of the role management provider's behaviors either in the `machine.config.comments` or from the `web.config` files. If you look in the `machine.config.comments` file, you see an entire section that deals with the role management service (see Listing 16-23).

Listing 16-23: Role management provider settings in the machine.config.comments file

```
<roleManager
 enabled="false"
 cacheRolesInCookie="false"
 cookieName=".ASPXROLES"
 cookieTimeout="30"
 cookiePath="/"
 cookieRequireSSL="false"
 cookieSlidingExpiration="true"
 cookieProtection="All"
 defaultProvider="AspNetSqlRoleProvider"
 createPersistentCookie="false"
 maxCachedResults="25">
   <providers>
      <clear />
      <add connectionStringName="LocalSqlServer" applicationName="/"
       name="AspNetSqlRoleProvider" type="System.Web.Security.SqlRoleProvider,
       System.Web, Version=2.0.0.0, Culture=neutral,
       PublicKeyToken=b03f5f7f11d50a3a" />
      <add applicationName="/" name="AspNetWindowsTokenRoleProvider"
       type="System.Web.Security.WindowsTokenRoleProvider, System.Web,
       Version=2.0.0.0, Culture=neutral, PublicKeyToken=b03f5f7f11d50a3a" />
```

```
      </providers>
   </roleManager>
```

The role management service defines its settings from within the machine.config.comments file, as shown in the previous code listing. You can make changes to these settings either directly in the machine.config.comments file or by overriding these settings in the web.config file (thereby making changes only to the application at hand).

The main settings are defined in the <roleManager> element. Some of the attributes of the <roleManager> element are defined in the following table.

Attribute	Description
enabled	Defines whether the role management service is enabled for the application. This attribute takes a Boolean value and is set to False by default. This means that the role management service is disabled by default. This is done to avoid breaking changes that would occur for users migrating from ASP.NET 1.0/1.1 to ASP.NET 2.0. Therefore, you must first change this value to True in either the machine.config or the web.config file.
cacheRolesInCookie	Defines whether the roles of the user can be stored within a cookie on the client machine. This attribute takes a Boolean value and is set to True by default. This is an ideal situation because retrieving the roles from the cookie prevents ASP.NET from looking up the roles of the user via the role management provider. Set it to False if you want the roles to be retrieved via the provider for all instances.
cookieName	Defines the name used for the cookie sent to the end user for role management information storage. By default, this cookie is named .ASPXROLES, and you probably won't change this.
cookieTimeout	Defines the amount of time (in minutes) after which the cookie expires. The default value is 30 minutes.
cookieRequireSSL	Defines whether you require that the role management information be sent over an encrypted wire (SSL) instead of being sent as clear text. The default value is False.
cookieSlidingExpiration	Specifies whether the timeout of the cookie is on a sliding scale. The default value is True. This means that the end user's cookie does not expire until 30 minutes (or the time specified in the cookieTimeout attribute) after the last request to the application has been made. If the value of the cookieSlidingExpiration attribute is set to False, the cookie expires 30 minutes from the first request.
createPersistentCookie	Specifies whether a cookie expires or if it remains alive indefinitely. The default setting is False because a persistent cookie is not always advisable for security reasons.

Table continued on following page

Attribute	Description
cookieProtection	Specifies the amount of protection you want to apply to the cookie stored on the end user's machine for management information. The possible settings include All, None, Encryption, and Validation. You should always attempt to use All.
defaultProvider	Defines the provider used for the role management service. By default, it is set to AspNetSqlRoleProvider.

Making Changes to the web.config File

The next step is to configure your web.config file so that it can work with the role management service. Certain pages or subsections of your application may be accessible only to people with specific roles. To manage this access, you define the access rights in the web.config file. The necessary changes are shown in Listing 16-24.

Listing 16-24: Changing the web.config file

```xml
<?xml version="1.0" encoding="utf-8"?>
<configuration>

    <system.web>
        <roleManager enabled="true"/>
        <authentication mode="Forms" />
        <authorization>
            <deny users="?" />
        </authorization>
    </system.web>

    <location path="AdminPage.aspx">
        <system.web>
            <authorization>
                <allow roles="AdminPageRights" />
                <deny users="*" />
            </authorization>
        </system.web>
    </location>

</configuration>
```

This web.config file is doing a couple of things. First, the function of the first <system.web> section is no different from that of the membership service shown earlier in the chapter. The <deny> element is denying all unauthenticated users across the board.

The second section of this web.config file is rather interesting. The <location> element is used to define the access rights of a particular page in the application (AdminPage.aspx). In this case, only users contained in the AdminPageRights role are allowed to view the page, whereas all other users — regardless whether they are authenticated — are not allowed to view the page. When using the asterisk (*) as a value of the users attribute of the <deny> element, you are saying that all users (regardless of whether they are authenticated) are not allowed to access the resource being defined. This overriding denial of access, however, is broken open a bit via the use of the <allow> element, which allows users contained within a specific role.

Adding and Retrieving Application Roles

Now that the machine.config.comments and the web.config files are in place, you can add roles to the role management service. The role management service, just like the membership service, uses data stores to store information about the users. These examples focus primarily on using Microsoft SQL Server Express Edition as the provider because it is the default provider.

One big difference between the role management service and the membership service is that no server controls are used for the role management service. You manage the application's roles and the user's role details through a new Roles API or through the Web Site Administration Tool provided with ASP.NET 2.0. Listing 16-25 shows how to use some of the new methods to add roles to the service.

Listing 16-25: Adding roles to the application

VB

```
<%@ Page Language="VB" %>

<script runat="server">
    Protected Sub Page_Load(ByVal sender As Object, ByVal e As System.EventArgs)
    If Not Page.IsPostBack Then
        ListBoxDataBind()
    End If
    End Sub

    Protected Sub Button1_Click(ByVal sender As Object, ByVal e As System.EventArgs)
        Roles.CreateRole(TextBox1.Text)
        ListBoxDataBind()
    End Sub

    Protected Sub ListBoxDataBind()
        ListBox1.DataSource = Roles.GetAllRoles()
        ListBox1.DataBind()
    End Sub
</script>

<html xmlns="http://www.w3.org/1999/xhtml" >
<head runat="server">
    <title>Role Manager</title>
</head>
<body>
    <form id="form1" runat="server">
        <h1>Role Manager</h1>
        Add Role:<br />
        <asp:TextBox ID="TextBox1" Runat="server"></asp:TextBox>
        <p><asp:Button ID="Button1" Runat="server" Text="Add Role to Application"
            OnClick="Button1_Click" /></p>
        Roles Defined:<br />
        <asp:ListBox ID="ListBox1" Runat="server">
        </asp:ListBox>
    </form>
</body>
</html>
```

(continued)

Listing 16-25: *(continued)*

C#

```csharp
<%@ Page Language="C#" %>

<script runat="server">
   protected void Page_Load(object sender, EventArgs e)
   {
   if (!Page.IsPostBack)
   {
      ListBoxDataBind();
   }

   protected void Button1_Click(object sender, EventArgs e)
   {
      Roles.CreateRole(TextBox1.Text.ToString());
      ListBoxDataBind();
   }

   protected void ListBoxDataBind()
   {
      ListBox1.DataSource = Roles.GetAllRoles();
      ListBox1.DataBind();
   }
</script>
```

This example enables you to enter roles into the text box and then to submit them to the role management service. The roles contained in the role management service are then displayed in the list box, as illustrated in Figure 16-21.

To enter the roles into the management service, you simply use the `CreateRole` method of the `Roles` class. Just as with the `Membership` class, you don't instantiate the `Roles` class. To add roles to the role management service, use the `CreateRole` method that takes only a single parameter — the name of the role as a `String` value:

```
Roles.CreateRole(rolename As String)
```

Figure 16-21

With this method, you can create as many roles as you want, but each role must be unique — otherwise an exception is thrown.

To retrieve the roles that are in the application's role management service (such as the list of roles displayed in the list box from the earlier example), you use the `GetAllRoles` method of the `Roles` class. This method returns a `String` collection of all the available roles in the service:

```
Roles.GetAllRoles()
```

Deleting Roles

It would be just great to sit and add roles to the service all day long. Every now and then, however, you might want to delete roles from the service as well. Deleting roles is just as easy as adding roles to the role management service. To delete a role, you use one of the `DeleteRole` method signatures. The first option of the `DeleteRole` method takes a single parameter — the name of the role as a `String` value. The second option takes the name of the role plus a `Boolean` value that determines whether to throw an exception when one or more members are contained within that particular role (so that you don't accidentally delete a role with users in it when you don't mean to):

```
Roles.DeleteRole(rolename As String)

Roles.DeleteRole(rolename As String, throwOnPopulatedRole As Boolean)
```

Listing 16-26 is a partial code example that builds on Listing 16-25. For this example, add an additional button, which initiates a second button-click event that deletes the role from the service.

Listing 16-26: Deleting roles from the application

VB
```
Protected Sub DeleteButton_Click(ByVal sender As Object, _
    ByVal e As System.EventArgs)

    For Each li As ListItem In ListBox1.Items
        If li.Selected = True Then
            Roles.DeleteRole(li.ToString())
        End If
    Next
    ListBoxDataBind()
End Sub
```

C#
```
protected void DeleteButton_Click(object sender, EventArgs e)
{
    foreach (ListItem li in ListBox1.Items) {
        if (li.Selected == true) {
            Roles.DeleteRole(li.ToString());
        }
    }
    ListBoxDataBind();
}
```

This example deletes the selected items from the ListBox control. If more than one selection is made (meaning that you have placed the attribute `SelectionMode="Multiple"` in the ListBox control), each of the roles is deleted from the service, in turn, in the `For Each` loop. Although `Roles.DeleteRole(li.ToString())` is used to delete the role, `Roles.DeleteRole(li.ToString(), True)` could also be used to make sure that no roles are deleted if that role contains any members.

Adding Users to Roles

Now that the roles are in place and it is also possible to delete these roles if required, the next step is adding users to the roles created. A role doesn't do much good if no users are associated with it. To add a single user to a single role, you use the following construct:

```
Roles.AddUserToRole(username As String, rolename As String)
```

To add a single user to multiple roles at the same time, you use this construct:

```
Roles.AddUserToRoles(username As String, rolenames() As String)
```

To add multiple users to a single role, you use the following construct:

```
Roles.AddUsersToRole(usernames() As String, rolename As String)
```

Then finally, to add multiple users to multiple roles, you use the following construct:

```
Roles.AddUsersToRoles(usernames() As String, rolenames() As String)
```

The parameters that can take collections, whether they are `usernames()` or `rolenames()`, are presented to the method as `String` arrays.

Getting All the Users of a Particular Role

Looking up information is easy in the role management service, whether you are determining which users are contained within a particular role or whether you want to know the roles that a particular user belongs to.

Methods are available for either of these scenarios. First, look at how to determine all the users contained in a particular role, as illustrated in Listing 16-27.

Listing 16-27: Looking up users in a particular role

VB

```vb
<%@ Page Language="VB" %>

<script runat="server">
    Protected Sub Page_Load(ByVal sender As Object, ByVal e As System.EventArgs)
    If Not Page.IsPostBack Then
        DropDownDataBind()
    End If
    End Sub

    Protected Sub Button1_Click(ByVal sender As Object, ByVal e As System.EventArgs)
        GridView1.DataSource = Roles.GetUsersInRole(DropDownList1.SelectedValue)
        GridView1.DataBind()
        DropDownDataBind()
    End Sub
```

```
      Protected Sub DropDownDataBind()
          DropDownList1.DataSource = Roles.GetAllRoles()
          DropDownList1.DataBind()
      End Sub

  </script>

  <html xmlns="http://www.w3.org/1999/xhtml" >
  <head runat="server">
      <title>Role Manager</title>
  </head>
  <body>
      <form id="form1" runat="server">
          Roles:
          <asp:DropDownList ID="DropDownList1" Runat="server">
          </asp:DropDownList>
          <asp:Button ID="Button1" Runat="server" Text="Get Users In Role"
           OnClick="Button1_Click" />
          <br />
          <br />
          <asp:GridView ID="GridView1" Runat="server">
          </asp:GridView>
      </form>
  </body>
  </html>
```

C#

```
<%@ Page Language="C#" %>

<script runat="server">
   protected void Page_Load(object sender, EventArgs e)
   if (!Page.IsPostBack)
   {
      DropDownDataBind();
   }

   protected void Button1_Click(object sender, EventArgs e)
   {
      GridView1.DataSource = Roles.GetUsersInRole(DropDownList1.SelectedValue);
      GridView1.DataBind();
      DropDownDataBind();
   }

   protected void DropDownDataBind()
   {
      DropDownList1.DataSource = Roles.GetAllRoles();
      DropDownList1.DataBind();
   }
</script>
```

This page creates a drop-down list that contains all the roles for the application. Clicking the button displays all the users for the selected role. Users of a particular role are determined using the GetUsersInRole method. This method takes a single parameter—a String value representing the name of the role:

```
Roles.GetUsersInRole(rolename As String)
```

When run, the page looks similar to the page shown in Figure 16-22.

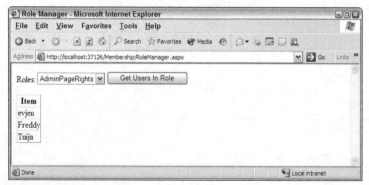

Figure 16-22

Getting All the Roles of a Particular User

To determine all the roles for a particular user, create a page with a single text box and a button. In the text box, you type the name of the user; and a button click initiates the retrieval and populates a GridView control. The button click event (where all the action is) is illustrated in Listing 16-28.

Listing 16-28: Getting all the roles of a specific user

VB

```
Protected Sub Button1_Click(ByVal sender As Object, ByVal e As System.EventArgs)
   GridView1.DataSource = Roles.GetRolesForUser(TextBox1.Text)
   GridView1.DataBind()
End Sub
```

C#

```
protected void Button1_Click(object sender, EventArgs e)
{
   GridView1.DataSource = Roles.GetRolesForUser(TextBox1.Text.ToString());
   GridView1.DataBind();
}
```

The preceding code produces something similar to what is shown in Figure 16-23.

To get the roles of a particular user, you simply use the GetRolesForUser method. This method has two possible signatures. The first is shown in the preceding example—a String value that represents the name of the user. The other option is an invocation of the method without any parameters listed. This returns the roles of the user who has logged into the membership service.

Figure 16-23

Removing Users from Roles

In addition to adding users to roles, you can also easily remove users from roles. To delete or remove a single user from a single role, you use the following construct:

```
Roles.RemoveUserFromRole(username As String, rolename As String)
```

To remove a single user from multiple roles at the same time, you use this construct:

```
Roles.RemoveUserFromRoles(username As String, rolenames() As String)
```

To remove multiple users from a single role, you use the following construct:

```
Roles.RemoveUsersFromRole(usernames() As String, rolename As String)
```

Then finally, to remove multiple users from multiple roles, you use the following construct:

```
Roles.RemoveUsersFromRoles(usernames() As String, rolenames() As String)
```

The parameters shown as collections, whether they are usernames() or rolenames(), are presented to the method as String arrays.

Checking Users in Roles

One final action you can take is checking whether a particular user is in a role. You can go about this in a couple of ways. The first is using the IsUserInRole method.

The IsUserInRole method takes two parameters — the username and the name of the role:

```
Roles.IsUserInRole(username As String, rolename As String)
```

This method returns a Boolean value on the status of the user, and it can be used as shown in Listing 16-29.

Listing 16-29: Checking a user's role status

VB

```vb
If (Roles.IsUserInRole(TextBox1.Text, "AdminPageRights")) Then
    ' perform action here
End If
```

C#

```csharp
if (Roles.IsUserInRole(TextBox1.Text.ToString(), "AdminPageRights"))
{
    // perform action here
}
```

The other option, in addition to the `IsUserInRole` method, is to use `FindUsersInRole`. This method enables you make a name search against all the users in a particular role. The `FindUsersInRole` method takes two parameters — the name of the role and the username, both as `String` values:

```
Roles.FindUsersInRole(rolename As String, username As String)
```

Listing 16-30 shows an example of this method.

Listing 16-30: Checking for a specific user in a particular role

VB

```vb
<%@ Page Language="VB" %>

<script runat="server">
    Protected Sub Button1_Click(ByVal sender As Object, ByVal e As System.EventArgs)
        GridView1.DataSource = _
            Roles.FindUsersInRole("AdminPageRights", TextBox1.Text)
        GridView1.DataBind()
    End Sub
</script>

<html xmlns="http://www.w3.org/1999/xhtml" >
<head runat="server">
    <title>Role Manager</title>
</head>
<body>
    <form id="form1" runat="server">
        <asp:TextBox ID="TextBox1" Runat="server"></asp:TextBox>
        <asp:Button ID="Button1" Runat="server" Text="Button"
         OnClick="Button1_Click" />
        <p><asp:GridView ID="GridView1" Runat="server">
        </asp:GridView></p>
    </form>
</body>
</html>
```

C#

```csharp
<%@ Page Language="C#" %>

<script runat="server">
    protected void Button1_Click(object sender, EventArgs e)
```

```
        {
            GridView1.DataSource =
                Roles.FindUsersInRole("AdminPageRights", TextBox1.Text.ToString());
            GridView1.DataBind();
        }
</script>
```

Understanding How Roles Are Cached

By default, after you retrieve a user's roles from the data store underlying the role management service, you can store these roles as a cookie on the client machine. This is done so you don't have to access the data store each and every time the application needs a user's role status. There is always a bit of risk in working with cookies because the end user can manipulate the cookie and thereby gain access to information or parts of an application that normally would be forbidden to that particular user.

Although roles are cached in a cookie, the default is that they are cached for only 30 minutes at a time. You can deal with this role cookie in several ways—some of which might help to protect your application better.

One protection for your application is to delete this role cookie, using the `DeleteCookie` method of the Role API, when the end user logs on to the site. This is illustrated in Listing 16-31.

Listing 16-31: Deleting the end user's role cookie upon authentication

VB
```
If Membership.ValidateUser(TextBox1.Text, TextBox2.Text) Then
    Roles.DeleteCookie()
    FormsAuthentication.RedirectFromLoginPage(TextBox1.Text, False)
Else
    Label1.Text = "You are not registered with the site."
End If
```

C#
```
if (Membership.ValidateUser(TextBox1.Text.ToString(), TextBox2.Text.ToString()) {
    Roles.DeleteCookie();
    FormsAuthentication.RedirectFromLoginPage(TextBox1.Text.ToString(), false);
}
else {
    Label1.Text = "You are not registered with the site.";
}
```

Using `Roles.DeleteCookie` does exactly what you would think—it deletes from the client machine any cookie that is used to define the user's roles. If the end user is re-logging into the site, no problem should arise with re-authenticating his exact roles within the application. There is no need to rely on the contents of the cookie. This step provides a little more protection for your site.

Using the Web Site Administration Tool

Many of the actions shown in this chapter can also be performed through the Web Site Administration Tool shown in Figure 16-24.

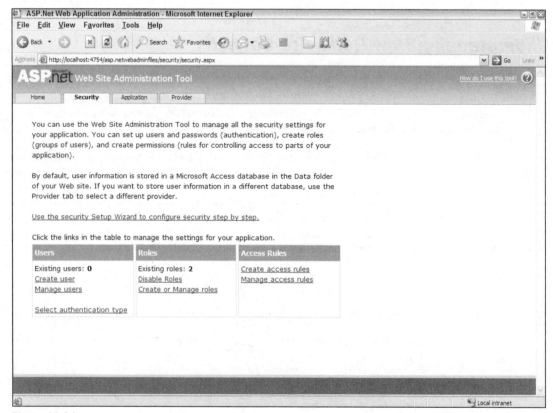

Figure 16-24

Although you can easily use this tool to perform all the actions for you, often you perform these actions through your own applications as well. It is important to know all the possibilities when programming an ASP.NET application.

The Web Site Administration Tool is detailed in Chapter 28.

Public Methods of the Membership API

The public methods of the Membership API are detailed in the following table. You would use this API when working with the authentication process of your application.

Membership Methods	Description
CreateUser	Adds a new user to the appointed data store.
DeleteUser	Deletes a specified user from the data store.
FindUsersByEmail	Returns a collection of users who have an e-mail address to match the one provided.
FindUsersByName	Returns a collection of users who have a username to match the one provided.
GeneratePassword	Generates a random password of a length that you specify.
GetAllUsers	Returns a collection of all the users contained in the data store.
GetNumberOfUsersOnline	Returns an Integer that specifies the number of users who have logged in to the application. The time window during which users are counted is specified in the machine.config or the web.config files.
GetUser	Returns information about a particular user from the data store.
GetUserNameByEmail	Retrieves a username of a specific record from the data store based on an e-mail address search.
UpdateUser	Updates a particular user's information in the data store.
ValidateUser	Returns a Boolean value indicating whether a specified set of credentials is valid.

Public Methods of the Roles API

The public methods of the Roles API are detailed in the following table. You would use this API when working with the authorization process of your application.

Roles Methods	Description
AddUsersToRole	Adds a collection of users to a specific role.
AddUsersToRoles	Adds a collection of users to a collection of roles.
AddUserToRole	Adds a specific user to a specific role.
AddUserToRoles	Adds a specific user to a collection of roles.
CreateRole	Adds a new role to the appointed data store.
DeleteCookie	Deletes the cookie on the client used to store the roles to which the user belongs.

Table continued on following page

Roles Methods	Description
DeleteRole	Deletes a specific role in the data store. Using the proper parameters for this method, you can also control if roles are deleted or kept intact whether or not that particular role contains users.
FindUsersInRole	Returns a collection of users who have a username to match the one provided.
GetAllRoles	Returns a collection of all the roles stored in the data store.
GetRolesForUser	Returns a collection of roles for a specific user.
IsUserInRole	Returns a Boolean value that specifies whether a user is contained in a particular role.
RemoveUserFromRole	Removes a specific user from a specific role.
RemoveUserFromRoles	Removes a specific user from a collection of roles.
RemoveUsersFromRole	Removes a collection of users from a specific role.
RemoveUsersFromRoles	Removes a collection of users from a collection of roles.
RoleExists	Returns a Boolean value indicating whether a role exists in the data store.

Summary

This chapter covered two outstanding new additions to ASP.NET 2.0. The membership and role management services that are now a part of ASP.NET make managing users and their roles almost trivial.

This chapter reviewed both the Membership and Roles APIs and the controls that also utilize these APIs. These new controls and APIs follow the same data provider models as the rest of ASP.NET 2.0. The examples were presented using Microsoft Access, but you can also use Microsoft SQL Server for the back-end storage.

17

Portal Frameworks and Web Parts

Internet and intranet applications have changed considerably since their introduction in the 1990s. Today's applications don't simply display the same canned information to every viewer; they do much more. Because of the wealth of information being exposed to end users, Internet and intranet applications must integrate large amounts of customization and personalization into their offerings.

Web sites that provide a plethora of offerings give end users the option to choose which parts of the site they want to view and which parts they want to hide. Ideally, end users can personalize the pages, deciding for themselves the order in which the content appears on the page. They should be able to move items around on the page as if it were a design surface.

In this situation, after pages are customized and established, end users need the capability to export their settings for storage. You certainly wouldn't want an end user who has highly customized a page or a series of pages in your portal to be forced to reapply the settings each time he visits the site. Instead, you want to retain these setting points by moving them to a data store for later exposure.

Adding this kind of functionality is expensive—*expensive* in the sense that it can take a considerable amount of work on the part of the developer. Before ASP.NET 2.0, the developer had to build a personalization framework to be used by each page requiring the functionality. This type of work is error prone and difficult to achieve, which is why in most cases it wasn't done.

But wait. . . .

Introducing Web Parts

To make it easier to retain the page customization settings that your end users apply to your page, Microsoft has included Web Parts in this release of ASP.NET. Web Parts, part of the larger Portal Framework, provide an outstanding way to build a modular Web site that can be customized with dynamically reapplied settings on a per-user basis. Web Parts are objects in the Portal Framework which the end user can open, close, minimize, maximize, or move from one part of the page to another.

The Portal Framework enables you to build pages that contain multiple Web Parts — which are part of the ASP.NET server control framework and are used like any other ASP.NET server controls. This means that you can also extend Web Parts if necessary.

The components of the Portal Framework provide the means to build a truly dynamic Web site, whether that site is a traditional Internet site, an intranet site, a browser-based application, or any other typical portal.

When you first look at Web Parts in ASP.NET 2.0, it may remind you of Microsoft's SharePoint offering. Be forewarned, however, that these two technologies are not the same. The ASP.NET team introduced Web Parts; the resulting Portal Framework, besides being offered in ASP.NET, is also used by the Windows SharePoint Services (WSS). Microsoft, as it often does, is simply creating singular technologies that can be used by other Microsoft offerings. In this process, Microsoft is trying to reach the Holy Grail of computing — *code reuse!*

The modular and customizable sites that you can build with the new Portal Framework enable you to put the Web page that is in view into several possible modes for the end user. The following list describes each of the available modes and what each means to the end user viewing the page:

❑ **Normal Mode:** Puts the page in a normal state, which means that the end user cannot edit or move sections of the page. This is the mode used for standard page viewing.

❑ **Edit Mode:** Enables end users to select particular sections on the page for editing. The selected section allows all types of editing capabilities from changing the part's title, the part's color, or even setting custom properties — such as allowing the end user to specify his zip code to pull up a customized weather report.

❑ **Design Mode:** Enables end users to rearrange the order of the page's modular components. The end user can bring items higher or lower within a zone, delete items from a zone, or move items from one page zone to another.

❑ **Catalog Mode:** Displays a list of available sections (Web Parts) that can be placed in the page. Catalog mode also allows the end user to select in which zone on the page the items should appear.

Figure 17-1 shows a screen shot of a sample portal utilizing the Portal Framework with the Edit mode selected.

The Portal Framework is a comprehensive and well-thought-out framework that enables you to incorporate everything you would normally include in your ASP.NET applications. You can apply security using either Windows Authentication or Forms Authentication. This framework also enables you to leverage the other new aspects of ASP.NET 2.0, such as applying role management, personalization, and membership features to any portal that you build.

To understand how to build your own application on top of the new Portal Framework, start by creating a simple page that uses this new framework's utilities.

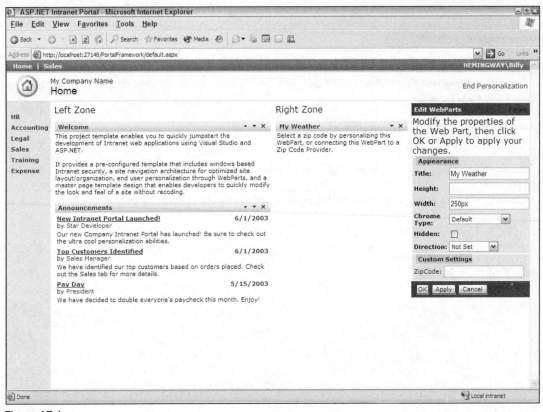

Figure 17-1

Building Dynamic and Modular Web Sites

As you begin using the new Portal Framework to build Web sites, note that the framework defines everything in *zones*. There are zones for both laying out and editing content. The zones that a page might incorporate are managed by a Portal Framework manager—you don't have to manage them in any fashion—which makes working with this new Portal Framework a breeze.

This framework contains a lot of moving parts (pieces that are dependent upon each other), so this section starts at the beginning by examining the Portal Framework manager control: WebPartManager.

Introducing the WebPartManager Control

The WebPartManager control is an ASP.NET server control that completely manages the state of the zones and the content placed in the zones on a per-user basis. This control, which has no visual aspect, can add and delete items contained within each zone of the page. The WebPartManager control can also manage the communications sometimes required between different elements contained in the zones. For example, you can pass a specific name/value pair from one item to another item within the same zone, or between items contained in entirely separate zones. The WebPartManager control provides the capabilities to make this communication happen.

The WebPartManager control must be in place on every page in your application that works with the Portal Framework. A single WebPartManager control does not manage an entire application; it manages on a per-page basis.

> *You can also place a WebPartManager server control on the master page (if you are using one) to avoid having to place one on each and every content page.*

Listing 17-1 shows a WebPartManager control added to an ASP.NET page.

Listing 17-1: Adding a WebPartManager control to an ASP.NET page

```
<%@ Page Language="VB" %>

<html xmlns="http://www.w3.org/1999/xhtml" >
<head runat="server">
    <title>Web Parts Example</title>
</head>
<body>
    <form id="form1" runat="server">
        <asp:WebPartManager ID="Webpartmanager1" runat="server">
        </asp:WebPartManager>
    </form>
</body>
</html>
```

If you want to work from the design surface of Visual Studio 2005, you can drag and drop the WebPartManager control from the Toolbox to the design surface — but remember, it does not have a visual aspect and appears only as a gray box. You can find the WebPartManager control (and the other server controls that are part of the Portal Framework) in the WebParts section of the Toolbox, as shown in Figure 17-2.

Working with Zone Layouts

After you place the WebPartManager control on the page, the next step is to create zones from which you can utilize the Portal Framework. You should give this step some thought because it contributes directly to the usability of the page you are creating. Web pages are constructed in a linear fashion — either horizontally or vertically. Web pages are managed in square boxes — usually through the use of tables that organize the columns and rows in which items appear on the page.

Web zones define specific rows or columns as individual content areas managed by the WebPartManager. For an example of a Web page that uses these zones, create a table similar to the one shown in Figure 17-3.

Figure 17-2

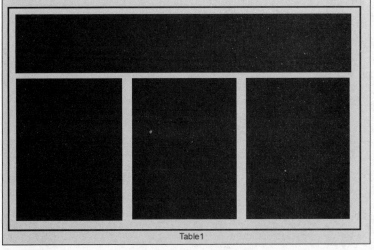

Figure 17-3

The black sections in Figure 17-3 represent Web zones. The code used to produce the table is shown in Listing 17-2.

Listing 17-2: Creating multiple Web zones

```
<%@ Page Language="VB"%>
<%@ Register Src="DailyLinks.ascx" TagName="DailyLinks" TagPrefix="uc1" %>

<html xmlns="http://www.w3.org/1999/xhtml" >
<head runat="server">
    <title>Web Parts Example</title>
</head>
<body>
    <form id="form1" runat="server">
        <asp:WebPartManager ID="Webpartmanager1" runat="server">
        </asp:WebPartManager>
        <table cellpadding="5" border="1">
            <tr>
                <td colspan="3">
                    <h1>Bill Evjen's Web Page</h1>
                    <asp:WebPartZone ID="WebPartZone1" runat="server"
                     LayoutOrientation="Horizontal">
                        <ZoneTemplate>
                            <asp:Label ID="Label1" runat="server" Text="Label"
                             Title="Welcome to my web page!">
                             Welcome to the page!
                            </asp:Label>
                        </ZoneTemplate>
                    </asp:WebPartZone>
                </td>
            </tr>
            <tr valign="top">
                <td>
                    <asp:WebPartZone ID="WebPartZone2" runat="server">
                        <ZoneTemplate>
                            <asp:Image ID="Image1" runat="server"
                             ImageUrl="~/Images/Kids.jpg" Width="150px"
                             Title="My Kids">
                            </asp:Image>
                            <uc1:DailyLinks ID="DailyLinks1" runat="server"
                             Title="Daily Links">
                            </uc1:DailyLinks>
                        </ZoneTemplate>
                    </asp:WebPartZone>
                </td>
                <td>
                    <asp:WebPartZone ID="WebPartZone3" runat="server">
                        <ZoneTemplate>
                            <asp:Calendar ID="Calendar1" runat="server"
                             Title="Calendar">
                            </asp:Calendar>
                        </ZoneTemplate>
                    </asp:WebPartZone>
```

```
                      </td>
                      <td><!-- Blank for now -->
                      </td>
                  </tr>
              </table>
          </form>
    </body>
    </html>
```

This page now has sections like the ones shown in Figure 17-3: a header section that runs horizontally and three vertical sections underneath the header. Running this page provides the result shown in Figure 17-4.

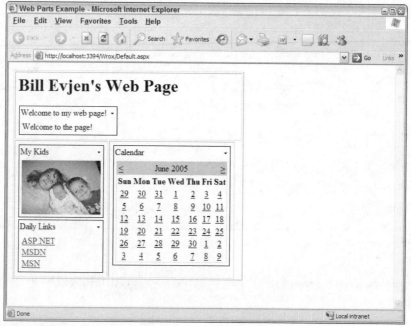

Figure 17-4

First, this page includes the `<asp:WebPartManager>` control that manages the items contained in the three zones on this page. Within the table, the `<asp:WebPartZone>` server control specifies three Web zones. You can declare each Web zone in one of two ways. You can use the `<asp:WebPartZone>` element directly in the code, or you can create the zones within the table by dragging and dropping WebPartZone controls onto the design surface at appropriate places within the table. In Figure 17-4, the table border width is intentionally turned on and set to 1 in order to show the location of the Web zones in greater detail. Figure 17-5 shows what the sample from Listing 17-2 looks like in the Design view of Visual Studio 2005.

When using Visual Studio 2005, note that by default this IDE creates a Microsoft SQL Server Express Edition file called `ASPNETDB.MDF` and stores it in the `App_Data` folder of your Web Project. This database file is where the Portal Framework stores all the customization points.

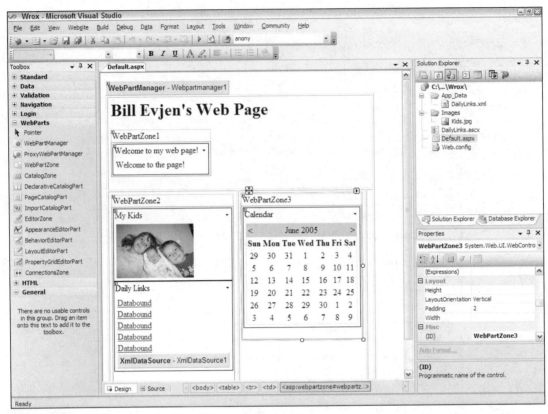

Figure 17-5

Now that you have seen the use of WebPartZone controls, which are managed by the WebPartManager control, the next section takes a closer look at the WebPartZone control itself.

Understanding the WebPartZone Control

The WebPartZone control defines an area of items, or Web Parts, that can be moved, minimized, maximized, deleted, or added based on programmatic code or user preferences. When you drag and drop WebPartZone controls onto the design surface using Visual Studio 2005, the WebPartZone control is drawn at the top of the zone, along with a visual representation of any of the items contained within the zone.

You can place almost anything in one of the Web zones. For example, you can include the following:

❏ HTML elements

❏ Raw text

❏ HTML server controls

❏ Web server controls

❏ User controls

❏ Custom controls

WebPartZone controls are declared like this:

```
<asp:WebPartZone ID="WebPartZone1" Runat="server"></asp:WebPartZone>
```

The LayoutOrientation Attribute

The Web Parts declared within a WebPartZone control can be displayed either horizontally or vertically. By default, all the items are displayed vertically, but to display the items horizontally, you simply add the LayoutOrientation attribute to the `<asp:WebPartZone>` element:

```
<asp:WebPartZone ID="WebPartZone1" Runat="server"
 LayoutOrientation="Horizontal"></asp:WebPartZone>
```

The first row in the table from Listing 17-2 uses horizontal orientation, whereas the other two zones use the default vertical orientation.

The ZoneTemplate Element

In order to include items within the templated WebPartZone control, you must include a `<ZoneTemplate>` element.

The ZoneTemplate element encapsulates all the items contained within a particular zone. The order in which they are listed in the ZoneTemplate section is the order in which they appear in the browser until changed by the end user or by programmatic code. The sample `<ZoneTemplate>` section used earlier is illustrated here:

```
<asp:WebPartZone ID="WebPartZone2" Runat="server">
   <ZoneTemplate>
      <asp:Image ID="Image1" Runat="server"
       ImageUrl="~/Images/kids.jpg" Width="150" Title="My Kids">
      </asp:Image>
      <uc1:DailyLinks ID="DailyLinks1" runat="server" Title="Daily Links">
      </uc1:DailyLinks>
   </ZoneTemplate>
</asp:WebPartZone>
```

This zone contains two items — a dynamic image and a user control consisting of a collection of links that come from an XML file.

Default Web Part Control Elements

By default, when you generate a page using the code from Listing 17-2, you discover that you can exert only minimal control over the Web Parts themselves. In the default view, which isn't the most artistic, you are able only to minimize or close a Web Part. You can see these options when you click on the down arrow that is presented next to the name of the Web Part.

Figure 17-6 shows what the Web Part that contains the Calendar control looks like after you minimize it. Notice also that if you opt to close one of the Web Parts, the item completely disappears. There seems to be no way to make it come back — even if you shut down the page and restart it. This is by design — so don't worry. I'll show you how to get it back!

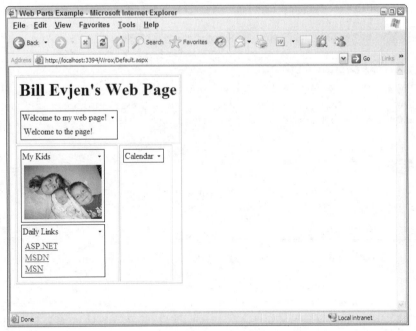

Figure 17-6

A few of the items included in the zones have new titles. By default, the title that appears at the top of the Web Part is the name of the control. For instance, you can see that the Calendar control is simply titled Calendar. If you add a Button control or any other control to the zone, at first it is simply titled Untitled. To give better and more meaningful names to the Web Parts that appear in a zone, you simply add a `Title` attribute to the control—just as was done with the Image control and the User control, which both appear on the page. In the preceding code example, the Image control is renamed to `My Kids`, and the user control is given the `Title` value `Daily Links`.

Besides this little bit of default functionality, you can do considerably more with the Web Parts contained within this page, but you have to make some other additions. These are reviewed next.

Allowing the User to Change the Mode of the Page

Working with the `WebPartManager` class either directly or through the use of the WebPartManager server control, you can have the mode of the page changed. Changing the mode of the page being viewed allows the user to add, move, or change the pages they are working with. The nice thing about the Web Part capabilities of ASP.NET is that these changes are then recorded to the `ASPNETDB.MDF` database file and are, therefore, re-created the next time the user visits the page.

Through the use of the `WebPartManager` object, you can enable the user to do the following, as defined in this list:

❑ **Add new Web Parts to the page:** Includes Web Parts not displayed on the page by default and Web Parts that the end user has previously deleted. This aspect of the control works with the catalog capabilities of the Portal Framework, which is discussed shortly.

❑ **Enter the Design mode for the page:** Enables the end user to drag and drop elements around the page. The end user can use this capability to change the order in which items appear in a zone or to move items from one zone to another.

❑ **Modify the Web Parts settings:** Enables the end user to customize aspects of the Web Parts, such as their appearance and behavior. It also allows the end user to modify any custom settings that developers apply to the Web Part.

❑ **Connect Web Parts on the page:** Enables the end user to make a connection between one or more Web Parts on the page. For example, when an end user working in a financial services application enters a stock symbol into an example Web Part, he can use a connection to another Web Part to see a stock chart change or news appear based on that particular stock symbol. All of this is based on the variable defined in the first Web Part.

Building on Listing 17-2, Listing 17-3 adds a DropDownList control to the table's header. This drop-down list provides a list of available modes the user can employ to change how the page is displayed. Again, the mode of the page determines the actions the user can initiate directly on the page (this is demonstrated later in this chapter).

Listing 17-3: Adding a list of modes to the page

VB

```vb
<%@ Page Language="VB"%>
<%@ Register Src="DailyLinks.ascx" TagName="DailyLinks" TagPrefix="uc1" %>

<script runat="server">
    Protected Sub DropDownList1_SelectedIndexChanged(ByVal sender As Object, _
      ByVal e As System.EventArgs)

      Dim wpDisplayMode As WebParts.WebPartDisplayMode = _
      Webpartmanager1.SupportedDisplayModes(DropDownList1.SelectedValue.ToString())
      Webpartmanager1.DisplayMode = wpDisplayMode
    End Sub

    Protected Sub Page_Init(ByVal sender As Object, ByVal e As System.EventArgs)
      For Each wpMode As WebPartDisplayMode In _
        Webpartmanager1.SupportedDisplayModes

        Dim modeName As String = wpMode.Name
        Dim dd_ListItem As ListItem = New ListItem(modeName, modeName)
        DropDownList1.Items.Add(dd_ListItem)
    Next
    End Sub
</script>

<html xmlns="http://www.w3.org/1999/xhtml" >
<head id="Head1" runat="server">
    <title>Web Parts Example</title>
</head>
<body>
    <form id="form1" runat="server">
        <asp:WebPartManager ID="Webpartmanager1" Runat="server">
        </asp:WebPartManager>
        <table cellpadding="5" border="1">
```

(continued)

Listing 17-3: *(continued)*

```
            <tr>
                <td colspan="2">
                    <h1>Bill Evjen's Web Page</h1>
                    <asp:WebPartZone ID="WebPartZone1" Runat="server"
                     LayoutOrientation="Horizontal">
                        <ZoneTemplate>
                            <asp:Label ID="Label1" Runat="server" Text="Label"
                             Title="Welcome to my web page!">
                             Welcome to the page!
                            </asp:Label>
                        </ZoneTemplate>
                    </asp:WebPartZone>
                </td>
                <td valign="top">
                    Select mode:
                    <asp:DropDownList ID="DropDownList1" runat="server"
                     AutoPostBack="True"
                     OnSelectedIndexChanged="DropDownList1_SelectedIndexChanged">
                    </asp:DropDownList>
                </td>
            </tr>
            <tr valign="top">
                <td>
                    <asp:WebPartZone ID="WebPartZone2" Runat="server">
                        <ZoneTemplate>
                            <asp:Image ID="Image1" Runat="server"
                             ImageUrl="~/Images/Kids.jpg" Width="150px"
                             Title="My Kids">
                            </asp:Image>
                            <uc1:DailyLinks ID="DailyLinks1" runat="server"
                             Title="Daily Links">
                             </uc1:DailyLinks>
                        </ZoneTemplate>
                    </asp:WebPartZone>
                </td>
                <td>
                    <asp:WebPartZone ID="WebPartZone3" Runat="server">
                        <ZoneTemplate>
                            <asp:Calendar ID="Calendar1" Runat="server"
                             Title="Calendar">
                            </asp:Calendar>
                        </ZoneTemplate>
                    </asp:WebPartZone>
                </td>
                <td><!-- Blank for now -->
                </td>
            </tr>
        </table>
    </form>
</body>
</html>
```

C#

```
<%@ Page Language="C#"%>
<%@ Register Src="DailyLinks.ascx" TagName="DailyLinks" TagPrefix="uc1" %>
```

```
<script runat="server">
    protected void DropDownList1_SelectedIndexChanged(object sender, EventArgs e)
    {
      WebParts.WebPartDisplayMode wpDisplayMode =
      Webpartmanager1.SupportedDisplayModes[DropDownList1.SelectedValue.ToString()];
      Webpartmanager1.DisplayMode = wpDisplayMode;
    }

    protected void Page_Init(object sender, EventArgs e)
    {
      foreach (WebPartDisplayMode wpMode in
        Webpartmanager1.SupportedDisplayModes)
      {
          string modeName = wpMode.Name;
          ListItem dd_ListItem = new ListItem(modeName, modeName);
          DropDownList1.Items.Add(dd_ListItem);
      }
    }
</script>
```

This adds a drop-down list to the top of the table, as shown in Figure 17-7. This drop-down list will allow the end user to switch between the Browse and Design modes.

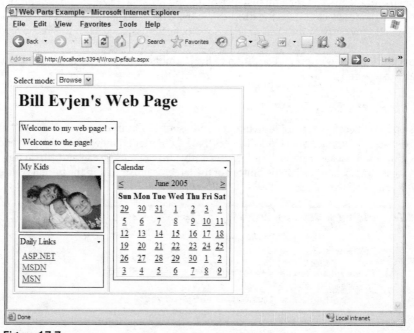

Figure 17-7

When the end user clicks open the link, a drop-down window of options appears, as shown in Figure 17-8.

Figure 17-8

Using the `Page_Init` event, the drop-down list is populated with a list of the available page modes that are accessible at this particular time. In this case, it is Browse and Design. The Browse mode is the default mode used when the page is first created. The Design mode causes the ASP.NET page to show the WebPartZone sections. In this mode, the user can drag and drop controls from one section to another with relative ease. Again, the positioning of the elements contained in the page is remembered from one application visit to the next.

The DropDownList control is populated by iterating through a list of available `WebPartDisplayMode` objects contained in the `SupportedDisplayModes` collection of modes. These modes are available through the `WebPartManager1` control, which was placed on the page and is in charge of managing the modes and change of modes of the page. These `WebPartDisplayMode` objects are then used to populate the DropDownList control.

When the end user selects one of the available modes displayed in the DropDownList control, using the `AutoPostBack` feature of the control, the page is then changed to the selected mode. This is done through the use of the first creating an instance of a `WebPartDisplayMode` object and populating it with the value of the mode selected from the drop-down list. Then, using this `WebPartDisplayMode` object, the `DisplayMode` property of the `WebPartManager` object is assigned with this retrieved value.

The next section covers an important addition to the Portal Framework — the capability to add Web Parts dynamically to a page.

Adding Web Parts to a Page

The next step is to rework the example so that the end user has a built-in way to add Web Parts to the page through the use of the Portal Framework. The ASP.NET 2.0 Portal Framework enables an end user to add Web Parts, but you must also provide the end user with a list of items he can add. To do this, simply add a Catalog Zone to the last table cell in the bottom of the table, as illustrated in the partial code example in Listing 17-4.

Listing 17-4: Adding a Catalog Zone

```
<tr valign="top">
   <td>
      <asp:WebPartZone ID="WebPartZone2" runat="server">
         <ZoneTemplate>
            <asp:Image ID="Image1" runat="server"
             ImageUrl="~/Images/Kids.jpg" Width="150px"
             Title="My Kids">
```

```
            </asp:Image>
            <uc1:DailyLinks ID="DailyLinks1" runat="server"
             Title="Daily Links">
            </uc1:DailyLinks>
        </ZoneTemplate>
      </asp:WebPartZone>
  </td>
  <td>
      <asp:WebPartZone ID="WebPartZone3" runat="server">
          <ZoneTemplate>
            <asp:Calendar ID="Calendar1" runat="server"
             Title="Calendar">
            </asp:Calendar>
          </ZoneTemplate>
      </asp:WebPartZone>
  </td>
  <td>
      <asp:CatalogZone ID="Catalogzone1" runat="server">
          <ZoneTemplate>
              <asp:PageCatalogPart ID="Pagecatalogpart1" runat="server" />
          </ZoneTemplate>
      </asp:CatalogZone>
  </td>
</tr>
```

Once a Catalog Zone section is present on the page, the page is enabled for the Catalog mode. You need to create a Catalog Zone section by using the `<asp:CatalogZone>` control. This is similar to creating a Web Part Zone, but the Catalog Zone is specifically designed to allow for categorization of the items that can be placed on the page. Notice that Catalog mode does not appear as an option in the drop-down list of available modes until a CatalogZone control is placed on the page. If no CatalogZone control is present on the page, this option is not displayed.

After the Catalog Zone is in place, the next step is to create a `<ZoneTemplate>` section within the Catalog Zone because this is also a templated control. Inside the `<ZoneTemplate>` element is a single control — the PageCatalogPart control. If you run the page after adding the PageCatalogPart control and change the mode to Catalog, you will see the results shown in Figure 17-9.

To get some items to appear in the list (since none do at present), close one or more items (any items contained on the page when viewing the page in the browser) from the page's default view and enter the Catalog mode by selecting Catalog from the drop-down list of modes.

At this point, you can see the deleted Web Parts in the Catalog Zone. The PageCatalogPart control contains a title and check box list of items that can be selected. The PageCatalogPart control also includes a drop-down list of all the available Web Part Zones on the page. From here, you can place the selected Web Parts into one of the Web Part Zones available from this list. After you select the Web Parts and the appropriate zone in which you want to place the item, you click the Add button and the items appear in the specified locations.

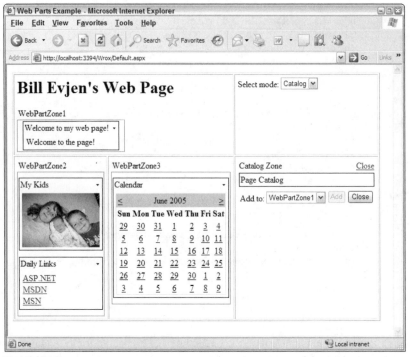

Figure 17-9

Moving Web Parts

Not only can the end user change the order in which Web Parts appear in a zone, he can also move Web Parts from one zone to another. By adding the capability to enter the Design mode through the drop-down list that you created earlier, you have already provided the end user with this capability. He simply enters the Design mode and this allows for this type of movement.

The Design option in the drop-down list changes the page so that the user can see the zones defined on the page, as illustrated in Figure 17-10.

From this figure, you can see the three zones (WebPartZone1, WebPartZone2, and WebPartZone3). At this point, the end user can select one of the Web Parts contained in one of these zones and either change its order in the zone or move it to an entirely different zone on the page. To grab one of the Web Parts, the user simply clicks and holds the left mouse button on the title of the Web Part. When done correctly, the cross-hair, which appears when the end user hovers over the Web Part's title, turns into an arrow. This means that the user has grabbed hold of the Web Part and can drag it to another part of the page. While the user drags the Web Part around the page, a visual representation of the item appears (see Figure 17-11). In this state, the Web Part is a bit transparent and its location in the state of the page is defined with a blue line (the darker line shown at the top of WebPartZone3). Releasing the left mouse button drops the Web Part at the blue line's location.

After the end user places all the items where he wants them, the locations of the items on the page are saved for later use.

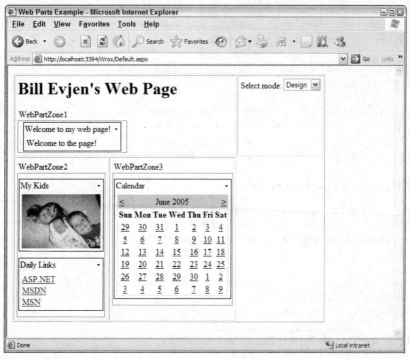

Figure 17-10

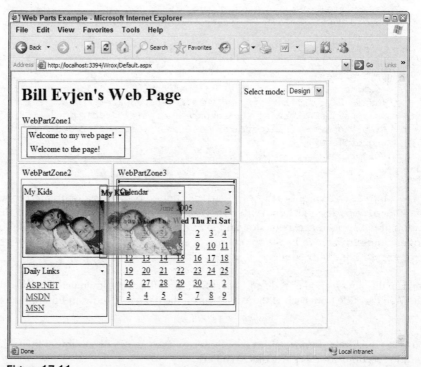

Figure 17-11

When he reopens the browser, everything is then drawn in the last state in which he left the page. This is done on a per-user basis, so any other users browsing to the same page see either their own modified results or the default view if it is a first visit to the page.

The user can then leave the Design view by opening the list of options from the drop-down list of modes and selecting Browse.

Another way to move Web Parts is to enter the Catalog mode of the page (which is now one of the options in the drop-down list due to the addition of the Catalog Zone section). The Catalog mode enables you to add deleted items to the page, but it also allows you to modify the location of the items on the page by providing the same drag-and-drop capability as the Design mode.

Modifying the Web Part Settings

Another option in the list of modes that can be added to the drop-down list is to allow your end users to edit the actual Web Parts themselves to a degree. This is done through the available Edit mode, and this enables the end user to modify settings determining appearance, behavior, and layout for a particular Web Part on the page.

To make this functionality work, you must add an Editor Zone to the page just as you add the Catalog Zone. This is illustrated in Listing 17-5. You place this bit of new code within the same table directly below the Catalog Zone declaration.

Listing 17-5: Adding an Editor Zone to the page

```
<td>
    <asp:CatalogZone ID="Catalogzone1" runat="server">
        <ZoneTemplate>
            <asp:PageCatalogPart ID="Pagecatalogpart1" runat="server" />
        </ZoneTemplate>
    </asp:CatalogZone>
    <asp:EditorZone ID="Editorzone1" runat="server">
        <ZoneTemplate>
            <asp:AppearanceEditorPart ID="Appearanceeditorpart1" runat="server" />
            <asp:BehaviorEditorPart ID="Behavioreditorpart1" runat="server" />
            <asp:LayoutEditorPart ID="Layouteditorpart1" runat="server" />
            <asp:PropertyGridEditorPart ID="PropertyGridEditorPart1" runat="server" />
        </ZoneTemplate>
    </asp:EditorZone>
</td>
```

Just like the `<asp:CatalogZone>`, the `<asp:EditorZone>` control is a templated control that requires a `<ZoneTemplate>` section. Within this section, you can place controls that allow for the modification of the appearance, behavior, and layout of the selected Web Part. These controls include `<asp:AppearanceEditorPart>`, `<asp:BehaviorEditorPart>`, `<asp:LayoutEditorPart>`, and `<asp:PropertyGridEditorPart>`.

When you run this new section of code and select Edit from the drop-down list of modes, the arrow that is next to the Web Part title from each of the Web Parts on the page will show an Edit option, as illustrated in Figure 17-12.

After you select the Edit option from this list of three options, the right column of the table shows the various editing sections for this particular Web Part.

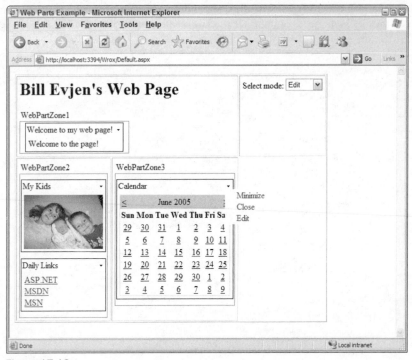

Figure 17-12

The Appearance section enables the end user to change the Web Part's details, including the title, how the title appears, and other appearance-related items such as the item's height and width. The Appearance section is shown in Figure 17-13.

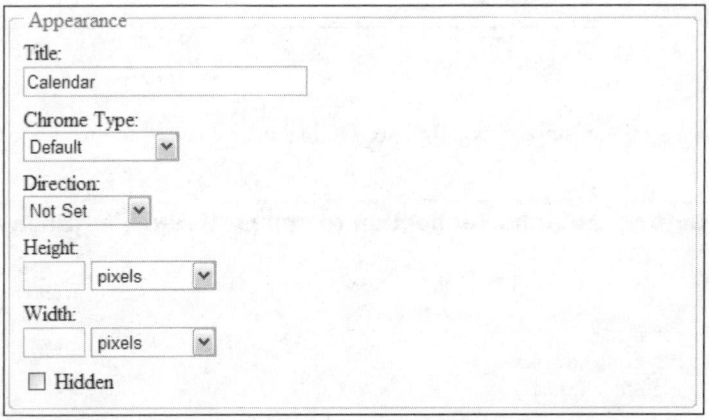

Figure 17-13

The Behavior section (shown in Figure 17-14) enables the end user to select whether the Web Part can be closed, minimized, or exported. This section allows you to change behavior items for either yourself only (a single user) or for everyone in the system (a shared view of the Web Part). Using the shared view, the Behavior section is generally used to allow site editors (or admins) to change the dynamics of how end users can modify Web Parts. General viewers of the page most likely won't see this section.

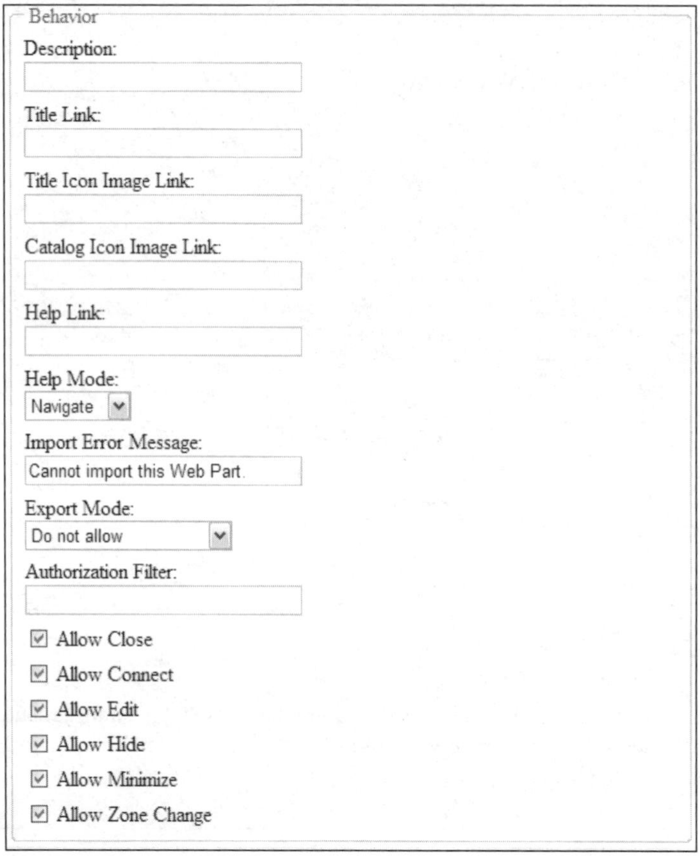

Figure 17-14

To get the Behavior section to appear, you first need to make the changes to the Web.config files presented in Listing 17-6.

Listing 17-6: Getting the Behavior section to appear through settings in the Web.config

```
<configuration>
    <system.web>
        <webParts>
            <personalization>
                <authorization>
                    <allow users="*" verbs="enterSharedScope" />
                </authorization>
            </personalization>
        </webParts>
    </system.web>
</configuration>
```

After the `Web.config` file is in place, the next step is to add a bit of code to your `Page_Load` event, as shown in Listing 17-7.

Listing 17-7: Adding some code to allow the Behavior section to appear

VB

```
If Webpartmanager1.Personalization.Scope = PersonalizationScope.User _
    AndAlso Webpartmanager1.Personalization.CanEnterSharedScope Then

        Webpartmanager1.Personalization.ToggleScope()
End If
```

C#

```
if (Webpartmanager1.Personalization.Scope == PersonalizationScope.User
    && Webpartmanager1.Personalization.CanEnterSharedScope)
{
        Webpartmanager1.Personalization.ToggleScope();
}
```

The Layout section (shown in Figure 17-15) enables the end user to change the order in which Web Parts appear in a zone or move Web Parts from one zone to another. This is quite similar to the drag-and-drop capabilities illustrated previously, but this section allows for the same capabilities through the manipulation of simple form elements.

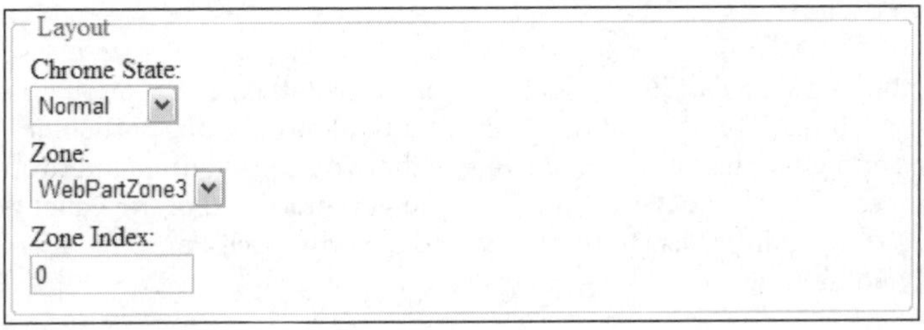

Figure 17-15

The PropertyGridEditorPart, though not demonstrated yet, allows end users to modify properties that are defined in your own custom server controls. At the end of this chapter, we will take a look at building a custom Web Part and using the PropertyGridEditorPart to allow end users to modify one of the publicly exposed properties contained in the control.

After you are satisfied with the appearance and layout of the Web Parts and have made the necessary changes to the control's properties in one of the editor parts, simply click OK or Apply.

Connecting Web Parts

One option you do have is to make a connection between two Web Parts using the `<asp:ConnectionsZone>` control. This control enables you to make property connections between two Web Parts on the same page. For example, within the Weather Web Part built into one of ASP.NET's pre-built applications, you can have a separate Web Part that is simply a text box and a button that allows the end user to input a zip code. This, in turn, modifies the contents in the original Weather Web Part.

Modifying Zones

One aspect of the Portal Framework that merits special attention is the capability to modify zones on the page. These zones allow for a high degree of modification — not only in the look-and-feel of the items placed in the zone, but also in terms of the behaviors of zones and the items contained in the zones as well. Following are some examples of what you can do to modify zones.

Turning Off the Capability for Modifications in a Zone

As you have seen, giving end users the capability to move Web Parts around the page is quite easy, whether within a zone or among entirely different zones. When working with the Portal Framework and multiple zones on a page, you do not always want to allow the end user to freely change the items that appear in every zone. You want the items placed in some zones to be left alone. Listing 17-8 shows an example of this.

Listing 17-8: Turning off the zone modification capability

```
<asp:WebPartZone ID="WebPartZone1" runat="server"
 LayoutOrientation="Horizontal" AllowLayoutChange="false">
    <ZoneTemplate>
        <asp:Label ID="Label1" runat="server" Text="Label"
         Title="Welcome to my web page!">
         Welcome to the page!
        </asp:Label>
    </ZoneTemplate>
</asp:WebPartZone>
```

In this example, the first Web Part Zone, WebPartZone1, uses the AllowLayoutChange attribute with a value of False, which turns off the end user's capability to modify this particular Web Part Zone. When you run this page and go to the design mode, notice that you cannot drag and drop any of the Web Parts from the other zones into WebPartZone1. Neither can you grab hold of the Label Web Part contained in WebPartZone1. No capability exists to minimize and close the Web Parts contained in this zone. It allows absolutely no modifications to the zone's layout.

You may notice another interesting change when you are working in the page catalog mode with the AllowLayoutChange attribute set to False. After you select items to add to the page through the page catalog, WebPartZone1 does not appear in the drop-down list of places where you can publish the Web Parts (see Figure 17-16). From this figure, you can see that only WebPartZone2 and WebPartZone3 appear and allow modifications.

Adding Controls through Other Means

Earlier in this chapter, you examined how to use the <asp:PageCatalogPart> control to restore controls to a page after they had been deleted. Although the <asp:PageCatalogPart> is ideal for this, you might also want to allow the end user to add Web Parts that are not on the page by default. You may want to enable the end user to add more than one of any particular Web Part to a page. For these situations, you work with the <asp:DeclarativeCatalogPart> control.

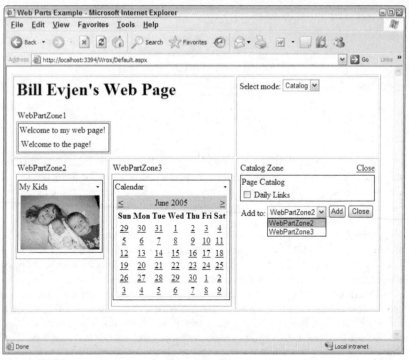

Figure 17-16

Listing 17-9 shows an example of using this type of catalog system in place of the `<asp:PageCatalogPart>` control.

Listing 17-9: Using the DeclarativeCatalogPart control

```
<asp:CatalogZone ID="Catalogzone1" Runat="server">
   <ZoneTemplate>
      <asp:DeclarativeCatalogPart ID="Declarativecatalogpart1" Runat="server">
        <WebPartsTemplate>
           <uc1:CompanyContactInfo ID="CompanyContact" Runat="Server"
            Title="Company Contact Info" />
           <uc1:PhotoAlbum ID="PhotoAlbum" Runat="Server" Title="Photo Album" />
           <uc1:Customers ID="Customers" Runat="Server" Title="Customers" />
           <uc1:Locations ID="Locations" Runat="Server" Title="Locations" />
        </WebPartsTemplate>
      </asp:DeclarativeCatalogPart>
   </ZoneTemplate>
</asp:CatalogZone>
```

Instead of using the `<asp:PageCatalogPart>` control, this catalog uses the `<asp:DeclarativeCatalogPart>` control. This templated control needs a `<WebPartsTemplate>` section where you can place all the controls you want available as options for the end user. The controls appear in the check box list in the same order in which you declare them in the `<WebPartsTemplate>` section. Figure 17-17 shows how the catalog looks in the Design view in Visual Studio 2005.

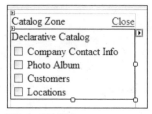

Figure 17-17

This catalog lets you select items from the list of Web Parts and assign the location of the zone in which they will be placed. After they are placed, notice that the option to add these Web Parts has not disappeared as it did with the earlier PageCatalogPart control. In fact, you can add as many of these items to the page as you deem necessary—even if it is to the same zone within the Portal Framework.

Using the DeclarativeCatalogPart control is not always a completely ideal solution. When the end user closes one of the Web Parts that initially appears on the page, he may not see that control listed in the DeclarativeCatalogPart control's list of elements. You must explicitly specify it should appear when you write the code for the DeclarativeCatalogPart control. In fact, the end user cannot re-add these deleted items. Using both the PageCatalogPart control and the DeclarativeCatalogPart control simultaneously is sometimes the best solution. The great thing about this framework is that it allows you to do that. The Portal Framework melds both controls into a cohesive control that not only enables you to add controls that are not on the page by default, but it also lets you add previously deleted default controls. Listing 17-10 shows an example of this.

Listing 17-10: Combining both catalog types

```
<asp:CatalogZone ID="Catalogzone1" Runat="server">
    <ZoneTemplate>
        <asp:PageCatalogPart ID="Pagecatalogpart1" Runat="server" />
        <asp:DeclarativeCatalogPart ID="Declarativecatalogpart1" Runat="server">
            <WebPartsTemplate>
                <uc1:CompanyContactInfo ID="CompanyContact" Runat="Server"
                 Title="Company Contact Info" />
                <uc1:PhotoAlbum ID="PhotoAlbum" Runat="Server" Title="Photo Album" />
                <uc1:Customers ID="Customers" Runat="Server" Title="Customers" />
                <uc1:Locations ID="Locations" Runat="Server" Title="Locations" />
            </WebPartsTemplate>
        </asp:DeclarativeCatalogPart>
    </ZoneTemplate>
</asp:CatalogZone>
```

In this example, both the PageCatalogPart control and the DeclarativeCatalogPart control are contained within the <ZoneTemplate> section. When this page is run, you see the results shown in Figure 17-18.

You can see that each catalog is defined within the Catalog Zone. Figure 17-18 shows the PageCatalogPart control's collection of Web Parts (defined as Page Catalog). Also note that a link to the Declarative Catalog is provided for that particular list of items. Note that the order in which the catalogs appear in the <ZoneTemplate> section is the order in which the links appear in the Catalog Zone.

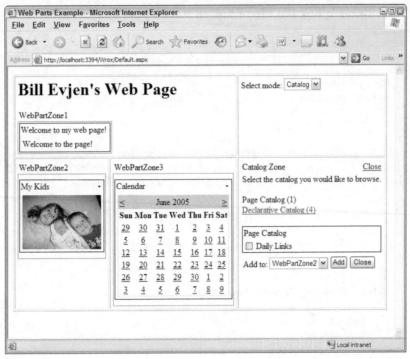

Figure 17-18

Web Part Verbs

Web Part verbs declare the actions of the items (such as Minimize and Close) that appear in the title. These verbs are basically links that initiate an action for a particular Web Part. The available list of Web Part verbs includes the following:

- ❑ <CloseVerb>
- ❑ <ConnectVerb>
- ❑ <EditVerb>
- ❑ <ExportVerb>
- ❑ <HelpVerb>
- ❑ <MinimizeVerb>
- ❑ <RestoreVerb>

The <asp:WebPartZone> control allows you to control these verbs by nesting the appropriate verb elements within the <asp:WebPartZone> element itself. After these are in place, you can manipulate how these items appear in all the Web Parts that appear in the chosen Web Part Zone.

For example, look at graying out the default Close link included with a Web Part. This is illustrated in Listing 17-11.

Listing 17-11: Graying out the Close link in a Web Part

```
<asp:WebPartZone ID="WebPartZone3" Runat="server">
    <CloseVerb Enabled="False" />
    <ZoneTemplate>
        <asp:Calendar ID="Calendar1" Runat="server">
        </asp:Calendar>
    </ZoneTemplate>
</asp:WebPartZone>
```

In this example, you can see that you simply need to set the `Enabled` attribute of the `<CloseVerb>` element to `False` in order to gray out the Close link in any of the generated Web Parts included in this Web Part Zone. If you construct the Web Part Zone in this manner, you achieve the results shown in Figure 17-19.

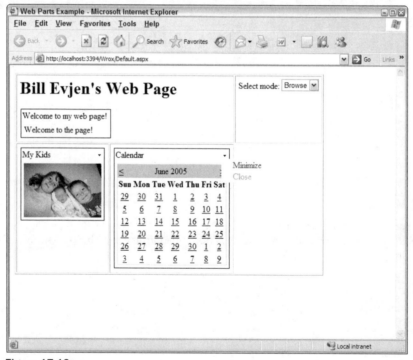

Figure 17-19

If you don't want to gray out the Close link (or any other verb link contained within the Web Part), you must instead use the `Visible` attribute of the appropriate verb (see Listing 17-12).

Listing 17-12: Removing the Close link in a Web Part

```
<asp:WebPartZone ID="WebPartZone3" Runat="server">
    <CloseVerb Visible="False" />
    <ZoneTemplate>
```

```
        <asp:Calendar ID="Calendar1" Runat="server">
        </asp:Calendar>
    </ZoneTemplate>
</asp:WebPartZone>
```

Using the `Visible` attribute produces the screen shown in Figure 17-20.

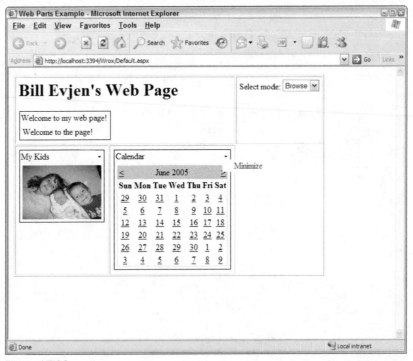

Figure 17-20

Verb elements provide another exciting feature: They give you the capability to use images that would appear next to the text of an item. Using images with the text makes the Web Parts appear more like the overall Windows environment. For instance, you can change the contents of `WebPartZone3` again so that it now uses images with the text for the Close and Minimize links. This is illustrated in Listing 17-13.

Listing 17-13: Using images for the Web Part verbs

```
<asp:WebPartZone ID="WebPartZone3" Runat="server">
    <CloseVerb ImageUrl="Images/CloseVerb.gif" />
    <MinimizeVerb ImageUrl="Images/MinimizeVerb.gif" />
    <ZoneTemplate>
        <asp:Calendar ID="Calendar1" Runat="server">
        </asp:Calendar>
    </ZoneTemplate>
</asp:WebPartZone>
```

To point to an image for the verb, use the `ImageUrl` attribute. This produces something similar to Figure 17-21, depending on the images you use.

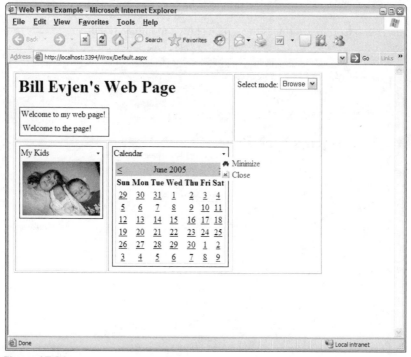

Figure 17-21

This chapter, thus far, has concentrated on creating completely customizable portal applications in a declarative manner using the capabilities provided by the ASP.NET Portal Framework. As with most aspects of ASP.NET, however, not only can you work with appearance and functionality in a declarative fashion, but you can also create the same constructs through server-side code.

Working with Classes in the Portal Framework

The Portal Framework provides three main classes for dealing with the underlying framework presented in this chapter: `WebPartManager`, `WebPartZone`, and `WebPart`.

The `WebPartManager` class allows you to perform multiple operations in your server-side code. The following table shows a partial listing of some of the properties that this class provides.

WebPartManager Class Properties	Description
Connections	Provides a collection of all the connections between Web Parts contained on the page.
DisplayMode	Allows you to change the page's display mode. Possible choices include CatalogDisplayMode, ConnectDisplayMode, DesignDisplayMode, EditDisplayMode, and BrowseDisplayMode.
SelectedWebPart	Allows you to perform multiple operations on the selected Web Part.
WebParts	Provides a collection of all the Web Parts contained on the page.
Zones	Provides a collection of all the Web Part Zones contained on the page.

Beyond the properties of the WebPartManager class, you also have an extensive list of available methods at your disposal. The following table outlines some of the available methods of the WebPartManager class.

WebPartManager Class Methods	Description
AddWebPart	Allows you to dynamically add new Web Parts to a particular zone on the page.
ConnectWebParts	Allows you to connect two Web Parts together via a common property or value.
DeleteWebPart	Allows you to dynamically delete new Web Parts from a particular zone on the page.
DisconnectWebParts	Allows you to delete a connection between two Web Parts.
MoveWebPart	Allows you to move a Web Part from one zone to another, or allows you to change the index order in which Web Parts appear in a particular zone.

Whereas the WebPartManager class allows you to manipulate the location, addition, and deletion of Web Parts that appear in the page as a whole, the WebPartZone class allows you to modify a single Web Part Zone on the page. The following table provides a list of some properties available to the WebPartZone class.

WebPartZone Class Properties	Description
AllowLayoutChange	Takes a `Boolean` value and either enables or disables the Web Part Zone's capability to accept or allow any changes in the Web Parts it contains.
BackColor, BackImageUrl, BorderColor, BorderStyle, BorderWidth	Enable you to modify the Web Part Zone's general appearance.
CloseVerb	References the Close verb for a particular Web Part Zone from which you can then manipulate the verb's `Description`, `Enabled`, `ImageUrl`, `Text`, and `Visible` properties.
ConnectVerb	References a Web Part Zone's Connect verb from which you can then manipulate the verb's `Description`, `Enabled`, `ImageUrl`, `Text`, and `Visible` properties.
DragHighlightColor	Takes a `System.Color` value that sets the color of the Web Part Zone's border if focused when the moving of Web Parts is in operation. This also changes the color of the line that appears in the Web Part Zone specifying where to drop the Web Part.
EditVerb	References a Web Part Zone's Edit verb from which you can then manipulate the verb's `Description`, `Enabled`, `ImageUrl`, `Text`, and `Visible` properties.
EmptyZoneText	Sets the text that is shown in the zone if a Web Part is not set in the zone.
HeaderText	Sets header text.
Height	Sets the height of the Web Part Zone.
HelpVerb	References a Web Part Zone's Help verb from which you can then manipulate the verb's `Description`, `Enabled`, `ImageUrl`, `Text`, and `Visible` properties.
MenuLabelStyle, MenuLabelText	Enable you to modify the drop-down menu that appears when end users edit a Web Part. These properties let you apply an image, alter the text, or change the style of the menu.
MinimizeVerb	References a Web Part Zone's Minimize verb from which you can then manipulate the verb's `Description`, `Enabled`, `ImageUrl`, `Text`, and `Visible` properties.
LayoutOrientation	Enables you to change the Web Part Zone's orientation from horizontal to vertical or vice versa.

WebPartZone Class Properties	Description
RestoreVerb	References a Web Part Zone's Restore verb, from which you can then manipulate the verb's Description, Enabled, ImageUrl, Text, and Visible properties.
VerbButtonType	Enables you to change the button style. Choices include ButtonType.Button, ButtonType.Image, or ButtonType.Link.
WebParts	Provides a collection of all the Web Parts contained within the zone.
Width	Sets the width of the Web Part Zone.

You have a plethora of options to manipulate the look-and-feel of the Web Part Zone and the items contained therein.

The final class is the WebPart class. This class enables you to manipulate specific Web Parts located on the page. The following table details some of the properties available in the WebPart class.

WebPart Class Properties	Description
AllowClose	Takes a Boolean value that specifies whether the Web Part can be closed and removed from the page.
AllowEdit	Takes a Boolean value that specifies whether the end user can edit the Web Part.
AllowHide	Takes a Boolean value that specifies whether the end user can hide the Web Part within the Web Part Zone. If the control is hidden, it is still in the zone, but invisible.
AllowMinimize	Takes a Boolean value that specifies whether the end user can collapse the Web Part.
AllowZoneChange	Takes a Boolean value that specifies whether the end user can move the Web Part from one zone to another.
BackColor, BackImageUrl, BorderColor, BorderStyle, BorderWidth	Enable you to modify the Web Part's general appearance.

Table continued on following page

WebPart Class Properties	Description
ChromeState	Specifies whether the Web Part chrome is in a normal state or is minimized.
ChromeType	Specifies the chrome type that the Web Part uses. Available options include BorderOnly, Default, None, TitleAndBorder, and TitleOnly.
Direction	Specifies the direction of the text or items placed within the Web Part. Available options include LeftToRight, NotSet, and RightToLeft. This property is ideal for dealing with Web Parts that contain Asian text that is read from right to left.
HelpMode	Specifies how the help items display when the end user clicks the Help verb. Available options include Modal, Modeless, and Navigate. Modal displays the help items within a modal window if the end user's browser supports modal windows. If not, a pop-up window displays. Modeless means that a pop-up window displays for every user. Navigate redirects the user to the appropriate help page (specified by the HelpUrl property) when he clicks on the Help verb.
HelpUrl	Used when the HelpMode is set to Navigate. Takes a String value that specifies the location of the page the end user is redirected to when he clicks on the Help verb.
ScrollBars	Applies scroll bars to the Web Part. Available values include Auto, Both, Horizontal, None, and Vertical.
Title	Specifies the text for the Web Part's title. Text appears in the title bar section.
TitleIconImageUrl	Enables you to apply an icon to appear next to the title by specifying to the icon image's location as a String value of the property.
TitleUrl	Specifies the location to direct the end user when the Web Part's title Web Part is clicked. When set, the title is converted to a link; when not set, the title appears as regular text.
Zone	Allows you to refer to the zone in which the Web Part is located.

Creating Custom Web Parts

When adding items to a page that utilizes the Portal Framework, you add the pre-existing ASP.NET Web server controls, user controls, or custom controls. In addition to these items, you can also build and incorporate custom Web Parts. Using the WebParts class, you can create your own custom Web Parts. Although similar to ASP.NET custom server control development, the creation of custom Web Parts adds some additional capabilities. Creating a class that inherits from the WebPart class instead of the Control class enables your control to use the new personalization features and to work with the larger Portal Framework, thereby allowing for the control to be closed, maximized, minimized, and more.

To create a custom Web Part control, the first step is to create a project in Visual Studio 2005. From Visual Studio, choose File ⇨ New Project. This pops open the New Project dialog. From this dialog, select Web Control Library. Name the project MyStateListBox and click OK to create the project. You are presented with a class that contains the basic framework for a typical ASP.NET server control. Ignore this framework; you are going to change it so that your class creates a custom Web Parts control instead of a ASP.NET custom server control. Listing 17-14 details the creation of a custom Web Part control.

Listing 17-14: Creating a custom Web Part control

VB

```vb
Imports System
Imports System.Web
Imports System.Web.UI.WebControls
Imports System.Web.UI.WebControls.WebParts


Namespace Wrox

    Public Class StateListBox
        Inherits WebPart

        Private _LabelStartText As String = " Enter State Name: "
        Dim StateInput As New TextBox
        Dim StateContents As New ListBox

        Public Sub New()
            Me.AllowClose = False
        End Sub

        <Personalizable(), WebBrowsable()> _
        Public Property LabelStartText() As String
            Get
                Return _LabelStartText
            End Get
            Set(ByVal value As String)
                _LabelStartText = value
            End Set
        End Property

        Protected Overrides Sub CreateChildControls()
            Controls.Clear()

            Dim InstructionText As New Label
```

(continued)

Listing 17-14: *(continued)*

```vb
            InstructionText.BackColor = Drawing.Color.LightGray
            InstructionText.Font.Name = "Verdana"
            InstructionText.Font.Size = 10
            InstructionText.Font.Bold = True
            InstructionText.Text = LabelStartText
            Me.Controls.Add(InstructionText)

            Dim LineBreak As New Literal
            LineBreak.Text = "<br />"
            Me.Controls.Add(LineBreak)

            Me.Controls.Add(StateInput)

            Dim InputButton As New Button
            InputButton.Text = "Input State"
            AddHandler InputButton.Click, AddressOf Me.Button1_Click
            Me.Controls.Add(InputButton)

            Dim Spacer As New Literal
            Spacer.Text = "<p>"
            Me.Controls.Add(Spacer)

            Me.Controls.Add(StateContents)

            ChildControlsCreated = True
        End Sub

        Public Sub Button1_Click(ByVal sender As Object, ByVal e As EventArgs)
            StateContents.Items.Add(StateInput.Text)
            StateInput.Text = String.Empty
            StateInput.Focus()
        End Sub

    End Class

End Namespace
```

C#

```csharp
using System;
using System.Web;
using System.Web.UI.WebControls;
using System.Web.UI.WebControls.WebParts;

namespace Wrox
{
    public class StateListBox : WebPart
    {
        private String _LabelStartText = " Enter State Name: ";
        TextBox StateInput = new TextBox();
        ListBox StateContents = new ListBox();

        public StateListBox()
        {
```

```
            this.AllowClose = false;
        }

        [Personalizable, WebBrowsable]
        public String LabelStartText
        {
            get { return _LabelStartText; }
            set { _LabelStartText = value; }
        }

        protected override void CreateChildControls()
        {
            Controls.Clear();

            Label InstructionText = new Label();
            InstructionText.BackColor = System.Drawing.Color.LightGray;
            InstructionText.Font.Name = "Verdana";
            InstructionText.Font.Size = 10;
            InstructionText.Font.Bold = true;
            InstructionText.Text = LabelStartText;
            this.Controls.Add(InstructionText);

            Literal LineBreak = new Literal();
            LineBreak.Text = "<br />";
            this.Controls.Add(LineBreak);

            this.Controls.Add(StateInput);

            Button InputButton = new Button();
            InputButton.Text = "Input State";
            InputButton.Click += new EventHandler(this.Button1_Click);
            this.Controls.Add(InputButton);

            Literal Spacer = new Literal();
            Spacer.Text = "<p>";
            this.Controls.Add(Spacer);

            this.Controls.Add(StateContents);

            ChildControlsCreated = true;
        }

        private void Button1_Click(object sender, EventArgs e)
        {
            StateContents.Items.Add(StateInput.Text);
            StateInput.Text = String.Empty;
            StateInput.Focus();
        }
    }
}
```

In review, you first import the `System.Web.UI.WebControls.WebParts` namespace. The important step in the creation of this custom control is to make sure that it inherits from the `WebPart` class instead of the customary `Control` class. As stated earlier, this gives the control access to the advanced functionality of the Portal Framework that a typical custom control wouldn't have.

VB
```
Public Class StateListBox
    Inherits WebPart

End Class
```

C#
```
public class StateListBox : WebPart
{

}
```

After the class structure is in place, a few properties are defined, and the constructor is defined as well. The constructor directly uses some of the capabilities that the `WebPart` class provides. These capabilities wouldn't be available if this custom control has the `Control` class as its base class and is making use of the `WebPart.AllowClose` property.

VB
```
Public Sub New()
    Me.AllowClose = False
End Sub
```

C#
```
public StateListBox()
{
    this.AllowClose = false;
}
```

This constructor creates a control that explicitly sets the control's `AllowClose` property to `False` — meaning that the Web Part will not have a Close link associated with it when generated in the page. Because of the use of the `WebPart` class instead of the `Control` class, you will find, in addition to the `AllowClose` property, other `WebPart` class properties such as `AllowEdit`, `AllowHide`, `AllowMinimize`, `AllowZoneChange`, and more.

In the example shown in Listing 17-14, you see a custom-defined property: `LabelStartText`. This property allows the developer to change the instruction text displayed at the top of the control. The big difference with this custom property is that it is preceded by the `Personalizable` and the `WebBrowsable` attributes.

The `Personalizable` attribute enables the property for personalization, whereas the `WebBrowsable` attribute specifies whether the property should be displayed in the Properties window in Visual Studio. The `Personalizable` attribute can be defined further using a `PersonalizationScope` enumeration. The only two possible enumerations — `Shared` and `User` — can be defined in the following ways:

VB
```
<Personalizable(PersonalizationScope.Shared), WebBrowsable()> _
Public Property LabelStartText() As String
    Get
        Return _LabelStartText
    End Get
    Set(ByVal value As String)
        _LabelStartText = value
    End Set
End Property
```

C#
```
[Personalizable(PersonalizationScope.Shared), WebBrowsable]
public String LabelStartText
{
    get { return _LabelStartText; }
    set { _LabelStartText = value; }
}
```

A `PersonalizationScope` of `User` means that any modifications are done on a per-user basis. This is the default setting and means that if a user makes modifications to the property, the changes are seen only by that particular user and not by the other users that browse the page. If the `PersonalizationScope` is set to `Shared`, changes made by one user can be viewed by others requesting the page.

After you have any properties in place, the next step is to define what gets rendered to the page by overriding the `CreateChildControls` method. From the example in Listing 17-14, the `CreateChildControls` method renders Label, Literal, TextBox, Button, and ListBox controls. In addition to defining the properties of some of these controls, a single event is associated with the Button control (`Button1_Click`) that is also defined in this class.

Now that the custom Web Part control is in place, build the project so that a DLL is created. The next step is to open up the ASP.NET Web project where you want to utilize this new control and, from the Visual Studio Toolbox, add the new control. You can quickly accomplish this task by right-clicking in the Toolbox on the tab where you want the new control to be placed. After right-clicking the appropriate tab, select Choose Items. Click the Browse button and point to the new `MyStateListBox.dll` that you just created. After this is done, the StateListBox control is highlighted and checked in the Choose Toolbox Items dialog, as illustrated in Figure 17-22.

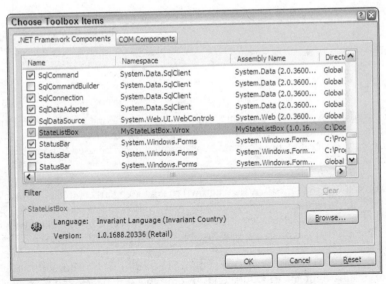

Figure 17-22

Clicking OK adds the control to your toolbox. Now you are ready to use this new control as a Web Part control. To do this, simply drag and drop the control into one of your Web Part Zone areas. This does a couple of things. First, it registers the control on the page using the Register directive:

```
<%@ Register TagPrefix="cc1" Namespace="MyStateListBox.Wrox"
    Assembly="MyStateListBox" %>
```

Once registered, the control can be used on the page. If dragged and dropped onto the page's design surface, you get a control in the following construct:

```
<cc1:StateListBox Runat="server" ID="StateListBox1"
 LabelStartText=" Enter State Name: " AllowClose="False" />
```

The two important things to notice with this construct is that the custom property, `LabelStartText`, is present and has the default value in place, and the `AllowClose` attribute is included. The `AllowClose` attribute is present only because earlier you made the control's inherited class `WebPart` and not `Control`. Because `WebPart` was made the inherited class, you have access to these Web-Part–specific properties. When the StateListBox control is drawn on the page, you can see that, indeed, it is part of the larger Portal Framework and allows for things such as minimization and editing. End users can use this custom Web Part control as if it were any other type of Web Part control. As you can see, you have a lot of power when you create your own Web Part controls.

And because `LabelStartText` uses the `WebBrowsable` attribute, you can use the PropertyGridEditorPart control to allow end users to edit this directly in the browser. With this in place, as was demonstrated earlier in Listing 17-5, an end user will see the following editing capabilities after switching to the Edit mode (see Figure 17-23).

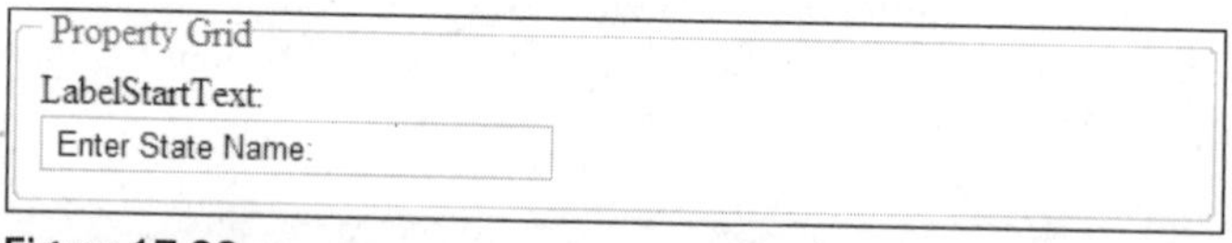

Figure 17-23

Summary

This chapter introduced you to the Web Part Manager, Web Part Zone, and the Web Part controls. Not only do these controls allow for easy customization of the look-and-feel of either the Web Parts or the zones in which they are located, but the framework provided can be used to completely modify the behavior of these items.

This chapter also showed you how to create your own custom Web Part controls. Creating your own controls was always one of the benefits provided by ASP.NET, and this benefit has been taken one step further with the capability to now create Web Part controls. Web Part controls enable you to take advantage of some of the more complex features that you don't get with custom ASP.NET server controls.

You may find the Portal Framework to be one of the more exciting new features of ASP.NET 2.0; you may like the idea of creating completely modular and customizable Web pages. End users like this feature, and it is quite easy for developers to implement. Just remember that you don't have to implement every feature explained in this chapter; with the framework provided, however, you can choose the functionality that you want.

18

Security

Not every page that you build with ASP.NET is meant to be open and accessible to everyone on the Internet. Sometimes, you want to build pages or sections of an application that are accessible to only a select group of your choosing. For this reason, you need the security measures explained in this chapter. They can help protect the data behind your applications and the applications themselves from fraudulent use.

Security is a very wide-reaching term. During every step of the application-building process, you must, without a doubt, be aware of how mischievous end users might attempt to bypass your lockout measures. You must take steps to ensure that no one can take over the application or gain access to its resources. Whether it involves working with basic server controls or accessing databases, you should be thinking through the level of security you want to employ to protect yourself.

How security is applied to your applications is truly a measured process. For instance, a single ASP.NET page on the Internet, open to public access, has different security requirements than does an ASP.NET application that is available to only selected individuals because it deals with confidential information such as credit card numbers or medical information.

The first step is to apply the appropriate level of security for the task at hand. Because you can take so many different actions to protect your applications and the resources, you have to decide for yourself which of these measures to employ. This chapter takes a look at some of the possibilities for protecting your applications.

Notice that security is discussed throughout this book. In addition, a couple chapters focus on new security frameworks provided by ASP.NET 2.0 that are not discussed in this chapter. Chapters 15 and 16 discuss ASP.NET's new membership and role management frameworks, as well as the new personalization features in this version. These topics are aspects of security that can make it even easier for you to build safe applications. Although these new security frameworks are provided with this latest release of ASP.NET, you can still build you own measures as you did in the previous versions of ASP.NET. This chapter discusses how to do so.

An important aspect of security is how you handle the authentication and authorization for accessing resources in your applications. Before you begin working through some of the authentication/authorization possibilities in ASP.NET, you should know exactly what we mean by those two terms.

Authentication and Authorization

As discussed in Chapter 16, *authentication* is the process that determines the identity of a user. After a user has been authenticated, a developer can determine if the identified user has authorization to proceed. It is impossible to give an entity authorization if no authentication process has been applied.

Authorization is the process of determining whether an authenticated user is permitted access to any part of an application, access to specific points of an application, or access only to specified datasets that the application provides. Authenticating and authorizing users and groups enable you to customize a site based on user types or preferences.

Applying Authentication Measures

ASP.NET provides many different types of authentication measures to use within your applications, including basic authentication, digest authentication, forms authentication, Passport, and Integrated Windows authentication. You also can develop your own authentication methods. You should never authorize access to resources you mean to be secure if you haven't applied an authentication process to the requests for the resources.

The different authentication modes are established through settings that can be applied to the application's web.config file or in conjunction with the application server's Internet Information Services (IIS) instance.

ASP.NET is configured through a series of .config files on the application server. These are XML-based files that enable you to easily change how ASP.NET behaves. This is an ideal way to work with the configuration settings you require. ASP.NET configuration files are applied in a hierarchal manner. The .NET Framework provides a server-level configuration file called the machine.config file, which can be found at C:\Windows\Microsoft.NET\Framework\v2.0xxxxx\CONFIG. The folder contains machine.config and machine.config.comments files. These files provide ASP.NET application settings at a server-level, meaning that the settings are applied to each and every ASP.NET application that resides on the particular server.

A web.config file is another XML-based configuration file that resides in the root of the Web application. The settings applied in the web.config file override the same settings applied in the higher-level machine.config file.

You can even nest the web.config files so that the main application web.config file is located in the root directory of your application, but additional web.config files reside in some of the application's subdirectories (see Figure 18-1). The web.config files contained in any of the subdirectories supersede the root directory's web.config file. Therefore, any settings applied through a subdirectory's web.config file change whatever was set in the application's main web.config file.

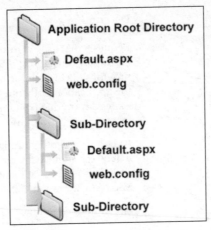

Figure 18-1

In a lot of the examples in this chapter, you use the web.config file to apply the authentication and authorization mechanics you want in your applications. You also can work with IIS to apply settings directly to your applications.

IIS is the Web server that handles all the incoming HTTP requests that come to into the server. You must modify IIS to perform as you want. IIS hands a request to the ASP.NET engine only if the page has a specific file extension (for example, .aspx). You learn how to work with IIS 5.0 and 6.0 later in this chapter.

The <authentication> Node

You use the <authentication> node in the application's web.config file to set the type of authentication your ASP.NET application requires:

```
<system.web>
    <authentication mode="Windows|Forms|Passport|None">

    </authentication>
</system.web>
```

The <authentication> node uses the mode attribute to set the form of authentication that is to be used. Options include Windows, Forms, Passport, and None. Each option is explained in the following table.

Provider	Description
Windows	Windows authentication is used together with IIS authentication. Authentication is performed by IIS in the following ways: basic, digest, or Integrated Windows Authentication. When IIS authentication is complete, ASP.NET uses the authenticated identity to authorize access. This is the default setting.

Table continued on following page

Provider	Description
Forms	Requests that are not authenticated are redirected to an HTML form using HTTP client-side redirection. The user provides his login information and submits the form. If the application authenticates the request, the system issues a form that contains the credentials or a key for reacquiring the identity.
Passport	A centralized authentication service provided by Microsoft that offers single login and core profile services for member sites. This mode of authentication was de-emphasized by Microsoft at the end of 2004.
None	No authentication mode is in place with this setting.

As you can see, a couple of methods are at your disposal for building an authentication/authorization model for your ASP.NET applications. We start by examining the Windows mode of authentication.

Windows-Based Authentication

Windows-based authentication is handled between the Windows server where the ASP.NET application resides and the client machine. In a Windows-based authentication model, the requests go directly to IIS to provide the authentication process. This type of authentication is quite useful in an intranet environment where you can let the server deal completely with the authentication process — especially in environments where users are already logged onto a network. In this scenario, you simply grab and utilize the credentials that are already in place for the authorization process.

IIS first takes the user's credentials from the domain login. If this process fails, IIS displays a pop-up a dialog box so the user can enter or re-enter his login information. To set up your ASP.NET application to work with Windows-based authentication, begin by creating some users and groups.

Creating Users

You use aspects of Windows-based authentication to allow specific users who have provided a domain login to access your application or parts of your application. Because it can use this type of authentication, ASP.NET makes it quite easy to work with applications that are deployed in an intranet environment. If a user has logged onto a local computer as a domain user, he won't need to be authenticated again when accessing a network computer in that domain.

The following steps show you how to create a user. It is important to note that you must have sufficient rights to be authorized to create users on a server. If you are authorized, the steps to create users are as follows:

1. Within your Windows XP or Windows Server 2003 server, choose Start ⇨ Control Panel ⇨ Administrative Tools ⇨ Computer Management. The Computer Management utility opens. It manages and controls resources on the local Web server. You can accomplish many things using this utility, but the focus here is on the creation of users.

2. Expand the System Tools node.

3. Expand the Local Users and Groups node.

4. Select the Users folder. You see something similar to the results shown in Figure 18-2.

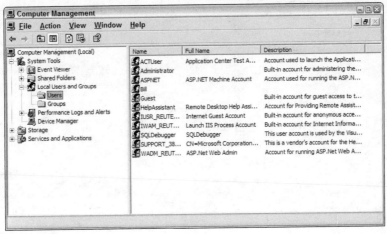

Figure 18-2

5. Right-click the Users folder and select New User. The New User dialog appears, as shown in Figure 18-3.

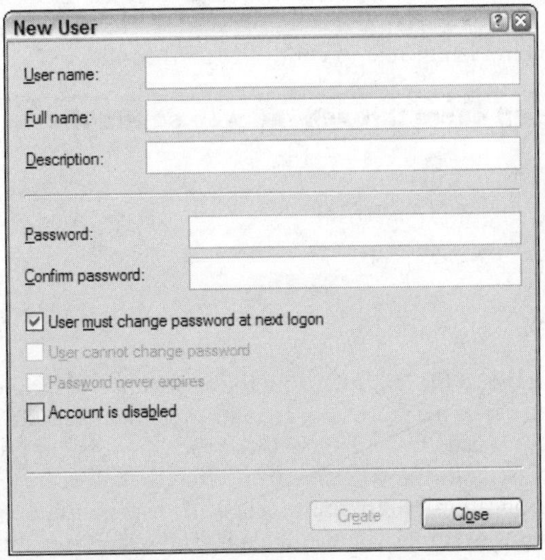

Figure 18-3

6. Give the user a name, password, and description stating that this is a test user. This example calls the user **Bubbles**.

7. Uncheck the check box that requires the user to change his password at the next login.

8. Click the Create button. Your test user is created and presented in the Users folder of the Computer Management utility, as shown in Figure 18-4.

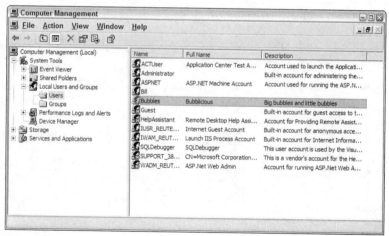

Figure 18-4

Now create a page to work with this user.

Authenticating and Authorizing a User

Now create an application that enables the user to enter it. You work with the application's web.config file to control which users are allowed to access the site and which users are not allowed.

Add the section presented in Listing 18-1 to your web.config file.

Listing 18-1: Denying all users through the web.config file

```
<system.web>
    <authentication mode="Windows" />
    <authorization>
        <deny users="*" />
    </authorization>
</system.web>
```

In this example, the web.config file is configuring the application to employ Windows-based authentication through the use of the <authentication> element's mode attribute. In addition, the <authorization> element is used to define specifics about the users or groups who are permitted access to the application. In this case, the <deny> element specifies that all users (even if they are authenticated) are denied access to the application. Not permitting specific users with the <allow> element doesn't make much sense, but for this example, leave it like it is. The results are illustrated in Figure 18-5.

Any end user—authenticated or not—who tries to access the site sees a large "Access is denied" statement in his browser window, which is just what you want for those not allowed to access your application!

In most instances, however, you want to allow at least some users to access your application. Use the <allow> element in the web.config file to allow a specific user. Here's the syntax:

```
<allow users="Domain\Username" />
```

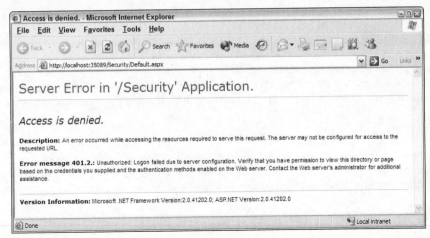

Figure 18-5

Listing 18-2 shows how the user is permitted access.

Listing 18-2: Allowing a single user through the web.config file

```
<system.web>
    <authentication mode="Windows" />
    <authorization>
        <allow users="REUTERS-EVJEN\Bubbles" />
        <deny users="*" />
    </authorization>
</system.web>
```

Even though all users (even authenticated ones) are denied access through the use of the <deny> element, the definitions defined in the <allow> element take precedence. In this example, a single user — Bubbles — is allowed.

Now, if you are logged on to the client machine as the user Bubbles and run the page in the browser, you get access to the application.

Looking Closely at the <allow> and <deny> Nodes

The <allow> and <deny> nodes enable you to work not only with specific users, but also with groups. The elements support the attributes defined in the following table.

Attribute	Description
users	Enables you to specify users by their domain and/or name.
roles	Enables you to specify access groups that are allowed or denied access.
verbs	Enables you to specify the HTTP transmission method that is allowed or denied access.

When using any of these attributes, you can specify all users with the use of the asterisk (*):

```
<allow roles="*" />
```

In this example, all roles are allowed access to the application. Another symbol you can use with these attributes is the question mark (?), which represents all anonymous users. For example, if you want to block all anonymous users from your application, use the following construction:

```
<deny users="?" />
```

When using `users`, `roles`, or `verbs` attributes with the `<allow>` or `<deny>` elements, you can specify multiple entries by separating the values with a comma. If you are going to allow more than one user, you can either separate these users into different elements as shown here

```
<allow users="MyDomain\User1" />
<allow users="MyDomain\User2" />
```

or you can use the following:

```
<allow users="MyDomain\User1, MyDomain\User2" />
```

Use the same construction when defining multiple roles and verbs.

Authenticating and Authorizing a Group

You can define groups of individuals allowed or denied access to your application or the application's resources. Your server can contain a number of different groups, each of which can have any number of users belonging to it. It's also possible for a single user to belong to multiple groups. Pull up the Computer Management utility (Start ⇨ Control Panel ⇨ Administrative Tools ⇨ Computer Management) to access the list of the groups defined on the server you are working with. Simply click the Groups folder in the Computer Management utility, and the list of groups is displayed, as illustrated in Figure 18-6.

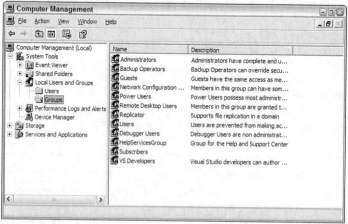

Figure 18-6

Right-click in the Groups folder to select New Group. The New Group dialog displays (see Figure 18-7).

Figure 18-7

To create a group, give it a name and description; then click the Add button and select the users whom you want to be a part of the group. After a group is created, you can allow it access to your application like this:

```
<allow roles="MyGroup" />
```

You can use the `roles` attribute in either the `<allow>` or `<deny>` element to work with a group that you have created or with a specific group that already exists.

Authenticating and Authorizing an HTTP Transmission Method

In addition to authenticating and authorizing specific users or groups of users, you can also authorize or deny requests that come via a specific HTTP transmission protocol. This is done using the `verb` attribute in the `<allow>` and `<deny>` elements.

```
<deny verbs="GET, DEBUG" />
```

In this example, requests that come in using the HTTP GET or HTTP DEBUG protocols are denied access to the site. Possible values for the `verbs` attribute include POST, GET, HEAD, and DEBUG.

Integrated Windows Authentication

So far, you've been using the default Integrated Windows authentication mode for the authentication/authorization process. This is fine if you are working with an intranet application and each of the clients is using Windows, the only system that the authentication method supports. This system of authentication also requires the client to be using Microsoft's Internet Explorer, which might not always be possible.

Integrated Windows authentication was previously known as NTLM or Windows NT Challenge/Response authentication. This authentication model has the client prove its identity by sending a hash of its credentials to the server that is hosting the ASP.NET application. Along with Microsoft's Active Directory, a client can also use Kerberos if it's using Microsoft's Internet Explorer 5 or higher.

Basic Authentication

Another option is to use Basic authentication, which also requires a username and password from the client for authentication. The big plus about Basic authentication is that it is part of the HTTP specification and therefore is supported by most browsers. The negative aspect of Basic authentication is that it passes the username and password to the server as clear text, meaning that the username and password are quite visible to prying eyes. For this reason, it is important to use Basic authentication along with SSL (*Secure Sockets Layer*).

To implement Basic authentication for your application, you must pull up IIS and open the Properties dialog for the Web site you are working with. Select the Directory Security tab and click the Edit button in the Anonymous Access and Authentication Control box. The Authentication Methods dialog box opens.

Uncheck the Integrated Windows Authentication check box at the bottom and check the Basic Authentication check box above it (see Figure 18-8). When you do, you are warned that this method transmits usernames and passwords as clear text.

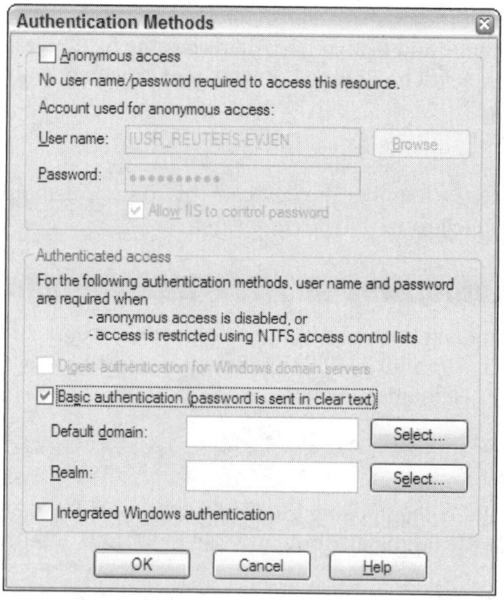

Figure 18-8

End by clicking OK in the dialog. Now your application uses Basic authentication instead of Integrated Windows authentication.

Digest Authentication

Digest authentication is the final mode you explore in this chapter. The model alleviates the Basic authentication problem of passing the client's credentials as clear text. Instead, Digest authentication uses an algorithm to encrypt the client's credentials before they are sent to the application server.

To use Digest authentication, you are required to have a Windows domain controller. One of the main issues that arises with Digest authentication is that it is not supported on all platforms and requires browsers that conform to the HTTP 1.1 specification. Digest authentication, however, not only works well with firewalls, but it is also compatible with proxy servers.

You can select Digest authentication as the choice for your application in the same Authentication Methods dialog—simply select the Digest Authentication check box.

Forms-Based Authentication

Forms-based authentication is a popular mode of authenticating users to access an entire application or specific resources within an application. Using it enables you to put the login form directly in the application so that the end user simply enters his username and password into an HTML form contained within the browser itself. One negative aspect of forms-based authentication is that the usernames and passwords are sent as clear text unless you are using SSL.

It's easy and relatively straightforward to implement forms-based authentication in your Web application. To begin with, you make some modifications to your application's web.config file, as illustrated in Listing 18-3.

Listing 18-3: Modifying the web.config file for forms-based authentication

```
<system.web>
    <authentication mode="Forms">
        <forms name="Wrox" loginUrl="Login.aspx" path="/" />
    </authentication>

    <authorization>
        <deny users="?" />
    </authorization>
</system.web>
```

This is the structure you must apply to the web.config file. First, using the <authorization> element described earlier, you are denying access to the application to all anonymous users. Only authenticated users are allowed to access any page contained within the application.

If the requestor is not authenticated, what is defined in the <authentication> element is put into action. The value of the mode attribute is set to Forms to employ forms-based authentication for your Web application. The next attribute specified is loginUrl, which points to the page that contains the application's login form. In this example, Login.aspx is specified as a value. If the end user trying to access the application is not authenticated, his request is redirected to Login.aspx so that the user can be authenticated and authorized to proceed. After valid credentials have been provided, the user is returned to the location in the application where he originally made the request. The final attribute used here is path. It simply specifies the location in which to save the cookie used to persist the authorized user's access token. In most cases, you want to leave the value as /. The following table describes each of the possible attributes for the <forms> element.

Attribute	Description
name	This is the name that is assigned to the cookie saved used to remember the user from request to request. The default value is .ASPXAUTH.
loginUrl	Specifies the URL to which the request is redirected for login if no valid authentication cookie is found. The default value is Login.aspx.
protection	Specifies the amount of protection you want to apply to the authentication cookie. The four available settings are: —All: The application uses both data validation and encryption to protect the cookie. This is the default setting. —None: Applies no encryption to the cookie. —Encryption: The cookie is encrypted but data validation isn't performed on it. Cookies used in this manner might be subject to plain text attacks. —Validation: The opposite of the Encryption setting. Data validation is performed, but the cookie is not encrypted.
path	Specifies the path for cookies issued by the application. In most cases you want to use /, which is the default setting.
timeout	Specifies the amount of time, in minutes, after which the cookie expires. The default value is 30.
cookieless	Specifies whether the forms-based authentication process should use cookies when working with the authentication/authorization process.
defaultUrl	Specifies the default URL.
domain	Specifies the domain name to be sent with forms authentication cookies.
slidingExpiration	Specifies whether to apply a sliding expiration to the cookie. If set to True, the expiration of the cookie is reset with each request made to the server. The default value is False.
enableCrossAppsRedirect	Specifies whether to allow for cross-application redirection.
requireSSL	Specifies whether a Secure Sockets Layer (SSL) connection is required when transmitting authentication information.

After the `web.config` file is in place, the next step is to create a typical page for your application that people can access. Listing 18-4 presents a simple page.

Listing 18-4: A simple page—Default.aspx

```
<%@ Page Language="VB" %>

<html xmlns="http://www.w3.org/1999/xhtml" >
<head runat="server">
    <title>The Application</title>
</head>
<body>
    <form id="form1" runat="server">
    <div>
       Hello World
    </div>
    </form>
</body>
</html>
```

As you can see, this page simply writes `Hello World` to the browser. The real power of forms authentication is shown in the `Login.aspx` page presented in Listing 18-5.

Listing 18-5: The Login.aspx page

VB
```
<%@ Page Language="VB" %>

<script runat="server">
    Protected Sub Button1_Click(ByVal sender As Object, _
    ByVal e As System.EventArgs)

        If (TextBox1.Text = "BillEvjen" And TextBox2.Text = "Bubbles") Then
            FormsAuthentication.RedirectFromLoginPage(TextBox1.Text, True)
        Else
            Response.Write("Invalid credentials")
        End If
    End Sub
</script>

<html xmlns="http://www.w3.org/1999/xhtml" >
<head runat="server">
    <title>Login Page</title>
</head>
<body>
    <form id="form1" runat="server">
    <div>
        Username<br />
        <asp:TextBox ID="TextBox1" runat="server"></asp:TextBox><br />
        <br />
        Password<br />
        <asp:TextBox ID="TextBox2" runat="server"
         TextMode="Password"></asp:TextBox><br />
        <br />
```

(continued)

Listing 18-5: *(continued)*

```
            <asp:Button ID="Button1" OnClick="Button1_Click" runat="server"
            Text="Submit" />
        </div>
        </form>
    </body>
    </html>
```

C#

```
<%@ Page Language="C#"%>

<script runat="server">
    protected void Button1_Click(object sender, EventArgs e)
    {
        if (TextBox1.Text == "BillEvjen" && TextBox2.Text == "Bubbles") {
            FormsAuthentication.RedirectFromLoginPage(TextBox1.Text, true);
        }
        else {
            Response.Write("Invalid credentials");
        }
    }
</script>
```

`Login.aspx` has two simple TextBox controls and a Button control that ask the user to submit his username and password. The `Button1_Click` event uses the `RedirectFromLoginPage` method of the `FormsAuthentication` class. This method does exactly what its name implies — it redirects the request from `Login.aspx` to the original requested resource.

`RedirectFromLoginPage` takes two arguments. The first is the name of the user, used for cookie authentication purposes. This argument doesn't actually map to an account name and is used by ASP.NET's URL authorization capabilities. The second argument specifies whether a durable cookie should be issued. If set to `True`, the end user does not need to log in again to the application from one browser session to the next.

Using the three pages you've constructed, each request for the `Default.aspx` page from Listing 18-4 causes ASP.NET to check that the proper authentication token is in place. If the proper token is not found, the request is directed to the specified login page (in this example, `Login.aspx`). Looking at the URL in the browser, you can see that ASP.NET is using a querystring value to remember where to return the user after he has been authorized to proceed:

```
http://localhost:35089/Security/Login.aspx?ReturnUrl=%2fSecurity%2fDefault.aspx
```

Here the querystring `ReturnUrl` is used with a value of the folder and page that was the initial request.

Look more closely at the `Login.aspx` page from Listing 18-5, and note that the values placed in the two text boxes are checked to make sure they abide by a specific username and password. If they do, the `RedirectFromLoginPage` method is invoked; otherwise, the `Response.Write` statement is used. In most cases, you don't want to hardcode a username and password in your code. Many other options exist for checking whether usernames and passwords come from authorized users. Some of the other options follow.

Authenticating Against Values Contained in the web.config File

The previous example is not the best approach for dealing with usernames and passwords offered for authentication. It is never a good idea to hardcode these things directly into your applications. Take a quick look at storing these values in the `web.config` file itself.

The `<forms>` element in `web.config` that you worked with in Listing 18-3 can also take a sub-element. The sub-element, `<credentials>`, allows you to specify username and password combinations directly in the `web.config` file. You can choose from a couple of ways to add these values. The simplest method is shown in Listing 18-6.

Listing 18-6: Modifying the web.config file to add username/password values

```
<system.web>
    <authentication mode="Forms">
        <forms name="Wrox" loginUrl="Login.aspx" path="/">
            <credentials passwordFormat="Clear">
                <user name="BillEvjen" password="Bubbles" />
            </credentials>
        </forms>
    </authentication>

    <authorization>
        <deny users="?" />
    </authorization>
</system.web>
```

The `<credentials>` element has been included to add users and their passwords to the configuration file. `<credentials>` takes a single attribute—`passwordFormat`. The possible values of `passwordFormat` are `Clear`, `MD5`, and `SHA1`. The following list describes each of these options:

❑ `Clear`: Passwords are stored in clear text. The user password is compared directly to this value without further transformation.

❑ `MD5`: Passwords are stored using a Message Digest 5 (MD5) hash digest. When credentials are validated, the user password is hashed using the MD5 algorithm and compared for equality with this value. The clear-text password is never stored or compared. This algorithm produces better performance than SHA1.

❑ `SHA1`: Passwords are stored using the SHA1 hash digest. When credentials are validated, the user password is hashed using the SHA1 algorithm and compared for equality with this value. The clear-text password is never stored or compared. Use this algorithm for best security.

In the example from Listing 18-6, you use a setting of `Clear`. This isn't the most secure method, but it is used for demonstration purposes. A sub-element of `<credentials>` is `<user>`; that's where you define the username and password for the authorized user with the attributes `name` and `password`.

The next step is to change the `Button1_Click` event on the `Login.aspx` page shown earlier. This is illustrated in Listing 18-7.

Listing 18-7: Changing the Login.aspx page to work with the web.config file

VB

```vb
<%@ Page Language="VB" %>

<script runat="server">
    Protected Sub Button1_Click(ByVal sender As Object, _
      ByVal e As System.EventArgs)

        If FormsAuthentication.Authenticate(TextBox1.Text, TextBox2.Text) Then
            FormsAuthentication.RedirectFromLoginPage(TextBox1.Text, True)
        Else
            Response.Write("Invalid credentials")
        End If
    End Sub
</script>
```

C#

```csharp
<%@ Page Language="C#"%>

<script runat="server">
    protected void Button1_Click(object sender, EventArgs e)
    {
        if (FormsAuthentication.Authenticate(TextBox1.Text, TextBox2.Text)) {
            FormsAuthentication.RedirectFromLoginPage(TextBox1.Text, true);
        }
        else {
            Response.Write("Invalid credentials");
        }
    }
</script>
```

In this example, you simply use the `Authenticate` method to get your ASP.NET page to look at the credentials stored in the `web.config` file for verification. The `Authenticate` method takes two parameters — the username and the password that you are passing in to be checked. If the credential lookup is successful, the `RedirectFromLoginPage` method is invoked.

It is best not to store your users' passwords in the `web.config` file as clear text as the preceding example did. Instead, use one of the available hashing capabilities so you can keep the end user's password out of sight of prying eyes. To do this, simply store the hashed password in the configuration file as shown in Listing 18-8.

Listing 18-8: Using encrypted passwords

```
<forms name="Wrox" loginUrl="Login.aspx" path="/">
    <credentials passwordFormat="SHA1">
        <user name="BillEvjen" password="58356FB4CAC0B801F011B397F9DFF45ADB863892" />
    </credentials>
</forms>
```

Using this kind of construct makes it impossible for even the developer to discover a password because the clear text password is never used. The `Authenticate` method in the `Login.aspx` page hashes the password using SHA1 (because it is the method specified in the `web.config`'s `<credentials>` node) and compares the two hashes for a match. If a match is found, the user is authorized to proceed.

When using SHA1 or MD5, the only changes you make are in the web.config file and nowhere else. You don't have to make any changes to the login page or to any other page in the application. To store hashed passwords, however, you use the FormsAuthentication.HashPasswordForStoringInConfigFile method (probably the longest method name in the .NET Framework). You accomplish this in the following manner:

```
FormsAuthentication.HashPasswordForStoringInConfigFile(TextBox2.Text, "SHA1")
```

Authenticating Against Values in a Database

Another common way to retrieve username/password combinations is by getting them directly from a datastore of some kind. This enables you, for example, to check the credentials input by a user against values stored in Microsoft's SQL Server. The code for this is presented in Listing 18-9.

Listing 18-9: Checking credentials in SQL Server (Login.aspx)

VB
```
<%@ Page Language="VB" %>
<%@ Import Namespace="System.Data" %>
<%@ Import Namespace="System.Data.SqlClient" %>

<script runat="server">
    Protected Sub Button1_Click(ByVal sender As Object, _
      ByVal e As System.EventArgs)

        Dim conn As SqlConnection
        Dim cmd As SqlCommand
        Dim cmdString As String = "SELECT [Password] FROM [AccessTable] WHERE" & _
            " (([Username] = @Username) AND ([Password] = @Password))"

        conn = New SqlConnection("Data Source=localhost;Initial " & _
            "Catalog=Northwind;Persist Security Info=True;User ID=sa")
        cmd = New SqlCommand(cmdString, conn)

        cmd.Parameters.Add("@Username", SqlDbType.VarChar, 50)
        cmd.Parameters("@Username").Value = TextBox1.Text
        cmd.Parameters.Add("@Password", SqlDbType.VarChar, 50)
        cmd.Parameters("@Password").Value = TextBox2.Text

        conn.Open()

        Dim myReader As SqlDataReader

        myReader = cmd.ExecuteReader(CommandBehavior.CloseConnection)

        If myReader.Read() Then
            FormsAuthentication.RedirectFromLoginPage(TextBox1.Text, False)
        Else
            Response.Write("Invalid credentials")
        End If

        myReader.Close()
    End Sub
</script>
```

(continued)

Listing 18-9: *(continued)*

C#

```
<%@ Page Language="C#"%>
<%@ Import Namespace="System.Data" %>
<%@ Import Namespace="System.Data.SqlClient" %>

<script runat="server">
    protected void Button1_Click(object sender, EventArgs e)
    {
        SqlConnection conn;
        SqlCommand cmd;
        string cmdString = "SELECT [Password] FROM [AccessTable] WHERE" +
            " (([Username] = @Username) AND ([Password] = @Password))";

        conn = new SqlConnection("Data Source=localhost;Initial " +
            "Catalog=Northwind;Persist Security Info=True;User ID=sa");
        cmd = new SqlCommand(cmdString, conn);

        cmd.Parameters.Add("@Username", SqlDbType.VarChar, 50);
        cmd.Parameters["@Username"].Value = TextBox1.Text;
        cmd.Parameters.Add("@Password", SqlDbType.VarChar, 50);
        cmd.Parameters["@Password"].Value = TextBox2.Text;

        conn.Open();

        SqlDataReader myReader;

        myReader = cmd.ExecuteReader(CommandBehavior.CloseConnection);

        if (myReader.Read()) {
            FormsAuthentication.RedirectFromLoginPage(TextBox1.Text, false);
        }
        else {
            Response.Write("Invalid credentials");
        }

        myReader.Close();
    }
</script>
```

Leave everything else from the previous examples the same, except for the Login.aspx page. You can now authenticate usernames and passwords against data stored in SQL Server. In the Button1_Click event, a connection is made to SQL Server. (For security reasons, you should store your connection string in the web.config file.) Two parameters are passed in — the inputs from TextBox1 and TextBox2. If a result is returned, the RedirectFromLoginPage method is invoked.

Using the Login Control with Forms Authentication

You have seen how to use ASP.NET forms authentication with standard ASP.NET server controls, such as simple TextBox and Button controls. You can also use the latest ASP.NET 2.0 server controls — such as the new Login server control — with your custom-developed forms-authentication framework instead of using other controls. This really shows the power of ASP.NET — you can combine so many pieces to construct the solution you want.

Listing 18-10 shows a modified `Login.aspx` page using the new Login server control.

Listing 18-10: Using the Login server control on the Login.aspx page

VB

```
<%@ Page Language="VB" %>

<script runat="server">
    Protected Sub Login1_Authenticate(ByVal sender As Object, _
      ByVal e As System.Web.UI.WebControls.AuthenticateEventArgs)

        If (Login1.UserName = "BillEvjen" And Login1.Password = "Bubbles") Then
            FormsAuthentication.RedirectFromLoginPage(Login1.UserName, _
                Login1.RememberMeSet)
        Else
            Response.Write("Invalid credentials")
        End If
    End Sub
</script>

<html xmlns="http://www.w3.org/1999/xhtml" >
<head runat="server">
    <title>Login Page</title>
</head>
<body>
    <form id="form1" runat="server">
    <div>
        <asp:Login ID="Login1" runat="server" OnAuthenticate="Login1_Authenticate">
        </asp:Login>
    </div>
    </form>
</body>
</html>
```

C#

```
<%@ Page Language="C#" %>

<script runat="server">
    protected void Login1_Authenticate(object sender, AuthenticateEventArgs e)
    {
        if (Login1.UserName == "BillEvjen" && Login1.Password == "Bubbles") {
            FormsAuthentication.RedirectFromLoginPage(Login1.UserName,
                Login1.RememberMeSet);
        }
        else {
            Response.Write("Invalid credentials");
        }
    }
</script>
```

Because no Button server control is on the page, you use the Login control's `OnAuthenticate` attribute to point to the authentication server-side event — `Login1_Authenticate`. The event takes care of the authorization lookup (although the values are hardcoded in this example). The username text box of the

Login control can be accessed via the `Login1.UserName` declaration, and the password can be accessed using `Login1.Password`. The `Login1.RememberMeSet` property is used to specify whether to persist the authentication cookie for the user so that he is remembered on his next visit.

This example is a bit simpler than creating your own login form using TextBox and Button controls. You can give the Login control a predefined look-and-feel that is provided for you. You can also get at the subcontrol properties of the Login control a bit more easily. In the end, it really is up to you as to what methods you employ in your ASP.NET applications.

Looking Closely at the FormsAuthentication Class

As you can tell from the various examples in the forms authentication part of this chapter, a lot of what goes on depends on the `FormsAuthentication` class itself. For this reason, you should learn what that class is all about.

`FormsAuthentication` provides a number of methods and properties that enable you to read and control the authentication cookie as well as other information (such as the return URL of the request). The following table details some of the methods and properties available in the `FormsAuthentictation` class.

Method/Property	Description
Authenticate	This method is used to authenticate credentials that are stored in a configuration file (such as the `web.config` file).
Decrypt	Returns an instance of a valid, encrypted authentication ticket retrieved from an HTTP cookie as an instance of a `FormsAuthenticationTicket` class.
Encrypt	Creates a string which contains a valid encrypted authentication ticket that can be used in an HTTP cookie.
FormsCookieName	Returns the name of the cookie for the current application.
FormsCookiePath	Returns the cookie path (the location of the cookie) for the current application.
GetAuthCookie	Provides an authentication cookie for a specified user.
GetRedirectUrl	Returns the URL to which the user is redirected after being authorized by the login page.
HashPasswordFor Storing InConfigFile	Creates a hash of a provided string password. This method takes two parameters — one is the password and the other is the type of hash to perform on the string. Possible hash values include SHA1 and MD5.
Initialize	Performs an initialization of the `FormsAuthentication` class by reading the configuration settings in the `web.config` file, as well as getting the cookies and encryption keys used in the given instance of the application.
RedirectFromLogin Page	Performs a redirection of the HTTP request back to the original requested page. This should be performed only after the user has been authorized to proceed.

Method/Property	Description
RenewTicketIfOld	Conditionally updates the sliding expiration on a FormsAuthenticationTicket instance.
RequireSSL	Specifies whether the cookie should be transported via SSL only (HTTPS).
SetAuthCookie	Creates an authentication ticket and attaches it to a cookie that is contained in the outgoing response.
SignOut	Removes the authentication ticket.
SlidingExpiration	Provides a Boolean value indicating whether sliding expiration is enabled.

Passport Authentication

Another method for the authentication of your end users is using Microsoft's Passport identity system. Users with a passport account can have a single sign-on solution, meaning that he needs only those credentials to log in to your site and into other Passport-enabled sites and applications on the Internet.

When your application is enabled for Passport authentication, the request is actually redirected to the Microsoft Passport site where the user can enter his credentials. If the authentication is successful, the user is then authorized to proceed, and the request is redirected back to your application.

Very few Internet sites and applications use Microsoft's Passport technologies. In fact, Microsoft has completely de-emphasized Passport in 2005, and most companies interested in global authentication/authorization standards are turning toward the Project Liberty endeavors for a solution (www.projectliberty.org).

Authenticating Specific Files and Folders

You may not want to require credentials for each and every page or resource in your application. For instance, you might have a public Internet site with pages anyone can access without credentials, although you might have an administration section as part of your application that may require authentication/authorization measures.

URL authorization enables you to use the web.config file to apply the settings you need. Using URL authorization, you can apply any of the authentication measures to only specific files or folders. Listing 18-11 shows an example of locking down a single file.

Listing 18-11: Applying authorization requirements to a single file

```
<configuration>
  <system.web>
```

(continued)

Listing 18-11: *(continued)*

```
        <authentication mode="None" />

        <!-- The rest of your web.config file settings go here -->

    </system.web>

    <location path="AdminPage.aspx">
        <system.web>
            <authentication mode="Windows" />

            <authorization>
                <allow users="ReutersServer\EvjenB" />
                <deny users="*" />
            </authorization>
        </system.web>
    </location>
</configuration>
```

This `web.config` construction keeps the Web application open to the general public while, at the same time, it locks down a single file contained within the application — the `AdminPage.aspx` page. This is accomplished through the `<location>` element. `<location>` takes a single attribute (`path`) to specify the resource defined within the `<system.web>` section of the `web.config` file.

In the example, the `<authentication>` and `<authorization>` elements are used to provide the authentication and authorization details for the `AdminPage.aspx` page. For this page, Windows authentication is applied, and the only user allowed access is `EvjenB` in the `ReutersServer` domain. You can have as many `<location>` sections in your `web.config` file as you want.

Programmatic Authorization

So far, you have seen a lot of authentication examples that simply provide a general authorization to a specific page or folder within the application. Yet, you may want to provide more granular authorization measures for certain items on a page. For instance, you might provide a link to a specific document only for users who have an explicit Windows role. Other users may see something else. You also might want additional commentary or information for specified users, while other users see a condensed version of the information. Whatever your reason, this role-based authorization practice is possible in ASP.NET by working with certain objects.

You can use the `Page` object's `User` property, which provides an instance of the `IPrincipal` object. The `User` property provides a single method and a single property:

❑ `Identity`: This property provides an instance of the `System.Security.Principal.IIdentity` object for you to get at specific properties of the authenticated user.

❑ `IsInRole`: This method takes a single parameter, a string representation of the system role. It returns a Boolean value that indicates whether the user is in the role specified.

Working with User.Identity

The User.Identity property enables you to work with some specific contextual information about the authorized user. Using the property within your ASP.NET applications enables you to make resource-access decisions based on the information the object provides.

With User.Identity, you can gain access to the user's name, his authentication type, and whether he is authenticated. The following table details the properties provided through User.Identity.

Attribute	Description
AuthenticationType	Provides the authentication type of the current user. Example values include Basic, NTLM, Forms, and Passport.
IsAuthenticated	Returns a Boolean value specifying whether the user has been authenticated.
Name	Provides the username of the user as well as the domain of the user (only if he logged on with a Windows account).

For some examples of working with the User object, take a look at checking the user's login name. To do this, you use code similar to that shown in Listing 18-12.

Listing 18-12: Getting the username of the logged-in user

VB
```
Dim UserName As String
UserName = User.Identity.Name
```

C#
```
string userName;
userName = User.Identity.Name;
```

Another task you can accomplish with the User.Identity object is checking whether the user has been authenticated through your application's authentication methods, as illustrated in Listing 18-13.

Listing 18-13: Checking whether the user is authenticated

VB
```
Dim AuthUser As Boolean
AuthUser = User.Identity.IsAuthenticated()
```

C#
```
bool authUser;
authUser = User.Identity.IsAuthenticated();
```

This example provides you with a Boolean value indicating whether the user has been authenticated. You can also use the IsAuthenticated method in an If/Then statement as shown in Listing 18-14.

Listing 18-14: Using an If/Then statement that checks authentication

VB
```
If (User.Identity.IsAuthenticated) Then
    ' Do some actions here for authenticated users
Else
    ' Do other actions here for unauthenticated users
End If
```

C#
```
if (User.Identity.IsAuthenticated()) {
    // Do some actions here for authenticated users
}
else {
    // Do other actions here for unauthenticated users
}
```

You can also use the User object to check the authentication type of the user. This is done with the AuthenticationType property illustrated in Listing 18-15.

Listing 18-15: Using the AuthenticationType property

VB
```
Dim AuthType As String
AuthType = User.Identity.AuthenticationType
```

C#
```
string authType;
authType = User.Identity.AuthenticationType;
```

Again, the result is Basic, NTLM, Forms, or Passport.

Working with User.IsInRole()

If you are using Windows-based authentication, you can check to make sure that an authenticated user is in a specific Windows role. For example, you might want to show specific information only for users in the Subscribers group in the Computer Management Utility. To accomplish that, you can use the User object's IsInRole method, as shown in Listing 18-16.

Listing 18-16: Checking whether the user is part of a specific role

VB
```
If (User.IsInRole("ReutersServer\Subscribers")) Then
    ' Private information for subscribers
Else
    ' Public information
End If
```

```csharp
if (User.IsInRole("ReutersServer\Subscribers") {
   // Private information for subscribers
}
else {
   // Public information
}
```

The `IsInRole` method's parameter provides a string value that represents the domain and the group (Windows role). In this case, you specify that any user in the `Subscribers` Windows role from the `ReutersServer` domain is permitted to see some information not available to users who don't belong to that specific role.

Another possibility is to specify some of the built-in groups available to you. Ever since Windows 2000, Windows has included a series of built-in accounts such as Administrator, Guest, PrintOperator, and User. You can access to these built-in accounts in a couple of ways. One is to specify the built-in account with the domain directly:

```
User.IsInRole("ReutersServer\Administrator")
```

The other possibility is to use the `BUILTIN` keyword:

```
User.IsInRole("BUILTIN\Administrator")
```

Pulling More Information with WindowsIdentity

So far, in working with the user's identity information, you've used the standard `Identity` object that is part of ASP.NET by default. If you are working with Windows-based authentication, you also have the option of using the `WindowsIdentity` object and other objects. To gain access to these richer objects, create a reference to the `System.Security.Principal` object in your application.

Used in combination with the `Identity` object from the preceding examples, these additional objects make certain tasks even easier. For instance, if you are working with roles, `System.Security.Principal` provides access to the `WindowsBuiltInRole` enumeration.

Listing 18-17 is an example of using the `WindowsBuiltInRole` enumeration.

Listing 18-17: Using the WindowsBuiltInRole enumeration

VB
```vb
Dim AdminUser As Boolean
AdminUser = User.IsInRole(WindowsBuiltInRole.Administrator.ToString())
```

C#
```csharp
bool adminUser;
adminUser = User.IsInRole(WindowsBuiltInRole.Administrator.ToString())
```

Instead of specifying a string value of the domain and the role, you can use the `WindowsBuiltInRole` enumeration to easily access specific roles on the application server. When working with this and other enumerations, you also have IntelliSense (see Figure 18-9) to help you make your selections easily.

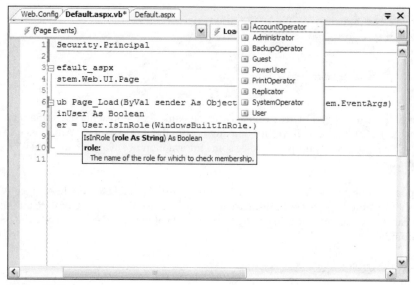

Figure 18-9

The roles in the `WindowsBuiltInRole` enumeration include the following:

- ❏ AccountOperator
- ❏ Administrator
- ❏ BackupOperator
- ❏ Guest
- ❏ PowerUser
- ❏ PrintOperator
- ❏ Replicator
- ❏ SystemOperator
- ❏ User

Using `System.Security.Principal`, you have access to the `WindowsIdentity` object—which is much richer than working with the default `Identity` object. Listing 18-18 lists some of the additional information you can get through the `WindowsIdentity` object.

Listing 18-18: Using the WindowsIdentity object

VB

```
<%@ Page Language="VB" %>
<%@ Import Namespace="System.Security.Principal" %>

<script runat="server">
    Protected Sub Page_Load(ByVal sender As Object, _
```

```
        ByVal e As System.EventArgs)

        Dim AuthUser As WindowsIdentity = WindowsIdentity.GetCurrent()
        Response.Write(AuthUser.AuthenticationType.ToString() & "<br>" & _
            AuthUser.ImpersonationLevel.ToString() & "<br>" & _
            AuthUser.IsAnonymous.ToString() & "<br>" & _
            AuthUser.IsAuthenticated.ToString() & "<br>" & _
            AuthUser.IsGuest.ToString() & "<br>" & _
            AuthUser.IsSystem.ToString() & "<br>" & _
            AuthUser.Name.ToString())
    End Sub
</script>
```

C#

```
<%@ Page Language="C#" %>
<%@ Import Namespace="System.Security.Principal" %>

<script runat="server">
    protected void Page_Load(object sender, EventArgs e)
    {
        WindowsIdentity AuthUser = WindowsIdentity.GetCurrent();
        Response.Write(AuthUser.AuthenticationType.ToString() + "<br>" +
            AuthUser.ImpersonationLevel.ToString() + "<br>" +
            AuthUser.IsAnonymous.ToString() + "<br>" +
            AuthUser.IsAuthenticated.ToString() + "<br>" +
            AuthUser.IsGuest.ToString() + "<br>" +
            AuthUser.IsSystem.ToString() + "<br>" +
            AuthUser.Name.ToString());
    }
</script>
```

In this example, an instance of the `WindowsIdentity` object is created and populated with the current identity of the user accessing the application. Then you have access to a number of properties that are written to the browser using a `Response.Write` statement. The displayed listing shows information about the current user's credentials, such as if the user is authenticated, anonymous, or running under a guest account or a system account. It also gives you the user's authentication type and login name. A result is shown in Figure 18-10.

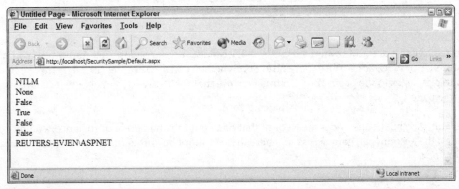

Figure 18-10

Identity and Impersonation

ASP.NET runs under a worker process that uses the credentials of a Windows account named ASPNET (without the period) when working from IIS 5.0, and an account named Network Service when working from IIS 6.0. For security purposes, it is always best to run everything using the fewest number of privileges possible, and that is specifically what ASP.NET is designed to do.

By default, the ASP.NET account has Read & Execute privileges on all ASP.NET pages. Look at the Security tab of a sample aspx page's properties, for example, and you see that the ASPNET or Network Service account is not listed. What is listed is the Everyone account, which is given Read & Execute privileges, as shown in Figure 18-11.

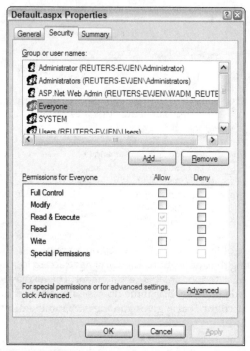

Figure 18-11

If you remove this account from the list, ASP.NET cannot run the pages. At a minimum, you have to give the ASPNET or Network Service (depending on whether you are running IIS 5.0 or IIS 6.0) Read & Execute privileges to the page. You also must ensure that the IUSR_MachineName account has access to the same page.

By default, ASP.NET runs under an account that has limited privileges. For instance, you may find that although the account can gain access to a network, it cannot be authenticated to any other computer on the network.

The account setting is provided in the `machine.config` file:

```
<processModel
 enable="true"
 userName="machine"
 password="AutoGenerate" />
```

These settings force ASP.NET to run under the system account (ASPNET or Network Service). This is really specified through the `userName` attribute that contains a value of `machine`. The other possible value you can have for this attribute is `system`. Here's what each entails:

❑ `machine`: The most secure setting. You should have good reasons to change this value. It's the ideal choice mainly because it forces the ASP.NET account to run under the fewest number of privileges possible.

❑ `system`: Forces ASP.NET to run under the local SYSTEM account, which has considerably more privileges to access networking and files.

It is also possible to specify an account of your choosing using the `<processModel>` element in either the `machine.config` or `web.config` files:

```
<processModel
 enable="true"
 userName="MySpecifiedUser"
 password="MyPassword" />
```

In this example, ASP.NET is run under a specified administrator or user account instead of the default ASPNET or Network Service account. It inherits all the privileges this account offers.

You can also change how ASP.NET behaves in whatever account it is specified to run under through the `<identity>` element in the `web.config` file. The `<identity>` element in the `web.config` file allows you to turn on *impersonation*. Impersonation provides ASP.NET with the capability to run as a process using the privileges of another user for a specific session. In more detail, impersonation allows ASP.NET to run under the account of the entity making the request to the application. To turn on this impersonation capability, you use the `impersonate` attribute in the `<identity>` element as shown here:

```
<configuration>
    <system.web>

       <identity impersonate="true" />

    </system.web>
</configuration>
```

By default, the `impersonate` attribute is set to `false`. Setting this property to `true` ensures that ASP.NET runs under the account of the person making the request to the application. If the requestor is an anonymous user, ASP.NET runs under the IUSR_MachineName account. To see this in action, run the example shown in Listing 18-18, but this time with impersonation turned on (`true`). Instead of getting a username of REUTERS-EVJEN\ASPNET as the user, you get the name of the user who is requesting the page — REUTERS-EVJEN\Administrator in this example, as shown in Figure 18-12.

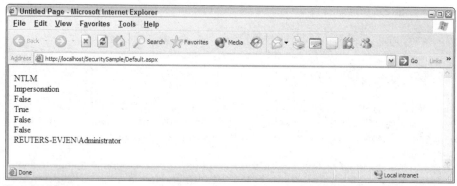

Figure 18-12

You also have the option of running ASP.NET under a specified account that you declare using the `<identity>` element in the `web.config` file:

```
<identity impersonate="true" userName="MySpecifiedUser" password="MyPassword" />
```

As shown, you can run the ASP.NET process under an account that you specify through the `userName` and `password` attributes. These values are stored as clear text in the `web.config` file.

Look at the `machine.config.comments` file, and you can see that ASP.NET runs under full trust, meaning that it has some pretty high-level capabilities to run and access resources. Here's the setting:

```
<system.web>

    <securityPolicy>
        <trustLevel name="Full" policyFile="internal" />
        <trustLevel name="High" policyFile="web_hightrust.config" />
        <trustLevel name="Medium" policyFile="web_mediumtrust.config" />
        <trustLevel name="Low"  policyFile="web_lowtrust.config" />
        <trustLevel name="Minimal" policyFile="web_minimaltrust.config" />
    </securityPolicy>

    <!--  level="[Full|High|Medium|Low|Minimal]" -->
    <trust level="Full" originUrl="" />

</system.web>
```

Five possible settings exist for the level of trust that you give ASP.NET — Full, High, Medium, Low, and Minimal. The level of trust applied is specified through the `<trust>` element's level attribute. By default it is set to Full. Each one points to a specific configuration file for the policy in which the level can find its trust level settings. The Full setting does not include a policy file because it simply skips all the code access security checks.

Securing Through IIS

ASP.NET works in conjunction with IIS; not only can you apply security settings directly in ASP.NET (through code or configuration files), but you can also apply additional security measures in IIS itself. IIS enables you to apply access methods you want by working with users and groups (which were discussed earlier in the chapter), working with restricting IP addresses, file extensions, and more. Security through IIS is deserving of a chapter in itself, but the major topics are explored here.

IP Address and Domain Name Restrictions

You can work with the restriction of IP addresses and domain names in Windows Server 2003, Windows 2000 Server, or Windows NT only. Through IIS, you can apply specific restrictions based on a single computer's IP address, a group of computers, or even a specific domain name.

To access this capability, pull up the Internet Information Services (IIS) Manager and right-click on either the Web site you are interested in working with or on the Default Web Site node to simply apply the settings to every Web application on the server. From the menu, choose Properties and select the Directory Security tab.

Click the Edit button in the IP Address and domain name restrictions box and a dialog appears. The resulting dialog enables you to grant or restrict access based on an IP address or domain name. These dialogs are shown in Figure 18-13.

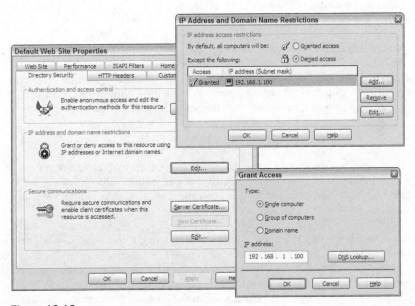

Figure 18-13

Think twice about restricting based on a domain name. It can hinder performance when the reverse DNS lookup is performed on each request to check the domain.

You not only can restrict specific IP addresses and domain names, but you can also restrict everyone and just allow specified entities based on the same items. Although Figure 18-13 shows restricting a specific IP address, you can restrict or grant access to an entire subnet as well. Figure 18-14 shows how to grant access just to the servers on the 192.168.1.0 subnet (defined by a Linksys router).

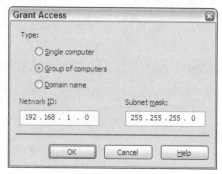

Figure 18-14

Working with File Extensions

You can work with many types of files in ASP.NET. These files are defined by their extensions. For example, you know that .aspx is a typical ASP.NET page, and .asmx is an ASP.NET Web service file extension. These files are actually mapped by IIS to the ASP.NET DLL, aspnet_isapi.dll.

To access the dialog in IIS that maps the file extensions, pull up the Properties dialog of your Web application in IIS or pull up the Default Web Site Properties. In a specific Web application, you must work from the Directory tab; but if you are working with the Default Web Site Properties dialog, you can instead use the Home Directory tab. From these tabs, click the Configuration button in the Application Settings box. The Application Configuration dialog includes a Mapping tab, where the mappings are configured. Highlight .aspx in the list of mappings and click the Edit button. Figure 18-15 shows the result.

In the Executable text box, you can see that all .aspx pages map to the aspnet_isapi.dll from ASP.NET 2.0, and that you can also specify which types of requests are allowed in the application. You can either allow all verbs (for example, GET or POST) or you can specify which verbs are allowed access to the application.

One important point regarding these mappings is that you don't see .html, .htm, .jpg, or other file extensions such as .txt in the list. Your application won't be passing requests for these files to ASP.NET. That might not be a big deal, but in working through the various security examples in this chapter, you might want to have the same type of security measures applied to these files as to .aspx pages. If, for instance, you want all .html pages to be included in the forms authentication model that you require for your ASP.NET application, you must add .html (or whatever file extension you want) to the list. To do so, click the Add button in the Application Configuration dialog.

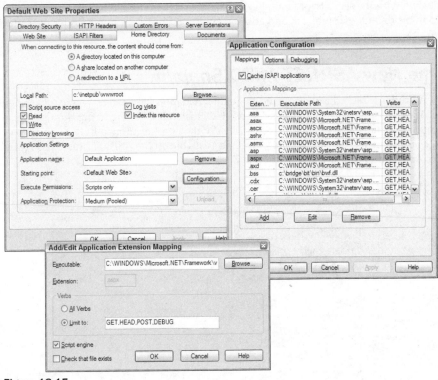

Figure 18-15

In the next dialog, you can add the ASP.NET DLL to the Executable text box, and the appropriate file extension and verbs to the list before adding the mapping to your application's mapping table. This example is illustrated in Figure 18-16.

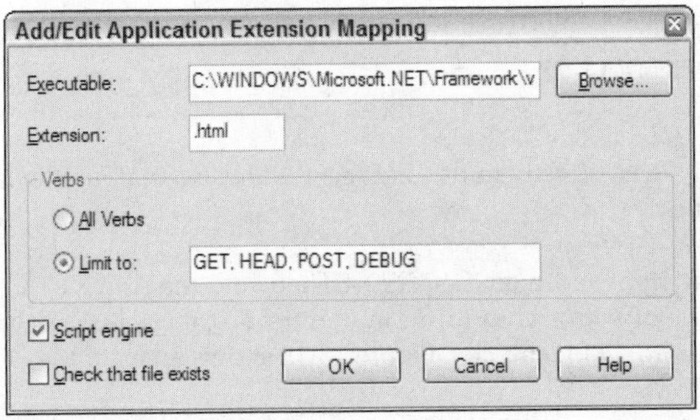

Figure 18-16

When dealing with the security of your site, you have to remember all the files that might not be included in the default mapping list and add the ones you think should fall under the same security structure.

Using the New ASP.NET MMC Snap-In

The new ASP.NET MMC console (covered in detail in Chapter 28) enables you to edit the `web.config` and `machine.config` files using an easy-to-use GUI instead of having to dig through the text of those files yourself to make the necessary changes. Most of the items examined in this book can also be modified and changed using this dialog. The plug-in is available on the ASP.NET tab (see Figure 18-17) of your Web application running under IIS.

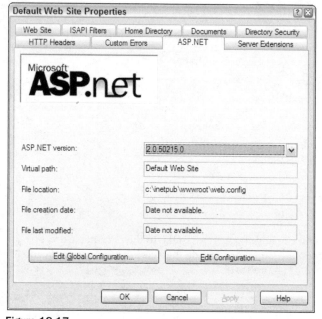

Figure 18-17

When you make the changes directly in the dialog, you are also making the hardcoded changes to the actual configuration files.

Click the Edit Configuration button on the ASP.NET tab, and the ASP.NET Configuration Settings dialog opens. There you can modify how your forms authentication model works in the GUI without going to the application's `web.config` file directly. Figure 18-18 shows an example of working with forms authentication in the GUI.

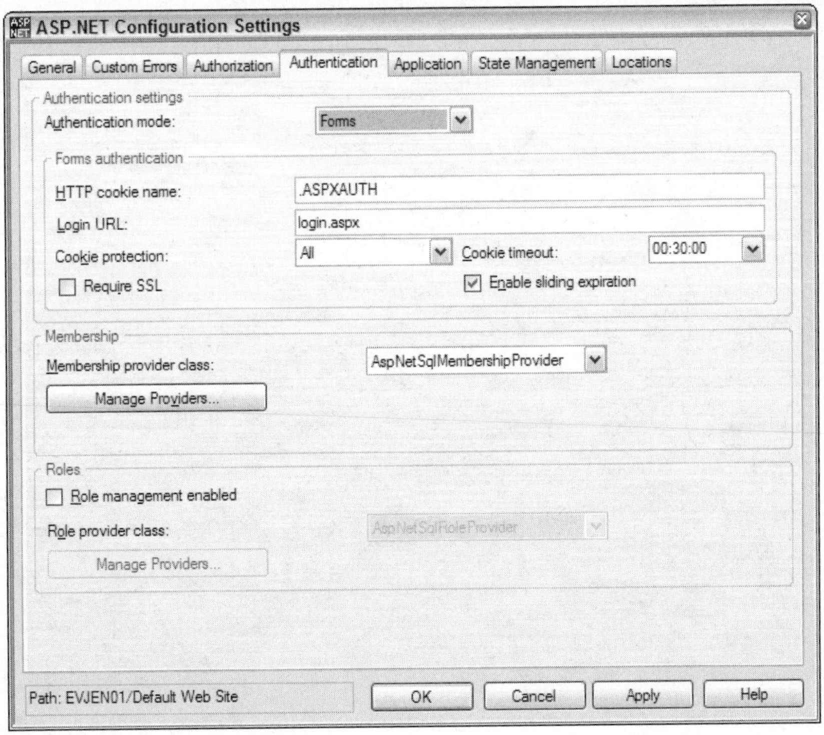

Figure 18-18

Summary

This chapter covered some of the foundation items of ASP.NET security and showed you how to apply both authentication and authorization to your Web applications. It reviewed some of the various authentication and authorization models at your disposal, such as Basic, Digest, and Windows Integrated Authentication. Other topics included forms-based authentication and how to construct your own forms-based authentication models outside of the new ones provided via ASP.NET 2.0 by using the new membership and role management capabilities it provides. The chapter also discussed how to use authentication properties within your applications and how to authorize users and groups based on those properties.

19

State Management

Why is state management such a difficult problem that it requires an entire chapter in a book on programming? In the old days (about 10 years ago), using standard client-server architecture meant using a fat client and a fat server. Perhaps your Visual Basic 6 application could talk to a database. The state was held either on the client-side or in the server-side database. Typically, you could count on a client having a little bit of memory and a hard drive of its own to manage state. The most important aspect of traditional client/server design, however, was that the client was *always* connected to the server. It's easy to forget, but HTTP is a stateless protocol. For the most part, a connection is built up and torn down each time a call is made to a remote server. Yes, HTTP 1.1 includes a keep-alive technique that provides optimizations at the TCP level. Even with these optimizations, the server has no way to determine that subsequent connections came from the same client.

Although the Web has the richness of DHTML, JavaScript, and HTML 4.0 on the client side, the average high-powered Pentium 4 with a gigabyte of RAM is still being used only to render HTML. It's quite ironic that such powerful computers on the client side are still so vastly underutilized when it comes to storing state. Additionally, although many individuals have broadband, it is not universally used. Developers must still respect and pay attention to the dial-up users of the world. When was the last time that your project manager told you that bandwidth was not an issue for your Web application?

The ASP.NET concept of a Session that is maintained over the statelessness of HTTP is not a new one, and it existed before ASP.NET and even before classic ASP. It is, however, a very effective and elegant way to maintain state. There are, however, a number of different choices available to you, of which the ASP.NET session is just one. There have been a few subtle changes between ASP.NET 1.*x* and 2.0 that will be covered in this chapter. The Session object remains as before, but the option is available now to plug in your own session state provider.

What Are Your Choices?

Given a relatively weak client, a stateless protocol such as HTTP, and ASP.NET 1.*x* or 2.0 on the server side, how do you manage state on the Web? Figure 19-1 is a generalized diagram that calls out the primary means available for managing state. The problem is huge, and the solution range is even larger. This chapter assumes that you are not using Java applets or ActiveX controls to manage state. Although these options are certainly valid (although complex) solutions to the state problem, they are beyond the scope of this book.

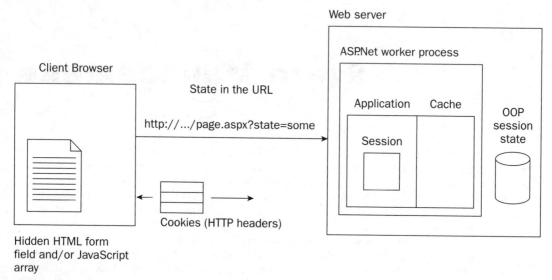

Figure 19-1

If you remember one thing about state management, remember this: There is no right answer. Some answers are more right than others, certainly; but there are many, many ways to manage state. Think about your last project. How many days were spent trying to decide where you should manage state? The trick is to truly understand the pros and cons of each method.

To make an educated decision about a method, you should understand the lifecycle of a request and the opportunities for state management at each point in the process:

1.   A Web browser makes an HTTP GET request for a page on your server http://myserver/ myapp/mypage.aspx. This client Web browser has *never* visited your site before.

2.   IIS and your ASP.NET application respond by returning HTML rendered by mypage.aspx. Additionally mypage.aspx returns a cookie with a unique ID to track this Web browser. Remember that a cookie is actually a slightly abstract concept. The cookie is set by returning a Set-Cookie HTTP Header to the client. The client then promises to return the values of the cookie in every subsequent HTTP call in the HTTP header. The *state* in this example is actually an agreement between the client and server to bounce the cookie back-and-forth on every request in response.

3. The HTML that is returned may contain hidden text boxes like `<input type= "hidden" value= "somestate" />`. These text boxes are similar to cookies because they are passed back to the server if the form on this page is submitted. Cookies are set per domain; hidden form fields are set per page.

4. Upon the next request, the previously set cookies are returned to the server. If this request was the submission of the form as an HTTP POST, all fields in the Form are returned—hidden or otherwise.

5. The unique identifier that was set earlier as a cookie can now be used as a key into any kind of server-side state mechanism. That state might be as simple as an in-memory hashtable, or as complicated as a SQL database.

One of the repeating themes you might notice is the agreement between the client and the server to pass information back and forth. That information can be in the URL, in HTTP headers, or even in the submitted Form as an input field.

On the server side, you have a few options available. You'll want to weigh the options based on the amount of memory you have available, the amount of data you want to store, and how often you'll require access to the data.

The following tables express each of the server-side and client-side options and list a few pros and cons for each.

Server-Side Option	Pros	Cons
Application State	Fast. Shared among all users.	State is stored once per server in multiple server configurations.
Cache Object (Application Scope)	Like the Application but includes expiration via Dependencies (see Chapter 20).	State is stored once per server in multiple server configurations.
Session State	Three choices: in process, out of process, DB-backed. Can be configured as cookieless.	Can be abused. You pay a serialization cost when objects leave the process. In process requires Web Server affinity. Cookieless configuration makes it easier to hijack.
Database	State can be accessed by any server in a Web farm.	Pay a serialization and persistence cost when objects leave the process. Requires a SQL Server license.

On the client side, every available option costs you in bandwidth. Each option involves passing data back and forth from client to server. Every byte of data you store will be paid for twice: once when it is passed to the server and once when it is passed back.

Client-Side Option	Pros	Cons
Cookie	Simple	Can be rejected by browser. Not appropriate for large amounts of data. Inappropriate for sensitive data. Size cost is paid on *every* HTTP Request and Response.
Hidden Field	Simple for page-scoped data	Not appropriate for large amounts of data. Inappropriate for sensitive data.
ViewState	Simple for page-scoped data	Encoding of serialized object as binary Base64-encoded data adds approximately 30 percent overhead. Small serialization cost. Has a negative reputation, particularly with DataGrids.
ControlState	Simple for page-scoped control-specific data	Like ViewState, but used for controls that require ViewState even if the developer has turned it off.
QueryString (URL)	Incredibly simple and often convenient if you want your URLs to be modified directly by the end user	Comparatively complex. Can't hold a lot of information. Inappropriate for sensitive data. Easily modified by the end user.

These tables provided you with some of the server-side and client-side options. The improvements to caching in ASP.NET 2.0 are covered in Chapter 20.

Understanding the Session Object in ASP.NET 2.0

In classic ASP, the `Session` object was held in-process (as was everything) to the IIS process. The user received a cookie with a unique key in the form of a GUID. The Session key was an index into a dictionary where object references could be stored.

In ASP.NET 2.0 the `Session` object still offers an in-process option, but also includes an out-of-process and database-backed option. Additionally, the developer has the option to enable a *cookieless* Session State where the Session key appears in the URL rather than being sent as a cookie.

Sessions and the Event Model

The HttpApplication object raises a series of events during the life of the HTTP protocol request:

- ❏ BeginRequest: This event fires at the beginning of every request.

- ❏ AuthenticateRequest: This event is used by the security module and indicates that a request is about to be authenticated. This is where the security module, or you, determines who the user is.

- ❏ AuthorizeRequest: This event is used by the security module and indicates that a request is about to be authorized. This is where the security module, or you, determines what the user is allowed to do.

- ❏ ResolveRequestCache: This event is used by the caching module to determine whether this now-authorized request can bypass any additional processing.

- ❏ AcquireRequestState: This event indicates that all session state associated with this HTTP request is about to be acquired.

> Session state is available to you, the developer, *after* the AcquireRequestState event fires. The session state key that is unique to each user is retrieved either from a cookie or from the URL.

- ❏ PreRequestHandlerExecute: This is the last event you get before the HttpHandler class for this request is called.

> Your application code, usually in the form of a Page, executes at this point in the process.

- ❏ PostRequestHandlerExecute: This is the event that fires just after the HttpHandler is called.

- ❏ ReleaseRequestState: Indicates that the session state should be stored. Session state is persisted at this point, using whatever Session-state module is configured in web.config.

- ❏ UpdateRequestCache: All work is complete, and the resulting output is ready to be added to the cache.

- ❏ EndRequest: This is the last event called during a request.

You can see from the preceding list that AcquireRequestState and ReleaseRequestState are two significant events in the life of the Session object.

By the time your application code executes, the Session object has been populated using the Session key that was present in the cookie, or as you see later, from the URL. If you want to handle some processing at the time the Session begins, rather than handling it in AcquireRequestState, you can define an event handler for the Start event of a SessionState HttpModule.

```
Sub Session_OnStart()
     'this fires after session state has been acquired by the SessionStateModule.
End Sub
```

> The Session object includes both Start and End events that you can hook event handlers to for your own needs. However, the Session_OnEnd event is supported only in the In-Process Session State mode. This event will not be raised if you use out-of-process State Server or SQL Server modes. The Session ends, but your handlers will never hear about it.

Pre- and post-events occur at almost every point within the life of an HTTP request. Session state can be manipulated at any point after AcquireRequestState, including in the Global.asax within the Session_OnStart event.

The HttpSessionState object can be used within any event in a subclass of the Page object. Because the pages you create in ASP.NET 2.0 derive from System.Web.UI.Page, you can access Session State as a collection because System.Web.SessionState.HttpSessionState implements ICollection.

The Page has a public property aptly named Session that automatically retrieves the Session from the current HttpContext. Even though it seems as if the Session object lives inside the page, it actually lives in the HttpContext, and the page's public Session property actually retrieves the reference to the Session State. This convenience not only makes it more comfortable for the classic ASP programmer, but saves you a little typing as well.

The Session object can be referred to within a page in this way:

```
Session["SomeSessionState"] = "Here is some data";
```

or

```
HttpContext.Current.Session["SomeSessionState"] = "Here is some data";
```

The fact that the Session object actually lives in the current HTTP context is more than just a piece of trivia. This knowledge enables you to access the Session object in contexts other than the page (such as in your own HttpHandler).

Configuring Session State Management

All the code within a page refers to the Session object using the dictionary-style syntax seen previously, but the HttpSessionState object uses a Provider Pattern to extract possible choices for session state storage. You can choose between the included providers by changing the sessionState element in web.config. ASP.NET ships with the following three storage providers:

❑ **In-Process Session State Store:** Stores sessions in the ASP.NET in-memory cache

❑ **Out-Of-Process Session State Store:** Stores sessions in the ASP.NET State Server service asp-net_state.exe

❑ **Sql Session State Store:** Stores sessions in Microsoft SQL Server database and is configured with aspnet_regsql.exe

The format of the `web.config` file's `sessionState` element is shown in the following code:

```
<configuration>
    <system.web>
        <sessionState mode="Off|InProc|StateServer|SQLServer|Custom" ../>
    </system.web>
...
```

Begin configuring session state by setting the `mode="InProc"` attribute of the `sessionState` element in the `web.config` of a new Web site. This is the most common configuration for session state within ASP.NET 2.0 and is also the fastest, as you see next.

In-Process Session State

When the configuration is set to `InProc`, session data is stored in the `HttpRuntime`'s internal cache in an implementation of `ISessionStateItemCollection` that implements `ICollection`. The session state key is a 120-bit value string that indexes this global dictionary of object references. When session state is in process, objects are stored as live references. This is an incredibly fast mechanism because no serialization occurs, nor do objects leave the process space. Certainly, your objects are not garbage-collected if they exist in the `In-Process Session` object because a reference is still being held.

Additionally, because the objects are stored (held) in memory, they use up memory until that Session times out. If a user visits your site and hits one page, he might cause you to store a 40MB `XmlDocument` in in-process session. If that user never comes back, you are left sitting on that large chunk of memory for the next 20 minutes or so (a configurable value) until the Session ends, even if the user never returns.

InProc Gotchas

Although the InProc Session model is the fastest, the default, and the most common, it does have a significant limitation. If the worker process or application domain recycles, all session state data is lost. Also, ASP.net application may restart for a number of reasons, such as the following:

❑   You've changed the `web.config` or `Global.asax` file or "touched" it by changing its modified date.

❑   You've modified files in the `\bin` or `\App_Code` directory.

❑   The `processModel` element has been set in the `web.config` or `machine.config` file indicating when the application should restart. Conditions that could generate a restart might be a memory limit or request-queue limit.

❑   Antivirus software modifies any of the previously mentioned files. This is particularly common with antivirus software that *innoculates* files.

This said, In-Process Session State works great for smaller applications that require only a single Web server, or in situations where IP load balancing is returning each user to the server where his original Session was created.

If a user already has a Session key, but is returned to a different machine than the one on which his session was created, a new Session is created on that new machine using the session ID supplied by the user. Of course, that new Session is empty and unexpected results may occur. However if `regenerateExpiredSessionId` is set to `True` in the `web.config` file, a new Session ID is created and assigned to the user.

Web Gardening

Web gardening is a technique for multiprocessor systems wherein multiple instances of the ASP.NET worker process are started up and assigned with processor affinity. On a larger Web server with as many as four CPUs, you could have anywhere from one to four worker processes hosting ASP.NET 2.0. *Processor affinity* means literally that an ASP.NET 2.0 worker process has an affinity for a particular CPU. It's "pinned" to that CPU. This technique is usually enabled only in very large Web farms.

Don't forget that In-Process Session State is just that — in-process. Even if your Web application consists of only a single Web server and all IP traffic is routed to that single server, you have no guarantee that each subsequent request will be served on the same processor. A Web garden must follow many of the same rules that a Web farm follows.

> If you're using Web gardening on a multiprocessor system, you must not use In-Process Session State or you lose Sessions. In-Process Session State is appropriate only where there is a 1:1 ratio of applications to application domains.

Storing Data in the Session Object

In the following simple example, in a `Button_Click` event the content of the text box is added to the `Session` object with a specific key. The user then clicks to go to another page within the same application, and the data from the `Session` object is retrieved and presented in the browser.

Note the use of the `<asp:HyperLink>` control. Certainly, that markup could have been hard coded as HTML, but this small distinction will serve us well later. Additionally, the URL is relative to this site, not absolute. Watch for it to help you later in this chapter.

Listing 19-1 illustrates how simple it is to use the `Session` object. It behaves like any other `IDictionary` collection and allows you to store keys of type `String` associated with any kind of object. The Retrieve.aspx file referenced will be added in Listing 19-2.

Listing 19-1: Setting values in session state

ASP.NET–C#
```
<%@ Page Language="C#" CodeFile="Default.aspx.cs" Inherits="_Default" %>
```

ASP.NET–VB.NET
```
<%@ Page Language="VB" AutoEventWireup="false" CodeFile="Default.aspx.vb"
    Inherits="_Default" %>
```

ASP.NET
```
<!DOCTYPE html PUBLIC "-//W3C//DTD XHTML 1.1//EN"
"http://www.w3.org/TR/xhtml11/DTD/xhtml11.dtd">
<html xmlns="http://www.w3.org/1999/xhtml" >
<head runat="server">
    <title>Session State</title>
</head>
<body>
    <form id="form1" runat="server">
```

```
        <div>
            <asp:TextBox ID="TextBox1" Runat="server"></asp:TextBox>
            <asp:Button ID="Button1" Runat="server" Text="Store in Session"
             OnClick="Button1_Click" />
            <br />
            <asp:HyperLink ID="HyperLink1" Runat="server"
             NavigateUrl="Retrieve.aspx">Next Page</asp:HyperLink>
        </div>
        </form>
</body>
</html>
```

VB

```
Partial Class _Default
    Inherits System.Web.UI.Page

    Protected Sub Button1_Click(ByVal sender As Object, _
            ByVal e As System.EventArgs)
        Session("mykey") = TextBox1.Text
    End Sub

End Class
```

C#

```
public partial class _Default : System.Web.UI.Page
{
    protected void Button1_Click(object sender, EventArgs e)
    {
        Session["mykey"] = TextBox1.Text;
    }
}
```

The page from Listing 19-1 renders in the browser as shown in Figure 19-2. The Session object is accessed as any dictionary indexed by a string key. See Chapter 10 for more on collections and lists.

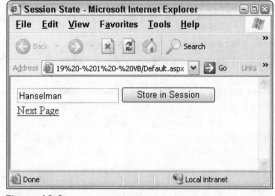

Figure 19-2

More details about the page and the `Session` object can be displayed to the developer if page tracing is enabled. You add this element to your application's `web.config` file inside the `<system.web>` element, as follows:

```
<trace enabled="true" pageOutput="true"/>
```

Now tracing is enabled, and the tracing output is sent directly to the page. More details on tracing and debugging are given in Chapter 21. For now, make this change and refresh your browser.

In Figure 19-3, the screen shot is split to show both the top and roughly the middle of the large amount of trace information that is returned when trace is enabled. Session State is very much baked into the fabric of ASP.NET. You can see in the Request Details section of the trace that not only was this page the result of an HTTP POST but the Session ID was as well—elevated to the status of first-class citizen. However, the ASP.NET Session ID lives as a cookie by default, as you can see in the `Cookies` collection at the bottom of the figure.

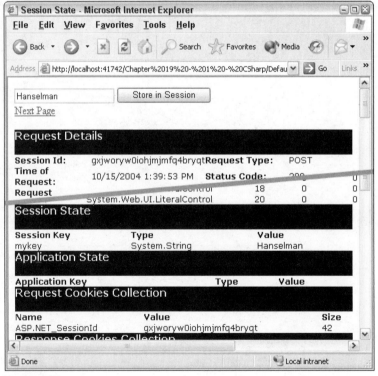

Figure 19-3

The default name for that cookie is `ASP.NET_SessionId`, but its name can be configured via the `cookieName` attribute of the `<sessionState>` element in `web.config`. Some large enterprises allow only certain named cookies past their proxies, so you might need to change this value when working on an extranet or a network with a gateway server; but this would be a very rare occurrence. The `cookieName` is changed to use the name "Foo" in the following example.

```
<sessionState cookieName="Foo" mode="InProc"></sessionState>
```

The trace output shown in Figure 19-3 includes a section listing the contents of the `Session State` collection. In the figure, you can see that the name `mykey` and the value `Hanselman` are currently stored. Additionally, you see the CLR data type of the stored value; in this case, it's `System.String`.

> The Value column of the trace output comes from a call to the contained object's `ToString()` method. If you store your own objects in the Session, you can override `ToString()` to provide a text-friendly representation of your object that might make the trace results more useful.

Now add the next page, `retrieve.aspx`, which pulls this value out of the session. Leave the `retrieve.aspx` page as the IDE creates it and add a `Page_Load` event handler, as shown in Listing 19-2.

Listing 19-2: Retrieving values from the session

VB

```
Partial Class Retrieve
    Inherits System.Web.UI.Page

    Protected Sub Page_Load(ByVal sender As Object, ByVal e As System.EventArgs) _
        Handles Me.Load

        Dim myValue As String = CType(Session("mykey"), String)
        Response.Write(myValue)
    End Sub
End Class
```

C#

```
public partial class Retrieve : System.Web.UI.Page
{
    protected void Page_Load(object sender, EventArgs e)
    {
        string myValue = (string)Session["mykey"];
        Response.Write(myValue);
    }
}
```

Because the session contains object references, the resulting object is converted to a string by way of a cast in C# or the `CType` function in VB.

Making Sessions Transparent

It is unfortunate that the cast to a string is required to retrieve data from the `Session` object. Combined with the string key used as an index, it makes for a fairly weak contract between the page and the `Session` object. You can create a session helper that is specific to your application to hide these details, or you can add properties to a base `Page` class that presents these objects to your pages in a friendlier way. Because the generic `Session` object is available as a property on `System.Web.UI.Page`, add a new class derived from `Page` that exposes a new property named `MyKey`.

Start by right-clicking your project and selecting Add New Item from the context menu to create a new class. Name it `SmartSessionPage` and click OK. The IDE may tell you that it would like to put this new class in the `/App_Code` folder to make it available to the whole application. Click Yes.

Your new base page is very simple. Via derivation, it does everything that `System.Web.UI.Page` does, plus it has a new property, as shown in Listing 19-3.

Listing 19-3: A more session-aware base page

VB

```vb
Imports Microsoft.VisualBasic
Imports System
Imports System.Web

Public Class SmartSessionPage
    Inherits System.Web.UI.Page

    Private Const MYSESSIONKEY As String = "mykey"
    Public Property MyKey() As String
        Get
            Return CType(Session(MYSESSIONKEY), String)
        End Get
        Set(ByVal value As String)
            Session(MYSESSIONKEY) = value
        End Set
    End Property
End Class
```

C#

```csharp
using System;
using System.Web;

public class SmartSessionPage : System.Web.UI.Page
{
    private const string MYKEY = "mykey";
    public string MyKey
    {
        get
        {
            return (string)Session[MYKEY];
        }
        set
        {
            Session[MYKEY] = value;
        }
    }
}
```

Now, return to your code from Listing 19-1 and derive your pages from this new base class. To do this, change the base class in the code-beside files to inherit from `SmartSessionPage`. Listing 19-4 shows how the class in the code-behind file derives from the `SmartSessionPage`, which in turn derives from `System.Web.UI.Page`. Listing 19-4 outlines the differences to make to Listing 19-1.

Listing 19-4: Deriving from the new base page

VB–ASPX

```
<%@ Page Language="VB" AutoEventWireup="false" CodeFile="Default.aspx.vb"
    Inherits="_Default" %>
```

VB–Default.aspx.vb Code

```
Partial Class _Default
    Inherits SmartSessionPage

    Protected Sub Button1_Click(ByVal sender As Object, ByVal e As System.EventArgs)
        ' Session("mykey") = TextBox1.Text
        MyKey = TextBox1.Text
    End Sub
End Class
```

C#–ASPX

```
<%@ Page Language="C#" CodeFile="Default.aspx.cs" Inherits="_Default" %>
```

C#–Default.aspx.cs Code

```
public partial class _Default : SmartSessionPage
{
    protected void Button1_Click(object sender, EventArgs e)
    {
        //Session["mykey"] = TextBox1.Text;
        MyKey = TextBox1.Text;
    }
}
```

In this code, you change the access to the `Session` object so it uses the new public property. After the changes in Listing 19-3, all derived pages have a public property called `MyKey`. This property can be used without any concern about casting or Session key indexes. Additional specific properties can be added as other objects are included in the Session.

Here's an interesting language note: In Listing 19-3 the name of the private string value collides with the public property in VB because they differ only in case. In C#, a private variable named MYKEY and a public property named MyKey are both acceptable. Be aware of things like this when creating APIs that will be used with multiple languages. Aim for CLS compliance.

Advanced Techniques for Optimizing Session Performance

By default, all pages have write access to the `Session`. Because it's possible that more than one page from the same browser client might be requested at the same time (using frames, more than one browser window on the same machine, and so on), a page holds a reader/writer lock on the same `Session` for the duration of the page request. If a page has a writer lock on the same `Session`, all other pages requested in the same `Session` must wait until the first request finishes. To be clear, the `Session` is locked only for that SessionID. These locks don't affect other users with different `Sessions`.

In order to get the best performance out of your pages that use Session, ASP.NET allows you declare exactly what your page requires of the Session object via the EnableSessionState @Page attribute. The options are True, False, or ReadOnly:

❑ EnableSessionState="True": The page requires read and write access to the Session. The Session with that SessionID will be locked during each request.

❑ EnableSessionState="False": The page does not require access to the Session. If the code uses the Session object anyway, an HttpException is thrown stopping page execution.

❑ EnableSessionState="ReadOnly": The page requires read-only access to the Session. A reader lock is held on the Session for each request, but concurrent reads from other pages can occur. If a page is requested requiring read-only access and two other requests are queued up, one requesting read-only access and one requesting read/write access, the read-only page is executed while the read/write access page waits.

By modifying the @Page direction in default.aspx and retrieve.aspx to reflect each page's actual need, you affect performance when the site is under load. Add the EnableSessionState attribute to the pages as shown in the following code:

VB–Default.aspx
```
<%@ Page Language="VB" EnableSessionState="True" AutoEventWireup="false"
    CodeFile="Default.aspx.vb" Inherits="_Default" %>
```

VB–Retrieve.aspx
```
<%@ Page Language="VB" EnableSessionState="ReadOnly" AutoEventWireup="false"
    CodeFile="Retrieve.aspx.vb" Inherits="Retrieve" %>
```

C#–Default.asp
```
<%@ Page Language="C#" EnableSessionState="True"
    CodeFile="Default.aspx.cs" Inherits="_Default"%>
```

C#–Retrieve.aspx
```
<%@ Page Language="C#" EnableSessionState="ReadOnly"
    CodeFile="Retrieve.aspx.cs" Inherits="Retrieve" %>
```

Under the covers, ASP.NET is using marker interfaces from the System.Web.SessionState namespace to keep track of each page's needs. When the partial class for default.aspx is generated, it implements the IRequiresSessionState interface, whereas Retrieve.aspx implements IReadOnlySessionState. All HttpRequests are handled by objects that implement IHttpHandler. Pages are handled by a PageHandlerFactory. You can find more on HttpHandlers in Chapter 23. Internally, the SessionStateModule is executing code similar to the pseudocode that follows:

```
If TypeOf HttpContext.Current.Handler Is IReadOnlySessionState Then
    Return SessionStateStore.GetItem(itemKey)
Else 'If TypeOf HttpContext.Current.Handler Is IRequiresSessionState
    Return SessionStateStore.GetItemExclusive(itemKey)
End If
```

As the programmer, you know things about the intent of your pages at compile time that ASP.NET can't figure out at runtime. By including the EnableSessionState attribute in your pages, you allow ASP.NET to operate more efficiently. Remember, ASP.NET always makes the most conservative decision unless you give it more information to act upon.

> *Performance Tip:* **If you're coding a page that doesn't require anything of the Session, by all means, set** `EnableSessionState="False"`. **This causes ASP.NET to schedule that page ahead of pages that require Session and helps with the overall scalability of your app. Additionally, if your application doesn't use Session at all, set** `Mode="Off"` **in your** `web.config` **file to reduce overhead for the entire application.**

Out-of-Process Session State

Out-of-process session state is held in a process called `aspnet_state.exe` that runs as a Windows Service. You can start the ASP.NET state service by using the Services MMC snap-in or by running the following `net` command from the command line:

```
net start aspnet_state
```

By default, the State Service listens on TCP port 42424, but this port can be changed at the registry key for the service, as shown in the following code. The State Service is not started by default.

```
HKEY_LOCAL_MACHINE\SYSTEM\CurrentControlSet\Services\
aspnet_state\Parameters\Port
```

Change the `web.config`'s settings from `InProc` to `StateServer`, as shown in the following code. Additionally, you must include the `stateConnectionString` attribute with the IP address and port on which the Session State Service is running. In a Web farm (a group of more than one Web server), you could run the State Service on any single server or on a separate machine entirely. In this example, the State Server is running on the local machine, so the IP address is the localhost IP 127.0.0.1. If you run the State Server on another machine, make sure the appropriate port is open — in this case, TCP port 42424.

```
<configuration>
    <system.web>
        <sessionState mode="StateServer"
            stateConnectionString="tcpip=127.0.0.1:42424"/>
    </system.web>
</configuration>
```

The State Service used is always the most recent one installed with ASP.NET. That means that if you are running ASP.NET 2.0 and 1.1 on the same machine, all the states stored in `Session` objects for any and all versions of ASP.NET are kept together in a single instance of the ASP.NET 2.0 State Service.

Because your application's code runs in the ASP.NET Worker Process (`aspnet_wp.exe`, or `w3wp.exe`) and the State Service runs in the separate `aspnet_state.exe` process, objects stored in the Session can't be stored as references. Your objects must physically leave the worker process via binary serialization.

> For a world-class, highly available, and scalable Web site, consider using a Session model other than InProc. Even if you can guarantee via your load-balancing appliance that your Sessions will be *sticky*, you still have application-recycling issues to contend with. The out-of-process state service's data is persisted across application pool recycles but not computer reboots. However, if your state is stored on a different machine entirely, it will survive Web Server recycles and reboots.

Only classes that have been marked with the [Serializable] attribute may be serialized. In the context of the Session object, think of the [Serializable] attribute as a permission slip for instances of your class to leave the worker process.

Update the SmartSessionPage file in your \App_Code directory to include a new class called Person, as shown in Listing 19-5. Be sure to mark it as Serializable or you will see the error shown in Figure 19-4.

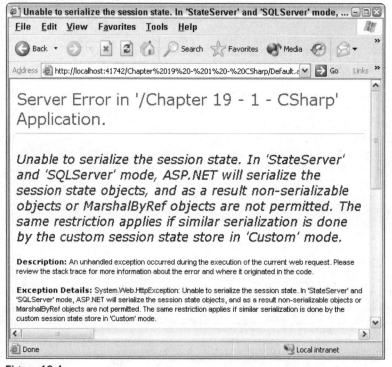

Figure 19-4

As long as you've marked your objects as [Serializable], they'll be allowed out of the ASP.NET process. Notice that the objects in Listing 19-5 are marked [Serializable].

Listing 19-5: A serializable object that can be used in the out-of-process Session

VB
```vb
<Serializable()> _
Public Class Person
    Public firstName As String
    Public lastName As String

    Public Overrides Function ToString() As String
        Return String.Format("Person Object: {0} {1}", firstName, lastName)
    End Function
End Class
```

C#
```csharp
[Serializable]
public class Person
{
    public string firstName;
    public string lastName;

    public override string ToString()
    {
        return String.Format("Person Object: {0} {1}", firstName, lastName);
    }
}
```

Because you put an instance of the `Person` class from Listing 19-5 into the `Session` object that is currently configured as `StateServer`, you should add a strongly typed property to the base `Page` class from Listing 19-3. In Listing 19-6 you see the strongly typed property added. Note the cast on the property `Get`, and the strongly typed return value indicating that this property deals only with objects of type `Person`.

Listing 19-6: Adding a strongly typed property to SmartSessionPage

VB
```vb
Public Class SmartSessionPage
    Inherits System.Web.UI.Page

    Private Const MYSESSIONPERSONKEY As String = "myperson"

    Public Property MyPerson() As Person
        Get
            Return CType(Session(MYSESSIONPERSONKEY), Person)
        End Get
        Set(ByVal value As Person)
            Session(MYSESSIONPERSONKEY) = value
        End Set
    End Property

End Class
```

C#
```csharp
public class SmartSessionPage : System.Web.UI.Page
{
    private const string MYPERSON = "myperson";

    public Person MyPerson
    {
        get
        {
            return (Person)Session[MYPERSON];
        }
        set
        {
        Session[MYPERSON] = value;
        }
    }
}
```

Now, add code to create a new `Person`, populate its fields from the text box, and put the instance into the now-out-of-process Session State Service. Then, retrieve the `Person` and write its values out to the browser using the overloaded `ToString()` method from Listing 19-5.

> Certain classes in the Framework Class Library are not marked as serializable. If you use objects of this type within your own objects, these objects are *not* serializable at all. For example, if you include a DataRow field in a class and add your object to the State Service, you receive a message telling you it ". . . is not marked as serializable" because the DataRow includes objects that are not serializable.

In Listing 19-7, the value of the `TextBox` is split into a string array and the first two strings are put into a `Person` instance. For example, if you entered `"Scott Hanselman"` as a value, `"Scott"` is put into `Person.firstName` and `"Hanselman"` is put into `Person.lastName`. The values you enter should appear when they are retrieved later in `Retrieve.aspx` and written out to the browser with the overloaded `ToString` method.

Listing 19-7: Setting and retrieving objects from the Session using State Service and a base page

VB–Default.aspx.vb
```vb
Partial Class _Default
    Inherits SmartSessionPage

    Protected Sub Button1_Click(ByVal sender As Object, ByVal e As System.EventArgs)
        Dim names As String()
        names = TextBox1.Text.Split(" "c) ' " "c creates a char
        Dim p As New Person()
        p.firstName = names(0)
        p.lastName = names(1)
        Session("myperson") = p
        }
    End Sub
End Class
```

VB–Retrieve.aspx.vb

```
Partial Class Retrieve
    Inherits SmartSession Page
    Protected Sub Page_Load(ByVal sender As Object, ByVal e As System.EventArgs) _
            Handles Me.Load
        Dim p As Person = MyPerson
        Response.Write(p) ' ToString will be called!
    End Sub
End Class
```

C#–Default.aspx.cs

```
public partial class _Default : SmartSessionPage
{
    protected void Button1_Click(object sender, EventArgs e)
    {
        string[] names = TextBox1.Text.Split(' ');
        Person p = new Person();
        p.firstName = names[0];
        p.lastName = names[1];

        Session["myperson"] = p;
    }
}
```

C#–Retrieve.aspx.cs

```
public partial class Retrieve : SmartSessionPage
{
    protected void Page_Load(object sender, EventArgs e)
    {
        Person p = MyPerson;
        Response.Write(p); //ToString will be called!
    }
}
```

Now, launch the browser, enter your name (or "Scott Hanselman" if you like), click the button to store it in the Session, and then visit Retrieve.aspx via the hyperlink. You see the result of the ToString() method via Response.Write, as shown in Figure 19-5.

The completed code and techniques shown in Listing 19-7 illustrate a number of best practices for session management:

❑ Mark your objects as Serializable if you might ever use non-In-Proc session state.

❑ Even better, do all your development with a local session state server. This forces you to discover non-serializable objects early, gives you a sense of the performance and memory usages of aspnet_state.exe, and allows you to choose from any of the session options at deployment time.

❑ Use a base Page class or helper object with strongly typed properties to simplify your code. It enables you to hide the casts made to session keys otherwise referenced throughout your code.

These best practices apply to all state storage methods, including SQL session state.

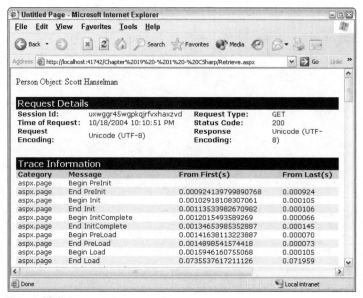

Figure 19-5

SQL-Backed Session State

ASP.NET sessions can also be stored in a SQL Server database. InProc offers speed, StateServer offers a resilience/speed balance, and storing sessions in SQL Server offers resilience that can serve sessions to a large Web farm that persists across IIS restarts, if necessary.

SQL-backed session state is configured with `aspnet_regsql.exe`. This tool adds and removes support for a number of ASP.NET features such as cache dependency (see Chapter 20) and personalization/membership (Chapters 15 and 16) as well as session support. When you run `aspnet_regsql.exe` from the command line without any options, surprisingly, it pops up a GUI as shown in Figure 19-6. This utility is located in the .NET Framework's installed directory, usually `c:\windows\microsoft.net\framework\<version>`.

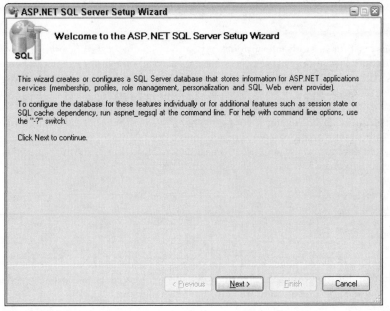

Figure 19-6

The text of the dialog shown in Figure 19-6 contains instructions to run `aspnet_regsql` from the command line with a "`-?`" switch. You have a huge number of options, so you'll want to pipe it through in a form like `aspnet_regsql -? | more`. You see the session-state–specific options shown here:

```
                            -- SESSION STATE OPTIONS --

-ssadd                      Add support for SQLServer mode session state.

-ssremove                   Remove support for SQLServer mode session state.

-sstype t|p|c               Type of session state support:

                            t: temporary. Session state data is stored in the
                            "tempdb" database. Stored procedures for managing
                            session are installed in the "ASPState" database.
                            Data is not persisted if you restart SQL. (Default)

                            p: persisted. Both session state data and the stored
                            procedures are stored in the "ASPState" database.

                            c: custom. Both session state data and the stored
                            procedures are stored in a custom database. The
                            database name must be specified.
```

```
-d <database>              The name of the custom database to use if -sstype is
                           "c".
```

Three options exist for session state support: t, p, and c. The most significant difference is that the
-sstype t option does not persist session state data across SQL Server restarts, whereas the -sstype p
option does. Alternatively, you can specify a custom database with the -c option and give the database
name with -d database.

The following command-line example configures your system for SQL session support with the SQL
Server on localhost with an sa password of *wrox* and a persistent store in the ASPState database (certainly,
you know not to deploy your system using sa and a weak password, but this simplifies the example). If
you're using SQL Express, replace "localhost" with ".\SQLEXPRESS".

```
C:\ >aspnet_regsql -S localhost -U sa -P wrox -ssadd -sstype p
Start adding session state.
..........
Finished.
```

Next, open up Enterprise Manager and look at the newly created database. Two tables are created —
ASPStateTempApplications and ASPStateTempSessions — as well as a series of stored procedures to
support moving the session back and forth from SQL to memory.

If your SQL Server has its security locked down tight, you might get an Error 15501 after executing
aspnet_regsql.exe that says "An error occurred during the execution of the SQL file
'InstallSqlState.sql'." The SQL error number is 15501 and the SqlException message is: This
module has been marked OFF. Turn on 'Agent XPs' in order to be able to access the module.
If the job does not exist, an error from msdb.dbo.sp_delete_job is expected. This is a
rather obscure message, but aspnet_regsql.exe is trying to tell you that the extended stored
procedures it needs to enable session state are not enabled for security reasons. You'll need to allow
them explicitly. To do so, execute the following commands within the SQL Server 2005 Query Analyzer
or the SQL Server 2005 Express Manager:

```
USE master
EXECUTE sp_configure 'show advanced options', 1
RECONFIGURE WITH OVERRIDE
GO
EXECUTE sp_configure 'Agent XPs', 1
RECONFIGURE WITH OVERRIDE
GO
EXECUTE sp_configure 'show advanced options', 0
RECONFIGURE WITH OVERRIDE
GO
```

Now, change the web.config <sessionState> element to use SQL Server, as well as the new
connection string:

```
<sessionState mode="SQLServer" sqlConnectionString="data source=127.0.0.1;user
id=sa;password=Wrox"/>
```

The session code shown in Listing 19-7 continues to work as before. However, if you open up the ASPStateTempSessions table, you see the serialized objects. Notice in Figure 19-7 that the Session ID from the trace appears as a primary key in a row in the ASPStateTempSessions table.

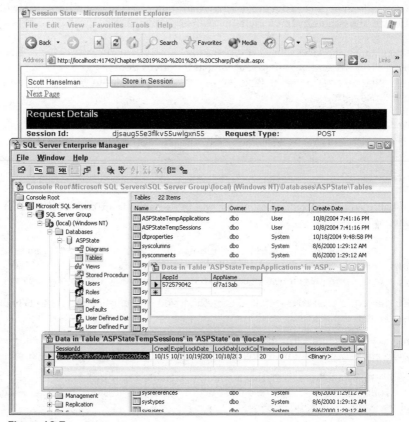

Figure 19-7

Figure 19-7 shows the SessionId as seen in the Request Details of ASP.NET tracing and how that SessionId appears in the SessionId column of the ASPStateTempSessions table in the ASPState database just created. Notice also the ASPStateTempApplications table that keeps track of each IIS application that may be using the same database to manage sessions.

If you want to use your own database to store session state, you specify the database name with the -d <database> switch of aspnet_regsql.exe and include the allowCustomSqlDatabase="true" attribute and the name of the database in the connection string:

```
<sessionState allowCustomSqlDatabase="true" mode="SQLServer"
sqlConnectionString="data source=127.0.0.1;database=MyCustomASPStateDatabase;"/>
```

The user ID and password can be included in the connection string; or Windows Integrated Security can be used if the ASP.NET Worker Process's identity is configured with access in SQL Server.

Extending Session State with Other Providers

ASP.NET 2.0 Session State is built on a new, extensible, provider-based storage model. You can implement custom providers that store session data in other storage mechanisms simply by deriving from SessionStateStoreProviderBase. This extensibility feature also allows you to generate session IDs via your own algorithms by implementing ISessionIDManager.

You start by creating a class that inherits from SessionStateStoreProviderBase. The session module will call methods on any session provider as long as it derives from SessionStateStoreProviderBase. Register your custom provider in your application's web.config, as in the following example:

```
<sessionState mode ="Custom" customProvider ="WroxProvider">
    <providers >
        <add name ="WroxProvider" type ="Wrox.WroxStore, WroxSessionSupplier"/>
    </providers>
</sessionState>
```

ASP.NET initializes the SessionStateModule, and these methods are called on any custom implementation:

❑   Initialize: This method is inherited ultimately from System.Configuration .Provider.ProviderBase and is called immediately after the constructor. With this method, you set your provider name and call up to the base implementation of Initialize.

❑   SetItemExpireCallback: With this method, you can register any methods to be called when a session item expires.

❑   InitializeRequest: This method is called by the SessionStateModule for each request. This is an early opportunity to get ready for any requests for data that are coming.

❑   CreateNewStoreData: With this method, you create a new instance of SessionStateStoreData, the data structure that holds session items, the session timeout values, and any static items.

When a session item is requested, ASP.NET calls your implementation to retrieve it. Implement the following methods to retrieve items:

❑   GetItemExclusive: This method is where you get SessionStateStoreData from your chosen store. You may have created an Oracle provider, stored data in XML, or wherever you like.

❑   GetItem: This is your opportunity to retrieve it as you did in GetItemExclusive except without exclusive locking. You may or may not care, depending on what backing store you've chosen.

When it's time to store an item, the following method is called:

❑   SetAndReleaseItemExculsive: Here you should save the SessionStateStoreData object to your custom store.

Expect to see a number of third-party session state providers available to both open source and for sale soon after the release of ASP.NET 2.0.

> ScaleOut Software released the first 3rd party ASP.NET 2.0 State Provider in the form of their StateServer product. It fills a niche between the ASP.NET included singleton StateServer and the SQL Server Database State Provider. ScaleOut Software's StateServer is an out-of-process service that runs on each machine in the Web Farm and ensures that session state is stored in a transparent and distributed manner among machines in the farm. You can learn more about StateServer and their ASP.NET 2.0 Session Provider at http://www.scaleoutsoftware.com/asp.net2.0.htm.

The derivation-based provider module for things such as session state will no doubt create a rich ecosystem of enthusiasts who will help push the functionality to new places Microsoft did not expect.

Cookieless Session State

In the previous example, the ASP.NET Session State ID was stored in a cookie. Some devices don't support cookies, or a user may have turned off cookie support in his browser. Cookies are convenient because the values are passed back and forth with every request and response. That means every HttpRequest contains cookie values, and every HttpResponse contains cookie values. What is the only other thing that is passed back and forth with every Request and Response? The URL.

If you include the cookieless="UseUri" attribute in the web.config, ASP.NET does not send the ASP.NET Session ID back as a cookie. Instead, it modifies every URL to include the Session ID just before the requested page:

```
<sessionState mode="SQLServer" cookieless="UseUri" sqlConnectionString="data
source=127.0.0.1;user id=sa;password=Wrox"></sessionState>
```

Notice that the Session ID appears in the URL as if it were a directory of its own situated between the actual Web site virtual directory and the page. With this change, server-side user controls such as the HyperLink control, used in Listing 19-1, have their properties automatically modified. The link in Listing 19-1 could have been hard-coded as HTML directly in the Designer, but then ASP.NET could not modify the target URL shown in Figure 19-8.

The Session ID is a string that contains only the ASCII characters allowed in a URL. That makes sense when you realize that moving from a cookie-based Session-State system to a cookieless system requires putting that Session State value in the URL.

Notice in Figure 19-8 that the request URL contains a Session ID within parentheses. One disadvantage to cookieless Sessions is how easily they can be tampered with. Certainly, cookies can be tampered with using HTTP sniffers, but URLS can be edited by anyone. The only way Session State is maintained is if *every* URL includes the Session ID in this way.

Figure 19-8

Additionally, all URLS *must* be relative. Remember that the Session ID appears as if it were a directory. The Session is lost if an absolute URL such as /myapp/retrieve.aspx is invoked. If you are generating URLs on the server side, use HttpResponse.ApplyAppPathModifier(). It changes a URL when the Session ID is embedded, as shown here:

```
Response.Write(Response.ApplyAppPathModifier("foo/bar.aspx"));
```

The previous line generates a URL similar to the following:

```
/myapp/(S(avkbnbml4n1n5mi5dmfqnu45))/foo/bar.aspx
```

Notice that not only was session information added to the URL, but it was also converted from a relative URL to an absolute URL, including the application's virtual directory. This method can be useful when you need to use Response.Redirect or build a URL manually to redirect from an HTTP page to an HTTPS page while still maintaining cookieless session state.

Choosing the Correct Way to Maintain State

Now that you're familiar with the variety of options available for maintaining state in ASP.NET 2.0, here's some real-world advice from production systems. The In-Process (InProc) Session provider is the fastest method, of course, because everything held in memory is a live object reference. This provider is held in the HttpApplication's cache and, as such, it is susceptible to application recycles. If you use Windows 2000 Server or Windows XP, the aspnet_wp.exe process manages the ASP.NET HTTP pipeline. If you're running Windows 2003 Server, w3wp.exe is the default process that hosts the runtime.

You must find a balance between the robustness of the out-of-process state service and the speed of the in-process provider. In my experience, generally the out-of-process state service is usually about 15 percent slower than the in-process provider because of the serialization overhead and marshaling. SQL Session State is about 25 percent slower than InProc. Of course your mileage will likely vary. Don't let these numbers concern you too much. Be sure to do scalability testing on your applications before you panic and make inappropriate decisions.

It's worth saying again: We recommend that all developers use Out-Of-Process Session State during development, even if this is not the way your application will be deployed. Forcing yourself to use the Out-Of-Process provider enables you to catch any potential problems with custom objects that do not carry the `Serializable` attribute. If you design your entire site using the In-Process provider and then discover, late in the project, that requirements force you to switch to the SQL or Out-Of-Process providers, you have no guarantee that your site will work as you wrote it. Developing with the Out-Of-Process provider gives you the best of both worlds and does not affect your final deployment method. Think of it as an insurance policy that costs you nothing upfront.

The Application Object

The `Application` object is the equivalent of a bag of global variables for your ASP.NET application. Global variables have been considered harmful for many years in other programming environments, and ASP.NET is no different. You should give some thought to what you want to put in the `Application` object and why. Often, the more flexible `Cache` object that helps you control an object's lifetime is the more useful. Caching is discussed in depth in Chapter 20.

The `Application` object is not global to the machine; it's global to the `HttpApplication`. If you are running in the context of a Web farm, each ASP.NET application on each Web server has its own `Application` object. Because ASP.NET applications are multithreaded and are receiving requests that are being handled by your code on multiple threads, access to the `Application` object should be managed using the `Application.Lock` and `Application.Unlock` methods. If your code doesn't call Unlock directly (which it should, shame on you) the lock is removed implicitly at the end of the `HttpRequest` that called Lock originally.

This small example shows locking the `Application` object just before inserting an object. Other threads that might be attempting to write to the `Application` will wait until it is unlocked. This example assumes there is an integer already stored in `Application` under the key `GlobalCount`.

VB
```
Application.Lock()
Application("GlobalCount") = CType(Application("GlobalCount"), Integer) + 1
Application.UnLock()
```

C#
```
Application.Lock();
Application["GlobalCount"] = (int)Application["GlobalCount"] + 1;
Application.UnLock();
```

Object references can be stored in the `Application`, as in the `Session`, but they must be cast back to their known types when retrieved (as shown in the preceding sample code).

QueryStrings

The URL, or QueryString, is the idea place for navigation-specific — not user-specific — data. The QueryString is the most hackable element on a Web site, and that fact can work for you or against you. For example, if your navigation scheme uses your own page IDs at the end of a query string (such as `/localhost/mypage.aspx?id=54`) be prepared for a user to play with that URL in his browser, and try every value for `id` under the sun. Don't blindly cast `id` to an int, and if you do, have a plan if it fails. A good idea is to return `Response.StatusCode = 404` when someone changes a URL to an unreasonable value. Another fine idea that Amazon.com implemented was the *Smart 404* — perhaps you've see these: They say "Sorry you didn't find what you're looking for. Did you mean _____?"

Remember, your URLs are the first thing your users may see, even before they see your HTML. *Hackable* URLs — hackable even by my mom — make your site more accessible. Which of these URLs is friendlier and more hackable (for the *right* reason)?

```
http://reviews.cnet.com/Philips_42PF9996/4505-6482_7-31081946.html?tag=cnetfd.sd
```

or

```
http://www.hanselman.com/blog/CategoryView.aspx?category=Movies
```

Cookies

Do you remember the great cookie scare of 1997? Most users weren't quite sure just what a cookie was, but they were all convinced that cookies were evil and were storing their personal information. Back then, it was likely personal information was stored in the cookie! Never, ever store sensitive information, like a user ID or password, in a cookie. Cookies should be used only to store non-sensitive information, or information that can be retrieved from an authoritative source. Cookies shouldn't be trusted, and their contents should be able to be validated. For example, if a Forms Authentication cookie has been tampered with, the user is logged out and an exception is thrown. If an invalid session ID cookie is passed in for an expired Session, a new cookie can be assigned.

When you store information in cookies, remember that it's quite different from storing data in the `Session` object:

- ❑ Cookies are passed back and forth on *every* request. That means you are paying for the size of your cookie during *every* HTTP GET and HTTP POST.

- ❑ If you have ten 1-pixel spacer GIFs on your page used for table layouts, the user's browser is sending the same cookie *eleven* times: once for the page itself, and once for each spacer GIF, even if the GIF is already cached.

- ❑ Cookies can be stolen, sniffed, and faked. If your code counts on a cookie's value, have a plan in your code for the inevitability that cookie will get corrupted or be tampered with.

- ❑ What is the expected behavior of your application if a cookie doesn't show? What if it's 4096 bytes? Be prepared. You should design your application around the "principle of least surprise." Your application should attempt to heal itself if cookies are found missing or if they are larger than expected.

- ❑ Think twice before Base64 encoding anything large and placing it in a cookie. If your design depends on this kind of technique, rethink using either the Session or another backing-store.

PostBacks and Cross-Page PostBacks

In classic ASP, in order to detect logical events like a button being clicked, developers had to inspect the `Form` collection of the `Request` object. Yes, a button was clicked in the user's browser, but no object model was built on top of stateless HTTP and HTML. ASP.NET 1.*x* introduced the concept of the postback, wherein a server-side event was raised to alert the developer of a client-side action. If a button is clicked on the browser, the Form collection is POSTed back to the server, but now ASP.NET allowed the developer to write code in events such as `Button1_Click` and `TextBox1_Changed`.

However, this technique of posting *back* to the same page is counter-intuitive, especially when you are designing user interfaces that aim to create wizards to give the user the sense of forward motion.

This chapter is about all aspects of state management. Postbacks and cross-page postbacks, however, are covered extensively in Chapter 3 so this chapter touches on them only in the context of state management. Postbacks were introduced in ASP.NET 1.*x* to provide an eventing subsystem for Web development. It was inconvenient to have only single-page postbacks in 1.*x*, however, and that caused many developers to store small objects in the `Session` on a postback and then redirect to the next page to pick up the stored data. With cross-page postbacks, data can be posted "forward" to a different page, often obviating the need for storing small bits of data that could be otherwise passed directly.

ASP.NET 2.0 adds the notion of a `PostBackUrl` to all the Button controls including LinkButton and ImageButton. The `PostBackUrl` property is both part of the markup when a control is presented as part of the ASPX page, as seen in the following, and is a property on the server-side component that's available in the code-behind:

```
<asp:Button PostBackUrl="url" ..>
```

When a button control with the `PostBackUrl` property set is clicked, the page does not post back to itself; instead, the page is posted to the URL assigned to the button control's `PostBackUrl` property. When a cross-page request occurs, the `PreviousPage` property of the current `Page` class holds a reference to the page that caused the postback. To get a control reference from the `PreviousPage`, use the `Controls` property or use the `FindControl` method.

Create a fresh site with a `Default.aspx` (as shown in Listing 19-8). Put a `TextBox` and a `Button` on it, and set the `Button PostBackUrl` property to `Step2.aspx`. Then create a `Step2.aspx` page with a single `Label` and add a `Page_Load` handler by double-clicking the HTML Designer.

Listing 19-8: Cross-page postbacks

Default.aspx

```
<!DOCTYPE html PUBLIC "-//W3C//DTD XHTML 1.1//EN"
"http://www.w3.org/TR/xhtml11/DTD/xhtml11.dtd">
<html xmlns="http://www.w3.org/1999/xhtml" >
<head runat="server">
    <title>Cross-page PostBacks</title>
</head>
<body>
    <form id="form1" runat="server">
    <div>
        <asp:TextBox ID="TextBox1" Runat="server"></asp:TextBox>
        <asp:Button ID="Button1" Runat="server" Text="Button"
```

(continued)

Listing 19-8: *(continued)*

```
                PostBackUrl="~/Step2.aspx" />
    </div>
    </form>
</body>
</html>
```

Step2.aspx

```
<!DOCTYPE html PUBLIC "-//W3C//DTD XHTML 1.0 Transitional//EN"
"http://www.w3.org/TR/xhtml1/DTD/xhtml1-transitional.dtd">
<html xmlns="http://www.w3.org/1999/xhtml" >
<head runat="server">
    <title>Step 2</title>
</head>
<body>
    <form id="form1" runat="server">
    <div>
        <asp:Label ID="Label1" runat="server" Text="Label"></asp:Label>
    </div>
    </form>
</body>
 </html>
```

VB–Step2.aspx.vb

```
Partial Class Step2
    Inherits System.Web.UI.Page

    Protected Sub Page_Load(ByVal sender As Object, ByVal e As System.EventArgs) _
            Handles Me.Load

        If PreviousPage IsNot Nothing AndAlso PreviousPage.IsCrossPagePostBack Then
            Dim text As TextBox = _
                    CType(PreviousPage.FindControl("TextBox1"), TextBox)
            If text IsNot Nothing Then
                Label1.Text = text.Text
            End If
        End If

    End Sub

End Class
```

CS–Step2.aspx.cs

```
using System;
using System.Web.UI.WebControls;

public partial class Step2 : System.Web.UI.Page
{
    protected void Page_Load(object sender, EventArgs e)
    {
        if (PreviousPage != null && PreviousPage.IsCrossPagePostBack)
        {
            TextBox text = PreviousPage.FindControl("TextBox1") as TextBox;
            if (text != null)
```

```
        {
            Label1.Text = text.Text;
        }
    }
}

}
```

In Listing 19-8, `Default.aspx` posts *forward* to `Step2.aspx`, which can then access the `Page`
`.PreviousPage` property and retrieve a populated instance of the `Page` that caused the postback. A call
to `FindControl` and a cast retrieves the `TextBox` from the previous page and copies its value into the
Label of `Step2.aspx`.

Hidden Fields, ViewState, and ControlState

Hidden input fields like `<input type="hidden" name="foo">` are sent back as name/value pairs in a
Form POST exactly like any other control, except they are not rendered. Think of them as hidden text
boxes. Figure 19-9 shows a HiddenField control on the Visual Studio Designer with its available
properties. Hidden fields are available in both ASP.NET 1.*x* and 2.0.

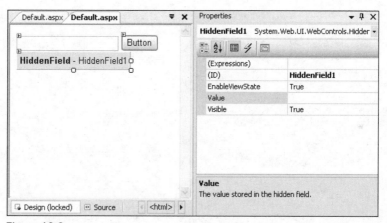

Figure 19-9

ViewState, on the other hand, exposes itself as a collection of key/value pairs like the `Session` object,
but renders itself as a hidden field with the name "`__VIEWSTATE`" like this:

```
<input type="hidden" name="__VIEWSTATE" value="/AAASSDAS...Y/lOI=" />
```

Any objects put into the ViewState must be marked `Serializable`. ViewState serializes the objects with
a special binary formatter called the LosFormatter. LOS stands for limited object serialization. It serializes
any kind of object, but it is optimized to contain strings, arrays, and hashtables.

To see this at work, create a new page and drag a `TextBox`, `Button`, and `HiddenField` onto it. Double-click
in the Designer to create a `Page_Load` and include the code from Listing 19-9. This example adds a string to
`HiddenField.Value`, but adds an instance of a `Person` to the `ViewState` collection. This listing illustrates
that while ViewState is persisted in a single HTML `TextBox` on the client, it can contain both simple types

such as strings, and complex types such as Person. This technique has been around since ASP.NET 1.*x* and continues to be a powerful and simple way to persist small pieces of data without utilizing server resources.

Listing 19-9: Hidden fields and ViewState

ASPX

```
<!DOCTYPE html PUBLIC "-//W3C//DTD XHTML 1.1//EN"
 "http://www.w3.org/TR/xhtml11/DTD/xhtml11.dtd">
<html xmlns="http://www.w3.org/1999/xhtml" >
<head runat="server">
    <title>Hidden Fields and ViewState</title>
</head>
<body>
    <form id="form1" runat="server">
    <div>
        <asp:TextBox ID="TextBox1" Runat="server"></asp:TextBox>
        <asp:Button ID="Button1" Runat="server" Text="Button"  />
        <asp:HiddenField ID="HiddenField1" Runat="server" />
    </div>
    </form>
</body>
</html>
```

VB

```
<Serializable> _
Public Class Person
    Public firstName As String
    Public lastName As String
End Class

Partial Class _Default
    Inherits System.Web.UI.Page

    Protected Sub Page_Load(ByVal sender As Object, ByVal e As System.EventArgs) _
            Handles Me.Load

        If Not Page.IsPostBack Then
            HiddenField1.Value = "foo"
            ViewState("AnotherHiddenValue") = "bar"

            Dim p As New Person
            p.firstName = "Scott"
            p.lastName = "Hanselman"
            ViewState("HiddenPerson") = p
        End If

    End Sub

End Class
```

C#

```
using System;
using System.Web.UI.WebControls;
using System.Web.UI.HtmlControls;
```

```
[Serializable]
public class Person
{
    public string firstName;
    public string lastName;
}
public partial class _Default : System.Web.UI.Page
{
    protected void Page_Load(object sender, EventArgs e)
    {
        if (!Page.IsPostBack)
        {
            HiddenField1.Value = "foo";
            ViewState["AnotherHiddenValue"] = "bar";

            Person p = new Person();
            p.firstName = "Scott";
            p.lastName = "Hanselman";
            ViewState["HiddenPerson"] = p;
        }
    }
}
```

In Listing 19-9, a string is added to a HiddenField and to the ViewState collection. Then a Person instance is added to the ViewState collection with another key. A fragment of the rendered HTML is shown in the following code:

```
<form method="post" action="Default.aspx" id="form1">
<div>
<input type="hidden" name="__VIEWSTATE"
value="/wEPDwULLTIxMjQ3OTEzODcPFgQeEkFub3RoZXJIaWRkZW5WYWx1ZQUDYmFyHgxIaWRkZW5QZXJz
b24ypwEAAQAAAP////8BAAAAAAAAAwCAAAAP3ZkcTVqYzdxLCBWZXJzaW9uPTAuMC4wLjAsIEN1bHR1cmU
9bmV1dHJhbCwgUHVibGljS2V5VG9rZW49bnVsbAUBAAAAE0RlZmF1bHRfYXNweCtQZXJzb24CAAAACWZpcn
N0TmFtZZQhsYXN0TmFtZQEBAgAAAAYDAAAABVNjb3R0BgQAAAAJSGFuc2VsbWFuC2RkI/CLauUviFo58BF8v
pSNsjY/lOI=" />
</div>
    <div>
        <input name="TextBox1" type="text" id="TextBox1" />
        <input type="submit" name="Button1" value="Button" id="Button1" />
        <input type="hidden" name="HiddenField1" id="HiddenField1" value="foo" />
    </div>
</form>
```

Notice that the ViewState value uses only valid ASCII characters to represent all its contents. Don't let the sheer mass of it fool you. It is big and it appears to be opaque. However, it's just a hidden text box and is automatically POSTed back to the server. The entire ViewState collection is available to you in the Page_Load. The value of the HiddenField is stored as plain text.

Neither ViewState nor Hidden Fields are acceptable for any kind of sensitive data.

> People often complain about the size of ViewState and turn if off completely
> without realizing its benefits. ASP.NET 2.0 cuts the size of serialized ViewState
> nearly in half. You can find a number of tips on using ViewState at http://
> www.hanselman.com/blog/SearchView.aspx?q=viewstate. Also, Fritz Onion's
> free ViewStateDecoder tool from http://www.pluralsight.com is a great way to
> gain insight into what's stored in your pages' ViewState.

By default, the ViewState field is sent to the client with a *salted hash* to prevent tampering. Salting means
that the ViewState's data has a unique value appended to it before it's encoded. As Keith Brown says
"Salt is just one ingredient to a good stew." The technique used is called HMAC, or hashed message
authentication code. As shown in the following code, you can use the `<machineKey>` element of the
`web.config file` to specify the `validationKey`, as well as the algorithm used to protect ViewState.
This section of the file and the `decryptionKey` attribute also affect how Forms Authentication cookies
are encrypted (see Chapter 18 for more on Forms Authentication).

```
<machineKey validationKey="AutoGenerate,IsolateApps"
  decryptionKey="AutoGenerate,IsolateApps" validation="SHA1" />
```

If you are running your application in a Web farm, `<validationKey>` and `<decryptionKey>` have to
be manually set to the same value. Otherwise, ViewState generated from one machine could be POSTed
back to a machine in the farm with a different key! The keys should be 128 characters long (the
maximum) and generated totally by random means. If you add `IsolateApps` to these values, ASP.NET
generates a unique encrypted key for each application using each application's application ID.

I like to use Security Guru Keith Brown's GenerateMachineKey tool, which you can find at http://
www.pluralsight.com/tools.aspx, *to generate these keys randomly.*

The `validation` attribute can be set to SHA1 or MD5 to provide tamper-proofing, but you can include
added protection by encrypting ViewState as well. In ASP.NET 1.1 you can only encrypt ViewState using
the value 3DES in the `validation` attribute, and ASP.NET 1.1 will use the key in the `decryptionKey`
attribute for encryption. However, ASP.NET 2.0 adds a new decryption attribute that is used exclusively
for specifying the encryption and decryption mechanisms for forms authentication tickets, and the
`validation` attribute is used exclusively for ViewState, which can now be encrypted using 3DES or
AES and the key stored in the `validationKey` attribute.

ASP.NET 2.0 also adds the `ViewStateEncryptionMode` attribute to the `<pages>` configuration element
with two possible values, `Auto` or `Always`. Setting the attribute to `Always` will force encryption of
ViewState, whereas setting it to `Auto` will encrypt ViewState only if a control requested encryption using
the new `Page.RegisterRequiresViewStateEncryption` method.

Added protection can be applied to ViewState by setting `Page.ViewStateUserKey` in the `Page_Init` to
a unique value such as the user's ID. This must be set in `Page_Init` because the key should be provided
to ASP.NET before ViewState is loaded or generated. For example:

```
protected void Page_Init (Object sender, EventArgs e)
{
    if (User.Identity.IsAuthenticated)
        ViewStateUserKey = User.Identity.Name;
}
```

When optimizing their pages, ASP.NET programmers often disable ViewState for many controls when that extra bit of state isn't absolutely necessary. However, in ASP.NET 1.*x*, disabling ViewState was a good way to break many third-party controls, as well as the included DataGrid's sorting functionality. ASP.NET 2.0 now includes a second, parallel ViewState-like collection called ControlState. This dictionary can be used for round-tripping crucial information of limited size that should not be disabled even when ViewState is. You should only store data in the ControlState collection that is absolutely critical to the functioning of the control.

Recognize that ViewState, and also ControlState, although not secure, is a good place to store small bits of a data and state that don't quite belong in a cookie or the Session object. If the data that must be stored is relatively small and local to that specific instance of your page, ViewState is a much better solution than littering the Session object with lots of transient data.

Using HttpContext.Current.Items for Very Short-Term Storage

The Items collection of HttpContext is one of ASP.NET's best-kept secrets. It is an IDictionary key/value collection of objects that's shared across the life of a single HttpRequest. That's a *single* HttpRequest. Why would you want to store state for such a short period of time? Consider these reasons:

❑ **When you share content between IHttpModules and IHttpHandlers.** If you write a custom IHttpModule, you can store context about the user for use later in a Page.

❑ **When you communicate between two instances of the same UserControl on the same page.** Imagine you are writing a UserControl that serves banner ads. Two instances of the same control could select their ads from HttpContext.Items to prevent showing duplicates on the same page.

❑ **When you store the results of expensive calls that might otherwise happen twice or more on a page.** If you have multiple UserControls that each show a piece of data from a large, more expensive database retrieval, those UserControls can retrieve the necessary data from HttpContext.Items. The database is hit only once.

❑ **When individual units within a single** HttpRequest **need to act on the same or similar data.**

The Items collection holds objects, just like many of the collections that have been used in this chapter. You need to cast those objects back to their specific type when they are retrieved.

Within a Web-aware Database Access Layer, per-request caching can be quickly implemented with the simple coding pattern shown in the following. Note that this sample code is a design pattern and there is no MyData class; it's for illustration.

```vb
VB
Public Shared Function GetExpensiveData(ID As Integer) As MyData
    Dim key as string = "data" & ID.ToString()
    Dim d as MyData = _
        CType(HttpContext.Current.Items(key), MyData)
    If d Is Nothing Then
```

```
      d = New Data()
      'Go to the Database, do whatever...
      HttpContext.Current.Items(key) = d
   End If
   Return d
End Function
```

C#
```
public static MyData GetExpensiveData(int ID)
{
   string key = "data" + ID.ToString();
   MyData d = (MyData) HttpContext.Current.Items[key];
   if (d == null)
   {
      d = new Data();
      //Go to the Database, do whatever...
      HttpContext.Current.Items[key] = d;
   }
   return d;
}
```

This code checks the Items collection of the current HttpContext to see if the data is already there. If not, the data is retrieved from the appropriate backing store and then stored in the Items collection. Subsequent calls to this function within the same HttpRequest receive the already-cached object.

As with all optimizations and caching, premature optimization is the root of all evil. Measure your need for caching, and measure your improvements. Don't cache just because it *feels right*; cache because it makes sense.

Summary

This chapter explored the many ways to manage State within your ASP.NET application. The Session object and its providers offer many choices. Each has its own pros and cons for managing state in the form of object references and serialized objects in a way that can be made largely transparent to the application. Server-side Session state data can have its unique identifying key stored in a cookie or the key can be carried along in the URL. Cookies can also be used independently to store small amounts of data and persist it between visits, albeit in much smaller amounts and with simpler types. Hidden fields, ViewState, ControlState, postbacks, and new cross-page postbacks offer new possibilities for managing small bits of state within a multi-page user experience. HttpContext.Current.Items offers a perfect place to hold transient state, living the life of only a single HttpRequest. QueryStrings are an old standby for holding non-private state that is appropriate for navigation.

ASP.NET 2.0 has improved on ASP.NET 1.1's state management options with a flexible Session State Provider module, the addition of Control State for user controls, and cross-page postbacks for a more mature programming model.

20

Caching

Performance is a key requirement for any application or piece of code that you develop. The browser helps with client-side caching of text and images, whereas the server-side caching you choose to implement is vital for creating the best possible performance. *Caching* is the process of storing frequently used data on the server to fulfill subsequent requests. You will discover that grabbing objects from memory is much faster than re-creating the Web pages or items contained in them from scratch each time they are requested. Caching increases your application's performance, scalability, and availability. The more you fine-tune your application's caching approach, the better it performs.

This chapter focuses on caching, including the new SQL invalidation caching capabilities that ASP.NET 2.0 provides. This chapter takes a close look at this unique aspect of caching. When you are using SQL cache invalidation, if the result set from SQL Server changes, the output cache can be triggered to change. This ensures that the end user always sees the latest result set, and the data presented is never stale. This is an outstanding new feature, so this chapter looks at SQL cache invalidation in-depth. This feature was frequently requested by developers using ASP.NET 1.0/1.1, so the ASP.NET team worked hard to bring it to ASP.NET 2.0. After introducing SQL cache invalidation, this chapter also covers other performance enhancements. It discusses the new Post-Cache Substitution feature, which caches entire pages while dynamically replacing specified bits of content. Last, the chapter covers a new capability that enables a developer to create custom dependencies.

Caching

In ASP.NET 1.0/1.1 and now in ASP.NET 2.0, developers deal with caching in several ways. First, you can cache an entire HTTP response (the entire Web page) using a mechanism called output caching. Two other methods are partial page caching and data caching. The following sections describe these methods.

Output Caching

Output caching is a way to keep the dynamically generated page content in the server's memory for later retrieval. After a cache is saved to memory, it can be used when any subsequent requests are made to the server. You apply output caching by inserting an `OutputCache` page directive at the top of an `.aspx` page, as follows:

```
<%@ OutputCache Duration="60" VaryByParam="None" %>
```

The `Duration` attribute defines the number of seconds a page is stored in memory. The `VaryByParam` attribute determines which versions of the page output are actually cached. You can generate different responses based on whether an HTTP-POST or HTTP-GET response is required. Other than the attributes for the `OutputCache` directive, ASP.NET includes the `VaryByHeader`, `VaryByCustom`, `VaryByControl`, and `Location` attributes. Additionally, the `Shared` attribute can affect UserControls, as you'll see later.

Caching in ASP.NET is implemented as an `HttpModule` that listens to all `HttpRequests` that come through the ASP.NET worker process. The `OutputCacheModule` listens to the application's `ResolveRequestCache` and `UpdateRequestCache` events, handles cache hits and misses, and returns the cached HTML, bypassing the Page Handler if need be.

VaryByParam

The `VaryByParam` attribute can specify which `QueryString` parameters cause a new version of the page to be cached:

```
<%@ OutputCache Duration="90" VaryByParam="pageId;subPageId" %>
```

For example, if you have a page called `navigation.aspx` that includes navigation information in the `QueryString`, such as `pageId` and `subPageId`, the `OutputCache` directive shown here caches the page for every different value of `pageId` and `subPageId`. In this example, the number of pages is best expressed with an equation:

```
cacheItems = (num of pageIds) * (num of subPageIds)
```

where `cacheItems` is the number of rendered HTML pages that would be stored in the cache. Pages are cached only after they're requested and pass through the `OutputCacheModule`. The maximum amount of cache memory in this case is used only after every possible combination is visited at least once. Although these are just *potential* maximums, creating an equation that represents your system's potential maximum is an important exercise.

If you want to cache a new version of the page based on any differences in the `QueryString` parameters, use `VaryByParam="*"`, as in the following code.

```
<%@ OutputCache Duration="90" VaryByParam="*" %>
```

It's important to "do the math" when using the VaryBy attributes. For example, you could add `VaryByHeader` and cache a different version of the page based on the browser's reported `User-Agent` HTTP Header.

```
<%@ OutputCache Duration="90" VaryByParam="*" VaryByHeader="User-Agent"%>
```

Literally dozens, if not hundreds, of `User-Agent` strings exist in the wild; this `OutputCache` directive could multiply into thousands of different versions of this page being cached, depending on server load. In this case, you should measure the cost of the caching against the cost of re-creating the page dynamically.

> Always cache what will give you the biggest performance gain, and prove that assumption with testing. Don't "cache by coincidence" using attributes like `VaryByParam="*"`. In order to see the most dramatic effects, cache the least possible amount of data.

VaryByControl

`VaryByControl` can be a very easy way to get some serious performance gains from complicated UserControls that render a lot of HTML that doesn't change often. For example, imagine a UserControl that renders a ComboBox showing the names of all the countries in the world. Perhaps those names are retrieved from a database and rendered in the combo box as follows:

```
<%@ OutputCache Duration="2592000" VaryByControl="comboBoxOfCountries" %>
```

Certainly the names of the world's countries don't change that often, so the `Duration` might be set to a month (in seconds).

VaryByCustom

Although the `VaryBy` attributes offer a great deal of power, sometimes you need more flexibility. If you want to take the `OutputCache` directive from the previous navigation example and cache by a value stored in a cookie, you can add `VaryByCustom`. The value of `VaryByCustom` is passed into the `GetVaryByCustomString` method that can be added to the `Global.asax.cs`. This method is called every time the page is requested, and it is the function's responsibility to return a value.

A different version of the page is cached for each unique value returned. For example, say your users have a cookie called `Language` that has three potential values: en, es, and fr. You want to allow users to specify their preferred language, regardless of their language reported by their browser. `Language` also has a fourth potential value—it may not exist! Therefore, the `OutputCache` directive in the following example caches many versions of the page, as described in this equation:

```
cacheItems = (num of pageIds) * (num of subPageIds) * (4 possible Language values)
```

To summarize, suppose there were ten potential values for `pageId`, five potential `subPageId` values for each `pageId`, and four possible values for `Language`. That adds up to 200 different potential cached versions of this single navigation page. This math isn't meant to scare you away from caching, but you should realize that with great (caching) power comes great responsibility.

The following `OutputCache` directive includes `pageId` and `subPageId` as values for `VaryByParam`, and `VaryByCustom` passes in the value of `"prefs"` to the `GetVaryByCustomString` callback function in Listing 20-1:

```
<%@ OutputCache Duration="90" VaryByParam="pageId;subPageId" VaryByCustom="prefs"%>
```

Caching in ASP.NET is a trade-off between CPU and memory: How hard is it to make this page, versus whether you can afford to hold 200 versions of it. If it's only 5KB of HTML, a potential megabyte of memory could pay off handsomely versus thousands and thousands of database accesses. Every page request served from the cache saves you a trip to the database. Efficient use of caching can translate into significant cost savings if fewer database servers and licenses are needed.

The code in Listing 20-1 returns the value stored in the `Language` cookie. The `arg` parameter to the `GetVaryByCustomString` method contains the string `"prefs"`, as specified in `VaryByCustom`.

Listing 20-1: GetVaryByCustomString callback method in the HttpApplication

VB
```
Overrides Function GetVaryByCustomString(ByVal context As HttpContext, _
        ByVal arg As String) As String
    If arg.ToLower() = "prefs" Then
        Dim cookie As HttpCookie = context.Request.Cookies("Language")
        If cookie IsNot Nothing Then
            Return cookie.Value
        End If
    End If
    Return MyBase.GetVaryByCustomString(context, arg)
End Function
```

C#
```
public override string GetVaryByCustomString(HttpContext context, string arg)
{
    if(arg.ToLower() == "prefs ")
    {
      HttpCookie cookie = context.Request.Cookies["Language"];
      if(cookie != null)
      {
          return cookie.Value;
      }
    }
    return base.GetVaryByCustomString(context, arg);
}
```

The `GetVaryByCustomString` method in Listing 20-1 is used by the `HttpApplication` and will be called for every page that uses the `VaryByCustom OutputCache` directive. If your application has many pages that use `VaryByCustom`, you can create a switch statement and a series of helper functions to retrieve whatever information you want from the user's HttpContext and to generate unique values for cache keys.

Partial Page (UserControl) Caching

Similar to output caching, *partial page caching* enables you to cache only specific blocks of a Web page. You can, for example, cache only the center of the page. Partial page caching is achieved with the caching of user controls. You can build your ASP.NET pages utilizing numerous user controls and then apply output caching to the user controls you select. This, in essence, caches only the parts of the page that you want, leaving other parts of the page outside the reach of caching. This is a nice feature and, if done correctly, it can lead to pages that perform better.

Typically, UserControls are placed on multiple pages to maximize reuse. However, when these UserControls (ASCX files) are cached with the @OutputCache directive's default attributes, they are cached on a per-page basis. That means that even if a UserControl outputs the identical HTML when placed on pagea.aspx as it does when placed on pageb.aspx, its output is cached twice. By enabling the Shared="true" attribute, the UserControl's output can be shared among multiple pages and on sites that make heavy use of shared UserControls:

```
<%@ OutputCache Duration="300" VaryByParam="*" Shared="true" %>
```

The resulting memory savings can be surprisingly large. As with all optimizations, test both for correctness of output as well as memory usage.

> If you have an ASCX UserControl using the OutputCache directive, remember that the UserControl *exists only for the first request*. If a UserControl has its HTML retrieved from the OutputCache, the control doesn't really exist on the ASPX page. Instead, a PartialCachingControl is created that acts as a proxy or *ghost* of that control.

Any code in the ASPX page that requires a UserControl to be constantly available will fail if that control is reconstituted from the OutputCache. So be sure to always check for this type of caching before using any control. The following code fragment illustrates the kind of logic required when accessing a potentially cached UserControl:

VB
```
Protected Sub Page_Load()
    If Not PossiblyCachedUserControl is Nothing Then
        ' Place code manipulating PossiblyCachedUserControl here.
    End If
End Sub
```

C#
```
protected void Page_Load()
{
    if (PossiblyCachedUserControl != null)
    {
        // Place code manipulating PossiblyCachedUserControl here.
    }
}
```

Post-Cache Substitution

Output caching has typically been an all-or-nothing proposition. The output of the entire page is cached for later use. However, often you want the benefits of output caching, but you also want to keep a small bit of dynamic content on the page. It would be a shame to cache a page but be unable to output a dynamic "Welcome, Scott!"

ASP.NET 2.0 adds post-cache substitution as an opportunity to affect the about-to-be-rendered page. A control is added to the page that acts as a placeholder. It calls a method that you specify after the cached content has been returned. The method returns any string output you like, but you should be careful not to abuse the feature. If your post-cache substitution code calls an expensive stored procedure, you could easily lose any performance benefits you might have gained with a little more thought.

Post-cache substitution is the easiest new feature to use. It gives you two ways to control the substitution:

❑ Call the new `Response.WriteSubstitution` method, passing it a reference to the desired substitution method callback.

❑ Add a `<asp:Substitution>` control to the page at the desired location, and set its `methodName` attribute to the name of the callback method.

To try this feature, create a new Web site with a `Default.aspx`. Drag a label control and a substitution control to the design surface. The code in Listing 20-2 updates the label to display the current time, but the page is cached immediately and future requests return that cached value. Set the `methodName` property in the substitution control to `GetUpdatedTime`, meaning the name of the static method that is called after the page is retrieved from the cache.

The callback function must be static because the page that is rendered doesn't really exist at this point (an instance of it doesn't). Because you don't have a page instance to work with, this method is limited in its scope. However, the current `HttpContext` is passed into the method, so you have access to the `Session`, `Request`, and `Response`. The string returned from this method is injected into the `Response` in place of the substitution control.

Listing 20-2: Using the substitution control

ASPX

```
<%@ Page Language="C#" CodeFile="Default.aspx.cs" Inherits="_Default" %>
<%@ OutputCache Duration="30" VaryByParam="None" %>

<html xmlns="http://www.w3.org/1999/xhtml" >
<head>
    <title>Substitution Control</title>
</head>
<body>
    <form id="form1" runat="server">
    <div>
        <asp:Label ID="Label1" Runat="server" Text="Label"></asp:Label>
        <br />
        <asp:Substitution ID="Substitution1" Runat="server"
            methodName="GetUpdatedTime" />
        <br />
    </div>
    </form>
</body>
</html>
```

VB

```
Partial Class _Default
        Inherits System.Web.UI.Page
        Public Shared Function GetUpdatedTime(ByVal context As HttpContext) As String
            Return DateTime.Now.ToLongTimeString() + " by " + _
                    context.User.Identity.Name
        End Function


        Protected Sub Page_Load(ByVal sender As Object, ByVal e As System.EventArgs) _
                Handles Me.Load
            Label1.Text = DateTime.Now.ToLongTimeString()
```

```
    End Sub
End Class
```

C#
```
public partial class _Default : System.Web.UI.Page
{
    public static string GetUpdatedTime(HttpContext context)
    {
        return DateTime.Now.ToLongTimeString() + " by " +
                context.User.Identity.Name;
    }
    protected void Page_Load(object sender, EventArgs e)
    {
        Label1.Text = DateTime.Now.ToLongTimeString();
    }
}
```

The ASPX page in Listing 20-2 has a label and a Post-Cache Substitution Control. The control acts a placeholder in the spot where you want fresh content injected after the page is returned from the cache. The very first time the page is visited only the label is updated because no cached content is returned. The second time the page is visited, however, the entire page is retrieved from the cache — the page handler isn't called and, consequently, none of the page-level events fire. However, the GetUpdatedTime method is called after the cache module completes its work. Figure 20-1 shows the result if the first line is cached and the second line is created dynamically.

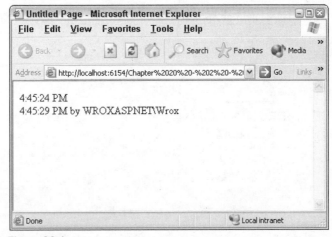

Figure 20-1

HttpCachePolicy and Client-Side Caching

Caching is more than just holding data in memory on the server-side. A good caching strategy should also include the browser and its client-side caches, controlled by the Cache-Control HTTP Header. HTTP Headers are hints and directives to the browser on how to handle a request.

Some people recommend using HTML <META> tags to control caching behavior. Be aware that neither the browsers nor routers along the way are obligated to pay attention to these directives. You might have more success using HTTP Headers to control caching.

Because HTTP Headers travel outside the body of the HTTP message, you have several options for viewing them. You can enable tracing (see Chapter 21) and view the Headers from the tracing output. We prefer to use a tool like IEHttpHeaders that shows the Headers in an IE Explorer Bar.

> Get the IEHttpHeaders Explorer Bar for free from Jonas Blunck at www.blunck.info. For background information on HTTP headers and controlling caching, see the document RFC 2616: Hypertext Transfer Protocol - HTTP/1.1, available on the World Wide Web Consortium's site at www.w3c.org.

Create a Default.aspx that writes the current time in its Load event. Now, view the default HTTP Headers used by ASP.NET, as in Figure 20-2. Note that one header, Cache-Control: private, indicates to routers and other intermediates that this response is intended only for you. Otherwise, no headers refer to caching.

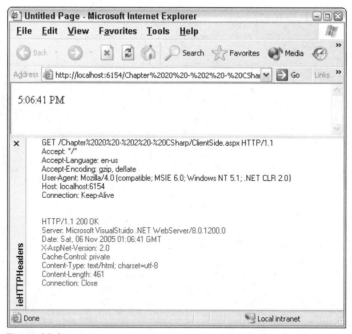

Figure 20-2

The HttpCachePolicy class gives you an object model for managing client-side state that insulates you from adding HTTP Headers yourself. Add the lines from Listing 20-3 to your Page_Load to influence the Response's Headers and the caching behavior of the browser. This listing tells the browser not to cache this Response in memory nor store it on disk. It also directs the Response to expire immediately.

Listing 20-3: Using HTTP Headers to force the browser not to cache on the client-side

VB

```
Protected Sub Page_Load(ByVal sender As Object, _
  ByVal e As System.EventArgs) Handles Me.Load

  Response.Cache.SetCacheability(HttpCacheability.NoCache)
  Response.Cache.SetNoStore()
  Response.Cache.SetExpires(DateTime.MinValue)

  Response.Write(DateTime.Now.ToLongTimeString())
End Sub
```

C#

```
protected void Page_Load(object sender, EventArgs e)
{
    Response.Cache.SetCacheability(HttpCacheability.NoCache);
    Response.Cache.SetNoStore();
    Response.Cache.SetExpires(DateTime.MinValue);

    Response.Write(DateTime.Now.ToLongTimeString());
}
```

Compare the results of running Listing 20-3 in the *before* Figure 20-2 and then in the *after* Figure 20-3. Two new HTTP Headers have been injected directing the client's browser and the `Cache-Control` Header has changed to `no-cache, no-store`. In this figure, the Request HTTP Headers are in the top grouping whereas the Response Headers are in the bottom group. The Output Caching HttpModule will respect these HTTP Headers, so sending `no-cache` to the browser also advises the HttpModule to record the response as a cache miss.

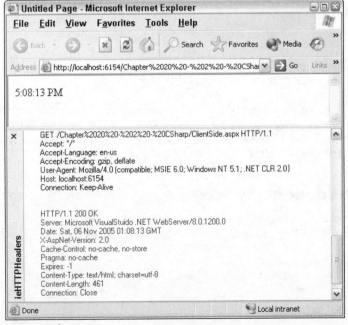

Figure 20-3

If your ASP.NET application contains a considerable number of relatively static or non–time-sensitive pages, consider what your client-side caching strategy is. It's better to take advantage of the disk space and the memory of your users' powerful client machines rather than burdening your server's limited resources.

Caching Programmatically

Output Caching is a very declarative business. UserControls and Pages can be marked up with `OutputCache` directives and dramatically change the behavior of your site. Declarative caching controls the life cycle of HTML markup, but ASP.NET also includes deep support for caching objects.

Data Caching Using the Cache Object

Another method of caching is to use the `Cache` object to start caching specific data items for later use on a particular page or group of pages. The `Cache` object enables you to store everything from simple name/value pairs to more complex objects like datasets and entire `.aspx` pages.

You use the `Cache` object in the following fashion:

VB
```
Cache("WhatINeedToStore") = myDataSet
```

C#
```
Cache["WhatINeedToStore"] = myDataSet;
```

After an item is in the cache, you can retrieve it later as shown here:

VB
```
Dim ds As New DataSet
ds = CType(Cache("WhatINeedToStore"), DataSet)
```

C#
```
DataSet ds = new DataSet();
ds = (DataSet)Cache["WhatINeedToStore"];
```

Using the `Cache` object is an outstanding way to cache your pages and is, in fact, what the `OutputCache` directive uses under the covers. This small fragment shows the simplest use of the `Cache` object. Simply put an object reference in it. However, the real power of the `Cache` object comes with its capability to invalidate itself. That's where cache dependencies come in.

Cache Dependencies

Using the `Cache` object, you can store and also invalidate items in the cache based on several different dependencies. In ASP.NET 1.0/1.1, the only possible dependencies were the following:

❑ File-based dependencies

❑ Key-based dependencies

❑ Time-based dependencies

When inserting items into the cache using the `Cache` object, you set the dependencies with the `Insert` method, as shown in the following example:

```
Cache.Insert("DSN", connectionString, _
    New CacheDependency(Server.MapPath("myconfig.xml")))
```

By using a *dependency* when the item being referenced changes, you remove the cache for that item from memory.

Cache Dependencies have been improved in ASP.NET 2.0 with the addition of the `AggregateCacheDependency` class, the newly extendable `CacheDependency` class, and the capability to create your own custom `CacheDependency` classes. These three things are discussed in the following sections.

The AggregateCacheDependency Class

The `AggregateCacheDependency` class is like the `CacheDependency` class but it allows you to create an association connecting an item in the cache with many disparate dependencies of *different types*. For example, if you have a cached data item that is built from XML from a file and you also have information from a SQL database table, you can create an `AggregateCacheDependency` with inserted `CacheDependency` objects for each subdependency. To do this, you call `Cache.Insert` and add the `AggregateCacheDependency` instance. For example:

```
Dim agg as new AggregateCacheDependency()
agg.Insert(New CacheDependency(Server.MapPath("myconfig.xml")))
agg.Insert(New SqlCacheDependency("Northwind", "Customers"))
Cache.Insert("DSN", connectionString, agg)
```

Note that `AggregateCacheDependency` is meant to be used with *different* kinds of `CacheDependency` classes. If you simply want to associate one cached item with multiple files, use an overload of `CacheDependency`, as in this example:

VB
```
Cache.Insert("DSN", yourObject, _
    New System.Web.Caching.CacheDependency( _
        New String() _
      { _
        Server.MapPath("foo.xml"), _
        Server.MapPath("bar.xml") _
      } _
    ) _
)
```

C#
```
Cache.Insert("DSN", yourObject,
    new System.Web.Caching.CacheDependency(
        new string[]
        {
            Server.MapPath("foo.xml"),
            Server.MapPath("bar.xml")
        }
    )
);
```

The `AggregateCacheDependency` class is made possible by the new support for extending the previously sealed `CacheDependency` class. You can use this innovation to create your own custom `CacheDependency`.

The Unsealed CacheDependency Class

A big change in caching in ASP.NET 2.0 is that the `CacheDependency` class has been refactored and unsealed (or made overrideable). You can now create classes that inherit from the `CacheDependency` class and create more elaborate dependencies that are not limited to the `Time`, `Key`, or `File` dependencies of the past.

When you create your own cache dependencies, you have the option to add procedures for such things as Web services data, only-at-midnight dependencies, or textual string changes within a file. The dependencies you create are limited only by your imagination. The unsealing of the `CacheDependency` class makes this possible.

Because of the unsealing of the `CacheDependency` class, the ASP.NET team has built a new SQL Server cache dependency — `SqlCacheDependency`. A SQL cache dependency was the caching feature most requested by ASP.NET 1.0/1.1 developers. When a cache becomes invalid because a table changes within the underlying SQL Server, you now know it immediately.

Because `CacheDependency` is now unsealed, you can derive your own custom Cache Dependencies; that's what you do in the next section.

Creating Custom Cache Dependencies

ASP.NET 2.0 ships with time-based, file-based, and now SQL-based `CacheDependency` support. You might ask yourself why you would write your own `CacheDependency`. Here are a few ideas:

❑ Invalidate the cache from the results of an Active Directory lookup query

❑ Invalidate the cache upon arrival of an MSMQ or MQSeries message

❑ Create an Oracle-specific `CacheDependency`

❑ Invalidate the cache using data reported from an XML Web service

❑ Update the cache with new data from a Stock Price service

The new version of the `CacheDependency` class, while introducing no breaking changes to existing ASP.NET 1.1 code, exposes three new members and a constructor overload that developers can use:

❑ `GetUniqueID`: When overridden, enables you to return a unique identifier for a custom cache dependency to the caller.

❑ `DependencyDispose`: Used for disposing of resources used by the custom cache dependency class. When you create a custom cache dependency, you are required to implement this method.

❑ `NotifyDependencyChanged`: Called to cause expiration of the cache item dependent on the custom cache dependency instance.

❑ New Public Constructor

Listing 20-4 creates a new `RssCacheDependency` that invalidates a cache key if an RSS (Rich Site Summary) XML Document has changed.

Listing 20-4: Creating an RssCacheDependency class

VB

```vb
Imports System
Imports System.Web
Imports System.Threading
Imports System.Web.Caching
Imports System.Xml

Public Class RssCacheDependency
        Inherits CacheDependency

    Shared backgroundThread As Timer
    Dim howOften As Integer = 900
    Dim RSS As XmlDocument
    Dim RSSUrl As String

    Public Sub New(ByVal URL As String, ByVal polling As Integer)
        howOften = polling
        RSSUrl = URL
        RSS = RetrieveRSS(RSSUrl)

        If backgroundThread Is Nothing Then
            backgroundThread = New Timer( _
                New TimerCallback(AddressOf CheckDependencyCallback), _
                Me, (howOften * 1000), (howOften * 1000))
        End If
    End Sub

    Function RetrieveRSS(ByVal URL As String) As XmlDocument
        Dim retVal As New XmlDocument
        retVal.Load(URL)
        Return retVal
    End Function

    Public Sub CheckDependencyCallback(ByVal Sender As Object)
        Dim CacheDepends As RssCacheDependency = _
            CType(Sender, RssCacheDependency)
        Dim NewRSS As XmlDocument = RetrieveRSS(RSSUrl)
        If Not NewRSS.OuterXml = RSS.OuterXml Then
            CacheDepends.NotifyDependencyChanged(CacheDepends, EventArgs.Empty)
        End If
    End Sub

    Protected Overrides Sub DependencyDispose()
        backgroundThread = Nothing
        MyBase.DependencyDispose()
    End Sub

    Public ReadOnly Property Document() As XmlDocument
        Get
            Return RSS
        End Get
    End Property
End Class
```

(continued)

Listing 20-4: *(continued)*

C#

```csharp
using System;
using System.Web;
using System.Threading;
using System.Web.Caching;
using System.Xml;

public class RssCacheDependency : CacheDependency
{
    static Timer backgroundThread;
    int howOften = 900;
    XmlDocument RSS;
    string RSSUrl;

    public RssCacheDependency(string URL, int polling)
    {
        howOften = polling;
        RSSUrl = URL;
        RSS = RetrieveRSS(RSSUrl);

        if (backgroundThread == null)
        {
            backgroundThread = new Timer(
                new TimerCallback(CheckDependencyCallback),
                this, (howOften * 1000), (howOften * 1000));
        }
    }

    public XmlDocument RetrieveRSS(string URL)
    {
        XmlDocument retVal = new XmlDocument();
        retVal.Load(URL);
        return retVal;
    }

    public void CheckDependencyCallback(object sender)
    {
        RssCacheDependency CacheDepends = sender as RssCacheDependency;
        XmlDocument NewRSS = RetrieveRSS(RSSUrl);
        if (NewRSS.OuterXml != RSS.OuterXml)
        {
            CacheDepends.NotifyDependencyChanged(CacheDepends, EventArgs.Empty);
        }
    }

    override protected void DependencyDispose()
    {
        backgroundThread = null;
        base.DependencyDispose();
    }

    public XmlDocument Document
```

```
    {
        get
        {
            return RSS;
        }
    }
}
```

Create a new Web site and put the RssCacheDependency class in a /Code folder. Create a default.aspx and drag two text boxes, a label, and a button onto the HTML Design view. Execute the Web site and enter an RSS URL for a blog (like mine at www.hanselman.com/blog/SyndicationService.asmx/GetRss), and click the button. The program checks the Cache object using the URL itself as a key. If the XmlDocument containing RSS doesn't exist in the cache, a new RssCacheDependency is created with a 10-minute (600-second) timeout. The XmlDocument is then cached, and all future requests to this page retrieve the RSS XmlDocument from the cache.

Next, your new RssCacheDependency class from Listing 20-4 is illustrated in the following fragment. The RssCacheDependency is created and passed into the call to Cache.Insert. The Cache object handles the lifetime and calling of the methods of the RssCacheDependency instance:

VB

```
<%@ Page Language="VB" ValidateRequest="false" %>

<html>
<head runat="server">
    <title>Custom Cache Dependency Example</title>
</head>
<body>
    <form runat="server"> RSS URL:
        <asp:TextBox ID="TextBox1" Runat="server"/>
        <asp:Button ID="Button1" onclick="Button1_Click" Runat="server"
        Text="Get RSS" />
        Cached:<asp:Label ID="Label2" Runat="server"></asp:Label><br />
        RSS:<br />
        <asp:TextBox ID="TextBox2" Runat="server" TextMode="MultiLine"
         Width="800px" Height="300px"></asp:TextBox>
    </form>
</body>
</html>

<script runat="server">
    Sub Button1_Click(ByVal sender As Object, ByVal e As System.EventArgs)
        Dim RSSUrl As String = TextBox1.Text
        Label2.Text = "Loaded From Cache"
        If Cache(TextBox1.Text) Is Nothing Then
            Label2.Text = "Loaded Fresh"
            Dim itDepends As New RssCacheDependency(RSSUrl, 600)
            Cache.Insert(RSSUrl, itDepends.Document, itDepends)
        End If
        TextBox2.Text = CType(Cache(TextBox1.Text), _
            System.Xml.XmlDocument).OuterXml
    End Sub
</script>
```

(continued)

Listing 20-4: *(continued)*

C#

```
<%@ Page Language="C#" ValidateRequest="false" %>
<script runat="server">
    void Button1_Click(object sender, System.EventArgs e)
    {
        string RSSUrl = TextBox1.Text;
        Label2.Text = "Loaded From Cache";
        if (Cache[TextBox1.Text] == null)
        {
            Label2.Text = "Loaded Fresh";
            RssCacheDependency itDepends = new RssCacheDependency(RSSUrl, 600);
            Cache.Insert(RSSUrl, itDepends.Document, itDepends);
        }
        TextBox2.Text = ((System.Xml.XmlDocument)Cache[TextBox1.Text]).OuterXml;
    }
</script>
```

The RssCacheDependency class creates a Timer background thread to poll for changes in the RSS feed. If it detects changes, the RssCacheDependency notifies the caching subsystem with the NotifyDependencyChanged event. The cached value with that key clears, and the next page view forces a reload of the requested RSS from the specified feed.

Using the SQL Server Cache Dependency

To utilize the new SQL Server Cache Dependency feature in ASP.NET 2.0, you must perform a one-time setup of your SQL Server database. To set up your SQL Server, use the aspnet_regsql.exe tool found at C:\Windows\Microsoft.NET\Framework\v2.0xxxxx\. This tool makes the necessary modifications to SQL Server so that you can start working with the new SQL cache invalidation features.

Follow these steps when using the new SQL Server Cache Dependency features:

1. Enable your database for SQL Cache Dependency support.

2. Enable a table or tables for SQL Cache Dependency support.

3. Include SQL connection string details in the ASP.NET application's web.config.

4. Utilize the SQL Cache Dependency features in one of the following ways:

    ❑ Programmatically create a SqlCacheDependency object in code.

    ❑ Add a SqlDependency attribute to an OutputCache directive.

    ❑ Add a SqlCacheDependency instance to the Response object via Response.AddCacheDependency.

This section explains all the steps required and the operations available to you.

To start, you need to get at the `aspnet_regsql.exe` tool. Open up the Visual Studio Command Prompt by choosing Start ⇨ All Programs ⇨ Microsoft Visual Studio 2005 ⇨ Visual Studio Tools ⇨ Visual Studio Command Prompt from the Windows Start menu. After the prompt launches, type this command:

```
aspnet_regsql.exe -?
```

This code outputs the help command list for this command-line tool, as shown in the following:

```
                  -- SQL CACHE DEPENDENCY OPTIONS --

    -d <database>         Database name for use with SQL cache dependency. The
                          database can optionally be specified using the
                          connection string with the -c option instead.
                          (Required)

    -ed                   Enable a database for SQL cache dependency.

    -dd                   Disable a database for SQL cache dependency.

    -et                   Enable a table for SQL cache dependency. Requires -t
                          option.

    -dt                   Disable a table for SQL cache dependency. Requires -t
                          option.

    -t <table>            Name of the table to enable or disable for SQL cache
                          dependency. Requires -et or -dt option.

    -lt                   List all tables enabled for SQL cache dependency.
```

The following sections show you how to use some of these commands.

Enabling Databases for SQL Server Cache Invalidation

To use SQL Server cache invalidation with SQL Server 7 or 2000, begin with two steps. The first step enables the appropriate database. In the second step, you enable the tables that you want to work with. You must perform both steps for this process to work. If you want to enable your databases for SQL cache invalidation and you are working on the computer where the SQL Server instance is located, you can use the following construct. If your SQL instance is on another computer, change `localhost` in this example to the name of the remote machine.

```
aspnet_regsql.exe -S localhost -U sa -P password -d Northwind -ed
```

This produces something similar to the following output:

```
Enabling the database for SQL cache dependency.

..
Finished.
```

From this command prompt, you can see that we simply enabled the Northwind database (the sample database that comes with SQL Server) for SQL cache invalidation. The name of the SQL machine was passed in with -S, the username with -U, the database with -d, and most importantly, the command to enable SQL cache invalidation was -ed.

Now that you have enabled the database for SQL cache invalidation, you can enable one or more tables contained within the Northwind database.

Enabling Tables for SQL Server Cache Invalidation

You enable or more tables by using the following command:

```
aspnet_regsql.exe -S localhost -U sa -P password -d Northwind -t Customers -et
```

```
aspnet_regsql.exe -S localhost -U sa -P password -d Northwind -t Products -et
```

You can see that this command is not much different from the one for enabling the database, except for the extra -t Customers entry and the use of -et to enable the table rather than -ed to enable a database. Customers is the name of the table that is enabled in this case.

Go ahead and enable both the Customers and Product tables. You run the command once per table. After a table is successfully enabled, you receive the following response:

```
Enabling the table for SQL cache dependency.
.
Finished.
```

After the table is enabled, you can begin using the SQL cache invalidation features. However, before you do, the following section shows you what happens to SQL Server when you enable these features.

Looking at SQL Server

Now that the Northwind database and the Customers and Products tables have all been enabled for SQL cache invalidation, look at what has happened in SQL Server. If you open up the SQL Server Enterprise Manager, you see a new table contained within the Northwind database — AspNet_SqlCacheTablesForChangeNotification (whew, that's a long one!). Your screen should look like Figure 20-4.

At the top of the list of tables in the right-hand pane, you see the AspNet_ SqlCacheTablesForChangeNotification table. This is the table that ASP.NET uses to learn which tables are being monitored for change notification and also to make note of any changes to the tables being monitored. The table is actually quite simple when you look at the details, as illustrated in Figure 20-5.

In this figure, you can see three columns in this new table. The first is the tableName column. This column simply shows a String reference to the names of the tables contained in the same database. Any table named here is enabled for SQL cache invalidation.

The second column, notificationCreated, shows the date and time when the table was enabled for SQL cache invalidation. The final column, changeId, is used to communicate to ASP.NET any changes to the included tables. ASP.NET monitors this column for changes and, depending on the value, either uses what is stored in memory or makes a new database query.

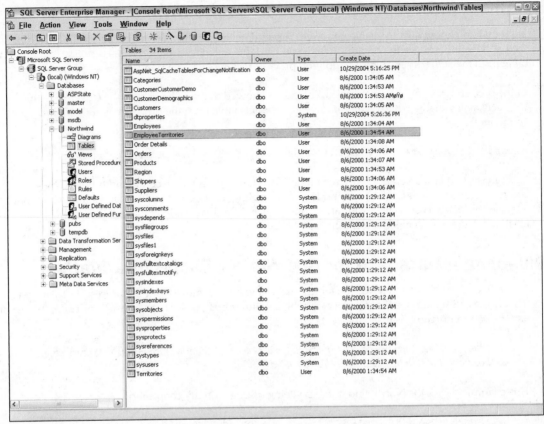

Figure 20-4

tableName	notificationCreated	changeId
Customers	10/29/2004 5:19:05 PM	0
Products	10/29/2004 5:17:07 PM	0

Figure 20-5

Looking at the Tables That Are Enabled

Using the aspnet_regsql.exe tool, you can see (by using a simple command) which tables are enabled in a particular database. If you are working through the preceding examples, you see that so far you have enabled the Customers and Products tables of the Northwind database. To get a list of the tables that are enabled, use something similar to the following command:

```
aspnet_regsql.exe -S localhost -U sa -P password -d Northwind -lt
```

The -lt command produces a simple list of tables enabled for SQL cache invalidation. Inputting this command produces the following results:

```
Listing all tables enabled for SQL cache dependency:
Customers
Products
```

Disabling a Table for SQL Server Cache Invalidation

Now that you know how to enable your SQL Server database for SQL Server cache invalidation, take a look at how you remove the capability for a specific table to be monitored for this process. To remove a table from the SQL Server cache invalidation process, use the -dt command.

In the preceding example, using the -lt command showed that you have both the Customers and Products tables enabled. Next, you remove the Products table from the process using the following command:

```
aspnet_regsql.exe -S localhost -U sa -P password -d Northwind -t Products -dt
```

You can see that all you do is specify the name of the table using the -t command followed by a -dt command (disable table). The command line for disabling table caching will again list the tables that are enabled for SQL Server cache invalidation; this time, the Products table will is not listed — instead, Customers, the only enabled table, is listed.

Disabling a Database for SQL Server Cache Invalidation

Not only can you pick and choose the tables that you want to remove from the process, but you can also disable the entire database for SQL Server cache invalidation. In order to disable an entire database, you use the -dd command (disable database).

> Note that disabling an entire database for SQL Server cache invalidation also means that every single table contained within this database is also disabled.

This example shows the Northwind database being disabled on my computer:

```
C:\>aspnet_regsql -S localhost -U sa -P wrox -d Northwind -dd
Disabling the database for SQL cache dependency.
..
Finished.
```

To ensure that the table is no longer enabled for SQL Server cache invalidation, we attempted to list the tables that were enabled for cache invalidation using the -lt command. We received the following error:

```
C:\ >aspnet_regsql -S localhost -U sa -P wrox -d Northwind -lt
An error has happened. Details of the exception:
The database is not enabled for SQL cache notification. To enable a database for
SQL cache notification, please use SQLCacheDependencyAdmin.EnableNotifications
method, or the command line tool aspnet_regsql.exe.
```

If you now open the Northwind database in the SQL Server Enterprise Manager, you can see that the AspNet_SqlCacheTablesForChangeNotification table has been removed for the database.

SQL Server 2005 Cache Invalidation

As you've seen, standard SQL Server 2000 cache invalidation uses a table-level mechanism using a polling model every few seconds to monitor what tables have changed.

SQL Server 2005 supports a different, more granular series of notification that doesn't require polling. Direct notification of changes are a built-in feature of SQL Server 2005 and are presented via the ADO.NET SqlCommand. For example:

```
Protected Sub Page_Load(ByVal sender as Object, ByVal e as System.EventArgs)

    Response.Write("Page created: " + DateTime.Now.ToLongTimeString())
        Dim connStr As String =
    ConfigurationManager.ConnectionStrings("AppConnectionString1").ConnectionString
    SqlDependency.Start(connStr)
    Dim connection As New SqlConnection(connStr)
    Dim command as New SqlCommand("Select * FROM Customers", connection)
    Dim depends as New SqlCacheDependency(command)

    Connection.Open
    GridView1.DataSource = command.ExecuteReader()
    GridView1.DataBind()

    Connection.Close

     'Now, do what you want with the sqlDependency object like:
    Response.AddCacheDependency(depends)

End Sub
```

SQL Server 2005 supports both programmatic and declarative techniques when caching. Use the string "CommandNotification" in the OutputCache directive to enable notification-based caching for a page as in this example. You can specify SQL caching options programmatically or declaratively, but not both. Note that you must first call System.Data.SqlClient.SqlDependency.Start, passing in the connection string, to start the SQL notification engine.

```
<%@ OutputCache Duration="3600" VaryByParam="none"
    SqlDependency="CommandNotification"%>
```

Or, if you're using a SqlDataSource control from within your ASP.NET page:

```
<asp:SqlDataSource EnableCaching="true" SqlCacheDependency="CommandNotification"
    CacheDuration="2600" />
```

As data changes within SQL Server 2005, SQL and ADO.NET automatically invalidate data cached on the web server.

Configuring Your ASP.NET Application

After you enable a database for SQL Server cache invalidation and also enable a couple of tables within this database, the next step is to configure your application for SQL Server cache invalidation.

To configure your application to work with SQL Server cache invalidation, the first step is to make some changes to the web.config file. In the web.config file, specify that you want to work with the Northwind database, and you want ASP.NET connected to it.

Listing 20-5 shows an example of how you should change your web.config file to work with SQL Server cache invalidation. The pollTime attribute isn't needed if you're using SQL Server 2005 notification.

Listing 20-5: Configuring the web.config file

```
<configuration xmlns="http://schemas.microsoft.com/.NetConfiguration/v2.0">

    <connectionStrings>
        <add name="AppConnectionString1" connectionString="Data Source=localhost;
            User ID=sa;Password=wrox;Database=Northwind;Persist Security Info=False"
            providerName="System.Data.SqlClient" />
    </connectionStrings>

    <system.web>

        <caching>
            <sqlCacheDependency enabled="true">
                <databases>
                    <add name="Northwind" connectionStringName="AppConnectionString1"
                        pollTime="500" />
                </databases>
            </sqlCacheDependency>
        </caching>

    </system.web>
</configuration>
```

From this listing, you can see that the first thing established is the connection string to the Northwind database using the <connectionStrings> element in the web.config file. Note of the name of the connection string because it is utilized later in the configuration settings for SQL Server cache invalidation.

The SQL Server cache invalidation is configured using the new <caching> element. This element must be nested within the <system.web> elements. Because you are working with a SQL Server cache dependency, you must use a <sqlCacheDependency> child node. You enable the entire process by using the enabled="true" attribute. After this attribute is enabled, you work with the <databases> section. You use the <add> element, nested within the <databases> nodes, to reference the Northwind database. The following table explains all the attributes of the <add> element.

Attribute	Description
Name	The name attribute provides an identifier to the SQL Server database.
connectionStringName	The connectionStringName attribute specifies the name of the connection. Because the connection string in the preceding example is called AppConnectionString1, you use this value for the connectionStringName attribute as well.
pollTime	The pollTime attribute specifies the time interval from one SQL Server poll to the next. The default is .5 seconds or 500 milliseconds (as shown in the example). This is not needed for SQL Server 2005 notification.

Now that the `web.config` file is set up correctly, you can start using SQL Server cache invalidation on your pages. ASP.NET makes a separate SQL Server request on a completely different thread to the `AspNet_SqlCacheTablesForChangeNotification` table to see if the `changeId` number has been incremented. If the number is changed, ASP.NET knows that an underlying change has been made to the SQL Server table and that a new result set should be retrieved. When it checks to see if it should make a SQL Server call, the request to the small `AspNet_SqlCacheTablesForChangeNotification` table has a single result. With SQL Server cache invalidation enabled, this is done so quickly that you really notice the difference.

Testing SQL Server Cache Invalidation

Now that the `web.config` file is set up and ready to go, the next step is to actually apply these new capabilities to a page. For an example of a page using the new SQL Server cache invalidation process, look at Listing 20-6.

Listing 20-6: An ASP.NET page utilizing SQL Server cache invalidation

VB

```
<%@ Page Language="VB" %>
<%@ OutputCache Duration="3600" VaryByParam="none"
    SqlDependency="Northwind:Customers"%>

<script runat="server">
    Protected Sub Page_Load(ByVal sender As Object, ByVal e As System.EventArgs)
        Label1.Text = "Page created at " & DateTime.Now.ToShortTimeString ()
    End Sub
</script>

<html xmlns="http://www.w3.org/1999/xhtml" >
<head runat="server">
    <title>Sql Cache Invalidation</title>
</head>
<body>
    <form id="form1" runat="server">
        <asp:Label ID="Label1" Runat="server"></asp:Label><br />
        <br />
        <asp:GridView ID="GridView1" Runat="server" DataSourceID="SqlDataSource1">
        </asp:GridView>
        <asp:SqlDataSource ID="SqlDataSource1" Runat="server"
         SelectCommand="Select * From Customers"
         ConnectionString="<%$ ConnectionStrings:AppConnectionString1 %>"
         ProviderName="<%$ ConnectionStrings:AppConnectionString1.providername %>">
        </asp:SqlDataSource>
    </form>
</body>
</html>
```

(continued)

Listing 20-6: *(continued)*

C#

```
<%@ Page Language="C#" %>
<%@ OutputCache Duration="3600" VaryByParam="none"
    SqlDependency="Northwind:Customers"%>

<script runat="server">
    protected void Page_Load(object sender, System.EventArgs e)
    {
        Label1.Text = "Page created at " + DateTime.Now.ToShortTimeString();
    }
</script>
```

The first and most important part of this page is the OuputCache page directive that is specified at the top of the file. Typically, the OutputCache directive specifies how long the page output is held in the cache using the Duration attribute. Next comes the VaryByParam attribute, which does not permit separate page outputs to be cached based on factors like the requestor's browser. The new addition is the SqlDependency attribute. This enables a particular page to use SQL Server cache invalidation. The following line shows the format of the value for the SqlDependency attribute:

```
SqlDependency="database:table"
```

The value of Northwind:Customers specifies that you want the SQL Server cache invalidation enabled for the Customers table within the Northwind database. The Duration attribute of the OutputCache directive shows you that, typically, the output of this page is stored in the cache for a long time — but this cache is disabled if the Customers table has any underlying changes made to the data that it contains.

A change to any of the cells in the Customers table of the Northwind database invalidates the cache, and a new cache is generated from the result, which now contains a new SQL Server database request. Figure 20-6 shows an example of the page generated the first time it is run.

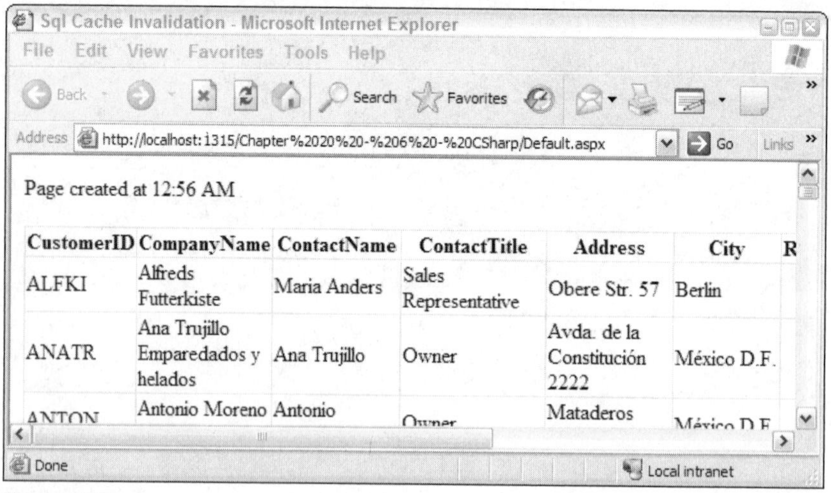

Figure 20-6

From this figure, you can see the contents of the customer with the `CustomerID` of `ALFKI`. For this entry, go to SQL Server and change the value of the `ContactName` from `Maria Anders` to `Mary Anders`. Before SQL Server cache invalidation, this change would have done nothing to the output cache. The original page output in the cache would still be present and the end user would still see the `Maria Anders` entry for the duration specified in the page's `OutputCache` directive. Because of SQL Server cache invalidation, after the underlying information in the table is changed, the output cache is invalidated, a new result set is retrieved, and the new result set is cached. When a change has been made, you see the results as shown in Figure 20-7.

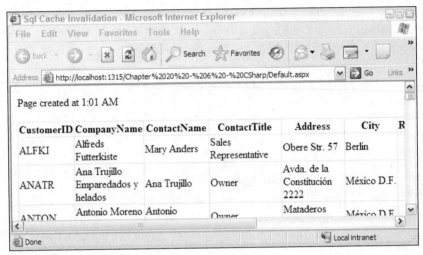

Figure 20-7

Notice also that the text "Page created at" includes an updated time indicating when this page was rendered. Need to stop working so late, eh?

Adding More Than One Table to a Page

The preceding example shows how to use SQL Server cache invalidation for a single table on the ASP.NET page. What do you do if your page is working with two or more tables?

To add more than one table, you use the `OutputCache` directive shown here:

```
SqlDependency="database:table;database:table"
```

From this example, you can see that the value of the `SqlDependency` attribute separates the databases and tables with a semicolon. If you want to work with both the Customers table and the Products table of the Northwind database, you construct the value of the `SqlDependency` attribute as follows:

```
SqlDependency="Northwind:Customers;Northwind:Products"
```

Attaching SQL Server Cache Dependencies to the Request Object

In addition to changing settings in the `OutputCache` directive to activate SQL Server cache invalidation, you can also set the SQL Server cache invalidation programmatically. To do so, use the `SqlCacheDependency` class, which is illustrated in Listing 20-7.

Listing 20-7: Working with SQL Server cache invalidation programmatically

VB

```vb
Dim myDependency As SqlCacheDependency = _
    New SqlCacheDependency("Northwind", "Customers")
Response.AddCacheDependency(myDependency)
Response.Cache.SetValidUntilExpires(true)
Response.Cache.SetExpires(DateTime.Now.AddMinutes(60))
Response.Cache.SetCacheability(HttpCacheability.Public)
```

C#

```csharp
SqlCacheDependency myDependency = new SqlCacheDependency("Northwind", "Customers");
Response.AddCacheDependency(myDependency);
Response.Cache.SetValidUntilExpires(true);
Response.Cache.SetExpires(DateTime.Now.AddMinutes(60));
Response.Cache.SetCacheability(HttpCacheability.Public);
```

You first create an instance of the `SqlCacheDependency` object, assigning it the value of the database and the table at the same time. The `SqlCacheDependency` class takes the following parameters:

```
SqlCacheDependency(databaseEntryName As String, tablename As String)
```

You use this parameter construction if you are working with SQL Server 7.0 or with SQL Server 2000. If you are working with SQL Server 2005 you use the following construction:

```
SqlCacheDependency(sqlCmd As System.Data.SqlClient.SqlCommand)
```

After the `SqlCacheDependency` class is in place, you add the dependency to the `Cache` object and set some of the properties of the `Cache` object as well. You can do this either programmatically or through the `OutputCache` directive.

Attaching SQL Server Cache Dependencies to the Cache Object

In addition to attaching SQL Server cache dependencies to the `Request` object, you can attach them to the `Cache` object. The `Cache` object is contained within the `System.Web.Caching` namespace, and it enables you to work programmatically with the caching of any type of objects. Listing 20-8 shows a page that utilizes the `Cache` object with the `SqlDependency` object.

Listing 20-8: Using the Cache object with the SqlDependency object

```vb
<%@ Page Language="VB" %>
<%@ Import Namespace="System.Data"%>
<%@ Import Namespace="System.Data.SqlClient"%>

<script runat="server">
    Protected Sub Page_Load(ByVal sender As Object, ByVal e As System.EventArgs)
        Dim myCustomers As DataSet
        myCustomers = CType(Cache("firmCustomers"), DataSet)

        If myCustomers Is Nothing Then
            Dim conn As SqlConnection = _
             New SqlConnection( _
    ConfigurationManager.ConnectionStrings("AppConnectionString1").ConnectionString)
            Dim da As SqlDataAdapter = _
             New SqlDataAdapter("Select * From Customers", conn)

            myCustomers = New DataSet
            da.Fill(myCustomers)

            Dim myDependency As SqlCacheDependency = _
                New SqlCacheDependency("Northwind", "Customers")
            Cache.Insert("firmCustomers", myCustomers, myDependency)

            Label1.Text = "Produced from database."
        Else
            Label1.Text = "Produced from Cache object."
        End If

        GridView1.DataSource = myCustomers
        GridView1.DataBind()
    End Sub
</script>

<html xmlns="http://www.w3.org/1999/xhtml" >
<head runat="server">
    <title>Sql Cache Invalidation</title>
</head>
<body>
    <form id="form1" runat="server">
        <asp:Label ID="Label1" Runat="server"></asp:Label><br />
        <br />
        <asp:GridView ID="GridView1" Runat="server"></asp:GridView>
    </form>
</body>
</html>
```

(continued)

Listing 20-8: *(continued)*

C#

```csharp
<%@ Page Language="C#" %>
<%@ Import Namespace="System.Data" %>
<%@ Import Namespace="System.Data.SqlClient" %>

<script runat="server">
    protected void Page_Load(object sender, System.EventArgs e)
    {
        DataSet myCustomers;
        myCustomers = (DataSet)Cache["firmCustomers"];

        if (myCustomers == null)
        {
            SqlConnection conn = new
             SqlConnection(
ConfigurationManager.ConnectionStrings["AppConnectionString1"].ConnectionString);
            SqlDataAdapter da = new
                SqlDataAdapter("Select * from Customers", conn);

            myCustomers = new DataSet();
            da.Fill(myCustomers);

            SqlCacheDependency myDependency = new
                SqlCacheDependency("Northwind", "Customers");
            Cache.Insert("firmCustomers", myCustomers, myDependency);

            Label1.Text = "Produced from database.";
        }
        else
        {
            Label1.Text = "Produced from Cache object.";
        }

        GridView1.DataSource = myCustomers;
        GridView1.DataBind();
    }
</script>
```

In this example, the `SqlCacheDependency` class associated itself to the Customers table in the Northwind database as before. This time, however, you use the `Cache` object to insert the retrieved dataset along with a reference to the `SqlCacheDependency` object. The `Insert` method of the `Cache` class is constructed as follows:

```
Cache.Insert(key As String, value As Object,
    dependencies As System.Web.Caching.CacheDependency)
```

You can also insert more information about the dependency using the following construct:

```
Cache.Insert(key As String, value As Object,
    dependencies As System.Web.Caching.CacheDependency
    absoluteExpiration As Date, slidingExpiration As System.TimeSpan)
```

And finally:

```
Cache.Insert(key As String, value As Object,
    dependencies As System.Web.Caching.CacheDependency
    absoluteExpiration As Date, slidingExpiration As System.TimeSpan)
    priority As System.Web.Caching.CacheItemPriority,
    onRemoveCallback As System.Web.Caching.CacheItemRemovedCallback)
```

The SQL Server cache dependency created comes into action and does the same polling as it would have done otherwise. If any of the data in the Customers table has changed, the `SqlCacheDependency` class invalidates what is stored in the cache. When the next request is made, the `Cache("firmCustomers")` is found to be empty and a new request is made to SQL Server. The `Cache` object again repopulates the cache with the new results generated.

When the ASP.NET page from Listing 20-8 is called for the first time, the results generated are shown in Figure 20-8.

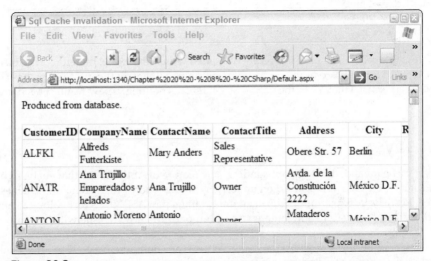

Figure 20-8

Because this is the first time that the page is generated, nothing is in the cache. The `Cache` object is, therefore, placed in the result set along with the association to the SQL Server cache dependency. Figure 20-9 shows the result for the second request. Notice that the HTML table is identical since it was generated from the identical `DataSet`, but the first line of the file has changed to indicate that this output was produced from cache.

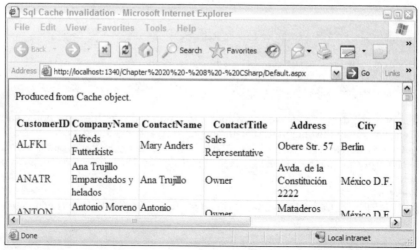

Figure 20-9

On the second request, the dataset is already contained within the cache; therefore, it is retrievable. You aren't required to hit SQL Server to get the full results again. If any of the information has changed within SQL Server itself, however, the `Cache` object returns nothing; a new result set is retrieved.

Summary

SQL Server cache invalidation is an outstanding new feature of ASP.NET 2.0 that enables you to invalidate items stored in the cache when underlying changes occur to the data in the tables being monitored. Post-Cache Substitution fills in an important gap in ASP.NET's technology, enabling you to have both the best highly dynamic content and a high-performance Web site with caching.

When you are monitoring changes to the database, you can configure these procedures easily in the `web.config` file, or you can work programmatically with cache invalidation directly in your code. These changes are possible because the `CacheDependency` object has been unsealed. You can now inherit from this object and create your own cache dependencies. The SQL Server cache invalidation process is the first example of this capability.

Debugging and Error Handling Techniques

Your code always runs exactly as you wrote it, and you will *never* get it right the first time. So, expect to spend about 30 percent of your time debugging and, to be a successful debugger, learn to use the available tools effectively. Visual Studio has upped the ante with version 2005, giving you a host of new features that greatly improve your debugging experience. So many of these new features, however, can be overwhelming at first. This chapter breaks down all the techniques available to you, one at a time, while presenting a holistic view of Visual Studio, the Common Language Runtime (CLR), and the Base Class Library (BCL).

> Everyone knows that debugging is twice as hard as writing a program in the first place. So if you're as clever as you can be when you write it, how will you ever debug it?
> — *Brian Kernighan*

Additionally, because debugging is more than stepping through code, this chapter talks about efficient error and exception handling, tracing and logging, and cross-language (C#, Visual Basic, client-side JavaScript, XSLT, and SQL Stored Procedure) debugging.

Design-Time Support

Visual Studio has always had excellent support for warning you of potential errors at design time. *Syntax notifications* or *squiggles* underline code that won't compile or that might cause an error before you have compiled the project. A *new error notification* pops up when an exception occurs during a debugging session and recommends a course of action that prevents the exception. At every step, Visual Studio tries to be smarter, anticipating your needs and catching common mistakes.

Rico Mariani, a performance architect on the CLR team, has used the term *The Pit of Success* to describe the experience Microsoft wants you to have with Visual Studio. When Microsoft designed these new features, they wanted the customer to simply fall into winning practices. The company tried to achieve this by making it more difficult for you to write buggy code or make common mistakes. Microsoft's developers put a great deal of thought into building APIs that point us in the right direction.

Syntax Notifications

Both the Visual Basic and C# editors show squiggles and tooltips for many syntax errors well before compilation, as illustrated in Figure 21-1. In prior releases of these language editors, Visual Basic had superior support for syntax errors, but in this latest release, a number of improvements have been made to C# to bring the syntax notifications up to par with what Visual Basic already offered.

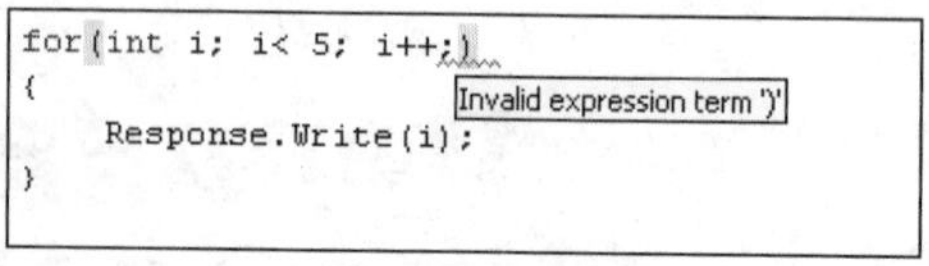

```
for (int i; i< 5; i++;)
{                  Invalid expression term ')'
    Response.Write(i);
}
```

Figure 21-1

Syntax notifications aren't just for CLR programming languages; Visual Studio has also greatly improved the XML Editor with enhancements like the following:

❑ Full XML 1.0 syntax checking

❑ Support for DTD as well as XSD validation

❑ Support for XSLT 1.0 syntax checking

Figure 21-2 shows a detailed tooltip indicating that the element `<junk>` doesn't have any business being in the `web.config` file. The editor knows this because of a combination of the XSD validation support in the XML Editor and the addition of schemas for configuration files like `web.config`. This is a welcome change for anyone who, when manually editing a `web.config` file, has wondered if he guessed the right elements.

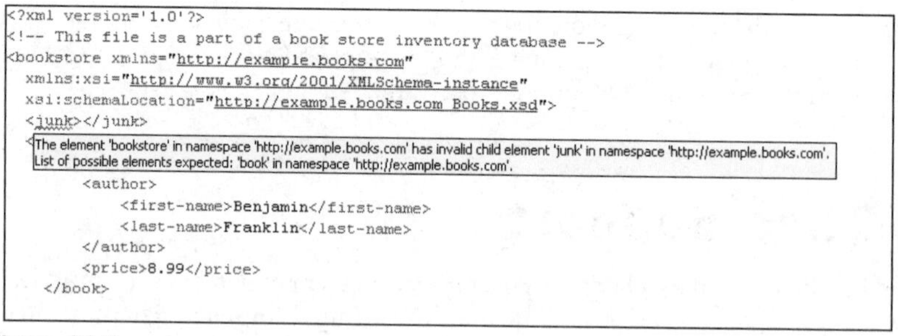

```
<?xml version='1.0'?>
<!-- This file is a part of a book store inventory database -->
<bookstore xmlns="http://example.books.com"
    xmlns:xsi="http://www.w3.org/2001/XMLSchema-instance"
    xsi:schemaLocation="http://example.books.com Books.xsd">
    <junk></junk>
    The element 'bookstore' in namespace 'http://example.books.com' has invalid child element 'junk' in namespace 'http://example.books.com'.
    List of possible elements expected: 'book' in namespace 'http://example.books.com'.
        <author>
            <first-name>Benjamin</first-name>
            <last-name>Franklin</last-name>
        </author>
        <price>8.99</price>
    </book>
```

Figure 21-2

The ASPX/HTML Editor benefits from these improvements as well; for example, Figure 21-3 shows a warning that the `<hanselman/>` element is not available in the active schema. Code that appears in `<script runat="Server"/>` blocks in ASP.NET pages is also parsed and marked with squiggles. This makes including code in your pages considerably easier. Notice also that the ASP.NET page in Figure 21-3 has an XHTML DOCTYPE declaration on the first line, and the HTML element has a default XHTML namespace. This HTML page is treated as XML because XHTML has been targeted.

> XHTML is the HTML vocabulary of markup expressed with all the syntax rules of XML. For example, in HTML you could create a <br> tag and never close it. In XHTML you use the closing tag <br />. XHTML documents look exactly like HTML documents because they in fact *are* expressing the same semantics. Because XHTML documents are XML, they require a namespace on their root element and should have a DOCTYPE as well.

To add a hanselman element, you must put it in its own namespace and add a namespace declaration in the root HTML element.

```
<!DOCTYPE html PUBLIC "-//W3C//DTD XHTML 1.0 Transitional//EN"
<html xmlns="http://www.w3.org/1999/xhtml" >
<head runat="server">
    <title>Untitled Page</title>
</head>
<body>
    <hanselman></hanselman>
    Validation (XHTML 1.0 Transitional): Element 'hanselman' is not supported.
    <div>

    </div>
    </form>
</body>
</html>
```

Figure 21-3

The Visual Basic Editor takes assistance to the next level with a *smart tag* like the pulldown/button that appears when you hover your mouse over a squiggle. A very nicely rendered modeless window appears with your code in a box along with some suggested changes to make your code compile. Figure 21-4 shows a recommendation to insert a missing End If; making the correction is simple—just click Insert the missing 'End If'.

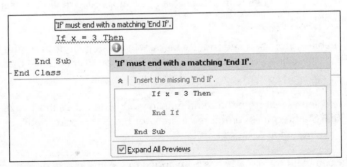

Figure 21-4

All these design-time features exist to help you ensure better code while it's being written, before it's been compiled and run. Two related features help you run arbitrary code within the development environment as well as organize the tasks still to be performed.

Immediate and Command Window

The Immediate Window lets you run arbitrary bits of code in Design mode without compiling your application. You can evaluate code at design time or while you're debugging. It can be a great way to test a line of code or a static method quickly. The Immediate mode of this window is used primarily for debugging.

Access the Immediate Window from Debug ➪ Windows ➪ Immediate. To evaluate a variable or run a method, simply click in the Immediate Window and type a question mark (**?**) followed by the expression, variable, or method you want to evaluate.

The immediate window can also be switched into the Command Window by prefacing commands with a greater-than sign (>). When you enter a greater-than sign in the Immediate/Command Window, an IntelliSense drop-down appears exposing the complete Visual Studio object model as well as any macros that you may have recorded. Command mode of this window is used for executing Visual Studio Commands without using the menus. You can also execute commands that may not have a menu item.

If you type **>alias** into the Command Window, you receive a complete list of all current aliases and their definitions. Some useful command aliases include the following:

❑   `>Log filename /overwrite /on|off`: The Log command starts logging all output from the command window to a file. If no filename is included for logging, go to `cmdline.log`. This is one of the more useful and least-used features of the debugger, and reason enough to learn a few things about the immediate/Command Window.

❑   `>Shell args /command /output /dir:folder`: The Shell command allows you to launch executable programs from within the Visual Studio Command Window such as utilities, command shells, batch files, and so on.

Task List

The Task List in Visual Studio is more useful than you might think. People who haven't given it much attention are missing out on a great feature. The Task List supports two views: User Tasks and Comments.

User Tasks view enables you to add and modify tasks, which can include anything from "Remember to Test" to "Buy Milk." These tasks are stored in the .SUO (solution user options) that is a parallel partner to the .SLN files.

The Comments view shows text from the comments in your code where those lines are prefixed with a specific token. Visual Studio comes configured to look for the TODO: token, but you can add your own in Tools ➪ Options ➪ Environment ➪ Task List.

In Figure 21-5, the comment token HACK has been added in the Options dialog. A comment appears in the source with HACK: preceding it, so that comment line automatically appears in the Task List in the docked window at the bottom of Visual Studio. The three circles in Figure 21-5 illustrate the connection between the word HACK added to the Options dialog and its subsequent appearance in the source code and Task List. You and your team can add as many of these tokens as you'd like.

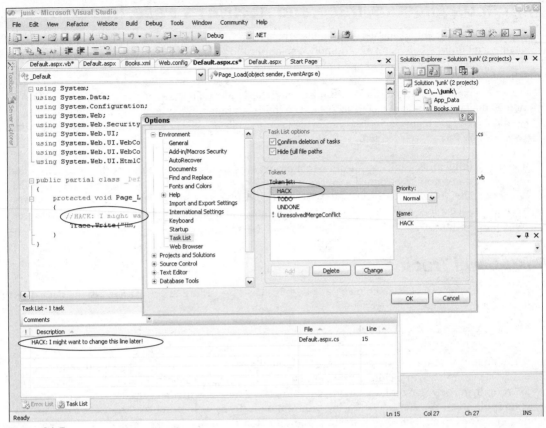

Figure 21-5

Tracing

Tracing is a way to monitor the execution of your ASP.NET application. You can record exception details and program flow in a way that doesn't affect the program's output. In classic ASP, tracing and debugging facilities were nearly nonexistent, forcing developers to use *got here* debugging in the form of many `Response.Write` statements that litter the resulting HTML with informal trace statements announcing to the programmer that the program "got here" and "got there" with each new line executed. This kind of intrusive tracing was very inconvenient to clean up and many programmers ended up creating their own informal trace libraries to get around these classic ASP limitations.

In ASP.NET 2.0, there is rich support for tracing. The destination for trace output can be configured with TraceListeners like the `EventLogTraceListener`. Configuration of TraceListeners is covered later in this section. ASP.NET 2.0 also includes a number of small improvements to tracing over ASP.NET 1.x, including trace forwarding between the ASP.NET page-specific `Trace` class and standard Base Class Library's (BCL) `System.Diagnostics.Trace` used by non–Web developers. Additionally, the resolution of the timing output by ASP.NET tracing has increased precision—from 6 digits to 18 digits for highly accurate profiling.

System.Diagnostics.Trace and ASP.NET's Page.Trace

There are multiple things named *Trace* in the whole of the .NET Framework, so it may appear that tracing isn't unified between Web and non-Web applications. Don't be confused because there is a class called `System.Diagnostics.Trace` and there is also a public property on `System.Web.UI.Page` called `Trace`. The `Trace` property on the `Page` class gives you access to the `System.Web.TraceContext` and the ASP.NET-specific tracing mechanism. The `TraceContext` class collects all the details and timing of a Web request. It contains a number of methods, but the one you'll use the most is `Write`. It also includes `Warn`, which simply calls `Write()`, and also ensures that the output generated by `Warn` is colored red.

If you're writing an ASP.NET application that has no supporting components or other assemblies that may be used in a non-Web context, you can usually get a great deal of utility using only the ASP.NET `TraceContext`. However, ASP.NET support tracing is different from the rest of the base class library's tracing. You'll explore ASP.NET's tracing facilities first, and then learn how to bridge the gap and see some new features in 2.0 that make debugging even easier.

Page-Level Tracing

ASP.NET tracing can be enabled on a page-by-page basis by adding `Trace="true"` to the Page directive in any ASP.NET page:

```
<%@ Page Language="C#" Inherits="System.Web.UI.Page" Trace="true" %>
```

Additionally, you can add the `TraceMode` attribute that sets `SortByCategory` or the default, `SortByTime`. You might include a number of categories, one per subsystem, and use `SortByCategory` to group them, or you might use `SortByTime` to see the methods that take up the most CPU time for your application. You can enable tracing programmatically as well, using the `Trace.IsEnabled` property. The capability to enable tracing programmatically means you can enable tracing via a querystring, cookie, or IP address; it's up to you.

Application Tracing

Alternatively, you can enable tracing for the entire application by adding tracing settings in `web.config`. In the following example, `pageOutput="false"` and `requestLimit="20"` are used, so trace information is stored for 20 requests, but not displayed on the page:

```
<configuration>
    <system.web>
        <trace enabled="true" pageOutput="false" requestLimit="20"
            traceMode="SortByTime" localOnly="true" />
    </system.web>
</configuration>
```

The page-level settings take precedence over settings in `web.config`, so if `enabled="false"` is set in `web.config` but `trace="true"` is set on the page, tracing occurs.

Viewing Trace Data

Tracing can be viewed for multiple page requests at the application level by requesting a special page (of sorts) called trace.axd. Note that trace.axd doesn't actually exist; it is actually provided by System.Web.Handlers.TraceHandler, a special IHttpHandler to which trace.axd is bound. When ASP.NET detects an HTTP Request for trace.axd, that request is handled by the TraceHandler rather than by a page.

Create a Web site and a page, and in the Page_Load event, call Trace.Write(). Enable tracing in the web.config as shown in Listing 21-1.

Listing 21-1: Tracing using Page.Trace

Web.config
```
<configuration>
    <system.web>
        <trace enabled="true" pageOutput="true" />
    </system.web>
</configuration>
```

VB
```
Protected Sub Page_Load(ByVal sender As Object, ByVal e As System.EventArgs)
    Handles Me.Load 'All on one line!
        Trace.Write("This message is from the START OF the Page_Load method!")
End Sub
```

C#
```
protected void Page_Load(object sender, EventArgs e)
{
    Trace.Write("This message is from the START of the Page_Load method!");
}
```

Hit the page in the browser a few times and notice that, although this page doesn't create any HTML to speak of, a great deal of trace information is presented in the browser, as shown in Figure 21-6, because the setting is pageOutput="true".

The message from Trace.Write appears after Begin Load and before End Load — it's right in the middle of the Page_Load method where you put it. Also, notice the timing from the Begin Load until the trace output. It takes nearly 6.5 seconds! The page was automatically JIT-compiled as you ran it, and that initial performance hit is over. Now that it's been compiled into native code, a subsequent run of this same page, performed by clicking Refresh in the browser, took only 0.017735 seconds on my laptop because the page had already compiled. It's easy to collect this kind of very valuable performance timing data between Trace statements.

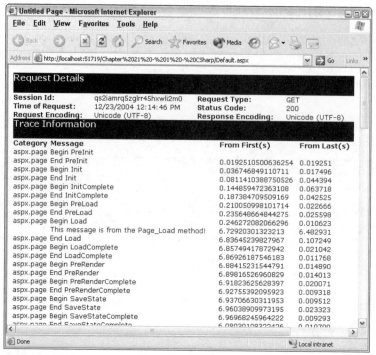

Figure 21-6

Eleven different sections of tracing information provide a great deal of detail and specific insight into the ASP.NET page-rendering process, as described in the following table.

Section	Description
Request Details	Includes the ASP.NET Session ID, the character encoding of the request and response, and the HTTP conversation's returned status code. Be aware of the request and response encoding, especially if you're using any non-Latin character sets. If you're returning languages other than English, you'll want your encoding to be UTF-8. Fortunately that is the default.
Trace Information	Includes all the `Trace.Write` methods called during the lifetime of the HTTP request and a great deal of information about timing. This is probably the most useful section for debugging. The timing information located here is valuable when profiling and searching for methods in your application that take too long to execute.

Section	Description
Control Tree	Presents an HTML representation of the ASP.NET Control Tree. Shows each control's unique ID, runtime type, the number of bytes it took to be rendered, and the bytes it requires in ViewState and ControlState. Don't undervalue the usefulness of these two sections, particularly of the three columns showing the weight of each control. The weight of the control indicates the number of bytes occupied in ViewState and/or ControlState by that particular Control. Be aware of the number of bytes that each of your controls uses, especially if you write your own custom controls, as you want your controls to return as few bytes as possible to keep overall page weight down.
Session State	Lists all the keys for a particular user's session, their types, and their values. Shows only the current user's Session State.
Application State	Lists all the keys in the current application's Application object and their types and values.
Request Cookies	Lists all the cookies passed in during the page's request.
Response Cookies	Lists all the cookies that were passed back during the page's response.
Headers Collection	Shows all the headers that might be passed in during the request from the browser, including Accept-Encoding, indicating whether the browser supports compressed HTTP responses; Accept-Languages, a list of ISO language codes that indicate the order of the user's language preferences; and User-Agent, the identifying string for the user's browser. The string also contains information about the user's operating system and the version or versions of the .NET Framework he is running.
Form Collection	Displays a complete dump of the Form collection and all its keys and values.
Querystring Collection	Displays a dump of the Querystring collection and all its contained keys and values.
Server Variables	A complete dump of name-value pairs of everything that the Web server knows about the application and the requesting browser.

Page output of tracing shows only the data collected for the current page request. However, when visiting `http://localhost/yoursite/trace.axd` you'll see detailed data collected for all requests to the site thus far. If you're using the built-in ASP.NET Development Server, remove the current page from the URL and replace it with `trace.axd`. Don't change the automatically selected port or path.

Again, `trace.axd` is an internal handler, not a real page. When it's requested from a local browser, as shown in Figure 21-7, it displays all tracing information for all requests up to a preset limit.

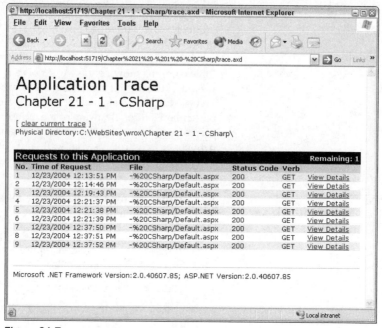

Figure 21-7

Figure 21-7 shows that nine requests have been made to this application and the right side of the header indicates "Remaining: 1". That means that there is one more request remaining before tracing stops for this application. After that final request, tracing data is not saved until an application recycle or until you click "Clear current trace" from the `trace.axd` page. The request limit can be raised in `web.config` at the expense of memory:

```
<trace requestLimit="100" pageOutput="true" enabled="true"/>
```

The maximum request limit value is 10000. If you try to use any greater value, ASP.NET uses 10000 anyway and gives you no error. However, a new property called `mostRecent` is added to the trace section in ASP.NET 2.0. When set to `true`, it shows the most recent requests that are stored in the trace log up to the request limit — instead of showing tracing in the order it occurs (the default) — without using up a lot of memory. Setting `mostRecent` to true causes memory to be used only for the trace information it stores and automatically throws away tracing information over the `requestLimit`.

Clicking "View Details" from `Trace.axd` on any of these requests takes you to a request-specific page with the same details shown in Figure 21-6.

Tracing from Components

The tracing facilities of ASP.NET are very powerful and can stand alone. However, previously we mentioned `System.Diagnostics.Trace`, the tracing framework in the Base Class Library that is not Web-specific and that receives consistent and complete tracing information when an ASP.NET application calls a non–Web-aware component. This can be confusing. Which should you use?

`System.Diagnostics.Trace` is the core .NET Framework tracing library. Along with `System.Diagnostics.Debug`, this class provides flexible, non-invasive tracing and debug output for any application. But, as mentioned earlier, there is rich tracing built into the `System.Web` namespace. As a Web developer, you'll find yourself using ASP.NET's tracing facilities. You may need to have ASP.NET-specific tracing forwarded to the base framework's `System.Diagnostics.Trace`, or more likely, you'll want to have your non–Web-aware components output their trace calls to ASP.NET so you can take advantage of `trace.axd` and other ASP.NET specific features.

Additionally, some confusion surrounds `Trace.Write` and `Debug.Write` functions. Look at the source code for `Debug.Write`, and you see something like this:

```
[Conditional("DEBUG")]
public static void Write(string message)
{
        TraceInternal.Write(message);
}
```

Notice that `Debug.Write` calls a function named `TraceInternal.Write`, which has a conditional attribute indicating that `Debug.Write` is compiled only if the debug preprocessor directive was set. In other words, you can put as many calls to `Debug.Write` as you want in your application without affecting your performance when you compile in Release mode. This enables you to be as verbose as you want to be during the debugging phase of development.

`TraceInternal` cycles through all attached trace listeners, meaning all classes that derive from the `TraceListener` base class and are configured in that application's configuration file. The default `TraceListener` lives in the aptly named `DefaultTraceListener` class and calls the Win32 API `OutputDebugString`. `OutputDebugString` sends your string into the abyss and, if a debugger is listening, it is displayed. If no debugger is listening, `OutputDebugString` does nothing. Everyone knows the debugger listens for output from `OutputDebugString` so this can be a very effective way to listen in on debug versions of your application.

> **For quick and dirty no-touch debugging, try using DbgView from SysInternals at** `http://www.sysinternals.com/ntw2k/freeware/debugview.shtml`. **DbgView requires no installation, works great with all your calls to Debug.Writer, and has lots of cool features such as highlighting and logging to a file.**

Now, if you look at the source code for `Trace.Write` (that's TRACE not DEBUG), you see something like this:

```
[Conditional("TRACE")]
public static void Write(string message)
{
        TraceInternal.Write(message);
}
```

The only difference between `Debug.Write` and `Trace.Write` given these two source snippets is the conditional attribute indicating the preprocessor directive TRACE . You can conditionally compile your assemblies to include tracing statements, debug statements, both, or neither. Most people keep TRACE defined even for release builds and use the configuration file to turn tracing on and off. More than likely, the benefits you gain from making tracing available to your users far outweigh any performance issues that might arise.

Because `Trace.Write` calls the `DefaultTraceListener` just like `Debug.Write`, you can use any debugger to tap into tracing information. So, what's the difference?

When designing your application, think about your deployment model. Are you going to ship debug builds or release builds? Do you want a way for end-users or systems engineers to debug your application using log files or the event viewer? Are there things you want only the developer to see?

Typically, you want to use tracing and `Trace.Write` for any formal information that could be useful in debugging your application in a production environment. `Trace.Write` gives you everything that `Debug.Write` does, except it uses the TRACE preprocessor directive and is not affected by debug or release builds.

This means you have four possibilities for builds: Debug On, Trace On, Both On, or Neither On. You choose what's right for you. Typically, use Both On for debug builds and Trace On for production builds. You can specify these conditional attributes in the property pages or the command line of the compiler, as well as with the C# #define keyword or #CONST keyword for Visual Basic.

Trace Forwarding

You often find existing ASP.NET applications that have been highly instrumented and make extensive use of the ASP.NET `TraceContext` class. ASP.NET version 2.0 introduces a new attribute to the `web.config` <trace> element that allows you to route messages emitted by ASP.NET tracing to `System.Diagnostics.Trace: writeToDiagnosticsTrace`.

```
<trace writeToDiagnosticsTrace="true" pageOutput="true" enabled="true"/>
```

When you set `writeToDiagnosticsTrace` to `true`, all calls to `System.Web.UI.Page.Trace.Write` (the ASP.NET TraceContext) also go to `System.Diagnostics.Trace.Write`, enabling you to use all the standard TraceListeners and tracing options that are covered later in this chapter. The simple `writeToDiagnoticsTrace` setting connects the ASP.NET tracing functionality with the rest of the base class library. I use this feature when I'm deep in debugging my pages, and it's easily turned off using this configuration switch. I believe that more information is better than less, but you may find the exact page event information too verbose. Try it and form your own opinion.

TraceListeners

Output from `System.Diagnostics.Trace` methods is routable by a TraceListener to a text file, to ASP.NET, to an external monitoring system, even to a database. This powerful facility was a woefully underused tool in many ASP.NET 1.1 developers' tool belts. In ASP.NET 1.1, some component developers who knew their components were being used within ASP.NET would introduce a direct reference to `System.Web` and call `HttpContext.Current.Trace`. They did this so that their tracing information would appear in the developer-friendly ASP.NET format. All components called within the context of an `HttpRequest` automatically receive access to that request's current context, enabling the components to talk directly to the request and retrieve cookies or collect information about the user.

However, assuming an `HttpContext` will always be available is dangerous for a number of reasons. First, you are making a big assumption when you declare that your component can be used only within the context of an HttpRequest. Notice that this is said within the context of *a request*, not within the context of *an application*. If you access `HttpContext.Current` even from within the `Application_Start`, you will be surprised to find that `HttpContext.Current` is null. Second, marrying your component's functionality to `HttpContext` makes it tricky if not impossible to use your application in any non-Web context, and unit testing becomes particularly difficult.

If you have a component that is being used by a Web page, but it also needs to be unit tested outside of Web context or must be called from any other context, don't call `HttpContext.Current.Trace`. Instead, use the standard `System.Diagnostics.Trace` and redirect output to the ASP.NET tracing facilities using the new WebPageTraceListener described in the next section. Using the standard trace mechanism means your component can be used in any context, Web or otherwise. You'll still be able to view the component's trace output with a TraceListener.

The framework comes with a number of very useful TraceListeners; you can add them programmatically or via a `.config` file. For example, you can programmatically add a TraceListener log to a file as shown in Listing 21-2. These snippets required the `System.Diagnostics` and `System.IO` namespaces.

Listing 21-2: Configuring TraceListeners

VB

```
Dim myTextListener As New TextWriterTraceListener(File.Create("c:\myListener.log"))
Trace.Listeners.Add(myTextListener)
```

C#

```
TextWriterTraceListener myTextListener = new
    TextWriterTraceListener(File.Create(@"c:\myListener.log"));
Trace.Listeners.Add(myTextListener);
```

You can do the same thing declaratively in `web.config` via an `add` element that passes in the type of TraceListener to use, along with any initializing data it might need. TraceListeners already configured in `machine.config` or a parent `web.config` can also be removed using the `remove` tag, along with their name:

```
<configuration>
  <system.diagnostics>
      <trace autoflush="false" indentsize="4">
```

```
                <listeners>
                    <add name="myListener"
                        type="System.Diagnostics.TextWriterTraceListener"
                        initializeData="c:\myListener.log" />
                    <remove name="Default" />
                </listeners>
            </trace>
        </system.diagnostics>
    </configuration>
```

TraceListeners, like `TextWriterTraceListener`, that access a resource (such as a file, event log, or database) require that the ASP.NET worker process be run as a user who has sufficient access. In order to write to `c:\foo\example.log`, for example, the ASP.NET worker process requires explicit write access in the Access Control List (ACL) of that file.

Notice the preceding example also optionally removes the default TraceListener. If you write your own TraceListener, you must provide a fully qualified assembly name in the `type` attribute.

The New ASP.NET WebPageTraceListener

The new ASP.NET 2.0 `WebPageTraceListener` derives from `System.Diagnostics` `.TraceListener` and automatically forwards tracing information from any component calls to `System.Diagnostics.Trace.Write`. This enables you to write your components using the most generic trace provider and to see its tracing output in the context of your ASP.NET application.

The `WebPageTraceListener` is added to the `web.config` as shown in the following example:

```
<configuration>
  <system.diagnostics>
     <trace autoflush="false" indentsize="4">
          <listeners>
              <add name="webListener"
                  type="System.Web.WebPageTraceListener, System.Web"/>
          </listeners>
      </trace>
  </system.diagnostics>
  <system.web>
        <trace enabled="true" pageOutput="false" localOnly="true" />
  </system.web>
</configuration>
```

Figure 21-8 shows output from a call to `System.Diagnostics.Trace.Write` from a referenced library. It appears within ASP.NET's page tracing. The line generated from the referenced library is circled in this figure.

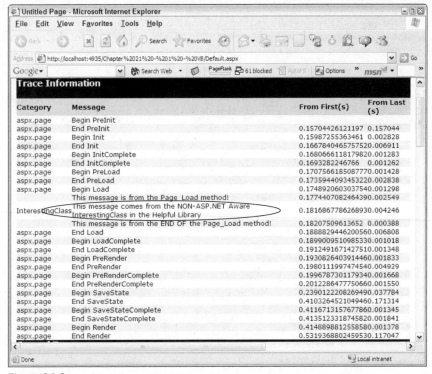

Figure 21-8

EventLogTraceListener

Tracing information can also be sent to the event log using the EventLogTraceListener. This can be a little tricky because ASP.NET requires explicit write access to the event log:

```
<configuration>
 <system.diagnostics>
     <trace autoflush="false" indentsize="4">
         <listeners>
            <add name="EventLogTraceListener"
                 type="System.Diagnostics.EventLogTraceListener"
                 initializeData="Wrox"/>
         </listeners>
     </trace>
 </system.diagnostics>
</configuration>
```

Notice that "Wrox" is passed in as a string to the initializeData attribute as the TraceListener is added. The string "Wrox" appears as the application or *source* for this event. This works fine when debugging your application; most likely, the debugging user has the appropriate access. However, when your application is deployed, it will probably run under a less privileged account, so you must give

explicit write access to a registry key such as `HKLM\System\CurrentControlSet\Services\`
`EventLog\Application\Wrox`, where "Wrox" is the same string passed in to `initializeData`.
Remember that registry keys have ACLs (Access Control Lists) just as files do. Use `RegEdit.exe` to
change the permissions on a registry key by right-clicking the key and selecting Properties, and setting
the ACL just like you would for a file.

Be careful when using the EventLogTraceListener because your event log can fill up fairly quickly if you
have a particularly chatty application. Figure 21-9 shows the same tracing output used in Figure 21-8,
this time in the event log.

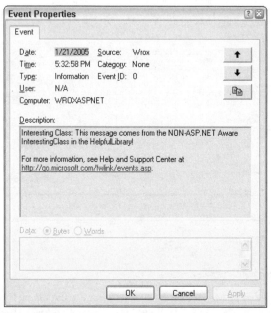

Figure 21-9

Other New Listeners

The .NET 2.0 Framework adds two TraceListeners in addition to the WebPageTraceListener:

❑ **XmlWriterTraceListener:** Derives from `TextWriterTraceListener` and writes out a strongly
typed XML file.

❑ **DelimitedListTraceListener:** Also derives from `TextWriterTraceListener`; writes out
comma-separated values (CSV) files.

One of the interesting things to note about the XML created by the XmlWriterTraceListener — it's not
well-formed XML! Specifically, it doesn't have a root node; it's just a collection of peer nodes as shown in
the following code. This may seem like it goes against many of the ideas you've been told about XML,
but think of each event as a document. Each stands alone and can be consumed alone. They just happen
to be next to each other in one file. Certainly the absence of an ultimate closing tag cleverly dodges the
issue of wellformedness and allows easy appending to a file.

```
<E2ETraceEvent xmlns=\"http://schemas.microsoft.com/2004/06/E2ETraceEvent\">
    <System xmlns=\"http://schemas.microsoft.com/2004/06/windows/eventlog/system\">
        <EventID>0</EventID>
        <Type>3</Type>
        <SubType Name="Information">0</SubType>
        <Level>8</Level>
        <TimeCreated SystemTime="2005-11-05T12:43:44.4234234Z">
        <Source Name="WroxChapter21.exe"/>
        <Correlation ActivityID="{00000000-0000-0000-0000-000000000000>
        <Execution ProcessName="WroxChapter21.exe" ProcessID="4234" ThreadID="1"/>
        <Channel/>
        <Computer>SCOTTPC</Computer>
    </System>
    <ApplicationData>Your Text Here</ApplicationData>
</E2ETraceEvent>
<E2ETraceEvent xmlns=\"http://schemas.microsoft.com/2004/06/E2ETraceEvent\">
    <System xmlns=\"http://schemas.microsoft.com/2004/06/windows/eventlog/system\">
        <EventID>0</EventID>
        <Type>3</Type>
...the XML continues...
```

The "E2E" in E2ETraceEvent stands for end-to-end. Notice that it includes information such as your computer name and a "correlation id." Microsoft will include TraceViewer tools with coming products, such as the product codenamed *Indigo* and the managed WinFX API that will consume this XML Schema and help you diagnose problems with operations that span multiple machines in a Web farm. If your ASP.NET application makes calls to an Indigo service, you may want your app to supply its tracing information in this format to make aggregated analysis easier.

Diagnostic Switches

It's often not convenient to recompile your application just because you want to change tracing characteristics. Sometimes you may want to change your configuration file to add and remove TraceListeners. At other times, you may want to change a configuration parameter or "flip a switch" to adjust the amount of detail the tracing produces. That's where Switch comes in. Switch is an abstract base class that supports a series of diagnostic switches that you can control by using the application's configuration file.

BooleanSwitch

To use a BooleanSwitch, create an instance and pass in the switch name that appears in the application's config file (see Listing 21-3).

Listing 21-3: Using diagnostic switches

```
<configuration>
 <system.diagnostics>
  <switches>
    <add name="ImportantSwitch" value="1" /> <!-- This is for the BooleanSwitch -->
    <add name="LevelSwitch" value="3" />     <!-- This is for the TraceSwitch -->
    <add name="SourceSwitch" value="4" />    <!-- This is for the SourceSwitch -->
  </switches>
 </system.diagnostics>
</configuration>
```

Switches can be used in an `if` statement for any purpose, but they are most useful in the context of tracing along with `System.Diagnostics.Trace.WriteIf`:

VB
```vb
Dim aSwitch As New BooleanSwitch("ImportantSwitch", "Show errors")
System.Diagnostics.Trace.WriteIf(aSwitch.Enabled, "The Switch is enabled!")
```

C#
```csharp
BooleanSwitch aSwitch = new BooleanSwitch("ImportantSwitch", "Show errors");
System.Diagnostics.Trace.WriteIf(aSwitch.Enabled, "The Switch is enabled!");
```

If `ImportantSwitch` is set to 1 in the `config` file, the call to `WriteIf` sends a string to trace output.

TraceSwitch

TraceSwitch offers five levels of tracing from 0 to 4, implying an increasing order: Off, Error, Warning, Info, and Verbose. You construct a `TraceSwitch` exactly as you create a `BooleanSwitch`:

VB
```vb
Dim tSwitch As New TraceSwitch("LevelSwitch", "Trace Levels")
System.Diagnostics.Trace.WriteIf(tSwitch.TraceInfo, "The Switch is 3 or more!")
```

C#
```csharp
TraceSwitch tSwitch = new TraceSwitch("LevelSwitch", "Trace Levels");
System.Diagnostics.Trace.WriteIf(tSwitch.TraceInfo, "The Switch is 3 or more!");
```

There are a number of properties on the `TraceSwitch` class that return `true` if the switch is at the same level or at a higher level than the property's value. For example, the `TraceInfo` property will return `true` if the switch's value is set to 3 or more.

SourceSwitch

New with .NET 2.0 is `SourceSwitch`, which is similar to `TraceSwitch` but provides a greater level of granularity. You call `SourceSwitch.ShouldTrace` with an EventType as the parameter:

VB
```vb
Dim sSwitch As New SourceSwitch("SourceSwitch", "Even More Levels")
System.Diagnostics.Trace.WriteIf(sSwitch.ShouldTrace(TraceEventType.Warning), _
                                 "The Switch is 3 or more!")
```

C#
```csharp
SourceSwitch sSwitch = new SourceSwitch("SourceSwitch", " Even More Levels");
System.Diagnostics.Trace.WriteIf(sSwitch.ShouldTrace(TraceEventType.Warning),
                                 "The Switch is 4 or more!");
```

Web Events

It doesn't exactly qualify as debugging, but a series of new application-monitoring and health-monitoring tools within the system has been added in ASP.NET's `System.Web.Management` namespace in ASP.NET 2.0. These tools can be as valuable as tracing information in helping you monitor, maintain, and diagnose the health of your application. The system has a whole new event model and event engine that can update your application with runtime details. There are a number of built-in events, including application lifetime events such as start and stop and a heartbeat event. You can take these base classes and events and build on them to create events of your own. For example, you might want to create an event that tells you when a user downloads a particularly large file or when a new user is created in your personalization database. You can have your application send an e-mail to you once a day with statistics.

For instance, you can create your own event by deriving from `System.Web.Management.WebBaseEvent`, as shown in Listing 21-4.

Listing 21-4: Web events

VB

```vb
Imports System
Imports System.Web.Management

Namespace Wrox
    Public Class WroxEvent
        Inherits WebBaseEvent

        Public Const WroxEventCode As Integer = WebEventCodes.WebExtendedBase + 1
        Public Sub New(ByVal message As String, ByVal eventSource As Object)
            MyBase.New(message, eventSource, WroxEventCode)
        End Sub
    End Class
End Namespace
```

C#

```csharp
namespace Wrox
{
    using System;
    using System.Web.Management;

    public class WroxEvent: WebBaseEvent
    {
        public const int WroxEventCode = WebEventCodes.WebExtendedBase + 1;
        public WroxEvent(string message, object eventSource) :
            base(message, eventSource, WroxEventCode){}
    }
}
```

Later, in a sample `Page_Load`, you raise this event to the management subsystem:

VB

```vb
Protected Sub Page_Load(sender As Object, e As EventArgs)
    ' Raise a custom event
    Dim anEvent As Wrox.WroxEvent = New Wrox.WroxEvent("Someone visited here", Me)
    anEvent.Raise()
  End Sub
```

C#

```csharp
protected void Page_Load(Object sender, EventArgs e)
{
    // Raise a custom event
    Wrox.WroxEvent anEvent = new Wrox.WroxEvent("Someone visited here!", this);
    anEvent.Raise();
}
```

The event is caught by the management subsystem and can be dispatched to different providers based on a number of rules. This is a much more formal kind of tracing than a call to `Trace.WriteLine`, so you create a strongly typed event class for events specific to your application:

Web.config

```xml
<?xml version="1.0"?>
<configuration>
    <system.web>
        <healthMonitoring enabled="true">
            <providers>
                <add name="WroxDatabaseLoggingProvider"
                    type="System.Web.Management.SqlWebEventProvider"
                    connectionStringName="QuickStartSqlServer"
                    maxEventDetailsLength="1073741823"
                    buffer="false"/>
            </providers>
            <rules>
                <add
                    name="Application Lifetime Events Rule"
                    eventName="All Events"
                    provider="WroxDatabaseLoggingProvider"
                    profile="Critical" />
            </rules>
        </healthMonitoring>
    </system.web>
</configuration>
```

Debugging

Visual Studio includes two configurations by default: *debug* and *release*. The debug configuration automatically defines the debug and trace constants, enabling your application to provide context to a troubleshooter. The option to generate debugging information is turned on by default, causing a program database (or debug) file (PDB) to be generated for each assembly and your solution. They appear in the same \bin folder as your assemblies. Remember, however, that the actual compilation to native code does not occur in Visual Studio, but rather at runtime using just-in-time compilation (JIT). The JIT will automatically optimize your code for speed. Optimized code, however, is considerably harder to debug because the operations that are generated may not correspond directly to lines in your source code. For debug purposes, this option is set to `false`.

What's Required

The PDBs are created when either the C# compiler (CSC.EXE) or Visual Basic compiler (VBC.EXE) is invoked with the /debug:full command lines switch. As an option, if you use /debug:pdbonly, you will generate PDBs but still direct the compiler to produce release-mode code.

Debug Versus Release

The debug and release configurations that come with Visual Studio are generally sufficient for your needs. However, these configurations control only the compilation options of the code behind files. Remember that, depending on how you've chosen to design your ASP.NET application, the ASP.NET

.aspx files may be compiled the first time they're hit, or the entire application may compile the first time a page is hit. You can control these compilation settings via the compilation elements within the <system.web> section of your application's web.config. Set <compilation debug="true"> to produce binaries as you do when using the /debug:full switches. PDBs are also produced.

The average developer is most concerned with the existence of PDB files. When these files exist in your ASP.NET applications \bin folder, the runtime provides you with line numbers. Of course, line numbers greatly assist in debugging. You can't step through source code during an interactive debugging session without these files.

> An interesting CLR Internals trick: Call System.Diagnostics.Debugger.Launch within your assembly, even if the assembly was compiled via /debug:pdbonly, and the debugger pops up. The JIT compiler compiles code on the first call to a method, and the code that it generates is debuggable because JIT knows that a debugger is attached.

Debugging and the JIT Dialog

When an unhandled error occurs in an ASP.NET application, the default error handler for the ASP.NET worker process catches it and tries to output some HTML that expresses what happened. However, when you are debugging components outside of ASP.NET, perhaps within the context of unit testing, the debug dialog appears when the .NET application throws an unhandled exception.

If something has gone horribly wrong with an ASP.NET application, it's conceivable that you may find a Web server with the dialog box popped up waiting for your input. This can be especially inconvenient if the machine has no keyboard or monitor hooked up. The day may come when you want to turn off the debug dialog that appears, and you have two options to do this:

❑ You can disable JIT Debugging from the registry. The proper registry key is HKLM\Software\ Microsoft\.NETFramework\DbgJITDebugLaunchSetting. There are three possible values for the option:

  ❑ 0: Prompts the user by means of a message box. The choices presented include Continue, which results in a stack dump and process termination, and Attach a Debugger, which means the runtime spawns the debugger listed in the DbgManagedDebugger registry key. If no key exists, the debugger releases control and the process is terminated.

  ❑ 1: Does not display a dialog. This results in a stack dump and then process termination.

  ❑ 2: Launches the debugger listed in the DbgManagedDebugger registry key.

  For this option, the registry entry must to be set to 0 for the dialog to show up.

❑ To disable the JIT debug dialog and still present an error dialog, within Visual Studio.NET, choose Tools ➪ Options ➪ Debugging ➪ Just-In-Time and deselect Common Language Runtime. Instead of the Select a Debugger dialog, an OK/Cancel dialog will appear during an unhandled exception.

IIS versus ASP.NET Development Server

ASP.NET greatly simplifies your Web developing experience by enabling you to develop applications without IIS (Internet Information Server — the Web server) on your developer machine. Rather than the traditional style of creating a virtual directory and mapping it to a physical directory, a directory can be opened as a Web site simply by telling Visual Studio that it is a Web site. When you open a Web site from the File menu, the first option on the list of places to open from is the file system. Visual Studio considers any folder that you open to be the root of a Web site. Other options, of course, are opening Web sites from your local IIS instance, FTP, or source control.

Using the IIS option works much as it does in previous versions of Visual Studio with a few convenient changes such as the capability to create a Web site or map a virtual directory directly from the Open Web Site dialog. However, more interesting stuff happens after you open a Web site from the file system.

By default, Web sites that exist only on the file system have a "just-in-time" Web server instantiated called the ASP.NET Development Server. The small Web server hosts the exact same ASP.NET page rendering at runtime that is hosted within IIS on a deployed production site. The page rendering behavior should be identical under the small server as it is under IIS. You should be aware of a few important differences and specific caveats to ensure a smooth transition from development to production.

Create a new Web site by selecting File ⇨ New Web Site and immediately pressing F5 to begin a debugging session. You are greeted with a Debugging Not Enabled dialog box. The first option automatically adds a new `web.config` file with debugging enabled. (Earlier versions of Visual Studio required a tedious manual process.) Click OK and balloon help appears in the system tray announcing that the ASP.NET Development Server has started up. It also shows what random high-number port the Web server has selected on the local host. When you close your browser and stop your debugging session, the tiny Web server shuts down.

The ASP.NET Development Server is an application, not a service. It is not a replacement for IIS, nor does it try to be. It's really just a broker that sits between the developer and the ASP.NET page renderer, and it contains very few, if any, of the security benefits that IIS includes. It is loosely based on a .NET 1.*x* project code-named Cassini that is downloadable from `http://asp.net/Projects/Cassini/Download/Default.aspx`. This project was a sample meant to illustrate how to use the `System.Web.Hosting` namespace. The Cassini project was the grandparent and now the ASP.NET Development Server is a first-class member of the Visual Studio product family. Including this tiny Web Server with the Development Environment also allows Visual Studio 2005 to be used on Windows XP Home systems that are unable to run IIS.

The small Web server runs under the same user context that runs Visual Studio. If your application requires a specific security context, such as an anonymous user or specific domain user, consider using IIS as your development Web server. Additionally, because the Web server starts up on a port other than port 80, be sure to use best practices while developing your site's navigation scheme. Often developers assume their site's URL will not include a port number (it will default to port 80), that their site may appear within a specific subdomain (`bar.foo.com`), or that their site will appear within a subdirectory (`www.foo.com/bar`). Consider making your navigation relative to the virtual root of your application so your application is resilient enough to be run in many contexts.

Starting a Debugging Session

There are a number of ways to enter an interactive debugging session with ASP.NET. Visual Studio can fire up the ASP.NET Worker Process, load your newly compiled Web site and attach the debugging to the Worker Process automatically. Or, you can attach a debugger to a site that is already running. Visual Studio also includes a new simpler remote debugging tool for cross-machine debugging.

F5 Debugging

When you start debugging an ASP.NET application, Visual Studio takes into consideration all the Start options within your project properties. Just as ASP.NET 1.*x* Visual Studio can be set to launch the browser on a specific page, the new version allows you to start debugging using the currently selected page. The specific page has been selected so that the Visual Studio debugger can automatically attach the correct process, which might be the Visual Studio Web Server, the ASP.NET Worker Process, or a remote debug monitor.

Attaching to a Process

It's often convenient to jump into an interactive debugging session of a Web site that is already running, and at known state, rather than starting an application from scratch each time you debug. To begin debugging a site that is already running, from Visual Studio's Debug menu, select Attach to Process. The dialog has been improved from previous versions of Visual Studio and now includes a Refresh button and simplifies most common debugging use cases by showing only those processes that belong to the user and that are in the currently running session.

Also included is a transport drop-down with the default transport selected. The default allows you to select processes on your computer or on a remote computer that's running the Remote Debugging Monitor. Other options are there for smart client or unmanaged debugging.

The only difference between starting a Debug session via F5 and attaching to a process manually is that when you debug via F5, Visual Studio automatically starts up a browser or external application for you. Remember that if you use Attach to Process, it is assumed that you have already done the work of starting up the process. The ASP.NET Worker Processes under IIS will start up when the site has been hit with an HttpRequest *at least once. The debugger can now attach to the running Worker Process.*

Sometimes you want to debug an ASP.NET application that is already running on your computer. If that application was not started by Visual Studio and you want to attach to it, select Attach to Process from the Debug menu and choose either ASPNET_WP.exe (if you're running Windows XP) or W3WP.exe (if you are running Windows 2003 server). Be careful that you are not trying to debug an application that is actively servicing other users or you may ruin their experience.

Simpler Remote Debugging

Remote debugging got simpler with this version of Visual Studio. However, in the interest of security, you must have the appropriate credentials to perform remote debugging. You'll find a Remote Debugger folder in C:\Program Files\Microsoft Visual Studio 8\Common7\IDE. In Figure 21-10, Explorer is shown open and the Remote Debugger folder is selected and has been configured as a shared directory for access over the local network.

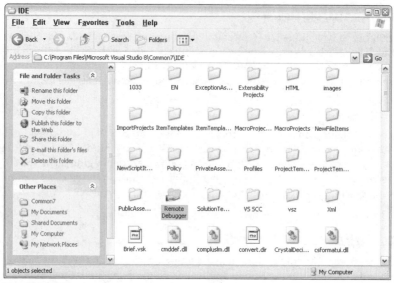

Figure 21-10

To begin, remote debugging must be set up on the machine that contains the application you want to debug. Rather than performing a complicated installation, you can now use the Remote Debug Monitor, and an application that can simply be run off a file share. The easiest scenario has you sharing these components directly from your Visual Studio machine and then running `msvsmon.exe` off the share, as seen in Figure 21-11.

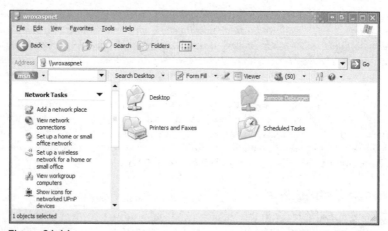

Figure 21-11

Simply running the Remote Debug Monitor executable off the file share can make remote ASP.NET debugging of an already-deployed applications much simpler, although you still need to manually attach to the ASP.NET worker process because automatic attaching is not supported.

You are allowed to debug a process that's running under your account and password without any special permissions. If you need to debug a process running under another account name, such as an ASP.NET worker process running as a user who is not you, you must be an administrator on the machine running the process.

The most important thing to remember when debugging remotely is this: You need to get the user account that is running as Visual Studio to map somehow to a legitimate user account on the machine running the Remote Debug Monitor (`msvsmon.exe`) machine and vice versa. The easiest way to do this is to create a local user account on both computers with the same username and password. To run `msvsmon` as a user other than Visual Studio, you must create two user accounts on each computer.

If one of the machines is located on a domain, be aware that domain account can be mapped to a local account. You create a local user account on both computers. However, if you pick the same username and password as your domain account, Visual Studio can be run as a domain account. Figure 21-12 shows the machine name is SCOTTPC and the username is *Wrox*. A Wrox user was created on both machines with the same password on each.

> *For Windows XP machines on a workgroup, the security option entitled Network Security: Shared and Security Model for Local Accounts affects your use of the Remote Debug Monitor. If this option is set to Guest Only — Local Users Authenticate As Guest, then remote debugging fails and shows you a dialog. Configure this via the Local Security Policy MMC-based administrative tool. The warning doesn't affect Windows 2000 or Windows Server 2003, or Windows XP-based computers that are joined to a domain.*

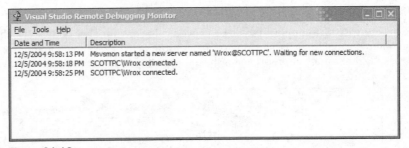

Figure 21-12

Debugging Running Windows XP Service Pack 2

Make sure that TCP Port 80 is set to allow ASP.NET and IIS to communicate with the remote machine. Try to keep the scope limited, using options such as Local Subnet Only, and avoid exposing your Web server to the Internet during development. Also include TCP Port 135, which allows DCOM to communicate with remote machines as well as with UDP Ports 4500 and 500 for IPSec-based security. Lastly, confirm that the Remote Debug Monitor (`msvsmon.exe`) is in the list of exceptions to the firewall. Again, avoid exposing your debugging session to the outside world. Remote debugging is usually a last resort if the bug isn't reproducible for whatever reason on the developer workstation.

New Tools to Help You with Debugging

The debugging experience in Visual Studio has improved arguably more than any other aspect of the environment. A number of new tools, some obvious, some more subtle, assist you in every step of the debug session.

Debugger Datatips

Previous versions of Visual Studio gave you tooltips when the user hovered the mouse over variables of simple types. Visual Studio 2005 offers *datatips*, allowing. complex types to be explored using a modeless tree-style view that acts like a tooltip and provides much more information. After you traverse the tree to the node that you're interested in, that simple type can be viewed using a visualizer by clicking the small magnifying glass icon, as seen in Figure 21-13.

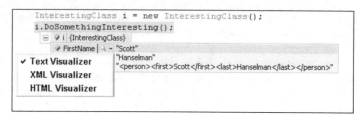

Figure 21-13

Data Visualizers

As you see in Figure 21-13, a simple type can be viewed using any number of data visualizers. For example, if a simple variable such as a string contains a fragment of XML, you might want to visualize that data in a style that's more appropriate for the data's native format, as shown in Figure 21-14.

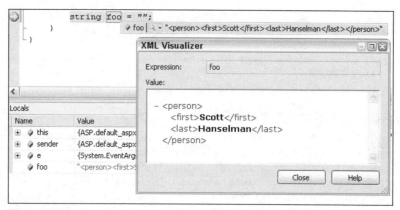

Figure 21-14

The visualizers are straightforward to write and, although Visual Studio ships with default visualizers for text, HTML, XML, and DataSets, expect to see a flood of new visualizers appearing on the Internet with support for images, collection classes, and more. The result is a rich, unparalleled debugging experience.

Error Notifications

During an interactive debugging session, Visual Studio now strives to assist you with informative Error Notifications. These notifications not only report on events like unhandled exceptions, but also offer context-sensitive troubleshooting tips and next steps for dealing with the situation. Figure 21-15 shows an unhandled `NullReferenceException` along with the good advice that we might try using the "new" keyword to create an object instance before using it. Oops!

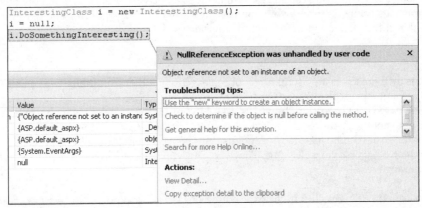

Figure 21-15

Edit and Continue (Lack of) Support, or Edit and Refresh

Visual Basic 6 was all about developing things quickly, and its most powerful feature was the Edit and Continue feature, which gave you capability to change code during a debugging session without restarting the session. In break mode, you could modify code fix bugs and move on. The 2.0 version of the CLR has restored this feature for both C# and Visual Basic. Although this has a large number of developers cheering, unfortunately this feature is not available to ASP.NET developers.

In ASP.NET, your assembly is compiled not by Visual Studio, but by the ASP.NET runtime using the same technique it does during a normal Web page request by a browser. To cooperate with the debugger and support Edit and Continue within ASP.NET, a number of fantastically complex modifications to ASP.NET runtime would have been required by the development team. Rather than including support for this feature, ASP.NET developers can use *page recycling*.

This means that code changes are made during a debugging session, and then the whole page is refreshed via F5, automatically recompiled, and re-executed. Basically, ASP.NET 2.0 includes much improved support for Edit and Refresh, but not for Edit and Continue.

Just My Code Debugging

A new concept in the .NET 2.0 CLR is called *Just My Code* debugging. Any method in code can be explicitly marked with the new attribute `[DebuggerNonUserCode]`. Using this explicit technique and a number of other heuristic methods internal to the CLR, the debugger silently skips over code that isn't important to the code at hand. You can find the new preference Enable Just My Code in Tools ⇨ Options ⇨ Debugging.

The [DebuggerHidden] attribute is still available in .NET 2.0 and hides methods from the debugger, regardless of the user's Just My Code preference. The 1.1 attribute [DebuggerStepThrough] tells the debugger to step through, rather than into, any method to which it's applied; the [DebuggerNonUserCode] attribute is a much more pervasive and complete implementation that works at runtime on delegates, virtual functions, and any arbitrarily complex code.

Be aware that these attributes and this new user option exist to help you debug code effectively and not be fooled by any confusing call stacks. While these can be very useful, be sure not to use them on your components until you're sure you won't accidentally hide the very error you're trying to debug. Typically these attributes are used for components such as proxies or thin shim layers.

Tracepoints

Breakpoints by themselves are useful for stopping execution either conditionally or unconditionally. Standard breakpoints break always. Conditional breakpoints cause you to enter an interactive debugging session based on a condition. Tracing is useful to output the value of a variable or assertion to the debugger or to another location. If you combine all these features, what do you get? Tracepoints, a new and powerful Visual Studio feature. Tracepoints can save you from hitting breakpoints dozens of times just to catch an edge case variable value. They can save you from covering your code with breakpoints to catch a strange case.

To insert a Tracepoint, right-click in the code editor and select Breakpoint ⇨ Insert Tracepoint. You'll get the dialog shown in Figure 21-16. The icon that indicates a breakpoint is a red circle, and the icon for a Tracepoint is a red diamond. Arbitrary strings can be created from the dialog using pseudo-variables in the form of keywords like $CALLSTACK or $FUNCTION, as well as the values of variables in scope placed in curly braces. In Figure 21-16 , the value of i.FirstName (placed in curly braces) is shown in the complete string with the Debug output of Visual Studio.

SQL Stored Proc Debugging

Database projects are file-based projects that let you manage and execute database queries. You can add your existing SQL scripts to the project or create new ones and edit them within Visual Studio. Database projects and SQL debugging are not available in the Express or Standard versions of Visual Studio. They are available only in the Professional or Team Edition Visual Studio SKUs/versions.

When debugging database applications, you can't use Step Into (F11) to step between code in the application tier into the code in SQL Server 2005 (be it T-SQL or CLR SQL). However, you can set a breakpoint in the stored procedure code and use Continue (F5) to execute code to that set break point.

When debugging SQL on SQL Server 2005, be aware of any software or hardware firewalls you may be running. Windows XP SP2's software firewall will warn you what you're trying to do. Be sure to select "unblock" in any warning dialogs to ensure that SQL Server 2005 and Visual Studio can communicate.

If you are using a SQL account to connect to the SQL Server, make sure the Windows User Account you run Visual Studio under is also an administrator on the SQL Server machine. You can add accounts to SQL Server's sysadmin privilege using the SQL command sp_addsrvrolemember 'Domain\Name', 'sysadmin'. Of course, never do this in production; and better yet, do your debugging on a machine with everything installed locally.

If you're using the NT Authentication model on the SQL Server 2005, make sure that account has permissions to run the `sp_enable_sql_debug` stored procedure. You can give account access to this stored procedure by using the SQL commands CREATE USER UserName FOR LOGIN 'Domain\Name' followed by GRANT EXECUTE ON `sp_enable_sql_debug` TO UserName. This creates a SQL user that is associated directly with a specific Windows User and then explicitly grants permissions to debug TSQL to that user. On SQL Server 2000, the user must have access to the extended stored procedure `sp_sdidebug`.

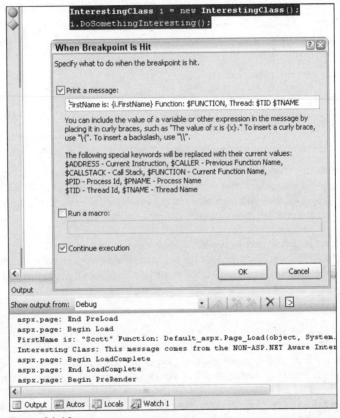

Figure 21-16

For slightly older installations such as Windows 2000 and Windows NT 4, or if you are using SQL 2000, be sure to visit MSDN for the latest details and tools in this space. The MSDN URL for debugging SQL Server is `http://msdn2.microsoft.com/library/zefbf0t6`.

Exception and Error Handling

When an exception occurs in your ASP.NET application code, you can handle it in a number of ways, but the best approach is a multi-pronged one:

❑ Catch what you expect:

  ❑ Use a `Try/Catch` around error-prone code. This can always catch specific exceptions that you can deal with, such as `System.IO.FileNotFoundException`.

  ❑ Rather than catching exceptions around specific chunks of code at the page level, consider using the page-level error handler to catch specific exceptions that might happen anywhere on the page.

❑ But prepare for unhandled exceptions:

  ❑ Set the `Page.Error` property if a specific page should show a specific error at page for any unhandled exception. This can also be done using the `<%@ Page %>` directive or the code behind the property.

  ❑ Have default error pages for 400 and 500 errors set in your `web.config`.

  ❑ Have a boilerplate `Application_OnError` handler that takes into consideration both specific exceptions that you can do something about, as well as all unhandled exceptions that you may want logged to either the event log, a text file, or other instrumentation mechanism.

The phrase *unhandled exception* may be alarming, but remember that you don't do anyone any good catching an exception that you can't recover from. Unhandled exceptions are okay if they are just that — exceptional. For these situations, rely on global exception handlers for logging and friendly error pages that you can present to the user.

> **Why try to catch an exception by adding code everywhere if you can catch and log exceptions all in one place? A common mistake is creating a try/catch block around some arbitrary code and catching the least specific exception type — `System.Exception`. A rule of thumb is, don't catch any exception that you can't do anything about. Just because an exception *can* be thrown by a particular method doesn't mean you have to catch it. It's *exceptional*, remember? Also, there are exception handlers at both the page and the application level. Catch exceptions in these two centralized locations rather than all over.**

Handling Exceptions on a Page

To handle exceptions at a page level, override the `OnError` method that `System.Web.UI.Page` inherits from the `TemplateControl` class (see Listing 21-5). Calling `Server.GetLastError` gives you access to the exception that just occurred. Be aware that a chain of exceptions may have occurred, and you can use the `ExceptionGetBaseException` method to return the root exception.

Listing 21-5: Page-level error handling

VB

```vb
Protected Overrides Sub OnError(ByVal e As System.EventArgs)
    Dim AnError As System.Exception = Server.GetLastError()
    If (TypeOf AnError.GetBaseException() Is SomeSpecificException) Then
        Response.Write("Something bad happened!")
        Response.StatusCode = 200
        Server.ClearError()
        Response.End()
    End If
End Sub
```

C#

```csharp
protected override void OnError(EventArgs e)
{
    System.Exception anError = Server.GetLastError();
    if (anError.GetBaseException() is SomeSpecificException)
    {
        Response.Write("Something bad happened!");
        Response.StatusCode = 200;
        Server.ClearError();
        Response.End();
    }
}
```

Handling Application Exceptions

The technique of catching exceptions in a centralized location can be applied to error handling at the application level in Global.asax, as shown in Listing 21-6. If an exception is not caught on the page, the web.config is checked for an alternate error page; if there isn't one, the exception bubbles up to the application and your user sees a complete call stack.

Listing 21-6: Application-level error handling

VB

```vb
Protected Sub Application_Error(sender as Object, ByVal e As System.EventArgs)
    Dim bigError As System.Exception = Server.GetLastError()
    'Example checking for HttpRequestValidationException
    If (TypeOf bigError.GetBaseException() Is HttpRequestValidationException) Then
        System.Diagnostics.Trace.WriteLine(bigError.ToString)
        Server.ClearError()
    End If
End Sub
```

C#

```csharp
protected void Application_Error(Object sender, EventArgs e)
{
    System.Exception bigError = Server.GetLastError();
    //Example checking for HttpRequestValidationException
    if(bigError.GetBaseException() is HttpRequestValidationException )
    {
```

(continued)

Listing 21-6: *(continued)*

```
        System.Diagnostics.Trace.WriteLine(bigError.ToString());
        Server.ClearError();
    }
}
```

Unhandled application errors turn into HTTP Status Code 500 and display errors in the browser. These errors, including the complete calls back and other technical details, may be useful during development, but are hardly useful at production time. Most often, you want to create an error handler (as shown previously) to log your error and to give the user a friendlier page to view.

> If you ever find yourself trying to catch exceptions of type System.Exception, take a look at the code to see whether you can avoid it. There's almost never a reason to do catch such a non-specific exception, and you're more likely to swallow exceptions that can provide valuable debugging. Check the API documentation for the framework method you are calling—a section specifically lists what exceptions an API call might throw. Never rely on an exception occurring to get a standard code path to work.

Http Status Codes

Every HttpRequest results in an HttpResponse, and every HttpResponse includes a status code. The following table describes 11 particularly interesting HTTP status codes.

Status Code	Explanation
200 OK	Everything went well.
301 Moved Permanently	Reminds the caller to use a new, permanent URL rather than the one he used to get here.
302 Found	Returned during a Response.Redirect. This is the way to say "No, no, look over here right now."
304 Not Modified	Returned as the result of a conditional GET when a requested document hasn't been modified. It is the basis of all browser-based caching. An HTTP message-body must not be returned when using a 304.
307 Temporary Redirect	Redirects calls to ASMX Web services to alternate URLs. Rarely used with ASP.NET.
400 Bad Request	Request was malformed.
401 Unauthorized	Request requires authentication from the user.
403 Forbidden	Authentication has failed, indicating that the server understood the requests but cannot fulfill it.

Status Code	Explanation
404 Not Found	The server has not found an appropriate file or handler to handle this request. The implication is that this may be a temporary state. This happens in ASP.NET not only because a file cannot be found, but also because it may be inappropriately mapped to an IHttpHandler that was not available to service the request.
410 Gone	The equivalent of a permanent 404 indicating to the client that it should delete any references to this link if possible. 404s usually indicate that the server does not know whether the condition is permanent.
500 Internal Server Error	The official text for this error is "The server encountered an unexpected condition which prevented it from fulfilling the request," but this error can occur when any unhandled exception bubbles all the way up to the user from ASP.NET.

Any status code greater than or equal to 400 is considered an error and, unless you configure otherwise, the user will likely see an unfriendly message in his browser. If you have not already handled these errors inside of the ASP.NET runtime by checking their exception types, or if the error occurred outside of ASP.NET and you want to show the user a friendly message, you can assign pages to any status code within web.config, as the following example shows:

```
<customErrors mode ="On" >
    <error statusCode ="500" redirect ="FriendlyMassiveError.aspx" />
</customErrors>
```

After making a change to the customer errors section of your web.config, make sure a page is available to be shown to the user. A classic mistake in error redirection is redirecting the user to a page that will cause an error, thereby getting him stuck in a loop. Use a great deal of care if you have complicated headers or footers in your application that might cause an error if they appear on an error page. Avoid hitting the database or performing any other backend operation that requires either user authorization or that the user's session be in any specific state. In other words, make sure that the error page is a reliable standalone.

> Any status code greater than or equal to 400 increments the ASP.NET Requests Failed performance counter. 401 increments Requests Failed and Requests Not Authorized. 404 and 414 increment both Requests Failed and Requests Not Found. Requests that result in a 500 status code increment Requests Failed and Requests Timed Out. If you're going to return status codes, you must realize their effects and their implications.

Summary

This chapter examined the debugging tools available to you for creating robust ASP.NET 2.0 applications. A successful debugging experience includes not only interactive debugging with new features like datatips, data visualizers, and error notifications, but also powerful options around configurable tracing and logging of information.

Remote debugging is easier than ever with ASP.NET 2.0, and the capability to write and debug ASP.NET pages without installing IIS removes yet another layer of complexity from the development process.

Visual Studio 2005 and its extensible new debugging mechanisms will no doubt be expanded in the coming months by intrepid bloggers and enthusiasts, making debugging even less like the tedious experience it has been in the past.

File I/O and Streams

Although most of this book concentrates specifically on learning and using the features of ASP.NET 2.0, .NET provides an enormous amount of additional functionality in other areas of the Base Class Library (BCL). This chapter examines a few of the common base classes that you can use to enhance your ASP.NET applications. First, you look at using the frameworks `System.IO` namespace to manage files on the local file system. Next, you explore how to use the various Stream classes within the framework to read from and write different data formats to memory and the local file system. Finally, you learn how to use the .NET Framework to communicate with other computers across the Internet using common protocols like HTTP and FTP.

A Word About I/O Security

Although this chapter is not specifically about ASP.NET security, you need to understand the impact of local system security on what the ASP.NET Worker Process is allowed to do inside of the IO namespace. Remember that generally, when your code is executed by IIS, it executes under the context of the ASP.NET Worker Process user account (ASPNET) and, therefore, your application may be restricted by that account's security rights. For example, by default, the ASP.NET Worker Process does not have rights to write to the local disk. The two main areas that you should look at to get a very basic understanding of the impact of security on an application are impersonation and user account ACLs. ASP.NET security is discussed thoroughly in Chapter 18.

Additionally, this chapter demonstrates how to use classes in the BCL to delete files and directories and to modify the permissions of directories and files. Recognize that it is entirely possible to permanently delete important data from your hard drive or change the permissions of a resource, which would result in you losing the ability to access the resource. *Be very careful* when using these classes against the file system.

Working with Drives, Directories, and Files

Many times in your ASP.NET applications, you need to interact with the local file system, reading directory structures, reading and writing to files, or performing many other tasks. The System.IO namespace within the .NET Framework makes working with file system directories and files very easy. While working with the classes in the System.IO namespace, keep in mind that because your ASP.NET applications are executing on the server, the file system you are accessing is the one your Web application is running on. You, of course, cannot use an ASP.NET application to access the end user's file system.

The DriveInfo Class

You can start working with the System.IO namespace at the top of the directory tree by using a great new addition to the .NET 2.0 class libraries, the DriveInfo class. This class supplements the GetLogicalDrives() method of the Directory class included in prior versions of the .NET Framework. It provides you with extended information on any drive registered with the server's local file system. You can get information such as the name, type, size, and status of each drive. Listing 22-1 shows you how to create a DriveInfo object and display local drive information on a Web page.

Listing 22-1: Displaying local drive information

VB

```
<script runat="server">
    Protected Sub Page_Load(ByVal sender As Object, ByVal e As System.EventArgs)
        Dim drive As New System.IO.DriveInfo("C:\")
        lblDriveName.Text = drive.Name
        lblDriveType.Text = drive.DriveType.ToString()
        lblAvailableFreeSpace.Text = drive.AvailableFreeSpace.ToString()
        lblDriveFormat.Text = drive.DriveFormat
        lblTotalFreeSpace.Text = drive.TotalFreeSpace.ToString()
        lblTotalSize.Text = drive.TotalSize.ToString()
        lblVolumeLabel.Text = drive.VolumeLabel
    End Sub
</script>

<html xmlns="http://www.w3.org/1999/xhtml" >
<head runat="server">
    <title>Displaying Drive Information</title>
</head>
<body>
    <form id="form1" runat="server">
    <div>
        <table>
            <tr><td>Drive Name:</td><td>
                <asp:Label ID="lblDriveName" runat="server" Text="Label" />
            </td></tr>
            <tr><td>Drive Type:</td><td>
                <asp:Label ID="lblDriveType" runat="server" Text="Label"/>
            </td></tr>
            <tr><td>Available Free Space:</td><td>
                <asp:Label ID="lblAvailableFreeSpace" runat="server" Text="Label" />
            </td></tr>
            <tr><td>Drive Format:</td><td>
```

```
                    <asp:Label ID="lblDriveFormat" runat="server" Text="Label" />
            </td></tr>
            <tr><td>Total Free Space:</td><td>
                <asp:Label ID="lblTotalFreeSpace" runat="server" Text="Label" />
            </td></tr>
            <tr><td>Total Size:</td><td>
                <asp:Label ID="lblTotalSize" runat="server" Text="Label" />
            </td></tr>
            <tr><td>Volume Label</td><td>
                <asp:Label ID="lblVolumeLabel" runat="server" Text="Label" />
            </td></tr>
        </table>
    </div>
    </form>
</body>
</html>
```

C#

```
<script runat="server">
    protected void Page_Load(object sender, EventArgs e)
    {
        System.IO.DriveInfo drive = new System.IO.DriveInfo(@"C:\");
        lblDriveName.Text = drive.Name;
        lblDriveType.Text = drive.DriveType.ToString();
        lblAvailableFreeSpace.Text = drive.AvailableFreeSpace.ToString();
        lblDriveFormat.Text = drive.DriveFormat;
        lblTotalFreeSpace.Text = drive.TotalFreeSpace.ToString();
        lblTotalSize.Text = drive.TotalSize.ToString();
        lblVolumeLabel.Text = drive.VolumeLabel;
    }
</script>
```

One of the more interesting properties in the sample is the `DriveType` enumeration. This read-only enumeration tells you what the drive type is, for example CD-ROM, Fixed, Ram, or Removable. Figure 22-1 shows you what the page looks like when you view it in a browser.

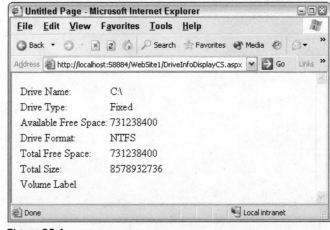

Figure 22-1

You can also enumerate through all the drives on the local file system by using the `DriveInfo`'s static `GetDrives()` method. Listing 22-2 shows an example of enumerating through the local file system drives and adding each drive as a root node to a TreeView control.

Listing 22-2: Enumerating through local file system drives

VB

```vb
<script runat="server">
    Protected Sub Page_Load(ByVal sender As Object, ByVal e As System.EventArgs)
        If (Not Page.IsPostBack) Then
        For Each drive As System.IO.DriveInfo In System.IO.DriveInfo.GetDrives()

            Dim node As TreeNode = New TreeNode()
            node.Value = drive.Name

            ' Make sure the drive is ready before we access it
            If (drive.IsReady) Then
                node.Text = drive.Name & _
                            " - (free space: " & drive.AvailableFreeSpace & ")"
            Else
                node.Text = drive.Name & " - (not ready)"
            End If

            Me.TreeView1.Nodes.Add(node)
        Next
        End If
    End Sub
</script>

<html xmlns="http://www.w3.org/1999/xhtml" >
<head runat="server">
    <title>Enumerate Local System Drives</title>
</head>
<body>
    <form id="form1" runat="server">
    <div>
        <table>
            <tr>
                <td style="width: 100px" valign="top">
                    <asp:TreeView ID="TreeView1" runat="server"></asp:TreeView>
                </td>
            </tr>
        </table>
    </div>
    </form>
</body>
</html>
```

C#

```csharp
<script runat="server">
    protected void Page_Load(object sender, EventArgs e)
    {
        if (!Page.IsPostBack)
        {
        foreach (System.IO.DriveInfo drive in System.IO.DriveInfo.GetDrives())
        {
            TreeNode node = new TreeNode();
```

```
                node.Value = drive.Name;

                //Make sure the drive is ready before we access it
                if (drive.IsReady)
                    node.Text = drive.Name +
                                " - (free space: " + drive.AvailableFreeSpace + ")";
                else
                    node.Text = drive.Name + " - (not ready)";

                this.TreeView1.Nodes.Add(node);
            }
        }
    }
</script>
```

Notice that, in this sample, the drive object's `IsReady` property is a read-only property used to test whether the drive is accessible. If you are enumerating drives, it's always a good idea to test for this before attempting to access any of the other drive properties because removable drives and network drives may not always be available when your code is executed. Figure 22-2 shows what the page looks like when viewed in the browser.

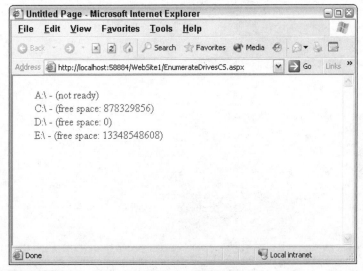

Figure 22-2

The Directory and DirectoryInfo Classes

Next, you can build on the previous examples and add the capability to browse through the system's directory structure. The `System.IO` namespace contains two classes for working with file system directories, the `Directory` and `DirectoryInfo` classes. The `Directory` class exposes static methods you can use to create, move, and delete directories. The `DirectoryInfo` represents a specific directory and lets you perform many of the same actions as the `Directory` class on the specific directory. Additionally, it enumerates child directories and files.

To continue the example, you can use the `GetDirectories()` method of the `DirectoryInfo` class to create a recursive method that loops through each system drive directory tree and adds the directories to a TreeView control to create a small directory browser. Listing 22-3 shows how to create a recursive `LoadDirectories()` method to walk through the local file system's directory structure.

Listing 22-3: Enumerating file system directories

VB

```
<script runat="server">

    Protected Sub Page_Load(ByVal sender As Object, ByVal e As System.EventArgs)
        If (Not Page.IsPostBack) Then
        For Each drive As System.IO.DriveInfo In System.IO.DriveInfo.GetDrives()

            Dim node As TreeNode = New TreeNode()
            node.Value = drive.Name

            If (drive.IsReady) Then
                node.Text = drive.Name & _
                                " - (free space: " & drive.AvailableFreeSpace & ")"

                LoadDirectories(node, drive.Name)
            Else
                node.Text = drive.Name & " - (not ready)"
            End If

            Me.TreeView1.Nodes.Add(node)
        Next
        End if

        Me.TreeView1.CollapseAll()

    End Sub

    Private Sub LoadDirectories(ByVal parent As TreeNode, ByVal path As String)

        Dim directory As System.IO.DirectoryInfo = _
                New System.IO.DirectoryInfo(path)

        Try
            For Each d As System.IO.DirectoryInfo In directory.GetDirectories()

                Dim node As TreeNode = New TreeNode(d.Name, d.FullName)

                parent.ChildNodes.Add(node)

                'Recurse the current directory
                LoadDirectories(node, d.FullName)
            Next
            End If
        Catch ex As System.UnauthorizedAccessException
            parent.Text += " (Access Denied)"
        Catch ex As System.IO.IOException
            parent.Text += " (Unknown Error: " + ex.Message + ")"
        End Try
    End Sub
</script>
```

C#

```csharp
<script runat="server">
    protected void Page_Load(object sender, EventArgs e)
    {
        if (!Page.IsPostBack)
        {
        foreach (System.IO.DriveInfo drive in System.IO.DriveInfo.GetDrives())
        {
            TreeNode node = new TreeNode();
            node.Value = drive.Name;

            if (drive.IsReady)
            {
                node.Text = drive.Name +
                            " - (free space: " + drive.AvailableFreeSpace + ")";

                LoadDirectories(node, drive.Name);
            }
            else
                node.Text = drive.Name + " - (not ready)";

            this.TreeView1.Nodes.Add(node);
        }
        }

        this.TreeView1.CollapseAll();
    }

    private void LoadDirectories(TreeNode parent, string path)
    {
        System.IO.DirectoryInfo directory = new System.IO.DirectoryInfo(path);

        try
        {
            foreach (System.IO.DirectoryInfo d in directory.GetDirectories())
            {
                TreeNode node = new TreeNode(d.Name, d.FullName);

                parent.ChildNodes.Add(node);

                //Recurs the current directory
                LoadDirectories(node, d.FullName);
            }
        }
        catch (System.UnauthorizedAccessException e)
        {
            parent.Text += " (Access Denied)";
        }
        catch (System.IO.IOException e)
        {
            parent.Text += " (Unknown Error: " + e.Message + ")";
        }
    }
</script>
```

Figure 22-3 shows what the page should look like in the browser. You should now be able to browse the directory tree, much as you do in Windows Explorer, by opening and closing the TreeView nodes.

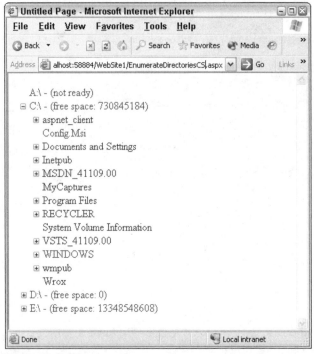

Figure 22-3

Notice that the example continuously creates new instances of the DirectoryInfo class each time the method executes in order to continue to enumerate the directory tree. You could also extend this example by displaying some additional properties as part of the Node text, such as the CreationTime or Attributes.

To perform only a specific action, you don't have to create an instance of the DirectoryInfo class. You can simply use the static methods exposed by the Directory class. These methods allow you to create, read properties from, and delete a directory. Rather than creating an object instance that represents a specific path and exposes methods that act on that path, the static methods exposed by the Directory class generally require you to pass the path as a method parameter. Listing 22-4 shows how you can use the static methods exposed by the Directory class to create, read properties from, and delete a directory.

> Remember to be very careful when deleting a folder from your hard drive. It is possible to permanently delete important data from your system or change the permissions of a resource, which would result in your losing the ability to access the resource.

Listing 22-4: Working with the static methods of the Directory class

VB

```
<script runat="server">

    Protected Sub Page_Load(ByVal sender As Object, ByVal e As System.EventArgs)

        Directory.CreateDirectory("C:\Wrox")

        If Directory.Exists("C:\Wrox") Then

            Me.Label1.Text = _
                    Directory.GetCreationTime("C:\Wrox").ToString()
            Me.Label2.Text = _
                    Directory.GetLastAccessTime("C:\Wrox").ToString()
            Me.Label3.Text = _
                    Directory.GetLastWriteTime("C:\Wrox").ToString()

            Directory.Delete("C:\Wrox")
        End If
    End Sub
</script>

<html xmlns="http://www.w3.org/1999/xhtml" >
<head runat="server">
    <title>Using Static Methods</title>
</head>
<body>
    <form id="form1" runat="server">
    <div>
        Creation Time:
                <asp:Label ID="Label1" runat="server" Text="Label"></asp:Label><br />
        Last Access Time:
                <asp:Label ID="Label2" runat="server" Text="Label"></asp:Label><br />
        Last Write Time:
                <asp:Label ID="Label3" runat="server" Text="Label"></asp:Label>
    </div>
    </form>
</body>
</html>
```

C#

```
<script runat="server">

    protected void Page_Load(object sender, EventArgs e)
    {
        Directory.CreateDirectory(@"C:\Wrox");

        if (Directory.Exists(@"C:\Wrox") )
        {
            this.Label1.Text =
                    Directory.GetCreationTime(@"C:\Wrox").ToString();
```

(continued)

Listing 12-4: *(continued)*

```
            this.Label2.Text =
                    Directory.GetLastAccessTime(@"C:\Wrox").ToString();
            this.Label3.Text =
                    Directory.GetLastWriteTime(@"C:\Wrox").ToString();

            Directory.Delete(@"C:\Wrox");
        }
    }
</script>
```

When you load this page in the browser, you will see that the Creation Time, Last Access Time, and Last Write Time are displayed. Additionally, if you open Windows Explorer, you will see that the Wrox directory has been deleted.

Using Relative Paths and Setting and Getting the Current Directory

When an ASP.NET page is executed, the thread used to execute the code that generates the page, by default, has a current working directory. It uses this directory as its base directory if you have specified relative paths in your application. Therefore, if you pass a relative file name into any System.IO class, the file is assumed to be located in the current working directory.

For example, the default working directory for the ASP.NET Development Server is a directory under your Visual Studio install root. If you installed Visual Studio in C:\Program Files, your ASP.NET Development Server working directory would be c:\Program Files\Microsoft Visual Studio 8\ Common7\IDE.

You can find the location of your working directory by using the Directory class's GetCurrentDirectory() method. In addition, you can change the current working directory using the Directory class's SetCurrentDirectory() method.

Listing 22-5 shows you how to set and then display your working directory.

Listing 22-5: Setting and displaying the application's working directory

VB

```
<script runat="server">

    Protected Sub Page_Load(ByVal sender As Object, ByVal e As System.EventArgs)
        Me.Label1.Text = Directory.GetCurrentDirectory()
        Directory.SetCurrentDirectory("C:\Wrox")
        Me.Label2.Text = Directory.GetCurrentDirectory()
    End Sub
</script>

<html xmlns="http://www.w3.org/1999/xhtml" >
<head runat="server">
    <title>Set and Display the Working Directory</title>
</head>
```

```
<body>
    <form id="form1" runat="server">
    <div>
        Old Working Directory:
            <asp:Label ID="Label1" runat="server" Text="Label"></asp:Label><br />
        New Working Directory:
            <asp:Label ID="Label2" runat="server" Text="Label"></asp:Label>
    </div>
    </form>
</body>
</html>
```

C#

```
<script runat="server">

    protected void Page_Load(object sender, EventArgs e)
    {
        this.Label1.Text = Directory.GetCurrentDirectory();
        Directory.SetCurrentDirectory(@"C:\Wrox");
        this.Label2.Text = Directory.GetCurrentDirectory();
    }
</script>
```

Note that the directory parameter you specify in the SetCurrentDirectory() method must already exist; otherwise, ASP.NET throws an exception. Knowing this, it would probably be a good idea to use the Exists() method of the Directory class to make sure the directory you are specifying does, in fact, already exist before you try to change the working directory.

When you execute this code, you should see that it displays the original working directory, and then displays the new working directory after you change it. Figure 22-4 shows what the page looks like when executed.

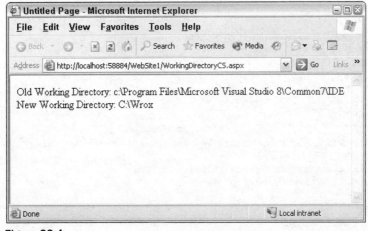

Figure 22-4

File and FileInfo

Now that you can effectively display and browse a directory tree, you can expand the example even further by displaying the files located in the directory that is currently selected in your TreeView control

The simplest way to display the files is to bind a `FileInfo` array to a `GridView`. This example uses the `GetFiles()` method of the `DirectoryInfo` class because it returns an array of `FileInfo` objects. You want to use this method because the `FileInfo` object enables you to display some properties of each file. (If you want to display only the file names, you could use the `Directory` class's `GetFiles()` method, which returns a simple string array of file names.)

Listing 22-6 shows how to use the TreeView control's `SelectedNodeChanged` event to bind your `GridView` with the file information.

Listing 22-6: Binding a GridView to directory files

```
VB
<script runat="server">

    Protected Sub Page_Load(ByVal sender As Object, ByVal e As System.EventArgs)
        If (Not Page.IsPostBack) Then
        For Each drive As System.IO.DriveInfo In System.IO.DriveInfo.GetDrives()

            Dim node As TreeNode = New TreeNode()
            node.Value = drive.Name

            If (drive.IsReady) Then
                node.Text = drive.Name & _
                            " - (free space: " & drive.AvailableFreeSpace & ")"

                LoadDirectories(node, drive.Name)
            Else
                node.Text = drive.Name & " - (not ready)"
            End If

            Me.TreeView1.Nodes.Add(node)
        Next
        End If

        Me.TreeView1.CollapseAll()

    End Sub

    Private Sub LoadDirectories(ByVal parent As TreeNode, ByVal path As String)

        Dim directory As System.IO.DirectoryInfo = _
                New System.IO.DirectoryInfo(path)

        Try
            For Each d As System.IO.DirectoryInfo In directory.GetDirectories()

                Dim node As TreeNode = New TreeNode(d.Name, d.FullName)

                parent.ChildNodes.Add(node)

                'Recurse the current directory
```

```
                LoadDirectories(node, d.FullName)
            Next
        Catch ex As System.UnauthorizedAccessException
            parent.Text += " (Access Denied)"
        Catch ex As Exception
            parent.Text += " (Unknown Error: " + ex.Message + ")"
        End Try
    End Sub


    Protected Sub TreeView1_SelectedNodeChanged _
        (ByVal sender As Object, ByVal e As System.EventArgs)

        Dim directory As System.IO.DirectoryInfo = _
                    New System.IO.DirectoryInfo(Me.TreeView1.SelectedNode.Value)

        Me.GridView1.DataSource = directory.GetFiles()
        Me.GridView1.DataBind()
    End Sub
</script>

<html xmlns="http://www.w3.org/1999/xhtml" >
<head runat="server">
    <title>Binding a Gridview </title>
</head>
<body>
    <form id="form1" runat="server">
    <div>
        <table>
            <tr>
                <td style="width: 100px" valign="top">
                    <asp:TreeView ID="TreeView1" runat="server"
                        OnSelectedNodeChanged="TreeView1_SelectedNodeChanged">
                    </asp:TreeView>
                </td>
                <td valign=top>
                    <asp:GridView ID="GridView1" runat="server"
                        AutoGenerateColumns=False GridLines=None CellPadding=3>
                        <Columns>
                            <asp:BoundField DataField="Name" HeaderText="Name"
                                HeaderStyle-HorizontalAlign=Left
                                HeaderStyle-Font-Bold=true />
                            <asp:BoundField DataField="Length" HeaderText="Size"
                                ItemStyle-HorizontalAlign=Right
                                HeaderStyle-HorizontalAlign=Right
                                HeaderStyle-Font-Bold=true />
                            <asp:BoundField DataField="LastWriteTime"
                                HeaderText="Date Modified"
                                HeaderStyle-HorizontalAlign=Left
```

(continued)

Listing 22-6: *(continued)*

```
                                    HeaderStyle-Font-Bold=true />
                        </Columns>
                    </asp:GridView>
                </td>
            </tr>
        </table>
    </div>
    </form>
</body>
</html>
```

C#
```csharp
<script runat="server">
    protected void Page_Load(object sender, EventArgs e)
    {
        if (!Page.IsPostBack)
        {
        foreach (System.IO.DriveInfo drive in System.IO.DriveInfo.GetDrives())
        {
            TreeNode node = new TreeNode();
            node.Value = drive.Name;

            // Make sure the drive is ready before we access it
            if (drive.IsReady)
            {
                node.Text = drive.Name +
                {
                        " - (free space: " + drive.AvailableFreeSpace + ")";
                LoanDirectories(node, drive.Name)
            }
            else
                node.Text = drive.Name + " - (not ready)";

            this.TreeView1.Nodes.Add(node);
        }
        }
    }

    private void LoadDirectories(TreeNode parent, string path)
    {
        System.IO.DirectoryInfo directory = new System.IO.DirectoryInfo(path);

        try
        {
            foreach (System.IO.DirectoryInfo d in directory.GetDirectories())
            {
                TreeNode node = new TreeNode(d.Name, d.FullName);

                parent.ChildNodes.Add(node);

                //Recurse the current directory
                LoadDirectories(node, d.FullName);
            }
        }
        catch (System.UnauthorizedAccessException e)
        {
            parent.Text += " (Access Denied)";
        }
```

```
        catch (Exception e)
        {
            parent.Text += " (Unknown Error: " + e.Message + ")";
        }
    }


    protected void TreeView1_SelectedNodeChanged(object sender, EventArgs e)
    {
        System.IO.DirectoryInfo directory =
                new System.IO.DirectoryInfo(this.TreeView1.SelectedNode.Value);

        this.GridView1.DataSource = directory.GetFiles();
        this.GridView1.DataBind();
    }
</script>
```

Figure 22-5 shows what your Web page looks like after you have selected a directory and your grid has been bound to the `FileInfo` array.

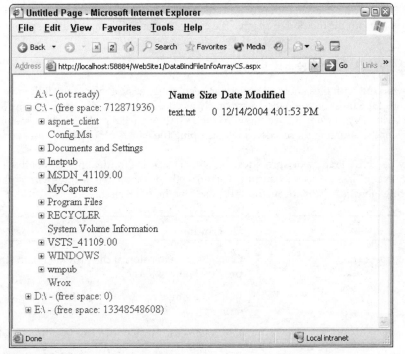

Figure 22-5

Keep in mind that, as in the Load Directory example, you can also enumerate though the `FileInfo` array to display the information. Listing 22-7 shows you how to enumerate through the `FileInfo` array and display the properties to the page.

Listing 22-7: Manually enumerating directory files

VB
```vb
Dim dir as New System.IO.DirectoryInfo("C:\")
For Each file as System.IO.FileInfo In dir.GetFiles("*.*"))
      Response.Write(file.Name & "<BR>")
      Response.Write(file.LastWriteTime.ToString() & "<BR>")
      Response.Write(file.Attributes.ToString() & "<BR>")
Next
```

C#
```csharp
System.IO.DirectoryInfo dir = new System.IO.DirctoryInfo(@"C:\");
foreach (System.IO.FileInfo file in dir.GetFiles("*.*"))
{
      Response.Write(file.Name + "<BR>");
      Response.Write(file.LastWriteTime.ToString() + "<BR>");
      Response.Write(file.Attributes.ToString() + "<BR>");
}
```

Listing 22-7 also shows that you can provide a file filter to the `GetFiles()` method. This allows you to limit the results from the method to specific file extensions or to files matching a specific file name part.

Working with Paths

Although working with files and directories has been pretty easy, even going all the way back to good old ASP, one of the most problematic areas has always been working with paths. Many lines of code have been written by developers to deal with concatenating partial paths together, making sure files have extensions, evaluating those extensions, stripping file names off of paths, and even more.

Thankfully, the .NET Framework provides you with a class just for dealing with paths. The `System.IO.Path` class exposes a handful of static methods that make dealing with paths a snap. The following table lists the static methods exposed by the `Path` class.

Method	Description
ChangeExtension	Changes the extension of the provided path string to the provided new extension.
Combine	Returns a single combined path from two partial path strings.
GetDirectoryName	Returns the directory or directories of the provided path.
GetExtension	Returns the extension of the provided path.
GetFileName	Returns the file name of the provided path.
GetFileNameWithoutExtension	Returns the file name without its extension of the provided path.
GetFullPath	Given a non-rooted path, returns a rooted pathname based on the current working directory. For example, if the path passed in is "temp" and the current working directory is c:\MyWebsite, the method returns C:\MyWebsite\temp.

Method	Description
GetInvalidFileNameChars	Returns an array of characters that are not allowed in file names for the current system
GetInvalidPathChars	Returns an array of characters that are not allowed in path-names for the current system.
GetPathRoot	Returns the root path.
GetTempFileName	Returns a temporary file name, located in the temporary directory returned by GetTempPath.
GetTempPath	Returns the temporary directory name.
HasExtension	Returns a Boolean value indicating whether a path has an extension.
IsPathRooted	Returns a Boolean indicating if a path is rooted.

As an example of using the Path class, the application shown in Figure 22-6 lets you enter a path and then displays the component parts of the path such as the root path (logical drive), the directory, file name, and extension.

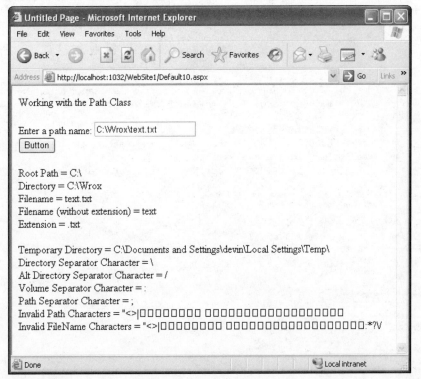

Figure 22-6

The GetInvalidPathChars *and* GetInvalidFileNameChars *methods return an array
of characters that are not allowed in path and file names, respectively. Although the specific invalid
characters are dependent on the platform the application is running on, the arrays returned by these
methods will most likely contain elements such as non-printable characters, special Unicode characters,
or characters from non-Latin–based character sets. The characters that your browser is capable of
rendering will depend on your specific platform setup. Characters that your browser is incapable of
rendering properly will display as the generic square box shown in Figure 22-6.*

The code in Listing 22-8 shows how the various methods and constant properties of the Path class have
been used to create the application shown in Figure 22-6.

Listing 22-8: Using the Path class

VB

```
<script runat="server">

    Protected Sub Page_Load(ByVal sender As Object, ByVal e As System.EventArgs)
        If Page.IsPostBack Then
            Me.lblRootPath.Text = Path.GetPathRoot(Me.txtPathName.Text)
            Me.lblDirectoryName.Text = Path.GetDirectoryName(Me.txtPathName.Text)
            Me.lblFileName.Text = Path.GetFileName(Me.txtPathName.Text)
            Me.lblFileNameWithoutExtension.Text = _
                    Path.GetFileNameWithoutExtension(Me.txtPathName.Text)
            Me.lblExtension.Text = Path.GetExtension(Me.txtPathName.Text)

            Me.lblTemporaryPath.Text = Path.GetTempPath()
            Me.lblDirectorySeparatorChar.Text =
                    Path.DirectorySeparatorChar.ToString()
            Me.lblAltDirectorySeparatorChar.Text =
                    Path.AltDirectorySeparatorChar.ToString()
            Me.lblVolumeSeparatorChar.Text = Path.VolumeSeparatorChar.ToString()
            Me.lblPathSeparator.Text = Path.PathSeparator.ToString()

            Me.lblInvalidChars.Text =
                    HttpUtility.HtmlEncode(New String(Path.GetInvalidPathChars()))
            Me.lblInvalidFileNameChars.Text =
                    HttpUtility.HtmlEncode(New String(Path.GetInvalidFileNameChars()))
        End If
    End Sub
</script>

<html xmlns="http://www.w3.org/1999/xhtml" >
<head runat="server">
    <title>Using the Path Class</title>
</head>
<body>
    <form id="form1" runat="server">
    <div>
        Working with the Path Class<br />
        <br />
        Enter a path name:
        <asp:TextBox ID="txtPathName" runat="server"></asp:TextBox><br />
        <asp:Button ID="Button1" runat="server" Text="Button" /><br />
        <br />
```

```
        Root Path =
        <asp:Label ID="lblRootPath" runat="server" Text="Label" />
        <br />
        Directory =
        <asp:Label ID="lblDirectoryName" runat="server" Text="Label" />
        <br />
        Filename =
        <asp:Label ID="lblFileName" runat="server" Text="Label" />
        <br />
        Filename (without extension) =
        <asp:Label ID="lblFileNameWithoutExtension" runat="server" Text="Label" />
        <br />
        Extension =
        <asp:Label ID="lblExtension" runat="server" Text="Label" />
        <br />
        <br />
        Temporary Directory =
        <asp:Label ID="lblTemporaryPath" runat="server" Text="Label" />
        <br />
        Directory Separator Character =
        <asp:Label ID="lblDirectorySeparatorChar" runat="server" Text="Label" />
        <br />
        Alt Directory Separator Character =
        <asp:Label ID="lblAltDirectorySeparatorChar" runat="server" Text="Label" />
        <br />
        Volume Separator Character =
        <asp:Label ID="lblVolumeSeparatorChar" runat="server" Text="Label" />
        <br />
        Path Separator Character =
        <asp:Label ID="lblPathSeparator" runat="server" Text="Label" />
        <br />
        Invalid Path Characters =
        <asp:Label ID="lblInvalidChars" runat="server" Text="Label" />
        <br />
        Invalid FileName Characters =
        <asp:Label ID="lblInvalidFileNameChars" runat="server" Text="Label" />

    </div>
    </form>
</body>
</html>
```

C#

```
<script runat="server">

    protected void Page_Load(object sender, EventArgs e)
    {
        if (Page.IsPostBack)
        {
            this.lblRootPath.Text =
                        Path.GetPathRoot(this.txtPathName.Text);
            this.lblDirectoryName.Text =
```

(continued)

Listing 22-8: *(continued)*

```
                         Path.GetDirectoryName(this.txtPathName.Text);
            this.lblFileName.Text =
                         Path.GetFileName(this.txtPathName.Text);
            this.lblFileNameWithoutExtension.Text =
                         Path.GetFileNameWithoutExtension(this.txtPathName.Text);
            this.lblExtension.Text =
                         Path.GetExtension(this.txtPathName.Text);

            this.lblTemporaryPath.Text = Path.GetTempPath();
            this.lblDirectorySeparatorChar.Text =
                         Path.DirectorySeparatorChar.ToString();
            this.lblAltDirectorySeparatorChar.Text =
                         Path.AltDirectorySeparatorChar.ToString();
            this.lblVolumeSeparatorChar.Text = Path.VolumeSeparatorChar.ToString();
            this.lblPathSeparator.Text = Path.PathSeparator.ToString();

            this.lblInvalidChars.Text =
               HttpUtility.HtmlEncode( new String(Path.GetInvalidPathChars() ) );
            this.lblInvalidFileNameChars.Text =
               HttpUtility.HtmlEncode( new String(Path.GetInvalidFileNameChars()));
        }
    }
</script>
```

File and Directory Properties, Attributes, and Access Control Lists

Finally, this section explains how you can access and modify file and directory properties, attributes, and Access Control Lists.

> *Samples in this section use a simple text file called* TextFile.txt *to demonstrate the concepts. You can either create this file or substitute your own file in the sample code. The samples assume the file has been added to the Web site and use the* Server.MapPath *method to determine the full filepath.*

Properties and Attributes

Files and directories share certain properties that you can use to determine the age of a file or directory, when it was last modified, and what attributes have been applied. These properties can be viewed by opening the file's Properties dialog. You can open this dialog from Windows Explorer by either right-clicking on the file and selecting Properties from the context menu, or selecting Properties from the File menu. Figure 22-7 shows the file's Properties window for the text document.

Both the DirectoryInfo and the FileInfo classes let you access these properties and modify them. Listing 22-9 shows you an example of displaying the file properties.

Listing 22-9: Displaying and modifying the file properties

VB

```vb
Dim file As New System.IO.FileInfo(Server.MapPath("TextFile.txt"))
Response.Write("Location: " & file.FullName)
Response.Write("Size: " & file.Length)
Response.Write("Created: " & file.CreationTime)
Response.Write("Modified: " & file.LastWriteTime)
Response.Write("Accessed: " & file.LastAccessTime)
Response.Write("Attributes: " & file.Attributes)
```

C#

```csharp
System.IO.FileInfo file = new System.IO.FileInfo(Server.MapPath("TextFile.txt"));
Response.Write("Location: " + file.FullName);
Response.Write("Size: " + file.Length);
Response.Write("Created: " + file.CreationTime);
Response.Write("Modified: " + file.LastWriteTime);
Response.Write("Accessed: " + file.LastAccessTime);
Response.Write("Attributes: " + file.Attributes);
```

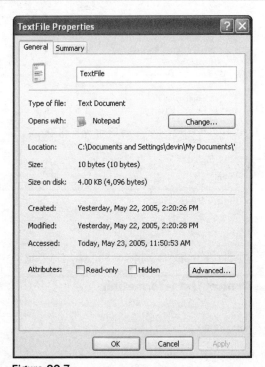

Figure 22-7

Access Control Lists

Although getting the properties and attributes is useful, what many developers need is the capability to actually change the Access Control Lists, or ACLs — pronounced *Ackels* — on directories and files. ACLs are the way resources such as directories and files are secured in the NTFS file system, which is the file system used by Windows XP, NT 4.0, 2000, and 2003. You can view a file's ACLs by selecting the Security tab from the file's Properties dialog. Figure 22-8 shows the ACLs set for the `TextFile.txt` file you created.

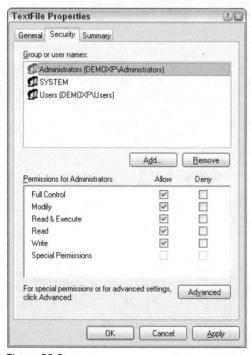

Figure 22-8

Using the new `System.AccessControl` namespace in the .NET Framework, you can query the file system for the ACL information or display it in a Web page, as shown in Listing 22-10.

Listing 22-10: Access Control List information

VB

```
<script runat="server">

    Protected Sub Page_Load(ByVal sender As Object, ByVal e As System.EventArgs)
        ' retrieve the AccessControl information for this file
        Dim sec As System.Security.AccessControl.FileSecurity = _
                sec = File.GetAccessControl(Server.MapPath("TextFile.txt"))

        Me.Label1.Text = _
                sec.GetOwner( GetType(System.Security.Principal.NTAccount) ).Value

        ' retrieve the collection of access rules
        Dim auth As System.Security.AccessControl.AuthorizationRuleCollection = _
```

```
                                    sec.GetAccessRules(true, true, _
                                    GetType (System.Security.Principal.NTAccount))

        Dim tc As TableCell
        ' loop through the rule collection and add a table row for each rule
        For Each (r As System.Security.AccessControl.FileSystemAccessRule In auth)

            Dim tr As New TableRow()

            tc = New TableCell()
            tc.Text = r.AcessControlType.ToString()   deny or allow
            tr.Cells.Add(tc)

            tc = New TableCell()
            tc.Text = r.IdentityReference.Value   who
            tr.Cells.Add(tc)

            tc = New TableCell()
            tc.Text = r.InheritanceFlags.ToString()
            tr.Cells.Add(tc)

            tc = New TableCell()
            tc.Text = r.IsInherited.ToString()
            tr.Cells.Add(tc)

            tc = New TableCell()
            tc.Text = r.PropagationFlags.ToString()
            tr.Cells.Add(tc)

            tc = New TableCell()
            tc.Text = r.FileSystemRights.ToString()
            tr.Cells.Add(tc)

            Table1.Rows.Add(tr)
        Next
    End Sub
</script>

<html xmlns="http://www.w3.org/1999/xhtml" >
<head runat="server">
    <title>Displaying ACL Information</title>
</head>
<body>
    <form id="form1" runat="server">
    <div>
        <p><b>File Owner:</b>
            <asp:Label ID="Label1" runat="server" Text="Label /></p>
        <p>
        Access Rules:<br />
        <asp:Table ID="Table1" runat="server" CellPadding="2" GridLines=Both>
            <asp:TableRow>
                <asp:TableHeaderCell>Control Type</asp:TableHeaderCell>
                <asp:TableHeaderCell>Identity</asp:TableHeaderCell>
                <asp:TableHeaderCell>Inheritance Flags</asp:TableHeaderCell>
                <asp:TableHeaderCell>Is Inherited</asp:TableHeaderCell>
```

(continued)

Listing 22-10: *(continued)*

```
                <asp:TableHeaderCell>Propagation Flags</asp:TableHeaderCell>
                <asp:TableHeaderCell>File System Rights</asp:TableHeaderCell>
            </asp:TableRow>
        </asp:Table>
        </p>
    </div>
    </form>
</body>
</html>
```

C#

```
<script runat="server">

    protected void Page_Load(object sender, EventArgs e)
    {
        // retrieve the AccessControl information for this file
        System.Security.AccessControl.FileSecurity sec =
                File.GetAccessControl(Server.MapPath("TextFile.txt"));

        this.Label1.Text =
                sec.GetOwner( typeof(System.Security.Principal.NTAccount) ).Value;

        // retrieve the collection of access rules
        AuthorizationRuleCollection auth =
                                    sec.GetAccessRules(true, true,
                                    typeof (System.Security.Principal.NTAccount))

        TableCell tc;
        // loop through the rule collection and add a table row for each rule
        foreach (FileSystemAccessRule r in auth)
        {
            TableRow tr = new TableRow();

            tc = new TableCell();
            tc.Text = r.AccessControlType.ToString(); // deny or allow
            tr.Cells.Add(tc);

            tc = new TableCell();
            tc.Text = r.IdentityReference.Value; // who
            tr.Cells.Add(tc);

            tc = new TableCell();
            tc.Text = r.InheritanceFlags.ToString();
            tr.Cells.Add(tc);

            tc = new TableCell();
            tc.Text = r.IsInherited.ToString();
            tr.Cells.Add(tc);

            tc = new TableCell();
            tc.Text = r.PropagationFlags.ToString();
```

```
                    tr.Cells.Add(tc);

                    tc = new TableCell();
                    tc.Text = r.FileSystemRights.ToString();
                    tr.Cells.Add(tc);

                    Table1.Rows.Add(tr);
            }
        }
</script>
```

Figure 22-9 shows what the page looks like when it is executed. Note that the Identity column might be different depending on whom you are logged in as when you run the page and what security mode the application is running under (Integrated Windows Authentication, Basic, or Anonymous).

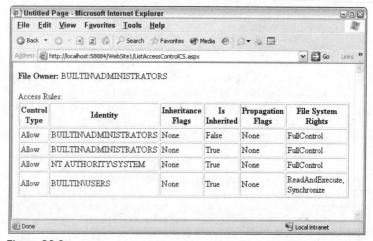

Figure 22-9

Now let's look at actually modifying the ACL lists. In this example, you give a user explicit Full Control rights over the TextFile.txt file. You can use either an existing user or create a new test User account in Windows to run this sample. Listing 22-11 shows how to add an access rule to the TextFile.txt file.

Listing 22-11: Adding a rule to the Access Control List

VB

```
Dim sec As System.Security.AccessControl.FileSecurity = _
        System.IO.File.GetAccessControl(Server.MapPath("TextFile.txt"))

sec.AddAccessRule( _
        New System.Security.AccessControl.FileSystemAccessRule( _
                "DEMOXP\TestUser", _
                System.Security.AccessControl.FileSystemRights.FullControl, _
                System.Security.AccessControl.AccessControlType.Allow _
                ) _
```

(continued)

Listing 22-11: *(continued)*

```
            )

File.SetAccessControl(Server.MapPath("TextFile.txt"),sec)
```

C#
```
System.Security.AccessControl.FileSecurity sec =
        System.IO.File.GetAccessControl(Server.MapPath("TextFile.txt"));

sec.AddAccessRule(
        new System.Security.AccessControl.FileSystemAccessRule(
                @"DEMOXP\TestUser",
                System.Security.AccessControl.FileSystemRights.FullControl,
                System.Security.AccessControl.AccessControlType.Allow
                )
        );

File.SetAccessControl(Server.MapPath("TextFile.txt"),sec);
```

There are several things to notice in this code sample. First, notice that you are passing three parameters to the `FileSystemAccessRule` constructor. The first parameter is the user you want to give rights to; change this value to a user on your specific system. Also notice that you must specify the full DOMAIN\USER-NAME for the user. Next, notice that, in the code, you are using the `FileSystemRights` enumeration to specify exactly which rights you want to give to this user. You can specify multiple rights by using a bitwise `Or` operator, as shown in the following:

```
new System.Security.AccessControl.FileSystemAccessRule(
    "DEMOXP\TestUser",
    System.Security.AccessControl.FileSystemRights.Read &
        System.Security.AccessControl.FileSystemRights.Write,
    System.Security.AccessControl.AccessControlType.Allow
)
```

After running this code, take a look at the Security tab in the file's Properties dialog and you should see that the user has been added to the Access Control List and allowed Full Control. Figure 22-10 shows what the dialog should look like.

Now remove the ACL you just added by running essentially the same code, but using the `RemoveAccessRule` method rather than the `AddAccessRule` method. Listing 22-12 shows this code.

Listing 22-12: Removing the rule from the Access Control List

VB
```
Dim sec As System.Security.AccessControl.FileSecurity = _
        System.IO.File.GetAccessControl(Server.MapPath("TextFile.txt"))

sec.RemoveAccessRule( _
        new System.Security.AccessControl.FileSystemAccessRule( _
                "DEMOXP\TestUser", _
                System.Security.AccessControl.FileSystemRights.FullControl, _
```

```
                System.Security.AccessControl.AccessControlType.Allow _
            ) _
    )

File.SetAccessControl(Server.MapPath("TextFile.txt"),sec)
```

C#
```
System.Security.AccessControl.FileSecurity sec =
        File.GetAccessControl(Server.MapPath("TextFile.txt"));

sec.RemoveAccessRule(
        new System.Security.AccessControl.FileSystemAccessRule(
            @"DEMOXP\TestUser",
            System.Security.AccessControl.FileSystemRights.FullControl,
            System.Security.AccessControl.AccessControlType.Allow)
        );

File.SetAccessControl(Server.MapPath("TextFile.txt"),sec);
```

If you open the file Properties dialog again, you see that the user has been removed from the Access Control List.

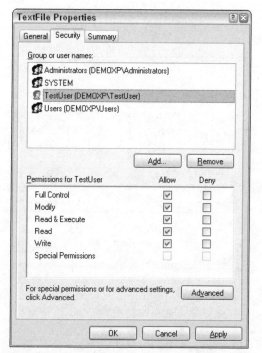

Figure 22-10

Reading and Writing Files

Now that you have learned how to manage the files on the local system, this section shows you how to use the .NET Framework to perform input/output (I/O) operations, such as reading and writing, on those files. The .NET Framework makes performing I/O very easy because it uses a common model of reading or writing I/O data; so regardless of the source, virtually the same code can be used. The model is based on two basic concepts, Stream classes and Reader/Writer classes. Figure 22-11 shows the basic I/O model .NET uses and how Streams, Readers, and Writers work together to make it possible to transfer data to and from any number of sources in any number of formats. Note that the diagram shows only some of the Streams and Reader/Writer pairs in the .NET Framework.

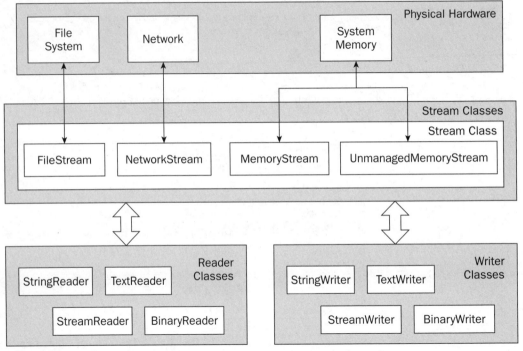

Figure 22-11

In this section, you dive deeper into learning how Streams, Readers, and Writers work and how .NET makes it easy to use them to transfer data.

Streams

Regardless of the type of I/O operation you are performing in .NET, if you want to read or write data you eventually use a stream of some type. Streams are the basic mechanism .NET uses to transfer data to and from its underlying source, be it a file, communication pipe, or TCP/IP socket. The `Stream` class provides the basic functionality to read and write I/O data, but because the `Stream` class is marked as abstract, you most likely need to use one of the several classes derived from `Stream`. Each `Stream` derivation is specialized to make it easy to transfer data from a specific source. The following table lists some of the classes derived from the `Stream` class.

Class	Description
`System.IO.FileStream`	Reads and writes files on a file system, as well as other file-related operating system handles (including pipes, standard input, standard output, and so on).
`System.IO.MemoryStream`	Creates streams that have memory as a backing store instead of a disk or a network connection. This can be useful in eliminating the need to write temporary files to disk or to store binary blob information in a database.
`System.IO.UnmanagedMemoryStream`	Supports access to unmanaged memory using the existing stream-based model and does not require that the contents in the unmanaged memory be copied to the heap.
`System.IO.BufferedStream`	Extends the `Stream` class by adding a buffering layer to read and write operations on another stream. The stream performs reads and writes in blocks (4096 bytes by default), which can result in improved efficiency.
`System.Net.Sockets.NetworkStream`	Implements the standard .NET Framework stream to send and receive data through network sockets. It supports both synchronous and asynchronous access to the network data stream.
`System.Security.Cryptography.CryptoStream`	Enables you to read and write data through cryptographic transformations.
`System.IO.Compression.GZipStream`	Enables you to compress data using the GZip data format.
`System.IO.Compression.DeflateStream`	Enables you to compress data using the `Deflate` algorithm. For more information, see the RFC 1951: DEFLATE 1.3 Specification.
`System.Net.Security.NegotiateStream`	Uses the Negotiate security protocol to authenticate the client, and optionally the server, in client-server communication.
`System.Net.Security.SslStream`	Necessary for client-server communication that uses the Secure Socket Layer (SSL) security protocol to authenticate the server and optionally the client.

As an example, you can use the `FileStream` to read a local system file from disk. To prepare for this sample, open the `TextFile.txt` you created for the samples in the previous section, enter some text, and save the file. Listing 22-13 shows the code to read this simple text file.

Listing 22-13: Using a FileStream to read a system file

VB

```vb
Dim fs As New FileStream (Server.MapPath("TextFile.txt"), FileMode.Open)
Dim data(fs.Length) As Byte
fs.Read(data, 0, fs.Length)
fs.Close()
```

C#

```csharp
FileStream fs = new FileStream(Server.MapPath("TextFile.txt"), FileMode.Open);
byte[] data = new byte[fs.Length];
fs.Read(data, 0, (int)fs.Length);
fs.Close();
```

There are several items of note in this code. First, notice that you are creating a byte array the length of the stream, using the `Length` property to properly size the array, and then passing it to the `Read` method. The `Read` method fills the byte array with the stream data, in this case reading the entire stream into the byte array. If you want to read only a chunk of the stream or to start at a specific point in the stream, just change the parameters you pass to the `Read` method.

Streams use byte arrays as the basic means of transporting data to and from the underlying data source. You use a byte array to read data in this sample and, later in the chapter, you learn how to create a byte array that contains data you can write to a stream.

Second, note that you are explicitly closing the `FileStream` using the `Close` method. Streams must always be explicitly closed in order to release the resources they are using, which in this case is the file. Failing to explicitly close the stream can cause memory leaks, and it may also deny other users and applications access to the resource.

A good way to ensure that your streams will always be closed once you are done using them is to wrap then in a `Using` statement. `Using` automatically calls the stream objects `Dispose()` method once the `Using` statement is closed. For the stream object, calling the `Dispose` method also automatically calls the streams `Close()` method. Utilizing the `Using` statement with stream objects is a good way to ensure that even if you do forget to explicitly add a call to close the stream, the object will be closed and the underlying resources released before the object is disposed.

Finally, notice that in the `FileStream` constructor, you are passing two parameters, the first being the path to the file you want to read and the other indicating the type of access you want to use when opening the file. The `FileMode` enumeration lets you specify how the stream should be opened, for reading, writing, or both reading and writing.

Thinking about *how* you will use the opened file can become very important. Here are some issues you might want to consider when working with files using `FileStream`:

❑ Will you be reading, writing, or both?

❑ Are you creating a new file, or appending or truncating an existing file?

❑ Should other programs be allowed to access the file while you are using it?

❑ How are you going to read or write the data in the file? Are you looking for a specific location in the file, or simply reading the entire file from beginning to end?

Thankfully, the `FileStream` constructor includes a number of overloads that let you explicitly specify how you will use the file. The IO namespace also includes four enumerations that can help you control how the `FileStream` accesses your file:

❑ **FileMode:** The `FileMode` enumeration lets you control whether the file is appended, truncated, created, or opened.

❑ **FileAccess:** The `FileAccess` enumeration controls whether the file is opened for reading, writing, or both.

❑ **FileOptions:** The `FileOptions` enumeration controls several other miscellaneous options, such as random or sequential access, file encryption, or asynchronous file writing.

❑ **FileShare:** The `FileShare` enumeration controls the access that other users and programs have to the file while your application is using it.

Listing 22-14 shows how you can use all these enumerations in the `FileStream` constructor to write data to the text file you created earlier. Notice that you are supplying the `FileStream` constructor with much more information on how you want to open the file. In this sample, you append another text string to the file you just read. To do this, set the `FileMode` to Append and the `FileAccess` to Write.

Listing 22-14: Using I/O enumerations to control file behavior when writing a file

VB
```vb
Dim fs As New FileStream(Server.MapPath("TextFile.txt"), FileMode.Append, _
             FileAccess.Write, FileShare.Read, 8, FileOptions.None)
Dim data() As Byte = _
             System.Text.Encoding.ASCII.GetBytes("This is an additional string")
fs.Write(data, 0, data.Length)
fs.Flush()
fs.Close()
```

C#
```csharp
FileStream fs = new FileStream(Server.MapPath("TextFile.txt"), FileMode.Append,
             FileAccess.Write, FileShare.Read, FileOptions.Asynchronous);
byte[] data = System.Text.Encoding.ASCII.GetBytes("This is an additional string");
fs.Write(data, 0, data.Length);
fs.Flush();
fs.Close();
```

You can write your text to the file by encoding a string to a byte array, which contains the information you want to write. Then, using the `Write` method, write your byte array to the `FileStreams` buffer and use the `Flush` method to instruct the `FileStream` to clear its buffer, causing any buffered data to be committed to the underlying data store. Finally, close the `FileStream`, releasing any resources it is using. If you open the `TextFile.txt` file in Notepad, you should see your string has been appended to the existing text in the file.

Note that using the `Flush` method in this scenario is optional because the `Close` method also calls `Flush` internally to commit the data to the data store. However, because the `Flush` method does not release the `FileStream` resources as `Close` does, it can be very useful if you are going to perform multiple write operations and do not want to release and then reacquire the resources for each write operation.

As you can see, so far reading and writing to files is really quite easy. The good thing is that, as mentioned earlier, because .NET uses the same basic `Stream` model for a variety of data stores, you can use these same techniques for reading and writing to any of the `Stream` derived classes. Listing 22-15 shows how you can use the same basic code to write to a `MemoryStream`, and Listing 22-16 demonstrates reading a Telnet server response using the `NetworkStream`.

Listing 22-15: Writing to a MemoryStream

VB

```
Dim data() As Byte = System.Text.Encoding.ASCII.GetBytes("This is a string")
Dim ms As New MemoryStream()
ms.Write(data, 0, data.Length)
ms.Close()
```

C#

```
byte[] data = System.Text.Encoding.ASCII.GetBytes("This is a string");
MemoryStream ms = new MemoryStream();
ms.Write(data, 0, data.Length);
ms.Close();
```

Listing 22-16: Reading from a NetworkStream

VB

```
Dim client As New TcpClient()

' Note: You can find a large list of Telnet accessible
' BBS systems at http://www.dmine.com/telnet/brieflist.htm

' The WCS Online BBS (http://bbs.wcssoft.com)
Dim addr As IPAddress = IPAddress.Parse("65.182.234.52")
Dim endpoint As New IPEndPoint(addr, 23)

client.Connect(endpoint)
Dim ns As NetworkStream = client.GetStream()

If (ns.DataAvailable) Then
    Dim data(client.ReceiveBufferSize) As Byte
    ns.Read(data, 0, client.ReceiveBufferSize)
    Dim response As String = System.Text.Encoding.ASCII.GetString(data)
End If
ns.Close()
```

C#

```
TcpClient client = new TcpClient();

// Note: You can find a large list of Telnet accessible
// BBS systems at http://www.dmine.com/telnet/brieflist.htm

// The WCS Online BBS (http://bbs.wcssoft.com)
IPAddress addr = IPAddress.Parse("65.182.234.52");
```

```
IPEndPoint endpoint = new IPEndPoint(addr,23);

client.Connect(endpoint);
NetworkStream ns = client.GetStream();

if (ns.DataAvailable)
{
    byte[] bytes = new byte[client.ReceiveBufferSize];
    ns.Read(bytes, 0, client.ReceiveBufferSize);
    string data = System.Text.Encoding.ASCII.GetString(bytes);
}
ns.Close();
```

Notice that the concept in both examples is virtually identical. You create a `Stream` object, read the bytes into a byte array for processing, and then close the stream. The code varies only in the implementation of specific Streams.

Readers and Writers

Other main parts of I/O in the .NET Framework are `Reader` and `Writer` classes. These classes help insulate you from having to deal with reading and writing individual bytes to and from Streams, enabling you to concentrate on the data you are working with. The .NET Framework provides a wide variety of reader and writer classes, each designed for reading or writing according to a specific set of rules. The first table following shows a partial list of the readers available in the .NET Framework. The second table lists the corresponding writer classes.

Class	Description
System.IO.TextReader	Abstract class that enables the reading of a sequential series of characters.
System.IO.StreamReader	Reads characters from a byte stream. Derived from `TextReader`.
System.IO.StringReader	Reads textual information as a stream of in-memory characters. Derived from `TextReader`.
System.IO.BinaryReader	Reads primitive data types as binary values from a stream.
System.Xml.XmlTextReader	Provides fast, non-cached, forward-only access to XML.

Class	Description
`System.IO.TextWriter`	Abstract class that enables the writing of a sequential series of characters.
`System.IO.StreamWriter`	Writes characters to a stream. Derived from `TextWriter`.
`System.IO.StringWriter`	Writes textual information as a stream of in-memory characters. Derived from `TextWriter`.
`System.IO.BinaryWriter`	Writes primitive data types in binary to a stream.
`System.Xml.XmlTextWriter`	Provides a fast, non-cached, forward-only way of generating XML streams or files

Now look at using several different types of readers and writers, starting with a simple example. Listing 22-17 shows you how to use a `StreamReader` to read a `FileStream`.

Listing 22-17: Reading and writing a text file with a StreamReader

VB
```
Dim streamwriter As New StreamWriter( File.Open("C:\Wrox\temp.txt",FileMode.Open) )
streamwriter.Write("This is a string")
streamwriter.Close()

Dim reader As New StreamReader( File.Open("C:\Wrox\temp.txt",FileMode.Open) )
Dim tmp As String = reader.ReadToEnd()
reader.Close()
```

C#
```
StreamWriter streamwriter =
            new StreamWriter( File.Open(@"C:\Wrox\temp.txt",FileMode.Open) );
streamwriter.Write("This is a string");
streamwriter.Close();

StreamReader reader =
            new StreamReader( File.Open(@"C:\Wrox\temp.txt",FileMode.Open) );
string tmp = reader.ReadToEnd();
reader.Close();
```

Notice that when you create a `StreamReader`, you must pass an existing stream instance as a constructor parameter. The reader uses this stream as its underlying data source. In this sample, you use the `File` class's static `Open` method to open a writable `FileStream` for your `StreamWriter`.

Also notice that you no longer have to deal with byte arrays. The `StreamReader` takes care of converting the data to a type that's more user-friendly than a byte array. In this case, you are using the `ReadToEnd` method to read the entire stream and convert it to a string. The `StreamReader` provides a number of different methods for reading data that you can use depending on exactly how you want to read the data, from reading a single character using the `Read` method, to reading the entire file using the `ReadToEnd` method.

Figure 22-12 shows the results of your write when you open the file in Notepad.

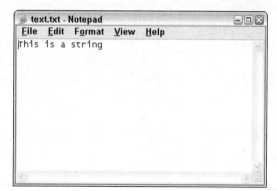

Figure 22-12

Now use the `BinaryReader` and `BinaryWriter` classes to read and write some primitive types to a file. The `BinaryWriter` writes primitive objects in their native format, so in order to read them using the `BinaryReader`, you must select the appropriate `Read` method. Listing 22-18 shows you how to do that; in this case, you are writing a value from a number of different primitive types to the text file, then reading the same value.

Listing 22-18: Reading and writing binary data

VB

```
Dim binarywriter As New BinaryWriter(File.Create("C:\Wrox\binary.dat"))
binarywriter.Write("a string")
binarywriter.Write(&H12346789ABCDEF)
binarywriter.Write(&H12345678)
binarywriter.Write("c"c)
binarywriter.Write(1.5F)
binarywriter.Write(100.2D)
binarywriter.Close()

Dim binaryreader As New BinaryReader( _
    File.Open("C:\Wrox\binary.dat", FileMode.Open))

Dim a As String = binaryreader.ReadString()
Dim l As Long = binaryreader.ReadInt64()
Dim i As Integer = binaryreader.ReadInt32()
Dim c As Char = binaryreader.ReadChar()
Dim f As Double = binaryreader.ReadSingle()
Dim d As Decimal = binaryreader.ReadDecimal()
binaryreader.Close()
```

C#

```
BinaryWriter binarywriter =
            new BinaryWriter( File.Create(@"C:\Wrox\binary.dat") );
binarywriter.Write("a string");
binarywriter.Write(0x12346789abcdef);
binarywriter.Write(0x12345678);0
```

(continued)

Listing 22-18: *(continued)*

```
binarywriter.Write('c');
binarywriter.Write(1.5f);
binarywriter.Write(100.2m);
binarywriter.Close();

BinaryReader binaryreader =
            new BinaryReader(File.Open(@"C:\Wrox\binary.dat", FileMode.Open));

string a = binaryreader.ReadString();
long l = binaryreader.ReadInt64();
int i = binaryreader.ReadInt32();
char c = binaryreader.ReadChar();
float f = binaryreader.ReadSingle();
decimal d = binaryreader.ReadDecimal();
binaryreader.Close();
```

If you open this file in Notepad, you should see that the `BinaryWriter` has written the nonreadable binary data to the file. Figure 22-13 shows what the content of the file looks like. The `BinaryReader` provides a number of different methods for reading various kinds of primitive types from the stream. In this sample, you use a different `Read` method for each primitive type that you write to the file.

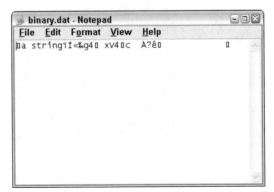

Figure 22-13

Finally, notice that the basic usage of both the `StreamReader`/`StreamWriter` and `BinaryReader`/ `BinaryWriter` classes is virtually identical. You can apply the same basic ideas to use any of the reader or writer classes.

Encodings

The `StreamReader` by default attempts to determine the encoding format of the file. If one of the supported encodings such as UTF-8 or UNICODE is detected, it is used. If the encoding is not recognized, the default encoding of UTF-8 is used. Depending on the constructor you call, you can change the default encoding used and optionally turn off encoding detection. The following example shows how you can control the encoding that the `StreamReader` uses.

```
StreamReader reader =
        new StreamReader(@"C:\Wrox\text.txt",System.Text.Encoding.Unicode);
```

The default encoding for the `StreamWriter` is also UTF-8, and you can override it in the same manner as the `StreamReader` class.

I/O Shortcuts

Although knowing how to create and use streams is always very useful and worth studying, the .NET Framework provides you with numerous shortcuts for common tasks like reading and writing to files. For instance, if you want to read the entire the entire file, you can simply use the static `ReadAll` method of the `File` class. Using this method, you cause .NET to handle the process of creating the `Stream` and `StreamReader` for you, and simply return the resulting string of data. This is just one example of the shortcuts that the .NET framework provides. Listing 22-19 shows some of the others, with explanatory comments. Keep in mind that Listing 22-19 is showing individual code snippets; do not try to run the listing as a single block of code.

Listing 22-19: Using the static method of the File and Directory classes

VB
```vb
' Opens a file and returns a FileStream
Dim fs As FileStream = System.IO.File.Open("C:\Wrox\temp.txt" ,FileMode.Open)


' Opens a file and returns a StreamReader for reading the data
Dim sr As StreamReader = System.IO.File.OpenText("C:\Wrox\temp.txt")


' Opens a filestream for reading
Dim fs As FileStream = System.IO.File.OpenRead("C:\Wrox\temp.txt")


' Opens a filestream for writing
Dim fs As FileStream = System.IO.File.OpenWrite("C:\Wrox\temp.txt")


' Reads the entire file and returns a string of data
Dim data As String = System.IO.File.ReadAllText("C:\Wrox\temp.txt")


' Writes the string of data to the file
File.WriteAllText("C:\Wrox\temp.txt", data)
```

(continued)

Listing 22-19: *(continued)*

C#

```csharp
// Opens a file and returns a FileStream
FileStream fs = System.IO.File.Open(@"C:\Wrox\temp.txt", FileMode.Open);


// Opens a file and returns a StreamReader for reading the data
StreamReader sr = System.IO.File.OpenText(@"C:\Wrox\temp.txt");


// Opens a filestream for reading
FileStream fs = System.IO.File.OpenRead(@"C:\Wrox\temp.txt");


// Opens a filestream for writing
FileStream fs = System.IO.File.OpenWrite(@"C:\Wrox\temp.txt");


// Reads the entire file and returns a string of data
string data = System.IO.File.ReadAllText(@"C:\Wrox\temp.txt");


// Writes the string of data to the file
File.WriteAllText(@"C:\Wrox\temp.txt", data);
```

Compressing Streams

A new and very welcome addition to the .NET 2.0 Framework is the introduction of the `System.IO` `.Compression` namespace. This namespace includes classes for compressing and decompressing data using either the `GZipStream` or the `DeflateStream` classes.

GZip Compression

Because both new classes are derived from the `Stream` class, using them should be relatively similar to using the other `Stream` operations you have examined so far in this chapter. Listing 22-20 shows an example of compressing your text file using the `GZipStream` class.

Listing 22-20: Compressing a file using GZipStream

VB

```vb
' Read the file we are going to compress into a FileStream
Dim filename As String = Server.MapPath("TextFile.txt")

Dim infile As FileStream = File.OpenRead(filename)
Dim buffer(infile.Length) As Byte
infile.Read(buffer, 0, buffer.Length)
infile.Close()

' Create the output file
Dim outfile As System.IO.FileStream = _
    File.Create(Path.ChangeExtension(filename, "zip"))

' Compress the input stream and write it to the output FileStream
```

```
Dim gzipStream As New GZipStream(outfile, CompressionMode.Compress)
gzipStream.Write(buffer, 0, buffer.Length)
gzipStream.Close()
```

C#

```csharp
// Read the file we are going to compress into a FileStream
string filename = Server.MapPath("TextFile.txt");

FileStream infile = File.OpenRead(filename);
byte[] buffer = new byte[infile.Length];
infile.Read(buffer, 0, buffer.Length);
infile.Close();

// Create the output file
FileStream outfile = File.Create(Path.ChangeExtension(filename, "zip"));

// Compress the input stream and write it to the output FileStream
GZipStream gzipStream = new GZipStream(outfile, CompressionMode.Compress);
gzipStream.Write(buffer, 0, buffer.Length);
gzipStream.Close();
```

Notice that the GZipStream constructor requires two parameters, the stream to write the compressed data to, and the CompressionMode enumeration, which tells the class if you want to compress or decompress data. After the code runs, be sure there is a file called text.zip in your website.

Deflate Compression

The Compression namespace also allows to you decompress a file using the GZip or Deflate methods. Listing 22-21 shows an example of decompressing a file using the Deflate method.

Listing 22-21: Decompressing a file using DeflateStream

VB

```
Dim filename As String = Server.MapPath("TextFile.zip")

Dim infile As FileStream = File.OpenRead(filename)
Dim deflateStream As New DeflateStream(infile, CompressionMode.Decompress)
Dim buffer(infile.Length + 100) As Byte

Dim offset As Integer = 0
Dim totalCount As Integer = 0
While True
    Dim bytesRead As Integer = deflateStream.Read(buffer, offset, 100)
    If bytesRead = 0 Then
        Exit While
    End If
    offset += bytesRead
    totalCount += bytesRead
End While

Dim outfile As FileStream = _
    File.Create(Path.ChangeExtension(filename, "txt"))
outfile.Write(buffer, 0, buffer.Length)
outfile.Close()
```

(continued)

Listing 22-21: *(continued)*

C#

```csharp
string filename = Server.MapPath("TextFile.zip");

FileStream infile = File.OpenRead(filename);
DeflateStream deflateStream =
    new DeflateStream(infile, CompressionMode.Decompress);
byte[] buffer = new byte[infile.Length + 100];

int offset = 0;
int totalCount = 0;
while (true)
{
    int bytesRead = deflateStream.Read(buffer, offset, 100);
    if (bytesRead == 0)
    { break; }

    offset += bytesRead;
    totalCount += bytesRead;
}

FileStream outfile = File.Create(Path.ChangeExtension(filename, "txt"));
outfile.Write(buffer, 0, buffer.Length);
outfile.Close();
```

Compressing HTTP Output

Besides compressing files, one other very good use of the new compression features of the .NET 2.0 Framework in an ASP.NET application is to implement your own `HttpModule` class that compresses the HTTP output of your application. This is easier than it might sound, and it will save you precious bandwidth by compressing the data that is sent from your Web server to the browsers that support the HTTP 1.1 Protocol standard (which most do). The browser can then decompress the data before rendering it.

> Note that IIS 6 does offer built-in HTTP compression capabilities, and there are several third-party HTTP compression modules available, such as the Blowery Http Compression Module (http://www.blowery.org).

Start by creating a Windows Class library project. Add a new class to your project called `CompressionModule`. This class is your compression `HttpModule`. Listing 22-22 shows the code for creating the class.

Listing 22-22: Compressing HTTP output with an HttpModule

VB

```vb
Imports System
Imports System.Collections.Generic
Imports System.Text
Imports System.Web
Imports System.IO
Imports System.IO.Compression


Namespace Wrox.Demo.Compression
Public Class CompressionModule
```

```
        Implements IHttpModule

        Public Sub Dispose() Implements System.Web.IHttpModule.Dispose
            Throw New Exception("The method or operation is not implemented.")
        End Sub

        Public Sub Init(ByVal context As System.Web.HttpApplication) _
            Implements System.Web.IHttpModule.Init
            AddHandler context.BeginRequest, AddressOf context_BeginRequest
        End Sub

        Public Sub context_BeginRequest(ByVal sender As Object, ByVal e As EventArgs)
            Dim app As HttpApplication = CType(sender, HttpApplication)

            'Get the Accept-Encoding HTTP header from the request.
            'The requesting browser sends this header which we will use
            ' to determine if it supports compression, and if so, what type
            ' of compression algorithm it supports
            Dim encodings As String = app.Request.Headers.Get("Accept-Encoding")

            If (encodings = Nothing) Then
                Return
            End If

            Dim s As Stream = app.Response.Filter

            encodings = encodings.ToLower()

            If (encodings.Contains("gzip")) Then
                app.Response.Filter = New GZipStream(s, CompressionMode.Compress)
                app.Response.AppendHeader("Content-Encoding", "gzip")
                app.Context.Trace.Warn("GZIP Compression on")
            Else
                app.Response.Filter = _
                        New DeflateStream(s, CompressionMode.Compress)
                app.Response.AppendHeader("Content-Encoding", "deflate")
                app.Context.Trace.Warn("Deflate Compression on")
            End If
        End Sub
    End Class
End Namespace
```

C#

```csharp
using System;
using System.Collections.Generic;
using System.Text;
using System.Web;
using System.IO;
using System.IO.Compression;

namespace Wrox.Demo.Compression
{
    public class CompressionModule : IHttpModule
```

(continued)

Listing 22-22: *(continued)*

```
    {

        #region IHttpModule Members

        void IHttpModule.Dispose()
        {
            throw new Exception("The method or operation is not implemented.");
        }

        void IHttpModule.Init(HttpApplication context)
        {
            context.BeginRequest += new EventHandler(context_BeginRequest);
        }

        void context_BeginRequest(object sender, EventArgs e)
        {
            HttpApplication app = (HttpApplication)sender;

            //Get the Accept-Encoding HTTP header from the request.
            //The requesting browser sends this header which we will use
            // to determine if it supports compression, and if so, what type
            // of compression algorithm it supports
            string encodings = app.Request.Headers.Get("Accept-Encoding");

            if (encodings == null)
                return;

            Stream s = app.Response.Filter;

            encodings = encodings.ToLower();

            if (encodings.Contains("gzip"))
            {
                app.Response.Filter = new GZipStream(s, CompressionMode.Compress);
                app.Response.AppendHeader("Content-Encoding", "gzip");
                app.Context.Trace.Warn("GZIP Compression on");
            }
            else
            {
                app.Response.Filter =
                            new DeflateStream(s, CompressionMode.Compress);
                app.Response.AppendHeader("Content-Encoding", "deflate");
                app.Context.Trace.Warn("Deflate Compression on");
            }
        }

        #endregion
    }
}
```

After you create and build the module, add the assembly to your Web site's `Bin` directory. After that's done, you let your Web application know that it should use the `HttpModule` when it runs. Do this by adding the module to the `web.confile` file. Listing 22-23 shows the nodes to add to the `web.config` `system.web` configuration section.

Listing 22-23: Adding an HttpCompression module to the web.config

```
<httpModules>
    <add name="HttpCompressionModule"
      type="Wrox.Demo.Compression.CompressionModule, HttpCompressionModule"/>
</httpModules>

<trace enabled="true" />
```

Notice that one other change you are making is to enable page tracing. You use this to demonstrate that the page is actually being compressed. When you run the page, you should see the trace output shown in Figure 22-14. Notice a new entry under the trace information showing that the GZip compression has been enabled on this page.

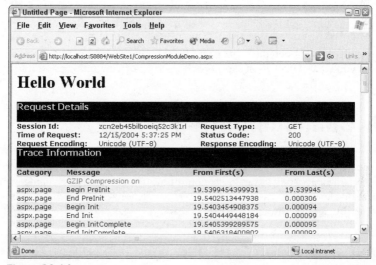

Figure 22-14

Working with Serial Ports

Another wonderful new addition to the .NET 2.0 Framework is the `System.IO.Ports` namespace. This namespace contains classes that enable you to work with and communicate through serial ports.

.NET provides a `SerialPort` component that you can add to the Component Designer of your Web page. Adding this component enables your application to communicate via the serial port. Listing 22-24 shows how to write some text to the serial port.

Listing 22-24: Writing text to the serial port

VB

```vb
Me.SerialPort1.PortName = "COM1"

If (Not Me.SerialPort1.IsOpen()) Then
    Me.SerialPort1.Open()
End If

Me.SerialPort1.Write("Hello World")
Me.SerialPort1.Close()
```

C#

```csharp
this.SerialPort1.PortName = "COM1";

if (!this.SerialPort1.IsOpen)
{
    this.SerialPort1.Open();
}

this.SerialPort1.Write("Hello World");
this.SerialPort1.Close();
```

This code simply attempts to open the serial port COM1 and write a bit of text. The `SerialPort` component gives you control over most aspects of the serial port, including baud rate, parity, and stop bits.

Network Communications

Finally, this chapter takes you beyond your own systems and talks about how you can use the .NET Framework to communicate with other systems. The .NET Framework contains a rich set of classes in the `System.Net` namespace that allow you to communicate over a network using a variety of protocols and communications layers. You can perform all types of actions, from DNS resolution to programmatic HTTP Posts to sending e-mail through SMTP.

WebRequest and WebResponse

The first series of classes to discuss are the `WebRequest` and `WebResponse` classes. You can use these two classes to develop applications that can make a request to a Uniform Resource Identifier (URI) and receive a response from that resource. The .NET Framework provides three derivatives of the `WebRequest` and `WebResponse` classes, each designed to communicate to a specific type of end point via HTTP, FTP, and file:// protocols.

HttpWebRequest and HttpWebResponse

The first pair of classes are the `HttpWebRequest` and `HttpWebResponse` classes. As you can probably guess based on their names, these two classes are designed to communicate using the HTTP protocol. Perhaps the most famous use of the `HttpWebRequest` and `HttpWebResponse` classes is to write applications that can make requests to other Web pages via HTTP and parse the resulting text to extract data. This is known as *screen scraping*.

For an example of using the `HttpWebRequest` and `HttpWebResponse` classes to screen scrape, you can use the following code to build a Web page that will serve as a simple Web browser. You also learn how another Web page can be displayed inside of yours using an `HttpWebRequest`. In this example, you scrape the Microsoft.com homepage and display it in a panel on your Web page. Listing 22-25 shows the code.

Listing 22-25: Using an HttpWebRequest to retrieve a Web page

VB

```vb
<%@ Page Language="VB" %>
<%@ Import Namespace=System.IO %>
<%@ Import Namespace=System.Net %>

<script runat="server">
    Protected Sub Page_Load(ByVal sender As Object, ByVal e As System.EventArgs)
        Dim uri As New Uri("http://www.microsoft.com/default.aspx")
        If (uri.Scheme = uri.UriSchemeHttp) Then
            Dim request As HttpWebRequest = HttpWebRequest.Create(uri)
            request.Method = WebRequestMethods.Http.Get
            Dim response As HttpWebResponse = request.GetResponse()
            Dim reader As New StreamReader(response.GetResponseStream())
            Dim tmp As String = reader.ReadToEnd()
            response.Close()

            Me.Panel1.GroupingText = tmp
        End If
    End Sub
</script>

<html xmlns="http://www.w3.org/1999/xhtml" >
<head runat="server">
    <title>Untitled Page</title>
</head>
<body>
    <form id="form1" runat="server">
    <div>
        <p>This is the microsoft.com website:</p>
        <asp:Panel ID="Panel1" runat="server"
            Height="355px" Width="480px" ScrollBars=Auto>
        </asp:Panel>
    </div>
    </form>
</body>
</html>
```

C#

```csharp
<script runat="server">
    protected void Page_Load(object sender, EventArgs e)
    {
        Uri uri = new Uri("http://www.microsoft.com/default.aspx");
        if (uri.Scheme == Uri.UriSchemeHttp)
        {
            HttpWebRequest request = (HttpWebRequest)HttpWebRequest.Create( uri );
            request.Method = WebRequestMethods.Http.Get;
            HttpWebResponse response = (HttpWebResponse)request.GetResponse();
```

(continued)

Listing 22-25: *(continued)*

```
            StreamReader reader = new StreamReader(response.GetResponseStream());
            string tmp = reader.ReadToEnd();
            response.Close();

            this.Panel1.GroupingText = tmp;
        }
    }
</script>
```

Figure 22-15 shows what the Web page look likes when you execute the code in Listing 22-25. The
`HttpWebRequest` to the microsoft.com home page returns a string containing the scraped HTML. The
sample assigns the value of this string to the `GroupingText` property of the Panel control. When the final
page is rendered, the browser renders the HTML that was scraped as literal content on the page.

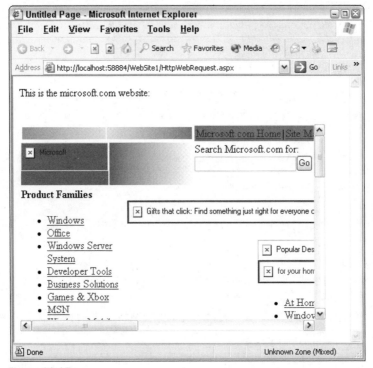

Figure 22-15

One other use of the `HttpWebRequest` and `HttpWebResponse` classes is to programmatically post data
to another Web page, as shown in Listing 22-26.

Listing 22-26: Using an HttpWebRequest to post data to a remote Web page

VB

```
<%@ Page Language="VB" %>
<%@ Import Namespace=System.IO %>
<%@ Import Namespace=System.Net %>

<!DOCTYPE html PUBLIC "-//W3C//DTD XHTML 1.1//EN"
"http://www.w3.org/TR/xhtml11/DTD/xhtml11.dtd">

<script runat="server">

    Protected Sub Page_Load(ByVal sender As Object, ByVal e As System.EventArgs)
        Dim uri As New Uri("http://www.amazon.com/" & _
                       "exec/obidos/search-handle-form/102-5194535-6807312")
        Dim data As String = "field-keywords=Professional ASP.NET 2.0"
        If (uri.Scheme = uri.UriSchemeHttp) Then

            Dim request As HttpWebRequest = HttpWebRequest.Create(uri)
            request.Method = WebRequestMethods.Http.Post
            request.ContentLength = data.Length
            request.ContentType = "application/x-www-form-urlencoded"

            Dim writer As New StreamWriter(request.GetRequestStream())
            writer.Write(data)
            writer.Close()

            Dim response As HttpWebResponse = request.GetResponse()
            Dim reader As New StreamReader(response.GetResponseStream())
            Dim tmp As String = reader.ReadToEnd()
            response.Close()

            Me.Panel1.GroupingText = tmp
        End If
    End Sub
</script>

<html xmlns="http://www.w3.org/1999/xhtml" >
<head runat="server">
    <title>Untitled Page</title>
</head>
<body>
    <form id="form1" runat="server">
    <div>
        <asp:Panel ID="Panel1" runat="server"
            Height="355px" Width="480px" ScrollBars=Auto>
        </asp:Panel>
    </div>
    </form>
</body>
</html>
```

(continued)

Listing 22-26: *(continued)*

```
<script runat="server">

    protected void Page_Load(object sender, EventArgs e)
    {
        Uri uri = new Uri("http://www.amazon.com/" +
                        "exec/obidos/search-handle-form/102-5194535-6807312");
        string data = "field-keywords=Professional ASP.NET 2.0";
        if (uri.Scheme == Uri.UriSchemeHttp)
        {
            HttpWebRequest request = (HttpWebRequest)HttpWebRequest.Create(uri);
            request.Method = WebRequestMethods.Http.Post;
            request.ContentLength = data.Length;
            request.ContentType = "application/x-www-form-urlencoded";

            StreamWriter writer = new StreamWriter( request.GetRequestStream() );
            writer.Write(data);
            writer.Close();

            HttpWebResponse response = (HttpWebResponse)request.GetResponse();
            StreamReader reader = new StreamReader(response.GetResponseStream());
            string tmp = reader.ReadToEnd();
            response.Close();

            this.Panel1.GroupingText = tmp;
        }
    }
</script>
```

You can see that the preceding code posts a search query to amazon.com and receives the HTML as the response. As in the example shown earlier in Listing 22-25, you can simply use a Panel to display the resulting text as HTML. The results of the query are shown in Figure 22-16.

FtpWebRequest and FtpWebResponse

The next pair of classes are the `FtpWebRequest` and `FtpWebResponse` classes. These two classes are new additions to the .NET 2.0 Framework, and they make it easy to execute File Transfer Protocol (FTP) commands from your Web page. Using these classes, it is now possible to implement an entire FTP client right from your Web application. Listing 22-27 shows an example of downloading a text file from the public Microsoft.com FTP site.

Listing 22-27: Using an FtpWebRequest to download a file from an FTP site

VB

```
<%@ Page Language="VB" %>
<%@ Import Namespace=System.IO %>
<%@ Import Namespace=System.Net %>

<script runat="server">

    Protected Sub Page_Load(ByVal sender As Object, ByVal e As System.EventArgs)
```

```
        Dim uri As New Uri("ftp://ftp.microsoft.com/SoftLib/ReadMe.txt")
         If (uri.Scheme = uri.UriSchemeFtp) Then
             Dim request As FtpWebRequest = FtpWebRequest.Create(uri)
             request.Method = WebRequestMethods.Ftp.DownloadFile
             Dim response As FtpWebResponse = request.GetResponse()
             Dim reader As New StreamReader(response.GetResponseStream())
             Dim tmp As String = reader.ReadToEnd()
             response.Close()

             Me.Panel1.GroupingText = tmp
         End If
    End Sub
</script>

<html xmlns="http://www.w3.org/1999/xhtml" >
<head runat="server">
    <title>Using FTP from an ASP.NET webpage</title>
</head>
<body>
    <form id="form1" runat="server">
    <div>
        <asp:Panel ID="Panel1" runat="server"
            Height="355px" Width="480px" ScrollBars=Auto>
        </asp:Panel>

    </div>
    </form>
</body>
</html>
```

C#

```
<script runat="server">

    protected void Page_Load(object sender, EventArgs e)
    {
        Uri uri = new Uri("ftp://ftp.microsoft.com/SoftLib/ReadMe.txt ");
        if (uri.Scheme == Uri.UriSchemeFtp)
        {
            FtpWebRequest request = (FtpWebRequest)FtpWebRequest.Create(uri);
            request.Method = WebRequestMethods.Ftp.DownloadFile;
            FtpWebResponse response = (FtpWebResponse)request.GetResponse();
            StreamReader reader = new StreamReader(response.GetResponseStream());
            string tmp = reader.ReadToEnd();
            response.Close();

            this.Panel1.GroupingText = tmp;
        }
    }
</script>
```

Figure 22-16

FileWebRequest and FileWebResponse

Next, look at the `FileWebRequest` and `FileWebResponse` classes. These classes provide a file system implementation of the WebRequest and WebResponse classes and are designed to make it easy to transfer files using the file:// protocol, as shown in Listing 22-28.

Listing 22-28: Using the FileWebRequest to write to a remote file

VB

```vb
Dim uri As New Uri("file://DEMOXP/Documents/lorum.txt")
If (uri.Scheme = uri.UriSchemeFile) Then
    Dim request As FileWebRequest = FileWebRequest.Create(uri)
    Dim response As FileWebResponse = request.GetResponse()
    Dim reader As New StreamReader(response.GetResponseStream())
    Dim tmp As String = reader.ReadToEnd()
    response.Close()
End If
```

C#

```csharp
Uri uri = new Uri("file://DEMOXP/Documents/lorum.txt ");
if (uri.Scheme == Uri.UriSchemeFile)
{
    FileWebRequest request = (FileWebRequest)FileWebRequest.Create(uri);
    FileWebResponse response = (HttpWebResponse)request.GetResponse();
```

```
    StreamReader reader = new StreamReader(response.GetResponseStream());
    string tmp = reader.ReadToEnd();
    response.Close();
}
```

In this listing, we are requesting the `lorum.txt` file that exists in the `Documents` folder on the DEMOXP machine on our local network.

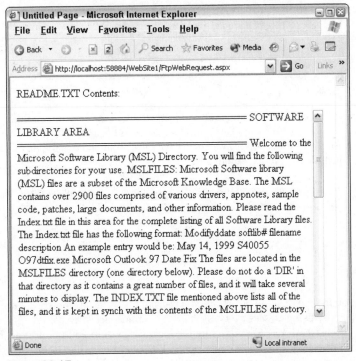

Figure 22-17

Sending Mail

Finally, consider a feature common to many Web applications—the capability to send e-mail from a Web page. The capability to send mail was part of the 1.0 Framework and located in the `System.Web.Mail` namespace. In the 2.0 Framework, this functionality has been enhanced and moved to the `System.Net.Mail` namespace. Listing 22-29 shows an example of sending an e-mail.

Listing 22-29: Sending mail from a Web page

VB
```
Dim message As _
    New System.Net.Mail.MailMessage("webmaster@ineta.org", "webmaster@ineta.org")
message.Subject = "Sending Mail with ASP.NET 2.0"
message.Body = _
```

(continued)

Listing 22-29: *(continued)*

```
     "This is a sample email which demonstrates sending email using ASP.NET 2.0"

Dim smtp As New System.Net.Mail.SmtpClient("localhost")
smtp.Send(message)
```

C#
```
System.Net.Mail.MailMessage message =
    new System.Net.Mail.MailMessage("webmaster@ineta.org","webmaster@ineta.org");
message.Subject = "Sending Mail with ASP.NET 2.0";
message.Body =
    "This is a sample email which demonstrates sending email using ASP.NET 2.0";
System.Net.Mail.SmtpClient smtp = new System.Net.Mail.SmtpClient("localhost");
smtp.Send(message);
```

In this sample, you first create a `MailMessage` object, which is the class that contains the actual message you want to send. The `MailMessage` class requires the To and From address be provided to its constructor, and you can either provide the parameters as strings, or you can use the `MailAddressCollection` class to provide multiple recipients' e-mail addresses.

After you create the `Message`, you use the `SmtpClient` class to actually send the message to your local SMTP server. The `SmtpClient` class allows you to specify the SMTP Server from which you want to relay your e-mail.

Summary

In this chapter, you looked at some of the other classes in the .NET Framework. You looked at managing the local file system by using classes in the `System.IO` namespace such as `DirectoryInfo` and the `FileInfo`, and you learned how to enumerate the local file system and manipulate both directory and file properties and directory and file Access Control Lists. Additionally, the chapter discussed the rich functionality .NET provides for working with paths.

The chapter also covered how the .NET framework enables you to read and write data to a multitude of data locations, including the local file system, network file system, and even system memory through a common `Stream` architecture. The Framework provides you with specialized classes to deal with each kind of data location. Additionally, the Framework makes working with streams even easier by providing `Reader` and `Writer` classes. These classes hide much of the complexity of reading from and writing to underlying streams. Here, too, the framework provides you with a number of different `Reader` and `Writer` classes that give you the power to control exactly how your data is read or written, be it character, binary, string, or XML.

You were also introduced to a new feature of the .NET 2.0 Framework that allows you to communicate with serial ports.

Finally, you learned about the variety of network communication options the .NET Framework provides. From making and sending Web requests over HTTP, FTP, and File, to sending mail, the .NET Framework offers you a full plate of network communication services.

User Controls, Server Controls, Modules, and HttpHandlers

In an object-oriented environment like .NET, the encapsulation of code into small, single-purpose, reusable objects is one of the keys to developing a robust system. For instance, if your application deals with customers, you might want to consider creating a customer's object that encapsulates all the functionality a customer might need. The advantage is that you create a single point with which other objects can interact, and you have only a single point of code to create, debug, deploy, and maintain. In this scenario, the customer object is typically known as a business object because it encapsulates all the business logic needed for a customer.

You can also create other types of reusable objects. In this chapter, we concentrate on discussing and demonstrating how you can create reusable visual components for an ASP.NET application. The two types of reusable components in ASP.NET are user controls and server controls.

A *user control* encapsulates existing ASP.NET controls into a single container control, which you can easily reuse throughout your Web project.

A *server control* encapsulates the visual design, behavior, and logic for an element that the user interacts with on the Web page.

Visual Studio ships with a large number of server controls that you are probably already familiar with, such as the Label, Button, and TextBox controls. This chapter talks about how you can create custom server controls and extend existing server controls.

Finally in this chapter, you look at two other types of objects: HttpHandlers, which allow you to intercept and process incoming HTTP requests much like an ISAPI filter does, and HttpModules, which allow you to modify incoming HTTP requests for Web application resources.

Because all four of these topics are so large, and because discussing the intricacies of each could easily fill an entire book by itself, you can't possibly investigate every option available to you. Instead, this chapter attempts to give you a brief overview of building and using user controls, server controls, HttpHandlers, and HttpModules. It demonstrates some common scenarios for each control. By the end of this chapter, you should have learned enough that you can get started building basic controls of each type and be able to continue to learn on your own.

User Controls

User controls represent the simplest form of ASP.NET control encapsulation. Because they are the simplest, they are also the easiest to create and use. Essentially a *user control* is the grouping of existing server controls into a single-container control. This enables you to create powerful objects that you can easily use throughout an entire Web project.

Creating User Controls

Creating user controls is very simple in Visual Studio 2005. To create a new user control, you first add a new User Control file to your Web site. From the Website menu, select the Add New Item option. After the Add New File dialog appears, select the Web User Control File template from the list and click OK. Notice that after the file is added to the project, the file has an .ascx extension. This extension signals to ASP.NET that this file is a user control. If you attempt to load the user control directly into your browser, ASP.NET returns an error telling you that this type of file cannot be served to the client.

If you look at the HTML source (shown in Listing 23-1) for the user control, you see several interesting differences from a standard ASP.NET Web page.

Listing 23-1: A Web user control file template

```
<%@ Control Language="VB" ClassName="WebUserControl1" %>

<script runat="server">

</script>
```

First, notice that the source uses the @Control directive rather than the @Page directive, which a standard Web page would use. Second, notice that unlike a standard ASP.NET Web page, no other HTML tags besides the <script> tags exist in the control. The Web page containing the user control provides the basic HTML, such as the <body> and <form> tags. In fact, if you try to add a server-side form tag to the user control, ASP.NET returns an error when the page is served to the client. The error message tells you that only one server-side form tag is allowed in your Web page.

To add controls to the form, simply drag them from the Toolbox onto your user control. Listing 23-2 shows the user control after a Label and a Button have been added.

Listing 23-2: Adding controls to the Web user control

```
<%@ Control Language="VB" ClassName="WebUserControl2" %>

<script runat="server">

</script>

<asp:Label ID="Label1" runat="server" Text="Label"></asp:Label>
<asp:Button ID="Button1" runat="server" Text="Button" />
```

After you add the controls to the user control, you put the user control onto a standard ASP.NET Web page. To do this, drag the file from the Solution Explorer onto your Web page.

If you are familiar with using user controls in prior versions of Visual Studio, you probably remember the gray control representation that appeared in the page designer when you dropped a user control onto a Web page. Visual Studio 2005 has improved this, and user controls are now fully rendered on the host Web page during design time. This allows you to see an accurate representation of what the entire page will look like after it is rendered to the client.

Figure 23-1 shows the user control after it has been dropped onto a host Web page.

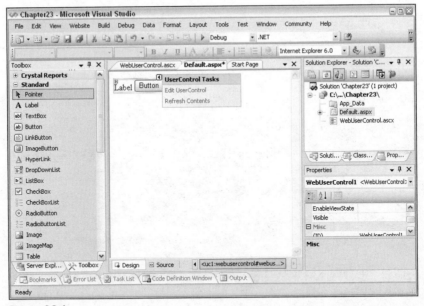

Figure 23-1

After you have placed the user control onto a Web page, open the page in a browser to see the fully rendered Web page.

User controls fully participate in the page-rendering lifecycle, and controls contained within a user control behave identically to controls placed onto a standard ASP.NET Web page. This means that the user control has its own page execute events (such as Init, Load, and Prerender) that execute as the page is processed. It also means that child control events, such as a button-click event, will behave identically. Listing 23-3 shows how to use the User Controls Page_Load event to populate the label and to handle the button-click event.

Listing 23-3: Creating control events in a user control

VB

```
<%@ Control Language="VB" ClassName="WebUserControl1" %>

<script runat="server">

    Protected Sub Page_Load(ByVal sender As Object, ByVal e As System.EventArgs)
        Me.Label1.Text = "The quick brown fox jumped over the lazy dog"
    End Sub

    Protected Sub Button1_Click(ByVal sender As Object, _
        ByVal e As System.EventArgs)
        Me.Label1.Text = "The quick brown fox clicked the button on the page"
    End Sub
</script>

<asp:Label ID="Label1" runat="server" Text="Label"></asp:Label>
<asp:Button ID="Button1" runat="server" Text="Button" OnClick="Button1_Click" />
```

C#

```
<%@ Control Language="C#" ClassName="WebUserControl1" %>

<script runat="server">

    protected void Page_Load(object sender, EventArgs e)
    {
        this.Label1.Text = "The quick brown fox jumped over the lazy dog";
    }

    protected void Button1_Click(object sender, EventArgs e)
    {
        this.Label1.Text = "The quick brown fox clicked the button on the page";
    }
</script>

<asp:Label ID="Label1" runat="server" Text="Label"></asp:Label>
<asp:Button ID="Button1" runat="server" Text="Button" OnClick="Button1_Click" />
```

Now when you render the Web page, you see that the text of the label changes as the user control loads, and again when you click the bottom of the page. In fact, if you put a breakpoint on either of these two events, you can see that ASP.NET does indeed break, even inside the user control code when the page is executed.

Interacting with User Controls

So far, you have learned how you can create user controls and add them to a Web page. You have also learned how user controls can execute their own code. Most user controls, however, are not islands on their parent page. Many scenarios require that the host Web page be able to interact with user controls that have been placed on it. For instance, you may decide that the text you want to load in the label must be given to the user control by the host page. To do this, you simply add a public property to the user control, and then assign text using the property. Listing 23-4 shows the modified user control.

Listing 23-4: Exposing user control properties

VB
```vb
<%@ Control Language="VB" ClassName="WebUserControl" %>

<script runat="server">

    Private _text As String

    Public Property Text() As String
        Get
            Return _text
        End Get
        Set(ByVal value As String)
            _text = value
        End Set
    End Property

    Protected Sub Page_Load(ByVal sender As Object, ByVal e As System.EventArgs)
        Me.Label1.Text = Me.Text
    End Sub

    Protected Sub Button1_Click(ByVal sender As Object, _
      ByVal e As System.EventArgs)
        Me.Label1.Text = "The quick brown fox clicked the button on the page"
    End Sub

</script>

<asp:Label ID="Label1" runat="server" Text="Label"></asp:Label>
<asp:Button ID="Button1" runat="server" Text="Button" OnClick="Button1_Click" />
```

C#
```csharp
<%@ Control Language="C#" ClassName="WebUserControl" %>

<script runat="server">

    private string _text;

    public string Text
    {
        get {
```

(continued)

Listing 23-4: *(continued)*

```
            return _text;
        }
        set {
            _text = value;
        }
    }

    protected void Page_Load(object sender, EventArgs e)
    {
        this.Label1.Text = this.Text;
    }

    protected void Button1_Click(object sender, EventArgs e)
    {
        this.Label1.Text = "The quick brown fox clicked the button on the page";
    }

</script>

<asp:Label ID="Label1" runat="server" Text="Label"></asp:Label>
<asp:Button ID="Button1" runat="server" Text="Button" OnClick="Button1_Click" />
```

After you modify the user control, you simply populate the property from the host Web page. Listing 23-5 shows how to set the Text property in code, but public properties exposed by user controls will also be exposed by the Property Browser.

Listing 23-5: Populating user control properties from the host Web page

VB
```
Protected Sub Page_Load(ByVal sender As Object, ByVal e As System.EventArgs)
    Me.WebUserControl1.Text = "The quick brown fox jumped over the lazy dog"
End Sub
```

C#
```
protected void Page_Load(object sender, EventArgs e)
{
    this.WebUserControl1.Text = "The quick brown fox jumped over the lazy dog";
}
```

User controls are simple ways of creating powerful, reusable components in ASP.NET. They are easy to create using the built-in templates. Because they participate fully in the page lifecycle, you can create controls that can interact with their host page and even other controls on the host page.

Server Controls

The power to create server controls in ASP.NET is one of the greatest tools you can have as an ASP.NET developer. Creating your own custom server controls and extending existing controls are actually both quite easy. All controls in ASP.NET are derived from two basic classes: `System.Web.UI.Control` or `System.Web.UI.WebControls.WebControl`. Classes derived from the `Control` class have the basic functionality required to participate in the Page framework. Additionally, because the `Control` class implements `IComponent`, classes derived from `Control` have the basic functionality to be a designable component. They can be added to the Visual Studio Toolbox, dragged onto the page designer, and have their properties and events displayed in the Property Browser.

Controls derived from the `WebControl` class build on the functionality that the `Control` class provides by adding much of the common functionality needed to create controls that render a visual HTML representation. Additionally, classes derived from the `WebControl` class have support for many of the basic styling elements such as Font, Height, and Width.

Project Setup

This section demonstrates just how easy it is to create custom server controls by creating a very simple server control that derives from the `WebControl` class. In order to create a new server control, you create a new Web Control Library project. You can use this project to demonstrate concepts throughout the rest of this chapter. In Visual Studio, choose File ➪ New Project to open the New Project dialog. From the Project Types tree, open either the Visual Basic or Visual C# nodes and select the Windows node. Figure 23-2 shows the New Project dialog with a Visual C# Web Control Library project template selected.

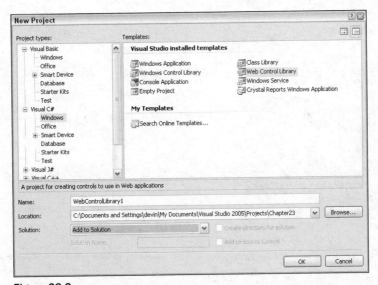

Figure 23-2

When you click OK in the New Project dialog, Visual Studio creates a new Web Control Library project for you. Notice that the project includes a template class that contains a very simple server control. Listing 23-6 shows the code for this template class.

Listing 23-6: The Visual Studio Web Control Library class template

VB

```vb
Imports System
Imports System.Collections.Generic
Imports System.ComponentModel
Imports System.Text
Imports System.Web
Imports System.Web.UI
Imports System.Web.UI.WebControls

<DefaultProperty("Text"), _
 ToolboxData("<{0}:WebCustomControl1 runat=server></{0}:WebCustomControl1>")> _
Public Class WebCustomControl1
    Inherits System.Web.UI.WebControls.WebControl

    Dim _text As String

    <Bindable(True), Category("Appearance"), DefaultValue("")> _
    Property [Text]() As String
        Get
            Return _text
        End Get

        Set(ByVal Value As String)
            _text = Value
        End Set
    End Property

    Protected Overrides Sub Render(ByVal output As System.Web.UI.HtmlTextWriter)
        output.Write([Text])
    End Sub

End Class
```

C#

```csharp
using System;
using System.Collections.Generic;
using System.ComponentModel;
using System.Text;
using System.Web.UI;
using System.Web.UI.WebControls;

namespace WebControlLibrary1
{
    [DefaultProperty("Text")]
    [ToolboxData("<{0}:WebCustomControl1 runat=server></{0}:WebCustomControl1>")]
    public class WebCustomControl1 : WebControl
    {
        private string text;

        [Bindable(true)]
        [Category("Appearance")]
        [DefaultValue("")]
        public string Text
        {
            get
```

```
        {
            return text;
        }
        set
        {
            text = value;
        }
    }

    protected override void Render(HtmlTextWriter output)
    {
        output.Write(Text);
    }
    }
}
```

This template class creates a basic server control that exposes one property called `Text` and renders the value of that property to the screen. Notice that you override the `Render` method of the control and write the value of the `Text` property to the pages output stream. We talk more about rendering output later in the chapter.

Now, take this class and use it in a sample Web application by adding a new Web Project to the existing solution. The default Web page, created by Visual Studio, serves as a test page for the server control samples in this chapter.

Visual Studio 2005 has greatly improved the process of using custom controls. Instead of having to manually add controls, as you had to do in prior Visual Studio versions, Visual Studio 2005 can automatically add the control to the Toolbox for you as long as the solution contains the Web Control Library project. To see this, simply build the project and then open the default Web page of the Web Project you just added. The Toolbox should contain a new section called WebControlLibrary1.Components, and the new server control should be listed in this section (see Figure 23-3).

New section

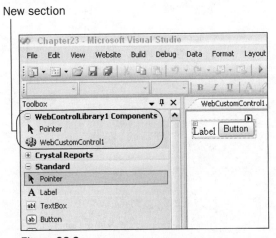

Figure 23-3

Now, all you have to do is drag the control onto the Web form, and the control's assembly is automatically added to the Web project for you. When you drag the control from the Toolbox onto the designer surface, the control adds itself to the Web page. Listing 23-7 shows you what the Web page source code looks like after you have added the control.

Listing 23-7: Adding a Web Control Library to a Web page

```
<%@ Register Assembly="ClassLibrary1" Namespace="ClassLibrary1" TagPrefix="cc1" %>

<!DOCTYPE html PUBLIC "-//W3C//DTD XHTML 1.1//EN"
"http://www.w3.org/TR/xhtml11/DTD/xhtml11.dtd">

<html xmlns="http://www.w3.org/1999/xhtml" >
<head runat="server">
    <title>Adding a Custom Web Control</title>
</head>
<body>
    <form id="form1" runat="server">
    <div>
        <cc1:WebCustomControl1 ID="WebCustomControl1_1" runat="server" />
    </div>
    </form>
</body>
</html>
```

After you drag the control onto the Web form, take a look at its properties in the Properties Window. Figure 23-4 shows the properties of your custom control.

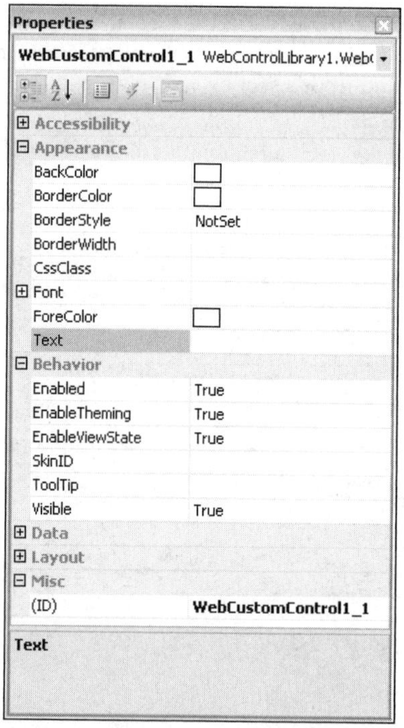

Figure 23-4

Notice that in addition to the `Text` property you defined in the control, the control has all the basic properties of a visual control, including various styling and behavior properties. The properties are exposed because the control was derived from the `WebControl` class. The control also inherits the base events exposed by `WebControl`.

Make sure the control is working by entering a value for the `Text` property and viewing the page in a browser. Figure 23-5 shows what the page looks like if you set the `Text` property to `"Hello World!"`.

Figure 23-5

As expected the control has rendered the value of the `Text` property to the Web page.

This sample demonstrates just how easy it is to create a simple server control. Of course, this control does not have much functionality and lacks many of the features of a server control. The following section shows how you can use attributes to enhance this server control to make it more useful and user-friendly.

Control Attributes

A key enhancement to the design-time experience for users utilizing server controls is achieved by adding attributes to the class level and to the control's classes and properties. Attributes define much of how the control behaves at design time in Visual Studio. For instance, when you look at the default control template from the previous section (Listing 23-6), notice that attributes have been applied to both the `Class` and to the `Text` property. In this section, you study these attributes and how they affect the behavior of the control.

Class Attributes

Class attributes generally control how the server control behaves in the Visual Studio Toolbox and when placed on the design surface. The class attributes can be divided into three basic categories: attributes that help the Visual Studio designer know how to render the control at design time, attributes that help you tell ASP.NET how to render nested controls, and attributes that tell Visual Studio how to display the control in the Toolbox. The following table describes some of these attributes.

Attribute	Description
Designer	Indicates the designer class this control should use to render a design-time view of the control on the Visual Studio design surface
Type Converter	Specifies what type to use as a converter for the object
DefaultEvent	Indicates the default event created when the user double-clicks the control on the Visual Studio design surface
DefaultProperty	Indicates the default property for the control
ControlBuilder	Specifies a ControlBuilder class for building a custom control in the ASP.NET control parser
ParseChildren	Indicates whether XML elements nested within the server controls tags will be treated as properties or as child controls
TagPrefix	Indicates the text the control is prefixed with in the Web page HTML

Property/Event Attributes

Property attributes are used to control a number of different aspects of server controls. You can use attributes to control how your properties and events behave in the Visual Studio Property Browser. You can also use attributes to control how properties and events are serialized at design time. The following table describes some of the property and event attributes you can use.

Attribute	Description
Bindable	Indicates that the property can be bound to a data source
Browsable	Indicates whether the property should be displayed at design time in the Property Browser
Category	Indicates the category this property should be displayed under in the Property Browser
Description	Displays a text string at the bottom of the Property Browser that describes the purpose of the property
EditorBrowsable	Indicates whether the property should be editable when shown in the Property Browser
DefaultValue	Indicates the default value of the property shown in the Property Browser

Attribute	Description
DesignerSerializationVisibility	Specifies the visibility a property has to the design-time serializer
NotifyParentProperty	Indicates that the parent property is notified when the value of the property is modified
PersistChildren	Indicates whether, at design-time, the child controls of a server control should be persisted as nested inner controls
PersistanceMode	Specifies how a property or an event is persisted to the ASP.NET page
TemplateContainer	Specifies the type of INamingContainer that will contain the template once it is created
Editor	Indicates the UI Type Editor class this control should use to edit its value
Localizable	Indicates that the property contains text that can be localized
Themable	Indicates whether this property can have a theme applied to it

Obviously, the class and property/event attribute tables present a lot of information upfront. You already saw a demonstration of some of these attributes in Listing 23-1; now, as you go through the rest of the chapter, you will spend time working with most of the attributes listed in the tables.

Control Rendering

Now that that you have seen the large number of options you have for working with a server control at design-time, look at what you need to know to manage how your server control renders its HTML at runtime.

The Page Event Lifecycle

Before we talk about rendering HTML, you must understand the lifecycle of a Web page. As the control developer, you are responsible for overriding methods that execute during the lifecycle and implementing your own custom rendering logic.

Remember that when a Web browser makes a request to the server, it is using HTTP, a stateless protocol. ASP.NET provides a page-execution framework that helps create the illusion of state in a Web application. This framework is basically a series of methods and events that execute every time an ASP.NET page is processed. You may have seen diagrams showing this lifecycle for ASP.NET 1.0, but ASP.NET 2.0 adds a variety of new events to give you more power over the behavior of the control. Figure 23-6 shows the events and methods called during the control's lifecycle.

Many events and members are executed during the control's lifecycle, but you should concentrate on the more important among them.

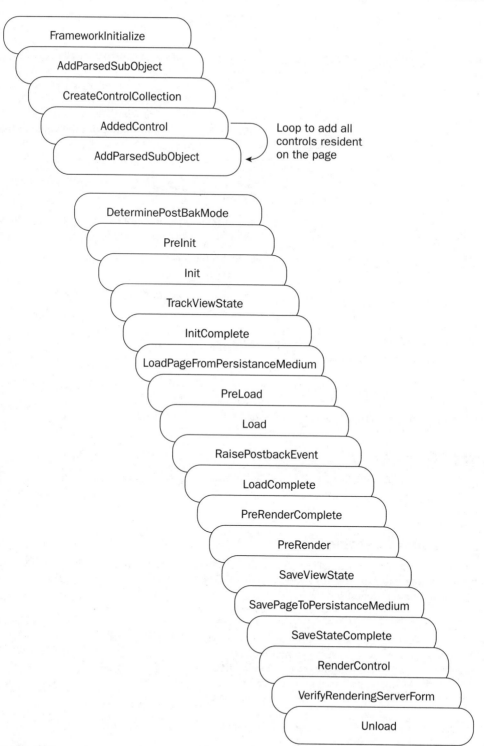

FrameworkInitialize

AddParsedSubObject

CreateControlCollection

AddedControl

AddParsedSubObject

Loop to add all controls resident on the page

DeterminePostBakMode

PreInit

Init

TrackViewState

InitComplete

LoadPageFromPersistanceMedium

PreLoad

Load

RaisePostbackEvent

LoadComplete

PreRenderComplete

PreRender

SaveViewState

SavePageToPersistanceMedium

SaveStateComplete

RenderControl

VerifyRenderingServerForm

Unload

Figure 23-6

Rendering Services

The main job of a server control is to render some type of markup language to the HTTP output stream, which is returned to and displayed by the client. If your client is a standard browser, the control should emit HTML; if the client is something like a mobile device, the control may need to emit a different type of markup, such as WAP, or WML. As I stated earlier, it is your responsibility as the control developer to tell the server control what markup to render. The overridden `Render` method, called during the control's lifecycle, is the primary location where you tell the control what you want to emit to the client. In Listing 23-8, notice that the `Render` method is used to tell the control to print the value of the `Text` property.

Listing 23-8: Overriding the Render method

VB

```
Protected Overrides Sub Render(ByVal output As System.Web.UI.HtmlTextWriter)
    output.Write([Text])
End Sub
```

C#

```
protected override void Render(HtmlTextWriter output)
{
    output.Write(Text);
}
```

Also notice that the `Render` method has one method parameter called `output`. This parameter is an `HtmlTextWriter` class, which is what the control uses to render HTML to the client. This special writer class is specifically designed to emit HTML 4.0–compliant HTML to the browser. The `HtmlTextwriter` class has a number of methods you can use to emit your HTML, including `RenderBeginTag` and `WriteBeginTag`. Listing 23-9 shows how you can modify the control's `Render` method to emit an HTML `<input>` tag.

Listing 23-9: Using the HtmlTextWriter to render an HTML tag

VB

```
Protected Overrides Sub Render(ByVal output As System.Web.UI.HtmlTextWriter)
    output.RenderBeginTag(HtmlTextWriterTag.Input)
    output.RenderEndTag()
End Sub
```

C#

```
protected override void Render(HtmlTextWriter output)
{
    output.RenderBeginTag(HtmlTextWriterTag.Input);
    output.RenderEndTag();
}
```

First, notice that the `RenderBeginTag` method is used to emit the HTML. The advantage of using this method to emit HTML is that it requires you to select a tag from the `HtmlTextWriterTag` enumeration. Using the `RenderBeginTag` method and the `HtmlTextWriterTag` enumeration enables you to have your control automatically support downlevel browsers that cannot understand HTML 4.0 syntax. If a downlevel browser is detected by ASP.NET, the control automatically emits HTML 3.2 syntax instead of HTML 4.0.

Second, notice that the `RenderEndTag` method is also used. As the name suggests, this method renders the closing tag. Notice, however, that you do not have to specify in this method which tag you want to close. The `RenderEndTag` automatically closes the last begin tag rendered by the `RenderBeginTag` method, which in this case is the `<input>` tag. If you want to emit multiple HTML tags, make sure you order your `Begin` and `End` render methods properly. In Listing 23-10, for example, you add a `<div>` tag to the control. The `<div>` tag surrounds the `<input>` tag when rendered to the page.

Listing 23-10: Using the HtmlTextWriter to render multiple HTML tags

VB

```vb
Protected Overrides Sub Render(ByVal output As System.Web.UI.HtmlTextWriter)
    output.RenderBeginTag(HtmlTextWriterTag.Div)
    output.RenderBeginTag(HtmlTextWriterTag.Input)
    output.RenderEndTag()
    output.RenderEndTag()
End Sub
```

C#

```csharp
protected override void Render(HtmlTextWriter output)
{
    output.RenderBeginTag(HtmlTextWriterTag.Div);
    output.RenderBeginTag(HtmlTextWriterTag.Input);
    output.RenderEndTag();
    output.RenderEndTag();
}
```

Now that you have a basic understanding of how to emit simple HTML, look at the output of your control. You can do this by viewing the test HTML page containing the control in a browser and choosing View ⇨ Source. Figure 23-7 shows the source for the page.

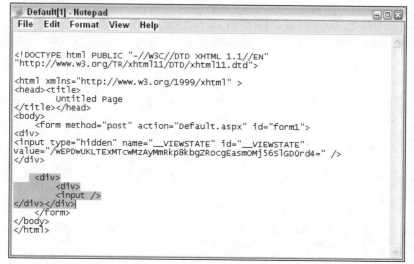

Figure 23-7

You can see that the control emitted some pretty simple HTML markup. Also notice (in the highlighted area) that the control was smart enough to realize that the input control did not contain any child controls and, therefore, the control did not need to render a full closing tag. Instead, it automatically rendered the shorthand `/>`, rather than `</input>`.

Adding Tag Attributes

Emitting HTML tags is a good start to building the control, but perhaps this is a bit simplistic. Normally, when rendering HTML you would emit some tag attributes (such as ID or Name) to the client in addition to the tag. Listing 23-11 shows how you can easily add tag attributes.

Listing 23-11: Rendering HTML tag attributes

VB

```vb
Protected Overrides Sub Render(ByVal output As System.Web.UI.HtmlTextWriter)
    output.RenderBeginTag(HtmlTextWriterTag.Div)

    output.AddAttribute(HtmlTextWriterAttribute.Type, "text")
    output.AddAttribute(HtmlTextWriterAttribute.Id, Me.ClientID)
    output.AddAttribute(HtmlTextWriterAttribute.Name, Me.ClientID)
    output.AddAttribute(HtmlTextWriterAttribute.Value, Me.Text)
    output.RenderBeginTag(HtmlTextWriterTag.Input)
    output.RenderEndTag()

    output.RenderEndTag()
End Sub
```

C#

```csharp
protected override void Render(HtmlTextWriter output)
{
    output.RenderBeginTag(HtmlTextWriterTag.Div);

    output.AddAttribute(HtmlTextWriterAttribute.Type, "text");
    output.AddAttribute(HtmlTextWriterAttribute.Id, this.ClientID);
    output.AddAttribute(HtmlTextWriterAttribute.Name, this.ClientID);
    output.AddAttribute(HtmlTextWriterAttribute.Value, this.Text);
    output.RenderBeginTag(HtmlTextWriterTag.Input);
    output.RenderEndTag();

    output.RenderEndTag();
}
```

You can see that by using the AddAttribute method, you have added three attributes to the `<input>` tag. Also notice that, once again, you are using an enumeration, HtmlTextWriterAttribute, to select the attribute you want to add to the tag. This serves the same purpose as using the HtmlTextWriterTag enumeration, allowing the control to degrade its output to downlevel browsers.

As with the Render methods, the order in which you place the AddAttributes methods is important. You place the AddAttributes methods directly before the RenderBeginTag method in the code. The AddAttributes method associates the attributes with the next HTML tag that is rendered by the RenderBeginTag method — in this case the `<input>` tag.

Now browse to the test page and check out the HTML source with the added tag attributes. Figure 23-8 shows the HTML source rendered by the control.

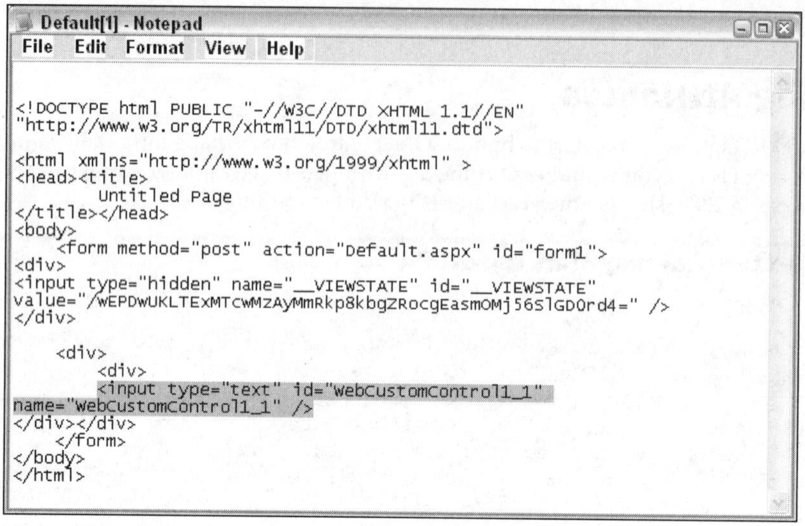

```
Default[1] - Notepad
File  Edit  Format  View  Help

<!DOCTYPE html PUBLIC "-//W3C//DTD XHTML 1.1//EN"
"http://www.w3.org/TR/xhtml11/DTD/xhtml11.dtd">

<html xmlns="http://www.w3.org/1999/xhtml" >
<head><title>
        Untitled Page
</title></head>
<body>
    <form method="post" action="Default.aspx" id="form1">
<div>
<input type="hidden" name="__VIEWSTATE" id="__VIEWSTATE"
value="/wEPDwUKLTExMTCwMzAyMmRkp8kbgZRocgEasmOMj56SlGDOrd4=" />
</div>

    <div>
        <div>
            <input type="text" id="webCustomControl1_1"
name="webCustomControl1_1" />
</div></div>
    </form>
</body>
</html>
```

Figure 23-8

You can see that the tag attributes you added in the server control are now included as part of the HTML tag rendered by the control.

A Word About Control IDs

Notice that in Listing 23-11 it's important to use the control's `ClientID` property as the value of both the `Id` and `Name` attributes. Controls that derive from the `WebControl` class automatically expose three different types of ID properties: `ID`, `UniqueID`, and `ClientID`. Each of these properties exposes a slightly altered version of the control's ID for use in a specific scenario.

The `ID` property is the most obvious. Developers use it to get and set the control's ID. It must be unique to the page at design time.

The `UniqueID` property is a read-only property generated at runtime that returns an ID that has been prepended with the containing control's ID. This is essential so that ASP.NET can uniquely identify each control in the page's control tree, even if the control is used multiple times by a container control such as a Repeater or GridView. For example, if you add this custom control to a repeater, the `UniqueID` for each custom control rendered by the Repeater is modified to include the Repeater's ID when the page executed:

```
MyRepeater:Ctrl0:MyCustomControl
```

The ClientID property is essentially identical to the UniqueID property with one important exception. The ClientID property always uses an underscore (_) to separate the ID values, rather than using the value of the IdSeparator property. This is because the ECMAScript standard disallows the use of colons in ID attribute values, which is the default value of the IdSeparator property. Using the underscore assures that a control can be used by client-side JavaScript.

Additionally, in order to ensure that controls can generate a unique ID, they should implement the INamingContainer interface. This is a marker interface only, meaning that it does not require any additional methods to be implemented; it does, however, ensure that the ASP.NET runtime guarantees the control always has a unique name within the page's tree hierarchy, regardless of its container.

Styling HTML

So far, you have seen how easy it is to build a simple HTML control and emit the proper HTML, including attributes. In this section, we discuss how you can have your control render style information. As mentioned at the very beginning of this section, you are creating controls that inherit from the WebControl class. Because of this, these controls already have the basic infrastructure for emitting most of the standard CSS-style attributes. In the Property Browser for this control, you should see a number of style properties already listed, such as background color, border width, and font. You can also launch the style builder to create complex CSS styles. These basic properties are provided by the WebControl class, but it is up to you to tell your control to render the values set at design time. To do this, you simply execute the AddAttributeToRender method. Listing 23-12 shows you how to do this.

Listing 23-12: Rendering style properties

VB
```vb
Protected Overrides Sub Render(ByVal output As System.Web.UI.HtmlTextWriter)
    output.RenderBeginTag(HtmlTextWriterTag.Div)

    output.AddAttribute(HtmlTextWriterAttribute.Type, "text")
    output.AddAttribute(HtmlTextWriterAttribute.Id, Me.ClientID)
    output.AddAttribute(HtmlTextWriterAttribute.Name, Me.ClientID)
    output.AddAttribute(HtmlTextWriterAttribute.Value, Me.Text)
    Me.AddAttributesToRender(output)

    output.RenderBeginTag(HtmlTextWriterTag.Input)
    output.RenderEndTag()

    output.RenderEndTag()
End Sub
```

C#
```csharp
protected override void Render(HtmlTextWriter output)
{
    output.RenderBeginTag(HtmlTextWriterTag.Div);

    output.AddAttribute(HtmlTextWriterAttribute.Type, "text");
```

(continued)

Listing 23-12: *(continued)*

```
        output.AddAttribute(HtmlTextWriterAttribute.Id, this.ClientID);
        output.AddAttribute(HtmlTextWriterAttribute.Name, this.ClientID);
        output.AddAttribute(HtmlTextWriterAttribute.Value, this.Text);
        this.AddAttributesToRender(output);

        output.RenderBeginTag(HtmlTextWriterTag.Input);
        output.RenderEndTag();

        output.RenderEndTag();
    }
```

Executing this method tells the control to render any style information that has been set. Using the Property Browser, you can set the background color of the control to Red and the font to Bold. When you set these properties, they are automatically added to the control tag in the ASP.NET page. After you have added the styles, the control tag looks like this:

```
<cc1:WebCustomControl1 BackColor="Red" Font-Bold=true
  ID="WebCustomControl1_1" runat="server" />
```

The style changes have been persisted to the control as attributes. When you execute this page in the browser, the style information should be rendered to the HTML, making the background of the text box red and its font bold. Figure 23-9 shows the page in the browser.

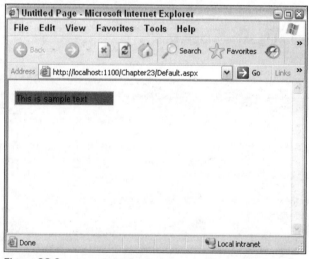

Figure 23-9

Once again, look at the source for this page. The style information has been rendered to the HTML as a style tag. Figure 23-10 shows the HTML emitted by the control.

Figure 23-10

Themes and Skins

A new feature in ASP.NET 2.0, introduced to you in Chapter 9, is themes and skins. This feature allows you to create visual styles for your Web applications. In this section, you learn what you need to know about themes and skins when creating a server control.

As you saw in Chapter 9, skins are essentially a way to set default values for the UI elements of controls in your Web application. You simply define the control and its properties in a .skin file and the values are applied to the control at runtime. Listing 23-13 shows a sample skin.

Listing 23-13: Sample ASP.NET 2.0 skin

```
<%@ Register Assembly="WebControlLibrary1" Namespace="WebControlLibrary1"
    TagPrefix="cc1" %>

<cc1:webcustomcontrol1 BackColor="Green" runat="server" />
```

By default, ASP.NET allows all control properties to be defined in the skin file, but obviously this is not always appropriate. Most exposed properties are non-UI related; therefore, you do not apply a theme to them. By setting the Themeable attribute to False on each of these properties, you prevent the application of a theme. Listing 23-14 shows how to do this in your control by disabling themes on the Text property.

Listing 23-14: Disabling theme support on a control property

VB

```
<Bindable(True), Category("Appearance"), DefaultValue(""), Themeable(False)> _
Property [Text]() As String
    Get
        Return _text
```

(continued)

877

Listing 23-14: *(continued)*

```
        End Get

        Set(ByVal Value As String)
            _text = Value
        End Set
    End Property
```

C#
```
[Bindable(true)]
[Category("Appearance")]
[DefaultValue("")]
[Themeable(false)]
public string Text
{
    get
    {
        return text;
    }
    set
    {
        text = value;
    }
}
```

Now, if a developer attempts to define this property in his skin file, he receives a compiler error when the page is executed.

Adding Client-Side Features

Although the capability to render and style HTML is quite powerful by itself, other resources can be sent to the client, such as client-side scripts, images, and resource strings. ASP.NET 2.0 provides you with some powerful new tools for using client-side scripts in your server controls and retrieving other resources to the client along with the HTML your control emits. Additionally, ASP.NET now includes an entire model that allows you to make asynchronous callbacks from your Web page to the server.

Emitting Client-Side Script

Having your control emit client-side script like VBScript or JavaScript enables you to add powerful client-side functionality to your control. Client-side scripting languages take advantage of the client's browser to create more flexible and easy-to-use controls. Although ASP.NET 1.0 provided some simple methods to emit client-side script to the browser, ASP.NET 2.0 has enhanced these capabilities and now provides a wide variety of methods for emitting client-side script that you can use to control where and how your script is rendered.

If you have already used ASP.NET 1.0 to render client-side script to the client, you are probably familiar with a few methods like the `Page.RegisterClientScriptBlock` and the `Page.RegisterStartupScript` methods. In ASP.NET 2.0, these classes have been deprecated. Instead, ASP.NET 2.0 now uses the `ClientScriptManager` class, which you can access using `Page.ClientScript`. This class exposes various static client-script rendering methods that you can use to render client-side script.

Listing 23-15 demonstrates how you can use the `RegisterStartupScriptMethod` method to render JavaScript to the client. This listing adds the code into the `OnPreRender` method, rather than into the `Render` method used in previous samples. This method allows every control to inform the page about the client-side script it needs to render. After the `Render` method is called, the page is able to render all the client-side script it collected during the `OnPreRender` method. If you call the client-side script registration methods in the `Render` method, the page has already completed a portion of its rendering before your client-side script can render itself.

Listing 23-15: Rendering a client-side script to the browser

VB

```
Protected Overrides Sub OnPreRender(ByVal e As System.EventArgs)
    Page.ClientScript.RegisterStartupScript(GetType(Page), _
        "ControlFocus", "document.getElementById('" & Me.ClientID & "').focus();", _
        True)
End Sub
```

C#

```
protected override void OnPreRender(EventArgs e)
{
    Page.ClientScript.RegisterStartupScript( typeof(Page),
        "ControlFocus","document.getElementById('" + this.ClientID + "').focus();",
        true);
}
```

In this listing, the code emits client-side script to automatically move the control focus to the TextBox control when the Web page loads. When you use the `RegisterStartupScript` method, notice that it now includes an overload that lets you specify if the method should render surrounding script tags. This can be handy if you are rendering more than one script to the page.

Also notice that the method requires a key parameter. This parameter is used to uniquely identify the script block; if you are registering more than one script block in the Web page, make sure that each block is supplied a unique key. You can use the `IsStartupScriptRegistered` method and the key to determine if a particular script block has been previously registered on the client using the `RegisterStatupScript` method.

When you execute the page in the browser, notice that the focus is automatically placed into a text box. If you look at the source code for the Web page, you should see that the JavaScript was written to the bottom of the page, as shown in Figure 23-11.

If you want the script to be rendered to the top of the page, you use the `RegisterClientScriptBlock` method that emits the script block immediately after the opening `<form>` element.

Keep in mind that the browser parses the Web page from top to bottom, so if you emit client-side script at the top of the page that is not contained in a function, any references in that code to HTML elements further down the page will fail. The browser has not parsed that portion of the page yet.

Being able to render script that automatically executes when the page loads is nice, but it is more likely that you will want the code to execute based on an event fired from an HTML element on your page, such as the Click, Focus, or Blur events. In order to do this, you add an attribute to the HTML element you want the event to fire from. Listing 23-16 shows you how you can modify your control's `Render` and `PreRender` methods to add this attribute.

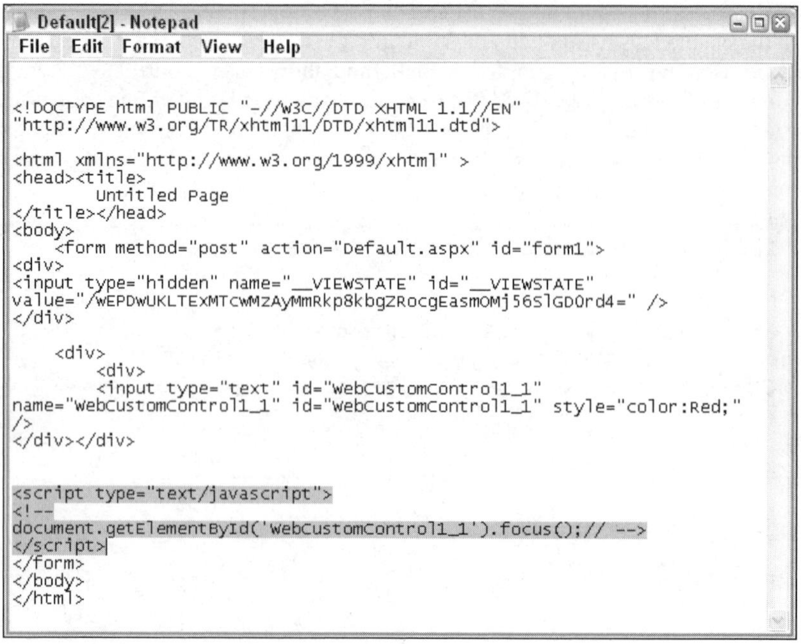

Default[2] - Notepad

File Edit Format View Help

```
<!DOCTYPE html PUBLIC "-//W3C//DTD XHTML 1.1//EN"
"http://www.w3.org/TR/xhtml11/DTD/xhtml11.dtd">

<html xmlns="http://www.w3.org/1999/xhtml" >
<head><title>
        Untitled Page
</title></head>
<body>
    <form method="post" action="Default.aspx" id="form1">
<div>
<input type="hidden" name="__VIEWSTATE" id="__VIEWSTATE"
value="/wEPDwUKLTExMTcwMzAyMmRkp8kbgZRocgEasmOMj56SlGD0rd4=" />
</div>

    <div>
        <div>
        <input type="text" id="WebCustomControl1_1"
name="WebCustomControl1_1" id="WebCustomControl1_1" style="color:Red;"
/>
</div></div>


<script type="text/javascript">
<!--
document.getElementById('WebCustomControl1_1').focus();// -->
</script>
</form>
</body>
</html>
```

Figure 23-11

Listing 23-16: Using client-side script and event attributes to validate data

VB

```
Protected Overrides Sub Render(ByVal output As System.Web.UI.HtmlTextWriter)
    output.RenderBeginTag(HtmlTextWriterTag.Div)

    output.AddAttribute(HtmlTextWriterAttribute.Type, "text")
    output.AddAttribute(HtmlTextWriterAttribute.Id, Me.ClientID)
    output.AddAttribute(HtmlTextWriterAttribute.Name, Me.ClientID)
    output.AddAttribute(HtmlTextWriterAttribute.Value, Me.Text)

    output.AddAttribute("OnBlur", "ValidateText(this)")
    Me.AddAttributesToRender(output)

    output.RenderBeginTag(HtmlTextWriterTag.Input)
    output.RenderEndTag()

    output.RenderEndTag()

End Sub

Protected Overrides Sub OnPreRender(ByVal e As System.EventArgs)
    Page.ClientScript.RegisterStartupScript(GetType(Page), _
       "ControlFocus", "document.getElementById('" & Me.ClientID & "').focus();", _
       True)
```

```vbnet
        Page.ClientScript.RegisterClientScriptBlock( _
            GetType(Page), _
            "ValidateControl", _
            "function ValidateText() {" & _
                "if (ctl.value=='') {" & _
                    "alert('Please enter a value.');ctl.focus(); }" & _
            "}", _
            True)
End Sub
```

C#

```csharp
protected override void Render(HtmlTextWriter output)
{
    output.RenderBeginTag(HtmlTextWriterTag.Div);
    output.AddAttribute(HtmlTextWriterAttribute.Type, "text");
    output.AddAttribute(HtmlTextWriterAttribute.Id, this.ClientID);
    output.AddAttribute(HtmlTextWriterAttribute.Name, this.ClientID);
    output.AddAttribute(HtmlTextWriterAttribute.Value, this.Text);

    output.AddAttribute("OnBlur", "ValidateText(this)");
    this.AddAttributesToRender(output);

    output.RenderBeginTag(HtmlTextWriterTag.Input);
    output.RenderEndTag();
    output.RenderEndTag();
}

protected override void OnPreRender(EventArgs e)
{
    Page.ClientScript.RegisterStartupScript(
        typeof(Page),
        "ControlFocus","document.getElementById('" + this.ClientID + "').focus();",
        true);

    Page.ClientScript.RegisterClientScriptBlock(
        typeof(Page),
        "ValidateControl",
        "function ValidateText(ctl) {" +
            "if (ctl.value=='') {" +
                "alert('Please enter a value.');ctl.focus(); }" +
        "}",
        true);
}
```

As you can see, the TextBox control is modified to check for an empty string. We have also included an attribute that adds the JavaScript OnBlur event to the text box. The OnBlur event fires when the control loses focus. When this happens, the client-side ValidateText method is executed, which we rendered to the client using RegisterClientScriptBlock.

The rendered HTML is shown in Figure 23-12.

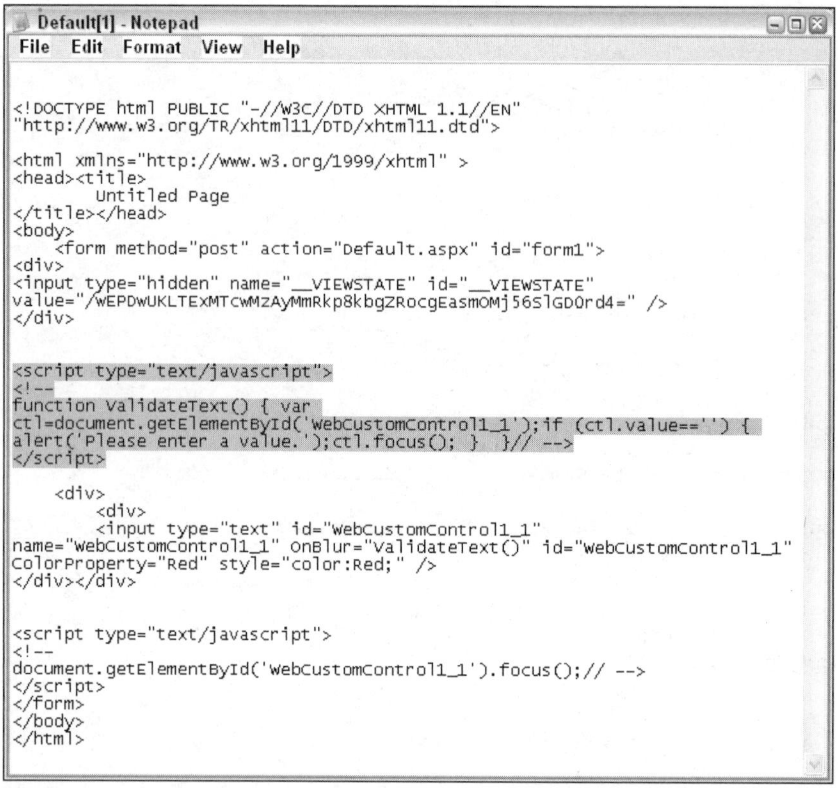

Figure 23-12

Embedding JavaScript in the page is powerful, but if you are writing large amounts of client-side code, you might want to consider storing the JavaScript in an external file. You can include this file in your HTML by using the `RegisterClientScriptInclude` method. This method renders a script tag using the URL you provide to it as the value of its `src` element.

```
<script src="[url]" type="text/javascript"></script>
```

Listing 23-17 shows how you can modify the validation added to the TextBox control in Listing 23-16; but this time, the JavaScript validation function is stored in an external file.

Listing 23-17: Adding client-side script include files to a Web page

VB

```vb
Protected Overrides Sub OnPreRender(ByVal e As System.EventArgs)
    Page.ClientScript.RegisterClientScriptInclude( _
        "UtilityFunctions", "JScript.js")

    Page.ClientScript.RegisterStartupScript(GetType(Page), _
        "ControlFocus", "document.getElementById('" & Me.ClientID & "').focus();", _
        True)
End Sub
```

C#
```
protected override void OnPreRender(EventArgs e)
{
    Page.ClientScript.RegisterClientScriptInclude(
        "UtilityFunctions", "JScript.js");

    Page.ClientScript.RegisterStartupScript(
        typeof(Page),
        "ControlFocus","document.getElementById('" + this.ClientID + "').focus();",
        true);
}
```

You have modified the `OnPreRender` event to register a client-side script file include, which contains the `ValidateText` function. You need to add a JScript file to the project and create the `ValidateText` function, as shown in Listing 23-18.

Listing 23-18: The validation JavaScript contained in the Jscript file

```
// JScript File

function ValidateText(ctl)
{
    if (ctl.value=='') {
        alert('Please enter a value.');
        ctl.focus();
    }
}
```

The `ClientScriptManager` also provides methods for registering hidden HTML fields and adding script functions to the `OnSubmit` event.

Accessing Embedded Resources

A great way to distribute application resources like JavaScript files, images, or resource files is to embed them directly into the compiled assembly. While this was possible in ASP.NET 1.0, it was very difficult to access these resources as part of the page request process. ASP.NET 2.0 solved this problem by including the RegisterClientScriptResource method as part of the ClientScriptManager.

This method makes it possible for your web pages to retrieve stored resources — like JavaScript files — from the compiled assembly at runtime. It works by using an HttpHandler to retrieve the requested resource from the assembly and return it to the client. The `RegisterClientScriptResource` method emits a `<script>` block whose `src` value points to this HttpHandler:

```
<script
    language="javascript"
    src="WebResource.axd?a=s&r=WebUIValidation.js&t=631944362841472848"
    type="text/javascript">
</script>
```

As you can see, the `WebResource.axd` handler is used to return the resource — in this case, the JavaScript file. You can use this method to retrieve any resource stored in the assembly, such as images or localized content strings from resource files.

Asynchronous Callbacks

Finally, a new addition to the client-side script rendering capabilities of ASP.NET 2.0 is *client-side callbacks*. Client-side callbacks enable you to take advantage of the XmlHttp components found in most modern browsers to communicate with the server without actually performing a complete postback. Figure 23-13 shows how client-side callbacks work in the ASP.NET framework.

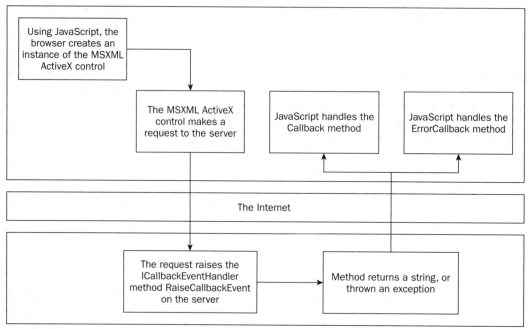

Figure 23-13

In order to enable callbacks in your server control, you implement the `System.Web.UI.ICallBackEventHander` interface. This interface requires you to implement a single method, `RaiseCallbackEvent`. This is the server-side event that fires when the client executes the callback. After you implement the interface, you want to tie your client-side events back to the server. You do this by using the `Page.ClientScript.GetCallbackEventReference` method. This method allows you to specify the two client-side functions: one to serve as the callback handler and one to serve as an error handler. Listing 23-19 demonstrates how you can modify the TextBox control's `Render` methods and add the `RaiseCallBackEvent` method to use callbacks to perform validation.

Listing 23-19: Adding an asynchronous callback to validate data

VB

```
Protected Overrides Sub Render(ByVal output As System.Web.UI.HtmlTextWriter)
    output.RenderBeginTag(HtmlTextWriterTag.Div)

    output.AddAttribute(HtmlTextWriterAttribute.Type, "text")
    output.AddAttribute(HtmlTextWriterAttribute.Id, Me.ClientID)
    output.AddAttribute(HtmlTextWriterAttribute.Name, Me.ClientID)
```

```vb
    output.AddAttribute(HtmlTextWriterAttribute.Value, Me.Text)

    output.AddAttribute("OnBlur", "ClientCallback();")
    Me.AddAttributesToRender(output)

    output.RenderBeginTag(HtmlTextWriterTag.Input)
    output.RenderEndTag()

    output.RenderEndTag()

End Sub

Protected Overrides Sub OnPreRender(ByVal e As System.EventArgs)
    Page.ClientScript.RegisterStartupScript(GetType(Page), _
        "ControlFocus", "document.getElementById('" & Me.ClientID & "').focus();", _
        True)

    Page.ClientScript.RegisterStartupScript( _
        GetType(Page), "ClientCallback", _
        "function ClientCallback() {" & _
            "args=document.getElementById('" & Me.ClientID & "').value;" & _
            Page.ClientScript.GetCallbackEventReference(Me, "args", _
                "CallbackHandler", Nothing, "ErrorHandler", True) + "}", _
        True)
End Sub

Public Sub RaiseCallbackEvent(ByVal eventArgument As String) _
    Implements System.Web.UI.ICallbackEventHandler.RaiseCallbackEvent
    Dim result As Int32
    If (Not Int32.TryParse(eventArgument, result)) Then
        Throw New Exception("The method or operation is not implemented.")
    End If
    End Sub

    Public Function GetCallbackResult() As String_
        ImplementsSystem.Web.UI.ICallBackEventHandler.GetCallbackResult

        Return "Valid Data"
    End Function
```

C#

```csharp
protected override void Render(HtmlTextWriter output)
{
    output.RenderBeginTag(HtmlTextWriterTag.Div);

    output.AddAttribute(HtmlTextWriterAttribute.Type, "text");
    output.AddAttribute(HtmlTextWriterAttribute.Id, this.ClientID);
    output.AddAttribute(HtmlTextWriterAttribute.Name, this.ClientID);
    output.AddAttribute(HtmlTextWriterAttribute.Value, this.Text);

    output.AddAttribute("OnBlur", "ClientCallback();");
    this.AddAttributesToRender(writer);

    output.RenderBeginTag(HtmlTextWriterTag.Input);
    output.RenderEndTag();

    output.RenderEndTag();
}

protected override void OnPreRender(EventArgs e)
```

(continued)

Listing 23-19: *(continued)*

```
    {
        Page.ClientScript.RegisterStartupScript(
            typeof(Page),
            "ControlFocus","document.getElementById('" + this.ClientID + "').focus();",
            true);

        Page.ClientScript.RegisterStartupScript(
            typeof(Page), "ClientCallback",
            "function ClientCallback() {" +
                "args=document.getElementById('" + this.ClientID + "').value;" +
                Page.ClientScript.GetCallbackEventReference(this, "args",
                    "CallbackHandler", null,"ErrorHandler",true) + "}",
            true);
    }

    #region ICallbackEventHandler Members

    {
        int result;
        if (!Int32.TryParse(eventArgument,out result) )
            throw new Exception("The method or operation is not implemented.");

    public string GetCallbackResult()
    {
    }
    }

    }
```

As you can see, the OnBlur attribute has again been modified, this time by simply calling the
ClientCallback method. This method is created and rendered during the PreRender event. The main
purpose of this event is to populate the client-side args variable and call the client-side callback method.

You are using the GetCallbackEventReference method to generate the client-side script that actually
initiates the callback. The parameters passed to the method indicate which control is initiating the callback, the names of the client-side callback method, and the name of the callback method parameters.
The following table provides more details on the GetCallbackEventReference arguments.

Parameter	Description
Control	Server control that initiates the callback.
Argument	Client-side variable used to pass arguments to the server-side event handler.
ClientCallback	Client-side function serving as the Callback method. This method fires when the server-side processing has completed successfully.
Context	Client-side variable that gets passed directly to the receiving client-side function. The context does not get passed to the server.
ClientErrorCallback	Client-side function serving as the Callback error-handler method. This method fires when the server-side processing encounters an error.

In the code, two client-side methods are called: `CallbackHandler` and `ErrorHandler`, respectively. The two method parameters are `args` and `ctx`.

In addition to the server control code changes, the two client-side callback methods have been added to the JavaScript file. Listing 23-20 shows these new functions.

Listing 23-20: The client-side callback JavaScript functions

```
// JScript File
var args;
var ctx;

function ValidateText(ctl)
{
    if (ctl.value=='') {
        alert('Please enter a value.');
        ctl.focus();
    }
}

function CallbackHandler(args,ctx)
{
    alert("The data is valid");
}

function ErrorHandler(args,ctx)
{
    alert("Please enter a number");
}
```

Now, when you view your Web page in the browser, as soon as the text box loses focus, you perform a client-side callback to validate the data. The callback raises the `RaiseCallbackEvent` method on the server, which validates the value of the text box that was passed to it in the `eventArguments`. If the value is valid, you return a string and the client-side `CallbackHandler` function fires. If the value is invalid, you throw an exception, which causes the client-side `ErrorHandler` function to execute.

Detecting and Reacting to Browser Capabilities

So far in the chapter we have described many powerful features, such as styling and emitting client-side scripts, that you can utilize when writing your own custom control. But if you are taking advantage of these features, you must also consider how you can handle certain browsers, often called downlevel browsers, that might not understand these advanced features or might not have them enabled. Being able to detect and react to downlevel browsers is an important consideration when creating your control. ASP.NET includes some powerful tools you can use to detect the type and version of the browser making the page request, as well as what capabilities the browser supports.

.browser files

ASP.NET 2.0 has introduced a new and highly flexible method for configuring, storing, and discovering browser capabilities. All browser identification and capability information is now stored in `.browser` files. ASP.NET stores these files in the `C:\Windows\Microsoft.NET\Framework\v2.0.[xxxx]\CONFIG\Browsers` directory. If you open this folder, you see that ASP.NET provides you with a variety of `.browser` files that describe the capabilities of most of today's common desktop browsers, as well as information on browsers in devices such as PDAs and cellular phones. Open one of the browser files, and you see that the file contains all the identification and capability information for the browser. Listing 23-21 shows you the contents of the WebTV capabilities file.

Listing 23-21: A sample browser capabilities file

```
<browsers>
    <!-- sample UA "Mozilla/3.0 WebTV/1.2(Compatible;MSIE 2.0)" -->
    <browser id="WebTV" parentID="IE2">
        <identification>
            <userAgent
            match="WebTV/(?'version'(?'major'\d+)(?'minor'\.\d+)(?'letters'\w*))" />
        </identification>

        <capture>
        </capture>

        <capabilities>
            <capability name="backgroundsounds"    value="true" />
            <capability name="browser"             value="WebTV" />
            <capability name="cookies"             value="true" />
            <capability name="isMobileDevice"      value="true" />
            <capability name="letters"             value="${letters}" />
            <capability name="majorversion"        value="${major}" />
            <capability name="minorversion"        value="${minor}" />
            <capability name="tables"              value="true" />
            <capability name="type"                value="WebTV${major}" />
            <capability name="version"             value="${version}" />
        </capabilities>

        <controlAdapters markupTextWriterType="System.Web.UI.Html32TextWriter">
    </controlAdapters>
    </browser>

    <browser id="WebTV2" parentID="WebTV">
        <identification>
            <capability name="minorversion" match="2" />
        </identification>

        <capture>
        </capture>

        <capabilities>
            <capability name="css1"                value="true" />
            <capability name="ecmascriptversion"   value="1.0" />
            <capability name="javascript"          value="true" />
        </capabilities>
    </browser>

    <gateway id="WebTVbeta" parentID="WebTV">
        <identification>
            <capability name="letters" match="^b" />
```

```
        </identification>

        <capture>
        </capture>

        <capabilities>
            <capability name="beta"      value="true" />
        </capabilities>
    </gateway>
</browsers>
```

The advantage of this new method for storing browser capability information is that as new browsers are created or new versions are released, developers simply create or update a .browser file to describe the capabilities of that browser.

Accessing Browser Capability Information

Now that you have seen how ASP.NET 2.0 stores browser capability information, we want to discuss how you can access this information at runtime and program your control to change what it renders based on the browser. To access capability information about the requesting browser, you can use the Page.Request.Browser property. This property gives you access to the System.Web.HttpBrowserCapabilities class, which provides information about the capabilities of the browser making the current request. The class provides you with a myriad of attributes and properties that describe what the browser can support and render and what it requires. Lists use this information to add capabilities to the TextBox control. Listing 23-22 shows how you can detect browser capabilities to make sure a browser supports JavaScript.

Listing 23-22: Detecting browser capabilities in server-side code

```vb
VB
Protected Overrides Sub OnPreRender(ByVal e As System.EventArgs)
    If (Page.Request.Browser.EcmaScriptVersion.Major > 0) Then
        Page.ClientScript.RegisterStartupScript( _
            GetType(Page), "ClientCallback", _
            "function ClientCallback() {" & _
                "args=document.getElementById('" & Me.ClientID & "').value;" & _
                Page.ClientScript.GetCallbackEventReference(Me, "args", _
                "CallbackHandler", Nothing, "ErrorHandler", True) + "}", _
            True)

        Page.ClientScript.RegisterStartupScript(GetType(Page), _
            "ControlFocus", "document.getElementById('" & _
            Me.ClientID & "').focus();", _
            True)
    End If
End Sub


C#
protected override void OnPreRender(EventArgs e)
{
    if (Page.Request.Browser.EcmaScriptVersion.Major > 0)
    {
        Page.ClientScript.RegisterClientScriptInclude(
```

(continued)

Listing 23-22: *(continued)*

```
                "UtilityFunctions", "JScript.js");
        Page.ClientScript.RegisterStartupScript(
            typeof(Page),
            "ControlFocus","document.getElementById('" +
                this.ClientID + "').focus();",
            true);

        Page.ClientScript.RegisterStartupScript(
            typeof(Page), "ClientCallback",
            "function ClientCallback() {" +
                "args=document.getElementById('" + this.ClientID + "').value;" +
                Page.ClientScript.GetCallbackEventReference(this, "args",
                    "CallbackHandler", null,"ErrorHandler",true) + "}",
            true);
    }
}
```

This is a very simple sample, but it gives you an idea of what is possible using the
HttpBrowserCapabilities class.

Using ViewState

When developing Web applications, remember that they are built on the stateless HTTP protocol. ASP.NET gives you a number of ways to give users the illusion that they are using a stateful application, including Session State and cookies. Additionally, ASP.NET 1.0 introduces a new way of creating the state illusion called ViewState. ViewState enables you to maintain the state of the objects and controls that are part of the Web page through the page's lifecycle by storing the state of the controls in a hidden form field that is rendered as part of the HTML. The state contained in the form field can then be used by the application to reconstitute the page's state when a postback occurs. Figure 23-14 shows how ASP.NET stores ViewState information in a hidden form field.

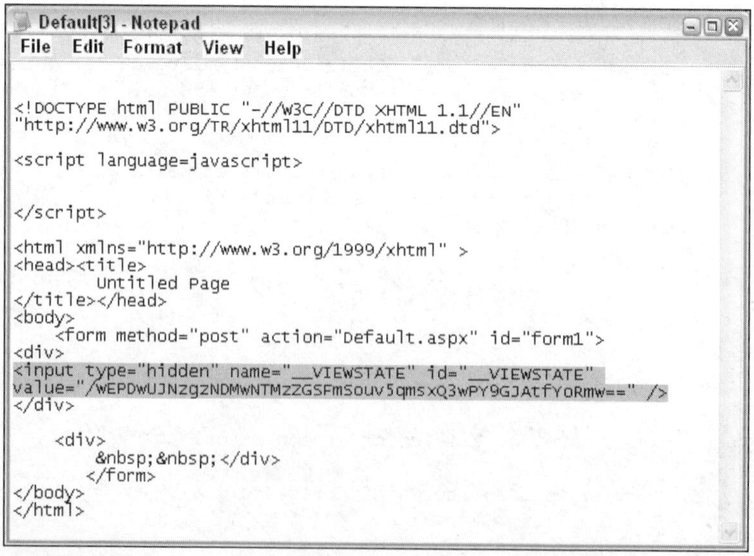

Figure 23-14

Notice that the page contains a hidden form field named __ViewState. The value of this form field is the ViewState for your Web page. By default, ViewState is enabled in all in-box server controls shipped with ASP.NET. If you write customer server controls, however, you are responsible for ensuring that a control is participating in the use of ViewState by the page.

The ASP.NET ViewState is basically a StateBag that enables you to save and retrieve objects as key/value pairs. As you see in Figure 23-14, these objects are then serialized by ASP.NET and persisted as an encrypted string, which is pushed to the client as a hidden HTML form field. When the page posts back to the server, ASP.NET can use this hidden form field to reconstitute the StateBag, which you can then access as the page is processed on the server.

Because the ViewState can sometimes grow to be very large and can therefore affect the overall page size, you might consider an alternate method of storing the ViewState information. You can create your own persistence mechanism by deriving a class from the System.Web.UI.PageStatePersister class and overriding its Load and Save methods.

To see the effects of ViewState, look at how the standard ASP.NET text box works in comparison to the customer server control's text box. To demonstrate this, add two buttons and a standard ASP.NET text box to your existing Web page. Listing 23-23 shows how you can modify the Web page.

Listing 23-23: The ViewState sample demonstration Web page

VB
```
<%@ Page Language="VB" %>

<%@ Register Assembly="WebControlLibrary1" Namespace="WebControlLibrary1"
    TagPrefix="cc1" %>

<!DOCTYPE html PUBLIC "-//W3C//DTD XHTML 1.1//EN"
    "http://www.w3.org/TR/xhtml11/DTD/xhtml11.dtd">

<script runat="server">
    Protected Sub Button1_Click(ByVal sender As Object, _
                                ByVal e As System.EventArgs)
        Me.WebCustomControl1_1.Text = "CustomControl"
        Me.TextBox1.Text = "StandardTextbox"
    End Sub
</script>

<html xmlns="http://www.w3.org/1999/xhtml" >
<head runat="server">
    <title>ViewState Sample</title>
</head>
<body>
    <form id="form1" runat="server">
    <div>
        My Control 
        <cc1:webcustomcontrol1 id="WebCustomControl1_1"
            runat="server"></cc1:webcustomcontrol1>
        <br />
        Reg Control
        <asp:TextBox ID="TextBox1" runat="server"></asp:TextBox><br />
```

(continued)

Listing 23-23: *(continued)*

```
            <asp:Button ID="Button1" runat="server" Text="Button" />
            <asp:Button ID="Button2" runat="server" Text="Button" /></div>
        </form>
    </body>
</html>
```

C#

```
<script runat="server">
    protected void Button1_Click(object sender, EventArgs e)
    {
        this.WebCustomControl1_1.Text = "CustomControl";
        this.TextBox1.Text = "StandardTextbox";
    }
</script>
```

Notice that you use the Button1 click event to assign a value to each text box. Now, see what happens when you execute the Web page in a browser. After the page has loaded, click the Populate button, and the text you assign should appear in each respective text box. Now click the Postback button and notice that when the page reloads after the postback, the text in your text box disappears, but the text in the standard text box is repopulated. This occurs because the request to the server re-initializes your server control and it rerenders itself to the client. Because you are not re-assigning the value, the control is empty. The standard ASP.NET text box uses ViewState to repopulate its value after the postback, whereas your custom control is not able to do that yet. Now modify your server control to take advantage of ViewState. Listing 23-24 shows how you make this modification.

Listing 23-24: Modifying control properties to use ViewState

VB

```
<Bindable(True), Category("Appearance"), DefaultValue(""), Themeable(False)> _
Property [Text]() As String
    Get
        _text = CStr(ViewState("ControlText"))
        If (_text = Nothing) Then
            Return String.Empty
        End If

        Return _text
    End Get

    Set(ByVal Value As String)
        ViewState("ControlText") = Value
    End Set
End Property
```

C#

```
[Bindable(true)]
[Category("Appearance")]
[DefaultValue("")]
[Themeable(false)]
public string Text
{
```

```
        get
        {
            text = (string)ViewState["ControlText"];
            if (text == null)
                return String.Empty;
            return text;
        }
        set
        {
            ViewState["ControlText"] = value;
        }
    }
}
```

After you make this change, rerun the previous sample using the modified server control. This time, you should see that both the standard ASP.NET text box and the custom server control now persist data across the postback because you stored the text property value in ViewState.

Note that the loading of ViewState happens after the OnInit event has been raised by the page. If your control makes changes to itself or another server control before the event has been raised, the changes are not saved to the ViewState.

Types and ViewState

As mentioned in the preceding section, the ViewState is basically a generic collection of objects, but not all objects can be added to the ViewState. Only types that can be safely persisted can be used in the ViewState, so objects such as database connections or file handles should not be added to the ViewState.

Additionally, certain data types are optimized for use in the ViewState. When adding data to the ViewState, try to package the data into these types:

❑ Primitive Types (Int32, Boolean, and so on)

❑ Arrays of Primitive Types

❑ ArrayList, HashTable

❑ Pair, Triplet

❑ Color, DataTime

❑ String, IndexedString

❑ HybridDictionary of these types

❑ Objects that have a TypeConverter available. Be aware, however, that there is a reduction in performance if you use these types.

❑ Objects that are serializable (marked with the Serializable attribute)

The .NET 2.0 ViewState also has some new features that improve performance. For example, the .NET 1.1 ViewState used the LosFormatter to serialize objects, but ViewState in .NET 2.0 does not. Instead, it uses the ObjectStateFormatter, and this results in dramatic improvements in the speed with which objects are serialized and deserialized. It also decreases the overall byte size of the resulting serialization. Additionally, the 2.0 ViewState has been modified to write out bytes rather than strings, thereby saving the cost of converting to a string.

Control State

At times, your control must store critical, usually private information across postbacks. In ASP.NET 1.0, you might have considered using ViewState, but a developer using your control could disable ViewState. ASP.NET 2.0 solves this problem by introducing a new kind of ViewState called ControlState. ControlState is essentially a private ViewState for your control only, and it is not affected when ViewState is turned off.

Two new methods, SaveViewState and LoadViewState, provide access to ControlState; however, the implementation of these methods is left up to you. Listing 23-25 shows how you can use the LoadControlState and SaveViewState methods.

Listing 23-25: Using ControlState in a server control

VB

```
Imports System.ComponentModel
Imports System.Web.UI

<DefaultProperty("Text")> _
<ToolboxData("<{0}:[WebCustomControl5] runat=server></{0}:[WebCustomControl5]>")> _
Public Class [WebCustomControl5]
    Inherits System.Web.UI.WebControls.WebControl

    Dim s As String
    Protected Overrides Sub OnInit(ByVal e As System.EventArgs)
        Page.RequiresControlState(Me)
        MyBase.OnInit(e)
    End Sub

    Protected Overrides Sub LoadControlState(ByVal savedState As Object)
        s = CStr(savedState)
    End Sub

    Protected Overrides Function SaveControlState() As Object
        Return CType("FOO", Object)
    End Function

    Protected Overrides Sub Render(ByVal output As System.Web.UI.HtmlTextWriter)
        output.Write("Control State: " & s)
    End Sub

End Class
```

C#

```
using System;
using System.Collections.Generic;
using System.ComponentModel;
using System.Text;
using System.Web.UI;
using System.Web.UI.WebControls;

namespace WebControlLibrary1
{
    [DefaultProperty("Text")]
```

```
[ToolboxData("<{0}:WebCustomControl5 runat=server></{0}:WebCustomControl5>")]
public class WebCustomControl5 : WebControl
{
    string s;
    protected override void OnInit(EventArgs e)
    {
        Page.RequiresControlState(this);
        base.OnInit(e);
    }

    protected override void LoadControlState(object savedState)
    {
        s = (string)savedState;
    }

    protected override object SaveControlState()
    {
        return (object)"FOO";
    }

    protected override void Render(HtmlTextWriter output)
    {
        output.Write("Control State: " + s);
    }
}
}
```

Controls intending to use ControlState must call the `Page.RegisterRequiresControlState` method before attempting to save control state data. Additionally, the `RegisterRequireControlState` method must be called for each page load because the value is not retained through page postbacks.

Raising PostBack Events

As you have seen in this chapter, ASP.NET provides a very powerful set of tools you can use to develop server controls and emit them to a client browser. But this is still one-way communication because the server only pushes data to the client. It would be useful if the server control could send data back to the server. The process of sending data back to the server is generally known as a *page postback*. You experience a page postback any time you click a form button or link that causes the page to make a new request to the Web server.

ASP.NET provides a rich framework for handling postbacks from ASP.NET Web pages. Additionally, ASP.NET attempts to give you a development model that mimics the standard Windows Forms event model. It enables you to use controls that, even though they are rendered in the client browser, can raise events in server-side code. It also provides an easy mechanism for plugging the server control into that framework, allowing you to create controls that can cause a page postback. Figure 23-15 shows the ASP.NET postback framework.

In order to initiate a postback, ASP.NET uses client-side scripting. You can add the proper script to your control by using the `GetPostBackEventReference` method and emitting the results to the client during the controls render method. Listing 23-26 shows how you can add that to a new server control that emits an HTML button.

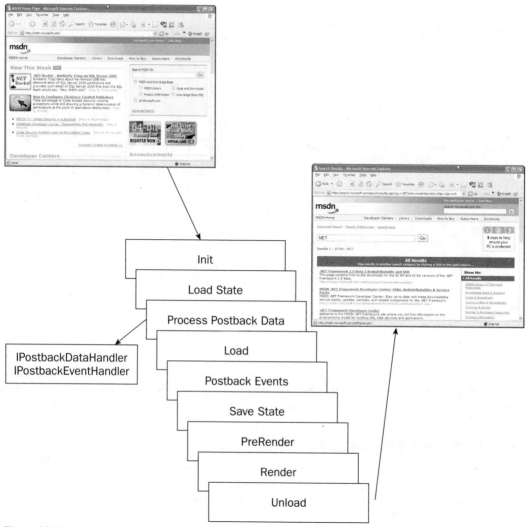

Figure 23-15

Listing 23-26: Adding PostBack capabilities to a server control

VB

```vb
Imports System.ComponentModel
Imports System.Web.UI

<DefaultProperty("Text")> _
<ToolboxData("<{0}:WebCustomControl3 runat=server></{0}:WebCustomControl3>")> _
Public Class WebCustomControl3
```

```
        Inherits System.Web.UI.WebControls.WebControl

    Protected Overrides Sub Render(ByVal output As System.Web.UI.HtmlTextWriter)
        Dim p As New PostBackOptions(Me)

        output.AddAttribute(HtmlTextWriterAttribute.Onclick, _
            Page.ClientScript.GetPostBackEventReference(p))

        output.AddAttribute(HtmlTextWriterAttribute.Value, "My Button")
        output.AddAttribute(HtmlTextWriterAttribute.Id, Me.ClientID)
        output.AddAttribute(HtmlTextWriterAttribute.Name, Me.ClientID)
        output.RenderBeginTag(HtmlTextWriterTag.Button)
        output.RenderEndTag()
    End Sub
End Class
```

C#

```
using System.ComponentModel;
using System.Text;
using System.Web.UI;
using System.Web.UI.WebControls;

namespace WebControlLibrary1
{
    [DefaultProperty("Text")]
    [ToolboxData("<{0}:WebCustomControl3 runat=server></{0}:WebCustomControl3>")]
    public class WebCustomControl3 : WebControl
    {
        protected override void Render(HtmlTextWriter output)
        {
            PostBackOptions p = new PostBackOptions(this);

            output.AddAttribute(HtmlTextWriterAttribute.Onclick,
                Page.ClientScript.GetPostBackEventReference(p));
            output.AddAttribute(HtmlTextWriterAttribute.Value, "My Button");
            output.AddAttribute(HtmlTextWriterAttribute.Id, this.ClientID);
            output.AddAttribute(HtmlTextWriterAttribute.Name, this.ClientID);
            output.RenderBeginTag(HtmlTextWriterTag.Button);
            output.RenderEndTag();
        }
    }
}
```

As you can see, this code adds the postback event reference to the client-side OnClick event, but you are not limited to that. You can add the postback JavaScript to any client-side event. You could even add the code to a client-side function if you want to include some logic code.

Now that you can create a postback, you may want to add events to your control that execute during the page postback. To raise server-side events from a client-side object, you implement the System.Web .IPostBackEventHandler interface. Listing 23-27 shows how to do this for a button control. You also create a server-side Click event you can handle when the page posts back.

Listing 23-27: Handling postback events in a server control

VB

```vb
Imports System.ComponentModel
Imports System.Web.UI

<DefaultProperty("Text")> _
<ToolboxData("<{0}:WebCustomControl3 runat=server></{0}:WebCustomControl3>")> _
Public Class WebCustomControl3
    Inherits System.Web.UI.WebControls.WebControl
    Implements IPostBackEventHandler _

    '. . . Code removed for clarity . . .

    Public Event Click()
    Public Sub OnClick(ByVal args As EventArgs)
        RaiseEvent Click()
    End Sub

    Public Sub RaisePostBackEvent(ByVal eventArgument As String)
      Implements System.Web.UI.IPostBackEventHandler.RaisePostBackEvent
        OnClick(EventArgs.Empty)
    End Sub
End Class
```

C#

```csharp
using System;
using System.Collections.Generic;
using System.ComponentModel;
using System.Text;
using System.Web.UI;
using System.Web.UI.WebControls;

namespace WebControlLibrary1
{
    [DefaultProperty("Text")]
    [ToolboxData("<{0}:WebCustomControl3 runat=server></{0}:WebCustomControl3>")]
    public class WebCustomControl3 : WebControl, IPostBackEventHandler
    {

        //. . . Code removed for clarity . . .

        #region IPostBackEventHandler Members
        public event EventHandler Click;

        public virtual void OnClick(EventArgs e)
        {
            if (Click != null)
            {
                Click(this,e);
            }
        }

        public void RaisePostBackEvent(string eventArgument)
```

```
        {
            OnClick(EventArgs.Empty);
        }

        #endregion
    }
}
```

Now, when the user clicks the button and the page posts back, the server-side Click event fires, allowing you to add server-side handling code to the event.

Handling PostBack Data

Now that you have learned how to store data in ViewState and add postback capabilities to a control, look at how you can enable the control to interact with data the user enters into one of its form fields. When a page is posted back to the server by ASP.NET, all the form data is also posted to the server. If the control can interact with data that is passed with a page, you can store the information in ViewState and complete the illusion of a stateful application.

To interact with postback data, your control must be able to access the data. To do this, it implements the System.Web.IPostBackDataHandler interface. This interface allows your control to examine the form data that is passed back to the server during the postback.

The IPostBackDataHandler interface requires that you implement two methods: LoadPostData and RaisePostBackDataChangedEvent. The LoadPostData method is called for all server controls on the page that have postback data. If a control does not have any postback data, the method is not called; however, you can explicitly ask for the method to be called by using the RegisterRequiresPostBack method.

Listing 23-28 shows how you implement the IPostBackDataHandler interface method in a text box.

Listing 23-28: Accessing Postback data in a server control

```vb
VB
Imports System.ComponentModel
Imports System.Web.UI

<DefaultProperty("Text")> _
<ToolboxData("<{0}:WebCustomControl3 runat=server></{0}:WebCustomControl3>")> _
Public Class WebCustomControl3
    Inherits System.Web.UI.WebControls.WebControl
    Implements IPostBackEventHandler, IPostBackDataHandler

    '. . . Code removed for clarity . . .

    Public Function LoadPostData(ByVal postDataKey As String, _
            ByVal postCollection As _
                System.Collections.Specialized.NameValueCollection) _
            As Boolean Implements System.Web.UI.IPostBackDataHandler.LoadPostData
        Me.Text = postCollection(postDataKey)
```

(continued)

Listing 23-28: *(continued)*

```
        Return False
    End Function

    Public Sub RaisePostDataChangedEvent() _
            Implements System.Web.UI.IPostBackDataHandler.RaisePostDataChangedEvent

    End Sub

End Class
```

C#
```
using System;
using System.Collections.Generic;
using System.ComponentModel;
using System.Text;
using System.Web.UI;
using System.Web.UI.WebControls;

namespace WebControlLibrary1
{
    [DefaultProperty("Text")]
    [ToolboxData("<{0}:WebCustomControl3 runat=server></{0}:WebCustomControl3>")]
    public class WebCustomControl3 : WebControl,
        IPostBackEventHandler, IPostBackDataHandler
    {

        //. . . Code removed for clarity . . .

        public bool LoadPostData(string postDataKey,
            System.Collections.Specialized.NameValueCollection postCollection)
        {
            this.Text = postCollection[postDataKey];
            return false;
        }

        public void RaisePostDataChangedEvent()
        {
        }
    }
}
```

As you can see, the LoadPostData method passes any form data submitted to the method as a name value collection that the control can access. The postDataKey parameter allows the control to access the postback data item specific to it. You use these parameters to save text to the Text property of the TextBox control. If you remember the earlier ViewState example, the Text property saves the new value to ViewState; when the page renders, the TextBox value automatically repopulates.

In addition to the input parameters, the LoadPostData method also returns a Boolean value. This value indicates whether the RaisePostBackDataChangedEvent method is also called after the LoadPostData method completes execution. In the sample, it returns false because no events exist, but if you create a TextChanged event to indicate the Textbox text has changed, you raise that event in the RaisePostDataChangedEvent method.

Composite Controls

So far, in looking at Server controls, you have concentrated on emitting a single HTML control; but this can be fairly limiting. Creating extremely powerful controls often requires that you nest several HTML elements together. ASP.NET allows you to easily create controls that serve as a container for other controls. These types of controls are called *composite controls*.

To demonstrate how easy creating a composite control can be, try to change an existing control into a composite control. Listing 23-29 shows how you can do this.

Listing 23-29: Creating a composite control

VB

```
Imports System.ComponentModel
Imports System.Web.UI
Imports System.Web.UI.WebControls

<DefaultProperty("Text")> _
<ToolboxData("<{0}:[WebCustomControl2] runat=server></{0}:[WebCustomControl2]>")> _
Public Class [WebCustomControl2]
    Inherits System.Web.UI.WebControls.CompositeControl

    Protected textbox As TextBox

    Protected Overrides Sub CreateChildControls()
        Me.Controls.Add(textbox)
    End Sub

End Class
```

C#

```
using System;
using System.Collections.Generic;
using System.ComponentModel;
using System.Text;
using System.Web.UI;
using System.Web.UI.WebControls;

namespace WebControlLibrary1
{
    [DefaultProperty("Text")]
    [ToolboxData("<{0}:WebCustomControl2 runat=server></{0}:WebCustomControl2>")]
    public class WebCustomControl2 : CompositeControl
    {
        protected TextBox textbox = new TextBox();

        protected override void CreateChildControls()
        {
            this.Controls.Add(textbox);
        }
    }
}
```

A number of things in this listing are important. First, notice that the control class is now inheriting from `CompositeControl`, rather than `WebControl`. Deriving from `CompositeControl` gives you a few extra features specific to this type of control.

Second, notice that no `Render` method appears in this code. Instead, you simply create an instance of another type of server control and add that to the `Controls` collection in the `CreateChildControls` method. When you run this sample, you see that it renders a text box just like the last control did. In fact, the HTML that it renders is almost identical.

Exposing Child Control Properties

When you drop a composite control (such as the text box from the last sample) onto the design surface, notice that even though you are using a powerful ASP.NET TextBox control within the control, none of that control's properties are exposed to you in the Properties Explorer. In order to expose child control properties through the parent container, you must create corresponding properties in the parent control. For example, if you want to expose the ASP.NET text box `Text` property through the parent control, you create a `Text` property. Listing 23-30 shows how to do this.

Listing 23-30: Exposing control properties in a composite control

VB
```vb
Imports System.ComponentModel
Imports System.Web.UI
Imports System.Web.UI.WebControls

<DefaultProperty("Text")> _
<ToolboxData("<{0}:[WebCustomControl2] runat=server></{0}:[WebCustomControl2]>")> _
Public Class [WebCustomControl2]
    Inherits System.Web.UI.WebControls.CompositeControl

    Protected textbox As TextBox

    Public Property Text() As String
        Get
            EnsureChildControls()
            Return textbox.Text
        End Get
        Set(ByVal value As String)
            EnsureChildControls()
            textbox.Text = value
        End Set
    End Property

    Protected Overrides Sub CreateChildControls()
        Me.Controls.Add(textbox)
        Me.ChildControlsCreated=True
    End Sub

End Class
```

C#
```csharp
using System;
using System.Collections.Generic;
using System.ComponentModel;
```

```
using System.Text;
using System.Web.UI;
using System.Web.UI.WebControls;

namespace WebControlLibrary1
{
    [DefaultProperty("Text")]
    [ToolboxData("<{0}:WebCustomControl2 runat=server></{0}:WebCustomControl2>")]
    public class WebCustomControl2 : CompositeControl
    {
        protected TextBox textbox = new TextBox();

        public string Text
        {
            get
            {
                EnsureChildControls();
                return textbox.Text;
            }
            set
            {
                EnsureChildControls();
                textbox.Text = value;
            }
        }

        protected override void CreateChildControls()
        {
            this.Controls.Add(textbox);
            this.ChildControlsCreated=true;
        }
    }
}
```

Notice that you use this property simply to populate the underlying control's properties. Also notice that before you access the underlying control's properties, you always call the EnsureChildControls method. This method ensures that children of the container control have actually been initialized before you attempt to access them.

Templated Controls

In addition to composite controls, you can also create templated controls. *Templated controls* allow the user to specify a portion of the HTML that is used to render the control, and to nest other controls inside of a container control. You might be familiar with the Repeater or DataList control. These are both templated controls that let you specify how you want the bound data to be displayed when the page renders.

To demonstrate a templated control, the following code gives you a simple example of displaying a message from a user on a Web page. Because the control is a templated control, the developer has complete control over how the message is displayed.

To get started, create the Message server control that will be used as the template inside of a container control. Listing 23-31 shows the class which simply extends the existing Panel control by adding two additional properties, Name and Text, and a new constructor.

Listing 23-31: Creating the templated control's inner control class

VB

```
Public Class Message
    Inherits System.Web.UI.WebControls.Panel
    Implements System.Web.UI.INamingContainer

    Private _name As String
    Private _text As String

    Public Sub New(ByVal name As String, ByVal text As String)
        _text = text
        _name = name
    End Sub

    Public ReadOnly Property Name() As String
        Get
            Return _name
        End Get
    End Property

    Public ReadOnly Property Text() As String
        Get
            Return _text
        End Get
    End Property
End Class
```

C#

```
using System;
using System.Text;
using System.Web;
using System.Web.UI;
using System.Web.UI.WebControls;

namespace WebControlLibrary1
{
    public class Message : Panel, INamingContainer
    {
        private string _name;
        private string _text;

        public Message(string name, string text)
        {
            _text = text;
            _name = name;
        }

        public string Name
        {
            get { return _name; }
        }

        public string Text
```

```
        {
            get { return _text; }
        }
    }
}
```

As you will see in a moment, you can access the public properties exposed by the Message class in order to insert dynamic content into the template. You will also see how you can display the values of the Name and Text properties as part of the rendered template control.

Next, create a new server control which will be the container for the Message control. This server control is responsible for rendering any template controls nested in it.

Listing 23-32: Creating the template control container class

VB

```
Imports System.ComponentModel
Imports System.Web.UI
Imports System.Web.UI.WebControls

<DefaultProperty("Text")> _
<ToolboxData("<{0}:TemplatedControl runat=server></{0}:TemplatedControl>")> _
Public Class TemplatedControl
    Inherits System.Web.UI.WebControls.WebControl

    Private _name As String
    Private _text As String

    Private _message As Message
    Private _messageTemplate As ITemplate

    <Browsable(True)> Public ReadOnly Property Message() As Message
        Get
            EnsureChildControls()
            Return _message
        End Get
    End Property

    <PersistenceMode(PersistenceMode.InnerProperty), _
        TemplateContainer(GetType(Message))> _
    Public Property MessageTemplate() As ITemplate
        Get
            Return _messageTemplate
        End Get
        Set(ByVal value As ITemplate)
            _messageTemplate = value
        End Set
    End Property

    <Bindable(True), DefaultValue("")> Public Property Name() As String
        Get
            Return _name
        End Get
```

(continued)

Listing 23-32: *(continued)*

```vb
        Set(ByVal value As String)
            _name = value
        End Set
    End Property

    <Bindable(True), DefaultValue("")> Public Property Text() As String
        Get
            Return _text
        End Get
        Set(ByVal value As String)
            _text = value
        End Set
    End Property

    Public Overrides Sub DataBind()
        CreateChildControls()
        ChildControlsCreated = True
        MyBase.DataBind()
    End Sub

    Protected Overrides Sub CreateChildControls()

        Me.Controls.Clear()

        _message = New Message(Name, Text)

        Dim template As ITemplate = MessageTemplate
        template.InstantiateIn(_message)
        Controls.Add(_message)
    End Sub

End Class
```

C#

```csharp
using System;
using System.Collections.Generic;
using System.ComponentModel;
using System.Text;
using System.Web.UI;
using System.Web.UI.WebControls;

namespace WebControlLibrary1
{
    [DefaultProperty("Text")]
    [ToolboxData("<{0}:TemplatedControl runat=server></{0}: TemplatedControl >")]
    public class TemplatedControl : WebControl
    {
        private string _name;
        private string _text;

        private Message _message;
        private ITemplate _messageTemplate;

        [Browsable(false)]
```

```
public Message Message
{
    get
    {
        EnsureChildControls();
        return _message;
    }
}

[PersistenceMode(PersistenceMode.InnerProperty)]
[TemplateContainer(typeof(Message))]
public virtual ITemplate MessageTemplate
{
    get { return _messageTemplate; }
    set { _messageTemplate = value; }
}

[Bindable(true)]
[DefaultValue("")]
public string Name
{
    get { return _name; }
    set { _name = value; }
}

[Bindable(true)]
[DefaultValue("")]
public string Text
{
    get { return _text; }
    set { _text = value; }
}

public override void DataBind()
{
    CreateChildControls();
    ChildControlsCreated = true;
    base.DataBind();
}

protected override void CreateChildControls()
{
    this.Controls.Clear();

    _message = new Message(Name,Text);

    ITemplate template = MessageTemplate;
    template.InstantiateIn(_message);
    Controls.Add(_message);
}

}
}
```

To start to dissect this sample, first notice the `MessageTemplate` property. This property allows Visual Studio to understand that the control can contain a template, and allows it to display the IntelliSense for that template. The property has been marked with the `PersistanceMode` attribute indicating that the template control should be persisted as an inner property within the control's tag in the ASPX page. Additionally, the property is marked with the `TemplateContainer` attribute, which helps ASP.NET figure out what type of template control this property represents. In this case, it's the Message template control you created earlier.

The container control exposes two public properties, Name and Text. These properties are used to populate the Name and Text properties of the Message control since that class does not allow developers to set the properties directly.

Finally, the `CreateChildControls` method, called by the `DataBind` method, does most of the heavy lifting in this control. It creates a new `Message` object, passing the values of `Name` and `Text` as constructor values. Once the CreateChildControls method completes, the base DataBind operation comtinues to execute. This is important because that is where the evaluation of the Name and Text properties occurs, which allows you to insert these properties values into the template control.

After the control and template are created, you can drop them onto a test Web page. Listing 23-33 shows how the control can be used to customize the display of the data.

Listing 23-33: Adding a templated control to a Web page

VB

```
<%@ Page Language="VB" %>

<%@ Register Assembly="WebControlLibrary1" Namespace="WebControlLibrary1"
    TagPrefix="cc1" %>

<script runat="server">
    Protected Sub Page_Load(ByVal sender As Object, ByVal e As System.EventArgs)
        Me.TemplatedControl1.DataBind()
    End Sub
</script>

<html xmlns="http://www.w3.org/1999/xhtml" >
<head runat="server">
    <title>Templated Web Controls</title>
</head>
<body>
    <form id="form1" runat="server">
    <div>
        <cc1:TemplatedControl Name="John Doe" Text="Hello World!"
            ID="TemplatedControl1" runat="server">
            <MessageTemplate>The user '<%# Container.Name %>'
                has a message for you: <br />"<%#Container.Text%>"
            </MessageTemplate>
        </cc1:TemplatedControl>
    </div>
    </form>
</body>
</html>
```

C#

```
<script runat="server">
    protected void Page_Load(object sender, EventArgs e)
    {
        this.TemplatedControl1.DataBind();
    }
</script>
```

As you can see in the listing, the `<cc1:TemplatedControl>` control contains a `MessageTemplate` within it, which has been customized to display the `Name` and `Text` values. Figure 23-16 shows this page after it has been rendered in the browser.

Figure 23-16

One item to consider when creating templated controls is what happens if the developer does not include a template control inside of the container control. In the previous example, if you removed the MessageTemplate control from the TemplateContainer, a NullReferenceException would occur when you tried to run your web page. This is because the container control's MessageTemplate property would return a null value. In order to prevent this, you can include a default template class as part of the container control. An example of a default template is shown in Listing 23-34.

Listing 23-34: Creating the templated control's default template class

VB

```
Private Class DefaultMessageTemplate
    Implements ITemplate

    Public Sub InstantiateIn(ByVal container As System.Web.UI.Control) _
            Implements System.Web.UI.ITemplate.InstantiateIn

        Dim l As New Literal()
        l.Text="No MessageTemplate was included."
        container.Controls.Add(l)
    End Sub
End Class
```

(continued)

Listing 23-34: *(continued)*

C#
```csharp
private sealed class DefaultMessageTemplate : ITemplate
{
    public void InstantiateIn(Control container)
    {
        Literal l = new Literal();
        l.Text="No MessageTemplate was included.";
        container.Controls.Add(l);
    }
}
```

Notice that the DefaultMessageTemplate implements the ITemplate interface. This interface requires that the InstantiateIn method be implemented, which we use to provide the default template content.

To include the default template, simply add the class to the TemplatedControl class. You will also need to modify the CreateChildControls method to detect the null MessageTemplate and instead create an instance of and use the default template.

VB
```vb
If template = Nothing Then
    template = New DefaultMessageTemplate()
End If
```

C#
```csharp
if (template == null)
{
    template = new DefaultMessageTemplate();
}
```

Creating Control Design-Time Experiences

So far in this chapter, you concentrated primarily on what gets rendered to the client's browser, but the browser is not the only consumer of server controls. Visual Studio and the developer using a server control are also consumers, and you need to consider their experiences when using your control.

ASP.NET 2.0 offers numerous improvements in the design-time experience you give to developers using your control. Some of these improvements require no additional coding, such as the WYSIWYG rendering of user controls and basic server controls; but for more complex scenarios, ASP.NET 2.0 includes a number of new tools that give the developer an outstanding design-time experience.

When you write server controls, a priority should be to give the developer a design-time experience that closely replicates the runtime experience. This means altering the appearance of the control on the design surface in response to changes in control properties and the introduction of other server controls onto the design surface. Three main components are involved in creating the design-time behaviors of a server control:

❑   Type Converters

❑   Designers

❑   UI Type Editors

Because a chapter can be written for each one of these topics, in this section I attempt to give you only an overview of each, how they tie into a control's design-time behavior, and some simple examples of their use.

Type Converters

TypeConverter is a class that allows you to perform conversions between one type and another. Visual Studio uses type converters at design time to convert object property values to String types so that they can be displayed on the Property Browser, and it returns them to their original types when the developer changes the property.

ASP.NET 2.0 includes a wide variety of type converters you can use when creating your control's design-time behavior. These range from converters that allow you to convert most number types, to converters that let you convert Fonts, Colors, DataTimes, and Guids. The easiest way to see what type converters are available to you in the .NET Framework is to search for types in the framework that derive from the TypeConverter class using the MSDN Library help.

After you have found a type converter that you want to use on a control property, mark the property with a TypeConverter attribute, as shown in Listing 23-35.

Listing 23-35: Applying the TypeConverter attribute to a property

VB
```
<Bindable(True)> _
<Category("Appearance")> _
<DefaultValue("")> _
<TypeConverter(GetType(GuidConverter))> _
Property BookId() As System.Guid
        Get
                Return _bookid
        End Get

        Set(ByVal Value As System.Guid)
            _bookid = Value
        End Set
    End Property
```

C#
```
[Bindable(true)]
[Category("Appearance")]
[DefaultValue("")]
[TypeConverter(typeof(GuidConverter))]
public Guid BookId
{
    get
    {
        return _bookid;
    }

    set
    {
        _bookid = value;
    }
}
```

In this example, a property is exposed that accepts and returns an object of type Guid. The Property Browser cannot natively display a Guid object, so you convert the value to a string so that it can be displayed properly in the property browser. Marking the property with the `TypeConverter` attribute and, in this case, specifying the GuidConverter as the type converter you want to use, allows complex objects like a Guid to display properly in the Property Browser.

Custom Type Converters

It is also possible to create your own custom type converters if none of the in-box converters fit into your scenario. Type converters derive from the `System.ComponentModel.TypeConverter` class. Listing 23-36 shows a custom type converter that converts a custom object called `Name` to and from a string.

Listing 23-36: Creating a custom type converter

```vb
VB
Imports System
Imports System.ComponentModel
Imports System.Globalization

Public Class Name

    Private _first As String
    Private _last As String

    Public Sub New(ByVal first As String, ByVal last As String)
        _first = first
        _last = last
    End Sub

    Public Property First() As String
        Get
            Return _first
        End Get
        Set(ByVal value As String)
            _first = value
        End Set
    End Property

    Public Property Last() As String
        Get
            Return _last
        End Get
        Set(ByVal value As String)
            _last = value
        End Set
    End Property
End Class

Public Class NameConverter
    Inherits TypeConverter

    Public Overrides Function CanConvertFrom(ByVal context As _
        ITypeDescriptorContext, ByVal sourceType As Type) As Boolean

        If (sourceType Is GetType(String)) Then
```

```
                    Return True
          End If

          Return MyBase.CanConvertFrom(context, sourceType)
      End Function

      Public Overrides Function ConvertFrom( _
              ByVal context As ITypeDescriptorContext, _
              ByVal culture As CultureInfo, ByVal value As Object) As Object
          If (value Is GetType(String)) Then
              Dim v As String() = (CStr(value).Split(New [Char]() {" "c}))
              Return New Name(v(0), v(1))
          End If
          Return MyBase.ConvertFrom(context, culture, value)
      End Function

      Public Overrides Function ConvertTo( _
              ByVal context As ITypeDescriptorContext, _
              ByVal culture As CultureInfo, ByVal value As Object, _
              ByVal destinationType As Type) As Object
          If (destinationType Is GetType(String)) Then
              Return (CType(value, Name).First + " " + (CType(value, Name).Last))
          End If
          Return MyBase.ConvertTo(context, culture, value, destinationType)
      End Function
  End Class
```

C#

```csharp
using System;
using System.ComponentModel;
using System.Globalization;

public class Name
{
    private string _first;
    private string _last;

    public Name(string first, string last)
    {
        _first=first;
        _last=last;
    }

    public string First
    {
        get{ return _first; }
        set { _first = value; }
    }
    public string Last
    {
        get { return _last; }
        set { _last = value; }
    }
```

(continued)

Listing 23-36: *(continued)*

```
    }

    public class NameConverter : TypeConverter
    {

        public override bool CanConvertFrom(ITypeDescriptorContext context,
            Type sourceType) {

            if (sourceType == typeof(string)) {
                return true;
            }
            return base.CanConvertFrom(context, sourceType);
        }

        public override object ConvertFrom(ITypeDescriptorContext context,
            CultureInfo culture, object value) {
            if (value is string) {
                string[] v = ((string)value).Split(new char[] {' '});
                return new Name(v[0],v[1]);
            }
            return base.ConvertFrom(context, culture, value);
        }

        public override object ConvertTo(ITypeDescriptorContext context,
            CultureInfo culture, object value, Type destinationType) {
            if (destinationType == typeof(string)) {
                return ((Name)value).First + " " + ((Name)value).Last;
            }
            return base.ConvertTo(context, culture, value, destinationType);
        }
    }
}
```

The `NameConverter` class overrides three methods, `CanConvertFrom`, `ConvertFrom`, and `ConvertTo`. The `CanConvertFrom` method allows you to control what types the converter can convert from. The `ConvertFrom` method converts the string representation back into a `Name` object, and `ConvertTo` converts the `Name` object into a string representation.

After you have built your type converter, you can use it to mark properties in your control with the `TypeConverter` attribute, as you saw in Listing 23-35.

Control Designers

Controls that live on the Visual Studio design surface depend on *control designers* to create the design-time experience for the end user. Control designers, for both WinForms and ASP.NET, are classes that derive from the `System.ComponentModel.Design.ComponentDesigner` class. .NET provides an abstracted base class specifically for creating ASP.NET control designers called the `System.Web.UI.Design.ControlDesigner`. In order to access these classes you will need to add a reference to the System.Design.dll assembly to your project.

.NET includes a number of in-box control designer classes that you can use when creating a custom control; but as you develop server controls, you see that .NET automatically applies a default designer. The designer it applies is based on the type of control you are creating. For instance, when you created your first TextBox control, Visual Studio used the ControlDesigner class to achieve the WYSIWYG design-time rendering of the text box. If you develop a server control derived from the ControlContainer class, .NET automatically use the ControlContainerDesigner class as the designer.

You can also explicitly specify the designer you want to use to render your control at design time using the Designer attribute on your control's class, as shown in Listing 23-37.

Listing 23-37: Adding a Designer attribute to a control class

VB

```vb
<DefaultProperty("Text")> _
<ToolboxData("<{0}:[WebCustomControl1] runat=server></{0}:[WebCustomControl1]>")> _
<Designer(GetType(ControlDesigner))> _
Public Class [WebCustomControl1]
    Inherits System.Web.UI.WebControls.WebControl
```

C#

```csharp
[DefaultProperty("Text")]
[ToolboxData("<{0}:WebCustomControl1 runat=server></{0}:WebCustomControl1>")]
[Designer(typeof(ControlDesigner))]
public class WebCustomControl1 : WebControl
```

Notice that the Designer attribute has been added to the WebCustomControl1 class. You have specified that the control should use the ControlDesigner class as its designer. Other in-box designers you could have specified are

- ❑ CompositeControlDesigner

- ❑ TemplatedControlDesigner

- ❑ DataSourceDesigner

Each designer provides a specific design-time behavior for the control, and you can select one that is appropriate for the type of control you are creating.

Design-Time Regions

As you saw earlier, ASP.NET allows you to create server controls that consist of other server controls and text. In ASP.NET 1.0, a server control developer could use the ReadWriteControlDesigner class to enable the user of the server control to enter text or drop other server controls into a custom server control at design time. An example of this is the ASP.NET Panel control, which enables developers to add content to the panel at design time.

In ASP.NET 2.0, however, creating a control with this functionality has changed. The ReadWriteControlDesigner class has been marked as obsolete in ASP.NET 2.0, and a new and improved way has been included to allow the developer to create server controls that have design-time editable portions. The new technique, called *designer regions*, is an improvement over the ReadWriteControlDesigner in several ways. First, unlike the ReadWriteControlDesigner class, which allowed only a single editable area, designer regions enables you to create multiple, independent regions defined within a single control. Second, designer classes can now respond to events raised by a design region. This might be the designer drawing a control on the design surface or the user clicking an area of the control or entering or exiting a template edit mode.

To show how you can use designer regions, create a container control to which you can apply a custom control designer (as shown in Listing 23-38).

Listing 23-38: Creating a composite control with designer regions

VB

```vb
<Designer(GetType(MultiRegionControlDesigner))> _
<ToolboxData("<{0}:MultiRegionControl runat=server width=100%>" & _
    "</{0}:MultiRegionControl>")> _
Public Class MultiRegionControl
    Inherits CompositeControl

    ' Define the templates that represent 2 views on the control
    Private _view1 As ITemplate
    Private _view2 As ITemplate

    ' These properties are inner properties
    <PersistenceMode(PersistenceMode.InnerProperty), DefaultValue("")> _
    Public Overridable Property View1() As ITemplate
        Get
            Return _view1
        End Get
        Set(ByVal value As ITemplate)
            _view1 = value
        End Set
    End Property

    <PersistenceMode(PersistenceMode.InnerProperty), DefaultValue("")> _
    Public Overridable Property View2() As ITemplate
        Get
            Return _view2
        End Get
        Set(ByVal value As ITemplate)
            _view2 = value
        End Set
    End Property

    ' The current view on the control; 0= view1, 1=view2, 2=all views
    Private _currentView As Int32 = 0
    Public Property CurrentView() As Int32
        Get
            Return _currentView
        End Get
        Set(ByVal value As Int32)
            _currentView = value
        End Set
    End Property

    Protected Overrides Sub CreateChildControls()
        MyBase.CreateChildControls()

        Controls.Clear()

        Dim template As ITemplate = View1
        If (_currentView = 1) Then
```

```
            template = View2
        End If

        Dim p As New Panel()
        Controls.Add(p)

        If (Not template Is Nothing) Then
            template.InstantiateIn(p)
        End If

    End Sub

End Class
```

C#

```csharp
[Designer(typeof(MultiRegionControlDesigner))]
[ToolboxData("<{0}:MultiRegionControl runat=\"server\" width=\"100%\">" +
    "</{0}:MultiRegionControl>")]
public class MultiRegionControl : CompositeControl {

    // Define the templates that represent 2 views on the control
    private ITemplate _view1;
    private ITemplate _view2;

    // These properties are inner properties
    [PersistenceMode(PersistenceMode.InnerProperty), DefaultValue(null)]
    public virtual ITemplate View1 {
        get { return _view1; }
        set { _view1 = value; }
    }

    [PersistenceMode(PersistenceMode.InnerProperty), DefaultValue(null)]
    public virtual ITemplate View2 {
        get { return _view2; }
        set { _view2 = value; }
    }

    // The current view on the control; 0= view1, 1=view2, 2=all views
    private int _currentView = 0;
    public int CurrentView {
        get { return _currentView; }
        set { _currentView = value; }
    }

    protected override void CreateChildControls()
    {
        Controls.Clear();

        ITemplate template = View1;
        if (_currentView == 1)
            template = View2;

        Panel p = new Panel();
        Controls.Add(p);
```

(continued)

Listing 23-38: *(continued)*

```
        if (template != null)
            template.InstantiateIn(p);
    }
  }
```

The container control creates two `ITemplate` objects, which serve as the controls to display. The `ITemplate` objects are the control containers for this server control, allowing you to drop other server controls or text into this control. The control also uses the `Designer` attribute to indicate to Visual Studio that it should use the `MultiRegionControlDesigner` class when displaying this control on the designer surface.

Now you create the control designer that defines the regions for the control. Listing 23-39 shows the designer class.

Listing 23-39: A custom designer class used to define designer regions

VB

```
Public Class MultiRegionControlDesigner
    Inherits CompositeControlDesigner

    Protected _currentView As Int32 = 0
    Private myControl As MultiRegionControl

    Public Overrides Sub Initialize(ByVal component As IComponent)
        MyBase.Initialize(component)
        myControl = CType(component, MultiRegionControl)
    End Sub

    Public Overrides ReadOnly Property AllowResize() As Boolean
        Get
            Return True
        End Get
    End Property

    Protected Overrides Sub OnClick(ByVal e As DesignerRegionMouseEventArgs)

        If (e.Region Is Nothing) Then
            Return
        End If

        If ((e.Region.Name = "Header0") And (Not _currentView = 0)) Then
            _currentView = 0
            UpdateDesignTimeHtml()
        End If

        If ((e.Region.Name = "Header1") And (Not _currentView = 1)) Then

            _currentView = 1
            UpdateDesignTimeHtml()
        End If
```

```
        End Sub

        Public Overrides Function GetDesignTimeHtml( _
                ByVal regions As DesignerRegionCollection) As String
            BuildRegions(regions)
            Return BuildDesignTimeHtml()
        End Function

        Protected Overridable Sub BuildRegions( _
                ByVal regions As DesignerRegionCollection)

            regions.Add(New DesignerRegion(Me, "Header0"))
            regions.Add(New DesignerRegion(Me, "Header1"))

            ' If the current view is for all, we need another editable region
            Dim edr0 As New EditableDesignerRegion(Me, "Content" & _currentView, False)
            edr0.Description = "Add stuff in here if you dare:"
            regions.Add(edr0)

            ' Set the highlight, depending upon the selected region
            If ((_currentView = 0) Or (_currentView = 1)) Then
                regions(_currentView).Highlight = True
            End If
        End Sub

        Protected Overridable Function BuildDesignTimeHtml() As String

            Dim sb As New StringBuilder()
            sb.Append(BuildBeginDesignTimeHtml())
            sb.Append(BuildContentDesignTimeHtml())
            sb.Append(BuildEndDesignTimeHtml())

            Return sb.ToString()
        End Function

        Protected Overridable Function BuildBeginDesignTimeHtml() As String
            ' Create the table layout
            Dim sb As New StringBuilder()
            sb.Append("<table ")

            ' Styles that we'll use to render for the design-surface
            sb.Append("height='" & myControl.Height.ToString() & "' width='" & _
                myControl.Width.ToString() & "'>")

            ' Generate the title or caption bar
            sb.Append("<tr height='25px' align='center' " & _
                "style='font-family:tahoma;font-size:10pt;font-weight:bold;'>" & _
                "<td style='width:50%' " & _
                DesignerRegion.DesignerRegionAttributeName & "='0'>")
            sb.Append("Page-View 1</td>")
            sb.Append("<td style='width:50%' " & _
                DesignerRegion.DesignerRegionAttributeName & "='1'>")
            sb.Append("Page-View 2</td></tr>")

            Return sb.ToString()
```

(continued)

)

Listing 23-39: *(continued)*

```
End Function
Protected Overridable Function BuildEndDesignTimeHtml() As String
    Return ("</table>")
End Function

Protected Overridable Function BuildContentDesignTimeHtml() As String

    Dim sb As New StringBuilder()
    sb.Append("<td colspan='2' style='")
    sb.Append("background-color:" & _
        myControl.BackColor.Name.ToString() & ";' ")

    sb.Append(DesignerRegion.DesignerRegionAttributeName & "='2'>")

    Return sb.ToString()
End Function

Public Overrides Function GetEditableDesignerRegionContent( _
        ByVal region As EditableDesignerRegion) As String

    Dim host As IDesignerHost =
        CType(Component.Site.GetService(GetType(IDesignerHost)), IDesignerHost)

    If (Not host Is Nothing) Then
        Dim template As ITemplate = myControl.View1
        If (region.Name = "Content1") Then
            template = myControl.View2
        End If

        If (Not template Is Nothing) Then
            Return ControlPersister.PersistTemplate(template, host)
        End If

    End If

    Return String.Empty
End Function

Public Overrides Sub SetEditableDesignerRegionContent( _
        ByVal region As EditableDesignerRegion, ByVal content As String)

    Dim regionIndex As Int32 = Int32.Parse(region.Name.Substring(7))

    If (content Is Nothing) Then

        If (regionIndex = 0) Then
            myControl.View1 = Nothing
        ElseIf (regionIndex = 1) Then
            myControl.View2 = Nothing
            Return
        End If

        Dim host As IDesignerHost =
```

```
                        CType(Component.Site.GetService(GetType(IDesignerHost)),
                            IDesignerHost)

                If (Not host Is Nothing) Then
                    Dim template = ControlParser.ParseTemplate(host, content)

                    If (Not template Is Nothing) Then
                        If (regionIndex = 0) Then
                            myControl.View1 = template
                        ElseIf (regionIndex = 1) Then
                            myControl.View2 = template
                        End If
                    End If
                End If
            End If
        End Sub
End Class
```

C#

```csharp
public class MultiRegionControlDesigner : CompositeControlDesigner {

    protected int _currentView = 0;

    private MultiRegionControl myControl;
    public override void Initialize(IComponent component)
    {
        base.Initialize(component);
        myControl = (MultiRegionControl)component;
    }

    public override bool AllowResize { get { return true; } }

    protected override void OnClick(DesignerRegionMouseEventArgs e)
    {
        if (e.Region == null)
            return;

        if (e.Region.Name == "Header0" && _currentView != 0) {
            _currentView = 0;
            UpdateDesignTimeHtml();
        }

        if (e.Region.Name == "Header1" && _currentView != 1) {
            _currentView = 1;
            UpdateDesignTimeHtml();
        }
    }

    public override String GetDesignTimeHtml(DesignerRegionCollection regions)
    {
        BuildRegions(regions);
        return BuildDesignTimeHtml();
    }
    protected virtual void BuildRegions(DesignerRegionCollection regions)
    {
```

(continued)

Listing 23-39: *(continued)*

```
        regions.Add(new DesignerRegion(this, "Header0"));
        regions.Add(new DesignerRegion(this, "Header1"));

        // If the current view is for all, we need another editable region
        EditableDesignerRegion edr0 = new
            EditableDesignerRegion(this, "Content" + _currentView, false);
        edr0.Description = "Add stuff in here if you dare:";
        regions.Add(edr0);

        // Set the highlight, depending upon the selected region
        if (_currentView ==0 || _currentView==1)
            regions[_currentView].Highlight = true;
    }

    protected virtual string BuildDesignTimeHtml()
    {
        StringBuilder sb = new StringBuilder();
        sb.Append(BuildBeginDesignTimeHtml());
        sb.Append(BuildContentDesignTimeHtml());
        sb.Append(BuildEndDesignTimeHtml());

        return sb.ToString();
    }

    protected virtual String BuildBeginDesignTimeHtml()
    {
        // Create the table layout
        StringBuilder sb = new StringBuilder();
        sb.Append("<table ");

        // Styles that we'll use to render for the design-surface
        sb.Append("height='" + myControl.Height.ToString() + "' width='" +
            myControl.Width.ToString() +  "'>");

        // Generate the title or caption bar
        sb.Append("<tr height='25px' align='center' " +
            "style='font-family:tahoma;font-size:10pt;font-weight:bold;'>" +
            "<td style='width:50%' " + DesignerRegion.DesignerRegionAttributeName +
            "='0'>");
        sb.Append("Page-View 1</td>");
        sb.Append("<td style='width:50%' " +
            DesignerRegion.DesignerRegionAttributeName + "='1'>");
        sb.Append("Page-View 2</td></tr>");

        return sb.ToString();
    }

    protected virtual String BuildEndDesignTimeHtml()
    {
        return ("</table>");
    }

    protected virtual String BuildContentDesignTimeHtml()
```

```
{
    StringBuilder sb = new StringBuilder();
    sb.Append("<td colspan='2' style='");
    sb.Append("background-color:" + myControl.BackColor.Name.ToString() +
        ";' ");

    sb.Append(DesignerRegion.DesignerRegionAttributeName + "='2'>");

    return sb.ToString();
}

public override string GetEditableDesignerRegionContent
    (EditableDesignerRegion region)
{
    IDesignerHost host =
        (IDesignerHost)Component.Site.GetService(typeof(IDesignerHost));

    if (host != null) {
        ITemplate template = myControl.View1;

        if (region.Name == "Content1")
            template = myControl.View2;

        if (template != null)
            return ControlPersister.PersistTemplate(template, host);
    }

    return String.Empty;
}

public override void SetEditableDesignerRegionContent
    (EditableDesignerRegion region, string content)
{
    int regionIndex = Int32.Parse(region.Name.Substring(7));

    if (content == null)
    {
        if (regionIndex == 0)
            myControl.View1 = null;
        else if (regionIndex == 1)
            myControl.View2 = null;
        return;
    }

    IDesignerHost host =
        (IDesignerHost)Component.Site.GetService(typeof(IDesignerHost));

    if (host != null)
    {
        ITemplate template = ControlParser.ParseTemplate(host, content);

        if (template != null)
        {
            if (regionIndex == 0)
```

(continued)

Listing 23-39: *(continued)*

```
                myControl.View1 = template;
        else if (regionIndex == 1)
                myControl.View2 = template;
        }
    }
  }
}
```

The designer overrides the `GetDesignTimeHtml` method, calling the `BuildRegions` and `BuildDesignTimeHtml` methods to alter the HTML that the control renders to the Visual Studio design surface.

The BuildRegions method creates three design regions in the control, two header regions and an editable content region. The regions are added to the `DesignerRegionCollection`. The `BuildDesignTimeHtml` method calls three methods to generate the actual HTML that will be generated by the control at design time.

The designer class also contains two overridden methods for getting and setting the editable designer region content: `GetEditableDesignerRegionContent` and `SetEditableDesignerRegionContent`. These methods get or set the appropriate content HTML, based on the designer region template that is currently active.

Finally, the class contains an `OnClick` method that it uses to respond to click events fired by the control at design time. This control uses the OnClick event to switch the current region being displayed by the control at design time.

When you add the control to a Web form, you see that you can toggle between the two editable regions, and each region maintains its own content. Figure 23-17 shows what the control looks like on the Visual Studio design surface.

As you can see in Figure 23-17, the control contains three separate design regions. When you click design regions 1 or 2, the `OnClick` method in the designer fires and redraws the control on the design surface, changing the template area located in design region 3.

Designer Actions

Another great new improvement in ASP.NET 2.0 is the introduction of control smart tags. Smart tags give developers using a control quick access to common control properties. Smart tags are actually a new and improved implementation of the Designer Verbs functionality that was available in ASP.NET 1.0.

To add menu items to a server control's smart tag, you create a new class that inherits from the `DesignerActionList` class. The `DesignerActionList` contains the list of designer action items that are displayed by a server control. Classes that derive from the `DesignerActionList` class can override the `GetSortedActionItems` method, creating their own `DesignerActionItemsCollection` object to which designer action items can be added.

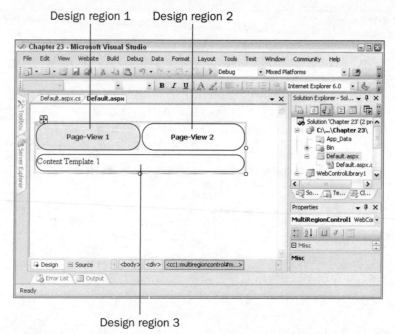

Figure 23-17

You can add several different types of `DesignerActionItems` types to the collection:

❑   `DesignerActionTextItem`

❑   `DesignerActionHeaderItem`

❑   `DesignerActionMethodItem`

❑   `DesignerActionPropertyItem`

Listing 23-40 shows a control designer class that contains a private class deriving from `DesignerActionList`.

Listing 23-40: Adding designer actions to a control designer

VB

```vb
Imports System.Web.UI.Design
Public Class TestControlDesigner
    Inherits ControlDesigner

    Public Overrides ReadOnly Property ActionLists() _
            As DesignerActionListCollection
        Get
            Dim lists As New DesignerActionListCollection()
            lists.AddRange(MyBase.ActionLists)
            lists.Add(New TestControlList(Me))
            Return lists
        End Get
```

(continued)

Listing 23-40: *(continued)*

```vb
    End Property

    Private NotInheritable Class TestControlList
        Inherits DesignerActionList

        Public Sub New(ByVal c As TestControlDesigner)
            MyBase.New(c.Component)
        End Sub

        Public Overrides Function GetSortedActionItems() _
                As DesignerActionItemCollection

            Dim c As New DesignerActionItemCollection()
            c.Add(New DesignerActionTextItem("FOO", "FOO"))
            Return c
        End Function
    End Class

End Class
```

C#

```csharp
using System.Web.UI.Design;
public class TestControlDesigner : ControlDesigner
{
    public override DesignerActionListCollection ActionLists
    {
        get
        {
            DesignerActionListCollection actionLists =
                new DesignerActionListCollection();
            actionLists.AddRange(base.ActionLists);
            actionLists.Add(new TestControlList(this));
            return actionLists;
        }
    }

    private sealed class TestControlList : DesignerActionList
    {
        public TestControlList(TestControlDesigner c) : base(c.Component)
        {
        }

        public override DesignerActionItemCollection GetSortedActionItems()
        {
            DesignerActionItemCollection c = new DesignerActionItemCollection();
            c.Add(new DesignerActionTextItem("FOO", "FOO"));
            return c;
        }
    }
}
```

The control designer class overrides the `ActionsLists` property. The property creates an instance of the `TextControlList` class, which derives from `DesignerActionList` and overrides the `GetSortedActionItems` method. The method creates a new `DesignerActionListCollection`, and a `DesignerActionTextItem` is added to the collection (see Figure 23-18). The `DesignerActionTextItem` class allows you to add text menu items to the smart tag.

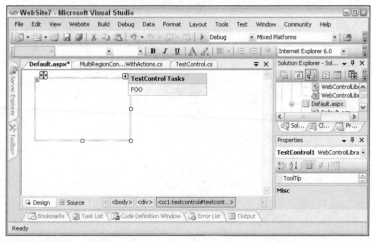

Figure 23-18

As shown in Figure 23-18, when you add the control to a Web page, the control now has a smart tag with the `DesignerActionTextItem` class as content.

UI Type Editors

A UI type editor is a way to provide users of your controls with a custom interface for editing properties directly from the Property Browser. One type of UI type editor you might already be familiar with is the Color Picker you see when you want to change the `ForeColor` attribute that exists on most ASP.NET controls. ASP.NET provides a wide variety of in-box UI type editors that make it easy to edit more complex property types. The easiest way to find what UI type editors are available in the .NET Framework is to search for types derived from the `UITypeEditor` class in the MSDN Library help.

After you find the type editor you want to use on your control property, you simply apply the UI Type Editor to the property using the `Editor` attribute. Listing 23-41 shows how to do this.

Listing 23-41: Adding a UI type editor to a control property

```vb
VB
<Bindable(True), Category("Appearance"), DefaultValue(""), _
Editor( _
        GetType(System.Web.UI.Design.UrlEditor), _
        GetType(System.Drawing.Design.UITypeEditor))> _
Public Property Url() As String
    Get
        Return _url
```

(continued)

Listing 23-41: *(continued)*

```
        End Get
        Set(ByVal value As String)
            _url = value
        End Set
End Property
```

C#
```
[Bindable(true)]
[Category("Appearance")]
[DefaultValue("")]
[Editor(typeof(System.Web.UI.Design.UrlEditor),
    typeof(System.Drawing.Design.UITypeEditor))]
public string Url
{
    get
    {
        return url;
    }
    set
    {
        url = value;
    }
}
```

In this sample, you have created a `Url` property for a control. Because you know this property will be a URL, you want to give the control user a positive design-time experience. You can use the UrlEditor type editor to make it easier for users to select a URL. Figure 23-19 shows the Url Editor that appears when the user edits the control property.

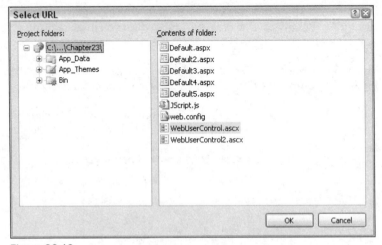

Figure 23-19

Modules and Handlers

Sometimes, just creating dynamic Web pages with the latest languages and databases just does not give you, the developer, enough control over an application. At times, you need to be able to dig deeper and create applications that can interact with the Web server itself. You want to be able to interact with the low-level processes, such as how the Web server processes incoming and outgoing HTTP requests.

Before ASP.NET, in order to get this level of control using IIS, you were forced to create ISAPI extensions or filters. This proved to be quite a daunting and painful task for many developers because creating ISAPI extensions and filters required knowledge of C/C++ and knowledge of how to create native Win32 DLLs. Thankfully, in the .NET world, creating these types of low-level applications is really no more difficult than most other tasks you would normally perform.

Now, take a high-level look at how ASP.NET processes HTTP requests and what options you have for plugging into those requests. ASP.NET processes HTTP requests using a pipeline model. This model has two core mechanisms for processing HTTP requests: HttpModules and HttpHandlers. ASP.NET uses those two mechanisms to process incoming ASP.NET requests, generate a response, and return that response to the client. In fact, you are probably already familiar with HttpModules and HttpHandlers—although you might not know it. If you have ever used the inbox caching or the authentication features of ASP.NET, you have used several different HttpModules. Additionally, if have ever served up an ASP.NET application, even something as simple as a *Hello World* Web page and viewed it in a browser, you have used an HttpHandler. ASP.NET uses handlers to process and render ASPX pages and many other file extensions. Modules and handlers allow you to plug into the request-processing pipeline at different points and interact with the actual requests being processed by IIS. Figure 23-20 shows how this model works.

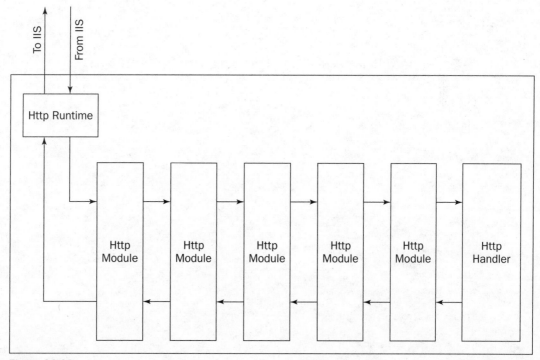

Figure 23-20

As you can see, ASP.NET passes each incoming request through a layer of HttpModules in the processing pipeline. ASP.NET allows multiple modules to exist in the pipeline for each request. After the incoming request has passed through each module, it is passed to the HttpHandler, which serves the request. Notice that although a single request may pass through many different modules, it can be processed by one handler only. The handler is generally responsible for creating a response to the incoming HTTP request. After the handler has completed execution and generated a response, the response is passed back through each module, before it is returned to the client.

You should now have a basic understanding of the ASP.NET request pipeline — and how you can use HttpModules and HttpHandlers to interact with the pipeline. The following sections take an in-depth look at each of these.

HttpModules

HttpModules are simple classes that can plug themselves into the request-processing pipeline. They do this by hooking into a handful of events thrown by the application as it processes the HTTP request. To create an HttpModule, you simply create a class that derives from the System.Web.IHttpModule interface. This interface requires you to implement two methods: Init and Dispose. Listing 23-42 shows the class stub created after you implement the IHttpModule interface.

Listing 23-42: Implementing the IHttpModule Interface

VB
```vb
Imports Microsoft.VisualBasic
Imports System.Web

Public Class AppendMessage
    Implements IHttpModule

    Public Overridable Sub Init(ByVal context As HttpApplication) _
            Implements IHttpModule.Init

    End Sub

    Public Overridable Sub Dispose() Implements IHttpModule.Dispose

    End Sub

End Class
```

C#
```csharp
using System;
using System.Collections.Generic;
using System.Text;
using System.Web;

namespace Demo
{
    class SimpleModule : IHttpModule
    {
        #region IHttpModule Members

        public void Dispose()
```

```
    {
        throw new Exception("The method or operation is not implemented.");
    }

    public void Init(HttpApplication context)
    {
        throw new Exception("The method or operation is not implemented.");
    }

    #endregion
  }
}
```

The `Init` method is the primary method you use to implement functionality. Notice that it has a single method parameter, an `HttpApplication` object named `context`. This parameter gives you access to the current `HttpApplication` context, and it is what you use to wire up the different events that fire during the request processing. The following table shows the events that you can register in the `Init` method.

Event Name	Description
AcquireRequestState	Raised when ASP.NET runtime is ready to acquire the Session State of the current HTTP request.
AuthenticateRequest	Raised when ASP.NET runtime is ready to authenticate the identity of the user.
AuthorizeRequest	Raised when ASP.NET runtime is ready to authorize the user for the resources user is trying to access.
BeginRequest	Raised when ASP.NET runtime receives a new HTTP request.
Disposed	Raised when ASP.NET completes the processing of HTTP request.
EndRequest	Raised just before sending the response content to the client.
Error	Raised when an unhandled exception occurs during the processing of HTTP request.
PostRequestHandlerExecute	Raised just after HTTP handler finishes execution.
PreRequestHandlerExecute	Raised just before ASP.NET begins executing a handler for the HTTP request. After this event, ASP.NET forwards the request to the appropriate HTTP handler.
PreSendRequestContent	Raised just before ASP.NET sends the response contents to the client. This event allows you to change the contents before it gets delivered to the client. You can use this event to add the contents, which are common in all pages, to the page output. For example, a common menu, header, or footer.
PreSendRequestHeaders	Raised just before ASP.NET sends the HTTP response headers to the client. This event allows you to change the headers before they get delivered to the client. You can use this event to add cookies and custom data into headers.

Modifying HTTP Output

Take a look at some examples of using HttpModules. The first example shows a useful way of modifying the HTTP output stream before it is sent to the client. This can be a simple and useful tool if you want to add text to each page served from your Web site, but you do not want to modify each page. For the first example, create a Web project in Visual Studio and add a class to the App_Code directory. The code for this first module is shown in Listing 23-43.

Listing 23-43: Altering the output of an ASP.NET Web page

VB

```vb
Imports Microsoft.VisualBasic
Imports System.Web

Public Class AppendMessage
    Implements IHttpModule

    Dim WithEvents _application As HttpApplication = Nothing

    Public Overridable Sub Init(ByVal context As HttpApplication) _
            Implements IHttpModule.Init
        _application = context
    End Sub

    Public Overridable Sub Dispose() Implements IHttpModule.Dispose

    End Sub

    Public Sub context_PreSendRequestContent(ByVal sender As Object, _
            ByVal e As EventArgs) Handles _application.PreSendRequestContent

        'alter the outgoing content by adding a HTML comment.
        Dim message As String = "<!-- This page has been post processed at " & _
                            System.DateTime.Now.ToString() & _
                            " by a custom HttpModule.-->"

        _application.Context.Response.Output.Write(message)

    End Sub

End Class
```

C#

```csharp
using System;
using System.Collections.Generic;
using System.Text;
using System.Web;

namespace Demo
{
    public class AppendMessage : IHttpModule
    {
        private HttpContext _current = null;

        #region IHttpModule Members
```

```
    public void Dispose()
    {
        throw new Exception("The method or operation is not implemented.");
    }

    public void Init(System.Web.HttpApplication context)
    {
        _current = context.Context;

        context.PreSendRequestContent +=
            new EventHandler(context_PreSendRequestContent);
    }

    void context_PreSendRequestContent(object sender, EventArgs e)
    {
        //alter the outgoing content by adding a HTML comment.
        string message = "<!-- This page has been post processed at " +
                         System.DateTime.Now.ToString() +
                         " by a custom HttpModule.-->";

        _current.Response.Output.Write(message);
    }

    #endregion
}
}
```

You can see that the class stub from Listing 23-42 is expanded here. In the `Init` method, you register the `PreSendRequestContent` event. This event fires right before the content is sent to the client, and you have one last opportunity to modify it.

In the `PreSendRequestContent` handler method, you simply create a string containing an HTML comment that contains the current time. You take this string and write it to the current HTTP requests output stream. The HTTP request is then sent back to the client.

In order to use this module, you must let ASP.NET know that you want to include the module in the request-processing pipeline. You do this is by modifying the `web.config` to contain a reference to the module. Listing 23-44 shows how you can add an httpModules section to your `web.config`.

Listing 23-44: Adding the httpModule configuration to web.config

```
<configuration>
    <system.web>
      <httpModules>
        <add name="AppendMessage" type="AppendMessage, App_code" />
      </httpModules>
    </system.web>
</configuration>
```

The generic format of the httpModules section is

```
<httpModules>
  <add name="modulename" type="namespace.classname, assemblyname" />
</httpModules>
```

If you have created your HttpModule in the `App_Code` directory of an ASP.NET, you might wonder how you know what the `assemblyname` value should be, considering ASP.NET now dynamically compiles this code at runtime. The solution is to use the text `App_Code` as the assembly name. This tells ASP.NET that your module is located in the dynamically created assembly.

You can also create HttpModules as a separate class library in which case you simply use the assembly name of the library.

After you have added this section to your `web.config` file, simply view one of the Web pages from your project in the browser. When you view the page in the browser, you should not notice any difference. But if you view the source of the page, notice the comment you added at the bottom of the HTML. Figure 23-21 shows what you should see when you view the page source.

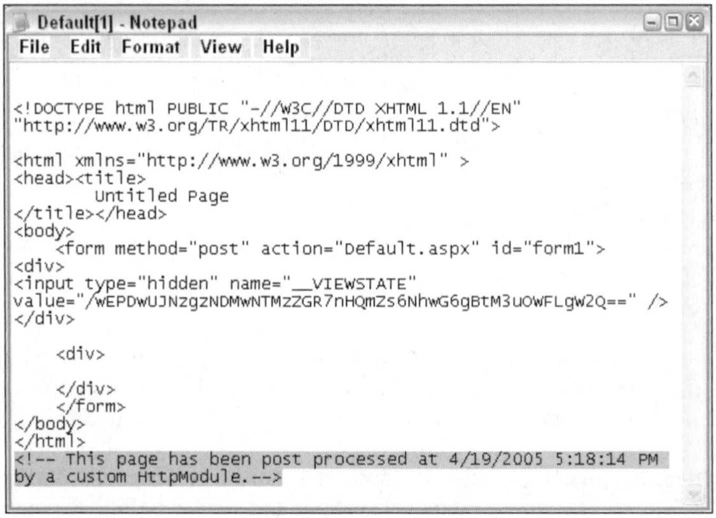

Figure 23-21

URL Rewriting

Another interesting use of an HttpModule is to perform URL rewriting. *URL rewriting* is a technique that allows you to intercept the HTTP request and change the path that was requested to an alternative one. This can be very useful for creating pseudo Web addresses that simplify a URL for the user. For example, the MSDN Library is well-known for its extremely long and cryptic URL paths, such as

```
http://msdn.microsoft.com/library/default.asp?url=/library/en-us/cpref/html/
frlrfSystemWebIHttpModuleClassTopic.asp
```

The problem with this URL is that it is not easy to remember; and even if you do somehow remember it, it is very difficult to type into the browser's Address field. URL rewriting allows you to create friendly URLs that you can parse and redirect to the appropriate resource. The MSDN Library now uses URL rewriting to create friendly URLs. Instead of the cryptic URL you saw previously, you can now use the following URL to access the same resource:

```
http://msdn2.microsoft.com/library/system.web.ihttpmodule.aspx
```

This URL is much shorter, easier to remember, and easier to type into a browser's Address field. You can create your own URL rewriter module to learn how this is done.

To demonstrate this, you create three new Web pages in your project. The first Web page is used to construct a URL using two text boxes. The second serves as the page that accepts the unfriendly querystring, like the MSDN URL shown previously. The third page is used to trick IIS into helping you serve the request. Shortly, we talk about this trick and how to get around it.

Listing 23-45 shows the first Web page you add to the project; it's called `friendlylink.aspx`.

Listing 23-45: The friendlylink.aspx Web page

```
<html xmlns="http://www.w3.org/1999/xhtml" >
<head runat="server">
    <title>Untitled Page</title>
</head>
<body>
    <form id="form1" runat="server">
    <div>
    <a href="John/Smith/trickiis.aspx">Click this friendly link</a>
    </div>
    </form>
</body>
</html>
```

As you can see, you simply created a hyperlink that links to a friendly, easily remembered URL.

Now, create the second page called `unfriendly.aspx`. This is the page that the handle actually executes when a user clicks the hyperlink in the `friendlylink.aspx` page. Listing 23-46 shows how to create `unfriendly.aspx`.

Listing 23-46: The unfriendly.aspx Web page

VB

```
<%@ Page Language="VB" %>

<script runat="server">
    Protected Sub Page_Load(ByVal sender As Object, _
            ByVal e As System.EventArgs) Handles Me.Load
        Label1.Text = Request("firstname").ToString() & _
            " " & Request("lastname").ToString()
    End Sub
</script>
<html xmlns="http://www.w3.org/1999/xhtml" >
<head runat="server">
    <title>Unfriendly Web Page</title>
</head>
<body>
    <form id="form1" runat="server">
        <div>
        Welcome to the unfriendly URL page <asp:Label ID="Label1"
            runat="server" Text="Label"></asp:Label>
```

(continued)

Listing 23-46: *(continued)*

```
            </div>
        </form>
    </body>
    </html>
```

C#
```
<script runat="server">
    protected void Page_Load(object sender, EventArgs e)
    {
        Label1.Text = Request("firstname").ToString() +
            " " + Request("lastname").ToString();
    }
</script>
```

Next, you create the directory and file that the hyperlink in `friendlyurl.aspx` points to. The
`trickiis.aspx` page can simply be an empty Web page because you are not really going to execute it.

Finally, you create a new module that parses the request path and rewrites the URL to the page you
want to execute. To do this, create another class in the `App_Code` directory called `SimpleRewriter`.
Listing 23-47 shows the code for this.

Listing 23-47: A sample URL rewriting HttpModule

VB
```
Imports Microsoft.VisualBasic
Imports System.Web

Public Class SimpleRewriter
    Implements System.Web.IHttpModule

    Dim WithEvents _application As HttpApplication = Nothing

    Public Overridable Sub Init(ByVal context As HttpApplication) _
            Implements IHttpModule.Init
        _application = context
    End Sub

    Public Overridable Sub Dispose() Implements IHttpModule.Dispose

    End Sub

    Public Sub context_BeginRequest(ByVal sender As Object, ByVal e As EventArgs) _
            Handles _application.BeginRequest

        Dim requesturl As String = _
            _application.Context.Request.Path.Substring(0, _
            _application.Context.Request.Path.LastIndexOf("/"c))

        'Here is where we parse the original request url to determine
        ' the querystring parameters for the unfriendly url
        Dim parameters() As String = _
```

```vb
                requesturl.Split(New [Char]() {"/"c}, _
                    StringSplitOptions.RemoveEmptyEntries)

        If (parameters.Length > 1) Then
            Dim firstname As String = parameters(1)
            Dim lastname As String = parameters(2)

            'Rewrite the request path
            _application.Context.RewritePath("~/unfriendly.aspx?firstname=" & _
                firstname & "&lastname=" & lastname)
        End If
    End Sub

End Class
```

C#

```csharp
using System.Web;

public class SimpleRewriter: System.Web.IHttpModule
{

    HttpApplication _application = null;

    public void Init(HttpApplication context)
    {
        context.BeginRequest+=new System.EventHandler(context_BeginRequest);
        _application = context;
    }

    public void Dispose()
    {
    }

    private void context_BeginRequest(object sender, System.EventArgs e)
    {
        string requesturl =
            _application.Context.Request.Path.Substring(0,
                _application.Context.Request.Path.LastIndexOf("//")
            );

        //Here is where we parse the original request url to determine
        //the querystring parameters for the unfriendly url
        string[] parameters = requesturl.Split(new char[] {'/'});
        if (parameters.Length > 1)
        {
            string firstname = parameters[1];
            string lastname = parameters[2];

            //Rewrite the request path
            _application.Context.RewritePath("~/unfriendly.aspx?firstname=" +
                firstname + "&lastname=" + lastname);
        }
    }
}
```

As you can see from the listing, in this sample you use the BeginRequest event in the HttpModule to parse the incoming HTTP request path and create a new URL that you execute. Normally, when you click the hyperlink on `friendlyurl.aspx`, an HTTP request is sent to the server for execution and then IIS returns the page asked for in the hyperlink. In this case, you make a request for this page:

```
http://localhost:1234/WebProject1/John/Smith/trickiis.aspx
```

But, because you put the HttpModule in the request-processing pipeline, you can modify the HTTP request and change its behavior. The code in the `BeginRequest` method of the module parses the request path to create a querystring that the `unfriendly.aspx` page can understand and execute. So when you execute the code in the listing, you convert the original path into the following:

```
http://localhost:1234/WebProject1/unfriendly.aspx?var1=John&var2=Smith
```

This URL is, as the page name states, not very friendly; and the user is less likely to remember and be able to type this URL. Finally, the module uses the `RewritePath` method to tell ASP.NET that you want to rewrite the path to execute for this request.

After you have completed creating the code for this sample, try loading `friendlyurl.aspx` into a browser. When you click the hyperlink on the page, you should notice two things. First, notice that the URL in the browser's address bar shows that you have been served the page you requested, `trickiis.aspx`, but the contents of the page show that you are actually served `unfriendly.aspx`. Figure 23-22 shows what the browser looks like.

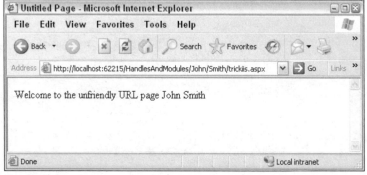

Figure 23-22

IIS WildCards

There is, however, a drawback to this type of URL rewriting. When IIS receives a request to serve a resource, it first checks to see if the resource exists. If the resource does exist, the request is passed to the appropriate handler; in this case, the handler is ASP.NET, which processes the request. IIS then returns the results to the client. However, if the requested resource does not exist, IIS returns a `404 File Not Found` error to the client. It never hands the request to ASP.NET. In order for a module to execute, you must create an endpoint that actually exists on the Web server.

In the case of this example, you actually create a `/WebProject1/John/Smith/trickiis.aspx` page in order to fool IIS. Otherwise, it simply returns a 404 error. This can be a problem if you find you are creating a large number of directories or resources just to enable URL rewriting. However, a solution to this problem exists in IIS: wildcards. *Wildcards* allow you tell IIS that it should use a particular executable to process all incoming requests, regardless of the requested paths or file extensions. In this sample, adding a wildcard fixes the problem of having to create a dummy endpoint for the module.

Adding Wildcards in IIS 5

To add a wildcard mapping in IIS 5, start by opening the IIS Management Console. After the console is open, right-click on the Web site you want to modify and select the Properties option from the context menu. When the Properties dialog opens, select the Configuration button from the Home Directory Tab. The Configuration dialog is where you can create new or modify existing application extension mappings. If you take a moment to look at the existing mappings, you see that most of the familiar file extensions (such as .aspx, .asp, and .html) are configured.

To add the wildcard that you need to create a new mapping, click the Add button. The Add Application Extension Mapping dialog is shown in Figure 23-23. You create a mapping that directs IIS to use the ASP.NET ISAPI DLL to process every incoming request. To do this, simply put the full path to the ISAPI DLL (usually something like C:\WINDOWS\Microsoft.NET\Framework\v1.1.4322\aspnet_isapi .dll) in the Executable field. For the extension, simply use .*, which indicates any file extension.

Additionally, you uncheck the Check That File Exists check box to tell IIS not to check whether the requested file exists before processing (because you know that it doesn't).

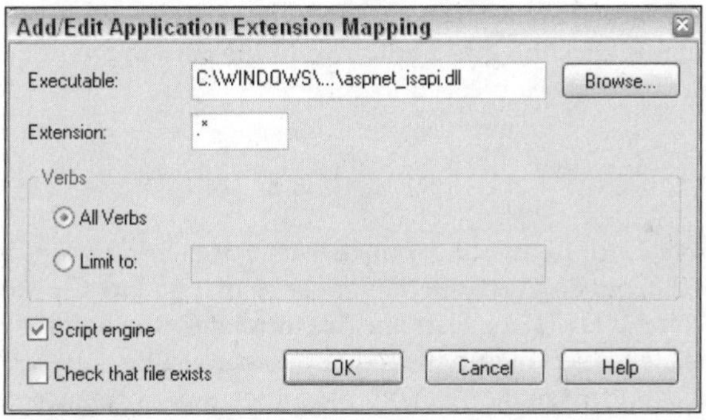

Figure 23-23

Now you don't have to add the stub file to your Web site. IIS will pass any request that it receives to ASP.NET for processing, regardless of whether the file exists.

Adding Wildcards in IIS 6

Adding Wildcards in IIS 6 is similar to adding wildcards in IIS 5. Open the IIS Management Console, and then open the Properties dialog for the Web site you want to modify. Next, click the Configuration button on the Home Directory tab.

The Application Extension Configuration dialog in IIS is slightly different. Wildcard application maps now have their own separate listing, as shown in Figure 23-24.

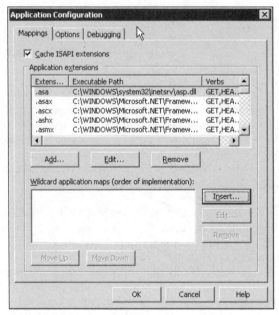

Figure 23-24

To add a wildcard mapping, click the Insert button, add the path to the ASP.NET ISAPI DLL, and make sure the Verify That File Exists check box is unchecked.

HttpHandlers

HttpHandlers differ from HttpModules, not only because of their positions in the request-processing pipeline (see Figure 23-20), but also because they must be mapped to a specific file extension. Handlers are the last stop for incoming HTTP requests and are ultimately the point in the request-processing pipeline that is responsible for serving up the requested content, be it an ASPX page, HTML, plain text, or an image. Additionally, HttpHandlers can offer significant performance gains

In this section, we demonstrate two different ways to create a simple HttpHandler that you can use to serve up dynamic images. First, you look at creating an HttpHandler using an ASHX file extension. Then you learn how you get even more control by mapping your HttpHandler to a custom file extension using IIS.

Generic Handlers

In previous versions of Visual Studio, HttpHandlers were somewhat hard to understand and create. This was because little documentation was included to help developers understand handlers, and Visual Studio did not provide any friendly methods for creating them.

This has changed in Visual Studio 2005, which comes with a standard template for HttpHandlers to help you get started. To add an HttpHandler to your project, you simply select the Generic Handler file type from the Add New Item dialog. Figure 23-25 shows this dialog with the file type selected.

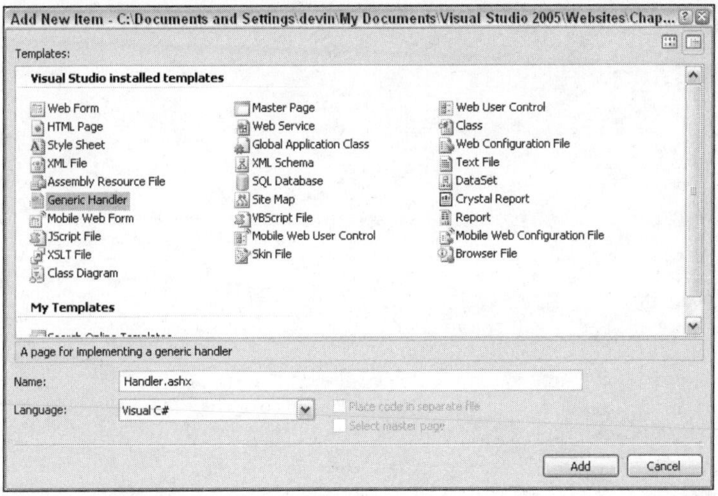

Figure 23-25

You can see that when you add the Generic Handler file to your project, it adds a file with an `.ashx` extension. The `.ashx` file extension is the default HttpHandler file extension set up by ASP.NET. Remember that HttpHandlers must be mapped to a unique file extension, so by default ASP.NET uses the `.ashx` extension. This is convenient because, otherwise, you would be responsible for adding the file extension yourself. This is obviously not always possible, nor is it practical. Using the Custom Handler file type helps you avoid any extra configuration.

Notice the class stub that the file type automatically creates for you. Listing 23-48 shows the class.

Listing 23-48: The IHttpHandler page template

VB

```vb
<%@ WebHandler Language="VB" Class="Handler" %>

Imports System.Web

Public Class Handler
    Implements IHttpHandler

    Public Sub ProcessRequest(ByVal context As HttpContext) _
            Implements IHttpHandler.ProcessRequest
        context.Response.ContentType = "text/plain"
        context.Response.Write("Hello World")
    End Sub

    Public ReadOnly Property IsReusable() As Boolean _
            Implements IHttpHandler.IsReusable
        Get
            Return False
        End Get
```

(continued)

941

Listing 23-48: *(continued)*

```
    End Property

End Class
```

C#
```
<%@ WebHandler Language="C#" Class="Handler" %>

using System.Web;

public class Handler : IHttpHandler {

    public void ProcessRequest (HttpContext context) {
        context.Response.ContentType = "text/plain";
        context.Response.Write("Hello World");
    }

    public bool IsReusable {
        get {
            return false;
        }
    }

}
```

Notice that the stub implements the IHttpHandler interface, which requires the `ProcessRequest` method and `IsReusable` property. The `ProcessRequest` method is the method we use to actually process the incoming HTTP request. By default, the class stub changes the content type to plain and then writes the `"Hello World"` string to the output stream. The `IsReusable` property simply lets ASP.NET know if incoming HTTP requests can reuse the sample instance of this HttpHandler.

By default, this handler is ready to run right away. Try executing the handler in your browser and see what happens. The interesting thing to note about this handler is that because it changes the content to text/plain, browsers handle the responses from this handler in potentially very different ways depending on a number of factors:

❑ Browser type and version

❑ Applications loaded on the system that may map to the MIME type

❑ Operating system and service pack level

Based on these factors, you might see the text returned in the browser, you might see Notepad open and display the text, or you might receive the Open/Save/Cancel prompt from IE. Make sure you understand the potential consequences of changing the ContentType header.

You can continue the example by modifying it to return an actual file. In this case, you use the handler to return an image. To do this, you simply modify the code in the `ProcessRequest` method, as shown in Listing 23-49.

Listing 23-49: Outputting an image from an HttpHandler

VB

```vb
<%@ WebHandler Language="VB" Class="Handler" %>

Imports System.Web

Public Class Handler : Implements IHttpHandler

    Public Sub ProcessRequest(ByVal context As HttpContext) _
            Implements IHttpHandler.ProcessRequest
        'Logic to retrieve the image file
        context.Response.ContentType = "image/jpeg"
        context.Response.WriteFile("Sunset.jpg")
    End Sub

    Public ReadOnly Property IsReusable() As Boolean _
            Implements IHttpHandler.IsReusable
        Get
            Return False
        End Get
    End Property

End Class
```

C#

```csharp
<%@ WebHandler Language="C#" Class="Handler" %>

using System.Web;

public class Handler : IHttpHandler {

    public void ProcessRequest (HttpContext context) {
        //Logic to retrieve the image file
        context.Response.ContentType = "image/jpeg"
        context.Response.WriteFile("Sunset.jpg")
    }

    public bool IsReusable {
        get {
            return false;
        }
    }
}
```

As you can see, you simply change the ContentType to image/jpeg to indicate that you are returning a JPEG image; then you use the `WriteFile()` method to write an image file to the output stream. Load the handler into a browser, and you see that the handler displays the image. Figure 23-26 shows the resulting Web page.

Now, you create a simple Web page to display the image handler. Listing 23-50 shows code for the Web page.

Figure 23-26

Listing 23-50: A sample Web page using the HttpHandler for the image source

```
<!DOCTYPE html PUBLIC "-//W3C//DTD XHTML 1.1//EN"
"http://www.w3.org/TR/xhtml11/DTD/xhtml11.dtd">

<html xmlns="http://www.w3.org/1999/xhtml" >
<head runat="server">
    <title>HttpHandler Serving an Image</title>
</head>
<body>
    <form id="form1" runat="server">
    <div>
        <img src="Handler.ashx" />
    </div>
    </form>
</body>
</html>
```

Although this sample is simple, you can enhance it by passing querystring parameters to your handler and using them to perform additional logic in the handler. For instance, you can pass an ID in to dynamically retrieve an image from a SQL database and return it to the client, like this:

```
<img src="ImageHandler.ashx?imageid=123" />
```

Mapping a File Extension in IIS

Although using the .ashx file extension is convenient, you might want to create an HTTP handler for a custom file extension or even for a commonly used extension. Use the code from the image handler to demonstrate this.

Create a new class in the App_Code directory of your Web project. You can simply copy the code from the existing image handler control into this class, as shown in Listing 23-51. Notice that you removed the WebHandler directive because this is only a class and not a generic handler control. Other than that, the code is the same.

Listing 23-51: The class-based image HttpHandler

VB
```vb
Imports System.Web

Public Class MappedHandler : Implements IHttpHandler

    Public Sub ProcessRequest(ByVal context As HttpContext) _
            Implements IHttpHandler.ProcessRequest
        context.Response.ContentType = "image/jpeg"
        context.Response.WriteFile("Sunset.jpg")
    End Sub

    Public ReadOnly Property IsReusable() As Boolean _
            Implements IHttpHandler.IsReusable
        Get
            Return False
        End Get
    End Property

End Class
```

C#
```csharp
using System.Web;

public class MappedHandler : IHttpHandler {

    public void ProcessRequest (HttpContext context) {
        //Logic to retrieve the image file
        context.Response.ContentType = "image/jpeg";
        context.Response.WriteFile("Sunset.jpg");
    }

    public bool IsReusable {
        get {
            return false;
        }
    }

}
```

After your class is added, configure the application to show which file extension this handler serves. You do this by adding an httpHandlers section to web.config. Listing 23-52 shows the section to add for the image handler.

Listing 23-52: Adding the HttpHandler configuration information to web.config

```
<httpHandlers>
    <add verb="*" path="ImageHandler.img" type="MappedHandler, App_Code" />
</httpHandlers>
```

In the configuration section, you direct the application to use the MappedHandler class to process incoming requests for ImageHandler.img. You can also specify wildcards for the path. Specifying *.img for the path indicates that you want the application to use the MappedHandler class to process any request with the .img file extension. Specifying * indicates that you want all requests to the application to be processed using the handler.

Load the ImageHandler.img file into a browser and, again, you should see that it serves up the image. Figure 23-27 shows the results. Notice the path in the browser's address bar leads directly to the ImageHandler.img file.

HttpHandler responds to custom file extension

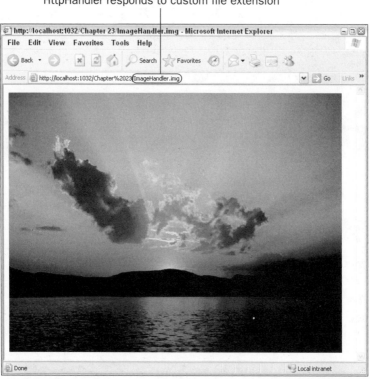

Figure 23-27

Summary

In this chapter, you learned a number of ways you can create reusable, encapsulated chunks of code. You first looked at user controls, the simplest form of control creation. You learned how to create user controls and how you can make them interact with their host Web page. Creating user controls is quite easy, but they lack the portability of other control-creation options.

Next, you saw how you can create your own custom server controls. You looked at many of the tools you can create by writing custom server controls, and these range from tools for emitting HTML and creating CSS styles and JavaScript to applying themes. The chapter also discussed the type of server controls you can create, ranging from server controls that simply inherit from the WebControl class to templated controls that give the control's user the power to define the display of the server control.

Next, I switched gears and talked about HttpModules. Modules give you the power to plug yourself directly into the ASP.NET page-processing pipeline. The events provided to an HttpModule give you great power and flexibility to customize your applications.

Finally, you looked at HttpHandlers. Handlers allow you to skip the ASP.NET page-processing pipeline completely and have 100 percent control over how the framework serves up requested data. You learned how to create your own image handler and then map the handler to any file or file extension you want.

As I said in the beginning of this chapter, an entire book could be written on these four topics alone; but I hope you have learned enough to feel motivated to continue exploring the topics discussed in this chapter.

Using Business Objects

One of the best practices in programming is to separate your application into workable and separate components — also known as *business objects*. This makes your applications far easier to manage and enables you to achieve the goal of code reuse because you can share these components among different parts of the same application or between entirely separate applications.

Using business components enables you to build your ASP.NET applications using a true 3-tier model where the business tier is in the middle between the presentation and data tiers. In addition, using business objects allows you to use multiple languages within your ASP.NET applications. Business objects can be developed in one programming language while the code used for the presentation logic is developed in another.

If you are moving any legacy applications or aspects of these applications to an ASP.NET environment, you might find that you need to utilize various COM components. This chapter shows you how to use both .NET and COM components in your ASP.NET pages and code.

This chapter also explains how you can mingle old ActiveX (COM) DLLs with new .NET components. So when all is said and done, you should feel somewhat relieved. You will see that you have not wasted all the effort you put into building componentized applications using the "latest" ActiveX technologies.

Using Business Objects in ASP.NET 2.0

Chapter 3 provides an introduction to using .NET business objects within your ASP.NET 2.0 applications. ASP.NET now includes a new folder, \App_Code, which you can place within your ASP.NET applications to hold all your .NET business objects. The nice thing about the App_Code folder is that you can simply place your uncompiled .NET objects (such as Calculator.vb or Calculator.cs) into this folder and ASP.NET takes care of compiling the objects into usable .NET business objects.

Chapter 3 also shows how you can place within the App_Code folder multiple custom folders that allow you to use business objects written in different programming languages. Using this method enables ASP.NET to compile each business object into the appropriate DLLs to be used by your ASP.NET applications.

Creating Precompiled .NET Business Objects

Even though the App_Code folder is there for your use, you might choose instead to precompile your business objects into DLLs to be used by your ASP.NET 2.0 applications. This is the method that was utilized prior to ASP.NET 2.0 and is still a method that is available today. You also might not have a choice if you are receiving your .NET business objects only as DLLs.

First look at how to create a simple .NET business object using Visual Studio 2005. The first step is not to create an ASP.NET project but to choose File ⇨ New Project from the Visual Studio menu. This launches the New Project dialog. From this dialog, select Class Library as the project type and name the project Calculator (see Figure 24-1).

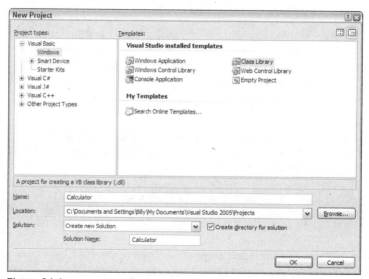

Figure 24-1

Using the Class1.vb or Class1.cs file that is created in the project for you, modify the class to be a simple calculator with Add, Subtract, Multiply, and Divide functions. This is illustrated using Visual Basic in Figure 24-2.

One point to pay attention to when you build your .NET components is the assembly's metadata that is stored along with the assembly. Looking at the project's properties, click the Application tab (the first tab available). On this tab's page, you will find a button labeled Assembly Information. Clicking this button gives you a dialog where you can put in all the business object's metadata, including the assembly's versioning information (see Figure 24-3).

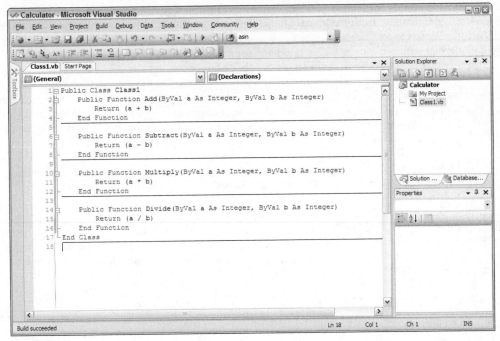

Figure 24-2

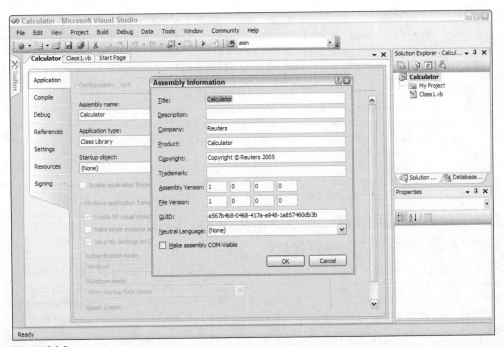

Figure 24-3

You are now ready to compile the business object into a usable object. To accomplish this task, choose Build ➪ Build Calculator from the Visual Studio menu. This process compiles everything contained in this solution down to a `Calculator.dll` file. You will find this DLL in your project's bin\debug folder. By default, that will be `C:\Documents and Settings\[user]\My Documents\Visual Studio 2005\Projects\Calculator\Calculator\bin\Debug\Calculator.dll`.

Besides using Visual Studio 2005 to build and compile your business objects into DLLs, you can also accomplish this yourself manually. In Notepad, you simply create the same class file as was shown in Figure 24-2 and save the file as `Calculator.vb` or `Calculator.cs` depending on the language you are using. After saving the file, you need to compile the class into an assembly (a DLL).

The .NET Framework provides you with a compiler for each of the targeted languages. This book focuses on the Visual Basic 2005 and C# 2005 compilers that come with the Framework.

To compile this class, open the Visual Studio 2005 Command Prompt found at All Programs ➪ Microsoft Visual Studio 2005 ➪ Visual Studio Tools ➪ Visual Studio 2005 Command Prompt. From the provided DOS prompt, navigate to the directory that is holding your `Calculator` class (an example navigation command is `cd c:\My Files`). From the DOS prompt, type the following command if you are using the Visual Basic compiler:

```
vbc /t:library Calculator.vb
```

If your class is in C#, you use the following command:

```
csc /t:library Calculator.cs
```

As stated, each language uses its own compiler. Visual Basic uses the `vbc.exe` compiler found at `C:\Windows\Microsoft.NET\Framework\v2.0xxxxx\`. You will find the C# compiler, `csc.exe`, contained in the same folder. In the preceding examples, `/t:library` states that you are interested in compiling the `Calculator.vb` (or `.cs`) class file into a DLL and not an executable (`.exe`), which is the default. Following the `t:/library` command is the name of the file to be compiled.

There are many different commands you can give the compiler, even more than Visual Studio 2005 offers. For example, if you want to make references to specific DLLs in your assembly, you will have to add commands such as `/r:system.data.dll`. To get a full list of all the compiler options, check out the MSDN documentation.

After you have run the commands through the compiler, the DLL is created and ready to go.

Using Precompiled Business Objects in Your ASP.NET Applications

To use any DLLs in your ASP.NET 2.0 project, you need to create a `Bin` folder in the root directory of your application by right-clicking on the project within the Solution Explorer and selecting Add Folder ➪ Bin Folder. In Visual Studio 2005, the `Bin` directory's icon appears as a gray folder with a gear next to it. Add your new DLL to this folder by right-clicking on the folder and selecting the Add Reference option from the menu provided. This launches the Add Reference dialog. From this dialog, select the Browse tab and browse till you find the `Calculator.dll`. When you find it, highlight the DLL and press OK to add it to the `Bin` folder of your project. This dialog is illustrated in Figure 24-4.

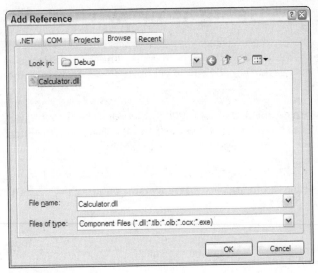

Figure 24-4

`Calculator.dll` is added to your project and is now accessible by the entire project. This means that you now have access to all the functions exposed through this interface. Figure 24-5 shows an example of how IntelliSense makes exploring this .NET component easier than ever.

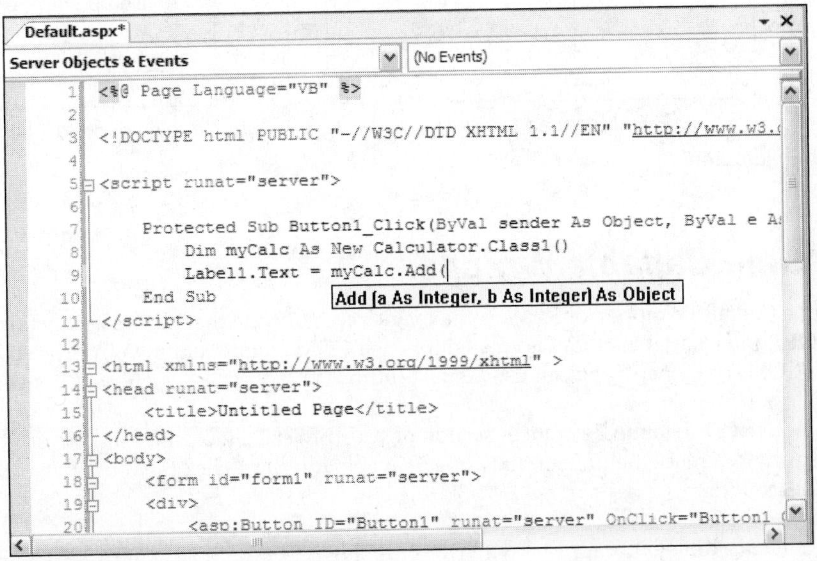

Figure 24-5

As you can see, it is rather simple to create .NET components and use them in your ASP.NET applications. Next, let's look at using COM components.

COM Interop: Using COM within .NET

Microsoft knows that every one of its legions of developers out there would be quite disappointed if they couldn't use the thousands of COM controls that it has built, maintained, and improved over the years. Microsoft knows that nobody would get up and walk away from these controls to a purely .NET world.

To this end, Microsoft has provided us with COM Interoperability. COM Interop (for short) is a technology that enables .NET to wrap the functionality of a COM object with the interface of a .NET component so that your .NET code can communicate with the COM object without having to use COM techniques and interfaces in your code.

Figure 24-6 illustrates the Runtime Callable Wrapper, the middle component that directs traffic between the .NET code and the COM component.

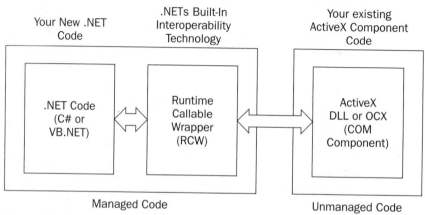

Figure 24-6

The Runtime Callable Wrapper

The Runtime Callable Wrapper, or RCW, is the magic piece of code that allows interaction to occur between .NET and COM. One RCW is created for each COM component in your project. To create an RCW for a COM component, you can use Visual Studio 2005.

To add an ActiveX DLL to the References section of your project, choose Website ➪ Add Reference or choose the Add Reference menu item that appears when you right-click the root node of your project in the Solution Explorer.

The Add Reference dialog box appears with five tabs: .NET, COM, Projects, Browse, and Recent, as shown in Figure 24-7. For this example, select the COM tab and locate the component that you want to add to your .NET project. After you have located the component, highlight the item and click OK to add a reference to the component to your project. The newly added component will then be found inside a newly created Bin folder in your project.

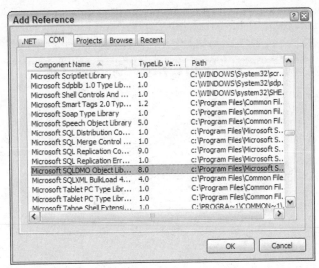

Figure 24-7

Your Interop library is automatically created for you from the ActiveX DLL that you told Visual Studio 2005 to use. This Interop library is the RCW component customized for your ActiveX control, as shown previously in Figure 24-6. The name of the Interop file is simply `Interop.OriginalName.DLL`.

It is also possible to create the RCW files manually instead of doing it through Visual Studio 2005. In the .NET Framework, you will find a method to create RCW Interop files for controls manually through a command-line tool called the Type Library Importer. You invoke the Type Library Importer by using the `tlbimp.exe` executable.

For example, to create the Interop library for the SQLDMO object used earlier, start up a Visual Studio 2005 Command Prompt from the Microsoft Visual Studio 2005 ⇨ Visual Studio Tools group within your Start Menu. From the comment prompt, type

```
tlbimp sqldmo.dll /out:sqldmoex.dll
```

In this example, the `/out:` parameter specifies the name of the RCW Interop library to be created. If you omit this parameter, you get the same name that Visual Studio would generate for you.

The Type Library Importer is useful when you are not using Visual Studio 2005 as your development environment, if you want to have more control over the assemblies that get created for you, or if you are automating the process of connecting to COM components.

The Type Library Importer is a wrapper application around the `TypeLibConvertor` class of the `System .Runtime.InteropServices` namespace.

Using COM objects in ASP.NET code

To continue working through some additional examples, you next take a look at a simple example of using a COM object written in Visual Basic 6 within an ASP.NET page.

In the first step, you create an ActiveX DLL that you can use for the upcoming examples. Add the Visual Basic 6 code shown in Listing 24-1 to a class called NameFunctionsClass and compile it as an ActiveX DLL called NameComponent.dll.

Listing 24-1: VB6 code for ActiveX DLL, NameComponent.DLL

```
Option Explicit

Private m_sFirstName As String
Private m_sLastName As String

Public Property Let FirstName(Value As String)
  m_sFirstName = Value
End Property

Public Property Get FirstName() As String
  FirstName = m_sFirstName
End Property

Public Property Let LastName(Value As String)
  m_sLastName = Value
End Property

Public Property Get LastName() As String
  LastName = m_sLastName
End Property

Public Property Let FullName(Value As String)
  m_sFirstName = Split(Value, " ")(0)
  If (InStr(Value, " ") > 0) Then
    m_sLastName = Split(Value, " ")(1)
  Else
    m_sLastName = ""
  End If
End Property

Public Property Get FullName() As String
  FullName = m_sFirstName + " " + m_sLastName
End Property

Public Property Get FullNameLength() As Long
  FullNameLength = Len(Me.FullName)
End Property
```

Now that you have created an ActiveX DLL to use in your ASP.NET pages, the next step is to create a new ASP.NET project using Visual Studio 2005. Replace the HTML code in the Default.aspx file with the HTML code illustrated in Listing 24-2. This adds a number of text boxes and labels to the HTML page, as well as the Visual Basic or C# code for the functionality.

Listing 24-2: Using the NameComponent.dll

VB

```
<%@ Page Language="VB" %>

<script runat="server">
  Protected Sub AnalyzeName_Click(ByVal sender As Object, _
     ByVal e As System.EventArgs)

    Dim Name As New NameComponent.NameFunctionsClass()

    If (FirstName.Text.Length > 0) Then
      Name.FirstName = FirstName.Text
    End If

    If (LastName.Text.Length > 0) Then
      Name.LastName = LastName.Text
    End If

    If (FullName.Text.Length > 0) Then
      Name.FullName = FullName.Text
    End If

    FirstName.Text = Name.FirstName
    LastName.Text = Name.LastName
    FullName.Text = Name.FullName
    FullNameLength.Text = Name.FullNameLength.ToString

  End Sub
</script>

<html xmlns="http://www.w3.org/1999/xhtml" >
  <head runat="server">
     <title>Using COM Components</title>
  </head>
  <body>
    <form id="form1" runat="server">
      <P>
        <asp:Label ID="Label1" runat="server">First Name:</asp:Label>
         
        <asp:TextBox ID="FirstName" runat="server"></asp:TextBox>
      </P>
      <P>
        <asp:Label ID="Label2" runat="server">Last Name:</asp:Label>
         
        <asp:TextBox ID="LastName" runat="server"></asp:TextBox>
      </P>
      <P>
        <asp:Label ID="Label3" runat="server">Full Name:</asp:Label>
         
        <asp:TextBox ID="FullName" runat="server"></asp:TextBox>
      </P>
      <P>
```

(continued)

Listing 24-2: *(continued)*

```
          <asp:Label ID="Label4" runat="server">Full Name Length:</asp:Label>
           
          <asp:Label ID="FullNameLength" runat="server"
           Font-Bold="True">0</asp:Label>
       </P>
       <P>
         <asp:Button ID="AnalyzeName" runat="server"
          OnClick="AnalyzeName_Click" Text="Analyze Name"></asp:Button>
       </P>
     </form>
   </body>
</html>
```

C#

```csharp
<%@ Page Language="C#" %>

<script runat="server">
  protected void AnalyzeName_Click(object sender, System.EventArgs e)
  {
    NameComponent.NameFunctionsClass Name =
       new NameComponent.NameFunctionsClass();

    if (FirstName.Text.Length > 0)
    {
      Name.FirstName = FirstName.Text.ToString();
      Name.set_FirstName(ref FirstName);
    }

    if (LastName.Text.Length > 0)
    {
      Name.LastName = LastName.Text.ToString();
      Name.set_LastName(ref LastName);
    }

    if (txtFullName.Text.Length > 0)
    {
      Name.FullName = FullName.Text.ToString();
      Name.set_FullName(ref FullName);
    }

    FirstName.Text = Name.get_FirstName();
    LastName.Text = Name.get_LastName();
    FullName.Text = Name.get_FullName();
    FullNameLength.Text = Name.FullNameLength.ToString();
  }
</script>
```

Now you need to add the reference to the ActiveX DLL that you created in the previous step. To do so, follow these steps:

1. Right-click your project in the Solution Explorer dialog.

2. Select the Add Reference menu item.

3. In the Add Reference dialog box, select the fourth tab, Browse.

4. Locate the `NameComponent.dll` by browsing to its location.

5. Click the OK button to add `NameComponent.dll` to the list of selected components and close the dialog.

> *If you are not using Visual Studio 2005 or code-behind pages, you can still add a reference to your COM control by creating the RCW manually using the Type Library Converter and then placing an* `Imports` *statement (VB) or* `using` *statement (C#) in the page.*

After you have selected your component using the Add Reference dialog, an RCW file is created for the component and added to your application.

That's all there is to it! Simply run the application to see the COM interoperability layer in action.

Figure 24-8 shows the ASP.NET page that you created. When the Analyze Name button is clicked, the fields in the First Name, Last Name, and Full Name text boxes are sent to the RCW to be passed to the `NameComponent.DLL` ActiveX component. Data is retrieved in the same manner to repopulate the text boxes and to indicate the length of the full name.

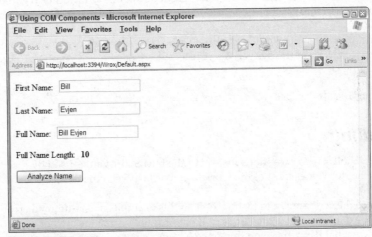

Figure 24-8

Accessing Tricky COM Members in C#

Sometimes, some members of COM objects do not expose themselves properly to C#. In the preceding examples, the `String` properties did not expose themselves, but the `Long` property (`FullNameLength`) did.

You know when there is a problem because, although you can see the property, you cannot compile the application. For instance, instead of the code shown in Listing 24-2 for C#, use the following piece of code to set the `FirstName` property of the `NameComponent.dll` ActiveX component:

```
if (FirstName.Text.Length > 0)
  Name.FirstName = FirstName.Text.ToString();
```

When you try to compile this code, you get the following error:

```
c:\inetpub\wwwroot\wrox\Default.aspx.cs(67): Property, indexer, or event
'FirstName' is not supported by the language; try directly calling accessor methods
'NameComponent.NameFunctionsClass.get_FirstName()' or
'NameComponent.NameFunctionsClass.set_FirstName(ref string)'
```

The `FirstName` property seems to be fine. It shows up in IntelliSense, but you can't use it. Instead, you must use `set_FirstName` (and `get_FirstName` to read). These methods do not show up in IntelliSense, but rest assured, they exist.

Furthermore, these methods expect a `ref string` parameter rather than a `String`. In the example from Listing 24-2, two steps are used to do this properly. First, `String` is assigned to a local variable, and then the variable is passed to the method using `ref`.

Releasing COM Objects Manually

One of the great things about .NET is that it has its own garbage collection — it can clean up after itself. This isn't always the case when using COM interoperability, however. .NET has no way of knowing when to release a COM object from memory because it doesn't have the built-in garbage collection mechanism that .NET relies on.

Because of this limitation, you should release COM objects from memory as soon as possible using the `ReleaseComObject` class of the `System.Runtime.InteropServices.Marshal` class:

C#
```
System.Runtime.InteropServices.Marshal.ReleaseComObject(Object);
```

Error Handling

Error handling in .NET uses exceptions instead of the HRESULT values used by Visual Basic 6 applications. Luckily, the RCW does most of the work to convert between the two.

Take for instance the code shown in Listing 24-3. In this example, a user-defined error is raised if the numerator or the denominator is greater than 1000. Also notice that we are not capturing a divide by zero error. Notice what happens when the ActiveX component raises the error on its own.

Begin this example by compiling the code listed in Listing 24-3 into a class named `DivideClass` within an ActiveX component called `DivideComponent.dll`.

Listing 24-3: Raising errors in VB6

```vb
Public Function DivideNumber(Numerator As Double, _
                            Denominator As Double) As Double

  If ((Numerator > 1000) Or (Denominator > 1000)) Then
      Err.Raise vbObjectError + 1, _
              "DivideComponent:Divide.DivideNumber", _
              "Numerator and denominator both have to " + _
              "be less than or equal to 1000."

  End If

  DivideNumber = Numerator / Denominator

End Function
```

Next, create a new ASP.NET project; add a reference to the `DivideComponent.dll` (invoking Visual Studio 2005 to create its own copy of the RCW). Remember, you can also do this manually by using the `tlbimp` executable.

Now add the code shown in Listing 24-4 to an ASP.NET page.

Listing 24-4: Error handling in .NET

VB

```vb
<%@ Page Language="VB" %>

<script runat="server">
  Protected Sub Calculate_Click(ByVal sender As Object, _
     ByVal e As System.EventArgs)

    Dim Divide As New DivideComponent.DivideClass()

    Try
       Answer.Text = Divide.DivideNumber(Numerator.Text, Denominator.Text)
    Catch ex As Exception
       Answer.Text = ex.Message.ToString()
    End Try

    System.Runtime.InteropServices.Marshal.ReleaseComObject(Divide)

  End Sub
</script>

<html xmlns="http://www.w3.org/1999/xhtml" >
  <body>
  <head runat="server">
     <title>Using COM Components</title>
  </head>
    <form id="form1" runat="server">
      <P>
         <asp:Label ID="Label1" runat="server">Numerator:</asp:Label>
          
         <asp:TextBox ID="Numerator" runat="server"></asp:TextBox>
      </P>
```

(continued)

Listing 24-4: *(continued)*

```
      <P>
        <asp:Label ID="Label2" runat="server">Denominator:</asp:Label>
         
        <asp:TextBox ID="Denominator" runat="server"></asp:TextBox>
      </P>
      <P>
        <asp:Label ID="Label3" runat="server">
         Numerator divided by Denominator:</asp:Label>
         
        <asp:Label ID="Answer" runat="server" Font-Bold="True">0</asp:Label>
      </P>
      <P>
        <asp:Button ID="Calculate"
         runat="server"
         OnClick="Calculate_Click"
         Text="Calculate">
        </asp:Button>
      </P>
    </form>
  </body>
</html>
```

C#

```
<%@ Page Language="C#" %>

<script runat="server">
  protected void Calculate_Click(object sender, System.EventArgs e)
  {

    DivideComponent.DivideClass myDivide = new DivideComponent.DivideClass();

    try
    {
      Answer.Text = Divide.DivideNumber(Numerator.Text, Denominator.Text);
    }

    catch (Exception ex)
    {
      Answer.Text = ex.Message.ToString();
    }

    System.Runtime.InteropServices.Marshal.ReleaseComObject(myDivide);

  }
</script>
```

The code in Listing 24-4 passes the user-entered values for the Numerator and Denominator to the DivideComponent.dll ActiveX component for it to divide. Running the application with invalid data gives the result shown in Figure 24-9.

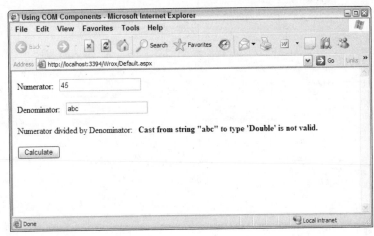

Figure 24-9

Depending on the language that you are using to run the ASP.NET application, you will see different values for different sets of data. For valid inputs, you will always see the correct result, of course, and for any input that is over 1000, you see the Visual Basic 6 appointed error description of Numerator and denominator both have to be less than or equal to 1000.

However, for invalid Strings, Visual Basic .NET reports Cast from string "abc" to type 'Double' is not valid. whereas C# reports Input string was not in a correct format.. For a divide by zero, they both report Divide by Zero because the error is coming directly from the Visual Basic 6 runtime.

Deploying COM Components with .NET Applications

Deploying COM components with your .NET applications is very easy; especially when compared to just deploying ActiveX controls. Two scenarios are possible when deploying .NET applications with COM components:

- ❑ Using private assemblies
- ❑ Using shared assemblies

Private Assemblies

Installing all or parts of the ActiveX component local to the .NET application is considered installing private assemblies. In this scenario, each installation of your .NET application on the same machine has, at least, its own copy of the Interop library for the ActiveX component you are referencing, as shown in Figure 24-10.

It is up to you whether you decide to install the ActiveX component as local to the application or in a shared directory for all calling applications.

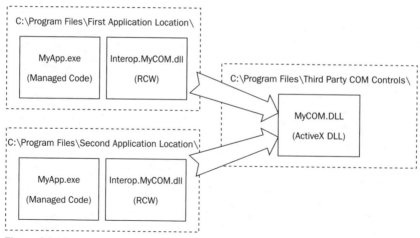

Figure 24-10

It was once considered proper practice to separate ActiveX components into their own directory so that if these components were referenced again by other applications, you did not have to register or install the file for a second time. Using this method meant that when you upgraded a component, you automatically upgraded all the utilizing applications. However, this practice didn't work out so well. In fact, it became a very big contributor to DLL hell and the main reason why Microsoft began promoting the practice of installing private .NET component assemblies.

After you have your components physically in place, the only remaining task is to register the ActiveX component using regsvr32, just as you would when deploying an ActiveX-enabled application.

Public Assemblies

The opposite of a private assembly is a public assembly. Public assemblies share the RCW Interop DLL for other applications. In order to create a public assembly, you must put the RCW file into the *Global Assembly Cache* (GAC), as shown in Figure 24-11.

You can find the GAC at C:\Windows\assembly. Installing items in the GAC can be as simple as dragging-and-dropping the item into this folder through Windows Explorer. Although the GAC is open to everyone, it is not recommended that you blindly install your components into this section unless you have a very good reason to do so.

You can also add items to the GAC from the command line using the Global Assembly Cache Tool (Gacutil.exe). It allows you to view and manipulate the contents of the global assembly cache and download cache. While the Explorer view of the GAC provides similar functionality, you can use Gacutil.exe from build scripts, makefile files, and batch files.

It is hard to find a very good reason to install your ActiveX Interop Assemblies into the GAC. If I had to pick a time to do this, it would be if and when I had a highly shared ActiveX component that many .NET applications would be utilizing on the same machine. In a corporate environment, this might occur when you are upgrading existing business logic from ActiveX to .NET enablement on a server that many applications use. In a commercial setting, I would avoid using the GAC.

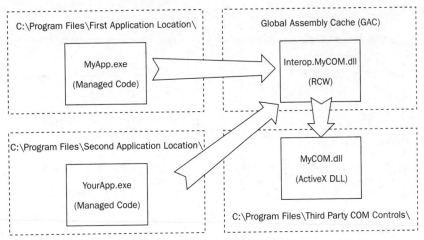

Figure 24-11

Using .NET from Unmanaged Code

.NET provides the opposite of COM interoperability by enabling you to use your newly created .NET components within unmanaged code. This section discusses using .NET components with Visual Basic 6 executables. The techniques shown in this section are identical when you are using ActiveX OCXs or DLLs instead of executables.

The COM-Callable Wrapper (CCW) is the piece of the .NET Framework that enables unmanaged code to communicate with your .NET component. The CCW, unlike the RCW, is not a separate DLL that you distribute with your application. Instead, the CCW is part of the .NET Framework that gets instantiated once for each .NET component that you are using.

Figure 24-12 shows how the CCW marshals the communication between the unmanaged code and the .NET component similarly to how the RCW marshals the code between managed code and COM code.

The COM-Callable Wrapper

The COM-Callable Wrapper or CCW, as previously stated, is not a separate DLL like the RCW. Instead, the CCW uses a specially created type library based on the .NET component. This type library is called an Interop Type Library. The Interop Type Library is statically linked with the unmanaged code so that this code can communicate with the CCW about the .NET component included in your application.

In order for a .NET component to generate an Interop Type Library, you tell Visual Studio 2005 to generate it when the component is built. Both Visual Basic and C# projects have a setting in the Compile properties section of the Class Library project's Property Pages dialog.

Right-click the project in the Solution Explorer and choose Properties to see the project's properties. Figure 24-13 shows the project's properties for a Visual Basic 2005 Class Library application. This is shown directly in the Visual Studio document window.

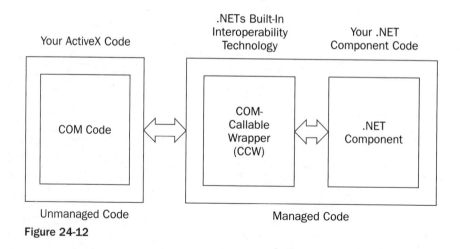

Figure 24-12

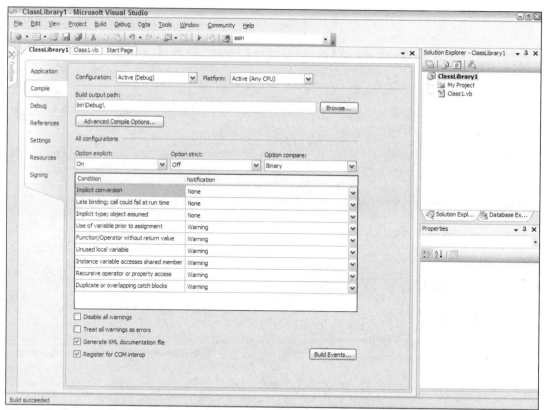

Figure 24-13

C# has a slightly different dialog, as shown in Figure 24-14. In both dialogs, the property is called Register for COM Interop. In Visual Basic, you can find this property on the Compile page; in C#, you can find it on the Build tab of the properties pages.

After you set this option by checking the check box, when you build the project a separate type library file (.tlb) is generated for the DLL that you are building. This .tlb file is your key to including .NET components in COM applications.

Normally in Visual Basic, when you add a reference to a DLL, you navigate from the References section of the Visual Basic project to find the ActiveX DLL that you want to add. If you use .NET components, they cannot be properly referenced in this manner because they are not ActiveX. Instead, you reference the Interop Type Library, which makes the functionality of the corresponding .NET component available to your application.

The .NET Framework also gives you a method to create Interop Type Library files manually for .NET components. You do this through a command-line tool called the Type Library Exporter (as compared to the Type Library Importer used for COM Interoperability). The Type Library Exporter is invoked using the tlbexp.exe executable.

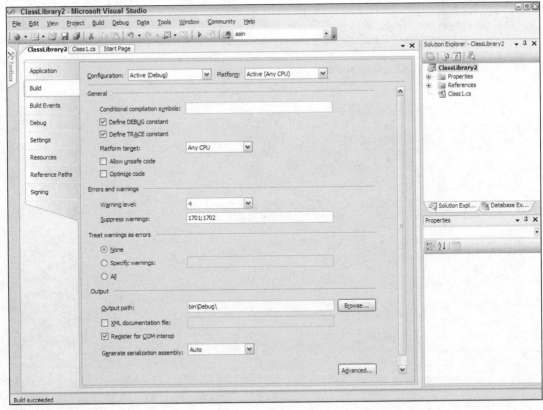

Figure 24-14

For example, to create the Interop Type Library for the `NameComponent.dll` in the next example, you use the following command:

```
tlbimp NameComponent.dll /out:NameComponentEx.tlb
```

The `/out:` parameter specifies the name of the Interop Type Library that is to be created. If you omit this parameter, you get a file with the same name as the ActiveX component, but with a `.tlb` extension.

The Type Library Exporter is useful when you are not using Visual Studio 2005 as your development environment, if you want to have more control over the assemblies that get created for you, or if you are automating the process of connecting to .NET components.

Using .NET Components within COM Objects

The next example illustrates how .NET components can be utilized within COM code. To begin, create and compile the .NET code found in Listing 24-5 in either Visual Basic or C#.

After you have typed your code into your Class Library project, build the component and call it `NameComponent`. Remember to choose to include the Register for the COM Interop setting of True (by checking the appropriate check box) from the project properties pages, as shown in Figure 24-13 for Visual Basic code and Figure 24-14 for C# code. If you aren't using Visual Studio 2005, you can use `tblimp.exe` to generate the Interop Type Library manually as described previously.

Listing 24-5: The .NET component

VB

```
Public Class NameFunctions

  Private m_FirstName As String
  Private m_LastName As String

  Public Property FirstName() As String
    Get
      Return m_FirstName
    End Get

    Set(ByVal Value As String)
      m_FirstName = Value
    End Set
  End Property

  Public Property LastName() As String
    Get
      Return m_LastName
    End Get

    Set(ByVal Value As String)
      m_LastName = Value
    End Set
  End Property

  Public Property FullName() As String
```

```vb
      Get
         Return m_FirstName + " " + m_LastName
      End Get

      Set(ByVal Value As String)
         m_FirstName = Split(Value, " ")(0)
         m_LastName = Split(Value, " ")(1)
      End Set
   End Property

   Public ReadOnly Property FullNameLength() As Long
      Get
         FullNameLength = Len(Me.FullName)
      End Get
   End Property

End Class
```

C#

```csharp
using System;
using System.Runtime.InteropServices;

namespace NameComponent
{
   [ComVisible(true)]
   public class NameFunctions
   {

      private string m_FirstName;
      private string m_LastName;

      public string FirstName
      {
         get
         {
            return m_FirstName;
         }
         set
         {
            m_FirstName=value;
         }
      }

      public string LastName
      {
         get
         {
            return m_LastName;
         }
         set
         {
            m_LastName=value;
         }
      }

      public string FullName
```

(continued)

Listing 24-5: *(continued)*

```
      {
        get
        {
          return m_FirstName + " " + m_LastName;
        }
        set
        {
          m_FirstName=value.Split(' ')[0];
          m_LastName=value.Split(' ')[1];
        }
      }

      public long FullNameLength
      {
        get
        {
          return this.FullName.Length;
        }
      }

    }
}
```

After you have created the .NET component, you can then create the consuming Visual Basic 6 code shown in Listing 24-6.

Listing 24-6: VB6 code using the .NET component

```
Option Explicit

Public Sub Main()

  Dim o As NameComponent.NameFunctions

  Set o = New NameComponent.NameFunctions

  o.FirstName = "Bill"
  o.LastName = "Evjen"

  MsgBox "Full Name is: " + o.FullName

  MsgBox "Length of Full Name is: " + CStr(o.FullNameLength)

  o.FullName = "Scott Hanselman"

  MsgBox "First Name is: " + o.FirstName

  MsgBox "Last Name is: " + o.LastName

  o.LastName = "Evjen"

  MsgBox "Full Name is: " + o.FullName
```

```
    Set o = Nothing

  End Sub
```

Remember to add a reference to the .NET component. You choose Project ➪ Project References and select the `.tlb` file for the .NET component that was created either by Visual Studio or manually using `tlbexp.exe`.

When you run the code in Listing 24-6, you see that Visual Basic 6 doesn't miss a beat when communicating with the .NET component.

It is also possible to register the assemblies yourself. Earlier I showed you how to manually create Interop Type Libraries with the Type Library Exporter. This tool does not register the assemblies created but instead generates only the type library.

To register the assemblies yourself, you use the Assembly Registration Tool (`regasm.exe`). This tool is like the `regsvr32.exe` for .NET components.

To use `regasm.exe`, use a command syntax similar to the following example:

```
regasm NameComponent.dll /tlb:NameComponentEx.tlb /regfile:NameComponent.reg
```

The `/tlb:` option specifies the name of the type library, and the `/regfile:` option specifies the name of a registry file to be created that can be used later in an installation and deployment application.

Early versus Late Binding

The preceding example illustrates the use of early binding, the technique most Visual Basic 6 developers are used to. However, in some cases, it is desirable to use late binding. Performing late binding with .NET components is no different than performing late binding with ActiveX components, as shown in Listing 24-7.

Listing 24-7: Late binding with VB6

```
Option Explicit

Public Sub Main()

  Dim o As Object

  Set o = CreateObject("NameComponent.NameFunctions")

  o.FirstName = "Bill"
  o.LastName = "Evjen"

  MsgBox "Full Name is: " + o.FullName

  MsgBox "Length of Full Name is: " + CStr(o.FullNameLength)
```

(continued)

Listing 24-7: *(continued)*

```
    o.FullName = "Scott Hanselman"

    MsgBox "First Name is: " + o.FirstName

    MsgBox "Last Name is: " + o.LastName

    o.LastName = "Evjen"

    MsgBox "Full Name is: " + o.FullName

    Set o = Nothing

End Sub
```

Error Handling

Handling errors that are raised from .NET components in Visual Basic 6 is easily accomplished via the Interop functionality. Listing 24-8 shows code for both Visual Basic and C# to throw exceptions for a custom error. When the Numerator or the Denominator parameters are greater than 1000 in the Divide function, a custom exception is thrown up to the calling code, which is Visual Basic 6 in this example.

Notice how I don't handle the divide by zero error possibility in this example. This is done intentionally to demonstrate how interoperability handles unhandled errors.

Listing 24-8: Raising errors

VB

```
Public Class CustomException
  Inherits Exception

  Sub New(ByVal Message As String)
    MyBase.New(Message)
  End Sub
End Class

Public Class DivideFunction

  Public Function Divide(ByVal Numerator As Double, _
                         ByVal Denominator As Double) As Double

    If ((Numerator > 1000) Or (Denominator > 1000)) Then
      Throw New CustomException("Numerator and denominator both " & _
                          "have to be less than or equal to 1000.")
    End If

    Divide = Numerator / Denominator

  End Function

End Class
```

C#

```csharp
using System;

namespace DivideComponent
{
    public class CustomException:Exception
    {
      public CustomException(string message):base(message)
      {
      }
    }

  public class DivideFunction
  {
    public double Divide(double Numerator, double Denominator)
    {
      if ((Numerator > 1000) || (Denominator > 1000))
        throw new CustomException("Numerator and denominator " +
                  "both have to be less than or equal to 1000.");

      return Numerator / Denominator;
    }
  }
}
```

Now that you have the code for the .NET component, compile it with the Register for COM Interop flag set to True in the project's Property Pages dialog and call the component DivideComponent.

The consuming Visual Basic 6 code is shown in Listing 24-9. Remember to add a reference to the Interop Type Library of the DivideComponent generated by Visual Studio.

Listing 24-9: VB6 experiencing .NET errors

```vb
Option Explicit

Public Sub Main()

  Dim o As DivideComponent.DivideFunction

  Set o = New DivideComponent.DivideFunction

  MsgBox "1 divided by 3: " + CStr(o.divide(1, 3))

  MsgBox "1 divided by 0: " + CStr(o.divide(1, 0))

  MsgBox "2000 divided by 3000: " + CStr(o.divide(2000, 3000))

  Set o = Nothing

End Sub
```

The Visual Basic 6 code example in Listing 24-9 does not handle the errors thrown by the .NET component, but it can easily do so using On Error, Visual Basic 6's method for trapping raised errors.

Instead of trapping the errors, make sure that the Error Trapping setting in the Options dialog of Visual Basic 6 is set to Break in Class Module.

When the application is run, the first example of 1 divided by 3 works fine; you see the output properly. The second example, which you would expect to end in a divide-by-zero error, does not. Instead, an invalid property value is returned to Visual Basic 6. The final example, which doesn't pass the custom error handling in the .NET component, raises a Visual Basic error as you would expect.

Deploying .NET Components with COM Applications

Deploying .NET components with COM applications is similar to deploying COM components. There are two scenarios in this deployment scheme:

❑ Using private assemblies

❑ Using shared assemblies

The following sections discuss these two scenarios.

Private Assemblies

Private assemblies mean the deployment of the .NET component is installed in each individual directory where the application is installed, within the same machine. The only needed component is the .NET DLL and the calling application. The Interop Type Library that you created earlier with Visual Studio 2005 or `tlbexp.exe` is statically linked with the component or application that references the .NET component.

The only additional task you must complete is to properly register the .NET assembly using `regasm.exe`. This is an extra step that is not needed in 100 percent .NET applications; it is required only for the interoperability for the unmanaged code to reference the managed code. Figure 24-15 illustrates using private assemblies.

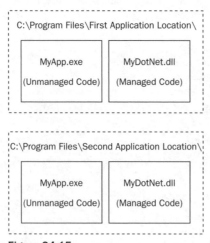

Figure 24-15

Public Assemblies

The use of a public assembly is illustrated in Figure 24-16. This scenario involves installing the .NET component into the Global Assembly Cache (GAC).

As with private assemblies, the .NET component and the consuming unmanaged code are the only requirements for deployment—besides the need to register the interop assembly using `regasm.exe`.

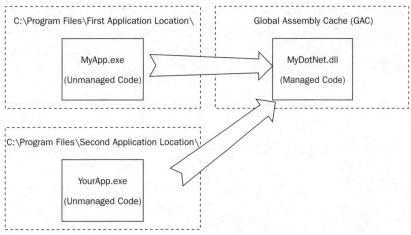

Figure 24-16

Summary

When .NET was introduced, there was some initial concern about existing ActiveX controls and their place in Microsoft's vision for the future of component development. Immediately, Microsoft stepped up to the bat and offered the robust and solid .NET Interop functionality to provide a means to communicate not only from .NET managed code to COM unmanaged code, but also from COM unmanaged code to .NET managed code. The latter was an unexpected, but welcome, feature for many Visual Basic 6 developers and future .NET component builders.

This layer of interoperability has given Microsoft the position to push .NET component development as a solution for not only newly created applications, but also applications that are currently in development and ones that have already been rolled out and are now in the maintenance phase.

Interoperability has given .NET developers a means to gradually update applications without rewriting them entirely, and it has given them a way to start new .NET projects without having to wait for all the supporting components to be developed in .NET

25

Mobile Development

We are entering an era of mobile applications. Mobile devices are getting better, faster, and cheaper every year. The bandwidth on these devices has improved significantly over the last few years and will continue to improve by leaps and bounds. Businesses are continually finding newer and more exciting ways to provide applications on mobile devices. If you haven't yet had the opportunity to program mobile Web applications, you can be sure that your time will come sooner than you might expect.

This book wouldn't be complete without a chapter showing you how to create mobile Web applications using ASP.NET 2.0. This chapter starts with the basics of mobile Web application development and goes deep enough to make you feel comfortable about starting your next mobile Web development project. The chapter first discusses how Visual Studio helps with the creation of mobile Web applications. It then shows you all available mobile Web controls and teaches you the appropriate ways of using them in your applications. Finally, you learn how to develop device-specific properties and manage ViewState and Sessions.

Creating a NEW ASP.NET Mobile Web Application

Visual Studio provides very powerful and user-friendly tools for creating mobile Web applications. If you are familiar with how to create a typical ASP.NET application with Visual Studio, you already know a lot about creating mobile Web applications. You simply create a Web site project and add a Mobile Web Form to your project. When you open this form in the Designer window, you see a set of mobile controls inside the Toolbox.

Follow these steps to create a new Visual Basic or Visual C# mobile Web application using Visual Studio 2005:

1. Choose File ⇨ New ⇨ Web Site.

2. From the Visual Studio Installed Templates list, select ASP.NET Web Site.

3. Provide the location, language, and path, and click OK (see Figure 25-1).

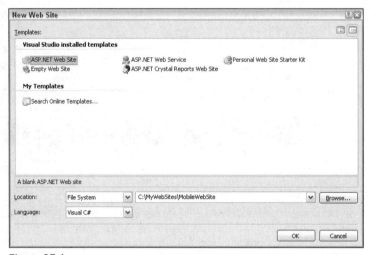

Figure 25-1

After you follow the preceding steps, you can see that Visual Studio creates a Web site project for you. Next, add Mobile Web Forms to your project by following these steps:

1. Right-click the ASP.NET Project you just created and select Add New Item.

2. In the Add New Item dialog, select Mobile Web Form from the Visual Studio Installed Templates list (see Figure 25-2).

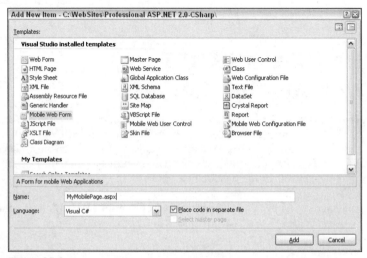

Figure 25-2

3. Provide a name for the Mobile Form, select a language, and click to check the Select Master Page check box if a master page is defined for your project. Be sure to check the Place Code in Separate File check box to use the code-behind model provided.

4. Click the Add button.

After you click the Add button, you can see that Visual Studio creates two files with the names `MyMobilePage.aspx` and `MyMobilePage.cs` (or `MyMobilePage.vb` if you selected Visual Basic). The `MyMobilePage.aspx` file contains the declarative format of the ASP.NET mobile controls. The `MyMobilePage.cs` file contains the code for handling events and performing other programmatic tasks.

After the Mobile Web Form is created, feel free to add controls from the Mobile Web Forms tab of the Toolbox. Just like other ASP.NET controls, the mobile controls provide properties and events that you can use to customize behaviors. You can also type these mobile controls directly into the Mobile Web Form source window by using the `<mobile: />` syntax shown here:

```
<mobile:TextBox ID="MyTextBox" runat="server"></mobile:TextBox>
<mobile:Label ID="MyLabel" runat="server">Label</mobile:Label>
```

Figure 25-3 shows a Mobile Web Form that contains Label, Text Box, and Command controls. This Mobile Web Form finds a customer record using the customer identifier provided in the text box.

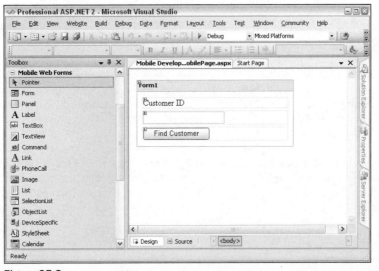

Figure 25-3

The HTML code generated by adding these controls is shown in Listing 25-1. You can see that all three mobile controls are reflected by the HTML tags that start with the `mobile:` prefix. Notice that the `mobile:` prefix is used with the form tag as well. In a typical ASP.NET page, you won't be required to treat forms as Web controls. However, the mobile Web page treats forms a little differently. The main difference is that the mobile Web page allows you to create multiple forms on one page and navigate among these forms without making a trip to the Web server. This flexibility allows you to reduce the number of roundtrips to the server because the bandwidth is typically slow on a mobile connection.

Listing 25-1: The source code for a simple mobile Web page

```
<%@ Page Language="C#" AutoEventWireup="true" CodeFile="MyMobilePage.aspx.cs"
    Inherits="_Default" %>
<%@ Register TagPrefix="mobile" Namespace="System.Web.UI.MobileControls"
    Assembly="System.Web.Mobile" %>

<html xmlns="http://www.w3.org/1999/xhtml" >
<body>
    <mobile:Form id="Form1" runat="server">
        <mobile:Label id="lblID" Runat="server">Customer ID</mobile:Label>
        <mobile:TextBox id="txtCustID" Runat="server"></mobile:TextBox>
        <mobile:Command id="cmdGetCustomer" Runat="server">
         Find Customer
        </mobile:Command>
    </mobile:Form>
</body>
</html>
```

Views of an ASP.NET Mobile Web Form

The ASP.NET Mobile Web Forms Designer provides three views in the Microsoft Visual Studio environment: Design view, HTML view, and Code view. These views are panes in the Visual Studio main window that you can access using a variety of mechanisms.

Design View

The Design view loads the Mobile Web Form and displays an automatic rendering of its controls using the default properties. You can add new controls by dragging and dropping them from the Toolbox. You can modify existing controls by using the Properties window or remove the controls by simply selecting them and pressing the Delete button on the keyboard.

The Design view is not a WYSIWYG editor, mainly because the actual appearance of a Mobile Web Form varies significantly from one device to another. For example, the Design view always displays one control per line, whereas some devices may be able to display multiple controls on the same line. You should also know that the ASP.NET Mobile Web Form does not support absolute positioning of Mobile Web Controls.

HTML View

The HTML view displays the source HTML. You can edit it directly if you want to gain total control of the layout and rendering of the form. You don't have to work directly in the HTML view; it is available mostly as a convenience for those who would rather not depend on automatic HTML generation. Otherwise, the designer does a very good job of allowing you to work in a user-friendly design environment.

You can switch between the Design view and the HTML view by clicking the appropriate tab at the bottom of each view.

Code View

The Code view manages the programming logic contained in the code-behind file. You can enter the Code view simply by right-clicking the mobile Web page in Solution Explorer and selecting the View Code menu option.

Event Handling with Mobile Web Controls

Just like regular Web controls, Mobile Web Controls also fire events. They provide default events for handling most commonly occurring scenarios. In addition, each control also raises a number of non-default events that can be handled as needed. You already know that events are raised by certain activities performed by the user on the browser. The mobile browser behaves in the same manner. It responds to the event by sending a post back to the server where the event is processed. The resulting HTML is sent back to the browser. Handling a default event fired by a mobile control is as simple as placing the control on the page and double-clicking it. You are presented with a code window where the event handler is already prewired for you, as shown in the following code. If you are interested in handling non-default events, you simply view the list of available events in the Properties window and double-click the event you want to handle.

VB
```vb
Private Sub cmdGetCustomer_Click(ByVal sender as System.Object, _
    ByVal e as System.EventArgs) Handles Command1.Click

End Sub
```

C#
```csharp
private void cmdGetCustomer_Click(object sender, System.EventArgs e)
{

}
```

Creating a non-default event handler is also quite easy. The steps are the same regardless of the programming language. If you have worked with previous versions of Visual Studio .NET, you may remember that wiring event handlers worked differently in Visual Basic .NET than in C#. The current version of Visual Studio unifies the steps in both languages.

Follow these steps to create a non-default event handler:

1. Select the desired control in Design view.

2. Click the Events button (the one with the lightning bolt) in the Properties window. Clicking this button shows a list of all available events for the selected control.

3. Double-click the event you want to handle. You are taken to the Code view with the event handler prewired for the selected event.

You have now created a non-default event handler.

Using Control Containers

Two kinds of container controls are provided for mobile Web pages: the Form control and the Panel control. All mobile controls in ASP.NET exist inside one of these container controls. Other than using these container controls for grouping together Mobile Web Controls, you can also use them to apply styles consistently to all controls inside them. The container controls are added to the page with a default size that changes as new controls are added to it. You can't resize a container control to a specific size.

Mobile Web Forms only support sequential placement of controls because of the diversity among the wide range of mobile devices—especially WML devices that, for the most part, can't support *side-by-side layout*—that is, having multiple controls reside next to each other sequentially. You can force ASP.NET to take advantage of side-by-side layout on devices that support it by setting the `BreakAfter` property of the mobile Web control to `False`. The ASP.NET Mobile Designer does not use the `BreakAfter` property. As a result, the Designer doesn't display controls side by side, even if `BreakAfter` is set to `False`.

The good news is that the ASP.NET Mobile Designer enables you to customize the appearance of Mobile Web Forms and controls for specific devices. This flexibility enables you to ensure that your application looks and functions as intended on the devices you specify. You can read more about customizing for specific devices a little later in this chapter in the section "Understanding Device Filters."

The Form Control

All content and all controls are contained inside a Form control. Every page is required to have at least one Form control. The page can contain multiple Form controls; however, it can display only one at a time. A default form is automatically created when you create a mobile Web page. You can add more forms by dragging and dropping them from the Toolbox.

When the page loads, it displays the first form placed inside it by default. You can write code in the `Page_Load` event to direct the user to a specific form if you want. You can also program to navigate users to other forms based on user input. Navigating between forms on the same page doesn't result in a trip to the Web server, thereby significantly improving your application's response time. Organizing pages into groups of forms also enables you to pass richer state information from one form to the next because all forms are contained inside the same physical page. All forms on a mobile page share the same code behind and, therefore, can share the same functions and member fields.

Because ASP.NET mobile Web applications usually run on devices with smaller screens, you might need to break a single ASP.NET Web page into several mobile Web pages so that each can fit on a smaller screen. Without the capability to put multiple logical groups of controls in mobile forms, you could have great difficulty maintaining a one-to-one mapping between ASP.NET Web Forms and ASP.NET Mobile Forms in the same application.

The real question to ask yourself is how to decide the appropriate groupings of forms on a mobile Web page. You should know that all forms on the page are instantiated when the page is loaded causing the page with many forms to take longer to load. However, navigating between these forms is speedy fast once all forms are loading in the device's memory. Another advantage you get by using multiple forms on a page is persistence of the state information while you are switching the user from one form to another.

The Panel Control

The Panel control provides an easy way to group related controls together while keeping them inside a Form control. You can easily apply styles to the panel to help you keep a consistent look-and-feel in your mobile applications. Another great benefit of panels is to keep related controls together on the same page because ASP.NET attempts to keep all controls in a panel on the screen at the same time.

You can show or hide a group of controls by keeping them inside a panel and making the panel either visible or invisible. You can optionally insert one panel inside another to create a composite group of controls.

Adding panels to your application is as simple as dragging and dropping them from the Toolbox. To add a Panel control, follow these steps:

1. Drag a Panel control from the Mobile Web Forms tab of the Toolbox.

2. Customize the Panel control by dragging other controls onto the panel from the Toolbox.

Using StyleSheets

You can use styles to customize the appearance of controls when they are rendered. You can do so by using StyleSheet controls, defining style information, and applying it to one or more controls on the same page. As mentioned earlier, you can apply styles not only to a specific control but also to container controls that consistently apply the styles to all controls inside the container.

A StyleSheet control should be placed outside the container control. In fact, this is the only type of control that can exist outside a container. You can define only one StyleSheet control for each page or mobile user control. After adding a StyleSheet control to a Mobile Web Forms page, you can open the StyleSheet Styles Editor and Templating Options dialog boxes to define these properties.

To create, customize, and apply a StyleSheet control to a Mobile Web Form, follow these steps:

1. Drag and Drop a StyleSheet control on the Mobile Web Form.

2. Right-click the StyleSheet control you just put in place and select the Templating Options menu. The Templating Options dialog box appears, as shown in Figure 25-4. This window allows you to create and edit multiple styles and device filters. Device filters are discussed a little later in this chapter.

Figure 25-4

3. Click the Edit button next to the Style drop-down box. The Styles Editor dialog box opens, as shown in Figure 25-5. This dialog box enables you to create as many styles as you want.

Figure 25-5

4. Click the desired style type from the left-hand list and click the > button. This action creates a new style in the right-hand list using the type you selected. You currently have two options in the Style Types list:

❑ **Pager Style type:** Provides styling elements for configuring pagination. This style is helpful if your Mobile Web Form has more controls than can fit on one screen. In this case, ASP.NET automatically creates pagination from viewable controls to others.

❑ **Style type:** Customizes styling for all mobile Web controls.

5. Right-click the styles shown in the Defined Styles list and select the Rename menu option. Rename these defined styles so that their names are more meaningful and easier to select from.

6. Click OK when you are done defining styles for your Mobile Web Form.

From Figure 25-5, you can see that your choice of style options is limited. Most of the restrictions are due to hardware limitations on mobile devices, especially WML-enabled phone devices. However, you still have a few good options to pick from. You can set background color, foreground color, alignment, font sizes, and font types. The good news is that the availability of StyleSheet controls makes it easy for you to apply these styles consistently throughout your mobile Web application.

After you have finished defining styles, the next step is to apply these styles to the mobile controls. You can do this by simply clicking the StyleReference property and selecting the desired style from the list. In Figure 25-6, the GrayBackground style has been applied to the Form control and the BlueBackground style to the Label control. You already know that applying a style to a Form control applies the style to all controls inside it. This is why all controls in this form have a light gray background. However, the Label control looks different. This is because we chose to override the style for the Label control by providing its own style reference.

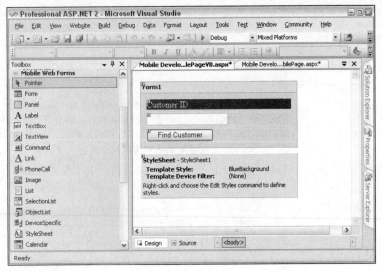

Figure 25-6

Creating a Single StyleSheet Control for All Mobile Web Forms

It is easy for you to create a `StyleSheet` control that can be used consistently for all mobile Web pages in your mobile Web application. You simply create a Mobile User control and place a `StyleSheet` control inside it. You can reuse the `StyleSheet` placed inside a Mobile User control by dropping a `StyleSheet` control on the Mobile Web Form and setting the `ReferencePath` property to the Mobile User Control. We talk more about the Mobile User Control a little later in this chapter.

You should know that Visual Studio doesn't understand the global style sheet reference and cannot assist you in applying these styles. Most notable is the lack of design-time style support for global styles. You also do not see the list of Styles in the `StyleReference` property of the Mobile Web control.

Using ASP.NET Mobile Controls

The ASP.NET Mobile Designer enables you to access a rich set of interactive development tools. This section discusses various mobile controls that are available for you to reuse. These controls provide functionality suitable for all your mobile Web development needs.

The AdRotator Control

The AdRotator mobile Web control is similar to the AdRotator control in ASP.NET Web Forms. It is capable of displaying and cycling through a random set of advertisement banners. This control automates the cycling process and changes the displayed advertisement every time the page is refreshed. You can customize this control to give more weight to certain advertisements and create a priority level for the banners. You can also provide a custom logic for cycling through the advertisements.

The AdRotator control provides a few very important properties that can be used to provide it a list of advertisements, image paths, and image links. The table that follows shows the important properties of this control.

Property	Description
AdvertisementFile	This read-write property receives a path to the advertisement file. This file should contain an XML-based definition of advertisement information, such as Image URL, Navigate URL, Number of Impressions, Start Date, and End Date.
ImageKey	This read-write property enables you to select a custom-defined tag in the advertisement XML file to find the URL for images.
NavigateUrlKey	This read-write property allows you to select a custom-defined tag in the advertisement XML file to find the URL link associated with each image.

Listing 25-2 shows the XML-based advertisement configuration file used for the AdRotator control shown in Figure 25-7. Save this file as Listing 25-02.xml. The AdRotator control selects a different image every time the page is loaded, so Figure 25-7 displays the same page showing two different images.

Listing 25-2: The advertisement configuration file Listing 25-02.xml

```xml
<?xml version="1.0" encoding="utf-8" ?>
<Advertisements>
  <Ad>
  <ImageUrl>images/RDLogo.jpg</ImageUrl>
  <NavigateUrl>http://www.MicrosoftRegionalDirectors.com</NavigateUrl>
  <AlternateText>Microsoft Regional Directors</AlternateText>
  <Keyword>Community Leader</Keyword>
  <Impressions>2000</Impressions>
  <StartDate>5/19/05</StartDate>
  <EndDate>7/18/05</EndDate>
  </Ad>
  <Ad>
  <ImageUrl>images/tcnug_logo.gif</ImageUrl>
  <NavigateUrl>http://www.ilmservice.com/twincitiesnet</NavigateUrl>
  <AlternateText>Twin Cities .NET User Group</AlternateText>
  <Keyword>User Group</Keyword>
  <Impressions>1000</Impressions>
  <StartDate>5/30/05</StartDate>
  <EndDate>7/5/05</EndDate>
  </Ad>
</Advertisements>
```

After the XML file that will be used by the AdRotator control is in place, you can reference this file directly from your mobile ASP.NET page, as illustrated in Listing 25-3.

Figure 25-7

Listing 25-3: Using the advertisement XML file with the AdRotator control

```
<%@ Page Language="C#" AutoEventWireup="true" CodeFile="Listing 25-03.aspx.cs"
        Inherits="Listing2503" %>
<%@ Register TagPrefix="mobile" Namespace="System.Web.UI.MobileControls"
        Assembly="System.Web.Mobile" %>

<html xmlns="http://www.w3.org/1999/xhtml" >
<body>
    <mobile:Form id="Form1" runat="server">
        <mobile:AdRotator ID="AdRotator1" Runat="server"
        AdvertisementFile="Listing 25-03.xml">
        </mobile:AdRotator>
        <mobile:Label id="lblID" Runat="server">ID
        </mobile:Label>
        <mobile:TextBox id="txtCustID" Runat="server">
        </mobile:TextBox>
        <mobile:Command id="cmdGetCustomer" Runat="server"
        OnClick="cmdGetCustomer_Click">Find
```

(continued)

987

Listing 25-3: *(continued)*

```
        </mobile:Command>
      </mobile:Form>
  </body>
  </html>
```

Once in place, you get the varying results shown in Figure 25-7.

The Calendar Control

The Calendar control offers date-picking functionality. You can add it to the Mobile Web Form by simply dragging and dropping from the Toolbox. The control starts by showing the current month by default. You can set the VisibleDate property to cause it to show a different month by default. The SelectedDate Property can be used to select a date on the calendar. The visible date can be changed irrespective of the SelectedDate property, causing the control to remember a selected date that may not be currently on display.

The SelectionMode property exposed by the Calendar control determines the manner in which the dates are selected. The default setting is Day, which allows the user to choose a single day. You can change this property to either DayWeek or DayWeekMonth. The DayWeek setting enables the user to select either a single day or a week. The DayWeekMonth setting allows the user to select a day, week, or month. You can change this setting at design time, or you can change it programmatically at runtime. This control raises an event with the name SelectionChanged. This event gets fired every time the user changes the currently selected date. The following table describes the Calendar control properties just mentioned.

Property	Description
FirstDayOfWeek	This read/write property enables the users to see the calendar starting from a given day.
SelectionMode	This read/write property allows you to configure the Calendar control to let the users select a day, a week, or the entire month. The available choices are None, Day, DayWeek, and DayWeekMonth.
SelectedDate	This read/write property enables you to pre-select a specific date. We can either set this property at design time, or alter its value at runtime. You should also know that if the selected date is set to a date that isn't currently visible on the screen, the Calendar control does not automatically change its appearance to show you the selected date.
VisibleDate	This read/write property allows you to set the date that should be visible on the screen when the calendar is displayed. This date doesn't have to be the same as the selected date.

Using the Calendar control is easy. You simply drag this control from the Toolbox, position it on the Mobile Web Form, and set the appropriate property to display the calendar in your favorite style. Interacting with the calendar is easy as well. For example, when a user selects a date on the calendar, you can read this date and populate a text box with it by writing just a single line of code in the Calendar control's `SelectionChange` event, as shown in Listing 25-4.

Listing 25-4: An example of using the Calendar control

Mobile page

```
<%@ Page Language="VB" AutoEventWireup="true" CodeFile="Calendar.aspx.vb"
        Inherits="Calendar" %>
<%@ Register TagPrefix="mobile" Namespace="System.Web.UI.MobileControls"
        Assembly="System.Web.Mobile" %>

<html xmlns="http://www.w3.org/1999/xhtml" >
<body>
    <mobile:Form id="Form1" runat="server">
        Event Date:
        <mobile:TextBox id="txtEventDate" runat="server">
        </mobile:TextBox>
        <mobile:Calendar id="EventCalendar"
         FirstDayOfWeek="Sunday" Runat="server"
         OnSelectionChanged="EventCalendar_SelectionChanged">
        </mobile:Calendar>
    </mobile:Form>
</body>
</html>
```

VB

```
Partial Class Calendar
    Inherits System.Web.UI.MobileControls.MobilePage

    Protected Sub EventCalendar_SelectionChanged(ByVal sender As Object, _
        ByVal e As System.EventArgs) Handles EventCalendar.SelectionChanged

        txtEventDate.Text = EventCalendar.SelectedDate.ToShortDateString()
    End Sub
End Class
```

C#

```
using System;
using System.Web.Mobile;
using System.Web.UI.MobileControls;

public partial class Calendar : System.Web.UI.MobileControls.MobilePage
{
    protected void EventCalendar_SelectionChanged(object sender, EventArgs e)
    {
        txtEventDate.Text = EventCalendar.SelectedDate.ToShortDateString();
    }
}
```

Figure 25-8 shows the Calendar control where the user can click on a certain date and then populate a text box.

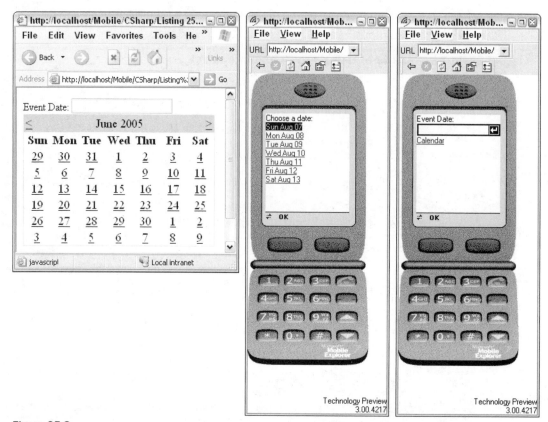

Figure 25-8

The Label Control

The Label control is used to display read-only, text-based information on the screen. You can set the string displayed by this control using the `Text` property in the Properties window, or you can change it programmatically. If the string is too long to fit entirely on the screen, be sure to set the `Wrapping` property to `Wrap`. This causes the label to display the information on multiple lines. The following table shows a few of the commonly used properties of the Label control.

Property	Description
Wrapping	This read/write property causes the control to display the text on multiple lines if the content is too large to display entirely on one line. The possible values are `NotSet`, `Wrap`, and `NoWrap`.
Alignment	This read/write property allows you to align the control on the screen. The possible values are `NotSet`, `Left`, `Right`, and `Center`.

Property	Description
BreakAfter	This read/write property allows you to specify whether you want to force a line break after this control when the control is rendered. This is useful on mobile browsers that are capable of displaying more than one control on a single line. The possible values are True and False.

The TextBox Control

You can use the TextBox control when you want to enable users to enter textual information. This information can also be programmatically set or retrieved using the Text property. You can prevent users from seeing sensitive information, such as a password, by setting the Password property to True. The following table shows a list of the TextBox control's common properties.

Property	Description
Text	This read/write property is used for reading and writing text-based information to and from this control. This property can either be set at design time or accessed during runtime.
Password	This read/write property is very useful for the cases where the information is sensitive, such as a password, and shouldn't be displayed on the screen. The possible values are True and False.
Size	This read/write property allows you to specify the width of the control.
MaxLength	This read/write property allows you to specify the maximum length of the string that the text box should accept.
Alignment	This read/write property allows you to position the control on the screen. The possible values are NotSet, Left, Right, and Center.

The code example in Listing 25-5 shows a simple calculator that uses two text boxes and a label. Users can enter two numbers using the TextBox controls and click the Add button. The result will be displayed using a Label control.

Listing 25-5: An example of using TextBox and Label controls

Mobile page

```
<%@ Page Language="VB" AutoEventWireup="false" CodeFile="LabelAndTextBoxVB.aspx.vb"
        Inherits="LabelAndTextBox" %>
<%@ Register TagPrefix="mobile" Namespace="System.Web.UI.MobileControls"
        Assembly="System.Web.Mobile" %>

<html xmlns="http://www.w3.org/1999/xhtml" >
<body>
    <mobile:Form id="Form1" runat="server"> 
        Add Two Numbers: 
        <mobile:TextBox ID="txtNumber1" Runat="server">
```

(continued)

Listing 25-5: *(continued)*

```
          </mobile:TextBox>
          <mobile:TextBox ID="txtNumber2" Runat="server">
          </mobile:TextBox>
          <mobile:Label ID="lblResult" Runat="server">Label
          </mobile:Label>
          <mobile:Command ID="cmdAdd" Runat="server" onClick="cmdAdd_Click">Add
          </mobile:Command>
      </mobile:Form>
  </body>
  </html>
```

VB

```
Partial Class LabelAndTextBox
    Inherits System.Web.UI.MobileControls.MobilePage

    Protected Sub cmdAdd_Click(ByVal sender As Object, _
        ByVal e As System.EventArgs) Handles cmdAdd.Click

        Dim Number1 As Integer
        Dim Number2 As Integer

        Number1 = Convert.ToInt32(txtNumber1.Text)
        Number2 = Convert.ToInt32(txtNumber2.Text)

        lblResult.Text = Convert.ToString(Number1 + Number2)
    End Sub
End Class
```

C#

```
using System;
using System.Web;
using System.Web.Mobile;
using System.Web.UI.MobileControls;

public partial class LabelAndTextBoxCSharp :
  System.Web.UI.MobileControls.MobilePage
{
    protected void cmdAdd_Click(object sender, EventArgs e)
    {
        int Number1;
        int Number2;

        Number1 = Convert.ToInt32(txtNumber1.Text);
        Number2 = Convert.ToInt32(txtNumber2.Text);

        lblResult.Text = Convert.ToString(Number1 + Number2);
    }
}
```

Figure 25-9 shows the calculator from Listing 25-5.

Figure 25-9

The TextView Control

The TextView control works much like the Label control except that it can display large fields of textual data. You can style the text to appear with normal, bold, and italic formatting; you can also use line breaks, paragraph markers, and hyperlinks.

In reality, this control doesn't offer anything different or better than the Label control. The earlier versions of the .NET Framework didn't allow the Label control to display its content on multiple lines by wrapping text. However, the 2.0 version of the .NET Framework enables the Label control to wrap, thereby causing the TextView control to be redundant with the Label control.

The following table shows the commonly used properties of the TextView control.

Property	Description
Wrapping	This read/write property causes the control to display the text on multiple lines if the content is too large to display entirely on one line. The possible values are NotSet, Wrap, and NoWrap.

Table continued on following page

Property	Description
Alignment	This read/write property allows you to align the control on the screen. The possible values are NotSet, Left, Right, and Center.
BreakAfter	This read/write property allows you to specify whether you want to force a line break after this control when the control is rendered. This is useful on mobile browsers that are capable of displaying more than one control on a single line. The possible values are True and False.

The Command Control

The Command control displays a button on the screen and is used for capturing user input and processing it on the server. When the user clicks on the button, this control automatically fires two events on the server with the names Click and ItemCommand. Both events can be handled in the same page. However, if this control is contained inside a container, the ItemCommand event is also propagated to the parent control.

You should know that the CausesValidation property of this control is set to True by default, which causes the validation controls to activate on the Mobile Web Form when the user clicks this control. You can disable this behavior by setting the CausesValidation property to False.

The following table shows the commonly used properties of the Command control.

Property	Description
Text	This read/write property displays textual information on the screen. The information is shown as a read-only caption on the control.
ImageUrl	This read/write property can be used to provide a link to an image that will be rendered instead of the default button.
CausesValidation	This property decides whether the validation controls on the Mobile Web Form should fire or not when the user clicks the control.
BreakAfter	This read/write property allows you to specify whether you want to force a line break after this control when the control is rendered. This is useful on mobile browsers that are capable of displaying more than one control on a single line. The possible values are True and False.

The Image Control

The Image control is useful for displaying an image on the screen by specifying the location of a bitmap file using the ImageUrl property. You can also cause this control to act as a hyperlink by setting the NavigateUrl property to a valid URL. The following table shows the Image control's commonly used properties.

Property	Description
NavigateUrl	This read/write property allows you to provide a link so that users can click on the image and get redirected to another Mobile Web Page or to another Mobile Web Form on the same page.
ImageUrl	This read/write property can be used to provide a link to an image that will be rendered when the Mobile Web Form is rendered.
AlternateText	This read/write property allows you to provide a textual description of the image. This description automatically renders if the Mobile Browser can't display the image.
Alignment	This read/write property allows you to position this control on the Mobile Web Form. The possible values are NotSet, Left, Right, and Center.
BreakAfter	This read/write property allows you to specify whether you want to force a line break after this control when the control is rendered. This is useful on mobile browsers that are capable of displaying more than one control on a single line. The possible values are True and False.

Listing 25-6 shows an example of how you can use this control,

Listing 25-6: An Image control on a Mobile Web Form

```
<%@ Page Language="C#" AutoEventWireup="true" CodeFile="ImageCSharp.aspx.cs"
        Inherits="ImageCSharp" %>
<%@ Register TagPrefix="mobile" Namespace="System.Web.UI.MobileControls"
        Assembly="System.Web.Mobile" %>

<html xmlns="http://www.w3.org/1999/xhtml" >
<body>
    <mobile:Form id="Form1" runat="server">
        <mobile:Image ID="Image1" Runat="server"
                AlternateText="Microsoft Regional Director"
                ImageUrl="~/Mobile Development/Images/RDLogo.JPG">
        </mobile:Image>

    </mobile:Form>
</body>
</html>
```

You can imagine the complexity of displaying an image on a wide variety of devices. The widely varying capabilities of mobile devices make it nearly impossible to display the same image on all devices. However, this control provides a powerful set of tools for overcoming this limitation. The device filters, for example, allow you to select an image to display from a group of images. Each image in the group can be targeted toward specific types of devices, such as a color image on handheld computers or a simplified monochrome image more suitable to the phone's display. The control chooses the most appropriate image to display by overriding its property values for specific hardware. Device filters are discussed in more detail in the section "Understanding Device Filters" a little later in this chapter.

The PhoneCall Control

The PhoneCall control is useful for those mobile devices that can originate a phone call, such as mobile phone devices. This control displays to the user a string that appears as a command the user can select. You can set the contents of the string with the `Text` property and use the `PhoneNumber` property to enter the number for the device to call.

The devices that can't originate a phone call simply display a text value according to the format string specified in the `AlternateFormat` property. By default, the `AlternateFormat` property contains `{0}` `{1}` as its formatting string. The control replaces the `{0}` with the string in the `Text` property and replaces the `{1}` with the contents of the `PhoneNumber` property.

The following table shows the commonly used properties of the PhoneCall control.

Property	Description
AlternateFormat	This read/write property allows you to format the way the phone number should appear in case the mobile device isn't capable of initiating a voice communication.
AlternateUrl	This read/write property allows you to provide a link in case the mobile device isn't capable of initiating a voice communication. This link redirects the user to another Mobile Web Page or to another Mobile Web Form on the same page.
Text	This read/write property allows you to provide a textual description of the image. This description automatically renders if the Mobile Browser can't display the image.
PhoneNumber	This read/write property allows you to position this control on the Mobile Web Form. The possible values are `NotSet`, `Left`, `Right`, and `Center`.
BreakAfter	This read/write property allows you to specify whether you want to force a line break after this control when the control is rendered. This is useful on mobile browsers that are capable of displaying more than one control on a single line. The possible values are `True` and `False`.

An example of using the PhoneCall control is shown in Listing 25-7.

Listing 25-7: A PhoneCall control

```
<%@ Page Language="C#" AutoEventWireup="true" CodeFile="PhoneCallCSharp.aspx.cs"
        Inherits="PhoneCallCSharp" %>
<%@ Register TagPrefix="mobile" Namespace="System.Web.UI.MobileControls"
        Assembly="System.Web.Mobile" %>

<html xmlns="http://www.w3.org/1999/xhtml" >
<body>
    <mobile:Form id="Form1" runat="server">
        <mobile:PhoneCall ID="PhoneCall1" Runat="server" Alignment="Left"
```

```
            AlternateUrl="~MyMS.aspx" PhoneNumber="1-800-555-1212">
            Call Microsoft
            </mobile:PhoneCall>

    </mobile:Form>
  </body>
</html>
```

Figure 25-10 shows the PhoneCall control.

The Link Control

The Link control displays a text string as a hyperlink that can lead to another form on the same Mobile Web Forms page or to any other URL. You can take advantage of the devices that support softkeys by specifying the `SoftKeyLabel` property and entering the link's text into the `Text` property. (A *softkey* is a key on a mobile device that lets a user execute a function; these keys can be used for multiple links. Softkeys generally correspond to a value that appears on the screen above the button.) You can customize the appearance of the Link control by setting the `Alignment`, `ForeColor`, `Font`, `StyleReference`, and `Wrapping` properties. The following table shows the Link control's commonly used properties.

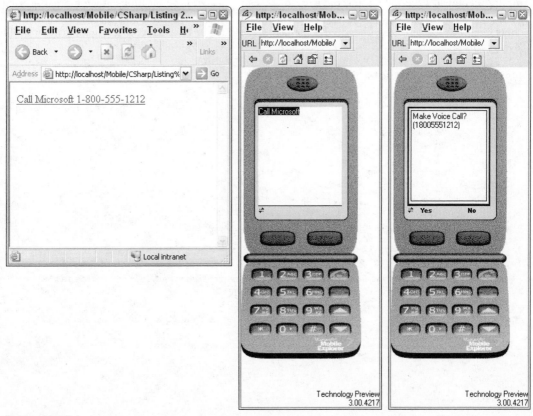

Figure 25-10

Property	Description
NavigateUrl	This read/write property allows you to provide a link to another Mobile Web Page or another Mobile Web Form on the same page. The user is taken to this URL when the Link control is clicked.
Text	This read/write property allows you to provide a textual description of the link that is displayed for users.
SoftKeyLabel	This read/write property allows you to provide a label for the softkey. This property is applicable only for mobile devices that provide softkey functionality. You can programmatically configure this key to be associated with any link control you prefer.
BreakAfter	This read/write property allows you to specify whether you want to force a line break after this control when the control is rendered. This is useful on mobile browsers that are capable of displaying more than one control on a single line. The possible values are True and False.

Link controls are very useful for creating menus on mobile devices. Mobile devices have very restricted input capabilities, especially phone devices, so you can make your applications much more user friendly by providing a menu of options for users to select from. The example shown in Listing 25-8 provides a short menu. Users can click either on the Contact, Candidate, or Hours link to navigate to other Mobile Web Forms.

Listing 25-8: A menu using Link controls

```
<%@ Page Language="C#" AutoEventWireup="true" CodeFile="LinkMenuCSharp.aspx.cs"
        Inherits="LinkMenuCSharp" %>
<%@ Register TagPrefix="mobile" Namespace="System.Web.UI.MobileControls"
        Assembly="System.Web.Mobile" %>

<html xmlns="http://www.w3.org/1999/xhtml" >
<body>
    <mobile:Form id="Shajar" runat="server">
        <mobile:Link ID="lnkContacts" Runat="server"
                NavigateUrl="/Contacts.aspx" SoftkeyLabel="Contacts">
                Search for Contacts
        </mobile:Link>
        <mobile:Link ID="lnkCandidates" Runat="server"
                NavigateUrl="/Candidates.aspx" SoftkeyLabel="Candidates">
                Search for Candidates
        </mobile:Link>
        <mobile:Link ID="lnkHours" Runat="server" NavigateUrl="/Hours.aspx"
                SoftkeyLabel="Hours">
                Hours Report
        </mobile:Link>

    </mobile:Form>
</body>
</html>
```

Figure 25-11 shows a menu built with Link controls.

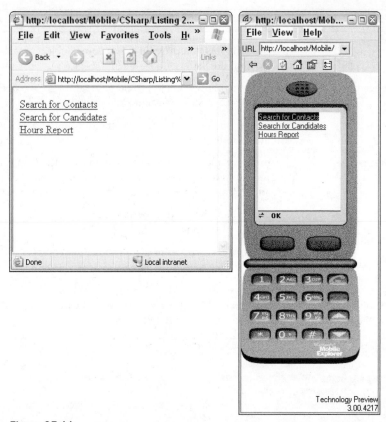

Figure 25-11

The List Control

The List control is very useful in displaying a list of items either as bullets, numbers, or a plain list. You can provide a static list of items or bind this control to a list retrieved from the database. The static list is provided by clicking the ellipsis (...) button next to the Items property in the Properties window. The list might paginate on some devices depending on the viewable area available. You can set the ItemsPerPage property to the preferred number of list items to display on each page. You should know that the Visual Studio Mobile Designer doesn't use this property when showing you a default rendering in the Design view.

Data binding this control to a list obtained from the database is quite easy. You simply specify the data source using the DataSource and DataMember properties. Be sure to provide appropriate values to the DataTextField and DataValueField properties so that the control manages the viewable column from the data source.

You can customize the appearance of this control by using the Alignment, ForeColor, Font, StyleReference, and Wrapping properties. You can cause the control to display the items as either bullets or numbers by providing the appropriate value for the Decoration property.

The following table shows the List control's commonly used properties.

Property	Description
DataSource	This property lets you provide a data source object that the control can use to obtain the list.
DataMember	This property allows you to provide the DataTable name if you choose to use the DataSet object as the data source.
DataTextField	This property allows you to select a field from the data source to be displayed on the screen.
DataValueField	This property allows you to select a field from the data source to be used as values for each item. The values aren't displayed on the screen. Instead, they are used to store identifiers for each displayed item.
Decoration	This property allows you to select the list style. The available choices are None, Bulleted, and Numbered.
Wrapping	This property allows you to display a list item on multiple lines if the content is too big to fit on one line.

Listing 25-9 shows how to bind the List control to a list obtained from the database. We chose to display the Company Name field from the data source in a bulleted-list format.

Listing 25-9: Binding to a List control

```
<%@ Page Language="VB" AutoEventWireup="true" CodeFile="List.aspx.vb"
        Inherits="List" %>
<%@ Register TagPrefix="mobile" Namespace="System.Web.UI.MobileControls"
        Assembly="System.Web.Mobile" %>

<html xmlns="http://www.w3.org/1999/xhtml" >
<body>
    <mobile:Form id="Form1" runat="server">
        <mobile:List ID="LResult" Runat="server" DataTextField="CompanyName"
                DataValueField="CustomerID" Decoration="Bulleted">
        </mobile:List>

    </mobile:Form>
</body>
</html>
```

VB

```
Imports System.Data
Imports System.Data.SqlClient
Imports System.Configuration

Partial Class List
    Inherits System.Web.UI.MobileControls.MobilePage

    Protected Sub Page_Load(ByVal sender As Object, _
        ByVal e As System.EventArgs) Handles Me.Load

        If Not Page.IsPostBack Then
```

```
            Dim MyConnection As SqlConnection
            Dim MyCommand As SqlCommand
            Dim MyReader As SqlDataReader

            MyConnection = New SqlConnection()
            MyConnection.ConnectionString = _
            ConfigurationManager.ConnectionStrings("DSN_Northwind").ConnectionString

            MyCommand = New SqlCommand()
            MyCommand.CommandText = " SELECT TOP 3 * FROM CUSTOMERS "
            MyCommand.CommandType = CommandType.Text
            MyCommand.Connection = MyConnection

            MyCommand.Connection.Open()
            MyReader = MyCommand.ExecuteReader(CommandBehavior.CloseConnection)

            ListControl.DataSource = MyReader
            ListControl.DataBind()

            MyCommand.Dispose()
            MyConnection.Dispose()
        End If

    End Sub
End Class
```

C#

```
using System;
using System.Data;
using System.Data.SqlClient;
using System.Web.Mobile;
using System.Web.UI.MobileControls;
using System.Configuration;

public partial class List : System.Web.UI.MobileControls.MobilePage
{
    protected void Page_Load(object sender, EventArgs e)
    {
        if (!Page.IsPostBack)
        {
         string conn;
         SqlConnection MyConnection;
         SqlCommand MyCommand;
         SqlDataReader MyReader;

         MyConnection = new SqlConnection();
         conn =

         ConfigurationManager.ConnectionStrings["DSN_Northwind"].ConnectionString;

         MyConnection.ConnectionString = conn;
         MyCommand = new SqlCommand();
         MyCommand.CommandText = " SELECT TOP 3 * FROM CUSTOMERS ";
         MyCommand.CommandType = CommandType.Text;
```

(continued)

Listing 25-9: *(continued)*

```
        MyCommand.Connection = MyConnection;

        MyCommand.Connection.Open();
        MyReader = MyCommand.ExecuteReader(CommandBehavior.CloseConnection);

        LResult.DataSource = MyReader;
        LResult.DataBind();

        MyCommand.Dispose();
        MyConnection.Dispose();

    }
  }
}
```

Figure 25-12 shows the result of compiling and executing the code in Listing 25-9.

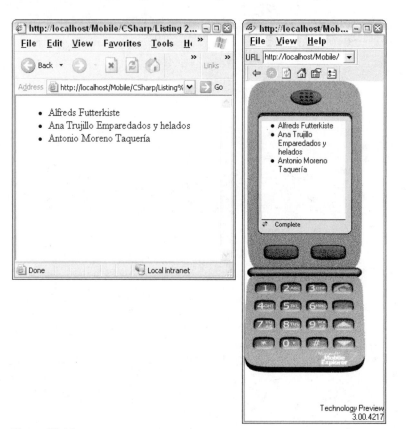

Figure 25-12

The ObjectList Control

The ObjectList control provides an easy-to-use way of viewing tabular information from a database. You can bind a list of records retrieved from the database. The control starts by showing you just a single column from the data source. You can select a record from the list to cause this control to post back to the server and display all columns for the selected record in a vertical list. The control also automatically provides a Back button, which takes you back to the screen showing a single column for all records. You can select the column that you want on the first screen by setting the LabelField property. Leaving this property alone causes this control to select the first column from the record to display on the first screen.

You can reuse the code shown in Listing 25-9 and modify it slightly to bind to an ObjectList control. The result of using this control is shown in Figure 25-13. Clicking the link in the screen on the left brings up the screen shown on the right.

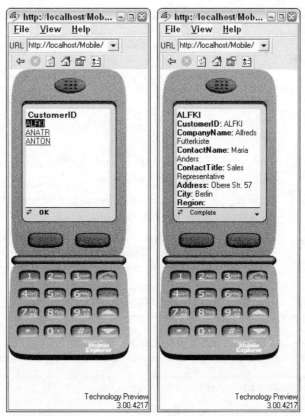

Figure 25-13

The SelectionList Control

The SelectionList control shows a list of items in the form of either a drop-down list, list box, check box list, or radio buttons list, enabling the user to select one or more items from the list. This control doesn't support pagination and is, therefore, a better choice for short lists.

Unlike its counterpart in the ASP.NET Web Forms, this control doesn't provide an auto post back property. Be sure to add a Command control, which causes the postback and fires a server-side event. This control, however, also fires a `SelectedIndexChanged` event on the server after the command object has initiated the postback process. The `SelectedIndexChanged` event, of course, fires only when the user changes the selected value prior to pushing the Command control.

Specifying that this control be rendered as a drop-down list, a list box, a check box list, or a radio-button list is as simple as setting the `SelectType` property. You also have the capability to provide static content to this control by using the `Items` property.

Property	Description
SelectType	This property lets you specify the type of selection list you desire. The available options are `DropDown`, `ListBox`, `Radio`, `MultiSelectListBox`, and `CheckBox`.
DataSource	This property lets you provide a data source object that the control can use to obtain the list.
DataMember	This property lets you provide the `DataTable` name if you choose to use the `DataSet` object as the data source.
DataTextField	This property allows you to select a field from the data source to be displayed on the screen.
DataValueField	This property allows you to select a field from the data source to be used as values for each item. The values aren't displayed on the screen. Instead, they are used to store identifiers for each displayed item.
Wrapping	This property allows you to display a list item on multiple lines if the content is too big to fit on one line.

The code shown in Listing 25-10 illustrates four different SelectionList controls; each control renders a different look, even though all of these controls are bound to the same data source.

Listing 25-10: Examples of SelectionList controls

```
<%@ Page Language="VB" AutoEventWireup="false" CodeFile="SelectionList.aspx.vb"
        Inherits="SelectionListVB" %>
<%@ Register TagPrefix="mobile" Namespace="System.Web.UI.MobileControls"
        Assembly="System.Web.Mobile" %>

<html xmlns="http://www.w3.org/1999/xhtml" >
<body>
```

```
    <mobile:Form id="Form1" runat="server">
        <mobile:SelectionList ID="slistDropDown" Runat="server"
                DataTextField="CompanyName" DataValueField="CustomerID">
        </mobile:SelectionList>
        <mobile:SelectionList ID="slistRadioButton" Runat="server"
                DataTextField="CompanyName" DataValueField="CustomerID"
                SelectType="Radio">
        </mobile:SelectionList>
        <mobile:SelectionList ID="slistCheckBoxes" Runat="server"
                DataTextField="CompanyName" DataValueField="CustomerID"
                SelectType="CheckBox">
        </mobile:SelectionList>
        <mobile:SelectionList ID="slistListBox" Runat="server"
                DataTextField="CompanyName" DataValueField="CustomerID"
                SelectType="ListBox">
        </mobile:SelectionList>

    </mobile:Form>
</html>
```

VB

```
Imports System.Data
Imports System.Data.SqlClient
Imports System.Configuration

Partial Class SelectionList
    Inherits System.Web.UI.MobileControls.MobilePage


    Protected Sub Page_Load(ByVal sender As Object, _
      ByVal e As System.EventArgs) Handles Me.Load

        If Not Page.IsPostBack Then
            Dim MyConnection As SqlConnection
            Dim MyCommand As SqlCommand
            Dim MyAdapter As SqlDataAdapter

            Dim MyDS As DataSet
            MyDS = New DataSet()

            MyConnection = New SqlConnection()
            MyConnection.ConnectionString = _
          ConfigurationManager.ConnectionStrings("DSN_Northwind").ConnectionString

            MyCommand = New SqlCommand()
            MyCommand.CommandText = "SELECT TOP 3 * FROM CUSTOMERS"
            MyCommand.CommandType = CommandType.Text
            MyCommand.Connection = MyConnection

            MyAdapter = New SqlDataAdapter()
            MyAdapter.SelectCommand = MyCommand
```

(continued)

Listing 25-10: *(continued)*

```
            MyAdapter.Fill(MyDS)
            MyCommand.Dispose()

            slistDropDown.DataSource = MyDS.Tables(0).DefaultView
            slistListBox.DataSource = MyDS.Tables(0).DefaultView
            slistRadioButton.DataSource = MyDS.Tables(0).DefaultView
            slistCheckBoxes.DataSource = MyDS.Tables(0).DefaultView

            slistDropDown.DataBind()
            slistListBox.DataBind()
            slistRadioButton.DataBind()
            slistCheckBoxes.DataBind()
        End If

    End Sub
End Class
```

C#

```csharp
using System;
using System.Configuration;
using System.Data;
using System.Data.SqlClient;
using System.Web.Mobile;
using System.Web.UI.MobileControls;

public partial class SelectionList : System.Web.UI.MobileControls.MobilePage
{
    protected void Page_Load(object sender, EventArgs e)
    {
        if (!Page.IsPostBack)
        {
            SqlConnection MyConnection;
            SqlCommand MyCommand;
            SqlDataAdapter MyAdapter;

            DataSet MyDS = new DataSet();

            MyConnection = new SqlConnection();
            MyConnection.ConnectionString =
          ConfigurationManager.ConnectionStrings["DSN_Northwind"].ConnectionString;

            MyCommand = new SqlCommand();
            MyCommand.CommandText = "SELECT TOP 3 * FROM CUSTOMERS";
            MyCommand.CommandType = CommandType.Text;
            MyCommand.Connection = MyConnection;

            MyAdapter = new SqlDataAdapter();
            MyAdapter.SelectCommand = MyCommand;

            MyAdapter.Fill(MyDS);
```

```
            MyCommand.Dispose();

            slistDropDown.DataSource = MyDS.Tables[0].DefaultView;
            slistListBox.DataSource = MyDS.Tables[0].DefaultView;
            slistRadioButton.DataSource = MyDS.Tables[0].DefaultView;
            slistCheckBoxes.DataSource = MyDS.Tables[0].DefaultView;

            slistDropDown.DataBind();
            slistListBox.DataBind();
            slistRadioButton.DataBind();
            slistCheckBoxes.DataBind();

        }

    }
}
```

Running the code shown in Listing 25-10 displays four SelectionList controls, each with a different style, as shown in Figure 25-14.

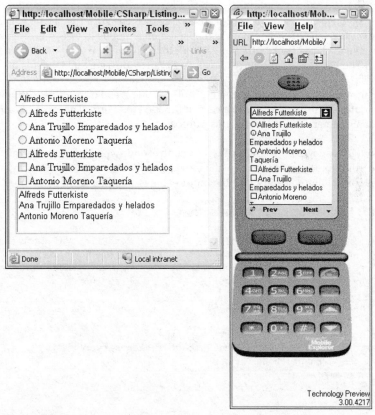

Figure 25-14

Using Validation Controls

The validation controls in mobile Web applications work similar to the way they function in standard ASP.NET Web applications. The RequiredFieldValidator, for instance, is meant to ensure the user provides information in the entry fields. The CompareValidator is used to compare the values of two fields. The RangeValidator is used to ensure that entry fields contain information within an acceptable range. The RegularExpressionValidator validates entry fields by using a custom format string, and the CustomValidator validates entry fields by using custom code.

There are, however, a few differences in the way the validation controls function on Mobile Web Forms. For example, the following properties are not supported for the ValidationSummary control:

❑ DisplayMode

❑ EnableClientScript

❑ ShowMessageBox

❑ ShowSummary

On the other hand, the ValidationSummary control supports two new properties that are not supported in the ASP.NET Web Forms. These properties are BackLabel and FormToValidate. Because of the small screen size, when the validation summary is displayed on a mobile device, it is often shown on a new screen. Users have to click a Back button to get back to the form they were using before the validation error occurred. The BackLabel property allows you to provide a custom label for this Back button.

Mobile Web pages are also capable of using multiple Mobile Web Forms. This feature requires you to assign the ValidationSummary control to a certain Mobile Web Form. The FormToValidate property of the ValidationSummary control serves this purpose.

The code shown in Listing 25-11 shows a TextBox control and two validation controls. The RequiredFieldValidator is meant to ensure the user doesn't leave the text box empty, and the RegularExpressionValidator ensures that the input value is a valid telephone number.

Listing 25-11: Validation controls in action

```
<%@ Page Language="VB" AutoEventWireup="false" CodeFile="Validation.aspx.vb"
        Inherits="Validation" %>
<%@ Register TagPrefix="mobile" Namespace="System.Web.UI.MobileControls"
        Assembly="System.Web.Mobile" %>

<html xmlns="http://www.w3.org/1999/xhtml" >
<body>
    <mobile:Form id="Form1" runat="server">
        <mobile:Label ID="lblPhoneNumber" Runat="server">
                Enter Phone Number:
        </mobile:Label>
        <mobile:TextBox ID="txtPhoneNumber" Runat="server">
        </mobile:TextBox>
        <mobile:RequiredFieldValidator ID="rfvPhone" Runat="server"
```

```
                ControlToValidate="txtPhoneNumber"
                ErrorMessage="Phone number must be provided">*
        </mobile:RequiredFieldValidator>
        <mobile:RegularExpressionValidator ID="revPhone" Runat="server"
                ControlToValidate="txtPhoneNumber"
                ErrorMessage="Invalid Phone Format"
                ValidationExpression="((\(\d{3}\) ?)|(\d{3}-))?\d{3}-\d{4}">*
        </mobile:RegularExpressionValidator>
        <mobile:Command ID="cmdPhoneNumber" Runat="server">OK</mobile:Command>
        <mobile:ValidationSummary ID="ValidationSummary1"
                Runat="server" BackLabel="Return to Entering Phone Number"
                FormToValidate="Form1">
        </mobile:ValidationSummary>

    </mobile:Form>
</body>
</html>
```

Figure 25-15 shows the result of executing the code shown in Listing 25-11.

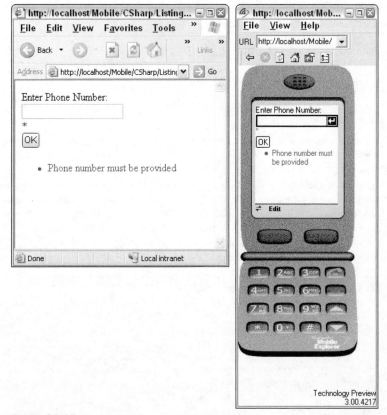

Figure 25-15

Navigating between Mobile Web Forms

A Mobile Web page can contain more than one Mobile Web Form, so you need to learn how to navigate between these forms. There are two ways you can navigate between Mobile Web Forms. You can either set the `ActiveForm` property of the Mobile Web page, or you can redirect using the Link control. If you are redirecting the Link control, you can create a navigation link to another Mobile Web Form on the same Mobile Web page by naming the form and prefixing it with the # symbol.

You can configure both these ways programmatically. While you are inside the class for the Mobile Web Form, you always have access to the `ActiveForm` property, which you can set at any time. You can also programmatically access the `NavigateUrl` property of the Link control and change its value to point to a different Mobile Web Form.

The Mobile Web User Control

A mobile user control is very similar to the ASP.NET Mobile Web Form. You create it in the same manner, fill it with controls and content, and then use it as a control in a page. Mobile Web user controls are stored in `.ascx` files and usually have an associated code-behind file. These controls inherit from the base class `MobileUserControl` in the namespace `System.Web.UI.MobileControls`.

To create a Mobile Web user control, follow these steps:

1. Right-click the project and select Add New Item.

2. In the Add New Item dialog, select Mobile Web User Control from the Visual Studio Installed Templates section.

3. Give the user control a name and select the programming language of your choice. Click the Add button.

The code example shown in Listing 25-13 displays a Mobile Web user control that asks the user to provide a Customer ID. Using the input Customer ID, this user control searches the database and displays a list of matching orders using an ObjectList control. The ObjectList control initially shows only a list of OrderID values. You can click a specific OrderID to see the details of that order.

Before that, though, Listing 25-12 shows a mobile page that is using this user control.

Listing 25-12: Utilizing a mobile user control

```
<%@ Page Language="VB" AutoEventWireup="false" CodeFile="Listing 25-12.aspx.vb"
        Inherits="UserControlSample" %>

<%@ Register Src="OrdersList.ascx" TagName="OrdersList" TagPrefix="uc1" %>
<%@ Register TagPrefix="mobile" Namespace="System.Web.UI.MobileControls"
        Assembly="System.Web.Mobile" %>

<html xmlns="http://www.w3.org/1999/xhtml" >
<body>
    <mobile:Form id="Form1" runat="server">
        <uc1:OrdersList ID="OrdersList1" runat="server" />
    </mobile:Form>
```

```
</body>
</html>
```

From this listing, you can see that first the user control is registered on the mobile page using the @Register page directive. You can also see that by using the attributes TagName and TagPrefix, you can define how you will declare the user control in your code. Finally, the Src attribute points to the location of the user control. You should review how this user control is constructed so you can actually use it in this simple page (see Listing 25-13).

Listing 25-13: Constructing the user control

.ASCX

```
<%@ Control Language="VB" AutoEventWireup="false" CodeFile="OrdersList.ascx.vb"
        Inherits="OrdersList" %>
<%@ Register TagPrefix="mobile" Namespace="System.Web.UI.MobileControls"
        Assembly="System.Web.Mobile" %>


    <mobile:Label ID="lblID" Runat="server">Customer ID</mobile:Label>
    <mobile:TextBox ID="txtCustID" Runat="server">
    </mobile:TextBox>
    <mobile:Command ID="cmdShowOrders" Runat="server"
            OnClick="cmdGetCustomer_Click">
            Show Orders
    </mobile:Command>
    <mobile:ObjectList ID="OLOrders" Runat="server"
            CommandStyle-StyleReference="subcommand"
            LabelStyle-StyleReference="title">
    </mobile:ObjectList>
```

VB

```
Imports System.Data
Imports System.Data.SqlClient
Imports System.Configuration

Partial Class OrdersList
    Inherits System.Web.UI.MobileControls.MobileUserControl

    Protected Sub cmdGetCustomer_Click(ByVal sender As Object, _
                ByVal e As System.EventArgs) Handles cmdShowOrders.Click

        Dim MyConnection As SqlConnection
        Dim MyCommand As SqlCommand
        Dim CustIDParam As SqlParameter
        Dim MyReader As SqlDataReader

        MyConnection = New SqlConnection()
        MyConnection.ConnectionString = _
            ConfigurationManager.ConnectionStrings("DSN_Northwind").ConnectionString

        MyCommand = New SqlCommand()
        MyCommand.CommandText = "SELECT * FROM ORDERS WHERE CustomerID = @CustID"
        MyCommand.CommandType = CommandType.Text
        MyCommand.Connection = MyConnection
        CustIDParam = New SqlParameter()
```

(continued)

Listing 25-13: *(continued)*

```
            CustIDParam.ParameterName = "@CustID"
            CustIDParam.SqlDbType = SqlDbType.NChar
            CustIDParam.Size = 5
            CustIDParam.Direction = ParameterDirection.Input
            CustIDParam.Value = txtCustID.Text

            MyCommand.Parameters.Add(CustIDParam)

            MyCommand.Connection.Open()
            MyReader = MyCommand.ExecuteReader(CommandBehavior.CloseConnection)

            OLOrders.DataSource = MyReader
            OLOrders.DataBind()

            MyCommand.Dispose()
            MyConnection.Dispose()

        End Sub
    End Class
```

C#

```
using System;
using System.Collections;
using System.ComponentModel;
using System.Data;
using System.Drawing;
using System.Web;
using System.Web.Mobile;
using System.Web.SessionState;
using System.Web.UI;
using System.Web.UI.MobileControls;
using System.Web.UI.WebControls;
using System.Web.UI.HtmlControls;

public partial class OrdersListCSharp :
System.Web.UI.MobileControls.MobileUserControl
{
    protected void cmdGetCustomer_Click(object sender, EventArgs e)
    {
        SqlConnection MyConnection ;
        SqlCommand MyCommand;
        SqlParameter CustIDParam;
        SqlDataReader MyReader;

        MyConnection = new SqlConnection();
        MyConnection.ConnectionString =
          ConfigurationManager.ConnectionStrings["DSN_Northwind"].ConnectionString;

        MyCommand = new SqlCommand();
        MyCommand.CommandText = "SELECT * FROM ORDERS WHERE CustomerID = @CustID";
        MyCommand.CommandType = CommandType.Text;
        MyCommand.Connection = MyConnection;

        CustIDParam = new SqlParameter();
```

```
        CustIDParam.ParameterName = "@CustID";
        CustIDParam.SqlDbType = SqlDbType.NChar;
        CustIDParam.Size = 5;
        CustIDParam.Direction = ParameterDirection.Input;
        CustIDParam.Value = txtCustID.Text;

        MyCommand.Parameters.Add(CustIDParam);

        MyCommand.Connection.Open();
        MyReader = MyCommand.ExecuteReader(CommandBehavior.CloseConnection);

        OLOrders.DataSource = MyReader;
        OLOrders.DataBind();

        MyCommand.Dispose();
        MyConnection.Dispose();
    }
}
```

This Mobile Web user control is now ready to be plugged into any Mobile Web Form (such as the one from Listing 25-13). You can create a new Mobile Web Form and drag and drop this Mobile Web user control onto it. You can see how easy it is to reuse it. Figure 25-16 shows the Mobile Web Form displaying its content using a mobile user control.

Figure 25-16

Using Emulators

So far, you have learned that you can develop mobile Web applications for a wide variety of mobile devices. Naturally, you want to be able to ensure that the application will look and function acceptably on the device on which you intend to use to access the application. The only sure ways of testing the application for various devices are either to deploy the application to a server with Internet access or to use a device emulator. Most developers are reluctant to deploy an untested application for Internet accessibility. Device emulators, therefore, provide an effective and practical way for testing an application's appearance and behavior on specific devices.

The manufacturers of most mobile devices provide emulators that simulate the operation of their hardware and browsers. Emulator software enables you to view your ASP.NET Mobile Web Forms application as it might appear on the manufacturer's hardware device. Viewing a Mobile Web Forms application on an emulator is simple. You compile the application and place the URL of the application's start page into the appropriate place in the emulator's browser. Your application operates on an emulator as it would on the actual hardware device.

There are many online sources from which you can download mobile emulators. A few of these sources are listed here:

❑ **OpenWave:** Download this emulator from `http://developer.openwave.com`. The Open Wave emulator supports WML, HTML, and XHTML.

❑ **Ericsson:** You can download this emulator (called WAPIDE) from `www.ericsson.com/developers`. The easiest way to find it is to search for WAPIDE on Ericsson's web site. This emulator requires Java Runtime.

❑ **Nokia:** You can download this emulator from `www.forum.nokia.com`. The easiest way to find it is to search for Mobile Internet Toolkit on Nokia's Web site. This emulator requires Java Runtime to be installed on the machine.

Microsoft Visual Studio uses a built-in browser as the default application browser. You can alter this default so that Visual Studio invokes a mobile device emulator instead. Visual Studio also enables you to easily select a different current device emulator to act as the default application browser. You can obtain the device emulators from mobile device hardware manufacturers and install them on your development computer.

To use an emulator as the Visual Studio application browser, follow these steps:

1. Install and test the mobile device emulator on your development computer as instructed in the emulator's documentation.

2. Right-click on any .ASPX page within a project displayed in the Solution Explorer and choose Browse With to open the Browse With dialog.

3. Click the Add button.

4. Browse to find the executable file for the emulator and provide a friendly name for it.

5. Click OK.

6. If you want to set the emulator as the default browser, highlight it from the list in the Browse With dialog and click the Set As Default button.

Understanding Devices Filters

Device filters give you the ultimate flexibility. You can customize the appearance of controls for either a specific device or for categories of devices. You can base the customization completely on the capability of devices. It helps you ensure that your application looks attractive and functions on all targeted devices.

You can accomplish a number of tasks by using device filters. For example, you can select styles based on the type of device, and you can render a richer presentation to the devices that support it and a toned-down presentation to devices that don't. The device filter stores specific information in the <deviceFilters> section of the web.config file.

There are two types of device filters: comparison-based and evaluator. You can use the comparison-based filter to determine whether a device supports a specific capability. You can accomplish this by comparing the current value of a device capability with a specific value.

The evaluator uses a delegate-based device filter. It allows you to provide a method that is called by the device filter so that you can write custom code to process complex evaluations yourself. You have the flexibility to define this method either in a separate assembly or in the code-behind page.

After you have defined one filter, you can apply it to any number of controls in your mobile Web application. This flexibility is possible because all comparison-based filters are automatically stored in the `web.config` file. The evaluator filters, however, are not declared in the configuration file.

To declare a comparison-based device filter, follow these steps:

1. From the Design View of a page, select the control to which you want to add a comparison-based device filter.

2. Click the ellipsis (...) button next to the `AppliedDeviceFilters` property in the Properties tool window. This action launches the Applied Device Filters dialog.

3. Click the Edit button to either create or modify filters.

4. In the Device Filter Editor dialog, click the New Device Filter button, type the name, and select the filter type.

5. In the Attributes section, select the attribute the device filter will use from the Compare drop-down box, and enter the value to compare against in the Argument text box.

6. Use the Up and Down arrows to set the filter order. The filters are stored in the `web.config` file in this order, and this is the order in which they are applied.

7. Click OK to save the device filter information.

After defining device filters, you can add them to the list of applied filters for a control. You simply click the ellipsis (...) button next to the `AppliedFilters` property of the control. This opens the Applied Device Filters dialog. Select your desired filter from the list of filters and click the Add button. Be sure to keep the filters in the order you need by using the Up Arrow and Down arrow buttons. At runtime, the mobile Web application tests the filters one by one from the top to the bottom. Consequently, the first device filter that results in a successful evaluation determines which property overrides or templates the application uses.

It is also a good practice to add the `(Default)` filter at the end of the list. This ensures that the device that doesn't match any of the filters receives the property values defined for the `(Default)` filter. This filter always results in a successful evaluation and blocks all other evaluations below it in the list.

Mobile Web controls differentiate between device filters by using the name and the argument value of each filter. This means that you can give two device filters the same name as long as they have different argument values.

Figure 25-17 shows the Applied Device Filter and Device Filter Editor dialogs.

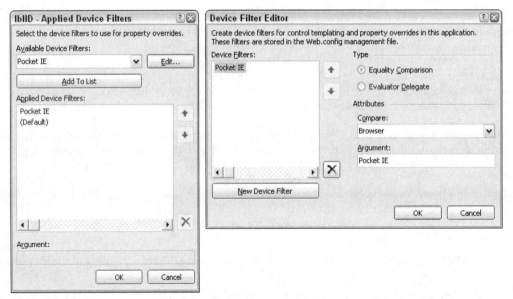

Figure 25-17

Now that you have determined the different kind of devices you want to support and have defined device filters for these devices, the next step is to define override properties for specific device filters. Defining property overrides is as simple as clicking the `PropertyOverrides` property of the Mobile Web control, selecting the device filter from the list, and providing the property value specific to the device filter.

Listing 25-13 shows a simple Mobile Web Form containing three controls. We want the Label and Command controls to display longer versions of the text if the application is accessed by an IE browser on a Pocket PC. We have already defined a device filter that checks to see if the incoming browser is Pocket IE.

Start by selecting the Label control on the Designer window and clicking the ellipsis (...) button next to the `PropertyOverrides` property. In the Property Override window, select the Pocket IE filter from the drop-down list and provide a longer version of the `Text` property to this Label control. Repeat these same steps for the Command control. Figure 25-18 shows the Property Override window for both controls. The title bars on these Windows show the selected control whose properties are being overridden.

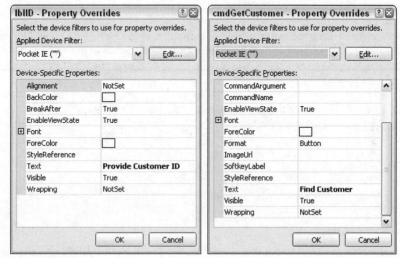

Figure 25-18

State Management in ASP.NET Mobile Applications

Mobile Web Forms provide elegant ways for managing user and page state. These state management mechanisms work in mobile applications in several ways, as the following sections explain.

ViewState in Mobile Web Controls

You already know that ASP.NET Web Forms are capable of maintaining their own state across multiple postbacks. They can do this because of the built-in support for ViewState. ViewState makes a Web Form's lifetime span multiple round trips to the server.

The ViewState in ordinary Web Forms is managed by the Web server using a hidden field in the form. This hidden field contains encoded ViewState data that gets submitted to the Web server every time the Web Form posts back.

However, ViewState in Mobile Web Forms functions in a completely different manner. The main goal for the mobile application is to avoid excessive network traffic due to limited bandwidth available on many mobile devices. As a result, ASP.NET does not send a page's ViewState to the client and, instead, stores it as part of a user's session on the server. A hidden field is still contained in the Mobile Web Form, but it contains an only identifier for the page's ViewState stored on the server.

You can imagine how easy it can be for the current ViewState to be out of synchronization with the current page displayed on the browser, especially if the user uses the Back button on the browser to go back in the history. Suppose you go to Page A, click a button to go to Page B, and then press the Back button to return to Page A. The current page displayed on your browser is now Page A, but the current state on the server is that of Page B.

ASP.NET Mobile Web Forms solve this problem by maintaining a history of ViewState information in the user's session. The identifier sent to the client corresponds to a position in this history. In the previous example, if you again post from Page A, the Mobile Web Form uses the identifier saved with Page A to synchronize the history.

You can configure the size of this history in order to tune your application. The default size is 6 and can be changed by adding a numeric attribute to a tag in the `web.config` file, as shown in the following code:

```
<configuration>
   <system.web>
      <mobileControls sessionStateHistorySize="8" />
   </system.web>
</configuration>
```

Because the ViewState is stored in the user's session, it is possible for it to expire if a page does not post back within the session expiration time. In such cases, the `OnViewStateExpire` method of the page is called. The default implementation of this method throws an exception indicating that the ViewState has expired. However, if you are able to restore ViewState manually after expiration, you can override this method at the page level and not call the base implementation.

Even though storing of ViewState in session has the advantage of reduced network traffic, it can also lead to poorer performance. It is usually a best practice to turn off ViewState on the controls when you don't need to retain the information. Disabling ViewState is as simple as setting the EnableViewState property on the control to `False`. You can also disable the ViewState for an entire page by adding the `EnableViewState="false"` attribute to the `@Page` directive. You should, however, be aware that some mobile controls save essential state information, such as active form, across client roundtrips even when the ViewState is disabled.

Mobile Web applications do not include a mobile control for writing out hidden variables. Instead, the Mobile Form provides a collection called `HiddenVariables` inside the `MobilePage` class that you can use to specify hidden variables. All name/value pairs stored in this collection are persisted as hidden variables. The `HiddenVariables` collection is automatically repopulated with these hidden variables when the form is submitted.

Managing Session State

The session management in ASP.NET functions the same way for mobile applications. It is scalable, robust, and can be used across Web farms. You are provided with a session object that you can use to save information about a user session across multiple requests.

The default behavior of the session management features of ASP.NET require the server to write out a session cookie to a client. The client submits the cookie on each request during the session, and the server looks up the Session State from this information. However, many mobile browsers do not support cookies. In such cases, the session management and the ViewState management require you to configure the application to use a `cookieless` session. `Cookieless` session management automatically inserts the session key in the application's URL.

Hidden Fields

ASP.NET 2.0 provides an elegant way of using hidden fields on a mobile Web application. Instead of providing a Mobile Web control that could be used for storing hidden information, ASP.NET 2.0 provides a collection object for every Mobile Web Form. This collection is called `HiddenVariables` and it is used to store key/value pair information. This information is automatically stored in hidden fields when the Mobile Web page is rendered. When the page is posted back, either to the same page or to a different page, ASP.NET 2.0 retrieves the hidden information from the page and restores the `HiddenVariables` collection. You can simply access the fields from within this collection without being concerned with the behind-the-scene details.

The code in Listing 25-14 shows a simple mobile Web application that lets the user add hidden fields by simply typing them on the screen and clicking the Add Hidden Fields button. The user can also view all the hidden fields by clicking the Show Hidden Fields button.

Listing 25-14: Ways to use hidden fields in mobile Web applications

ASPX Page

```
<%@ Page Language="VB" AutoEventWireup="false" CodeFile="HiddenVariable.aspx.vb"
        Inherits="HiddenVariable" %>
<%@ Register TagPrefix="mobile" Namespace="System.Web.UI.MobileControls"
        Assembly="System.Web.Mobile" %>

<html xmlns="http://www.w3.org/1999/xhtml" >
<body>
    <mobile:Form id="Form1" runat="server">
        <mobile:Label ID="lblKeyName" Runat="server">
         Provide Key Name</mobile:Label>
        <mobile:TextBox ID="txtKeyName" Runat="server">
        </mobile:TextBox>
        <mobile:Label ID="lblVariable" Runat="server">
         Provide Variable Value</mobile:Label>
        <mobile:TextBox ID="txtHiddenField" Runat="server">
        </mobile:TextBox>
        <mobile:Command ID="cmdAddHidden" Runat="server"
        OnClick="cmdAddHidden_Click">
```

(continued)

Listing 25-14: *(continued)*

```
            Add Hidden Fields</mobile:Command><br />
          <mobile:Command ID="cmdShowHidden" Runat="server"
          OnClick="cmdAddHidden_Click">
           Show Hidden Fields</mobile:Command><br />
          <mobile:List ID="lsHiddenFields" Runat="server">
          </mobile:List>
      </mobile:Form>
</body>
</html>
```

VB
```
Partial Class HiddenVariable
    Inherits System.Web.UI.MobileControls.MobilePage

    Protected Sub cmdAddHidden_Click(ByVal sender As Object, _
            ByVal e As System.EventArgs) Handles cmdAddHidden.Click
        Me.HiddenVariables.Add(txtKeyName.Text, txtHiddenField.Text)
    End Sub

    Protected Sub cmdShowHidden_Click(ByVal sender As Object, _
            ByVal e As System.EventArgs) Handles cmdShowHidden.Click
        lsHiddenFields.DataSource = Me.HiddenVariables.Values
        lsHiddenFields.DataBind()
    End Sub
End Class
```

C#
```
using System;
using System.Collections;
using System.Web.Mobile;
using System.Web.SessionState;
using System.Web.UI.MobileControls;

public partial class HiddenVariable : System.Web.UI.MobileControls.MobilePage
{
    protected void cmdShowHidden_Click(object sender, EventArgs e)
    {
        lsHiddenFields.DataSource = this.HiddenVariables.Values;
        lsHiddenFields.DataBind();
    }
    protected void cmdAddHidden_Click(object sender, EventArgs e)
    {
        this.HiddenVariables.Add(txtKeyName.Text, txtHiddenField.Text);
    }
}
```

Figure 25-19 shows the result of executing the code shown in Listing 25-14.

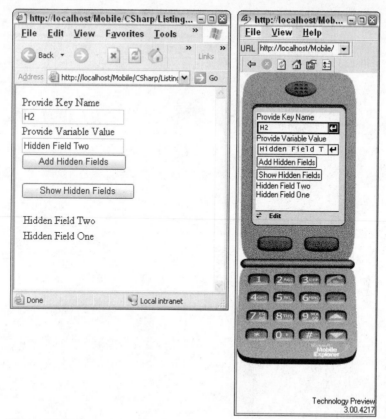

Figure 25-19

Summary

You should now have the knowledge to be successful with your mobile Web development projects. You have learned how you can use various feature-rich mobile Web controls. These controls encapsulate all the details related with rendering to a mobile device by providing an easy-to-use programming interface. The Web Control architecture for Mobile Web Controls enables you to reuse all your business logic and data access code from the ASP.NET Web application, hence providing a highly productive programming environment.

This chapter showed you how to create device-specific displays. The fast-evolving mobile device industry produces new devices with more capability at a more rapid pace than ever before. Programmers needed the capability to customize the rendering of a Mobile Web Control to a specific device to take full advantage of that device's capability. The device filters support provided for mobile Web controls now gives you this capability.

You also learned how you can effectively manage Session State and ViewState. It's important for you to understand how Session State and ViewState are handled differently in Mobile Web applications so that you can take full advantage of these features.

26

Building and Consuming XML Web Services

When the .NET Framework 1.0 was first introduced, much of the hype around its release was focused on XML Web services. In fact, Microsoft advertised that the main purpose of the newly released .NET Framework 1.0 was to enable developers to build and consume XML Web services with ease. Unfortunately, the new Web services model was slow to be accepted by the development community because it was so radically different from those that came before. Decision makers in the development community regarded this new Web services model with a cautious eye.

Since then, Microsoft has stopped trumpeting that .NET is all about Web services and instead has really expanded the power of .NET and its relation to applications built within the enterprise. Still, the members of the IT community continued to look long and hard at the Web services model (Microsoft is no longer alone in hyping this new technology), examining how it could help them with their current issues and problems.

This chapter looks at building XML Web services and how you can consume XML Web service interfaces and integrate them into your ASP.NET applications. It begins with the foundations of XML Web services in the .NET world by examining some of the underlying technologies such as SOAP, WSDL, and more.

Communication Between Disparate Systems

It's a diverse world. In a major enterprise, very rarely do you find that the entire organization and its data repositories reside on a single vendor's platform. In most instances, organizations are made up of a patchwork of systems—some based on Unix, some on Microsoft, and some on other systems.

There probably won't be a day when everything resides on a single platform where all the data moves seamlessly from one server to another. For that reason, these various systems must be able to talk to one another. If disparate systems can communicate easily, moving unique datasets around the enterprise becomes a simple process—alleviating the need for replication systems and data stores.

When XML (eXtensible Markup Language) was introduced, it became clear that the markup language would be the structure to bring the necessary integration into the enterprise. XML's power comes from the fact that it can be used regardless of the platform, language, or data store of the system using it to expose DataSets.

XML has its roots in the Standard Generalized Markup Language (SGML), which was created in 1986. Because SGML was so complex, something a bit simpler was needed—thus the birth of XML.

XML is considered ideal for data representation purposes because it enables developers to structure XML documents as they see fit. For this reason, it is also a bit chaotic. Sending self-structured XML documents between dissimilar systems doesn't make a lot of sense—you would have to custom build the exposure and consumption models for each communication pair.

Vendors and the industry as a whole soon realized that XML needed a specific structure that put some rules in place to clarify communication. The rules defining XML structure make the communication between the disparate systems just that much easier. Tool vendors can now automate the communication process, as well as provide for the automation of the possible creation of all the components of applications using the communication protocol.

The industry settled on using SOAP (Simple Object Access Protocol) to make the standard XML structure work. Previous attempts to solve the communication problem that arose included component technologies such as Distributed Component Object Model (DCOM), Remote Method Invocation (RMI), Common Object Request Broker Architecture (CORBA), and Internet Inter-ORB Protocol (IIOP). These first efforts failed because each of these technologies was either driven by a single vendor or (worse yet) very vendor-specific. It was, therefore, impossible to implement them across the entire industry.

SOAP enables you to expose and consume complex data structures, which can include items such as DataSets, or just tables of data that have all their relations in place. SOAP is relatively simple and easy to understand. Like ASP.NET, XML Web services are also primarily engineered to work over HTTP. The DataSets you send or consume can flow over the same Internet wires (HTTP), thereby bypassing many firewalls (as they move through port 80).

So what's actually going across the wire? ASP.NET Web services generally use SOAP over HTTP using the HTTP Post protocol. An example SOAP request (from the client to the Web service residing on a Web server) takes the structure shown in Listing 26-1.

Listing 26-1: A SOAP request

```
POST /MyWebService/Service.asmx HTTP/1.1
Host: www.wrox.com
Content-Type: text/xml; charset=utf-8
Content-Length: 19
SOAPAction: "http://tempuri.org/HelloWorld"

<?xml version="1.0" encoding="utf-8"?>
```

```
<soap:Envelope xmlns:xsi="http://www.w3.org/2001/XMLSchema-instance"
 xmlns:xsd="http://www.w3.org/2001/XMLSchema"
 xmlns:soap="http://schemas.xmlsoap.org/soap/envelope/">
  <soap:Body>
    <HelloWorld xmlns="http://tempuri.org/" />
  </soap:Body>
</soap:Envelope>
```

The request is sent to the Web service to invoke the `HelloWorld` WebMethod (WebMethods are discussed later in this chapter). The SOAP response from the Web service is shown in Listing 26-2.

Listing 26-2: A SOAP response

```
HTTP/1.1 200 OK
Content-Type: text/xml; charset=utf-8
Content-Length: 14

<?xml version="1.0" encoding="utf-8"?>
<soap:Envelope xmlns:xsi="http://www.w3.org/2001/XMLSchema-instance"
 xmlns:xsd="http://www.w3.org/2001/XMLSchema"
 xmlns:soap="http://schemas.xmlsoap.org/soap/envelope/">
  <soap:Body>
    <HelloWorldResponse xmlns="http://tempuri.org/">
      <HelloWorldResult>Hello World</HelloWorldResult>
    </HelloWorldResponse>
  </soap:Body>
</soap:Envelope>
```

In the examples from Listings 26-1 and 26-2, you can see that what is contained in this message is an XML file. In addition to the normal XML declaration of the `<xml>` node, you see a structure of XML that is the SOAP message. A SOAP message uses a root node of `<soap:Envelope>` that contains the `<soap:Body>` or the body of the SOAP message. Other elements that can be contained in the SOAP message include a SOAP header, `<soap:Header>`, and a SOAP fault — `<soap:Fault>`.

For more information about the structure of a SOAP message, be sure to check out the SOAP specifications. You can find them at the W3C Web site, `http://www.w3.org/tr/soap`.

Building a Simple XML Web Service

Building an XML Web service means that you are interested in exposing some information or logic to another entity either within your organization, to a partner, or to your customers. In a more granular sense, building a Web service means that you, as a developer, simply make one or more methods from a class you create that is enabled for SOAP communication.

You can use Visual Studio 2005 to build an XML Web service. The first step is to actually create a new Web Site by selecting File ➪ New ➪ Web Site from the IDE menu. The New Web Site dialog opens. Select ASP.NET Web Service, as shown in Figure 26-1.

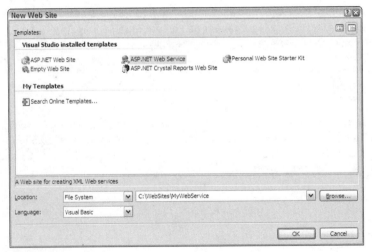

Figure 26-1

Visual Studio creates a few files you can use to get started. In the Solution Explorer of Visual Studio (see Figure 26-2) is a single XML Web service named `Service.asmx`; its code-behind file, `Service.vb`, is located in the `App_Code` folder.

Figure 26-2

Check out the `Service.asmx` file. All ASP.NET Web service files use the `.asmx` file extension instead of the `.aspx` extension used by typical ASP.NET pages.

The WebService Page Directive

Open the `Service.asmx` file in Visual Studio, and you see that the file contains only the `WebService` page directive, as illustrated in Listing 26-3.

Listing 26-3: Contents of the Service.asmx file

```
<%@ WebService Language="VB" CodeBehind="~/App_Code/Service.vb"
    Class="Service" %>
```

You use the @WebService directive instead of the @Page directive.

The simple WebService directive has only four possible attributes. The following list explains these attributes:

- ❑ Class: Required. It specifies the class used to define the methods and data types visible to the XML Web service clients.

- ❑ CodeBehind: Required only when you are working with an XML Web service file using the code-behind model. It enables you to work with Web services in two separate and more manageable pieces instead of a single file. The CodeBehind attribute takes a string value that represents the physical location of the second piece of the Web service — the class file containing all the Web service logic. In ASP.NET 2.0, it is best to place the code-behind files in the App_Code folder, starting with the default Web service created by Visual Studio when you initially opened the Web service project.

- ❑ Debug: Optional. It takes a setting of either True or False. If the Debug attribute is set to True, the XML Web service is compiled with debug symbols in place; setting the value to False ensures that the Web service is compiled without the debug symbols in place.

- ❑ Language: Required. It specifies the language that is used for the Web service.

Looking at the Base Web Service Class File

Now look at the WebService.vb or WebService.cs file — the code-behind file for the XML Web. By default, a structure of code is already in place in the WebService.vb or WebService.cs file, as shown in Listing 26-4.

Listing 26-4: Default code structure provided by Visual Studio for your Web service

```vb
VB
Imports System.Web
Imports System.Web.Services
Imports System.Web.Services.Protocols

<WebService(Namespace := "http://tempuri.org/")> _
<WebServiceBinding(ConformsTo:=WsiProfiles.BasicProfile1_1)> _
Public Class Service
     Inherits System.Web.Services.WebService

    Public Sub Service

    End Sub

    <WebMethod()> _
    Public Function HelloWorld() As String
        Return "Hello World"
    End Function

End Class
```

(continued)

Listing 26-4: *(continued)*

C#

```csharp
using System;
using System.Web;
using System.Web.Services;
using System.Web.Services.Protocols;

[WebService(Namespace = "http://tempuri.org/")]
[WebServiceBinding(ConformsTo = WsiProfiles.BasicProfile1_1)]
public class Service : System.Web.Services.WebService
{

    public Service () {

    }

    [WebMethod]
    public string HelloWorld() {
        return "Hello World";
    }

}
```

Some minor changes to the structure have been made since the .NET 2.0 release. First, the `System.Web.Services.Protocols` namespace is included by default. Therefore, in working with SOAP headers and other capabilities provided via this namespace, you don't need to worry about including it.

The other addition in the 2.0 release is the new `<WebServiceBinding>` attribute. It builds the XML Web service responses that conform to the WS-I Basic Profile 1.0 release (found at `http://www.ws-i.org/Profiles/BasicProfile-1.0-2004-04-16.html`).

Besides these minor changes, very little has changed in this basic *Hello World* structure.

Exposing Custom Datasets as SOAP

To build your own Web service example, delete the `Service.asmx` file and create a new file called `Customers.asmx`. This Web service will expose the Customers table from SQL Server. Then jump into the code shown in Listing 26-5.

Listing 26-5: An XML Web service that exposes the Customers table from Northwind

VB

```vbnet
Imports System.Web
Imports System.Web.Services
Imports System.Web.Services.Protocols
Imports System.Data
Imports System.Data.SqlClient

<WebService(Namespace := "http://www.wrox.com/customers")> _
```

```vbnet
<WebServiceBinding(ConformsTo:=WsiProfiles.BasicProfile1_1)> _
Public Class Customers
    Inherits System.Web.Services.WebService

    <WebMethod()> _
    Public Function GetCustomers() As DataSet
        Dim conn As SqlConnection
        Dim myDataAdapter As SqlDataAdapter
        Dim myDataSet As DataSet
        Dim cmdString As String = "Select * From Customers"

        conn = New SqlConnection("Server=localhost;uid=sa;pwd=;database=Northwind")
        myDataAdapter = New SqlDataAdapter(cmdString, conn)

        myDataSet = New DataSet()
        myDataAdapter.Fill(myDataSet, "Customers")

        Return myDataSet
    End Function

End Class
```

C#

```csharp
using System;
using System.Web;
using System.Web.Services;
using System.Web.Services.Protocols;
using System.Data;
using System.Data.SqlClient;

[WebService(Namespace = "http://www.wrox.com/customers")]
[WebServiceBinding(ConformsTo = WsiProfiles.BasicProfile1_1)]
public class Customers : System.Web.Services.WebService
{

    [WebMethod]
    public DataSet GetCustomers() {
        SqlConnection conn;
        SqlDataAdapter myDataAdapter;
        DataSet myDataSet;
        string cmdString = "Select * From Customers";

        conn = new SqlConnection("Server=localhost;uid=sa;pwd=;database=Northwind");
        myDataAdapter = new SqlDataAdapter(cmdString, conn);

        myDataSet = new DataSet();
        myDataAdapter.Fill(myDataSet, "Customers");

        return myDataSet;
    }

}
```

The WebService Attribute

All Web services are encapsulated within a class. The class is defined as a Web service by the `WebService` attribute placed before the class declaration. Here's an example:

```
<WebService(Namespace := "http://www.wrox.com/customers")> _
```

The `WebService` attribute can take a few properties. By default, the `WebService` attribute is used in your Web service along with the `Namespace` property, which has an initial value of `http://tempuri.org/`. This is meant to be a temporary namespace and should be replaced with a more meaningful and original name, such as the URL where you are hosting the XML Web service. In the example, the `Namespace` value was changed to `http://www.wrox.com/customers`. Remember that it doesn't have to be an actual URL; it can be any string value you want. The idea is that it should be unique. It is common practice is to use a URL because a URL is always unique.

Notice that the two languages define their properties within the `WebService` attribute differently. Visual Basic 2005 uses a colon and an equal sign to set the property:

```
Namespace:="http://www.wrox.com/customers"
```

C# uses just an equal sign to assign the properties within the `WebService` attribute values:

```
Namespace="http://www.wrox.com/customers"
```

Other possible `WebService` properties include `Name` and `Description`. `Name` enables you to change how the name of the Web service is presented to the developer via the ASP.NET test page (the test page is discussed a little later in the chapter). `Description` allows you to provide a textual description of the Web service. The description is also presented on the ASP.NET Web service test page. If your `WebService` attribute contains more than a single property, separate the properties using a comma. Here's an example:

```
<WebService(Namespace:="http://www.wrox.com/customers", Name:="GetCustomers")> _
```

The WebMethod Attribute

In Listing 26-5, the class called `Customers` has only a single `WebMethod`. A `WebService` class can contain any number of `WebMethods`, or a mixture of standard methods along with methods that are enabled to be `WebMethods` via the use of the attribute preceding the method declaration. The only methods that are accessible across the HTTP wire are the ones to which you have applied the `WebMethod` attribute.

Like the `WebService` attribute, `WebMethod` can also contain some properties, which are described in the following list:

❑ **BufferResponse:** When `BufferResponse` is set to `True`, the response from the XML Web service is held in memory and sent as a complete package. If it is set to `False`, the default setting, the response is sent to the client as it is constructed on the server.

- ❑ CacheDuration: Specifies the number of seconds that the response should be held in the system's cache. The default setting is 0, which means that caching is disabled. Putting an XML Web service's response in the cache increases the Web service's performance.

- ❑ Description: Applies a text description to the WebMethod that appears on the .aspx test page of the XML Web service.

- ❑ EnableSession: Setting EnableSession to True enables session state for a particular WebMethod. The default setting is False.

- ❑ MessageName: Applies a unique name to the WebMethod. This is a required step if you are working with overloaded WebMethods (discussed later in the chapter).

- ❑ TransactionOption: Specifies the transactional support for the WebMethod. The default setting is Disabled. If the WebMethod is the root object that initiated the transaction, the Web service can participate in a transaction with another WebMethod that requires a transaction. Other possible values include NotSupported, Supported, Required, and RequiresNew.

The XML Web Service Interface

The Customers Web service from Listing 26-5 has only a single WebMethod that returns a DataSet containing the complete Customers table from the SQL Server Northwind database.

Running Customers.asmx in the browser pulls up the ASP.NET Web service test page. This visual interface to your Web service is really meant for either testing purposes or as a reference page for developers interested in consuming the Web services you expose. The page generated for the Customers Web service is shown in Figure 26-3.

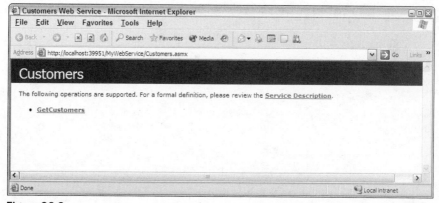

Figure 26-3

The interface shows the name of the Web service in the blue bar (the dark bar in this black and white image) at the top of the page. By default, the name of the class is used unless you changed the value through the `Description` property of the `WebService` attribute, as defined earlier. A bulleted list of links to all the Web service's `WebMethods` is displayed. In this example, there's only one `WebMethod`: `GetCustomers`.

A link to the Web service's Web Services Description Language (WSDL) document is also available (the link is titled Service Description in the figure). The WSDL file is the actual interface with the Customers Web service. The XML document (shown in Figure 26-4) is not really meant for human consumption; it's designed to work with tools such as Visual Studio, informing the tool what the Web service requires to be consumed. Each Web service requires a request that must have parameters of a specific type. When the request is made, the Web service response comes back with a specific set of data defined using specific data types. Everything you need for the request and a listing of exactly what you are getting back in a response (if you are the consumer) is described in the WSDL document.

Clicking the `GetCustomers` link gives you a new page, shown in Figure 26-5, that not only describes the `WebMethod` in more detail, but it also allows you to test the `WebMethod` directly in the browser.

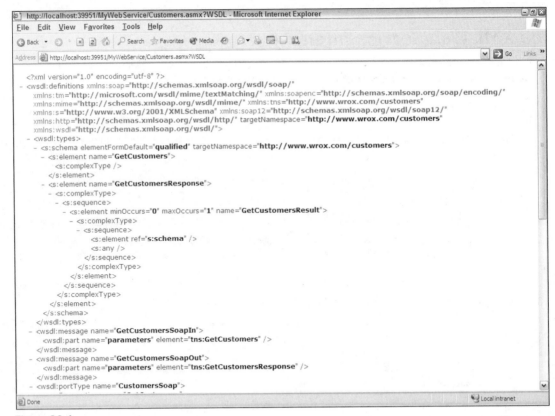

Figure 26-4

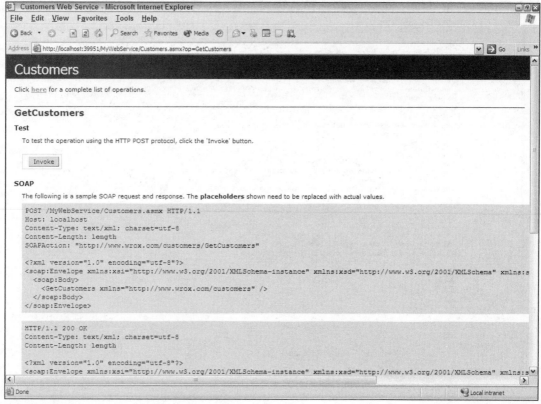

Figure 26-5

At the top of the page is the name of the XML Web service (Customers); below that is the name of this particular WebMethod (GetCustomers). The page shows you the structure of the SOAP messages that are required to consume the WebMethod, as well as the structure the SOAP message takes for the response. Below the SOAP examples is an example of consuming the XML Web service using HTTP Post (with name/value pairs). It is possible to use this method of consumption instead of using SOAP. (This is discussed later in the "Transport Protocols for Web Services" section of this chapter.)

You can test the WebMethod directly from the page. In the Test section, you find a form. If the WebMethod you are calling requires an input of some parameters to get a response, you see some text boxes included so you can provide the parameters before clicking the Invoke button. If the WebMethod you are calling does not require any parameters, you see only the Invoke button and nothing more.

Clicking Invoke is actually sending a SOAP request to the Web service, causing a new browser instance with the result to appear, as illustrated in Figure 26-6.

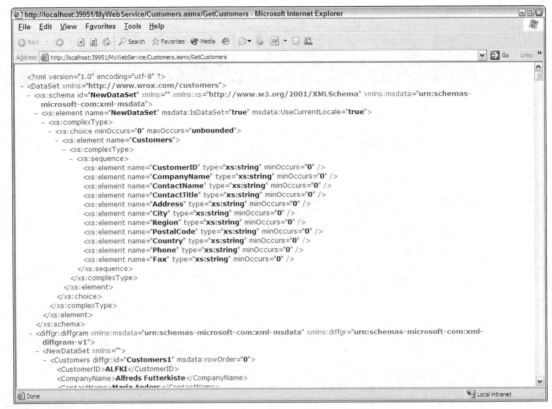

Figure 26-6

Now that everything is in place to expose the XML Web service, you can consume it in an ASP.NET application.

Consuming a Simple XML Web Service

So far, you have seen only half of the XML Web service story. Exposing data and logic as SOAP to disparate systems across the enterprise or across the world is a simple task using .NET and particularly ASP.NET. The other half of the story is the actual consumption of an XML Web service into an ASP.NET application.

You are not limited to consuming XML Web services only into ASP.NET applications; but because this is an ASP.NET book, it focuses on that aspect of the consumption process. Consuming XML Web services into other types of applications is not that difficult and, in fact, is rather similar to how you would consume them using ASP.NET. Remember that the Web services you come across can be consumed in Windows Forms, mobile applications, databases, and more. You can even consume XML Web services with other Web services so you can have a single Web service made up of what is basically an aggregate of other Web services.

Adding a Web Reference

To consume the Customers Web service that you created earlier in this chapter, create a new ASP.NET Web site called `CustomerConsumer`. The first step in consuming an XML Web service in an ASP.NET application is to make a reference to the remote object — the Web service. This is done by right-clicking on the root node of your solution from within the Solution Explorer of Visual Studio and selecting Add Web Reference. This pulls up the Add Web Reference dialog box, shown in Figure 26-7.

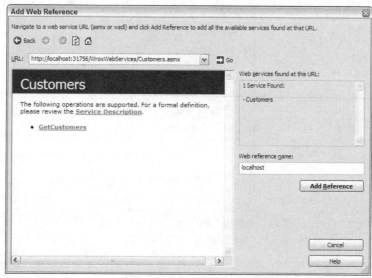

Figure 26-7

The Add Web Reference dialog box enables you to point to a particular `.asmx` file to make a reference to it. Understand that the Add Web Reference dialog is really looking for WSDL files. Microsoft's XML Web services automatically generate WSDL files based on the `.asmx` files themselves. To pull up the WSDL file in the browser, simply type in the URL of your Web service's `.asmx` file and add a `?WSDL` at the end of the string. For example, you might have the following construction:

```
http://www.wrox.com/MyWebService/Customers.asmx?WSDL
```

Because the Add Web Reference dialog automatically finds where the WSDL file is for any Microsoft-based XML Web service, you should simply type in the URL of the actual WSDL file for any non–Microsoft-based XML Web service.

> *If you are using Microsoft's Visual Web Developer Express Edition and its built-in Web server instead of IIS, you will be required to also interject the port number the Web server is using into the URL. In this case, your URL would be structured similar to* `http://localhost:5444/ MyWebService/Customers.asmx?WSDL`.

In the Add Web Reference dialog, change the reference from the default name to something a little more meaningful. If you are working on a single machine, the Web reference might have the name of `localhost`; if you are actually working with a remote Web service, the name is the inverse of the

URL, such as `com.wrox.www`. In either case, it is best to rename it so that the name makes a little more sense and is easy to use within your application. In the example here, the Web reference is renamed `WroxCustomers`.

Clicking the Add Reference button causes Visual Studio to make an actual reference to the Web service from the `web.config` file of your application (shown in Figure 26-8). You may find some additional files under the `App_WebReferences` folder — such as a copy of the Web service's WSDL file.

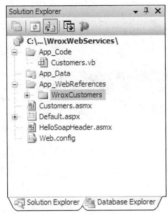

Figure 26-8

Your consuming application's `web.config` file contains the reference to the Web service in its `<appSettings>` section. The addition is shown in Listing 26-6.

Listing 26-6: Changes to the web.config file after making a reference to the Web service

```
<configuration xmlns="http://schemas.microsoft.com/.NetConfiguration/v2.0">
    <appSettings>
        <add key="WroxCustomers.Customers"
          value="http://www.wrox.com/MyWebService/Customers.asmx"/>
    </appSettings>
</configuration>
```

You can see that the `WroxCustomers` reference has been made along with the name of the Web service, providing a key value of `WroxCustomers.Customers`. The `value` attribute takes a value of the location of the Customers Web service, which is found within the `Customers.asmx` page.

Invoking the Web Service from the Client Application

Now that a reference has been made to the XML Web service, you can use it in your ASP.NET application. Create a new Web Form in your project. With this page, you can consume the Customers table from the remote Northwind database directly into your application. The data is placed in a GridView control.

On the design part of the page, place a Button and a GridView control so that your page looks something like the one shown in Figure 26-9.

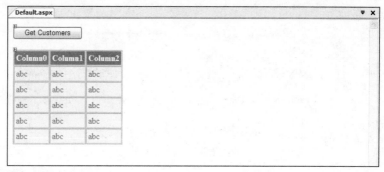

Figure 26-9

The idea is that, when the end user clicks the button contained on the form, the application sends a SOAP request to the Customers Web service and gets back a SOAP response containing the Customers table, which is then bound to the GridView control on the page. Listing 26-7 shows the code for this simple application.

Listing 26-7: Consuming the Customers Web service in an ASP.NET page

VB

```
<%@ Page Language="VB" %>

<script runat="server">
   Protected Sub Button1_Click(ByVal sender As Object, ByVal e As System.EventArgs)
       Dim ws As New WroxCustomers.Customers()
       GridView1.DataSource = ws.GetCustomers()
       GridView1.DataBind()
   End Sub
</script>

<html xmlns="http://www.w3.org/1999/xhtml" >
<head runat="server">
    <title>Web Service Consumer Example</title>
</head>
<body>
    <form id="form1" runat="server">
    <div>
        <asp:Button ID="Button1" Runat="server" Text="Get Customers"
         OnClick="Button1_Click" />
        <br />
        <br />
        <asp:GridView ID="GridView1" Runat="server" BorderWidth="1px"
         BackColor="#DEBA84" CellPadding="3" CellSpacing="2" BorderStyle="None"
         BorderColor="#DEBA84">
            <FooterStyle ForeColor="#8C4510" BackColor="#F7DFB5"></FooterStyle>
            <PagerStyle ForeColor="#8C4510" HorizontalAlign="Center"></PagerStyle>
            <HeaderStyle ForeColor="White" Font-Bold="True"
             BackColor="#A55129"></HeaderStyle>
            <SelectedRowStyle ForeColor="White" Font-Bold="True"
             BackColor="#738A9C"></SelectedRowStyle>
            <RowStyle ForeColor="#8C4510" BackColor="#FFF7E7"></RowStyle>
```

(continued)

Listing 26-7: *(continued)*

```
            </asp:GridView>
        </div>
        </form>
    </body>
    </html>
```

C#

```
<%@ Page Language="C#" %>

<script runat="server">
    protected void Button1_Click(Object sender, EventArgs e) {
        WroxCustomers.Customers ws = new WroxCustomers.Customers();
        GridView1.DataSource = ws.GetCustomers();
        GridView1.DataBind();
    }
</script>
```

The end user is presented with a simple button. Clicking it causes the ASP.NET application to send a SOAP request to the remote XML Web service. The returned DataSet is bound to the GridView control, and the page is redrawn, as shown in Figure 26-10.

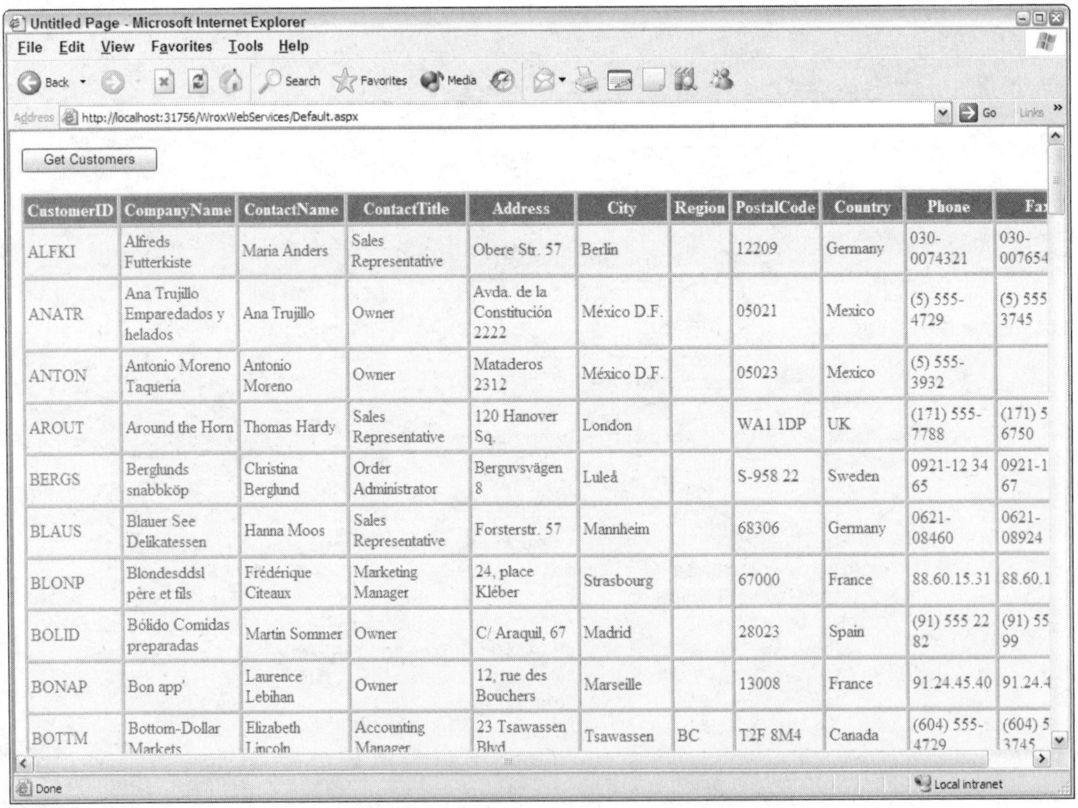

Figure 26-10

The Customers Web service is invoked by the instantiation of the `WroxCustomers.Customers` proxy object:

```
Dim ws As New WroxCustomers.Customers()
```

Then you can use the `ws` object like any other object within your project. In the code example from Listing 26-7, the results of the `ws.GetCustomers()` method call is assigned to the `DataSource` property of the GridView control:

```
GridView1.DataSource = ws.GetCustomers()
```

As you develop or consume more Web services within your applications, you will see more of their power and utility.

Transport Protocols for Web Services

XML Web services use standard wire formats such as HTTP for transmitting SOAP messages back and forth, and this is one of the reasons for the tremendous popularity of Web services. Using HTTP makes using Web services one of the more accessible and consumable messaging protocols when working between disparate systems.

The transport capabilities of Web services are a fresh new addition to the evolutionary idea of a messaging format to use between platforms. DCOM, an older messaging technology that was developed to address the same issues, uses a binary protocol that consists of a method-request layer riding on top of a proprietary communication protocol. One of the problems with using DCOM and similar methods for calling remote objects is that the server's firewall usually gets in the way because DCOM flows through some odd port numbers.

Web services, on the other hand, use a port that is typically open on almost every server — port 80. It's the port that is used for HTTP or Internet traffic. Moving messages from one system to another through port 80 over HTTP is sensible and makes consumption of Web services easy.

An interesting note about XML Web services is that, although many people still think of Web services as SOAP going over HTTP, you can actually consume the Web service in a couple of different ways. Three wire-formats are available to Web services: HTTP-GET, HTTP-POST, and SOAP.

Listing 26-8 shows how to work with these different wire formats by consuming a simple Addition Web service.

Listing 26-8: The Addition Web service

VB

```
Imports System.Web
Imports System.Web.Services
Imports System.Web.Services.Protocols

<WebService(Namespace := "http://www.wrox.com/addition/")> _
<WebServiceBinding(ConformsTo:=WsiProfiles.BasicProfile1_1)> _
Public Class WroxMath
    Inherits System.Web.Services.WebService
```

(continued)

Listing 26-8: *(continued)*

```
    <WebMethod()> _
    Public Function Addition(ByVal a As Integer, ByVal b As Integer) As Integer
        Return (a + b)
    End Function

End Class
```

C#

```
using System;
using System.Web;
using System.Web.Services;
using System.Web.Services.Protocols;

[WebService(Namespace = "http://www.wrox.com/addition/")]
[WebServiceBinding(ConformsTo = WsiProfiles.BasicProfile1_1)]
public class WroxMath : System.Web.Services.WebService
{

    [WebMethod]
    public int Addition(int a, int b) {
        return a + b;
    }

}
```

The Addition Web service takes two parameters: a and b. The Web service then adds these numbers and returns the result in a SOAP message. You might typically consume this Web service by sending a request SOAP message to the service. But now look at some of the other means of consumption.

HTTP-GET

The use of HTTP-GET has been rather popular for quite awhile. It enables you to send your entire request, along with any required parameters, all contained within the URL submission. Here is an example of a URL request that is passing a parameter to the server that will respond:

```
http://www.reuters.com?newscategory=world
```

In this example, a request from the Reuters.com Web site is made, but in addition to a typical Web request, it is also passing along a parameter. Any parameters that are sent along using HTTP-GET can only be in a name/value pair construction — also known as querystrings. This means that you can have only a single value assigned to a single parameter. You can't provide hierarchal structures through querystrings. As you can tell from the previous URL construction, the name/value pair is attached to the URL by ending the URL string with a question mark, followed by the variable name.

Using querystrings, you can also pass more than a single name/value pair with the URL request as the following example shows:

```
http://www.reuters.com?newscategory=world&language=en
```

In this example, the URL construction includes two name/value pairs. The name/value pairs are separated with an ampersand (&).

Now turn your attention to working with the Addition Web service using HTTP-GET. To accomplish this task, you must enable HTTP-GET from within the Web service application because it is disabled by default.

> *HTTP-GET requests have been disabled by default since ASP.NET 1.1. ASP.NET 1.0 did allow for HTTP-GET and even ran the Web service test interface page using it.*

To enable HTTP-GET, make changes to your `web.config` file as shown in Listing 26-9.

Listing 26-9: Enabling HTTP-GET in your Web service applications

```
<configuration xmlns="http://schemas.microsoft.com/.NetConfiguration/v2.0">
   <system.web>
      <webServices>
         <protocols>
            <add name="HttpGet"/>
         </protocols>
      </webServices>
   </system.web>
</configuration>
```

Creating a `<protocols>` section in your `web.config` file enables you to add or remove protocol communications. For example, you can add missing protocols (such as HTTP-GET) by using the syntax shown previously, or you can remove protocols as the following example shows:

```
<configuration xmlns="http://schemas.microsoft.com/.NetConfiguration/v2.0">
   <system.web>
      <webServices>
         <protocols>
            <remove name="HttpGet"/>
            <remove name="HttpPost"/>
            <remove name="HttpSoap"/>
            <remove name="Documentation"/>
         </protocols>
      </webServices>
   </system.web>
</configuration>
```

You don't want to remove everything shown in this code because that would leave your Web service with basically no capability to communicate; but you can see the construction required for any of the protocols that you do want to remove. HTTP-POST and SOAP are covered shortly, but the node removing `Documentation` is interesting in that it can eliminate the ability to invoke the Web services interface test page if you don't want to make that page available.

After you have enabled your Web service to receive HTTP-GET requests, you build a page that uses that protocol to communicate with the Addition Web service. The Web page is shown in Listing 26-10.

Listing 26-10: Invoking the Addition Web service using HTTP-GET

```
<html>
<head>
    <title>HTTP-GET Example</title>
</head>
<body>
    <a href="http://www.wrox.com/WroxMath.asmx/Addition?a=5&b=2">
      http://www.wrox.com/WroxMath.asmx/Addition?a=5&b=2</a>
</body>
</html>
```

This is a simple page with the single hyperlink pointing at the Addition Web service. When the page is run, you get the result shown in Figure 26-11.

Figure 26-11

To call a Web service using HTTP-GET, you call the actual file (`WroxMath.asmx`), followed by the method name (in this case, `/Addition`), followed by a querystring list of required parameters. In the example, values for a and b are passed in the URL. The diagram in Figure 26-12 details the construction of the URL.

Figure 26-12

Pull up the `WroxMath.aspx` page and click the link to produce the following text result in the browser:

```
<?xml version="1.0" encoding="utf-8" ?>
<int xmlns="http://wrox.com/addition/">7</int>
```

One little caveat when constructing your URL string is that the `WebMethod` name in the URL construction is case-sensitive. If you type `addition` instead of `Addition`, you get an error. Also, be sure to consider when it makes sense to use HTTP-GET; it can be a security risk. It is quite easy to alter values in the query-string to either input false values or values that might cause harm to a server. That's why HTTP-GET capabilities were removed from the default settings of the Web services model.

HTTP-POST

The HTTP-POST protocol is similar to HTTP-GET in that you are sending name/value pairs to the server for processing. The big difference is that HTTP-POST places these name/value pairs within a request header so that they are not visible; HTTP-GET sends these same items within a viewable, open URL string.

Setting up a standard HTML page to communicate with the Addition Web service using HTTP-POST is relatively simple, as illustrated in Listing 26-11.

Listing 26-11: Using HTTP-POST to send a request to an XML Web service

```
<html>
<head>
   <title>HTTP-POST Example</title>
</head>
<body>
   <form method="post" action="http://www.wrox.com/WroxMath.asmx/Addition">
       <p><input type="text" name="a"></p>
       <p><input type="text" name="b"></p>
       <p><input type="submit" value="Call Web Service"></p>
   </form>
</body>
</html>
```

This example puts two text boxes and a button on the form. In order to provide the form elements to be posted in the request, the construction of the text boxes and the `<form>` element are important when working with an XML Web service using HTTP-POST. The `<form>` element here contains two attributes. The first is `method`, which specifies that the form is using HTTP-POST for the request. The `action` attribute provides a link to the `WebMethod` that will be called. As with HTTP-GET, the construction of the URL takes the format of the `.asmx` page followed by the name of the `WebMethod` (`Addition`).

The two text boxes are typical text boxes. This process uses the `name` attribute, giving it a value of the parameter name required by the Web service. In the example, the two required parameters are a and b.

Posting this page (by clicking the Submit button), produces the same results as the HTTP-GET request:

```
<?xml version="1.0" encoding="utf-8" ?>
<int xmlns="http://tempuri.org/">7</int>
```

SOAP

The final method of communicating with an XML Web service is by using SOAP, which was discussed earlier in the chapter. The SOAP message is actually sent in an HTTP request, but does not use the name/value pair construction.

Representing data as SOAP messages brings a lot more value than the simple construction of name/value pairs. SOAP enables you to represent data in a hierarchical manner — something you cannot do when using name/value pairs. For instance, how would you send the Customers table from the Northwind database if you were limited to using name/value pairs? It would be impossible to represent the data properly. SOAP permits this type of data representation. Also, as you get into more advanced Web service scenarios, you can expand the SOAP messages and allow for authentication/authorization capabilities, SOAP routing, partial encryption capabilities, and more. The expandability of SOAP is a powerful feature.

> *Web Services Enhancements (WSE) is a powerful toolset from Microsoft that enables you to build advanced Web services for specialized situations, as described previously. You can find more information on the WSE at* `http://msdn.microsoft.com/webservices/`*.*

Overloading WebMethods

In the object-oriented world of .NET, it is quite possible to use method overloading in the code you develop. A true object-oriented language has support for *polymorphism* of which method overloading is a part. Method overloading enables you to have multiple methods that use the same name but have different signatures. With method overloading, one method can be called, but the call is routed to the appropriate method based on the full signature of the request. An example of standard method overloading is illustrated in Listing 26-12.

Listing 26-12: Method overloading in .NET

VB
```
Public Function HelloWorld() As String
    Return "Hello"
End Function

Public Function HelloWorld(ByVal FirstName As String) As String
    Return "Hello " & FirstName
End Function
```

C#
```
public string HelloWorld() {
    return "Hello";
}

public string HelloWorld(string FirstName) {
    return "Hello " + FirstName;
}
```

In this example, both methods have the same name, `HelloWorld`. So, which one is called when you invoke `HelloWorld`? Well, it depends on the signature you pass to the method. For instance, you might provide the following:

```
Label1.Text = HelloWorld()
```

This yields a result of just `Hello`. However, you might invoke the `HelloWorld()` method using the following signature:

```
Label1.Text = HelloWorld("Bill Evjen")
```

Then you get back a result of `Hello Bill Evjen`. As you can see, method overloading is a great feature that can be effectively utilized by your ASP.NET applications — but how do you go about overloading `WebMethods`?

If you have already tried to overload any of your WebMethods, you probably got the following error when you pulled up the Web service in the browser:

```
Both System.String HelloWorld(System.String) and System.String HelloWorld() use the
message name 'HelloWorld'. Use the MessageName property of the WebMethod custom
attribute to specify unique message names for the methods.
```

As this error states, the extra step you have to take to overload `WebMethods` is to use the `MessageName` property. Listing 26-13 shows how.

Listing 26-13: WebMethod overloading in .NET

VB
```
<WebMethod(MessageName:="HelloWorld")> _
Public Function HelloWorld() As String
    Return "Hello"
End Function

<WebMethod(MessageName:="HelloWorldWithFirstName")> _
Public Function HelloWorld(ByVal FirstName As String) As String
    Return "Hello " & FirstName
End Function
```

C#
```
[WebMethod(MessageName="HelloWorld")]
public string HelloWorld() {
    return "Hello";
}

[WebMethod(MessageName="HelloWorldWithFirstName")]
public string HelloWorld(string FirstName) {
    return "Hello " + FirstName;
}
```

In addition to adding the `MessageName` property of the `WebMethod` attribute, you have to disable your Web service's adherence to the WS-I Basic Profile 1.0 specification — which it wouldn't be doing if you perform WebMethod overloading with your Web services. You can disable the conformance to the WS-I Basic Profile specification in a couple of ways. The first way is to add the `<WebServiceBinding>` attribute to your code, as illustrated in Listing 26-14.

Listing 26-14: Changing your Web service so it does not conform to the WS-I Basic Profile spec

VB
```
<WebServiceBinding(ConformsTo := WsiProfiles.None)> _
Public Class MyOverloadingExample
    ' Code here
End Class
```

C#
```
[WebServiceBinding(ConformsTo = WsiProfiles.None)]
public class WroxMath : System.Web.Services.WebService
{
    // Code here
}
```

The other option is to turn off the WS-I Basic Profile 1.0 capability in the `web.config` file, as shown in Listing 26-15.

Listing 26-15: Turning off conformance using the web.config file

```
<configuration>
  <system.web>
    <webServices>
      <conformanceWarnings>
        <remove name="BasicProfile1_1" />
      </conformanceWarnings>
    </webServices>
  </system.web>
</configuration>
```

After you have enabled your Web service to overload `WebMethods`, you can see both `WebMethods` defined by their `MessageName` value properties when you pull up the Web service's interface test page in the browser (see Figure 26-13).

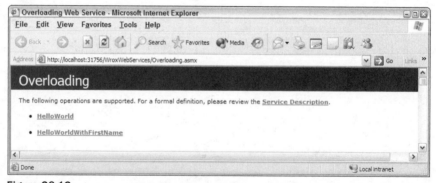

Figure 26-13

Although you can see the names of the `WebMethods` as distinct (based on the `MessageName` property values you assigned in your code through the Web service's test page), when the developer consuming the Web service makes a Web reference to your Web service, he sees only a single method name available (in this example, `HelloWorld`). This is shown in the IntelliSense of Visual Studio 2005 in the application consuming these methods (see Figure 26-14).

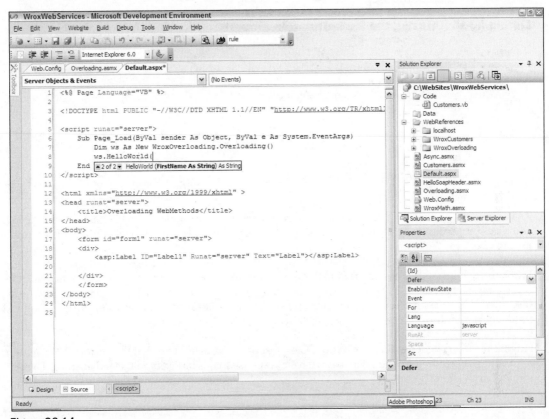

Figure 26-14

In the yellow box that pops up to guide developers on the signature structure, you can see two options available — one is an empty signature, and the other requires a single string.

Caching Web Service Responses

Caching is an important feature in almost every application that you build with .NET. Most of the caching capabilities available to you in ASP.NET are discussed in Chapters 19 and 20, but a certain feature of Web services in .NET enables you to cache the SOAP response sent to any of the service's consumers.

First, by way of review, remember that caching is the capability to maintain an in-memory store where data, objects, and various items are stored for reuse. This feature increases the responsiveness of the applications you build and manage. Sometimes, returning cached results can greatly affect performance.

XML Web services use an attribute to control caching of SOAP responses — the CacheDuration property. Listing 26-16 shows its use.

Listing 26-16: Utilizing the CacheDuration property

VB

```
<WebMethod(CacheDuration:=60)> _
Public Function GetServerTime() As String
    Return DateTime.Now.ToLongTimeString()
End Function
```

C#

```
[WebMethod(CacheDuration=60)]
public string GetServerTime() {
    return DateTime.Now.ToLongTimeString();
}
```

As you can see, CacheDuration is used within the WebMethod attribute much like the Description and Name properties. CacheDuration takes an Integer value that is equal to the number of seconds during which the SOAP response is cached.

When the first request comes in, the SOAP response is cached by the server, and the consumer gets the same timestamp in the SOAP response for the next minute. After that minute is up, the stored cache is discarded, and a new response is generated and stored in the cache again for servicing all other requests for the next minute.

Among the many benefits of caching your SOAP responses, you will find that the performance of your application is greatly improved when you have a response that is basically re-created again and again without any change.

SOAP Headers

One of the more common forms of extending the capabilities of SOAP messages is to add metadata of the request to the SOAP message itself. The metadata is usually added to a section of the SOAP envelope called the *SOAP header*. Figure 26-15 shows the structure of a SOAP message.

Figure 26-15

The entire SOAP message is referred to as a *SOAP envelope*. Contained within the SOAP message is the *SOAP body* — a piece of the SOAP message that you have been working with in every example thus far. It is a required element of the SOAP message.

The one optional component of the SOAP message is the SOAP header. It is the part of the SOAP message in which you can place any metadata about the overall SOAP request instead of incorporating it in the signature of any of your `WebMethods`. It is important to keep metadata separate from the actual request.

What kind of information? It could include a lot of things. One of the more common items placed in the SOAP header is any authentication/authorization functionality required to consume your Web service or to get at specific pieces of logic or data. Placing usernames and passwords inside the SOAP headers of your messages is a good example of what you might include.

Building a Web Service with SOAP Headers

You can build upon the sample `HelloWorld` Web service that is presented in the default `.asmx` page when it is first pulled up in Visual Studio (from Listing 26-4). Name the new `.asmx` file `HelloSoapHeader.asmx`. The initial step is to add a class that is an object representing what is to be placed in the SOAP header by the client, as shown in Listing 26-17.

Listing 26-17: A class representing the SOAP header

VB
```
Public Class HelloHeader
    Inherits System.Web.Services.Protocols.SoapHeader

    Public Username As String
    Public Password As String
End Class
```

C#
```
public class HelloHeader : SoapHeader
{
    public string Username;
    public string Password;
}
```

The class, representing a SOAP header object, has to inherit from the `SoapHeader` class from `System.Web.Services.Protocols.SoapHeader`. The `SoapHeader` class serializes the payload of the `<soap:header>` element into XML for you. In the example in Listing 26-17, you can see that this SOAP header requires two elements — simply a username and a password, both of type `String`. The names you create in this class are those used for the subelements of the SOAP header construction, so it is important to name them descriptively.

Listing 26-18 shows the Web service class that instantiates an instance of the `HelloHeader` class.

Listing 26-18: A Web service class that utilizes a SOAP header

VB

```vb
<WebService(Namespace:="http://www.wrox.com/helloworld")> _
<WebServiceBinding(ConformsTo:=WsiProfiles.BasicProfile1_1, _
  EmitConformanceClaims:=True)> _
Public Class HelloSoapHeader
    Inherits System.Web.Services.WebService

    Public myHeader As HelloHeader

    <WebMethod(), SoapHeader("myHeader")> _
    Public Function HelloWorld() As String
        If (myHeader Is Nothing) Then
            Return "Hello World"
        Else
            Return "Hello " & myHeader.Username & ". " & _
                "<br>Your password is: " & myHeader.Password
        End If
    End Function

End Class
```

C#

```csharp
[WebService(Namespace = "http://www.wrox.com/helloworld")]
[WebServiceBinding(ConformsTo = WsiProfiles.BasicProfile1_1)]
public class HelloSoapHeader : System.Web.Services.WebService
{

    public HelloHeader myHeader;

    [WebMethod]
    [SoapHeader("myHeader")]
    public string HelloWorld() {
        if (myHeader == null) {
            return "Hello World";
        }
        else }
        }
            return "Hello " + myHeader.Username + ". " +
                "<br>Your password is: " + myHeader.Password;
    }
        }


}
        }
```

The Web service, `HelloSoapHeader`, has a single `WebMethod`—`HelloWorld`. Within the Web service class, but outside of the `WebMethod` itself, you create an instance of the `SoapHeader` class. This is done with the following line of code:

```
Public myHeader As HelloHeader
```

Now that you have an instance of the `HelloHeader` class that you created earlier called `myHeader`, you can use that instantiation in your `WebMethod`. Because Web services can contain any number of `WebMethods`, it is not a requirement that all `WebMethods` use an instantiated SOAP header. You specify whether a `WebMethod` will use a particular instantiation of a SOAP header class by placing the `SoapHeader` attribute before the WebMethod declaration.

```
<WebMethod(), SoapHeader("myHeader")> _
Public Function HelloWorld() As String
    ' Code here
End Function
```

In this example, the `SoapHeader` attribute takes a `string` value of the name of the instantiated `SoapHeader` class — in this case, `myHeader`.

From here, the `WebMethod` actually makes use of the `myHeader` object. If the `myHeader` object is not found (meaning that the client did not send in a SOAP header with his constructed SOAP message), a simple "`Hello World`" is returned. However, if values are provided in the SOAP header of the SOAP request, those values are used within the returned `string` value.

Consuming a Web Service Using SOAP Headers

It really isn't difficult to build an ASP.NET application that makes a SOAP request to a Web service using SOAP headers. Just as with the Web services that don't include SOAP headers, you make a Web Reference to the remote Web service directly in Visual Studio.

For the ASP.NET page, create a simple page with a single Label control. The output of the Web service is placed in the Label control. The code for the ASP.NET page is shown in Listing 26-19.

Listing 26-19: An ASP.NET page working with an XML Web service using SOAP headers

VB
```
<%@ Page Language="VB" %>

<script runat="server">
    Protected Sub Page_Load(ByVal sender As Object, ByVal e As System.EventArgs)
        Dim ws As New localhost.HelloSoapHeader()
        Dim wsHeader As New localhost.HelloHeader()

        wsHeader.Username = "Bill Evjen"
        wsHeader.Password = "Bubbles"
        ws.HelloHeaderValue = wsHeader

        Label1.Text = ws.HelloWorld()
    End Sub
</script>

<html xmlns="http://www.w3.org/1999/xhtml" >
<head runat="server">
    <title>Working with SOAP headers</title>
</head>
<body>
    <form id="form1" runat="server">
    <div>
        <asp:Label ID="Label1" Runat="server"></asp:Label>
    </div>
    </form>
</body>
</html>
```

(continued)

Listing 26-19: *(continued)*

C#

```
<%@ Page Language="C#" %>

<script runat="server">
    protected void Page_Load(object sender, System.EventArgs e) {
        localhost.HelloSoapHeader ws = new localhost.HelloSoapHeader();
        localhost.HelloHeader wsHeader = new localhost.HelloHeader();

        wsHeader.Username = "Bill Evjen";
        wsHeader.Password = "Bubbles";
        ws.HelloHeaderValue = wsHeader;

        Label1.Text = ws.HelloWorld();
    }
</script>
```

Two objects are instantiated. The first is the actual web service, HelloSoapHeader. The second, which is instantiated as wsHeader, is the SoapHeader object. After both of these objects are instantiated and before making the SOAP request in the application, you construct the SOAP header. This is as easy as assigning values to the Username and Password properties of the wsHeader object. After these properties are assigned, you associate the wsHeader object to the ws object through the use of the HelloHeaderValue property. After you have made the association between the constructed SOAP header object and the actual WebMethod object (ws), you can make a SOAP request just as you would normally do:

```
Label1.Text = ws.HelloWorld()
```

Running the page produces the result in the browser shown in Figure 26-16.

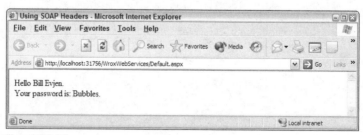

Figure 26-16

What is more interesting, however, is that the SOAP request reveals that the SOAP header was indeed constructed into the overall SOAP message, as shown in Listing 26-20.

Listing 26-20: The SOAP request

```
<?xml version="1.0" encoding="utf-8" ?>
<soap:Envelope xmlns:soap="http://schemas.xmlsoap.org/soap/envelope/"
 xmlns:xsi="http://www.w3.org/2001/XMLSchema-instance"
 xmlns:xsd="http://www.w3.org/2001/XMLSchema">
```

```
    <soap:Header>
       <HelloHeader xmlns="http://www.wrox.com/helloworld/">
          <Username>Bill Evjen</Username>
          <Password>Bubbles</Password>
       </HelloHeader>
    </soap:Header>
    <soap:Body>
       <HelloWorld xmlns="http://www.wrox.com/helloworld/" />
    </soap:Body>
 </soap:Envelope>
```

This returns the SOAP response shown in Listing 26-21.

Listing 26-21: The SOAP response

```
<?xml version="1.0" encoding="utf-8" ?>
<soap:Envelope xmlns:soap="http://schemas.xmlsoap.org/soap/envelope/"
 xmlns:xsi="http://www.w3.org/2001/XMLSchema-instance"
 xmlns:xsd="http://www.w3.org/2001/XMLSchema">
   <soap:Body>
      <HelloWorldResponse xmlns="http://www.wrox.com/helloworld/">
         <HelloWorldResult>Hello Bill Evjen. Your password is:
         Bubbles</HelloWorldResult>
      </HelloWorldResponse>
   </soap:Body>
</soap:Envelope>
```

Requesting Web Services Using SOAP 1.2

Most Web services out there use SOAP version 1.1 for the construction of their messages. With that said, SOAP 1.2 became a W3C recommendation in June 2003 (see www.w3.org/TR/soap12-part1/). The nice thing about XML Web services in the .NET Framework 2.0 platform is that they are capable of communicating in both the 1.1 and 1.2 versions of SOAP.

In an ASP.NET application that is consuming a Web service, you can control whether the SOAP request is constructed as a SOAP 1.1 message or a 1.2 message. Listing 26-22 changes the previous example so that the request uses SOAP 1.2 instead of the default setting of SOAP 1.1.

Listing 26-22: An ASP.NET Application Making a SOAP Request Using SOAP 1.2

VB
```
<%@ Page Language="VB" %>

<script runat="server">
    Protected Sub Page_Load(ByVal sender As Object, ByVal e As System.EventArgs)
        Dim ws As New localhost.HelloSoapHeader()
        Dim wsHeader As New localhost.HelloHeader()

        wsHeader.Username = "Bill Evjen"
        wsHeader.Password = "Bubbles"
        ws.HelloHeaderValue = wsHeader
```

(continued)

Listing 26-22: *(continued)*

```
        ws.SoapVersion = System.Web.Services.Protocols.SoapProtocolVersion.Soap12

        Label1.Text = ws.HelloWorld()
    End Sub
</script>
```

C#

```
<%@ Page Language="C#" %>

<script runat="server">
    protected void Page_Load(object sender, System.EventArgs e) {
        localhost.HelloSoapHeader ws = new localhost.HelloSoapHeader();
        localhost.HelloHeader wsHeader = new localhost.HelloHeader();

        wsHeader.Username = "Bill Evjen";
        wsHeader.Password = "Bubbles";
        ws.HelloHeaderValue = wsHeader;

        ws.SoapVersion = System.Web.Services.Protocols.SoapProtocolVersion.Soap12;

        Label1.Text = ws.HelloWorld();
    }
</script>
```

In this example, you first provide an instantiation of the Web service object and use the new
`SoapVersion` property. The property takes a value of `System.Web.Services.Protocols.`
`SoapProtocolVersion.Soap12` to work with SOAP 1.2 specifically.

With this bit of code in place, the SOAP request takes the structure shown in Listing 26-23.

Listing 26-23: The SOAP request using SOAP 1.2

```
<?xml version="1.0" encoding="utf-8"?>
<soap:Envelope xmlns:soap="http://www.w3.org/2003/05/soap-envelope"
 xmlns:xsi="http://www.w3.org/2001/XMLSchema-instance"
 xmlns:xsd="http://www.w3.org/2001/XMLSchema">
   <soap:Header>
      <HelloHeader xmlns="http://www.wrox.com/helloworld/">
         <Username>Bill Evjen</Username>
         <Password>Bubbles</Password>
      </HelloHeader>
   </soap:Header>
   <soap:Body>
      <HelloWorld xmlns="http://www.wrox.com/helloworld/" />
   </soap:Body>
</soap:Envelope>
```

One difference between the two examples is the `xmlns:soap` namespace that is used. The difference actually resides in the HTTP header. When you compare the SOAP 1.1 and 1.2 messages, you see a difference
in the `Content-Type` attribute. In addition, the SOAP 1.2 HTTP header does not use the `soapaction`
attribute because this is now combined with the `Content-Type` attribute.

You can turn off either SOAP 1.1 or 1.2 capabilities with the Web services that you build by making the proper settings in the `web.config` file, as shown in Listing 26-24.

Listing 26-24: Turning off SOAP 1.1 or 1.2 capabilities

```
<configuration xmlns="http://schemas.microsoft.com/.NetConfiguration/v2.0">
   <system.web>
      <webServices>
         <protocols>
            <remove name="HttpSoap"/> <!-- Removes SOAP 1.1 abilities -->
            <remove name="HttpSoap1.2"/> <!-- Removes SOAP 1.2 abilities -->
         </protocols>
      </webServices>
   </system.web>
</configuration>
```

Consuming Web Services Asynchronously

All the Web services that you have been working with in this chapter have been done *synchronously*. This means that after a request is sent from the code of an ASP.NET application, the application comes to a complete standstill until a SOAP response is received.

The process of invoking a `WebMethod` and getting back a result can take some time for certain requests. At times, you are not in control of the Web service from which you are requesting data and, therefore, you are not in control of the performance or response times of these services. For these reasons, you should consider consuming Web services *asynchronously*.

An ASP.NET application that makes an asynchronous request can work on other programming tasks while the initial SOAP request is awaiting a response. When the ASP.NET application is done working on the additional items, it can return to get the result form the Web service.

The great news is that to build an XML Web service that allows asynchronous communication, you don't have to perform any additional actions. All `.asmx` Web services have the built-in capability for asynchronous communication with consumers. The Web service in Listing 26-25 is an example.

Listing 26-25: A slow Web service

VB
```
<%@ WebService Language="VB" Class="Async" %>

Imports System.Web
Imports System.Web.Services
Imports System.Web.Services.Protocols

<WebServiceBinding(ConformsTo:=WsiProfiles.BasicProfile1_1,
   EmitConformanceClaims:=True)> _
Public Class Async
    Inherits System.Web.Services.WebService
```

(continued)

Listing 26-25: *(continued)*

```vb
    <WebMethod()> _
    Public Function HelloWorld() As String
        System.Threading.Thread.Sleep(1000)
        Return "Hello World"
    End Function

End Class
```

C#

```csharp
using System;
using System.Web;
using System.Web.Services;
using System.Web.Services.Protocols;

[WebService(Namespace = "http://www.wrox.com/AsyncHelloWorld")]
[WebServiceBinding(ConformsTo = WsiProfiles.BasicProfile1_1)]
public class Async : System.Web.Services.WebService
{

    [WebMethod]
    public string HelloWorld() {
        System.Threading.Thread.Sleep(1000);
        return "Hello World";
    }

}
```

This Web service returns a simple `Hello World` as a string, but before it does, the Web service makes a 1000-millisecond pause. This is done by putting the Web service thread to sleep using the `Sleep` method.

Next, take a look at how an ASP.NET application can consume this slow Web service asynchronously, as illustrated in Listing 26-26.

Listing 26-26: An ASP.NET application consuming a Web service asynchronously

VB

```vb
<%@ Page Language="VB" %>

<script runat="server">
    Protected Sub Page_Load(ByVal sender As Object, ByVal e As System.EventArgs)
        Dim ws As New localhost.Async()
        Dim myIar As IAsyncResult

        myIar = ws.BeginHelloWorld(Nothing, Nothing)

        Dim x As Integer = 0

        Do Until myIar.IsCompleted = True
            x += 1
        Loop
```

```
        Label1.Text = "Result from Web service: " & ws.EndHelloWorld(myIar) & _
            "<br>Local count while waiting: " & x.ToString()
    End Sub
</script>

<html xmlns="http://www.w3.org/1999/xhtml" >
<head runat="server">
    <title>Async consumption</title>
</head>
<body>
    <form id="form1" runat="server">
    <div>
        <asp:Label ID="Label1" Runat="server"></asp:Label>
    </div>
    </form>
</body>
</html>
```

C#

```
<%@ Page Language="C#" %>

<script runat="server">
    protected void Page_Load(object sender, System.EventArgs e) {
        localhost.Async ws = new localhost.Async();
        IAsyncResult myIar;

        myIar = ws.BeginHelloWorld(null, null);

        int x = 0;

        while (myIar.IsCompleted == false) {
            x += 1;
        }

        Label1.Text = "Result from Web service: " + ws.EndHelloWorld(myIar) +
            "<br>Local count while waiting: " + x.ToString();
    }
</script>
```

When you make the Web reference to the remote Web service in the consuming ASP.NET application, you not only see the HelloWorld WebMethod available to you in IntelliSense, you also see a BeginHelloWorld and an EndHelloWorld. To work with the Web service asynchronously, you must utilize the BeginHelloWorld and EndHelloWorld methods.

Use the BeginHelloWorld method to send a SOAP request to the Web service, but instead of the ASP.NET application waiting idly for a response, it moves on to accomplish other tasks. In this case, it is not doing anything that important—just counting the amount of time it is taking in a loop.

After the SOAP request is sent from the ASP.NET application, you can use the IAsyncResult object to check whether a SOAP response is waiting. This is done by using myIar.IsCompleted. If the asynchronous invocation is not complete, the ASP.NET application increases the value of x by one before making the same check again. The ASP.NET application continues to do this until the XML Web service is ready to return a response. The response is retrieved using the EndHelloWorld method call.

Results of running this application are similar to what is shown in Figure 26-17.

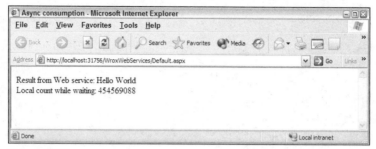

Figure 26-17

Summary

This chapter was a whirlwind tour of XML Web services in the .NET platform. It is definitely a topic that merits an entire book of its own. The chapter showed you the power of exposing your data and logic as SOAP and also how to consume these SOAP messages directly in the ASP.NET applications you build.

In addition to pointing out the power you have for building and consuming basic Web services, the chapter spent some time helping you understand caching, performance, the use of SOAP headers, and more. A lot of power is built into this model; every day the Web services model is starting to make stronger inroads into various enterprise organizations. It is becoming more likely that to get at some data or logic you need for your application, you will employ the tactics presented here.

Configuration

27

Those of you who remember the "Classic" ASP days know that ASP's configuration information was stored in a binary repository called the Internet Information Services (IIS) metabase. To configure a classic ASP application, you modify the metabase, either through script or, more commonly, through the IIS Microsoft Management Console snap-in.

Unlike classic ASP, ASP.NET versions 1.0 and above don't require extensive use of the IIS metabase. Instead, ASP.NET uses an XML-based configuration system that is much more flexible, accessible, and easier to use.

ASP.NET 2.0 moves up on the value chain and makes configuring ASP.NET 2.0 applications much easier and simpler than before. This chapter covers the following:

❑   Introduction to the ASP.NET configuration file

❑   An overview of the ASP.NET configuration settings

❑   An examination of the new ASP.NET 2.0 configuration APIs

❑   How to store and retrieve sensitive information

The journey into these new configuration enhancements begins with an overview.

Configuration Overview

ASP.NET configuration is stored in two primary XML-based files. XML is used to describe the properties and behaviors of various aspects of ASP.NET applications.

The ASP.NET configuration system supports two kinds of configuration files:

❑   `machine.config`: Server or machine-wide configuration file

❑   `web.config`: Application configuration file

Because the configuration files are based on XML, the elements that describe the configuration are case-sensitive. Moreover, the ASP.NET configuration system follows camel-casing naming conventions. If you look at the Session State configuration example shown in Listing 27-1, for example, you can see that the Session State XML element is presented as sessionState.

Listing 27-1: Session State configuration

```
<?xml version="1.0" encoding="UTF-8" ?>
<configuration>
<system.web>
    <sessionState
        mode="InProc"
        stateConnectionString="tcpip=127.0.0.1:42424"
        stateNetworkTimeout="10"
        sqlConnectionString="data source=127.0.0.1; user id=sa; password=P@55worD"
        cookieless="false"
        timeout="20"
    />
  </system.web>
</configuration>
```

The benefits of having an XML configuration file instead of a binary metabase include the following:

❑   The configuration information is human-readable and can be modified using a plain text editor such as Notepad, although it's recommended to use Visual Studio 2005 or another XML-aware editor Unlike a binary metabase, the configuration file can be easily copied from one server to another, as with any simple file. This feature is extremely helpful in a Web farm scenario.

❑   When some settings are changed in the configuration file, ASP.NET automatically detects the changes and applies them to the running ASP.NET application. ASP.NET accomplishes this by creating a new instance of the ASP.NET application and directing end users to this new application.

❑   The configuration changes are applied to the ASP.NET application without the need for the administrator to stop and start the Web server. This is completely transparent to the end user.

❑   The ASP.NET configuration system is extensible, and application-specific information can be stored and retrieved very easily.

❑   The sensitive information stored in the ASP.NET 2.0 configuration system can optionally be encrypted to keep it from prying eyes.

Server Configuration File

Every ASP.NET server installation includes a configuration file named machine.config, and this file is installed as a part of .NET Framework installation. You can find machine.config in C:\Windows\Microsoft.NET\Framework\v2.0xxxxx\, and the file represents the default settings used by all ASP.NET Web applications installed on the server.

The system-wide configuration file, machine.config, is used to configure common .NET Framework settings for all applications on the machine. As a general rule, it's not a good idea to edit or manipulate the machine.config file unless you know what you are doing. Changes to this file can affect all applications on your computer (Windows, Web, and so on).

Because the .NET Framework supports side-by-side execution mode, you might find more than one installation of the `machine.config` *file if you have multiple versions of the .NET Framework installed on the server. If you have .NET Framework versions 1.0, 1.1, and 2.0 running on the server, for example, each .NET Framework installation has its own* `machine.config` *file. This means that you'll find three* `machine.config` *file installations on that particular server.*

In addition to the `machine.config` file, the .NET Framework installer also installs two more files called `machine.config.default` and `machine.config.comments`. The `machine.config.default` file acts as a backup for the `machine.config` file. If you want to revert to the factory setting for `machine.config`, simply copy the settings from the `machine.config.default` to `machine.config`.

The `machine.config.comments` file contains a description for each configuration section and explicit settings for the most commonly used values. `machine.config.default` and `machine.config.comment` files are not used by the .NET Framework runtime; they're installed in case you want to revert back to default factory settings and default values.

Application Configuration File

Unlike `machine.config`, each and every ASP.NET application has its own copy of configuration settings stored in a file called `web.config`. If the Web application spans multiple subfolders, each subfolder has its own `web.config` file that inherits or overrides the parent's file settings.

To update servers in your farm with these new settings, you simply copy this `web.config` file to the appropriate application directory. ASP.NET takes care of the rest — no server restarts and no local server access is required — and your application continues to function normally, except now it uses the new settings.

How Configuration Is Applied

When ASP.NET runtime applies configuration settings for a given Web request, `machine.config` (as well as any `web.config` files configuration information) is merged into a single unit, and that information is applied to the given application. Configuration settings are inherited from parent Web applications; `machine.config` is the root or "ultimate" parent. A sample ASP.NET Web application is shown in Figure 27-1.

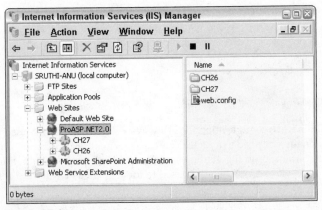

Figure 27-1

The configuration for each Web application is unique; however, settings are inherited from the parent. For example, if the web.config file in the root of your Web site /ProASP.NET2.0 defines a session time-out as 10 minutes, that setting overrides the default ASP.NET setting inherited from machine.config. The web.config files in the child folders /CH26 and /CH2 do not override these settings; rather, both /CH26/ and /CH27/configuration/Session/ inherit the settings of the 10-minute session timeout, in addition to applying their own settings for their respective applications.

> *The configuration settings for virtual directories are independent of the physical directory structure. Unless the manner in which the virtual directories are organized is exclusively specified, configuration problems can result.*

Detecting Configuration File Changes

ASP.NET automatically detects when configuration files, such as machine.config or web.config, are changed. This logic is implemented based on listening for file-change notification events provided by the operating system.

When an ASP.NET application is started, the configuration settings are read and stored in the ASP.NET cache. A file dependency is then placed on the entry within the cache in the machine.config and/or web.config configuration file. When the configuration file update is detected in the machine.config, ASP.NET creates a new application domain to service new requests. The old application domain is destroyed as soon as it completes servicing all its outstanding requests.

Configuration File Format

The main difference between machine.config and web.config is the file name. Other than that, their schemas are the same. Configuration files are divided into multiple sections, with each section being a top-level XML element. The root-level XML element in a configuration file is named <configuration>. A typical pseudo web.config file has a section to control ASP.NET, as shown in Listing 27-2.

Listing 27-2: A pseudo web.config file

```
<?xml version="1.0" encoding="UTF-8"?>
<configuration>
  <configSections>
    <section name="[sectionSettings]" type="[Class]"/>
    <sectionGroup name="[sectionGroup]">
      <section name="[sectionSettings]" type="[Class]"/>
    </sectionGroup>
  </configSections>
</configuration>
```

> *Values within brackets [ ] have unique values within the real configuration file.*

The root element in the XML configuration file is always <configuration>. Each of the section handlers and settings are optionally wrapped in a <sectionGroup>. A <sectionGroup> provides an organizational function within the configuration file. It allows you to organize configuration into unique groups — for instance, the <system.web> section group is used to identify areas within the configuration file specific to ASP.NET.

Config Sections

The `<configSections>` section is the mechanism to group the configuration section handlers associated with each configuration section. When you want to create your own section handlers, you must declare them in the `<configSections>` section. The `<httpModules>` section has a configuration handler that is set to `System.Web.Caching.OutputCacheModule`, and the `<sessionState>` section has a configuration handler that is set to `System.Web.SessionState.SessionStateModule` classes, as shown in Listing 27-3.

Listing 27-3: HTTP Module configuration

```
<configSections>
<httpModules>
  <section name="System.Web.Caching.OutputCacheModule" />
  <section name="System.Web.SessionState.SessionStateModule" />
</httpModules>
</configSections>
```

Common Configuration Settings

The ASP.NET 2.0 applications depend on a few common configuration settings. These settings are common to both the `web.config` and `machine.config` files. In this section, you look at some of these common configuration settings.

Connecting Strings

In ASP.NET 1.0 and 1.1, all the connection string information was stored in the `<appSettings>` section. However, ASP.NET 2.0 introduces a new section called `<connectionStrings>` that stores all kinds of connection-string information. Even though this method works fine, it poses the following challenges:

❑ When connection strings are stored in `appSettings` section, it is impossible for a data-aware control such as `SqlCacheDependency` or `MembershipProvider` to discover the information.

❑ Securing connection strings using cryptographic algorithms is a challenge.

❑ Last, but not least, this feature does not apply to ASP.NET only; rather, it applies to all the .NET applications including Windows Forms, Web Services, and so on.

Because the connection-string information is stored independently of the `appSettings` section, it can be retrieved using the strongly typed collection method `ConnectionStrings`. Listing 27-4 gives an example of how to store connecting strings.

Listing 27-4: Storing a connection string

```
<configuration>
  <connectionStrings>
    <add
        name = "401kApp"
        connectionString = "server=401kServer;database=401kDB;
        uid=WebUser;pwd=P@$$worD9" />
  </connectionStrings>
</configuration>
```

Listing 27-5 shows how to retrieve the method for a 401K retirement application.

Listing 27-5: Retrieving a connection string

VB
```
Public Sub Page_Load (sender As Object, e As EventArgs)
    ...
    Dim dbConnection as New _
        SqlConnection(ConfigurationManager.ConnectionStrings("401kApp"))
    ...
End Sub
```

C#
```
public void Page_Load (Object sender, EventArgs e)
{
    ...
    SqlConnection dbConnection = new
        SqlConnection(ConfigurationManager.ConnectionStrings["401kApp"]);
    ...
}
```

Configuring Session State

Because Web-based applications follow the stateless HTTP protocol, you must store the application-specific state or user-specific state where it can persist. The Session object is the common store where user-specific information is persisted. Session store is implemented as a Hashtable and stores data based on key/value pair combinations.

ASP.NET 1.0 and 1.1 had the capability to persist the session store data in InProc, StateServer, and SqlServer. ASP.NET 2.0 adds one more capability called "Custom". The "Custom" setting gives the developer a lot more control regarding how the Session State is persisted in a permanent store. For example, out of the box ASP.NET 2.0 doesn't support storing session data on Non-Microsoft databases such as Oracle, DB2, or Sybase. If you want to store the session data in any of these databases or in a custom store such as an XML file, you can implement that by writing a custom provider class. (See the section "Custom State Store" later in this chapter and Chapter 19 to learn more about the new Session State features in ASP.NET 2.0.)

You can configure the session information using the <sessionState> element:

```
<sessionState
  mode="StateServer"
  cookieless="false"
  timeout="20"
  stateConnectionString="tcpip=401kSessionStore:42424"
  stateNetworkTimeout="60"
  sqlConnectionString=""
/>
```

The following list describes each of the attributes for the <sessionState> element shown in the preceding code:

❏ mode: Specifies whether the session information should be persisted. The mode setting supports five options: Off, InProc, StateServer, SQLServer, and Custom. The default option is InProc.

❏ cookieless: Specifies whether HTTP cookieless Session key management is supported.

❏ timeout: Specifies the Session lifecycle time. The timeout value is a sliding value; at each request, the timeout period is reset to the current time plus the timeout value. For example, if the timeout value is 20 minutes and a request is received at 10:10 AM, the timeout occurs at 10:30 AM.

❏ stateConnectionString: When mode is set to StateServer, this setting is used to identify the TCP/IP address and port to communicate with the Windows Service providing state management.

❏ stateNetworkTimeout: Specifies the timeout value (in seconds) while attempting to store state in an out-of-process session store such as StateServer.

❏ sqlConnectionString: When mode is set to SQLServer, this setting is used to connect to the SQL Server database to store and retrieve session data.

Web Farm Support

Multiple web servers working as a group are called a Web Farm. If you'd like to scale out your ASP.NET application into multiple servers inside a Web Farm, ASP.NET supports this kind of deployment out of the box. However, the session data needs to be persisted in an out-of-process Session State such as StateServer or SQLServer.

State Server

Both StateServer and SQLServer support the out-of-process Session State. However, the StateServer stores all the session information in a Windows Service, which stores the session data in memory. Using this option, if the server that hosts the Session State service goes down in the Web farm, all the ASP.NET clients that are accessing the Web site fail; there is no way to recover the session data.

You can configure the Session State service using the Services and Applications Microsoft Management Console (MMC) snap-in available by choosing Start ➪ Settings ➪ ControlPanel ➪ AdministrativeTools ➪ ComputerManagement (as shown in Figure 27-2).

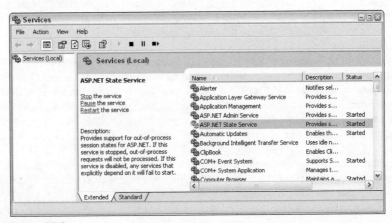

Figure 27-2

Alternatively, you can start the Session State service by using the command prompt and entering the `net start` command, like this:

```
C:\Windows\Microsoft.NET\Framework\v2.0xxxxx\> net start aspnet_state

The ASP.NET State Service service is starting.

The ASP.NET State Service service was started successfully.
```

All compatible versions of ASP.NET share a single state service instance, which is the service installed with the highest version of ASP.NET. For example, if you've installed ASP.NET 2.0 on a server where ASP.NET 1.0 and 1.1 are already running, the ASP.NET 2.0 installation replaces the ASP.NET 1.1's state server instance. The ASP.NET 2.0 service is guaranteed to work for all previous compatible versions of ASP.NET.

SQL Server

When you choose the `SQLServer` option, session data is stored in SQL Server tables. Even if SQL Server goes down, the built-in SQL Server recovery features enable you to recover all the session data. Configuring ASP.NET to support SQL Server for Session State is just as simple as configuring the Windows Service. The only difference is that you run a T-SQL script that ships with ASP.NET, `InstallSqlState.sql`. The T-SQL script that uninstalls ASP.NET SQL Server support, called `UninstallSqlState.sql`, is also included. The install and uninstall scripts are available in the Framework folder.

```
<configuration>
  <system.web>
    <sessionState
      mode="SQLServer"
      sqlConnectionString="data source=401kSessionServer;
      user id=401kWebUser;password=P@55worD"
      cookieless="false"
      timeout="20"
    />
  </system.web>
</configuration>
```

ASP.NET accesses the session data stored in SQL Server via stored procedures. By default, all the session data is stored in the Temp DB database. However, you can modify the stored procedures so they are stored in tables in a full-fledged database other than Temp DB.

Even though the SQL Server–based Session State provides a scalable use of Session State, it could become the single point of failure. This is because SQL Server Session State uses the same SQL Server database for all applications in the same ASP.NET process. This problem has been fixed in ASP.NET 2.0, and you can configure different databases for each application. Now you can use the `aspnet_regsql.exe` utility to configure this. However, if you're looking for a solution for older .NET Frameworks, a fix is available at `http://support.microsoft.com/default.aspx?scid=kb;EN-US;836680`.

Because the connection strings are stored in the strongly typed mode, the connection string information can be referenced in other parts of the configuration file. For example, when configuring Session State to be stored in SQL Server, you can specify the connection string in the `connectionStrings` section, and then you can specify the name of the connection string in the `sessionState` element, as shown in Listing 27-6.

Listing 27-6: Configuring Session State with a connection string

```
<configuration>
  <connectionStrings>
    <add name = "401kSqlSessionState"
        connectionString = "data source=401kSessionServer;
        user id=401kWebUser;password=P@55worD" />
  </connectionStrings>
  <system.web>
    <sessionState
      mode="SQLServer"
      sqlConnectionString="401kSqlSessionState"
      cookieless="false"
      timeout="20"
    />
  </system.web>
</configuration>
```

Custom State Store

The Session State in ASP.NET 2.0 is based on a pluggable architecture with different providers that inherit the `SessionStateStoreProviderBase` class. If you want to create your own custom provider or use a third-party provider, you must set the mode to `"Custom"`.

> ScaleOut Software released the first 3rd party ASP.NET 2.0 State Provider in the form of their StateServer product. It fills a niche between the ASP.NET included singleton StateServer and the SQL Server Database State Provider. ScaleOut Software's StateServer is an out-of-process service that runs on each machine in the Web Farm and ensures that session state is stored in a transparent and distributed manner among machines in the farm. You can learn more about StateServer and their ASP.NET 2.0 Session Provider at `http://www.scaleoutsoftware.com/asp.net2.0.htm`.

You specify the custom provider assembly that inherits the `SessionStateStoreProviderBase` class, as shown here:

```
<configuration>
  <system.web>
    <sessionState
        mode="Custom"
        CustomProvider="CustomStateProvider">
      <providers>
        <add name="CustomStateProvider"
        type="CustomStateProviderAssembly,
        customStateProviderNamespace.CustomStateProvider"/>
      </providers>
    </sessionState>
  </system.web>
</configuration>
```

In the previous example, you've configured the Session State mode as custom because you have specified the provider name as `"CustomStateProvider"`. Next, you add the provider element and include the type of the provider with namespace and class name.

Compilation Configuration

ASP.NET supports the dynamic compilation of ASP.NET pages, Web services, http handlers, and ASP.NET application files (`Global.asax`), source files, and so on. These files are automatically compiled on demand when first required by a Web application.

Any changes to a dynamically compiled file cause all affected resources to be automatically invalidated and recompiled. This system enables developers to quickly develop applications with a minimum of process overhead because they can just press Save to immediately cause code changes to take effect within their applications.

The ASP.NET 1.0 and 1.1 features are extended in ASP.NET 2.0 to account for other file types, including class files. The ASP.NET compilation settings can be configured using the `<compilation>` section in `web.config` or `machine.config`. The ASP.NET engine compiles the page when necessary and saves the generated code in code cache. This cached code is used when executing the ASP.NET pages. Listing 27-7 shows the syntax for the `<compilation>` section.

Listing 27-7: The compilation section

```
<!-- compilation Attributes -->
<compilation
  tempDirectory="directory"
  debug="[true|false]"
  strict="[true|false]"
  explicit="[true|false]"
  batch="[true|false]"
  batchTimeout="timeout in seconds"
  maxBatchSize="max number of pages per batched compilation"
  maxBatchGeneratedFileSize="max combined size in KB"
  numRecompilesBeforeAppRestart="max number of recompilations "
  defaultLanguage="name of a language as specified in a <compiler/> element below"
    <compilers>
        <compiler language="language"
                  extension="ext"
                  type=".NET Type"
                  warningLevel="number"
                  compilerOptions="options"/>
    </compilers>
    <assemblies>
        <add assembly="assembly"/>
    </assemblies>
    <codeSubDirectories>
      <codeSubDirectory directoryName="sub-directory name"/>
    </codeSubDirectories>
    <buildproviders>
      <buildprovider
        extension="file extension"
        type="type reference"/>
    </buildproviders>
</compilation>
```

Now take a more detailed look at these <compilation> attributes:

❏ batch: Specifies whether the batch compilation is supported. The default value is True.

❏ maxBatchSize: Specifies the maximum number of pages/classes that can be compiled into a single batch. Default value is 1000.

❏ maxBatchGeneratedFileSize: Specifies the maximum output size of a batch assembly compilation. Default value is 3000KB.

❏ batchTimeout: Specifies the amount of time (seconds) granted for batch compilation to occur. If this timeout elapses without compilation being completed, an exception is thrown. Default value is 15 seconds.

❏ debug: Specifies whether to compile production assemblies or debug assemblies. The default is False.

❏ defaultLanguage: Specifies the default programming language, such as VB or C#, to use in dynamic compilation files. Language names are defined using the <compiler> child element. Default is VB.

❏ explicit: Specifies whether the Microsoft Visual Basic code compile option is explicit. The default is True.

❏ numRecompilesBeforeAppRestart: Specifies the number of dynamic recompiles of resources that can occur before the application restarts.

❏ strict: Specifies the setting of the Visual Basic strict compile option.

❏ tempDirectory: Specifies the directory to use for temporary file storage during compilation. By default, ASP.NET creates the temp file in the [WinNT\Windows]\Microsoft.NET\ Framework\[version]\Temporary ASP.NET Files folder.

❏ compilers: The <compilers> section can contain multiple <compiler> subelements, which are used to create a new compiler definition:

  ❏ The language attribute specifies the languages (separated by semicolons) used in dynamic compilation files. For example, C#; VB.

  ❏ The extension attribute specifies the list of file name extensions (separated by semi-colons) used for dynamic code. For example, .cs; .vb.

  ❏ The type attribute specifies .NET type/class that implements the ICompiler interface used to compile all resources that use either the specified language or the file extension.

  ❏ The warningLevel attribute specifies how the .NET compiler should treat compiler warnings as errors. Five levels of compiler warnings exist, numbered 0 through 4. When the compiler transcends the warning level set by this attribute, compilation fails. The meaning of each warning level is determined by the programming language and compiler you're using; consult the reference specification for your compiler to get more information about the warning levels associated with compiler operations and what events trigger compiler warnings.

  ❏ The compilerOptions attribute enables you to include compiler's command line switches while compiling the ASP.NET source.

  ❏ assemblies: Specifies ASP.NET compilation processing directives.

❑ codeSubDirectories: Specifies an ordered collection of subdirectories containing files compiled at runtime. Adding the codeSubDirectories section creates separate assemblies.

❑ buildproviders: Specifies a collection of build providers used to compile custom resource files.

Browser Capabilities

Identifying and using the browser's capabilities is essential for Web applications. The browser capabilities component was designed for the variety of desktop browsers, such as Microsoft Internet Explorer, Netscape, Opera, and so on. The <browserCaps> attribute enables you to specify the configuration settings for the browser capabilities component. The <browserCaps> element can be declared at the machine, site, application, and subdirectory level.

The HttpBrowserCapabilities class contains all the browser properties. The properties can be set and retrieved in this section.

When a request is received from a browser, the browser capabilities component identifies the browser's capabilities from the request headers.

For each browser, compile a collection of settings relevant to applications. These settings may either be statically configured or gathered from request headers. Allow the application to extend or modify the capabilities settings associated with browsers and to access values through a strongly typed object model. The ASP.NET mobile capabilities depend on the browser capabilities component.

In ASP.NET 2.0, all the browser capability information is represented in browser definition files. The browser definitions are stored in *.browser file types and specified in XML format. A single file may contain one or more browser definitions. The *.browser files are stored in the Config\Browsers subdirectory of the Framework installation directory (for example, [WinNT\Windows]\Microsoft.NET\ Framework\xxxxx\CONFIG\Browsers), as shown in Figure 27-3. Application-specific browser definition files are stored in the /Browsers subdirectory of the application.

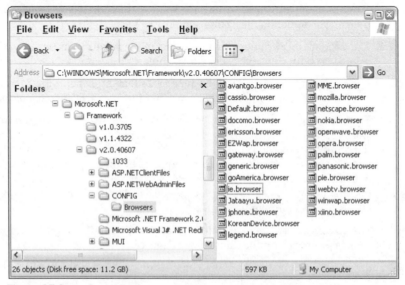

Figure 27-3

In ASP.NET 1.0 and 1.1, the browser cap information was stored in the `machine.config` *and* `web.config` *files.*

The browser definition file format defines each browser as an entity, self-contained in a `<browser>` XML element. Each browser has its own id that describes a class of browser and its parent class. The root node of a browser definition file is the `<browsers>` element and multiple browser entries identified using the id attribute of the `<browser>` element.

Listing 27-8 shows part of the IE.browser file.

Listing 27-8: Content of IE.browser file

```
<browsers>
    <browser id="IE" parentID="Mozilla">
        <identification>
            <userAgent match="^Mozilla[^(]*\([C|c]ompatible;\s*MSIE
            (?'version'(?'major'\d+)(?'minor'\.\d+)(?'letters'\w*))(?'extra'[^)]*)" />
            <userAgent nonMatch="Opera" />
            <userAgent nonMatch="Go\.Web" />
            <userAgent nonMatch="Windows CE" />
            <userAgent nonMatch="EudoraWeb" />
        </identification>
        <capture>
        </capture>
        <capabilities>
            <capability name="browser"          value="IE" />
            <capability name="extra"            value="${extra}" />
            <capability name="isColor"          value="true" />
            <capability name="letters"          value="${letters}" />
            <capability name="majorversion"     value="${major}" />
            <capability name="minorversion"     value="${minor}" />
            <capability name="screenBitDepth"   value="8" />
            <capability name="type"             value="IE${major}" />
            <capability name="version"          value="${version}" />
        </capabilities>
    </browser>
    ...
```

The id attribute of the `<browser>` element uniquely identifies the class of browser. The parentID attribute of the `<browser>` element specifies the unique ID of the parent browser class. Both the id and the parentID are required values.

Before running an ASP.NET application, the framework compiles all the browser definitions into an assembly and installs the compilation in GAC. When the browser definition files at the system level are modified, they do not automatically reflect the change in each and every ASP.NET application. Therefore, it becomes the responsibility of the developer or the installation tool to update this information. You can send the updated browser information to all the ASP.NET applications by running the `aspnet_regbrowsers.exe` *utility provided by the framework. When the* `aspnet_regbrowsers.exe` *utility is called, the browser information is recompiled and the new assembly is stored in the GAC; this assembly is reused by all the ASP.NET applications. Nevertheless, browser definitions at the application level are automatically parsed and compiled on demand when the application is started. If any changes are made to the application's* `/Browsers` *directory, the application is automatically recycled.*

Custom Errors

When the ASP.NET application fails, the ASP.NET page can show the default error page with the source code and line number of the error. However, this approach has a few problems:

❑ The source code and error message may not make any sense to a less experienced end user.

❑ If the same source code and the error messages are displayed to a hacker, subsequent damage could result.

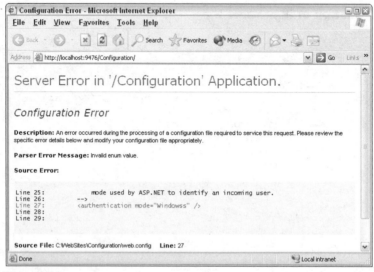

Figure 27-4

However, ASP.NET provides excellent infrastructure to prevent this kind of error information. The <customErrors> section provides a means for defining custom error messages in an ASP.NET application. The syntax is as follows:

```
<customErrors defaultRedirect="[url]" mode="[on/off/remote]">
<error statusCode="[statuscode]" redirect="[url]" />
</customErrors>
```

❑ defaultRedirect: Specifies the default URL to which the client browser should be redirected if an error occurs. This is an optional setting.

❑ mode: Specifies if the status of the custom errors is enabled, disabled, or shown only to remote machines. The possible values are On, Off, RemoteOnly. On indicates that the custom errors are enabled. Off indicates that the custom errors are disabled. RemoteOnly indicates that the custom errors are shown only to remote clients.

❑ customErrors: The <customErrors> section supports multiple <error> subelements that are used to define custom errors. Each <error> subelement can include a statusCode attribute and a URL.

Authentication

In Chapter 18, you've seen the authentication process in detail. In this section, you can review configuration-specific information. Authentication is a process that verifies the identity of the user and establishes the identity between the server and a request. Because HTTP is a stateless protocol, the authentication information is persisted somewhere in the client or the server; ASP.NET supports both of these.

You can store the server-side information in Session objects. When it comes to client side, you have many options:

❑ Cookies

❑ ViewState

❑ URL

❑ Hidden fields

ASP.NET 2.0 supports following authentication methods out of the box:

❑ Windows authentication

❑ Passport authentication

❑ Forms Authentication

If you'd like to disable authentication, you can use the setting mode="None":

```
<authentication mode="None">
```

Windows Authentication

ASP.NET relies on IIS's infrastructure to implement Windows authentication, and Windows authentication enables you to authenticate requests using Windows Challenge/Response semantics. When the Web server receives a request, it initially denies access to the request (which is a challenge). This triggers the browser to pop up a window to collect the credentials; the request responds with a hashed value of the Windows credentials, which the server can then choose to authenticate.

To implement Windows authentication, you configure the appropriate Web site or virtual directory using IIS. You can then use the <authentication> element to mark the Web application or virtual directory with Windows authentication.

```
<configuration>
   <system.web>
      <authentication>
            <authentication mode="Windows">
      </authentication>
   </system.web>
</configuration>
```

The <authentication> element can be declared only at the machine, site, or application level. Any attempt to declare it in a configuration file at the subdirectory or page level results in a parser error message.

Passport Authentication

The ASP.NET 2.0 relies on the Passport SDK to implement Passport authentication, which is promoted by Microsoft Corporation. Passport is a subscription-based authentication mechanism that allows end users to remember a single username/password pair across multiple Web applications that implement Passport authentication.

ASP.NET 2.0 authenticates users based on the credentials presented by users. The Passport service sends a token back to authenticate. The token is stored in a site-specific cookie after it has been authenticated with `login.passport.com`. Using the `redirectUrl` attribute of the `<passport>` authentication option, you can control how non-authenticated Passport users are directed, as in the following example:

```
<passport redirectUrl="/Passport/SignIn.aspx">
```

Forms Authentication

Forms Authentication is the widely used authentication mechanism right from Amazon.com. Forms Authentication can be configured using the `<authentication>` section along with the `<forms>` subsection.

```
<configuration>
    <system.web>
        <authentication mode="Forms">
            <forms
                name="[name]"
                loginUrl="[url]"
                protection="[All|None|Encryption|Validation]"
                timeout="30"
                path="/"
                requireSSL="[true|false]"
                slidingExpiration="[true|false]"
                cookieless="UseCookies|UseUri|AutoDetect|UseDeviceProfile"
                defaultUrl="[url]"
                domain="string"
                >
                <credentials passwordFormat="[Clear, SHA1, MD5]">
                  <user name="[UserName]" password="[password]"/>
                </credentials>
            </forms>
        </authentication>
    </system.web>
</configuration>
```

Each attribute is shown in detail in the following list:

❑   name: Specifies the name of the HTTP authentication ticket. The default value is .ASPXAUTH.

❑   loginUrl: Specifies the URL to which the request is redirected if the current request doesn't have a valid authentication ticket.

❑   protection: Specifies the method used to protect cookie data. Valid values are All, None, Encryption, and Validation.

❏   Encryption: Specifies that content of the cookie is encrypted using TripleDES or DES cryptography logarithms in the configuration file. However, the data validation is not done on the cookie.

❏   Validation: Specifies that content of the cookie is not encrypted, but validates that the cookie data hasn't been altered in transit.

❏   All: Specifies that content of the cookie is protected using both data validation and encryption. The configured data validation algorithm is used based on the <machineKey> element, and Triple DES is used for encryption. The default value is All, and it indicates the highest protection available.

❏   None: Specifies no protection mechanism is applied on the cookie. Web applications that don't store any sensitive information and potentially use cookies for personalization can look at this option. When None is specified, both encryption and validation are disabled.

❏   timeout: Specifies cookie expiration time in terms of minutes. The timeout attribute is a sliding value, which expires N minutes from the time the last request was received. Default value is 30 minutes.

❏   path: Specifies the path to use for the issued cookie. The default value is / to avoid difficulties with mismatched case in paths because browsers are strictly case-sensitive when returning cookies.

❏   requireSSL: Specifies whether Forms Authentication should happen in a secure HTTPS connection.

❏   slidingExpiration: Specifies whether valid cookies should be updated periodically when used. When false, a ticket is good for only the duration of the period for which it is issued, and a user must re-authenticate even during an active session.

❏   cookieless: Specifies whether cookieless authentication is supported. Supported values are UseCookies, UseUri, Auto, and UseDeviceProfile. The default value is UseDeviceProfile.

❏   defaultUrl: Specifies the default URL used by the login control to control redirection after authentication.

❏   domain: Specifies the domain name string to be attached in the authentication cookie. This attribute is particularly useful when the same authentication cookie is shared among multiple sites across the domain.

It is strongly recommended that the loginUrl *should be an SSL URL (*https://*) to keep secure credentials secure from prying eyes.*

Anonymous Identity

When you are building e-commerce Web applications, your site must support both anonymous and authenticated users. When anonymous users are browsing the site and adding items to a shopping cart, the Web application needs a way to uniquely identify these users. For example, if you take a look at busy e-commerce Web sites such as Amazon.com or BN.com, they don't have a concept called anonymous users. Rather these sites assign a unique identity to each user.

In ASP.NET 1.0 and 1.1, no out-of-the box feature existed to enable a developer to achieve this identification of users. Most developers used `SessionID` to identify users uniquely. They experienced a few pitfalls inherent in this method. ASP.NET 2.0 adds anonymous identity support using the `<anonymous Identification>` section. The following listing shows the `<anonymousIdentification>` configuration section settings:

```
<configuration>
  <system.web>
    <anonymousIdentification
                enabled="false"
                cookieName=".ASPXANONYMOUS
                cookieTimeout="100000"
                cookiePath="/"
                cookieRequireSSL="false"
                cookieSlidingExpiration = "true"
                cookieProtection = "Validation"
                cookieLess="UseCookies|UseUri|AutoDetect|UseDeviceProfile"
                domain="...."    />
  </system.web>
</configuration>
```

The `enable` property specifies whether the anonymous access is enabled. The other attributes are comparable to the Forms Authentication attribute discussed in the previous section. When cookies are not enabled, the identity is stored in the URL.

Authorization

The authorization process verifies whether a user has access to the resource he is trying to access. ASP.NET 2.0 supports both File and URL authorization. The authorization for an application can be controlled by using the `<authorization>` section. The `<authorization>` section, as shown in the following code example, can contain subsections that either allow or deny permission to a user or a role. Optionally, you can also use the `<location>` section to grant special authorization permission.

```
<authorization>
 <allow roles="" />
 <allow users="" />
 <deny users="" />
</authorization>
```

URL Authorization

The URL Authorization is a service provided by `URLAuthorizationModule` (inherited from `HttpModule`) to control the access to resources such as `.aspx` files. The URL Authorization is very useful if you want to allow or deny certain parts of your ASP.NET application to certain people or roles.

For example, you may want to restrict the administration part of your ASP.NET application only to administrators and deny access to others. You can achieve this very easily with URL Authorization. URL Authorization can be configurable based on the user, the role, or HTTP verbs such as HTTP GET request or HTTP POST request.

You can configure URL Authorization in the `web.config` file with `<allow>` and `<deny>` attributes. For example, the following code shows how you can allow the user `Ssivakumar` and deny the groups `Sales` and `Marketing` from using the application:

```
<system.web>
    <authorization>
        <allow users="Ssivakumar" />
        <deny roles="Sales, Marketing" />
    </authorization>
</system.web>
```

The `<allow>` and `<deny>` attributes support `users`, `roles`, and `verb` values. As you can see from the previous code example, you can add multiple users and groups by separating them with commas.

Two special characters, asterisk (*) and question mark (?), are supported by `URLAuthorizationModule`. The asterisk (*) represents all users and the question mark (?) represents anonymous users. The following code denies access to all anonymous users and grants access to the Admin group:

```
<system.web>
    <authorization>
        <allow roles="Admin" />
        <deny users="?" />
    </authorization>
</system.web>
```

You can also grant or deny access to the users or groups in regard to the HTTP methods that they can use. In the following example, the HTTP `GET` method is denied access to the `"Admin"` group and access to the HTTP `POST` method is denied to all users.

```
<system.web>
    <authorization>
        <deny verbs="GET" roles="Admin" />
        <deny verbs="POST" users="*" />
    </authorization>
</system.web>
```

File Authorization

The authorization information can also be set to a file or directory using the `<location>` attribute. For example, you have a root directory called `"Home"` and underneath that you have a subdirectory called `"Documents"`. Suppose you want to grant access (to the `"Documents"` subdirectory) only to the `"Admin"` group members:

```
<location path="Documents">
    <system.web>
        <authorization>
            <allow roles="Admin" />
        </authorization>
    </system.web>
</location>
```

The ASP.NET application doesn't verify the path specified in the path attribute. If the given path is invalid, ASP.NET does not apply the security setting.

You can also set the security for a single file like this:

```
<configuration>
    <location path="Documents/Default.aspx">
        <system.web>
            <authorization>
                <allow roles="Admin" />
            </authorization>
        </system.web>
    </location>
</configuration>
```

Locking-Down Configuration Settings

ASP.NET's configuration system is very flexible in terms of applying configuration information to a specific application or folder. Even though the configuration system is flexible, in some cases, you may want to limit the configuration options that a particular application can control. For example, you could decide to change the way ASP.NET session information is stored. The lock-down can be achieved using the `<location>` attributes `allowOverride` and `allowDefinition`, and also the `path` attributes.

In the following example, a location section identifies `"Default Web Site/401KApp"` and allows any application to override the trace setting in `machine.config`:

```
<configuration>
    <location path="Default Web Site/401KApp" allowOverride="true">
        <trace enabled="false"/>
    </location>
</configuration>
```

Because the trace attribute can be overridden, you can enable tracing in the `web.config` file of the `401KApp` virtual directory.

However, if you have selected `allowOverride="false"` in the `<location>` settings of the `machine.config` file, the `web.config` file for `401KApp` cannot override that.

ASP.NET Page Configuration

When an ASP.NET application has been deployed, the page configuration settings enable you to control some of the default behaviors for all ASP.NET pages. These behaviors include options such as whether you should buffer the output before sending it or whether the Session State should be enabled for the entire application:

```
<configuration>
  <system.web>
    <pages buffer="true"
           enableSessionState="true"
           enableViewState="true"
           enableViewStateMac="false"
           autoEventWireup="true"
           smartNavigation="false"
           masterPageFile="~/401kMasterPage.master"
```

```
            pageBaseType="System.Web.UI.Page"
            userControlBaseType="System.Web.UI.UserControl"
            compilationMode="Auto"
            validateRequest="true" >
        <namespaces>
            <add namespace="Wrox.401kApp"/>
        </namespaces>
        <registerTagPrefixes>
            <add tagPrefix="401kCtrls" namespace="Wrox.401kApp.Controls"/>
        </registertagPrefixes>
    </pages>
  </system.web>
</configuration>
```

The following list gives you the ASP.NET page configuration information elements in detail:

❑ buffer: Specifies whether the requests must be buffered on the server before it is sent it to the client.

❑ enableSessionState: Specifies whether the Session State for the current ASP.NET application should be enabled. The possible values are "true", "false", or "readonly". The "readonly" value means that the application can read the session values but can't modify them.

❑ enableViewState: Specifies whether the ViewState is enabled for all the controls. If the application does not use ViewState, you can set the value to false in the application's web.config file.

❑ autoEventWireup: Specifies whether ASP.NET can automatically wire-up common page events such as Load or Error.

❑ smartNavigation: Smart navigation is a feature that takes advantage of IE as a client's browser to prevent the redrawing that occurs when a page is posted back to itself. Using smart navigation, the request is sent through an IFRAME on the client, and IE redraws only the sections of the page that have changed. By default, this option is set to false. When it is enabled, it is available only to Internet Explorer browsers — all other browsers get the standard behavior.

❑ masterPageFile: Identifies the master page for the current ASP.NET application. If you wish to apply the master page template to only a specific subset of pages (such as pages contained within a specific folder of your application), you can use the <location> element within the web.config file:

```
<configuration>
    <location path="401kAdmin">
        <system.web>
            <pages masterPageFile="~/401kAdminMasterPage.master" />
        </system.web>
    </location>
</configuration>
```

❑ pageBaseType: Specifies the base class for all the ASP.NET pages in the current ASP.NET application. By default, this option is set to System.Web.UI.Page. However, if you want all ASP.NET pages to inherit from some other base class, you can change the default via this setting.

❏   `userControlBaseType`: Specifies the base class for all the ASP.NET user controls in the current ASP.NET application. The default is `System.Web.UI.UserControl`. You can override the default option using this element.

❏   `validateRequest`: Specifies whether ASP.NET should validate all the incoming requests that are potentially dangerous like the cross-site script attack and the script injection attack. This feature provides out-of-the-box protection against cross-site scripting and script injection attacks by automatically checking all parameters in the request, ensuring that their content does not include HTML elements. For more information about this setting, visit `http://www.asp.net/faq/RequestValidation.aspx`.

❏   `namespaces`: Optionally, you can import a collection of directives that can be included in the precompilation process

❏   `compilationMode`: Specifies how ASP.NET should compile the current Web application. Supported values are `Never`, `Always` and `Auto`. When you set `compilationMode="Never"`, this means that the pages should never be compiled. A part error occurs if the page has constructs that require compilation. When you set `compilationMode="Always"`, this means that the pages are always compiled. When you set `compilationMode="Auto"`, ASP.NET does not compile the pages if that is possible.

❏   `registertagprefixes`: Optionally, you can register collections of directives and the namespaces where the `tagPrefix` resides.

Include Files

Unlike ASP.NET 1.0 and 1.1, ASP.NET 2.0 supports *include* files in both `machine.config` and `web.config` files. When configuration content is to be included in multiple places or inside the location elements, an include file is an excellent way to encapsulate the content.

Any section in a configuration file can include content from a different file using the `configSource` attribute, and the value of the attribute indicates a virtual relative file name to the include file. Listing 27-9 is an example of such a directive.

Listing 27-9: Adding additional content to the web.config file

```
<configuration>
    <system.web>
        <pages configSource="SystemWeb.config" />
    </system.web>
</configuration>
```

The configuration include files can contain information that applies to a single section, and a single include file cannot contain more than one configuration section or a portion of a section. If the `configExternalSource` attribute is present, the section element in the source file should not contain any other attribute or any child element.

Nevertheless, the include file is not a full configuration file. It should contain only the include section, as shown in Listing 27-10.

Listing 27-10: The SystemWeb.config file

```
<pages authentication mode="Forms" />
```

The `configExternalSource` attribute cannot be nested. An include file cannot nest another file inside it using the `configExternalSource` attribute.

> *When an ASP.NET configuration file is changed, the application is restarted at runtime. When an external include file is used within the configuration file, the configuration reload happens without restarting the application.*

Configuring ASP.NET Runtime Settings

The general configuration settings are those that specify how long a given ASP.NET resource, such as a page, is allowed to execute before being considered timed-out. The other settings specify the maximum size of a request or whether to use fully qualified URLs in redirects. These settings can be specified using the `<httpRuntime>` setting. The `<httpRuntime>` attribute is applied at the ASP.NET application on the folder level:

```
<configuration>
  <system.web>
    <httpRuntime
      useFullyQualifiedRedirectUrl="false"
      enable="true"
      executionTimeout="90"
      maxRequestLength="4096"
      requestLengthDiskThreshold="512"
      appRequestQueueLimit="5000"
      minFreeThreads="8"
      minLocalRequestFreeThreads="4"
      enableKernelOutputCache="true"
    />
  </system.web>
</configuration>
```

Enabling and Disabling ASP.NET Applications

The `enable` attribute specifies whether the current ASP.NET application is enabled. When set to `false`, the current ASP.NET application is disabled, and all the clients trying to connect to this site receive the HTTP 404 — File Not Found exception. This value should be set only at the machine or application level. If you set this value in any other level (such as subfolder level), it is ignored. This is a great feature that allows the administrators to bring down the application for whatever reason without starting or stopping IIS. The default value is `true`. This is a new setting included in ASP.NET 2.0.

Fully Qualified Redirect URLs

The `useFullyQualifiedRedirectUrl` attribute specifies whether the client-side redirects should include the fully qualified URL. When you are programming against the mobile devices, some devices require specifying fully qualified URLs. The default value is `false`.

Request Time-Out

The `executionTimeout` setting specifies the timeout option for an ASP.NET request time-out. The value of this attribute is the amount of time in seconds during which a resource can execute before ASP.NET times the request out. The default setting is 90 seconds. If you have a particular ASP.NET page or Web service that takes longer than 90 seconds to execute, you can extend the time limit in the configuration.

Maximum Request Length

The `maxRequestLength` attribute specifies the maximum file-size upload accepted by ASP.NET runtime. For example, if the ASP.NET application is required to process huge files, it is better to change this setting. The default is 4096KB (4MB).

Web applications are prone to attacks these days. The attacks range from a script injection attack to a Denial of Service (DoS) attack. The DoS is a typical attack that bombards the Web server with requests for large files. This huge number of requests ultimately brings down the Web server. The `maxRequest Length` attribute could save you from a DoS attack by setting a restriction on the size of requests.

Buffer Uploads

In ASP.NET 1.0 or 1.1, when a HTTP post is made (either a normal ASP.NET form post, file upload, or an XMLHTTP client-side post), the entire content is buffered in memory. This works out fine for smaller posts. However, when memory-based recycling is enabled, a large post can cause the ASP.NET worker process to recycle before the upload is completed. To avoid the unnecessary worker process recycling, ASP.NET 2.0 includes a new setting called `requestLengthDiskThreshold`. This setting enables an administrator to configure the file upload buffering behavior without affecting the programming model. Administrators can configure a threshold below which requests will be buffered into memory. After a request exceeds the limit, it is transparently buffered on disk and consumed from there by whatever mechanism is used to consume the data. The valid values for this setting are numbers between 1 and `Int32.MaxSize` in KB.

When file buffering is enabled, the files are uploaded to the `codegen` folder. The default path for the `codegen` folder is the following:

```
[WinNT\Windows]\Microsoft.NET\Framework\[version]\Temporary ASP.NET
Files\[ApplicationName]
```

The files are buffered using a random name in a subfolder within the codegen folder called Uploads. The location of the codegen folder can be configured on a per-application basis using the tempDirectory attribute of the <compilation> section.

This is not a change in ASP.NET; rather it is an internal change. When an ASP.NET 1.0 or 1.1 application is migrated to the new framework, the ASP.NET application automatically takes advantage of this feature.

Thread Management

ASP.NET runtime uses free threads available in its thread pool to fulfill requests. The minFreeThreads attribute indicates the number of threads that ASP.NET guarantees are available within the thread pool. The default number of threads is eight. For complex applications that require additional threads to complete processing, this simply ensures that the threads are available and that the application will not be blocked while waiting for a free thread to schedule more work. The minLocalRequestFreeThreads attribute controls the number of free threads dedicated for local request processing; the default is four.

Application Queue Length

The appRequestQueueLimit attribute specifies the maximum number of requests that ASP.NET queues for the current ASP.NET application. ASP.NET queues requests when it does not have enough free threads to process them. The minFreeThreads attribute specifies the number of free threads the ASP.NET application should maintain, and this setting affects the number of items stored in the queue.

When the number of requests queued exceeds the limit set in the appRequestQueueLimit setting, all the incoming requests are rejected and an HTTP 503 - Server Too Busy error is thrown back to the browser.

Managing Queue Limits

The appRequestQueueLimit attribute controls the number of client requests that may be queued — in other words, how many can wait to be processed. Queuing occurs when the server is receiving requests faster than it can process those requests. When the number of requests in the queue reaches the threshold determined by this attribute, the server begins sending an HTTP status code 503 to indicate that the server is too busy to handle any more requests. If this occurs, you should consider adding another server to handle the load or isolate and improve the performance of poorly performing ASP.NET pages or Web services.

Request Priority

When ASP.NET receives requests, they are queued to be processed by available threads. When no free threads are available, the requests remain queued. What if certain ASP.NET pages have higher priority than others, and you want them to be processed first before the other requests are processed? The requestPriority attribute allows you to do just that.

All typical ASP.NET Web sites have home pages, and when the Web server is stressed out, the entire ASP.NET site takes a longer time to process. If you want the home page to come up very quickly, regardless of the time needed for the other pages, you can set a different priority level for the home page. You can do this by using the requestPriority attribute.

Although this attribute appears in the httpRuntime documentation, VisualStudio 2005 throws a compilation error saying requestPriority is not a valid attribute.

The supported enumeration values are Normal, High, and Critical. This enumeration is available in the HttpRequestPriority that is available in the System.Web namespace. The following list explains these values in more detail:

❑   Normal: Specifies that the request be placed in the normal queue and processed as a normal priority. This is the default setting.

❑   High: Specifies that the request be placed at the tail end of the high-priority queue that is to be processed before the normal queue. If the application queue is full, this request is rejected. The application queue setting is then specified using the appRequestQueueLimit attribute.

❑   Critical: Specifies that the request be inserted at the tail end of the high-priority queue and is processed before the normal queue. However, requests with Critical priority are not rejected even though the managed queue is full. This is the biggest difference between the High and Critical settings.

The Critical marked requests can also be rejected if the ISAPI threshold queue limit has been exceeded. The requestQueueLimit attribute of the <processModel> tag allows you to configure the ISAPI threshold queue limit. The default value is 5000.

In a busy Web site, if you want to process the home page requests in the Web application as the highest priority, you do it in conjunction with the location tag.

```
<location path="Default.aspx">
 <httpRuntime requestPriority="Critical"/>
</location>
```

In the preceding example, you marked the Default.aspx with Critical request priority. This ensures that home page requests are processed with highest priority by the ASP.NET runtime.

Output Caching

The enableKernelOutputCache specifies whether the output caching is enabled at the IIS kernel level (Http.sys). At present, this setting applies only to Web servers IIS6 and higher.

Configuring ASP.NET Worker Process

When a request for an ASP.NET page is received by IIS, it passes the request to an unmanaged DLL called aspnet_isapi.dll. The aspnet_isapi.dll further passes the request to a separate worker process, aspnet_wp.exe under IIS5, which runs all the ASP.NET applications. Under IIS6 and higher, all the ASP.NET applications are run by the w3wp.exe process. The ASP.NET worker process can be configured using the <processModel> section in the machine.config file.

All the configuration sections talked about so far are read by managed code. On the other hand, the <processModel> section is read by the aspnet_isapi.dll unmanaged DLL. Because the configuration information is read by an unmanaged DLL, the changed process model information is applied to all ASP.NET applications only after an IIS restart.

The following code shows the default format for the `<processModel>` section:

```
<processModel
    enable="true|false"
    timeout="hrs:mins:secs|Infinite"
    idleTimeout="hrs:mins:secs|Infinite"
    shutdownTimeout="hrs:mins:secs|Infinite"
    requestLimit="num|Infinite"
    requestQueueLimit="num|Infinite"
    restartQueueLimit="num|Infinite"
    memoryLimit="percent"
    cpuMask="num"
    webGarden="true|false"
    userName="username"
    password="password"
    logLevel="All|None|Errors"
    clientConnectedCheck="hrs:mins:secs|Infinite"
    responseDeadlockInterval="hrs:mins:secs|Infinite"
    responseRestartDeadlockInterval="hrs:mins:secs|Infinite"
    comAuthenticationLevel="Default|None|Connect|Call|
    Pkt|PktIntegrity|PktPrivacy"
    comImpersonationLevel="Default|Anonymous|Identify|
    Impersonate|Delegate"
    maxWorkerThreads="num"
    maxIoThreads="num"
/>
```

Look at each of these attributes in detail:

❑ `enable`: Specifies whether the process model is enabled. When set to `false`, the ASP.NET applications run under IIS's process model.

When ASP.NET is running under IIS6 or higher in native mode, the IIS6 or higher process model is used and the `<processModel>` section is ignored.

❑ `timeout`: Specifies how long the worker process lives before a new worker process is created to replace the current worker process. This value can be extremely useful if a scenario exists where the application's performance starts to degrade slightly after running for several weeks, as in the case of a memory leak. Rather than your having to manually start and stop the process, ASP.NET can restart automatically. The default value is `Infinite`.

❑ `idleTimeout`: Specifies how long the worker process should wait before it is shut down. You can shut down the ASP.NET worker process automatically using the `idleTimeout` option. The default value is `Infinite`. You can also set this value to a time using the format, HH:MM:SS:

❑ `shutdownTimeout`: Specifies how long the worker process is given to shut itself down gracefully before ASP.NET calls the `Kill` command on the process. `Kill` is a low-level command that forcefully removes the process. The default value is five seconds.

❑ `requestLimit`: Specifies when the ASP.NET worker process should be recycled before a certain number of requests are served. The default value is `Infinite`.

❑ `requestQueueLimit`: Instructs ASP.NET to recycle the worker process if the limit for queued requests is exceeded. The default setting is 5000.

❑ memoryLimit: Specifies how much physical memory the worker process is allowed to consume before it is considered to be misbehaving or leaking memory. The default value is 60 percent of available physical memory.

❑ username and password: By default, all ASP.NET applications are executed using the ASPNET identity. If you want an ASP.NET applications to run with a different account, you can provide the username and the password pair.

❑ logLevel: Specifies how the ASP.NET worker process logs events. The default setting is to log errors only. However, you can also disable logging by specifying None or Log Everything. All the log items are written to the Windows Application Event Log.

❑ clientConnectedCheck: The clientConnectedCheck setting enables you to check whether the client is still connected at timed intervals before performing work. The default setting is five seconds.

❑ responseDeadlockInterval: Specifies how frequently the deadlock check should occur. A deadlock is considered to exist when requests are queued and no responses have been sent during this interval. After a deadlock, the process is restarted. The default value is three minutes.

❑ responseRestartDeadlockInterval: Specifies, when a deadlock is detected by the runtime, how long the runtime should wait before restarting the process. The default value is nine minutes.

❑ comAuthenticationLevel: Controls the level of authentication for DCOM security. The default is set to Connect. Other values are Default, None, Call, Pkt, PktIntegrity, and PktPrivacy.

❑ comImpersonationLevel: Controls the authentication level for COM security. The default is set to Impersonate. Other values are Default, Anonymous, Identify, Impersonate, and Delegate.

❑ webGarden: Specifies whether Web Garden mode is enabled. The default setting is false. A Web Garden lets you host multiple ASP.NET worker processes on a single server, thus providing the application with better hardware scalability. Web Garden mode is supported only on multiprocessor servers.

❑ cpuMask: Specifies which processors should be affinities to ASP.NET worker processes when webGarden="true". The cpuMask is a hexadecimal value. The default value is all processors, shown as 0xFFFFFFFF.

❑ maxWorkerThreads: Specifies the maximum number of threads that exist within the ASP.NET worker process thread pool. The default is 25.

❑ maxIoThreads: Specifies the maximum number of I/O threads that exist within the ASP.NET worker process. The default is 25.

Running Multiple Web Sites with Multiple Versions of Framework

In the same context, multiple Web sites within the given Web server can host multiple Web sites, and each of these sites can be bound to a particular version of a .NET framework. This is typically done using the aspnet_regiis.exe utility. The aspnet_regiis.exe utility is shipped with each version of the framework.

This utility has multiple switches. Using the -s switch allows you to install the current version of the .NET framework runtime on a given Web site. Listing 27-11 shows how to install .NET Framework version 1.1 on the 401KApp Web site.

Listing 27-11: Installing .NET Framework version 1.1 on the 401KApp Web site

```
C:\WINDOWS\Microsoft.NET\Framework\v1.1.4322>aspnet_regiis -s W3SVC/1ROOT/401KApp
```

Storing Application-Specific Settings

Every Web application must store some application-specific information for its runtime use. The `<appSettings>` section of the `Web.config` file provides a way to define custom application settings for an ASP.NET application. The section can have multiple `<add>` subelements. Its syntax is as follows:

```
<appSettings>
    <add Key="[key]" Value="[value]"/>
</appSettings>
```

The `<add>` subelement supports two attributes:

- ❑   `Key`: Specifies the key value in an `appSettings` hash table
- ❑   `Value`: Specifies the value in an `appSettings` hash table

Listing 27-12 shows how to store an application-specific connection string. The `Key` value is set to `ApplicationInstanceID`, and the `Value` is set to the ASP.NET application instance and the name of the server on which the application is running.

Listing 27-12: Application instance information

```
<appSettings>
    <add Key="ApplicationInstanceID" Value="Instance1onServerOprta"/>
</appSettings>
```

Programming Configuration Files

In ASP.NET 1.0 and 1.1 versions of the Framework provided APIs that enabled you only to read information from the configuration file. You had no way to write information into the configuration file because no out-of-the-box support was available. However, some advanced developers wrote their own APIs to write the information back to the configuration files. Because the `web.config` file is an XML file, developers were able to open configuration file using the `XmlDocument` object, modify the settings, and write it back to the disk. Even though this approach worked fine, the way to access the configuration settings were not strongly typed. Therefore, validating the values was always a challenge.

However, ASP.NET 2.0 includes APIs (ASP.NET Management Objects) to manipulate the configuration information settings in `machine.config` and `web.config` files. ASP.NET Management Objects provide a strongly typed programming model that addresses targeted administrative aspects of a .NET Web Application Server. They also govern the creation and maintenance of the ASP.NET Web configuration. Using the ASP.NET Management Objects, you can manipulate the configuration information stored in the configuration files in the local or remote computer. These can be used to script any common administrative tasks or the writing of installation scripts.

All of the ASP.NET Management Objects are stored in the `System.Configuration` and `System.Web` `.Configuration` namespaces. You can access the configuration using the `WebConfigurationManager`

1087

class. The System.Configuration.Configuration class represents a merged view of the configuration settings from the machine.config and hierarchical web.config files. The System.Configuration and System.Web.Configuration namespaces have multiple classes that enable you to access pretty much all the settings available in the configuration file. The main difference between System.Configuration and System.Web.Configuration namespaces is that the System.Configuration namespace contains all the classes that apply to all the .NET applications. On the other hand, the System.Web.Configuration namespace contains the classes that are applicable only to ASP.NET Web applications. The following table shows the important classes in System.Configuration and their uses.

Class Name	Purpose
Configuration	Enables you to manipulate the configuration stored in the local computer or a remote one.
ConfigurationElementCollection	Enables you to enumerate the child elements stored inside the configuration file.
AppSettingsSection	Enables you to manipulate the <appSettings> section of the configuration file.
ConnectionStringSettings	Enables you to manipulate the <connectionStrings> section of the configuration file.
ProtectedConfigurationSection	Enables you to manipulate the <protectedConfiguration> section of the configuration file.
ProtectedDataSection	Enables you to manipulate the <protectedData> section of the configuration file.

The next table shows classes from the System.Web.Configuration and their uses.

Class Name	Purpose
AuthenticationSection	Enables you to manipulate the <authentication> section of the configuration file.
AuthorizationSection	Enables you to manipulate the <authorization> section of the configuration file.
CompilationSection	Enables you to manipulate the <compilation> section of the configuration file.
CustomErrorsSection	Enables you to manipulate the <customErrors> section of the configuration file.
FormsAuthenticationConfiguration	Enables you to manipulate the <forms> section of the configuration file.
GlobalizationSection	Enables you to manipulate the <Globalization> section of the configuration file.
HttpHandlersSection	Enables you to manipulate the <httpHandlers> section of the configuration file.

Class Name	Purpose
HttpModulesSection	Enables you to manipulate the `<httpModules>` section of the configuration file.
HttpRuntimeSection	Enables you to manipulate the `<httpRuntime>` section of the configuration file.
MachineKeySection	Enables you to manipulate the `<machineKeys>` section of the configuration file.
MembershipSection	Enables you to manipulate the `<membership>` section of the configuration file.
PagesSection	Enables you to manipulate the `<pages>` section of the configuration file.
ProcessModelSection	Enables you to manipulate the `<processModel>` section of the configuration file.
WebPartsSection	Enables you to manipulate the `<webParts>` section of the configuration file.

All the configuration classes are implemented based on simple object-oriented based architecture that has an entity class that holds all the data and a collection class that has methods to add, remove, enumerate, and so on. Start your configuration file programming with a simple connection string enumeration, as shown in the following section.

Enumerating Connection Strings

In a Web application, you can store multiple connection strings. Some of them are used by the system and the others may be application-specific. You can write a very simple ASP.NET application that enumerates all the connection strings stored in the web.config file, as shown in Listing 27-13.

Listing 27-13: The web.config file

```
<?xml version="1.0" ?>
<configuration xmlns="http://schemas.microsoft.com/.NetConfiguration/v2.0">
    <appSettings>
        <add key="symbolServer" value="10.200.241.10" />
    </appSettings>
    <connectionStrings>
        <add name="401kApp"
        connectionString="server=401kServer;
        database=401kDB;uid=WebUser;pwd=P@$$worD9"
        providerName="System.Data.SqlClient"
        />
    </connectionStrings>
    <system.web>
        <compilation debug="false" />
        <authentication mode="None" />
    </system.web>
</configuration>
```

As shown in Listing 27-13, one application setting points to the symbol server, and one connection string is stored in the `web.config` file. Use the `ConnectionStrings` collection of the `System.Web.Configuration.WebConfigurationManager` class to read the connection strings, as seen in Listing 27-14.

Listing 27-14: Enum.aspx

VB

```
Protected Sub Page_Load(ByVal sender As Object, ByVal e As System.EventArgs)
    GridView1.DataSource = _
        System.Web.Configuration.WebConfigurationManager.ConnectionStrings
    GridView1.DataBind()
End Sub
```

C#

```
protected void Page_Load(object sender, EventArgs e)
{
    GridView1.DataSource =
    System.Web.Configuration.WebConfigurationManager.ConnectionStrings;
    GridView1.DataBind();
}
```

As shown in Listing 27-14, you've bound the `ConnectionStrings` property collection of the `WebConfigurationManager` class into the GridView control. The `WebConfigurationManager` class returns an instance of the `Configuration` class and the `ConnectionStrings` property is a static (shared in Visual Basic) property. Therefore, you're just binding the property collection into the GridView control. Figure 27-5 shows the list of connection strings stored in the ASP.NET application.

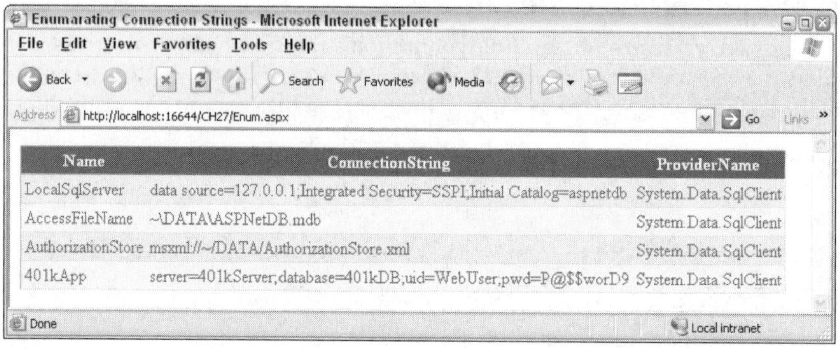

Figure 27-5

Adding a connection string at runtime is also a very easy task. If you do it as shown in Listing 27-13, you get an instance of the configuration object. Then you create a new `connectionStringSettings` class. You add the new class to the collection and call the update method. Listing 27-15 shows examples of this in both VB and C#.

Listing 27-15: Adding a connection string

VB

```vb
Protected Sub Button1_Click(ByVal sender As Object, ByVal e As System.EventArgs)
    ' Get the file path for the current web request
    Dim webPath As String = Request.CurrentExecutionFilePath

    'Parse the leading forward slash
    webPath = webPath.Substring(0, webPath.LastIndexOf("/"))

    Try
        'Get configuration object of the current web request
        Dim config As Configuration = _
    System.Web.Configuration.WebConfigurationManager.OpenWebConfiguration(webPath)

        'Create new connection setting from text boxes
        Dim newConnSetting As New _
        ConnectionStringSettings(txtName.Text, txtValue.Text, txtProvider.Text)

        'Add the connection string to the collection
        config.ConnectionStrings.ConnectionStrings.Add(newConnSetting)

        'Save the changes
        config.Save()
    Catch cEx As ConfigurationErrorsException
        lblStatus.Text = "Status: " + cEx.ToString()
    Catch ex As System.UnauthorizedAccessException
        'The ASP.NET process account must have read/write access to the directory
        lblStatus.Text = "Status: " + "The ASP.NET process account must have
        read/write access to the directory"
    Catch eEx As Exception
        lblStatus.Text = "Status: " + eEx.ToString()
    End Try

    ShowConnectionStrings()
End Sub
```

C#

```csharp
protected void Button1_Click(object sender, EventArgs e)
{
    //Get the file path for the current web request
    string webPath = Request.CurrentExecutionFilePath;

    //Parse the leading forward slash
    webPath = webPath.Substring(0, webPath.LastIndexOf('/'));

    //Get configuration object of the current web request
    Configuration config =
    System.Web.Configuration.WebConfigurationManager.OpenWebConfiguration(webPath);

    //Create new connection setting from text boxes
    ConnectionStringSettings newConnSetting = new
```

(continued)

Listing 27-15 *(continued)*

```
        ConnectionStringSettings(txtName.Text, txtValue.Text, txtProvider.Text);

        try
        {
            //Add the connection string to the collection
            config.ConnectionStrings.ConnectionStrings.Add(newConnSetting);

            //Save the changes
            config.Save();
        }
        catch (ConfigurationErrorsException cEx)
        {
            lblStatus.Text = "Status: " + cEx.ToString();
        }
        catch (System.UnauthorizedAccessException uEx)
        {
            //The ASP.NET process account must have read/write access to the directory
            lblStatus.Text = "Status: " + "The ASP.NET process account must have
            read/write access to the directory";
        }
        catch (Exception eEx)
        {
            lblStatus.Text = "Status: " + eEx.ToString();
        }

        //Reload the connection strings in the list box
        ShowConnectionStrings();
}
```

Manipulating a machine.config File

The `OpenMachineConfiguration` method of the `System.Web.Configuration`
`.WebConfigurationManager` class provides a way to manipulate the `machine.config` file. The
`OpenMachineConfiguration` method is a static method, and it has multiple overloads.

Listing 27-16 shows a simple example that enumerates all the section groups stored in the `machine`
`.config` file. As shown in this listing, you're getting an instance of the configuration object using the
`OpenMachineConfiguration` method. Then you're binding the `SectionGroups` collection with
the GridView control.

Listing 27-16: Configuration groups from machine.config

VB
```
Protected Sub Button2_Click(ByVal sender As Object, ByVal e As System.EventArgs)
    'List all the SectionGroups in Machine.Config file
    Dim configSetting As Configuration = _
    System.Configuration.ConfigurationManager.OpenMachineConfiguration()
    GridView1.DataSource = configSetting.SectionGroups
    GridView1.DataBind()
End Sub
```

```
C#
protected void Button2_Click(object sender, EventArgs e)
{
    //List all the SectionGroups in Machine.Config file
    Configuration configSetting =
    System.Configuration.ConfigurationManager.OpenMachineConfiguration();
    GridView1.DataSource = configSetting.SectionGroups;
    GridView1.DataBind();
}
```

In the same way, you can list all the configuration sections using the `Sections` collections, as shown in Listing 27-17.

Listing 27-17: Configuration sections from machine.config

```
VB
Protected Sub Button2_Click(ByVal sender As Object, ByVal e As System.EventArgs)
    'List all the SectionGroups in Machine.Config file
    Dim configSetting As Configuration = _
    System.Configuration.ConfigurationManager.OpenMachineConfiguration()
    GridView1.DataSource = configSetting.Sections
    GridView1.DataBind()
End Sub
```

```
C#
protected void Button2_Click(object sender, EventArgs e)
{
    //List all the SectionGroups in Machine.Config file
    Configuration configSetting =
    System.Configuration.ConfigurationManager.OpenMachineConfiguration();
    GridView1.DataSource = configSetting.Sections;
    GridView1.DataBind();
}
```

Manipulating machine.config from Remote Servers

The ASP.NET Management Objects also provide a way to read configuration information from remote servers. Both `GetWebConfiguration` and `GetMachineConfiguration` methods have overloads to support this functionality.

For example, if you'd like to manipulate the Expense Web application's configuration file located on the `Optra.Microsoft.com` site, you can do so as shown in Listing 27-18.

Listing 27-18: Manipulating a remote server's web.config

```
VB
' Connect to the web application Expense on Optra.Microsoft.com server
Configuration configSetting = Configuration.GetWebConfiguration("/Expense", "1", _
    "Optra.Microsoft.com")

' Change the authentication mode to Forms Authentication
configSetting.Web.Authentication.AuthenticationMode = AuthenticationMode.Forms

' Save the changes
configSetting.Update()
```

(continued)

Listing 27-18 *(continued)*

C#
```csharp
// Connect to the web application Expense on Optra.Microsoft.com server
Configuration configSetting = Configuration.GetWebConfiguration("/Expense", "1",
    "Optra.Microsoft.com");

// Change the authentication mode to Forms Authentication
configSetting.Web.Authentication.AuthenticationMode = AuthenticationMode.Forms;

// Save the changes
configSetting.Update();
```

If you look at the code shown in Listing 27-18, the only change from the previous example is that you've given the machine address in the constructor method to connect to the remote server. Then you changed its `authenticationMode` to Forms Authentication and saved the changes.

Listing 27-19 shows how to manipulate the remote server's `machine.config` file.

Listing 27-19: Manipulating a remote server's machine.config

VB
```vb
' Connect to the web application Expense on Optra.Microsoft.com server
Configuration configSetting = _
    Configuration.GetMachineConfiguration("Optra.Microsoft.com")

' Change the authentication mode to Forms Authentication
configSetting.Web.Authentication.AuthenticationMode = AuthenticationMode.Forms

' Save the changes
configSetting.Update()
```

C#
```csharp
// Connect to the web application Expense on Optra.Microsoft.com server
Configuration configSetting = Configuration.
    GetMachineConfiguration("Optra.Microsoft.com");

// Change the authentication mode to Forms Authentication
configSetting.Web.Authentication.AuthenticationMode = AuthenticationMode.Forms;

// Save the changes
configSetting.Update();
```

When using the `GetMachineConfiguration` *method, it uses the DCOM protocol to connect to the remote server. To open or modify a configuration file on the remote server, the caller must have administrative privileges on the remote computer. To open local configuration files, the caller needs to have only read and/or write privileges for the configuration files in the hierarchy and read access to the metabase to resolve IIS paths.*

When manipulating configuration information stored on a remote server, the ASP.NET configuration API uses an optimistic concurrency model for modifying configuration. If two callers simultaneously open the same configuration, they get unique copies of the Configuration object. If a caller attempts to modify the configuration by calling the Update method, and the underlying configuration file has been modified since the caller obtained the Configuration object, the caller gets an exception. The underlying file may have been modified by another caller updating the configuration or by some other change to the file, independent of the configuration API.

Protecting Configuration Settings

When ASP.NET 1.0 was introduced, all the configuration information were stored in human-readable, clear-text format. However, ASP.NET 1.1 introduced a way to store the configuration information inside the registry using the Data Protection API (or DPAPI).

For example, Listing 27-20 shows how you can store a process model section's username and password information inside the registry.

Listing 27-20: Secure Machine.Config

```
<processModel
    userName="registry:HKLM\SOFTWARE\401kApp\Identity\ASPNET_SETREG,userName"
    password="registry:HKLM\SOFTWARE\401kApp\Identity\ASPNET_SETREG,password"
/>
```

ASP.NET 1.0 also acquired this functionality as a fix. Visit the following URL for more information:
http://support.microsoft.com/default.aspx?scid=kb;en-us;329290.

ASP.NET 2.0 introduces a system for protecting sensitive data stored in the configuration system. It uses industry-standard XML encryption to encrypt administrator-specified sections of configuration that contain any sensitive data.

Editing Configuration Files

So far in this chapter, you have learned about configuration files and what each configuration entry means. Even though the configuration entries are in an easy, human-readable XML format, editing these entries can be cumbersome. To help with editing, Microsoft ships three tools:

❑   Visual Studio 2005 IDE

❑   Web Site Administration Tool

❑   ASP.NET Snap-In for IIS

Unlike with previous versions of Visual Studio .NET, the Visual Studio 2005 IDE supports IntelliSense-based editing for configuration files, as shown in Figure 27-6.

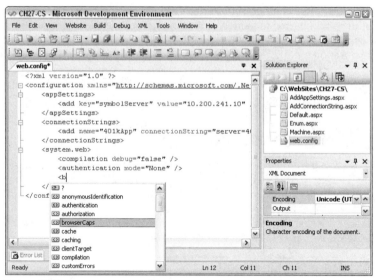

Figure 27-6

The Visual Studio 2005 IDE also supports XML element syntax checking, as shown in Figure 27-7.

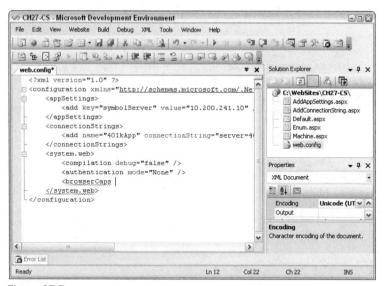

Figure 27-7

XML element syntax checking and IntelliSense for XML elements are accomplished using the XSD-based XML validation feature available for all the XML files inside Visual Studio 2005. The configuration XSD file is located at <drive>:\Program Files\Microsoft Visual Studio 8\Xml\Schemas\ dotnetconfig.xsd.

The Visual Studio 2005 IDE also adds two new useful features via the XML toolbar options that can help you with formatting the configuration settings:

❏   **Reformat Selection:** This option reformats the current XML notes content.

❏   **Format the whole document:** This option formats the entire XML document.

The Web Site Administration Tool and the ASP.NET Snap-In for IIS allow you to edit the configuration entries without knowing the XML element names and their corresponding values. Chapter 28 talks about both the Web Site Administration Tool and the ASP.NET Snap-In for IIS in more detail.

Summary

In this chapter, you have seen the ASP.NET configuration system and learned how it does not rely on the IIS metabase. Instead, ASP.NET uses an XML configuration system that is human-readable.

You also looked at the two different ASP.NET XML configuration files:

❏   `machine.config`

❏   `web.config`

The `machine.config` file applies default settings to all Web applications on the server. However, if the server has multiple versions of the Framework installed, the `machine.config` file applies to a particular Framework version. On the other hand, a particular Web application can customize or override its own configuration information using `web.config` files. Using a `web.config` file, you can also configure the applications on an application-by-application or folder-by-folder basis.

Next, you looked at some typical configuration settings that can be applied to an ASP.NET application, such as configuring connecting strings, Session State, browser capabilities, and so on. Then you looked at an overview of new ASP.NET Admin Objects and learned how to program configuration files. Finally, you learned how to protect the configuration section using cryptographic algorithms.

Administration and Management

You have almost reached the end of this book; you have been introduced to ASP.NET 2.0 with its wonderful new features designed to help you become a better and more efficient programmer. However, with all advancement comes complexity, as is the case in the areas of ASP.NET configuration and management. The good news is that the ASP.NET 2.0 development team realized this and provided tools and APIs that enable developers to configure and manage ASP.NET 2.0–based applications with reliability and comfort.

This chapter covers these tools in great detail in an effort to educate you about all the options available to you. Two powerful configuration tools are explored: WAT (Web Site Administration Tool), a Web-based application, and the MMC ASP.NET Snap-In, a plug-in for IIS.

The Web Site Administration Tool

When ASP.NET was first released, it introduced the concept of an XML-based configuration file for Web applications. The file is called `web.config` and is located in the same directory as the application. It's used to store a number of configuration settings, some of which could override configuration settings defined in `machine.config` file. Previous versions of ASP.NET, however, didn't provide an administration tool to make it easy to configure the settings. A large number of developers around the world ended up creating their own configuration tools to avoid having to make the configuration changes manually.

The Web Site Administration Tool (WAT) enables you to manage Web site configuration through a simple, easy-to-use Web interface. It eliminates the need for manually editing the `web.config` file. If no `web.config` file exists when you use the WAT for the first time, it creates one. By default, the WAT also creates a database in the `App_Data` folder of your Web site to store application data. The changes made to most settings in the WAT take effect immediately and are reflected in the `web.config` file.

The default settings are automatically inherited from any configuration files that exist in the root folder of a Web server. WAT enables you to create or update your own settings for your Web application. You can also override the settings inherited from uplevel configuration files, if an override for those settings is allowed. (If overriding isn't permitted, the setting appears dimmed in the WAT.)

The WAT is automatically installed during installation of the .NET Framework version 2.0. To use the WAT to administer your Web site, you must be logged in as a registered user of your site and you must have Read and Write permissions to `web.config`.

You can access the WAT by opening a browser, typing the URL of your application, and appending `Webadmin.axd`. For example, if the name of the application is DemoApp, the URL to administer your Web site is as follows:

```
http://localhost/DemoApp/Webadmin.axd
```

If you are working in Visual Studio, click ASP.NET Configuration in the Website menu. You can also get to this page by clicking the ASP.NET Configuration button in the Visual Studio Solution Explorer. Figure 28-1 shows WAT's welcome page.

Figure 28-1

WAT features a tabbed interface that groups related configuration settings. The tabs and the configuration settings that they manage are described in the following sections.

The Home Tab

The Home tab is a summary that supplies some basic information about the application you are monitoring or modifying. It provides the name of the application and the current user context in which you are accessing the application. In addition, you see links to the other WAT tabs that provide you with summaries of their settings. To make changes to your application, click the appropriate tab or link.

Remember that most changes to configuration settings made using the WAT take effect immediately, causing the application to be restarted and currently active sessions to be lost if you are using an InProc session. The best practice for administrating ASP.NET is to make configuration changes to a staged version of your application and later publish these changes to your production application.

Some settings (those in which the WAT interface has a dedicated Save button) don't save automatically. You can lose the information typed in these windows unless you click the Save button. The WAT times out after a period of inactivity. Any settings that do not take effect immediately and are not saved will be lost.

As extensive as WAT is, it manages only some of the configuration settings that are available for your Web application. All other settings require modification of configuration files manually, by using the Microsoft Management Console (MMC) snap-in for ASP.NET, or by using the configuration API.

The Security Tab

Use the Security tab to manage access permissions to secure sections of your Web application, user accounts, and roles. You can select whether your Web application is accessed on an intranet or from the Internet. If you specify the intranet, Windows-based authentication is used; otherwise, forms-based authentication is configured. The latter mechanism relies on you to manage users in a custom data store, such as SQL Server database tables. The Windows-based authentication employs the user's Windows logon for identification.

> **User information is stored in a SQL Express database by default. The database is automatically created in the App_Data folder of the Web application. I recommend that you store such sensitive information on a different and more secure database. You can simply use the Provider tab to select a different data provider. The Provider tab is covered later in this chapter.**

You can configure security settings on this tab in two ways: select the Setup Wizard, or simply use the links provided for the Users, Roles, and Access Management sections. Figure 28-2 shows the Security tab.

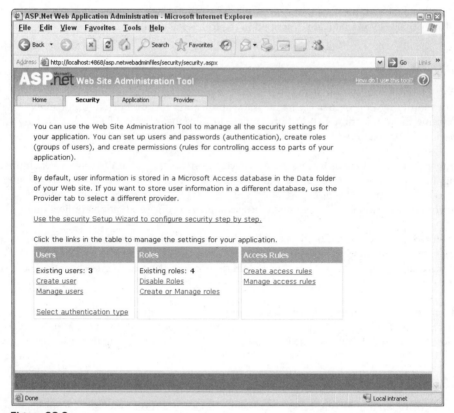

Figure 28-2

You can use the Wizard to configure initial settings. Later, you learn other ways to create and modify security settings.

The Security Setup Wizard

The Security Setup Wizard provides a seven-step process ranging from selecting the way the user will be authenticated to selecting a data source for storing user information. This is followed by definitions of roles, users, and access rules.

> **Be sure to create all folders that need special permissions *before* you engage the wizard.**

Follow these steps to use the Security Setup Wizard:

1. The wizard welcome screen (shown in Figure 28-3) is informational only. It educates you on the basics of security management in ASP.NET. When you finish reading the screen, click Next.

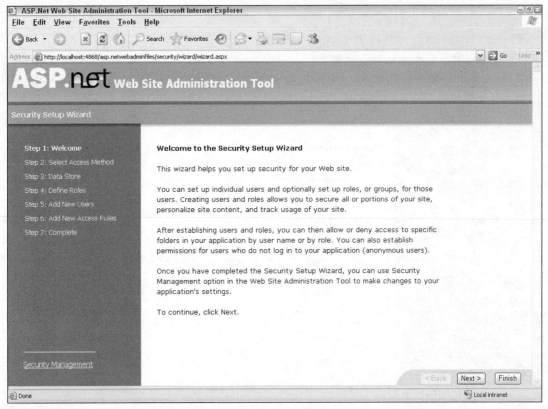

Figure 28-3

2. Select your access method (authentication mechanism). You have two options:

    ❏   **From the Internet:** Indicates you want forms-based authentication. You must use your own database of user information. This option works well in scenarios where nonemployees need to access the Web application.

    ❏   **From a Local Area Network:** Indicates users of this application are already authenticated on the domain. You don't have to use your own user information database. Instead, you can use the currently logged-in domain user information.

    Figure 28-4 shows the screen for Step 2.

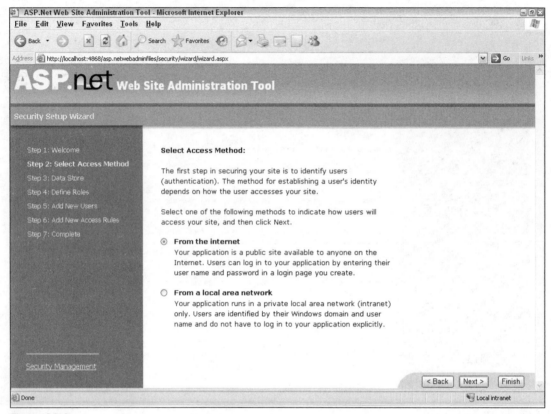

Figure 28-4

Select From the Internet, and click the Next button.

3. Select the data source provider. As mentioned earlier, the WAT uses SQL Express by default. You can configure additional providers on the Providers tab. In the Step 3 screen shown in Figure 28-5, only the Access Provider is displayed because no other providers have been configured yet. Click Next.

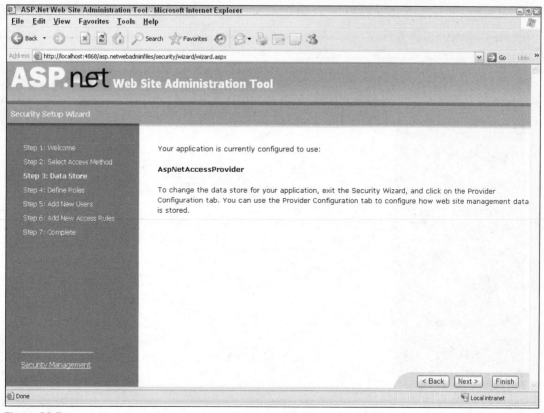

Figure 28-5

4. Define roles. If you are happy with all users having the same access permission, you can simply skip this step by deselecting the Enable Roles for This Web Site check box. If this box isn't checked, clicking the Next button takes you directly to the User Management screens. Check this box to see how to define roles using this wizard.

The first screen of Step 4 is shown in Figure 28-6. When you're ready, click Next.

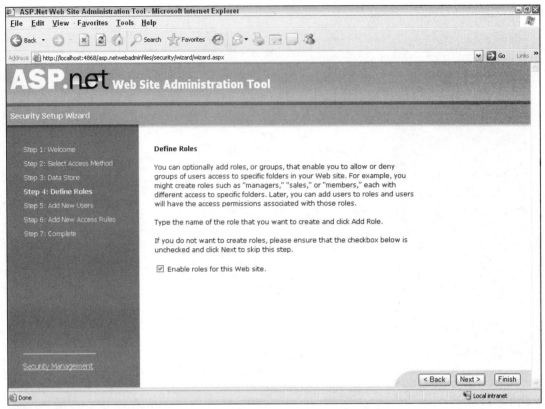

Figure 28-6

The next screen (see Figure 28-7) in the wizard enables you to create and delete roles. The roles simply define categories of users. Later, you can provide users and access rules based on these roles. Click Next.

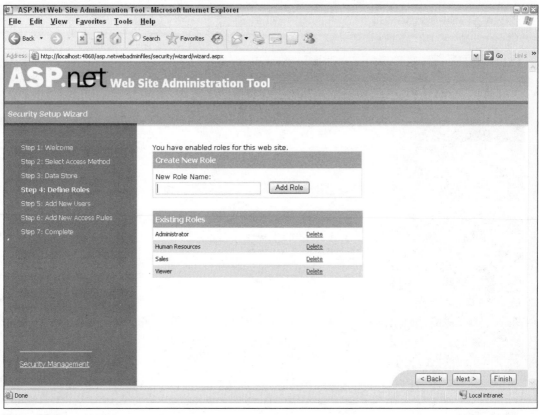

Figure 28-7

5. Create users for the Web application. Earlier, you selected the From the Internet option, so the wizard assumes that you want to use forms authentication and provides you with the option of creating and managing users. (The From a Local Area Network choice, remember, uses Windows-based authentication.)

The Add New Users screen (see Figure 28-8) enables you to enter the username, password, e-mail address, and security question and answer.

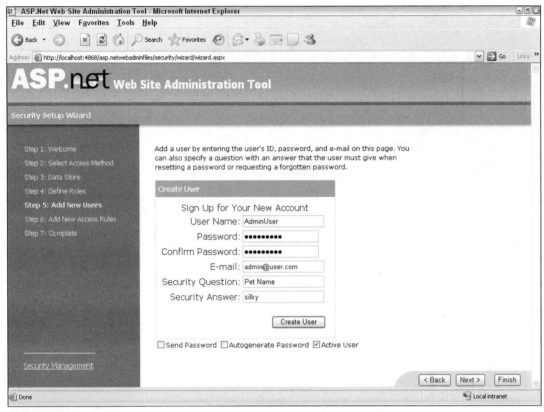

Figure 28-8

You can create as many users as you like; but to delete or update information for users, you must leave the wizard and manage the users separately. As mentioned earlier, the wizard is simply for creating the initial configuration for future management.

The Autogenerate Password option (at the bottom of the screen) is helpful when you want the Web application to create an initial password and e-mail it to the user. Be sure to check the Send Password option, too.

Click Next.

6. Create access rules (see Figure 28-9). First, select the folder in the Web application that needs special security settings. Then choose the role or user(s) to whom the rule will apply. Select the permission (Allow or Deny) and click the Add This Rule button. For example, selecting the Secure folder, the Administrator role, and the Allow radio button would permit all users in the Administrator role access to the Secure folder.

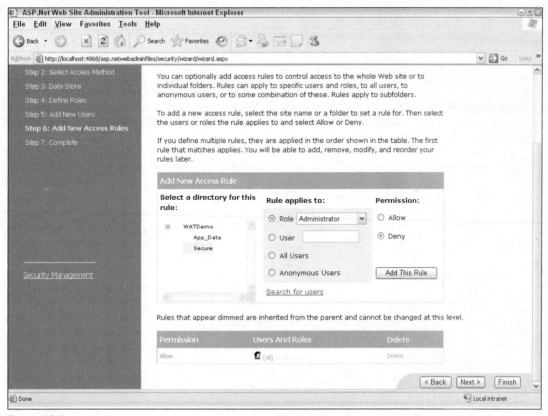

Figure 28-9

All folders that need special permissions must be created ahead of time. The information shown in the wizard is cached and is not updated if you decide to create a new folder inside your Web application when you are already on this screen.

The wizard gives you the capability to apply access rules to either roles or specific users. The Search for Users option is handy if you have defined a lot of users for your Web site and want to search for a specific user.

All access rules are shown at the bottom on the screen, and you can delete a specific rule and start again. Rules are shown dimmed if they are inherited from the parent configuration and can't be changed here.

When you're ready, click Next.

7.   The last screen in the Security Setup wizard is an information page. Click the Finish button to exit the wizard.

Creating New Users

The WAT Security tab provides ways to manage users without using the wizard and is very helpful for ongoing maintenance of users, roles, and access permissions.

To create a new user, simply click the Create User link on the main page of the Security tab (as you saw earlier in Figure 28-2). The Create User screen, shown in Figure 28-10, is displayed, enabling you to provide username, password, confirmation of password, e-mail, and the security question and answer. You can assign a new user to any number of roles in the Roles list; these are roles currently defined for your Web application.

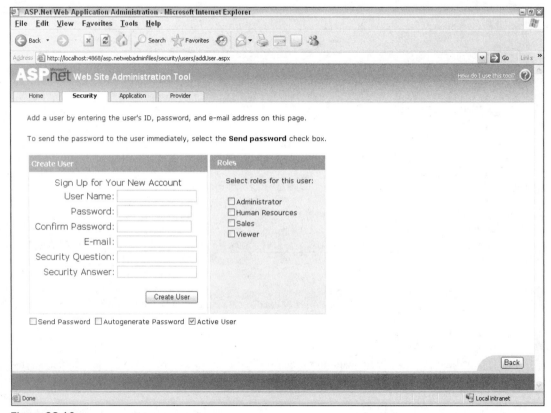

Figure 28-10

Managing Users

You can manage existing users by clicking the Manage Users link on the Security tab. A new screen displays a list of all existing users (see Figure 28-11). A search option is available, which makes it easier to find a specific user if the list is long.

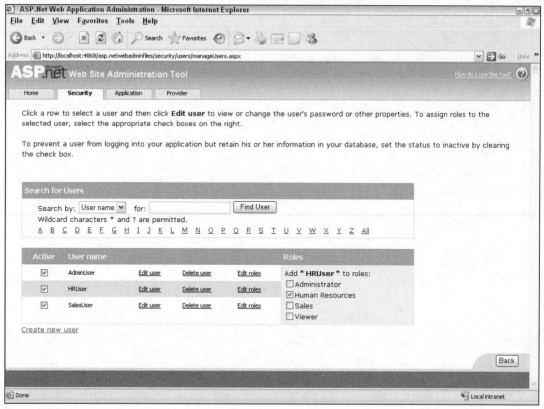

Figure 28-11

Find the user you want to manage, update his information, delete the user, reassign roles, or set the user to active or inactive.

Managing Roles

Two links are provided in the Security tab for managing roles: Disable Roles and Create or Manage Roles. Clicking Disable Roles does just that — disables role management in the Web application; it also dims the other link.

Click the Create Or Manage Roles link to start managing roles and user assignments to specific roles. A screen displays all roles you have defined so far. You have options to add new roles, delete existing roles, or manage specific roles.

Click the Manage link next to a specific role, and a screen shows all the users currently assigned to that role (see Figure 28-12). You can find other users by searching for their names, and you can then assign them to or remove them from a selected role.

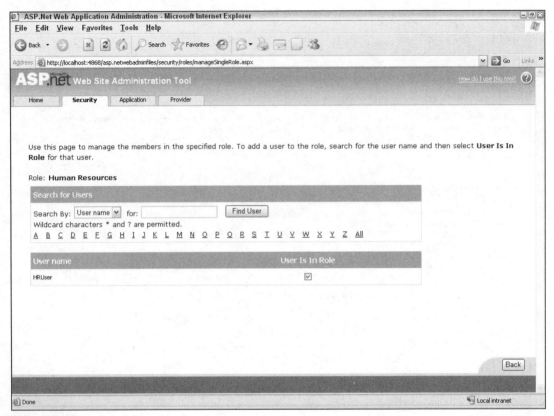

Figure 28-12

Managing Access Rules

The Security tab provides options for creating and managing access rules. Access rules are applied either to an entire Web application or to specific folders inside it. Clicking the Create Access Rules link takes you to a screen where you can view a list of the folders inside your Web application. You can select a specific folder, select a role or a user, and then choose whether you want to enable access to the selected folder. Figure 28-13 shows the Add New Access Rule screen.

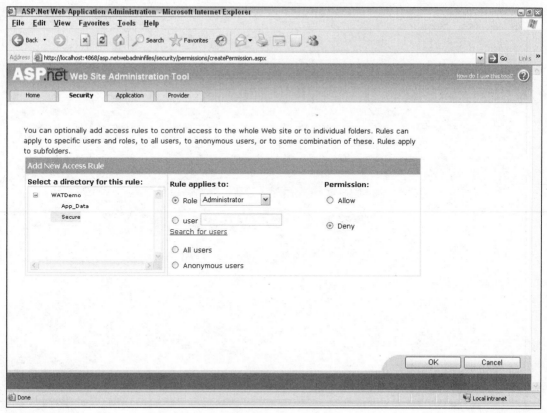

Figure 28-13

Clicking Manage Access Rules on the Security tab takes you to a screen that shows all existing access rules. You can remove any of these rules and add new ones. You can also readjust the list of access rules if you want to apply them in a specific order. The Manage Access Rules screen is shown in Figure 28-14.

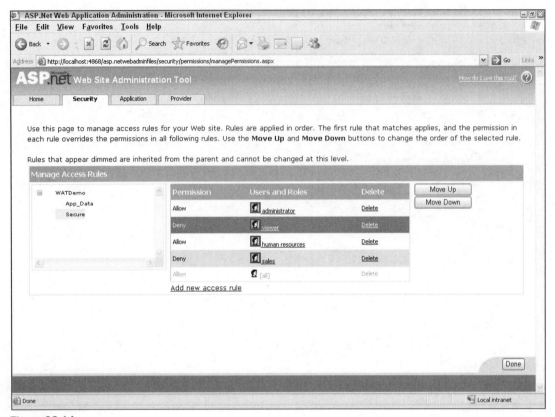

Figure 28-14

The Application Tab

The Application tab provides a number of application-specific configurations, including the configuration of appSettings, SMTP mail server settings, debugging and trace settings, and starting/stopping the entire Web application.

Managing Application Settings

The left side of the screen shows links for creating and managing application settings. The settings are stored in the `<appSettings>` tag. Most ASP.NET programmers are used to manually modifying this tag in previous versions of ASP.NET. Figure 28-15 shows the Application tab.

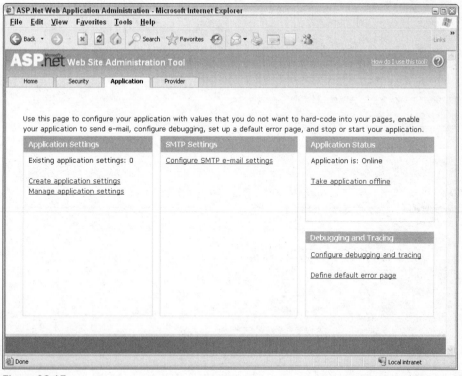

Figure 28-15

Clicking the Create Application Settings link takes you to a screen where you can provide the name and the value information. Clicking Manage Application Settings takes you to a screen where you can view existing settings and edit or delete them. You can also create new setting from this screen.

Managing SMTP Configuration

Click the Configure SMTP E-Mail Settings link to view a screen like the one shown in Figure 28-16. The configure SMTP mail settings feature is usable if your Web application can send autogenerated e-mails. Instead of denoting SMTP server configuration in the code, you can spell it out in the configuration file here in the WAT.

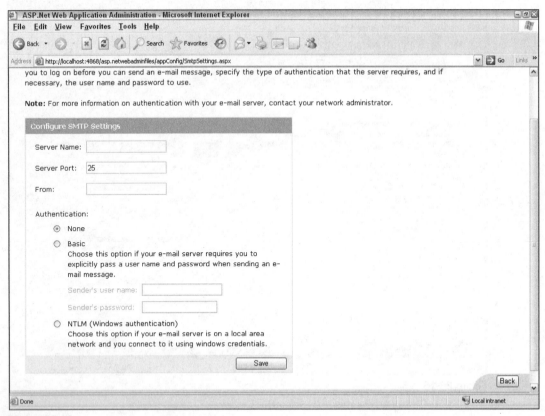

Figure 28-16

Specify the server name, port, sender e-mail address, and authentication type.

Managing Tracing and Debugging Information

Clicking the Application tab's Configure Debugging and Tracing link takes you to a screen (see Figure 28-17) where you can enable or disable tracing and debugging. Select whether you want to display trace information on each page. You can also specify whether tracking just local requests or all requests, as well as trace sorting and caching configuration.

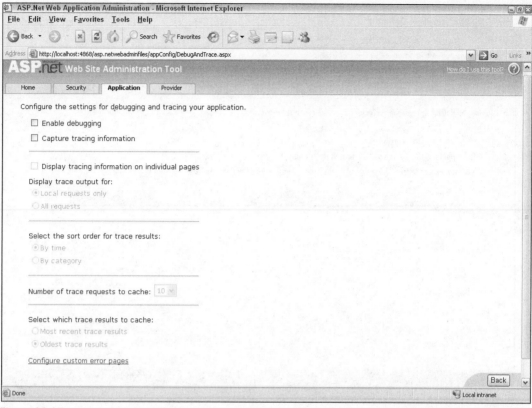

Figure 28-17

To configure default error pages, you simply click Define Default Error Page on the screen you saw in Figure 28-15. This takes you to a screen where you can select a URL that is used for redirection in case of an error condition (see Figure 28-18).

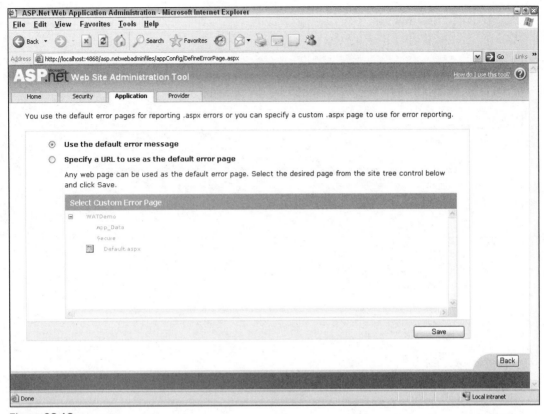

Figure 28-18

Taking an Application Offline

You can take your entire Web application offline simply by clicking the Take Application Offline link (again, refer to Figure 28-15). The link stops the app domain for your Web application. It is useful if you want to perform a scheduled maintenance for an application that is hosted at an ISP.

The Provider Tab

The final tab in the Web Admin tool is Provider, shown in Figure 28-19. You use it to set up additional providers and to determine the providers your application will use.

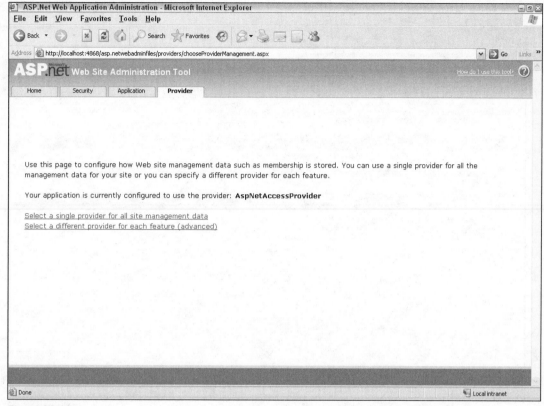

Figure 28-19

The Provider page is simple, but it contains an important piece of information: the default data provider with which your application is geared to work. In Figure 28-19, the application is set up to work with the AspNetAccessProvider, the default data provider.

The two links on this tab let you set up either a single data provider or a specific data provider for each of the features in ASP.NET that requires a data provider. If you click the latter, you are presented with the screen shown in Figure 28-20. It enables you to pick either an Access or SQL server provider separately for Membership and Role management.

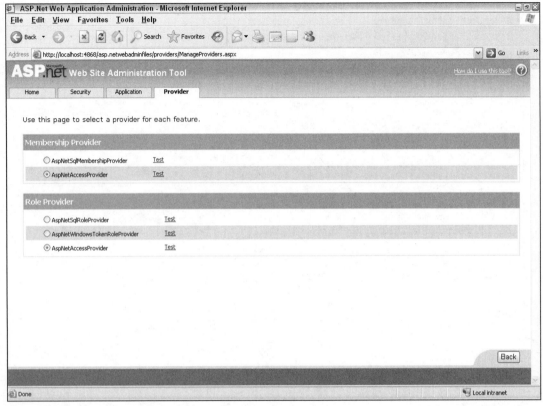

Figure 28-20

As you can see from the screen shots and brief explanations provided here, you can now handle a large portion of the necessary configurations through a GUI. You no longer have to figure out which setting must be placed in the web.config file. This functionality becomes even more important as the web .config file grows. In ASP.NET 1.0/1.1, the web.config file was a reasonable size, but with all the new features now provided by ASP.NET 2.0, the web.config file has the potential to become very large. The new GUI-based tools are an outstanding way to manage it.

The MMC ASP.NET Snap-In

If you are using IIS as the basis of your ASP.NET applications, you'll find the new ASP.NET tab in the Microsoft Management Console (MMC) a great addition. To access the tab, open IIS and expand the Web Sites folder, which contains all the sites configured to work with IIS. Remember that not all your Web sites are configured to work in this manner. It is also possible to create ASP.NET applications that make use of the new ASP.NET built-in Web server.

Right-click one of the applications in the Web Sites folder and select Properties from the context menu (see Figure 28-21).

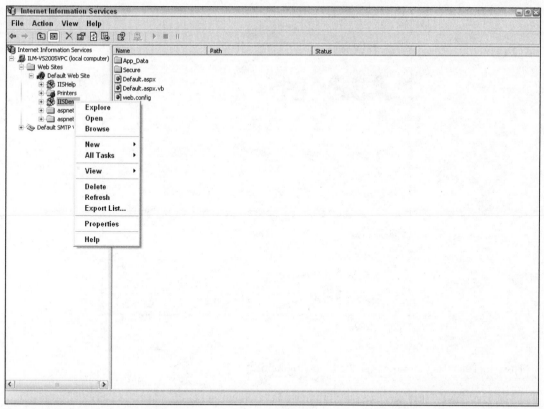

Figure 28-21

The MMC opens. Click the ASP.NET tab. A configuration panel similar to the one shown in Figure 28-22 appears.

> *Selecting one of the application folders enables you to edit the* `web.config` *file from the MMC snap-in; selecting Properties for the default Web site (the root node) lets you edit the* `machine.config` *file.*

Figure 28-22

The panel enables you to change the following items:

❑ **ASP.NET version:** The .NET Framework version number on which the ASP.NET application is to run. Be careful about switching versions of the application. Some minor breaking changes may cause errors in different versions of the framework.

❑ **Virtual path:** The virtual path of the application. In this example, Visual Studio creates an application titled IISDemo with an IISDemo virtual directory.

❑ **File location:** The location of the file being altered by the MMC console. In most cases, the configuration GUIs alter the web.config file. In this example, the file location is the web.config file in the IISDemo application.

❑ **File creation date:** The date when the web.config file was created.

❑ **File last modified:** The date when the web.config file was last modified either manually, using the MMC console, or by the ASP.NET Web Site Administration Tool.

In addition, the ASP.NET tab also includes an Edit Global Configuration (if working from the Default Web Site root) and an Edit Configuration button that provides a tremendous number of modification capabilities to use in the machine.config or web.config files. Click the button to access the multi-tabbed GUI titled ASP.NET Configuration Settings. The following sections review each of the tabs available through this MMC console.

General

The General tab enables you to manage connection strings and app settings for your application. Figure 28-23 shows an example of one setting for an application.

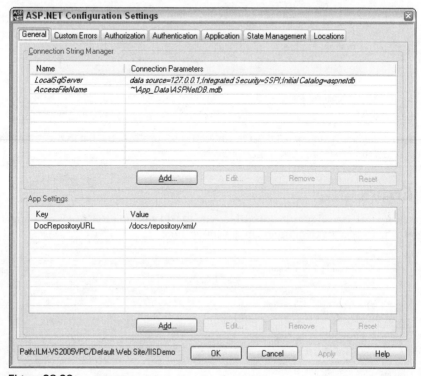

Figure 28-23

The General tab has two sections. First is the Connection String Manager. To add a connection string to your application, just click its Add button. You also can edit or remove existing connection strings. Figure 28-24 shows the Edit/Add Connection String dialog.

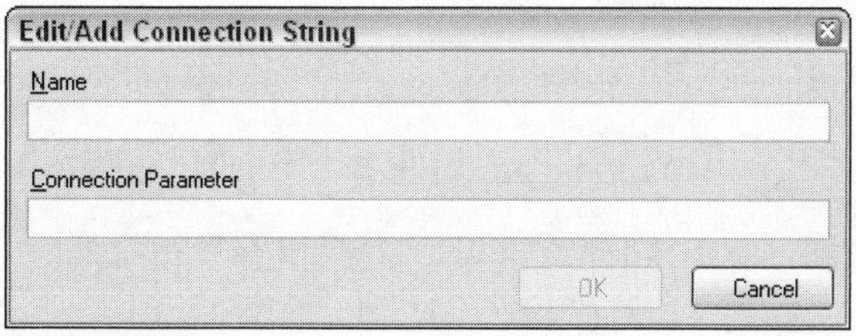

Figure 28-24

Supply a name and connection parameter and click OK to provide your application with a connection string.

The General tab's other section is App Settings. Click its Add or Edit button, and the Edit/Add Application Settings dialog opens (see Figure 28-25).

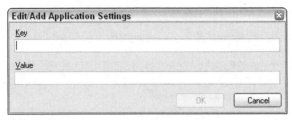

Figure 28-25

After you enter a key and value pair, click OK; the settings appear in the list in the main dialog. Then you can edit or delete the settings from the application.

Custom Errors

The Custom Errors tab (see Figure 28-26) enables you to add custom error pages or redirect users to particular pages when a specific error occurs in the application.

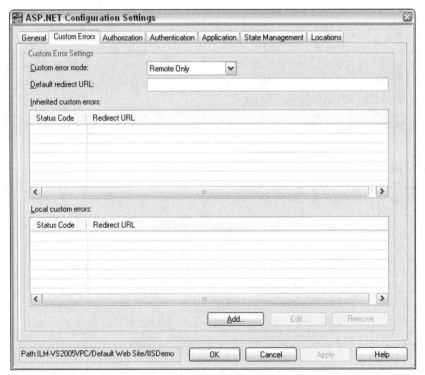

Figure 28-26

The tab allows you to work with the following items:

❑ **Custom error mode:** A drop-down list applies custom error modes for particular users of the application. The default option is Remote Only, which ensures that errors are redirected only for users who are on a remote machine. The other settings include On, which turns on error redirection for all users, and Off, which turns off error redirecting.

❑ **Default redirect URL:** The URL to which all errors are redirected.

❑ **Inherited custom errors:** All the errors that have been inherited from server defaults. These can be redirections for custom errors that are set in the `machine.config` file and all parent `web.config` files.

❑ **Local custom errors:** The errors that are set by you for this particular application. Error redirections are set using a name/value pair for the Status Code/Redirect URL.

Authorization

The MMC's Authorization tab enables you to authorize specific users or groups for the application (see Figure 28-27).

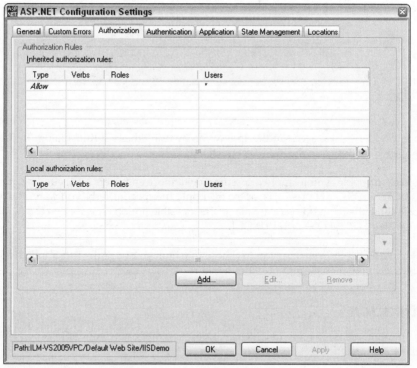

Figure 28-27

This dialog contains two items:

- **Inherited authorization rules:** All the authorization rules inherited from server defaults. These can be roles that are established in the `machine.config` file of the server.

- **Local authorization rules:** The authorization rules that you set for this particular application.

From this dialog, you can add, edit, or remove roles. Click the Add button and the Edit Rule dialog shown in Figure 28-28 appears.

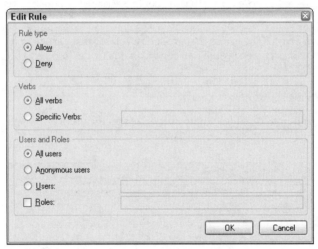

Figure 28-28

You can allow or deny users access to the application by using the Edit Rule dialog. To use this feature, click the appropriate option in the Rule Type section.

The Verbs section enables you to apply a specific rule to those end users retrieving the page via all possible means (HTTP-POST or HTTP-GET), or to cover only the specific verbs you want. Remember that the verb specifies how the request is actually made. The possible options specify that the request can be made using either HTTP-POST or HTTP-GET.

The Users and Roles section enables you to choose to whom you want the rule applied: all users that come to the site, anonymous users only, specific users, or users in specific groups.

Authentication

The Authentication tab (see Figure 28-29) enables you to modify how your application authenticates users for later authorization.

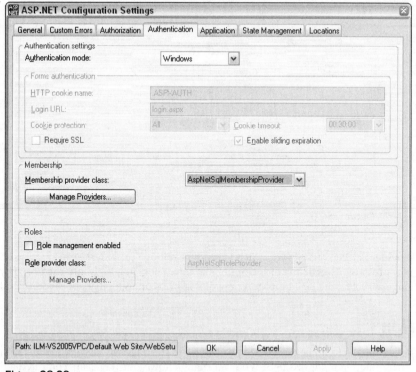

Figure 28-29

The dialog contains many options because you can work with the authorization of your end users in so many ways. The following list describes some of the items in this dialog:

❑ **Authentication Settings:** Here's where you set the authentication mode of your application. The options in the drop-down list include Windows, Forms, Passport, or None. If you select Forms, the grayed-out options are available and enable you to modify all the settings that determine how forms authentication is applied.

❑ **Membership:** You can tie the membership process to one of the available data providers available on your server. Click the Manage Providers button to add, edit, or remove providers.

❑ **Roles:** You can enable role-based management by checking the check box. From here, you can also tie the role management capabilities to a particular data provider.

Clicking the Manage Providers button opens the Provider Settings dialog (see Figure 28-30), which enables you to work with the data providers on the server.

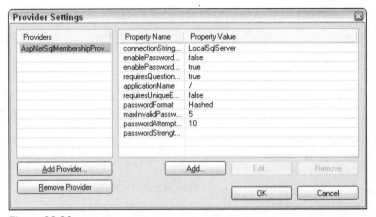

Figure 28-30

From the Provider Settings dialog, you can add, edit, or remove providers. You can also edit the settings of a particular provider. To edit any of the options in the dialog, just highlight the property that you want to change and click the Edit button. A new dialog pops up, which enables you to make changes.

Application

Use the Application tab to make more specific changes to the pages in the context of your application. From this dialog, shown in Figure 28-31, you can change how your pages are compiled and run. You can also make changes to global settings in your application.

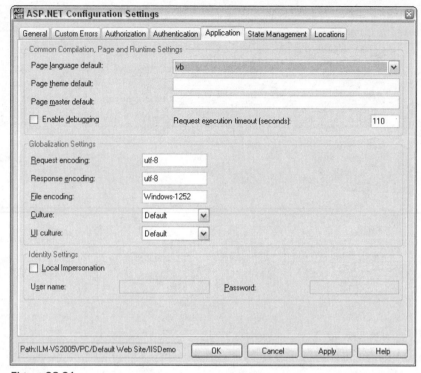

Figure 28-31

The dialog provides you with a wealth of options for modifying how the pages are run in a specific application, as well as how your applications, in general, are built and run. The following list briefly describes some of these options:

❑ **Common Compilation, Page, and Runtime Settings:** Includes a number of items that are very page-specific. From the first drop-down list, you can select the default language of your application. The available options include all the Microsoft .NET–compliant languages — C#, VB, JS, VJ#, and CPP. Other settings enable you to set the default theme or master page that ASP.NET pages use during construction.

❑ **Globalization Settings:** Enables you to set the default encodings and the cultures for your application.

❑ **Identity Settings:** Enables you to run the ASP.NET worker-process under a specific user account.

State Management

ASP.NET applications, being stateless in nature, are highly dependent on how state is stored. The State Management tab (see Figure 28-32) enables you to change a number of different settings that determine how state management is administered.

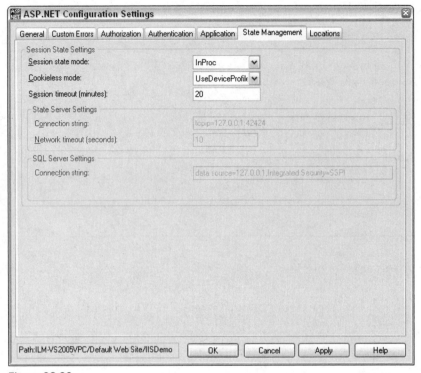

Figure 28-32

You can apply state management to your applications in a number of ways, and this dialog allows for a number of different settings — some of which are enabled or disabled based on what is selected. The following list describes the items available in the Session State Settings section:

❑ **Session state mode:** Determines how the sessions are stored by the ASP.NET application. The default option (shown in Figure 28-32) is InProc. Other options include Off, StateServer, and SQLServer. Running sessions in-process (InProc) means that the sessions are stored in the same process as the ASP.NET worker process. Therefore, if IIS is shut down and then brought up again, all the sessions are destroyed and unavailable to end users. StateServer means that sessions are stored out-of-process by a Windows service called ASPState. SQLServer is by far the most secure way to deal with your sessions — it stores them directly in SQL Server itself. StateServer is also the least performance-efficient method.

❑ **Cookieless mode:** Changes how the identifiers for the end user are stored. The default setting uses cookies (UseCookies). Other possible settings include UseUri, AutoDetect, and UseDeviceProfile.

❑ **Session timeout:** Sessions are stored for only a short period of time before they expire. For years, the default has been 20 minutes. Modifying the value here changes how long the sessions created by your application are valid.

Locations

The Locations tab allows you to specify configuration details for a particular folder or file in the web .config file. There may be cases where you are interested in applying specific details to only a file or folder using the <location> element in the web.config file. To accomplish this, click the Add button in the dialog and simply use the folder name (e.g., MyFolder) or the file (e.g., Admin.aspx) whose behavior you are interested in controlling. Once added, you can then highlight that added item and click the Edit Configuration button to launch another dialog that allows you to apply configuration settings to only the specified item. Figure 28-33 shows the Locations tab.

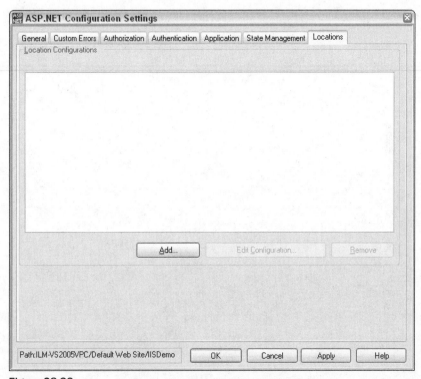

Figure 28-33

If you are an administrator of ASP.NET applications, gone are the days when you were required to go to XML files to fiddle with the settings. Fiddling is an error-prone method of administration and is effectively eliminated through the new administration GUIs — one of which is the new ASP.NET MMC snap-in.

Summary

This chapter showed you some of the new management tools that come with the latest release of ASP.NET. These tools make the ever-increasing size of the `web.config` file more manageable because they take care of setting the appropriate values in the application's configuration file.

The ASP.NET snap-in to the Microsoft Management Console is a welcome addition for managing applications that are configured to work with IIS. The ASP.NET Web Site Administration Tool provides even more value to administrators and developers by enabling them to remotely manage settings.

Packaging and Deploying ASP.NET Applications

Packaging and deploying ASP.NET applications are topics that usually receive little attention. This chapter is going to take a more in-depth look at how you can package and deploy your ASP.NET applications after they are built. It is rare (at least, it should be) that you build your ASP.NET applications on a production server. Usually, after you have built your ASP.NET application on a development computer, you deploy the finished product to a production server.

An important reason to consider the proper packaging and deploying of your ASP.NET applications is that many applications are built as either saleable products, starter kits, or solutions. You allow complete strangers to download and install these products in their own environments — environments that you have absolutely no control over. If this is the case, it is ideal to give the consumer a single installer file that ensures proper installation of the application in any environment.

Before you start, you should understand the basics of packaging and deploying ASP.NET applications. In the process of packaging your ASP.NET applications, you are putting your applications into a package and utilizing a process of deployment that is initiated through a deployment procedure, such as using a Windows installer.

The nice thing about the packaging and deployment process in ASP.NET 2.0 is that it is even easier than in previous versions of ASP.NET.

Deployment Pieces

So what are you actually deploying? ASP.NET contains a lot of pieces that are all possible parts of the overall application and need to be deployed with the application in order for it to run properly. The following list details some of the items that are potentially part of your ASP.NET application and need deployment consideration when you are moving your application:

- ❏ .aspx pages

- ❏ The code-behind pages for the .aspx pages (.aspx.vb or .aspx.cs files)

- ❏ User controls (.ascx)

- ❏ Web service files (.asmx and .wsdl files)

- ❏ .htm or .html files

- ❏ Image files such as .jpg or .gif

- ❏ ASP.NET system folders such as App_Code and App_Themes

- ❏ JavaScript files (.js)

- ❏ Cascading Style Sheets (.css)

- ❏ Configuration files such as the web.config file

- ❏ .NET components and compiled assemblies

- ❏ Data files such as .mdb files

Steps to Take before Deploying

Before deploying your ASP.NET Web applications, you should take some basic steps to ensure that your application is *ready* for deployment. These steps are often forgotten and are mentioned here to remind you of how you can ensure that your deployed application performs at its best.

The first step you should take is to *turn off* debugging in the web.config file. You do this by setting the debug attribute in the <compilation> element to false, as shown in Listing 29-1.

Listing 29-1: Setting debug to false before application deployment

```
<configuration xmlns="http://schemas.microsoft.com/.NetConfiguration/v2.0">
   <system.web>

      <compilation debug="false" />

   </system.web>
</configuration>
```

By default, most developers set the debug attribute to true when developing their applications. Doing this inserts debug symbols into the compiled ASP.NET pages. These symbols degrade the performance of any application. After the application is built and ready to be deployed, it is unnecessary to keep these debug symbols in place.

The second step is to build your application in Release mode. You can accomplish this by changing the Active Solution Configuration from Debug to Release through the drop-down list in the Visual Studio menu. This is illustrated in Figure 29-1.

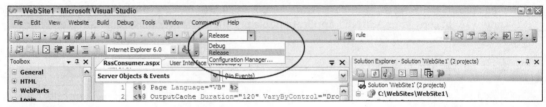

Figure 29-1

Methods of Deploying Web Applications

Remember that deployment is the last step in a process. The first is setting up the program—packaging the program into a component that is best suited for the deployment that follows. You can actually deploy a Web application in a number of ways. You can use the XCopy capability that simply wows audiences when demonstrated (because of its simplicity). A second method is to use Visual Studio 2005's capability to copy a Web site from one location to another using the Copy Web Site feature, as well as an alternative method that uses Visual Studio to deploy a precompiled Web application. The final method uses Visual Studio to build an installer program that can be launched on another machine. After reviewing each of the available methods, you can decide which is best for what you are trying to achieve. Start by looking at the simplest of the three methods: XCopy.

Using XCopy

Because of the nature of the .NET Framework, it is considerably easier to deploy .NET applications now than it was to deploy applications constructed using Microsoft's predecessor technology—COM. Applications in .NET compile down to assemblies, and these assemblies contain code that is executed by the Common Language Runtime (CLR). The great thing about assemblies is that they are self-describing. All the details about the assembly are stored within the assembly itself. In the Windows DNA world, COM stored all its self-describing data within the server's registry, so installing (as well as uninstalling) COM components meant shutting down IIS. Because a .NET assembly stores this information within itself, XCOPY functionality is possible. Installing an assembly is as simple as copying it to another server, and you don't need to stop or start IIS while this is going on.

We mention XCOPY here because it is the command-line way of basically doing a copy-and-paste of the files you want to move. XCOPY, however, provides a bit more functionality than just a copy-and-paste, as you will see shortly. XCOPY enables you to move files, directories, and even entire drives from one point to another.

The default syntax of the XCOPY command is as follows:

```
xcopy [source] [destination] [/w] [/p] [/c] [/v] [/q] [/f] [/l] [/g]
    [/d[:mm-dd-yyyy]] [/u] [/i] [/s [/e]] [/t] [/k] [/r] [/h] [{/a|/m}] [/n] [/o]
    [/x] [/exclude:file1[+[file2]][+file3]] [{/y|/-y}] [/z]
```

To see an example of using the XCOPY feature, suppose you are working from your developer machine (C:\) and want to copy your ASP.NET application to a production server (Z:\). In its simplest form, the following command would do the job:

```
xcopy c:\Websites\WebSite1 z:\Websites\ /f /e /k /h
```

This move copies the files and folders from the source drive to the destination drive. Figure 29-2 shows an example of this use on the command line.

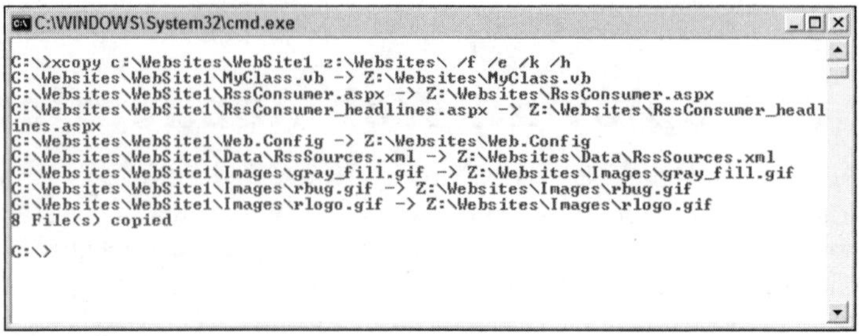

Figure 29-2

When you copy files using XCOPY, be aware that this method does not allow for the automatic creation of any virtual directories in IIS. To copy a new Web application, you create a virtual directory in the destination server and associate this virtual directory with the application you are copying. It is a simple process, but you must take these extra steps to finalize the site copy actions.

You can provide a number of parameters to this XCOPY command to get it to behave as you want it to. The following table details these parameters.

Parameter	Description
/w	Displays the message: Press any key to begin copying file(s). It waits for your response to start the copying process.
/p	Asks for a confirmation on each file being copied. This is done in a file-by-file manner.
/c	Ignores errors that might occur in the copying process.
/v	Performs a verification on the files being copied to make sure they are identical to the source files.
/q	Suppresses any display of the XCOPY messages.
/f	Displays the file names for the source and destination files while the copying process is occurring.
/l	Displays a list of the files to be copied to the destination drive.
/g	Builds decrypted files for the destination drive.

Parameter	Description
/d	When used as simply /d, the only files copied are those newer than the existing files located in the destination location. Another alternative is to use /d[:mm-dd-yyyy], which copies files that have been modified either on or after the specified date.
/u	Copies only source files that already exist in the destination location.
/i	If what is being copied is a directory or a file that contains wildcards and the same item does not exist in the destination location, a new directory is created. The XCOPY process also copies all the associated files into this directory.
/s	Copies all directories and their subdirectories only if they contain files. All empty directories or subdirectories are not copied in the process.
/e	Copies all subdirectories regardless of whether these directories contain files.
/t	Copies the subdirectories only and not the files they might contain.
/k	By default, the XCOPY process removes any read-only settings that might be contained in the source files. Using /k ensures that these read-only settings remain in place during the copying process.
/r	Copies only the read-only files to the destination location.
/h	Specifies that the hidden and system files, which are usually excluded by default, are included.
/a	Copies only files that have their archive file attributes set, and leaves the archive file attributes in place at the XCOPY destination.
/m	Copies only files that have their archive file attributes set, and turns off the archive file attributes.
/n	Copies using the NTFS short file and short directory names.
/o	Copies the discretionary access control list (DACL) in addition to the files.
/x	Copies the audit settings and the system access control list (SACL) in addition to the files.
/exclude	Allows you to exclude specific files. The construction used for this is exclude:File1.aspx+File2.aspx+File3.aspx.
/y	Suppresses any prompts from the XCOPY process that ask whether to overwrite the destination file.
/-y	Adds prompts in order to confirm an overwrite of any existing files in the destination location.
/z	Copies files and directories over a network in restartable mode.
/?	Displays help for the XCOPY command.

Using XCOPY is an easy way to move your applications from one server to another with little work on your part. If you have no problem setting up your own virtual directories, this mode of deployment should work just fine for you.

When the Web application is copied (and if placed in a proper virtual directory), it is ready to be called in a browser.

Using the VS Copy Web Site Option

The next option for copying a Web site is to use a GUI provided by Visual Studio 2005. This GUI enables you to copy Web sites from your development server to either the same server or a remote server (as you can when you use the XCOPY command).

You can pull up this Copy Web Site dialog in Visual Studio in two ways. The first way is to click in the Copy Web Site icon in the Visual Studio Server Explorer. This icon is shown in Figure 29-3.

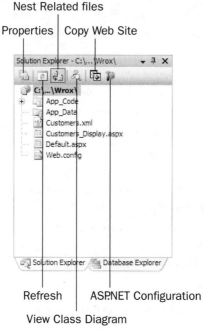

Figure 29-3

The other way to open the Copy Web Site GUI is to choose Website ➪ Copy Web Site from the Visual Studio menu. Using either method pulls up the Copy Web Site GUI in the Document window, as illustrated in Figure 29-4.

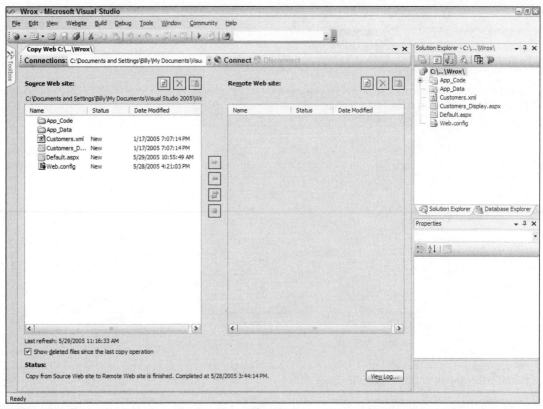

Figure 29-4

From this GUI, you can click the Connect To a Remote Server button (next to the Connections text box). This action brings up the Open Web Site dialog shown in Figure 29-5.

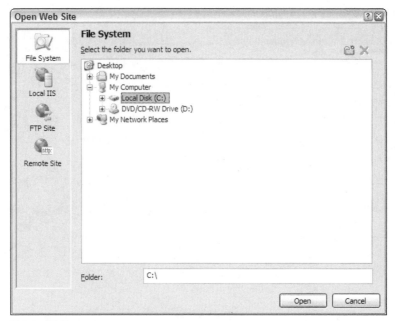

Figure 29-5

As you can see from this dialog, you have a couple of options to connect to and copy your Web application. These options include the following:

❑ **File System:** This option allows you to navigate through a file explorer view of the computer. If you are going to install on a remote server from this view, you must have already mapped a drive to the installation location.

❑ **Local IIS:** This option enables you to use your local IIS in the installation of your Web application. From this part of the dialog, you can create new applications as well as new virtual directories directly. You can also delete applications and virtual directories from the same dialog. The Local IIS option does not permit you to work with IIS installations on any remote servers.

❑ **FTP Site:** This option enables you to connect to a remote server using FTP capabilities. From this dialog, you can specify the server that you want to contact using a URL or IP address, the port you are going to use, and the directory on the server that you will work with. From this dialog, you can also specify the username and password that may be required to access the server via FTP. Note that if you access this server with this dialog via FTP and provide a username and password, the items are transmitted in plain text.

❑ **Remote Site:** This option enables you to connect to a remote site using FrontPage Server Extensions. From this option in the dialog, you can also choose to connect to the remote server using Secure Sockets Layer (SSL).

After being connected to a server, you can copy the contents of your Web application to it by selecting all or some of the files from the Source Web Site text area. After you select these files in the dialog, some of the movement arrows become enabled. Clicking the right-pointing arrow copies the selected files to the destination server. In Figure 29-6 you can see that, indeed, the files have been copied to the remote destination.

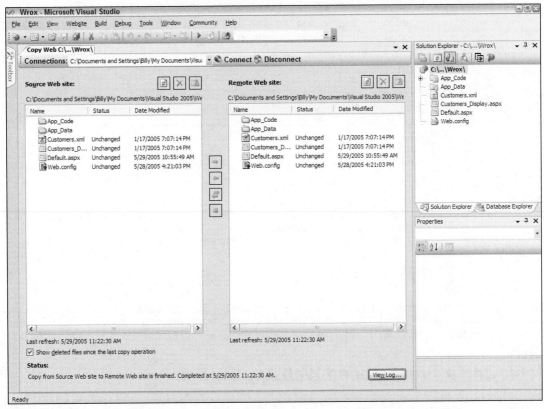

Figure 29-6

If you pull up the same copy dialog later, after working on the files, you see an arrow next to the files that have been changed in the interim and are, therefore, newer than those on the destination server (see Figure 29-7).

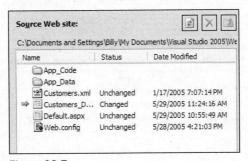

Figure 29-7

These arrows enable you to select only the files that must be copied again and nothing more. All the copying actions are recorded in a log file. You can view the contents of this log file from the Copy Web Site dialog by clicking the View Log button at the bottom of the dialog. This pulls up the CopyWebSite .log text file. From the copy that you made previously, you can see the transaction that was done. An example log entry is shown here:

```
Copy from 'C:\Documents and Settings\Billy\My Documents\Visual Studio
2005\WebSites\Wrox' to 'C:\Documents and Settings\Billy\My Documents\Visual Studio
2005\WebSites\Copy Here' started at 1/29/2006 11:22:30 AM.
        Create folder App_Data in the remote Web site.

        Create folder App_Code in the remote Web site.


        Copy file Customers.xml from source to remote Web site.
        Copy file Customers_Display.aspx from source to remote Web site.
        Copy file Default.aspx from source to remote Web site.
        Copy file Web.config from source to remote Web site.

        App_Code
        Copy file MyClass.vb from source to remote Web site.

Copy from 'C:\Documents and Settings\Billy\My Documents\Visual Studio
2005\WebSites\Wrox' to 'C:\Documents and Settings\Billy\My Documents\Visual Studio
2005\WebSites\Copy Here' is finished. Completed at 1/29/2006 11:22:30 AM.
```

Deploying a Precompiled Web Application

In addition to using Visual Studio to copy a Web application from one location to another, it is also possible to use this IDE to deploy a precompiled application. The process of precompiling a Web application is explained in Chapter 3. ASP.NET 2.0 introduces a new precompilation process that allows for a process referred to as *precompilation for deployment*.

What happens in the precompilation for deployment process is that each page in the Web application is built and compiled into a single application DLL and some placeholder files. These files can then be deployed together to another server and run from there. The nice thing about this precompilation process is that it obfuscates your code by placing all page code (as well as the page's code-behind code) into the DLL, thereby making it more difficult for your code to be stolen or changed if you select this option in the compilation process. This is an ideal situation when you are deploying applications your customers are paying for, or applications that you absolutely don't want changed in any manner after deployment.

Chapter 3 showed you how to use the command-line tool aspnet_compiler.exe to accomplish the task of precompilation. Although this is a great method for precompiling your Web applications and deploying them to remote servers, you can also use Visual Studio 2005 to accomplish the precompilation and deployment process.

To accomplish this task, open up the project you want to deploy and get the application ready for deployment by turning off the debugging capabilities as described earlier in the chapter. Then pull up the precompilation and deployment dialog by choosing Build ⇨ Publish in the Visual Studio menu. This opens the Publish Web Site dialog shown in Figure 29-8.

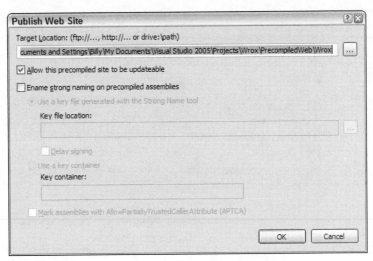

Figure 29-8

Using the Browse (...) button in this dialog, you can choose any remote location to which you want to deploy the application. As in earlier examples, your options are a file system location, a place in the local IIS, a location accessed using FTP, or a location accessed via FrontPage Server Extensions.

Other options in this dialog include the Allow This Precompiled Site to be Updateable check box. When checked, the site will be compiled and copied without any changes to the .aspx pages. This means that after the precompilation process, you can still make minor changes to the underlying pages and the application will work and function as normal. If this check box is unchecked, all the code from the pages is stripped out and placed inside a single DLL. In this state, the application is not updateable because it is impossible to update any of the placeholder files from this compilation process.

Another option in this dialog is to assign a strong name to the DLL that is created in this process. You can select the appropriate check box and assign a key to use in the signing process. The created DLL from the precompilation will then be a strong-assembly — signed with the key of your choice.

When you are ready to deploy, click OK in the dialog and then the open application is built and published. *Published* means that the application is deployed to the specified location. Looking at this location, you can see that a bin directory has now been added that contains the precompiled DLL, which is your Web application. This is illustrated in Figure 29-9.

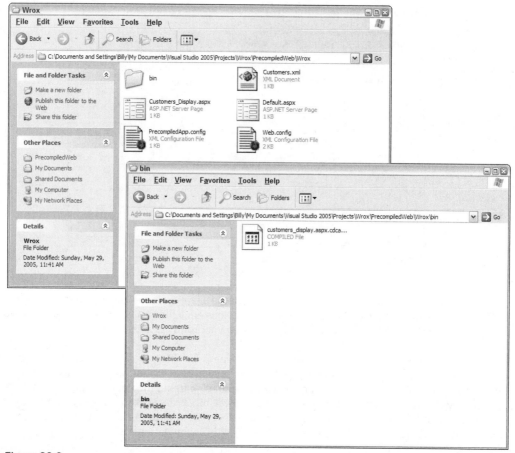

Figure 29-9

In this state, the code contained in any of the ASP.NET-specific pages is stripped out and placed inside the DLL. The files that you see are actually just placeholders that the DLL needs for reference.

Building an Installer Program

The final option you should look at is how to use Visual Studio to build an installation program. After the program is constructed, a consumer can run the installation program on a server where it performs a series of steps to install the Web application.

Packaging your Web application into an installer program works in many situations. For instance, if you sell your Web application, one of the simpler ways for the end user to receive the application is as an executable that can be run on the his computer and installed — all without much effort on his part.

The Windows Installer

The Windows Installer service was introduced with Windows 2000, although it is also available in Windows XP and Windows Server 2003. The Windows Installer service can also be used on previous versions of Windows (prior to Windows 2000) if desired. The Windows Installer service was introduced to make the installation process for your Windows-based applications as easy as possible.

You use the Windows Installer technology not only for ASP.NET applications but also for any type of Windows-based application. The Windows Installer service works by creating a set of rules that determine how the application is to be installed. These rules are packaged into a Windows Installer Package File that uses the `.msi` file extension.

The Windows Installer service considers all applications to be made up of three parts:

❑ **Products:** The large-bucket item being installed, also known as the application itself. An example of this is the ASP.NET Web application.

❑ **Features:** Features are subsets of products. Products are made up of one or more features.

❑ **Components:** Components make up features. A feature is made up of one or more components. A single component can be utilized by several features in the product.

The Windows Installer service is a powerful offering and can be modified in many ways. Not only does the Windows Installer technology detail the product, features, and components of what is to be installed, but it can also take other programmatic actions or show a sequence of user interfaces as the installation process proceeds. For detailed information on the Windows Installer, be sure to view the MSDN documentation on the Windows Installer SDK.

With that said, working with the Windows Installer SDK is complicated at best; that was the reason for the release of the Visual Studio Installer (VSI) as an add-on with Visual Studio 6. This addition made the steps for building an installer much easier to follow. Visual Studio 2005 continues to expand on this capability. You have quite a few options for the deployment projects you can build with Visual Studio 2005. Such projects include the following:

❑ **Setup Project:** This project type allows you to create a standard Windows Installer setup for a Windows application.

❑ **Web Setup Project:** This is the project type covered in this chapter. It's the type of setup project you use to create an installer for an ASP.NET Web application.

❑ **Merge Module Project:** This project type creates a merge module similar to a cabinet file. A merge module, like a cabinet file, allows you to package a group of files for distribution but not for installation. The idea is that you use a merge module file with other setup programs. This project type produces a file type with an extension of `.msm`.

❑ **Setup Wizard:** This selection actually gives you a wizard to assist you through one of the other defined project types.

❑ **Cab Project:** This project type creates a cabinet file (`.cab`) that packages a group of files for distribution. It is similar to a merge module file, but the cabinet file is different in that it allows for installation of the files contained in the package.

❑ **Smart Device Cab Project:** This new project type allows for the creation of a cabinet file that is installed on a smart device instead of on a typical operating system.

Although you have a number of different setup and deployment project types at your disposal, the Web Setup Project is the only one covered in this chapter because it is the project you use to build an installer for an ASP.NET Web application.

Actions of the Windows Installer

You might already be thinking that using the Windows Installer architecture for your installation program seems a lot more complicated than using the methods shown previously in this chapter. Yes, it is a bit more complicated — mainly because of the number of steps required to get the desired result; but in the end, you are getting a lot more control over how your applications are installed.

Using an installer program gives you programmatic logic over how your applications are installed. You also gain other advantages, such as:

❑ The capability to check if the .NET Framework is installed, as well as which version of the Framework is installed

❑ The capability to read or write values to the registry

❑ The capability to collect information from the end user during the installation process

❑ The capability to run scripts

❑ The capability to include such features such as dialogs and splash screens during the installation process

Creating a Basic Installation Program

You can apply a tremendous amount of customization to the installation programs you build. Let's start, however, by looking at how to create a basic installation program for your ASP.NET Web application. To create an installer for your application, first open up the project for which you want to create a deployment project in Visual Studio. The next step is to add an installer program to the solution. To do this, you add the setup program as a new project contained within the same solution. Choose File ➪ New ➪ Project from the Visual Studio menu. This launches the New Project dialog.

From the New Project dialog, first expand Other Project Types from the left-hand pane in the dialog and then select Setup and Deployment. This provides you with a list of all the available setup and deployment projects in Visual Studio. For our purposes, select Web Setup Project (shown in Figure 29-10).

Figure 29-10

Clicking OK in this dialog adds the Web Setup Project type to your solution. It uses the default name of `WebSetup1`. Visual Studio also opens up the File System Editor in the document window, which is shown in Figure 29-11.

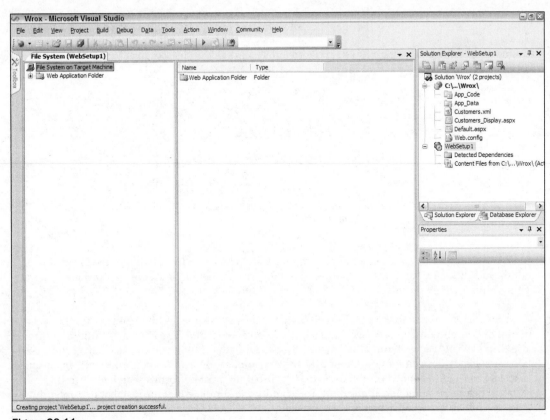

Figure 29-11

The File System Editor shows a single folder: the Web Application Folder. This is a representation of what is going to be installed on the target machine. The first step is to add the files from the WebSite1 project to this folder. You do this by choosing Project ➪ Add ➪ Project Output from the Visual Studio menu. This pulls up the Add Project Output Group dialog. This dialog (shown in Figure 29-12) enables you to select the items you want to include in the installer program.

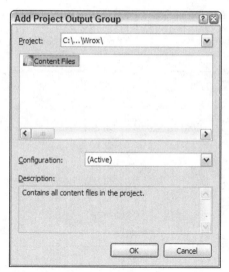

Figure 29-12

From this dialog, you can see that the project, Wrox, is already selected. Highlight the Content Files option and click OK. This adds all the files from the Wrox project to the WebSetup1 installer program. This addition is then represented in the File System Editor as well.

After the files are added to the installer program, the next step is to click the Launch Conditions Editor button in the Solution Explorer (see Figure 29-13) to open the editor. The Launch Conditions Editor is also displayed in Visual Studio's document window. From this editor, you can see that a couple of conditions are already defined for you. Obviously, for Web applications, it is important that IIS be installed. Logically, one of the defined conditions is that the program must perform a search to see if IIS is installed before installing the application. You should also stipulate that the installation server must have version 2.0 of the .NET Framework installed.

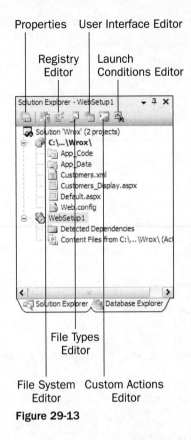

Figure 29-13

To establish this condition, right-click the Requirements On Target Machine node. Then select Add .NET Framework Launch Condition (as shown in Figure 29-14).

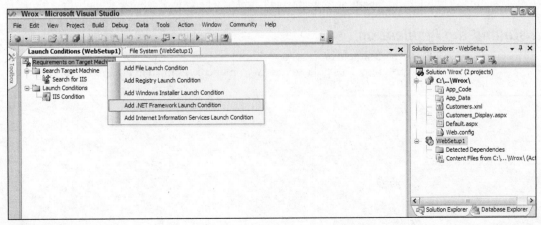

Figure 29-14

This adds the .NET Framework requirement to the list of launch conditions required for a successful installation of the Web application.

As a final step, highlight the WebSetup1 program in the Visual Studio Solution Explorer so you can modify some of the properties that appear in the Properties window. For now, you just change some of the self-explanatory properties, but you will review these again later in this chapter. For this example, however, just change the following properties:

- ❑ `Author`: Wrox
- ❑ `Description`: This is a test project.
- ❑ `Manufacturer`: Wrox
- ❑ `ManufacturerUrl`: http://www.wrox.com
- ❑ `SupportPhone`: 1-800-555-5555
- ❑ `SupportUrl`: http://www.wrox.com/support/

Now the installation program is down to its simplest workable instance. Make sure Release is selected as the active solution configuration in the Visual Studio toolbar; then build the installer program by choosing Build ⇨ Build WebSetup1 from the menu.

Looking in `C:\Documents and Settings\Administrator\My Documents\Visual Studio\ Projects\Wrox\WebSetup1\Release`, you find the following files:

- ❑ `Setup.exe`: This is the installation program. It is meant for machines that don't have the Windows Installer service installed.
- ❑ `WebSetup1.msi`: This is the installation program for those that have the Windows Installer service installed on their machine.

That's it! You now have your ASP.NET Web application wrapped up in an installation program that can be distributed in any manner you want. It can then be run and installed automatically for the end user. Take a quick look in the following section at what happens when the consumer actually fires it up.

Installing the Application

Installing the application is a simple process (as it should be). Double-click the `WebSetup1.msi` file to launch the installation program. This pulls up the Welcome screen shown in Figure 29-15.

Figure 29-15

From this dialog, you can see that the name of the program being installed is WebSetup1. Clicking Next gives you the screen shown in Figure 29-16.

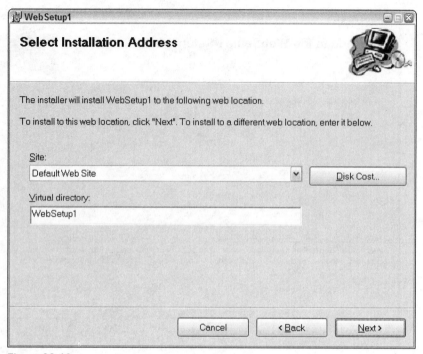

Figure 29-16

This screen tells you what you are installing (the Default Web Site) as well as the name of the virtual directory created for the deployed Web application. The consumer can feel free to change the name of the virtual directory in the provided text box. A button in this dialog allows for an estimation of the disk cost (space required) for the installed application. The next series of screens install the WebSetup1 application (shown in Figure 29-17).

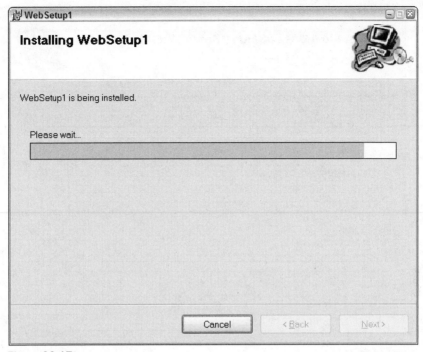

Figure 29-17

After the application is installed, you can find the WebSetup1 folder and application files located in the C:\Inetpub\wwwroot folder (within IIS). The application can now be run on the server from this location.

Uninstalling the Application

To uninstall the application, the consumer has a couple of options. First, he can relaunch the .msi file and use the option to either repair the current installation or to remove the installation altogether (as shown in Figure 29-18).

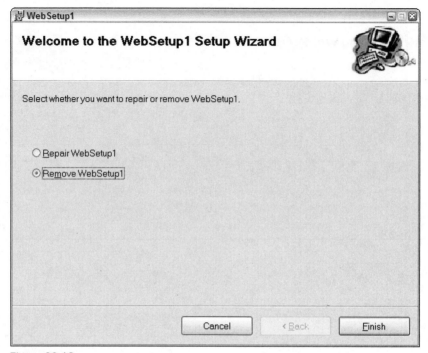

Figure 29-18

The other option is to pull up the Add/Remove Programs dialog from the server's Control Panel. On the Control Panel, you see WebSetup1 listed (as shown in Figure 29-19).

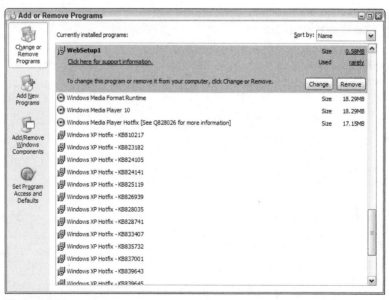

Figure 29-19

This dialog holds information about the size of the installed application and how often the application is used. Clicking the support link pulls up the Support Info dialog, which shows the project's properties that you entered a little earlier (see Figure 29-20).

Figure 29-20

From the Add/Remove Programs dialog, you can remove the installation by clicking the Remove button of the selected program.

Looking More Closely at Installer Options

The Windows Installer service easily installs a simple ASP.NET Web application. The installer takes care of packaging the files into a nice `.msi` file from which it can then be distributed. Next, the `.msi` file takes care of creating a virtual directory and installing the application files. The installer also makes it just as easy to uninstall the application from the server. All these great services are provided with very little work on the user's part.

Even though this approach addresses almost everything needed for an ASP.NET installer program, the setup and deployment project for Web applications provided by Visual Studio really provides much more in the way of options and customizations. This next section looks at the various ways you can work with modifying the installer program.

Working with the Deployment Project Properties

You can work with the project properties of the installer from Visual Studio in several ways. The first way is by right-clicking the installer project from the Solution Explorer of Visual Studio and selecting Properties from the menu. This pulls up the WebSetup1 Properties Pages dialog shown in Figure 29-21.

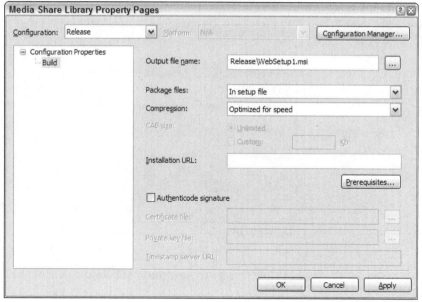

Figure 29-21

This dialog has some important settings for your installer application. Notice that, like other typical projects, this setup and deployment project allows for different active build configuration settings. For instance, you can have the active build configuration set to either Release or Debug. You can also click on the Configuration Manager button to get access to configuration settings for all the projects involved. In addition, this dialog enables you to add or remove build configurations from the project.

The Output File Name

The Output File Name setting lets you set the name of the .msi file that is generated. By default, it is the name of the project, but you can change this value to anything you want. This section also allows you to modify the location where the built .msi is placed on the system after the build process occurs.

Package Files

The Package files section of this properties page enables you to specify how the application files are packaged in the .msi file. The available options include the following:

❑ **As loose, uncompressed files:** This option builds the project so that a resulting .msi file is created without the required application files. Instead, these application files are kept separate from the .msi file but copied to the same location as the .msi file. With this type of structure, you must distribute both the .msi file and the associated application files.

❑ **In setup file:** This option (which is the default option) packages the application files inside the .msi file. This makes distribution an easy task because only a single file is distributed.

❑ **In cabinet file(s):** This option packages all the application files into a number of cabinet files. The size of the cabinet files can be controlled through this same dialog (discussed shortly). This is an ideal type of installation process to use if you have to spread the installation application over a number of DVDs, CDs, or floppy disks.

Installation URL

Invariably, the ASP.NET applications you build have some component dependencies. In most cases, your application depends on some version of the .NET Framework. The installation of these dependencies, or components, can be made part of the overall installation process. This process is also referred to as *bootstrapping*. Clicking the Prerequisites button next to the Installation URL text box gives you a short list of available components that are built into Visual Studio in order to bootstrap to the installation program you are constructing (see Figure 29-22).

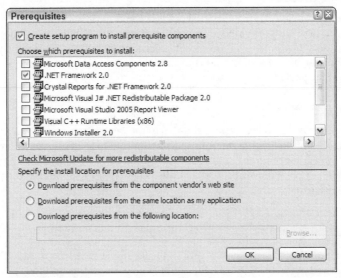

Figure 29-22

As you can see from when you first enter this settings dialog, the .NET Framework 2.0 is enabled by default, and you check the other components (thereby enabling them) only if your Web application has some kind of dependency on them.

From this dialog, you can also set how the dependent components are downloaded to the server where the installation is occurring. The options include downloading from Microsoft, from the server where the application originated, or from a defined location (URL) specified in the provided text box.

Compression

The Windows Installer service can work with the compression of the application files included in the build process so that they are optimized for either speed or size. You also have the option to turn off all compression optimizations. The default setting is Optimized for Speed.

CAB Size

The CAB Size section of the properties page is enabled only if you select In Cabinet File(s) from the Package Files drop-down list, as explained earlier. If this is selected, it is enabled with the Unlimited radio button selected. As you can see from this section, the two settings are Unlimited and Custom:

❏   `Unlimited`: This selection means that only a single cabinet file is created. The size of this file is dependent on the size of the collection of application files in the Web application and the type of compression selected.

❏   `Custom`: This selection allows you to break up the installation across multiple cabinet files. If the `Custom` radio button is selected, you can enter the maximum size of the cabinet files allowed in the provided text box. The measure of the number you place in the text box is in kilobytes (KB).

Authenticode Signature

The last option in the WebSetup1 property dialog allows you to provide an Authenticode signature. To use this option, you select the Authenticode Signature check box. When this is selected, you are asked for three possible items to complete the process: the certificate file used to sign the package, a private key file that contains the encryption key used to sign the file, and the timestamp server URL used to provide the time when the package is signed.

Additional Properties

You learned one place where you can apply settings to the installer program; however, at another place in Visual Studio you can find even more properties pertaining to the entire installer program. By selecting the `WebSetup1` installer program in the Solution Explorer, you can work with the installer properties directly from the Properties window of Visual Studio. The following table lists the properties that appear in the Properties window.

Property	Description
AddRemoveProgramsIcon	Defines the location of the icon used in the Add/Remove Programs dialog found through the system's Control Panel.
Author	The author of the installer. This could be the name of a company or individual.
Description	Allows for a textual description of the installer program.
DetectNewerInstalledVersion	Instructs the installer to make a check on the installation server if a newer version of the application is present. If one is present, the installation is aborted. The default setting is `True` (meaning that the check will be made).
Keywords	Defines the keywords used when a search is made for an installer.
Localization	Defines the locale for any string resources and the runtime user interface. An example setting is `English (United States)`.
Manufacturer	Defines the name of the company that built or provided the installer program.
ManufacturerUrl	Defines the URL of the company that built or provided the installer program.
PostBuildEvent	Specifies a command line executed after the build ends.

Property	Description
PreBuildEvent	Specifies a command line executed before the build begins.
ProductCode	Defines a string value that is the unique identifier for the application. An example value is {885D2E86-6247-4624-9DB1-50790E3856B4}.
ProductName	Defines the name of the program being installed.
RemovePreviousVersions	Specifies as a Boolean value whether any previous versions of the application should be uninstalled prior to installing the fresh version. The default setting is False.
RestartWWWService	Specifies as a Boolean value whether or not IIS should be stopped and restarted for the installation process. The default value is False.
RunPostBuildEvent	Defines when to run the post-build event. The default setting is On successful build. The other possible value is Always.
SearchPath	Defines the path to use to search for any files, assemblies, merge modules on the development machine.
Subject	Allows you to provide additional descriptions for the application.
SupportPhone	Specifies the support telephone number for the installed program.
SupportUrl	Specifies the URL by which the end user can get support for the installed application.
TargetPlatform	Defines the target platform of the installer. Possible values include x86, x64, and Itanium.
Title	Defines the title of the installer program.
UpgradeCode	Defines a shared identifier that can be used from build to build. An example value is {A71833C7-3B76-4083-9D34-F074A4FFF544}.
Version	Specifies the version number of the installer, cabinet file, or merge module. An example value is 1.0.1.

The following sections look at the various editors provided to help you build and customize the construction of the installer. You can get at these editors by clicking the appropriate icon in the Solution Explorer in Visual Studio or by choosing View ⇨ Editor in the Visual Studio menu. These editors are explained next.

The File System Editor

The first editor that comes up when you create your installer program is the File System Editor. The File System Editor enables you to add folders and files that are to be installed on the destination server. In addition to installing folders and files, it also facilitates the creation of shortcuts. This editor is shown in Figure 29-23.

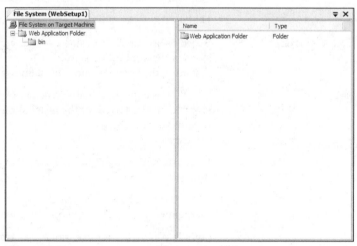

Figure 29-23

The File System Editor has two sections. The left section is the list of folders to be installed during the installation process. By default, only the Web Application Folder is shown. Highlighting this folder, or one of the other folders, gives you a list of properties for that folder in the Properties window of Visual Studio. The following table details some of the properties you might find in the Properties window.

Property	Description
AllowDirectoryBrowsing	Allows browsing of the selected directory in IIS. The default value is `False`.
AllowReadAccess	Specifies whether the selected folder should have Read access. The default value is `True`.
AllowScriptSourceAccess	Specifies the script source access of the selected folder. The default value is `False`.
AllowWriteAccess	Specifies whether the selected folder should have Write access. The default value is `False`.
ApplicationProtection	Defines the IIS Application Protection property for the selected folder. Possible values include `vsdapLow`, `vsdapMedium`, and `vsdapHigh`. The default value is `vsdapMedium`.
AppMappings	Enables you to define the IIS application mappings for the selected folder.

Property	Description
DefaultDocument	Defines the default document of the selected folder. The default value is Default.aspx.
ExecutePermissions	Defines the IIS Execute Permissions property. Possible values include vsdepNone, vsdepScriptsOnly, vsdepScriptsAndExecutables. The default value is vsdepScriptsOnly.
Index	Specifies the IIS Index of this resource property for the selected folder. The default value is True.
IsApplication	Specifies whether an IIS application root is created for the installed application. The default value is True.
LogVisits	Specifies the IIS Log Visits property for the selected folder. The default value is True.
VirtualDirectory	Defines the name of the virtual directory created. The default value is the name of the project.

Adding Items to the Output

You can add files, folders, and assemblies to the installer output quite easily. To add some of these items to the output list, right-click the folder and select Add from the menu. You have four choices: Web Folder, Project Output, File, and Assembly.

If you want to add a custom folder to the output (for example, an Images folder), you can select Web Folder and provide the name of the folder. This enables you to create the folder structure you want.

If you want to add system folders, you highlight the File System on Target Machine node and then choose Action ⇨ Add Special Folder. This provides you with a large list of folders that are available for you to add to the installer program. You can also get at this list of folders by simply right-clicking a blank portion of the left pane of the File System Editor (see Figure 29-24).

Figure 29-24

The following table defines the possible folders you can add to the installer structure you are building.

Folders and Menus	Description
Common Files Folder	Meant for non–system files not shared by multiple applications.
Common Files (64-bit) Folder	Meant for non–system files on a 64-bit machine not shared by multiple applications.
Fonts Folder	Meant for only fonts you want installed on the client's machine.
Program Files Folder	A Windows Forms application would be a heavy user of this folder because most applications are installed here.
Program Files (64-bit) Folder	A Programs Files folder meant for 64-bit machines.
System Folder	Meant for storing files considered shared system files.
System (64-bit) Folder	Meant for storing files on 64-bit machines considered shared system files.
User's Application Data Folder	A hidden folder meant for storing data that is application- and user-specific.

Folders and Menus	Description
User's Desktop	Meant for storing files on a user's desktop (also stores these files in the My Desktop folder).
User's Favorites Folder	Meant for storing files in a user's Favorites folder (browser-specific).
User's Personal Data Folder	Meant for storing personal data specific to a single user. This is also referred to as the My Documents folder.
User's Programs Menu	Meant for storing shortcuts, which then appear in the user's program menu.
User's Send To Menu	Meant for storing files that are presented when a user attempts to send a file or folder to a specific application (by right-clicking the folder or file and selecting Send To).
User's Start Menu	Meant for storing files in the user's Start menu.
User's Startup Folder	Meant for storing files that are initiated whenever a user logs into his machine.
User's Template Folder	Meant for storing templates (applications like Microsoft's Office).
Windows Folder	Meant for storing files in the Windows root folder. These are usually system files.
Global Assembly Cache Folder	Meant for storing assemblies that can then be utilized by all the applications on the server (shared assemblies).
Custom Folder	Another way of creating a unique folder.
Web Custom Folder	Another way of creating a unique folder that also contains a bin folder.

Creating a Desktop Shortcut to the Web Application

For an example of using one of these custom folders, take a look at placing a shortcut to the Web application on the user's desktop. The first step is to right-click on a blank portion of the left-hand pane in the File System Editor and choose Add Special Folder ➪ User's Desktop. This adds that folder to the list of folders presented in the left-hand pane.

Because you want to create a desktop shortcut to the Web Application Folder and not to the desktop itself, the next step is to right-click the Web Application folder and select Create Shortcut to Web Application Folder. The created shortcut appears in the right-hand pane. Right-click the shortcut and rename it to something a little more meaningful, such as Wrox Application. Because you don't want to keep the shortcut in this folder, drag the shortcut from the Web Application Folder and drop it onto the User's Desktop folder.

With this structure in place, this installer program not only installs the application (as was done previously), but it also installs the application's shortcut on the user's desktop.

The Registry Editor

The next editor is the Registry Editor. This editor enables you to work with the client's registry in an easy and straightforward manner. Using this editor, you can perform operations such as creating new registry keys, providing values for already existing registry keys, and importing registry files. The Registry Editor is presented in Figure 29-25.

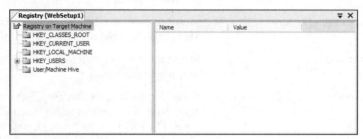

Figure 29-25

From this figure, you can see that the left-hand pane provides the standard registry folders, such as HKEY_CLASSES_ROOT and HKEY_LOCAL_MACHINE, as well as others. Right-clicking one of these folders, you can add a new key from the menu selection. This creates a new folder in the left-hand pane where it is enabled for renaming. By right-clicking this folder, you can add items such as those illustrated in Figure 29-26.

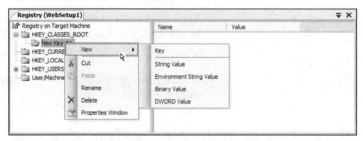

Figure 29-26

As you can see in the figure, you can add items such as the following:

❑ Key

❑ String Value

❑ Environment String Value

❑ Binary Value

❑ DWORD Value

Selecting String Value allows you to apply your settings for this in the right-hand pane as illustrated in Figure 29-27.

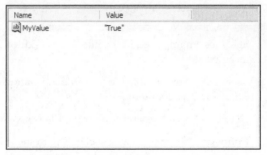

Figure 29-27

The other values work in a similar manner.

The File Types Editor

All files on a Windows operating system use file extensions to uniquely identify themselves. A file such as Default.aspx, for example, uses the file extension .aspx. This file extension is then associated with ASP.NET. Another example is .xls. This file extension is associated with Microsoft Excel. When someone attempts to open an .xls file, the file is passed to the Excel program because of mappings that have been made on the computer to associate these two entities.

Using the File Types Editor in Visual Studio, you can also make these mappings for the applications you are trying to install. Right-clicking the File Types On Target Machine allows you to add a new file type. From here, you can give your file type a descriptive name and provide a file extension (shown in Figure 29-28).

Figure 29-28

Highlighting the defined file type provides some properties that you can set in the Visual Studio Properties window, as shown in the following table.

Property	Description
Name	Specifies a name used in the File System Editor to identify a file type and its associated settings.
Command	Specifies the executable file (.exe) that is launched when the specified file extension is encountered.
Description	Defines a textual description for the file type.
Extensions	Defines the file extension associated with the executable through the Command property. An example is .wrox.
Icon	Defines the icon used for this file extension.
MIME	Specifies the MIME type associated with this file type. An example is application/msword.

The User Interface Editor

The User Interface Editor defines the dialogs used in the installation process. You can change the installation process greatly with the dialogs you decide to use or not use. By default, these dialogs (shown in Figure 29-29) are presented in your installer.

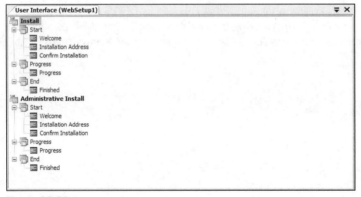

Figure 29-29

From this figure, you can see how the dialogs are divided into two main sections. The first section, labeled Install, is the dialog sequence used for a typical install. However, because some applications might require it, a second installation process is defined through the Administrative Install. The Administrative Install process is initiated only if the user is logged onto the machine under the Administrator account. If this is not the case, the Install section is used instead.

By default, the Install and Administrative Install sections are exactly the same. Both the Install and Administrative Install sections are further divided into three subsections: Start, Progress, and End. These sections are defined in the following list:

❑ **Start:** A sequence of dialogs that appears before the installation occurs. By default, the Start section includes a welcome screen, a definition stating where the application is to be installed, and a dialog asking for an installation confirmation.

❑ **Progress:** The second stage, the Progress stage, is the stage in which the actual installation occurs. Throughout this stage no interaction occurs between the installer program and the end user. This is the stage where the end user can watch the installation progress through a progress bar.

❑ **End:** The End stage specifies to the end user whether the installation was successful. Many installer programs use this stage to present the customer with release notes and `ReadMe.txt` files, as well as the capability to launch the installed program directly from the installer program itself.

Adding Dialogs to the Installation Process

Of course, you are not limited to just the dialogs that appear in the User Interface Editor by default. You have a number of other dialogs that can be added to the installation process. For instance, right-click the Start node and select Add Dialog (or highlight the Start node and choose Action ➪ Add Dialog). This pulls up the Add Dialog dialog, as shown in Figure 29-30.

Figure 29-30

As you can see from this image, you can add quite a number of different steps to the installation process, such as license agreements and splash screens. After adding a dialog to the process, you can highlight the dialog to get its properties to appear in the Properties window so that you can assign the items needed. For example, you can assign the image to use for the splash screen or the `.rtf` file to use for the license agreement.

When you add an additional dialog to the installation process (for instance, to the Install section), be sure to also install the same dialog on the Administrative Install (if required). If no difference exists between the two user types in the install process, be sure to add the dialogs in unison in order to keep them the same.

Changing the Order in Which the Dialogs Appear in the Process

In working with the dialogs in the Start, Process, and End sections of the User Interface Editor, you can always determine the order in which these dialogs appear. Even if you are working with the default dialogs, you can easily change their order by right-clicking the dialog and selecting Move Up or Move Down, as shown in Figure 29-31.

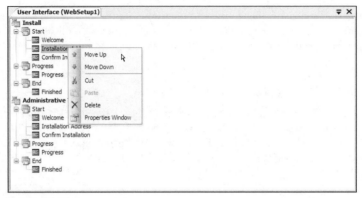

Figure 29-31

The Custom Actions Editor

The Custom Actions Editor is a powerful editor that enables you to take the installer one step further and perform custom actions during various events of the installation cycle (but always *after* the installation process is completed) such as: Install, Commit, Rollback, and Uninstall. The Custom Actions Editor is presented in Figure 29-32.

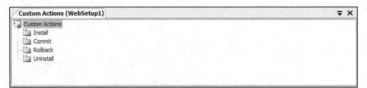

Figure 29-32

The idea is that you can place a reference to a .dll, .exe, or .vbs file from one of the folders presented here in the Custom Actions Editor to perform a custom action. For example, you can insert a custom action to install a database into Microsoft's SQL Server in the Commit folder (after the install has actually been committed).

The four available folders are explained in the following list:

- **Install:** This is the point at which the installation of the files for the Web application are finished being installed. Although the files are installed, this point is right before the installation has been committed.

- **Commit:** This is the point at which the actions of the installation have been actually committed (taken) and are considered successful.

- **Rollback:** This is the point at which the installation has failed and the computer must return to the same state that it was in before the installation occurred.

- **Uninstall:** This is the point at which a successfully installed application is uninstalled for a machine.

Using these capabilities, you can take the installation process to the level of complexity you need for a successfully installed application.

The Launch Conditions Editor

Certain conditions are required in order for your Web application to run on another server automatically. Unless your application is made up of HTML files only, you must make sure that the .NET Framework is installed on the targeted machine in order to consider the install a success. The Launch Conditions Editor is an editor that you can use to make sure that everything that needs to be in place on the installation computer for the installation to occur is there. The Launch Conditions Editor is presented in Figure 29-33.

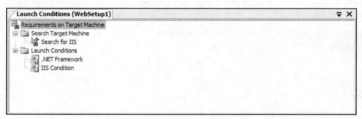

Figure 29-33

From this image, you can see some of the conditions required in this instance. The first folder defines the items that must be in place on the computer where the installation is to occur. A search is done on the computer to see whether IIS is installed. It can also check if any files or registry keys are present on the computer before the installation occurs.

The second folder is an important one because certain conditions must be in place before the installation. This folder shows two conditions. One is that the .NET Framework must be installed, and the second is that IIS must be installed. You can add these types of launch conditions by right-clicking the Requirements On Target Machine node in the dialog. You are then presented with a short list of conditions.

After a condition is in place, you can highlight the condition to see the property details of this condition in the Properties window. For instance, highlighting the IIS Condition gives you some basic properties in the Properties window. One of these is the `Condition` property. By default, for an IIS Condition, the value of the `Condition` property is the following:

```
IISVERSION >= "#4"
```

This means that the requirement for this installation is that IIS must be equal to or greater than version 4. If it is not, the installation fails. If the IIS version is 4, 5, or 6, the installation can proceed. You can feel free to change this value to whatever you deem necessary. You can change the value to `IISVERSION >="#5"`, for example, to ensure it is either IIS 5.0 or 6.0 at a minimum.

Another example of fine-tuning these launch conditions is the .NET Framework condition that enables you to set the minimum version of the .NET Framework you want to allow. You do this by setting the `Version` property of the condition.

Summary

As you can see, you have many possibilities for installing your ASP.NET applications! From the simplest mode of just copying the files to a remote server — sort of a save-and-run mode — to building a complex installer program that can run side events, provide dialogs, and even install extra items such as databases and more.

Just remember that when working on the installation procedures for your Web applications, you should be thinking about making the entire process logical and easy for your customers to understand. You don't want to make people's lives too difficult when they are required to programmatically install items on another machine.

Visual Basic 8.0 and C# 2.0 Language Enhancements

A lot has changed with the 2.0 release of .NET. Not only are there dramatic changes to ASP.NET (shown throughout this book), but also considerable changes have been made to the IDE, Windows Forms, Visual Basic, C#, and more. This chapter focuses on the changes to Visual Basic and C# languages because these are the two languages most commonly used for ASP.NET development. Because of their heavy use in Web application development, it is vital to understand the capabilities of these languages and the direction they are taking.

One of the greatest changes to Web application development in the Microsoft world is .NET's use of true object-oriented languages such as Visual Basic .NET and C# to build Web applications. No longer are you limited to working with interpreted languages such as VBScript. Although they have only recently been introduced to the Web application world, these object-oriented languages are continuing to evolve, bringing new features to Web application development.

This appendix focuses on some of the important changes that have occurred to both Visual Basic and C# with this latest release of the .NET Framework. Although not all language changes are covered here, what is covered can be applied directly to your ASP.NET 2.0 applications.

Overview of the Changes

Both Visual Basic and C# have undergone changes with the release of the .NET Framework 2.0. Some of the changes have occurred in both of the languages, whereas other changes have occurred in only one.

Notice that, throughout the book, I have referred to the VB language as Visual Basic. With this release of the .NET Framework, the language has reverted to the name Visual Basic (minus the .NET at the end of the name). This version of the VB language is called Visual Basic 8.0, whereas the newest version of C# is 2.0.

Some new features of these two languages include those described in the following table.

New Language Feature	Visual Basic 8.0	C# 2.0
Generics	Yes	Yes
Iterators	No	Yes
Anonymous methods	No	Yes
Operator Overloading	Yes	Yes (already present)
Partial Classes	Yes	Yes
XML documentation	Yes	Yes (already present)
Static Classes	No	Yes
Property Accessor Accessibility	Yes	Yes
Namespace Alias Qualifier	Yes	Yes
Unsigned Types	Yes	Yes (already present)
Default Instances	Yes	No

Take a look at some of these new features and how to use them in your applications.

Generics

In order to make collections a more powerful feature and also increase their efficiency and usability, generics were introduced to both Visual Basic and C#. The idea of generics is nothing new. They are similar to C++ templates. You can also find generics in other languages, such as Java. Their introduction into the .NET Framework 2.0 languages is a huge benefit for the user.

Generic Collections

Generics enable you to create generic collections of objects that are still strongly typed, providing fewer chances for errors (because they occur at runtime), increasing performance, and giving you IntelliSense features when you are working with the collections.

Creating generic collections of objects in .NET is not necessarily a new concept. Several different methods can be used to create generic object collections in .NET 1.0. Look at a sample that uses two generic object containers, the Stack and Array classes. Can you tell why using generics provides an advantage? Listing A-1 shows a simple use of the Stack and Array classes.

Listing A-1: A collection that is not using generics

VB

```vb
Sub Page_Load(ByVal sender As Object, ByVal e As System.EventArgs)
    Dim myStack As New Stack
    myStack.Push("St. Louis Rams")
    myStack.Push(5)

    Dim myArray As Array
    myArray = myStack.ToArray()

    For Each item As String In myArray
        Label1.Text += item.ToString() & "<br />"
    Next
End Sub
```

C#

```csharp
void Page_Load(object sender, EventArgs e)
{
    Stack myStack = new Stack();
    myStack.Push("St. Louis Rams");
    myStack.Push(5);

    Array myArray;
    myArray = myStack.ToArray();

    foreach (string item in myArray)
    {
        Label1.Text += item.ToString() + "<br />";
    }
}
```

The `Stack` class represents a simple first-in, first-out collection of objects. In this code example, you can see two member variables are added to the `Stack` collection using the `Push` method, a string with the value of `St. Louis Rams` and an integer with a value of `5`. This is also known as pushing items onto the stack. A number of performance issues, however, can arise when you use the `Stack` class in this scenario. First, each time you add a value type such as an integer to the stack, the value must be *boxed* before it is added.

> *Boxing is an implicit conversion of a value type such as int, bool or byte, to the type object or to any interface type implemented by this value type. Boxing a value type allocates an object on the stack that contains a reference to the value type contained on the heap. Although boxing and unboxing are beyond the scope of this book, it is important to know how both work. You can find more information on these topics on the MSDN Web site.*

Second, because every item added to the stack is stored as an object type, when you want to retrieve an item off of the stack, you have to explicitly cast the object back to its original type. This is demonstrated in the code sample in the `For Each` loop. Notice that you have to explicitly convert each object to a string in order to add it to the Label.

All this boxing and casting creates performance problems in your application. This is where generics give you an advantage. Generics enable you to create type-specific collections. The `System.Collections` `.Generic` namespace gives you access to generic versions of the `Stack`, `Dictionary`, `SortedDictionary`, `List`, and `Queue` classes. Again, you can make these collections type-specific to produce collections that avoid the boxing and casting problems for improved performance, have design-time type-checking to avoid runtime type exceptions, and provide you better IntelliSense features inside Visual Studio.

Look at a sample which demonstrates how to create a generic version of the `Stack` class that includes a collection of strings in Listing A-2.

Listing A-2: A generic Stack class

VB

```
<%@ Page Language="VB" %>

<script runat="server">
    Sub Page_Load(ByVal sender As Object, ByVal e As System.EventArgs)
        Dim myStack As New System.Collections.Generic.Stack(Of String)
        myStack.Push("St. Louis Rams")
        myStack.Push("Indianapolis Colts")
        myStack.Push("Minneapolis Vikings")

        Dim myArray As Array
        myArray = myStack.ToArray()

        For Each item As String In myArray
            Label1.Text += item & "<br />"
        Next
      End Sub
</script>

<html xmlns="http://www.w3.org/1999/xhtml" >
<head runat="server">
    <title>Untitled Page</title>
</head>
<body>
    <form id="form1" runat="server">
    <div>
        <asp:Label runat="server" ID="Label1"></asp:Label>
    </div>
    </form>
</body>
</html>
```

C#

```
<%@ Page Language="C#" %>

<script runat="server">
    void Page_Load(object sender, EventArgs e)
    {
        Stack<string> myStack = new Stack<string>();
        myStack.Push("St. Louis Rams");
        myStack.Push("Indianapolis Colts");
```

```
        myStack.Push("Minneapolis Vikings");

        Array myArray;
        myArray = myStack.ToArray();

        foreach (string item in myArray)
        {
            Label1.Text += item + "<br />";
        }
    }
}
</script>
```

Notice in the example in Listing A-2, the Stack class is explicitly cast to be a collection of type string. In Visual Basic, you do this by following the collection class with (Of String) or (Of Integer) or whatever type you want to use for your collection. In C#, you specify the collection type with the use of brackets. You cast the Stack class to type string using Stack<string>. If you want to cast it to a Stack collection of type int, you specify Stack<int>.

Because the Stack class is now considered strongly typed, it does not allow you to add items to the collection that are not of type string and, therefore, all its items need not be cast to type object. Additionally, in the For Each loop, the collection values need not be cast back to type string. Because you can specify the collection types up front, you increase performance for your collections.

Remember that when working with generic collections (as shown in the previous code example) you must import the System.Collections.Generic namespace into your ASP.NET page.

Now, change the Stack class from Listing A-2 so that instead of working with string objects, it uses integer objects in the collection. This change is illustrated in Listing A-3.

Listing A-3: A generic Stack class using integers

VB

```
<%@ Page Language="VB" %>

<script runat="server">
    Sub Page_Load(ByVal sender As Object, ByVal e As System.EventArgs)
        Dim myStack As New Stack(Of Integer)
        myStack.Push(5)
        myStack.Push(3)
        myStack.Push(10)

        Dim myArray As Array
        myArray = myStack.ToArray()

        Dim x As Integer = 0
        For Each item As Integer In myArray
            x += item
        Next

        Label1.Text = x.ToString()
    End Sub
```

Listing A-3 *(continued)*

```
</script>

<html xmlns="http://www.w3.org/1999/xhtml" >
<head runat="server">
    <title>Untitled Page</title>
</head>
<body>
    <form id="form1" runat="server">
    <div>
        <asp:Label runat="server" ID="Label1"></asp:Label>
    </div>
    </form>
</body>
</html>
```

C#
```
<%@ Page Language="VB" %>

<script runat="server">
    void Page_Load(object sender, EventArgs e)
    {
        Stack<int> myStack = new Stack<int>();
        myStack.Push(5);
        myStack.Push(3);
        myStack.Push(10);

        Array myArray;
        myArray = myStack.ToArray();

        int x = 0;
        foreach (int item in myArray)
        {
            x += item;
        }

        Label1.Text = x.ToString();
    }
</script>
```

The `Stack` class used in Listing A-3 specifies that everything contained in its collection must be type integer. In this example, the numbers are added together and displayed in the Label control.

Generic Methods

Another exciting way of utilizing Generics is using them with delegates and methods. For example, you can create a method that defines generic type parameters. This can be very useful for utility classes because it allows you to call the method with a different type every time. Listing A-4 demonstrates creating a method using generics.

Listing A-4: A generic method

VB

```
Public Function GenericReturn(Of T)(ByVal input As T) As T
    Return input
End Function
```

C#

```
public T GenericReturn<T>(T t)
{
    return t;
}
```

This simple method accepts a parameter of any type and returns the value that is passed to it regardless of type. To construct a generic method, you must follow the method name with (Of T) in Visual Basic or <T> declaration in C#. This specifies that the method is indeed a generic method.

The single parameter passed into the method is also of T, and the return value is the same as the type that is established when the method is called. In Listing A-5, note how you go about calling this generic method.

Listing A-5: Invoking the generic method

VB

```
Sub Page_Load(ByVal sender As Object, ByVal e As System.EventArgs)
    Label1.Text = GenericReturn(Of String)("Hello there!")
    Label2.Text = (GenericReturn(Of Integer)(5) + 5).ToString()
End Sub
```

C#

```
void Page_Load(object sender, EventArgs e)
{
    Label1.Text = GenericReturn<string>("Hello there!");
    Label2.Text = (GenericReturn<int>(5) + 5).ToString();
}
```

This little example in Listing A-5 shows two separate invocations of the GenericReturn method. The first instance populates the Label1 control and invokes the GenericReturn method as a string, which is quickly followed by the string value that is passed in as the item parameter. When called in this manner, the method is invoked as if it were constructed in the following way:

```
Public Function GenericReturn(ByVal item As String) As String
    Return item
End Function
```

Or:

```
public string GenericReturn(string item)
{
    return item;
}
```

The second invocation of the GenericReturn method passes in an object of type integer, adds 5, and then uses that value to populate the Label2 control. When called in this manner, the method is invoked as if it were constructed in the following way:

```
Public Function GenericReturn(ByVal item As Integer) As Integer
    Return item
End Function
```

Or:

```
public int GenericReturn(int item)
{
    return item;
}
```

As you can see, you gain a lot of power using generics. You see generics used in both of the main .NET languages because they can be built into the underlying framework.

Iterators

Iterators enable you to specify how your classes or collections work when they are dissected in a foreach loop. The iterators are used only in C#. Visual Basic 8.0 developers do not have a similar feature at present.

You can iterate through a collection of items just as you have always been able to do in C# 1.0 because the item implements the GetEnumerator function. For instance, you can just run a foreach loop over an ArrayList, as shown in Listing A-6.

Listing A-6: Running the foreach loop over an ArrayList

```
void Page_Load(object sender, EventArgs e)
{
    ArrayList myList = new ArrayList();

    myList.Add("St. Louis Rams");
    myList.Add("Indianapolis Colts");
    myList.Add("Minneapolis Vikings");

    foreach (string item in myList)
    {
        Response.Write(item.ToString() + "<br />");
    }
}
```

This code writes all three values that were added to the ArrayList to the browser screen. Iterators enable you to run a foreach loop on your own items such as classes. To do this, you create a class that implements the IEnumerable interface.

The first step is to create a class in your Web solution. To do this, create a folder in your solution and give it the name Code. Then place a new .cs class file in the Code directory. This class is illustrated in Listing A-7.

Listing A-7: Creating a class that works with a foreach loop

```csharp
using System;
using System.Collections;

public class myList
{
  internal object[] elements;
  internal int count;

  public IEnumerator GetEnumerator()
  {
        yield return "St. Louis Rams";
        yield return "Indianapolis Colts";
        yield return "Minneapolis Vikings";
  }
}
```

This class, myList, imports the System.Collections namespace so that it can work with the IEnumerable interface. In its simplest form, the myList class implements the enumerator pattern with a method called GetEnumerator(), which returns a value defined as IEnumerable. Then each item in the collection is returned with the yield return command.

Now that the class myList is in place, you can instantiate the class and iterate through the class collection using the foreach loop. This is illustrated in Listing A-8.

Listing A-8: Iterating through the myList class

```csharp
void Page_Load(object sender, EventArgs e)
{
    myList IteratorList = new myList();

    foreach (string item in IteratorList)
    {
        Response.Write(item.ToString() + "<br />");
    }
}
```

This ASP.NET Page_Load event simply creates an instance of the myList collection and iterates through the collection using a foreach loop. This is all possible because an IEnumerable interface was implemented in the myList class. When you run this page, each of the items returned from the myList class using the yield return command displays in the browser.

One interesting change you can make in the custom myList class is to use the new generics capabilities provided by C#. Because you know that only string types are being returned from the myList collection, you can define that type immediately to avoid the boxing and unboxing that occurs using the present construction. Listing A-9 shows the changes you can make to the class that was first presented in Listing A-7.

Listing A-9: Creating a class that works with a foreach loop using generics

```
using System;
using System.Collections;
using System.Collections.Generic;

public class myList : IEnumerable<string>
{
 internal object[] elements;
 internal int count;

 public IEnumerator<string> GetEnumerator()
 {
    yield return "St. Louis Rams";
    yield return "Indianapolis Colts";
    yield return "Minneapolis Vikings";
 }
}
```

Anonymous Methods

Another new feature of C# is anonymous methods. Anonymous methods enable you to put programming steps within a delegate that you can later execute instead of creating an entirely new method. This can be handled in a couple different ways.

Without using anonymous methods, create a delegate that is referencing a method found elsewhere in the class file. In the example from Listing A-10, when the delegate is referenced (by a button-click event), the delegate invokes the method that it points to.

Listing A-10: Using delegates in a traditional manner

```
void Page_Load(object sender, EventArgs e)
{
    this.Button1.Click += ButtonWork;
}

void ButtonWork(object sender, EventArgs e)
{
    Label1.Text = "Welcome to the camp, I guess you all know why you're here.";
}
```

In the example in Listing A-10, you see a method in place called ButtonWork, which is called only by the delegate in the Page_Load event. Anonymous methods now enable you to avoid creating a separate method and allow you to place the method directly in the delegate declaration instead. An example of the use of anonymous methods is shown in Listing A-11.

Listing A-11: Using delegates with an anonymous method

```
void Page_Load(object sender, EventArgs e)
{
    this.Button1.Click += delegate(object myDelSender, EventArgs myDelEventArgs)
    {
        Label1.Text = "Welcome to the camp, I guess you all know why you're here.";
    };
}
```

When you use anonymous methods, you don't create a separate method. Instead you place necessary code directly after the delegate declaration. The statements and steps to be executed by the delegate are placed between curly braces and closed with a semicolon.

Using anonymous methods, you can also work with variables or classes. This is illustrated in Listing A-12.

Listing A-12: Using items that are out of scope

```
string myString = "Out of scope item.";

void Page_Load(object sender, EventArgs e)
{
    this.Button1.Click += delegate(object myDelSender, EventArgs myDelEventArgs)
    {
        Label1.Text = myString;
    };
}
```

Although this anonymous method just used a variable that was outside of the Page_Load event, you can also use it to work with other classes and functions elsewhere in your solution.

Operator Overloading

Operator overloading enables you to define the +, -, *, / and other operators in your classes just as you can in system classes. This is a feature that has always been present in C#, but is now available in Visual Basic 8.0 as well. It gives you the capability to ensure that the objects in your classes, when used with operators, have the feel that they are simply of type string or integer.

Giving your classes this extended capability is a matter of simply creating a new method using the Operator keyword followed by the operator that you wish to overload. An example of the Operator functions is illustrated in Listing A-13.

Listing A-13: An example of Operator overloading functions

```
Public Shared Operator +(ByVal Left As Point, ByVal Right As Size) As Point
    Return New Point(Left.X + Right.Width, Left.Y + Right.Height)
End Operator

Public Shared Operator -(ByVal Left As Point, ByVal Right As Size) As Point
    Return New Point(Left.X - Right.Width, Left.Y - Right.Height)
End Operator
```

Two different types of operators can be overloaded from Visual Basic, unary and binary operators.

Overloadable unary operators include

```
+    -    Not    IsTrue    IsFalse    Widening    Narrowing
```

Overloadable binary operators include

```
+    -    *    /    \    &    Like    Mod    And    Or    Xor    ^    <<    >>    =
<>    >    <    >=    <=
```

Global Namespace Qualifiers

A problem in the .NET 1.0 languages was that a developer, or more commonly a code-generation tool, could not search for types at the root namespace level. Both Visual Basic 8.0 and C# 2.0 have provided solutions to this problem with new keywords. In Visual Basic the `Global` keyword has added a top-root namespace to avoid any namespace conflicts that might arise from similarly named namespaces. An example of the use of the `Global` keyword is the following:

```
Global.System.String
```

In C# the global namespace qualifier has introduced the `::` keyword.

```
::System.String
```

The advantage to the global namespace qualifiers is that you can now create namespaces that mimic the Framework namespaces without causing a conflict with the .NET Frameworks namespaces. For example, you can now create the following namespace in your application:

```
namespace MyCompany
{
    namespace System
    {
        class String
        {
            static void Main()
            {
                ::System.String copy = ::System.String.Copy("Hello");
            }
```

```
            }
        }
    }
```

Using the qualifiers allows the application to distinguish between the root namespaces.

Partial Classes

Partial classes are a new feature included with the .NET Framework 2.0 and available to both C# and Visual Basic 8.0. These classes allow you to divide up a single class into multiple class files, which are later combined into a single class when compiled.

Partial classes are the secret of how ASP.NET keeps the new code-behind model simple. In ASP.NET 1.0/1.1, the code-behind model included quite a bit of code labeled as machine-generated code (code generated by the designer) and hidden within #REGION tags. Now, however the code-behind file for ASP.NET 2.0 looks rather simple. A sample of the new code-behind model that uses partial classes is shown in Listing A-14.

Listing A-14: The new code-behind model using partial classes

VB
```
Imports Microsoft.VisualBasic

Namespace ASP

    Partial Class TestPage
        Sub Button1_Click(ByVal sender As Object, ByVal e As System.EventArgs)
            Label1.Text = "Hello " & Textbox1.Text
        End Sub
    End Class

End Namespace
```

C#
```
using System;

namespace ASP {

    public partial class TestPage
    {
        void Button1_Click (object sender, System.EventArgs e)
        {
            Label1.Text = "Hello " + Textbox1.Text;
        }
    }
}
```

This code-behind file contains a simple button-click event and nothing else. If you compare it to the designer-code (as it was called) from the code-behind files found in ASP.NET 1.0/1.1, you notice a big difference between the two. What happened to all that code in the original code-behind file? It is still there, but now, with the use of partial classes, all that necessary (but untouchable) code is kept in a separate class file. Upon compilation, the class file that is shown in Listing A-14 is merged with the other class file. The result shows you that the code-behind files in ASP.NET 2.0 can consist simply of objects that you actually work with.

Partial classes are created with the use of the `Partial` keyword in Visual Basic and with the `partial` keyword in C# for any classes that are to be joined with a different class. The `Partial` keyword precedes the `Class` keyword for the classes to be combined with the original class. Besides using partial classes with every code-behind page that you work with in ASP.NET 2.0, you can also employ the same techniques in your own class files. You can associate two or more classes as part of the same class using the procedure shown in Listings A-15 and A-16.

Listing A-15: The first class

VB

```
Public Class Calculator
    Public Function Add(ByVal a As Integer, ByVal b As Integer)
        Return (a + b)
    End Function
End Class
```

C#

```
public class Calculator
{
    public int Add(int a, int b)
    {
        return a + b;
    }
}
```

Listing A-16 shows the second class that utilizes the partial classes functionality.

Listing A-16: The second class

VB

```
Partial Class Calculator
    Public Function Subtract(ByVal a As Integer, ByVal b As Integer)
        Return (a - b)
    End Function
End Class
```

C#

```
public partial class Calculator
{
    public int Subtract(int a, int b)
    {
        return a - b;
    }
}
```

When the two separate files are compiled, the two class files appear as a single object. The first class shown in Listing A-15 is constructed just as a normal class is, whereas any additional classes that are to be made a part of this original class use the new `Partial` keyword. A consumer using the compiled `Calculator` class will see no difference. After the consumer of the `Calculator` class creates an instance of this class, this single instance has both an `Add` and a `Subtract` method in it. This is illustrated in Figure A-1.

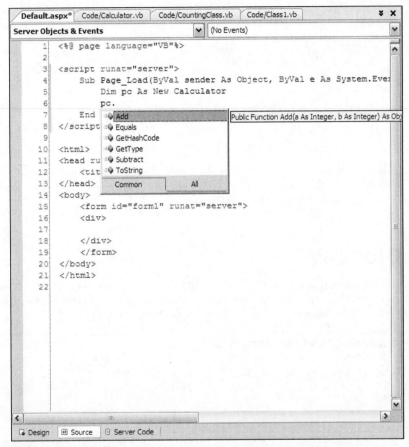

Figure A-1

Visual Basic XML Documentation

Like C#, Visual Basic 8.0 now includes the capability to create XML documentation from comments that are left in your VB files. Visual Basic denotes XML documentation remarks in code with the use of the three successive comment marks ('''). This is similar to how C# does it. C# uses three backslashes for XML documentation (///). Comments left in VB code can then be converted to documentation. Listing A-17 shows the use of XML documentation in code.

Listing A-17: Visual Basic code with comments for XML documentation

```vb
Imports Microsoft.VisualBasic

''' <summary>My Calculator Class</summary>
Public Class Class1

    ''' <summary>This Add method returns the value of two numbers
    '''  added together</summary>
    ''' <param name="a">First number of the collection of numbers to
    '''  be added</param>
    ''' <param name="b">Second number of the collection of numbers to
    '''  be added</param>
    Public Function Add(ByVal a As Integer, ByVal b As Integer)
        Return (a + b)
    End Function

End Class
```

The Visual Basic 8.0 compiler now includes a new /doc command that is similar to the way C# works with XML documentation. Compiling your VB code using the /doc command causes the compiler to produce the XML documentation with the compilation.

Static Classes

C# now supports the notion of a static class, where all members of the class must be declared as static. The static class is meant to replace the design pattern of creating a sealed class with a private constructor that contains only static members. Listing A-18 shows you how to create a static class.

Listing A-18: Creating a static class in C#

```csharp
public sealed static class Settings
{
    // class methods
}
```

Creating a static class means that the compiler can now catch any instance methods that might be accidentally declared in the class.

Property Accessors

When writing properties with .NET 1.0 languages, both the setter and getter portions of the properties were required to have the same level of access. This created problems if you wanted to create a read-only public property, but still be able to take advantage of using private setter's logic internally in the class.

In .NET 2.0, both C# and Visual Basic now allow you to explicitly set individual accessors on the getter and setter, as shown in Listing A-19.

Listing A-19: Using property accessors

VB
```
Private firstname As String
Public Property FirstName() As String
    Get
        Return _firstname
    End Get

    Friend Set(ByVal value As String)
        If value.Trim.Length > 0 Then
            _firstname = value.Trim
        Else
            value = "Default Name"
        End If
    End Set
End Property
```

C#
```
private string firstname;
public string FirstName
{
    get
    {
        return_firstname;
    }

    internal set
    {
        if (value.Trim().Length > 0)
        {
            _firstname = value.Trim();
        }
        else
        {
            value = "Default Name";
        }
    }
}
```

Unsigned Types

New to Visual Basic is support for unsigned types such as SByte, UShort, UInteger, and ULong. An unsigned type works like regular types do, except that they can store only positive numbers.

Unsigned types are most useful when making Win32 API calls. Listing A-20 shows how you can call the MessageBox function directly from the Windows API. This function requires a UInteger type method parameter be passed in and also returns a UInteger type.

Listing A-20: Using unsigned types in Visual Basic

```
Private Const uintOK As UInteger = 0

Private Declare Auto Function WinMessageBox Lib _
    "user32.dll Alias "MessageBox" _
    (ByVal hWnd As Integer, ByVal lpText As String, _
    ByVal lpCaption As String, ByVal uType As UInteger) _
    As UInteger

Public Function DirectMessageBox(ByVal message As String, _
    ByVal caption As String) As String

    Dim r As UInteger = WinMessageBox(0, message, caption, uintOK)

    If (r=0) Then
        Return "OK"
    End If

    If (r=8) Then
        Return "Cancel"
    End If

End Function
```

Default Instances

Another change to Visual Basic .NET that has tripped up many developers migrating from Visual Basic 6.0 is the lack of a default instance for forms. In order to use a specific form, you create an instance of it first.

```
Dim frm As New Form2
frm.Show()
```

Visual Basic now supports form default instances, so you can use the familiar syntax:

```
Form2.Show()
```

New Visual Basic Keywords

Visual Basic 8.0 introduces a couple of new keywords that can be utilized in your ASP.NET 2.0 applications. The keywords were brought to the language to make it easier to perform some common tasks such as working in loops or destroying resources as early as possible. Look at a couple of the new additions to the Visual Basic language.

Continue

The Continue statement is an outstanding new addition to the Visual Basic language that was brought on board to enable you to work through loops more logically in some specific situations. When working in a loop, it is sometimes beneficial to stop the conditional flow and move onto the next item in the collection if the item being examined simply doesn't fit your criteria. This logic can now be implemented better because of the new Continue statement. Listing A-21 shows an example of the use of the Continue statement.

Listing A-21: Using the new Continue statement

```
Sub Page_Load(ByVal sender As Object, ByVal e As System.EventArgs)
    Dim myString As String
    Dim count As Integer = 0
    myString = "The St. Louis Rams will go to the Superbowl this year."

    For i As Integer = 0 To (myString.Length() - 1)
        If (myString(i).Equals(" "c)) Then Continue For
            count += 1
    Next

    Label1.Text = "There are " & count.ToString() & _
        " characters used (minus spaces)."
End Sub
```

This little example counts each character in a complete string that is not a space. If a space is encountered, the Continue statement finds this in the check and immediately stops execution of the loop for that particular item in the collection. It then hands over the execution of the loop to the next item in the collection. In this example, you could easily check for the characters with a nested If statement, but using multiple nested If statements can get confusing. The use of the Continue statement makes the logic contained within the For loop very evident and clean.

The Continue statement is not only meant to be used within a For loop, but you can also use this new keyword with other language features that loop through a collection of items, such as the Do and While statements. The following section shows how to use the Continue statement with the four available options:

```
For [statement]
    ...

    If [statement] Then Continue For

    ...
Next

For Each [statement]
    ...

    If [statement] Then Continue For

    ...
```

```
    Next

Do While [statement]
    ...

    If [statement] Then Continue Do

    ...
Loop

While [statement]
    ...

    If [statement] Then Continue While

    ...
End While
```

As you can see, you have many ways to use this new keyword to make your code easier to read and manage.

Using

Although C# developers have been able to take advantage of the using keyword in C# to define an object scope, the new Visual Basic Using keyword gives VB developers the same feature. The Using keyword in Visual Basic ensures that expensive resources get destroyed as soon as possible instead of remaining in memory until the method is executed. You can now destroy expensive resources, such as connection objects and COM wrappers, immediately when you have finished using them instead of waiting for the garbage collector to make its rounds. An example of working with the Using keyword is illustrated in Listing A-22.

Listing A-22: Working with the Using keyword

```
Using myConn As New SqlConnection

    ' Work with the SqlConnection object

End Using
```

In Listing A-22, you can see that instead of using the Dim keyword to create a new instance of the SqlConnection object, the Using keyword is used in its place. If you utilize the Using keyword, you must close the Using statement with an End Using statement. The End Using statement is located at the point where the SqlConnection object is destroyed from memory.

My

One of the most challenging issues a developer faces when using the .NET Framework is the sheer size of the class library. Knowing where to find the proper class for a particular function in the Framework can prove challenging. If you do find it, figuring out its usage can be just as challenging. In order to help developers overcome this problem, Visual Basic has added the My keyword. This new keyword is a novel concept that is designed to quickly give you access to a large variety of resources you may need to access when developing your applications.

The My keyword is divided into several main areas of functionality, but using the keyword can be a bit deceiving depending on the type of project you are working with. For example, if you are working in an ASP.NET project and you use the My keyword, you see five objects available for you to use. If you switch to working in a Windows Forms application, the objects available to you using the My keyword are slightly different. The My keyword understands the type of project you are working with and can present you the appropriate objects based on the resources available to you in that project type. Figure A-2 shows how IntelliSense for the My keyword differs for an ASP.NET project type.

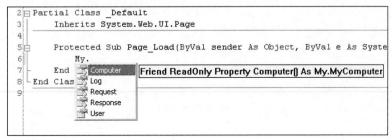

Figure A-2

Figure A-3 shows the IntelliSense for the My keyword in a Windows Forms project type.

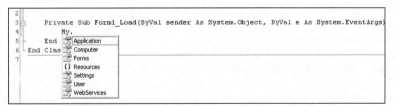

Figure A-3

Because the focus is on ASP.NET in this book, look at the My objects available to you in a Web project. In an ASP.NET application, the My keyword gives you access to five different objects, which are listed in the following table.

Object	Description
Computer	Accessing the host computer and its resources, services, and data
Log	Accessing the application log
Request	Accessing the current Web request
Response	Accessing the current Web response
User	Accessing the current user's security context

Look at how you can use these objects. The following section shows how you can use several different My objects to perform a variety of operations.

```
'Retrieve the computer name
Dim computername As String = My.Computer.Info.OSFullName

'Write a message to the applications event log listeners
My.Log.WriteEntry("This page has loaded.", Diagnostics.TraceEventType.Information)

'Retrieve the requesting browsers User-Agent string
Dim agent As String = My.Request.Browser.Browser

'Set the CacheControl proerty to allow
'proxy servers to cache this content
My.Response.CacheControl = "Public"

'Retrieve the current ahtuenticated users name
Dim username As String = My.User.Name
```

Keep in mind that all the functionality exposed by the My keyword is actually provided by underlying Framework classes.

IsNot

The IsNot operator is the opposite of the Is operator. It allows you to eliminate the Not operator from comparison expressions:

```
If myObject1 IsNot myObject2 Then
```

TryCast

In Visual Basic .NET, you have two different methods for casting objects, the CType or the DirectCast methods. The problem with both these methods is that if the object cannot be converted or cast, you raise an exception.

The TryCast statement allows you to attempt a cast without having to handle the invalid cast exception. Instead, if the cast is invalid you are simply returned a Nothing value, as shown in Listing A-23.

Listing A-23: Using TryCast in Visual Basic 8.0

```
cust = TryCast(obj, Customer)
If cust IsNot Nothing Then

     ' use the Customer object

End If
```

This keyword is the equivalent to the C# as keyword.

ASP.NET Online Resources

Author Blogs

Bill Evjen: `www.geekswithblogs.net/evjen`

Scott Hanselman: `www.hanselman.com/blog/`

Devin Rader: `www.geekswithblogs.net/devin`

ASP.NET Influential Blogs

Kent Sharkey: `weblogs.asp.net/ksharkey`

Rob Howard: `weblogs.asp.net/rhoward/`

Scott Guthrie: `weblogs.asp.net/scottgu`

Steve Smith: `blogs.aspadvice.com/ssmith/`

G. Andrew Duthie: `blogs.msdn.com/gduthie/`

Scott Mitchell: `www.scottonwriting.net/`

Scott Watermasysk: `scottwater.com/blog/default.aspx`

Nikhil Kothari: `www.nikhilk.net/`

Alex Homer: `www.daveandal.net/alshed.asp`

Dave Sussman: `www.daveandal.net/daveroom/diary.asp`

Mike Pope: `mikepope.com/blog/`

Web Sites

123ASPX Directory: `www.123aspx.com`

4 Guys from Rolla: `www.4guysfromrolla.com`

Angry Coder: `www.angrycoder.com`

ASP 101: `www.asp101.com`

ASP Alliance: `www.aspalliance.com`

ASP Alliance Lists: `www.aspadvice.com`

The ASP.NET Developer Portal: `msdn.microsoft.com/asp.net`

ASP.NET Homepage: `www.asp.net`

ASP.NET Resources: `www.aspnetresources.com`

ASP.NET World: `www.aspnetworld.com`

DotNetJunkies: `www.dotnetjunkies.com`

GotDotNet: `www.gotdotnet.com`

International .NET Association: `www.ineta.org`

Microsoft's Classic ASP Site: `http://msdn.microsoft.com/library/default.asp?url=/library/en-us/dnanchor/html/activeservpages.asp`

Microsoft Developer Centers: `msdn.microsoft.com/developercenters`

Microsoft Forums: `forums.microsoft.com`

Microsoft Newsgroups: `msdn.microsoft.com/newsgroups/`

.NET 247: `www.dotnet247.com`

RegExLib: `www.regexlib.com`

Server Side Code: `www.serversidecode.net`

The ServerSide .NET: `www.theserverside.net`

XML for ASP.NET: `www.xmlforasp.net`

Index

C